Essentials of Entrepreneurship and Small Business Management

SIXTH EDITION

Essentials of Entrepreneurship and Small Business Management

Norman M. Scarborough
Presbyterian College

Prentice Hall

Boston Columbus Indianapolis New York San Francisco Upper Saddle River
Amsterdam Cape Town Dubai London Madrid Milan Munich Paris Montreal Toronto
Delhi Mexico City Sao Paulo Sydney Hong Kong Seoul Singapore Taipei Tokyo

Editorial Director: Sally Yagan
Editor in Chief: Eric Svendsen
Acquisitions Editor: Kim Norbuta
Editorial Project Manager: Claudia Fernandes
Director of Marketing: Patrice Lumumba Jones
Marketing Manager: Nikki Ayana Jones
Marketing Assistant: Ian Gold
Senior Managing Editor: Judy Leale
Senior Production Project Manager: Kelly Warsak
Senior Operations Supervisor: Arnold Vila
Operations Specialist: Ilene Kahn
Creative Design Director: Christy Mahon
Senior Art Director: Janet Slowik
Art Director, Cover and Interior: Steven Firm
Text and Cover Designer: Dina Curro

Manager, Visual Research: Beth Brenzel
Photo Researcher: Melinda Alexander
Permissions Project Manager: Shannon Barbe
Image Permission Coordinator: Kathy Gavilanes
Manager, Cover Visual Research & Permissions: Karen Sanatar
Cover Art: iStockphoto Vetta™ Collection Dollar Bin
Media Project Manager: Lisa Rinaldi
Media Editor: Ashley Lulling
Full-Service Project Management: Elm Street Publishing Services
Composition: Integra Software Services Pvt. Ltd.
Printer/Binder: Courier/Kendallville
Cover Printer: Lehigh-Phoenix Color/Hagerstown
Text Font: 10/12 Times

Credits and acknowledgments borrowed from other sources and reproduced, with permission, in this textbook appear on appropriate page within text.

Library of Congress Cataloging-in-Publication Data
Scarborough, Norman M.
    Essentials of entrepreneurship and small business management / Norman M. Scarborough.—6th ed.
      p. cm.
    Rev. ed. of: Essentials of entrepreneurship and small business management / Thomas W. Zimmerer, Norman M. Scarborough with Doug Wilson. 5th ed. copyright 2008. ISBN-13: 978-0-13-229438-6 ISBN-10: 0-13-229438-9
    ISBN-10: 0-13-610959-4
    1. Small business—Management.   2. New business enterprises—Management.   3. Entrepreneurship.
  I. Title.
    HD62.7.Z55 2010   2009032859
    658.02'2—dc22

10 9 8 7 6 5

Prentice Hall
is an imprint of

www.pearsonhighered.com

ISBN 13: 978-0-13-610959-4
ISBN 10: 0-13-610959-4

To Cindy, whose patience is always tested during a writing project of this magnitude. Your love, support, and understanding are a vital part of every book. You are the love of my life.

—NMS

"May your own dreams be your only boundaries."
—*The Reverend Purlie Victorious Judson, in*
"Purlie," Broadway Theater, 1970

Brief Contents

Contents

Preface

What's New to This Edition?

Entrepreneurship is a fast-growing and ever-changing discipline. This edition includes many new features that reflect this dynamic and exciting field of study.

- Almost all of the real-world examples in this edition are new and are easy to spot because they are set off in italics within margin markers. These examples allow you to see how entrepreneurs are putting into practice the concepts that you are learning about in the book and in class. They are designed to help you to remember the key concepts in the course. The business founders in these examples also reflect the diversity that makes entrepreneurship a vital part of the global economy.

- Several new "Ethics and Entrepreneurship" features have been added that give you the opportunity to wrestle with some of the ethical dilemmas that entrepreneurs face in business. Encouraging you to think about and discuss these issues now prepares you for making the right business decisions later.

- A new sample business plan for a real business, Think Archimedes, an innovative student development business, is included both in the text and on the Companion Web site. You also have access to other sample business plans at Palo Alto's *Business Plan Pro*™ Web site, www.paloalto.com/ps/bp/samples.cfm. Many courses in entrepreneurship and small business management require students to write business plans. If creating a business plan is part of your class, you will find that having a model to guide you as you build your own plan to be quite helpful. This sample plan serves as a good model.

- To emphasize the practical nature of this book, the content of the very popular "Hands on...How to" feature has been updated. This feature selects a concept from each chapter and explains how you can put it to practice in your own company. These features include such topics as how to "Launch a Successful Business While You Are Still in College," "Protect Your Company's Intellectual Property," "Control Your Company's Accounts Receivable," "Make Your Small Business a Great Place to Work," and many others.

- Another feature that is popular with both students and professors is "You Be the Consultant." Every chapter contains at least two of these inserts that describe a decision that an entrepreneur faces and asks you to play the role of consultant and advise the entrepreneur on the best course of action. This feature includes the fascinating stories of entrepreneurs who are creating their dream jobs (including Jesse James of West Coast Choppers), running a global e-commerce business from a tiny village in rural England (Heather Gorringe of Wiggly Wigglers), and looking for capital to fuel a fast growing business (Warren Tracy of the Busted Knuckle Garage). Each one poses a problem or an opportunity and includes questions that focus your attention on key issues and helps you to hone your analytical and critical thinking skills.

- This edition includes 10 new brief cases that cover a variety of topics (see the Case Matrix that appears on the inside cover). All of the cases are about small companies, and most are companies that you can research online. These cases challenge you to think critically about a variety of topics that are covered in the text—from developing a business strategy and building a brand to protecting intellectual property and financing a business. In three of these cases, the winners of a national case writing contest sponsored by Vision Forward's Hot Mommas/Cool Daddies tell their own inspiring entrepreneurial stories and how they struggled to overcome obstacles to achieve success.

- The content of every chapter reflects the most recent statistics, studies, surveys, and research about entrepreneurship and small business management. You will learn how to launch and manage a business the *right* way by studying the most current concepts in entrepreneurship and small business management.

Entrepreneurship has become a major force in the global economy. Policymakers across the world are discovering that economic growth and prosperity lie in the hands of entrepreneurs—those dynamic, driven men and women who are committed to achieving success by creating and marketing innovative, customer-focused new products and services. Not only are these entrepreneurs creating economic prosperity, but many of them are also striving to make the world a better place in which to live. Those who possess this spirit of entrepreneurial leadership continue to lead the economic revolution that has proved time and again its ability to raise the standard of living for people everywhere. I hope that by using this book in your small business management or entrepreneurship class, you will join this economic revolution to bring about lasting, positive changes in their community and around the world. If you are interested in launching a business of your own, *Essentials of Entrepreneurship and Small Business Management* is the ideal book for you!

This sixth edition of *Essentials of Entrepreneurship and Small Business Management* introduces you to the process of creating a new venture and provides you with the knowledge you need to launch a business that has the greatest chance for success. One of the hallmarks of every edition of this book has been a very practical, "hands-on" approach to entrepreneurship. I strive to equip you with the tools you will need for entrepreneurial success. By combining this textbook with your professor's expertise, I believe that you will be prepared to follow your dreams of becoming successful entrepreneurs.

Other Text Features

- This edition once again emphasizes the importance of creating a business plan for a successful new venture. Chapter 4 offers comprehensive coverage of how to conduct a feasibility study for a business idea and then how to create a sound business plan for the ideasthat pass the feasibility test. Your professor may choose to bundle Prentice Hall's *Business Feasibility Analysis Pro* or Palo Alto's *Business Plan Pro*^{TM} software with this edition of *Essentials of Entrepreneurship and Small Business Management* at a special package price. These programs will guide you as you conduct a feasibility analysis or build a business plan.
- This edition features an updated, attractive, full-color design and a layout that includes an in-margin glossary and learning objectives and is designed to be user-friendly. Each chapter begins with learning objectives, which are repeated as in-margin markers within the chapter to guide you as you study.
- Chapter 2, "Inside the Entrepreneurial Mind: From Ideas to Reality," explains the creative process entrepreneurs use to generate business ideas and to recognize entrepreneurial opportunities. This chapter helps you learn to think like an entrepreneur.
- Chapter 9, "E-Commerce and the Entrepreneur," serves as a practical guide to using the Web to conduct business in the twenty-first century.
- *Business Plan Pro*^{TM}, the best-selling business planning software package from Palo Alto Software, is a valuable tool that has helped thousands of entrepreneurs (and students) to build winning business plans for their entrepreneurial ideas. Every chapter contains an updated *Business Plan Pro*^{TM} exercise that enables you to apply the knowledge you have gained from this book and your class to build a business plan with *Business Plan Pro*^{TM}.

Supplements

- A useful companion Web site, www.pearsonhighered.com/scarborough, offers free access to learning resources, including multiple-choice quizzes, Web essays, and links to relevant small business sites, that many students find useful.
- CourseSmart eTextbook - CourseSmart is an exciting new choice for students who are looking to save money. As an alternative to purchasing a printed textbook, you can purchase an electronic version of the same content and save up to 50 percent off the suggested list price of the print text. With a CourseSmart e-textbook, you can search the text, make notes online, print out reading assignments that incorporate lecture notes, and bookmark important passages for later review. For more information, or to purchase access to the CourseSmart e-textbook version of this text, visit www.coursesmart.com.

Beyond the Textbook

Essentials of Entrepreneurship and Small Business Management, Sixth Edition has stood the test of time and contains a multitude of both student- and instructor-friendly features. I trust that this edition will help the next generation of entrepreneurs reach their full potential and achieve their dreams of success as independent business owners. It is their dedication, perseverance, and creativity that keep the world's economy moving forward.

Acknowledgments

Supporting every author is a staff of professionals who work extremely hard to bring a book to life. They handle the thousands of details involved in transforming a rough manuscript into the finished product you see before you. Their contributions are immeasurable, and I appreciate all they do to make this book successful. I have been blessed to work with the following outstanding publishing professionals:

- Kim Norbuta, acquisitions editor, whose wisdom and guidance throughout this project were invaluable. I appreciate her creativity, integrity, honesty, and leadership.
- Claudia Fernandes, our exceptionally capable project manager, who was always just an e-mail away when I needed her help with a seemingly endless number of details. She did a masterful job of coordinating the many aspects of this project. Her ability to juggle many aspects of multiple projects at once is amazing!
- Kelly Warsak, production editor, who skillfully guided the book through the long and sometimes difficult production process with a smile and a "can-do" attitude. She is always a pleasure to work with and a good friend.
- Melinda Alexander, photo researcher, who took my ideas for photos and transformed them into the meaningful images you see on these pages. Her job demands many hours of research and hard work, which she did with aplomb.
- Nikki Jones, marketing manager, whose input helped focus this edition in an evolving market.

I also extend a big "Thank You" to the corps of Prentice Hall sales representatives, who work so hard to get my books into customers' hands and who represent the front line in our effort to serve customers' needs. They are the unsung heroes of the publishing industry.

Special thanks to the following academic reviewers, whose ideas, suggestions, and thought-provoking input have helped to shape this and previous editions of my two books, *Essentials of Entrepreneurship and Small Business Management* and *Effective Small Business Management*. I always welcome feedback from customers!

Lon Addams, Weber State University
Sol Ahiarah, Buffalo State College
Professor M. Ala, California State University–Los Angeles
Annamary Allen, Broome Community College
Jay Azriel, York College of Pennsylvania
Bruce Bachenheimer, Pace University
Kevin Banning, University of Florida
Tom Bergman, Northeastern State University
Nancy Bowman, Baylor University
Jeff Brice, Texas Southern University
Michael S. Broida, Miami University
James Browne, University of Southern Colorado
Rochelle Brunson, Alvin Community College
John E. Butler, University of Washington
R. D. Butler, Trenton State College
Pamela Clark, Angelo State University
Richard Cuba, University of Baltimore
Kathy J. Daruty, L. A. Pierce College
Gita DeSouza, Pennsylvania State University

Stuart Devlin, New Mexico State University
John deYoung, Cumberland Community College
Michael Dickson, Columbus State Community College
Judy Dietert, Southwest Texas State University
Art Elkins, University of Massachusetts
W. Bruce Erickson, University of Minnesota
Jan Feldbauer, Austin Community College
George J. Foegen, Metropolitan State College of Denver
Caroline E. W. Glackin, Delaware State University
Stephen O. Handley, University of Washington—Bothell
Charles Hubbard, University of Arkansas
Fred Hughes, Faulkner University
Ralph Jagodka, Mt. San Antonio College
Theresa Janeczek, Manchester Community College
E. L. (Betty) Kinarski, Seattle University
Kyoung-Nan Kwon, Michigan State University
Dick LaBarre, Ferris State University
Paul Lamberson, Riverton, WY
Mary Lou Lockerby, College of DuPage
Martin K. Marsh, California State University–Bakersfield
Charles H. Matthews, University of Cincinnati
John McMahon, Mississippi County Community College
Michael L. Menefee, Purdue University
Julie Messing, Kent State University
William Meyer, TRICOMP
Milton Miller, Carteret Community College
John Moonen, Daytona Beach Community College
Linda Newell, Saddleback College
Marcella Norwood, University of Houston
David O'Dell, McPherson State College
John Phillips, University of San Francisco
Louis D. Ponthieu, University of North Texas
Ben Powell, University of Alabama
Matthew W. Rutherford, Virginia Commonwealth University
Joseph Salamone, State University of New York at Buffalo
Manhula Salinath, University of North Texas
Nick Sarantakes, Austin Community College
Khaled Sartawi, Fort Valley State University
Terry J. Schindler, University of Indianapolis
Thomas Schramko, University of Toledo
Peter Mark Shaw, Tidewater Community College
Jack Sheeks, Broward Community College
Lakshmy Sivaratnam, Johnson Community College
Bill Snider, Cuesta College
Deborah Streeter, Cornell University
Ethné Swartz, Fairleigh Dickinson University
Yvette Swint-Blakely, Lansing Community College
John Todd, University of Arkansas
Charles Toftoy, George Washington University
Barry L. Van Hook, Arizona State University
Ina Kay Van Loo, WVU Institute of Technology
William Vincent, Mercer University
Jim Walker, Moorhead State University
Bernard W. Weinrich, St. Louis Community College
Donald Wilkinson, East Tennessee State University
Gregory Worosz, Schoolcraft College
Bernard Zannini, Northern Essex Community College

Many thanks to Michelle Carl and Andrew Turner, founder of Think Archimedes, for allowing us to use the plan that they created for Andrew's company as the sample business plan in this edition. Andrew has proved that he has what it takes to be a successful entrepreneur, and I appreciate his willingness to allow his plan to serve as a model for other entrepreneurs as they build their plans.

I also am grateful to my colleagues who support me in the often grueling process of writing a book: Foard Tarbert, Sam Howell, Jerry Slice, Suzanne Smith, Jody Lipford, and Kristy Hill of Presbyterian College.

Finally, I thank Cindy Scarborough for her love, support, and understanding while I worked many long hours to complete this book. For her, this project represents a labor of love.

Norman M. Scarborough
William H. Scott III Associate Professor of Information Science
Presbyterian College
Clinton, South Carolina

Special Note to the Students

I trust that this edition of *Essentials of Entrepreneurship and Small Business Management* will encourage and challenge you to fulfill your aspirations as an entrepreneur and to make the most of your talents, experience, and abilities. I hope that you find this book to be of such value that it becomes a permanent addition to your personal library. I look forward to the day when your personal success story appears on these pages.

Norman Scarborough

SuperJam/www.superjam.co.uk

CHAPTER

The Foundations of Entrepreneurship

Entrepreneurs are simply those who understand that there is little difference between obstacle and opportunity and are able to turn both to their advantage.
—Niccolò Machiavelli

Entrepreneurs are the new rock stars.
—Cindy Boyd

Learning Objectives

On completion of this chapter, you will be able to:

1. Define the role of the entrepreneur in the United States and across the world.

2. Describe the entrepreneurial profile and evaluate your potential as an entrepreneur.

3. Describe the benefits and drawbacks of entrepreneurship.

4. Explain the forces that are driving the growth of entrepreneurship.

5. Explain the cultural diversity of entrepreneurship.

6. Describe the important role small businesses play in our nation's economy.

7. Put failure into proper perspective.

8. Explain how an entrepreneur can avoid becoming another failure statistic.

LO 1

Define the role of the entrepreneur in the United States and across the world.

The World of the Entrepreneur

Welcome to the world of the entrepreneur! Around the world, growing numbers of people are realizing their dreams of owning and operating their own businesses. Entrepreneurship continues to thrive in nearly ever corner of the world. Globally, one in eleven adults is actively engaged in launching a business.[1] Research by the Kauffman Foundation shows that in the United States alone, entrepreneurs launch 550,000 businesses each month![2] This entrepreneurial spirit is the most significant economic development in recent business history. In the United States and around the globe, these heroes of the new economy are reshaping the business environment and creating a world in which their companies play an important role in the vitality of the global economy. With amazing vigor, their businesses have introduced innovative products and services, pushed back technological frontiers, created new jobs, opened foreign markets, and, in the process, provided their founders with the opportunity to do what they enjoy most.

Entrepreneurial activity is essential to a strong global economy. Many of the world's largest companies continue to engage in massive downsizing campaigns, dramatically cutting the number of employees on their payrolls. This flurry of "pink slips" has spawned a new population of entrepreneurs: "castoffs" from large corporations (in which many of these individuals thought they would be lifetime ladder-climbers) with solid management experience and many productive years left before retirement. According to the Small Business Administration, during a recent one-year period, the largest companies in the United States shed 214,000 net jobs; during the same period, small businesses with fewer than 20 employees created 1,625,000 net jobs![3]

One casualty of this downsizing has been the long-standing notion of job security in large corporations. As a result, members of Generation X (those born between 1965 and 1981) and Generation Y (those born between 1982 and 1995) no longer see launching a business as being a risky career path. Having watched large companies lay off their parents and grandparents after many years of service, these young people see entrepreneurship as the ideal way to create their own job security and success! They prefer to control their own destinies by building their own businesses.

The downsizing trend among large companies has created a more significant philosophical change. It has ushered in an age in which "small is beautiful." Twenty-five years ago, competitive conditions favored large companies with their hierarchies and layers of management; today, with the pace of change constantly accelerating, fleet-footed, agile, small companies have the competitive advantage. These nimble competitors can dart into and out of niche markets as they emerge and recede; they can move faster to exploit market opportunities; and they can use modern technology to create within a matter of weeks or months products and services that once took years and all of the resources a giant corporation could muster. The balance has tipped in favor of small, entrepreneurial companies. Howard Stevenson, Harvard's chaired professor of entrepreneurship, says, "Why is it so easy [for small companies] to compete against giant corporations? Because while they [the giants] are studying the consequences, [entrepreneurs] are changing the world."[4]

One of the most comprehensive studies of global entrepreneurship conducted by the Global Entrepreneurship Monitor (GEM) shows significant variation in the rate of new business formation among the nations of the world when measured by total entrepreneurial activity, or TEA (see Figure 1.1). The study reports that 18.7 percent of the adult population in the United States—nearly one in five people—is working to start a business. The GEM study also reports that globally men are twice as likely to start a business as women; that the majority of entrepreneurs turn to family members, friends, and other informal investors for external capital; and that entrepreneurs are most likely to launch their companies between the ages of 25 and 44.[5] The health of the global economy and the level of entrepreneurial activity are intertwined. "The world economy needs entrepreneurs," says GEM researcher Kent Jones, "and increasingly, entrepreneurs depend on an open and expanding world economy for new opportunities and growth—through trade, foreign investment, and finance."[6]

The United States and many other nations are benefiting from this surge in global entrepreneurial activity. Eastern European countries, China, Vietnam, and many other nations whose economies were state-controlled and centrally planned are now fertile ground for growing small businesses. Even in Scotland, a country not traditionally recognized as a hotbed of entrepreneurial activity, entrepreneurs of all ages are hard at work.

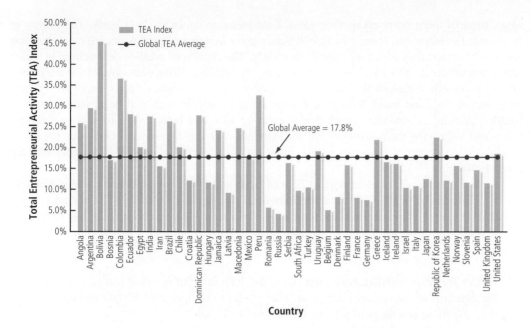

FIGURE 1.1

Entrepreneurial Activity Across the Globe

Source: Based on Niels Bosma, Kent Jones, Erkko Autio, and Jonathan Levie, Global Entrepreneurship Monitor 2007 Executive Report, Babson College, London School of Business, and Global Entrepreneurship Research Consortium, 2008, p.16.

Fraser Doherty, a student at the University of Strathclyde in Glasgow, started making jams using a secret family recipe that had been handed down through the generations and then selling them at local shops, farmers markets, and online when he was just 14 years old. Four years later, Doherty's company, Doherty's Preserves, was producing—from his parents' home—1,000 jars of jams and marmalades each week under the brand SuperJam. As sales grew beyond the capacity of the family kitchen, Doherty decided to move his business into a small factory in Herefordshire. SuperJam products now appear on the shelves of more than 600 supermarkets in the United Kingdom, and Doherty, just 19, recently won first place in the Global Student Entrepreneur Award competition. "[Going into business] is a huge learning opportunity and a lot of fun," he says.[7]

ENTREPRENEURIAL PROFILE

Fraser Doherty: Doherty's Preserves

Wherever they may choose to launch their companies, these business builders continue to embark on one of the most exhilarating—and one of the most frightening—adventures ever known: launching a business. It's never easy, but it can be incredibly rewarding, both financially and emotionally. It can be both thrilling and dangerous, like living life without a safety net. Still, true entrepreneurs see owning a business as the real measure of success. Indeed, entrepreneurship often provides the only avenue for success to those who otherwise might have been denied the opportunity.

Who are these entrepreneurs, and what drives them to work so hard with no guarantee of success? What forces lead them to risk so much and to make so many sacrifices in an attempt to achieve an ideal? Why are they willing to give up the security of a steady paycheck working for someone else to become the last person to be paid in their own companies? This chapter will examine the entrepreneur, the driving force behind the American economy.

What Is an Entrepreneur?

LO 2

Describe the entrepreneurial profile.

An **entrepreneur** is one who creates a new business in the face of risk and uncertainty for the purpose of achieving profit and growth by identifying significant opportunities and assembling the necessary resources to capitalize on them. Although many people come up with great business

Entrepreneur
one who creates a new business in the face of risk and uncertainty for the purpose of achieving profit and growth by identifying significant opportunities and assembling the necessary resources to capitalize on them.

ideas, most of them never act on their ideas. Entrepreneurs do. In his 1911 book, *The Theory of Economic Development*, economist Joseph Schumpeter said that entrepreneurs are more than just business creators; they are change agents in society. The process of creative destruction, in which entrepreneurs create new ideas and new businesses that make existing ones obsolete, is a sign of a vibrant economy. Although this constant churn of businesses—some rising, others sinking, new ones succeeding, and many failing—concerns some people, in reality, it is an indication of a healthy, growing, economic system that is creating new and better ways of serving people's needs and improving their quality of life and standard of living. Schumpeter compared the list of leading entrepreneurs to a popular hotel's guest list: "always full of people, but people who are forever changing."[8]

Researchers have invested a great deal of time and effort over the last few decades trying to paint a clear picture of "the entrepreneurial personality." Although these studies have identified several characteristics entrepreneurs tend to exhibit, none of them has isolated a set of traits required for success. We now turn to a brief summary of the entrepreneurial profile.[9]

1. *Desire for responsibility.* Entrepreneurs feel a deep sense of personal responsibility for the outcome of the ventures they start. They prefer to be in control of their resources, and they use those resources to achieve self-determined goals.

2. *Preference for moderate risk.* Entrepreneurs are not wild risk takers but are instead calculated risk takers. A study of the founders of the businesses listed as *Inc.* magazine's fastest-growing companies found no correlation between risk tolerance and entrepreneurship. "The belief that entrepreneurs are big risk takers just isn't true," says researcher and former *Inc.* 500 CEO Keith McFarland.[10] Unlike "high-rolling, riverboat" gamblers, entrepreneurs rarely gamble. Their goals may appear to be high—even impossible—in others' eyes, but entrepreneurs see the situation from a different perspective and believe that their goals are realistic and attainable. They usually spot opportunities in areas that reflect their knowledge, backgrounds, and experiences, which increases their probability of success. One writer observes

   > Entrepreneurship is not the same thing as throwing darts and hoping for the best. It is about planning and taking calculated risks based upon knowledge of the market, the available resources or products, and a predetermined measure of the potential for success.[11]

   In other words, successful entrepreneurs are not as much risk *takers* as they are risk *eliminators*, removing as many obstacles to the successful launch of their ventures as possible. One of the most successful ways of eliminating risks is to build a solid business plan for a venture.

3. *Confidence in their ability to succeed.* Entrepreneurs typically have an abundance of confidence in their ability to succeed and are confident that they chose the correct career path. A recent American Express Open Ages Survey reports that 90 percent of Baby Boomer business owners and 76 percent of Generation *Y* business owners said that their decision to go into business was the right one.[12] Entrepreneurs' high levels of optimism may explain why some of the most successful entrepreneurs have failed in business–often more than once–before finally succeeding.

4. *Desire for immediate feedback.* Entrepreneurs enjoy the challenge of running a business, and they like to know how they are doing and are constantly looking for feedback. "I love being an entrepreneur," says Nick Gleason, co-founder of CitySoft Inc., a Web site design firm based in Cambridge, Massachusetts. "There's something about the sheer creativity and challenge of it that I like."[13]

5. *High level of energy.* Entrepreneurs are more energetic than the average person. That energy may be a critical factor given the incredible effort required to launch a start-up company. Long hours and hard work are the rule rather than the exception, and the pace can be grueling. According to the American Express Open study, 66 percent of Generation *Y* business owners and 58 percent of Baby Boomer owners work 10 or more hours a day and do so six days a week.[14]

6. *Future orientation.* Entrepreneurs have a well-defined sense of searching for opportunities. They look ahead and are less concerned with what they did yesterday than with what they might do tomorrow. Not satisfied to sit back and revel in their success, real entrepreneurs stay focused on the future.

Tom Stemberg, founder of the Staples office supply chain, went on to start Zoots, a 54-store dry cleaning chain (he came up with the idea after a dry cleaners lost one of his Brooks Brothers dress shirts) and Olly Shoes, a small chain of children's shoe stores (he came up with the idea after a frustrating experience shopping for shoes for his four boys).

Entrepreneurs see potential where most people see only problems or nothing at all, a characteristic that often makes them the objects of ridicule (at least until their ideas become huge successes). Whereas traditional managers are concerned with managing available *resources*, entrepreneurs are more interested in spotting and capitalizing on *opportunities*. In the United States 62 percent of those engaged in entrepreneurial activity are **opportunity entrepreneurs,** those who start businesses because they spot an opportunity in the marketplace, compared to **necessity entrepreneurs,** those who start businesses because they cannot find work any other way. (Denmark leads the world with 81 percent opportunity entrepreneurs.)[15]

opportunity entrepreneurs
entrepreneurs who start businesses because they spot an opportunity in the marketplace.

necessity entrepreneurs
entrepreneurs who start businesses because they cannot find work any other way.

Serial entrepreneurs, those who repeatedly start businesses and grow them to a sustainable size before striking out again, push this characteristic to the maximum. The majority of serial entrepreneurs are *leapfroggers*, people who start a company, manage its growth until they get bored, and then sell it to start another. A few are *jugglers* (or *parallel entrepreneurs*), people who start and manage several companies at once. The American Express Open study reports that 59 percent of Generation Y business owners and 33 percent of Baby Boomer owners are or plan to be serial entrepreneurs.

serial entrepreneurs
entrepreneurs who repeatedly start businesses and grow them to a sustainable size before striking out again.

Jen Groover is a classic serial entrepreneur. After launching a wellness and fitness center, Groover has gone on to build other businesses around her ability to generate ideas. She markets the Butler Bag, an attractive bag of her own design that doubles as a purse or as a carry-on bag and that provides compartments to keep contents organized. Groover also operates Jen Groover Productions, a company that creates ideas on a multitude of topics–from toys and tools to strategies and speeches. The Broomall, Pennsylvania-based company has several dozen projects in various stages of development, and Groover also has signed a licensing agreement with a brand management company. She also is an author and manages to devote time to help young girls learn leadership skills through the Girls Take Charge program. Discussing her work, Groover says, "Every day, I feel like I am going to play. There's so much happiness and reward that it outweighs any stress."[16]

Jen Groover Productions

It's almost as if serial entrepreneurs are addicted to launching businesses. "Starting a company is a very imaginative, innovative, energy-driven, fun process," says Dick Kouri, who has started 12 companies in his career and now teaches entrepreneurship at the University of North Carolina. "Serial entrepreneurs can't wait to do it again."[17]

7. *Skill at organizing.* Building a company "from scratch" is much like piecing together a giant jigsaw puzzle. Entrepreneurs know how to put the right people together to accomplish

a task. Effectively combining people and jobs enables entrepreneurs to transform their visions into reality.

8. *Value of achievement over money.* One of the most common misconceptions about entrepreneurs is that they are driven wholly by the desire to make money. To the contrary, *achievement* seems to be entrepreneurs' primary motivating force; money is simply a way of "keeping score" of accomplishments—a symbol of achievement. What drives entrepreneurs goes much deeper than just the desire for wealth. Economist Joseph Schumpeter claimed that entrepreneurs have "the will to conquer, the impulse to fight, to prove oneself superior to others, to succeed for the sake, not of the fruits of success, but of success itself." Entrepreneurs experience "the joy of creating, of getting things done, or simply of exercising one's energy and ingenuity."[18]

Other characteristics frequently exhibited by entrepreneurs include:

High degree of commitment. Entrepreneurship is hard work, and launching a company successfully requires total commitment from an entrepreneur. Business founders often immerse themselves completely in their companies. Most entrepreneurs have to overcome seemingly insurmountable barriers to launch a company and to keep it growing. That requires commitment.

Tolerance for ambiguity. Entrepreneurs tend to have a high tolerance for ambiguous, ever-changing situations, the environment in which they most often operate. This ability to handle uncertainty is critical because these business builders constantly make decisions using new, sometimes conflicting information gleaned from a variety of unfamiliar sources. Based on his research, entrepreneurial expert Amar Bhidé says that entrepreneurs exhibit "a willingness to jump into things when it's hard to even imagine what the possible set of outcomes will be."[19]

Flexibility. One hallmark of true entrepreneurs is their ability to adapt to the changing demands of their customers and their businesses. In this rapidly changing global economy, rigidity often leads to failure. As our society, its people, and their tastes change, entrepreneurs also must be willing to adapt their businesses to meet those changes. When their ideas fail to live up to their expectations, successful entrepreneurs change them!

ENTREPRENEURIAL PROFILE _____

Ed Cox: S.O.S.

In 1917, Ed Cox invented a pre-soaped steel-wool scouring pad that was ideal for cleaning pots, and he used it as a "calling card" in his sales calls. Although his efforts at selling pots proved futile, Cox noticed how often his prospects asked for the soap pads. He quickly forgot about selling pots, shifted his focus to selling the scouring pads, which his wife had named S.O.S. ("Save Our Saucepans"), and went on to start a business that still thrives.[20]

Tenacity. Obstacles, obstructions, and defeat typically do not dissuade entrepreneurs from doggedly pursuing their visions. They simply keep trying. Noting the obstacles that entrepreneurs must overcome, economist Joseph Schumpeter argued that success is "a feat not of intellect but of will." Milton Hershey's first three candy-making businesses failed before he created the Lancaster Caramel Company, which became very successful and allowed him to build the chocolate manufacturing business that still carries his name and that remains one of the best known candy makers in the world.[21]

What conclusion can we draw from the volumes of research conducted on the entrepreneurial personality? Entrepreneurs are not of one mold; no one set of characteristics can predict who will become entrepreneurs and whether or not they will succeed. Indeed, *diversity* seems to be a central characteristic of entrepreneurs. One astute observer of the entrepreneurial personality explains, "Business owners are a culture unto themselves—strong, individualistic people who scorn convention—and nowadays, they're driving the global economy."[22] Indeed, entrepreneurs tend to be nonconformists, a characteristic that seems to be central to their views of the world and to their success.

As you can see from the examples in this chapter, *anyone*, regardless of age, race, gender, color, national origin, or any other characteristic, can become an entrepreneur (although not everyone should). There are no limitations on this form of economic expression. Entrepreneurship is not a mystery; it is a practical discipline. Entrepreneurship is not a genetic trait; it is a skill that most people can learn. It has become a very common vocation. The editors of *Inc.* magazine claim, "Entrepreneurship is more mundane than it's sometimes portrayed.... You don't need to be a person of mythical proportions to be very, very successful in building a company."[23]

The Benefits of Entrepreneurship

Surveys show that owners of small businesses believe they work harder, earn more money, and are more satisfied than if they worked for someone else. Before launching any business venture, every potential entrepreneur should consider the benefits of small business ownership.

Opportunity to Create Your Own Destiny

Owning a business provides entrepreneurs the independence and the opportunity to achieve what is important to them. Entrepreneurs want to "call the shots" in their lives, and they use their businesses to make that desire a reality.

The youngest of three children, Vivek Ranadive grew up in Mumbai, India, and dreamed of studying in the United States, at MIT. Raised to be competitive and to excel at whatever he did, Ranadive achieved his goal and enrolled at MIT. While there, he launched his first business in which he scouted ads for companies looking to hire computer programmers and then contacted the companies to offer the programming services of MIT students whom he had recruited. After earning an MBA from Harvard, Ranadive started a computer consulting company and then launched Tibco Finance Technology, a company that provides a variety of business applications software, which he still manages. A successful author, Ranadive says that at a very early age, he decided that "I don't want to work for somebody else. Instead, I want to be the master of my own destiny."[24]

ENTREPRENEURIAL PROFILE

Vivek Ranadive: Tibco Finance Technology

Entrepreneurs: Creating Their Own Dream Jobs

Although a career in corporate America can be rewarding, entrepreneurs discover that owning their own companies, controlling their own destinies, and working in their dream jobs can be even more so. Consider the following examples.

An Ocean in the Desert

Linda Nelson and her husband, George Sanders, are world-class scuba divers who own a dive shop near Grantsville, Utah, which is 4,250 feet above sea level and 900 miles away from the nearest ocean! The couple wanted to find a way to offer classes at a training facility that would complement their dive shop, but rather than build a traditional pool, they built their own "ocean" in the desert. Looking at geothermal maps, Nelson realized that saltwater springs ran beneath the ground that they had chosen as

their location. Sanders, who also owned a construction company, had the equipment to excavate the site, and the couple set out to build their desert ocean. "Nobody thought we could do it," laughs Nelson.

The geo-thermally heated man-made ocean, named Bonneville Seabase, is 200 yards across at its widest point, contains bays as deep as 62 feet, and is home to saltwater species such as nurse sharks, angel fish, tangs, puffers, and others. Scuba divers and snorkelers come to Bonneville Seabase from across the United States, and Nelson and Sanders have hosted guests from as far away as Australia and Thailand. Annual sales exceed $300,000.

Dream Cars

Fractional ownership, in which a person buys the right to use an asset for a certain number of days each year, started years ago in real estate before moving into private jets, yachts, and other luxury items. Blas Garcia Moros, a retired Microsoft executive, saw the opportunity to apply fractional ownership to one of his passions, exotic cars. Shortly after retiring, Moros was shopping for a new Ferrari but was so impressed with other makes of high performance cars that he had difficulty deciding which one to buy. He soon realized that he was not the only exotic car buff who faced the same issue and, with his friend Larry Murrah, a former owner of several luxury car dealerships, he decided to launch Collexium, a company that offers upscale customers the chance to purchase fractional ownership in ten luxury and high performance sports cars, including two Ferraris, two Lamborghinis, a Lotus Elise, and two Bentleys. For an initiation fee of $15,000 and an annual subscription rate $15,000, Collexium members can drive any of the ten cars whenever they want up to 30 days a year. Currently, Moros operates only in South Florida but has plans to expand into other warm-weather cities with significant populations of wealthy residents. "Collexium offers auto enthusiasts what wine enthusiasts have: great variety and an easy way to enjoy it," says Moros.

Custom Motorcycles

Jesse James, a distant relative of the famous outlaw from the 1880s, has become quite famous in his own right and also has a bit of a "bad boy" reputation. Unlike his bandit relative, however, the modern James is most famous for building custom motorcycles at his 250,000-square-foot shop in Long Beach, California. James, who starred in the hit television show *Monster Garage*, started West Coast Choppers in 1993 in a corner of his mother's garage. "I'm just a glorified welder," says James, shrugging his wide shoulders as if brushing off any attempt at imposing fame on him. "I build things."

He *does* build things. Today, James custom-builds motorcycles for clients from across the globe, including a recent $300,000 version of gleaming silver with a sidecar for Robert Wheeler, the CEO of Airstream, the company that makes the classic travel trailers, to commemorate the company's seventy-fifth anniversary. James's company has hand-built custom motorcycles for well-known clients such as Kid Rock, Shaquille O'Neal, and Keanu Reeves as well as for average citizens. Doing what he loves to do and doing it well have resulted in a three-year backlog of customer orders. James actually started on his career at age nine, when he took a Schwinn Straight Bar bicycle that his father had given him and decked it out with fresh chrome and pinstriping and sold it at a collector's show for $850. "It's not that different from what I do now," James says, "except now I get 125 grand each." Indeed, each bike that West Coast Choppers builds is like a Savile Row suit, custom-fit to its owner and his or her personality, and prices typically range from $50,000 to $150,000. West Coast Choppers generates $5 million in annual sales.

1. Explain how these entrepreneurs exhibit the entrepreneurial spirit.
2. What benefits do these entrepreneurs reap from owning their own businesses? What disadvantages do they face?
3. What career lessons can you learn from these entrepreneurs?

Sources: Adapted from Jessica Chen, "Smart Ideas: Swell on Wheels," *Entrepreneur*, October 2007, pp. 134-136; Dan Eldridge, "The Candywoman Can," *Paste*, April 2008, p. 16; Sara Wilson, "More Than a Mirage," *Entrepreneur*, July 2007, p. 110; Jeff Garigliano, "Own a Lamborghini–Part-Time," *FSB*, February 2007, pp. 90-93; Arlyn Tobias Gajilan, "The Outlaw," *FSB*, March 2003, http://money.cnn.com/magazines/fsb/fsb_archive/2003/03/01/338769/index.html; Dirk Smillie, "Hooligan Chic," *Forbes*, December 24, 2007, pp. 87–92.

Like Vivek Ranadive, entrepreneurs reap the intrinsic rewards of knowing they are the driving forces behind their businesses.

Opportunity to Make a Difference

social entrepreneurs
people who start businesses that seek innovative solutions to some of society's most vexing problems.

Increasingly, entrepreneurs are starting businesses because they see an opportunity to make a difference in a cause that is important to them. Known as **social entrepreneurs,** these business builders seek innovative solutions to some of society's most vexing problems. Whether it is providing low-cost, sturdy housing for families in developing countries or establishing a recycling program to preserve Earth's limited resources, these entrepreneurs are finding ways to combine their concerns for social issues and their desire to earn a good living.

ENTREPRENEURIAL PROFILE

Bob Shallenberger & John Cavanaugh: Highland Homes

Bob Shallenberger and John Cavanaugh, former fraternity brothers at St. Louis University, launched Highland Homes in St. Louis in 2003 with the idea of differentiating their business from the competition by focusing on building environmentally friendly houses. Not only do their construction methods reduce the impact on the environment by using "green" techniques, but the houses they build also benefit from the increased efficiency with which they use energy, water, and other materials. "[Green building] is difficult, and it's expensive to learn," says Cavanaugh. "It's challenging, but we see it as a big growth segment of the market. Being recognized as the top green residential builder in the country is the goal for us."[25]

Opportunity to Reach Your Full Potential

Too many people find their work boring, unchallenging, and unexciting. But not entrepreneurs! To them, there is little difference between work and play; the two are synonymous. Entrepreneurs' businesses become their instruments for self-expression and self-actualization. They know that the only boundaries on their success are those imposed by their own creativity, enthusiasm, and vision. Owning a business gives them a sense of empowerment.

Opportunity to Reap Impressive Profits

Although money is not the primary force driving most entrepreneurs, the profits their businesses can earn are an important motivating factor in their decisions to launch companies. Most entrepreneurs never become super-rich, but many of them do become quite wealthy. In fact, nearly 75 percent of those on the *Forbes* list of the 400 richest Americans are first-generation entrepreneurs![26] People who own their own businesses are more likely to be millionaires than those who are employed by others. According to Russ Alan Prince and Lewis Schiff, authors of *The Middle Class Millionaire*, more than 80 percent of middle class millionaires, those people with a net worth between $1 million and $10 million, own their own businesses or are part of professional partnerships. (They also work an average of 70 hours a week.)[27] Indeed, the typical millionaire's business is not a glamorous, high-tech enterprise; more often, it is something much less glamorous—scrap metal, welding, auctioneering, garbage collection, and the like.

Friends since high school, Kelly Flatley and Brendan Synnott in 2003 launched Bear Naked, a Connecticut-based small company that sells all-natural granola products. Flatley and Synnott moved in with their parents and invested $3,500 each to rent space in a commercial kitchen. Using the recipe that Flatley had developed while in college to make a healthy granola mix, the pair handed out samples of their product at triathlons and called on managers at grocery stores in Connecticut to create "buzz" about their granola. Flatley and Synnott achieved a major breakthrough when they showed up at the headquarters of Stew Leonard's, a local chain of grocery stores, at 7 a.m. with their granola, milk, fruit, and yogurt and announced to CEO Stew Leonard, "We brought you breakfast!" After spending two hours with the young entrepreneurs, Leonard agreed to put Bear Naked granola on his store shelves. Today, Bear Naked produces more than 40,000 pounds of granola each day, and its products are sold at Kroger, Costco, Safeway, Target, Whole Foods, and other retailers. Flatley and Synnott recently sold Bear Naked to industry giant Kellogg's Kashi subsidiary for $122 million, making them both millionaires before they turned 30![28]

ENTREPRENEURIAL PROFILE

Kelly Flatley & Brendan Synnott: Bear Naked

Opportunity to Contribute to Society and Be Recognized for Your Efforts

Often, small business owners are among the most respected and most trusted members of their communities. Business deals based on trust and mutual respect are the hallmark of many established small companies. These owners enjoy the trust and recognition they receive from the customers and the communities they have served faithfully over the years. A Harris Interactive survey that measures the level of confidence people have in different institutions shows that small business topped the list and were the only institution to win the trust of a majority of Americans.[29]

Playing a vital role in their local business systems and knowing that their work has a significant impact on how smoothly our nation's economy functions is yet another reward for small business managers. One survey reports that 72 percent of business owners say that what they enjoy most about being a business owner is contributing to the local community.[30]

Opportunity to Do What You Enjoy and Have Fun at It

A common sentiment among small business owners is that their work really isn't work. Most successful entrepreneurs choose to enter their particular business fields because they have an interest in them and enjoy those lines of work. They have made their avocations (hobbies) their vocations (work) and are glad they did! These entrepreneurs are living Harvey McKay's advice: "Find a job doing what you love, and you'll never have to work a day in your life." The journey rather than the destination is the entrepreneur's greatest reward. "Starting a company is very hard to do," says entrepreneur and small business researcher David Birch. "The risks are enormous; the anxiety is enormous. The only business you should start is one in which have a huge interest, or else you won't have the persistence to stick with it. Get into [a business] because you're fanatically interested in it."[31]

John Knox was managing a farm equipment company in which he owned a part interest, but he and his son Brian really enjoyed competitive tractor pulling, a sport in which souped-up tractors compete to pull weighted sleds the greatest distance. Knox and his wife, Rodalyn, had a background in drag racing, and in 1981 John and Brian built a 1,200 horsepower engine for a Massey Ferguson tractor and named it the "Sassy Massey." Soon, John decided to sell his share of the farm equipment company and pursue his passion of building engines for tractor pulling competitions, monster truck exhibitions, and drag racing full time. Each engine takes about 40 hours to build, and the Knox's family-owned business, Sassy Engines, builds about 15 engines a year for customers all across the globe, bringing in sales of $1.3 million.[32]

Not only have the Knoxes found a way to make a living, but what is more important, they are doing something they love!

The Potential Drawbacks of Entrepreneurship

Although owning a business has many benefits and provides many opportunities, anyone planning to enter the world of entrepreneurship should be aware of its potential drawbacks. Individuals who prefer the security of a steady paycheck, a comprehensive benefit package, a two-week paid vacation, and the support of a corporate staff probably should not go into business for themselves. Some of the disadvantages of entrepreneurship include the following:

Uncertainty of Income

Opening and running a business provides no guarantee that an entrepreneur will earn enough money to survive. Some small businesses barely earn enough to provide the owner-manager with an adequate income. In the early days of a start-up, a business often cannot provide an attractive salary for its owner and meet all of its financial obligations, which means that the entrepreneur may have to live on savings. The steady income that comes with working for someone else is absent because the owner is always the last one to be paid. One California couple left their corporate jobs that together brought in $120,000 a year to start a small vineyard; their combined income in their first year of business: $30,000.

Risk of Losing Your Entire Investment

Business failure can lead to financial ruin for an entrepreneur, and the small business failure rate is relatively high. According to a study by the National Federation of Independent Businesses (NFIB), 35 percent of new businesses fail within two years, and 54 percent shut down within four years. Within six years, 64 percent of new businesses will have folded. Studies also show that when a company creates at least one job in its early years, the probability of failure after six years plummets to 35 percent![33]

Before "reaching for the golden ring," entrepreneurs should ask themselves if they can cope psychologically with the consequences of failure:

- What is the worst that could happen if I open my business and it fails?
- How likely is the worst to happen? (Am I truly prepared to launch my business?)
- What can I do to lower the risk of my business failing?
- If my business were to fail, what is my contingency plan for coping?

Long Hours and Hard Work

Business start-ups often demand long hours from their owners. The average small business owner works 52 hours a week, compared to the 41.1 hours per week the typical U.S. production employee works.[34] In many start-ups, six- or seven-day workweeks with no paid vacations are the norm. In fact, a survey by American Express found that only 59 percent of small business owners were planning to take a summer vacation (and one-third of those planned to combine their vacations with a business trip). The primary reason entrepreneurs don't take vacations? "Too busy."[35] The demands of owning a business make achieving work-life balance difficult for entrepreneurs. "You must have stamina to see it through," says Chantelle Ludski, founder of London-based fresh!, an organic food company. "I put in many 16-hour workdays. Holidays and time off are things that go out the window!"[36]

Lower Quality of Life Until the Business Gets Established

The long hours and hard work needed to launch a company can take their toll on the other aspects of an entrepreneur's life. Business owners often find that their roles as husbands or wives and fathers or mothers take a back seat to their roles as company founders. In fact, according to a survey by American Express, 67 percent of entrepreneurs say that owning a business requires them to make sacrifices, most often in the areas of family relationships and friendships.[37] Part of the problem is that half of all entrepreneurs launch their businesses between the ages of 25 and 39, just when they start their families (see Figure 1.2). As a result, marriages, families, and friendships are too often casualties of small business ownership.

High Levels of Stress

Starting and managing a business can be an incredibly rewarding experience, but it also can be a highly stressful one. Entrepreneurs often have made significant investments in their companies, have left behind the safety and security of a steady paycheck, and have mortgaged everything they own to get into business. Failure may mean total financial ruin, and that creates intense levels of stress and anxiety! Sometimes entrepreneurs unnecessarily bear the burden of managing alone because they cannot bring themselves to delegate authority and responsibility to others in the company, even though their employees are capable.

Complete Responsibility

It's great to be the boss, but many entrepreneurs find that they must make decisions on issues about which they are not really knowledgeable. Many business owners have difficulty finding

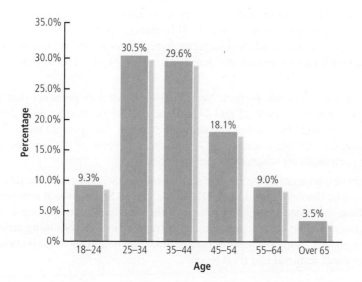

FIGURE 1.2

Entrepreneur's Age at Business Formation

Source: Based on Global Entrepreneurship Monitor, 2007.

advisors. A recent national small business poll conducted by the NFIB found that 34 percent of business owners have no one person to turn to for help when making a critical business decision.[38] When there is no one to ask, the pressure can build quickly. The realization that the decisions they make are the cause of their company's success or failure has a devastating effect on some people.

Discouragement

Launching a business is a substantial undertaking that requires a great deal of dedication, discipline, and tenacity. Along the way to building a successful business, entrepreneurs will run headlong into many different obstacles, some of which appear to be insurmountable. In the face of such difficulties, discouragement and disillusionment are common emotions. Successful entrepreneurs know that every business encounters rough spots along the way, and they wade through difficult times with lots of hard work and an abundant reserve of optimism.

Despite the challenges that starting and running a business pose, entrepreneurs are very satisfied with their career choices. The Wells Fargo/Gallup Small Business Index reports that 84 percent of small business owners say that if they were choosing a career again, they would still become small business owners.[39] Most entrepreneurs are so happy with their work that they want to continue it indefinitely. In fact, just 11 percent of entrepreneurs in a recent survey say that they intend to retire at all.[40]

Behind the Boom: What's Feeding the Entrepreneurial Fire

LO 4

Explain the forces that are driving the growth of entrepreneurship.

What forces are driving this entrepreneurial trend in our economy? Which factors have led to this age of entrepreneurship? Some of the most significant ones include the following:

Entrepreneurs as heroes. An intangible but very important factor is the attitude that Americans have toward entrepreneurs. As a nation we have raised them to hero status and have held out their accomplishments as models to follow. Business founders such as Bill Gates (Microsoft Corporation), Oprah Winfrey (Harpo Productions and Oxygen Media), Jeff Bezos (Amazon.com), Steve Jobs (Apple), and Phil Knight (Nike) are to entrepreneurship what Tiger Woods and Kevin Garnett are to sports.

Entrepreneurial education. Colleges and universities have discovered that entrepreneurship is an extremely popular course of study. Disillusioned with corporate America's downsized job offerings and less promising career paths, a rapidly growing number of students sees owning a business as their best career option. Growing numbers of students enroll in college knowing that they want to start their own companies rather than considering entrepreneurship as a possibility later in life; indeed, many are starting companies while they are in college. Today more than 3,000 colleges and universities offer courses in entrepreneurship and small business, up from just 16 in 1970. More than 200,000 students are enrolled in entrepreneurship courses, and many colleges and universities have difficulty meeting the demand for courses in entrepreneurship and small business.[41]

Demographic and economic factors. Nearly two-thirds of entrepreneurs start their businesses between the ages of 25 and 44, and the number of Americans in that age range currently is 85 million! In addition, the economic growth that spanned most of the last 25 years created a significant amount of wealth among people of this age group and many business opportunities on which they can capitalize.

Shift to a service economy. The service sector produces 80 percent of the jobs and 68 percent of the Gross Domestic Product (GDP) in the United States, which represents a sharp rise from just a decade ago.[42] Because of their relatively low start-up costs, service businesses have become very popular among entrepreneurs. The booming service sector continues to provide many business opportunities, from health care and computer maintenance to pet waste removal and iPod repair.

While tinkering with his iPod, Ben Levy broke it and began searching online forums for repair sources. He discovered that many other iPod owners faced the same problem and that Apple's warranty did not cover the repairs and the repairs were very expensive. Sensing an opportunity, Levy and his friend Aaron Vronko bought several broken iPods and taught themselves to repair them. Before long, they hired other repair workers and launched a Web site, RapidRepair.com, with $1,500 from their personal savings. Today, the 15-employee company, which is based in Kalamazoo, Michigan, receives 500 iPods and other small electronic devices each week from all across the United States and 65 countries around the world and generates annual sales of more than $3 million.[43]

Technology advancements. With the help of modern business machines such as personal computers, laptop computers, fax machines, copiers, color printers, answering machines, and voice mail, even one person working at home can look like a big business. At one time, the high cost of such technological wizardry made it impossible for small businesses to compete with larger companies that could afford the hardware. Today, however, powerful computers and communication equipment are priced within the budgets of even the smallest businesses. Although entrepreneurs may not be able to manufacture heavy equipment in their spare bedrooms, they can run a service- or information-based company from their homes—or almost anywhere—very effectively and look like any *Fortune* 500 company to customers and clients. Jimbo Wales, founder of Wikipedia, says, "Wherever my laptop is, that's my office."[44]

Independent lifestyle. Entrepreneurship fits the way Americans want to live—independent and self-sustaining. People want the freedom to choose where they live, the hours they work, and what they do. Although financial security remains an important goal for most entrepreneurs, many place top priority on lifestyle issues such as more time with family and friends, more leisure time, and more control over work-related stress.

E-Commerce and the World Wide Web. The proliferation of the **World Wide Web,** the vast network that links computers around the globe via the Internet and opens up oceans of information to its users, has spawned thousands of entrepreneurial ventures since its beginning in 1993. Online retail sales, which currently account for five percent of total retail sales, are forecast to continue to grow rapidly (see Figure 1.3), creating many opportunities for Web-savvy entrepreneurs. Travel services, computer hardware and software, books, music, videos, and consumer electronics are among the best-selling items on the Web, but entrepreneurs are learning that they can use this powerful tool to sell just about anything! In fact, entrepreneurs are using the Web to sell services, such as tours to the sites of their favorite television shows and movies (including *Sex and the City* and *The Sopranos*) and pajama parties for women, and products, such as crocheted cotton

ENTREPRENEURIAL
PROFILE_____

Ben Levy & Aaron
Vronko:
RapidRepair.com

World Wide Web
the vast network that links computers around the globe via the Internet and opens up oceans of information to its users and is a major business opportunity for entrepreneurs.

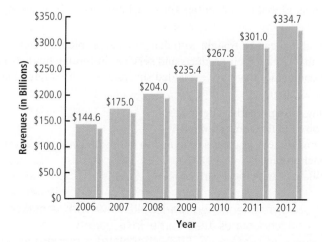

FIGURE 1.3

U.S. Retail E-Commerce Revenues

Source: Based on Forrester Research, 2008.

thong underwear and recordings by musicians who perform for tips in the subway of New York City.[45]

Unfortunately, many small business owners have not yet tapped the power of the Web. According to a study by the National Small Business Association, 60 percent of small businesses have Web sites, nearly double the number that had Web sites in 1997. Among those small companies that have created Web sites, only 35 percent are actually engaged in e-commerce.[46] Small companies that do conduct e-commerce typically reap benefits quickly, however, in the form of new customers and increased sales. These "net-preneurs" are using the Web to connect with their existing customers and, ultimately, to attract new ones.

ENTREPRENEURIAL PROFILE

Georgette Blau: On Location Tours

In 1999, Georgette Blau was living in New York City and working as an editor for a publishing house. On her way home, she often walked by the apartment building that was featured on the television show *The Jefferson's*, from the 1970s and 80s. Blau came up with the idea of offering tours to sites around the city that had been featured in television shows and movies. Blau discovered that New York City is one of the most filmed cities in the world and has been the location for many hit television shows and movies. In addition, the city hosts 43.8 million tourists a year, each spending an average of $190 per day. Using $3,000 from her savings, she launched a weekend business, the Scene on TV Tour, in which she served as owner and tour guide. In 2001, Blau quit her job as an editor and launched a tour based on the popular television show *The Sopranos*, a move that generated plenty of buzz and sales for her company. Blau's company, now called On Location Tours, books most of its tours, including its popular *Sex and the City* Tour, through its Web site and generates annual sales of more than $1 million. Now with 31 employees, Blau no longer conducts tours, choosing instead to manage her company's growth, which she plans to fuel by launching similar tours in Washington, DC.[47]

International opportunities. No longer are small businesses limited to pursuing customers within their own borders. The shift to a global economy has opened the door to tremendous business opportunities for entrepreneurs willing to reach across the globe. Although the United States is an attractive market for entrepreneurs, approximately 95 percent of the world's population lives outside its borders. The emergence of potential markets across the globe and crumbling barriers to international business because of trade agreements have opened the world to entrepreneurs who are looking for new customers. Whereas companies once had to grow into global markets, today small businesses can have a global scope from their inception. Small companies comprise 97 percent of all businesses engaged in exporting, yet they account for only 29 percent of the nation's export sales.[48] Most small companies do not take advantage of export opportunities, often because their owners don't know how or where to start an export initiative. Although terrorism and regional recessions remain challenges to international trade, global opportunities for small businesses have a long-term positive outlook.

Although going global can be fraught with dangers and problems, many entrepreneurs are discovering that selling their products and services in foreign markets is really not so difficult. Small companies that have expanded successfully into foreign markets tend to rely on the following strategies:

- Researching foreign markets thoroughly.
- Focusing on a single country initially.
- Utilizing government resources designed to help small companies establish an international presence.
- Forging alliances with local partners.

ENTREPRENEURIAL PROFILE

Maribel Lieberman: MarieBelle New York

In 2001, Maribel Lieberman launched MarieBelle New York, a maker of high-quality, exquisitely decorated chocolates that come in a variety of exotic flavors such as cinnamon, Earl Grey, and cardamom. "[My chocolate] is modern in both design and flavor because I infuse MarieBelle chocolate with exotic ingredients like saffron and passion fruit," she says. Even though the upscale chocolates are considered pricey for most chocolate lovers ($37 for a one-pound tin and $15 for a single chocolate bar), MarieBelle's domestic sales have increased steadily as the company's reputation has grown. Lieberman's goal was to take her company into foreign markets as well. While staying at the ritzy George W hotel in Paris, Lieberman approached the food and beverage manager and the chef about selling her company's products. One sip of her company's hot chocolate convinced them to carry MarieBelle's chocolates. In addition to her company's two New York City locations, Lieberman now has outlets in several countries. "I sell them at Bergdorf's, the Four Seasons Hotel, Japan, France, and all over Europe," says Lieberman, a former fashion designer and self-taught chef.[49]

College: A Great Place to Launch a Business

For growing numbers of students, college is not just a time of learning, partying, and growing into young adulthood; it is fast becoming a place for building a business. More than 3,000 colleges and universities offer courses in entrepreneurship and small business management to more than 200,000 students, and many of them have trouble keeping up with demand for these classes. "Students used to come to college and assume that five to ten years down the road, they'd start a business," says Gerry Hills, co-founder of the Collegiate Entrepreneurs Organization (CEO). "[Today], they come in preparing to get ideas and launch."

Many of these collegiate entrepreneurs' ideas come from their college experience itself. Russell D'Souza and Jon Groetzinger, students at Dartmouth College, watched fellow students discard perfectly good dorm furniture at the end of each academic year rather than move it or pay to store it over the summer. "We realized there's a great market for a furniture rental company that provides everything students need for their dorms," says D'Souza. The two student entrepreneurs used their personal savings to launch their company, Evolving Vox, and to purchase modern dorm room essentials such as flat-screen televisions, DVD players, compact refrigerators, lamps, telephones, chairs, and futons. Students place orders through the Evolving Vox Web site and receive free delivery. D'Souza and Groetzinger were overwhelmed by the initial response to their business; Dartmouth students flocked to their Web site, and sales quickly exceeded $250,000. They have expanded Evolving Vox to Brandeis University and Cornell University and have plans to open offices on 10 other campuses soon.

During his freshman year at the University of Central Florida, David Lopez was participating in an internship program with a *Fortune* 500 business. After being marched into the company cafeteria with his co-workers, who were informed that their jobs were being eliminated on the spot, Lopez decided that a career in corporate America was not for him. "I wanted the American dream," he says, "but I didn't think I'd achieve it with a corporation." Having worked for two fruit smoothie stores in high school, Lopez spotted the opportunity to open a smoothie kiosk on the campus of a

nearby community college. The initial barriers he faced were getting permission from college officials to open the kiosk and finding the financing to get the business running. Lopez badgered the college's cafeteria manager until he finally won approval to open a smoothie kiosk on campus. To get the capital he needed to set up the kiosk, Lopez maxed out his student loans (which he now admits may not have been legal) and used the $20,000 to buy equipment and cover start-up costs. Today, Lopez, who married his college sweetheart (who also was his business partner in the smoothie kiosk business), is the CEO of Froots Smoothie and has sold more than 100 franchises in the United States and abroad.

1. In addition to the normal obstacles of starting a business, what other barriers do collegiate entrepreneurs face?
2. What advantages do collegiate entrepreneurs have when launching a business?
3. What advice would you offer a fellow college student about to start a business?
4. Work with a team of your classmates to develop ideas about what your college or university could do to create a culture of entrepreneurship on your campus or in your community.

Sources: Adapted from Glenn Rifkin, "A Classroom Path to Entrepreneurship," *New York Times*, May 1, 2008, http://www.nytimes.com/2008/05/01/business/smallbusiness/01sbiz.html?_r=1&pagewanted=print&oref=slogin; Jessica Chen, "Lair Necessities," *Entrepreneur*, September 2007, p. 126; Julia Hecht, "Evolving Vox Makes Move-In Easier," *Dartmouth*, September 21, 2006, http://thedartmouth.com/2006/09/21/news/evolving/print/; Diana Ransom, "Starting Up: University Incubators," *SmartMoney's Small Biz*, January 28, 2008, http://www.smsmallbiz.com/capital/University_Incubators.html; Jenny Staletovich, "Froots Smoothie Stores Take Off," *Miami Herald*, December 3, 2007, www.miamiherald.com/business_monday/story/327485.html; Nichole L. Torres, "Big Biz on Campus," *Entrepreneur B.Y.O.B.*, December 2004, p. 130; Nichole L. Torres, "Hit the Floor," *Entrepreneur*, May 2005, p. 122; Nichole L. Torres, "Inside Job," *Entrepreneur*, March 2005, p. 132; Nichole L. Torres, "Class Acts," *Entrepreneur*, June 2003, www.entrepreneur.com/article/print/0,2361,309005,00.html; Ellen McCarthy, "A Dorm for Dreamers," *Washington Post*, October 30, 2002, p. E1; "Hinman CEOs Living-Learning Entrepreneurship Program," http://www.hinmanceos.umd.edu/.

LO 5

Explain the cultural diversity of entrepreneurship.

The Cultural Diversity of Entrepreneurship

As we have seen, virtually anyone has the potential to become an entrepreneur. Indeed, diversity is a hallmark of entrepreneurship. We now explore the diverse mix of people who make up the rich fabric of entrepreneurship.

Young Entrepreneurs

Young people are setting the pace in starting businesses. Disenchanted with their prospects in corporate America and willing to take a chance at controlling their own destinies, scores of young people are choosing entrepreneurship as their primary career path. Teenagers and those in their 20s (the Millenial Generation or Generation Y) show high levels of interest in entrepreneurship. Many members of this diverse generation, 70 million strong, are deciding that owning their own companies is the best way to create job security and to achieve the work-life balance that they seek. According to the Global Entrepreneurship Monitor (GEM), people in the United States in the 18- to 24-year-old range are launching businesses at a faster rate than those in the 35- to 44-year old range.[50] "People are realizing [that] they don't have to go to work in suits and ties and don't have to talk about budgets every day," says Ben Kaufman, founder of Mophie, a company that he named after his Golden Retrievers, Molly and Sophie, and that makes iPod accessories such as cases, armbands, and belt clips. "They can have a job they like. They can create a job for themselves." Kaufman, who founded Mophie at age 18 while still in high school, eventually landed $2 million in venture capital for his company, which was generating annual sales of $5 million before he sold it to mStation. Kaufman is now working on Kluster, a business based on a collaborative decision-making platform.[51] Because of young people such as Kaufman, the future of entrepreneurship looks very bright.

Women Entrepreneurs

Despite years of legislative effort, women still face discrimination in the work force. However, small business has been a leader in offering women opportunities for economic expression through entrepreneurship. Increasing numbers of women are discovering that the best way to break the "glass ceiling" that prevents them from rising to the top of many organizations is to start their own companies. Women entrepreneurs have even broken through the comic strip barrier. Blondie Bumstead, long a typical suburban housewife married to Dagwood, now owns her own catering business with her best friend and neighbor, Tootsie Woodly!

Although more than 83 percent of women-owned businesses are concentrated in services and retailing (as are most small businesses), female entrepreneurs are branching out rapidly into other industries. According to the Center for Women's Business Research, the fastest-growing industries for women-owned companies are wholesale, health care, arts and entertainment, and

Source: The Wall Street Journal, permission Cartoon Features Syndicate.

"Another start-up."

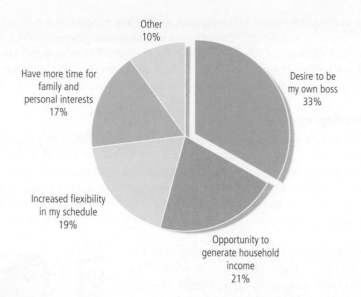

FIGURE 1.4

Why Women Start Businesses

Source: Based on MasterCard Worldwide Survey, Fall 2006.

professional, scientific, and technical services.[52] Figure 1.4 shows the reasons women give for starting businesses.

Although the businesses women start tend to be smaller and require half as much start-up capital as those men start, their impact is anything but small. The nearly 10.5 million women-owned companies in the United States employ more than 12.8 million workers and generate sales of $1.9 trillion a year! Women now own 41 percent of all privately-held businesses in the United States.[53] Although their businesses tend to grow more slowly than those owned by men, women-owned businesses have a higher survival rate than U.S. small businesses overall.

The inspiration for Brenda Dronkers's business came on a rainy day when she watched her three children gleefully bounce on two inflatable games at her church's fall festival. "I looked at the kids bouncing, the drizzle outside, and my brain started ticking," she recalls. Her idea was to create a permanent indoor playground filled with inflatable play spaces so that kids could have a place to play on rainy days or have a special place to celebrate their birthdays and other special events. In January 2000, Dronkers and a friend put up $25,000 in start-up capital, located inexpensive warehouse space in her hometown of Pleasanton, California, and filled it with inflatable games. In its first month, Pump It Up booked 90 kids' parties; by the second month, the company was profitable and has been so ever since. Dronkers began franchising the company in 2002, and today, Pump It Up has 160 franchises in 38 states, generates annual sales of $55 million, and recently made *Inc.* magazine's list of the 500 fastest-growing small companies in the United States.[54]

ENTREPRENEURIAL PROFILE

Brenda Dronkers: Pump It Up

Minority Enterprises

Another rapidly growing segment of the small business population is minority-owned businesses. Hispanics, Asians, and African-Americans, respectively, are the minority groups that are most likely to become entrepreneurs.[55] Hispanics, who now make up the largest minority population in the United States, own 6.6 percent of all businesses. African-Americans, who comprise about 13 percent of the U.S. population, own 5 percent of all businesses, and Asians own 4.7 percent of all businesses.[56] Minority-owned businesses have come a long way in the last two decades, however, and their success rate is climbing.

A former college basketball star at Notre Dame, Lavetta Willis always has had a fierce competitive streak. While in law school, Willis and two partners created a company called DaDa that sold hats and T-shirts aimed at the urban market. Inspired by her background in sports, Willis decided to launch a footwear business, LL International Shoe Company, with another partner under the DaDa brand. Her company's product line now covers a wide range of athletic performance footwear and includes a shoe called Code M that contains an MP3 player and speakers! LL International Shoe's annual sales have surpassed $15 million.[57]

ENTREPRENEURIAL PROFILE

Lavetta Willis: LL International Shoe Company

A study by the Small Business Administration reports that minorities own 18 percent of all businesses, but their impact is significant.[58] Minority-owned businesses generate $668.4 billion in annual revenues and employ more than 4.73 million workers with a payroll of more than $116.3 billion.[59] The future is promising for this new generation of minority entrepreneurs, who are better educated, have more business experience, and are better prepared for business ownership than their predecessors.

Immigrant Entrepreneurs

The United States has always been a melting pot of diverse cultures, and many immigrants have been drawn to this nation by its promise of economic freedom. Unlike the unskilled "huddled masses" of the past, today's immigrants arrive with more education and experience and often a desire to start a business of their own. In fact, immigrants are significantly more likely to start businesses than are native-born U.S. citizens. Although many of them come to the United States with few assets, their dedication and desire to succeed enable them to achieve their entrepreneurial dreams.

ENTREPRENEURIAL PROFILE

Lana Fertelmeister: Lana Jewelry

Lana Unlimited

Lana Fertelmeister's parents emigrated from Russia to the United States with their six-year-old daughter, whom they taught that with hard work, anything is possible. She put that lesson to work in 2003 when she launched Lana Jewelry, a company that designs fine jewelry for everyday wear. Fertelmeister's line of signature three-color gold and diamond jewelry is available in more than 100 of the most exclusive retailers in the world, including Neiman Marcus, Saks Fifth Avenue, Borsheims, and Holt Renfrew, and the company is expanding into stores in Europe and Asia. Lana Jewelry designs have received plenty of buzz from celebrity clients such as Halle Berry, Sandra Bullock, Cameron Diaz, and Kate Hudson and from appearances in movies and television shows such as *American Idol*, *Sex and the City*, and *Cashmere Mafia*. Lana Jewelry's annual sales recently hit $6 million.[60]

Part-Time Entrepreneurs

Starting a part-time business is a popular gateway to entrepreneurship. Part-time entrepreneurs have the best of both worlds: They can ease into business for themselves without sacrificing the security of a steady paycheck and benefits. The Internet (and particularly eBay) makes establishing and running a part-time business very easy; many part-time entrepreneurs run online businesses from a spare bedroom in their homes. For instance, Janice Ford-Freeman, who works full-time at the University of Alabama at Birmingham, enjoys shopping at garage sales and Goodwill outlets for vintage clothing, which she resells on her eBay store. Her part-time eBay business not only brings in extra income but also gives her a sense of enjoyment. "[eBay] gives me a fabulous outlet to market the bargains I find," Ford-Freeman says.[61]

According to the Panel Study of Entrepreneurial Dynamics, 50 percent of entrepreneurs work full-time and 20 percent have part-time work in addition to their businesses.[62] A major advantage of going into business part-time is the lower risk in case the venture flops. Many part-timers are "testing the entrepreneurial waters" to see whether their business ideas will work, whether there is sufficient demand for their products and services, and whether they enjoy being self-employed. As they grow, many part-time enterprises absorb more of entrepreneurs' time until they become full-time businesses.

Home-Based Businesses

Home-based businesses are booming! More than 12 percent of the households in the United States operate home-based businesses, generating $427 billion a year in sales.[63] Fifty-three percent of all small businesses are home-based, but most of them are very small with no employees.[64] Several factors make the home the first choice location for many entrepreneurs:

- Operating a business from home keeps start-up and operating costs to a minimum.
- Home-based companies allow owners to maintain a flexible lifestyle and work style. Many home-based entrepreneurs relish being part of the "open-collar workforce."

- Technology, which is transforming many ordinary homes into "electronic cottages," allows entrepreneurs to run a wide variety of businesses from their homes.
- Many entrepreneurs use the Internet to operate e-commerce businesses from their homes, businesses that literally span the globe.

In the past, home-based businesses tended to be rather unexciting cottage industries such as making crafts or sewing. Today's home-based businesses are more diverse; modern home-based entrepreneurs are more likely to be running high-tech or service companies with millions of dollars in sales. The average home-based business generates revenues of $62,523 and earns a net income of $22,569.[65]

Family Businesses

A **family-owned business** is one that includes two or more members of a family with financial control of the company. Family businesses are an integral part of our economy. Of the 30.23 million businesses in the United States, 90 percent are family-owned and managed. These companies account for 62 percent of total U.S. employment and 78 percent of all new jobs, pay 65 percent of all wages, and generate 64 percent of the nation's GDP. Not all of them are small; 37 percent of the *Fortune 500* companies are family businesses.[66]

"When it works right," says one writer, "nothing succeeds like a family firm. The roots run deep, embedded in family values. The flash of the fast buck is replaced with long-term plans. Tradition counts."[67] Indeed, in the typical family business, the family owns the company for an average of 78 years.[68] Despite their magnitude, family businesses face a major threat, a threat from within: management succession. Only 30 percent of family businesses survive to the second generation, just 12 percent make it to the third generation, and only 3 percent survive into the fourth generation and beyond. Business periodicals are full of stories describing bitter feuds among family members that have crippled or destroyed once thriving businesses.

To avoid such senseless destruction of valuable assets, founders of family businesses should develop plans for management succession long before retirement looms before them.

family-owned business
one that includes two or more members of a family with financial control of the company.

ENTREPRENEURIAL PROFILE _____

Kurt Schmidt: A.E. Schmidt Company

Kurt Schmidt, 49, is the fifth generation owner of A.E. Schmidt Company, a manufacturer of pool tables that was founded in 1850 in St. Louis, Missouri. Schmidt's great-great-great-grandfather emigrated from Germany and started the business with just one lathe. In its nearly 160 years of operation, the family business has survived several catastrophes. "We've had several brushes with oblivion over the years, but good relationships with vendors, a strong customer base, good employees, hard work, and some help from above have pulled us through," he says. Schmidt has expanded the company's product line to include "virtually everything you could want for a game room" and already is grooming the sixth generation to take over the family business. Schmidt's son Michael has been working for the company part-time while he finishes college, and daughters Stephanie and Rachel are learning about the company by working in the factory and office after school.[69]

Copreneurs

"Copreneurs" are entrepreneurial couples who work together as co-owners of their businesses. Unlike the traditional "Mom and Pop" (Pop as "boss" and Mom as "subordinate"), copreneurs "are creating a division of labor that is based on expertise as opposed to gender," says one expert.[70] Managing a small business with a spouse may appear to be a recipe for divorce, but most copreneurs say not. "There is nothing like sharing an intense, life-changing experience with someone to bring you closer," says Caterina Fake, who with her husband, Sewart Butterfield, launched Flickr, a photo-sharing Web site. "Late nights, early mornings, laughter, terror, white-knuckle meetings with people you desperately need to give you money, getting your first check from a paying user—how can you beat it?"[71] Successful copreneurs learn to build the foundation

copreneurs
entrepreneurial couples who work together as co-owners of their businesses.

for a successful working relationship before they ever launch their companies. Some of the characteristics they rely on include:

- An assessment of whether their personalities will mesh—or conflict—in a business setting.
- Mutual respect for each other and one another's talents.
- Compatible business and life goals—a common vision.
- A view that they are full and equal partners, not a superior and a subordinate.
- Complementary business skills that each acknowledges and appreciates and that lead to a unique business identity for each spouse.
- The ability to keep lines of communication open, talking and listening to each other.
- A clear division of roles and authority, ideally based on each partner's skills and abilities, to minimize conflict and power struggles.
- The ability to encourage each other and to lift up a disillusioned partner.
- Separate work spaces that allow them to escape when the need arises.
- Boundaries between their business life and their personal life so that one doesn't consume the other.
- A sense of humor.
- The realization that not every couple can work together.

Although copreneuring isn't for everyone, it works extremely well for many couples and often leads to successful businesses. "Both spouses are working for a common purpose but also focusing on their unique talents," says a family business counselor. "With all these skills put together, one plus one equals more than two."[72]

ENTREPRENEURIAL PROFILE

Ben & Mena Trott: Six Apart

Ben and Mena Trott started dating in high school and after marrying launched Six Apart, a company that makes popular Internet blogging tools, from a spare bedroom in their home. For four years, the copreneurs worked long days from desks that were just five feet apart. Today, Ben and Mena not only have separate offices, but they also have divided the responsibilities of running their company. Ben focuses on behind-the-scenes activities such as product development, and Mena handles marketing and serves as Six Apart's spokesperson. Under their combined leadership, Six Apart continues to grow.[73]

Six Apart, Ltd.

Corporate Castoffs

Concentrating on shedding the excess bulk that took away their flexibility and speed, many large American corporations have been downsizing in an attempt to regain their competitive edge. For decades, one major corporation after another has announced layoffs—and not just among blue-collar workers. According to placement firm Challenger, Gray, and Christmas, corporations lay off an average of 75,000 employees per month.[74] Executives and production workers alike have experienced job cuts. Millions of people have lost their jobs, and these corporate castoffs have become an important source of entrepreneurial activity. Some 20 percent of these discharged corporate managers have become entrepreneurs, and many of those left behind in corporate America would like to join them.

Many corporate castoffs are deciding that the best defense against future job insecurity is an entrepreneurial offense. Accustomed to the support in the corporations they left, many corporate castoffs decide to purchase franchises, where there is a built-in management system already in place. *Entrepreneur* magazine surveyed the companies on its Franchise 500 list recently and discovered that 77 percent of franchisors report that "second-career executives" (i.e., corporate castoffs) were among the primary purchasers of their franchises.[75]

Corporate Dropouts

The dramatic downsizing of corporate America has created another effect among the employees left after restructuring: a trust gap. The result of this trust gap is a growing number of dropouts from the corporate structure who then become entrepreneurs. Although their workdays may grow longer and their incomes may shrink, those who strike out on their own often find their work more rewarding and more satisfying because they are doing what they enjoy. Other entrepreneurs are inspired to launch their companies after being treated unfairly by large impersonal corporate entities.

In the 1950s, Marion Kauffman was so successful as a salesman for a pharmaceutical company that his pay exceeded that of the company president, who promptly cut Kauffman's sales territory. Kauffman managed to rebuild sales so that he once again earned more than the boss, who then cut Kauffman's commission rate. Outraged, Kauffman left to start his own business, Marion Laboratories, which he sold to Dow Chemical Company in 1989 for $5.2 billion! Before his death in 1993, Kauffman established the Ewing Marion Kauffman Foundation in Kansas City, Missouri to promote entrepreneurship.[76]

Because they have college degrees, a working knowledge of business, and years of management experience, both corporate dropouts and castoffs may ultimately increase the small business survival rate. A survey by Richard O'Sullivan found that 64 percent of people starting businesses have at least some college education, and 14 percent have advanced degrees.[77] Better-trained, more experienced entrepreneurs are more likely to succeed.

Social Entrepreneurs

Social entrepreneurs use their skills not only to create profitable business ventures but also to achieve social and environmental goals for society as a whole. Their businesses often have a triple bottom line that encompasses economic, social, and environmental objectives. These entrepreneurs see their businesses as mechanisms for achieving social goals that are important to them as individuals.

social entrepreneurs
entrepreneurs who use their skills not only to create profitable businesses but also to achieve social and environmental goals for the common good.

Ron Gonen, a former consultant, saw a way to create a business that could both address the vexing problem of garbage disposal and the limited landfill space in which to put it and also generate a profit. Gonen's company, RecycleBank, provides homeowners with recycling carts that are equipped with radio frequency identification (RFID) tags. When a truck picks up a cart, it weighs the recycled material and an RFID scanner records the information, which is sent to RecycleBank. Each household earns points based on how much material it recycles, and residents can redeem their RecycleBank points at retailers such as Starbucks, Patagonia, Stonyfield Farm, Dunkin' Donuts, and others. So far, RecycleBank says that it has more than doubled the recycling rates in the communities with which it has partnered, saving more than 277,000 trees and 15 million gallons of oil and diverted more than 19,500 tons of waste from landfills. Its customers have redeemed more than 3 million reward points. RecycleBank, which generates its income by taking a percentage of the money that cities save by producing less landfill space, recently received $30 million in venture capital to expand its presence in the United States and to market its service in Europe.[78]

Retiring Baby Boomers

Because people are living longer and are remaining active as they grow older, the ranks of older entrepreneurs are growing. In fact, according to studies by the Ewing Marion Kauffman Foundation, the level of entrepreneurial activity among people ages 55 to 64 actually exceeds that of people ages 20 to 34. One advantage that older entrepreneurs have is wisdom that has been forged by experience.

ENTREPRENEURIAL PROFILE

Lisa Gable: L.G. Accessories

At age 70, Lisa Gable, who had been frustrated by drooping bra straps all of her life, designed a clever solution to the problem and launched a company to market the Strap-Mate. Today, at age 84, Gable is still running her company, L.G. Accessories, from her home in East Windsor, New Jersey. Gable applied for and received a patent for her invention, and because no one would finance a 70-year-old entrepreneur, she launched her company using credit cards. In addition to selling the Strap-Mate on the L.G. Accessories Web site, Gable also has managed to get her product into major retailers such as Nordstrom and J.C. Penney.[79]

L.G. Accessories, Inc.

HANDS ON... HOW TO

Launch a Successful Business While You Are Still in College

Collegiate entrepreneurs are becoming increasingly common as colleges and universities offer more courses and a greater variety of courses in the areas of entrepreneurship and small business management. Launching a business while in college offers many advantages, including access to research and valuable advice, but starting an entrepreneurial career also poses challenges, including a lack of financial resources, business experience, and time. What are some of the most common myths that prevent young people (not just college students) from launching businesses?

- *I don't have enough money to launch a business.* One of the greatest benefits of the shift in the United States to a service economy is that service businesses usually are very inexpensive to start. One young entrepreneur worked with a friend to launch a Web development company while in high school, and their total start-up cost was just $80.
- *I don't have enough time.* Many companies that have grown into very successful, mature businesses were started by entrepreneurs in their spare time. Everyone has the same 24 hours in a day. What matters is what you do with those hours.
- *I'm not smart enough to start a company.* SAT scores and grades have little correlation to one's ability to launch a successful business. Quite a few successful entrepreneurs, including Michael Dell (Dell Inc.), Richard Branson (Virgin), Walt Disney (Disney), Mark Zuckerberg (FaceBook) and Debbi Fields (Mrs. Fields Cookies), dropped out of college to start their businesses.
- *I'm not creative enough to come up with a good idea for a business.* As you will learn in Chapter 2, *everyone* has the potential to be creative. Some of the most successful businesses are the result of an entrepreneur who recognized a simple need that people had and created a business to meet that need.
- *I don't have any experience.* Neither did Bill Gates (Microsoft) and Michael Dell (Dell Inc.) when they launched their companies, and things worked out pretty well for both of them. Business experience can be an important factor in a company's success, but every entrepreneur has to start somewhere to gain that experience.
- *I might fail.* Failure is a possibility. In fact, the survival rate of new companies after four years is 44 percent. Ask yourself:

What is the worst that can happen if I launch a business and it fails? Entrepreneurs do not allow the fear of failure to stop them from trying to realize their dreams.

If you want to become a successful collegiate entrepreneur, what can you do to increase the chances of your success? The following tips will help:

Recognize that starting a business at an early age may be to your advantage

Young people tend to be highly creative, and that can provide your company with a competitive advantage. In addition, young people often accomplish things simply because they don't know that they are not supposed to be able to do them!

Build a business plan

One of the best ways to lower the probability that your business will fail is to create a business plan. Doing so forces you to ask and then answer some tough questions about your idea and your proposed venture.

Use all of the resources that are available to you

Many colleges and universities now offer courses in entrepreneurship and small business management and have faculty members who are experts in the field. In many cases, the people who are teaching these classes are veteran entrepreneurs themselves with tremendous reservoirs of knowledge and experience. Some colleges provide special dorms for budding entrepreneurs that serve as business incubators. Smart collegiate entrepreneurs tap into the pool of resources that their campuses offer.

Find a mentor

Most young entrepreneurs have not had the opportunity to gain a wealth of business experience, but they do have access to mentors who do. Mike Brown, who recently won the top prize at the annual Global Student Entrepreneur Awards for his company ModBargains.com, a business that sells aftermarket products for modifying cars and trucks, says that his first boss, who owns several businesses, served as his mentor. ModBargains.com, which Brown started with fellow car enthusiast Ron Hay, now has more than 4,000 products available and has surpassed annual sales of $1 million.

Learn to be a guerrilla marketer

Because they lack the deep pockets of their larger rivals, entrepreneurs must use their creativity, ingenuity, and street smarts to market their companies effectively. For example, the owner of a company that provided investigative services for law firms slipped his business cards into books in the legal section of the local library. Attorneys and paralegals doing research in the library assumed that other law firms used the company's services and began hiring the investigator. You will learn more about guerrilla marketing tactics in Chapter 8.

Learn to be a "bootstrapper"

Learning to start and manage a company with few resources is good training for any entrepreneur. In the early days of their start-ups, many successful entrepreneurs find creative ways to finance their businesses and to keep their operating expenses as low as possible.

Manage your time wisely

Taking college classes and running a business places a large workload on any collegiate entrepreneur, one that demands good time management skills. The most successful entrepreneurs recognize the importance of controlling their schedules (as much as possible) and working as efficiently as they can.

Remember to have fun

College is supposed to be one of the best times of your life! Starting and running a business also can be one of the most rewarding experiences of your life. Doing both can double the fun, but it also can create a great deal of stress. Balance is the key.

Sources: Adapted from Robert Sherman, "Student Entrepreneur Shares Hard-Won Lessons at YoungMoney.com," *Orange Entrepreneur*, Syracuse University, Fall 2007, p. 5; Daniel Jimenez, "The Best College Entrepreneurs of 2006," *Young Money*, July 2007, http://www.youngmoney.com/entrepreneur/student_entrepreneurs/070126; Michael Simmons, "Why Starting a Business Now May Be the Best Way to Achieve Your Dreams," *Young Money*, July 2003, http://www.youngmoney.com/entrepreneur/student_entrepreneurs/031010_01; Scott Reeves, "How to Swing with Guerrilla Marketing," *Forbes*, June 8, 2006, http://www.forbes.com/2006/06/08/entrepreneurs-marketing-harley-davidson-cx_sr_0608askanexpert.html.

The Power of "Small" Business

Of the 30.23 million businesses in the United States, approximately 30.14 million, or 99.7 percent, are considered "small." Although there is no universal definition of a small business (the U.S. Small Business Administration has more than 800 definitions of a small business based on industry categories), a common delineation of a **small business** is one that employs fewer than 100 people. They thrive in virtually every industry, although the majority of small companies are concentrated in the service and retail industries (see Figure 1.5). Although they may be small businesses, their contributions to the economy are anything but small. For example, small companies employ 51 percent of the nation's private sector workforce, even though they possess less than one-fourth of total business assets. Almost 90 percent of small businesses employ fewer than 20 workers, but small companies pay more than 45 percent of total private payroll in the United States. Because they are primarily labor intensive, small businesses actually create more jobs than do big businesses. In fact, over the last decade small companies have created 60 percent to 80 percent of the net new jobs in the U.S. economy.[80]

Researcher David Birch says that the ability to create jobs is not distributed evenly across the small business sector, however. His research shows that just 3 percent of small companies create 70 percent of the net new jobs in the economy, and they do so across all industry sectors, not just in "hot" industries. Birch calls these job-creating small companies "**gazelles**," those growing at 20 percent or more per year for four years with at least

small business
one that employs fewer than 100 people.

gazelles
small companies that are growing at 20 percent or more per year with at least $100,000 in annual sales; they create 70 percent of net new jobs in the economy.

FIGURE 1.5

Small Businesses by Industry

Source: U.S. Small Business Administration, 2007.

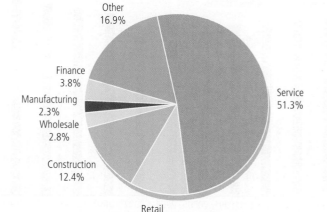

Other 16.9%
Finance 3.8%
Manufacturing 2.3%
Wholesale 2.8%
Construction 12.4%
Retail 10.3%
Service 51.3%

$100,000 in annual sales. His research also identified "mice," small companies that never grow much and don't create many jobs. The majority of small companies are "mice." Birch tabbed the country's largest businesses "elephants," which have continued to shed jobs for several years.[81]

Small businesses also produce 51 percent of the country's private GDP and account for 47 percent of business sales.[82] In fact, the U.S. small business sector is the world's second-largest "economy," trailing only the entire U.S. economy! Small companies also are incubators of new ideas, products, and services. Small firms actually create 13 times more patents per employee than large companies.[83] Traditionally, small businesses have played a vital role in innovation, and they continue to do so today. Many important inventions trace their roots to an entrepreneur, including the zipper, FM radio, the laser, the brassiere, air conditioning, the escalator, the light bulb, the personal computer, and the automatic transmission.

Putting Failure into Perspective

LO 6

Put failure into the proper perspective.

Because of their limited resources, inexperienced management, and lack of financial stability, small businesses suffer relatively high mortality rates. A recent study reports that after two years, 34 percent of new companies have failed and that after four years 56 percent have failed.[84] Figure 1.6 shows the number of business births and business terminations in recent years, clear evidence of the constant "churn" that exists as entrepreneurs create new businesses as others close.

Because they are building businesses in an environment filled with uncertainty and shaped by rapid change, entrepreneurs recognize that failure is likely to be part of their lives, but they are not paralyzed by that fear. "The excitement of building a new business from scratch is greater than the fear of failure," says one entrepreneur who failed in business several times before finally succeeding.[85] Entrepreneurs use their failures as a rallying point and as a means of refocusing their business ventures for success. They see failure for what it really is: an opportunity to learn what does not work! Successful entrepreneurs have the attitude that failures are simply stepping stones along the path to success. Basketball legend Michael Jordan displayed the same attitude. "I've missed more than 9,000 shots in my career," he says. "I lost almost 300 games. Twenty-six times, I've been trusted to take the game-winning shot and *missed*. I've failed over and over and over again in my life. And that is why I succeed."[86]

Failure is a natural part of the creative process. The only people who never fail are those who never do anything or never attempt anything new. Baseball fans know that babe Ruth held the record for career home runs (714) for many years, but how many know that he also held the record for strikeouts (1,330)? Successful entrepreneurs know that hitting an entrepreneurial home run requires a few strikeouts along the way, and they are willing to accept them. Failure is an inevitable part of being an entrepreneur, and true entrepreneurs don't quit

FIGURE 1.6

Number of Business Starts and Closures of Employer Firms

Source: Small Business Administration, 2007.

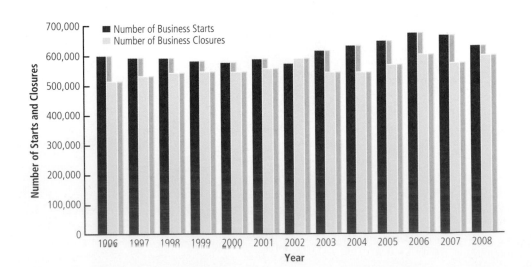

when they fail. One entrepreneur whose business burned through $800 million of investors' money before folding says, "If you're an entrepreneur, you don't give up when times get tough."[87]

One hallmark of successful entrepreneurs is the ability to fail *intelligently*, learning why they failed so that they can avoid making the same mistake again. James Dyson, whose company makes one of the best selling vacuum cleaners in the world, made 5,127 prototypes of his bagless vacuum cleaner before he hit upon one that worked. "There were 5,126 failures," he says, "but I learned from each one. That's how I came up with a solution. So I don't mind failure."[88] Like Dyson, entrepreneurs know that business success does not depend on their ability to avoid making mistakes but to be open to the lessons each mistake teaches. They learn from their failures and use them as fuel to push themselves closer to their ultimate target. Entrepreneurs are less worried about what they might lose if they try something and fail than about what they might lose if they fail to try.

Entrepreneurial success requires both persistence and resilience, the ability to bounce back from failure. Thomas Edison discovered about 1,800 ways not to build a light bulb before hitting on a design that worked. Walt Disney was fired from a newspaper job because, according to his boss, he "lacked imagination and had no good ideas." Disney also went bankrupt several times before he created Disneyland. R. H. Macy failed in business seven times before his retail store in New York City became a success. In the spirit of true entrepreneurship, these visionary business leaders refused to give up in the face of failure; they simply kept trying until they achieved success. When it comes to failure, entrepreneurs' motto seems to be: Failure is temporary; quitting is permanent.

ENTREPRENEURIAL PROFILE

Michelle Long:
Sustainable Connections

Michelle Long launched World2Market, an online company that linked entrepreneurs in developing countries with buyers in the United States, and raised several million dollars from private investors and venture capital companies. World2Market folded in 2001, but Long learned many valuable lessons from the failed business and decided to give entrepreneurship another try in 2002, when she launched Sustainable Connections, a social network that is designed to help small businesses that use sustainable business practices to grow. Long is making sure she does not make the same mistakes with her current venture that she made with World2Market. Her plan is working, and many of the investors who lost money in Long's first venture decided to back Sustainable Connections.[89]

How to Avoid the Pitfalls

Although failure can be a valuable part of the entrepreneurial process, no one sets out to fail in business. Now we must examine the ways to avoid becoming another failure statistic and gain insight into what makes a successful business.

Know Your Business in Depth

We have already emphasized the need for the right type of experience in the business you plan to start. Get the best education in your business area you possibly can *before* you set out on your own. Become a serious student of your industry. Read everything you can—trade journals, business periodicals, books, research reports—relating to your industry and learn what it takes to succeed in it. Personal contact with suppliers, customers, trade associations, and others in the same industry is another excellent way to get that knowledge. Smart entrepreneurs join industry trade associations and attend trade shows to pick up valuable information and to make key contacts before they open their doors for business.

ENTREPRENEURIAL PROFILE

Laura Bennett: Embrace Pet Insurance

Laura Bennett worked in the insurance industry for years as an actuary and an executive before she launched her own company targeting an interesting niche in the same industry—pet insurance. Bennett also tapped the expertise of a former co-worker, Bill Acton, to help her launch Embrace Pet Insurance. Acton was so impressed with Bennett's business plan that he invested $50,000 in the start-up.

Bennett is the only pet insurance actuary in the United States, and because her company specializes in insurance policies for pets, she can offer customized packages for her clients and their pets. Embrace wrote its first policy in 2006 but already has passed the $2 million mark in policies written. Bennett's success shows that successful entrepreneurs are like sponges, soaking up as much knowledge as they can from a variety of sources.[90]

Develop a Solid Business Plan

For any entrepreneur, a well-written business plan is a crucial ingredient in preparing for business success. Without a sound business plan, a firm merely drifts along without any real direction. Yet entrepreneurs, who tend to be people of action, too often jump right into a business venture without taking time to prepare a written plan outlining the essence of the business. Not only does a plan provide a pathway to success, but it also creates a benchmark against which an entrepreneur can measure actual company performance. Building a successful business begins with implementing a sound business plan with laser-like focus.

A business plan allows entrepreneurs to replace sometimes faulty assumptions with facts before making the decision to go into business. The planning process forces entrepreneurs to ask and then answer some difficult, challenging, and crucial questions.

ENTREPRENEURIAL PROFILE

Tom Szaky: TerraCycle

In his freshman year at Princeton, Tom Szaky created a business plan that helped him launch TerraCycle International, a company that uses red worms to compost food waste into potting soil and liquid all-natural fertilizers guaranteed not to burn plants. Szaky's ingenious plan was to sell waste disposal services to restaurants, schools, penitentiaries, and other institutions and to allow the worms to transform the waste into vermicompost, which the company turns into potting soil and fertilizers and sells to garden centers, nurseries, home superstores, and other retail outlets. Szaky's research told him that the organic segments of the fertilizer and potting soil industry are multibillion-dollar businesses and have been growing at double-digit rates for the last several years. TerraCycle sells its all-natural plant foods and other products through retail outlets across the United States and is planning to expand into global markets as well. Szaky not only used his business plan to make TerraCycle a success, but, in the early days of the company, he used it as a source of financing, entering numerous business plan competitions to win prize money that kept the young company afloat.[91]

We will discuss the process of developing a business plan in Chapter 4, "Conducting a Feasibility Analysis and Crafting a Winning Business Plan."

Manage Financial Resources

The best defense against financial problems is to develop a practical information system and then use this information to make business decisions. No entrepreneur can maintain control over a business unless he or she is able to judge its financial health.

The first step in managing financial resources effectively is to have adequate start-up capital. Too many entrepreneurs begin their businesses with too little capital. One experienced business owner advises, "Estimate how much capital you need to get the business going and then double that figure." His point is well taken; it almost always costs more to launch a business than any entrepreneur expects.

The most valuable financial resource to any small business is *cash*. Although earning a profit is essential to its long-term survival, a business must have an adequate supply of cash to pay its bills and obligations. Some entrepreneurs count on growing sales to supply their company's cash needs, but this almost never happens. Growing companies usually consume more cash than they generate, and the faster they grow, the more cash they gobble up! Business history is littered with failed companies whose founders had no idea how much cash their businesses were generating and were spending cash as if they were certain there was "plenty more where that came from." We will discuss cash management techniques in Chapter 13, "Managing Cash Flow."

Understand Financial Statements

Every business owner must depend on records and financial statements to know the condition of his or her business. All too often entrepreneurs use these only for tax purposes and not as vital management control devices. To truly understand what is going on in their business, an owner must have at least a basic understanding of accounting and finance.

When analyzed and interpreted properly, these financial statements are reliable indicators of a small firm's health. They can be quite helpful in signaling potential problems. For example, declining sales, slipping profits, rising debt, and deteriorating working capital are all symptoms of potentially lethal problems that require immediate attention. We will discuss financial statement analysis in Chapter 12, "Creating a Successful Financial Plan."

Learn to Manage People Effectively

No matter what kind of business you launch, you must learn to manage people. Every business depends on a foundation of well-trained, motivated employees. No business owner can do everything alone. The people an entrepreneur hires ultimately determine the heights to which the company can climb—or the depths to which it can plunge. Attracting and retaining a corps of quality employees is no easy task, however. It remains a challenge for every small business owner. "In the end, your most dominant sustainable resource is the quality of the people you have," says one small business expert.[92] We will discuss the techniques of managing and motivating people effectively in Chapter 16, "Building a New Venture Team and Planning for the Next Generation."

Set Your Business Apart from the Competition

The formula for almost certain business failure involves becoming a "me-too business"— merely copying whatever the competition is doing. Most successful entrepreneurs find a way to convince their customers that their companies are superior to their competitors even if they sell similar products or services. It is especially important for small companies going up against larger, more powerful rivals with greater financial resources. Ideally, the basis for differentiating a company from its competitors is founded in what it does best. For small companies, that basis often is customer service, convenience, speed, quality, or whatever else is important to attracting and keeping happy customers. We will discuss the strategies for creating a unique footprint in the marketplace in Chapter 3, "Designing a Competitive Business Model and Building a Solid Strategic Plan" and in Chapter 8, "Building a Guerrilla Marketing Plan."

Maintain a Positive Attitude

Achieving business success requires an entrepreneur to maintain a positive mental attitude toward business and the discipline to stick with it. Successful entrepreneurs recognize that their most valuable resource is their time, and they learn to manage it effectively to make themselves and their companies more productive. None of this, of course, is possible without passion—passion for their businesses, their products or services, their customers, their communities. Passion is what enables a failed business owner to get back up, try again, and make it to the top! One business writer says that growing a successful business requires entrepreneurs to have great faith in themselves and their ideas, great doubt concerning the challenges and inevitable obstacles they will face as they build their businesses, and great effort—lots of hard work—to make their dreams become reality.[93]

Conclusion

As you can see, entrepreneurship lies at the heart of this nation's free enterprise system; small companies truly are the backbone of our economy. Their contributions are as many and as diverse as the businesses themselves. Indeed, diversity is one of the strengths of the U.S. small business sector. Although there are no secrets to becoming a successful entrepreneur, there are steps that entrepreneurs can take to enhance the probability of their success. The remainder of this book will explore those steps and how to apply them to the process of launching a successful business with an emphasis on building a sound business plan.

- The next chapter, "Inside the Entrepreneurial Mind: From Ideas to Reality," explores the creative process that lies at the heart of entrepreneurship and offers practical tips on how you can stimulate your own creativity.
- Section 2, "Building the Business Plan: Beginning Considerations" (Chapters 3–7), discusses the classic start-up questions every entrepreneur faces, particularly conducting a feasibility analysis, developing a strategy, choosing a form of ownership, alternative methods for becoming a business owner (franchising and buying an existing business), and building a business plan.
- Section 3, "Building the Business Plan: Marketing and Financial Considerations" (Chapters 8–11), focuses first on creating an effective marketing plan for a small company. These chapters address creating an effective e-commerce strategy, establishing pricing and credit strategies, and penetrating global markets.
- Section 4, "Building the Business Plan: Financial Matters" (Chapters 12–14), explains how to develop the financial component of a business plan, including creating projected financial statements and forecasting cash flow. These chapters also offer existing business owners practical financial management tools and explain how to find the sources of funding, both debt and equity, necessary to launch a business.
- Section 5, "Putting the Business Plan to Work: Source of Funds" (Chapters 15–16), discusses how entrepreneurs can select the right location and layout for their businesses. This section also provides useful techniques for assembling a strong new venture team and leading its members to success and discusses the importance of creating a management succession plan to ensure that a company successfully makes the transition to the next generation of owners.

As you can see, the journey down the road of entrepreneurship will be an interesting and exciting one. Let's get started!

Chapter Summary

1. Define the role of the entrepreneur in business in the United States and around the world.

Entrepreneurship is thriving in the United States, but the current wave of entrepreneurship is not limited to the United States; many nations across the globe are seeing similar growth in their small business sectors. A variety of competitive, economic, and demographic shifts have created a world in which "small is beautiful."

Capitalist societies depend on entrepreneurs to provide the drive and risk-taking necessary for the system to supply people with the goods and services they need.

2. Describe the entrepreneurial profile and evaluate your potential as an entrepreneur.

Entrepreneurs have some common characteristics, including a desire for responsibility, a preference for moderate risk, confidence in their ability to succeed, desire for immediate feedback, a high energy level,

a future orientation, skill at organizing, and a value of achievement over money. In a phrase, they are tenacious high achievers.

3-A. Describe the benefits of entrepreneurship.

Driven by these personal characteristics, entrepreneurs establish and manage small businesses to gain control over their lives, make a difference in the world, become self-fulfilled, reap unlimited profits, contribute to society, and do what they enjoy doing.

3-B. Describe the drawbacks of entrepreneurship.

Entrepreneurs also face certain disadvantages, including: uncertainty of income, the risk of losing their investments (and more), long hours and hard work, a lower quality of life until the business gets established, high stress levels, and complete decision-making responsibility.

4. Explain the forces that are driving the growth of entrepreneurship.

Several factors are driving the boom in entrepreneurship, including: the portrayal of entrepreneurs as heroes, better entrepreneurial education, economic and demographic factors, a shift to a service economy, technological advances, more independent lifestyles, and increased international opportunities.

5. Explain the cultural diversity of entrepreneurship.

Several groups are leading the nation's drive toward entrepreneurship: young people, women, minorities, immigrants, part-timers, home-based business owners, family business owners, copreneurs, corporate castoffs, corporate dropouts, social entrepreneurs, and retired baby boomers.

6. Describe the important role small businesses play in our nation's economy.

The small business sector's contributions are many. They make up 99.7 percent of all businesses, employ 51 percent of the private sector workforce, have created two-thirds to three-fourths of the net new jobs in the economy, produce 51 percent of the country's private gross domestic product (GDP), and account for 47 percent of all business sales.

7. Put failure into the proper perspective.

Entrepreneurs recognize that failure is a natural part of the creative process. Successful entrepreneurs have the attitude that failures are simply stepping stones along the path to success, and they refuse to be paralyzed by a fear of failure.

8. Explain how entrepreneurs can avoid becoming another business failure statistic.

Entrepreneurs can employ several general tactics to avoid these pitfalls. They should know their businesses in depth, prepare a solid business plan, manage financial resources effectively, understand financial statements, learn to manage people, set their businesses apart from the competition, and maintain a positive attitude.

Discussion Questions

1. What forces have led to the boom in entrepreneurship in the United States and across the globe?
2. What is an entrepreneur? Give a brief description of the entrepreneurial profile.
3. *Inc.* magazine claims, "Entrepreneurship is more mundane than it's sometimes portrayed...you don't need to be a person of mythical proportions to be very, very successful in building a company." Do you agree? Explain.
4. What are the major benefits of business ownership?
5. Which of the potential drawbacks to business ownership are most critical?
6. Briefly describe the role of the following groups in entrepreneurship: young people, women, minorities, immigrants, "part-timers," home-based business owners, family business owners, copreneurs, corporate castoffs, corporate dropouts, social entrepreneurs, and retired baby boomers.
7. What is a small business? What contributions do they make to our economy?
8. Describe the small business failure rate.
9. Outline the causes of business failure. Which problems cause most business failures?
10. How does the typical entrepreneur view the possibility of business failure?
11. How can the small business owner avoid the common pitfalls that often lead to business failures?
12. Why is it important to study the small business failure rate and to understand the causes of business failures?
13. Explain the typical entrepreneur's attitude toward risk.
14. Are you interested in someday launching a small business? If so, when? What kind of business? Describe it. What can you do to ensure its success?

Business PlanPro™

This book may include the best-selling business planning software, *Business Plan Pro*™ by Palo Alto Software, Inc. This software can assist you in four ways as you begin to build your business plan.

1. *Structure: Business Plan Pro*™ provides a structure to the process of creating a business plan. There are general business plan standards and expectations and *Business Plan Pro*™ has a recognized and well received format that lends credibility to your plan. A comprehensive plan that follows a generally recognized outline adds credibility and, if it is a part of the plan's purpose, of being funded.
2. *Efficiency: Business Plan Pro*™ will save you time. Once you become familiar with the interface, *Business Plan Pro*™ creates all of the essential financial statements for you based on the information the software prompts you to enter. The software automatically formats the income statement, balance sheet, and the profit and loss statement.

3. *Examples: Business Plan Pro*™ includes a variety of sample business plans. Seeing examples of other plans can be a helpful learning tool as you create a plan that is unique based on your product or service and your market.

4. *Appearance: Business Plan Pro*™ automatically incorporates relevant tables and graphs into your text. The result is a cohesive business plan that combines text, tables and charts to enhance the impact of your plan.

Writing a business plan is more than just creating a document. The process itself can be the most valuable benefit of all. A business plan "tells the story" about your business. It address why your business concept is viable, who your market is, what you offer to that market, why your offer represents a unique value, how you are going to reach them, how your business is going to be funded and, based on your projections, how it will result in financial success.

Creating a business plan is a learning process. For the start-up business, completing a business plan allows the entrepreneur to gain insight before the business launches. The current business owner benefits from writing a business plan to better address challenges and optimize opportunities. *Business Plan Pro*™ is a tool to assist with this process.

The *EasyPlan Wizard*™ within the software guides you through the process by asking a series of questions to bring the vision of the business to paper. The wizard will skip from section to section as you build concepts about your business, the products and services you offer, the markets you will serve, and your financial information. You can use the wizard or follow the sections of the outline based on the guidance from each chapter. Both options will lead you through the entire process and help you create a comprehensive business plan.

At the end of each chapter in this book, you will find a *Business Plan Pro*™ activity that applies the concepts discussed. These activities will enable you to build your plan one step at a time in manageable components. You will be able to assemble your plan in a way that captures the information you know about your business and also raise key questions that will push you to learn more in areas you may not have considered. *Business Plan Pro*™ will guide you through each step to complete you plan as you progress through this book. This step represents a critical step toward launching a business or establishing a better understanding of an existing business.

Business Plan Exercises

The following set of exercises leads you through the process of creating your own business plan. If you or your planning team does not have a business concept in mind, select a business idea and work through these steps. Future chapters will ask you to review, validate and change this concept as needed.

On the Web

Visit the companion Web site designed for this book at http://www.pearsonhighered.com/scarborough. Find the cover of this book, the 6th edition of *Essentials of Small Business*

Management and click on the Companion Site link. Find the Business Plan Resource tab in the left-hand navigation The information and links here will be a resource for you as you progress through each chapter to develop your business plan.

Sample Plans

Click on the Sample Plan Browser and review these two plans: The Supreme Courts and InteliChild.com.

- Compare the table of contents of each plan. What differences do you notice?
- Review the executive summary of each plan. What is the key difference in these two business concepts?
- What similarities do the plans share?
- What are common tables and charts within the text? What value do these tables and charts offer?

In the Software

Follow the instructions included on the CD to install *Business Plan Pro*™. After opening *Business Plan Pro*™— preferably on a PC with an Internet connection—open the Sample Plan Browser. The Sample Plan Browser allows you to preview a library of sample business plans. You will find numerous business plan examples ranging from restaurants to non-profit organizations. A search tool will help sort through these plans based on a specific industry or key words. Don't be concerned about finding a plan that is identical your business concept. Look for plans that contain parallels characteristics, such as a product or service plan, or one that targets consumers versus business customers. Review several of these plans to get a better idea of the outline and content. This may give you a clearer vision of how your finished business plan may look.

Building Your Business Plan

Open *Business Plan Pro*™ and select the choice that starts a new plan. Optional resources help you throughout the experience of creating a business plan. For example, the movie offers an animated and audio overview of the software. Using the *EasyPlan Wizard*™ asks about your start date, the title of your plan, and other basic information such as:

- Do you sell products or services?
- Is your business a profit of a nonprofit organization?
- Is your business a start-up operation or an ongoing business?
- What kind of business plan do you want to create?
- Do you want to include the SWOT analysis?
- Will the business have a Web site?
- A series of revenue and expense questions structure the financial aspects of your plan with assistance throughout.
- Do you want to prepare a plan for three years (a standard plan) or a longer term plan of five years?

Save these decisions by using the drop down menu under File and clicking on Save or by clicking on the save icon at the top right of the menu bar. You can change your response to these decisions at any time. Review the plan outline by clicking on the Preview icon on the top of your screen, or by clicking on File, Print and then Preview within the Print window to see the outline of your business plan. *Business*

Plan Pro™ will enable you to change and modify the plan outline in any way you choose as you progress through each chapter.

Beyond the Classroom...

1. Choose an entrepreneur in your community and interview him or her. What's the "story" behind the business? How well does the entrepreneur fit the entrepreneurial profile described in this chapter? What advantages and disadvantages does the owner see in owning a business? What advice would he or she offer to someone considering launching a business?
2. Select one of the categories under the section "The Cultural Diversity of Entrepreneurship" in this chapter and research it in more detail. Find examples of business owners in that category. Prepare a brief report for your class.
3. Search through recent business publications (especially those focusing on small companies) and find an example of an entrepreneur, past or present, who exhibits the entrepreneurial spirit of striving for success in the face of failure. Prepare a brief report for your class.

Hey Buddy LLC

CHAPTER 2

Inside the Entrepreneurial Mind: From Ideas to Reality

The world is but a canvas to the imagination.
—*Henry David Thoreau*

The best way to have a good idea is to have lots of ideas.
—*Linus Pauling*

Learning Objectives

On completion of this chapter, you will be able to do the following:

1. Explain the differences among creativity, innovation and entrepreneurship.

2. Describe why creativity and innovation are such an integral part of entrepreneurship.

3. Understand how the two hemispheres of the human brain function and what role they play in creativity.

4. Explain the 10 "mental locks" that limit individual creativity.

5. Understand how entrepreneurs can enhance the creativity of their employees as well as their own creativity.

6. Describe the steps in the creative process

7. Discuss techniques for improving the creative process.

8. Describe the protection of intellectual property through patents, trademarks, and copyrights.

One of the tenets of entrepreneurship is the ability to create new and useful ideas that solve the problems and challenges people face every day. Entrepreneurs achieve success by creating value in the marketplace when they combine resources in new and different ways to gain a competitive edge over rivals. From Alexander Fleming's pioneering work that resulted in a cure for infections (penicillin) and the founders of the Rocket Chemical Company's fortieth try to create an industrial lubricant (WD-40) to Jeff Bezos's innovative use of the World Wide Web in retailing (Amazon.com) and Ted Turner's unique approach to the availability of television news (CNN), entrepreneurs' ideas have transformed the world.

As you learned in Chapter 1, entrepreneurs can create value in a number of ways—inventing new products and services, developing new technology, discovering new knowledge, improving existing products or services, finding different ways of providing more goods and services with fewer resources, and many others. Indeed, finding new ways of satisfying customers' needs, inventing new products and services, putting together existing ideas in new and different ways, and creating new twists on existing products and services are hallmarks of the entrepreneur!

ENTREPRENEURIAL PROFILE_____

Roger Adams: Heelys Inc.

Roger Adams grew up around skating because as a kid, he worked in his parents' skating rink, repairing skates and performing odd jobs. Inspired by James Bond movies, he also invented unusual devices in his spare time. To help pay for college, Adams designed sound and lighting systems for skating rinks. Given his background in the skating industry, it was only natural that Adams would turn there for inspiration years later as an adult when he was visiting a friend and watching roller skaters, skateboarders, and bicyclists on Manhattan Beach in California. "It seemed to me that there had to be some new way to have fun on wheels," he recalls. He took an old pair of Nike athletic shoes into his friend's workshop and, using a heated butter knife, cut them apart began experimenting with metal balls and wheels. Adams "cannibalized at least four pairs," he recalls, before hitting on a design that would allow the wearer to walk normally and then roll as if on roller skates by placing his or her weight on the rear of the shoe and placing one foot in front of the other for proper balance. Convinced he had invented a product that would sell, Adams invested $150,000 of his own money to secure a patent and perfect his design. Seven shoe companies and six sporting goods companies showed no interest in Adams's skate-shoe, and so he decided to launch his own company, Heelys Inc., to market them. Adams finally secured financing from a venture capital firm and ended up making an initial public offering in December 2006. Adams has turned over the management responsibilities of Heelys to others so that he can focus on his role as the company's "chief tinkerer" in his workspace, which he refers to as the "Lunatic Lab."[1]

Like many innovators, Adams created a successful business by taking everyday items that had existed for many years and looking at them in a different way.

Creativity, Innovation, and Entrepreneurship

LO 1

Explain the differences among creativity, innovation, and entrepreneurship.

According to the National Science Foundation, U.S. companies, government agencies, and universities invest nearly $343 billion annually in research and development (R&D). Small companies are an important part of the total R&D picture.[2] One study by the Small Business Administration reports that small companies produce 13 to 14 times more patents per employee than their larger rivals. Small businesses also produce more economically and technically important innovations than larger firms.[3] What is the entrepreneurial "secret" for creating value in the marketplace? In reality, the "secret" is no secret at all: it is applying creativity and innovation to solve problems and to exploit opportunities that people face every day. **Creativity** is the ability to develop new ideas and to discover new ways of looking at problems and opportunities. **Innovation** is the ability to *apply* creative solutions to those problems and opportunities to enhance or to enrich people's lives. Harvard's Ted Levitt says that creativity is *thinking* new things, and innovation is *doing* new things. In short, entrepreneurs succeed by *thinking and doing* new things or old things in new ways. Simply having a great new idea is not enough; transforming

creativity
the ability to develop new ideas and to discover new ways of looking at problems and opportunities.

innovation
the ability to apply creative solutions to problems and opportunities to enhance or to enrich people's lives.

the idea into a tangible product, service, or business venture is the essential next step. As management legend Peter Drucker said, "Innovation is the specific instrument of entrepreneurs, the means by which they exploit change as an opportunity for a different business or a different service."[4]

Successful entrepreneurs come up with ideas and then find ways to make them work to solve a problem or to fill a need. In a world that is changing faster than most of us ever could have imagined, creativity and innovation are vital to a company's success—and survival. That's true for businesses in every industry—from automakers to tea growers—and for companies of all sizes. However, creativity and innovation are the signatures of small, entrepreneurial businesses. Creative thinking has become a core business skill, and entrepreneurs lead the way in developing and applying that skill. In fact, creativity and innovation often lie at the heart of small companies' ability to compete successfully with their larger rivals. Even though they cannot outspend their larger rivals, small companies can create powerful, effective competitive advantages over big companies by "out-creating" and "out-innovating" them! If they fail to do so, entrepreneurs don't stay in business very long. Leadership expert Warren Bennis says, "Today's successful companies live and die according to the quality of their ideas."[5]

Sometimes innovation involves generating something from nothing. However, innovation is more likely to result from elaborating on the present, from putting old things together in new ways, or from taking something away to create something simpler or better. An experiment designed to improve the adhesive on tape resulted in a glue that hardly stuck at all. Although most researchers might have considered the experiment a total failure and scrapped it, this researcher asked a simple, creative question: What can you do with a glue when you take away most of its stickiness? The answer led to the invention of one of the most popular office products of all time: the Post-It note.

More often, creative ideas arise when entrepreneurs look at something old and think something new or different. Legendary Notre Dame football coach Knute Rockne, whose teams dominated college football in the 1920s, got the idea for his constantly shifting backfields while watching a burlesque chorus routine! Rockne's innovations in the backfield (which included the legendary "Four Horsemen") and his emphasis on the forward pass (a legal but largely unused tactic in this era) so befuddled opposing defenses that his teams compiled an impressive 105-12-5 record.[6]

ENTREPRENEURIAL PROFILE

Jerry Knoblach: Space Data Corporation

More recently, Jerry Knoblach, founder of Space Data Corporation, developed a new way to use old technology—weather balloons. Space Data uses large latex balloons that are inflated with hydrogen to lift shoebox-size payloads of electronics 20 miles into the stratospheres to serve as floating cellular telephone towers capable of providing thousands of square miles of coverage. Currently, Space Data's primary customers are utilities, oil and gas explorers, and trucking companies. Knoblach, however, came up with the idea of using his company's balloons, which burst after about 24 hours in the thin air of the upper atmosphere (the electronics float safely back to earth with the help of parachutes and are recovered later), to provide wireless Internet access to the 36 percent of the U.S. population that lives in rural areas and has no Internet connection. In another stroke of creative genius, Knoblach intends to use dairy farmers to launch the balloons each day. "They're very reliable people," he says, "and they have to milk the cows 24/7, 365 days a year, so they're great people to use as a launch crew."[7]

Entrepreneurship is the result of a disciplined, systematic process of applying creativity and innovation to needs and opportunities in the marketplace. It involves applying focused strategies to new ideas and new insights to create a product or a service that satisfies customers' needs or solves their problems. It is much more than random, disjointed tinkering with a new gadget. Millions of people come up with creative ideas for new or different products and services; most of them, however, never do anything with them. Entrepreneurs are people who connect their creative ideas with the purposeful action and structure of a business. Thus, successful entrepreneurship is a constant process that relies on creativity, innovation, and application in the marketplace.

Innovation must be a constant process because most ideas don't work and most innovations fail. One writer explains, "Trial—and lots of error—is embedded in entrepreneurship."[8] Karen

Anne Zien, co-founder of Polaroid Corporation's Creativity and Innovation Lab, estimates that for every 3,000 new product ideas, four make it to the development stage, two are actually launched, and only one becomes a success in the market. These new products are crucial to companies' success, however. According to Robert Cooper, a researcher who has analyzed thousands of new product launches, on average, new products account for a whopping 40 percent of companies' sales.[9] Still, successful entrepreneurs recognize that many failures will accompany innovations, and they are willing to accept their share of failures because they know that failure is merely part of the creative process. Rather than quit when they fail, entrepreneurs simply keep trying. While working as a textbook editor, James Michener had an idea for a book based on his experiences in the Solomon Islands during World War II. He sent the manuscript to a publisher and received the following note: "You are a good editor. Don't throw it all away trying to be a writer. I read your book. Frankly, it's not really that good." Michener persisted and went on to publish *South Pacific*, for which he won a Pulitzer Prize and which became the basis for one of Broadway's most successful musicals of all time.[10]

Entrepreneurship requires business owners to be bold enough to try their new ideas, flexible enough to throw aside those that do not work, and wise enough to learn about what will work based on their observations of what did not. We now turn our attention to creativity, the creative process, and methods of enhancing creativity.

Creativity—A Necessity for Survival

LO 2

Describe why creativity and innovation are such an integral part of entrepreneurship.

In this fiercely competitive, fast-paced, global economy, creativity is not only an important source for building a competitive advantage, but it also is a necessity for survival. When developing creative solutions to modern problems, entrepreneurs must go beyond merely relying on what has worked in the past. Past experiences shape the ways in which we perceive the world around us ("We've always done it this way"). That's why children are so creative and curious about new possibilities; society has not yet brainwashed them into an attitude of conformity, nor have they learned to accept *traditional* solutions as the *only* solutions. Retaining their creative "inner child," entrepreneurs are able to throw off the shackles on creativity and see opportunities for creating viable businesses where most people see what they've always seen (or, worse yet, see nothing). Creative exercises such as the one in Figure 2.1 can help adults reconnect with the creativity they exhibited so willingly as children.

Many years ago, during an international chess competition, Frank Marshall made what has become known as one of the most beautiful—and one of the most creative—moves ever made on a chess board. In a crucial game in which he was evenly matched with a Russian master player, Marshall found his queen under serious attack. Marshall had several avenues of escape for his queen available. Knowing that the queen is one of the most important offensive players on the chessboard, spectators assumed that Marshall would make a conventional move and push his queen to safety.

Using all the time available to him to consider his options, Marshall picked up his queen—and paused—and put it down on the most *illogical* square of all—a square from which the queen could easily be captured by any one of three hostile pieces. Marshall had done the unthinkable! He had sacrificed his queen, a move typically made only under the most desperate of circumstances. All the spectators—even Marshall's opponent—groaned in dismay. Then, the Russian, and finally the crowd, realized that Marshall's move was, in reality, a brilliant one. No matter how the Russian opponent took the queen, he would eventually be in a losing position. Seeing the inevitable outcome, the Russian conceded the game. Marshall had won the match in a rare and daring fashion: he had won by sacrificing his queen![11]

What lesson does this story hold for entrepreneurs? By suspending conventional thinking long enough to even consider the possibility of such a move, Marshall was able to throw off the usual paradigms constraining most chess players. He had looked beyond the traditional and orthodox strategies of the game and was willing to take the risk of trying an unusual tactic to win. The result: he won. Successful entrepreneurs, those who are constantly pushing technological and economic boundaries forward, constantly ask: "Is it time to sacrifice the queen?"

Merely generating one successful creative solution to address a problem or a need usually is not good enough to keep an entrepreneurial enterprise successful in the long run, however. Success—even survival—in this fiercely competitive, global environment requires entrepreneurs to tap their creativity (and that of their employees) constantly. Entrepreneurs can be sure that if

FIGURE 2.1

"How Creative Are You?"

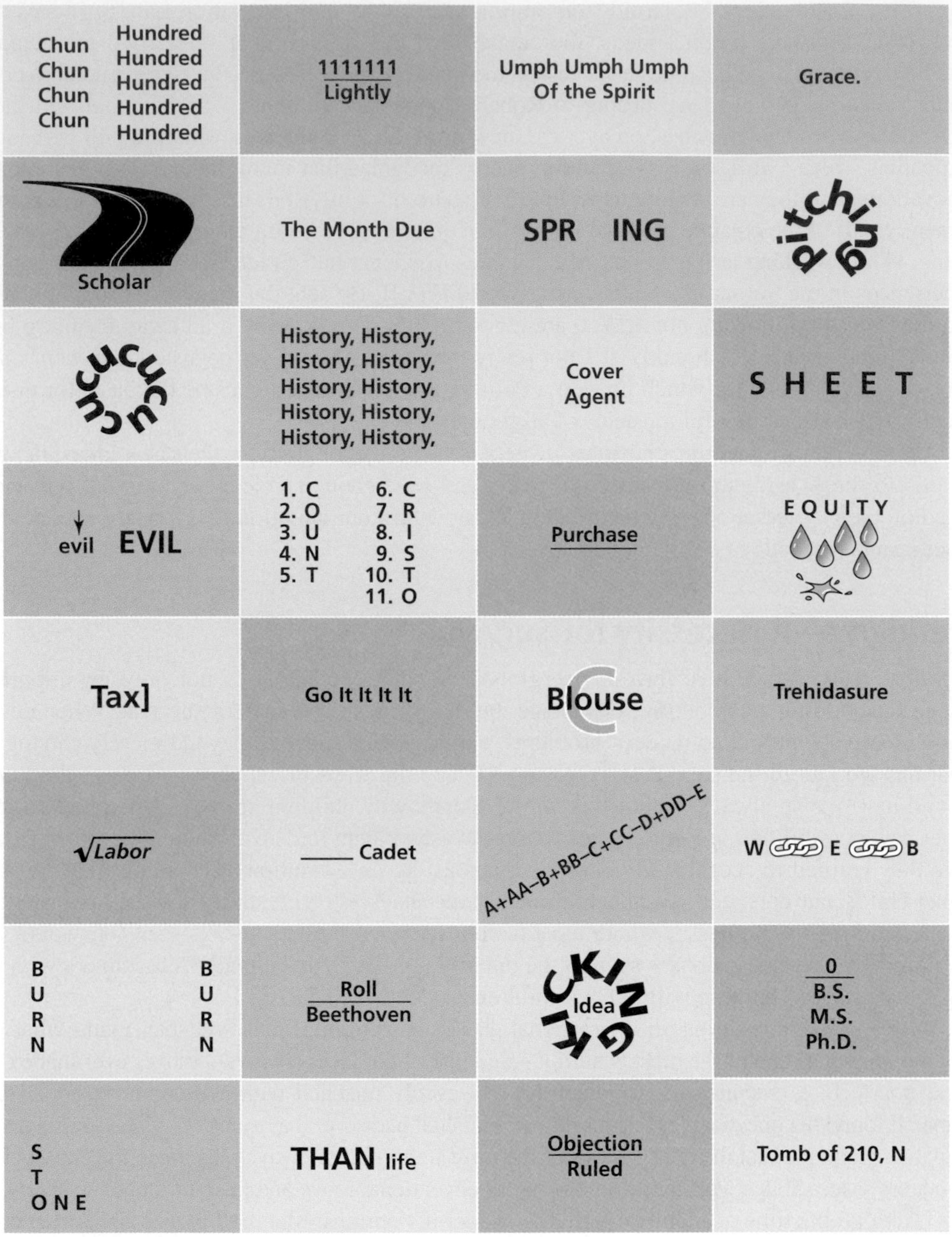

Chun Chun Chun Chun Hundred Hundred Hundred Hundred Hundred	1111111 Lightly	Umph Umph Umph Of the Spirit	Grace.
Scholar	The Month Due	SPR ING	pitching
cucucuc	History, History, History, History, History, History, History, History, History, History, History, History,	Cover Agent	S H E E T
↓ evil EVIL	1. C 6. C 2. O 7. R 3. U 8. I 4. N 9. S 5. T 10. T 11. O	Purchase	E Q U I T Y
Tax]	Go It It It It	Blouse	Trehidasure
√Labor	_____ Cadet	A+AA–B+BB–C+CC–D+DD–E	W E B
BURN BURN	Roll Beethoven	KICKING Idea	0 B.S. M.S. Ph.D.
S T O N E	THAN life	Objection Ruled	Tomb of 210, N

they have developed a unique, creative solution to solve a problem or to fill a need, a competitor (perhaps one six times zones away) is hard at work developing an even more creative solution to render theirs obsolete. This extremely rapid and accelerating rate of change has created an environment in which staying in a leadership position requires constant creativity, innovation, and entrepreneurship. A company that has achieved a leadership position in an industry but then ceases to innovate is soon toppled from its number one perch.

Creative Thinking

Research into the operation of the human brain shows that each hemisphere of the brain processes information differently and that one side of the brain tends to be dominant over the other. The human brain develops asymmetrically, and each hemisphere tends to specialize in certain functions. The left-brain is guided by linear, vertical thinking (from one logical conclusion to the next) whereas the right-brain relies on kaleidoscopic, lateral thinking (considering a problem from all sides and jumping into it at different points). The left-brain handles language, logic, and symbols; the right-brain takes care of the body's emotional, intuitive, and spatial functions.

The left-brain processes information in a step-by-step fashion, but the right-brain processes it intuitively—all at once, relying heavily on images.

Left-brained vertical thinking is narrowly focused and systematic, proceeding in a highly logical fashion from one point to the next. Right-brained lateral thinking, on the other hand, is somewhat unconventional, unsystematic, and unstructured, much like the image of a kaleidoscope, whirling around to form one pattern after another. It is this right-brain driven, lateral thinking that lies at the heart of the creative process. Those who have learned to develop their right-brained thinking skills tend to:

- Always ask the question, "Is there a better way?"
- Challenge custom, routine, and tradition.
- Be reflective, often staring out windows, deep in thought. (How many traditional managers would stifle creativity by snapping these people out of their "daydreams," chastise them for "loafing," and admonish them to "get back to work?")
- Be prolific thinkers. They know that generating lots of ideas increases the likelihood of coming up with a few highly creative ideas.
- Play mental games, trying to see an issue from different perspectives.
- Realize that there may be more than one "right answer."
- See mistakes as mere "pit stops" on the way to success.
- See problems as springboards for new ideas.
- Understand that failure is a natural part of the creative process. James Dyson spent 15 years and nearly his entire savings before he succeeded in developing the bagless vacuum cleaner that made him rich and famous. "If you want to discover something that other people haven't." he says, "you need to do things the wrong way. You don't learn from success."[12]
- Relate seemingly unrelated ideas to a problem to generate innovative solutions.
- Have "helicopter skills," the ability to rise above the daily routine to see an issue from a broader perspective and then swoop back down to focus on an area in need of change.

With 80 percent of the world's available farmland already in use and the global population expected to increase by 3 billion (almost all of it in cities) by 2050, experts are looking for new ways to grow enough food to feed everyone. As environmental scientist Dickson Despommier thought about how skyscrapers changed the concept of office buildings, he used right-brain thinking to contemplate how skyscrapers might change the future of farming. Using a skyscraper as inspiration, he began sketching a vertical farm equipped with rooftop solar panels that would power special "grow lights," making the farm capable of producing as much food as 588 acres of land! His research revealed existing technology from NASA that would capture evaporating water for irrigating the crops. In addition, because the vertical farm could be built in the heart of a city, the cost of transporting the food grown there (typically a significant part of the final cost of a food item) would be minimal. "Vertical farming will free the world from worrying about where our next meal will come from," says Despommier, who says that fifteen 30-story vertical farms could feed one million people.[13]

Although each hemisphere of the brain tends to dominate in its particular functions, the two halves normally cooperate, with each part contributing its special abilities to accomplish those tasks best suited to its mode of information processing. Sometimes, however, the two hemispheres may even compete with each other, or one half may choose not to participate. Some researchers have suggested that each half of the brain has the capacity to keep information from the other! The result, literally, is that "the left hand doesn't know what the right hand is doing."

Successful entrepreneurship requires both left- and right-brain thinking. Right-brain thinking draws on the power of divergent reasoning, which is the ability to create a multitude of original, diverse ideas. Left-brain thinking counts on convergent reasoning, the ability to evaluate multiple ideas and choose the best solution to a given problem. Entrepreneurs rely on right-brain thinking to generate innovative product, service, or business ideas. Then, they must use left-brain thinking to judge the market potential of the ideas they generate. Successful entrepreneurs have learned to coordinate the complementary functions of each hemisphere of the brain, using their brains' full creative power to produce pragmatic innovation. Otherwise, entrepreneurs, who

YOU BE THE CONSULTANT

The Spirit of Entrepreneurship in the Olympics

Entrepreneurs aren't the only ones who use creativity to create competitive advantages for themselves. Throughout history, Olympic athletes have pushed back the frontiers of their sports by developing new techniques, improved training methods, and innovative solutions to existing problems. One of the best examples of applying creativity to her sport was figure skater Sonja Henie, who relied on the creative process to throw off the paradigms that bound the other athletes competing in her sport.

Before Sonja Henie came along, figure skating routines were exactly that—routine. In competitions, skaters performed a series of precise moves that emphasized accuracy and control. But when the young Norwegian glided onto the ice, skating changed forever. Bringing the beauty and movement of ballet to the skating rink, Henie transformed the sport into the graceful combination of motion, music, and muscle that it remains today. From 1927 to 1936, Henie dominated ice skating by creatively blending her graceful ballet skills with her strength on the ice. She won 10 straight world championships, eight European titles, and a record three Olympic gold medals. Trained in both dance and ballet as a child, Henie cast aside the existing paradigms of what ice skating was as she recognized the possibilities of transferring dance movements onto the ice.

After winning her last world championship in 1936, Henie used her dance and skating skills to get into show business. She became an international star in movies and in traveling ice shows that gave her the freedom to use her creative genius on the ice. Even her glamorous and daring (for the 1930s) costumes proved to be an exciting innovation in ice skating as they emphasized the grace and flow of her movements. Later generations of ice skaters would push the sport even farther. Tenley Albright (1956 Olympics) and Peggy Fleming (1968 Olympics) introduced spins, twirls, and leaps. More recently, Tara Lipinsky, Kristi Yamaguchi, Nancy Kerrigan, Katarina Witt, and others have injected an element of gymnastics to ice skating, performing triple jumps and double and triple axels. Yet every one of these champions owes a debt of gratitude to Sonja Henie, the daring young skater who had the creativity and the courage to make innovations on the ice.

Sonja Henie became a champion by applying creativity and innovation to the sports she loved so much. Similarly, entrepreneurs can become "champions" in their industries by using their creative spirit to come up with new ideas, better products and services, and innovative techniques. Successful entrepreneurs rely on their ability to see the same things everyone else sees and to dream what no one else dreams.

1. What is a paradigm? How does a paradigm stifle creativity?
2. Work with a small group of your classmates to identify a local business that is bound by a paradigm. What impact is this paradigm having on the business? Identify the paradigm and then generate as many creative suggestions as you can in 20 minutes that would change this paradigm.
3. What can entrepreneurs do to throw off existing paradigms?

Based on "Innovations of the Olympic Games," *Fortune*, January 27, 1992, pp. 28–29.

Sculptor's block

rarely can be accused of being "half-hearted" about their business ideas, run the risk of becoming "half-headed."

How can entrepreneurs learn to tap their innate creativity more readily? The first step is to break down the barriers to creativity that most of us have erected over the years. We now turn our attention to these barriers and some suggested techniques for tearing them down.

Barriers to Creativity

LO 4
Understand the ten "mental locks" that limit individual creativity.

The number of potential barriers to creativity is virtually limitless—time pressures, unsupportive management, pessimistic co-workers, overly rigid company policies, and countless others. Perhaps the most difficult hurdles to overcome, however, are those that individuals impose on themselves. In his book *A Whack on the Side of the Head*, Roger von Oech identifies ten "mental locks" that limit individual creativity:[14]

1. *Searching for the one "right" answer.* Deeply ingrained in most educational systems is the assumption that there is one "right" answer to a problem. The average student who has completed four years of college has taken more than 2,600 tests; therefore, it is not unusual for this one-correct-answer syndrome to become an inherent part of our thinking. In reality, however, most problems are ambiguous. Depending on the questions one asks, there may be (and usually are) several "right" answers.

When Jeff Peri discovered that his young daughter suffered from multiple chemical sensitivities, he began searching for chemical-free products for his family. His wife, Lisa, jokingly said, "While you're at it, see if you can find a waterless carwash." Peri did find waterless carwash products, but they contained chemicals. He began working with a chemist and, after raising $100,000 in capital from family and friends, developed an organic carwash that lifts dirt from a car's surface, which can then be wiped down—without using any water. Had Peri not taken the time to reconsider the assumption that washing a car requires water, he never would have had the opportunity to launch Lucky Earth LLC, which now generates annual sales of $2 million.[15]

Tonya McCahon Photographs, LLC

ENTREPRENEURIAL PROFILE

Jeff & Lisa Peri: Lucky Earth LLC

2. *Focusing on "being logical."* Logic is a valuable part of the creative process, especially when evaluating ideas and implementing them. However, in the early imaginative phases of the process, logical thinking can restrict creativity. Focusing too much effort on being logical also discourages the use of one of the mind's most powerful creations: intuition. Von Oech advises us to "think something different" and to use non-logical thinking freely, especially in the imaginative phase of the creative process. Intuition, which is based on the accumulated knowledge and experiences a person encounters over the course of a lifetime and resides in the subconscious, can be unlocked. It is a crucial part of the creative process because using it often requires one to tear down long-standing assumptions that limit creativity and innovation.

Jerry Mix, chairman of a maker of swimming gear called Finis, loved to swim for exercise, but he often had trouble staying focused. Like many swimmers, Mix wished that he could listen to his MP3 player while he swam just like he did when he was on dry land. Inspired by his idea, Mix began working with an engineer to develop a waterproof MP3 player. Their early attempts to make earbuds waterproof failed because the water that enters a swimmer's ear distorts traditional sound waves. The two made a major breakthrough when they came up with a non-traditional idea of transmitting sound: "Why not use bone conduction?," a technique that uses vibrations to transmit sound through a person's skull and facial bones. They discovered that the water that naturally

SwiMP3 Finis Inc.

ENTREPRENEURIAL PROFILE

Jerry Mix: Finis

enters a swimmer's ear actually improves the quality of sound transmitted this way by sealing it in. Within two years, Finis was selling the SwiMP3, a pair of goggles equipped with a waterproof MP3 player and special cheekpads that transmit the music. The SwiMP3 now accounts for 20 percent of Finis's sales.[16]

3. *Blindly following the rules.* We learn at a very early age not to "color outside the lines," and we spend the rest of our lives blindly obeying such rules. Sometimes creativity depends on our ability to break the existing rules so that we can see new ways of doing things. Consider, for example, the top row of letters on a standard typewriter or computer keyboard:

Q W E R T Y U I O P

In the 1870s, Sholes & Company, a leading manufacturer of typewriters, began receiving numerous customer complaints about its typewriter keys sticking together when typists' fingers were practiced enough to go really fast. Company engineers came up with an incredibly creative solution to eliminate the problem of sticking keys. They designed a less efficient keyboard configuration, placing the letters O and I (the third and sixth most commonly used letters of the alphabet) so that the weakest fingers (the ring and little fingers) would strike them. By slowing down typists with this inefficient keyboard, the engineers solved the sticking keys problem. Today, despite the fact that computer technology has eliminated all danger of sticking keys, this same inefficient keyboard configuration remains the industry standard!

4. *Constantly being practical.* Imagining impractical answers to "what if" questions can be powerful stepping stones to creative ideas. Suspending practicality for awhile frees the mind to consider creative solutions that, otherwise, might never arise. Whenever Thomas Edison hired an assistant to work in his creative laboratory, he would tell the new employee, "Walk through town and list 20 things that interest you." When the worker returned, Edison would ask him to split the list into two columns. Then he would say, "Randomly combine objects from column A and column B and come up with as many inventions as you can." Edison's methods for stimulating creativity in his lab proved to be successful; he holds the distinction of being the only person to have earned a patent every year for 65 consecutive years![17]

Periodically setting aside practicality allows entrepreneurs to consider taking a product or a concept from one area and placing it in a totally different application.

ENTREPRENEURIAL PROFILE

Richard Dyson: the Dyson Airblade

Richard Dyson spent ten years developing the motor that powers his unique bagless vacuum cleaner and finally came up with one that runs at 110,000 revolutions per minute, three times faster than competitors' motors. While studying ways to apply that same technology to another product, Dyson discovered that he could squirt air at 400 miles per hour through a tiny slot, creating an "air blade." Dyson asked himself: "How can we use this concept?" The creative answer he came up with: a revolutionary hand dryer for use in restrooms, in which the blade safely wipes water off of the hands in a mere 10 seconds rather than the average 40 seconds required for a traditional hand dryer. Not only do users get dry hands faster, but the device also cuts energy use by 75 percent.[18]

5. *Viewing play as frivolous.* A playful attitude is fundamental to creative thinking. There is a close relationship between the "haha" of humor and the "aha" of discovery. Play gives us the opportunity to reinvent reality and to reformulate established ways of doing things. Children learn when they play, and so can entrepreneurs. Watch children playing and you will see them invent new games, create new ways of looking at old things, and learn what works (and what doesn't) in their games.

Entrepreneurs can benefit from playing in the same way that children do. They, too, can learn to try new approaches and discover what works and what doesn't. Creativity results when entrepreneurs take what they have learned at play, evaluate it, corroborate it with other knowledge, and put it into practice. Employees who have fun when solving problems are more likely to push the boundaries and come up with a genuinely creative solution than those who do not. What kind of invention would Wile E. Coyote, who seems to have an inexhaustible supply of ideas for catching the roadrunner in those cartoons, create in this situation? How might the Three Stooges approach this problem? What would *Seinfeld*'s Kramer suggest? What would a six-year-old do? The idea is to look at a problem or situation from different perspectives.

6. *Becoming overly specialized.* Defining a problem as one of "marketing" or "production," or some other area of specialty limits the ability to see how it might be related to other issues. Creative thinkers tend to be "explorers," searching for ideas outside their areas of specialty. The idea for the roll-on deodorant stick came from the ballpoint pen. The famous Mr. Potato Head toy was invented by a father sitting with his family at the dinner table who noted how much fun his children had playing with their food.

7. *Avoiding ambiguity.* Ambiguity can be a powerful creative stimulus; it encourages us to "think something different." Being excessively detailed in an imaginative situation tends to stifle creativity. Ambiguity, however, requires us to consider at least two different, often contradictory notions at the same time, which is a direct channel to creativity. Ambiguous situations force us to stretch our minds beyond their normal boundaries and to consider creative options we might otherwise ignore. Although ambiguity is not a desired element when entrepreneurs are evaluating and implementing ideas, it is a valuable tool when they are searching for creative ideas and solutions. Entrepreneurs are famous for asking a question and then going beyond the first answer to explore other possible answers. The result is that they often find business opportunities by creating ambiguous situations.

Copreneurs Tom and Sally Fegley, owners of Tom and Sally's Handmade Chocolates, considered the possibility of other answers to the question "What uses exist for chocolate sauce?" Although most people see chocolate sauce merely as a topping for ice cream or other desserts, their friend Larry (whom they have nicknamed "Dirty Larry") came up with a different idea. The Fegleys were trying to come up with an innovative recipe that would keep their string of awards at a local fund-raising event devoted to celebrating chocolate, the Brown-Out. Their fun-loving friend suggested they shoot for the Most Decadent Award. "I'll go naked," he said. "You paint melted chocolate all over my body, and you'll win!" Although the Fegleys declined Larry's offer, his suggestion got them thinking. Before long, Tom had whipped up a batch of chocolate dessert topping, labeled it "Chocolate Body Paint" and included the following directions on the bottle: "Heat to 98.6 degrees, apply liberally, and let your imagination run wild." Today, Chocolate Body Paint is the Fegleys' best-selling product, and it has won awards and has been featured in publications ranging from *The Wall Street Journal* to *Playboy* magazine. "Never judge an idea by its source," advises Sally.[19]

ENTREPRENEURIAL PROFILE _____

Tom & Sally Fegley:
Tom & Sally's Handmade Chocolates

8. *Fearing looking foolish.* Creative thinking is no place for conformity! New ideas rarely are born in a conforming environment. People tend toward conformity because they don't want to look foolish. The fool's job is to whack at the habits and rules that keep us thinking in the same old ways. In that sense, entrepreneurs are top-notch "fools." They are constantly questioning and challenging accepted ways of doing things and the assumptions that go with them. The noted entrepreneurship theorist, Joseph Schumpeter, wrote that entrepreneurs perform a vital function—"creative destruction"—in which they rethink conventional assumptions and discard those that are no longer useful. According to Schumpeter, "The function of entrepreneurs is to reform or revolutionize the pattern of production by exploiting an invention or, more generally, an untried technological possibility for producing a new commodity or producing an old one in a new way, by opening up a new source of supply of materials or a new outlet for products, by reorganizing an industry or so on."[20] In short, entrepreneurs look at old ways of doing things and ask, "Is there a better way?" By destroying the old, they create the new.

9. *Fearing mistakes and failure.* Creative people realize that trying something new often leads to failure; however, they do not see failure as an end. It represents a learning experience on

the way to success. As you learned in Chapter 1, failure is an important part of the creative process; it signals entrepreneurs when to change their course of action. Entrepreneurship is all about the opportunity to fail! Many entrepreneurs failed numerous times before they succeeded. Despite their initial setbacks, they were able to set aside the fear of failure and kept trying.

The key, of course, is to see failure for what it really is: a chance to learn how to succeed. Entrepreneurs who willingly risk failure and learn from it when it occurs have the best chance of succeeding at whatever they try. Successful entrepreneurs equate failure with innovation rather than with defeat.

10. *Believing that "I'm not creative."* Some people limit themselves because they believe creativity belongs only to the Einsteins, Beethovens, and da Vincis of the world.

Unfortunately, this belief often becomes a self-fulfilling prophecy. People who believe they are not creative will, in all likelihood, behave that way and will make that belief come true. Some people who are considered geniuses, visionaries, and inventors actually are no smarter and have no more innate creative ability than the average person; however, they have learned how to think creatively and are persistent enough to keep trying until they succeed.

By avoiding these ten mental locks, entrepreneurs can unleash their own creativity and the creativity of those around them as well. Successful entrepreneurs are willing to take some risks, explore new ideas, play a little, ask "What if?" and learn to appreciate ambiguity. By doing so, they develop the skills, attitudes, and motivation that make them much more creative—one of the keys to entrepreneurial success. Table 2.1 lists some questions designed to spur imagination.

TABLE 2.1 Questions to Spur the Imagination

People learn at an early age to pursue answers to questions. Creative people, however, understand that good *questions* are extremely valuable in the quest for creativity. Some of the greatest breakthroughs in history came as a result of creative people asking thought-provoking questions. Bill Bowerman, contemplating a design for the soles of running shoes over a breakfast of waffles, asked, "What would happen if I poured rubber into my waffle iron?" He did, and that's how Nike shoes came to be. (The Bowerman's rubber-coated waffle iron is on display in the Nike Town superstore and museum in Chicago.) Albert Einstein, creator of the theory of relativity, asked, "What would a light wave look like to someone keeping pace with it?" Masura Ibuka, who created the Sony Walkman, asked, "Why can't we remove the recording function and speaker and put headphones on the recorder?"

To jump-start creativity, Steve Gillman suggests writing a short list of adjectives, such as light, cheap, fast, big, short, small, fun, and others, and then use them to ask "what if" questions. What if this product could be lighter? What if this process could be faster? What if this service could be cheaper?

The following questions can help spur your imagination:

1. Is there a new way to do it?	10. Can you put it to other uses?
2. Can you borrow or adapt it?	11. What else could we make from this?
3. Can you give it a new twist?	12. Are there other markets for it?
4. Do you merely need more of the same?	13. Can you reverse it?
5. Less of the same?	14. Can you eliminate it?
6. Is there a substitute?	15. Can you put it to another use?
7. Can you rearrange the parts?	16. What idea seems impossible but, if
8. What if you do just the opposite?	executed, would revolutionize your
9. Can you combine ideas?	business?

Sources: Adapted from David Lidsky, "Brain Calisthenics," *Fast Company*, December 2004, p. 95; Thea Singer, Christopher Caggiano, Ilan Mochari, and Tahl Raz, "If You Come, They Will Build It," *Inc.*, August 2002, p. 70; Creativity Web, "Question Summary," http://www.ozemail.com.au/~caveman/Creative/Techniques/osb_quest.html; *Bits & Pieces*, February 1990, p.20; *Bits & Pieces*, April 29, 1993, "Creativity Quiz, " *In Business*, November/December 1991, p.18; Doug Hall, *Jump Start Your Brain*, (New York: Warner Books, Inc., 1995), pp. 86–87; Christine Canabou, "Imagine That," *Fast Company*, January 2001, p. 56; Steve Gillman, "Step Out of Business Mode to Solve Problems," *Regan's Manager's eBulletin*, May 22, 2008, p. 1.

How to Enhance Creativity

Enhancing Organizational Creativity

LO 5

Understand how entrepreneurs can enhance their own creativity and that of their employees as well.

Creativity doesn't just happen in organizations; entrepreneurs must establish an environment in which creativity can flourish—for themselves and for their workers. "Everyone has a creative spark, but many factors can inhibit its ignition," says one writer. "Part of an [entrepreneur's] role is to see the spark in his or her people, encourage its ignition, and champion its success."[21] New ideas are fragile creations, but the right company culture can encourage people to develop and cultivate them. Ensuring that workers have the freedom and the incentive to be creative is one of the best ways to achieve innovation. "Developing a corporate culture that both fosters and rewards creativity…is critical because companies must be able to churn out innovations at a fast pace since technology has shortened product life cycles," says Geoff Yang, successful entrepreneur and venture capitalist.[22] Entrepreneurs can stimulate their own creativity and encourage it among workers by following these suggestions, which are designed to create a culture of innovation.

INCLUDE CREATIVITY AS A CORE COMPANY VALUE Innovative companies do not take a passive approach to creativity; they are proactive in their search for new ideas. One of the best ways to do this is to establish an innovative company culture, and setting a creative tone in an organization begins with the company's mission statement. Entrepreneurs should incorporate creativity and innovation into their companies' mission statements and affirm their commitment to them in internal communications. Innovation allows a company to shape, transform, and create its future, and the natural place to define that future is in the mission statement. Because creativity and innovation are vital to a company's success, they also should be a natural part of the performance appraisal process.

Innovation can be a particularly powerful competitive weapon in industries that are resistant to change and are populated by companies that cling to the same old ways of doing business. Even small companies that are willing to innovate can have a significant impact on entire industries by shaking up the status quo with their creative approaches. The result often is growing market share and impressive profits for the innovator. Apple's introduction of the iPod in 2001 and the iTunes Music Store in 2003 revolutionized the staid music business, sent CD sales plummeting by 35 percent, and allowed the company to increase its profits by more than 3,000 percent over the next three years.[23]

EMBRACING DIVERSITY One of the best ways to cultivate a culture of creativity is to hire a diverse workforce. When people solve problems or come up with ideas, they do so within the framework of their own experience. Hiring people from different backgrounds, cultural experiences, hobbies, and interests provides a company with a crucial raw material needed for creativity. Smart entrepreneurs enhance organizational creativity by hiring beyond their own comfort zones.

Focusing the talent and creativity of a diverse group of employees on a problem or challenge is one of the best ways to generate creative solutions. Research by Harvard Business School professor Karim Lakhani concludes that the experiences, viewpoints, and thought processes of diverse groups of people are powerful tools for solving problems creatively. "It's very counterintuitive," says Lakhani, "but not only did the odds of a [problem] solver's success actually increase in fields outside his expertise, but also the further a challenge was from his specialty, the greater was the likelihood of success."[24] The lesson for entrepreneurs: To increase the odds of a successful creative solution to a problem, involve in the process people whose background and experience lies *outside* of the particular problem area.

EXPECTING CREATIVITY Employees tend to rise—or fall—to the level of expectations entrepreneurs have of them. One of the best ways to communicate the expectation of creativity is to give employees permission to be creative. At one small company that manufactures industrial equipment, the owner put a "brainstorming board" in a break area. Anyone facing a sticky problem simply posts it on a brightly colored piece of paper on the board. Other workers are invited to share ideas and suggestions by writing them on white pieces of paper and posting them around the problem. The board has generated many creative solutions that otherwise would not have come up.

EXPECTING AND TOLERATING FAILURE Creative ideas will produce failures as well as successes. People who never fail are not being creative. Creativity requires taking chances, and managers must remove employees' fear of failure. The surest way to quash creativity throughout an organization is to punish employees who try something new and fail. Cambridge Consultants, a company that creates products for clients in five industries, allows employees to spend a portion of their time working on "pet projects" that they find exciting and believe have potential. In addition, Cambridge sets aside 10 percent of its annual revenue to provide seed capital for spin-off companies based on employees' most promising ideas. If the spin-off succeeds, the employee gets to operate it and enjoy the profits, in which Cambridge shares. If it fails, the employee gets his or her old job back, and Cambridge simply writes off the investment as a loss.[25]

CREATING AN ORGANIZATIONAL STRUCTURE THAT NOURISHES CREATIVITY John Kao, an economist whose nickname is "Mr. Creativity," says that innovative companies are structured like spaghetti rather than a traditional pyramid. In a spaghetti-style organization, employees are encouraged to mix and mingle constantly so that creative ideas flow freely throughout the company.[26] A well-planned physical layout that encourages interaction and collaboration among employees from all parts and all levels of a company also boosts a company's creative capacity.

ENCOURAGING CURIOSITY Entrepreneurs and their employees constantly should ask "what if…" questions and to take a "maybe we could…" attitude. Challenging standing assumptions about how something should be done ("We've always done it that way.") is an excellent springboard for creativity. Doing so allows people to break out of assumptions that limit creativity. Encouraging employees to "think big" also helps. "Incremental innovation is not a winner's game," says creativity expert John Kao. "The opportunity these days is to become a disruptive inventor," striving for major changes that can revolutionize an entire industry and give the company creating it a significant competitive advantage.[27]

CREATE A CHANGE OF SCENERY PERIODICALLY The physical environment in which people work has an impact on their level of creativity. The cubicles made so famous in the Dilbert cartoon strip can suck the creativity right out of a workspace. Transforming a typical office space—even one with cubicles—into a haven of creativity does not have to be difficult or expensive. Covering bland walls with funny posters, photographs, murals, or other artwork, adding splashes of color, and incorporating live plants can enliven a workspace and enhance creativity. Because creativity is at the heart of their jobs, employees at Davison Design and Development, a product design company, work in a setting that more closely resembles an amusement park than an office complex. CEO George Davison designed the office, known as Inventionland™, to get employees out of their offices, to interact with one another, and to be inspired by a fun, whimsical environment. The 60,000-square-foot space includes a pirate ship where employees design toys and games for clients and a Thinktank Treehouse for hardware designers. Davison calls Inventionland™ "the world's most innovative workplace" and says that the unusual design has helped the company grow by 10 percent in just 15 months.[28] Even though creating their own version of Inventionland™ may not be not practical for every business, entrepreneurs can still stimulate creativity by starting meetings with some type of short, fun exercise designed to encourage participants to think creatively.

VIEWING PROBLEMS AS OPPORTUNITIES Every problem offers the opportunity for innovation. One of the best ways to channel a company's innovative energy productively is to address questions that focus employees' attention on customers' problems and how to solve them.

ENTREPRENEURIAL PROFILE

Nick Bayss: Smart Lid Systems

While working in his family's café, Nick Bayss began thinking about the danger that a cup of coffee or tea that is too hot poses to consumers and the liability issues it creates for the companies that serve hot beverages. He came up with the idea for a cup lid that changes color depending on the temperature of the liquid it contains. Using a food-grade compliant color-changing additive, Bayss perfected the temperature sensitive lid and launched Smart Lid Systems. If the lid turns red, it means that the contents are too hot to drink safely, but a rich-brown lid means the drink is the perfect temperature. He also added another important safety feature: The lid turns a mottled color if it is not securely fastened to the cup. Smart Lid Systems already sells more than 100 million lids annually, and Bayss says that the global hot lid market is between 80 and 100 billion units per year.[29]

PROVIDING CREATIVITY TRAINING Almost everyone has the capacity to be creative, but developing that capacity requires training. One writer claims, "What separates the average person from Edison,

Picasso, or even Shakespeare isn't creative capacity—it's the ability to tap that capacity by encouraging creative impulses and then acting upon them."[30] Training accomplished through books, seminars, workshops, and professional meetings can help everyone learn to tap their creative capacity.

PROVIDING SUPPORT Entrepreneurs must give employees the tools and the resources they need to be creative. Entrepreneurs should remember that creativity often requires non-work phases, and giving employees time to "daydream" is an important part of the creative process. The creativity that employees display when they know that managers value innovation can be amazing—and profitable. These **intrapreneurs,** entrepreneurs who operate within the framework of an existing business, sometimes can transform a company's future or advance its competitive edge. Jim Lynch, an electrical engineer at iRobot, a leading maker of robotic devices including the Roomba vacuum cleaner, was cleaning the gutters on his house one day and thought, "This is the perfect job for a robot because it fits our company's three criteria: dumb, dirty, and dangerous." Lynch began tinkering and built a gutter-cleaning robot using a spaghetti ladle and an electric screwdriver. At the company's "Idea Bake-Off," an event at which employees have 10 minutes to pitch a new product idea, Lynch's idea received solid support and became an official project. Fellow employees volunteered to work on Lynch's team, and within one year, iRobot introduced the Looj, the world's first gutter-cleaning robot![31]

intrapreneurs
entrepreneurs who operate within the framework of an existing business.

DEVELOPING A PROCEDURE FOR CAPTURING IDEAS Small companies that are outstanding innovators do not earn that mantle by accident; they have a process in place to solicit and then collect new ideas. When workers come up with creative ideas, however, not every organization is prepared to capture them. The unfortunate result is that ideas that might have vaulted a company ahead or made people's lives better simply evaporate. Clever entrepreneurs establish processes within their companies that are designed to harvest the results of employees' creativity. Marissa Mayer, a top manager at Google, frequently holds informal "office hours" like a college professor for employees who want to pitch new ideas. At one session, Mayer learned about one employee's pet project—a search engine for his own computer. Mayer assembled a team to work with the employee, provided the resources they needed, and in just two months, the team had created Google Desktop.[32]

TALKING WITH CUSTOMERS—OR BETTER YET INTERACTING WITH THEM Innovative companies take the time to get feedback about how customers use the companies' products or services, listening for new ideas. The voice of the customer (VOC) can be an important source of creative ideas, and the Internet allows entrepreneurs to hear their customers' voices quickly and inexpensively. Some companies go even further, observing their customers actually using their products or services to glean ideas that may lead to improvements and new features.

Employees at IDEO, a creative development company in San Francisco, filmed kids brushing their teeth with Gillette's Oral-B toothbrushes. Because the brush handles were too long for their small hands, the children held the brushes in their fists rather than in their fingertips like an adult would. This simple observation led IDEO to work with Gillette to develop a children's toothbrush with a fat, squishy handle that fit their small hands well. Shortly after its release, the Squish-Grip became the best-selling children's toothbrush in the world.[33]

LOOKING FOR USES FOR YOUR COMPANY'S PRODUCTS OR SERVICES IN OTHER MARKETS Focusing on the "traditional" uses of a product or service limits creativity—and a company's sales. Entrepreneurs can boost sales by finding new applications, often in unexpected places, for their products and services.

In 2002, Neil Wadhawan and Raj Raheja launched Heartwood Studios, a company that produced 3-D renderings and animations of buildings and products for architects and designers. Their business was successful, but a brainstorming session helped the entrepreneurs to realize that their company's 3-D renderings had applications in other industries as well. Today Heartwood Studios has clients in the defense and aerospace industries as well as in the fields of entertainment and sports. In fact, the company creates animations for use on the giant screens in sports arenas for the Dallas Cowboys and the New Jersey Nets.[34]

REWARDING CREATIVITY Entrepreneurs can encourage creativity by rewarding it when it occurs. Financial rewards can be effective motivators of creative behavior, but non-monetary rewards such as praise, recognition, and celebration usually offer more powerful incentives for creativity.

ENTREPRENEURIAL PROFILE ___

IDEO: Gillette

ENTREPRENEURIAL PROFILE ___

Neil Wadhawan & Raj Raheja: Heartwood Studios

ENTREPRENEURIAL PROFILE

Digital Communications Corporation

Digital Communications Corporation, a small company that develops advanced wireless technologies, recognizes employees who develop patentable inventions with stock options, cash awards, and honors at an Inventors' Dinner. The reward system works; within two years after implementing it, the number of patent applications Digital Communications filed increased by a factor of five![35]

Modeling creative behavior. Creativity is "caught" as much as it is "taught." Companies that excel at innovation find that the passion for creativity starts at the top. Entrepreneurs who set examples of creative behavior, taking chances, and challenging the status quo will soon find their employees doing the same.

ENTREPRENEURIAL PROFILE

Mark Constantine: Lush Cosmetics

For example, at Lush Cosmetics, a fast-growing maker of soaps, shampoos, lotions, and moisturizers, founder Mark Constantine understands that a constant stream of innovative new products is one key to his company's success. That's why he holds annual "Mafia meetings," at which Constantine and his staff mark one-third of the company's products for elimination. Although dropping one-third of Lush's product line every year is risky and means that the product development team must come up with at least 100 new products annually, it gives team members incredible freedom and fearlessness to dream. CEO Constantine himself works on new product development for Lush, and most of his ideas, like those of other team members, are never made into finished products. By modeling creative behavior, Constantine encourages creativity among his staff.[36]

Enhancing Individual Creativity

Just as entrepreneurs can cultivate an environment of creativity in their organizations by using the techniques described above, they can enhance their own creativity by using the following techniques:

ALLOW YOURSELF TO BE CREATIVE   As we have seen, one of the biggest obstacles to creativity occurs when a person believes that he or she is not creative. Giving yourself the permission to be creative is the first step toward establishing a pattern of creative thinking. Refuse to give in to the temptation to ignore ideas simply because you fear that someone else may consider them "stupid." When it comes to creativity, there are no stupid ideas!

GIVE YOUR MIND FRESH INPUT EVERY DAY   To be creative, your mind needs stimulation. Do something different each day—listen to a new radio station, take a walk through a park or a shopping center, or pick up a magazine you never read.

ENTREPRENEURIAL PROFILE

Doris Raymond: The Way We Wore

The Way We Wore, a huge vintage clothing store in Los Angeles started by Doris Raymond in 2004 that stocks garments from the Victorian era to the 1980s, has become a destination for designers from many fashion houses and retailers, ranging from Marc Jacobs to Forever 21, who are looking for inspiration for their clothing collections. Recognizing that meeting customers' demand for fresh designs gives their clothing lines a competitive advantage, many designers are looking to the past for creative ideas, taking note not only of fabrics and patterns but also the smallest details such as buttons and the type of stitching used on pockets. For instance, New York fashion designer Zac Posen recently came across a piece of colorful ribbon from the early 1920s that became the inspiration for many of the items in his collection. These fashion experts have discovered that exposing their minds to "new" designs is a great way to stimulate their own creativity.[37]

OBSERVE THE PRODUCTS AND SERVICES OF OTHER COMPANIES, ESPECIALLY THOSE IN COMPLETELY DIFFERENT MARKETS   Creative entrepreneurs often borrow ideas from companies that are in businesses totally unrelated to their own. In the 1950s, Ruth and Elliott Handler, cofounders of Mattel Inc., drew the inspiration for the best-selling doll of all time, Barbie (named after the Handler's daughter), from a doll called Lilli that was based on a shapely character in a German comic strip, and then borrowed the idea of dressing her in stylish outfits from cardboard cutout games that were popular in that era.[38] One day as Tariq and Kamran Farid were thinking about ways to increase sales at their flower shop, the brothers came up with the creative idea of combining fresh fruits such as melons, strawberries, pineapples, and others into artistic, floral-like arrangements. The Farid brothers launched Edible Arrangements in 1999 with $16,000 of their own money, and the business became a hit. Today, Edible Arrangements has more than 870 franchised outlets around the world and generates annual sales of $26 million.[39]

RECOGNIZE THE CREATIVE POWER OF MISTAKES Innovations sometimes are the result of serendipity, finding something while looking for something else, and sometimes they arise as a result of mistakes. Creative people recognize that even their errors may lead to new ideas, products, and services. Charles Goodyear worked for five years trying to combine rubber with a variety of chemicals to prevent it from being too soft in hot weather and too brittle in cold weather. One cold night in 1839, Goodyear was combining rubber, sulfur, and white lead when he accidentally spilled some of the mixture on a work stove. The substances melted together to form a new compound that had just the properties Goodyear was looking for! Goodyear named the process he discovered accidentally "vulcanization," and today practically every product made from rubber depends upon it.[40]

NOTICE WHAT IS MISSING Sometimes entrepreneurs spot viable business opportunities by noticing what is *missing*. The first step is to determine whether a market for the missing product or service actually exists (perhaps the reason it does not exist is that there is not market potential), which is one of the objectives of building a business plan.

While living in Miami, Florida, dog-lover and fashion model Carlotta Lennox noticed that when people walked their dogs in the local park, they lacked most of the supplies their pets needed. Thinking about the prevalence of soft drink vending machines, Lennox came up with the idea for a successful business: vending machines that sell dog supplies. "There was a need for pickup bags, toys, and water," she says. Lennox spent the next several years researching the idea and developing a business plan. In 2005, she received a patent for her doggie

Hey Buddy LLC

ENTREPRENEURIAL PROFILE_____

Carlotta Lennox: Hey Buddy! Vending

vending machine and trademarks for her company logos and launched Hey Buddy! She placed her first Hey Buddy! vending machine—stocked with lots of doggie necessities such as treats, tennis balls, frisbees, dog sun glasses, water, bowls, and other items—in Bark Park Central in Dallas, Texas, and now has dozens of the machines across the United States.[41]

KEEP A JOURNAL HANDY TO RECORD YOUR THOUGHTS AND IDEAS Creative ideas are too valuable to waste so always keep a journal nearby to record them as soon as you get them. Leonardo Da Vinci was famous for writing down ideas as they struck him. Patrick McNaughton invented the neon blackboards that restaurants use to advertise their specials. In addition to the neon blackboard, McNaughton has invented more than 30 new products, many of which are sold through the company that he and his sister, Jamie, own. McNaughton credits much of his creative success to the fact that he writes down every idea he gets and keeps it in a special folder. "There's no such thing as a crazy idea," he insists.[42]

LISTEN TO OTHER PEOPLE No rule of creativity says that an idea has to be your own! Sometimes the best business ideas come from someone else, but entrepreneurs are the ones to act on them.

While working at Microsoft, Brenda Cannon went to a family reunion with her son, Davon. "We came home and started talking about how much fun it would be to have a Web site with pictures from the reunion, news from family members, and so on," she says. "So we built one." Soon, the site morphed into a place where far-flung relatives were posting blogs, adding family recipes, and uploading videos. Before long, several of Cannon's friends asked her to build similar sites for them. After listening to them, Cannon realized that the site had business potential. She and

Andréanna Seymore Photography

ENTREPRENEURIAL PROFILE_____

Brenda & Davon Cannon: FamilyLobby.com

Davon launched FamilyLobby.com, and within several months, the company had signed on 1,500 customers, keeping Cannon so busy that she quit her job at Microsoft to run Family Lobby.com from her home.[43]

LISTEN TO CUSTOMERS Some of the best ideas for new products and services or new applications of an existing product or service come from a company's customers. Entrepreneurs who take the time to listen to their customers often receive ideas they may never have come up with on their own. At Lush Cosmetics, founder Mark Constantine routinely draws ideas for new products or product names from the company's loyal customers (affectionately known as "Lushies") in the company's chat room.[44]

TALK TO A CHILD As we grow older, we learn to conform to society's expectations about many things, including creative solutions to problems. Children place very few limitations on their thinking; as a result, their creativity is practically boundless. (Remember all of the games you and your friends invented when you were young?) Frustrated at not being able to use the small pieces of broken crayons, eleven-year-old Cassidy Goldstein invented a plastic crayon holder now sold in stores across the United States. Inspired by the plastic tubes that keep roses fresh in transport, Goldstein developed a plastic device capable of holding a crayon, no matter how small it is.[45]

DO SOMETHING ORDINARY IN AN UNUSUAL WAY Experts say that simply doing something out of the ordinary can stimulate creativity. To stimulate his own creativity, Scott Jones, an entrepreneur who is known as "the guy who invented voicemail" (and many other items as well), often engages in what other people might consider bizarre behavior—eating without utensils, watching TV sitting one foot away from the screen, or taking a shower with his eyes closed. "Anything I normally do, I'll do differently just to see what happens," says Jones.[46]

KEEP A TOY BOX IN YOUR OFFICE Your box might include silly objects such as wax lips, a yo-yo, a Slinky, fortune cookie sayings, feathers, a top, a compass, or a host of other items. When you are stumped, pick an item at random from the toy box and think about how it relates to your problem.

DO NOT THROW AWAY SEEMINGLY "BAD" IDEAS Some creative ideas prove to be impractical, too costly, or too silly to work. Creative entrepreneurs, however, do not discard these seemingly bad ideas. Instead, they ask, "What part of this idea can I build on?" and "What could I change about this idea to make it work?" They realize that seemingly bad ideas can be the nucleus of a really good idea.

READ BOOKS ON STIMULATING CREATIVITY OR TAKE A CLASS ON CREATIVITY Creative thinking is a technique that anyone can learn. Understanding and applying the principles of creativity can improve dramatically the ability to develop new and innovative ideas.

TAKE SOME TIME OFF Relaxation is vital to the creative process. Getting away from a problem gives the mind time to reflect on it. It is often during this time, while the subconscious works on a problem, that the mind generates many creative solutions. One study reports that 35 percent of entrepreneurs say that they come up with their best ideas during down time, when they are away from work.[47]

BE PERSISTENT Entrepreneurs know that one secret to success is persistence and a "don't quit" attitude. Twelve publishers rejected J. K. Rowling's manuscript about the adventures of a boy wizard and his friends, which she started writing at age 25 when she was a single mother trying to raise her children on Welfare. Then Bloomsbury, a small London publishing house, agreed to publish 1,000 copies of *Harry Potter and the Philosopher's Stone.* Rowling's six-part Harry Potter book series went on to sell more than 400 million copies worldwide, making the author a billionaire.[48]

The Creative Process

LO 6

Describe the steps in the creative process.

Although creative ideas may appear to strike as suddenly as a bolt of lightning, they are actually the result of the creative process, which involves seven steps:

1. Preparation
2. Investigation
3. Transformation
4. Incubation

5. Illumination
6. Verification
7. Implementation

Step 1. Preparation

This step involves getting the mind ready for creative thinking. Preparation might include a formal education, on-the-job training, work experience, and taking advantage of other learning opportunities. This training provides a foundation on which to build creativity and innovation. As one writer explains, "Creativity favors the prepared mind."[49] For example, Dr. Hamel Navia, a scientist at tiny Vertex Pharmaceuticals, was working on a promising new drug to fight the AIDS virus. His preparation included earning an advanced degree in the field of medicine and learning to use computers to create 3-D images of the protein molecules he was studying.[50] How can you prepare your mind for creative thinking?

- Adopt the attitude of a lifelong student. Realize that educating yourself is a never-ending process. Look at every situation you encounter as an opportunity to learn.

Anthony Cialone, founder of Lehigh Technologies, spent years studying the process of cryogenically freezing materials and began to think about how to apply the process to old tires, which pose an environmental problem. Cialone co-developed a new technology that uses liquid nitrogen to freeze scrap tire material and then grinds it into a fine powder that can be used to enhance a variety of products. Products made with his company's rubber powder take on some of the powder's qualities, such as elasticity and impact resistance. Cialone's 83,000-square-foot factory can produce 100 million pounds of rubber powder annually, the equivalent of removing six million scrap tires from the environment.[51]

- Read...a lot...and not just in your field of expertise. Many innovations come from blending ideas and concepts from different fields in science, engineering, business, and the arts. Reading books, magazines, and papers covering a variety of subject matter is a great way to stimulate your creativity.
- Clip articles of interest to you and create a file for them. Over time, you will build a customized encyclopedia of information from which to draw ideas and inspiration.
- Take time to discuss your ideas with other people, including those who know little about it as well as experts in the field. Sometimes, the apparently simple questions an "unknowledgeable" person asks lead to new discoveries and to new approaches to an old problem.[52]
- Join professional or trade associations and attend their meetings. There you have the chance to brainstorm with others who have similar interests. Learning how other people have solved a particular problem may give you fresh insight into solving it.
- Invest time in studying other countries and their cultures; then travel there. Our global economy offers incredible business opportunities for entrepreneurs with the necessary knowledge and experience to recognize them. One entrepreneur began a lucrative business exporting a variety of consumer products to Latvia after he accompanied his daughter there on a missionary trip. He claims that he never would have seen the opportunity had he not traveled to Latvia with his daughter.
- Develop listening skills. It's amazing what you can learn if you take the time to listen to other people—especially those who are older and have more experience. Try to learn something from everyone you meet.
- Eliminate creative distractions. Interruptions from telephone calls, e-mails, and visitors can crush creativity. Allowing employees to escape to a quiet, interruption-free environment enhances their ability to be creative.

Step 2. Investigation

This step requires one to develop a solid understanding of the problem, situation, or decision at hand. To create new ideas and concepts in a particular field, an individual first must study the problem and understand its basic components. Creative thinking comes about when people make careful observations of the world around them and then investigate the way things work (or fail to work). For example, Dr. Navia and another scientist at Vertex had spent several years conducting research on viruses and on a protein that blocks a virus enzyme called protease. His exploration of the various ways to block this enzyme paved the way for his discovery.

Step 3. Transformation

convergent thinking
the ability to see similarities and the connections among various data and events.

Transformation involves viewing the similarities and the differences among the information collected. This phase requires two types of thinking: convergent and divergent. **Convergent thinking** is the ability to see the *similarities* and the connections among various and often diverse data and events.

ENTREPRENEURIAL PROFILE

Chris Savarese: RadarGolf

With a handicap of 17, Chris Savarese lost a lot of golf balls, a common problem among golfers. After hitting a particularly bad slice one day, Savarese began searching through patents for ideas for an effective way to track errant golf balls. He discovered patents as far back as 1925, but none provided an ideal solution. Then one day while he was shopping at a department store, Savarese saw someone set off the alarm when a clerk forgot to remove the electronic security tag from a sweater the customer had purchased. "That technology might work in a golf ball," he remembers thinking. Savarese acquired some of the security tags, took them apart, and discovered that they rely on radio frequency identity (RFID) tags. He quit his job and launched RadarGolf, a company that sells RFID-equipped golf balls and a hand-held tracking device that can detect lost balls up to 100 feet away. Annual sales now exceed $1 million—all because Savarese used convergent thinking to blend several existing products into one creative idea.[53]

divergent thinking
the ability to see among various data and events.

Divergent thinking is the ability to see the *differences* among various data and events. While developing his AIDS-fighting drug, Dr. Navia studied the work of other scientists whose attempts at developing an enzyme-blocking drug had failed. He was able to see the similarities and the differences in his research and theirs and to build on their successes while avoiding their failures.

How can you increase your ability to transform the information collected into a purposeful idea?

- Evaluate the parts of the situation several times, trying to grasp the "big picture." Getting bogged down in the details of a situation too early in the creative process can diminish creativity. Look for patterns that emerge.
- Rearrange the elements of the situation. By looking at the components of an issue in a different order or from a different perspective, you may be able to see the similarities and the differences among them more readily. Rearranging them also may help uncover a familiar pattern that had been masked by an unfamiliar structure.
- Try using synectics (a term derived from the Greek words for "to bring together" and "diversity"), taking two seemingly nonsensical ideas and combining them. For instance, why not launch a bookstore with no physical storefront and no books—an accurate description of what Jeff Bezos did when he came up with the idea for Amazon.com.[54]
- Before locking into one particular approach to a situation, remember that several approaches might be successful. If one approach produces a deadend, don't hesitate to jump quickly to another. Considering several approaches to a problem or opportunity simultaneously is like rolling a bowling ball down each of several lanes in quick succession. The more balls you roll down the lanes, the greater is the probability of hitting at least one strike. Resist the temptation to make snap judgments on how to tackle a problem or opportunity. The first approach may not be the best one.

Step 4. Incubation

The subconscious needs time to reflect on the information collected. To an observer, this phase of the creative process would be quite boring; it looks as though nothing is happening! In fact, during this phase, it may appear that the creative person is *loafing*. Incubation occurs while the individual is away from the problem, often engaging in some totally unrelated activity.

Dr. Navia's creative powers were working at a subconscious level even when he was away from his work, not even thinking about his research on AIDS-fighting drugs.

How can you enhance the incubation phase of the creative process, letting ideas marinate in your mind?

- Walk away from the situation. Time away from a problem is vital to enhancing creativity. A study by Wilson Brill, an expert on creativity, of how 350 great ideas became successful products shows that two-thirds of the ideas came to people while they were *away* from work—in the shower, in their cars, in bed, on a walk, and other non-work situations.[55] Doing something totally unrelated to the problem gives your subconscious mind the chance to work on the problem or opportunity. Indeed, the "three b's"—bath, bed, and bus—are conducive to creativity.
- Take the time to daydream. Although it may *look* as if you're doing nothing, daydreaming is an important part of the creative process. That's when your mind is most free from paradigms and other self-imposed restrictions on creativity. Feel free to let your mind wander, and it may just stumble onto a creative solution.
- Relax—and play—regularly. Perhaps the worst thing you can do for creativity is to work on a problem or opportunity constantly. Soon enough, fatigue walks in, and creativity walks out! Great ideas often are incubated on the golf course, on the basketball court, in the garden, or in the hammock.
- Dream about the problem or opportunity. Although you may not be able to dream on command, thinking about an issue just before you drift off to sleep can be an effective way to encourage your mind to work on it while you sleep, a process called lucid dreaming. When he gets in bed, prolific inventor, serial entrepreneur, and author Ray Kurzweil focuses on a particular problem, sometimes imagining that he is giving a speech about his success at solving it. "This has the purpose of seeding your subconscious to influence your dreams," he explains. Often, while he is asleep, ideas and potential solutions to the problem drift into his dreams.[56]
- Work on the problem or opportunity in a different environment–somewhere other than the office. Take your work outside on a beautiful fall day or sit on a bench in a mall. The change of scenery will likely stimulate your creativity.

Step 5. Illumination

This phase of the creative process occurs at some point during the incubation stage when a spontaneous breakthrough causes "the light bulb to go on." It may take place after five minutes—or five years. In the illumination stage, all of the previous stages come together to produce the "Eureka factor"—the creation of the innovative idea. In one study of 200 scientists, 80 percent said that at least once a solution to a problem had "just popped into their heads"—usually when they were away from the problem.[57] For Dr. Navia, the illumination stage occurred one day while he was reading a scientific journal. As he read, Dr. Navia says he was struck with a "hallucination" of a novel way to block protease.

Although the creative process itself may last for months or even years, the suddenness with which the illumination step occurs can be deceiving, making the process appear to occur much faster than it actually does. Dr. Michael Clarke had been researching cures for cancer for years, but his "eureka" moment came one day while he was showing University of Michigan medical students a slide of cancer cells. He pointed out that some of them were mature cells and others were immature stem cells. Traditional cancer treatments traditionally focus on attacking the mature cells, and current research was focused on using stem cells as a possible treatment. As he pointed out the cells to his students, Clarke thought, "What if it were the other way around? What if the stem cells are *causing* the cancer?" He changed the focus of his research to reflect his new idea, and early results look promising. Clarke recently launched a company, OncoMed, to focus on this line of research and landed an investment from pharmaceutical giant GlaxoSmithKline that ultimately could grow to $1.4 billion.[58]

Step 6. Verification

For entrepreneurs, validating an idea as realistic and useful may include conducting experiments, running simulations, test marketing a product or service, establishing small-scale pilot programs, building prototypes, and many other activities designed to verify that the new idea will work and is practical to implement. The goal is to subject the innovative idea to the test of cold, hard reality. At this phase, appropriate questions to ask include:

- Is it *really* a better solution to a particular problem or opportunity? Sometimes an idea that appears to have a bright future in the lab or on paper dims considerably when put to the test of reality.
- Will it work?
- Is there a need for it?
- If so, what is the best application of this idea in the marketplace?
- Does this product or service idea fit into our core competencies?
- How much will it cost to produce or to provide?
- Can we sell it at a reasonable price that will produce adequate sales, profit, and return on investment for our business?

To test the value of his new drug formulation, Dr. Navia used power computers at Vertex Pharmaceuticals to build 3-D Tinkertoy-like models of the HIV virus and then simulated his new drug's ability to block the protease enzyme. Subsequent testing of the drug verified its safety. "I was convinced that I had an insight that no one else had," he recalls.[59]

Step 7. Implementation

The focus of this step is to transform the idea into reality. Plenty of people come up with creative ideas for promising new products or services, but most never take them beyond the idea stage. What sets entrepreneurs apart is that they *act* on their ideas. An entrepreneur's philosophy is "Ready, aim, fire," not "Ready, aim, aim, aim, aim…" NCT Group, a small company, had developed a system that sent mirror images of sound waves through ceramic tiles to cancel out noise. One day, an engineer wondered what would happen if he sent music instead of "anti-noise" through the tiles. He connected a radio to the unit, and from the flat tiles came the sound of the Beatles! The company took the engineer's discovery and developed two-inch-thick wall-mounted speakers that produce high-quality audio for the consumer market! Another small business, Cygnus Inc., had created a patch that was designed to deliver drugs through the wearer's skin. Wile taking apart a patch one day, a researcher realized that not only did it deliver drugs, but it also absorbed material from the body. Cygnus transformed the discovery into a line of watch-like devices that monitor the glucose levels of diabetic patients.[60] The key to both companies' success was their ability to take a creative idea for a useful new product and turn it into a reality. As one creativity expert explains, "Becoming more creative is really just a matter of paying attention to that endless flow of ideas you generate, and learning to capture and act upon the new that's within you."[61]

For Dr. Navia and Vertex Pharmaceuticals, the implementation phase required testing the drug's ability to fight the deadly virus in humans. If it proved to be effective, Vertex would complete the process by bringing the drug to market. In this final phase of testing, Navia was so certain that he was on the verge of a major breakthrough in fighting AIDS that he couldn't sleep at night. Unfortunately the final critical series of tests proved that Dr. Navia's flash of creativity was, as he now says, "completely, totally, and absolutely incorrect." Although his intuition proved to be wrong this time, Dr. Navia's research into fighting AIDS continues. Much of the current work at Vertex is based on Dr. Navia's original idea. Although it proved to be incorrect, his idea has served a valuable purpose: generating new ideas. "We are now applying a powerful technology in HIV research that wasn't used before, one inspired by a hunch," he says.[62]

A Wave of Opportunity

The rising cost of oil and other fossil fuels and their negative impact on the environment have stimulated a global interest in alternative energy sources that are less expensive and more environmentally friendly. Creative entrepreneurs see plenty of business opportunities in these alternative energy sources and are working hard to create companies to provide them. George Taylor, founder of Ocean Power Technology, is one of those entrepreneurs. Taylor, a former surfer who grew up in Australia, used his training as an electrical engineer to become an inventor and a serial entrepreneur. In 1970, he and several other engineers started a company that designed flat-panel liquid crystal displays before selling it to a larger business. (The technology they developed is the foundation of the flat-panel screens used in everything from televisions to cell phones.)

More recently, Taylor was pondering the future of the world's energy supply and demand and saw the potential for demand to outstrip supply. "In 20 years, China alone will be consuming all of the energy that the entire world uses now," he says. He began thinking about ways to generate clean, inexpensive electricity and considered researching wind power but ruled it out because it is intermittent and unpredictable and requires constructing large, unsightly turbines. He realized that the world's oceans are a huge source of potential energy. He began tinkering and invented the PowerBuoy, a high-tech buoy that captures the up-and-down, mechanical motion that ocean waves create, converts it into electricity using a piston-like device and a generator, and transfers it through cables on the sea floor to power grids onshore. The buoys, which are designed to be deployed in 100 to 150 feet of water and can be linked together into large "farms" a mile or more offshore, are 50 feet tall, but only about 9 feet of the buoy extends above the ocean surface. The buoys pose almost no threat to the environment because they are barely visible from the shore, emit no greenhouse gases, and have no negative impact on ocean life. What makes Ocean Power's buoys unique is the bank of sophisticated sensors that measure each wave in the first one-tenth of a second, allowing an onboard computer to adjust the internal piston to capture the maximum amount of energy from the wave.

Researchers at Oregon State University concur with Taylor's wave energy idea; their studies show that the ocean's wave energy has the potential to supply a significant portion of the world's demand for electricity. In addition, because 60 percent of the world's population lives within 40 miles of the coast, transporting electricity generated by the ocean would be simple enough. Taylor's Company has installed several buoys in demonstration projects around the world—from Hawaii to Spain—for a variety of customers, including the U.S. Navy and the New Jersey Board of Public Utilities. Taylor says that PowerBuoys can generate electricity at 5 cents per kilowatt hour, a rate that is comparable to coal, which currently is the cheapest way to generate electricity, but without creating the pollutants that come from burning coal.

As experienced entrepreneurs, Taylor and his partner, Joseph Burns (who died in 2001) were selective in choosing their investors. Because they knew that their business model would most likely take years to come to fruition, they wanted patient investors who would take a long-term view. "We wanted friends, high net worth individuals, and customers with long-range goals who were willing to be long-term strategic partners," says Taylor. In 2003, Taylor guided Ocean Power through an initial public offering (IPO), but he had to go to the London Stock Exchange because at the time, there was little interest in the United States in investing in an alternative energy company. In 2007, the tide had turned in the United States, and OPT made a second public offering, this time on the NASDAQ in New York. Taylor's strategy has been to perfect the company's technology on a small scale before taking on larger projects. Ocean Power's installed its first PowerBuoy in 1997 off the coast of New Jersey, a project that generated one kilowatt of electricity. Recent projects have grown larger, including a buoy field off the cost of Oregon that is capable of generating up to 50 megawatts of electricity, enough to power 50,000 homes.

Ocean Power Technologies

Like most entrepreneurs who are constantly looking into the future, Taylor has plans to build a 37-foot wide, 100-ton super PowerBuoy capable of generating 500 kilowatts, which he says is the "magic number" for alternative sources of electricity. At that point, economies of scale kick in, and a field of super buoys could generate huge amounts of electricity at a cost that is less than that of generating an equivalent amount of power using coal. As he stares wistfully over the ocean, Taylor, now 75, says, "It's a very exciting thing to come late in one's career. It keeps me young."

1. On a scale of 1 (low) to 10 (high), how would you rate George Taylor's creative idea? Explain. On a scale 1 (very simple) to 10 (highly complex), how would you rate Taylor's idea?

2. Visit the Ocean Power Technologies Web site at www.oceantechnologies.com to learn more about the company. Explain how Taylor applied the steps of the creative process described in this chapter to come up with the idea of using ocean wave energy to generate electricity.

3. Would you be willing to invest in Ocean Power Technologies? Explain.

Sources: Adapted from Dan Drollette, "The Next Little Thing: Electricity from Wave Power," *FSB*, December 2006/January 2007, pp. 26–38; David Erlich, "Ocean Power Tech Gets Oregon Contract," *Cleantech*, August 21, 2007, http://media.cleantech.com/1638/ocean-power-tech-gets-oregon-contract.

LO 7

Discuss techniques for improving the creative process.

Techniques for Improving the Creative Process

Teams of people working together usually can generate more and more creative ideas. Five techniques that are especially useful for improving the quality of creative ideas from teams are brainstorming, mind-mapping, force field analysis, Triz, and rapid prototyping.

Brainstorming

Brainstorming

a process in which a small group of people interact with very little structure with the goal of producing a large quantity of novel and imaginative ideas.

Brainstorming is a process in which a small group of people interact with very little structure with the goal of producing a large *quantity* of novel and imaginative ideas. The goal is to create an open, uninhibited atmosphere that allows members of the group to "free-wheel" ideas. Participants should suggest any ideas that come to mind *without evaluating or criticizing them*. As group members interact, each idea sparks the thinking of others, and the spawning of ideas becomes contagious. The free-flowing energy generated by the team becomes the genesis of a multitude of ideas, some of which may be impractical; however, those impractical ideas may lead to one idea that results in a breakthrough product or service for a company. For a brainstorming session to be successful, entrepreneurs should follow these guidelines:

- Keep the group small—just five to eight members. Amazon founder Jeff Bezos uses the "two-pizza rule"—if a brainstorming group can eat two pizzas, it's too big.[63]
- Make the group as diverse as possible. Include people with different backgrounds, disciplines, and perspectives. At Joe Designer Inc., a product development and graphic communications company in New York City, every employee takes part in brainstorming sessions. "We bring in everybody from the bookkeeper to the office manager because they see things completely differently than we do," says cofounder Joe Raia.[64]
- Encourage participants to engage in some type of aerobic exercise before the session. One study found that people who exercised—walking, bicycling, swimming, or running—before brainstorming sessions were more creative than those who did not exercise.[65]
- Emphasize that company rank and department affiliation are irrelevant. Every member of the brainstorming team is on equal ground.
- Have a well-defined problem for the group to address. Stating the problem in the form of a "Why," "How," or "What" question often helps.
- Rather than waste precious group meeting time getting participants up to speed, provide everyone involved in the session with relevant background material about the problem to be solved. Invite participants to submit at least three ideas by e-mail before the brainstorming session takes place. This gets people's minds focused on the issue.
- Limit the session to 40 to 60 minutes. Beyond that, participants grow weary, and creativity flags because brainstorming is an intense activity.
- Take a field trip. Visit the scene of the problem, if possible. Research shows that brainstorming teams that go "onsite" actually come up with more and better ideas.[66]
- Appoint someone (preferably not a brainstorming participant) the job of recorder. The recorder should write every idea on a flip chart or board so that everyone can see it.
- Use a seating pattern that encourages communication and interaction (e.g., circular or U-shaped arrangements).
- Throw logic out the window. The best brainstorming sessions are playful and anything but logical.
- Encourage *all* ideas from the team, even wild and extreme ones. Discourage participants from editing their ideas. Not only can ideas that initially seem crazy get the group's creative juices flowing, but they also can spread creativity like wildfire. In addition, the group often can polish some of these wild ideas into practical, creative solutions!
- Establish a goal of *quantity* of ideas over *quality* of ideas. There will be plenty of time later to evaluate the ideas generated. At Ideo Inc., a Silicon Valley design firm, brainstorming teams shoot for at least 150 ideas in a 30-to 45-minute session.[67] When chemist Linus Pauling received his second Nobel Prize, someone asked him how he came up with so many great ideas. Pauling replied simply, "I come up with *lots* of ideas."[68]
- Forbid evaluation or criticism of any idea during the brainstorming session. No idea is a bad idea. Criticism slams the brakes on the creative process instantly!

- Encourage participants to use "idea hitch-hiking," building new ideas on those already suggested. Often, some of the best solutions are those that are piggybacked on others.
- Dare to imagine the unreasonable. Creative ideas often arise when people suspend conventional thinking to consider far-fetched solutions.

At Nottingham-Spirk, an industrial design firm whose success depends on the creativity of its people, employees routinely use brainstorming to come up with new product ideas and designs. The focus of these sessions is to generate a large quantity of ideas, "from mild to wild," says co-founder John Nottingham, rather than to emphasize the quality of the ideas. By the end of the session, the walls are covered with pieces of paper containing scribbles, sketches, and notes, representing 100 or more ideas. Only after the brainstorming session do employees begin to focus on the quality of the ideas generated. In these meetings, employees judge each idea using a simple scale. Each person can display one of three cards: "Who Cares?," "Nice," or "Wow!" (All participants display their cards simultaneously.) A consensus of "Who Cares?" cards means that the group discards the idea, but a strong showing of "Wow!" cards means the idea moves forward for refinement. A vote of "Nice" usually means that the idea goes back for more brainstorming, hopefully transforming it into a "Wow!" idea. An idea for a Christmas tree stand that uses a swivel joint and a locking pedal initially received a "Nice" rating from the group. The idea's champion kept tinkering with it, ultimately adding a self-regulating automatic watering device and other features before returning to the group. In its second pass, the idea went from "Nice" to "Wow!" Since 2002, the SwivelStraight tree stand has sold one million units.[69]

Mind-Mapping

Another useful tool for jump-starting creativity is mind-mapping, an extension of brainstorming. One strength of mind-mapping is that it reflects the way the brain actually works. Rather than throwing out ideas in a linear fashion, the brain jumps from one idea to another. In many creative sessions ideas are rushing out so fast that many are lost if a person attempts to shove them into a linear outline. Creativity suffers. **Mind-mapping** is a graphical technique that encourages thinking on both sides of the brain, visually displays the various relationships among ideas, and improves the ability to view a problem from many sides.

The mind-mapping process works this way:

- Start by writing down or sketching a picture symbolizing the problem or area of focus in the center of a large blank page. Tony Buzan, originator of the mind-mapping technique, suggests using ledger paper or covering an entire wall with butcher paper to establish a wide open attitude toward creativity.
- Write down *every* idea that comes into your mind, connecting each idea to the central picture or words with a line. Use key words and symbols to record ideas in shorthand. Work as quickly as possible for no more than 20 minutes, doing your best to capture the tide of ideas that flows from your brain. Just as in brainstorming, do not judge the quality of your ideas; just get them onto the paper. Build new ideas on the backs of existing ones. If you see a connection between a new idea and one already on the paper, connect them with a line. If not, simply connect the idea to the center symbol. You will organize your ideas later in the process.
- When the flow of ideas slows to a trickle, stop! Don't try to force creativity.
- Allow your mind to rest for a few minutes and then begin to integrate the ideas on the page into a mind map. Use colored pens and markers to connect ideas with similar themes or to group ideas into related clusters. As you organize your thoughts, look for new connections among your ideas. Sometimes the brain needs time to process the ideas in a mind map. (Recall the incubation stage of the creative process.) Walking away from the mind map and the problem for a few minutes or a few hours may lead to several new ideas or to new relationships among ideas. One entrepreneur created the format for his company's business plan with a mind map rather than with a traditional linear outline. When he finished, he not only knew what he should include in his plan but he also had a clear picture of the order in which to sequence the elements.

mind-mapping
a graphical technique that encourages thinking on both sides of the brain, visually displays the various relationships among ideas, and improves the ability to view a problem from many sides.

Force Field Analysis

Force field analysis is a useful technique for evaluating the forces that support and oppose a proposed change. It allows entrepreneurs to weigh both the advantages and the disadvantages of a particular decision and to maximize the variables that support it and minimize those that work against it. The process, which, like brainstorming, works well with a group, begins by making three columns and listing the problem to be addressed in the center column. In the column on the left, the group should list driving forces, those that support the issue and move it forward. In the column on the right, the group should list the restraining forces, those that hold back the company from implementing the idea. The specific forces the group may come up with are almost limitless, but some of the factors the team should consider include people, values, costs, trends, traditions, politics, costs, revenues, environmental impact, regulations, and attitudes.

Once the group has identified a reasonable number of driving and restraining forces (four to ten is typical), the next task is to assign a numerical value that reflects the strength of that particular force. For the driving forces column, scores range from 1 (weak) to 4 (strong), and in the restraining forces column, scores range from -1 (weak) to -4 (strong). Adding the scores for the driving forces column and the restraining forces column shows which set of forces dominates the issue. The higher the total score, the more feasible is the idea. If the decision is a "go," the group can focus on ideas to create new driving forces, strengthen existing driving forces, and minimize the impact of restraining forces.

Force field analysis produces many benefits, particularly when it is combined with other creativity enhancing techniques. It helps entrepreneurs judge the practicality of a new idea, identify resources the company can use to bring the idea to market, recognize obstacles that the company must overcome to implement the idea, and suggest ways to conquer those obstacles.

Figure 2.2 shows a sample force field analysis for a small liberal arts college that is considering an entrepreneurial venture, launching a pharmacy school.

Triz

Developed in 1946 by Genrich Altshuller, a 22-year-old naval officer in the former Soviet Union, TRIZ (pronounced "trees") is a systematic approach designed to help solve any technical problem, whatever its source. The name is derived from the acronym for the Russian phrase that translates as "theory of inventive problem solving." Unlike brainstorming and mind-mapping, which are right-brained activities, TRIZ is a left-brained, scientific, step-by-step process that is based on the study of hundreds of the most innovative patents across the globe. Altshuller claimed that these innovations followed a particular set of patterns. Unlocking the principles behind those patterns allows one not only to solve seemingly insurmountable problems but also to predict where the next challenges would arise.

FIGURE 2.2

Sample Force Field Analysis

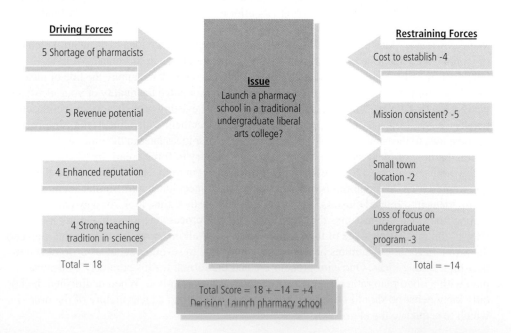

Driving Forces
- 5 Shortage of pharmacists
- 5 Revenue potential
- 4 Enhanced reputation
- 4 Strong teaching tradition in sciences

Total = 18

Issue
Launch a pharmacy school in a traditional undergraduate liberal arts college?

Restraining Forces
- Cost to establish -4
- Mission consistent? -5
- Small town location -2
- Loss of focus on undergraduate program -3

Total = −14

Total Score = 18 + −14 = +4
Decision: Launch pharmacy school

Altshuller and his colleagues developed 40 principles underlying these innovative patents and then developed the "TRIZ contradiction matrix," a tool that combines these principles to solve a problem. They recognized that innovations come about when someone is able to overcome the inherent contradictions in a process. For instance, in the packaging industry, a contradiction exists between the effectiveness of child-proof safety caps for medicine containers and making those containers easy for authorized users to open. Manufacturers of mattresses face the contradiction of making mattresses that are both hard and soft. Too often, companies rely on a very unimaginative solution to contradictions such as these; they compromise. Rather than settle for a mediocre compromise, the TRIZ contradiction matrix is designed to *resolve* these conflicts using the 40 principles Altshuller developed. One axis of the matrix displays the characteristic of the process to be improved, and the other axis displays the conflicting characteristic that is becoming worse.

For example, suppose that a candy maker wants to make syrup-filled, bottle-shaped chocolates by molding the chocolate bottles and then pouring syrup into the mold. To speed production of the finished product to meet demand, the business owner tries heating the syrup to allow for faster pouring, but the heated syrup melts the molded chocolate bottles and distorts their shape (the contradiction – see figure 2.3). Using the TRIZ contradiction matrix, the candy maker recognizes the problem as a conflict between speed and shape. Speed is the characteristic to be improved, and shape is the characteristic that

| | Characteristic that is getting worse | | | | | |
	Volume of stationary object	Speed	Force	Stress or pressure	Shape	Stability of the object
Volume of stationary object	—	*	Taking out Mechanical vibration Thermal expansion	Intermediary Parameter changes	Nested doll Taking out Parameter changes	Discarding and recovering Mechanics substitution Parameter changes Composite materials
Speed	*	—	The other way round Mechanics substitution Dynamics Periodic action	Universality Mechanical vibration Strong oxidants Composite materials	Dynamics Discarding and recovering Mechanical vibration Parameter changes	Mechanics substitution Homogeneity Segmentation Mechanical vibration
Force	Taking out Phase transitions Mechanical vibration Thermal expansion	The other way round Mechanics substitution Dynamics Equipotentiality	—	Mechanical vibration Skipping Beforehand cushioning	Preliminary action Parameter changes Composite materials Discarding and recovering	Parameter changes Preliminary action Skipping
Stress or pressure	Parameter changes Intermediary	Universality Parameter changes Phase transitions	Phase transitions Parameter changes Skipping	—	Parameter changes Asymmetry Dynamics Preliminary action	Parameter changes Homogeneity Taking out Composite materials
Shape	Nested doll Taking out Parameter changes	Parameter changes Discarding and recovering Mechanical vibration	Parameter changes Preliminary action Thermal expansion Composite materials	Discarding and recovering Dynamics Preliminary action Spheroidality and curvature	—	Homogeneity Segmentation Mechanical vibration Asymmetry

Characteristic to be improved

FIGURE 2.3

TRIZ Contradiction Matrix

Source: © 2006. www.TRIZ40.com.

is getting worse. The principles that the matrix suggests for solving this problem include: (1) changing the dynamics of the object or the environment (e.g., making a rigid part flexible), (2) discarding or recovering parts of an object (e.g., dissolving a protective case when it is no longer needed), (3) causing an object to vibrate or oscillate (e.g., transforming a standard knife into a electric knife by introducing oscillating blades), and (4) changing the properties of the object (e.g., freezing the chocolate syrup and then molding the bottles around the syrup).

Choosing principle number 4, the candy maker decides to change the properties of the chocolate syrup by adding a compound that causes it to solidify when exposed to air, making it easier and faster to coat with chocolate. Once enclosed inside the chocolate, the syrup once again becomes a liquid. Problem solved![70]

Rapid Prototyping

Generating creative ideas is a critical step in the process of taking an idea for a product or a service successfully to the market. However, recall that many (perhaps most) ideas that entrepreneurs come up with fail. Inventor and serial entrepreneur Scott Jones says that his kids still enjoy teasing him about one of his offbeat ideas that flopped: a pair of microturbines imbedded in the soles of shoes that would propel the wearer forward. (Jones abandoned the idea after seeing a similar concept fail flamboyantly in the movie *Jackass*.)[71] Rapid prototyping plays an important part in the creative process because it serves as a way to screen ideas that are not practical or just won't work so that entrepreneurs can focus their creative energy on other ideas. The premise behind **rapid prototyping** is that transforming an idea into an actual model will point out flaws in the original idea and will lead to improvements in its design. "If a picture is worth a thousand words, a prototype is worth ten thousand," says Steve Vassallo of Ideo Inc.[72]

rapid prototyping
the process of creating a model of an idea, enabling an entrepreneur to discover flaws in the idea and to make improvements in the design.

The three principles of rapid prototyping are the three *R*'s: rough, rapid, and right. Models do not have to be perfect; in fact, in the early phases of developing an idea, perfecting a model usually is a waste of time. The key is to make the model good enough to determine what works and what does not. Doing so allows an entrepreneur to develop prototypes rapidly, moving closer to a successful design with each iteration. The final *R*, "right," means building lots of small models that focus on solving particular problems with an idea. "You're not trying to build a complete model," says Vassallo. "You're just focusing on a small section of it."[73]

LO 8

Describe the protection of intellectual property rights involving patents, trademarks, and copyrights.

Intellectual Property: Protecting Your Ideas

Once entrepreneurs come up with innovative ideas for a product or service that has market potential, their immediate concern should be to protect them from unauthorized use. The U.S. Chamber of Commerce estimates that intellectual property theft, piracy, and counterfeiting of goods cost businesses $250 billion a year.[74] The World Trade Organization estimates that between 5 percent and 7 percent of all goods traded globally are counterfeit.[75] To protect their businesses, entrepreneurs must understand how to put intellectual property—patents, trademarks, and copyrights—to work for them.

Patents

patent
a grant from the federal government's Patent and Trademark Office to the inventor of a product, giving the exclusive right to make, use, or sell the invention in this country for 20 years from the date of filing the patent application.

A **patent** is a grant from the United States Patent and Trademark Office (PTO) to the inventor of a product, giving the exclusive right to make, use, or sell the invention in this country for 20 years from the date of filing the patent application. The purpose of giving an inventor a 20-year monopoly over a product is to stimulate creativity and innovation. After 20 years, the patent expires and cannot be renewed. Most patents are granted for new product inventions (called utility patents), but *design patents*, extending for 14 years beyond the date the patent is issued, are given to inventors who make new, original, and ornamental changes in the design of existing products that enhance their sales. To be patented, a device must be new (but not necessarily better!), not obvious to a person of ordinary skill or knowledge in the related field, and useful. A device *cannot* be patented if it has been publicized in print anywhere in the world or if it has been used or offered for sale in this country prior to the date of the patent

Source: From *The Wall Street Journal*, permission Cartoon Features Syndicate.

application. A U.S. patent is granted only to the true inventor, not a person who discovers another's invention, and is effective only in the United States and its territories.* Inventors who want to sell their inventions abroad must file for patents in each country in which they plan to do business. Once a product is patented, no one can copy or sell it without getting a license from its creator. A patent does not give one the right to make, use, or sell an invention, but the right to exclude others from making, using, or selling it.

Although inventors are never assured of getting a patent, they can enhance their chances considerably by following the basic steps suggested by the PTO. Before beginning the often lengthy and involved procedure, inventors should obtain professional assistance from a patent practitioner—a patent attorney or a patent agent—who is registered with the PTO. Only those attorneys and agents who are officially registered may represent an inventor seeking a patent. A list of registered attorneys and agents is available at the PTO's Web site. Approximately 98 percent of all inventors rely on these patent experts to steer them through the convoluted process. Legal fees for filing a patent application range from $4,000 to $25,000, depending on the complexity of the product.

THE PATENT PROCESS. Since George Washington signed the first patent law in 1790, the U.S. Patent and Trademark Office (www.uspto.gov) has issued patents on everything imaginable (and some unimaginable items, too), including mouse traps (of course!), Robert Fulton's steamboat, animals (genetically engineered mice), Thomas Edison's light bulb, golf tees (764 different patents), games, and various fishing devices. The J.M. Smucker Company even holds a patent issued in 1999 on a "sealed, crustless sandwich," a peanut butter and jelly sandwich it markets very successfully under the name "Uncrustables."[76] The PTO also has issued patents on business processes—methods of doing business—including Amazon.com's controversial patent on its "1-Click" technology, which allows users to store their customer information in a file and then recall it with one mouse click at checkout. To date the PTO has issued more than 7 million patents, and it receives more than 400,000 new applications each year (see Figure 2.4)![77] To receive a patent, an inventor must follow these steps:

Establish the invention's novelty. An invention is not patentable if it is known or has been used in the United States or has been described in a printed publication in this or a foreign country.

---

*Proposed legislation currently before Congress would change the "first to invent" rule now in place to "first to file," which means that a patent would go to the first person to *file* a patent application.

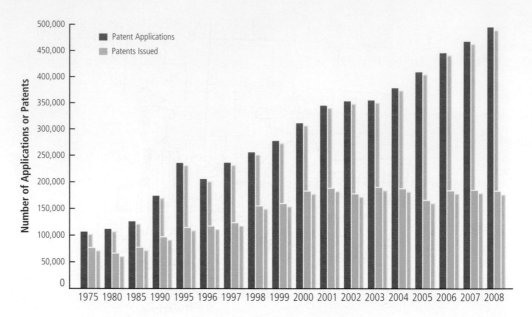

FIGURE 2.4

**Trademark Applications
and Trademarks Issued**

Document the device. To protect their patent claims, inventors should be able to verify the date on which they first conceived the idea for their inventions. Inventors should document a device by keeping dated records (including drawings) of their progress on the invention and by having knowledgeable friends witness these records.

Search existing patents. To verify that the invention truly is new, not obvious, and useful, an inventor must conduct a search of existing patents on similar products. The purpose of the search is to determine whether the inventor has a chance of getting a patent. Most inventors hire professionals trained in conducting patent searches to perform the research. Inventors themselves can conduct an online search of all patents granted by the PTO since 1976 from the office's Web site. An online search of these patents does not include sketches; however, subscribers to Delphion's Research Intellectual Property Network can access patents, including sketches, as far back as 1971 at: http://www.delphion.com/.

Study search results. Once the patent search is finished, inventors must study the results to determine their chances of getting a patent. To be patentable, a device must be sufficiently different from what has been used or described before and must not be obvious to a person having ordinary skill in the area of technology related to the invention.

Complete a patent application. If an inventor decides to seek a patent, he or she must file an application describing the invention with the PTO. The patent application must include specific *claims*, which describe the invention, what it does, and how it works and any drawings that are necessary to support the claims. The typical patent application runs 20 to 40 pages although some, especially those for biotech or high-tech products, are tens of thousands of pages long. The longest patent application to date is one for a gene patent that was 6 million pages long![78] Most inventors hire patent attorneys or agents to help them complete their patent applications. Figure 2.5 shows a portion of the application for a rather unusual patent, number 5,830,035.

Inventors also can file a provisional application for a patent for a fee of just $105. Filing for a provisional patent does not require the inventor to file any claims but does give him or her the right to use the phrase "patent pending" on the device. After filing for a provisional patent, an inventor has one year to file a standard patent application.

File the patent application. Before the PTO will issue a patent, one of its examiners studies the application to determine whether the invention warrants a patent. Approval of a patent normally takes on average 32 months (and growing) from the date of filing. If

US005830035A

FIGURE 2.5

United States Patent

United States Patent [19]

Budreck

[11] **Patent Number:**   **5,830,035**

[45] **Date of Patent:**   **Nov. 3, 1998**

[54] **TOE PUPPET**

[76] Inventor: **David J. Budreck**, 109 E. Woodruff
St., Port Washington, Wis. 53074

[21] Appl. No.: **794,294**

[22] Filed: **Feb. 3, 1997**

Related U.S. Application Data

[63] Continuation of Ser. No. 553,885, Nov. 6, 1995, abandoned.

[51] **Int. Cl.**[6] **A63H 03/14**
[52] **U.S. Cl.** **446/366**; 446/26; 446/327
[58] **Field of Search** 446/26, 327, 328,
446/329, 486, 359, 365, 366, 367

[56]   **References Cited**

U.S. PATENT DOCUMENTS

D. 292,811	11/1987	Fogarty et al.	D21/153
D. 304,052	10/1989	Dickens	D21/153
752,607	2/1904	Thowless .	
1,008,619	11/1911	Spear	446/99
1,269,056	6/1918	Criest	446/366
1,545,120	7/1925	Boggio	446/366
2,155,665	4/1939	Leeper .	
2,187,407	1/1940	Stone .	
2,621,440	12/1952	Stone .	
2,624,155	1/1953	Boyce	446/367
3,226,849	1/1966	Rosen	446/329
3,442,267	5/1969	Krygier	446/26
3,501,144	3/1970	Schmidt .	
3,611,628	10/1971	Noble et al. .	
3,911,618	10/1975	Gerst .	
3,918,180	11/1975	Chamberlin	446/327
4,148,151	4/1979	Ulrich	446/367
4,173,842	11/1979	Bahner .	
4,518,366	5/1985	Fultz et al.	446/366
4,992,070	2/1991	Mullen et al.	446/327
5,299,967	4/1994	Gilbert	446/366

FOREIGN PATENT DOCUMENTS

7644	5/1922	Germany	446/366
1301966	8/1969	Germany	446/366
21268	of 1900	United Kingdom	446/367

OTHER PUBLICATIONS

"Finger Fun", Washington Post, Mar. 22, 1959, p. c8.

Primary Examiner—Robert A. Hafer
Assistant Examiner—Jeffrey D. Carlson
Attorney, Agent, or Firm—Andrus, Sceales, Starke &
Sawall

[57]   **ABSTRACT**

A puppet is adapted to be mounted on a single human digit
for providing animated motion of a figurine responsive to
movement of the single human digit. The puppet comprises
a hollow, elastic cap having an interior wall defining a cavity
into which the single human digit is snugly received. The
cap includes a resilient neck portion for supporting the
figurine at a distance spaced from the single human digit
such that movement of the single human digit causes the
neck portion and the figurine to oscillate to and fro under the
influence of the weight of the figurine.

11 Claims, 1 Drawing Sheet

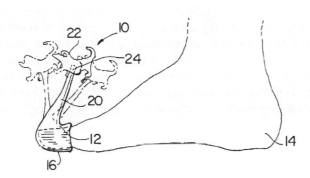

the PTO rejects the application, the inventor can amend his or her application and resub-
mit it to the PTO.

Defending a patent against "copycat producers" can be expensive and time-consuming but
often is necessary to protect an entrepreneur's interest. The median cost of a patent infringement lawsuit when the amount in dispute is between $1 million and $25 million is about
$2.6 million if the case goes to trial (about 95 percent of patent infringement lawsuits are set-
tled out of court), but the odds of winning are in the patent holder's favor. More than 60 percent
of those holding patents win their infringement suits.[79] Knockoffs of Apple's popular iPhone,
which look almost exactly like the real thing, have cost the company hundreds of thousands of
dollars in lost sales. Known as "iClones," the fake phones began showing up in Asia six months
before Apple introduced the iPhone, proving just how fast counterfeiters work.[80] With its
global reach and speedy convenience, the Internet has compounded the problem of counterfeit
sales, especially among luxury items such as Luis Vuitton and Coach bags, Cartier jewelry, and
Chanel perfumes.

Trademarks

trademark

any distinctive word, phrase, symbol, design, name, logo, slogan, or trade dress that a company uses to identify the origin of a product or to distinguish it from other goods on the market.

A **trademark** is any distinctive word, phrase, symbol, design, name, logo, slogan, or trade dress that a company uses to identify the origin of a product or to distinguish it from other goods on the market. (A **service mark** is the same as a trademark except that it identifies and distinguishes the source of a service rather than a product.) A trademark serves as a company's "signature" in the marketplace. A trademark can be more than just a company's logo, slogan, or brand name; it can also include symbols, shapes, colors, smells, or sounds. For instance, Coca Cola holds a trademark on the shape of its bottle, and NBC owns a trademark on its three-toned chime. Motorcycle maker Harley-Davidson has applied for trademark protection for the shape of its oil tanks and the throaty rumbling sound its engines make![81]

service mark

offers the same protection as a trademark but identifies and distinguishes the source of a service rather than a product.

ENTREPRENEURIAL PROFILE

Jennifer Cassetta: Health and the City

Fitness training instructor Jennifer Cassetta came up with what she thought was the perfect name for her exercise and martial arts business located in the heart of New York City: Health and the City. To protect the name, she paid a $484 trademark application fee to register the name with the Patent and Trademark Office. Then she received notice from cable television company HBO, owner of the *Sex and the City* television series and movie, that the company intended to oppose Cassetta's application because it infringed on the profitable HBO franchise. Previously, HBO had successfully challenged companies that had wanted to use names such as Scents in the City, Pets in the City, and Handbags and the City. Attorneys representing HBO suggested that Cassetta change the name of her company from Health in the City, but Cassetta refused, pointing out that the change would cost at least $10,000 and the name was already a registered trademark. "They know I am a small business owner and I don't have the money to fight them," says Cassetta. Ultimately, HBO chose not to challenge Cassetta's trademark application, giving her the right to use Health and the City as her company's name.[82]

trade dress

the unique combination of elements that a company uses to create a product's image and to promote it.

Components of a product's identity such as these are part of its **trade dress,** the unique combination of elements that a company uses to create a product's image and to promote it. For instance, a Mexican restaurant chain's particular décor, color schemes, design, and overall "look and feel" would be its trade dress. To be eligible for trademark protection, trade dress must be inherently unique and distinctive to a company, and another company's use of that trade dress must be likely to confuse customers.

HANDS ON... HOW TO

Protect Your Company's Intellectual Property

John Anton, founder of Anton Sport, a Tempe, Arizona-based company that sells customized clothing such as T-shirts, sweatshirts, caps, and casual shirts, could not believe what he was seeing on his computer screen: a Web site that was a duplicate of the site that he had spent $500,000 and hundreds of hours designing for his business, DesignAShirt.com. Not only had the thief stolen the html code that drove the site, but he also had lifted Anton's proprietary graphics and images, including photos of himself and his nine-year-old daughter modeling some of the company's products! A few more searches produced a half-dozen other sites that were clones of DesignAShirt.com.

Anton's Web site was one of the first that allowed customers to use a simple drag-and-drop system to order products customized with, say, a company logo and was a major competitive advantage

for his business. In just three years, sales for DesignAShirt had hit $6 million. Now, some pirate had stolen Anton's entire Web site and was selling his intellectual property for a flat fee of just $1,200. "I felt sick to my stomach every time I clicked on another site and saw my own double chin," he recalls. After digging online for a while, Anton was able to trace the theft to someone named Kumar Sudhir, who owned a company in India called Infogate. The only contact information Anton could find was an e-mail address for a technical support center. Outraged, Anton sent an e-mail to Infogate that said, "I demand that you cease and desist from selling this application immediately or we will have no other choice than to involve our legal team." No one at Infogate responded to his e-mail.

Anton contacted his lawyers and received mixed news. It was clear that Infogate had violated international copyright law, and Anton had a right to threaten Sudhir and his company with legal action. However, his attorneys advised, filing a lawsuit would be very expensive and time consuming. In addition, even if he won the lawsuit, they believed that the probability that an Indian court would actually enforce a ruling against Infogate was small. However, Anton learned that he could take action for copyright infringement against any company that was operating in the United States and using the code that Infogate had stolen from Anton. He decided to pursue that option and went after two companies, whose founders it turned out, had no idea that they were using stolen intellectual property to power their Web sites. Both entrepreneurs agreed to shut down their Web sites and to pay restitution to Anton. The settlements totaled just $3,800, and Anton already had spent $12,000 in legal fees! In addition, he was still frustrated by the fact that Infogate was continuing to sell the code it had stolen from Anton. He estimated that Infogate's piracy had cost him at least $500,000 in lost sales.

What lessons can other entrepreneurs learn from Anton's unfortunate experience about protecting their intellectual property?

1. **Recognize that intellectual property (IP), the rights that result when a person uses his or her knowledge and creativity to produce something of value, can be immensely valuable, even for small companies.** Experts estimate that in the United States alone, 30 to 40 percent of all gains in productivity over the course of the twentieth century were due to IP in the forms discussed in this chapter. In short, IP matters!

2. **Understand the basics of patent, trademark, and copyright protection.** By understanding the features of each of these shields for IP you can protect your rights for at least 14 years, often longer.

3. **Use the appropriate method to file for protection of your IP and do so promptly.** The processes of filing for a patent, a trademark, and a copyright are different; make sure you know which tool is right for you and how to get maximum protection for your IP. You may be able to apply for more than one type of protection. For instance, an entrepreneur may be able to trademark a company logo and, if it is a form of artistic expression, copyright it as well.

4. **Use qualified, experienced IP attorneys to gain the proper protection.** The time to involve attorneys in protecting the product of your knowledge and creativity is *before* you have to bring them in to take action against someone who has stolen your IP. Filing for patents, trademarks, and copyrights can be intimidating if you have never done it before, and doing it incorrectly may mean that you have no protection at all.

5. **If you do business globally, register your company's patents, trademarks, and copyrights in the countries in which you do business.** Although enforcing IP laws in some countries can be difficult, the chances that you will be successful rise significantly if you have registered your IP with the proper offices in those nations.

6. **Protect your rights vigorously.** If you discover that someone is using your IP without permission, pursue your rights vigorously. Recognize that the costs of taking legal action, especially in foreign lands, may outweigh the benefits, at least in the short run. Like John Anton, entrepreneurs must decide whether pursuing costly legal action to protect their IP rights will yield long-term benefits.

Sources: Adapted from Darren Dahl, "Case Study: A Hacker in India Hijacked His Website Design and Was Making Good Money Selling It. The Question Was, How to Fight Back?" *Inc.*, December 2007, pp. 77–80; David Hirschmann, "Intellectual Property Theft: Big Problem, Real Solutions, *The ChamberPost*, March 2008, www.chamberpost.com/2008/03/intellectual-pr.html; Merrill Matthews, Jr. and Tom Giovanetti, "Why Intellectual Property Is Important," *Ideas*, Institute for Policy Innovation, July 8, 2002, p. 1; Nichole L. Torres, "Getting Intellectual," *Entrepreneur*, December 2007, p. 110.

There are 1.5 million trademarks registered in the United States, 900,000 of which are in actual use (see Figure 2.6). Federal law permits a manufacturer to register a trademark, which prevents other companies from employing a similar mark to identify their goods. Before 1989, a business could not reserve a trademark in advance of use. Today the first party who either uses a trademark in commerce or files an application with the PTO has the ultimate right to register that trademark. Unlike patents and copyrights, which are issued for limited amounts of time, trademarks last indefinitely as long as the holder continues to use it. (Five years after a trademark's registration date, the entrepreneur must file an affidavit of use with the United States PTO.) However, a trademark cannot keep competitors from producing the same product or and selling it under a different name. It merely prevents others from using the same or confusingly similar trademark for the same or similar products.

Many business owners are confused by the use of the symbols "™" and "®." Anyone who claims the right to a particular trademark (or service mark) can use the "™" (or "SM") symbols without having to register the mark with the PTO. The claim to that trademark or service mark may or may not be valid, however. Only those businesses that have registered their marks with the PTO can use the "®" symbol. Entrepreneurs do not have to register trademarks or service marks to establish their rights to those marks; however, registering a mark with the PTO does give entrepreneurs greater power to protect their marks. Filing an application to register a trademark or service mark is relatively easy, but it does require a search of existing names.

An entrepreneur may lose the exclusive right to a trademark if it loses its unique character and becomes a generic name. Aspirin, escalator, thermos, brassiere, super glue, yo-yo, and cellophane all were once enforceable trademarks that have become common words in the English language. These generic terms can no longer be licensed as trademarks.

FIGURE 2.6

Trademark Applications and Trademarks and Renewals Issued

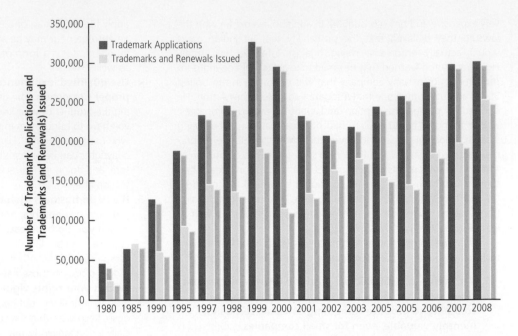

copyright

an exclusive right that protects the creators of original works of authorship such as literary, dramatic, musical, and artistic works.

Copyrights

A **copyright** is an exclusive right that protects the creators of original works of authorship such as literary, dramatic, musical, and artistic works (e.g., art, sculptures, literature, software, music, videos, video games, choreography, motion pictures, recordings, and others). The internationally recognized symbol © denotes a copyrighted work. A copyright protects only the form in which an idea is expressed, not the idea itself. A copyright on a creative work comes into existence the moment its creator puts that work into a tangible form. Just as with a trademark, obtaining basic copyright protection does *not* require registering the creative work with the U.S. Copyright Office (www.copyright.gov).

Registering a copyright does give creators greater protection over their work, however. Copyright applications must be filed with the Copyright Office in the Library of Congress for a fee of $45 per application ($35 online). A valid copyright on a work lasts for the life of the creator plus 70 years after his or her death. When a copyright expires, the work becomes public property and can be used by anyone free of charge.

Because they are so easy to duplicate, computer software programs, CDs, and DVDs are among the most-often pirated items by copyright infringers. The Business Software Alliance estimates that the global software industry loses $47.8 billion each year to pirates who illegally copy programs.[83] The Motion Picture Association of America reports that the global movie industry loses more than $11 billion to those who forge counterfeit movies and sell them. (Piracy rates are highest in China [90 percent], Russia [79 percent], and Thailand [79 percent].) Because they are so adept at plying their trade, video pirates often manage to beat genuine distributors to the market with movies![84]

Table 2.2 provides a summary of the characteristics of patents, trademarks, and copyrights.

TABLE 2.2 Characteristics of Patents, Trademarks, and Copyrights

Type of Protection	What It Covers	Time Required	Cost
Copyright	Works of original authorship such as books or software	About two weeks	About $35
Trademark	Logos, names, phrases	Six months to one year	$900 to $1,500
Design patent	The look of an original product	Up to two years	$5,000 to $20,000
Utility patent	How an original product works	Two to five years	$5,000 to $20,000
Business method patent	A business process or procedure	Two to five years	$5,000 to $20,000

Source: Anne Field, "How to Knock Out Knock Offs," *Business Week*, March 14, 2005, http://www .businessweek.com/@@7oPzclQQnlWLqxsA/magazine/content/05_11/b3021446.htm

Chapter Summary

1. Explain the differences among creativity, innovation, and entrepreneurship.

The entrepreneur's "secret" for creating value in the marketplace is applying creativity and innovation to solve problems and to exploit opportunities that people face every day. Creativity is the ability to develop new ideas and to discover new ways of looking at problems and opportunities. Innovation is the ability to apply creative solutions to those problems and opportunities to enhance or to enrich people's lives. Entrepreneurship is the result of a disciplined, systematic process of applying creativity and innovation to needs and opportunities in the marketplace.

2. Describe why creativity and innovation are such an integral part of entrepreneurship.

Entrepreneurs must always be on guard against paradigms—preconceived ideas of what the world is, what it should be like, and how it should operate—because they are logjams to creativity. Successful entrepreneurs often go beyond conventional wisdom as they ask "Why not...?"

Success—even survival—in this fiercely competitive, global environment requires entrepreneurs to tap their creativity (and that of their employees) constantly.

3. Understand how the two hemispheres of the human brain function and what role they play in creativity.

For years, people assumed that creativity was an inherent trait. Today, however, we know better. Research shows that almost anyone can learn to be creative. The left hemisphere of the brain controls language, logic, and symbols, processing information in a step-by-step fashion. The right hemisphere handles emotional, intuitive, and spatial functions, processing information intuitively. The right side of the brain is the source of creativity and innovation. People can learn to control which side of the brain is dominant in a given situation.

4. Explain the 10 "mental locks" that limit individual creativity.

The number of potential barriers to creativity is limitless, but entrepreneurs commonly face 10 "mental locks" on creativity: Searching for the one "right" answer; focusing on "being logical;" blindly following the rules; constantly being practical; viewing play as frivolous; becoming overly specialized; avoiding ambiguity; fearing looking foolish; fearing mistakes and failure; and believing that "I'm not creative."

5. Understand how entrepreneurs can enhance the creativity of their employees as well as their own creativity.

Entrepreneurs can stimulate creativity in their companies by: expecting creativity; expecting and tolerating failure; encouraging curiosity; viewing problems as challenges; providing creativity training; providing support; rewarding creativity; and modeling creativity.

Entrepreneurs can enhance their own creativity by using the following techniques: allowing themselves to be creative; giving their minds fresh input every day; keeping a journal handy to record their thoughts and ideas; reading books on stimulating creativity or taking a class on creativity; taking some time off to relax.

6. Describe the steps in the creative process.

The creative process consists of seven steps: Step 1. Preparation—involves getting the mind ready for creative thinking; Step 2. Investigation—requires the individual to develop a solid understanding of the problem or decision; Step 3. Transformation—involves viewing the similarities and the differences among the information collected; Step 4. Incubation—allows the subconscious mind to reflect on the information collected; Step 5. Illumination—occurs at some point during the incubation stage when a spontaneous breakthrough causes "the light bulb to go on;" Step 6. Verification—involves validating the idea as accurate and useful; and Step 7. Implementation—involves transforming the idea into a business reality,

7. Discuss techniques for improving the creative process.

Five techniques that are especially useful for improving the creative process:

- Brainstorming is a process in which a small group of people interact with very little structure with the goal of producing a large *quantity* of novel and imaginative ideas.
- Mind-mapping is a graphical technique that encourages thinking on both sides of the brain, visually displays the various relationships among ideas, and improves the ability to view a problem from many sides.
- Force field analysis is a useful technique for evaluating the forces that support and oppose a proposed change. It allows entrepreneurs to weigh both the advantages and the disadvantages of a particular decision and to maximize the variables that support it and minimize those that work against it.
- TRIZ is a systematic approach designed to help solve any technical problem, whatever its source. Unlike brainstorming and mind-mapping, which are right-brained activities, TRIZ is a left-brained, scientific, step-by-step process that is based on the study of hundreds of the most innovative patents across the globe.
- Rapid prototyping is based on the premise that transforming an idea into an actual model will point out flaws in the original idea and will lead to improvements in its design.

8. Describe the protection of intellectual property involving patents, trademarks, and copyrights.

A patent is a grant from the federal government that gives an inventor exclusive rights to an invention for 20 years.

A trademark is any distinctive word, symbol, or trade dress that a company uses to identify its product and to distinguish it from other goods. It serves as a company's "signature" in the marketplace.

A copyright protects original works of authorship. It covers only the form in which an idea is expressed and not the idea itself and lasts for 70 years beyond the creator's death.

Discussion Questions

1. Explain the differences among creativity, innovation, and entrepreneurship.
2. How are creativity, innovation, and entrepreneurship related?
3. Why are creativity and innovation so important to the survival and success of a business?
4. One entrepreneur claims, "Creativity unrelated to a business plan has no value," What does he mean? Do you agree?
5. What is a paradigm? What impact do paradigms have on creativity?
6. Can creativity be taught or is it an inherent trait? Explain.
7. How does the human brain function? What operations does each hemisphere specialize in? Which hemisphere is the "seat" of creativity?
8. Briefly outline the 10 "mental locks" that can limit individual creativity. Give an example of a situation in which you subjected yourself to one of these mental locks.
9. What can entrepreneurs do to stimulate their own creativity and to encourage it among workers?
10. Explain the steps of the creative process. What can an entrepreneur do to enhance each step?
11. Explain the differences among a patent, a trademark, and a copyright. What form of intellectual property does each protect?

Business PlanPro™

The creative process can help you to develop your business concept and add dimension to an existing business venture. The process of creating your business plan will enable you to refine and test your creative ideas.

Business Plan Exercises

Select one of the creative processes mentioned in this chapter. You may want to consider mind-mapping, TRIX, or brainstorming if you are in a group. Apply this technique to your business concept. If your business idea is in the embryonic stage, use this exercise to bring focus to the business. If you have a solid grasp on your business concept, use one of these creative techniques to address a specific business challenge or to explore a potential opportunity for your business.

On the Web

Identify at least three key words or phrases that you associate with your business concept. For example, if your business is a specialty retail and online store selling wakeboards, you may consider the terms "wakeboards," "water sports," and "boards." Enter terms relevant to your business in your favorite search engine and see what information appears.

1. What companies advertise under those terms?
2. What are the top three listings?
3. How is your business unique from those businesses listed, including the fact that your business may offer a local presence?
4. What other attributes set your business apart from what you see on the Web?

Make note of anything that you learned or observed from what you saw online.

In the Software

Open *Business Plan Pro*™ and the business plan you began in Chapter 1. If this exercise has changed any of your initial concepts or produced an entirely different business concept, think about why the exercise led you down a different path. If that venture is different, select the Create a new business plan option and work through the wizards as you did before. Once again, you can view the outline created based on those responses by clicking on the Preview icon or going to File, Print, and then Print Preview.

Sample Plans

Open the Sample Plan Browser in *Business Plan Pro*™; it will be helpful to have an Internet connection when you do. Enter one or more of the search terms you selected in the exercise in the search window of the Sample Plan Browser. Do any sample plans appear based on the term you entered? If so, review those plans. Will one of those plans be a potential resource for you as create your business plan? Remember, the sample plan does not have to be identical to your business concept. With even distant similarities, sample plans may be a resource for you based on its general content or layout.

Building Your Business Plan

Open your business plan and go to the section titled "Product and Service Description." You can do that by clicking on the Plan Outline icon at the top of your screen or clicking on View and selecting Outline from the drop-down menu. Within that section, begin to describe the products or services your business will offer. Notice that you have the option to view that section of a sample plan by clicking on Examples in the upper right hand section of the screen. Now, go to the "Market Needs" section of the plan. Make a few notes here regarding the needs that your products and services satisfy. We will revisit these sections, so just make comments that will help you develop your thoughts as you progress through the chapters.

Beyond the Classroom...

1. Your dinner guests are to arrive in five minutes, and you've just discovered that you forgot to chill the wine! Wanting to maintain your reputation as the perfect host/hostess, you must tackle this problem with maximum creativity. What could you do? Generate as many solutions as you can in five minutes working alone. Then work with two or three students in a small group to brainstorm the problem.

2. Work with a group of your classmates to think of as many alternative uses for the commercial lubricant, WD-40, as you can. Remember to think *fluidly* (generating a quantity of ideas) and *flexibly* (generating unconventional ideas).

3. Review the following list of household appliances. Working with a small group of your classmates, select one and use the brainstorming technique to develop as many alternative uses for the appliance as you can in 15 minutes. Remember to abide by the rules of brainstorming! The appliances: dishwasher, clothes dryer, curling iron, toaster oven, iron, microwave oven, coffeemaker, and any others you want to use.

4. A major maker of breakfast cereals was about to introduce a new multigrain cereal. Its principal selling point is that it features "three great tastes" in every bowl: corn, rice, and wheat. Because a cereal's name is an integral part of its marketing campaign, the company hired a very costly consulting firm to come up with the right name for the new product. The consulting firm tackled the job using "a combination of structural linguistics and personal creativity." One year and many dollars later, the consulting firm gave its recommendation.

   Take 20 minutes to list names that you think would be appropriate for this cereal. Make brief notes about why you think each name is appropriate. Your professor may choose to prepare a list of names from all of the members of your class and may take a vote to determine the "winner."

5. Every quarter, Inventables, a creative design company in Chicago, sends its clients a package called a DesignAid that contains 20 items, each with "unexpected properties," as a way to stimulate innovation and ideas for new products or services. One Inventables's recent DesignAid package included the following items:

   - Translucent concrete–concrete that contains thin layers of fiber optics, which create semi-transparent stripes in the concrete.
   - Sound-recording paper–a piece of cardboard-like paper that records and plays sounds with the help of ultrathin electronics imbedded in the page.
   - Impact-absorbing silicon–silicon that, despite being only one inch thick, absorbs impact, including microvibrations. If you drop an egg on it, the egg won't break.
   - Wireless battery-free speaker–a solar-powered speakers receives sound via infrared waves rather than radio frequencies and is capable of producing directional sound. In other words, only the person at whom the speaker is aimed can hear the sound coming from it.

   Select one of these items and work with a small group of your classmates to brainstorm as many alternative uses for the item as you can in 15 minutes. Remember to abide by the rules of brainstorming!

6. Each hemisphere of the brain processes information differently, and one hemisphere tends to dominate the other. Consider the following lists of words and decide which one best describes the way you make decisions and solve problems:

Metaphor	Logic
Dream	Reason
Humor	Precision
Ambiguity	Consistency
Play	Work
Approximate	Exact
Fantasy	Reality
Paradox	Direct
Diffuse	Focused
Hunch	Analysis
Generalization	Specific
Child	Adult

   If you chose the list on the left, you tend to engage in "soft" thinking, which suggests a right-brain orientation. If you chose the list on the right, you tend to engage in "hard" thinking, which suggests a left-brain orientation.

Creativity relies on both "soft" and "hard" thinking. Each plays an important role in the creative process but at different phases.

A. Identify which type of thinking—"soft" or "hard"—would be most useful in each of the seven stages of the creative process.

B. List five things you can do to develop your thinking skills in the area ("soft" or "hard") that least describes your decision making style.

7. Interview at least two entrepreneurs about their experiences as business owners. Where did their business ideas originate? How important are creativity and innovation to their success? How do they encourage an environment of creativity in their businesses?

Michael Cogliantry Inc.

CHAPTER 3

Designing a Competitive Business Model and Building a Solid Strategic Plan

Think little goals and expect little achievements. Think big goals and win big success.
—*David Joseph Schwartz*

Strategy without tactics is the slowest route to victory. Tactics without strategy is the noise before the defeat.
—*General Sun Tzu*

Learning Objectives

On completion of this chapter, you will be able to:

1. Understand the importance of strategic management to a small business.

2. Explain why and how a small business must create a competitive advantage in the market.

3. Develop a strategic plan for a business using the nine steps in the strategic planning process.

4. Discuss the characteristics of three basic strategies: low-cost, differentiation, and focus and know when to employ them.

5. Understand the importance of controls such as the balanced scorecard in the planning process.

Few activities in the life of a business are as vital—or as overlooked—as that of developing a strategy for success. Too often, entrepreneurs brimming with optimism and enthusiasm launch businesses destined for failure because their founders never stop to define a workable strategy that sets them apart from their competition. Because they tend to be people of action, entrepreneurs often find the process of developing a strategy dull and unnecessary. Their tendency is to start a business, try several approaches, and see what works. Without a cohesive plan of action, however, these entrepreneurs have as much chance of building a successful business as a defense contractor attempting to build a jet fighter without blueprints. Companies lacking clear strategies may achieve some success in the short run, but as soon as competitive conditions stiffen or an unanticipated threat arises, they usually "hit the wall" and fold. Without a basis for differentiating itself from a pack of similar competitors, the best a company can hope for is mediocrity in the marketplace.

In today's global competitive environment, any business, large or small, that is not thinking and acting strategically is extremely vulnerable. Every business is exposed to the forces of a rapidly changing competitive environment, and in the future small business executives can expect even greater change and uncertainty. From sweeping political changes around the planet and rapid technological advances to more intense competition and newly emerging global markets, the business environment has become more turbulent and challenging to business owners. Although this market turbulence creates many challenges for small businesses, it also creates opportunities for those companies that have in place strategies to capitalize on them. Entrepreneurs' willingness to adapt, to create change, to experiment with new business models, and to break traditional rules has become more important than ever. "It's not the strongest or the most intelligent [companies that] survive," says American Express CEO Ken Chenault, "but those most adaptive to change."[1]

Perhaps the biggest change that entrepreneurs face is unfolding now: the shift in the world's economy from a base of *financial to intellectual* capital. "Knowledge is no longer just a factor of production," says futurist Alvin Toffler. "It is the *critical* factor of production."[2] Today, a company's intellectual capital is likely to be the source of its competitive advantage in the marketplace. **Intellectual capital** is comprised of three components:[3]

intellectual capital

a key source of a company's competitive advantage that is comprised of 1) human capital, 2) structural capital, and 3) customer capital.

1. *Human capital,* the talents, creativity, skills, and abilities of a company's workforce, shows up in the innovative strategies, plans, and processes that the people in an organization develop and then passionately pursue.
2. *Structural capital,* is the accumulated knowledge and experience that a company possesses. It can take many forms including processes, software, patents, copyrights, and, perhaps most importantly, the knowledge and experience of the people in a company.
3. *Customer capital,* includes the established customer base, positive reputation, ongoing relationships, and goodwill a company builds up over time with its customers.

Increasingly, entrepreneurs are recognizing that the capital stored in these three areas forms the foundation of their ability to compete effectively and that they must manage this intangible capital base carefully. Every business uses all three components in its strategy, but the emphasis they place on each one varies.

ENTREPRENEURIAL PROFILE _____

Whole Foods

For example, Whole Foods, a highly successful retailer of natural and organic foods with more than 270 stores in North America and the United Kingdom, emphasizes human capital in its strategy for achieving a competitive advantage in the marketplace. The company subjects all job applicants to a thorough screening process, carefully selecting only those who demonstrate a passion for what lies at the heart of its competitive edge: a love of food and dedication to customer service. Unlike most of its competitors in the supermarket industry, Whole Foods invests heavily in training its workers (called Team Members inside the company) so that they can demonstrate and explain to customers the features and the benefits of the company's natural foods. In addition, managers recognize that food preferences vary from one region of a nation to another, and they give Team Members at the local level a great deal of autonomy in the selection of foods they stock. Because the company's core customers prefer to purchase locally grown products, Whole Foods is expanding that component of its product mix rapidly. The company recognizes the role that Team Members play in the company's success and its employee-friendly policies have landed it on Fortune's "100 Best Companies to Work For" list consistently. Even though its cost structure is not the lowest in the industry, the company is growing rapidly because owners know that its loyal customers do not shop there searching for the lowest prices.[4]

The rules of the competitive game of business are constantly changing. To be successful, entrepreneurs can no longer do things in the way they've always done them. Fortunately, successful entrepreneurs have at their disposal a powerful weapon to cope with a hostile, ever-changing environment: the process of strategic management. **Strategic management** involves developing a game plan to guide a company as it strives to accomplish its vision, mission, goals, and objectives and to keep it from straying off its desired course. The idea is to give an entrepreneur a blueprint for matching the company's strengths and weaknesses to the opportunities and threats in the environment.

strategic management
the process of developing a game plan to guide a company as it strives to accomplish its vision, mission, goals, and objectives and to keep it from straying off course.

Building a Competitive Advantage

The goal of developing a strategic plan is to create for the small company a **competitive advantage**—the aggregation of factors that sets a small business apart from its competitors and gives it a unique position in the market that is superior to its competition. It is the differentiating factor that makes customers want to buy from your business rather than from your competitors. From a strategic perspective, the key to business success is to develop a unique competitive advantage, one that creates value for customers and is difficult for competitors to duplicate. For example, Whole Foods competes successfully with giant chains such as Wal-Mart and Kroger not on price but by emphasizing superior customer service, higher quality products, a more extensive inventory of local and organic products, and a commitment to fair-trade suppliers. Its stores are well organized, attractive, and entertaining. Asked to describe his recently-opened Whole Foods store, team leader Matthew Mell says, "It's a Disney World for foodies."[5] Companies that fail to define their competitive advantage fall into "me too" strategies that never set them apart from their competitors and do not allow them to become market leaders or to achieve above-average profits.

LO 2

Explain why and how a small business must create a competitive advantage in the market.

competitive advantage
the aggregation of factors that sets a small business apart from its competitors and gives it a unique position in the market superior to its competition.

Entrepreneurs should examine four aspects of their businesses to define their companies' competitive advantages:

1. *Products they sell.* What is unique about the products the company sells? Do they save customers time or money? Are they more reliable and more dependable than those that competitors sell? Do they save energy, protect the environment, or provide more convenience for customers? By identifying the unique customer benefits of their companies' products, entrepreneurs can differentiate their businesses.

2. *Service they provide.* Many entrepreneurs find that the service they provide their customers is an excellent way to differentiate their companies. Because they are small, friendly, and close to their customers, small businesses are able to provide customer service that is superior to that which their larger competitors can provide. What services does the company provide (or which ones can it provide) to deliver added value and a superior shopping experience for customers?

3. *Pricing they offer.* As we will see later in this chapter, some small businesses differentiate themselves using price. Price can be a powerful point of differentiation; offering the lowest price gives some customers a great incentive to buy. However, offering the lowest price is not always the best way to create a unique image. Small companies that do not offer the lowest prices may be able to emphasize the value that their products offer.

4. *Way they sell.* Customers today expect to be able to conduct business when they want to, which means that companies that offer extended hours—even 24-hour service seven days a week (perhaps with the Web)—have the basis for an important competitive advantage. Zoots, a small chain of dry cleaning stores in the Northeast, offers customers extended hours seven days a week and allows a secure 24-hour pick-up and drop-off service. The company also offers a home pick-up and delivery service that customers can book online and an environmentally friendly cleaning process, all of which maximizes customers' convenience.[6]

ENTREPRENEURIAL PROFILE _____

Jason Lander: ShiftWise

Recognizing that a shortage of registered nurses had created a national vacancy rate of 8.1 percent, Jason Lander began a part-time business that provided temporary nurses to understaffed hospitals. When his customers complained about the burdensome paperwork that scheduling temporary nurses required, Lander saw an opportunity to create a company that offered customers a compelling competitive advantage. He quit his job and raised $6 million to launch ShiftWise, a company that allows hospitals and medical providers to fill gaps in their nursing staffs as easily as booking a hotel by using a much more efficient real-time, Web-based staffing management system. The system also saves hospitals money; one hospital using ShiftWise reports an annual savings of $1.2 million! More than 300 hospitals in 14 states now use ShiftWise, which, despite facing several competitors, is the industry leader.[7]

core competencies

a unique set of capabilities that a company develops in key operational areas that allow it to vault past competitors.

Building a competitive advantage alone is not enough; the key to success over time is building a *sustainable* competitive advantage. In the long run, a company gains a sustainable competitive advantage through its ability to develop a set of core competencies that enable it to serve its selected target customers better than its rivals. **Core competencies** are a unique set of capabilities that a company develops in key areas, such as superior quality, customer service, innovation, team-building, flexibility, responsiveness, and others that allow it to vault past competitors. As the phrase suggests, they are central to a company's ability to compete successfully and are usually the result of important skills and lessons a business has learned over time.

Typically, a company develops core competencies in no more than five or six (often fewer) areas. These core competencies become the nucleus of a company's competitive advantage and are usually quite enduring over time. Markets, customers, and competitors may change, but a company's core competencies are more durable, forming the building blocks for everything a company does. To be effective strategically, these core competencies should be difficult for competitors to duplicate, and they must provide customers with an important perceived benefit. Small companies' core competencies often have to do with the advantages of their size—such as agility, speed, closeness to their customers, superior service, or the ability to innovate. According to Scott Cook, founder of Intuit, agility is what matters most. "Agile firms will win," he says. "Rigid firms will disappear."[8] Smart entrepreneurs use their companies' size to their advantage, recognizing that it allows them to do things that their larger rivals cannot. The key to success is building the company's strategy on its core competencies and then using core competencies to provide superior service and value for its target customers (see Figure 3.1).

Successful small companies are able to build strategies that exploit all of the competitive advantages that their size gives them by:

- Responding quickly to customers' needs
- Providing personalized customer service
- Remaining flexible and willing to change
- Constantly searching for new, emerging market segments
- Building and defending market niches
- Erecting "switching costs," the costs a customer incurs by switching to a competitor's product or service, through personal service and loyalty
- Remaining entrepreneurial and willing to take risks and act with lightning speed
- Constantly innovating

FIGURE 3.1

Building a Sustainable Competitive Advantage

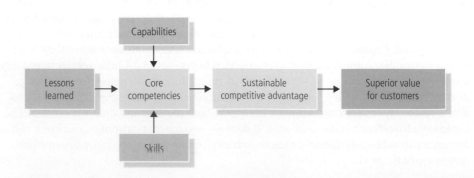

Although Monster.com, CareerBuilder, and HotJobs account for 75 percent of the revenue in the online job listing market, tiny Jobster is gaining ground fast by building on its core competencies to gain a competitive edge. Rather than try to compete by building an even bigger résumé database than its rivals have amassed, Jobster uses the popularity of social networking to help recruiters find the best job candidates. With Jobster, recruiters build a network of job contacts by sending job descriptions to their existing employees, who then use the e-mail's "send to friends" button to pass the information on to people in their network of contacts. The recipients of these e-mails can join the company's referral network and apply—again with just a mouse click. Jobster's software allows managers to track where their best leads originate by creating a customized dashboard. "It's really, really easy," says the recruiting manager at Automatic Data Processing (ADP), who says that Jobster has allowed ADP to cut its job-board recruiting budget in half! More important, Jobster's social networking system produces high-quality applicants. In a recent Booz Hamilton survey, 88 percent of employers say their best job applicants come from referrals, yet fewer than 20 percent of their hires came from a referral. "Posting the job is not the value," says Jobster CEO Jason Goldberg, who came up with the idea for Jobster and its networking approach after becoming frustrated with the flood of unqualified applicants in his job at T-Mobile USA. "It's matching the right person to the job. That's the real business problem."[9]

No business can be everything to everyone. In fact, one of the biggest pitfalls many entrepreneurs stumble into is failing to differentiate their companies from the crowd of competitors. Entrepreneurs often face the challenge of setting their companies apart from their larger, more powerful competitors (who can easily outspend them) by using their creativity and the special abilities their businesses offer customers. Developing core competencies does *not* necessarily require a company to spend a great deal of money. It does, however, require an entrepreneur to use creativity, imagination, and vision to identify those things that it does best and that are most important to its target customers. Businesses have an infinite number of ways to create a competitive edge, but building strategy around a company's core competencies allows it to gain a sustainable competitive based on what it does best.

Advanced Composite Materials (ACM) has transformed its technological know-how into a competitive advantage. ACM, a small company whose management team, led by Tom Quantrille, executed a leveraged buyout of a division of a large corporation in 2006, has developed a unique product line that has restaurateurs lining up to purchase. The products, called Silar, are innovative ceramic composite inserts for microwave ovens that allow restaurants to cook foods amazingly fast without drying them out. For instance, the Silar grill can cook a panini sandwich and grill the bread in just 80 seconds. Flipping the grill over reveals a flatstone surface that can cook a pizza in just 90 seconds compared to the usual 20 to 30 minutes. The National Restaurant Association recently awarded ACM a Kitchen Innovation Award for Silar. ACM is more than tripling its manufacturing capacity to meet soaring demand for its products.[10]

Strategic management can increase a small company's effectiveness, but entrepreneurs first must have a process designed to meet their needs and their business's special characteristics. It is a mistake to attempt to apply a big business's strategic development techniques to a small business because a small business is not merely "a little big business." Because of their size and their particular characteristics—a small resource base, flexible managerial style, informal organizational structure, and adaptability to change—small businesses need a different approach to the strategic management process. The strategic management procedure for a small business should include the following features:

- Use a relatively short planning horizon—two years or less for most small companies.
- Be informal and not overly structured; a shirt-sleeve approach is ideal.
- Encourage the participation of employees and outside parties to improve the reliability and creativity of the resulting plan.

- Do not begin with setting objectives because extensive objective-setting early on may interfere with the creative process of strategic management.
- Maintain flexibility; competitive conditions change too rapidly for any plan to be considered permanent.
- Focus on strategic *thinking*, not just planning, by linking long-range goals to day-to-day operations.
- Ensure that the development process is ongoing because businesses and the competitive environment in which they operate constantly change.

LO 3

Develop a stategic plan for a business using the nine steps of the stategic management process.

The Strategic Management Process

Strategic management is a continuous process that consists of nine steps:

Step 1. Develop a clear vision and translate it into a meaningful mission statement.
Step 2. Assess the company's strengths and weaknesses.
Step 3. Scan the environment for significant opportunities and threats facing the business.
Step 4. Identify the key factors for success in the business.
Step 5. Analyze the competition.
Step 6. Create company goals and objectives.
Step 7. Formulate strategic options and select the appropriate strategies.
Step 8. Translate strategic plans into action plans.
Step 9. Establish accurate controls.

Step 1. Develop a Clear Vision and Translate It Into a Meaningful Mission Statement

VISION Throughout history, the greatest political and business leaders have been visionaries. Whether the vision is as grand as Martin Luther King Jr.'s "I have a dream" speech or as simple as Ray Kroc's devotion to quality, service, cleanliness, and value at McDonald's, the purpose is the same: to focus everyone's attention on the same target and to inspire them to reach it. The vision is future-oriented and touches everyone associated with the company—for instance, employees, investors, lenders, customers, and the community. The vision is an expression of what an entrepreneur stands for and believes in. Highly successful entrepreneurs are able to communicate their vision and their enthusiasm about that vision to those around them.

A vision is the result of an entrepreneur's dream of something that does not exist yet and the ability to paint a compelling picture of that dream for everyone to see. It answers the question "Where are we going?" A clearly defined vision helps a company in four ways:

1. *Vision provides direction.* Entrepreneurs who spell out the vision for their company focus everyone's attention on the future and determine the path the business will take to get there.
2. *Vision determines decisions.* The vision influences the decisions, no matter how big or how small, that owners, managers, and employees make every day in a business. This influence can be positive or negative, depending on how well defined the vision is.
3. *Vision motivates people.* A clear vision excites and ignites people to action. People want to work for a company that sets its sights high.
4. *Vision allows for perseverance in the face of adversity.* Young companies, their founders, and their employees often face many hardships from a multitude of sources. Having a vision that serves as a company's "guiding star" enables people to overcome imposing obstacles.

Vision is based on an entrepreneur's values. Explaining how an entrepreneur's values are the nucleus around which a company grows, author and consultant Ken Blanchard says, "Winning companies first emphasize values—the beliefs that you, as the business owner, have about your employees, customers, quality, ethics, integrity, social responsibility, growth, stability, innovation, and flexibility. Managing by values—not by profits—is a powerful process."[11] Successful entrepreneurs build their businesses around a set of three to six core values, which might range from respect for the individual and innovation to creating satisfied customers and making the world a better place. Indeed, truly visionary entrepreneurs see their companies' primary purpose as more than just "making money." One writer explains, "Almost all workers are making decisions, not just filling out weekly sales reports or tightening screws. They will do what they think best. If you want them to do as the company thinks best too, then you must [see to it that they have] an inner gyroscope aligned with the corporate compass."[12] That gyroscope's alignment depends on the entrepreneur's values and how well he or she transmits them throughout the company.

The best way to put values into action is to create a written mission statement that communicates those values to everyone the company touches.

MISSION The **mission statement** addresses another basic question of any business venture: "What business are we in?" Establishing the purpose of the business in writing must come first in order to give the company a sense of direction. "If you don't reduce [your company's purpose] to paper, it just doesn't stick," says the owner of an architecture firm. "Reducing it to paper really forces you to think about what you are doing."[13] As an enduring declaration of a company's purpose, a mission statement is the mechanism for making it clear to everyone the company touches "why we are here" and "where we are going."

mission statement
an enduring declaration of a company's purpose that addresses the first question of any business venture: What business am I in?

ENTREPRENURIAL PROFILE _____

Truett Cathy: Chick-Fil-A

Truett Cathy, founder of the highly successful restaurant chain Chick-Fil-A, recalls a time when his business was struggling because of intensifying competition from big hamburger chains. The company, with 200 outlets at the time, was struggling to keep operating costs under control as inflation threatened to push them ever higher. Cathy scheduled an executive retreat at a lake outside of Atlanta, where managers could relax and talk about their concerns and ideas for the company. His oldest son, Dan, then director of operations, asked, "Why are we in business? Why are we here?" Cathy was about to tell his son that this retreat was no time to dwell on philosophical issues because there were bigger problems to solve. "Then," recalls Cathy, "I realized he was serious. His question both challenged and inspired us." In the ensuing brainstorming session, the group defined values that became Chick-Fil-A's mission statement: "To glorify God by being faithful stewards of all that is entrusted to our care. To have a positive influence on all who come in contact with Chick-Fil-A." With their purpose clearly defined, the management team went on to lead the company in a growth spurt, in which sales climbed 30 percent a year. Today, the company has nearly 1,400 restaurants in 37 states and the District of Columbia (none of which are open on Sundays) and generates annual sales of more than $2.6 billion.[14]

Without a concise, meaningful mission statement, a small business risks wandering aimlessly in the marketplace, with no idea of where to go or how to get there. A great mission statement sets the tone for the entire company and focuses its attention in the right direction.

ELEMENTS OF A MISSION STATEMENT A sound mission statement need not be lengthy to be effective. Three key issues entrepreneurs and their employees should address as they develop a mission statement for their businesses include:

- The _purpose_ of the company: What are we in business to accomplish?
- The _business_ we are in: How are we going to accomplish that purpose?
- The _values_ of the company: What principles and beliefs form the foundation of the way we do business?

ENTREPRENEURIAL PROFILE _____

Eric Ryan & Adam Lowry: Method

At Method, a San Francisco—based company that makes a line of all natural, non-toxic household and personal cleaning products and sells them in attractive bottles that were created by designer Karim Rashid, co-founders Eric Ryan and Adam Lowry identify five core values that support their unique small company's mission: collaboration, innovation, care, "what would McGyver do?," and keeping Method weird. Ryan and Lowry's vision is to build a company that creates a better cleaning experience for their customers by providing safe, environmentally friendly products in cleverly designed packages, constantly engaging in product innovation, and creating a fun work environment for employees.[15]

A company's mission statement may be the most essential and basic communication that it puts forward. If the people on the plant, shop, retail, or warehouse floor don't know what a company's mission is, then, for all practical purposes, it does not have one! The mission statement expresses a company's character, identity, and scope of operations, but writing it is only half the battle, at best. The most difficult part is *living* that mission every day. *That's* how employees decide what really matters. To be effective, a mission statement must become a natural part of the organization, embodied in the minds, habits, attitudes, and decisions of everyone in the company every day. One business writer claims, "If what you say about your firm's values and mission isn't true, you're in worse trouble than if you'd never articulated it in the first place."[16]

A well-used mission statement serves as a strategic compass for a small company, guiding both managers and employees as they make decisions in the face of uncertainty. Some companies use short, one- or two-sentence mission statements, and others create longer mission statements with multiple components. Consider the following examples:

- Google, the world's leading search engine, says its mission "is to organize the world's information and make it universally accessible and useful."[17]
- The mission of Great Harvest Bread Company, which Pete and Laura Wakeman co-founded in Great Falls, Montana, in 1976, conveys both the fun personality of the company and the values that are important to its founders: "Be loose and have fun. Bake phenomenal bread. Run fast to help customers. And give generously to others."[18]
- Eileen Fisher, a women's clothing company known for its simple, comfortable styles, uses a longer four-part mission statement that addresses its purpose, its products, its practices, and its profitability.[19]

A company may have a powerful competitive advantage, but it is wasted unless (1) the owner has communicated that advantage to workers, who, in turn, work hard to communicate it to customers and potential customers, and (2) customers recommend the company to their friends because they understand the benefits they are getting from it that they cannot get elsewhere. *That's* the real power of a mission statement. Table 3.1 offers some useful tips on writing a mission statement.

TABLE 3.1 Tips for Writing a Powerful Mission Statement

A mission statement is a useful tool for getting everyone fired up and heading in the same direction, but writing one is not as easy as it may first appear. Here are some tips for writing a powerful mission statement:

- *Keep it short.* The best mission statements are just a few sentences long. If they are short, people will tend to remember them better.
- *Keep it simple.* Avoid using fancy jargon just to impress outsiders such as customers or suppliers. The first and most important use of a mission statement is inside a company.
- *Know what makes your company different.* Your competitors are trying to reach the same customers that you are. A mission statement should address what is unique about your company and what sets it apart from the competition.
- *Take a broad view, but not too broad.* If it is too specific, a mission statement can limit a company's potential. Similarly, a mission statement is too broad if it applies to any company in the industry. When asked what business his company was in, Rob Carter, a top manager at FedEx, did not mention shipping packages quickly; instead, his response was, "We're in the business of engineering time."
- *Get everyone involved.* If the boss writes the company mission statement, who is going to criticize it? Although the entrepreneur has to be the driving force behind the mission statement, everyone in the company needs the opportunity to have a voice in creating it. Expect to write several drafts before you arrive at a finished product.
- *Keep it current.* Mission statements can get stale over time. As business and competitive conditions change, so should your mission statement. Make a habit of evaluating your mission periodically so that it stays fresh.
- *Make sure your mission statement reflects the values and beliefs you hold dear.* They are the foundation on which your company is built.

- *Make sure your mission includes values that are worthy of your employees' best efforts.* One entrepreneur says that a mission statement should "send a message to employees, suppliers, and customers as to what the purpose of the company is aside from just making profits."

- *Make sure your statement reflects a concern for the future.* Business owners can get so focused on the present that they forget about the future. A mission statement should be the first link to the company's future.

- *Keep the tone of the statement positive and upbeat.* No one wants to work for a business with a pessimistic outlook of the world.

- *Use your mission statement to lay an ethical foundation for your company.* This is the ideal time to let employees know what your company stands for—and what it won't stand for.

- *Look at other companies' mission statements to generate ideas for your own.* Two books, *Say It and Live It: The 50 Corporate Mission Statements That Hit the Mark* (Currency/Doubleday) and *Mission Statements: A Guide to the Corporate and Nonprofit Sectors* (Garland Publishing), are useful resources.

- *Make sure that your mission statement is appropriate for your company's culture.* Although you should look at other companies' missions, do not make the mistake of trying to copy them. Your company's mission is unique to you and your company.

- *Revise it when necessary.* No business is static, which means that your company's mission statement should change as your company changes. Work with a team of your employees on a regular basis to review and revise your company's mission statement.

- *Use it.* Don't go to all of the trouble of writing a mission statement just to let it collect dust. Post it on bulletin boards, print it on buttons and business cards, stuff it into employees' pay envelopes. Talk about your mission often, and use it to develop your company's strategic plan. That's what it's for!

Sources: Adapted from "Ten Tips for Writing a Mission Statement," AllBusiness, http://www.allbusiness. com/marketing/advertising-copywriting/12185-1.html; Ken Blanchard, "The New Bottom Line," *Entrepreneur*, February 1998, pp. 127–131; Alan Farnham, "Brushing Up Your Vision Thing," *Fortune*, May 1, 1995, p. 129; Sharon Nelton, "Put Your Purpose in Writing," *Nation's Business*, February 1994, pp. 61–64; Jacquelyn Lynn, "Single-Minded," *Entrepreneur*, January 1996, p. 97.

Step 2: Assess the Company's Strengths and Weaknesses

Having defined the vision she has for her company and translated that vision into a meaningful mission statement, an entrepreneur can turn her attention to assessing company strengths and weaknesses. Building a successful competitive strategy requires a business to magnify its strengths and overcome or compensate for its weaknesses. **Strengths** are positive internal factors that a company can draw on to accomplish its mission, goals, and objectives. They might include special skills or knowledge, a positive public image, an experienced sales force, an established base of loyal customers, and many other factors. **Weaknesses** are negative internal factors that inhibit a company's ability to accomplish its mission, goals, and objectives. A lack of capital, a shortage of skilled workers, the inability to master technology, and an inferior location are examples of weaknesses.

Identifying strengths and weaknesses helps owners understand their businesses as they exist (or, for start-ups, will exist). An organization's strengths should originate in the core competencies that are essential to gaining an edge in each of the market segments in which the firm competes. The key to building a successful strategy is using the company's underlying strengths as its foundation and matching those strengths against competitors' weaknesses.

One effective technique for taking this strategic inventory is to prepare a "balance sheet" of the company's strengths and weaknesses . The positive side should reflect important skills, knowledge, or resources that contribute to the firm's success. The negative side should record honestly any limitations that detract from the company's ability to compete. This balance sheet should analyze all key performance areas of the business—human resources, finance, production, marketing, product development, organization, and others. This analysis should give owners a more realistic perspective of their businesses, pointing out foundations on which they can build future strengths and obstacles that they must remove for the business to progress. This exercise can help entrepreneurs move from their current position to future actions.

strengths
positive internal factors that a company can use to accomplish its mission, goals, and objectives.

weaknesses
negative internal factors that inhibit the accomplishment of a company's mission, goals, and objectives.

Step 3: Scan the Environment for Significant Opportunities and Threats Facing the Business

OPPORTUNITIES   Once entrepreneurs have taken an internal inventory of company strengths and weaknesses, they must turn to the external environment to identify any opportunities and threats that might have a significant impact on the business. **Opportunities** are positive external options that a firm can exploit to accomplish its mission, goals, and objectives. The number of potential opportunities is limitless, so entrepreneurs need analyze only those that are most significant to the business (probably two or three at most). The key is to focus on the most promising opportunities that fit most closely with the company's strengths and core competencies.

Opportunities arise as a result of factors that are beyond entrepreneurs' control. Constantly scanning for those opportunities that best match their companies' strengths and core competencies and then pouncing on them ahead of competitors is the key to success.

opportunities

positive external options that a firm can exploit to accomplish its mission, goals, and objectives.

ENTREPRENEURIAL PROFILE

Cott Corporation: Fortifido

Managers at Cott Corporation, a maker of private-label drinks for humans, recognized that Americans spend $43.4 billion each year on their pets, more than the gross domestic product of all but 64 countries in the world, and decided to capitalize on the opportunity by introducing a line of vitamin-infused beverages for dogs. They believed that a trend toward people trying to select healthier food and beverages for themselves would carry over to their food and beverage choices for their pets. Sensing an opportunity, the company spent 18 months on research and development with veterinarians and food scientists to create a line of drinks that meet the nutritional needs of dogs. Cott's "Fortifido" vitamin-infused waters for dogs include varieties designed to strengthen bones (peanut butter flavored formula with calcium), joints (lemon grass flavor with amino acids and minerals), and skin (parsley flavor with zinc), and a spearmint flavor for fresh breath.[20]

Cott Beverages Inc.

THREATS   **Threats** are negative external forces that inhibit a company's ability to achieve its mission, goals, and objectives. Threats to the business can take a variety of forms, such as new competitors entering the local market, a government mandate regulating a business activity, an economic recession, rising interest rates, mounting energy prices, technological advances that make a company's product obsolete, and many others. For instance, video on demand and digital downloading of movies pose a serious threat to both retailers of DVDs and to companies that rent them from storefronts (e.g., Blockbuster) or online (e.g., Netflix). Both video on demand and DVD rentals, when coupled with large-screen, high-definition television sets and home theater sound systems, are a threat to movie theaters because many people prefer to sit on their own couches to watch movies rather than go to the theater. In fact, in 1946, the average person in the United States went to the movies 28 times per year; today, the average person goes to a movie theater fewer than five times per year! As a result, several theater chains, including Muvico, Cinema de Lux, CineBistro, and others, are changing their strategies to encourage movie fans to return to the big screen. These chains have added on-site restaurants, some offering traditional movie fare such as pizza, hamburgers, hot dogs, and nachos but others offering upscale dinners such as shrimp scampi and duck quesadillas. Their theaters boast valet parking, full bars, stadium seating with plush leather chairs with extra leg room, digital projection systems that provide crisp images, interactive game rooms for children, and child care services. "We're competing with a million things for people's time," says Jeremy Welman, COO of CineBistro Theaters. "We have to give them an experience that's worth going out to."[21]

Many small retailers face a threat from "big-box" retailers such as Wal-Mart, Home Depot, Circuit City, and others offering lower prices because of their high-volume purchasing power, huge advertising budgets, and mega-stores that attract customers for miles around. However, small businesses with the proper strategies in place do *not* have to fold in the face of intense competition. The accompanying "Hands On: How To . . ." feature explains that with the proper strategy, small companies can not only survive but thrive in the shadow of larger, more powerful rivals.

HANDS ON...
HOW TO

Beat Big-Box Competitors

It's the news that sends shivers down the spines of small business owners everywhere: Wal-Mart (or any other "big-box" retailer) is coming to town. "How can my small business compete against the largest company in the world?" they wonder. "Can my business survive?"

Although no business owner welcomes a threat of this magnitude from a giant competitor with greater buying power, more name recognition, and a reputation for driving small companies out of business, it is no reason to fold up the tent and go home. Smart entrepreneurs know that, by formulating and executing the proper strategy, they not only can survive in the face of big-box competitors, but they also can *thrive* in their presence.

Rule 1. Don't play their game

A fundamental concept in strategy is to avoid matching your company's weaknesses against a competitor's strengths. For instance, because Wal-Mart buys in such huge volume from its suppliers, it can extract the lowest prices from them. Small companies purchasing from those same suppliers cannot; therefore, it makes little sense for small companies to try to compete with Wal-Mart and other giant retailers on price. Unless your small company has another more significant cost advantage, competing on the basis of price is a recipe for disaster. Entrepreneurs who compete successfully emphasize features that giant discounters cannot provide—extensive product knowledge, better selection, superior customer service, a hassle-free buying experience, product warranties, and others.

Rule 2. Emphasize what is unique about your company and how it benefits your customers

When Brian Kelly, owner of City Beans, a coffee shop with two stores in northern New Jersey, learned that Starbucks was opening a location in the same building that housed one of his shops, he knew that he had to take action to save his business. Because Kelly purchased coffee beans from a local coffee roaster who made deliveries within 24 hours of roasting, he realized that the coffee City Beans sold was much fresher than Starbucks coffee. Kelly began a "served fresh daily" promotion that gave customers an important benefit and provided City Beans with a competitive advantage. He also re-energized his company's loyalty card program (Buy 11 cups of coffee and get one free), which provided him with important information about his customers, including their e-mail addresses. Kelly, whose stores also serve a selection of sandwiches, salads, and soups, began e-mailing customers in the loyalty program about daily lunch and coffee specials, and sales increased.

Rule 3. Hit 'em where they ain't

Big chains aim at big markets and often ignore small but profitable niche markets, which are ideal targets for small companies. When Home Depot moved into town, the owner of a small nursery began changing his company's product mix, emphasizing selections of unusual plants that were quite different from the inexpensive but rather typical plants its big-box rival sold. In addition, he added a section in his store dedicated to all-natural, organic gardening. Free weekend "workshops" that taught customers how to build different types of gardens brought in existing customers more often and attracted new ones. Two years after Home Depot opened, the small nursery was generating record sales that were higher than they were before its big-box competitor appeared!

Rule 4. Hire the best...and train them

Jeff Brotman, founder of Costco, a discount warehouse that goes up against Wal-Mart's Sam's Club discount warehouses, has been competing in competition with the industry giant for two decades. Costco pays its workers at rates well above the industry average, which keeps turnover rates low (in fact the lowest in the industry) and productivity high, giving it another edge over Wal-Mart. Small companies cannot always afford to pay the highest wages in an area; however, because their companies are small, entrepreneurs have the opportunity to create a work environment in which employees can thrive. For instance, one small company attracts and retains quality workers by allowing them to use flexible work schedules that make it easier for them to manage their busy lives. The owner also invests heavily in training workers so that they can move up the organization—and the pay scale—faster. The training pays off in the form of greater productivity, lower turnover, increased customer satisfaction, and higher sales per employee. Paying attention to seemingly small details such as more communication, frequent recognition for jobs well done, less bureaucracy, and flexible benefits enables small companies to build a loyal, motivated workforce that can outperform those at larger companies.

Rule 5. Bring back what the big boys have eliminated

Many companies in the supermarket industry have taken a beating as discount mass retailers have expanded their superstore concepts into more markets across the United States. Yet, many small supermarket chains have thrived by taking a completely different strategic approach, building small stores that allow shoppers to make their purchases quickly and conveniently. A Wal-Mart supercenter, for instance, adds about 40,000 grocery items to the already mind-boggling 116,000 items in its outlets. Customers have a wide selection of products at low prices, but many have grown weary of the time they have to invest to navigate these cavernous stores just to find the items they need. That's exactly what small grocers such as Save-a-Lot are counting on. Going back to the days of the old corner grocer, the St. Louis-based chain keeps its 1,250 stores small—operated by no more than 25 employees—and sells no more than 1,250 grocery items in each one. To keep its costs and prices low, Save-a-Lot carefully selects neighborhood locations and emphasizes private label items. (In fact, private label items make up 75 percent of the company's inventory.)

Rule 6. Beat them at the service game

In tennis, the serve is one of the most important parts of the game; so it is in the retail game. Small companies can differentiate themselves from their larger, more powerful rivals by emphasizing superior, friendly, personal service, something their size makes them uniquely capable of doing. One of the best ways to determine exactly how to provide superior service is identify your top five customers and periodically ask them, "How can we serve you better?"

1. Why do many small businesses fail when a big discount retailer such as Wal-Mart becomes a competitor?
2. Work with a team of your classmates to identify a local small business that competes with a big discounter. Which of these strategies has the small company employed to become a stronger competitor? What other strategies would you recommend to the owner of this business?
3. Based on your work in question number two, develop a one-page report summarizing your strategic suggestions.

Sources: Adapted from Norm Brodsky, "How Independents Can Hold Their Ground," *Inc.*, August 2007, pp. 65–66; Thomas M. Box, Kent Byus, Chris Fogliasso, and Warren D. Miller, "Hardball and OODA Loops: Strategy for Small Firms, *Proceedings of the Academy of Strategic Management*, Volume 6, Number 1, 2007, pp. 5–10; Matthew Maier, "How to Beat Wal-Mart," *Business 2.0*, May 2005, pp. 108–114; Rhonda Abrams, "Small Businesses Can Compete with the Big Guys," *Business*, September 26, 2004, p. 8; Ann Zimmerman, "Behind the Dollar-Store Boom: A Nation of Bargain Hunters," *Wall Street Journal*, December 13, 2004, pp. A1, A10; Barry Cotton, and Jean-Charles Cachon, "Resisting the Giants: Small Retail Entrepreneurs Against Mega-Retailers—An Empirical Study, Presented at the International Council for Small Business 2005 World Conference, June 2005; Amy Merrick, Gary McWilliams, Ellen Byron, and Kortney Stringer, "Targeting Wal-Mart," *Wall Street Journal*, December 1, 2004, pp. B1, B2.

Figure 3.2 illustrates that opportunities and threats are products of the interactions of forces, trends, and events outside the direct control of the business. These external forces have direct impact on the behavior of the markets in which the business operates, the behavior of competitors, and the behavior of customers. The number of potential threats facing a business is huge, but entrepreneurs should focus on the three or four most significant threats confronting their companies.

The interactions of strengths and weaknesses and opportunities and threats [SWOT] can be the most revealing aspects of using a SWOT analysis as part of a strategic plan. This analysis also requires entrepreneurs to take an objective look at their businesses and the environment in which they operate as they address many issues fundamental to their companies' success in the future.

Step 4: Identify the Key Factors for Success in the Business

KEY SUCCESS FACTORS Every business is characterized by controllable variables that determine the relative success of market participants. Identifying and manipulating these variables is how a small business gains a competitive advantage. By focusing efforts to maximize their companies' performance on these key success factors, entrepreneurs can achieve dramatic market advantages over their competitors. Companies that understand these key success factors tend to be leaders of the pack, whereas those that fail to recognize them become also-rans.

key success factors

the factors that determine a company's ability to compete successfully in an industry.

Key success factors (KSFs) come in a variety of different patterns depending on the industry. Simply stated, they are the factors that determine a company's ability to compete successfully in an industry. Every company in an industry must understand the key success factors driving the industry; otherwise, they are likely to become industry "also-rans" like the horses trailing the pack in the Kentucky Derby. Many of these sources of competitive advantages are based on cost factors such as manufacturing cost per unit, distribution cost per unit, or development cost per unit. Some are less tangible and less obvious but are just as important, such as superior product quality, solid relationships with dependable suppliers, superior customer service, a highly trained and knowledgeable sales force, prime store locations,

FIGURE 3.2

The Power of External Market Forces

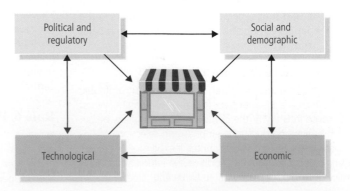

readily available customer credit, and many others. For example, one restaurant owner identified the following key success factors:

- Experience in the industry
- Sufficient start-up capital
- Tight cost control (labor costs, 15–18 percent of sales and food costs, 35–40 percent of sales)
- Accurate sales forecast, which minimizes wasted food
- Proper inventory control
- Meticulous cash management
- Careful site selection (the right location)
- High food quality
- Consistency
- Cleanliness
- Friendly and attentive service from a well-trained wait staff
- A clear definition of the restaurant's distinctive concept—its food, décor, service, and ambiance

These controllable variables determine the ability of any restaurant in his market segment to compete. Restaurants lacking these KSFs are not likely to survive, but those that build their strategies with these factors in mind will prosper. However, before entrepreneurs can build a strategy around the industry's KSFs, they must identify them. Identifying the KSFs in an industry allows entrepreneurs to determine where they should focus their companies' resources strategically. It is unlikely that a company, even a large one, can excel on every KSF it identifies. Therefore, as they begin to develop their strategies, most entrepreneurs focus on surpassing their rivals on one or two KSFs to build a sustainable competitive edge. As a result, KSFs become the cornerstones of a company's strategy.

For instance, the John H. Daniel Company, a custom tailor of high-end men's suits in Knoxville, Tennessee, understands that attracting and retaining skilled master tailors is crucial to its success. The company, founded in 1928, produces 75,000 to 80,000 made-to-measure suits a year that retail at prices ranging from $800 to $3,000, and sells them under a variety of labels. Unfortunately, the number of master tailors in the United States has fallen to only a dozen (learning the necessary skills usually takes an apprentice at least 10 years), and the family-owned business dedicates a significant portion of its budget to searching them out in foreign countries such as Italy, Turkey, and Vietnam. Owners Richard and Benton Bryant send scouts on recruiting trips to these countries and then pay to relocate the master tailors they hire along with their families to Tennessee. The company provides low-interest loans to help families get settled, and a company attorney handles all of the paperwork necessary to get visas for the tailors and their families. The strategy has paid off; today, more than 200 master tailors from 17 nations turn out luxurious custom-fitted garments, including the famous green jacket that is presented to the winner of the Master's Golf Tournament.[22]

ENTREPRENEURIAL PROFILE

Richard & Benton Bryant: John H. Daniel Company

Step 5: Analyze the Competition

Ask most small business owners to identify the greatest challenge their companies face and the most common response is *competition*. One study of small business owners by the National Federation of Independent Businesses (NFIB) reports that small business owners believe they operate in a highly competitive environment and that the level of competition is increasing.[23] The Internet and e-commerce have increased the ferocity and the scope of the competition that entrepreneurs face and have forced many business owners to change completely the ways in which they do business. Figure 3.3 shows the competitive strategies that small business owners rely on most heavily to compete with their rivals.

FIGURE 3.3

How Small Businesses Compete

Based on: William J. Dennis, Jr., *National Small Business Poll: Competition* (Washington, DC: National Federation of Independent Businesses, 2003), Vol. 3, Issue 8, p. 1.

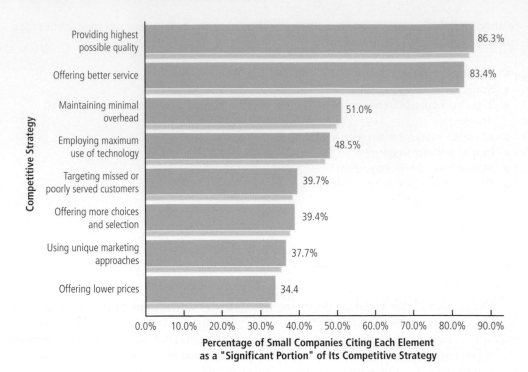

Percentage of Small Companies Citing Each Element as a "Significant Portion" of Its Competitive Strategy

---

ENTREPRENEURIAL PROFILE

Shawn Gupta & Reman Child: Expensr

When entrepreneurs Shawn Gupta and Reman Child decided to create a personal finance software package, they knew that they would be facing tough competition from the market leaders, Quicken and Microsoft Money. To be successful, Gupta and Reman knew that they would have to take a different approach to helping customers unravel the complexities of personal finance. After talking with people who used existing personal finance software, the entrepreneurs decided to pursue a "simpler is better" strategy for their product, which they named Expensr. First, they made Expensr a Web-based application rather than a traditional software package that customers had to install on their computers. Second, they made the program extremely intuitive and easy to use. Expensr not only helps users analyze their spending and set up a budget, but it also shows how much they are spending on average each day and offers money-saving tips. Gupta and Remen also added a social component to Expensr. Users can add a tag, such as "in my twenties" or "a young professional" to their profiles and compare their financial positions to that of the typical person in the same category. "That's the idea behind the social network," says Gupta, "to help you do better by making you aware of what other people like you are doing." Typical serial entrepreneurs, Gupta and Child recently sold Expensr to technology company Strands so that they could begin work on their next business start-up.[24]

Keeping tabs on rivals' movements through competitive intelligence programs is a vital strategic activity. "Business is like any battlefield. If you want to win the war, you have to know who you're up against," says one small business consultant.[25] Unfortunately, most businesses are not very good at competitive intelligence; 97 percent of U.S. businesses do not systematically track the progress of their key competitors.[26] A study of business executives around the world by McKinsey and Company reports that just 23 percent of their companies discovered a major competitive innovation by a competitor in time to be able to plan a response before the innovation hit the market.[27] The primary goals of a competitive intelligence program include the following:

- Avoiding surprises from existing competitors' new strategies and tactics.
- Identifying potential new competitors.
- Improving reaction time to competitors' actions.
- Anticipating rivals' next strategic moves.

ETHICS AND ENTREPRENEURSHIP

Diving for Information?

Nate Anderson had been working for six months on the business plan for the fitness center that he was trying to start in his hometown. Nate was growing increasingly frustrated because his full-time job commitments meant that he could work on the plan only part-time. He had hoped to be finished by now and presenting his plan to potential lenders and investors. Still, he could not afford to quit his full-time job just yet. He and his wife, Heather, had just had their first child, Matthew, 18 months ago, and she had stopped working, at least temporarily, which meant that he was the sole income earner in the household.

At first, Nate found writing the business plan to be easy. He was able to create a mission statement, set goals and objectives, and define a workable strategy for his company. He had visited the Web site of the International Health, Racquet and Sportsclub Association (IHRSA) and had gathered reams of research on the industry and its key success factors. Using his research, Nate had compiled a comprehensive profile of his target customers and had developed a guerrilla marketing plan designed to reach them. He had started to develop the financial forecasts for the business but knew that he had more information to gather before he could complete them. He knew how many employees it would take to operate the fitness center and already had approached a few outstanding candidates about working there when he opened for business. He was unsure of what his monthly operating expenses would be, however. "How much will I have to pay my employees?" he wondered. "What about employee benefits? How much will they cost? Utilities? Insurance? What other expenses am I overlooking that might have a significant impact on my company's profitability?"

As he looked over the plan, Nate noticed that the biggest gap in his plan dealt with operating cost estimates and competitor analysis. There were two competing fitness clubs already in operation in the town of 98,000 people, but Nate really did not know much about their operations. One was a locally owned fitness center, and the other was a franchised unit of a national chain. He had been a member of the locally owned center, but that was years ago, before he discovered his desire to open a fitness center of his own. Nate has visited the two companies' Web sites but found only basic information there. "How can I find information about these companies?" he thought to himself.

After a long day at work, Nate came home and took over caring for Matthew so that Heather could have some time for herself. By the time he fed Matthew and put him to bed, Nate was too tired to work on his business plan and sat down to watch television. He flipped to the PBS station and saw that *The History Detectives* was just beginning. One of the episodes involved a letter from President Ronald Reagan and some other historic material that led to a fascinating investigation of the history of Camp David, the Presidential retreat in the mountains of nearby Maryland. The viewer who submitted the story said that he had found the letter and material while "Dumpster diving," sifting through the trash in a dumpster. "Aha!" thought Nate. "That's it! I can start sifting through the trash that these two companies throw out. There should be a gold mine of information in there."

The next day Nate was telling his friend Jackson about his idea. "Yeah, that might work, but I have a better idea," he said. "I noticed an ad in the newspaper that said the franchised fitness club was offering a free 60-day trial membership. If you really want to get some good information about that operation, you should join for 60 days. It won't cost you a thing, and who knows what kinds of reports you may come across once you're inside. In addition, you can always pump unsuspecting employees for information as part of 'casual conversations.'" Jackson emphasized the last two words with air quotes and a clever grin.

"That's the company that concerns me the most," admitted Nate. "They've got the benefit of that national advertising campaign, and I'll bet that brings in a lot of customers."

"Well now you can find out just how many of them there are and how much they pay to be members," laughed Jackson.

"It certainly would speed up my ability to finish my plan," thought Nate. As he walked away, Nate realized that he had to make some decisions about completing his business plan.

1. Is gathering competitive intelligence unethical? Explain.
2. Visit the Web site for the Society of Competitive Intelligence Professionals (www.scip.org) and review the organization's code of ethics. How do the actions that Nate is considering taking to learn about his competitors measure up to the code?
3. Does gathering information on their competitors mean that entrepreneurs must violate ethical standards? Explain.
4. What suggestions can you offer Nate for gathering the information he needs to complete his business plan *without* violating any laws or ethical standards?

COMPETITOR ANALYSIS Sizing up the competition gives a business owner a more realistic view of the market and her company's position in it. Yet not every competitor warrants the same level of attention in the strategic plan. *Direct competitors* offer the same products and services, and customers often compare prices, features, and deals from these competitors as they shop. *Significant competitors* offer some of the same products and services. Although their product or service lines may be somewhat different, there is competition with them in several key areas. *Indirect competitors* offer the same or similar products or services only in a small number of areas, and their target customers seldom overlap with yours. Entrepreneurs should monitor closely the actions of their direct competitors, maintain a solid grasp of where their significant competitors are heading, and spend only minimal resources tracking their indirect competitors.

A competitive intelligence exercise enables entrepreneurs to update their knowledge of competitors by answering the following questions:

- Who are your primary competitors? Where are they located? (The *Yellow Pages* is a great place to start.)
- What distinctive core competencies have they developed?
- How do their cost structures compare to yours? Their financial resources?
- How do they market their products and services?
- What do customers say about them? How do customers describe their products or services; their way of doing business; the additional services they might supply?
- What are their key strategies?
- What are their strengths? How can your company surpass them?
- What are their major weaknesses? How can your company capitalize on them?
- Are new competitors entering the business?

According to the Society of Competitive Intelligence, 95 percent of the competitive intelligence information is available from public sources that anyone can access—if they know how.[28] Gathering information on competitors does not require entrepreneurs to engage in activities that are unethical, illegal, or unsavory (such as dumpster diving). One expert says that competitive intelligence (CI) involves "taking information from the public domain, adding it to what you know about your company and your industry, and looking for patterns."[29]

competitive profile matrix

a tool that allows a business owners to evaluate their companies against major competitors using the key success factors for that market.

Entrepreneurs can use the results of their competitive intelligence efforts to construct a competitive profile matrix for their direct competitors. A **competitive profile matrix** allows owners to evaluate their firms against major competitors using the key success factors for that market segment. The first step is to list the key success factors identified in Step 4 of the strategic planning process (refer to Table 3.4) and to attach weights to them reflecting their relative importance. (For simplicity, the weights in this matrix sum add up to 1.00.) In this example, notice that product quality is weighted twice as heavily (twice as important) as is price competitiveness.

The next step is to identify the company's major competitors and to rate each one (and your company) on each of the key success factors:

If factor is a:	Rating is:
Major weakness	1
Minor weakness	2
Minor strength	3
Major strength	4

Once the rating is completed, the owner simply multiplies the weight by the rating for each factor to get a weighted score, and then adds up each competitor's weighted scores to get a total weighted score. Table 3.2 shows a sample competitive profile matrix for a small company. The results should show which company is strongest, which is weakest, and which of the key success factors each one is best and worst at meeting. By carefully studying and interpreting the results, an entrepreneur can begin to envision the ideal strategy for building a competitive edge in her market segment.

Step 6. Create Company Goals and Objectives

Before entrepreneurs can build a comprehensive set of strategies, they must first establish business goals and objectives, which give them targets to aim for and provide a basis for evaluating their companies' performance. Without them, it is impossible to know where a business is going or how well it is performing. The following conversation between Alice and the Cheshire Cat,

TABLE 3.2 Sample Competitive Profile Matrix

Key Success Factors (from Step 4)	Weight	Your Business		Competitor 1		Competitor 2	
		Rating	Weighted Score	Rating	Weighted Score	Rating	Weighted Score
Quality	0.25	4	1.00	2	0.50	2	0.50
Customer Retention	0.20	3	0.60	3	0.60	3	0.60
Location	0.15	4	0.60	3	0.45	4	0.60
Perception of Value	0.20	4	0.80	2	0.40	3	0.60
Cost Control	0.20	3	0.60	1	0.20	4	0.80
Total	1.00		3.60		2.15		3.10

taken from Lewis Carroll's *Alice in Wonderland*, illustrates the importance of creating meaningful goals and objectives as part of the strategic management process: [30]

> "Would you tell me please, which way I ought to go from here?" asked Alice.
> "That depends a good deal on where you want to get to," said the Cat.
> "I don't much care where…," said Alice.
> "Then it doesn't matter which way you go," said the Cat.

A small business that "doesn't much care where" it wants to go (i.e., one that has no goals and objectives) will find that "it really doesn't matter which way" it chooses to go (i.e., its strategy is irrelevant).

GOALS **Goals** are the broad, long-range attributes that a business seeks to accomplish; they tend to be general and sometimes even abstract. Goals are not intended to be specific enough for a manager to act on, but simply state the general level of accomplishment sought. Do you want to boost your market share? Does your cash balance need strengthening? Would you like to enter a new market or increase sales in a current one? Do you want to develop new products or services? Researchers Jim Collins and Jerry Porras studied a large group of businesses and determined that one of the factors that set apart successful companies from unsuccessful ones was the formulation of very ambitious, clear, and inspiring long-term goals. Collins and Porras called them BHAGs ("Big Hairy Audacious Goals," pronounced "bee-hags") and say that their main benefit is to inspire and focus a company on important actions that are consistent with its overall mission.[31]

Addressing these broad issues will help you focus on the next phase—developing specific, realistic objectives.

goals
the broad, long-range attributes a business seeks to accomplish; they tend to be general and sometimes even abstract.

OBJECTIVES **Objectives** are more specific targets of performance. Common objectives concern profitability, productivity, growth, efficiency, markets, financial resources, physical facilities, organizational structure, employee welfare, and social responsibility. Because some of these objectives might conflict with one another, it is important to establish priorities. Which objectives are most important? Which are least important? Arranging objectives in a hierarchy according to their priority can help an entrepreneur resolve conflicts when they arise. Well-written objectives have the following characteristics:

objectives
more specific targets of performance, commonly addressing areas such as profitability, productivity, growth, and other key aspects of a business.

They are specific. Objectives should be quantifiable and precise. For example, "to achieve a healthy growth in sales" is not a meaningful objective; however, "to increase retail sales by 12 percent and wholesale by 10 percent in the next fiscal year" is precise and spells out exactly what management wants to accomplish.

They are measurable. Managers should be able to plot the organization's progress toward its objectives; this requires a well-defined reference point from which to start and a scale for measuring progress.

They are assignable. Unless an entrepreneur assigns responsibility for an objective to an individual, it is unlikely that the company will ever achieve it. Creating objectives without giving someone responsibility for accomplishing it is futile. Accountability is the key.

They are realistic, yet challenging. Objectives must be within the reach of the organization or motivation will disappear. In any case, managerial expectations must remain high. In other words, the more challenging an objective is (within realistic limits), the higher the performance will be. Set objectives that will challenge your business and its employees.

They are timely. Objectives must specify not only what is to be accomplished but also when it is to be accomplished. A time frame for achievement is important.

They are written down. Writing down objectives makes them more concrete and makes it easy to communicate them to everyone in the company. The process of setting and writing down objectives does not have to be complex; in fact, an entrepreneur should keep the number of objectives relatively small, from five to ten.

No Copycats Here!

In his book *Break from the Pack*, Oren Harari explains how business owners can escape the problems of the "Copycat Economy, where everyone has access to the same resources and talent, where the Web is the great equalizer, and where the market's twin foundations are imitation and commoditization." He argues that too many businesses are stuck in the pack with "me-too" products and services that customers see as commodities. The danger of being stuck in the pack is becoming what entrepreneur Terry Brock calls "disgustingly generic." What can small companies, which often lack the resources that large companies have, do to break from the pack? Consider the lessons we can learn from the following small businesses.

MotoArt LLC

Donovan Fell and Dave Hall were co-workers in an architectural sign business when they saw several greasy, beat-up propellers from a B-17 bomber from World War II on a scrap metal truck that were destined to be melted down. They rescued the propellers and began transforming them into works of art known as Propeller Sculptures. The entrepreneurs quickly realized that other people were interested in these historic pieces of art, quit their jobs, and launched MotoArt LLC, a company that salvages parts from retired airplanes and transforms them into beautiful pieces of artwork and furniture. One of their recently completed pieces is a stylish couch made from the pontoon float of a 1950 Grumman Albatross. MotoArt, with annual sales that exceed $2 million, has a growing list of customers that includes celebrities, history buffs, and *Fortune* 500 companies such as Microsoft and Boeing.

MotoArt

Blink, Inc.

Calfee Designs

When Craig Calfee's 60-pound dog playfully grabbed a bamboo stick, Calfee was amazed that the bamboo was strong enough to allow him to lift his dog off of the ground. Calfee, who pioneered the use of carbon fiber in bicycle frames, began wondering how bamboo bicycle frames would perform. His research showed that bamboo has greater tensile strength than steel, withstands compression better than concrete, and is lightweight, characteristics that make it an ideal material for a bicycle frame. In addition to its performance potential, bamboo is a renewable resource, which appeals to environmentally sensitive customers. Calfee believes that bamboo is the next "big thing" in bicycle design and has added bamboo-frame models to his company's line of high-performance bicycles. Although the company's bamboo bikes are priced at $2,700, sales are growing so fast that they now make up 25 percent of the company's $1 million in annual sales. One champion bicyclist, who now uses a bamboo-frame bicycle in competitions, says that riding his bamboo bike "is like wearing comfortable loafers and having the efficiency of track spikes."

Calfee Design

XV Motorsports

John Buscema and Sean Hyland, both car buffs, started XV Motorsports in 2005 with a unique twist on the idea of selling classic Chrysler and Dodge muscle cars from the 1960s and 1970s: to completely re-engineer the cars, installing modern high-performance engines, disc brakes, alloy wheels, modern suspensions and steering

components, cutting edge electronics, and safety features, and retain only the original body shell. The result: a classic muscle car reborn and updated with hi-tech modern parts. Their re-engineered cars typically are priced between $140,000 and $230,000, and each one requires six to eight months to complete. Currently, XV Motorsports, which is based in Irvington, New York, can handle up to 18 orders a year, and customers keep its craftsmen busy.

1. Which of the strategies discussed in this chapter are these companies using? Explain.
2. What competitive advantages does the successful execution of their strategies produce for these businesses?
3. What are the risks associated with these companies' strategies?

Sources: Adapted from Oren Harari, Break from the Pack, Wharton School Publishing, (Philadelphia, PA: 2007); Terry Brock, "Avoid Being 'Disgustingly Generic,'" *Biz Journals*, July 2, 2008, http://www.bizjournals.com/extraedge/consultants/succeeding_today/2007/07/02/column476.html; Jim Champy, "Arm Yourself to Win," *FSB*, May 2008, pp. 81–84; "Looking Buff," *Forbes Life*, Fall 2007, p. 128; Jason Harper, "Classic '70 Dodge Challenger Gets Remake as $176,000 Muscle Car," *Bloomberg News*, August 14, 2007, http://www.bloomberg.com/apps/news?pid=20601096&refer=auto&sid=aWNEg_Nzvug8; Lily Huang, "Stronger Than Steel," Newsweek, April 12, 2008, http://www.newsweek.com/id/131702; Mina Kimes, "Bamboo on Wheels," *FSB*, February 2008, p. 24; Sara Wilson, "Make It a Reality," *Entrepreneur*, August 2007, p. 65; "About Us," MotoArt, http://www.motoart.com/motoartabout.php.

Step 7. Formulate Strategic Options and Select the Appropriate Strategies

By this point in the strategic management process, entrepreneurs should have a clear picture of what their businesses do best and what their competitive advantages are. They also should understand their firms' weaknesses and limitations as well as those of its competitors. The next step is to evaluate strategic options and then prepare a game plan designed to achieve the stated mission, goals, and objectives.

LO 4

Discuss the three basic strategies—low-cost, differentiation, and focus—and know when and how to employ them.

STRATEGY A **strategy** is a road map of the actions an entrepreneur draws up to accomplish a company's mission, goals, and objectives. In other words, the mission, goals, and objectives spell out the ends, and the strategy defines the means for reaching them. A strategy is the master plan that covers all of the major parts of the organization and ties them together into a unified whole. The plan must be action-oriented; it should breathe life into the entire planning process. An entrepreneur must build a sound strategy based on the preceding steps that uses the company's core competencies and strengths as the springboard to success. Joseph Picken and Gregory Dess, authors of *Mission Critical: The 7 Strategic Traps that Derail Even the Smartest Companies*, write, "A flawed strategy—no matter how brilliant the leadership, no matter how effective the implementation—is doomed to fail. A sound strategy, implemented without error, wins every time."[32] A successful strategy is comprehensive and well-integrated, focusing on establishing the key success factors that the entrepreneur identified in Step 4. For instance, because maximum shelf space is a key success factor for a small manufacturer's product, the strategy must identify techniques for gaining more in-store shelf space (e.g., offering higher margins to distributors and brokers than competitors do, assisting retailers with in-store displays, or redesigning a wider, more attractive package).

strategy
a road map of the actions an entrepreneur draws up to fulfill a company's mission, goals, and objectives.

THREE STRATEGIC OPTIONS Obviously, the number of strategies from which the small business owner can choose is infinite. When all the glitter is stripped away, however, three basic strategies remain. In his classic book, *Competitive Strategy*, Michael Porter defines these strategies: (1) cost leadership, (2) differentiation, and (3) focus (see figure 3.4). [33]

FIGURE 3.4

Three Strategic Options

cost leadership strategy
a strategy in which a company strives to be the low-cost producer relative to its competitors in the industry.

COST LEADERSHIP A company pursuing a **cost leadership strategy** strives to be the lowest-cost producer relative to its competitors in the industry. Low-cost leaders have a competitive advantage in reaching buyers whose primary purchase criterion is price, and they have the power to set the industry's price floor. This strategy works well when buyers are sensitive to price changes, when competing firms sell the same commodity products and compete on the basis of price, and when companies can benefit from economies of scale. Not only is a low-cost leader in the best position to defend itself in a price war, but it also can use its power to attack competitors with the lowest price in the industry.

There are many ways to build a low-cost strategy, but the most successful cost leaders know where they have cost advantages over their competitors, and they use these as the foundation for their strategies. Successful cost leaders often find low-cost suppliers (or use a vertical integration strategy to produce their own products), eliminate the efficiencies in their channels of distribution, use the Internet to cut costs, and operate more efficiently than their competitors. They are committed to squeezing unnecessary costs out of their operations.

ENTREPRENEURIAL PROFILE

Chuck Runyon, Jeff Klinger, & Dave Mortensen: Anytime Fitness

In 1995, fitness instructors Chuck Runyon, Jeff Klinger, and Dave Mortensen purchased a run-down gym in St. Paul, Minnesota, for $100,000 and refurbished it. Their fitness club was profitable, but containing the costs of operation proved to be a constant challenge. That's when the entrepreneurs began asking their customers what they looked for in a fitness club. Two reasons stood out: convenience and affordability. In 2002, Runyon, Klinger, and Mortensen sold the club for $1 million and launched Anytime Fitness, a franchise that offers customers access to a "no frills" exercise facility that includes treadmills, weight machines, and free weights with minimal staff but no upscale amenities, not even a pool. "We don't have smoothie bars and aerobics," says Runyon. "[Our customers] want to get in, get out, and get on with the rest of their lives." As it names implies, Anytime Fitness locations are open 24 hours a day and are staffed from 11 a.m. to 7 p.m. with a skeleton crew, which keeps labor costs down to just 10 percent of sales compared to 45 percent or more of revenues for full-service gyms. During the rest of the day, the doors are locked, but customers can get in using computerized cards. A security system includes surveillance cameras and personal security devices that customers wear as necklaces while working out and can alert a security company that responds in less than one minute or 911 dispatchers. "It's all about finding populations of 7,000 to 10,000 people, where the big-box centers can't compete," says Runyon. "We've found a sweet spot between the intimidating environment at Gold's Gym and the 100,000-square-foot, gargantuan fitness emporiums." With its low cost strategy, Anytime Fitness has been profitable from the start and now generates sales of more than $15 million, with nearly 700 franchises in 45 states and Canada.[34]

Of course, there are dangers in following a cost leadership strategy. Sometimes a company focuses exclusively on lower manufacturing costs, without considering the impact of purchasing, distribution, or overhead costs. Another danger is incorrectly identifying the company's true cost drivers. Although their approach to managing is characterized by frugality, companies that understand cost leadership are willing to invest in those activities that drive costs out of doing business, whether it is technology, preventive maintenance, or some other factor. In addition, over time, competitors may erode a company's cost advantage by finding ways to lower their own costs. Finally, a firm may pursue a low cost leadership strategy so zealously that in its drive to push costs downward, it eliminates product or service features that customers consider to be essential.

Under the right conditions, a cost-leadership strategy executed properly can be an incredibly powerful strategic weapon. Small discount retailers that live in the shadows of Wal-Mart but thrive even when the economy slows succeed by relentlessly pursuing low-cost strategies. Small chains such as Fred's, Dollar General, Family Dollar, and 99 Cents Only cater to low- and middle-income customers who live in inner cities or rural areas. They offer inexpensive products such as food, health and beauty products, cleaning supplies, clothing, and seasonal merchandise, and many of the items they stock are closeout buys (purchases made as low as 10 cents on the dollar) on brand name merchandise. These companies also strive to keep their overhead costs as low as possible. For instance, 99 Cents Only, whose name describes its merchandising strategy, is housed in a no-frills warehouse in an older section of City of Commerce, California.[35] The success of these stores proves that companies pursuing a cost leadership strategy must emphasize cost containment in *every* decision, from where to locate the company headquarters to which items to stock.

DIFFERENTIATION A company following a **differentiation strategy** seeks to build customer loyalty by selling goods or services that provide unique attributes and that customers perceive to be superior to competing products. That, in turn, enables the business to command higher prices for its products or services than competitors. There are many ways to create a differentiation strategy, but the key is to be unique at something that is important to the customer. In other words, a business strives to be better than its competitors at something that customers value.

differentiation strategy
a strategy in which a company seeks to build customer loyalty by positioning its goods or services in a unique or different fashion.

The Markoff Group

After graduating from the famous culinary school, Le Cordon Bleu, in Paris, Katrina Markoff took a cooking mentor's advice and began traveling the world to expand her passion for combining unusual flavors in creative ways. "I noticed a lack of creativity in chocolate," she says. "I thought I could do something." In 1998, from her Chicago apartment, Markoff launched Vosges-Haut Chocolat, a company that makes gourmet chocolates in exotic combinations such as wasabi and ginger-infused black pearl chocolate bars and Krug champagne-filled Hip-Hop truffles topped with gold leaves as well as more standard creations such as organic peanut butter bonbons. Markoff devises her company's unique recipes ("I create the flavors," she says) from the extensive notes she took on her travels in Europe, Southeast Asia, and Australia, allowing her customers to experience flavors from around the world. "It's about much more than just doing interesting flavors with chocolate," she says. "It's about telling a story of a different culture through the medium of chocolate." With a $50,000 loan from the U.S. Small Business Administration, Markoff opened a retail store in Chicago, launched the company's Web site, www.vosgeschocolate.com, and landed upscale retailer Neiman Marcus as a customer. In addition to selling a unique chocolate experience, Markoff, who recently was named *Entrepreneur* magazine's Woman of the Year, also sets her company apart from the competition by managing it in an environmentally sustainable manner. Company headquarters operates with 100 percent renewable energy. She also supports several nonprofit organizations through her company, even creating special truffle collections from which she donates a portion of profits to help women around the world. Markoff's differentiation strategy works well; Vosges-Haut Chocolat has opened stores in Japan and England and generates annual sales of $12 million.[36]

If a small company can improve a product's (or service's) performance, reduce the customer's cost and risk of purchasing it, or provide intangible benefits that customers value (such as status, prestige, a sense of safety, among others), it has the potential to be a successful differentiator. Companies that execute a differentiation strategy successfully can charge premium prices for their products and services, increase their market share, and reap the benefits of customer loyalty and retention. To be successful, a business must make its product or service truly different, at least in the eyes of its customers.

ENTREPRENEURIAL PROFILE

Ice Hotel

Entrepreneur Yngve Bergqvist has no trouble setting his hotel in Jukkasjärvi, Sweden, apart from others. Located 125 miles above the Arctic Circle, the aptly-named Ice Hotel offers travelers a unique experience. Everything in the hotel—walls, beds, night tables, chairs, cinema, bars—is made from 30,000 tons of snow and 10,000 tons of crystal clear ice harvested from the Torne River! Each of the 60 rooms is unique, designed by a different artist from around the world. Guests sleep in insulated sleeping bags on ice beds covered with thin mattresses and plenty of reindeer blankets. Because temperatures inside the hotel typically hover at 5 degrees below zero (centigrade), guests cannot take their luggage to their ice rooms; it will freeze! Amenities include an ice bar, an ice chapel, an ice cinema, and an ice art exhibition. The 30,000 square-foot Ice Hotel is open from December through April (it melts in the spring), but during its brief existence, it will accommodate some 5,000 guests at rates ranging from $200 to $500 per night! Countless rock groups, including Van Halen, have shot music videos at the Ice Hotel. "It's not about comfort," says co-owner Arne Bergh. "It's a journey, an adventure."[37]

Although few businesses are innately as unique as the ice hotel, the goal for a company pursuing a differentiation strategy is to create that kind of uniqueness in the minds of its customers. The key to a successful differentiation strategy is to build it on a core competency, something a small company is uniquely good at doing in comparison to its competitors. Common bases for differentiation include superior customer service, special product features, complete product lines, instantaneous parts availability, absolute product reliability, supreme product quality, and extensive product knowledge. To be successful, a differentiation strategy must create the perception of value in the customer's eyes. No customer will purchase a good or service that fails to produce its perceived value, no matter how real that value may be. One business consultant advises, "Make sure you tell your customers and prospects what it is about your business that makes you different. Make sure that difference is on the form of a true benefit to the customer."[38]

ENTREPRENEURIAL PROFILE

Scott Leonard & Matt Reynolds: Indigenous Designs

In 1993, 26-year-old Scott Leonard traveled to Ecuador, where a friend introduced him to a fair-trade knitting cooperative that was created to help local women lift themselves out of poverty. When he retuned to California, Leonard decided to sell his surf shop and open a business that would earn a profit while supporting women like the ones he met in Ecuador. In 1994, Leonard and business partner, Matt Reynolds, launched Indigenous Designs, a company that markets stylish women's clothing made from all-natural, sustainable fabrics such as organic cotton, silk, alpaca, tencel, and wool. However, Indigenous Designs is more than just a "green" clothing company. The company's marketing message to upscale retail customers, which include Whole Foods, Sundance, Eileen Fisher, Dillard's and many others, emphasizes fashion, style, design, price—and then sustainability. "It's all about the product, but P.S., there is this story behind it," says Leonard. "Our design mantra is 'Never let customers feel like they are sacrificing quality or fashion sense to be a good corporate citizen.'" As part of its socially responsible heritage, Indigenous Designs monitors its suppliers to make sure that they abide by fair-trade standards, powers its office with solar energy, and gives employees incentives to ride their bicycles to work. Indigenous Design's differentiation strategy has allowed the company to increase the number of stores selling its merchandise by 75 percent and to double its annual sales to $4 million within just 18 months.[39]

Small companies encounter risks when pursuing a differentiation strategy. One danger is trying to differentiate a product or service on the basis of something that does not boost its performance or lower its cost to customers. Another pitfall is trying to differentiate on the basis of something that customers do not see as important. Business owners also must consider how long they can sustain a product's or service's differentiation; changing customer tastes may make the basis for differentiation temporary. Imitations and "knockoffs" from competitors also pose a threat to a successful differentiation strategy. For instance, entrepreneurs in Finland have built an ice hotel in Finland to compete with the original ice hotel in Sweden. Designers of high-priced original clothing see much cheaper knockoff products on the market shortly after their designs hit the market. Another pitfall is over-differentiating and charging so much that the company prices its products out of the market. The final risk is focusing only on the physical characteristics of a product or service and ignoring important psychological factors such as status, prestige, and image, which can be powerful sources of differentiation.

FOCUS A **focus strategy** recognizes that not all markets are homogeneous. In fact, in any given market, there are many different customer segments, each having different needs, wants, and characteristics. The principal idea of a focus strategy is to select one (or more) segment(s), identify customers' special needs, wants, and interests, and provide them with a good or service designed to excel in meeting these needs, wants, and interests. Focus strategies build on *differences* among market segments. Because they are small, flexible, and attentive to their customers' particular needs, small companies can be successful in niches that are too narrow for their larger competitors to enter profitably. These companies focus on a narrow segment of the overall market and set themselves apart by becoming either cost leaders in the segment or by differentiating themselves from competitors.

> **focus strategy**
> a strategy in which a company selects one or more market segments, identifies customers' special needs, wants, and interests, and approaches them with a good or service designed to excel in meeting those needs, wants, and interests.

Focus strategies will become more prevalent among small businesses in the future as industries increasingly become dumbbell-shaped, with a few large companies dominating one end, a relatively small number of mid-size businesses in the middle, and a large number of small businesses operating at the other end. A study by Intuit and the Institute for the Future on the small business environment in 2018, *The Intuit Future of Small Business Report*, cites increasingly fragmented markets, customers who demand products and services that are tailored to their specific needs, and advancements that give small companies affordable access to increasingly sophisticated technology as key factors that will make narrow markets increasingly suitable for small businesses to thrive. The report concludes that "there will be increasing opportunities for small businesses to flourish in niches left untouched by global giants."[40]

In fact, serving specific target segments or niches rather than attempting to reach the total market is the essence of a focus strategy, which makes it ideally suited to small businesses, which often lack the resources to reach the overall market. Their goal is to serve their narrow target markets more effectively and efficiently than do competitors that pound away at the broad market. Common bases for building a focus strategy include zeroing in on a small geographic area, targeting a group of customers with similar needs or interests (e.g., left-handed people), specializing in a specific product or service (e.g. Batteries Plus, a store that sells and services every kind of battery imaginable), or selling specialized knowledge (e.g., restoring valuable and priceless works of art).

ENTREPRENEURIAL PROFILE _____

Anthony & Elizabeth Trento: American Plume and Fancy Feather

Anthony and Elizabeth Trento own American Plume and Fancy Feather, a family business that sells feathers and was started by Anthony's uncle in 1921, when women's hats decorated with feathers were the rage. Changing fashion trends required the company to search out new customers, however, and today, American Plume selects, dyes, trims, and sells individual feathers or assembles them into finished products such as boas and fans. Although the company's customer base includes Broadway theaters, cruise ships, Las Vegas show girls, movie makers, party planners, ballroom dancers, and even makers of fishing flies, its primary niche is show business. American Plume recently sold $80,000 of feathers for the costumes for 40 showgirls in a Las Vegas show and has been supplying feathers to Broadway shows (including the hit musical *Wicked*) for more than 25 years. Trento's celebrity customers include Uma Thurman, the model Iman, and John Travolta, who sported an American Plume boa in the movie *Hairspray*. Perhaps American Plume's most famous customer is *Sesame Street's* Big Bird, the eight-foot-tall inspiration for generations of kids (who has been played by Caroll Spinney for the last four decades). American Plume dyes large turkey feathers two shades of yellow and then ships them to the Sesame Workshop, where they are assembled into the famous feathered costume.[41]

Because of their size and agility, small companies are particularly well suited for serving niche markets. The most successful focusers build a competitive edge by concentrating on specific market niches and serving them better than competitors—even powerful giants—can. "They can establish close, personal, one-on-one bonds with customers that large companies can't match," says Norm Brodsky, a highly successful serial entrepreneur. "Small companies also can outmaneuver giants. That's especially important if they're competing against a chain with a cookie-cutter approach to managing its stores." Brodsky says that with the right focus strategy, entrepreneurs "can do things that [large companies] won't be able to respond to for months, if ever."[42]

A focus strategy depends on creating value for customers either by being the lowest-cost producer or by differentiating the product or service in a unique fashion but doing it in a narrow target segment. To be worth targeting, a niche must be large enough to be profitable, reachable with marketing media, and capable of sustaining a business over time (i.e., not a passing fad). Many small companies operate quite successfully in small, yet profitable, niches. Damon Carson, founder of Kiddie Rides USA, purchases the coin-operated kiddies rides that once resided outside supermarkets, retail stores, and shopping malls, refurbishes them, and sells them at prices ranging from $1,000 to $6,000, a fraction of their original cost. The refurbished rides can remain coin-operated or can be modified to run at the push of a button. Carson's customers include parents and grandparents who feel a sense of nostalgia and want to introduce a new generation of kids to the rides and businesses that want an inexpensive promotional tool or simply a way to build goodwill with customers. Banks have bought them for their lobbies, dentists have purchased them for their offices, and Scott Innes, who founded a chain of ice cream shops called Scoop 'N Doos (Innes is the voice of Scooby Doo on the Cartoon Network) in Baton Rouge, Louisiana, purchased several rides for his shops. The rides proved to be a hit with children—and their parents and grandparents. "I couldn't keep the adults out of them," he says.[43]

Although it can be a highly profitable strategy, pursuing a focus strategy is not without risks. Companies sometimes must struggle to capture a large enough share of a small market to be profitable. If a small company is successful in a niche, there is also the danger of larger competitors entering the market and eroding it. Entrepreneurs following this strategy often face a constant struggle to keep costs down; the small volume of business that some niches support pushes production costs upward, making a company vulnerable to lower-cost competitors as their prices spiral higher. Sometimes a company with a successful niche strategy gets distracted by its success and tries to branch out into other areas. As it drifts farther away from its core strategy, it loses its competitive edge and runs the risk of confusing or alienating its customers. Muddying its image with customers puts a company in danger of losing its identity.

YOU BE THE CONSULTANT

Floating Luxury

Rising fuel prices represent a serious threat to many industries, but they do not seem to have an impact on the demand for mega-yachts (yachts that are more than 80 feet in length), which serve as symbols of achievement for many super-rich people. Because the prices of these yachts start at $30 million, the price of the fuel to power them is the least of their owners' worries. "Nobody is buying these yachts because they need them," says Billy Smith, vice-president of Trinity Yachts, one of the leading companies in the industry. "They're buying them because they want them." More than 5,000 mega-yachts are sailing the seas around the world, and 3,000 of those were built after 2000. "There are a lot of people with new wealth looking for relaxation and enjoyment," says John Dane III, president of Trinity Yachts.

That surging demand creates a tremendous opportunity for the companies that build mega-yachts, a process that can take two years or more, depending on size and the design. Despite being forced temporarily out of its 38-acre shipyard in New Orleans by Hurricane Katrina, Trinity Yachts is well positioned to capitalize on the opportunity. After the hurricane destroyed almost all of its manufacturing operation, Trinity moved its headquarters and manufacturing to Gulfport, Mississippi. When the company reopened its shipyard in New Orleans in 2006, the move doubled its manufacturing capacity just as demand for

mega-yachts was taking off. "It's a great time to be in the super-yacht business," says Dane. Industry trackers say that 90,000 families in the world have a net worth of at least $360 million, a level of wealth that enables them to purchase a mega-yacht. By 2011, the number of super-rich families is expected to grow to nearly 120,000.

With 19 acres of covered workspace and ceiling heights up to 90 feet at its New Orleans and Gulfport shipyards, Trinity has enough manufacturing capacity to build eight to ten mega-yachts of up to 330 feet in length a year. The company currently has 24 yachts under contract ranging in size from 122 feet to 242 feet, enough to keep the company busy for three years. One of those is the New Horizon, which at 242 feet, is the longest yacht that Trinity has built to date. Powered by two 2,682 horsepower engines, the yacht has four decks, a pool (of course!), and every amenity that a luxury home could contain. The price tag: more than $90 million.

Trinity Yachts has set itself apart from the competition by developing expertise in marine engineering as well as in yacht design and manufacturing. By submerging Trinity's equipment underwater, Hurricane Katrina forced the company to install brand new, state-of-the-art equipment and the most modern manufacturing processes in its Gulfport and New Orleans shipyards. That move has enabled Trinity to build some of the highest-quality, best-performing mega-yachts in the world. The company has a reputation for constant innovation, finding ways to integrate the latest technology advances and construction methods into its yachts. Teams of engineers and designers use the latest computer-aided design tools, including 3-D modeling, for every Trinity yacht, a process that yields the most efficient hull designs and propulsion and stabilizing systems. The company's experience building high-speed patrol boats for the U.S. Navy and other customers also is an important factor in its success. Many of the lessons that employees learned over the years building those boats show up in Trinity's mega-yachts. A recent edition of *Superyacht Industry* included a glowing review of Trinity Yachts and its latest projects:

> Every Trinity yacht consistently outperforms the competition in its sea-keeping ability and structural integrity. Coupled with an innate sense of practicality, each Trinity yacht is a hybrid of the finest in marine technology and exquisite styling. Intelligent space planning allows for maximum enjoyment and a minimum of crew intrusion. Striking exterior lines blend with well-appointed interior volume and spacious, feature-filled areas.

Through every aspect of project execution, Trinity's expertise in shipbuilding assures a level of impeccable coordination between designers, technicians, and subcontractors.

1. Visit Trinity Yacht's Web site at www.trinityyachts.com to learn more about the company. Identify at least three of the company's core competencies.
2. How does Trinity Yachts use its core competencies to gain a competitive advantage in the market for luxury yachts?
3. How did the threat of Hurricane Katrina turn out to be a strength for Trinity Yachts? Work with a team of your classmates to identify the strengths, weaknesses, opportunities, and threats facing Trinity.

Sources: Adapted from Alan Sayre, "Yacht Builders Can't Keep Up," *Greenville News*, July 5, 2008, p. 6A; Alan Sayre, "Smooth Sailing for Yacht Builders Despite Economy," *Washington Post*, July 5, 2008, http://www.washingtonpost.com/wp-dyn/content/article/2008/07/04/AR2008070401650.html; Lisa Hoogerwerf Knapp, "Southern Roots," *Boat International USA*, July 2006, pp. 118–122; "Trinity Yachts," *Superyachts Industry*, Volume 3, Number 1, May 2008, pp. 76–81.

Step 8. Translate Strategic Plans into Action Plans

LO 5

Understand the importance of controls such as the balanced scorecard in the planning process.

No strategic plan is complete until it is put into action; planning a company's strategy and implementing it go hand-in-hand. Entrepreneurs must convert strategic plans into operating plans that guide their companies on a daily basis and become a visible, active part of the business. No small business can benefit from a strategic plan sitting on a shelf collecting dust. Unfortunately, failure to implement a strategy effectively is a common problem. In a survey conducted by Marakon Associates and the Economist Intelligence Unit, senior executives reported that their companies had achieved only 63 percent of the results expected in their strategic plans.[44] The lesson is that even sound strategies, unless properly implemented, will fail.

IMPLEMENT THE STRATEGY Implementing a strategy successfully requires both a process that fits a company's culture and the right people committed to making that process work. Getting the right people in place starts with the selection process but includes every other aspect of the human resources function—from job design and training to motivational methods and compensation. To make their strategic plans workable, entrepreneurs should divide them into projects, carefully defining each one by the following:

Purpose. What is the project designed to accomplish?

Scope. Which areas of the company will be involved in the project?

Contribution. How does the project relate to other projects and to the overall strategic plan?

Resource requirements. What human and financial resources are needed to complete the project successfully?

Timing. Which schedules and deadlines will ensure project completion?

Involving employees and delegating adequate authority to them is essential because these projects affect them most directly. If an organization's people have been involved in the strategic management process to this point, they will have a better grasp of the steps they must take to achieve the organization's goals as well as their own professional goals. Early involvement of the workforce in the strategic management process is a luxury that larger businesses cannot achieve. Commitment to reaching the company's objectives is a powerful force, but involvement is a prerequisite for achieving total employee commitment.

Step 9. Establish Accurate Controls

So far, the planning process has created company objectives and has developed a strategy for reaching them, but rarely, if ever, will the company's actual performance match stated objectives. Entrepreneurs quickly realize the need to control actual results that deviate from plans.

CONTROLLING THE STRATEGY   Planning without control has little operational value; therefore, a sound planning program requires a practical control process. The plans and objectives created in the strategic planning process become the standards against which actual performance is measured. It is important for everyone in the organization to understand—and to be involved in—the planning and controlling process. Unless entrepreneurs measure progress against the goals and objectives established in step 6, their companies makes little progress toward accomplishing them.

Controlling plans and projects and keeping them on schedule means that an entrepreneur must identify and track key performance indicators. The source of these indicators is the operating data from the company's normal business activity; they are the guideposts for detecting deviations from established standards. Financial, production, sales, inventory, quality, customer service and satisfaction, and other operating records are primary sources of data managers can use to control activities. For example, on a customer service project, performance indicators might include the number of customer complaints, the number of orders returned, the percentage of on-time shipments, and a measure of order accuracy.

The most commonly used indicators of a company's performance are financial measures; however, judging a company's performance solely on the basis of financial measures can lead to strategic myopia. To judge the effectiveness of their strategies, many companies are developing **balanced scorecards**, a set of multidimensional measurements that are unique to a company and that incorporate both financial and operational measures to give managers a quick yet comprehensive picture of the company's overall performance. One writer says that a balanced scorecard:

> is a sophisticated business model that helps a company understand what's really driving its success. It acts a bit like the control panel on a spaceship—the business equivalent of a flight speedometer, odometer, and temperature gauge all rolled into one. It keeps track of many things, including financial progress and softer measurements—everything from customer satisfaction to return on investment—that need to be managed to reach the final destination: profitable growth.[45]

Rather than sticking solely to the traditional financial measures of a company's performance, the balanced scorecard gives managers a comprehensive view from *both* a financial and an operational perspective. The premise behind such a scorecard is that relying on any single measure of company performance is dangerous. Just as a pilot in command of a jet cannot fly safely by focusing on a single instrument, an entrepreneur cannot manage a company by concentrating on a single measurement. The complexity of managing a business demands that an entrepreneur be able to see performance measures in several areas simultaneously. "Knowing whether an enterprise is viable or not doesn't mean looking at just the bottom line," says one manager.[46] Scoreboards that combine relevant results from all aspects of the operation allow everyone in the organization to see how their job performance connects to a company's mission, goals, and objectives.

When creating a balanced scorecard for their companies, entrepreneurs should establish goals for each critical indicator of company performance and then create meaningful measures for each one. If used properly, a balanced scorecard serves as a call to action. When a key indicator is out of control, everyone in the company knows it and can work together to do something about it quickly. The keys to using scorecards successfully are making sure that the measures included are important to your company's success and that each one tells a different story.

balanced scorecard

a set of multidimensional measurements that are unique to a company and that incorporate both financial and operational measures to give managers a quick yet comprehensive picture of a company's overall performance.

ENTREPRENEURIAL PROFILE _____

Alex Phinn: Griff Paper and Film

Alex Phinn, president of Griff Paper and Film, a maker of protective films, silicone-coated liners, and specialty labeling materials, looks over his company's balanced scorecard with his morning cup of coffee. Rather than use one of the many balanced scorecard software packages available, Phinn designed his own scorecard. His one-page report includes operating data such as new orders received, the number of quotations submitted to potential customers (both measures of future sales), the number of customer complaints, employee absentee rates (both quality indicators), and financial data such as daily accounts eceivables, accounts payables, and cash balances. Phinn's easy-to-use scorecard gives him and his employees the ability to spot problem areas and positive trends in the company quickly.[47]

Ideally, a balanced scorecard looks at a business from five important perspectives (see Figure 3.5):[48]

CUSTOMER PERSPECTIVE How do customers see us? Customers judge companies by at least four standards: time (how long it takes the company to deliver a good or service), quality (how well a company's product or service performs in terms of reliability, durability, and accuracy), performance (the extent to which a good or service performs as expected), and service (how well a company meets or exceeds customers' expectations of value). Because customer-related goals are external, managers must translate them into measures of what the company must do to meet customers' expectations.

INTERNAL BUSINESS PERSPECTIVE At what must we excel? The internal factors on which managers should focus are those that have the greatest impact on customer satisfaction and retention and on company effectiveness and efficiency. Developing goals and measures for factors such as quality, cycle time, productivity, costs, and others that employees directly influence is essential.

INNOVATION AND LEARNING PERSPECTIVE Can we continue to improve and create value? This view of a company recognizes that the targets required for success are never static; they are constantly changing. If a company wants to continue its pattern of success, it cannot stand still; it must continuously improve. A company's ability to innovate, learn, and improve determines its

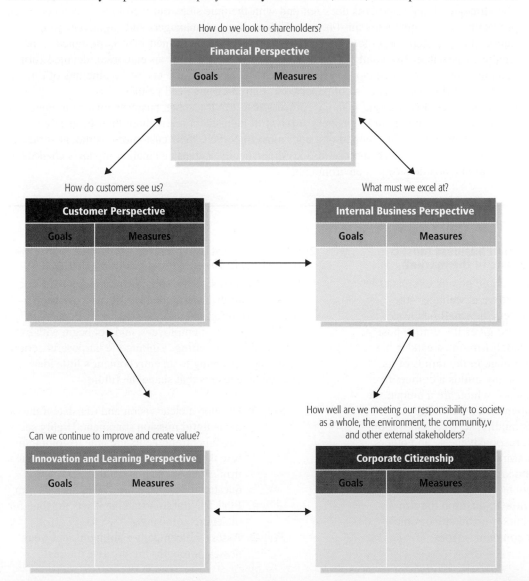

FIGURE 3.5

The Balanced Scorecard Links Performance Measures

future. These goals and measures emphasize the importance of continuous improvement in customer satisfaction and internal business operations.

FINANCIAL PERSPECTIVE How do we look to shareholders? Financial standards, the most traditional performance measures, tell how much the company's overall strategy and its execution are contributing to its bottom line. These measures focus on factors such as profitability, growth, and shareholder value. On balanced scorecards, companies often break their financial goals into three categories: survival, success, and growth.

CORPORATE CITIZENSHIP How well are we meeting our responsibility to society as a whole, the environment, the community, and other external stakeholders? Even small companies must recognize that they must be good business citizens.

Although the balanced scorecard is a vital tool that helps managers keep their companies on track, it is also an important tool for changing behavior in an organization and for keeping everyone focused on what really matters. Used properly, balanced scorecards allow managers to see how actions in each of the four dimensions of performance influence actions in the others. As competitive conditions and results change, managers can use the balanced scorecard to make corrections in plans, policies, strategies, and objectives to get performance back on track. A practical control system is also economical to operate. Most small businesses have no need for a sophisticated, expensive control system. The system should be so practical that it becomes a natural part of the management process.

Conclusion

The strategic planning process does *not* end with the nine steps outlined here; it is an ongoing procedure that entrepreneurs must repeat. With each round, managers and employees gain experience, and the steps become easier. The planning process outlined here is designed to be as simple as possible. No small business should be burdened with an elaborate, detailed formal planning process that it cannot easily use. Such processes require excessive amounts of time to operate, and they generate a sea of paperwork. Entrepreneurs need neither.

What does this strategic planning process lead to? It teaches business owners a degree of discipline that is important to business survival. It helps them learn about their businesses, their core competencies, their competitors, and, most important, their customers. Although strategic planning cannot guarantee success, it does dramatically increase a small company's chances of survival in a hostile business environment.

Chapter Summary

1. Explain why and how a small business must create a competitive advantage in the market.

The goal of developing a strategic plan is to create for the small company a competitive advantage—the aggregation of factors that sets the small business apart from its competitors and gives it a unique position in the market. Every small firm must establish a plan for creating a unique image in the minds of its potential customers. A company builds a competitive edge on its core competencies, which are a unique set of capabilities that a company develops in key operational areas, such as quality, service, innovation, team-building, flexibility, responsiveness, and others, that allow it to vault past competitors. They are what the company does best and are the focal point of the strategy. This step must identify target market segments and determine how to position the firm in those markets. Entrepreneurs must identify some way to differentiate their companies from competitors.

2. Develop a strategic plan for a business using the nine steps in the strategic planning process.

Small businesses need a strategic planning process designed to suit their particular needs. It should be relatively short, informal, and not structured, encourage the participation of employees, and not begin with extensive objective setting. Linking the purposeful action of strategic planning to an entrepreneur's little ideas can produce results that shape the future.

Step 1. Develop a clear vision and translate it into a meaningful mission statement. Highly successful entrepreneurs are able to communicate their vision to those around them. The firm's mission statement answers the first question of any venture: What business am I in? The mission statement sets the tone for the entire company.

Step 2. Assess the company's strengths and weaknesses. Strengths are positive internal factors; weaknesses are negative internal factors.

Step 3. Scan the environment for significant opportunities and threats facing the business. Opportunities are positive external options; threats are negative external forces.

Step 4. Identify the key factors for success in the business. In every business, key factors determine the success of the firms in it, and so they must be an integral part of a company's strategy. Key success factors are relationships between a controllable variable and a critical factor influencing the firm's ability to compete in the market.

Step 5. Analyze the competition. Business owners should know their competitors almost as well as they know their own companies. A competitive profile matrix is a helpful tool for analyzing competitors' strengths and weaknesses.

Step 6. Create company goals and objectives. Goals are the broad, long-range attributes that the firm seeks to accomplish. Objectives are quantifiable and more precise; they should be specific, measurable, assignable, realistic, timely, and written down. The process works best when managers and employees are actively involved.

Step 7. Formulate strategic options and select the appropriate strategies. A strategy is the game plan the firm plans to use to achieve its objectives and mission. It must center on establishing for the firm the key success factors identified earlier.

Step 8. Translate strategic plans into action plans. No strategic plan is complete until the owner puts it into action.

Step 9. Establish accurate controls. Actual performance rarely, if ever, matches plans exactly. Operating data from the business assembled into a comprehensive scorecard serves as an important guidepost for determining how effective a company's strategy is. This information is especially helpful when plotting future strategies.

The strategic planning process does not end with these nine steps; rather, it is an ongoing process that an entrepreneur will repeat.

3. Establish meaningful goals and objectives.

Goals are broad, long-range attributes a company seeks to accomplish; objectives are quantifiable and more precise. They should be specific, measurable, assignable, realistic, timely, and in writing.

4. Discuss the characteristics of three basic strategies: low-cost, differentiation, and focus.

Three basic strategic options are cost leadership, differentiation, and focus. A company pursuing a cost leadership strategy strives to be the lowest-cost producer relative to its competitors in the industry.

A company following a differentiation strategy seeks to build customer loyalty by positioning its goods or services in a unique or different fashion. In other words, the firm strives to be better than its competitors at something that customers value.

A focus strategy recognizes that not all markets are homogeneous. The principal idea of this strategy is to select one (or more) segment(s), identify customers' special needs, wants, and interests, and approach them with a good or service designed to excel in meeting these needs, wants, and interests. Focus strategies build on *differences* among market segments.

5. Understand the importance of controls such as the balanced scorecard in the planning process.

Just as a pilot in command of a jet cannot fly safely by focusing on a single instrument, an entrepreneur cannot manage a company by concentrating on a single measurement. The balanced scorecard is a set of multidimensional measurements unique to a company that includes both financial and operational measures and gives managers a quick yet comprehensive picture of the company's total performance.

Discussion Questions

1. Why is strategic planning important to a small company?

2. What is a competitive advantage? Why is it important for a small business to establish one?

3. What are the steps in the strategic management process?

4. "Our customers don't just like our ice cream," write Ben Cohen and Jerry Greenfield, co-founders of Ben and Jerry's Homemade. Inc. "They like what our company stands for. They like how doing business with us makes them feel." What do they mean?

5. What are strengths, weaknesses, opportunities, and threats? Give an example of each.

6. Explain the characteristics of effective objectives. Why is setting objectives important?

7. What are business strategies?

8. Describe the three basic strategies available to small companies. Under what conditions is each most successful?

9. "It's better to be a company with a great strategy in a crummy business than to be a company with a crummy

strategy in a great business," says one business expert. Do you agree? Explain.

10. Explain how a company can gain a competitive advantage using each of the three strategies described in this chapter: cost-leadership, differentiation, and focus. Give an example of a company that is using each strategy.

11. How is the controlling process related to the planning process?

12. What is a balanced scorecard? What value does it offer entrepreneurs who are evaluating the success of their current strategies?

Business PlanPro™

We are now going to think about your business plan from a strategic perspective. This involves describing your business objectives, drafting your mission statement, identifying "keys to success," conducting a SWOT analysis, and making initial comments about your strategy and your competitive advantage.

Business Plan Exercises

On the Web

Visit http://www.pearsonhighered.com/scarborough, click on the Companion Site link, and go to the Business Plan Resources tab. Scroll down to find the Standard Industry Classification codes heading to identify the SIC code associated with your industry. Next, review the information associated with the Competitor Analysis section. This information may provide insight about your industry competitors on a global, national, or possibly on a local basis.

In the Software

Open your business plan in *Business Plan Pro*™. You are now going to add text to the strategic areas mentioned in this chapter. Don't worry about perfecting this information. Simply capture your thoughts and ideas so you can revisit these topics, add detail, and make certain that the sections are congruent with your entire plan.

Sample Plans

Review the following sections, as they appear, in the sample plans that you identified earlier:

Mission Statement
Objectives
SWOT Analysis
Keys to Success
Competition, Buying Patterns, and Main Competitors
Value Proposition
Competitive Edge
Strategy and Implementation Summary

Note the information captured in these sections of the plans. Some areas may be in a narrative style and others may contain only bullet points. As you look at each plan, determine if it provides the needed information under each topic.

Building Your Business Plan

Here are some tips you may want to consider as you tackle each of these sections:

Mission Statement

The mission statement establishes the fundamental goals for the quality of the business offering. The mission statement represents the opportunity to answer the questions "What business are you in?" and "Why does your business exist?" This may include the value you offer and the role customers, employees, and owners play in providing and benefiting from that value. A mission statement is a critical element in defining your business and communicating this definition to key stakeholders including investors, partners, employees, and customers.

Objectives

Each objective should be specific, quantifiable and measurable. Setting measurable objectives will enable you to track your progress and measure your results.

SWOT Analysis

What are the internal strengths and weaknesses of your business? What are the external opportunities and threats? List the strengths and weaknesses and assess what insight this offers about your business. How can you leverage your strengths to take advantage of the opportunities ahead? How can you further develop or minimize the areas of weaknesses?

Keys to Success

Virtually every business has critical aspects that make the difference between success and failure. These may be brief bullet point comments that capture those key elements that will make a difference in realizing your mission and accomplishing your stated objectives.

Competition, Buying Patterns, and Main Competitors

Discuss your ideal position in the market. Think about specific kinds of features and benefits your business offers and how that is unique compared to what is available to your market today. Why do people buy your products and services instead of other services your competitor offer? Discuss your primary competitors' strengths and weaknesses. Consider their service offering, pricing, reputation, management, financial position, brand awareness, business development, technology, and any other factors that may be important. What market segments do they occupy? What strategy to they appear to pursue? How much of a competitive threat do they present?

Value Proposition

A value proposition is a clear and concise statement that describes the tangible value-based result a customer receives from using your product or service. How effectively does your value proposition communicate and fulfill your promise to your customers or clients?

Your Competitive Edge

A competitive edge will build on your value proposition and capture the unique value—in whatever terms the customer defines that value—that your business offers. Your competitive edge may result from a product, customer service, method of distribution, pricing, or promotional methods. It describes how your business is uniquely different from all others in a sustainable manner.

Strategy and Implementation

Make initial comments that capture your strategies for the business. This strategic game plan provides the focus required to realize your venture's objectives and mission. Based on your initial strategic analysis, which of the three business strategies—low-cost, differentiation, or focus—will you use to give your company a competitive advantage? How will this strategy capitalize on your company's strengths and appeal to your customer's need? You will later build on this information as you formulate action plans to bring the strategy section of your plan to life.

Capture your ideas in each of these sections and continually review this information. If it does not add value to your business plan, there is no need to include this information.

Beyond the Classroom...

1. Contact the owner of a small business that competes directly with an industry giant (such as Home Depot, Wal-Mart, Barnes & Noble, or others). What does the owner see as his or her competitive advantage? How does the business communicate this advantage to its customers? What competitive strategy is the owner using? How successful is it? What changes would you suggest the owner make?

2. In his book, *The HP Way*, Dave Packard, co-founder of Hewlett Packard, describes the seven commitments of the HP Way:

   - Profit—the ultimate source of corporate strength.
   - Customers—constant improvement in the value of the products and services the company offers them.
   - Field of interest—seeking new opportunities but limiting them to complementary products and services based on company core competencies.
   - Growth—a measure of strength and a requirement for survival.
   - Employees—provide opportunities for advancement, share in their success, and offer job security based on performance.
   - Organization—foster individual motivation, initiative and creativity by giving employees the freedom to work toward established goals and objectives.
   - Citizenship—contribute in a positive way toward the community and society at large.

   In what ways do these values help HP define its vision? Its competitive edge? How important is it for entrepreneurs to define a system of values to guide their companies?

3. Contact a local entrepreneur and help him or her devise a balanced scorecard for his or her company. What goals did you and the owner establish in each of the four perspectives? What measures did you use to judge progress towards those goals?

4. Use the strategic tools provided in this chapter to help a local small business owner discover his or her firm's strengths, weaknesses, opportunities, and threats; identify the relevant key success factors; and analyze its competitors. Help the owner devise a strategy for success for his or her business.

5. Choose an entrepreneur in your community and interview him or her. Does the company have a strategic plan? A mission statement? Why or why not? What does the owner consider the company's strengths and weaknesses to be? What opportunities and threats does the owner perceive? What image is the owner trying to create for the business? Has the effort been successful? (Do you agree?) Which of the generic competitive strategies is the company following? Who are the company's primary competitors? How does the owner rate his or her chances for success in the future (use a low (1) to high (10) scale). When you have completed the interview, use the following evaluation questionnaire to rate the company's strategic orientation. Compare your evaluation with other classmates. What, if any, generalizations can you draw from the interview?

CHAPTER 4

Conducting a Feasibility Analysis and Crafting a Winning Business Plan

> Planning is bringing the future into the present so that
> you can do something about it now.
> —*Alan Lakein*

> If you wait until all the lights are "green" before you leave home,
> you'll never get started on your trip to the top.
> —*Zig Ziglar*

Learning Objectives

Upon completion of this chapter, you will be able to:

1. Discuss the steps involved in subjecting a business idea to a feasibility analysis.

2. Explain why every entrepreneur should create a business plan as well as the benefits of developing a plan.

3. Describe the elements of a solid business plan.

4. Explain the "5 Cs of Credit" and why they are important to potential lenders and investors reading business plans.

5. Describe the keys to making an effective business plan presentation.

For many entrepreneurs, the easiest part of launching a business is coming up with an idea for a new business concept or approach. As you learned in Chapter 2, entrepreneurs do not lack creativity and are responsible for some of the world's most important innovations. Business success, however, requires much more than just a great new idea. Once entrepreneurs develop an idea for a business, the next step is to subject it to a feasibility analysis to determine whether they can transform the idea into a viable business. A **feasibility analysis** is the process of determining whether or not an entrepreneur's idea is a viable foundation for creating a successful business. Its purpose is to determine whether or not a business idea is worth pursuing. If the idea passes the feasibility analysis, the entrepreneur's next step is to build a solid business plan for capitalizing on the idea. If the idea fails to pass muster, the entrepreneur drops it and moves on to the next opportunity. He or she has not wasted valuable time, money, energy, and other resources creating a full-blown business plan, or worse, launching a business that is destined to fail because it is based on a flawed concept. One aspiring entrepreneur wanted to start a business that created custom scrapbooks until a feasibility study revealed that she would earn far below the minimum wage on her investment of time.[1] Although it is impossible for a feasibility study to guarantee an idea's success, conducting a study reduces the likelihood that entrepreneurs will waste their time pursuing fruitless business ventures.

A feasibility study is *not* the same as a business plan; both play important, but separate, roles in the start-up process. A feasibility study answers the question, "Should we proceed with this business idea?" Its role is to serve as a filter, screening out ideas that lack the potential for building a successful business, *before* an entrepreneur commits the necessary resources to building a business plan. A feasibility study primarily is an *investigative* tool. It is designed to give an entrepreneur a picture of the market, sales, and profit potential of a particular business idea. Will a ski resort located here attract enough customers to be successful? Will customers in this community support a sandwich shop with a retro rock-'n'-roll theme? Can we build the product at a reasonable cost and sell it at a price customers are willing and able to pay? Does this entrepreneurial team have the ability to implement the idea successfully?

A business plan, on the other hand, is a planning tool for transforming an idea into reality. It builds on the foundation of the feasibility study but provides a more comprehensive analysis than a feasibility study. It functions primarily as a planning tool, taking an idea that has passed the feasibility analysis and describing how to turn it into a successful business. Its primary goals are to guide entrepreneurs as they launch and operate their businesses and to help them acquire the financing needed to launch.

Feasibility studies are particularly useful when entrepreneurs have generated multiple ideas for business concepts and must winnow their options down to the "best choice." They enable entrepreneurs to explore quickly the practicality of each of several potential paths for transforming an idea into a successful business venture. Sometimes the result of a feasibility study is the realization that an idea simply won't produce a viable business—no matter how it is organized. In other cases, a study shows an entrepreneur that the business idea is a sound one but it must be organized in a different fashion to be profitable.

Conducting a Feasibility Analysis

A feasibility analysis consists of three interrelated components: an industry and market feasibility analysis, a product or service feasibility analysis, and a financial feasibility analysis (see Figure 4.1).

feasibility analysis
the process of determining whether or not an entrepreneur's idea is a viable foundation for creating a successful business.

LO 1
Discuss the steps involved in subjecting a business idea to a feasibility analysis.

FIGURE 4.1

Elements of a Feasibility Analysis

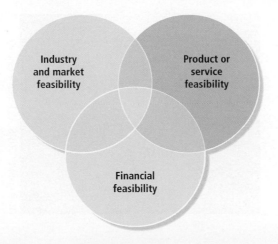

Industry and market feasibility

Product or service feasibility

Financial feasibility

Industry and Market Feasibility Analysis

When evaluating the feasibility of a business idea, entrepreneurs find a basic analysis of the industry and targeted market segments to be a good starting point. The focus in this phase is two-fold: (1) To determine how attractive an industry is overall as a "home" for a new business, and (2) to identify possible niches a small business can occupy profitably.

The first step in assessing industry attractiveness is to paint a picture of the industry with broad strokes, assessing it from a "macro" level. Answering the following questions will help:

- How large is the industry?
- How fast is it growing?
- Is the industry as a whole profitable?
- Is the industry characterized by high profit margins or razor-thin margins?
- How essential are its products or services to customers?
- What trends are shaping the industry's future?
- What threats does the industry face?
- What opportunities does the industry face?
- How crowded is the industry?
- How intense is the level of competition in the industry?
- Is the industry young, mature, or somewhere in between?

Addressing these questions helps entrepreneurs determine whether or not the potential for sufficient demand for their products and services exists.

A useful tool for analyzing an industry's attractiveness is the **five forces model** developed by Michael Porter of the Harvard Business School (see Figure 4.2). Five forces interact with one another to determine the setting in which companies compete and hence the attractiveness of the industry: (1) The rivalry among the companies competing in the industry, (2) the bargaining power of suppliers to the industry, (3) the bargaining power of buyers, (4) the threat of new entrants to the industry, and (5) the threat of substitute products or services.

RIVALRY AMONG COMPANIES COMPETING IN THE INDUSTRY The strongest of the five forces in most industries is the rivalry that exists among the businesses competing in a particular market. Much like the horses running in the Kentucky Derby, businesses in a market are jockeying for position in an attempt to gain a competitive advantage. When a company creates an innovation or develops a unique strategy that transforms the market, competing companies must adapt or run the risk of being forced out of business. This force makes markets a dynamic and highly competitive place. Generally, an industry is more attractive when:

- The number of competitors is large, or, at the other extreme, quite small (fewer than five).
- Competitors are not similar in size or capability.
- The industry is growing at a fast pace.
- The opportunity to sell a differentiated product or service exists.

BARGAINING POWER OF SUPPLIERS TO THE INDUSTRY The greater the leverage that suppliers of key raw materials or components have, the less attractive is the industry. For instance, because they supply the chips that serve as the "brains" of PCs and because those chips make up a sizeable

five forces model
a model that recognizes the power of five forces—rivalry among competing firms, bargaining power of suppliers, bargaining power of buyers, threat of new entrants, and threat of substitute products or services—on an industry.

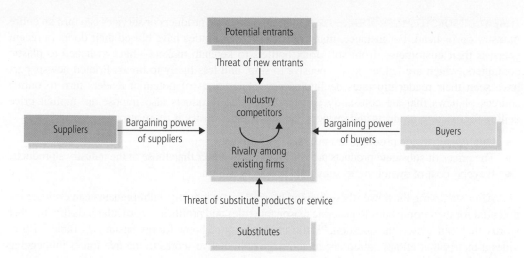

FIGURE 4.2
Five Forces Model

Source: Adapted from Michael E. Porter, "How Competitive Forces Shape Strategy," Harvard Business Review, Volume 57, No. 2, March-April, 1979, pp. 137–145.

portion of the cost of a computer, chip makers such as Intel and Advanced Micro Devices (AMD) exert a great deal of power over computer manufacturers such as Dell, Hewlett-Packard, and Gateway. Generally, an industry is more attractive when:

- Many suppliers sell a commodity product to the companies in it.
- Substitute products are available for the items that suppliers provide.
- Companies in the industry find it easy to switch from one supplier to another or to substitute products (i.e., "switching costs" are low).
- When the items supplied to the industry account for a relatively small portion of the cost of the industry's finished products.

BARGAINING POWER OF BUYERS Just as suppliers to an industry can be a source of pressure, buyers also have the potential to exert significant power over an industry, making it less attractive. When the number of customers is small and the cost of switching to competitors' products is low, buyers' influence on companies is high. Famous for offering its customers low prices, Wal-Mart, the largest company in the world, is also well known for applying relentless pressure to its 21,000 suppliers for price concessions, which it almost always manages to get.[2] Generally, an industry is more attractive when:

- Industry customers' "switching costs" to competitors' products or to substitutes are relatively high.
- The number of buyers in the industry is large.
- Customers demand products that are differentiated rather than purchase commodity products that they can obtain from any supplier (and subsequently can pit one company against another to drive down price).
- Customers find it difficult to gather information on suppliers' costs, prices, and product features—something that is becoming much easier for customers in many industries to do by using the Web.
- When the items companies sell to the industry account for a relatively small portion of the cost of their customers' finished products.

THREAT OF NEW ENTRANTS TO THE INDUSTRY New entrants to an industry can erode existing companies' market share and profits. The larger the pool of potential new entrants to an industry, the greater is the threat to existing companies in it. This is particularly true in industries where the barriers to entry, such as capital requirements, specialized knowledge, access to distribution channels, and others, are low. Generally, an industry is more attractive to new entrants when:

- The advantages of economies of scale are absent. Economies of scale exist when companies in an industry achieve low average costs by producing huge volumes of items (e.g., computer chips).
- Capital requirements to enter the industry are low.
- Cost advantages are not related to company size.
- Buyers are not extremely brand-loyal, making it easier for new entrants to the industry to draw customers away from existing businesses.
- Governments, through their regulatory and international trade policies, do not restrict new companies from entering the industry.

THREAT OF SUBSTITUTE PRODUCTS OR SERVICES   Substitute products or services can turn an entire industry on its head. For instance, many makers of glass bottles have closed their doors in recent years as their customers—from soft drink bottlers to ketchup makers—have switched to plastic containers, which are lighter, less expensive to ship, and less likely to break. Printed newspapers have seen their readership rates decline as new generations of potential readers turn to online sources of news that are constantly updated. Substitute products also impose an implicit price ceiling for existing products and services. Generally, an industry is more attractive when:

- Quality substitute products are not readily available.
- The prices of substitute products are not significantly lower than those of the industry's products.
- Buyers' cost of switching to substitute products is high.

After surveying the power these five forces exert on an industry, entrepreneurs can evaluate the potential for their companies to generate reasonable sales and profits in a particular industry. In other words, they can answer the question, "Is this industry a good home for my business?" Table 4.1 provides a matrix that allows entrepreneurs to assign quantitative scores to the five forces influencing industry attractiveness. Note that the lower the score for an industry, the more attractive it is.

The next step in assessing an industry is to identify potentially attractive niches that exist in the industry. As you learned in Chapter 2, many small businesses prosper by sticking to niches in a market that are too small to attract the attention of large competitors. Occupying an industry niche enables a business to shield itself to some extent from the power of the five forces. The key question entrepreneurs address here is "Can we identify a niche that is large enough to produce a profit, or can we position our company uniquely in the market to differentiate it from the competition in a meaningful way?" Entrepreneurs who have designed successful focus or differentiation strategies for their companies can exploit these niches to their advantage.

Questions entrepreneurs should address in this portion of the feasibility analysis include:

- Which niche(s) in the market will we occupy?
- How large is this market segment, and how fast is it growing?
- What is the basis for differentiating our product or service from competitors?
- Do we have a superior business model that will be difficult for competitors to reproduce?

Companies can shield themselves from some of the negative impact of these five forces by finding a niche and occupying it.

TABLE 4.1 Five Forces Matrix

Assign a value to rate the importance of each of the five forces to the industry on a 1 (not important) to 5 (very important) scale. Then assign a value to reflect the threat that each force poses to the industry. Multiply the importance rating in column 2 by the threat rating in column 3 to produce a weighted score. Add the weighted scores in column 3 to get a total weighted score. This score measures the industry's attractiveness. The matrix is a useful tool for comparing the attractiveness of different industries.

Maximum Score = 125 (Very unattractive)

Force	Importance (1 to 5) (1 = Not Important, 5 = Very Important)	Threat to Industry (1 to 5) (1 = Low 3 = Medium 5 = High)	Weighted Score Col 2 × Col 3
Rivalry among companies competing in the industry	5	3	15
Bargaining power of suppliers in the industry	2	2	4
Bargaining power of buyers	2	4	8
Threat of new entrants to the industry	3	4	12
Threat of substitute products or services	4	3	12
		Total	51

Because of their experience in the beleaguered textile industry, Patrick Methven and Robert Lazarus spotted a lucrative niche and in 2002, launched Pinnacle Textiles, a small maker and distributor of table linens, uniforms, and kitchen clothing (aprons, coats, pants, and hats) for the restaurant industry. Although the textile industry as a whole scores quite low in industry attractiveness, the niche that Pinnacle targets has few competitors and is characterized by low bargaining power of both customers and suppliers. Pinnacle's primary customer base is in the East and the Midwest, but Methven has plans to expand into the fastest-growing areas on the West Coast. The company's niche strategy has allowed it to push annual sales, which are growing steadily at 18 percent a year, to more than $15 million.[3]

ENTREPRENEURIAL PROFILE

Patrick Methven & Robert Lazarus: Pinnacle Textiles

One technique for gauging the quality of a company's business model involves **business prototyping,** in which entrepreneurs test their business models on a small scale before committing serious resources to launch a business that might not work. Business prototyping recognizes that every business idea is a hypothesis that needs to be tested before an entrepreneur takes it to full scale. If the test supports the hypothesis and its accompanying assumptions, it is time to launch a company. If the prototype flops, the entrepreneur scraps the business idea with only minimal losses and turns to the next idea.

business prototyping
a process in which entrepreneurs test their business models on a small scale before committing serious resources to launch a business that might not work.

The Web makes business prototyping practical, fast, and easy. Entrepreneurs can test their ideas by selling their products on established sites such as eBay or by setting up their own Web sites to gauge customers' response.

Jake Rockwell, founder of Rockwell Products LLC, has launched several successful companies using this approach. Rockwell first looks for a product that faces limited competition and that customers will purchase repeatedly. One of Rockwell's first ventures involved a product that met his criteria, soft vinyl nail caps that prevent cats from ruining their owners' furniture. Rockwell's next screening criterion is whether he can start the business for less than $20,000, an amount that fits within his financial comfort zone. To minimize his level of risk, Rockwell prefers products for which he can make drop-shipping arrangements with suppliers (to avoid having to carry inventory himself). When he realized that the nail caps passed his feasibility analysis, Rockwell set up a Web site, SafePetProducts.com, and purchased pay-per-click ads to drive traffic to the site. His analysis was accurate; Rockwell's company generates more than $3 million in annual sales. Rockwell's feasibility analysis does not end there, however. He evaluates each new product launch constantly. "If I'm not making money right away, I'm not going to continue," he says.[4]

ENTREPRENEURIAL PROFILE

Jake Rockwell: Rockwell Products LLC

Does Your Business Model GEL?

Don Debelak, author of *Business Models Made Easy*, has developed a **GEL** analysis for evaluating business models: **G**reat Customers, **E**asy Sales, and **L**ong Life.

- Four factors make for Great Customers:
  1. *Number of customers.* There should be a sufficient number of customers to allow a business to reach its break-even point.
  2. *Easy to find.* A company should not have to saturate the market or "beat the bushes," both of which are expensive, to reach potential customers.
  3. *Spending patterns.* A company's customers are willing to spend freely on its products or services.
  4. *Ongoing sales support.* Ideally, a company does not have to spend large sums of money for ongoing sales support of its product or service.

Businesses that sell organic food and beverages, a market that is growing at 15 to 20 percent a year, have access to Great Customers because they score high on all four factors.

- Three factors determine whether a business model will have Easy Sales, which Debelak says is the most important GEL factor:
  1. *Importance to potential customers.* Unless customers perceive a company's product as important to them, they are not likely to make buying it a priority. This is where having a clear and compelling competitive advantage makes a difference.
  2. *Customers are easy and inexpensive to acquire.* A business that finds customers easy and inexpensive to acquire usually can reach them in many ways, including retail stores, Web sites, catalogs, home shopping networks, and others.
  3. *Product or service requires minimal promotional activity.* Like ongoing sales support, promotional activities can require a great deal of effort and money. However, if customers are easy to find (see GEL factor number one), a business should not have to spend disproportionate sums of money to advertise and promote its product or service.

Many companies in the pet care business have the advantage of Easy Sales because 63 percent of households in the United States (that's 71.1 million households) have pets and 80 percent of pet owners consider themselves to be "pet parents" who are willing to spend freely across multiple channels to indulge their four-legged "children."

- Five factors influence a company's capacity for Long Life:
  1. *Initial investment required.* The lower the initial investment required to enter a business, the more attractive it is because the risk is lower.
  2. *Cost of staying in business.* Two of the major costs of staying in business are fighting off competitors and investing in technology or product updates to maintain market share.
  3. *Profit margins.* The most important factor in a company's staying power is its profit margins because high profit margins can make up for deficiencies in other GEL factors. The higher the profit margins a business model generates, the more attractive it is.
  4. *Potential for cross-selling.* Acquiring a new customer costs seven to nine times as much as selling to an existing one; therefore, a business model that provides the opportunity to sell other products or services to existing customers yields a big advantage.
  5. *Ongoing product costs.* Ongoing product costs, such as providing follow-up sales support or keeping customers informed about changes to a product or service, reduce profits and make a business model less attractive.

Debelak says that a business start-up that does not score high on the GEL factors is likely to struggle to get established and to succeed. Try your hand at applying the model by evaluating the following actual business ideas using the GEL approach. (You may want to establish a 1 [low] to 5 [high] scoring system for each factor to make your analysis more quantifiable.) When you are done, compare your answers to those of some of your classmates. Be ready to justify the reasoning behind your scores.

PAYJr

David Jones noted that teenagers and young kids are spending more time online, but they lacked a convenient way to pay for their iTunes downloads and Webkinz subscriptions. Jones launched PAYJr, which sells Visa Buxx, a prepaid debit card for teens that costs $3.95 per month plus 50 cents for each reload. His company also sells a prepaid card aimed at children under the age of 12 that has no monthly fee. Jones is forecasting annual sales of $3.7 million, a 420 percent increase over the previous year. He has raised $4.5 million from private investors and is seeking another $5 million to $7 million in capital to hire several key executives and a sales force.

MyPunchbowl

Matt Douglas and Sean Conta launched MyPunchbowl to help users plan parties using the latest technology to select a date with their guests, send invitations, and share photos and videos after the event. Although they are competing with industry giant Evite, Douglas and Conta say that their user base is increasing 50 percent each month. The company has not yet generated any sales revenue, and Douglas and Conta forecast revenue of less than $100,000 next year. They claim that the party-supply industry is large and fragmented and that they see MyPunchbowl becoming a centralized source for party-supply companies. They are seeking $3 million in capital for marketing, developing partnerships with other companies, and hiring engineers and a sales force.

1. Use Debelak's GEL analysis to evaluate the quality of PAYJr's and MyPunchbowl's business models. (You may have to do more research to evaluate each company more accurately.)
2. Based on your analysis in question number 1, would you invest in these businesses? Explain.
3. What steps could the founders of these businesses take to improve the quality of their business models?

Source: Adapted from Nichole L. Torres, "Does It GEL?" *Entrepreneur*, February 2007 p. 93; Don Debelak, "Having a Hard Time Getting Your Product Launched? Maybe It's Your Business Model," *Inventor Help*, 2008, http://dondebelak.net/index.php?page=Online_Article_77; Don Debelak, "GEL Factors–Part 1: Great Customers, *Inventor Help*, 2008, http://dondebelak.net/index.php?page=Online_Article_78; Don Debelak, "GEL Factors–Part 2: Easy Sales, *Inventor Help*, 2008, http://dondebelak.net/index.php?page=Online_Article_81; Don Debelak, "Does Your Business Have Staying Power? GEL Factors–Part 3: Long Life," *Inventor Help*, 2008, http://dondebelak.net/index.php?page=Online_Article_84; Dalia Fahmy, "PAYJr Gets Kids and Teens to Pay with Plastic. Can It Raise $7.5 Million?" *Inc.*, May 2008, p. 46; Ryan McCarthy, "MyPunchbowl Is Aiming to Knock Evite Off Its Party Pedestal," *Inc.*, December 2007, p. 42.

Product or Service Feasibility Analysis

product or feasibility analysis
an analysis that determines the degree to which a product or service idea appeals ot potential customers and identifies the resources necessary to produce the product or provide the service.

primary research
information that an entrepreneur collects firsthand and analyzes.

secondary research
information that has already been compiled and is available for use, often at a very reasonable cost or sometimes even free.

Once entrepreneurs discover that sufficient market potential for their product or service idea actually exists, they sometimes rush in with their exuberant enthusiasm ready to launch a business without actually considering whether or not they can actually produce the product or provide the service at a reasonable cost. A **product or service feasibility analysis** determines the degree to which a product or service idea appeals to potential customers and identifies the resources necessary to produce the product or provide the service. This portion of the feasibility analysis addresses two questions:

- Are customers willing to purchase our goods and services?
- Can we provide the product or service to customers at a profit?

To answer these questions, entrepreneurs need feedback from potential customers. Getting that feedback might involve engaging in primary research such as customer surveys and focus groups, gathering secondary customer research, building prototypes, and conducting in-home trials.

Conducting **primary research** involves collecting data firsthand and analyzing it; **secondary research** involves gathering data that has already been compiled and is available, often at a very reasonable cost or sometimes even free. In both types of research, gathering both quantitative and qualitative information is important to drawing accurate conclusions about a product's or service's market potential. Primary research techniques include:

CUSTOMER SURVEYS AND QUESTIONNAIRES Keep them short. Word your questions carefully so that you do not bias the results and use a simple ranking system (e.g., a 1-to-5 scale, with 1 representing "definitely would not buy" and 5 representing "definitely would buy"). Test your survey for problems on a small number of people before putting it to use. Web surveys using tools such as Survey Monkey are inexpensive, easy to conduct, and provide feedback fast. Monster.com, the online job search company, recently conducted an online survey of 30,000 customers and integrated the results from the survey into every aspect of the company's operation. "The survey results impact policy, process, product development and marketing efforts," says Chip Henry, Monster.com's, vice president, voice of the customer (note the unique job title). "There's nothing in the company that isn't touched as a result of the surveys."[5]

FOCUS GROUPS A **focus group** involves enlisting a small number of potential customers (usually eight to twelve) to give you feedback on specific issues about your product or service (or the business idea itself). Listen carefully for what focus group members like and don't like about your product or service as they tell you what is on their minds. The founders of one small snack food company that produced apple chips conducted several focus groups to gauge customers' acceptance of the product and to guide many key business decisions, ranging from the product's name to its packaging. Once again, consider creating virtual focus groups on the Web; one small bicycle retailer conducts 10 online focus groups each year at virtually no cost and gains valuable marketing information from them. Feedback from online customers is fast, convenient, and real-time.

focus group
a market research technique that involves enlisting a small number of potential customers (usually eight to twelve) to give an entrepreneur feedback on specific issues about a product or service (or the business idea itself).

Secondary research, which is usually less expensive to collect than primary data, includes the following sources:

TRADE ASSOCIATIONS AND BUSINESS DIRECTORIES To locate a trade association, use *Business Information Sources* (University of California Press), the *Encyclopedia of Associations,* or the *World Directory of Trade and Business Associations* (Gale Research). To find suppliers, use *The Thomas Register of American Manufacturers* (Thomas Publishing Company) or *Standard and Poor's Register of Corporations, Executives, and Industries* (Standard and Poor Corporation). *The American Wholesalers and Distributors Directory* (Gale Research) includes details on more than 18,000 wholesalers and distributors.

DIRECT MAIL LISTS You can rent mailing lists for practically any type of business. *The Standard Rates and Data Service (SRDS) Directory of Mailing Lists* (Standard Rates and Data), which includes more than 60,000 lists for rent, is a good place to start looking.

DEMOGRAPHIC DATA To learn more about the demographic characteristics of customers in general, use *The Statistical Abstract of the United States* (Government Printing Office). Profiles of more specific regions are available in *The State and Metropolitan Data Book* (Government Printing Office). *The Sourcebook of Zip Code Demographics* (ESRI, Inc.) provides detailed breakdowns of the population in every zip code in the country. *Sales and Marketing Management's Survey of Buying Power* (Nielsen Business Media) contains comprehensive statistics, rankings, and projections on consumer, retail, and industrial purchasing, including its popular buying power index.

CENSUS DATA The Bureau of the Census publishes a wide variety of reports that summarize the wealth of data found in its census database, which is available at most libraries and at the Census Bureau's Web site (www.census.gov). Located on the Census Bureau's Web site, the American Factfinder allows entrepreneurs to collect important demographic data ranging from income levels and educational attainment to age and home value for every county and most towns and cities in the United States.

MARKET RESEARCH Someone may already have compiled the market research you need. MarketResearch.com lists more than 160,000 research reports from more than 600 sources available for purchase. Other sources of market research include Experian Consumer Research (formerly Simmons Market Research Bureau Inc.), which covers more than 8,000 product categories and the *A.C. Neilsen Retail Index* (A.C. Neilsen Company).

ARTICLES Magazine and journal articles pertinent to your business are a great source of information. Use the *Reader's Guide to Periodical Literature*, the *Business Periodicals Index* (similar to the Reader's Guide but focuses on business periodicals), and *Ulrich's Guide to International Periodicals* to locate the ones you need.

LOCAL DATA Your state Department of Commerce and your local Chamber of Commerce will very likely have useful data on the local market of interest to you. Call to find out what is available.

WORLD WIDE WEB Most entrepreneurs are astounded at the marketing information that is available on the Web. Using one of the search engines, you can gain access to a world of information–literally!

Prototypes

prototype
an original, functional model of a new product that entrepreneurs can put into the hands of potential customers so they can see it, test it, and use it.

One of the most effective ways to gauge the viability of a product is to build a prototype of it. A **prototype** is an original, functional model of a new product that entrepreneurs can put into the hands of potential customers so that they can see it, test it, and use it. Prototypes usually point out potential problems in a product's design, giving inventors the opportunity to fix them even before they put the prototype into customers' hands. The feedback customers give entrepreneurs based on prototypes often leads to design improvements and new features, some of which the entrepreneurs might never have discovered on their own. Makers of computer software frequently put prototypes of new products into customers' hands as they develop new products or improve existing ones. Known as *beta tests*, these trials result in an iterative design process in which software designers collect feedback from users and then incorporate their ideas into the product for the next round of tests.

ENTREPRENEURIAL PROFILE

Shawn Donegan & Mike Puczkowski: Trac Tool Inc.

Entrepreneur Shawn Donegan teamed up with inventor Mike Puczkowski to launch Trac Tool Inc., a Cleveland, Ohio–based business that markets Speed Rollers, a paint application system aimed at professional paint contractors. Puczkowski's invention features an airless paint pump that feeds paint onto one of two rollers, eliminating the need to dip the rollers into a paint tray and making the system four to five times faster than using traditional rollers. Donegan and Puczkowski built several models of the system before they had a prototype that worked. Early prototypes pointed out several problems the entrepreneurs had to fix, including a valve that could handle only a fraction of the pressure that a typical airless system delivers and coupling joints that leaked paint. "Once we redesigned the components, we tested them thoroughly," says Donegan. "We wanted to ensure worker safety and product quality before proceeding." They used the prototype to conduct focus groups with paint contractors, industry experts, and property managers to get feedback on the product and its features. The response from the focus groups was very positive, leading Donegan and Puczkowski to launch Trac Tool Inc., which now generates more than $3 million in sales of the Speed Rollers system.[6]

In-Home Trials

in-home trial
a research technique that involves sending researchers into customers' homes to observe them as they use the company's product or service.

One technique that reveals some of the most insightful information into how customers actually use a product or service is also the most challenging to coordinate: in-home trials. An **in-home trial** involves sending researchers into customers' homes to observe them as they use the company's product or service.

ENTREPRENEURIAL PROFILE

Scott Cook: Intuit®

Intuit®, the software company that produces popular programs such as Quicken®, QuickBooks, and TurboTax, was one of the first companies to adopt in-home trials as part of its product development process in 1989. In the company's follow-me-home program, software engineers would hang around a retail store, waiting for customers to buy an Intuit product. They would then ask to go into customers' homes, where they watch how customers install and use the software and listen to their suggestions in a natural setting. The company also combs through blogs and Intuit online communities, looking for comments and feedback about its software products. The process works; the latest version of Quicken® included 121 customer-recommended improvements.[7]

Financial Feasibility Analysis

The final component of a feasibility analysis involves assessing the financial feasibility of a proposed business venture. At this stage of the process, a broad financial analysis is sufficient. If the business concept passes the overall feasibility analysis, an entrepreneur should conduct a more thorough financial analysis when creating a full-blown business plan. The major elements to be included in a financial feasibility analysis include the initial capital requirement, estimated earnings, and the resulting return on investment.

CAPITAL REQUIREMENTS Just as a Boy Scout needs fuel to start a fire, an entrepreneur needs capital to start a business. Some businesses require large amounts of capital, but others do not. Typically, service businesses require less capital to launch than do manufacturing or retail businesses. Start-up companies often need capital to purchase equipment, buildings, technology, and other tangible assets as well as to hire and train employees, promote their products and services, and establish a presence in the market. A good feasibility analysis provides an estimate of the amount of start-up capital an entrepreneur will need to get the business up and running. For instance, Shawn Donegan and Mike Puczkowski needed $150,000 to launch Trac Tool Inc. and bring the Speed Rollers paint system to market. They spent most of that start-up capital to develop and test the prototype and to introduce the product at the Painting and Decorating Contractors of America trade show.[8]

You will learn more about finding sources of business funding, both debt and equity, in Chapter 14, Sources of Financing: Debt and Equity.

ESTIMATED EARNINGS In addition to producing an estimate of the start-up company's capital requirements, an entrepreneur also should forecast the earning potential of the proposed business. Industry trade associations and publications such as the *RMA Annual Statement Studies* offer guidelines on preparing sales and earnings estimates. From these, entrepreneurs can estimate the financial results they and their investors can expect to see from the business venture.

RETURN ON INVESTMENT The final aspect of the financial feasibility analysis combines the estimated earnings and the capital requirements to determine the rate of return the venture is expected to produce. One simple measure is the rate of return on the capital invested, which is calculated by dividing the estimated earnings the business yields by the amount of capital invested in the business. Although financial estimates at the feasibility analysis stage typically are rough, they are an important part of the entrepreneur's ultimate "go/no go" decision about the business ventures. A venture must produce an attractive rate of return relative to the level of risk it requires. This risk-return tradeoff means that the higher the level of risk a prospective business involves, the higher the rate of return it must provide to the entrepreneur and investors. Why should an entrepreneur take on all of the risks of starting and running a business that produces a mere three or four percent rate of return when he or she could earn that much in a risk-free investment at a bank or other financial institution? You will learn more about developing detailed financial forecasts for a business start-up in Chapter 12, Creating a Successful Financial Plan.

Wise entrepreneurs take the time to subject their ideas to a feasibility analysis like the one described here, whatever outcome it produces. If the study suggests that transforming the idea into a viable business is not feasible, the entrepreneur moves on to the next idea, confident that he or she has not wasted valuable resources launching a business destined to fail. If the analysis shows that the idea has real potential as a profitable business, the entrepreneur can pursue it, using the information gathered during the feasibility analysis as the foundation for building a sound business plan. We now turn our attention to that process.

Why Develop a Business Plan?

Any entrepreneur who is in business or is about to launch a business needs a well-conceived and factually based business plan to increase the likelihood of success. For decades, research has proved that companies that engage in business planning outperform those that do not. Unfortunately, studies also show that small companies are especially lackadaisical in their approach to developing business plans. Many entrepreneurs never take the time to develop plans for their businesses; unfortunately, the implications of the lack of planning are all too evident in the high failure rates that small companies experience.

LO 2

Explain why every entrepreneur should create a business plan, as well as benefits of a plan.

business plan
a written summary of an entrepreneur's proposed business venture, its operational and financial details, its marketing opportunities and strategy, and its managers' skills and abilities.

A **business plan** is a written summary of an entrepreneur's proposed business venture, its operational and financial details, its marketing opportunities and strategy, and its managers' skills and abilities. There is no substitute for a well-prepared business plan, and there are no shortcuts to creating one. The plan serves as an entrepreneur's road map on the journey toward building a successful business. As a small company's guidebook, a business plan describes the direction the company is taking, what its goals are, where it wants to be, and how it's going to get there. The plan is written proof that an entrepreneur has performed the necessary research, has studied the business opportunity adequately, and is prepared to capitalize on it with a sound business model. One business planning expert says that a business plan is "a written description of your business's future."[9] In short, a business plan is an entrepreneur's best insurance against launching a business destined to fail or mismanaging a potentially successful company.

A business plan serves two essential functions. First and most important, it guides an entrepreneur by charting the company's future course of action and devising a strategy for success. The plan provides a battery of tools—a mission statement, goals, objectives, market analysis, budgets, financial forecasts, target markets, strategies—to help entrepreneurs lead a company successfully. It gives managers and employees a sense of direction, but only if everyone is involved in creating, updating, or revising it. As more team members become committed to making the plan work, the plan takes on special meaning. It gives everyone targets to shoot for, and it provides a yardstick for measuring actual performance against those targets, especially in the crucial and chaotic start-up phase. Creating a plan also forces entrepreneurs to subject their ideas to the test of reality. Can this business idea actually produce a profit?

Owners of existing businesses also can reap the benefits of creating a business plan.

ENTREPRENEURIAL PROFILE

Rhonda Abrams: The Planning Shop

Rhonda Abrams, founder of The Planning Shop, a small publisher of books and tools for entrepreneurs, says that the business plan that she and her employees craft every year has been a key to her company's success. "Developing a business plan is a strategy for recognizing what's going on in your industry and in the world and responding to that in your business," she says. "The process will save you a lot of money by liberating your firm from unfruitful directions and by setting your priorities for the year." To prepare for the business planning sessions, Abrams's office manager collects key financial data and industry statistics, trends, and forecasts, and every employee submits a list of key issues. In their sessions, Abrams and her employees compare the company's performance to industry averages and to the goals they established the previous year before painting a picture for its future. "Make the process strategic so you're thinking through larger business issues and so everyone can focus on the agreed-upon goals you set collectively," she advises.[10]

The second function of the business plan is to attract lenders and investors. Too often small business owners approach potential lenders and investors without having prepared to sell themselves and their business concept. Simply scribbling a few rough figures on a note pad to support a loan application is not enough. Applying for loans or attempting to attract investors without a solid business plan rarely attracts needed capital. Rather, the best way to secure the necessary capital is to prepare a sound business plan, which enables an entrepreneur to communicate to potential lenders and investors the potential the business opportunity offers. Entrepreneur must pay attention to details because they are germane to their sales presentations to potential lenders and investors. The quality of the firm's business plan weighs heavily in the decision to lend or invest funds. It is also potential lenders' and investors' first impression of the company and its managers. Therefore, the finished product should be highly polished and professional in both form and content.

Building a plan forces a potential entrepreneur to look at his or her business idea in the harsh light of reality. It also requires the entrepreneur to assess the venture's chances of success more objectively. A well-assembled plan helps prove to outsiders that a business idea can be successful. To get external financing, an entrepreneur's plan must pass three tests with potential lenders and investors: (1) the reality test, (2) the competitive test, and (3) the value test. The first two tests have both an external and internal component:

REALITY TEST The external component of the reality test revolves around proving that a market for the product or service really does exist. It focuses on industry attractiveness, market niches, potential customers, market size, degree of competition, and similar factors. Entrepreneurs who pass this part of the reality test prove in the marketing portion of their business plan that there is strong demand for their business idea.

The internal component of the reality test focuses on the product or service itself. Can the company *really* build it for the cost estimates in the business plan? Is it truly different from what competitors are already selling? Does it offer customers something of value?

COMPETITIVE TEST The external part of the competitive test evaluates the company's relative position to its key competitors. How do the company's strengths and weaknesses match up with those of the competition? Do competitors' reactions threaten the new company's success and survival?

The internal competitive test focuses on management's ability to create a company that will gain an edge over existing rivals. To pass this part of the competitive test, a plan must prove the quality, skill, and experience of the venture's management team. What other resources does the company have that can give it a competitive edge in the market?

VALUE TEST To convince lenders and investors to put their money into the venture, a business plan must prove to them that it offers a high probability of repayment or an attractive rate of return. Entrepreneurs usually see their businesses as good investments because they consider the intangibles of owning a business—gaining control over their own destinies, freedom to do what they enjoy, and others; lenders and investors, however, look at a venture in colder terms: dollar-for-dollar returns. A plan must convince lenders and investors that they will earn an attractive return on their money.

Sometimes the greatest service a business plan provides an entrepreneur is the realization that "it just won't work." The time to find out a potential business idea won't succeed is in the planning stages *before* an entrepreneur commits significant resources to a venture. In other cases it reveals important problems to overcome before launching a company.

The real value in preparing a business plan is not so much in the plan itself as it is in the *process* an entrepreneur goes through to create the plan. Although the finished produce is useful, the process of building a plan requires an entrepreneur to subject his or her idea to an objective, critical evaluation. What an entrepreneur learns about his or her company, its target market, its financial requirements, and other factors can be essential to making the venture a success. Simply put, building a business plan reduces the risk and uncertainty in launching a company by teaching the entrepreneur to do it the right way! Scott Shane, who has conducted studies on entrepreneurs' use of business plans, says:

> The data show that writing business plans increases the odds that a venture will undertake other organizational activities and product development as well as continue in business. Completing a business plan also increases the pace of initiating product development, obtaining inputs, starting marketing, talking to customers, and asking for external funds.[11]

A business plan should reflect the fire and passion an entrepreneur has for the venture. For this reason an entrepreneur cannot allow others to prepare the business plan because outsiders cannot understand the business nor envision the proposed company as well as he or she can. The entrepreneur is the driving force behind the business idea and is the one who can best convey the vision and the enthusiasm needed to transform that idea into a successful business.

Perhaps the best way to understand the need for a business plan is to recognize the validity of the "two-thirds rule," which says that only two-thirds of the entrepreneurs with a sound and viable new business venture will find financial backing. Those who do find financial backing will only get two-thirds of what they initially requested, and it will take them two-thirds longer to get the financing than they anticipated.[12] The most effective strategy for avoiding the two-thirds rule is to build a business plan!

Apparently, wild hopes and dreams,
re-enacted by Barbie and Ken, are no
substitute for a solid business plan.

Source: www.cartoonstock.com

LO 3

Describe the elements of a solid
business plan.

The Elements of a Business Plan

Smart entrepreneurs recognize that every business plan is unique and must be tailor-made. They avoid the off-the-shelf, "cookie-cutter" approach that produces look-alike plans. The elements of a business plan may be standard, but the way entrepreneurs tell their stories should be unique and reflect their enthusiasm for the new venture. If this is a first attempt at writing a business plan, it may be very helpful to seek the advice of individuals with experience in this process. Accountants, business professors, attorneys, and consultants with Small Business Development Centers (SBDC) can be excellent sources of advice in creating and refining a plan. (For a list of Small Business Development Center locations, see the Small Business Administration's Web SBDC Web page at http://www.sba.gov/SBDC/) Entrepreneurs also can use business planning software available from several companies to create their plans. Some of the most popular programs include *Business Plan Pro*™* (Palo Alto Software), BizPlan Builder (Jian Tools), PlanMaker (Power Solutions for Business), and Plan Write (Business Resources Software). These planning packages help entrepreneurs organize the material they have researched and gathered, and they provide helpful tips on writing business plans and templates for creating financial statements. These planning packages produce professional-looking business plans, but entrepreneurs who use them face one drawback: the plans they produce often look the same, as if they came from the same mold. That can be a turn-off for professional investors, who see hundreds of business plans each year.

Initially, the prospect of writing a business plan may appear to be overwhelming. Many entrepreneurs would rather launch their companies and "see what happens" than invest the necessary time and energy defining and researching their target markets, defining their strategies, and mapping out their finances. After all, building a plan is hard work! However, it is hard work that pays many dividends—not all of them immediately apparent. Although building a business plan does not *guarantee* success, it *does* raise an entrepreneur's chances of succeeding in business.

A business plan typically ranges from 25 to 40 pages in length. Shorter plans usually are too sketchy to be of any value, and those much longer than this run the risk of never getting used or read! This section explains the most common elements of a business plan. However, entrepreneurs must recognize that, like every business venture, every business plan is unique. An entrepreneur should view the following elements as a starting point for building a plan and should modify them as needed to better tell the story of his or her new venture.

Business Plan Pro™ is available at a nominal cost with this textbook.

YOU Be the CONSULTANT

Battle of the Plans

In 1984, two MBA students at the University of Texas thought that it would be a good idea to teach and experience entrepreneurship in the same comprehensive way that "moot court" competitions taught law. They approached some of their professors and soon launched Moot Corp., the country's first business plan competition in which students competed not only for pride but also for start-up capital to launch their businesses. In 1989, the Massachusetts Institute of Technology started the MIT $10K (now $100K) Entrepreneurship Competition, and many other colleges and universities have followed suit with business plan competitions of their own. Today hundreds of colleges, universities, and other organizations across the United States sponsor business plan competitions. About 85 colleges and universities sponsor major competitions in which the prizes are tens of thousands of dollars, and it is not uncommon for winners of these competitions to attract serious capital of venture capital from judges. "I have been amazed at the quality of the plans and the companies coming out of these competitions," says Steve Kaplan of the University of Chicago. The richest business plan competition, the Global Security Challenge, is sponsored by the London Business School and the U.S. Defense Department and emphasizes security-focused start-ups. Clifford King recently won the prestigious competition with a business plan for his company, Noblepeak Vision, which has developed the TriWave™ camera, a revolutionary night-vision camera with applications in the security, transportation, and defense markets. Noblepeak received a $500,000 grant and a mentoring relationship with venture capital firm, Paladin Capital Group. King says that the intense competition "was like [being on] a reality TV show."

While Karan Goel was an MBA student at the University of Chicago, he won $20,000 in the University of Chicago New Venture Challenge for his business plan for PrepMe, an online SAT preparation service that uses a diagnostic test to create a customized course of study and adapts it to the learner's progress using artificial intelligence. PrepMe (whose motto is "Prepare. Relax. Ace.") also offers online tutors, all of whom mastered the important college admissions test; the average PrepMe tutor's SAT score is an impressive 2,312 out of 2,400! Since winning the competition, PrepMe's sales have skyrocketed. More than 37,000 students have used PrepMe's service, which Goel launched in 2005 with partners Joe Jewell and Avichal Garg, and more than 100 high schools have integrated the course into their curricula. "We [don't] focus on test-taking tricks," says Goel. "We actually try to improve [students'] math or English skills." PrepMe has launched a similar service to help students prepare for the ACT, and Goel plans to expand the model into other standardized entrance tests, such as the LSAT (law school) and the MCAT (medical school) once he knows that the preparation course PrepMe develops is " the best on the market."

Faculty and students alike find the idea of business plan competitions appealing because they provide an all-encompassing educational experience. As they prepare their plans, students learn a comprehensive set of business skills, ranging from conducting industry and market research and assembling a new venture team to developing realistic financial forecasts and writing mission statements. They also learn valuable skills as they present their plans to panels of judges that often comprise successful entrepreneurs, bankers, venture capitalists, and other business heavy-hitters. Two

Callie Lipkin Photography, Inc.

valuable lessons that often come from business plan competitions are that it takes more than just a good idea to build a successful business venture and that building a business is hard work.

Competition winners say that the start-up capital they receive is just one of the many benefits they gain. The feedback they receive from the judges, the recognition and credibility they earn as winners, and the contacts they make with private investors and venture capitalists may be worth more in the long run. "If you win one of the competitions, you'll have [venture capitalists] banging down your door," says Jay Mullis, who finished in the money in a recent Moot Corp competition. While working on his MBA at the University of Georgia, Mullis took a formula for a safe, all-natural roach poison that his grandfather had left him, and launched Mullis Enterprises to bring the product, which he named Green Dragon Roach Kill, to market. Mullis devised a straw-shaped plastic container for dispensing the roach bait and has applied for patents on both the formula and the dispenser. He recently negotiated a deal with a private investor he met at the Moot Corp competition to give up 25 percent ownership in his company in exchange for a $750,000 investment. Mullis is using the money to obtain approval from the Food and Drug Administration for Green Dragon Roach Kill. Once he does, his plan calls for setting up a production facility in Danville, Georgia, and targeting large pest-control companies that treat residential and commercial properties. He says that he already has orders totaling $200,000 from four pest-control companies in the Southeast. "Their customers are asking for a green solution," says Mullis. "I've got it."

Mullis Enterprises GDPS, Inc.

According to one business writer, "Business plan competitions remind would-be entrepreneurs that success requires a solid business plan even more than a bountiful bank balance. Once students have truly learned that business basic, they're not only better prepared to play the entrepreneurial game, they're more likely to end up as winners."

1. If your school does not already have a business plan competition, work with a team of your classmates in a brainstorming session to develop ideas for creating one. What would you offer as a prize? How would you finance the competition? Whom would you invite to judge it? How would you structure the competition?

2. Use the Web to research business plan competitions at other colleges and universities across the nation. Using the competitions at these schools as benchmarks and the ideas you generated in the previous question, develop a format for a business plan competition at your school.

3. Assume that you are a member of a team of entrepreneurial students competing in a prestigious business plan competition. Outline your team's strategy for winning the competition.

Sources: Adapted from: Alina Dizik, "Where Big Ideas Win Big Bucks," *Business Week*, November 13, 2007, http://www.businessweek.com/bschools/content/nov2007/bs20071113_247178.htm?chan=search; Jeffrey Gangemi, "The Afterlife of Business Plan Contest Winners," *Business Week*, December 12, 2006, http://www.businessweek.com/smallbiz/content/dec2006/sb20061212_4 10722.htm?chan=smallbiz_smallbiz+index+page_today's+top+stories; Alison Damast, "How to Win a B-School Competition," *Business Week*, May 30, 2007, http://www.businessweek.com/bschools/content/may2007/bs20070530_80086 0.htm; Kelly K. Spors, "Business Plan Contests Become '*American Idol* Meets Trump,'" *Wall Street Journal*, December 11, 2007, pp. B1, B4; Amy Haimerl, "Killer Start-Ups," *FSB*, November 2007, pp. 75–80; Zak Stambor, "Venture Prone," *University of Chicago Magazine*, March/April 2008, Volume 100, Issue 4, http://magazine.uchicago.edu/0834/features/venture.shtml; Tricia Bisoux, "Winning Ways," *BizEd*, September/October 2004, pp. 26–32; Suzanne Isack, "Search for Next Google on America's College Campuses," The National Institute for Entrepreneurship, May 12, 2004, pp.1–2; Nichole L. Torres, "Planning for Gold," *Entrepreneur B.Y.O.B.*, November 2004, pp. 112–118; "Eight Great Business Plans, But Only One Is the Winner," Knowledge@Wharton, May 5, 2005, http://knowledge.wharton.upenn.edu/index.cfm?fa=printArticle&ID=1190.

TITLE PAGE AND TABLE OF CONTENTS A business plan is a professional document and should contain a title page with the company's name, logo, and address as well as the names and contact information of the company founders. Many entrepreneurs also include the copy number of the plan and the date on which it was issued on the title page.

Business plan readers appreciate a table of contents that includes page numbers so that they can locate the particular sections of the plan in which they are most interested.

EXECUTIVE SUMMARY To summarize the presentation to each potential financial institution or investors, the entrepreneur should write an executive summary. It should be concise—a maximum of two pages–and should summarize all of the relevant points of the business venture. The executive summary is a synopsis of the entire plan, capturing its essence in a capsulized form. It should briefly describe:

- The company's business model and the basis for its competitive edge.
- The company's target market(s) and the benefits its products or services will provide customers.
- The qualifications of the founders and key employees.
- Key financial highlights (e.g., sales and earnings projections, capital required, rates of return on the investment, and when any loans will be repaid).

The executive summary is a written version of what is known as "the elevator pitch." Imagine yourself on an elevator with a potential lender or investor. Only the two of you are on the elevator, and you have that person's undivided attention for the duration of the ride, but the building is not very tall! To convince the investor that your business is a great investment, you must boil your message down to its essence—key points that you can communicate in just a matter of one or two minutes: What your company does and why it matters.

Dave Yewman, co-owner of Elevator Speech, a company that helps executives hone their elevator pitches, shows a video to his clients that features what he says is "the worst elevator speech ever." When asked what his e-commerce consulting company did, the founder replied, "We've asked our clients to reconceptualize their business. We've reconceptualized what it is to be in the service business." When asked once again to explain what his company did *in English*, the CEO replied, "We provide services to companies that help them win." A third attempt produced no better results: "We radically transform businesses to invent and reinvent them."[13]

An entrepreneur must make sure that the company's elevator pitch is fine-tuned and on target because an executive summary *must* capture the reader's attention. If it misses the mark,

Corbis RF

the chances of the remainder of the plan being read are minimal. Although the executive summary is the first part of the business plan, it should be the last section written.

VISION AND MISSION STATEMENT As you learned in Chapter 3, a mission statement expresses in words an entrepreneur's vision for what his or her company is and what it is to become. It is the broadest expression of a company's purpose and defines the direction in which it will move. It anchors a company in reality and serves as the thesis statement for the entire business plan. Every good plan captures an entrepreneur's passion and vision for the business, and the mission statement is the ideal place to express them.

COMPANY HISTORY The owner of an existing small business who is creating a business plan should prepare a brief history of the operation, highlighting the significant financial and operational events in the company's life. This section should describe when and why the company was formed, how it has evolved over time, and what the owner envisions for the future. It should highlight the successful accomplishment of past objectives such as developing prototypes, earning patents, achieving market-share targets, or securing long-term customer contracts. This section also should describe the company's current image in the marketplace.

BUSINESS AND INDUSTRY PROFILE To acquaint lenders and investors with the industry in which a company competes, an entrepreneur should describe it in the business plan. This section should provide the reader with an overview of the industry or market segment in which the new venture will operate. Industry data such as market size, growth trends, and the relative economic and competitive strength of the major firms in the industry all set the stage for a better understanding of the viability of the new product or service. Strategic issues such as ease of market entry and exit, the ability to achieve economies of scale or scope, and the existence of cyclical or seasonal economic trends further help readers evaluate the new venture. This part of the plan also should describe significant industry trends and key success factors as well as an overall outlook for its future. Information about the evolution of the industry helps the reader comprehend its competitive dynamics.

FIGURE 4.3

Mission, Goals, and Objectives

This section should contain a statement of the company's general business goals and then work down to a narrower definition of its immediate objectives. Together they should spell out what the business plans to accomplish, how, when, and who will do it. **Goals** are broad, long-range statements of what a company plans to achieve in the future that guide its overall direction. In other words, they address the question, "What do I want my company to look like in three to five years?"

Objectives, on the other hand, are short-term, specific performance targets that are attainable, measurable, and controllable. Every objective should reflect some general business goal and should include a technique for measuring progress toward its accomplishment. To be meaningful, an objective must have a time frame for achievement. Both goals and objectives should relate to the company's basic mission (see Figure 4.3).

BUSINESS STRATEGY Another important part of a business plan is the owner's view of the strategy needed to meet—and beat—the competition. In the previous section, the entrepreneur defined *where* to take the business by establishing goals and objectives. This section addresses the question of *how* to get there—the business strategy. Here entrepreneurs must explain how they plan to gain a competitive edge in the market and what sets the business apart from the competition. They should comment on how they plan to achieve business goals and objectives in the face of competition and government regulation and should identify the image that the business will try to project. An important theme in this section is what makes the company unique in the eyes of its customers. One of the quickest routes to business failure is trying to sell "me-too" products or services that offer customers nothing new, better, bigger, faster, more convenient, or different from existing products or services.

goals

broad, long-range statements of what a company plans to achieve in the future that guide its overall direction.

objectives

short-term specific performance targets that are attainable, measurable, and controllable.

ENTREPRENEURIAL PROFILE_____

Håkan & Annika Olsson: First Penthouse

While renovating their top-floor apartment in Stockholm, Sweden, civil engineers Håkan and Annika Olsson came up with a unique idea for creating high-quality modular penthouses that could be manufactured in factories and installed atop existing flat-roof buildings. When the couple moved to London, they purchased aerial photographs of the city and marked all of the flat-roof buildings in red ink. "We knew we had a good business idea when the whole picture was red," says Håkan. After conducting more research and building a business plan, the Olssons launched First Penthouse, a company specializing in rooftop development. Their business model adds value both for tenants, who get ritzy penthouse living quarters where none existed before, and for landlords, whose property values are enhanced by the addition of the modular penthouses. First Penthouse offers the convenience of one-day installation of its penthouses and guarantees no disturbances to existing residents. Like most entrepreneurs, the Olssons had to overcome obstacles, including banks that were hesitant to extend credit "because the idea was so new," says Håkan. (To get the capital they needed, the Olssons used angel financing, a topic you will learn more about in Chapter 13, when they convinced a wealthy friend to put up most of the $400,000 they needed to create and install the first penthouse.) To convince balking regulators, the Olssons agreed to use special "quiet" tools and to place soundproof mats over the roofs they worked on. Sales of the company's penthouses are growing, and the Olssons are planning to take their concept into other large urban markets around the world, including New York City.[14]

The strategy section of the business plan should outline the methods the company can use to satisfy the key success factors required to thrive in the industry. If, for example, a strong, well-trained sales force is considered critical to success, the owner must devise a plan of action for assembling one. The foundation for this part of the business plan comes from the material in Chapter 3, Strategic Management and the Entrepreneur.

DESCRIPTION OF THE COMPANY'S PRODUCT OR SERVICE An entrepreneur should describe the company's overall product line, giving an overview of how customers use its goods or services. Drawings, diagrams, and illustrations may be required if the product is highly technical. It is best to write product and service descriptions in a jargon-free style so that laypeople can understand them. A statement of a product's position in the product life cycle might also be helpful. An entrepreneur should include a summary of any patents, trademarks, or copyrights protecting the product or service from infringement by competitors. Finally, it is helpful provide an honest comparison of the company's product or service with those of competitors, citing specific advantages or improvements that make the entrepreneur's goods or services unique and indicating plans for creating the next generation of goods and services that will evolve from the present product line.

The emphasis of this section should be on defining the unique characteristics of the company's products or services and the *benefits* customers get by purchasing them, rather than on just a "nuts and bolts" description of the *features* of those products or services. A **feature** is a descriptive fact about a product or service ("An ergonomically-designed, more comfortable handle"). A **benefit** is what a customer gains from the product or service feature ("Fewer problems with carpal tunnel syndrome and increased productivity"). Advertising legend Leo Burnett once said, "Don't tell the people how good you make the goods; tell them how good your goods make them." This part of the plan must describe how a business will transform tangible product or service *features* into important, but often intangible, customer *benefits*—for example, lower energy bills, faster access to the Internet, less time writing checks to pay monthly bills, greater flexibility in building floating structures, shorter time required to learn a foreign language, or others. Remember: Customers buy benefits, *not* product or service features.

feature
a descriptive fact about a product or service.

benefit
what a customer gains from the product or service.

MARKETING STRATEGY One crucial concern of entrepreneurs and the potential lenders and investors who finance their companies is whether or not there is a real market for the proposed good or service. Every entrepreneur must therefore describe the company's target market and its characteristics. Defining the target market and its potential is one of the most important—and most challenging—parts of building a business plan. Creating a successful business depends on an entrepreneur's ability to attract real customers who are willing and able to spend real money to buy its products or services. Perhaps the worst marketing error an entrepreneur can commit is failing to define the target market and trying to make his or her business "everything to everybody." Small companies usually are much more successful focusing on a specific market niche where they can excel at meeting customers' special needs or wants.

One technique for identifying potential target markets is to list all of the features your company's product or service provides and then translate those features into a list of benefits (refer to the previous section). The next step is to develop a list of the types of people who need or could use those benefits. Be creative, and let your mind roam free. Once you have identified potential target markets, you can begin to research them to narrow the list down to the most promising one or two. Those are the markets your company should pursue.

One growing and evolving target market for small businesses is the U.S. Hispanic market, which is the second largest in the world, behind only Mexico. With 47.6 million people, the Hispanic market makes up 15 percent of the total U.S. population, is expected to grow by 29 percent (compared to 9 percent for the population as a whole) by 2015, and has purchasing power that exceeds $1 trillion.[15] "If you want your company to grow, you had better market to Latinos or you are missing the boat," says Hispanic marketing expert Chiqui Cartagena.[16]

In 1989, copreneurs Hipolito and Ana Maria Anaya moved from Jalisco, Mexico, to Las Vegas to open a small tortilla factory, which they soon expanded to include a deli and a line of authentic Mexican grocery items. Sales grew steadily, and in 2002, the Anayas purchased and renovated a 32,000-square-foot building, transforming it into a grocery store named Mariana's aimed squarely at Hispanic customers (particularly Mexican customers), who spend more on groceries than the average consumer and who see shopping as a fiesta. Hipolito's son, Ruben, director of operations, says that the three-store chain's customer base

ENTREPRENEURIAL PROFILE_____

Hipolito & Ana Maria Anaya: Mariana's

is 90 percent Hispanic, and everything in the store, from the products to the layout, is designed to appeal to them. Mariana's newest store is divided into sections to make it feel more like a series of interconnected specialty shops than a full-service grocery store. The bakery carries a full line of products that shoppers would find in small bakeries in Mexico, including cochitas (small ginger cookies) and pan dulce, a Mexican sweet bread. La Cocina ("The Kitchen") offers hungry shoppers authentic Mexican fare, ranging from homemade tamales to chile verde, and a catering service. The store also features a fresh juice bar, Mariachi bands, and a one-day Los Posadas celebration (based on a Mexican Christmas tradition) with prizes, music, and gifts for children.[17]

Defining a company's target market involves using the techniques described in more detail in Chapter 6, Building a Marketing Plan, but a business plan should address the following questions:

- Who are my target customers (age, gender, income level, and other demographic characteristics)?
- Where do they live, work, and shop?
- How many potential customers are in my company's trading area?
- Why do they buy? What needs and wants drive their purchase decisions?
- What can my business do to meet those needs and wants better than my competitors?
- Knowing my customers' needs, wants, and habits, what should be the basis for differentiating my business in their minds?

Proving that a profitable market exists involves two steps: documenting market claims and showing customer interest.

DOCUMENTING MARKET CLAIMS Too many business plans rely on vague generalizations such as "This market is so huge that if we get just 1 percent of it, we will break even in 8 months." Statements such as this are not backed by facts and usually reflect an entrepreneur's unbridled optimism. In most cases, they are also unrealistic, and potential lenders and investors quickly dismiss them. Market share determination is not obtained by "shoot from the hip" generalizations; on the contrary, sophisticated investors expect to see research that supports the claims an entrepreneur makes about the market potential of a product or service.

Providing facts about the sales potential of a product or service requires market research. Results of market surveys, customer questionnaires, and demographic studies lend credibility of an entrepreneur's frequently optimistic sales projections. (You will learn more about market research techniques and resources in Chapter 8, Building a Guerrilla Marketing Plan.)

ENTREPRENEURIAL PROFILE

James Poss: Seahorse Power

In his business plan, James Poss, founder of Seahorse Power, a company that makes solar-powered trash compactors, identified the primary target customer as resorts and amusement parks and included market research on them. Today Poss admits that the plan was off "by a long shot"; in reality, the company's major customers turned out to be cities and municipal governments. "We were out there selling a boxy-looking, ugly machine for close to two years," he says. "I could have shown [potential customers] a picture and said, 'Would you buy this?' and saved myself a lot of money." Although Seahorse Power now generates sales of more than $3 million, Poss learned a valuable lesson about "actually getting out in the field and talking to people."[18]

SHOWING CUSTOMER INTEREST As important as providing convincing market research is, proving that a significant group of target customers actually needs or wants a company's good or service and would be willing to pay for it is even more so. Two of the most reliable techniques involve building a working prototype of a product so that customers can see how it works and producing a small number of products so that customers can actually use them. An entrepreneur might offer a prototype or an actual product to several potential customers to get written testimonials and evaluations to show investors.

That's the approach that Nate Alder took for his company, Klymit, that makes a temperature-adjustable jacket for snow skiers. Alder, a scuba diver, knew that divers used inert gases such as argon as insulation in dry suits during cold water dives and thought the same concept could keep skiers comfortable on the slopes. "It's inconvenient to wear bulky layers for the summit just to peel them off at the base, where it is warmer," he says. Alder, a student at Brigham Young University, created a prototype jacket that contains a series of airtight chambers and a lipstick case-sized cartridge of pressurized argon. At cold temperatures, the wearer turns a knob to fill the chambers with argon, which has properties that seal in heat and block out cold. Turning the valve the other way releases the harmless gas, cooling the skier. A cartridge lasts for 10 days on the slopes. Before approaching potential lenders and investors, Alder used the prototype to acquire letters of intent from three top sports companies that want to license the technology for use in their products. "Like Velcro, [Klymit] is a simple solution to a big problem," says Alder.[19]

Another way to get useful feedback is to sell the product to several customers at a discount. This proves that potential customers for the product do exist and allows for demonstrations of the product in operation. Getting a product into customers' hands early in the process also is an excellent way to get valuable feedback that can lead to significant design improvements and increased sales down the road.

One of the goals of the marketing strategy section of the business plan is to lay the foundation for the financial forecasts that come later in the plan. A start-up company's financial forecasts must be based on more than just wishful thinking. As much as possible, they should be built on research and facts. Many entrepreneurs build financial models for their potential business by applying information collected from trade or professional associations, local chambers of commerce, articles in magazines and newspapers, market studies conducted by themselves or others, government agencies, and, of course, the Web. With the availability of this volume of information, the sales, cost, and net income projections in a business plan should be a great deal more accurate than sketchy estimates scribbled on the backs of napkins.

This section of the business plan should address the company's plans for advertising, pricing its products and services, distributing them, and choosing a location, topics we will discuss in later chapters.

COMPETITOR ANALYSIS An entrepreneur should discuss the new venture's competition. Failing to assess competitors realistically makes entrepreneurs appear to be poorly prepared or dishonest, especially to potential lenders and investors. Entrepreneurs who believe they have no competitors are only fooling themselves and are raising a huge red flag to potential lenders and investors. Gathering information on direct competitors' market shares, products, and strategies is usually not difficult. Trade associations, customers, industry journals, marketing representatives, and sales literature are valuable sources of data. This section of the plan should focus on demonstrating that the entrepreneur's company has an advantage over its competitors. Who are the company's key competitors? What are their strengths and weaknesses? What are their strategies? What images do they have in the marketplace? How successful are they? What distinguishes the entrepreneur's product or service from others already on the market, and how will these differences produce a competitive edge? This section of the plan should demonstrate that the firm's strategies are customer-focused.

Frustrated with her job as a Website designer, Shelly Gardner-Alley decided to launch an e-commerce business with her husband. The couple did not have a particular product in mind, so they invested considerable time in researching markets that would be most suitable for e-commerce and would allow them to differentiate their business from the competition. They finally settled on an online business selling high-end, decorative paper from all over the world—ranging from silk paper from Japan to translucent vellum from

France—at prices ranging from $2 to $16 per sheet. Before launching their business, Paper Mojo, one of their first tasks was to study their competition. Gardner-Alley discovered that most companies lacked extensive product lines, and she decided to use that as one differentiating point for her business. As a former Website designer, Gardner-Alley also noted that the few companies that did have broad product lines suffered from poorly designed Web sites that made shopping a chore for customers. A well-designed Web site that would be easy to navigate became another basis for differentiating her company from the competition. Paper Mojo's sales took off after Gardner-Alley submitted the site to search engine Yahoo!, which featured the new business in a newsletter. Gardner-Alley's extensive research and the decision to build her business model on a platform of outperforming the competition in ways that directly benefit customers are paying off.[20]

DESCRIPTION OF THE MANAGEMENT TEAM The most important factor in the success of a business venture is the quality of its management, and financial officers and investors weigh heavily the ability and experience of the company's managers in their financing decisions. Thus, a plan should describe the qualifications of business officers, key directors, and any person with at least 20 percent ownership in the company. *Remember: Lenders and investors prefer experienced managers.* A management team with industry experience and a proven record of success goes a long way in adding credibility to the new venture.

ENTREPRENEURIAL PROFILE _____

Jason Henry, Anil Nair, & Heath Seymour: Inkwell FineArts LLC

When Jason Henry, Anil Nair, and Heath Seymour wrote the business plan for their company, Inkwell Fine Arts, LLC, a company that sells customized, high-quality art prints to interior designers over the Web, they emphasized the diverse and complementary backgrounds of their management team as well as their business experience. Seymour, an artist, manages the artistic and creative aspects of the business, Henry handles daily operations, and Nair oversees the Web site and the information technology components. With the three founders working in tandem, Inkwell Fine Arts is able to offer interior designers prints made to their specifications—the exact size, colors, and medium they need for to decorate a client's living or workspace.[21]

Résumés in a plan should summarize each key person's education, work history (emphasizing managerial responsibilities and duties), and relevant business experience. Entrepreneurs should not cover up previous business failures. Failing in business no longer has a terrible stigma attached to it. In fact, many investors are suspicious of entrepreneurs who have never experienced a business failure.

When considering investing in a business, lenders and investors look for the experience, talent, and integrity of the people who will breathe life into the plan. This portion of the plan should show that the company has the right people organized in the right fashion for success. One experienced private investor advises entrepreneurs to remember the following:

- Ideas and products don't succeed; people do. Show the strength of your management team. A top-notch management team with a variety of proven skills is crucial.
- Show the strength of key employees and how you will retain them. Most small companies cannot pay salaries that match those at large businesses, but stock options and other incentives can improve employee retention.
- A board of directors or advisers consisting of industry experts lends credibility and can enhance the value of the management team.[22]

PLAN OF OPERATION To complete the description of the business, the owner should construct an organization chart identifying the business's key jobs and the qualifications of the people occupying them. Assembling a management team with the right stuff is difficult, but keeping it together until the company is established may be harder. Thus, the entrepreneur should describe the steps taken to encourage important officers to remain with the company. Employment contracts, shares of ownership, and perks are commonly used to keep and motivate these employees.

Finally, a description of the form of ownership (partnership, joint venture, S Corporation, LLC) and of any leases, contracts, and other relevant agreements pertaining to the business is helpful. (You will learn more about this topic in Chapter 5, Organizational Issues and Forms of Ownership.)

PRO FORMA (PROJECTED) FINANCIAL STATEMENTS One of the most important sections of the business plan is an outline of the proposed company's financial statements–the "dollars and cents" of the proposed venture. In fact, one survey found that 74 percent of bankers say that financial documentation is the most important aspect of a business plan for entrepreneurs seeking loans.[23] For an existing business, lenders and investors use past financial statements to judge the health of the company and its ability to repay loans or generate adequate returns; therefore, an owner should supply copies of the firm's financial statements from the past three years

Whether assembling a plan for an existing business or for a start-up, an entrepreneur should carefully prepare monthly projected (or pro forma) financial statements for the operation for the next year (and for two more years by quarter) using past operating data, published statistics, and research to derive three sets of forecasts of the income statement, balance sheet, cash forecast (always!), and a schedule of planned capital expenditures. (You will learn more about creating projected financial statements in Chapter 12, Creating a Successful Financial Plan, and cash forecasts in Chapter 13, Managing Cash Flow.) The forecasts should cover pessimistic, most likely, and optimistic conditions to reflect the uncertainty of the future. When in doubt, be up front and include some contingencies for any costs that you are unsure about.

It is essential that all three sets of forecasts be realistic. Entrepreneurs must avoid the tendency to "fudge the numbers" just to make their businesses look good. Lenders and investors compare these projections against published industry standards and can detect unrealistic forecasts. In fact, some venture capitalists automatically discount an entrepreneur's financial projections by as much as 50 percent. After completing these forecasts, an entrepreneur should perform a break-even analysis and a ratio analysis on the projected figures.

It is also important to include a statement of the *assumptions* on which these financial projections are based. Potential lenders and investors want to know how an entrepreneur derived forecasts for sales, cost of goods sold, operating expenses, accounts receivable, collections, accounts payable, inventory, taxes, and other items. Spelling out realistic assumptions gives a plan more credibility and reduces the tendency to include overly optimistic estimates of sales growth and profit margins. Greg Martin, a partner in the venture capital company Redpoint Ventures, says, "I have problems with start-ups making unrealistic assumptions–how much money they need or how quickly they can ramp up revenue. Those can really kill a deal for me."[24]

In addition to providing valuable information to potential lenders and investors, projected financial statements help entrepreneurs run their businesses more effectively and more efficiently after the start-up. They establish important targets for financial performance and make it easier for an entrepreneur to maintain control over routine expenses and capital expenditures.

THE LOAN OR INVESTMENT PROPOSAL The loan or investment proposal section of the business plan should state the purpose of the financing, the amount requested, and the plans for repayment or, in the case of investors, an attractive exit strategy. When describing the purpose of the loan or investment, an entrepreneur must specify the planned use of the funds. General requests for funds using terms such as "for modernization," "working capital," or "expansion" are unlikely to win approval. Instead, entrepreneurs should use more detailed descriptions such as "to modernize production facilities by purchasing five new, more efficient looms that will boost productivity by 12 percent" or "to rebuild merchandise inventory for fall sales peak, beginning in early summer." Entrepreneurs should state the precise amount requested and include relevant backup data, such as vendor estimates of costs or past production levels. Entrepreneurs should not hesitate to request the amount of money needed but should not inflate the amount anticipating the financial officer to "talk them down." Remember: Lenders and investors are normally very familiar with industry cost structures.

Another important element of the loan or investment proposal is the repayment schedule and exit strategy. A lender's main consideration in granting a loan is the reassurance that the applicant will repay, whereas an investor's major concern is earning a satisfactory rate of return. Financial projections must reflect a company's ability to repay loans and produce adequate returns. Without this proof, a request for funding stands little chance of being approved. It is necessary for the entrepreneur to produce tangible evidence showing the ability to repay loans or to generate attractive returns. "Plan an exit for the investor," advises the owner of a financial consulting company. "Generally, the equity investor's objective with early stage funding is to earn a 30% to 50% annual return over the life of the investment. To enhance the investor's interest in your enterprise, show how they can 'cash out' perhaps through a public offering or acquisition."[25]

Finally, an entrepreneur should have a timetable for implementing the proposed plan. He should present a schedule showing the estimated start-up date for the project and noting any significant milestones along the way. Entrepreneurs tend to be optimistic, so document how and why the timetable of events is realistic.

There is a difference between a *working* business plan—the one the entrepreneur is using to guide her business—and the *presentation* business plan—the one she is using to attract capital. Although coffee rings and penciled-in changes in a working plan don't matter (in fact, they're a good sign that the entrepreneur is actually using the plan), they have no place on a plan going to someone outside the company. A plan is usually the tool that an entrepreneur uses to make a first impression on potential lenders and investors. To make sure that impression is a favorable one, an entrepreneur should follow these tips:

- Realize that first impressions are crucial. Make sure the plan has an attractive (not necessarily expensive) cover.
- Make sure the plan is free of spelling and grammatical errors and "typos." It is a professional document and should look like one.
- Make it visually appealing. Use color charts, figures, and diagrams to illustrate key points. Don't get carried away, however, and end up with a "comic book" plan.
- Include a table of contents with page numbers to allow readers to navigate the plan easily. Reviewers should be able to look through a plan and quickly locate the sections they want to see.
- Make it interesting. Boring plans seldom get read.
- A plan must prove that the business will make money. In one survey of lenders, investors, and financial advisors, 81 percent said that, first and foremost, a plan should prove that a venture will earn a profit.[26] Start-ups do not necessarily have to be profitable immediately, but sooner or later (preferably sooner), they must make money.
- Use computer spreadsheets to generate financial forecasts. They allow entrepreneurs to perform valuable "what if" (sensitivity) analysis in just seconds.
- *Always* include cash flow projections. Entrepreneurs sometimes focus excessively on their proposed venture's profit forecasts and ignore cash flow projections. Although profitability is important, lenders and investors are much more interested in cash flow because they know that's where the money to pay them back or to cash them out comes from.
- The ideal plan is "crisp," long enough to say what it should but not so long that it is a chore to read. It is a good idea, however, to prepare a five- to ten-page summary that features the highlights of your plan for investors who do not want to wade through the detail of a full-blown plan.
- Tell the truth. Absolute honesty is always critical when preparing a business plan.

What Lenders and Investors Look For in a Business Plan

LO 4

Explain the "five *C*'s of credit" and why they are important to potential lenders and investors reading business plans.

Banks usually are not a new venture's sole source of capital because a bank's return is limited by the interest rate it negotiates, but its risk could be the entire amount of the loan if the new business fails. Once a business is operational and has established a financial track record, however, banks become a regular source of financing. For this reason the small business owner needs to be aware of the criteria lenders and investors use when evaluating the creditworthiness of entrepreneurs seeking financing. Lenders and investors refer to these criteria as the **five *C*s of credit**: capital, capacity, collateral, character, and conditions.

Capital

A small business must have a stable capital base before any lender is willing to grant a loan. Otherwise the lender would be making, in effect, a capital investment in the business. Most banks refuse to make loans that are capital investments because the potential for return on the investment is limited strictly to the interest on the loan, and the potential loss would probably exceed the reward. In fact, the most common reasons that banks give for rejecting small business loan applications are undercapitalization or too much debt. Banks expect a small company to have an equity base of investment by the owner(s) that will help support the venture during times of financial strain, which are common during the start-up and growth phases of a business. Lenders and investors see capital as a risk-sharing strategy with entrepreneurs.

Capacity

A synonym for capacity is cash flow. Lenders and investors must be convinced of the firm's ability to meet its regular financial obligations and to repay loans, and that takes cash. In Chapter 9, you will learn that more small businesses fail from lack of cash than from lack of profit. It is possible for a company to be showing a profit and still have no cash—that is, to be bankrupt. Lenders expect small businesses to pass the test of liquidity, especially for short-term loans. Potential lenders and investors examine closely a small company's cash flow position to decide whether it has the capacity necessary to survive until it can sustain itself.

Collateral

Collateral includes any assets an entrepreneur pledges to a lender as security for repayment of a loan. If the company defaults on the loan, the lender has the right to sell the collateral and use the proceeds to satisfy the loan. Typically, banks make very few unsecured loans (those not backed by collateral) to business start-ups. Bankers view the entrepreneurs' willingness to pledge collateral (personal or business assets) as an indication of their dedication to making the venture a success. A sound business plan can improve a banker's attitude toward venture.

Character

Before extending a loan to or making an investment in a small business, lenders and investors must be satisfied with an entrepreneur's character. The evaluation of character frequently is based on intangible factors such as honesty, integrity, competence, polish, determination, intelligence, and ability. Although the qualities judged are abstract, this evaluation plays a critical role in the decision to put money into a business or not.

Lenders and investors know that most small businesses fail because of incompetent management, and they try to avoid extending loans to high-risk entrepreneurs. A solid business plan and a polished presentation by the entrepreneur can go far in convincing the banker of the owner's capability.

Conditions

The conditions surrounding a funding request also affect an entrepreneur's chances of receiving financing. Lenders and investors consider factors relating to a business's operation such as potential growth in the market, competition, location, strengths, weaknesses, opportunities, and threats. Again, the best way to provide this relevant information is in a business plan. Another important condition influencing the banker's decision is the shape of the overall economy, including interest rate levels, inflation rate, and demand for money. Although these factors are beyond an entrepreneur's control, they still are an important component in a banker's decision.

The higher a small business scores on these five Cs, the greater its chance will be of receiving a loan.

Table 4.2 describes eight mistakes that entrepreneurs often make in their business plans.

five C's of credit
criteria lenders and investors use to evaluate the creditworthiness of entrepreneurs seeking financing: capital, capacity, collateral, character, and conditions.

TABLE 4.2 Don't Make These Business Plan Mistakes

Profit Dynamics Inc. conducted a survey of 500 of the most active venture capital companies in the United States, and the results revealed eight critical mistakes that entrepreneurs most often commit in their business plans.

Mistake 1: Failure to explain the business opportunity clearly. Too many entrepreneurs fail to explain why their business ideas make sense and why their business models will be successful. This is one reason that a concise, meaningful elevator pitch that tells a compelling story is so important.

Mistake 2: Unrealistic projections. Entrepreneurs tend to be optimistic, sometimes overly so, and it shows up in the form of unrealistic financial projections. Make sure that your forecasts are *realistic* by comparing them to industry averages and verifying them with people who have experience in the industry.

Mistake 3: Overly simplistic assumptions. Some business plans gloss over complex areas that are vital to business success. For instance, if a reliable supply chain is a key to your company's success, make sure that your plan includes a strategy for assembling one.

Mistake 4: Weak competitor analysis. One sure path to having your business plan rejected is to say, "We have no competition." Experienced business people know better! Other entrepreneurs run into problems when they underestimate their competitors' strengths. Take the time to identify your primary competitors and to learn about what makes them successful and where their weaknesses lie.

Mistake 5: Failure to describe the company's competitive advantage. A business plan must explain the way in which a company will set itself apart from the competition. What factors will give your business an edge in attracting and retaining customers?

Mistake 6: A sloppy plan that contains errors. A business plan is a reflection of its creator. A plan that is filled with errors and mistakes sends up warning signals to potential lenders and investors. Make sure your document is polished and professional.

Mistake 7: Exaggerating the qualifications of the management team. Venture capitalists invest in management, and they investigate thoroughly the backgrounds of the managers in the start-up companies in which they are considering investing. A business plan should highlight the management team's experience and accomplishments but should not overstate them. Few mistakes will destroy a deal faster.

Mistake 8: A plan that is incomplete. Venture capitalists tend to trash business plans that are missing key sections or that have insufficient financial data. Although every entrepreneur should tell the story of his or her business in a unique fashion, every plan should include the basic elements described in this chapter.

Source: Adapted from "Don't Make These Mistakes in Your Business Plans," The Capital Connection, 2008, http://www.capital-connection.com/vcsurvey.html.

LO 5

Describe the keys to making an effective business plan presentation.

Making the Business Plan Presentation

Lenders and investors are favorably impressed by entrepreneurs who are informed and prepared when requesting a loan or investment. When attempting to secure funds from professional venture capitalists or private investors, the written business plan almost always precedes the opportunity to meet "face-to-face". Typically, an entrepreneur's time for presenting her business opportunity will be limited. (When presenting a plan to a venture capital forum, the allotted time is usually no more than 15 to 20 minutes, and at some forums, the time limit is a mere five or six minutes.) When the opportunity arises, an entrepreneur must be well prepared. It is important to rehearse, rehearse, and then rehearse more. It is a mistake to begin by leading the audience into a long-winded explanation about the technology on which the product or service is based. Within minutes most of the audience will be lost and so is any chance the entrepreneur has of obtaining the necessary financing for her new venture. Entrepreneur-turned-venture-capitalists Guy Kawasaki is famous for his 10/20/30 Rule: A business plan presentation should have ten slides, last no more than 20 minutes, and contain no font smaller than 30 points.

Some helpful tips for making a business plan presentation to potential lenders and investors include:

- Demonstrate enthusiasm about the venture, but don't be overemotional.
- Know your audience thoroughly, and work to establish a rapport with them.
- "Hook" investors quickly with an up-front explanation of the new venture, its opportunities, and the anticipated benefits to them.
- Hit the highlights; specific questions will bring out the details later. Don't get caught up in too much detail in early meetings with lenders and investors.
- Keep your presentation simple by limiting it to the two or three (no more) major points you must get across to your audience.
- Avoid the use of technological terms that will likely be above most of the audience. Do at least one rehearsal before someone who has no special technical training. Tell him to stop you anytime he does not understand what you are talking about. When this occurs (and it likely will), rewrite that portion of your presentation.
- Use visual aids. They make it easier for people to follow your presentation, but do not make the visual aids the "star" of the presentation. They should merely support and enhance your message.
- Close by reinforcing the nature of the opportunity. Be sure you have sold the benefits the investors will realize when the business is a success.
- Be prepared for questions. In many cases, there is seldom time for a long "Q&A" session, but interested investors may want to get you aside to discuss the details of the plan.
- Follow up with every investor to whom you make a presentation. Don't sit back and wait; be proactive. They have what you need—investment capital. Demonstrate that you have confidence in your plan and have the initiative necessary to run a business successfully.

The accompanying "Hands On: How To" feature describes the 12 questions that every business plan presentation must answer to convince potential investors to put their money into a business venture.

HANDS ON... HOW TO

Answer Twelve Questions That Your Business Plan Presentation MUST Address If You Are to Get Financing

Addressing the following 12 questions in your business plan presentation increases the probability of landing the capital your start-up business needs.

1. **What is the problem?** A clear illustration of the problem that your company intends to solve is essential to a successful presentation. During a recent business plan competition, Raymond Sekula, founder of NeuroBank, told potential investors that his business can extract neural stem cells through a spinal tap procedure and store them for use in cutting-edge treatments later in life for individuals who experience brain injuries, strokes, or diseases such as Alzheimer's or Parkinson's.

2. **What is your company's solution to the problem?** How does your company's product or service provide a unique or improved solution to the problem? Your presentation should emphasize the competitive advantage that your business offers. Lenders and investors shy away from businesses that offer "me-too" solutions that offer no benefits over existing solutions to a problem. Ajay Chawan, founder of Saatwic

Foods, invented a food additive that cuts the human body's absorption of calories from carbohydrates by 50 percent, a feature that gives his company the potential to differentiate its products from those of other companies in the eyes of calorie-counting customers and diabetics.

3. **What is your company's business model?** In other words, what is your strategy for building a successful and sustainable business? A company's strategy determines its success in its attempt to capitalize on a market opportunity. The wrong strategy, even though a management team may execute it to perfection, will cause a company to fail every time. Be sure that your presentation shows how your company will generate sales and a profit, both of which are very important to potential lenders and investors.

4. **What is your company's underlying technology or "magic"?** Has your company developed unique technology, approach to the market, or some other "magic"? If so, explain it in simple, nontechnical terms. Do you have patents, trademarks, or copyrights to protect the "magic" component of your company? How long will it take competitors to replicate your company's "magic"?

5. **What is your company's marketing strategy?** Who are the target customers at whom your company is aiming its products or services? How much do you know about them?

What drives their purchase decisions? How will you reach them? Although market research reports are important and can provide the foundation of a marketing plan, convincing potential lenders and investors requires providing feedback or firm commitments from actual customers. What surveys or test marketing efforts have you conducted? Lenders and investors want solid proof that a strong base of customers exists for your company's product or service. The marketing strategy question is the one that most entrepreneurs fail to answer sufficiently. Don't let it happen to you.

6. **What is your company's sales strategy?** In other words, how will you connect with (and stay connected with) your customers? One helpful tool when answering this question is to explain how you will communicate your company's unique selling proposition (USP), the key customer benefit of a product or service that sets it apart from the competition, to your customers and why it matters to them. Is your product or service a luxury, a "nice to have," or a "must have"? Which channels of distribution will your company use? How important are repeat sales? What will you do to capture them?

7. **Who are your competitors and what can you learn from them?** Every business has competitors, and entrepreneurs who claim that their companies face no competition make lenders and investors nervous. What do your competitors do well? What can your company do better than the competition? Be specific. When discussing the competition, be sure to point out (again) your company's competitive advantage.

8. **Who are the members of your team and what makes them uniquely qualified to create this business?** Lenders and investors want to see a sound business strategy aimed at solving a real customer problem, but what they really put their money in is the management team. In your presentation, be sure to emphasize your management team's qualifications and experience. Have you or your co-founders launched other companies? If your organization chart has holes in it, be honest about it but be prepared to address how you plan to fill those holes. Inexperienced entrepreneurs should consider creating a board of advisors who can bring experience and expertise to the venture. Sarah Endline, founder of Sweetriot, a company that sells gourmet candy (cacao beans covered in dark chocolate) in attractive tin canisters through several large retailers, hired an experienced executive from Sony's Zomba music label because she believes that his experience in a creative industry fits perfectly with the creative culture at her start-up company.

9. **What are your financial forecasts?** Business plans once included five years of financial forecasts. Today potential lenders and investors know that any long-range financial forecasts usually are just guesses and are unreliable. You should include a summary of your company's income statements for three years (no more), focusing on sales, major expenses, and net income. You also should demonstrate an understanding of the importance of cash flow to your company's future. Make sure that all of your financial forecasts are realistic; otherwise, you lose all credibility with lenders and investors—and with it all hope of receiving financing.

10. **How much capital will your company require now and three years in the future?** How much money have you raised to date? Where did it come from? How much money does your company need and how do you intend to use it? At Sweetriot, founder Sarah Endline recently raised $1.5 million from private investors ("angels") and plans to use the money to boost her company's visibility by creating partnerships with other outlets, including *Good* magazine. Make sure that you explain how lenders' and investors' money will add value to your business.

11. **What is the exit strategy?** Before potential lenders and investors put money into a business, they want to know how they will get it back out—preferably with an attractive rate of return. Depending on the type of investor with whom you are dealing (make sure you know!), the time frame for executing the exit strategy may be from three to ten years or more. Two common exit strategies include selling the company to a larger business and making an initial public offering (IPO), but only a handful of small companies will qualify for the latter.

12. **What are the risk factors?** Every business involves risk. Entrepreneurs must walk a fine line with this question, however. Dwelling too much on the risks associated with the business can dissuade potential lenders and investors. Ignoring the risks altogether makes an entrepreneur appear to be unprepared, unrealistic, or dishonest. What market, financial, technological, and management risks does your company face?

Once you have answered these 12 questions, it is time for you to summarize the key points of your presentation (This is your "elevator pitch") and to "make the ask." In other words, this is your opportunity to extend a call to action to the potential lenders and investors in your audience.

A presentation that addresses these twelve questions should take between 20 and 30 minutes, which for most potential lenders and investors is in the ideal range.

Sources: Adapted from David E. Gumpert, "Impress Potential Investors in 12 Steps," *Business Week*, January 7, 2008, http://www.businessweek .com/smallbiz/content/jan2008/sb2008017_066659.htm?chan=smallbiz_spe cial+report+ — +the+abcs+of+business+plans_the+abcs+of+business+plans; Adriana Gardella, "Tickets, Anyone?" *FSB*, May 2008, pp. 61-67; Guy Kawasaki, "Rule of Thumb," *Entrepreneur*, May 2008, p. 44.

Conclusion

Although there is no guarantee of success when launching a business, the best way to protect against failure is create a business plan. A good plan serves as an entrepreneurial strategic compass that keeps a business on course as it travels into an uncertain future. Will the business that an entrepreneur actually creates look exactly like the company described in the business plan? Of course not. One experienced entrepreneur who has created several business plans for the companies that he has launched says, "A start-up business plan is a piece of good fiction filled with great ideas."[27] The *real* value in preparing a business plan is not so much in the finished document itself but in the *process* the entrepreneur goes through to create it, a process in which he or she learns how to compete successfully in the marketplace. In addition, a solid plan is essential to raising the capital needed to start a business; lenders and investors demand it.

YOU BE THE CONSULTANT

The Presentation

Dick Bardow sat quietly in his car, pondering why he had failed to convince Pat Guinn, managing partner of Next Century Venture Capital, to provide the start-up capital he needed to launch the business that would present his new high-tech medical invention. Bardow had spent the past three-and-a-half years researching and developing the concept, and now that he had a product in hand, he was ready to take it to the market. The idea for Bardow's new venture had been simmering for many years during his stints as a researcher for a major medical lab and as a technical advisor for a medical products company. Bardow had learned a great deal about use of the end product in his technical job, which he took after earning a Master's degree in Biomedical Engineering. But it was during his tenure at the medical lab that Bardow saw the importance of staying on the cutting edge of technology in the field of medicine. He also saw the tremendous profit potential of successful medical products.

Driving home, Bardow replayed his meeting with Guinn in his mind. "How could those venture capitalists have missed the tremendous opportunity right in front of them?" he mused. During his 45-minute meeting with Guinn and her staff, Bardow had spent 30 minutes explaining how the technology had evolved over time, how he had developed the product, and why it was technologically superior to anything currently on the market. "I've got them where I want then, now," he remembers thinking. "They can't help but see the incredible power of this technology." Throughout his corporate career, Bardow had earned a reputation for his ability to explain abstract ideas and highly technical concepts to his fellow scientists. Over the years, he had made dozens of presentations at scientific professional meeting, all of which were well received.

Bardow had to admit, however, that he was puzzled by all of the questions Guinn had asked him toward the end of their meeting. They weren't at all what he was expecting! "She never asked a single question about my product, its design, the technology behind it, or the patent I have pending," he muttered. He remembered her questioning him about a "market analysis" and how and to whom he planned to market his product. "How foolish!" he thought. "You can't forecast exact sales for a new product. Once this product is on the market and the medical industry sees what it can do, we'll have all the sales we'll need—and more." Bardow was convinced that Guinn simply didn't understand that new, innovative products create their own markets. "I've seen it dozens of times," he said. Dick was beginning to believe that venture capital firms were too focused on revenues, profits, and return on investment. "Don't they know that those things are outcomes?" he thought. "They come…in time."

1. Identify the possible problems with Dick Bardow's presentation of his business plan to Pat Guinn and the other venture capitalists.
2. Should potential lenders and investors evaluate new ventures that are based on cutting-edge technology differently from other business ventures? Explain.
3. List at least five suggestions you would make to Dick Bardow to improve his business plan and his presentation of it.

Business Plan Format

Although every company's business plan will be unique, reflecting its individual circumstances, certain elements are universal. The following outline summarizes these components:

I. Executive Summary (not to exceed two pages)
   A. Company name, address, and phone number
   B. Name(s), addresses, and phone number(s) of all key people
   C. Brief description of the business, its products and services, and the customer problems they solve
   D. Brief overview of the market for your products and services
   E. Brief overview of the strategies that will make your firm a success
   F. Brief description of the managerial and technical experience of key people
   G. Brief statement of the financial request and how the money will be used
   H. Charts or tables showing highlights of financial forecasts

II. Vision and Mission statement
   A. Entrepreneur's vision for the company
   B. "What business are we in?"
   C. Values and principles on which the business stands
   D. What makes the business unique? What is the source of its competitive advantage?

III. Company History (for existing businesses only)
   A. Company founding
   B. Financial and operational highlights
   C. Significant achievements

IV. Business and Industry Profile
  A. Industry Analysis
      1. Industry background and overview
      2. Significant trends
      3. Growth rate
      4. Key success factors in the industry
  B. Outlook for the future
  C. Stage of growth (start-up, growth, maturity)
  D. Company goals and objectives
      1. Operational
      2. Financial
      3. Other

V. Business Strategy
  A. Desired image and position in market
  B. SWOT analysis
      1. Strengths
      2. Weaknesses
      3. Opportunities
      4. Threats
  C. Competitive strategy
      1. Cost-leadership
      2. Differentiation
      3. Focus

VI. Company Products and Services
  A. Description
      1. Product or service features
      2. Customer benefits
      3. Warranties and guarantees
      4. Unique Selling Proposition (USP)
  B. Patent or trademark protection
  C. Description of production process (if applicable)
      1. Raw materials
      2. Costs
      3. Key suppliers
  D. Future product or service offerings

VII. Marketing Strategy
  A. Target market
      1. Complete demographic profile
      2. Other significant customer characteristics
  B. Customers' motivation to buy
  C. Market size and trends
      1. How large is the market?
      2. Is it growing or shrinking? How fast?
  D. Advertising and promotion
      1. Media used—reader, viewer, listener profiles
      2. Media costs
      3. Frequency of usage
      4. Plans for generating publicity
  E. Pricing
      1. Cost structure
          a. Fixed
          b. Variable

      2. Desired image in market

      3. Comparison against competitors' prices

   F. Distribution strategy

      1. Channels of distribution used

      2. Sales techniques and incentives

VIII. Location and Layout

   A. Location

      1. Demographic analysis of location vs. target customer profile

      2. Traffic count

      3. Lease/Rental rates

      4. Labor needs and supply

      5. Wage rates

   B. Layout

      1. Size requirements

      2. Americans with Disabilities compliance

      3. Ergonomic issues

      4. Layout plan (suitable for an appendix)

IX. Competitor Analysis

   A. Existing competitors

      1. Who are they? Create a competitive profile matrix.

      2. Strengths

      3. Weaknesses

   B. Potential competitors: Companies that might enter the market

      1. Who are they?

      2. Impact on your business if they enter

X. Description of management team

   A. Key managers and employees

      1. Their backgrounds

      2. Experience, skills, and know-how they bring to the company

   B. Resumes of key managers and employees (suitable for an appendix)

XI. Plan of Operation

   A. Form of ownership chosen and reasoning

   B. Company structure (organization chart)

   C. Decision making authority

   D. Compensation and benefits packages

XII. Financial Forecasts (suitable for an appendix)

   A. Financial statements

      1. Income statement

      2. Balance sheet

      3. Cash flow statement

   B. Break-even analysis

   C. Ratio analysis with comparison to industry standards (most applicable to existing businesses)

XIII. Loan or Investment Proposal

   A. Amount requested

   B. Purpose and uses of funds

   C. Repayment or "cash out" schedule (exit strategy)

   D. Timetable for implementing plan and launching the business

XIV. Appendices—Supporting documentation, including market research, financial statements, organization charts, resumes, and other items.

Chapter Summary

1. Discuss the steps involved in subjecting a business idea to a feasibility analysis.

A feasibility analysis consists of three interrelated components: an industry and market feasibility analysis, a product or service feasibility analysis, and a financial feasibility analysis. The goal of the feasibility analysis is to determine whether or not an entrepreneur's idea is a viable foundation for creating a successful business.

2. Explain why every entrepreneur should create a business plan.

A business plan serves two essential functions. First and most important, it guides the company's operations by charting its future course and devising a strategy for following it. The second function of the business plan is to attract lenders and investors. Applying for loans or attempting to attract investors without a solid business plan rarely attracts needed capital

3. Explain the benefits of preparing a plan.

Preparing a sound business plan clearly requires time and effort, but the benefits greatly exceed the costs. Building the plan forces a potential entrepreneur to look at her business idea in the harsh light of reality. It also requires the owner to assess the venture's chances of success more objectively. A well-assembled plan helps prove to outsiders that a business idea can be successful.

The *real* value in preparing a business plan is not so much in the plan itself as it is in the process the entrepreneur goes through to create the plan. Although the finished product is useful, the process of building a plan requires an entrepreneur to subject his idea to an objective, critical evaluation. What the entrepreneur learns about his company, its target market, its financial requirements, and other factors can be essential to making the venture a success.

4. Describe the elements of a solid business plan.

Although a business plan should be unique and tailor-made to suit the particular needs of a small company, it should cover these basic elements: an executive summary, a mission statement, a company history, a business and industry profile, a description of the company's

business strategy, a profile of its products or services, a statement explaining its marketing strategy, a competitor analysis, owners' and officers' resumes, a plan of operation, financial data, and the loan or investment proposal.

5. Understand the keys to making an effective business plan presentation.

Lenders and investors are favorably impressed by entrepreneurs who are informed and prepared when requesting a loan or investment.

Tips include: Demonstrate enthusiasm about the venture, but don't be overemotional; "hook" investors quickly with an up-front explanation of the new venture, its opportunities, and the anticipated benefits to them; use visual aids; hit the highlights of your venture; don't get caught up in too much detail in early meetings with lenders and investors; avoid the use of technological terms that will likely be above most of the audience; rehearse your presentation before giving it; close by reinforcing the nature of the opportunity; and be prepared for questions.

6. Explain the "Five Cs of Credit" and why they are important to potential lenders and investors reading business plans.

Small business owners needs to be aware of the criteria bankers use in evaluating the credit-worthiness of loan applicants—the five Cs of credit: capital, capacity, collateral, character, and conditions.

Capital—Lenders expect small businesses to have an equity base of investment by the owner(s) that will help support the venture during times of financial strain.

Capacity—A synonym for capacity is cash flow. The bank must be convinced of the firm's ability to meet its regular financial obligations and to repay the bank loan, and that takes cash.

Collateral—Collateral includes any assets the owner pledges to the bank as security for repayment of the loan.

Character—Before approving a loan to a small business, the banker must be satisfied with the owner's character.

Conditions—The conditions—interest rates, the health of the nation's economy, industry growth rates, etc.—surrounding a loan request also affect the owner's chance of receiving funds.

Discussion Questions

1. Explain the steps involved in conducting a feasibility analysis.
2. Why should an entrepreneur develop a business plan?
3. Describe the major components of a business plan.
4. How can an entrepreneur seeking funds to launch a business convince potential lenders and investors

that a market for the product or service really does exist?
5. How would you prepare to make a formal presentation of your business plan to a venture capital forum?
6. What are the five Cs of credit? How does a potential lender use them to evaluate a loan request?

Business PlanPro™

This chapter discusses the importance of testing your business concept. Does the idea represent a viable business concept? A comprehensive business plan can help answer this question.

Business Plan Exercises

The following exercises will assist you in validating or challenging your business concept. You will also begin to work through the situation analysis part of your plan to better understand your market. Be as objective as you work through these exercises. Rely on your ability to gather information and make realistic assessments and projections

On the Web

Go to http://www.pearsonhighered.com/scarborough to the Business Plan Resource tab. If you have not done this yet, find the Standard Industry Classification (SIC) code associated with your industry. You will find a link in the SIC code information that will connect you to a resource. Explore the information and links that are available to you on that site to learn more about the size of the industry and its growth, trends, and issues. Based on the industry you have selected and the associated SIC code, apply Porter's five forces model. Consider the five forces—the bargaining power of buyers, the power of suppliers, the threat of new entrants, the threat of substitute products, and the level of rivalry. You will find additional information on Porter's five forces model in the Strategy section of this same site. Look for information on the Web that may assist you with this analysis. Based on this information, how attractive do you consider this industry? How would you assess the opportunity this industry presents? Does this information encourage you to become involved in this industry, or does it highlight significant challenges?

In the Software

Your text may include Business Feasibility Analysis Pro. This software steps you through assessing the feasibility of your business concept. It addresses the overall feasibility of your product or service, helps you to conduct an industry assessment, reviews your management skills, and takes you through a preliminary financial analysis. The software provides initial "feedback" based on your input of four components of the feasibility analysis with a numeric assessment. You can then export this information directly into *Business Plan Pro™*. *Business Plan Pro™* will also help assess the feasibility of your business concept in the areas of product, service, market organization, and financial feasibility. For example, you can enter the initial capital requirements for the business in the start-up and expenses section.

Combined with a sales forecast, the software calculates your return on investment. If you have these estimates available, enter those into your plan. Next, refer to the Profit and Loss statement. At what point, if any, does that statement indicate that your venture will begin generating a profit based on those forecasts and expenses. In what year does that occur? Do you find that amount of time acceptable? If you are seeking investors, will they find that timeframe acceptable? Is the return on investment promising, and does this venture merit taking on the associated level of risk? We will talk more about these sections of your plan as you progress through the chapters.

Sample Plans

Review the start-up sample plans called InteliChild.com and Corporate Fitness.

1. What was the total amount of the start-up investment for each of these plans?
2. What is the monthy revenue break-even point?
3. What is the total profit that was projected in the year following this point?
4. Based on the break-even point, which of these ventures do you find most attractive?
5. Based the profit projections by year three, which plan appears to offer the greatest financial potential?
6. How does the scale and potential of these two opportunities compare to those in your plan?

Building Your Business Plan

Review the information in the Market Analysis section. Continue to build your information in this section based on the outline. You will find information to help project your expenses in the Sales Strategy section. Enter numbers directly in the table itself or use the wizard that will pop up to assist you. Manipulate the visual graph to build that forecast based on a visual growth curve or enter the actual data. If your business is a start-up venture, your expenses will include those figures along with your ongoing expense projections. Don't worry about the accuracy of your projections. Get some numbers entered into the software; you can change those numbers at any time. Look at the Profit and Loss statement. Do you find that acceptable? At what point in time will your business begin making a profit? As you build your plan, check to see that the outline and structure of your plan are a good fit to tell your story. Although the outline in *Business Plan Pro™* is not identical to the outline presented in the chapter, by right clicking on the outline, you can move, add, and delete any topic you choose to modify the plan you create.

Beyond the Classroom...

1. Contact a local entrepreneur who recently launched a business. Did he or she prepare a business plan before starting the company? Why or why not? If the entrepreneur did not create a plan, is he or she considering doing so now? If the entrepreneur did create a plan, what benefits did he or she gain from the process? How long did it take to complete the plan? How did he or she put the plan to use during the start-up phase? Does he or she intend to keep the business plan updated? What advice does he or she have to offer another entrepreneur about to begin writing a business plan?

2. Interview a local banker who has experience in making loans to small businesses. Ask him or her the following questions.
   a. How important is a well-prepared business plan?
   b. How important is a smooth presentation?
   c. How does the banker evaluate the owner's character?
   d. How heavily does the bank weigh the five Cs of credit?
   e. What percentage of small business owners are well prepared to request a bank loan?
   f. What are the most common reasons the bank rejects small business loan applications?

3. Interview a small business owner who has requested a bank loan or an equity investment from external sources. Ask him or her these questions:
   a. Did you prepare a written business plan before approaching the financial officer?
   b. If the answer is "yes" to part a, did you have outside or professional help in preparing it?
   c. How many times have your requests for additional funds been rejected? What reasons were given for the rejection?

(Morris)/CORBIS All Rights Reserved

CHAPTER 5

Forms of Business Ownership

A friendship founded on business is a good deal better than a business founded on friendship.
—*John D. Rockefeller*

Over a long distance, you learn about the strength of your horse; over a long time, you learn about the character of your friend.
—*Chinese Proverb*

Learning Objectives

On completion of this chapter, you will be able to:

1. Explain the advantages and the disadvantages of the three major forms of ownership: the sole proprietorship, the partnership, and the corporation.

2. Discuss the advantages and the disadvantages of the S corporation, the limited liability company, the professional corporation, and the joint venture.

Once an entrepreneur makes the decision to launch a business, one of the first issues he or she faces is choosing a form of ownership. Too often entrepreneurs invest insufficient time and effort evaluating the impact that the various forms of ownership will have on them and on their businesses. They simply select a form of ownership by default or choose the form that appears to be most popular at the time. Choosing a form of ownership is important because it is a decision that has far-reaching effects for both the entrepreneur and the business. Although the decision is not irreversible, changing from one ownership form to another can be difficult, time consuming, complicated, and expensive. In many instances, switching an existing business from one form of ownership to another can trigger onerous tax consequences for the owners. Therefore, it is important for entrepreneurs to get it right the first time.

There is no one "best" form of ownership. The form of ownership that is best for one entrepreneur may not be suitable at all for another. Choosing the "right" form of ownership means that entrepreneurs must understand the characteristics of each form and how well those characteristics match their business and personal circumstances. Only then can an entrepreneur make an informed decision about a form of ownership. "Choose a structure that gives you the protection you need but with as few rules as possible," advises one attorney. "Entrepreneurs should move up the complexity chain only when it is necessary because each step up means more requirements and more paperwork."[1] The following are some of the most important issues entrepreneurs should consider when they are evaluating the various forms of ownership:

Tax considerations. The amount of net income an entrepreneur expects the business to generate and the tax bill the owner must pay are important factors when choosing a form of ownership. The graduated tax rates that apply to each form of ownership, the government's constant tinkering with the tax code, and the year-to-year fluctuations in a company's income make some forms of ownership more attractive than others.

Liability exposure. Certain forms of ownership offer business owners greater protection from personal liability that might result from financial problems, faulty products, and a host of other difficulties. Entrepreneurs must decide the extent to which they are willing to assume personal responsibility for their companies' financial obligations. Two entrepreneurs who started a company with a portable climbing wall formed a limited liability company (LLC) to limit their personal liability exposure because of the high-risk nature of their business.

Start-up and future capital requirements. Forms of ownership differ in their ability to raise start-up capital. Depending on how much capital an entrepreneur needs and where he or she plans to get it, some forms are superior to others. In addition, as a business grows, so does its appetite for capital, and some forms of ownership make it easier to attract external growth capital than others.

Control. By choosing certain forms of ownership, an entrepreneur automatically gives up some control over the company. Entrepreneurs must decide early on how much control they are willing to sacrifice in exchange for help from other people to build a successful business.

Managerial ability. Entrepreneurs must assess their skills and abilities to manage a business effectively. If they lack ability or experience in key areas, they may choose a form of ownership that allows them to bring in other owners who can provide the necessary skills for the company to succeed.

Business goals. How big and how profitable an entrepreneur plans for the business to become will influence the form of ownership chosen. Businesses often switch forms of ownership as they grow, but moving from some formats to others can be extremely complex and expensive.

Management succession plans. When choosing a form of ownership, business owners must look ahead to the day when they will pass their companies on to the next generation or to a buyer. Some forms of ownership make this transition much easier than others.

Cost of formation. Some forms of ownership are much more costly and involved to create. Entrepreneurs must weight carefully the benefits and the costs of the particular form they choose.

When it comes to organizing their businesses, entrepreneurs have a wide choice of forms of ownership, including a sole proprietorship, a general partnership, a limited partnership, a corporation, an S corporation, and a limited liability company. Figure 5.1 provides a breakdown of these forms of ownership. Notice that sole proprietorships account for the greatest percentage of businesses, but corporations generate the largest portion of business sales and profits. This chapter discusses the key features of these various forms of ownership, beginning with the three most basic forms (from simplest to most complex): the sole proprietorship, the partnership, and the corporation.

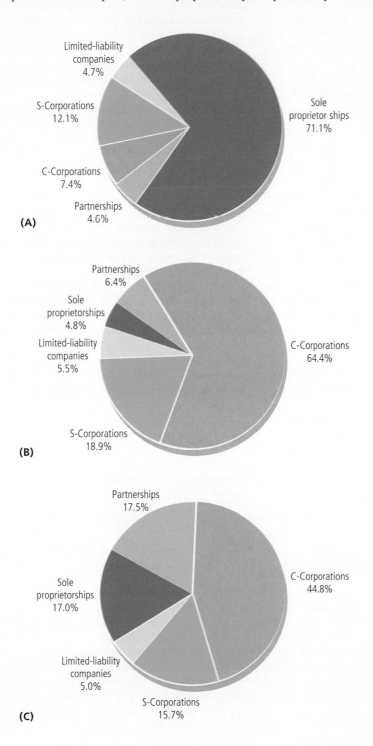

FIGURE 5.1

Forms of Business Ownership (A) Percentage of Business; (B) Percentage of Sales; (C) Percentage of Profits

HANDS ON... HOW TO

Come Up with the Perfect Moniker for Your Business

When Mike Rohan started a financial software company in 2002, he came up with what he thought was a clever business name: Aucent. Within two years, Rohan realized that the company's name had become a liability. It failed to suggest to potential customers exactly what Aucent could do for them, it was hard to spell, its pronunciation was unclear, and it was not particularly memorable. Rohan decided to hire a San Francisco naming company, Igor International, to help him come up with a better name for his company. After much research and analysis, Rohan settled on Rivet. Because it is reminiscent of the sound that a frog makes ("ribbet"), the name has a friendly tone and is easy to remember. Before adopting the new name, Rohan tested it on existing customers and others; almost all were enthusiastic about it.

For another company in Stamford, Connecticut, the choice of a business name became the company's worst enemy. GHB Marketing Communications started getting numerous e-mails and phone calls requesting a certain product. Sounds harmless, right? Wrong! The product that many of those customers were seeking was GHB, an illegal drug also known as ecstasy. "Imagine having a 30-year-old company named LSD, Inc. in the late 60s," explains company President Mark Bruce. "Then you can begin to understand what we went through." The new name (HiTechPR) cost the owners $20,000.

Choosing a memorable name can be one of the most fun—and most challenging—aspects of starting a business. It also is an extremely important task because it has long-term implications, is the single most visible attribute of a company, and has the capacity to either engage or repel customers. The business name is the first connection that many customers will have with a company, and it should create an appropriate image in their minds. "A name is a cornerstone for branding," says the president of one small design firm specializing in branding. If done properly, a company's name will portray the business's personality, will stand out in a crowd, and will stick in the minds of consumers. Large companies may spend hundreds of thousands of dollars in their search for just the right name. Although entrepreneurs don't have the resources to enable them to spend that kind of money finding the ideal name, they can use the following process to come up with the perfect name for their businesses.

1. Decide on the image you want your company to project to customers, suppliers, bankers, the press, the community, and others. Do you want to create an air of sophistication, the suggestion of a bargain, a sense of adventure, the implication of trustworthiness and dependability, or a spirit of fun and whimsy? The right name can go a long way toward communicating the right image for a company.

2. Make a list of your competitors' business names. The idea is *not* to borrow from their ideas but to try to come up with a name that is unique. Do you notice any trends among competitors' names? What are the similarities? What are the differences?

3. Work with a group of the most creative people you know to brainstorm (refer to Chapter 2 for details on the brainstorming

process) potential names for your business. One entrepreneur called on 10 customers and 10 vendors to help him come up with a business name. Don't worry about quality at this point; the goal is to generate a large quantity of names. The idea is to come up with at least 100 potential names. Having a dictionary, a thesaurus, and samples (or graphics) of your company's products and services will help stimulate creativity. When brothers Tariq and Kamran Farid decided to start a company to sell fruit baskets that looked like floral arrangements, they asked their employees to help come up with a company name. To stimulate creativity, the group began describing their product and soon came up with a catchy name that has proved to be a hit, Edible Arrangements.

4. Evaluate the names generated in the brainstorming session, after allowing the names to percolate a bit. Narrow the list of choices to ten or so names with the greatest potential. Print each name in large font on a single page and look at them. Which ones are visually appealing? Which ones lend themselves to being paired with a clever logo?

5. Reassemble your creative group, present each name you have printed, and discuss its merits and challenges. Having a designated person to record the group's comments helps. The group may come to a consensus on a preferred name; if not, you can use a round-by-round voting process to move the group toward a consensus.

6. Conduct a search at the U.S. Patent and Trademark Office Web site (www.uspto.gov) to see whether the leading names on your list are already registered trademarks for existing businesses. Remember, however, that the same name can be registered as a trademark as long as the product, service, or company's business does not overlap. If your company conducts e-commerce, you also should check with one of the name registration services to see if a "dot com" version of the name is available.

7. Make your choice. Including input from others is useful when selecting a business name, but the final choice is yours.

8. Register your company name with the U.S. Patent and Trademark Office. Doing so gives you maximum protection from others using the name that you worked so hard to create.

Other helpful tips for creating the ideal business name include:

- Look at your name from your potential customer's perspective. Do customers need reassurance (Gentle Dentistry), or do they prefer a bit of humor (Barkingham Palace Doggie Daycare)? Other options include using a name that conveys an image to your customers that expresses your business strategy. For example: Discount Hair Products, Quality Muffler, or Pay-Less Auto Detailing.

- Decide the most appropriate single quality of the business that you want to convey and incorporate it into your business name. Avoid sending a mixed or inappropriate message. Avoid business names that might leave potential customers confused about what your business does. Remember: The company name will be displayed on all of your advertising and printed material.

- Avoid names that are hard to spell, pronounce, or remember. This is especially true if your business is an Internet company or if you plan to have a Web site.
- Select a name that is short, fun, attention getting, and memorable. Not only is Google fun to say, it is also quite memorable. Naming experts say that a great name has "emotional hang time," a football metaphor to describe a name that stays in your mind.
- Be creative but maintain good taste! Lisa Rothstein found the perfect name for her business that sells fresh-baked gourmet brownies as corporate gifts: Brownie Points. Rothstein's company name recently won the "Name to Fame" contest sponsored by *Entrepreneur* magazine and the Small Business Television Network.
- Be careful that the name, while catchy and cute, doesn't create a negative image. Ask yourself: Does Rent-a-Wreck attract you because you think you'll save money on a car rental or does the name put you off because you question the reliability of their cars?
- Finally, after all is said and done and you are comfortable with your choice, conduct a name search to make sure that no one else in your jurisdiction has already claimed the name. This is an especially tedious chore if you are starting an Internet company. Registering a domain name sometimes can be daunting because you will find that your brilliant idea is already registered.

There are millions of names in the marketplace. Coming up with the one that is just right for your business can help greatly in creating a brand image for your business. Choosing a name that is distinctive, memorable, and positive can go a long way toward helping you achieve success in your business venture. What's in a name? Everything!

Sources: Adapted from Scott Trimble, "18 Strategies and Tools for Naming Your Business or Product," *Marketing Profs*, January 24, 2008, https://www.marketingprofs.com/login/join.asp?adref=rdblk&source=%2F8%2Fhow%2Dto%2Dname%2Dproducts%2Dcompanies%2Dtrimble%2Easp; Alex Frankel, "The New Science of Naming," *Business 2.0*, December 2004, pp. 53–55; Rhonda Abrams, "Sometimes Business Success Is All in the Name," *Business*, July 23, 2000, p. 3; Elizabeth Weinstein, "GHB Marketing Finds Its Name Is One Thing It Doesn't Want To Plug," *Wall Street Journal*, June 7, 2001, p. B1; Andrew Raskin, "The Name of the Game," *Inc.*, February 2000, pp. 31–32; Rhonda Adams "Sometimes Business Success Is All In The Name," *Business*, July 23, 2000, p. 3; Tomima Edmark, "What's In A Name?" *Entrepreneur*, October 1999, pp. 163–165; Jeff Wuorio, "'Oedipus Wrecks' and Other Business Names to Avoid," *bCentral*, www.bCentral.com/articles/wuorio/153.asp; Suzanne Barlyn, "Name That Firm," *Wall Street Journal*, March 17, 2008, p. R7.

The Sole Proprietorship

The simplest and most popular form of ownership remains the **sole proprietorship**. The sole proprietorship, as its name implies, is a business owned and managed by one individual. Sole proprietorships make up more than 71 percent of all businesses in the United States.

The Advantages of a Proprietorship

SIMPLE TO CREATE One of the most attractive features of a proprietorship is how fast and simple it is to begin. If an entrepreneur wants to operate a business under his own name (e.g., Strossner's Bakery), he simply obtains the necessary licenses from state, county, and/or local governments and begins operation! For most entrepreneurs, it is possible to start a proprietorship in a single day.

LEAST COSTLY FORM OF OWNERSHIP TO BEGIN In addition to being easy to begin, the proprietorship is generally the least expensive form of ownership to establish. There is no need to create and file legal documents that are recommended for partnerships and required for corporations. An entrepreneur simply goes to the city or county government, states the nature of the business he will start, and purchases a business license. The Small Business Administration provides a list of Web sites where entrepreneurs in every state can get information about purchasing a business license.

LO 1-A

Explain the advantages and disadvantages of the sole proprietorship.

sole proprietorship

a business owned and managed by one individual; the business and the owner are one and the same in the eyes of the law.

AGE Fotostock America, Inc.—Royalty-free

Sole proprietorships are flexible
and can move fast.

An entrepreneur planning to conduct business under a trade name should acquire a Certificate of Doing Business under an Assumed Name from the secretary of state. The fee for filing this certificate usually is nominal. Acquiring this certificate involves conducting a legal search to ensure that the name chosen is not already registered as a trademark or a service mark with the secretary of state. Filing this certificate also notifies the state who owns the business. In a sole proprietorship, the owner *is* the business.

PROFIT INCENTIVE One major advantage of proprietorships is that once owners pay all of their companies' expenses, they can keep the remaining profits (less taxes, of course). The profit incentive is a powerful one, and profits represent an excellent way of "keeping score" in the game of the business. Sole proprietors report the net income of their businesses on Schedule C of IRS Form 1040, and the amount is taxed at the entrepreneur's personal tax rate. Because they are self-employed, sole proprietors' income from their business activities also is subject to the self-employment tax, which currently stands at 15.3 percent (an amount equal to the 7.65 percent employers pay plus the 7.65 percent employees contribute toward the Social Security and Medicare programs) of the proprietor's income. A ceiling on the Social Security portion of the self-employment tax does apply.

TOTAL DECISION-MAKING AUTHORITY Because the sole proprietor is in total control of operations, he or she can respond quickly to changes, which is an asset in a rapidly shifting market. The freedom to set the company's course of action is a major motivational force. For those who thrive on the enjoyment of seeking new opportunities in business, the freedom of fast, flexible decision making is vital. Many sole proprietors thrive on the feeling of control they have over their personal financial futures and the recognition they earn as the owners of their businesses.

NO SPECIAL LEGAL RESTRICTIONS The proprietorship is the least regulated form of business ownership. In a time when government regulation seem never-ending, this feature has much merit.

EASY TO DISCONTINUE If an entrepreneur decides to discontinue operations, he or she can terminate the business quickly even though he or she will still be personally liable for any outstanding debts and obligations that the business cannot pay.

The Disadvantages of a Proprietorship

Entrepreneurs considering the sole proprietorship as a form of ownership also must be aware of its disadvantages.

unlimited personal liability
a situation in which the sole proprietor is personally liable for all of the business's debts.

UNLIMITED PERSONAL LIABILITY Probably the greatest disadvantage of a sole proprietorship is the **unlimited personal liability** of the owner, which means that the sole proprietor is personally liable for all of the business's debts. Remember: In a proprietorship, the owner *is* the business. He or she owns all of the business's assets, and if the business fails, creditors can force the sale of these assets to cover its debts. If unpaid business debts remain, creditors can also force the sale of the proprietor's *personal* assets to recover payment. In short, the company's debts are the owner's debts. Laws vary from one state to another, but most states require creditors to leave the failed business owner a minimum amount of equity in a home, a car, and some personal items. The reality is that failure of a business can ruin a sole proprietor financially. When Max Baer started a production studio in Memphis, Tennessee, he chose to operate as a sole proprietor. Then a former employee sued Baer. Although he negotiated a modest out-of-court settlement in the case, Baer realized that a sole proprietorship left all of his personal assets at risk and converted his company into a corporation to gain the benefit of limited personal liability.[2]

LIMITED SKILLS AND CAPABILITIES A sole proprietor has total decision-making authority, but that does not mean that he or she has the range of skills that running a successful business requires. Each of us has areas in which our education, training, and work experiences have taught us a great deal; yet there are other areas in which our decision-making ability is weak. Many business failures occur because owners lack the skills, knowledge, and experience in areas that are vital to business success. Owners tend to push aside problems they don't understand or don't feel comfortable with in favor of those they can solve more easily. Unfortunately, the problems they set aside seldom solve themselves. By the time an owner decides to ask for help in addressing these problems, it may be too late to save the company.

FEELINGS OF ISOLATION Running a business alone gives an entrepreneur maximum flexibility, but it also creates feelings of isolation; there is no one else to turn to for help when solving problems or getting feedback on a new idea. Most sole proprietors will admit that there are times when they feel the pressure of being alone and fully and completely responsible for every major business decision. Learning what one needs to know about running a business can be challenging, especially in areas in which an entrepreneur may have had little or no previous experience.

LIMITED ACCESS TO CAPITAL If a business is to grow and expand, a sole proprietor often needs additional financial resources. However, many proprietors have already put all they have into their businesses and have used their personal resources as collateral to acquire loans, making it difficult to borrow additional funds. A sole proprietorship is limited to whatever capital the owner can contribute and whatever money he or she can borrow. In short, proprietors find it difficult to raise additional money and maintain sole ownership. Most banks and other lending institutions have well-defined formulas for determining borrowers' eligibility. Unfortunately, many sole proprietors cannot meet those borrowing requirements, especially in the early days of business.

LACK OF CONTINUITY OF THE BUSINESS Lack of continuity is inherent in a sole proprietorship. If the proprietor dies, retires, or becomes incapacitated, the business automatically terminates. Unless a family member or employee can take over (which means that person is now a sole proprietor), the business could be in jeopardy. Because people look for secure employment and an opportunity for advancement, proprietorships often have trouble recruiting and retaining good employees. If no one is willing to step in to run the business in the founder's absence, creditors can petition the courts to liquidate the assets of the dissolved business to pay outstanding debts.

Some entrepreneurs find that forming partnerships is one way to overcome the disadvantages of the sole proprietorship. For instance, when one person lacks specific managerial skills or has insufficient access to needed capital, he or she can compensate for these weaknesses by forming a partnership with someone with complementary management skills or money to invest.

The Partnership

A **partnership** is an association of two or more people who co-own a business for the purpose of making a profit. In a partnership, the co-owners (partners) share the business's assets, liabilities, and profits according to the terms of a previously established partnership agreement (if one exists).

The law does not require a partnership agreement (also known as the articles of partnership), but it is wise to work with an attorney to develop one that spells out the exact status and responsibility of each partner. All too often the parties think they know what they are agreeing to, only to find later that no real meeting of the minds took place. A **partnership agreement** is a document that states in writing the terms under which the partners agree to operate the partnership and protects each partner's interest in the business. Every partnership should be based on a written agreement. "When two entrepreneurial personalities are combined, there is a tremendous amount of strength and energy, but it must be focused in the same direction, or it will tear the relationship apart," explains one business writer. "A good partnership agreement will guide you through the good times, provide you with a method for handling problems, and serve as the infrastructure for a successful operation."[3]

LO 1-B

Explain the advantages and disadvantages of the partnership.

partnership
an association of two or more people who co-own a business for the purpose of making a profit.

partnership agreement
a document that states in writing the terms under which the partners agree to operate the partnership and protects each partner's interest in the business.

When no partnership agreement exists, the Revised Uniform Partnership Act (RUPA) governs a partnership, but its provisions may not be as favorable as a specific agreement hammered out among the partners. Creating a partnership agreement is not necessarily costly. In most cases the partners can discuss their preferences for each of the provisions in advance. Once they have reached an agreement, an attorney can draft the formal document. Bankers often want to see a copy of a partnership agreement before lending money to a partnership. Probably the most important feature of the partnership agreement is that it resolves potential sources of conflict that, if not addressed in advance, could later result in partnership battles and the dissolution of an otherwise successful business. Spelling out details—in particular, sticky ones such as profit splits, contributions, workloads, decision-making authority, dispute resolution, dissolution, and others—in a written agreement at the outset will help avoid damaging tension in a partnership that could lead to a business "divorce." Business divorces, like marital ones, are almost always costly and unpleasant for everyone involved.

Generally, a partnership agreement can include any terms the partners want (unless they are illegal). The standard partnership agreement will likely include the following:

1. *Name of the partnership.*
2. *Purpose of the business.* What is the reason the business was brought into being?
3. *Domicile of the business.* Where will the principal business be located?
4. *Duration of the partnership.* How long will the partnership last?
5. *Names of the partners and their legal addresses.*
6. *Contributions of each partner to the business*, at the creation of the partnership and later. This includes each partner's investment in the business. In some situations a partner may contribute assets that are not likely to appear on a balance sheet. Experience, sales contacts, or a good reputation in the community may be reasons for asking a person to join in partnership.
7. Agreement on *how the profits or losses will be distributed.*
8. Procedure for *expansion through the addition of new partners.*
9. *Agreement on the distribution of assets if the partners voluntarily dissolve the partnership.*
10. *Sale of partnership interest.* The articles of partnership should include terms that define how a partner can sell his or her interest in the business.
11. *Salaries, draws, and expense accounts for the partners.* How much money will each partner draw from the business? Under what circumstances? How often?
12. *Absence or disability of one of the partners.* If a partner is absent or disabled for an extended period of time, should the partnership continue? Will the absent or disabled partner

receive the same share of profits as she did prior to the absence or disability? Should the absent or disabled partner be held responsible for debts incurred while unable to participate?

13. *Dissolution of the partnership.* Under what circumstances will the partnership dissolve? How will the assets of the business be valued for dissolution?

14. *Alternations or modifications of the partnership agreement.* No document is written to last forever. Partnership agreements should contain provisions for alterations or modifications.

THE UNIFORM PARTNERSHIP ACT The Uniform Partnership Act (UPA) codifies the body of law dealing with partnerships in the United States. Under the UPA, the three key elements of any partnership are common ownership interest in a business, sharing the business's profits and losses, and the right to participate in managing the operation of the partnership. Under the act each partner has the *right* to:

1. Participate in the management and operations of the business.
2. Share in any profits the business might earn from operations.
3. Receive interest on loans made to the business.
4. Be compensated for expenses incurred in the name of the partnership.
5. Have access to the business's books and records.
6. Receive a formal accounting of the partnership's business affairs.

The UPA also sets forth the partners' general obligations. Each partner is *obligated* to:

1. Share in any losses sustained by the business.
2. Work for the partnership without salary.
3. Submit differences that may arise in the conduct of the business to majority vote or arbitration.
4. Give the other partner(s) complete information about all business affairs.
5. Give a formal accounting of the partnership's business affairs.
6. Live up to a fiduciary responsibility of the partnership and place the interest of the partnership above his or her personal interests.

David Gage, a partnership mediator, suggests that partners also create a "partnership charter," a document that "serves as a guide for running the business and dealing with one another." Whereas a partnership agreement addresses the legal and business issues of running a business, a partnership charter covers the interpersonal aspects of the partners' relationships and serves as a helpful tool for managing the complexity of partnership relations.[4] Even with a partnership charter and a partnership agreement, a partnership must have two more essential elements above all others: mutual trust and respect. Any partnership missing these elements is destined to fail.

The Advantages of the Partnership

EASY TO ESTABLISH Like the proprietorship, the partnership is easy and inexpensive to establish. The owner must obtain the necessary business licenses and submit a minimal number of forms. In most states, partners must file a Certificate for Conducting Business as Partners if the business is run under a trade name.

COMPLEMENTARY SKILLS In a sole proprietorship, the owner must wear lots of different hats, and not all of them will fit well. In successful partnerships, the parties' skills and abilities usually complement one another, strengthening the company's managerial foundation. For years, entrepreneur Norm Brodsky, founder of CitiStorage, a successful document storage company in New York City, thought that partnerships were a recipe for disaster in business—until he had the chance to work with Sam Kaplan. Over time, Brodsky saw how Kaplan's values and philosophies were similar to his own and that Kaplan's strengths were skills that he lacked. The two became business partners, and with their combined skills, CitiStorage went on to achieve record levels of success. "Alone I might be right six or seven times out of ten," says Brodsky. "With Sam, I can be right nine times out of ten. That's a big advantage."[5]

In his book *The Illusions of Entrepreneurship*, Scott Shane says that businesses that are founded by teams of entrepreneurs (not necessarily partners) are more likely to succeed than those that are founded by a single entrepreneur.[6]

After David Wu graduated from Wharton West in San Francisco, he took an idea for Rotohog, an interactive fantasy sports community to one of his former professors, Kent Smetters, for advice. Smetters was impressed with Wu's idea and the market opportunity and said, "I can be your advisor, or we can be partners." For Wu, the choice was easy. "I said, 'Let's be partners,' and it really took off from there." Smetters agrees, pointing out that their skill sets complement one another. "I'm the nuts and bolts guy, and he is the bigger vision person," he says. The partnership is proving to be profitable; Rotohog now generates annual sales of more than $2.5 million.[7]

DIVISION OF PROFITS There are no restrictions on how partners distribute the company's profits as long as they are consistent with the partnership agreement and do not violate the rights of any partner. The partnership agreement should articulate the nature of each partner's contribution and proportional share of the profits. If the partners fail to create an agreement, the UPA says that the partners share equally in the partnership's profits, even if their original capital contributions were unequal.

LARGER POOL OF CAPITAL The partnership form of ownership can significantly broaden the pool of capital available to a business. Each partner's asset base enhances the business's pool of capital and improves its ability to borrow needed funds; together, partners' personal assets support greater borrowing capacity.

ABILITY TO ATTRACT LIMITED PARTNERS When partners share in owning, operating, and managing a business, they are **general partners**. General partners have unlimited liability for the partnership's debts and usually take an active role in managing the business. Every partnership must have at least one general partner although there is no limit on the number of general partners a business can have.

    Limited partners are financial investors in a partnership, cannot participate in the day-to-day management of a company, and have limited liability for the partnership's debts. If the business fails, they lose only what they have invested in it and no more. A limited partnership can attract investors by offering them limited liability and the potential to realize a substantial return on their investments if the business is successful. Many individuals find it very profitable to invest in high-potential small businesses but only if they avoid the disadvantages of unlimited liability while doing so. If limited partners are "materially and actively" engaged in a business (defined as spending more than 500 hours per year in the company) or if they hold themselves out as general partners, they will be treated as general partners and will lose their limited liability protection. Two types of limited partners are silent partners and dormant partners. **Silent partners** are not active in a business but generally are known to be members of the partnership. **Dormant partners** are neither active nor generally known to be associated with the business. We will discuss limited partnerships in the next section of this chapter.

MINIMAL GOVERNMENT REGULATION Like the sole proprietorship, partnerships are not burdened with red tape.

FLEXIBILITY Although not as flexible as sole ownership, a partnership can generally react quickly to changing market conditions because the partners can respond quickly and creatively to new opportunities. In large partnerships, however, getting partners' approval can slow a company's strategic actions.

TAXATION A partnership itself is not subject to federal taxation. It serves as a conduit for the profit or losses it earns or incurs; its net income or losses are passed through to the partners as personal income, and the partners pay income tax on their distributive shares based on their individual tax rates. The partnership files an informational return, Form 1065, with the IRS that reports its net income for the tax year and the percentages of the business that each partner owns. The partnership provides each partner with a Schedule K-1 that shows his or her share of partnership's net income (or loss). Partners must pay taxes on their respective shares of the partnership's net income, even if none of that income actually is distributed to them. A partnership, like a sole proprietorship, avoids the "double taxation" disadvantage associated with the corporate form of ownership.

The Disadvantages of the Partnership

A partnership is like a business marriage, and before entering into one, an entrepreneur should be aware of the disadvantages.

general partners
partners who share in owning, operating, and managing a business and who have unlimited personal liability for the partnership's debts.

limited partners
partners who make financial investments in a partnership, do not take an active role in managing a business, and whose liability for the partnership's debts is limited to the amount they have invested.

silent partners
limited partners who are not active in a business but generally are known to be members of the partnership.

dormant partners
limited partners who are neither active in a business nor generally known to be associated with the business.

UNLIMITED LIABILITY OF AT LEAST ONE PARTNER At least one member of every partnership must be a general partner. A general partner has unlimited personal liability for any debts that remain after the partnerships assets are exhausted. In addition, a general partner's liability is *joint and several*, which means that creditors can hold all general partners equally responsible for the partnership's debts or they can collect the entire debt from just one partner.

CAPITAL ACCUMULATION Although the partnership form of ownership is superior to the proprietorship in its ability to attract capital, it is generally not as effective as the corporate form of ownership, which can raise capital by selling shares of ownership to outside investors.

DIFFICULTY IN DISPOSING OF PARTNERSHIP INTEREST WITHOUT DISSOLVING THE PARTNERSHIP Most partnership agreements restrict how partners can dispose of their shares of the business. Often, an agreement requires a partner to sell his or her interest to the remaining partner(s). Even if the original agreement contains such a requirement and clearly delineates how the value of each partner's ownership will be determined, there is no guarantee that the other partner(s) will have the financial resources to buy the seller's interest. When the money is not available to purchase a partner's interest, the other partner(s) may be forced to either accept a new partner or to dissolve the partnership, distribute the remaining assets, and begin again.

Unless the partnership agreement states otherwise, a partner may sell his or her interest in the business to another person without the consent of the remaining partners. However, that person does *not* automatically become a partner in the business. The transferee has the right to receive the former partner's share of the company's net income (or loss), but he or she does not have the right to take an active role in managing the business, gain access to the business's books, or demand a formal accounting of the partnership's business affairs.

When a general partner dies, becomes incompetent, or withdraws from the business, the partnership automatically dissolves, although it may not terminate. When a business consists of numerous partners and one chooses to disassociate from the business, the remaining partners can form a new partnership.

LACK OF CONTINUITY If one partner dies, complications arise. Partnership interest is often nontransferable through inheritance because the remaining partner(s) may not want to be in a partnership with the person who inherits the deceased partner's interest. Partners can make provisions in the partnership agreement to avoid dissolution due to death if all parties agree to accept as partners those who inherit the deceased's interest.

A similar problem arises when a partner chooses to leave the business. Buying out an exiting partner can be difficult financially, and the emotional pain of the separation can destroy friendships and personal relationships. Brad Powell says that he lost a longtime friend when he decided to leave the software company they had co-founded because of differences over how to manage the business. Powell entered into a new partnership with another friend, but this time, the two invested a great deal of time creating a partnership agreement that covers everything from the partners' roles and responsibilities to an exit strategy and a buy-sell agreement. "I didn't want to repeat the past," he says.[8]

POTENTIAL FOR PERSONALITY AND AUTHORITY CONFLICTS Being in a partnership is much like being in a marriage. Making sure partners' work habits, goals, ethics, and general business philosophy are compatible is an important step in avoiding a nasty business divorce. Engaging in serious discussions with potential partners before launching a business together is a valuable and revealing exercise. A better way to "test drive" a potential partnership is to work with a prospective partner on a joint project to get a sense of how compatible your work styles, business philosophies, and personalities really are. That project might be a small business venture or working together to create a business plan for the proposed partnership. The idea is to work together before committing to a partnership to determine how compatible the potential partners' values, goals, personalities, views, and ethics are.

No matter how compatible partners are, friction among them is inevitable. They key is to have a mechanism such as a partnership agreement and open lines of communication for managing conflict. The demise of many partnerships can be traced to interpersonal conflicts and the lack of a procedure to resolve those conflicts.

PARTNERS ARE BOUND BY THE LAW OF AGENCY Each partner is an agent for the business and can legally bind the partnership and, hence, the other partners, to contracts—even without the remaining partners' knowledge or consent. Because of this agency power, all partners must exercise good faith and reasonable care when performing their responsibilities. For example, if a partner signs a three-year lease for a business jet, a move that only worsens the small company's cash flow struggles, the partnership is legally bound by the agreement even though the remaining partners may not be in favor of the decision.

Some partnerships survive a lifetime while others suffer from many of the preceding problems. In a general partnership, the continued exposure to unlimited personal liability for partners' actions can wear an entrepreneur down. Knowing that they could lose their personal assets because of a partner's bad business decision is a fact of life in partnerships. Conflicts between or among partners can force an otherwise thriving business to close. Too many partnerships never put into place a mutually agreed upon method of conflict resolution such as a partnership agreement. Without such a mechanism, disagreements can escalate to the point where the partnership is dissolved and the business ceases to operate.

Limited Partnerships

limited partnership

a partnership composed of at least one general partner and at least one limited partner.

A **limited partnership** is composed of at least one general partner and at least one limited partner. In a limited partnership the general partner is treated, under the law, exactly as in a general partnership. Limited partners are treated as investors in the business venture, and they have limited liability for the partnership's debts. They can lose only the amount they have invested in the business. Because of this advantage, limited partnerships own many professional sports teams.

Most states have ratified the Revised Uniform Limited Partnership Act. Forming a limited partnership requires its founders to file a Certificate of Limited Partnership with the Secretary of

Keeping a Partnership Thriving

A fast-growing sector in the field of entrepreneurship is copreneurs (see Chapter 1), couples who share not only a home but also a business. Although owning a business together sounds like a recipe for divorce (and it sometimes is), researcher Glenn Muske says that one-third of family businesses in the United States are owned by couples. Many couples who work as business partners find that their personal relationship improves their business relationship and, in turn, their business relationship strengthens their personal relationship. "I love sharing our 'firsts,'" says Robert LePera, who owns Acorn Food Services with his wife, Deborah. "Our first-ever client, our first really large contract. It's all about shared memories." Acorn Food Services employs 100 full-time workers and competes against billion-dollar corporations for administering food service contracts for corporate and military clients, but the LePeras have strict rules about separating their work and personal lives: Dinner marks the end of the workday. No business discussions around the dinner table. We take weekends off to enjoy family life.

In another move that experts recommend, the LaPeras have assumed distinct roles in the business and avoid treading on the other's turf. Robert handles the behind-the-scenes management tasks, and Deborah is the company's lead sales person. "I'm the face of the business," she says. Since adopting twins, the LaPeras decided that Deborah should cut back to just 30 hours a week and became more selective in the contracts they accepted. As they anticipated, sales dropped somewhat but remain a healthy $7 million, and the company's profit margins have held steady.

The LaPeras demonstrate several important lessons for the ingredients to a successful business partnership:

- Have a strong, healthy romantic relationship. This is the foundation of any copreneurial relationship because

couples will have to work their way through many business challenges together.

- Respect each other's abilities. Just like regular business partners, spouses should focus on what they do best in the business and trust and respect the other person's ability to do his or her job.
- Give each other sufficient space. Couples that live and work together must be sure to spend some time away from one another. Too much togetherness can put a strain on any relationship.
- Separate their opinions about work from feelings about each other. Successful copreneurs are careful not to allow disputes about business to spill over into their personal feelings for each other.
- Feel free to talk about money openly and honestly. Unless couples can discuss personal and business finances comfortably, going into business together may not be the best idea.

1. Research relationships between copreneurs and add at least three guidelines to those listed here.
2. Develop a list of the types of behavior that is almost certain to destroy a partnership.
3. Locate a business that is operated by a couple and interview the copreneurs. What are the keys to their success in maintaining sound business and personal relationships?

Sources: Adapted from Phaedra Hise and Joanne Chen, "Unlimited Partnership," *Inc.*, February 2008, pp. 68–79; Dimitra Kessenides, "Happy Together," *Inc.*, November 2004, pp. 54–56; Rosabeth Moss Kanter , "Six Rules for a Happy Marriage…Uh, Partnership", *Business 2.0*, April 2002 p. 114; Maggie Jackson, 'Copreneurs' Brave Work-Life Challenges," Boston Globe, March 9, 2008, http://www.boston.com/jobs/news/articles/2008/03/09/co_preneurs_brave_work_life_challenges/.

State's office. Although the requirements vary from one state to another, the Certificate of Limited Partnership typically includes the following information:

- The name of the limited partnership.
- The general character of its business.
- The address of the office of the firm's agent authorized to receive summonses or other legal notices.
- The name and business address of each partner, specifying which ones are general partners and which are limited partners.
- The amount of cash contributions actually made, and agreed to be made in the future, by each partner.
- A description of the value of non-cash contributions made or to be made by each partner.
- The times at which additional contributions are to be made by any of the partners.
- Whether and under what conditions a limited partner has the right to grant limited partner status to an assignee of his or her interest in the partnership.
- If agreed upon, the time or the circumstances when a partner may withdraw from the firm (unlike the withdrawal of a general partner, the withdrawal of a limited partner does *not* automatically dissolve a limited partnership).
- If agreed upon, the amount of, or the method of determining, the funds to be received by a withdrawing partner.
- Any right of a partner to receive distributions of cash or other property from the firm, and the times and circumstances for such distributions.
- The time or circumstances when the limited partnership is to be dissolved.
- The rights of the remaining general partners to continue the business after withdrawal of a general partner.
- Any other matters the partners want to include.

Every limited partnership must have at least one general partner, but there is no limit to the number of general or limited partners allowed. The general partner has the same rights and duties as under a general partnership: the right to make decisions for the business, to act as an agent for the partnership, to use the property of the partnership for normal business, and to share in the business's profits. The limited partner does not have the right to engage actively in managing the business. In fact, limited partners who take an active part in managing the business (more than 500 hours per year) forfeit their limited liability status and are treated just like general partners. Limited partners can, however, make management suggestions to the general partners, inspect the business, and make copies of business records. A limited partner is, of course, entitled to a share of the business's profits as specified in the Certificate of Limited Partnership. The primary disadvantage of limited partnerships is the complexity and the cost of establishing and maintaining them.

ENTREPRENEURIAL PROFILE _____

Wolfgang Puck & Barbara Lazaroff: Food Company

Wolfgang Puck, the Austrian-born chef who has won national acclaim for his unique food combinations such as scrambled egg pizza with smoked salmon, and banana chocolate chip soufflé, and his wife, Barbara Lazaroff, operate three dozen upscale restaurants across the United States. The largest division of their business, the Food Company, is a corporation, but Puck and Lazaroff rely on limited partnerships to operate the restaurants in their Fine Dining Group. For instance, each of the company's various Spago's (Beverly Hills, Palo Alto, Maui, and Las Vegas) has a distinct collection of owners as do the other restaurants in the group such as Postrio and Chinois.[9]

Limited Liability Partnerships

Many states now recognize **limited liability partnerships (LLPs)** in which *all* partners in a business are limited partners, which gives them the advantage of limited liability for the debts of the partnership. Most states restrict LLPs to certain types of professionals such as attorneys, physicians, dentists, accountants, and others.

Just as with any limited partnership, the partners must file a Certificate of Limited Partnership in the state in which the partnership will conduct business, and the partnership must identify itself as an LLP to those with whom it does business. In addition, like every partnership, an LLP does not pay taxes; its income is passed through to the limited partners, who pay taxes on their shares of the company's income.

limited liability partnership
a special type of limited partnership in which *all* partners, who in many states must be professionals, are limited partners.

"*It's a swell offer, Brad, and you're a great guy, but I've just got out of a bad limited partnership, and I'm not ready for that kind of commitment yet.*"

master limited partnership
a partnership whose shares are traded on stock exchanges, just like a corporation's.

Master Limited Partnerships

A relatively new form of business structure, **master limited partnerships (MLPs)**, are just like regular limited partnerships, except their shares are traded just like shares of common stock. They provide most of the same advantages to investors as a corporation, including limited liability. Operationally, a master limited partnership behaves like a corporation, and some even trade on major stock exchanges. In 1987, congressional legislation provided that any MLP not involved in natural resources such as oil, natural gas, or real estate would be taxed as a corporation and consequently eliminated their ability to avoid the disadvantage of double taxation that corporations experience.

LO 1-C

Explain the advantages and disadvantages of the corporation.

corporation
a separate legal entity apart from its owners that receives the right to exist from the state in which it is incorporated.

domestic corporation
a corporation doing business in the state in which it is incorporated.

foreign corporation
a corporation doing business in a state other than the one in which it is incorporated.

alien corporation
a corporation formed in another country but doing business in the United States.

closely held corporation
a corporation whose shares are controlled by a relatively small number of people, often family members, relatives, friends, or employees.

publicly held corporation
a corporation that has a large number of shareholders and whose stock usually is traded on one of the large stock exchanges.

Corporations

The corporation is the most complex of the three major forms of business ownership. It is a separate entity apart from its owners, and may engage in business, make contracts, sue and be sued, own property, and pay taxes. The Supreme Court has defined the **corporation** as "an artificial being, invisible, intangible, and existing only in contemplation of the law."[10] Because the life of the corporation is independent of its owners, the shareholders can sell their interests in the business without affecting its continuation.

Corporations (also known as "C Corporations") are creations of the states. When a corporation is founded, it accepts the regulations and restrictions of the state in which it is incorporated and any other state in which it chooses to do business. A corporation doing business in the state in which it is incorporated is a **domestic corporation**. When a corporation conducts business in another state, that state considers it to be a **foreign corporation**. A corporation that is formed in another country but does business in the United States is called an **alien corporation**.

Corporations have the power to raise large amounts of capital by selling shares of ownership to outside investors, but many corporations have only a handful of shareholders. A **closely held corporation** has shares that are controlled by a relatively small number of people, often family members, relatives, friends, or employees. Its stock is not traded on any stock exchange but instead is passed from one generation to the next. Most small corporations are closely held. A **publicly held corporation** has a large number of shareholders, and its stock usually is traded on one of the large stock exchanges.

A corporation must report annually its financial operations to its home state's secretary of state. These financial reports become public record. If a corporation's stock is sold in more than one state, the corporation must comply with federal regulations governing the sale of corporate securities. There are substantially more reporting requirements for a corporation than for the other forms of ownership.

How to Incorporate

Most states allow entrepreneurs to incorporate without the assistance of an attorney. Some states even provide incorporation kits to help in the incorporation process. Although it is cheaper for entrepreneurs to complete the process themselves, it is not always the best idea. In some states, the application process is complex, and the required forms are confusing. The price for filing incorrectly can be high. If an entrepreneur completes the incorporation process improperly, it is generally invalid.

Once entrepreneurs decide to form a corporation, they must choose a state in which to incorporate. If the business will operate within a single state, it is most logical to incorporate in that state. States differ—sometimes dramatically—in the requirements they place on the corporations they charter and how they treat the corporations created within their borders. They also differ in the tax rates they impose on corporations, the restrictions they place on their activities, the capital they require for a company to incorporate, and the fees or organization taxes they charge to incorporate. Delaware, for instance, offers low incorporation fees, favorable laws, low taxes, and minimal legal requirements, and many corporations are chartered there. Vermont has undertaken a similar strategy to attract virtual corporations, those that operate exclusively online. A new Vermont law allows a private corporation anywhere in the world to register in Vermont without opening a physical location there, holding a face-to-face stockholder's meeting, or filing any paperwork. Instead, companies can meet all of these requirements by using e-mail, instant messaging, or other online tools, which greatly simplifies the incorporation process. "This is going to allow for ways of doing business that we can't even imagine yet," says an entrepreneurship researcher at the Kuaffman Foundation.[11]

To create a corporation, every state requires a Certificate of Incorporation or charter to be filed with the secretary of state. The following information is generally required to be in the Certificate of Incorporation:

The corporation's name. The corporation must choose a name that is not so similar to that of another firm in that state that it causes confusion or lends itself to deception. It must also include a term such as "corporation," "incorporated," "company," or "limited" to notify the public that they are dealing with a corporation.

The corporation's statement of purpose. The incorporators must state in general terms the intended nature of the business. The purpose must, of course, be lawful. An illustration might be "to engage in the sale of office furniture and fixtures." The purpose should be broad enough to allow for some expansion in the activities of the business as it develops.

The corporation's time horizon. Most corporations are formed with no specific termination date; they are formed "for perpetuity." However, it is possible to incorporate for a specific duration, for example, 50 years.

Names and addresses of the incorporators. The incorporators must be identified in the articles of incorporation and are liable under the law to attest that all information in the articles of incorporation is correct. Some states require one or more of the incorporators to reside in the state in which the corporation is being created.

Place of business. The street and mailing addresses of the corporation's principal office must be listed. For a domestic corporation, this address must be in the state in which incorporation takes place.

Capital stock authorization. The articles of incorporation must include the amount and class (or type) of capital stock the corporation wants to be authorized to issue. This is *not* the number of shares it must issue; a corporation can issue any number of shares up to the total number authorized. This section also must define the different classification of stock and any special rights, preferences, or limits each class has.

Capital required at the time of incorporation. Some states require a newly formed corporation to deposit in a bank a specific percentage of the stock's par value prior to incorporating.

Provisions for preemptive rights, if any, that are granted to stockholders. If a corporation later issues more shares of the stock it is authorized to issue, its original investors' shares of ownership would be diluted. To prevent this dilution, some corporations grant **preemptive rights** to shareholders, which give them the ability to purchase enough shares to maintain their original percentage of ownership in the company.

Restrictions on transferring shares. Many closely held corporations—those owned by a few shareholders, often family members—require shareholders who are interested in selling their stock to offer it first to the corporation. (Shares the corporation itself owns are called **treasury stock**.) To maintain control over their ownership, many closely held corporations exercise this right, known as the **right of first refusal**.

preemptive rights
the rights of a corporation's original investors to purchase enough shares of future stock issues to maintain their original percentage of ownership in the company.

treasury stock
the shares of its own stock that a corporation owns.

right of first refusal
a provision requiring shareholders who want to sell their stock to offer it first to the corporation.

bylaws
the rules and regulations the officers and directors establish for a corporation's internal management and operation.

Names and addresses of the officers and directors of the corporation.

Rules under which the corporation will operate. **Bylaws** are the rules and regulations the officers and directors establish for the corporation's internal management and operation.

Once the secretary of state of the incorporating state has approved a request for incorporation and the corporation pays its fees, the approved articles of incorporation become its charter. With the charter in hand, the next order of business is to hold an organizational meeting for the stockholders to formally elect directors who, in turn, will appoint the corporate officers.

The Advantages of the Corporation

LIMITED LIABILITY OF STOCKHOLDERS Because it is a separate legal entity, a corporation allows investors to limit their liability to the total amount of their investment in the business. In other words, creditors of the corporation cannot lay claim to shareholders' personal assets to satisfy the company's unpaid debts. The legal protection of personal assets from business creditors is of critical concern to many potential investors. John Gazzola, founder of Toyopolis, a company that sells toys, games, and collectibles online, chose the corporate form of ownership because of his desire to limit his personal liability and for "peace of mind."[12]

This shield of limited liability may not be impenetrable, however. Because start-up companies are so risky, lenders and other creditors often require the founders of corporations to personally guarantee loans made to the business. Experts estimate that 95 percent of small business owners have to sign personal guarantees to get the financing they need. By making these guarantees, owners are putting their personal assets at risk (just as in a proprietorship) despite choosing the corporate form of ownership.

The corporate form of ownership also does not protect its owners from being held personally liable for fraudulent or illegal acts. Court decisions have extended the personal liability of the owners of small corporations beyond the financial guarantees that banks and other lenders require, "piercing the corporate veil" much more than ever before. Courts increasingly are holding entrepreneurs *personally* liable for environmental, pension, and legal claims against their corporations. Courts will pierce the corporate veil and hold entrepreneurs liable for the company's debts and obligations if the owners deliberately commit criminal or negligent acts when handling corporate business. Courts ignore the limited liability shield the corporate form of ownership provides when an entrepreneur:

1. Uses corporate assets for personal reasons or commingles them with his or her personal assets.
2. Fails to act in a responsible manner and creates an unwarranted level of financial risk for the stockholders.
3. Makes financial misrepresentations, such as operating with more than one set of books.
4. Takes actions in the name of the corporation that were not authorized by the board of directors.

Liability problems associated with piercing the corporate veil almost always originate from actions and decisions that fail to maintain the integrity of a corporation. The most common cause of these problems, especially in closely held corporations, is corporate owners and officers failing to keep their personal funds and assets separate from those of the corporation.

Table 5.1 offers some useful suggestions for avoiding legal tangles in a corporation.

Sergey Brin and Larry Page raised $1.67 billion in an initial public offering for Google, the company they founded in a college dorm room.

AP Wide World Photos

TABLE 5.1 Avoiding Legal Tangles in a Corporation

Steps that entrepreneurs should take to avoid legal problems if they own a corporation include the following:

- *Identify the company as a corporation by using "Inc." or "Corporation" in the business name.* This alerts all who do business with a company that it is a corporation.

- *File all reports and pay all necessary fees required by the state in a timely manner.* Most states require corporations to file reports with the secretary of state on an annual basis. Failing to do so will jeopardize the validity of your corporation and will open the door for personal liability problems for its shareholders.

- *Hold annual meetings to elect officers and directors.* In a closely held corporation, the officers elected may *be* the shareholders, but that does not matter. Corporations formed by an individual are not required to hold meetings, but the sole shareholder must file a written consent form.

- *Keep minutes of every meeting of the officers and directors, even if it takes place in the living room of the founders.* It is a good idea to elect a secretary who is responsible for recording the minutes.

- *Make sure that the corporation's board of directors makes all major decisions.* Problems arise in closely held corporations when one owner makes key decisions alone without consulting the elected board.

- *Make it clear that the business is a corporation by having all officers sign contracts, loan agreements, purchase orders, and other legal documents in the corporation's name rather than their own names.* Failing to designate their status as agents of the corporation can result in the officers' being held personally liable for agreements they think they are signing on the corporation's behalf.

- *Keep corporate assets and the personal assets of the owner's separate.* Few actions make courts more willing to hold shareholders personally liable for a corporation's debts than commingling corporate and personal assets. In some closely held corporations, owners have been known to use corporate assets to pay their personal expenses (or vice versa) or to mix their personal funds with corporate funds into a single bank account. Protect the corporation's identity by keeping it completely separate from the owner's personal identities.

ABILITY TO ATTRACT CAPITAL Because of the limited liability they offer their investors, corporations have proved to be the most effective form of ownership for accumulating large amounts of capital. Limited only by the number of shares authorized in its charter (which can be amended), a corporation can raise money to begin business and expand by selling shares of its stock to investors. A corporation can sell its stock to a limited number of private investors in a **private placement** or to the public through an **initial public offering (or IPO)**. One of the most successful initial public offerings in recent years was Google's IPO. When founders Sergey Brin and Larry Page, who founded the company in their college dorm room, took their company public, they sold 19.6 million shares at $85 per share, raising $1.67 billion to fund Google's growth and expansion.[13] You will learn more about IPOs in Chapter 14, Sources of Financing: Debt and Equity.

private placement
a fund-raising tool in which a company sells shares of its stock to a limited number of private investors.

initial public offering (IPO)
a fund-raising tool in which a company sells shares of its stock to the public.

ABILITY TO CONTINUE INDEFINITELY Unless a corporation fails to pay its taxes or is limited to a specific length of life by its charter, it can continue indefinitely. The corporation's existence does not depend on the fate of any single individual. Unlike a proprietorship or partnership in which the death of a founder ends the business, a corporation lives beyond the lives of those who gave it life. This perpetual life gives rise to the next major advantage—transferable ownership.

TRANSFERABLE OWNERSHIP Unlike an investment in a partnership, shares of ownership in a corporation are easily transferable. If stockholders want to liquidate their shares of ownership in a corporation, they can sell their shares to someone else. Millions of shares of stock representing ownership in companies are traded daily on the world's stock exchanges. Shareholders can also transfer their stock through inheritance to a new generation of owners. During all of these transfers of ownership, the corporation continues to conduct business as usual. The market for stock of closely held corporations, which often are held by company founders, family members, or employees, is limited, which can make transfer of ownership difficult.

The Disadvantages of the Corporation

COST AND TIME INVOLVED IN THE INCORPORATION PROCESS Corporations can be costly and time-consuming to establish and to maintain. The owners are giving birth to an artificial legal entity, and the gestation period can be prolonged, especially for a novice. Many entrepreneurs hire attorneys to handle the incorporation process, but in most states entrepreneurs can complete all of the required forms, most of which are online, themselves. However, entrepreneurs must exercise great caution when incorporating without the help of an attorney. Incorporating a business requires a variety of fees that are not applicable to proprietorships or partnerships. The average cost to create a corporation is around $1,000, but, depending on the complexity of the organization, fees can range from $500 to $5,000. In addition, a corporation must have a board of directors, and the board must conduct an annual meeting and maintain written records of that meeting even if the entity is a single-shareholder corporation.

double taxation

a disadvantage of the corporate form of ownership in which a corporation's profits are taxed twice: at the corporate rate and at the individual rate (on the portion of profits distributed as dividends).

DOUBLE TAXATION Because a corporation is a separate legal entity, it must pay taxes on its net income at the federal level, in most states, and to some local governments as well. Before stockholders receive a penny of its net income as dividends, a corporation must pay these taxes at the *corporate* tax rate, a graduated tax on corporate profits. Then, stockholders must pay taxes on the dividends they receive from these same profits at their *individual* tax rates. Thus, a corporation's profits are taxed twice. This **double taxation** is a distinct disadvantage of the corporate form of ownership.

POTENTIAL FOR DIMINISHED MANAGERIAL INCENTIVES As corporations grow, they often require additional managerial expertise beyond that which the founder can provide. Because they often have most of their personal wealth tied up in their companies, entrepreneurs have an intense interest in making them a success and are willing to make sacrifices for them. Professional managers the entrepreneur brings in to help run the business as it grows do not always have the same degree of interest in or loyalty to the company. As a result, the business may suffer without the founder's energy, attention, and devotion. One way to minimize this potential problem is to link managers' (and even employees') compensation to the company's financial performance through a profit-sharing or bonus plan. Corporations can also stimulate managers' and employees' incentive on the job by creating an employee stock ownership plan (ESOP) in which managers and employees become part or whole owners in the company.

LEGAL REQUIREMENTS AND REGULATORY RED TAPE Corporations are subject to more legal, reporting, and financial requirements than other forms of ownership. Corporate officers must meet more stringent requirements for recording and reporting management decisions and actions. They must also hold annual meetings and consult the board of directors about major decisions that are beyond day-to-day operations. Managers may be required to submit some major decisions to the stockholders for approval. Corporations that are publicly held must file quarterly (10-Q) and annual (10-K) reports with the Securities and Exchange Commission (SEC). These reports are available to the public, and anyone, including competitors, can access them.

POTENTIAL LOSS OF CONTROL BY THE FOUNDER(S) When entrepreneurs sell shares of ownership in their companies, they relinquish some control. Especially when they need large capital infusions for start-up or growth, entrepreneurs may have to give up *significant* amounts of control, so much, in fact, that the founder becomes a minority shareholder. Losing majority ownership—and therefore control—in a company leaves the founder in a precarious position. He or she no longer has the power to determine the company's direction; "outsiders" do. In some cases, founders' shares have been so diluted that majority shareholders actually vote them out of their jobs!

In 1975, Bill Gates and Paul Allen founded Microsoft as a partnership. At that time, Bill Gates owned 50 percent of the business. As the entrepreneurs needed additional capital, they made an initial public offering. Later, to fund the business's rapid growth, Gates sold additional shares of common stock. The result has been a dilution of co-founder Bill Gates's percentage of ownership to 9 percent. (Gates is still Microsoft's largest shareholder.) However, there is no reason to feel sorry for Gates; the value of his Microsoft stock has pushed his net worth to $58 billion, making him the third wealthiest person in the world![14]

ENTREPRENEURIAL PROFILE _____

Bill Gates & Paul Allen: Microsoft

Other Forms of Ownership

In addition to the sole proprietorship, the partnership, and the corporation, entrepreneurs can choose from other forms of ownership, including the S corporation, the limited liability company, the professional corporation, and the joint venture.

LO 2

Discuss the advantages and disadvantages of the S corporation, the limited liability company, the professional corporation, and the joint venture.

The S Corporation

In 1954 the Internal Revenue Service Code created the Subchapter S corporation. In recent years the IRS has shortened the title to S corporation and has made some modifications in its qualifications. An **S corporation** is only a distinction that is made for federal income tax purposes, and is, in terms of its legal characteristics, no different from any other corporation. A corporation seeking "S" status must meet the following criteria:

1. It must be a domestic (U.S.) corporation.
2. It cannot have a nonresident alien as a shareholder.
3. It can issue only one class of common stock, which means that all shares must carry the same rights (e.g., the right to dividends or liquidation rights). The exception is voting rights, which may differ. In other words, an S corporation can issue voting and nonvoting common stock.
4. It must limit its shareholders to individuals, estates, and certain trusts, although tax-exempt creations such as employee stock ownership plans (ESOPs) and pension plans can be shareholders.
5. It cannot have more than 100 shareholders (increased from 75), which is an important benefit for family businesses making the transition from one generation of owners to another. Members of one family are treated as a single shareholder.
6. Less than 25 percent of the corporation's gross revenues during three successive tax years must be from passive sources.

S corporation

a corporation that retains the legal characteristics of a regular (C) corporation but has the advantage of being taxed as a partnership if it meets certain criteria.

If a corporation meets the criteria of an S corporation, its shareholders must actually elect to be treated as one. An S corporation election may be filed at any time during the 12 months that precede the taxable year for which the election is to be effective. (The corporation must have been eligible for S status for the entire year.) To make the election of S status effective for the current tax year, entrepreneurs must file Form 2553 with the IRS within the first 75 days of the corporation's fiscal year. *All* shareholders must consent to have the corporation treated as an S corporation.

THE ADVANTAGES OF AN S CORPORATION An S corporation retains all of the advantages of a regular corporation, such as continuity of existence, transferability of ownership, and limited personal liability for its owners. The most notable provision of the S corporation is that it serves as a conduit for its net income, passing all of its profits or losses through to the individual shareholders, which means that its income is taxed only once at the individual tax rate. Thus, electing S corporation status avoids a primary disadvantage of the regular (or "C") corporation—double taxation. In essence, the tax treatment of an S corporation is exactly like that of a partnership. The corporation files an informational return (1120-S) with the IRS and provides its shareholders with Schedule K-1, which reports their proportionate shares of the company's profits. The shareholders report their portions of the S corporation's earnings on their individual income tax returns (Form 1040) and pay taxes on those profits at the individual tax rates (even if they never take the money out of the business). This tax treatment can cause problems for individual shareholders, however. If an S corporation earns a profit but managers choose to plow that income back into the business in the form of retained earnings to fuel its growth and expansion, shareholders still must pay taxes on their share of the company's net income. In that case, shareholders pay taxes on "phantom income" they never actually receive.

Another advantage the S corporation offers is avoiding the tax C corporations pay on assets that have appreciated in value and are sold. S corporations' earnings also are not subject to the self-employment tax that sole proprietors and general partners must pay; however, they are responsible for payroll taxes (for Social Security and Medicare) on the wages and salaries the S corporation pays its employees. Therefore, owners of S corporations must be sure that the salaries they draw are reasonable; salaries that are too low or too high draw scrutiny from the IRS.

One significant change to the laws governing S corporations that benefits entrepreneurs involves subsidiary companies. Before 1998, if an entrepreneur owned separate but affiliated companies, he or she had to maintain each one as a distinct S corporation with its own accounting records and tax return. Under current law, business owners can set up all of these affiliated companies as qualified S corporation subsidiaries ("Q Subs") under the umbrella of a single company, each with its own separate legal identity, and still file a single tax return for the parent company. For entrepreneurs with several lines of businesses, this change means greatly simplified tax filing. Owners also can use losses from one subsidiary company to offset profits from another to minimize their tax bills.

DISADVANTAGES OF AN S CORPORATION When the Tax Reform Act (TRA) of 1986 restructured individual and corporate tax rates, many business owners switched to S corporations to lower their tax bills. For the first time since Congress enacted the federal income tax in 1913, the maximum individual rate was lower than the maximum corporate rate. However, Congress later realigned the tax structure by raising the maximum individual tax rate to 39.6 percent from 31 percent. This new rate was 4.6 percent *higher* than the maximum corporate tax rate of 35 percent, making S corporation status less attractive than before. Currently, marginal tax rates for corporations with net incomes between $75,000 and $335,000 are higher than the marginal tax rates for individuals with similar earnings, which makes S corporations appealing again. Because Congress constantly tinkers with both the corporate and individual tax rates, entrepreneurs who are considering both C corporation and S corporation status must review the impact of the decision on their companies, especially the tax implications (including the impact of the C corporation's double taxation penalty on the portion of its net income distributed as dividends).

Another disadvantage of the S corporation is that the costs of many benefits—insurance, meals, lodging, and others—paid to shareholders with 2 percent or more of stock cannot be deducted as business expenses for tax purposes; these benefits are then considered to be taxable income. In addition, S corporations offer shareholders only a limited range of retirement benefits, while regular corporations make a wide range of retirement plans available.

WHEN IS AN S CORPORATION A WISE CHOICE? Choosing S corporation status is usually beneficial to start-up companies anticipating net losses because their founders can use the loss to offset other income, thus lowering their tax bills. At the other extreme, founders who expect their companies to earn more than $75,000 in net income consistently should consider S corporation status. Companies that plan to reinvest most of their earnings to finance growth also find S corporations favorable. Small business owners who intend to sell their companies in the near future will prefer "S" over "C" status because the taxable gains on the sale of an S corporation are generally lower than those of a C corporation.

ENTREPRENEURIAL PROFILE_____

Kathy Colby: Financial Independents

Kathy Colby, owner of Financial Independents, a three-employee investment advisory company, formed her business as an S corporation because she wanted the benefits of limited liability and the ability to control her own salary (and therefore her employment taxes). Because of the current tax rate structure, Colby estimates that she pays $5,000 to $6,000 less per year in taxes than she would if she had formed a C corporation.[15]

Small companies with the following characteristics are *not* likely to benefit from S corporation status:

- highly profitable personal service companies with large numbers of shareholders, in which most of the profits are passed on to shareholders as compensation or retirement benefits.
- fast-growing companies that must retain most of their earnings to finance growth and capital spending.
- corporations in which the loss of benefits to shareholders exceeds tax savings.
- corporations in which the income before any compensation to shareholders is less than $100,000 per year.
- corporations with sizable net operating losses that cannot be used against S corporation earnings.

The Limited Liability Company (LLC)

The **limited liability company (LLC)** is, like an S corporation, a cross between a partnership and a corporation. Like S corporations, LLCs offer their owners limited personal liability for the debts of the business, providing a significant advantage over sole proprietorships and partnerships. LLCs, however, are not subject to many of the restrictions currently imposed on S corporations and offer more flexibility than S corporations. For example, S corporations cannot have more than 100 shareholders, none of whom can be foreigners or corporations. S corporations are also limited to only one class of stock. LLCs eliminate those restrictions. In most states an LLC can have just one owner, but a few states require LLC to have at least two owners (called "members"). LLCs offer their owners limited liability without imposing any requirements on their characteristics or any ceiling on their numbers. LLC members can include non-U.S. citizens, partnerships and corporations. Unlike a limited partnership, which prohibits limited partners from participating in the day-to-day management of the business, an LLC does not restrict its members' ability to become involved in managing the company.

In addition to offering its members the advantage of limited liability, LLCs also avoid the double taxation imposed on C corporations. Like an S corporation, an LLC does not pay income taxes; its income flows through to the members, who are responsible for paying income taxes on their shares of the LLC's net income. Because they are not subject to the many restrictions imposed on other forms of ownership, LLCs offer entrepreneurs another significant advantage: flexibility. An LLC permits its members to divide income (and thus tax liability) as they see fit, including allocations that differ from their percentages of ownership. Like an S corporation, the members' share of an LLC's earnings is not subject to self-employment tax. However, the managing member's share of the LLC's earnings is subject to the self-employment tax (15.3 percent) just as a sole proprietor's or a general partner's earned income is.

These advantages make the LLC an ideal form of ownership for many small companies across many industries—retail, wholesale, manufacturing, real estate, or service. Because it offers the tax advantage of a partnership, the legal protection of a corporation, and maximum operating flexibility, the LLC is the fastest growing form of business ownership. Michael Pritz and Bruce Harrison chose to form an LLC when they launched their telecommunications and advisory services company, JRP Partners. "We wanted [liability] protection and simplicity of structure, given the size of our firm," says Pritz. Pritz and Harrison also found the LLC's tax treatment to be an advantage.[16]

Creating an LLC is much like creating a corporation. Forming an LLC requires an entrepreneur to create two documents: the articles of organization (which must be filed with the secretary of state) and the operating agreement. The LLC's **articles of organization**, similar to the corporation's articles of incorporation, actually creates the LLC by establishing its name and address, its method of management (board-managed or member-managed), its duration, and the names and addresses of each organizer. In most states the company's name must contain the words "limited liability company," "limited company," or the letters "L.L.C." or "L.C." Unlike a corporation, an LLC does not have perpetual life; in most states an LLC's charter may not exceed 30 years. However, the same factors that would cause a partnership to dissolve would also cause the dissolution of an LLC before its charter expires.

The **operating agreement**, similar to a corporation's bylaws, outlines the provisions that govern the way the LLC will conduct business, such as members' capital contributions to the

limited liability company (LLC)
a relatively new form of ownership that, like an S corporation, is a cross between a partnership and a corporation; it is not subject to many of the restrictions imposed on S corporations.

articles of organization
the document that creates an LLC by establishing its name, its method of management, its duration, and other details.

operating agreement
the document that establishes for an LLC the provisions governing the way it will conduct business.

LLC; members' rights, roles, and responsibilities; the admission or withdrawal of members; distributions from the business; and how the LLC will be managed. To ensure that their LLCs are classified as a partnership for tax purposes, entrepreneurs must draft the operating agreement carefully. The operating agreement must create an LLC that has more characteristics of a partnership than of a corporation to maintain this favorable tax treatment. Specifically, an LLC cannot have any more than *two* of the following four corporate characteristics:

1. *Limited liability.* Limited liability exists if no member of the LLC is personally liable for the debts or claims against the company. Because entrepreneurs choosing this form of ownership usually do so to get limited liability protection, the operating agreement almost always includes this characteristic.
2. *Continuity of Life.* Continuity of life exists if the company continues to exist in spite of changes in ownership. To avoid continuity of life, any LLC member must have the power to dissolve the company. Most entrepreneurs choose to omit this characteristic from their LLC's operating agreements.
3. *Free transferability of interest.* Free transferability of interest exists if each LLC member has the power to transfer his ownership to another person freely and without the consent of other members. To avoid this characteristic, the operating agreement must state that a recipient of a member's LLC stock cannot become a substitute member without the consent of the remaining members.
4. *Centralized management.* Centralized management exists if a group that does not include all LLC members has the authority to make management decisions and to conduct company business. To avoid this characteristic, the operating agreement must state that the company elects to be "member-managed" rather than board managed.

Despite their universal appeal to entrepreneurs, LLCs suffer some disadvantages. They can be expensive to create, often costing between $1,500 and $5,000. Some states also impose annual fees on LLCs. Unlike corporations, which can operate "for perpetuity," LLCs have limited life spans. Entrepreneurs who want to provide attractive benefits to themselves and their employees will not find this form of ownership appealing because the cost of those benefits is not tax deductible in an LLC. Because there is no stock involved, this form of ownership also is not suitable for companies whose owners plan to raise money through an initial public offering or who want to use stock options or an employee stock ownership plan (ESOP) as incentives for employees.

ENTREPRENEURIAL PROFILE

Richard Burke: Trek Bicycle

Trek Bicycle, the company that became famous for making the carbon fiber bicycles that Lance Armstrong rode to an unprecedented seven victories in the Tour de France, switched to an S corporation so that it could create an employee stock ownership plan. Selecting S status, says founder Richard Burke, "has been good for my family; everyone owns 3 percent to 4 percent. It's been good for the ESOP, which holds about 25 percent of the company's stock. We tie a lot of direct and indirect compensation to company performance. If you're making money, you ought to share it."[17]

Although an LLC may be ideally suited for an entrepreneur launching a new company, it may pose problems for business owners considering converting an existing business to an LLC. Switching to an LLC from a general partnership, a limited partnership, or a sole proprietorship reorganizing to bring in new owners is usually not a problem. However, owners of corporations and S corporations would incur large tax obligations if they converted their companies to LLCs.

The Professional Corporation

Professional corporations are designed to offer professionals—lawyers, doctors, dentists, accountants, and others—the advantages of the corporate form of ownership. They are ideally suited for professionals, who must always be concerned about malpractice lawsuits, because they offer limited liability. For example, if three doctors formed a professional corporation, none of them would be liable for the others' malpractice. (Of course, each would be liable for his or her own actions.) Creating a professional corporation is no different from creating a regular corporation. Professional corporations are often identified by the abbreviations P.C. (professional

Which Form Is Best?

Watoma Kinsey and her daughter Katrina are about to launch a business that specializes in children's parties. Their target audience is upscale families who want to throw unique, memorable parties to celebrate special occasions for their children between the ages of 5 and 15. The Kinseys have leased a large building and have renovated it to include many features designed to appeal to kids, including special gym equipment, a skating rink, an obstacle course, a mockup of a pirate ship, a ball crawl, and even a moveable haunted house. They can offer simple birthday parties (cake and ice cream included) or special theme parties as elaborate as the customer wants. Their company will provide magicians, clowns, comedians, jugglers, tumblers, and a variety of other entertainers.

Watoma and Katrina each have invested $45,000 to get the business ready to launch. Based on the quality of their business plan and their preparation, the Kinseys have negotiated a $40,000 bank loan. Because they both have families and own their own homes, the Kinseys want to minimize their exposure to potential legal and financial problems. A significant portion of their start-up costs went to purchase a liability insurance policy to cover the Kinseys in case a child is injured at a party. If their business plan is

accurate, the Kinseys will earn a small profit in their first year (about $1,500), and a more attractive profit of $16,000 in their second year of operation. Within five years, they expect their company to generate as much as 50,000 in profits. The Kinseys have agreed to split the profits—and the workload—equally.

If the business is as successful as they think it will be, the Kinseys eventually want to franchise their company. That, however, is part of their long-range plan. For now, they want to perfect their business system and prove that it can be profitable before they try to duplicate it in the form of franchises.

As they move closer to the launch date for their business, the Kinseys are reviewing the different forms of ownership. They know that their decision has long-term implications for themselves and for their business, but they aren't sure which form of ownership is best for them.

1. Which form(s) of ownership would you recommend to the Kinseys? Explain.
2. Which form(s) of ownership would you recommend the Kinseys *avoid*? Explain.
3. What factors should the Kinseys consider as they evaluate the various forms of ownership?

---

corporation), P.A. (professional association), or S.C. (service corporation). A professional corporation has the following additional limitations beyond the standard corporation:

- All shares of stock of the corporation must be owned and held by individuals licensed in the profession of the corporation.
- At least one of the incorporators must be licensed in the profession.
- At least one director and one officer must be licensed must be licensed in the profession.
- The articles of incorporation, in addition to all other requirements, must designate the personal services to be provided by the corporation.
- The professional corporation must obtain from the appropriate licensing board a certification that declares the shares of stock are owned by individuals who are duly licensed in the profession.

The Joint Venture

A joint venture is very much like a partnership, except that it is formed for a specific purpose. For instance, suppose that you own a 500-acre tract of land 60 miles from Chicago that has been cleared and is normally used in agricultural production. You have a friend who has solid contacts among major musical groups and would like to put on a concert. You expect prices for your agricultural products to be low this summer, and you and your friend form a joint venture for the specific purpose of staging a three-day concert. Your contribution will be the exclusive use of the land for one month, and your friend will provide all the performers as well as technicians, facilities, and equipment. All costs will be paid out of receipts and the profits will be split with you receiving 20 percent for the use of your land. When the concert is over, the facilities removed, and the accounting for all costs completed, you and your friend split the profits 20-80, and the joint venture terminates.

In any endeavor in which neither party can effectively achieve the purpose alone, a joint venture is a common choice. The "partners" form a new joint venture for each new project they undertake. The income derived from a joint venture is taxed as if it arose from a partnership.

Table 5.2 provides a summary of the key features of the major forms of ownership discussed in this chapter.

TAELE 5.2 Characteristics of the Major Forms of Ownership

Characteristic	Sole Proprietorship	General Partnership	Limited Partnership	C Corporation	S Corporation	Limited Liability Company
Definition	A for profit business owned and operated by one person	A for profit business jointly owned and operated by two or more people	One general partner and one or more partners with limited liability and no rights of management	An artificial legal entity separate from its owners and formed under state and federal laws	An artificial legal entity that is structured like a C corporation but taxed by the federal government like a partnership	A business entity that provides limited liability like a corporation but is taxed like a partnership. Owners are referred to as members
Ease of Formation	Easiest form of business to set up. If necessary, acquire licenses and permits, register fictitious name, and obtain taxpayer identification	Easy to set up and operate. A written partnership agreement is highly recommended. Must acquire an Employer ID number. If necessary, register fictitious name.	File a Certificate of Limited Partnership with the Secretary of State. Name must show that business is a limited partnership. Must have written agreement, and must keep certain records.	File articles of incorporation and other required reports with the Secretary of State. prepare bylaws and follow corporate formalities	Must meet all criteria to file as an S corporation. Must file timely election with the IRS (within $2\frac{1}{2}$ months of first taxable year.	File articles of organization with the Secretary of State. Adopt operating agreement, and file necessary reports with Secretary of State. The name must show it is limited liability company.
Owner's Personal Liability	Unlimited	Unlimited for general partners, Limited for limited partners	Unlimited for general partners, Limited for limited partners	Limited	Limited	Limited
Number of Owners	One	2 or More	At least one general partner and any number of limited partners	Any number	Maximum of 100 with restrictions on who they are	One (A few states require two or more)
Tax Liability	Single tax: Personal tax rate	Single Tax: Partners pay on their proportional shares at their individual rates	Same as General Partnership	Double tax: corporation pays tax and shareholders pay tax on dividends distributed	Single tax: owners pay on their proportional shares at individual rates	Single tax: members pay on their proportional shares at individual rates
Current Maximum Tax Rate	35%	35%	35%	39% corporate plus 35% individual	35%	35%
Transferability of Ownership	Fully transferable through sale or transfer of company assets	May require consent of all partners	Same as General Partnership	Fully transferable	Transferable (but transfer may affect S status)	Usually requires consent of all members
Continuity of the Business	Ends on death or insanity of proprietor or upon termination by proprietor	Dissolves upon death, insanity, or retirement of a general partner (business may continue)	Same as General Partnership	Perpetual Life	Perpetual Life	30 years in most states
Cost of Formation	Low	Moderate	Moderate	High	High	High
Liquidity of the Owner's Investment in the Business	Poor to Average	Poor to Average	Poor to Average	High	High	High
Ability to raise capital	Low	Moderate	Moderate to High	Very High	High	High
Formation Procedure	No special steps required other than buying necessary licenses	No written partnership agreement required (but highly advisable)	Must comply with state laws regarding limited partnerships	Must meet formal requirements specified by state law	Must follow same procedures as C corporation, then elect S status with IRS	Must meet formal requirements specified by state law

Chapter Summary

1-A. Explain the advantages and the disadvantages of the sole proprietorship.

A sole proprietorship is a business owned and managed by one individual and is the most popular form of ownership.

Sole proprietorships offer these *advantages*: They are simple to create; they are the least costly form to begin; the owner has total decision-making authority; there are no special legal restrictions; and they are easy to discontinue.

They also suffer from these *disadvantages*: unlimited personal liability of owner; limited managerial skills and capabilities; limited access to capital; lack of continuity.

1-B. Explain the advantages and the disadvantages of the partnership.

A partnership is an association of two or more people who co-own a business for the purpose of making a profit. Partnerships offer these *advantages*: ease of establishing; complementary skills of partners; division of profits; larger pool of capital available; ability to attract limited partners; little government regulation flexibility; and tax advantages.

Partnerships suffer from these *disadvantages*: unlimited liability of at least one partner; difficulty in disposing of partnership; interest lack of continuity; potential for personality and authority conflicts; and partners bound by the law of agency.

1-C. Explain the advantages and the disadvantages of the corporation.

A corporation, the most complex of the three basic forms of ownership, is a separate legal entity. To form a corporation, an entrepreneur must file the articles of incorporation with the state in which the company will incorporate. Corporations offer these *advantages*: limited liability of stockholders; ability to attract capital; ability to continue indefinitely; and transferable ownership.

Corporations suffer from these *disadvantages*: cost and time involved in incorporating; double taxation; potential for diminished managerial incentives; legal requirements and regulatory red tape; and potential loss of control by the founder(s).

2. Discuss the advantages and the disadvantages of the S corporation, the Limited Liability Company, the professional corporation, and the joint venture.

Entrepreneurs can also choose from several other forms of ownership, including S corporations, and limited liability companies. An S corporation offers its owners limited liability protection but avoids the double taxation of C Corporations.

A Limited Liability Company, like an S corporation, is a cross between a partnership and a corporation, yet is operates without the restrictions imposed on an S corporation. To create an LLC, an entrepreneur must file the articles of organization and the operating agreement with the secretary of state.

A professional corporation offers professionals the benefits of the corporate form of ownership.

A joint venture is like a partnership, except that it is formed for a specific purpose.

Discussion Questions

1. What factors should an entrepreneur consider before choosing a form of ownership?
2. Why are sole proprietorships so popular as a form of ownership?
3. How does personal conflict affect partnerships?
4. What issues should the articles of partnership address? Why are the articles important to a successful partnership?
5. Can one partner commit another to a business deal without the other's consent? Why?
6. What issues should the Certificate of Incorporation cover?
7. How does an S Corporation differ from a regular corporation?
8. What role do limited partners play in a partnership? What happens if a limited partner takes an active role in managing the business?
9. What advantages does a Limited Liability Company offer over an S Corporation? A partnership?
10. How is an LLC created? What criteria must an LLC meet to avoid double taxation?
11. Briefly outline the advantages and disadvantages of the major forms of ownership.

Business PlanPro™ Selecting the form of ownership is an important decision. This chapter discusses how this decision will affect the number of business owners, tax obligations, the time and cost to form the entity, the ability to raise capital, and options for transferring ownership.

Business Plan Exercises

The Company Ownership section in the business plan is where you will discuss the form of business ownership and will impact other areas including the management and finance sections.

On the Web

Go to http://www.pearsonhighered.com/scarborough and review the business entity links for Chapter 5. This provides additional information and resources to assist with selecting the optimal form of business. Search for the term "business entity" in your favorite search engine and note the resources and information it generates.

Sample Plans

Go to the Sample Plan Browser in *Business Plan Pro*™ and look at these three business plans: Calico Computer Consulting is a sole proprietorship, Lansing Aviation is a limited liability company, and Southeast Health Plans, Inc. is a corporation. After reviewing the executive summaries of each of these plans, answer these questions:

- Why might the owners select this form of ownership?
- What are the advantages and disadvantages do each of these business entities offer the business owners?
- Why are these choices a good match for the business relating to the ease of starting, liability, control, ability to raise capital, and transfer of ownership?

In the Software

Go to the section of *Business Plan Pro*™ called Company Ownership. Look at the comparison matrix of the Characteristics of Major Forms of Ownership, Table 5.2 on page 156, and consider the ramifications of your choice.

- If a sole proprietorship or a partnership is sued, you may be personally liable. Is the nature of your business one that may present this type of risk? Is this an appropriate business entity based on that potential outcome?
- Once your business becomes profitable, what is the potential tax ramifications compared to your current situation?
- What is your ideal situation regarding the long-term ownership of the business and what are the possible choices based on that preference?
- What should you budget for legal fees and other expenditures to form the business?
- How much time do you estimate you will need to invest to establish this business entity?
- If you need to raise capital, how much money will the venture require? Is this form of ownership optimal for accomplishing that objective?

As you review the instructions provided within *Business Plan Pro*™, refer back to the "Characteristics of Major Forms of Ownership" matrix to help you select the form of ownership that is best for you and your venture.

Building Your Business Plan

Review the work that you have completed on your business plan to date. Does your chosen form of ownership fit the vision and the scope of the business? Will this choice of business entity offer the type of protection and flexibility you desire for your business? You may also want to include comments in your plan regarding changing factors that may require you to reexamine your form of ownership in the future.

Beyond the Classroom...

1. Interview five local small business owners. What form of ownership did each choose? Why? Prepare a brief report summarizing your findings, and explain advantages and disadvantages those owners face because of their choices. Do you think that these business owners have chosen the form of ownership that is best for their particular situations? Explain.

2. Invite entrepreneurs who operate as partners to your classroom. Do they have a written partnership agreement? Are their skills complementary? How do they divide responsibility for running their company? How do they handle decision making? What do they do when disputes and disagreements arise?

(Lehman)/CORBIS All Right Reserved

CHAPTER 6

Franchising and the Entrepreneur

There is nothing so easy to learn as experience and nothing so hard to apply.
—*Josh Billings*

Where else [but franchising] can we find a job creator, an economic growth stimulator, and a personal wealth creator that gives [people] the opportunity to realize their dreams and financial security for their families beyond their wildest expectations?
—*Don DeBolt*

Learning Objectives

Upon completion of this chapter, you will be able to:

1. Describe the three types of franchising: trade name, product distribution, and pure.

2. Explain the benefits and the drawbacks of buying a franchise.

3. Understand the laws covering franchise purchases.

4. Discuss the right way to buy a franchise.

5. Outline the major trends shaping franchising.

At age 16, Catherine Peña took on a part-time job at a Smoothie King franchise in her hometown of Friendswood, Texas. By the time she was 18, Peña was the youngest person ever to complete the company's management training program and had become the store's manager. At 22, Peña convinced her mother, a retired schoolteacher, to become her partner and put up $200,000 so that she could open her own franchise outlet in Corpus Christi, Texas, making Peña the youngest franchisee in Smoothie King franchise history. "I thought, 'If she can manage a store the way she does, she can do it,'" says Catherine's mother Ernestina. Now in her mid-twenties, Peña is still the youngest franchisee in the chain, and her goal is to open four more outlets within 10 years. "It's a little surreal sometimes," says Peña about owning her own franchise. "I've thought about this from the time I was 16, and I look around a say, 'This is mine.'"[1]

Like Peña's store, most franchised outlets are small, but as a whole they have a significant impact on the U.S. economy. More than 3,000 franchisors operate more than 909,000 franchise outlets in the United States alone, and more are opening at an incredible pace both in the United States and around the world. In fact, a new franchise opens somewhere in the world every eight minutes! Each year, franchises in the United States produce goods and services that are worth about $881 billion, which represents 4.4 percent of the nation's gross domestic product. They also employ one in every 12 workers in the United States in more than 230 major industries.[2] The total economic impact of franchising on the U.S. economy is an impressive $2.3 trillion.[3] Much of the popularity of franchising stems from its ability to offer those who lack business experience the chance to own and operate a business with a high probability of success. This booming industry has moved far beyond the traditional boundaries of fast-food and hotels into fields as diverse as automotive airbag replacement, used clothing, dating services, and pet-sitting.

franchising

a system of distribution in which semi-independent business owners (franchisees) pay fees and royalties to a parent company (franchisor) in return for the right to become identified with its trademark, to sell its products or services, and often to use its business format and system.

In **franchising**, semi-independent business owners (franchisees) pay fees and royalties to a parent company (franchisor) in return for the right to become identified with its trademark, to sell its products or services, and often to use its business format and system. Franchisees do not establish their own autonomous businesses; instead, they buy a "success package" from the franchisor, who shows them how to use it. Franchisees, unlike independent business owners, don't have the freedom to change the way they run their businesses—for example, shifting advertising strategies or adjusting product lines—but they do have access to a formula for success that the franchisor has worked out. Fundamentally, when they buy their franchises, franchisees are purchasing a successful business model. Many successful franchisors claim that neglecting to follow the formula is one of the chief reasons that franchisees fail. "If you are overly entrepreneurial and you want to invent your own wheel, or if you are not comfortable with following a system, then don't go down [the franchise] path," says Don DeBolt, former head of the International Franchise Association.[4]

Franchising is built on an ongoing relationship between a franchisor and a franchisee. The franchisor provides valuable services such as a proven business system, training and support, name recognition, and many other forms of assistance; in return, the franchisee pays an initial franchise fee as well as an ongoing percentage of his or her outlet's sales to the franchisor as a royalty and agrees to operate the outlet according to the franchisor's terms. Because franchisors develop the business systems their franchisees use and direct their distribution

McDonald's franchisees learn the intricacies of operating a successful franchise at Hamburger University.

Olivier Vidal/ZUMA Press-Gamma.

FIGURE 6.1

The Franchising Relationship

Source: Adapted from National Economic Consulting Practice of PricewaterhouseCoopers, *Economic Impact of Franchised Businesses:A tudy for the International Franchise Association* (New York: IFA Education Foundation, 2004), pp. 3, 5.

Element	The Franchisor	The Franchisee
Site selection	Oversees and approves; may choose site.	Chooses site with franchisor's approval.
Design	Provides prototype design.	Pays for and implements design.
Employees	Makes general recommendations and training suggestions.	Hires, manages, and fires employees.
Products and services	Determines product or service line.	Modifies only with franchisor's approval.
Prices	Can only recommend prices.	Sets final prices.
Purchasing	Establishes quality standards; provides list of approved suppliers; may require franchisees to purchase from the franchisor.	Must meet quality standards; must purchase only from approved suppliers; must purchase from supplier if required.
Advertising	Develops and coordinates national ad campaign; may require minimum level of spending on local advertising.	Pays for national ad campaign; complies with local advertising requirements; gets franchisor approval on local ads.
Quality control	Sets quality standards and enforces them with inspections; trains franchisees.	Maintains quality standards; trains employees to implement quality systems.
Support	Provides support through an established business system.	Operates business on a day-to-day basis with franchisor's support.

methods, they maintain substantial control over their franchisees. This standardization lies at the core of franchising's success as a method of distribution (see Figure 6.1).

Types of Franchising

There are three basic types of franchising: trade name franchising, product distribution franchising, and pure franchising. **Trade name franchising** involves a brand name such as True Value Hardware or Western Auto. Here, the franchisee purchases the right to use the franchisor's trade name without distributing particular products exclusively under the franchisor's name. **Product distribution franchising** involves a franchisor licensing a franchisee to sell specific products under the franchisor's brand name and trademark through a selective, limited distribution network. This system is commonly used to market automobiles (Chevrolet, Lexus, Ford), gasoline products (ExxonMobil, Sunoco, Texaco), soft drinks (Pepsi Cola, Coca Cola), bicycles (Schwinn), appliances, cosmetics, and other products. These two methods of franchising allow franchisees to acquire some of the parent company's identity.

    Pure (or **comprehensive** or **business format**) **franchising** involves providing the franchisee with a complete business format, including a license for a trade name, the products or services to be sold, the physical plant, the methods of operation, a marketing plan, a quality control process, a two-way communication system, and the necessary business support services. In short, the franchisee purchases the right to use all of the elements of a fully integrated business operation. Business format franchising is the most common and the fastest growing of the three types of franchising and accounts for 85.1 percent of all franchise outlets in the United States.[5] It is common among fast-food restaurants, hotels, business service firms, car rental agencies, educational institutions, beauty aid retailers, and many other types of businesses.

LO 1

Describe the three types of franchising: trade name, product distribution, and pure.

trade name franchising
a system of franchising in which a franchisee purchases the right to use the franchisor's trade name without distributing particular products under the franchisor's name.

product distribution franchising
a system of franchising in which a franchisor licenses a franchisee to sell its products under the franchisor's brand name and trademark through a selective, limited distribution network.

pure franchising
a system of franchising in which a franchisor sells a franchisee a complete business format and system.

Figure 6.2 shows a breakdown of the number of outlets franchisors operate; note that 25 percent of franchise systems have no more than 10 outlets, which is another indicator of the franchising industry's fast growth.

The Benefits of Buying a Franchise

LO 2

Explain the benefits of buying a franchise.

A franchisee gets the opportunity to own a small business relatively quickly, and, because of the identification with an established product and brand name, a franchise often reaches the break-even point faster than an independent business would. Still, most new franchise outlets don't break even for at least six to eighteen months.

Franchisees also benefit from the franchisor's business experience. In fact, experience is the essence of what a franchisee is buying from a franchisor. Many entrepreneurs go into business by themselves and make many costly mistakes. Given the thin margin for error in the typical start-up, a new business owner cannot afford to make many mistakes. In a franchising arrangement, the franchisor already has worked out the kinks in the system by trial-and-error, and franchisees benefit from that experience. A franchisor has climbed up the learning curve and can share with franchisees the secrets of success they have discovered in the industry. "A great franchisor has developed all of the tools that you need to start a business," says Lori Kiser-Block, president of a franchise consulting firm. "They've developed the marketing system, the training and operation system, the brand, and the marketing tools you need. They've made all of the mistakes for you."[6]

FIGURE 6.2

U. S. Franchisors Numbers of Franchised Units

Source: FRANdata, 2007.

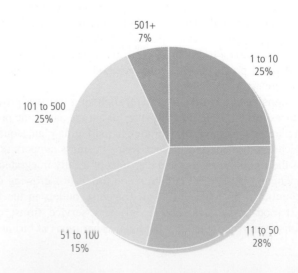

For many first-time entrepreneurs, access to a business model with a proven track record is the safest way to own a business. Still, every potential franchisee must consider the answer to one important question: "What can a franchise do for me that I cannot do for myself?" The answer to this question depends on one's particular situation and requires a systematic evaluation of a franchise opportunity. Franchisees often cite the following advantages:

A Business System

One of the biggest benefits of buying a franchise is gaining access to a business system that has a proven record of success. In many cases, the business system that a franchisor provides allows franchisees to get their businesses up and running faster than if they had tried to launch them on their own. Using the franchisor's business system as a guide, franchisees can be successful even though they may have little or no experience in the industry.

When Gina Schaefer decided to quit her job at a technology company to open an Ace Hardware franchise with her husband, Marc Friedman (also a "techie"), she was confident that they could succeed even though they had no prior experience in the hardware business. Her research and firsthand knowledge told her that customers in her Washington, D.C., neighborhood needed a hardware store, and she was confident that the Ace Hardware system would give them the support and the name recognition they needed. After attending the company's Top Gun management training school, Schaefer and Friedman opened a smaller-than-average 6,500-square-foot store with assistance from franchise headquarters. The store was so successful that Schaefer and Friedman since have opened four more Ace Hardware stores that generate annual sales of nearly $10 million.[7]

Susan Biddle/Washington Post Writers Group

ENTREPRENEURIAL PROFILE

Gina Schaefer & Marc Friedman: Ace Hardware

Management Training and Support

Franchisors want to give their franchisees a greater chance for success than independent businesses and offer management training programs to franchisees prior to opening a new outlet. Many franchisors, especially the well-established ones, also provide follow-up training and consulting services. This service is vital because most franchisors do not require a franchisee to have experience in the business. These programs teach franchisees the details they need to know for day-to-day operations as well as the nuances of running their businesses successfully. Because Jerry Heath's neighbor was the president of Hungry Howie's Pizza, it was only natural for Heath to become one of the company's franchisees, particularly after he spent a year managing a Hungry Howie's outlet. With financial backing from his father, Heath, just 23 years old, moved from Detroit to Jenison, Michigan, to open his own pizza franchise. "[The franchisor] offered quite a bit of support," recalls Heath. "If I had a question or problem, I'd call them and they would help me out."[8]

Training programs often involve both classroom and on-site instruction to teach franchisees the basic operations of the business. Before beginning operations, McDonald's franchisees spend 14 days in Illinois at Hamburger University where they learn everything from how to scrape the grill correctly to the essential elements of managing a business with high community visibility and great profit potential. MAACO franchisees spend four weeks at the company's headquarters delving into a five-volume set of operations manuals and learning to run an auto services shop, and Ben & Jerry's Homemade franchisees study at Scoop University at the company's headquarters in Burlington, Vermont. Shortly after Adam Wyatt graduated from the University of Kentucky, he purchased a Wing Zone franchise, a chain of buffalo wing delivery stores, with financing help from his parents and attended the company's 14-day training program, in which he took classes and worked in a company-owned store.[9]

To ensure franchisees' continued success, many franchisors supplement their start-up training programs with ongoing instruction and support. For instance, Ben & Jerry's sends regional trainers to new franchisees' locations for additional training before they open their stores. Once they are up and running, franchisees also benefit from ongoing training programs from Ben & Jerry's field-based support team.[10] When Adam Wyatt opened his Wing Zone store, the franchisor sent two representatives to help with the grand opening. Franchisors offer these training programs because they realize that their ultimate success depends on the franchisee's success.

Brand Name Appeal

A licensed franchisee purchases the right to use a nationally known and advertised brand name for a product or service. Thus, the franchisee has the advantage of identifying his business with a widely recognized trademark, which provides a great deal of drawing power, particularly for franchisees of established systems. Customers recognize the identifying trademark, the standard symbols, the store design, and the products of an established franchise. Because of the franchise's name recognition, franchisees who have just opened their outlets often discover a ready supply of customers eager to purchase their products or services. Entrepreneurs who launch independent businesses may have to work for years and spend many thousands of dollars in advertising to build a customer base of equivalent size. "One of the reasons I bought an AAMCO [transmission repair] franchise was its name recognition," says Stephen Rogers, who owns a franchise in Lockport, New York.[11]

Standardized Quality of Goods and Services

Because a franchisee purchases a license to sell the franchisor's product or service and the privilege of using the associated brand name, the quality of the goods or service sold determines the franchisor's reputation. Building a sound reputation in business is not achieved quickly, although destroying a good reputation takes no time at all. If some franchisees were allowed to operate at substandard levels, the image of the entire chain would suffer irreparable damage; therefore, franchisors normally demand compliance with uniform standards of quality and service throughout the entire chain. In many cases, the franchisor conducts periodic inspections of local facilities to assist in maintaining acceptable levels of performance.

ENTREPRENEURIAL PROFILE

John Schnatter: Papa John's

For instance, John Schnatter, founder of Papa John's, a fast-growing pizza franchise with nearly 3,000 outlets in 49 states and 20 global markets, makes personal visits to some of his franchisees' stores four to five times each week to make sure they are performing up to the company's high quality standards. Franchisees say that Schnatter, known for his attention to detail, often checks pizzas for air bubbles in the crust or tomato sauce for freshness. "Pizza is Schnatter's life, and he takes it very seriously," says one industry analyst.[12]

Maintaining quality is so important that most franchisors retain the right to terminate the franchise contract and to repurchase the outlet if the franchisee fails to comply with established standards.

National Advertising Programs

An effective advertising program is essential to the success of virtually all franchise operations. Marketing a brand name product or service over a wide geographic area requires a far-reaching advertising campaign. A regional or national advertising program benefits all franchisees, and most franchisors have one. Typically, these advertising campaigns are organized and controlled by the franchisor, but franchisees actually pay for the campaigns. In fact, a recent study reports that 79 percent of franchisors require franchisees to contribute to a national advertising fund (the amount ranges from 1 to 5 percent of sales, and the average amount is 2 percent of sales).[13] For example, Subway franchisees pay 3.5 percent of gross revenues to the Subway national advertising program. These funds are pooled and used for a cooperative advertising program, which has more impact than if the franchisees spent the same amount of money separately.

Many franchisors also require franchisees to spend a minimum amount on local advertising. In fact, 41 percent of franchisors require their franchisees to invest in local advertising (once again, the average amount is 2 percent of sales).[14] To supplement their national advertising efforts, both Wendy's and Burger King require franchisees to spend at least 3 percent of gross sales on local advertising. Some franchisors assist franchisees in designing and producing their local ads. Many companies help franchisees create promotional plans and provide press releases and advertisements for grand openings.

Financial Assistance

Purchasing a franchise can be just as expensive (if not more so) than launching an independent business. Although franchisees typically invest a significant amount of their own money in their businesses, most of them need additional financing. In some cases, the franchisor provides at least some of that additional financing. A basic principle of franchising is to use franchisees' money to grow their businesses, but some franchisors realize that because start-up costs have reached breathtakingly high levels, they must provide financial help for franchisees. In fact, a study by FRANdata, a franchising research company, reports that 20 percent of franchisors offer direct financing to their franchisees (see Figure 6.3).[15] Small franchise systems are more likely to provide direct financial assistance to franchisees than are larger, more established franchisors. In addition, franchisors rarely make loans to enable franchisees to pay the initial franchise fee. However, once a franchisor locates a suitable prospective franchisee, it may offer the qualified candidate direct financial assistance in specific areas, such as purchasing equipment, inventory, or even the franchise fee.

In most instances, financial assistance from franchisors takes a form other than direct loans, leases, or short-term credit. Franchisors usually are willing to assist qualified franchisees in establishing relationships with banks, nonbank lenders, and other sources of funds. The support and connections from the franchisor enhance a franchisee's credit standing because lenders recognize the lower failure rate among established franchises. For instance, Papa John's, the pizza franchise, has established relationships with 10 different lenders to whom it refers franchisees in search of financing.[16]

The Small Business Administration (SBA) has created a program called the Franchise Registry that is designed to provide financing for franchisees through its loan guarantee programs (more on these in Chapter 13, Sources of Debt and Equity Financing). The Franchise Registry streamlines and expedites the loan application process for franchisees who pass the screening tests at franchises that are members of the Registry. More than 1,000 franchises ranging from AAMCO Transmissions (automotive repair) to Zaxby's (fast-food chicken restaurants) participate in the Franchise Registry program. Approximately 6.3 percent of all SBA loan guarantees go to franchisees, and the amount typically ranges from $250,000 to $500,000.[17] Franchisees interested in the Franchise Registry program should visit its Web site at www.franchiseregistry.com.

Proven Products and Business Formats

As we have seen, franchisees essentially purchase a franchisor's experience in the form of a business system. A franchise owner does not have to build the business from scratch. Instead of being forced to rely solely on personal ability to establish a business and attract a clientele, a franchisee can depend on the methods and techniques of an established business. These standardized procedures and operations greatly enhance the franchisee's chances of success and avoid the most inefficient type of learning—trial and error. In addition, a franchisee does not have to struggle for recognition in the local marketplace as much as an independent owner might.

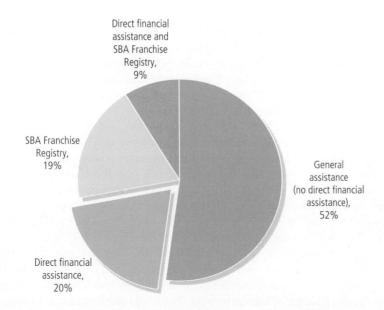

FIGURE 6.3

Franchisor Financial Assistance

Source: The Profile of Franchising 2006, International Franchise Association (Washington, DC: 2007), p. 70.

Steven Taylor, just 29 years old and with little business experience, realized that the best way for him to realize his goal of owning his own business was to purchase a franchise. "I knew the power behind [franchising]," he says. Taylor began investigating franchise options, focusing on Subway and Moe's Southwest Grill, a quick-service Mexican restaurant that he frequented. One of the Subway franchisees whom Taylor interviewed, a man who owned 45 outlets, was so impressed with Taylor's ambition and enthusiasm that he agreed to help finance the initial cost of a franchise. Within a year, Taylor and business partner Chris Smith had opened their first Moe's Southwest Grill in Columbia, South Carolina, and have since added four more locations. Their stores have won numerous company awards, but Taylor and Smith credit following the franchisor's system for their success. They rely on a battery of tools ranging from activity checklists, time-and-temperature logs, and food cost and labor cost calculators to make sure their stores run smoothly and efficiently. "In the same way the franchisor gave us a system to run, we, in turn, create systems that we expect the managers to run," says Taylor. "As long as they're running the systems, we're running an A-plus store."[18]

Moe's Corporate HQ Southwest Grill

Centralized Buying Power

A significant advantage a franchisee has over an independent small business owner is participation in the franchisor's centralized and large-volume buying power. If franchisors sell goods and supplies to franchisees (not all do), they may pass on to franchisees any cost savings from quantity discounts they earn by buying in volume. For example, it is unlikely that a small, independent ice cream parlor could match the buying power of Baskin-Robbins with its 5,800-plus retail ice cream stores. In many instances, economies of scale simply preclude an independent business owner from competing head-to-head with a franchise operation.

Site Selection and Territorial Protection

A proper location is critical to the success of any small business, and franchises are no exception. In fact, franchise experts consider the three most important factors in franchising to be *location*, *location*, and *location*. Sometimes, entrepreneurs discover that becoming affiliated with a franchisor is the best way to get into prime locations. Many franchisors conduct an extensive location analysis for each new outlet, including researching traffic patterns, zoning ordinances, accessibility, and population density. Although choosing a location usually is the franchisee's responsibility, some franchisors control the site selection process. Stephen Rogers decided to leave a family business to purchase an AAMCO transmission service franchise and relied on the franchisor to select a location for his service center because of the company's experience in selecting prime locations for their outlets. (AAMCO has been selling franchises since 1963.)[19] Even when the franchisee makes the location decision, the franchisor reserves the right to approve the final site. Choosing a suitable location requires a thorough location analysis, including studies of traffic patterns, zoning ordinances, accessibility, population density, and demographics. Experienced franchisors know that selecting a location in a high-traffic area but on the "wrong" side of the street can doom a unit from the outset, and they do everything they can to help franchisees avoid bad locations.

Some franchisors offer franchisees territorial protection, which gives existing franchisees the right to exclusive distribution of brand name goods or services within a particular geographic area. A clause establishing such a protective zone that bars other outlets from the same franchise gives franchisees significant protection and security. The size of a franchisee's territory varies from industry to industry. For example, one national fast-food restaurant agrees not to license another franchisee within a mile and one-half of existing locations, but, one ice cream franchisor defines its franchisees' territories on the basis of zip code designations. The purpose of this protection is to prevent an invasion of the existing franchisee's territory and the accompanying dilution of sales. A recent study of successful franchises reports that the failure rate for franchisees is lower in systems that offer exclusive territories than in those that do not.[20]

As existing markets have become increasingly saturated with franchise outlets, the placement of new outlets has become a source of friction between franchisors and franchisees. Existing franchisees complain that franchisors are encroaching on their territories by granting new franchises so close to them that their sales are diluted. Before signing a franchise contract, every prospective franchisee must know exactly what kind of territorial protection, if any, the franchisor guarantees. Why invest years building a successful franchise in a particular location only to have the franchisor allow another franchisee to open nearby, siphoning off sales of your existing outlet?

Greater Chance for Success

Investing in a franchise is not risk-free. In a typical year, between 200 and 300 new franchise companies enter the market, and not all of them survive. For instance, 138 franchisee-owned restaurants faced an uncertain future when their franchisor Bennigan's filed for bankruptcy. Although they no longer have the support of a franchisor, the restaurateurs are trying to stay open.[21] Scott Shane, who has conducted extensive research on both entrepreneurs and franchises, says that the failure rate for young franchise systems is higher than that of older, more established ones. "Twenty years from their start, less than 20 percent of the franchisers will still be around," he says.[22]

Despite the fact that franchising offers no guarantees of success, experts contend that franchising is less risky than building a business from the ground up. The tradition of success for franchises is attributed to the broad range of services, assistance, guidelines, and the comprehensive business system the franchisor provides. Statistics regarding the success of a given franchise must be interpreted carefully, however. For example, sometimes when a franchise is in danger of failing, the franchisor often repurchases or relocates the outlet and does not report it as a failure.* As a result, some franchisors boast of never experiencing a failure.

A recent study of franchises reports that the success rate of franchisees is higher when a franchise system:

- Requires franchisees to have prior industry experience.
- Requires franchisees to actively manage their stores (no "absentee" owners).
- Has built a strong brand name.
- Offers training programs designed to improve franchisees' knowledge and skills.[23]

The risk involved in purchasing a franchise is two-pronged: success—or failure—depends on the franchisee's managerial skills and motivation and on the franchisor's business experience, system, and support. Many franchisees are convinced that franchising has been the key to their success in business. Their success is proof of the common sentiment that franchising offers the opportunity to be in business *for* yourself but not *by* yourself. "[Franchising is] the perfect combination of having an independently owned and operated office, but with support," says Olivier Hecht, who left his corporate job to open a Handyman Matters home repair franchise.[24]

The Drawbacks of Buying a Franchise

The benefits of franchising can mean the difference between success and failure for some entrepreneurs. Prospective franchisees must understand the disadvantages of franchising before choosing this method of doing business. Perhaps the biggest drawback of franchising is that a franchisee must sacrifice some freedom to the franchisor. Other disadvantages include the following.

Franchise Fees and Ongoing Royalties

Virtually every franchisor imposes some type of fees and demands a share of franchisees' sales revenue in return for the use of the franchisor's name, products or services, and business system. The fees and the initial capital requirements vary among the different franchisors. The total investment required for a franchise varies from around $1,000 for some home-based service franchises to $6.5 million or more for hotel and motel franchises. For example, Jazzercise, an aerobics exercise franchise, requires a capital investment that ranges from just $3,000 to $33,100, and Quizno's, the Italian-style submarine sandwich and salad chain, estimates that the total cost of opening a franchise ranges from $29,100 for a kiosk location to $323,900 for a traditional restaurant. Culver's, a fast-growing regional chain that sells sandwiches (including the delicious ButterBurger®), salads, dinners, and frozen custard, requires an investment of $341,000 to $2,923,000, depending on land acquisition and building construction costs.

LO 3

Explain the drawbacks of buying a franchise.

---

*As long as an outlet's doors never close, most franchisors do not count it as a failure even if the outlet has struggled for survival and has been through a series of owners who have tried unsuccessfully to turn around its performance.

Start-up costs for franchises often include a variety of fees. Most franchises impose an up-front franchise fee for the right to use the company name. The average upfront fee that franchisers charge is $25,147.[25] Culver's, the fast-food chain, charges a franchise fee that ranges from $30,000 to $50,000, depending upon the franchisee's territory. Other franchise start-up costs might include a location analysis, site purchase and preparation, construction, signs, fixtures, equipment, management assistance, and training. Some franchise fees include these costs, but others do not. For example, Closets by Design, a company that designs and installs closet- and garage-organizers, entertainment centers, and home office systems, charges a franchise fee ranging from $24,500 to $39,900, which includes both a license for an exclusive territory and management training and support. Before signing any contract, a prospective franchisee should determine the total cost of a franchise, something every franchisor is required to disclose in item 10 of its Franchise Disclosure Document (see the "Franchising and the Law" section later in this chapter).

Franchisors also impose continuing royalty fees as revenue-sharing devices. The royalty usually involves a percentage of gross sales with a required minimum, or a flat fee levied on the franchise. (In fact, 82 percent of franchisors charge a royalty based on a percentage of franchisees' sales.[26]) Royalty fees range from 1 percent to 11 percent, and the average royalty rate is 6.7 percent.[27] The Atlanta Bread Company charges franchisees a royalty of 5 percent of gross sales, which is payable weekly, and Cold Stone Creamery charges a royalty of 6 percent of gross sales. These ongoing royalties increase a franchisee's overhead expenses significantly. Because the franchisor's royalties and fees (the total fees the average franchisor collects amount to 8.4 percent of a franchisee's sales) are calculated as a percentage of a franchisee's sales, the franchisor gets paid—even if the franchisee fails to earn a profit.[28] Sometimes unprepared franchisees discover (too late) that a franchisor's royalties and fees are the equivalent of the normal profit margin for a franchise.

Strict Adherence to Standardized Operations

Although franchisees own their businesses, they do not have the autonomy that independent owners have. To protect its image, a franchisor requires that franchisees maintain certain operating standards. In fact, conformity is standard operating procedure in franchising. The franchisor controls the layout and the color schemes its franchisees use in their stores, the products they sell, the personnel, and operating policies they use, and many other aspects of running the business. At McDonald's franchisees must operate their businesses by the franchise manual, which specifies nearly every detail of running a franchise—including how many hamburger patties per pound of beef (10), how long to toast a bun (17 seconds), and how much sanitizer to use when cleaning the milkshake machine (1 packet for 2.5 gallons of water).

If a franchise constantly fails to meet the minimum standards established for the business, the franchisor may terminate its license. Many franchisors determine compliance with standards with periodic inspections and mystery shoppers. Mystery shoppers work for a survey company and, although they look like any other customer, are trained to observe and then later record on a checklist a franchise's performance on key standards such as cleanliness, speed of service, employees' appearances and attitudes, and others. McDonald's, a long-time user of mystery shoppers, even posts franchisees' mystery shoppers' scores on an internal Web site so that owners can compare their scores with regional averages.[29]

Restrictions on Purchasing

In the interest of maintaining quality standards, franchisors may require franchisees to purchase products, special equipment, or other items from the franchisor or from a list of "approved" suppliers. For example, KFC requires that franchisees use only seasonings blended by a particular company because a poor image could result from franchisees using inferior products to cut costs. Under some conditions, these purchase arrangements may be challenged in court as a violation of antitrust laws, but generally franchisors have a legal right to ensure that franchisees maintain acceptable quality standards. Franchisees of one ice cream franchise have complained that their profit margins suffer because the franchisor requires them to purchase costly ingredients from a single supplier.[30]

A franchisor legally may set the prices it charges for the products it sells to franchisees but cannot control the retail prices franchisees charge for the products they sell. A franchisor can *suggest* retail prices for a franchisee's products and services but cannot force the franchisee to abide by them. To do so would be a violation of the Robinson-Patman Act. For instance, even though many fast-food franchisors promote their "dollar menus," many franchisees charge more than $1 for those items. One long-time franchisee, who charges $1.29 for a double cheeseburger says that if he had to price them at $1, he "couldn't stay in business."[31] Franchisors do influence the prices that their franchisees charge in other ways, however. A common technique is to offer discount coupons that franchisees must honor. One company's franchisee's complained that the franchisor's "two-for-one" coupons were cutting into their profit margins so severely that the franchisor agreed to stop distributing them.[32]

Limited Product Line

In most cases, the franchise agreement stipulates that the franchise can sell only those products approved by the franchisor. Unless they are willing to risk the cancellation of their licenses, franchisees must avoid selling unapproved products through the franchise. A franchise may be required to carry an unpopular product or be prevented from introducing a desirable one by the franchise agreement. A franchisee's freedom to adapt a product line to local market conditions is restricted. However, some franchisors actively solicit innovations and product suggestions from their franchisees. In fact, some of McDonald's most successful products did not come from the corporate kitchen but from franchisees such as Jim Delligatti, who invented the legendary Big Mac in 1972. Today, McDonald's sells 550 million Big Macs each year—an average of 17 sandwiches per second![33]

Contract Terms and Renewal

Because they are written by the franchisor's attorneys, franchise contracts always are written in favor of the franchisor. Some franchisors are willing to negotiate the terms of their contracts, but many of the well-established franchisors are not because they know that they don't have to. The franchise contract is extremely important because it governs the franchisor-franchisee relationship over its life, which may last as long as 20 years. In fact, the average length of a franchise contract is 10.3 years.[34] Yet one study conducted by the Federal Trade Commission found that 40 percent of new franchisees signed their contracts without reading them![35]

Franchisees also should understand the terms and conditions under which they may renew their franchise contracts at the expiration of the original agreement. In most cases, franchisees are required to pay a renewal fee and to repair any deficiencies in their outlets or to modernize and upgrade them. A recent study of franchising by the International Franchise Association and FRANdata reports that the renewal rate of franchise agreements is 94 percent.[36]

Jim Delligatti, creator of the Big Mac, with a 14-foot tall replica of McDonald's best-selling sandwich in the Big Mac Museum.

Unsatisfactory Training Programs

A major benefit of purchasing a franchise is the training that the franchisor provides franchisees so that they are able to run successful operations. The quality of franchise training programs can vary dramatically, however. "Many franchisees think they will get a lot of training but find out it's a one-week crash course," says Marko Grunhagen, a franchising expert at Southern Illinois University.[37] Before signing on with a franchise, it is wise to find out the details of the training program the franchisor provides to avoid unpleasant surprises.

Market Saturation

Franchisees in fast-growing systems reap the benefits of the franchisor's expanding reach, but they also may encounter the downside of a franchisor's aggressive growth strategy: market saturation. As the owners of many fast-food, sandwich shops, and yogurt and ice cream franchises have discovered, market saturation is a very real danger. Subway, for example, has grown from just 166 outlets in 1981 to more than 30,000 outlets today![38] Any franchise growing that rapidly runs the risk of having outlets so close together that they cannibalize sales from one another. Franchisees of one fast-growing ice cream chain claim that the franchisor's rapid expansion has resulted in oversaturation in some markets, causing them to struggle to reach their break-even points. Some franchisees saw their sales drop precipitously and were forced to close their outlets.

Although some franchisors offer franchisees territorial protection, others do not. Territorial encroachment has become a hotly contested issue in franchising as growth-seeking franchisors have exhausted most of the prime locations and are now setting up new franchises in close proximity to existing ones. In some areas of the country, franchisees are upset, claiming that their markets are oversaturated and their sales are suffering.

Less Freedom

When franchisees sign a contract, they agree to sell the franchisor's product or service by following its prescribed formula. This feature of franchising is the source of the system's success, but it also gives many franchisees the feeling that they are reporting to a "boss." Franchisors want to ensure franchisees' success, and most monitor their franchisees' performances closely to make sure franchisees follow the system's specifications. "Everything you do in a franchise will be dictated [by the franchisor] from the moment you turn the key in the door in the morning," warns Eric Karp, a Boston attorney who teaches franchising at Babson College.[39]

Strict uniformity is the rule rather than the exception. "There is no independence," says one writer. "Successful franchisees are happy prisoners."[40] As a result, highly independent, "go-my-own-way" entrepreneurs often are frustrated with the basic "go-by-the-rules" philosophy of franchising. Table 6.1 describes ten myths of franchising.

TABLE 6.1 Ten Myths of Franchising

Myth #1. Franchising is the safest way to go into business because franchises never fail. Although the failure rate for franchises is lower than that of independent businesses, there are no guarantees of success. Franchises can— and do—fail. Potential franchisees must exercise the same degree of caution in judging the risk of a franchise as they would any other business.

Myth #2. I'll be able to open my franchise for less money than the franchisor estimates. Launching a business, including a franchise, normally takes more money and more time than entrepreneurs estimate. Be prepared. One franchisee of a retail computer store advises, "If a franchiser tells you you'll need $100,000 to get started, you better have $150,000."

Myth #3. The bigger the franchise organization, the more successful I'll be. Bigger is not always better in the franchise business. Some of the largest franchise operations are struggling to maintain their growth rates because the best locations are already taken and their markets have become saturated. Market saturation is a significant problem for many large franchises, and smaller franchises are accounting for much of the growth in the industry. Early franchisees in new franchise systems often can negotiate better deals and receive more individual attention from the franchisor than those who purchase units in well-established systems.

Myth #4. I'll use 80 percent of the franchisor's business system, but I'll improve on it by substituting my experience and know-how. When franchisees buy a franchise, they are buying, in essence, the franchisor's experience and knowledge. Why pay all of that money to a franchisor if you aren't willing to use their system? When franchisors screen potential franchisees, they look for people who are willing to fit into their systems rather than fiercely independent entrepreneurs. "[franchisors] have spent years building the company," says Jeff Elgin, founder of FranChoice, a franchise referral consulting firm. "They don't want someone who will come in and try to innovate because that produces chaos." Ideally, franchisors look for franchisees who exhibit a balance between the free-wheeling entrepreneurial spirit and a system-focused approach.

Myth #5. All franchises are basically the same. Each franchise has its own unique personality, requirements, procedures, and culture. Naturally, some will suit you better than others. Avoid the tendency to select the franchise that offers the lowest cost. If the franchise does not fit your needs, it is not a bargain, no matter how inexpensive it is. Ask the franchisor and existing franchisees lots of questions to determine how well you will fit into the system. One of the best ways to get a feel for a franchise's personality is to work in a unit for a time.

Myth #6. I don't have to be a hands-on manager. I can be an absentee owner and still be very successful. Most franchisors shy away from absentee owners, and some simply do not allow them in their systems at all. They know that franchise success requires lots of hands-on attention, and the franchise owner is the best person to provide that.

Myth #7. Anyone can be a satisfied, successful franchise owner. With more than 3,000 franchises available, the odds of finding a franchise that appeals to your tastes is high. However, not everyone is cut out to be a franchisee. Those "free spirits" who insist on doing things their way most likely will be miserable in a franchise.

Myth #8. Franchising is the cheapest way to get into business for yourself. Although bargains do exist in franchising, the price tag for buying into some well-established systems is breathtaking, sometimes running into millions of dollars. Franchisors look for candidates who are on solid financial footing.

Myth #9. The franchisor will solve my business problems for me; after all, that's why I pay an ongoing royalty. Although franchisors offer franchisees start-up and ongoing training programs, they will not run their franchisees' businesses for them. As a franchisee, your job is to take the formula that the franchisor has developed and make it work in your location. Expect to solve many of your own problems.

Myth #10. Once I open my franchise, I'll be able to run things the way I want to. Franchisees are not free to run their businesses as they see fit. Every franchisee signs a contract that requires him or her to run the business according to the franchisor's requirements. Franchisees who violate the terms of that agreement run the risk of having their franchise relationship terminated.

Sources: Adapted from April Y. Pennington, "The Right Stuff," *Entrepreneur B.Y.O.B.*, September 2004, pp. 90–100; Andrew A. Caffey, "There's More to a Franchise Than Meets the Eye," *Entrepreneur*, May 1998, http://www.entrepreneur.com/article/0,4621,228443,00.html; Andrew A. Caffey, "Myth vs. Reality," *Entrepreneur*, October 1998, http://www.entrepreneur.com/mag/article/0,1539,229435,00.html; Chieh Chieng, "Do You Want to Know a Secret?" *Entrepreneur*, January 1999, pp. 174–178; "Ten Most Common Mistakes Made by Franchise Buyers," Franchise Doctor, www.franchisedoc.com/mistakes.html; Devlin Smith, "The Sure Thing," *Entrepreneur B.Y.O.B.*, May 2004, p. 100.

Franchising and the Law

LO 4

Explain the laws covering franchise purchases.

The franchising boom spearheaded by McDonald's and others in the late 1950s brought with it many prime investment opportunities. However, the explosion of legitimate franchises also ushered in with it numerous fly-by-night franchisors who defrauded their franchisees. By the 1970s, franchising was rife with fraudulent practitioners. Thousands of people lost millions of dollars to criminals and unscrupulous operators who sold flawed business concepts and phantom franchises to unsuspecting investors. In an effort to control the rampant fraud in the industry and the potential for deception inherent in a franchise relationship, California in 1971 enacted the first Franchise Investment Law. The law (and those of 14 other states that passed similar laws) required franchisors to register a Uniform Franchise Offering Circular (UFOC) and deliver a copy to prospective franchisees before any offer or sale of a franchise. In October 1979, the Federal Trade Commission (FTC) adopted similar legislation at the national level that established full

Franchise Disclosure Document (FDD)

a document that every franchisor is required by law to give prospective franchisees before any offer or sale of a franchise; it outlines 23 important pieces of information.

disclosure guidelines for any company selling franchises and was designed to give potential franchisees the information they needed to protect themselves from unscrupulous franchisors.

In 2008, the FTC replaced the UFOC with a similar document, the **Franchise Disclosure Document (FDD)**, which requires all franchisors to disclose detailed information on their operations at least 14 days before a franchisee signs a contract or pays any money. The FDD applies to all franchisors, even those in the 35 states that lack franchise disclosure laws. The purpose of the regulation is to assist potential franchisees' investigations of a franchise deal and to introduce consistency into the franchisor's disclosure statements. The FTC also established a "plain English" requirement for the FDD that prohibits legal and technical jargon and makes a document easy to read and understand. The FTC's philosophy is not so much to prosecute abusers as to provide information to prospective franchisees and help them to make intelligent decisions.

The Trade Regulation Rule requires a franchisor to include 23 major topics in its disclosure statement:

1. Information identifying the franchisor and its affiliates and describing the franchisor's business experience and the franchises being sold.
2. Information identifying and describing the business experience of each of the franchisor's officers, directors, and managers responsible for the franchise program.
3. A description of the lawsuits in which the franchisor and its officers, directors, and managers have been involved. Although most franchisors will have been involved in some type of litigation, an excessive number of lawsuits, particularly if they relate to the same problem, is alarming. Another red flag is an excessive number of lawsuits brought against the franchisor by franchisees. "The history of the litigation will tell you the future of your relationship [with the franchisor]," says the founder of a maid-service franchise.[41]
4. Information about any bankruptcies in which the franchisor and its officers, directors, and managers have been involved.
5. Information about the initial franchise fee and other payments required to obtain the franchise, the intended use of the fees, and the conditions under which the fees are refundable.
6. A table that describes all of the other fees that franchisees are required to make after start-up, including royalties, service fees, training fees, lease payments, advertising or marketing charges, and others. The table also must include the due dates for the fees.
7. A table that shows the components of a franchisee's total initial investment. The categories covered are pre-opening expenses, the initial franchise fee, training expenses, equipment, opening inventory, initial advertising fee, signs, real estate (purchased or leased), equipment, opening inventory, security deposits, business licenses, initial advertising fees, and other expenses, such as working capital, legal and accounting fees. These estimates, usually stated as a range, give prospective franchisees an idea of how much their total start-up costs will be.
8. Information about quality requirements of goods, services, equipment, supplies, inventory, and other items used in the franchise and where franchisees may purchase them, including required purchases from the franchisor.
9. A cross-reference table that shows the location in the FDD and in the franchise contract of the description of the franchisee's obligations under the franchise contract.
10. A description of any financial assistance available from the franchisor in the purchase of the franchise. Although many franchisors do not offer direct financial assistance to franchisees, they may have special arrangements with lenders who help franchisees find financing.
11. A description of all obligations the franchisor must fulfill in helping a franchisee prepare to open and operate a unit, including site selection, advertising, computer systems, pricing, training (a table describing the length and type of training is required), and other forms of assistance provided to franchisees. This usually is the longest section of the FDD.
12. A description of any territorial protection that the franchisee receives and a statement as to whether the franchisor may locate a company-owned store or other franchised outlet in that territory. The franchisor must specify whether it offers exclusive or non-exclusive territories. Given the controversy in many franchises over market saturation, franchisees should pay close attention to this section.
13. All relevant information about the franchisor's trademarks, service marks, trade names, logos, and commercial symbols, including where they are registered. Prospective franchisees should look for a strong trade or service mark that is registered with the U.S. Patent and Trademark Office.

14. Similar information on any patents, copyrights, and proprietary processes the franchisor owns and the rights franchisees have to use them.

15. A description of the extent to which franchisees must participate personally in the operation of the franchise. Many franchisors look for "hands-on" franchisees and discourage or even prohibit "absentee owners."

16. A description of any restrictions on the goods or services that franchises are permitted to sell and with whom franchisees may deal. The agreement usually restricts franchisees to selling only those items that the franchisor has approved.

17. A table that describes the conditions under which the franchise may be repurchased or refused renewal by the franchisor, transferred to a third party by the franchisee, and terminated or modified by either party. This section also addresses the method established for resolving disputes between franchisees and the franchisor.

18. A description of the involvement of celebrities and public figures in the franchise.

19. A complete statement of the basis for any earnings claims made to the franchisee, including the percentage of existing franchises that have actually achieved the results that are claimed. Franchisors that make earnings claims must include them in the FDD, and the claims must "have a reasonable basis" at the time they are made. However, franchisors are *not* required to make any earnings claims at all; in fact, 81.7 percent of franchisors do not, primarily because of liability concerns about committing such numbers to writing.[42]

20. A table that displays system-wide statistical information about the expansion or the contraction of the franchise over the last three years. This section also includes the current number of franchises, the number of franchises projected for the future and the states in which they are to be sold, the number of franchises terminated, the number of agreements the franchisor has not renewed, the number of franchises that have been sold to new owners, the number of outlets the franchisor has repurchased, and a list of the addresses (organized by state) of other franchisees in the system and of those who have left the system within the last year. Contacting some of the franchisees who have left the system alerts would-be franchisees to potential problems with the franchise.

21. The franchisor's audited financial statements.

22. A copy of all franchise and other contracts (leases, purchase agreements, and others) that the franchisee will be required to sign.

23. A standardized, detachable "receipt" to prove that the prospective franchisee received a copy of the FDD. The FTC now allows franchisors to provide the FDD to prospective franchisees electronically.

The typical FDD is from 100 to 200 pages long, but every potential franchisee should read and understand it. Unfortunately, many do not, which often results in unpleasant surprises for franchisees. The information contained in the FDD neither fully protects a potential franchisee from deception nor does it guarantee success. The FDD does, however, provide enough information to begin a thorough investigation of the franchisor and the franchise deal, and prospective franchisees should use it to their advantage.

The Opportunity of a Lifetime

"Honey, I think I've found it!" said Joe Willingham to his wife, Allie, as he rushed through the door. "This is just what I've been looking for, and just in time, too. My severance package from the company runs out next month. The man said that if we invested in this franchise now, we could be bringing in good money by then. It's that easy!"

Allie knew that Joe had been working hard at finding another job since he had become a victim of his company's latest downsizing, but that jobs were scarce even for someone with his managerial experience and background in manufacturing. "Nobody wants to hire a 51-year-old man with experience when they can hire 23-year-old college graduates at less than half the salary and teach them what they need to know," Joe told her after months of fruitless job hunting. That's when Joe got the idea of setting up his own business. Rather than start an independent business from scratch, Joe felt more comfortable, given his 26-year corporate career, opening a franchise. "A franchiser can give me the support I need," he told Allie.

"Tell me about this franchise," Allie said.

"It's a phenomenal opportunity for us," Joe said, barely able to contain his excitement. "I saw this booth for American Speedy Print at the Business Expo this morning. There were all kinds of franchises represented there, but this one really caught my eye," Joe said as he pulled a rather plain-looking photocopy of a brochure from his briefcase.

"Is that their brochure?" asked Allie.

"Well, the company is growing so fast that they have temporarily run out of their normal literature. This is just temporary."

"Oh... You would think that a printing franchise could print flashier brochures even on short notice, but I guess...," said Allie.

"The main thing is the profit potential this business has," said Joe. "I met one of their franchisees. I tell you the guy was wearing a $2,000 suit if ever there was one, and he had expensive jewelry dripping from his fingers. He's making a mint with this franchise, and he said we could too!"

Joe continued, "With the severance package I have from the company, we could pay the $10,000 franchise fee and lease most of the equipment we need to get started. It'll take every penny of my package, but, hey, it's an investment in our future. The representative said the company would help us with our grand opening, and would help us compile a list of potential customers."

"What would you print?" asked Allie.

"Anything!" said Joe. "The franchisee I talked to does fliers, posters, booklets, newsletters, advertising pieces...you name it!"

"Oh my! It seems like you'd need lots of specialized equipment to do all of that." How much does the total franchise package cost?" asked Allie.

"Well, I'm not exactly sure. He never gave me an exact figure, but we can lease all the equipment we need from the franchiser!"

"Is this all of the material they gave you? I thought franchisers were supposed to have some kind of information packet to give to people." said Allie.

"Yeah, I asked him about that," said Joe. "He said that American Speedy Print is just a small franchise. They'd rather put their money

into building a business and helping their franchisees succeed than into useless paperwork that nobody reads anyway. It makes sense to me."

"I guess so...," Allie said reluctantly.

"I think we need to take this opportunity, Hon," Joe said, with a look that spoke of determination and enthusiasm." Besides, he said that there was another couple in this county that is already looking at this franchise, and that the company will license only one franchisee in this area. They don't want to saturate the market. He thinks they may take it. I think we have to move on this now, or we'll lose the opportunity of a lifetime."

Allie had not seen Joe exhibit this much enthusiasm and excitement for anything since he had lost his job at the plant. Piles of rejection letters from his job search had sapped Joe's zest for life. Allie was glad to see "the old Joe" return, but she still had her doubts about the franchise opportunity Joe was describing.

"It might just be the opportunity of a lifetime, Joe," she said. "But don't you think we need to find out a little more about this franchise before we invest that much money? I mean..."

"Hon, I'd love to do that, but like the man said, we may miss out on the opportunity of a lifetime if we don't sign today. I think we've got to move on this thing now!"

1. What advice would you offer Joe about investing in this franchise? Explain.
2. Map out a plan for Joe to use in finding the right franchise for him. What can Joe do to protect himself from making a bad franchise investment?
3. Summarize the advantages and disadvantages Joe can expect if he buys a franchise.

LO 5

Discuss the *right* way to buy a franchise.

The *Right* Way to Buy a Franchise

Not every franchise "horror story" is the result of would-be franchisees being duped by dishonest franchisors. More often than not, the problems that arise in franchising have more to do with franchisees who buy legitimate franchises without proper research and analysis. They end up in businesses they don't enjoy and that they are not well-suited to operate. How can you avoid this mistake? The following steps will help you to make the right choice:

Evaluate Yourself

Before looking at any franchise, entrepreneurs should study their own traits, goals, experience, likes, dislikes, risk-orientation, income requirements, time and family commitments, and other characteristics. Knowing how much you can invest in a franchise is important, but it is not the only factor to consider. "You not only have to understand simple things such as what kind of investment you're willing to make, but also what kind of risks you are willing to take, how hard you want to work, how many hours you want to work, and what kind of environment you want to work in," advises Lori Kiser-Block, head of franchise consulting service FranChoice.[43] Will you be comfortable working in a structured environment? In what region of the country or world do you want to live and work? What is your ideal job description? Do you want to sell a product or a service? What hours do you expect to work? Do you want to work with people or do you prefer to work alone? Knowing what you enjoy doing (and what you *don't* want to do) will help you to narrow your search. Which franchises are a good match for your strengths, weaknesses, interests, and professional experience? The goal is to find the franchise that is right—for *you*!

**ENTREPRENEURIAL
PROFILE**_____

Todd & Bambi Stringham:
Signs by Tomorrow

After spending 15 years in the corporate world, Todd and Bambi Stringham grew disillusioned and decided to make a career change. After evaluating their experience, strengths, and finances, they decided to transform their dream of owning a business into a reality by buying a franchise. The Stringhams spent months reviewing the features of more than 30 franchisors that matched their profile of what they were looking for in a franchise before settling on Signs By Tomorrow, a Maryland-based company with nearly 200 outlets that makes a variety of signs, primarily for businesses. They wanted a franchisor that would support their operation with a solid business system and that would allow them to use their own creativity. "I have always wanted to own my own business," says Todd. "After a lot of research, we found that Signs by Tomorrow had the business model and support system we were looking for."[44]

Table 6.2 is designed to help prospective franchisees to evaluate their potential as successful franchisees.

TABLE 6.2 Are You Franchisee Material?

Not everyone is cut out to be a franchisee. What characteristics do successful franchise owners have?

- **Commitment.** Like all entrepreneurs, successful franchisees must be committed to making their businesses successful. For franchisees, that means learning how the franchisor's system works and how to apply it in their individual markets.
- **Learning attitude.** Franchisees must exhibit a learning attitude and be willing to learn from the franchisor, other franchisees, and other experts.
- **Willingness to work with others.** Franchising success requires a willingness to work with the franchisor in a close, mutually beneficial relationship.
- **Patience.** Franchisees must understand that franchising is *not* a ticket to overnight success; success often requires years of hard work.
- **Positive attitude.** Franchisors look for franchisees who have a positive outlook and are focused on success.
- **General business skills.** Although franchisors usually do not require franchisees to have years of experience in the particular industry in which they operate, they do look for people who have general business experience. Sound leadership and communication skills are important in every industry.
- **Leadership ability.** To get a franchise up and running successfully requires every ounce of leadership ability that a franchisee has.
- **Coachability.** In addition to being successful leaders, franchisees also must be good followers. Franchisors say that their most successful franchisees are coachable and are willing to learn from the experience of others. Reaping the advantages of the franchisor's experience is one of the primary benefits of franchising, and franchisees should take advantage of it. "Be prepared to listen to others who have blazed the path for you," says John Hewitt, founder of the Jackson Hewitt Tax Service franchise.
- **Perseverance.** Successful franchisees are dedicated to making their franchises successful and work hard to get the job done.
- **Solid people skills.** Whatever field they enter, successful franchisees require good people skills because they will be managing employees and working with customers.
- **Adequate capital.** Franchisors look for franchisees who have adequate financial resources to launch their businesses and to keep them going until they can generate enough cash flow to support themselves.
- **Compatible values.** Successful franchisees have values systems that are compatible with those of the franchisor.
- **Willingness to follow the system.** Some people enter the world of franchising because they have an entrepreneurial streak, which could be a mistake. Although creativity and a fresh approach are valuable assets in any business, franchising boils down to following the system that the franchisor has established. Why pay a franchisor for the benefit of experience if you are not willing to put that experience to work for yourself?

Sources: Jeff Elgin, "Are You Franchisee Material?" *Entrepreneur*, April 4, 2005, www.entrepreneur.com/franchises/buyingafranchise/franchisecolumnistjeffelgin/article76896.html; Kim Ellis, "Key Characteristics of Successful Franchise Owners," *Bison*, July 1, 2007, http://www.bison.com/articles_investigationellis_07012007; Jennifer Openshaw, "Five Keys to Success as a Franchise Owner," *AOL Small Business*, October 8, 2007, http://smallbusiness.aol.com/article/_a/five-keys-to-success-as-a-franchise/2007101217280999000; Sara Wilson, "Show Me the Way," *Entrepreneur*, September 2006, p. 120.

Research Your Market

Before shopping for a franchise, research the market in the area you plan to serve. How fast is the overall area growing? How many competitors already operate in the area? How strong is the competition? In which areas is that growth occurring fastest? Investing some time at the library and online to develop a profile of the customers in your target area is essential; otherwise, you will be flying blind. Who are your potential customers? How many of them are in your proposed trading area? What are their characteristics? What are their income and education levels? What kinds of products and services do they buy? What gaps exist in the market? These gaps represent potential franchise opportunities for you. Market research also should confirm that a franchise is not merely part of a fad that will quickly fade. Steering clear of fads and into long-term trends is one way to sustain the success of a franchise. Before Papa John's Pizza allows franchisees to open a franchise, the company requires them to spend six months to a year evaluating the market potential of the local area. "We don't just move into an area and open up 200 stores," says one manager. "We do it one store at a time."[45]

Consider Your Franchise Options

Small business magazines (and their Web sites) such as *Entrepreneur*, *Inc.*, *FSB*, and others devote at least one issue to franchising, in which they often list hundreds of franchises. These guides can help you to find a suitable franchise within your price range. The Web is another valuable tool for gathering information on franchises. The Web sites of organizations such as the International Franchise Association, the American Association of Franchisees and Dealers, the Canadian Franchise Association, and others offer valuable resources and advice for prospective franchisees. In addition, many cities host franchise trade shows throughout the year, where hundreds of franchisors gather to sell their franchises. Attending one of these franchise showcases is a convenient, efficient way to collect information about a variety of available opportunities.

Get a Copy of the Franchisor's FDD

Once you narrow down your franchise choices, you should contact each franchise (at least two in the industry that you have selected) and get a copy of its FDD. Then read it! This document is an important tool in your search for the right franchise, and you should make the most of it. When evaluating a franchise opportunity, what should a potential franchisee look for? Although there is never a guarantee of success, the following characteristics make a franchise stand out:

- A unique concept or marketing approach. "Me-too" franchises are no more successful than "me-too" independent businesses. Pizza franchisor Papa John's has achieved an impressive growth rate by emphasizing the quality of its ingredients, while Domino's is known for its fast delivery.
- Profitability. A franchisor should have a track record of profitability and so should its franchisees. If a franchisor is not profitable, its franchisees are not likely to be either. Franchisees who follow the business format should expect to earn a reasonable rate of return.
- A registered trademark. Name recognition is difficult to achieve without a well-known and protected trademark.
- A business system that works. A franchisor should have in place a system that is efficient and is well-documented in its manuals.
- A solid training program. One of the most valuable components of a franchise system is the training that it offers franchisees. The system should be relatively easy to teach.
- Affordability. A franchisee should not have to take on an excessive amount of debt to purchase a franchise. Being forced to borrow too much money to open a franchise outlet can doom a business from the outset. Respectable franchisors verify prospective franchisees' financial qualifications as part of the screening process.
- A positive relationship with franchisees. The most successful franchises are those that see their franchisees as partners...and treat them accordingly.

The FDD covers the 23 items discussed in the previous section and includes a copy of the company's franchise agreement and any contracts accompanying it. Although the law requires a FDD to be written in plain English rather than "legalese," it is best to have an attorney experienced in franchising to review the FDD and discuss its provisions with you. Watch for clauses that give the franchisor absolute control and discretion. The franchise contract summarizes the details that will govern the franchisor-franchisee relationship over its life. It outlines *exactly* the rights and the obligations of each party and sets the guidelines that govern the franchise relationship. Because franchise contracts typically are long-term (50 percent run for 15 years or more), it is extremely important for prospective franchisees to understand their terms *before* they sign them.

One of the most revealing items in the FDD is the **franchisee turnover rate**, the rate at which franchisees leave the system. If the turnover rate is less than 5 percent, the franchise is probably sound. However, a double-digit franchise turnover rate is cause for concern, and one approaching 20 percent is a sign of serious, underlying problems in a franchise. Satisfied franchisees are not inclined to leave a successful system.

franchisee turnover rate
the rate at which franchisees leave a franchise system.

Another important aspect of investigating a potential franchise is judging how well you fit into the company culture. Unfortunately, the FDD isn't much help here. The best way to determine this is to actually work for a unit for a time (even if it's without pay). Doing so not only gives prospective franchisees valuable insight into the company culture, but it also enables them to determine how much they enjoy the daily activities involved in operating the franchise. "Many people don't do enough research, digging into what a company is about, what they believe in, what they're trying to accomplish, and whether they will fit into the culture," says Kevin Hogan, a consultant who works with the Whattaburger franchise.[46]

Talk to Existing Franchisees

One of the best ways to evaluate the reputation of a franchisor is to visit several franchise owners who have been in business at least one year and interview them about the positive and the negative features of the agreement and whether the franchisor delivered what was promised. Did the franchise estimate their start-up costs accurately? Do they get the support the franchisor promised them? Was the training the franchisor provided helpful? How long did it take to reach the break-even point? Have they incurred any unexpected expenses? What risks are involved in purchasing a franchise? Has the franchise met their expectations concerning sales, profitability, and return on investment? What is involved in operating the franchise on a typical day? How many hours do they work in a typical week? What do they like best (and least) about their work? Knowing what they know now, would they buy the franchise again? When you are on site, note the volume of customer traffic and the average transaction size. Are they large enough for an outlet to be profitable? How well-managed are the franchises you visit? Michael Whalen, who left a management position with a large office supply chain after 20 years to purchase a Huntington Learning Center franchise, says that the most helpful part of his franchise evaluation process "was meeting with current franchise owners."[47] Table 6.3 offers a list of questions prospective franchisees should ask existing franchisees.

Interviewing past franchisees to get their perspectives on the franchisor-franchisee relationship is also helpful. (Their contact information is available in the FDD.) Why did they leave? Franchisees of some companies have formed associations that might provide prospective franchisees with valuable information. Other sources of information include the American Association of Franchisees and Dealers, the American Franchise Association, and the International Franchise Association.

Ask the Franchisor Some Tough Questions

Take the time to ask the franchisor questions about the company and its relationship with its franchisees. As a franchisee, you will be in this relationship a long time, and you need to know as much about it as you possibly can beforehand. What is the franchisor's philosophy

TABLE 6.3 Questions to Ask Existing Franchisees

One of the most revealing exercises for entrepreneurs who are evaluating potential franchises is to visit and interview franchisees who already are operating outlets for a franchise. This is the chance to get "the inside scoop" from people who know best how a particular franchise system works. Following are some questions to ask:

1. Are you happy with your relationship with the franchisor? Explain.

2. How much control does the franchisor exercise over you and the way you run your franchise?

3. What did it actually cost you to get your franchise running? How close was the actual amount to the amount the franchisor told you it would cost?

4. Is your franchise profitable? How long did it take for your franchise to earn a profit? How much does your franchise earn? Are the earnings consistent with your expectations?

5. Did the franchisor estimate accurately the amount of working capital necessary to sustain your business until it began generating positive cash flow?

6. What is the training program like? Were you pleased with the training you received from the franchisor? Did the training prepare you adequately for operating your franchise successfully?

7. Did you encounter any unexpected franchise fees or hidden costs? If so, what were they?

8. Are you pleased with the size of your territory? Is it large enough for you to reach your sales and profitability goals? What kind of territorial protection does the franchisor offer?

9. What restrictions do you face on the products and services that you can sell? Are you required to purchase from approved suppliers? Are their prices reasonable?

10. Does the franchisor advertise as much as it said it would? Is the advertising effective in producing sales?

11. What kind of education and business experience do you have? How important have they been to your success in the franchise?

12. Given what you know now, would you purchase this franchise again?

Sources: Adapted from: Sara Wilson, "Final Answer," *Entrepreneur*, December 2007, pp. 122-126; "Ten Questions to Ask Other Franchisees in the Franchise Chain," *AllBusiness*, 2006, http://www.allbusiness.com/buying-exiting-businesses/franchising-franchises/2188-1.html.

concerning the relationship? What is the company culture like? How much input do franchisees have into the system? What are the franchise's future expansion plans? How will they affect your franchise? Are you entitled to an exclusive territory? Under what circumstances can either party terminate the franchise agreement? What happens if you decide to sell your franchise in the future? Under what circumstances would you not be entitled to renew the agreement? What kind of earnings can you expect? (If the franchisor made no earnings claims in item 19 of the FDD, why not?) Does the franchisor have a well-formulated strategic plan? How many franchisees own multiple outlets? (A significant percentage of multi-unit franchisees is a good sign that a franchise's brand name and business system are strong.) Has the franchisor terminated any franchisee's contracts? If so, why? Have any franchisees failed? If so, why? How are disputes between the franchisor and franchisees settled?

Make Your Choice

The first lesson in franchising is, "Do your homework *before* you get out your checkbook." Once you have done your research, you can make an informed choice about which franchise is right for you. Then it is time to put together a solid business plan that will serve as your road map to success in the franchise you have selected. The plan is also a valuable tool to use as you arrange the financing for your franchise.

Appendix A at the end of this chapter offers a checklist of questions a potential franchisee should ask before entering into any franchise agreement.

HANDS ON... HOW TO

Select the Ideal Franchise – *For You*!

After working extra hours and many weekends as a buyer in the retail industry, Gina Frerich began to think that she should be the beneficiary of her hard work rather than some corporate giant. She was confident that her work ethic and business experience would help her succeed in business but because she did not know how to launch a business from scratch, Frerich began looking at franchises as the gateway to business ownership. "[Franchises] already have the proven product, they do marketing, and, [sometimes] they provide a lot of training and support," she says. Following is a chronicle of how Frerich made her franchise selection and lessons that every prospective franchisee can learn from her experience.

Lesson 1. Don't be in a rush; start with a self-evaluation and then research the most suitable franchise opportunities thoroughly

After examining the activities and work that she enjoyed most, Frerich decided that she did not want a franchise in the clothing or fashion business. Over the course of a year, she and her husband, Kevin, considered their franchise options. Frerich did not rush into a decision; she and Kevin spent more than two years studying and researching before narrowing their choice down to an ice cream franchise.

Lesson 2. Use power of the Internet in your research

From their New Jersey home, the Frerichs used the Internet to research several franchise operations in the retail ice cream industry. Based on the research, Gina was intrigued by the Cold Stone Creamery franchise, a retail ice cream shop that features freshly made ice cream to which customers can add a multitude of toppings. Because the chain had not yet established any outlets in the New Jersey area, Frerich did almost all of her preliminary research online. It wasn't until she was visiting family in San Diego that she actually went into a Cold Stone Creamery franchise and tasted the product. That visit confirmed all of her research about the franchise, clinching the decision. "I called my husband and said, 'You know that Cold Stone [concept] we were looking at? I just had it, and it's amazing super-premium ice cream.' It was so good."

Lesson 3. Review the Franchise Disclosure Document (FDD) with the help of an experienced attorney

Frerich found the franchiser's FDD to be an extremely useful, comprehensive document. Poring over the document alone can be frustrating, however, because it covers so much. "The typical FDD is about the size of a telephone book," says Eric Karp, an attorney who teaches franchising courses at Babson College. "It is enormously complex because it is so multifaceted." Karp says that some franchisees are so overwhelmed by the size of the FDD that they make the mistake of not reading it at all.

Lesson 4. Don't be shy about asking LOTS of questions

When Frerich returned from San Diego, she contacted the Cold Stone Creamery headquarters in Scottsdale, Arizona, and asked plenty of questions. She was excited to hear that the company was about to open a flagship store in New York City's famous Times Square. Frerich thought that opening this high profile store would increase the awareness of the Cold Stone Creamery brand name in the Northeast, benefiting any stores that she might open in nearby New Jersey. She submitted her official application to become a Cold Stone Creamery franchisee.

In the meantime, of course, the franchiser was evaluating Frerich to make sure that she met the company's criteria for its franchisees. "The Creamery is very selective [to] whom they award franchises," she explains. "They had to make sure it was the right fit."

Lesson 5. Talk to existing franchisees about what it's like to operate a franchise

Frerich was able to attend the Cold Stone Creamery annual franchise convention, a gathering of franchisees from all across the country. The convention was a prime opportunity for Frerich to spend a week talking to lots of veteran franchisees about the advantages and the disadvantages of owning and operating a Cold Stone Creamery franchise. "It was one of the greatest experiences throughout this adventure," she says.

Lesson 6. Take an active role in the training program

After attending the convention, Frerich enrolled in the franchiser's Ice Cream University in Scottsdale, where she spent two weeks immersed in the details of making ice cream and running a successful franchise. The course involved both classroom instruction and hands-on experience operating a real store. Most evenings she spent studying for the final exam, which paid off when Frerich made the highest score on the exam, garnering her "Scoopa Cum Laude" status. Franchisees must recognize that they are paying the franchiser to train them to operate their outlets successfully and it is their responsibility to make the most of the opportunity to learn.

Lesson 7. Utilize the franchiser's experience and support

Smart franchisees use their franchiser's experience to their benefit. For instance, Stone Cold Creamery helped Frerich with one of the most important tasks in retail operations: finding an ideal location for her store. She also drew on the franchiser's support when it came to hiring and training her staff.

Despite Frerich's thorough analysis, research, and preparation, opening day for her franchise brought unexpected challenges. A walk-in freezer went into defrost mode and refused to come out, posing a huge threat to the store's inventory of freshly-made ice cream. Despite the glitch, Frerich's grand opening was a success, as is her store, whose sales exceeded the chain's average unit volume of $375,000 within two years. Although some days are stressful, Frerich believes that franchising was the right choice for her. In fact, she already has opened two more Stone Cold Creamery franchises in New Jersey, one in Madison and the other in Summit.

Sources: Adapted from *Franchisee Profiles*, Cold Stone Creamery, http://www.coldstonecreamery.com/images/news/Franchisee_Profiles_737.pdf; Anne Fisher, "Risk Reward," *FSB*, December 2005/January 2006, pp. 45–61; Nichole L. Torres, The Inside Scoop," *Entrepreneur*, January 2005, pp.96–102.

Trends Shaping Franchising

Franchising has experienced three major growth waves since its beginning. The first wave occurred in the early 1970s when fast-food restaurants used the concept to grow rapidly. The fast-food industry was one of the first to discover the power of franchising, but other businesses soon took notice and adapted the franchising concept to their industries. The second wave took place in the mid-1980s as the U.S. economy shifted heavily toward the service sector. Franchises followed suit, springing up in every service business imaginable—from maid services and copy centers to mailing services and real estate. The third wave began in the early 1990s and continues today. It is characterized by new, low-cost franchises that focus on specific market niches. In the wake of major corporate downsizing and the burgeoning costs of traditional franchises, these new franchises allow would-be entrepreneurs to get into proven businesses faster and at reasonable costs. These companies feature startup costs in the $2,000 to $250,000 range and span a variety of industries—from leak detection in homes and auto detailing to daycare and tile glazing.

Other significant trends affecting franchising include:

The Changing Face of Franchisees

Franchisees today are a more diverse group than in the past. A study by the International Franchise Association reports that minorities own 19.3 percent of all franchises and women own 25 percent of them.[48] To encourage diversity among their franchisees, some franchisors have established special programs that offer special deals to members of minority groups. Focus Brands, a company that operates several franchises including Cinnabon, Carvel, Moe's Southwest Grill, and Schlotsky's, has a Growth Through Diversity program that gives minority franchisees discounts on the initial franchise fee and operating fees. Focus Brands also is a member of MinorityFran, a program sponsored by the International Franchise Association that has the goal of recruiting minority franchisees.[49]

ENTREPRENEURIAL PROFILE

Jessy Watson: Domino's Pizza

Jessy Watson, an African-American franchise owner, started as a delivery man at Domino's Pizza, worked hard, and soon was promoted to general manager of a store. Six years after he started, Watson purchased a Domino's franchise in LaGrande, Oregon, with co-owners Dennis Poe and Rebecca Johnston, with the help of a $180,000 loan guarantee through Domino's Delivering the Dream program, which is designed to help minority general managers to become franchise owners. Watson's franchise has been so successful that he has since opened a second one.[50]

Modern franchisees also are better educated, are more sophisticated, have more business acumen, and are more financially secure than those of just 20 years ago. People of all ages and backgrounds are choosing franchising as a way to get into business for themselves. A survey by Franchise Business Review reports that 13 percent of franchisees are between the ages of 18 and 34.[51] Franchising also is attracting skilled, experienced businesspeople who are opening franchises in their second careers and whose goal is to own multiple outlets that cover entire states or regions. Many of them are former corporate managers—either corporate castoffs or corporate dropouts—looking for a new start on a more meaningful and rewarding career. They have the financial resources, management skills and experience, and motivation to operate their franchises successfully.

Multiple-Unit Franchising

multiple-unit franchising
a method of franchising in which a franchisee opens more than one unit in a broad territory within a specific time period.

Twenty years ago, the typical franchisee operated a single outlet. Today, however, modern franchisees increasingly have as a goal operating multiple franchise units. In **multiple-unit franchising (MUF)**, a franchisee opens more than one unit in a broad territory within a specific time period. It is no longer unusual for a single franchisee to own 25, 75, or even 100 units. According to FRANdata, 52 percent of franchise units are operated by multiple-unit owners, and that number is expected to continue to grow over the next several years.[52] Frank Carney, who with his brother Dan started Pizza Hut in 1958, before selling the company to PepsiCo in 1977, has returned to franchising—this time as a franchisee. Carney owns 116 Papa John's Pizza franchises in five different markets![53]

Franchisors are finding it is far more efficient in the long run to have one well-trained franchisee operate a number of units than to train many franchises to operate that same number of outlets. A multiple-unit strategy also accelerates a franchise's growth rate. For instance, to reach its goal of adding 5,000 new outlets within five years, Allied Domecq Quick Service Restaurants, the company that sells Baskin-Robbins, Dunkin' Donuts, and Togo's franchises, began recruiting multi-unit franchisees in 17 major markets in the United States. Many of the franchisees the company selected were existing franchisees looking to expand their businesses, but others were newcomers to the chain.[54]

The popularity of multiple-unit franchising has paralleled the trend toward increasingly experienced, sophisticated franchisees, who set high performance goals that a single outlet cannot meet. The typical multi-unit franchisee owns between three and six units, but some franchisees own many more.

ENTREPRENEURIAL PROFILE

Bill Welter: Buffalo Wild Wings

After working as executive vice-president of marketing for Wendy's and then operating his own advertising agency for 18 years, Bill Welter moved to Las Vegas, Nevada. When he arrived, he noticed the absence of his favorite restaurant back East, Buffalo Wild Wings, a franchise with which he had become familiar while working at Wendy's. Sensing an opportunity, Welter investigated the franchise and the local market thoroughly and, at age 52, decided to launch a new career as a Buffalo Wild Wings franchisee. Welter purchased the license for the entire Las Vegas area and has already opened six franchises in the area with plans to open four more within the next few years. "The most satisfying thing to me," says Welter, "is to wear a Buffalo Wild Wings shirt anywhere in this town, and people come up and say, "'That's my favorite place.' That means more to me than anything."[55]

Although operating multiple units offers advantages for both franchisors and franchisees, there are dangers. Franchisees must be aware of the dangers of losing their focus and becoming distracted if they take on too many units. In addition, operating multiple units means more complexity because the number of business problems franchisees face also is multiplied.

International Opportunities

One of the major trends in franchising is the internationalization of American franchise systems. Increasingly, franchising is becoming a major export industry for the United States; in fact, since 1997, nearly half of all franchises sold by U.S.–based franchisors have been located in other countries.[56] Increasingly, U.S. franchises are moving into international markets to boost sales and profits as the domestic market becomes saturated. A survey by the International Franchise Association reports that 52 percent of U.S.–based franchisors have an international presence, and more domestic franchisors are looking to expand abroad. For example, Yum! Brands, franchisor of Taco Bell, Long John Silver's, Pizza Hut, KFC, and A&W, has more than 8,000 foreign franchises and, on average, opens three restaurants each day *outside* the United States.[57] Burger King projects that 80 percent of its future growth will come from expansion in international markets, with the growth rate in Asia surpassing that in Europe, the Middle East, and Latin America.[58] In 1980, McDonald's had restaurants in 28 countries; today, the company operates more than 31,300 outlets in 118 nations.[59] Europe is the primary market for U.S. franchisors, with Pacific Rim countries, Canada, and South America following, but China is becoming a franchising "hot spot."[60] These markets are most attractive to franchisors because they are similar to the U.S. market—rising personal incomes, strong demand for consumer goods, growing service economies, and spreading urbanization.

As they venture into foreign markets, franchisors have learned that adaptation is one key to success. Although a franchise's overall business format may not change in foreign markets, some of the details of operating its local outlets must. For instance, fast-food chains in other countries often must make adjustments to their menus to please locals' palates. In Japan, McDonald's (known as "Makudonarudo") outlets sell teriyaki burgers, rice burgers, and katsu burgers (cheese wrapped in a roast pork cutlet topped with katsu sauce and shredded cabbage) in addition to their traditional American fare. McDonald's has eliminated beef and pork from its menu and has substituted mutton for beef in its burgers in India, where it sells sandwiches such as the Maharaja Mac

(two specially seasoned chicken patties with locally flavored condiments) and the McAloo (a patty made from potatoes, peas, and special spices).[61] In the Philippines, the McDonald's menu includes a spicy Filipino-style burger, spaghetti, and chicken with rice. In China, KFC quickly learned that residents were not interested in cole slaw, so the company dropped the item from its menu and added local delicacies such as shredded carrots, fungus, and bamboo shoots.[62]

As China's economy continues to grow and its capital markets expand, increasing numbers of franchisors are opening locations there. Currently, more than 2,000 franchise systems operate some 120,000 outlets in China.[63] Fast-growing Subway Sandwiches is the third largest U.S.-based fast-food chain in China behind McDonald's and KFC. In China, Subway, known as Sai Bei Wei (which translates as "tastes better than others" in Mandarin), has learned the importance of patience in building a franchise presence in challenging international markets.

China: The Next Franchise Frontier

Since its beginning in the United States more than 125 years ago, franchising has become an important part of the both the U.S. and the global economy. As franchisors have found it increasingly difficult to continue to wring impressive growth rates from the domestic market, they have begun to export their franchises to international markets, including those with developing economies. Indeed, franchising is ideally suited for developing economies because it allows people with limited business experience and financial resources to become part of an established business. China, with a population of nearly 1.4 billion people whose annual incomes are growing and creating what is potentially the largest consumer market in the world, is becoming a target for many franchisors. Many experts are calling China the most important consumer market of the twenty-first century. "China is a fast-growing market where 1.4 billion people are getting wealthier every day," says Peter Tan, president of Burger King's Asia Pacific division. A burgeoning tourist industry also is attracting franchisors. In 2007, China was the fourth most popular destination country in the world for tourists, and by 2015, the World Tourism Organization forecasts that it will be the leading tourist destination.

Franchising is relatively new to China, but fast-food franchisors see a bright future there because the fast-food industry is in its infancy and is growing very fast. KFC (formerly Kentucky Fried Chicken) established the first outlet in 1987, but it was a company-owned store rather than a true franchise. The first fran-

chised KFC store opened in the city of Xi'an in 1993. Yum! Brands, the owner of KFC, Pizza Hut, and other franchises, has more than 2,200 KFC and 360 Pizza Hut restaurants in China. "We're the number one brand in China," says Yum! Brands CEO David Novak. "KFC makes almost as much money in China today as it makes in the U.S."

McDonald's entered China in 1992 when it opened a store in Beijing as part of a joint venture with a local Chinese company. Working with this local partner, McDonald's has expanded to more than 1,000 locations across China. Meng Sun, a Chinese national who took a part-time job at a McDonald's while working on her MBA at the University of Calgary in Canada, opened McDonald's first franchised store in 2004 in Tianjin, a city of 10 million people about 70 miles southeast of Beijing. Meng Sun used $360,000 (about three million yuan) she had saved from working as a financial consultant to open her franchised store. "I thought it was a very good start for an aspiring entrepreneur," she says of her busy mall-based restaurant.

When entering foreign markets, patience is a must for franchisors. Traditionally, Chinese people conduct business on the principle of *guanxi*, interpersonal trust, which takes time to build. InterContinental Hotels Group recently announced that it will open its first Holiday Inn Express franchise after three years of planning and 24 years of operating Holiday Inn and Crowne Plaza hotels there. Both Yum! Brands and McDonald's have expanded their franchising operations in China slowly, as have most other successful franchisors. Jim Bryant, an international development manager for Subway, the sandwich franchise, says that when he started developing franchises in China in 1995, there was no word in the Chinese language for "franchise." (Today, there is a Chinese word for "franchise"—"*jia meng*," which roughly translates into "person joins group of other people.") U.S. franchisors are anxious to tap into the knowledge of the nuances of doing business in the diverse market segments that native Chinese franchisees have developed. They understand that intimate knowledge of local markets is central to their operations' success in China.

U.S. franchisors operating in China know that it will take time for their investments to come to fruition, but they believe the payoffs will be worth the wait. "We are planting the seeds for a bigger future," says Sam Su, president of Yum! Restaurants China.

1. What steps should U.S.–based franchisors take when establishing outlets in foreign countries?

2. Describe the opportunities and the challenges franchisors face when entering emerging markets such as China.

3. Use the Web as a resource to develop a list of at least five suggestions that will help new franchisors looking to establish outlets in China.

Sources: Adapted from Dexter Roberts, "China: Tops in Tourism Too?" *Business Week*, April 3, 2008, http://www.businessweek.com/globalbiz/content/apr2008/gb2008043_908497.htm; Carlye Adler, "How China Eats a Sandwich," *Fortune*, March 21, 2005, pp. 210[B]—210[D]; Julia Boorstin, "Yum Isn't Chicken of China – or Atkins," *Fortune*, March 8, 2004, p. 50; "Burger King Plans Rapid China Growth Over 3 Years," *FlexNews*, April 21, 2008, http://www.flex-news-food.com/pages/15888/Burger-King/burger-king-plans-rapid-china-growth-years.html; "Loretta Chao," IHG to Franchise Hotels in China," *Wall Street Journal*, January 29, 2008, http://online.wsj.com/article_print/SB120154569108322845.html.

When the company opened its first outlet in China, managers had to print signs explaining how to order a sandwich. Sales of tuna salad were dismal because residents, accustomed to seeing their fish whole, did not believe the salad was made from fish at all. In addition, because Chinese diners do not like to touch their food, many of them held their sandwiches vertically, peeled the paper wrapper away gradually, and ate the contents as they would eat a banana! [64]

Master Franchising

A **master franchise** (or **subfranchise**) gives a franchisee the right to create a semi-independent organization in a particular territory to recruit, sell, and support other franchises. A master franchisee buys the right to develop subfranchise within a broad geographic area or, sometimes, an entire country. Subfranchising, also known as area development, "turbocharges" a franchisor's growth. Many franchisors use it to open outlets in international markets more quickly and efficiently because the master franchisees understand local laws and the nuances of selling in local markets. For instance, Dunkin' Donuts plans to open 100 locations in China over the next decade with the help of a master franchisee, Mercuries and Associates, a company with which Dunkin' Donuts had worked to establish franchises in Taiwan. The outlets will sell traditional items such as doughnuts, coffee, and espresso but will be customized to reflect local tastes and will add items that are popular in the region such as mocha rings, cake doughnuts made from rice flour.[65]

master franchise
a method of franchising that gives a franchisee the right to create a semi-independent organization in a particular territory to recruit, sell, and support other franchises.

Smaller, Non-traditional Locations

As the high cost of building full-scale locations continues to climb, more franchisors are searching out non-traditional locations in which to build smaller, less expensive outlets. Based on the principle of **intercept marketing**, the idea is to put a franchise's products or services directly in the paths of potential customers, wherever that may be. Franchises are putting scaled-down outlets on college campuses, in high school cafeterias, sports arenas, zoos, and on airline flights. The Subway sandwich chain has more than 6,400 franchises in nontraditional locations that range from airports and military bases to college campuses and convenience stores.[66] Many franchisees have discovered that smaller outlets in these nontraditional locations generate nearly the same sales volume as full-sized outlets at just a fraction of the cost! Camille's Sidewalk Café, a fast-casual restaurant chain with 84 locations in 24 states, is opening outlets in Wal-Mart Supercenters across the United States. Although the in-store outlets will be smaller than a typical Camille's Café, the franchisor expects their sales per square foot to be significantly higher because of the millions of customers who visit Wal-Mart Supercenters each day.[67] Locations that emphasize convenience by being close to their customers will be a key to continued franchise growth in the domestic market.

intercept marketing
the principle of putting a franchise's products or services directly in the paths of potential customers, wherever they may be.

conversion franchising
a franchising trend in which owners of independent businesses become franchisees to gain the advantage of name recognition.

Conversion franchising

The recent trend toward **conversion franchising**, in which owners of independent businesses become franchises to gain the advantage of name recognition, will continue. One study reports that 72 percent of franchisors in North America use conversion franchising as a growth strategy.[68] In a franchise conversion, the franchisor gets immediate entry into new markets and experienced operators; franchisees get increased visibility and often a big sales boost. It is not unusual for entrepreneurs who convert their independent stores into franchises to experience an increase of 20 percent or more in sales because of the instant name recognition the franchise offers. The biggest force in conversion franchising has been Century 21, the real estate sales company, which converts independent real estate agencies into franchised units and gives them brand recognition and increased visibility.

Piggybacking (or Combination or Multi-branded Franchising)

piggybacking
a method of franchising in which two or more franchises team up to sell complementary products or services under one roof.

Some franchisors also are discovering new ways to reach customers by teaming up with other franchisors selling complementary products or services. A growing number of companies are **piggybacking** outlets—combining two or more distinct franchises under one roof. This "buddy system" approach works best when the two franchise ideas are compatible and appeal to similar customers. For example, Yum! Brands, whose stable of franchises includes Taco Bell, KFC, Pizza Hut, A&W, and Long John Silver, is building hundreds of combination outlets, a concept that has proved to be highly successful. About 15 percent of the company's restaurants involve multi-branding, with two or more concepts in the same location. "We find customers prefer a double-branded concept to a single brand six to one," says Yum! Brands CEO David Novak.[69]

Properly planned, piggybacked franchises can magnify many times over the sales and profits of individual, self-standing outlets. One Baskin Robbins franchisee saw his sales climb 25 percent when he added a Blimpie Subs and Salads franchise to his existing ice cream shop. Another enterprising franchisee who combined Shell Oil (gas station), Charley's Steakery (sandwich shop), and TCBY (frozen yogurt) franchises under one roof in Columbus, Ohio, says that sales are running 10 percent more than the three outlets would generate in separate locations.[70]

Serving Dual-Career Couples and Aging Baby Boomers

Now that dual career couples have become the norm, the market for franchises offering convenience and time-saving devices is booming. Customers are willing to pay for products and services that will save them time or trouble, and franchises are ready to provide them. Franchisees of Around Your Neck go into the homes and offices of busy male executives to sell men's apparel and accessories ranging from shirts and ties to custom–made suits. Other areas in which franchising is experiencing rapid growth include home delivery of meals, house-cleaning services, continuing education and training (especially computer and business training), leisure activities (such as hobbies, health spas, and travel-related activities), products and services aimed at home-based businesses, and health care. Franchises that cater to pets are growing rapidly because most Americans treat their pets as family members and spend more than $41 billion a year caring for them. Terri Sassone, who owns a Camp Bow Wow pet boarding and daycare franchise in Temecula, California, says that "extras" such as alarm systems, comfy cots (elevated beds with fleece blankets), and Camper Cams that allow owners to watch their pets online appeal to her company's clientele. In just two years, sales for the entire Camp Bow Wow chain, which has more than 60 franchisees, grew from $2 million to $18 million.[71]

A number of franchises are aiming at one of the nation's largest population segments: aging baby boomers. About 36.8 million people, 12.4 percent of the U.S. population, are 65 or older, and by 2030 that number is expected to double to 72 million. An AARP survey shows that 90 percent of senior citizens want to remain in their homes as they age, which is creating a great business opportunity for franchises such as Home Instead Senior Care, a company that provides in-home non–health care services to senior citizens.[72]

Conclusion

Franchising has proved its viability in the U.S. economy and has become a key part of the small business sector because it offers many would-be entrepreneurs the opportunity to own and operate a business with a greater chance for success. Despite its impressive growth rate to date, the franchising industry still has a great deal of room to grow. "Franchising is really small business at its best," says Don DeBolt, former president of the International Franchise Association.[73]

Chapter Summary

1. Describe the three types of franchising: trade name, product distribution, and pure.

- Trade name franchising involves a franchisee purchasing the right to become affiliated with a franchisor's trade name without distributing its products exclusively.
- Product distribution franchising involves licensing a franchisee to sell products or services under the franchisor's brand name through a selective, limited distribution network.
- Pure franchising involves a franchisor selling a franchisee a complete business format.

2. Explain the benefits and the drawbacks of buying a franchise.

- Franchises offer many benefits: management training and support, brand name appeal, standardized quality of goods and services, national advertising programs, financial assistance, proven products and business formats, centralized buying power, territorial protection, and a greater chance of success.
- Franchising also suffers from certain drawbacks: franchise fees and profit sharing, strict adherence to standardized operations, restrictions on purchasing, limited product lines, unsatisfactory training programs, market saturation, and less freedom.

3. Explain the laws covering franchise purchases.

The Federal Trade Commission (FTC) requires all franchisors to disclose detailed information on their operations in a Franchise Disclosure Document (FDD) at the first personal meeting or at least 14 days before a franchise contract is signed or before any money is paid. The FTC rule covers *all* franchisors. The FDD requires franchisors to provide information on 23 topics in their disclosure statements. The FDD is an extremely helpful tool for prospective franchisees.

4. Discuss the right way to buy a franchise.

The following steps will help you make the right franchise choice: Evaluate yourself, research your market, consider your franchise options, get a copy of the franchisor's FDD, talk to existing franchisees, ask the franchisor some tough questions, make your choice.

5. Outline the major trends shaping franchising.

Key trends shaping franchising today include: the changing face of franchisees, international franchise opportunities, smaller, non-traditional locations, conversion franchising, multiple-unit franchising, master franchising, and piggybacking (or combination franchising).

Discussion Questions

1. What is franchising?
2. Describe the three types of franchising and give an example of each.
3. Discuss the advantages and the limitations of franchising for the franchisee.
4. Why might an independent entrepreneur be dissatisfied with a franchising arrangement?
5. What kinds of clues should alert a prospective franchisee that he is dealing with a disreputable franchisor?

6. What steps should a potential franchisee take before investing in a franchise?

7. Two franchising experts recently debated the issue of whether new college graduates should consider franchising as a pathway to entrepreneurship. Jeff Elgin said that recent college graduates are not ready to be franchise owners. "First, most recent college graduates don't have the financial resources to fund a franchise start-up. Second, many lack the life experience and the motivation to run a business effectively and stick with it when times get tough." Jennifer Kushell, on the other hand, says that franchising is the perfect career choice for many recent college graduates, and she cites several reasons: (1) The support system that franchising provides is ideal for young entrepreneurs; (2) young people have grown up with franchising and understand it well; (3) many college graduates already have launched businesses of their own; and (4) they think big. Which view do you think is correct? Explain.

8. What is the function of the FTC's Trade Regulation Rule? Outline the protection the Trade Regulation Rule gives all prospective franchisees.

9. Describe the current trends in franchising.

10. One franchisee says, "Franchising is helpful because it gives you somebody [the franchisor] to get you going, nurture you, and shove you along a little. But, the franchisor won't make you successful. That depends on what you bring to the business, how hard you are prepared to work, and how committed you are to finding the right franchise for you." Do you agree? Explain.

Business PlanPro™

Most franchises will require you to submit a business plan with the application process. In many cases, the franchiser will specify what the business plan should include and may even require you follow an established business plan outline. If you are planning to purchase a franchise, investigate all of the application requirements.

Business Plan Exercises

Submitting a business plan is often a major milestone in the franchise application process. The business plan is another assessment of your ability to become a successful franchisee.

On the Web

Go to http://www.pearsonhighered.com/scarborough and click on the Chapter 6 tab. Review the online franchise resources and find the link "The World Franchise Directory." Click on that link and enter the first letter of a familiar franchise, the letter "S," for example. The number of franchise systems that will appear, many of them with an international presence, is staggering. If you plan to purchase a franchise, visit the franchise system's Web site and request information. In most cases, the franchise will expect you to respond to a set of initial questions before you receive detailed franchise information. As you proceed through the process, note the specific questions regarding your sources of capital. Your access to capital will be a major qualification in determining whether you are "franchise worthy" in addition to other criteria.

Sample Plans

Find the Tennis Master Pro Shops, Inc. plan in *Business Plan Pro's*™ sample plan browser. Read the Executive Summary, Objectives, Mission and Keys to Success and note the information about franchising. Review the sales forecast and note the projected revenue sources.

In the Software

If you plan to own a franchise with specific business plan requirements, modify the outline in *Business Plan Pro*™ to match the franchise's recommendation. To view the outline in the left-hand navigation, click on the Plan Outline icon, or go to the "View" menu and click on "Outline." Then, right-click on each topic that you need to change, move or delete to meet the franchise's requirement. You may move topics up or down the outline with the corresponding arrows. To change topics from headings to subheadings, you "demote" the topic. When you "promote" a topic, you move a subheading to the left to a more dominant position.

Building Your Business Plan

Continue building your franchise business plan based on that outline. Determine the expectations regarding the content and structure of the franchise business plan. Inquire whether the franchiser has a recommended outline, example plan, or an actual business plan from another franchisee that is available for review. Use the information and verbiage that is familiar to the franchise system whenever possible. Your plan may be one of dozens received that week, and you want the plan to demonstrate your knowledge, competence, and credibility. Your franchise business plan can be a sales tool to position you as an informed, attractive and capable future franchise owner.

Beyond the Classroom...

1. Visit a local franchise operation. Is it a trade name, product distribution, or pure franchise? To what extent did the franchisee investigate before investing? What assistance does the franchisor provide? How does the franchisee feel about the franchise contract he or she signed? What would he or she do differently now?

2. Use the Web to locate several franchises that interest you. Contact the franchisors and ask for their franchise packages. Write a report comparing their treatment of the topics covered by the Trade Regulation Rule. Analyze the terms of their franchise contracts. What are the major differences? Are some terms more favorable than others? If you were about to invest in the franchise, which terms would you want to change?

3. Ask a local franchisee to approach his or her regional franchise representative about leading a class discussion on franchising.

APPENDIX A. A FRANCHISE EVALUATION CHECKLIST

Yourself

1. Are you qualified to operate a franchise successfully? Do you have adequate drive, skills, experience, education, patience, and financial capacity? Are you prepared to work hard?

2. Are you willing to sacrifice some autonomy in operating a business to own a franchise?

3. Can you tolerate the financial risk? Would business failure wipe you out financially?

4. Can you juggle multiple tasks simultaneously and prioritize various projects so that you can accomplish those that are most important?

5. Are you genuinely interested in the product or service you will be selling? Do you enjoy this kind of business? Do you like to sell?

6. Do you enjoy working with and managing people? Are you a "team player"?

7. Will the business generate enough profit to suit you?

8. Has the franchiser investigated your background thoroughly enough to decide if you are qualified to operate the franchise?

9. What can this franchiser do for you that you cannot do for yourself?

The Franchiser and the Franchise

1. Is the potential market for the product or service adequate to support your franchise? Will the prices you charge be in line with the market?

2. Is the market's population growing, remaining static, or shrinking? Is the demand for your product or service growing, remaining static, or shrinking?

3. Is the product or service safe and reputable?

4. Is the product or service a passing "fad," or is it a durable business idea?

5. What will the competition, direct or indirect, be in your sales territory? Do any other franchisees operate in this general area?

6. Is the franchise international, national, regional, or local in scope? Does it involve full- or part-time involvement?

7. How many years has the franchiser been in operation? Does it have a sound reputation for honest dealings with franchisees?

8. How many franchise outlets now exist? How many will there be a year from now? How many outlets are company-owned?

9. How many franchises have failed? Why?

10. How many franchisees have left the system within the past year? What were their reasons for leaving?

11. What service and assistance will the franchiser provide? What kind of training program does the franchiser offer? How long does it last? What topics does it cover? Does the franchiser offer ongoing assistance and training?

12. Will the franchise perform a location analysis to help you find a suitable site? If so, is there an extra charge for doing so?

13. Will the franchiser offer you exclusive distribution rights for the length of the agreement, or may it sell to other franchises in this area?

14. What facilities and equipment are required for the franchise? Who pays for construction? Is there a lease agreement?

15. What is the total cost of the franchise? What are the initial capital requirements? Will the franchiser provide financial assistance? Of what nature? What is the interest rate? Is the franchiser financially sound enough to fulfill all its promises?

16. How much is the franchise fee? Exactly what does it cover? Are there any confining fees? What additional fees are there?

17. Does the franchiser provide an estimate of expenses and income? Are they reasonable for your particular area? Are they sufficiently documented?

18. How risky is the franchise opportunity? Is the return on the investment consistent with the risks?

19. Does the franchiser offer a written contract that covers all the details of the agreement? Have your attorney and your accountant studied its terms and approved it? Do you understand the implications of the contract?

20. What is the length of the franchise agreement? Under what circumstances can it be terminated? If you terminate the contract, what are the costs to you? What are the terms and costs of renewal?

21. Are you allowed to sell your franchise to a third party? Does the franchiser reserve the right to approve the buyer?

22. Is there a national advertising program? How is it financed? What media are used? What help is provided for local advertising?

23. Once you open for business, *exactly* what support will the franchiser offer you?

24. How does the franchise handle complaints from and disputes with franchisees? How well has the system worked?

The Franchisees

1. Are you pleased with your investment in this franchise?

2. Has the franchiser lived up to its promises?

3. What was your greatest disappointment after getting into this business?

4. How effective was the training you received in helping you run the franchise?

5. What are your biggest challenges and problems?

6. What is your franchise's cash flow like?

7. How much money are you making on your investment?

8. What do you like most about being a franchisee? Least?

9. Is there a franchisee advisory council that represents franchisees?

10. Knowing what you know now, would you buy this franchise again?

CHAPTER

7

Buying an Existing Business

Goodwill, like a good name, is gotten by many actions, and lost by one.
—Lord Jeffrey

There is nothing so easy to learn as experience and nothing so hard to apply.
—Josh Billings

Learning Objectives

On completion of this chapter, you will be able to:

1. Understand the advantages and disadvantages of buying an existing business.

2. Define the steps involved in the *right* way to buy a business.

3. Explain the process of evaluating an existing business.

4. Describe the various techniques for determining the value of a business.

5. Understand the seller's side of the buyout decision and how to structure the deal.

6. Understand how the negotiation process works and identify the factors that affect it.

Rather than launch their own businesses or purchase a franchise, some entrepreneurs opt for a more direct route to business ownership: They buy an existing business. In fact, in a typical year, between 500,000 and one million small businesses are bought and sold. Over the next 10 years, there will be a wave of retiring entrepreneurial baby boomers whose family members are not interested in running a business—which means that about 10 million small companies in the United States will hang "for sale" signs in their windows.[1] Each circumstance is unique, but the process of evaluating a potential business acquisition is not. The due diligence process that involves analyzing and evaluating an existing business for possible purchase is no less time consuming than developing a comprehensive business plan for a start-up. Done correctly, this due diligence process reveals both the negative and the positive aspects of an existing business. Glossing over or skipping altogether the due diligence process is a mistake because a business that looks good on the surface may have serious flaws hidden at its core. Investigating a business to discover its real condition and value requires time, dedication, and, as the name implies, diligence, but the process is worthwhile because it can prevent an entrepreneur from purchasing a business destined for failure.

When considering purchasing a business, the first rule is "Do not rush into a deal." Taking shortcuts when investigating a potential business acquisition almost always leads to nasty—and expensive—surprises. Prospective buyers must be sure that they discover the answers to the following fundamental questions:

- Is the right type of business for sale in a market in which you want to operate?
- What experience do you have in this particular business and the industry in which it operates? How critical to your ultimate success is experience in the business?
- What is the company's potential for success?
- What changes will you have to make—and how extensive will they be—to realize the business's full potential?
- What price and payment method are reasonable for you and acceptable to the seller?
- Will the company generate sufficient cash to pay for itself and leave you with a suitable rate of return on your investment?
- Should you be starting a business and building it from the ground up rather than buying an existing one?

Figure 7.1 shows a profile of the four major categories of buyers and their characteristics that business brokers have identified.

FIGURE 7.1

Types of Business Buyers

Source: Darren Dahl, "Meet the Buyers," *Inc.,* April 2008, pp. 98–99

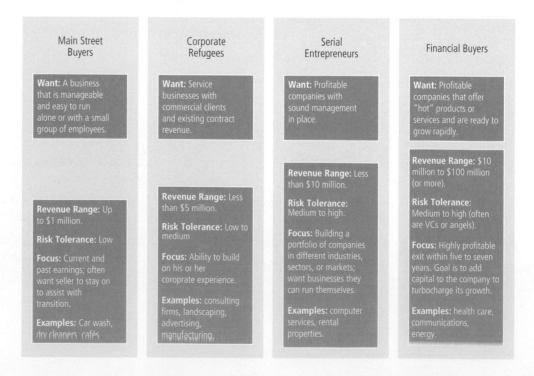

Main Street Buyers

Want: A business that is manageable and easy to run alone or with a small group of employees.

Revenue Range: Up to $1 million.

Risk Tolerance: Low

Focus: Current and past earnings; often want seller to stay on to assist with transition.

Examples: Car wash, dry cleaners, cafés.

Corporate Refugees

Want: Service businesses with commercial clients and existing contract revenue.

Revenue Range: Less than $5 million.

Risk Tolerance: Low to medium

Focus: Ability to build on his or her corporate experience.

Examples: consulting firms, landscaping, advertising, manufacturing.

Serial Entrepreneurs

Want: Profitable companies with sound management in place.

Revenue Range: Less than $10 million.

Risk Tolerance: Medium to high.

Focus: Building a portfolio of companies in different industries, sectors, or markets; want businesses they can run themselves.

Examples: computer services, rental properties.

Financial Buyers

Want: Profitable companies that offer "hot" products or services and are ready to grow rapidly.

Revenue Range: $10 million to $100 million (or more).

Risk Tolerance: Medium to high (often are VCs or angels).

Focus: Highly profitable exit within five to seven years. Goal is to add capital to the company to turbocharge its growth.

Examples: health care, communications, energy.

Buying an Existing Business

The Advantages of Buying an Existing Business

Over the next decade, entrepreneurs looking to buy existing businesses will have ample opportunities to consider. Those who purchase an existing business may reap the following benefits.

A SUCCESSFUL EXISTING BUSINESS MAY CONTINUE TO BE SUCCESSFUL Purchasing a thriving business at an acceptable price increases the likelihood of success. Although buying an existing business brings with it certain risks, it tends to be less risky than starting a company from scratch. The previous management team already has established a customer base, built supplier relationships, and set up a business system. The customer base inherited in a business purchase can carry an entrepreneur while he or she learns how to build on the company's success. The new owner's objective should be to make those modifications that will attract new customers while retaining the company's existing customers. Maintaining the proper balance of old and new is not an easy task, however.

AN EXISTING BUSINESS MAY ALREADY HAVE THE BEST LOCATION When the location of the business is critical to its success (as is often the case in retailing), it may be wise to purchase a business that is already in the right place. Opening in a second-choice location and hoping to draw customers usually proves fruitless. In fact, an existing business's biggest asset may be its prime location. As part of its expansion plans, one fast-food chain recently purchased a smaller chain, not so much for its customer base or other assets as for its prime store locations.

EMPLOYEES AND SUPPLIERS ARE ESTABLISHED An existing business already has experienced employees who can help the new owner through the transition phase. Experienced employees enable a company to continue to earn money while a new owner learns the business. Many new owners find it valuable to solicit ideas from employees about methods for increasing sales or reducing costs. In many cases, the previous owner may not have involved employees in this fashion and never gained the advantages found in their wisdom and experience. Few people know a job better than the people who perform it every day.

In addition, an existing business has an established set of suppliers with a history of business dealings. Those vendors can continue to supply the business while the new owner investigates the products and services of other suppliers. However, suppliers may want to ensure that the new owners are capable of running the business successfully.

When Reid Chase and Scott Semel purchased Cole-Kramer Imports, a high-end candy company that imported and distributed Swiss mint candies, they invested $100,000 of their own money and borrowed the remaining $500,000. The new owners soon discovered that the previous owners had no written contracts with the company's key suppliers. When Chase and Semel attempted to negotiate a formal supply contract, their suppliers refused, insisting that the new owners first prove their ability to operate the candy company successfully. Chase and Semel expanded their product line beyond mints and landed several major retail accounts in the process. Convinced that the new owners could manage the business, the Swiss suppliers forged long-term contracts with Cole-Kramer Imports, whose sales climbed from $600,000 to more than $40 million in just seven years.[2]

ENTREPRENEURIAL PROFILE

Reid Chase & Scott Semel: Cole-Kramer Imports

EQUIPMENT IS INSTALLED AND PRODUCTIVE CAPACITY IS KNOWN Acquiring and installing new equipment exerts a tremendous strain on a fledgling company's financial resources. In an existing business, a potential buyer can determine the condition of the plant and equipment and its capacity before buying. The previous owner may have established an efficient production operation through trial and error, although the new owner may need to make modifications to improve it. In many cases, entrepreneurs can purchase physical facilities and equipment at prices significantly below their replacement costs.

INVENTORY IS IN PLACE AND TRADE CREDIT IS ESTABLISHED The proper amount of inventory is essential to both controlling costs and generating adequate sales volume. If a business has too little inventory, it will not have the quantity and variety of products to satisfy customer demand.

However, if a business has too much inventory, it ties up excessive capital unnecessarily, thereby increasing costs and reducing profitability. Owners of successful established businesses have learned the proper balance between these extremes. In addition, previous owners have established trade credit relationships with vendors that can benefit the new owner. No supplier wants to lose a good customer.

THE NEW BUSINESS OWNER HITS THE GROUND RUNNING Entrepreneurs who purchase existing businesses avoid the time, costs, and energy required to launch a new business. The day they take over an ongoing business is the day their revenues begin. Entrepreneurs who buy existing successful businesses do not have to invest a lifetime building a company to enjoy its success.

ENTREPRENEURIAL PROFILE

Lania D'Agostino: Mannequin Service Company

Lania D'Agostino, a sculptor who moved from Michigan to Baltimore, Maryland, to attend the Maryland Institute College of Art, began working at Mannequin Service Company, a business that specializes in designing and creating custom mannequins for museums, special events, and entertainment companies. D'Agostino spent three years learning the business before buying it from the founder, who had built the business by making display mannequins for major retail stores. After buying the business, D'Agostino shifted the strategy to focus on highly specialized, artistic projects. A big break came for the company when D'Agostino landed a contract with Lucasfilm Inc., the company that produced the Star Wars trilogies, to provide mannequins depicting the characters from the films, from Obi-Won Kenobi and Princess Leia to Padme and Chewbacca, the Wookiee. Requiring as many as 80 hours to create, the company's character mannequins sell for $7,500 and up.[3]

THE NEW OWNER CAN USE THE EXPERIENCE OF THE PREVIOUS OWNER Even if the previous owner is not around after the sale, the new owner will have access to all of the business's records to guide him or her until he or she becomes acclimated to the business and the local market. The new owner can trace the impact on costs and revenues of the major decisions that the previous owner made and can learn from his mistakes and profit from his achievements. In many cases, the previous owner spends time with the new owner during the transition period, giving the new manager the opportunity to learn about the policies and procedures in place and the reasons for them. Previous owners also can be extremely helpful in unmasking the unwritten rules of business in the area, critically important intangibles such as how to keep customers happy and whom one can trust and cannot trust. After all, most owners who sell out want to see the buyer succeed in carrying on their businesses.

FINANCING IS EASIER TO OBTAIN Attracting financing to purchase an existing business often is easier than finding the money to launch a company from scratch. Many existing businesses already have established relationships with lenders, which may open the door to financing through traditional sources such as banks. As we will see later in this chapter, many business buyers also have access to another important source of financing: the seller.

IT'S A BARGAIN Some existing businesses may be real bargains. The current owner may need to sell on short notice, which may lead him or her to sell the business at a bargain price. Many small companies operate in profitable but tiny niches, making it easy for potential buyers to overlook them. The more specialized a business is, the greater the likelihood is that a buyer can find a bargain. If special skill or training is required to operate a business, the number of potential buyers will be significantly smaller. If the seller wants a substantial down payment or the entire selling price in cash, few buyers may qualify; however, those who do may be able to negotiate a good deal.

Disadvantages of Buying an Existing Business

LO 1-B

Understand the disadvantages of buying an existing business.

IT'S A "LOSER" A business may be for sale because it is struggling and the owner wants out. In these situations, a prospective buyer must be wary. Business owners sometimes attempt to disguise the facts and employ creative accounting techniques to make the company's financial picture appear much brighter than it really is. Few business sellers honestly state "It's losing money" as the reason for putting their companies up for sale. If there is one area of business where the maxim "let the buyer beware" still prevails, it is in the purchase of an existing business. Any buyer unprepared to do a complete and thorough analysis of a business may be stuck with a real loser.

Although buying a money-losing business is risky, it is not necessarily taboo. If an analysis of a company shows that it is poorly managed or suffering from neglect, a new owner may be able to turn it around. However, a prospective buyer who does not have a well-defined plan for improving a struggling business should *not* consider buying it!

Stephen Julius, who worked for a private equity firm in London, and Steve Heese, who had just sold his global construction products business, discovered Chris-Craft, a company that manufactured luxury boats for American society's upper crust during the first half of the twentieth century. The once prestigious brand languished after several buyers mismanaged the company, but Julius and Heese had experience turning around troubled companies and saw real potential in Chris-Craft. They were able to purchase the company's assets for $5 million and the rights to the Chris-Craft name for another $5 million and set out to reinvigorate the company by introducing new models and incorporating modern technology into Chris-Craft's classic style. Within three years, the company had boosted sales to $30 million and was profitable. After their successful turnaround at Chris-Craft, Julius and Heese purchased another struggling classic business, the Indian Motorcycle Company, and are in the process of turning it around as well.[4]

Chris Craft

THE PREVIOUS OWNER MAY HAVE CREATED ILL WILL Just as ethical, socially responsible business dealings create goodwill for a company, improper business behavior creates ill will. A buyer's due diligence process may reveal that customers, suppliers, creditors, or employees may have negative feelings about a company's reputation because of the unethical actions of its current owner. Business relationships may have begun to deteriorate, but their long-term effects may not yet appear in the business's financial statements. Ill will can permeate a business for years.

EMPLOYEES INHERITED WITH THE BUSINESS MAY NOT BE SUITABLE Previous managers may have kept marginal employees because they were close friends or because they started with the company. A new owner, therefore, may have to make some very unpopular termination decisions. For this reason, employees often do not welcome a new owner because they feel threatened by change. Some employees may not be able to adapt to the new owner's management style, and a culture clash may result. If the due diligence efforts reveals that existing employees are a significant cause of the problems a business faces, the new owner will have no choice but to terminate them and make new hires.

THE BUSINESS LOCATION MAY HAVE BECOME UNSATISFACTORY What was once an ideal location may have become obsolete as market and demographic trends change. Large shopping malls, new competitors, or highway re-routings can spell disaster for small retail shops. Prospective buyers should always evaluate the existing market in the area surrounding an existing business as well as its potential for expansion. Buyers must remember that they are buying the future of a business, not its past. If business success is closely linked to a good location, acquiring a business in a declining area or where demographic trends are moving downward is not a good idea. The value of the business can erode faster than the neighborhood surrounding it.

EQUIPMENT AND FACILITIES MAY BE OBSOLETE OR INEFFICIENT Potential buyers sometimes neglect to have an expert evaluate a company's facilities and equipment before they purchase it. Only later do they discover that the equipment is obsolete and inefficient and that the business may suffer losses from excessively high operating costs. The equipment may have been well suited to the business they purchased but not to the business they want to build. Modernizing equipment and facilities is seldom inexpensive.

CHANGE AND INNOVATION ARE DIFFICULT TO IMPLEMENT It is easier to plan for change than it is to implement it. Methods, policies, and procedures the previous owner used in a business may have established precedents that a new owner finds difficult to modify. Customers may resist changes the new owner wants to make to the business.

For instance, when Charles Usry purchased the landmark Esso Club in Clemson, South Carolina, he quickly discovered that the bar's regulars were skeptical of the changes he had planned to implement. Originally begun as a gas station/grocery store in 1935, the Esso Club eventually was converted into a bar and became a legendary destination for sports fans when *ESPN The Magazine* named it one of the top must-visit locations for sports fans. When Usry announced his plans to upgrade the décor of the no-frills, cinder-block building and to transform the club into a sports bar, long-time customers and loyal visitors howled in protest. "It's the ambiance of the place that really does it for us," says David Ford, an Esso Club regular, only half-joking. "The closest thing [to the Esso Club] is Cheers," says another long-time customer.[5]

Reversing a downward slide in an existing company's sales can be just as difficult as implementing change. Making changes that bring in new business and convince former clients to return can be an expensive, time-consuming, and laborious process. A business buyer must be aware of the effort, time, and expense it takes to change the negative momentum of a business in trouble. Before a business can go forward, it must stop going backward.

INVENTORY MAY BE OUTDATED OR OBSOLETE Inventory is valuable only if it is salable. Smart buyers know better than to trust the inventory valuation on a firm's balance sheet. Some of it may actually appreciate in value in periods of rapid inflation, but inventory is more likely to depreciate. A prospective buyer must judge inventory by its market value, *not* by its book value.

ACCOUNTS RECEIVABLE MAY BE WORTH LESS THAN FACE VALUE Like inventory, accounts receivable rarely are worth their face value. The prospective buyer should age the company's accounts receivable (a breakdown of accounts 30, 60, 90, and 120 days old and beyond) to determine their collectibility. The older the receivables are, the less likely they are to be collected, and, consequently, the lower their value is. Table 7.1 shows a simple but effective method of evaluating accounts receivable once they have been aged, using the estimated probabilities of collecting the accounts.

TABLE 7.1 Valuing Accounts Receivable

A prospective buyer asked the current owner of a business about the value of her accounts receivable. The owner's business records showed $101,000 in receivables. But when the prospective buyer aged the accounts and multiplied them by his estimated collection probabilities, he discovered their *real* value:

Age of Accounts	Amount	Collection Probability	Value
0–30 days	$40,000	95%	$38,000
31–60 days	$25,000	88%	$22,000
61–days	$14,000	70%	$9,800
91–120 days	$10,000	40%	$4,000
121–150 days	$7,000	25%	$1,750
151-plus days	$5,000	10%	$500
Total	$101,000		$76,050

Had he blindly accepted the seller's book value of these accounts receivable, this prospective buyer would have overpaid nearly $25,000 for them!

When one buyer was considering purchasing an existing business, his research showed that a substantial volume of accounts receivable were well past due. Further investigation revealed that the company and its largest customer were locked in a nasty dispute over outstanding account balances. The buyer decided to withdraw his preliminary offer.

THE BUSINESS MAY BE OVERPRICED   Each year, many people purchase businesses at prices far in excess of their value, which can impair the companies' ability to earn a profit and generate a positive cash flow. If a buyer accurately values a business's accounts receivable, inventories, and other assets, he or she will be in a better position to negotiate a price that will allow the business to be profitable. Making payments on a business that is overpriced is a millstone around the new owner's neck, making it difficult to keep the business afloat.

Although most buyers do not realize it, the price they pay for a company typically is not as crucial to its continued success as the terms on which they make the purchase. Of course, wise business buyers will try to negotiate a fair and reasonable price, but they are often equally interested in the more specific terms of the deal, such as how much cash they must pay out and when; how much of the price the seller is willing to finance and for how long; the interest rate at which the deal is financed; and other terms that can make or break a deal from the buyer's perspective. A buyer's primary concern is making sure that the terms of the deal do not endanger the company's future financial health and that they preserves the company's cash flow.

The Saga of Selling My Business: Part 1

Norm Brodsky is a serial entrepreneur who owns three businesses— a records storage company, a document destruction business, and a trucking company—and all of them are successful. Over the years, Brodsky had received many offers from people interested in buying his companies, but he had refused them all. Now at age 60, Brodsky has received an offer that has his attention, one that is "by far the best I've ever gotten," he says. "It has always been my belief that I would ultimately sell my company. You'd think I'd be thrilled, but the prospect of selling a business raises a whole range of emotional issues. When you've been in business as long as I have, the company becomes part of your identity, even your personality. You're no longer quite sure where the business ends and you begin. I feel a certain anxiety at the thought of separating from the business. What will be left of me if I no longer own it?"

Following is a chronicle of the ups and downs that Brodsky experienced as he considered selling his company when faced with "an offer that might be the best I'll ever get, the opportunity of a lifetime." His story offers valuable lessons to both business sellers and business buyers.

"Selling your business is especially difficult if, like me, you're not sure you're ready to sell, you're enjoying your life as it is, you don't have the slightest interest in retiring, and you don't know what you'll do after the sale." Several years ago, when people asked Brodsky about selling his companies, he told them that he had "a number" in mind, one that was considerably higher than the company was worth at the time. As his company grew, however, Brodsky realized that its value was approaching his number. Cintas, a large company that wanted to get into the documents storage business, contacted Brodsky and expressed interest in buying his business. Brodsky quoted a price that was one-third higher than his original "number," and to his surprise, "the Cintas

people didn't blink," which meant that he had a big decision to make: to sell or not. "I agonized over it," says Brodsky. "Finally, I told the Cintas people that we just weren't ready to sell."

Brodsky had put aside the idea of selling his company until he met venture capitalists Chris Debbas of CD Ventures in Berwyn, Pennsylvania, at an industry trade conference the next year. During the course of a conversation, Debbas said, "I think it's time for us to buy your company. What's it going to take?"

Brodsky laughed and then told Debbas, "We'll do it as a multiple of EBITDA (earnings before interest, taxes, depreciation, and amortization), but there's one thing: I won't negotiate. I'll give you the multiple, but I won't discuss it. If you're interested in buying us under those conditions, I'll talk to you. If you're not, you'll still be my friend."

Like the representative from Cintas, Debbas didn't blink at Brodsky's terms. "Can you get me some financials?" he asked.

"Of course," replied Brodsky. "You'll just have to sign a confidentiality agreement."

"No problem," said Debbas.

As fast as that, Brodsky's company was back on the market. "CD Ventures would buy our records storage, document-shredding, and deliver businesses for a lot more money than we had ever been offered before," he says. "One thing I can be pretty sure of: I will never get a deal like this again. Therein lies the paradox: The less interest you have in doing a deal, the more likely you are to get one you'll find difficult to refuse."

As Brodsky and Debbas began working on a potential deal, Brodsky began having second thoughts about selling his business. "Part of the problem is not knowing what I'll do if I sell the business," he says. "I certainly won't retire. What's going to happen to me when I sell my business? The frightening part is going from a somebody to a former somebody. In a way, I really want to do the sale, and in a way, I really don't. I am about as conflicted as a person can be."

1. Is the deal that Brodsky and CD Ventures are working on typical of most business sales? Is it common for buyers and sellers to determine the value of a company by using a multiple of earnings? What are the advantages and the disadvantages of using this approach?

2. Brodsky says, "Therein lies the paradox: The less interest you have in doing a deal, the more likely you are to get one you'll find difficult to refuse." What does he mean? Do you agree?

3. Brodsky also says, "One thing I can be pretty sure of: I will never get a deal like this again." How does that mindset affect an entrepreneur's decision to sell his or her company?

4. Is it typical for a business owner to ask a prospective buyer to sign a confidentiality agreement before opening up his or her business to the buyer? Explain.

Source: Adapted from Norm Brodsky, "The Offer, Part One," *Inc.*, November 2006, pp. 55–56; Norm Brodsky, "The Offer, Part Two," *Inc.*, December 2006, pp. 59–61; Norm Brodsky, "The Offer, Part Three," *Inc.*, January 2007, pp. 67–68.

LO 2

Define the steps involved in the *right* way to buy a business.

The Steps in Acquiring a Business

Buying an existing business can be risky if approached haphazardly. Kevin Mulvaney, a professor of entrepreneurship at Babson College and a consultant to business sellers, says that 50 to 75 percent of all business sales that are initiated fall through.[6] To avoid blowing a deal or making costly mistakes, an entrepreneur-to-be should follow a methodical approach:

- Analyze your skills, abilities, and interests to determine what kind(s) of businesses you should consider.
- Prepare a list of potential candidates.
- Investigate those candidates and evaluate the best one(s).
- Explore financing options.
- Ensure a smooth transition.

Analyze Your Skills, Abilities, and Interests

The first step in buying a business is *not* searching out potential acquisition candidates. Every entrepreneur considering buying a business should begin by conducting a self-audit to determine the ideal business for him or her. The primary focus is to identify the type of business *you* will be happiest and most successful owning. Consider, for example, the following questions:

- What business activities do you enjoy most? Least? Why?
- Which industries or markets offer the greatest potential for growth?
- Which industries interest you most? Least? Why?
- What kind of business would you enjoy running?
- What kinds of businesses do you want to *avoid*?
- What do you expect to get out of the business?
- How much time, energy, and money can you put into the business?
- What business skills and experience do you have? Which ones do you lack?
- How easily can you transfer your skills and experience to other types of businesses? In what kinds of businesses would that transfer be easiest?
- How much risk are you willing to take?
- Are you willing and able to turn around a struggling business?
- What size company do you want to buy?
- Is there a particular geographic location you desire?

Answering these and other questions beforehand allows you to develop a list of criteria a company must meet to become a purchase candidate. Addressing these issues early in the process will also save a great deal of time, trouble, and confusion as you wade through a multitude of business opportunities. The better you know yourself and your skills, competencies, and interests, the more likely you will be to find and manage a successful business.

Prepare a List of Potential Candidates

Once you know what your goals are for acquiring a business, you can begin your search. Do *not* limit yourself to only those businesses that are advertised as being "for sale." In fact, the "**hidden market**" of companies that might be for sale but are not advertised as such is one of the richest sources of top-quality businesses. Many businesses that can be purchased are not publicly

hidden market

Low-profile companies that might be for sale but are not advertised as such.

advertised but are available either through the owners themselves or through business brokers and other professionals. Although they maintain a low profile, these hidden businesses represent some of the most attractive purchase targets a prospective buyer may find.

For example, when brothers Art and Alan McCraw, two enterprising college graduates, returned to their hometown, they approached the owners of B. W. Burdette and Sons, a local hardware store that had been founded by the current owners' father 80 years earlier, about buying the business. The company was not listed for sale, but because the McCraws were familiar with the business, they knew that the current owners might be interested in selling. After several months of due diligence and negotiations, the young entrepreneurs closed the deal. They have since expanded the business to include two more locations, expanded its market reach, and increased its profitability many times over.

How can you tap into this hidden market of potential acquisitions? Typical sources include the following:

- Business brokers—to locate a broker near you, visit the Web site for the International Business Brokers Association at www.ibba.org
- Professionals who provide business services such as bankers, accountants, attorneys, investment bankers, and others
- Industry contacts—suppliers, distributors, customers, insurance brokers, and others
- "Networking"—social and business contact with friends and relatives
- Knocking on the doors of businesses you would like to buy (even if they're not advertised as being "for sale")
- Trade associations
- Newspapers and trade journals listing businesses for sale

In recent years, the Web also has become an important tool for entrepreneurs looking to buy businesses. In the past, the market for businesses was highly fragmented and unstructured, making it difficult for entrepreneurs to conduct an organized, thorough search for companies that might meet their purchase criteria. Today, hundreds of business brokers have established Web sites that list thousands of companies for sale in practically every industry imaginable, enabling entrepreneurs to search the entire country for that perfect business from the comfort of their own homes. BizBuySell, BizQuest, BusinessesForSale, BusinessMart, and Acquireo are among the most popular Web sites for entrepreneurs looking to buy a business online.[7] Using sites such as these, potential buyers can eliminate the companies that do not suit them and can conduct preliminary research on those that look most promising. The more opportunities an entrepreneur has to find and evaluate potential acquisitions, the greater the likelihood of finding a match that meets his or her criteria.

Investigate and Evaluate Candidate Businesses and Evaluate the Best One

Finding the right company requires patience. Although some buyers find a company after only a few months of looking, the typical search takes much longer, sometimes as long as two or three years. Once you have a list of prospective candidates, it is time to do your homework. The next step is to investigate the candidates in more detail:

- What are the company's strengths? Weaknesses?
- Is the company profitable? What is its overall financial condition?
- What is its cash flow cycle? How much cash will the company generate?
- Who are its major competitors?
- How large is the customer base? Is it growing or shrinking?
- Are the current employees suitable? Will they stay?
- What is the physical condition of the business, its equipment, and its inventory?
- What new skills must you learn to be able to manage this business successfully?

Determining the answers to these and other questions addressed in this chapter allow a prospective buyer to develop a list of the most attractive prospects and to prioritize them in descending order of attractiveness. This process also will make the task of valuing the business much easier.

When Mark Forst and his father decided to leave the corporate life and go into business for themselves, they knew that they wanted to buy an existing business rather than start their own. "We wanted a company that could use better marketing and service, one that we could take from the local to the national level," says Forst. Forst spent weeks poring over the business listings in Fort Lauderdale newspapers and hired a business broker to help uncover potential purchase candidates. One day he noticed a listing in the newspaper for a business called Rip's Uniforms that specialized in providing uniforms for postal workers. Forst and his father thought the asking price of $100,000 was reasonable, and they began researching the industry. Their research was encouraging. They discovered that the uniform supply industry had solid growth rates and that although a number of local uniform distributors were scattered across the United States, only five operated on a national level. Forst and his father began the due diligence process, talking with the small company's owners, studying the industry, and interviewing the company's vendors and its sole employee. They even conducted market research, talking with postal workers to glean ideas about how they could win them as customers and integrating what they learned into their business plan for the company. Their research of the company revealed that Rip's Uniforms had much more debt and far less inventory than the current owners believed, but the Forsts still believed in the company's potential. Using the information they had gathered, the Forsts purchased Rip's Uniforms after they were able to whittle the purchase price down to just $10,000. They renamed the company A.M.E.'s Uniforms, and sales, which now top $3 million annually, are growing so fast that the company has made *Inc.* magazine's list of the 500 fastest growing small companies twice.[8]

Explore Financing Options

Placing a value on an existing business (a topic you will learn more about later in this chapter) represents a major hurdle for many would-be entrepreneurs. The next challenging task in closing a successful deal is financing the purchase. Although financing the purchase of an existing business usually is easier than financing a new one, some traditional lenders shy away from deals involving the purchase of an existing business. Those that are willing to finance business purchases normally lend only a portion of the value of the assets, and buyers often find themselves searching for alternative sources of funds. Fortunately, most business buyers have access to a ready source of financing: the seller. Seller financing often is more flexible, faster, and easier to obtain than loans from traditional lenders.

Once a seller finds a suitable buyer, he or she typically will agree to finance anywhere from 25 percent to 80 percent of the purchase price. Dan Steppe, a serial entrepreneur who leads the University of Houston's Center for Entrepreneurship, tells his college students, "You will soon be talking to a 67-year-old guy who is a bit tired of what he's doing, who's already talked to his son and his daughter, and the family options don't exist. The seller will enable the buyer to buy his company fairly inexpensively. You can buy a $10 million company for $2 million and the seller will finance the other $8 million."[9]

Usually, a deal is structured so that the buyer makes a sizeable down payment to the seller, who then finances a note for the balance. The buyer makes regular principal and interest payments over five to ten years—perhaps with a larger balloon payment at the end—until the note is paid off. The terms and conditions of such a loan are a vital concern to both buyer and seller. They cannot be so burdensome that they threaten the company's continued existence; that is, the buyer must be able to make the payments to the seller out of the company's cash flow. At the same time, the deal must give the seller the financial security he or she is seeking from the sale. Defining reasonable terms is the result of the negotiation process between the buyer and the seller.

Tim Johnstone's experience in conducting due diligence for his former employer gave him an advantage when he was considering buying Anywhere Shoe Company, a Seattle-based maker and distributor of professional footwear. Johnstone's thorough analysis of the company revealed several factors that caused him concern, including a wrongful termination lawsuit filed by a former employee. Consequently, these discoveries caused him to assign a lower value to the business than the seller's asking price. Johnstone's offer included a "holdback" clause that allowed him to deduct from the purchase price the value of any undisclosed claims against Anywhere. To avoid paying off the seller at the expense of the security of the company's financial future, he also stipulated that the payout the seller was to receive would be based on the company's financial performance. Finally, Johnstone's terms required the seller to finance 55 percent of the purchase price. Initially, the owner balked at the terms but agreed to them rather than risk losing a viable buyer. "If we had not used seller financing, the deal probably wouldn't have come together," says Johnstone. His foresight paid off when, 14 months after the purchase, he discovered that a customer had filed a lawsuit against the company before he had signed the contract to buy the business. "Having seller financing gives you some protection that you otherwise might not have," says Johnstone. "It turned out to be the smartest thing I ever did."[10]

Ensure a Smooth Transition

Once the parties strike a deal, the challenge of making a smooth transition immediately arises. No matter how well planned the sale is, there are *always* surprises. For instance, the new owner may have ideas for changing the business—sometimes radically—that cause a great deal of stress and anxiety among employees and the previous owner. Charged with such emotion and uncertainty, the transition phase is always difficult and frustrating—and sometimes painful. To avoid a bumpy transition, a business buyer should do the following:

- Concentrate on communicating with employees. Business sales are fraught with uncertainty and anxiety, and employees need reassurance.
- Be honest with employees. Avoid telling them only what they want to hear. Share with the employees your vision for the business in the hope of generating a heightened level of motivation and support.
- Listen to employees. They have first-hand knowledge of the business and its strengths and weaknesses and usually can offer valuable suggestions for improving it.
- Consider asking the seller to serve as a consultant until the transition is complete. The previous owner can be a valuable resource, especially to an inexperienced buyer.

Evaluating an Existing Business—The Due Diligence Process

When evaluating an existing business, a buyer can quickly feel overwhelmed by the tremendous number and complexity of the issues involved. Therefore, a smart buyer will assemble a team of specialists to help investigate a potential business opportunity. This team is usually composed of a banker, an accountant familiar with the particular industry, an attorney, and perhaps a small business consultant or a business broker. The cost of assembling a team can range from $3,000 to $20,000, but most buyers agree that using a team significantly lowers the likelihood of making a bad purchase. Because making a bad purchase will cost many times the expense of a team of experts, most buyers see it as a wise investment. It is important for a buyer to trust the members of the business evaluation team. With this team assembled, the potential buyer is ready to explore the business opportunity by examining five critical areas.

1. Why does the owner want to sell?
2. What is the physical condition of the business?
3. What is the potential for the company's products or services?
4. What legal aspects should be considered?
5. Is the business financially sound?

Evaluating these five areas of a business is known as performing **due diligence**. A prospective buyer should never consider purchasing a business without conducting the necessary due diligence to learn about the strengths, weaknesses, opportunities, and threats facing the company. "There are so many ugly stories," explains Robert Strang, president of Strang Hayes Consulting, a firm that specializes in helping prospective buyers through the due diligence process. For one of its clients, Strang Hayes discovered that the CEO of a company that one of its clients was considering purchasing had hidden five sexual harassment lawsuits that had been filed against him. Another search revealed that the business another buyer was considering purchasing had been banned from doing business in Florida, which was a major market for the prospective buyer.[11] The message is clear: Those buyers who neglect thorough due diligence do so at their own peril.

LO 3

Explain the process of evaluating an existing business.

due diligence
the process of investigating the details of a company that is for sale to determine the strengths, weaknesses, opportunities, and threats facing it.

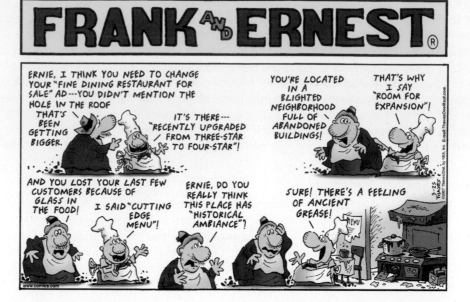

Source: FRANK & ERNEST: ©
Thaves/Dist. by Newspaper Enterprise
Association, Inc.

Why Is the Business for Sale?

WHY DOES THE OWNER WANT TO SELL? Every prospective business buyer should investigate the *real* reason the business owner wants to sell. A study by DAK Group and Rutgers University found that the most common reason that owners of small businesses cite for selling their companies is to reduce the risk of having most of their personal assets tied up in their businesses.[12] Their goal is to cash out their business investments and diversify into other types of assets. Many owners tell buyers that they have become bored or burned out and want to move on to other business ventures, but is that really the case? Note that market competition and external pressures are the next most common reasons owners give for selling their companies.

Smart business buyers know that the biggest and most unpleasant surprises can crop up outside the company's financial records and may never appear on the spreadsheets designed to analyze a company's financial position. For instance, a business owner might be looking to sell his or her business because a powerful new competitor is about to move into the market, a major highway re-routing will cause customer traffic to evaporate, the lease agreement on the ideal location is about to expire, or the primary customer base is declining. Every prospective buyer should investigate thoroughly any reason a seller gives for wanting to sell a business.

Businesses do not last forever, and smart entrepreneurs know when the time has come to sell. Some owners consider their behavior ethical only if they do not make false or misleading statements. Buyers should not expect to get a full disclosure of the whole story behind the reasons for a business being offered for sale. In most business sales, the buyer bears the responsibility of determining whether the business is a good value. The best way to do that is to get out into the local community, talk to people, and ask a lot of questions. Visiting local business owners may reveal general patterns about the area and its overall vitality. The local chamber of commerce also may have useful information. Suppliers, customers, and even competitors may be able to shed light on why a business is up for sale. By combining this information with an analysis of the company's financial records, a potential buyer should be able to develop a clear picture of the business and its real value.

The Condition of the Business

WHAT IS THE PHYSICAL CONDITION OF THE BUSINESS? A prospective buyer should evaluate the business's assets to determine their value. Are they reasonably priced? Are they obsolete? Will they need to be replaced soon? Do they operate efficiently? The potential buyer should check the condition of both the equipment and the building. It may be necessary to hire a professional to evaluate the major components of the building—its structure and its plumbing, its electrical, heating, and cooling systems, and other elements. Unexpected renovations are rarely inexpensive or simple and can punch a gaping hole in a buyer's financial plans.

How fresh is the company's inventory? Is it consistent with the image the new owner wants to project? How much of it would the buyer have to sell at a loss? A potential buyer may need an independent appraisal to determine the value of the company's inventory and other assets because the current owner may have priced them far above their actual value. These items typically comprise the largest portion of a business's value, and a potential buyer should not accept the seller's asking price blindly. Remember: *Book value is not the same as market value.* Usually, a buyer can purchase equipment and fixtures at substantially lower prices than book value. Value is determined in the marketplace, not on a balance sheet.

Other important factors that the potential buyer should investigate include the following:

Accounts Receivable. If the sale includes accounts receivable, the buyer should check their quality before purchasing them. How creditworthy are the accounts? What portion of them is past due? How likely are you to be able to collect them? By aging the accounts receivable, a buyer can judge their quality and determine their value. (Refer to Table 7.1.)

Lease Arrangements. Is the lease included in the sale? When does it expire? What restrictions does it have on renovation or expansion? The buyer should determine *beforehand* any restrictions the landlord has placed on the lease and negotiate any change prior to purchasing the business.

Business Records. Well-kept business records can be a valuable source of information and can tell a prospective buyer a lot about the company's pattern of success (or lack of it). Typically, buyers should expect to see financial statements documenting revenues and net income, operating budgets, and cash flow statements for at least five years. Sales and earnings forecasts from the seller for at least three years also can be helpful when trying to determine the value of a business.

Unfortunately, many business owners are sloppy recordkeepers. Consequently, the potential buyer and his or her team may have to reconstruct some critical records. It is important to verify as much information about the business as possible. For instance, does the owner have customer mailing lists? These lists can be a valuable marketing tool for a new business owner. Has the owner created an operations manual outlining the company's policies and procedures?

Intangible Assets. Does the sale include any intangible assets such as trademarks, patents, copyrights, or goodwill? How long do patents have left to run? Is the trademark threatened by lawsuits for infringement? Does the company have logos or slogans that are unique or widely recognized? Determining the value of such intangibles is much more difficult than computing the value of the tangible assets.

Location and Appearance. The location and the overall appearance of a business are important factors for a prospective buyer to consider. What had been an outstanding location in the past may be totally unacceptable today. Even if the building and equipment are in good condition and are fairly priced, the business may be located in a declining area. What other businesses operate in the surrounding area? Every buyer should consider the location's suitability not only for the present but also for several years into the future.

Products and Services

HOW CURRENT IS THE COMPANY'S PRODUCT LINE? A company with no new products in the pipeline may falter in the future.

WHAT IS THE POTENTIAL FOR THE COMPANY'S PRODUCTS OR SERVICES? No one wants to buy a business with a shrinking customer base. A thorough market analysis helps a buyer to develop his or her own sales forecast for an existing business (in addition to the one he or she should ask the seller to prepare). This research will reveal important trends in the business's sales and customer base.

WHAT ARE THE CUSTOMERS' CHARACTERISTICS AND COMPOSITION? Before purchasing an existing business, a buyer should analyze both existing and potential customers. Discovering why customers buy from the business and developing a profile of the company's existing customer base help the buyer to identify a company's strengths and weaknesses and discover how to market more effectively. A potential buyer should determine the answers to the following questions:

- How is the community's population changing? Is it growing or shrinking? How is the composition of the population changing?
- Who are the company's target customers? What are their race, age, gender, and income levels? What is their demographic profile?

- What do customers want the business to do for them? What needs are they satisfying when they make a purchase?
- How often do customers buy? Do they buy in seasonal patterns?
- How loyal are present customers?
- Is it practical to attract new customers at a reasonable cost?
- Does the business have a well-defined customer base? Is it growing? Do these customers come from a large geographic area or do they all live near the business?

Analyzing the answers to these questions helps a potential buyer to create and implement a more powerful marketing plan. The goal is to keep the business attractive to existing customers while changing some features of its marketing plan to attract new ones.

WHAT ARE THE COMPETITORS' CHARACTERISTICS AND COMPOSITION? A potential buyer must identify the company's direct competition—those businesses in the immediate area that sell the same or similar products or services. The potential profitability and survival of the business may well depend on the behavior of these competitors. Important factors to consider are the number of competitors and the intensity of the competition. How many competitors have opened in recent years? How many have closed in the last five years? What caused them to fail? Has the market already reached the saturation point? Being a latecomer in an already saturated market is not the pathway to long-term success.

Legal Aspects

WHAT LEGAL ASPECTS SHOULD YOU CONSIDER? Business buyers must be careful to avoid several legal pitfalls as they negotiate the final deal. The biggest potential legal traps include liens, bulk transfers, contract assignments, covenants not to compete, and ongoing legal liabilities.

lien
a creditor's claim against an asset.

Liens. The key legal issue in the sale of any asset is typically the proper transfer of good title from seller to buyer. However, because most business sales involve a collection of assorted assets, the transfer of a good title is more complex. Some business assets may have **liens** (creditors' claims) against them and unless the lien is satisfied before the sale, the buyer must assume it and is financially responsible for it. One way to reduce this potential problem is to include a clause in the sales contract stating that any liability not shown on the balance sheet at the time of sale remains the responsibility of the seller. A prospective buyer should have an attorney thoroughly investigate all of the assets for sale and their lien status before buying any business.

bulk transfer
protects the buyer of a business's assets from the claims unpaid creditors might have against those assets.

Bulk Transfers. To protect against surprise claims from the seller's creditors after purchasing a business, the buyer should meet the requirements of a **bulk transfer** under Section 6 of the Uniform Commercial Code. Suppose that an owner owing many creditors sells his business to a buyer. The seller, however, does not use the proceeds of the sale to pay his debts to business creditors. Instead, he pockets them to use for his own benefit. Without the protection of a bulk transfer, those creditors could make claim to the assets that the buyer purchased to satisfy the previous owner's debts (within six months). To be effective, a bulk transfer must meet the following criteria:

- The seller must give the buyer a signed, sworn list of existing creditors.
- The buyer and the seller must prepare a list of the property included in the sale.
- The buyer must keep the list of creditors and the list of property for 6 months.
- The buyer must give written notice of the sale to each creditor at least 10 days before he or she takes possession of the goods or pays for them (whichever is first).

By meeting these criteria, a buyer acquires free and clear title to the assets purchased, which are not subject to prior claims from the seller's creditors. Because Section 6 can create quite a burden on a business buyer, 16 states have repealed it, and more may follow. About a half-dozen states have revised Section 6 to make it easier for buyers to notify creditors. Under the revised rule, if a business has more than 200 creditors, the buyer may notify them by public notice rather than by contacting them individually.

Contract Assignments. Buyers must investigate the rights and the obligations they would assume under existing contracts with suppliers, customers, employees, lessors, and others. To continue the smooth operation of the business, the buyer must assume the rights of the seller under many existing contracts. Assuming these rights and obligations requires the seller to assign existing contracts to the new owner. For example, the current owner may have four years left on a 10-year lease and will assign this contract to the buyer. To protect his or her interest, the buyer (who is the assignee) should notify the other party involved in the contract (in this case, the landlord) of the assignment. Generally, the seller can assign any contractual right to the buyer unless the contract specifically prohibits the assignment or the contract is personal in nature. For instance, loan contracts sometimes prohibit assignments with a **due-on-sale clause**. These clauses require the buyer to pay the full amount of the remaining loan balance or to finance the balance at prevailing interest rates. Thus, the buyer cannot assume the seller's loan (which may be at a lower interest rate than the prevailing rate on a loan). In addition, a seller usually cannot assign his or her credit arrangements with suppliers to the buyer because they are based on the seller's business reputation and are personal in nature. If such contracts are crucial to the business operation and cannot be assigned, the buyer must renegotiate new contracts. A prospective buyer also should evaluate the terms of any other unique contracts the seller has, including exclusive agent or distributor contracts, real estate leases, financing and loan arrangements, and union contracts.

Covenants Not to Compete. One of the most important and most often overlooked legal considerations for a prospective buyer is negotiating a **covenant not to compete** (or a **restrictive covenant** or a **noncompete agreement**) with the seller. Under one of these covenants, the seller agrees not to open a new, competing business within a specific time period and geographic area of the existing one. (The covenant should be negotiated with the *owner*, not with the corporation, because if the corporation signs the agreement, the owner may not be bound.) However, the covenant must be a part of a business sale and must be reasonable in scope to be enforceable. Although some states place limitations on the enforceability of restrictive covenants, business buyers should insist on the seller signing one. Without this protection, a buyer may find his or her new business eroding beneath his or her feet. For instance, suppose that Bob purchases a tire business from Alexandra, whose reputation in town for selling tires in unequaled. If Bob fails to negotiate a restrictive covenant, nothing can stop Alexandra from opening a new shop next to her old one and keeping all of her customers, thereby driving Bob out of business. A reasonable covenant in this case might restrict Alexandra from opening a tire store within a three-mile radius for three years. Every business buyer should negotiate a covenant not to compete with the seller.

To be enforceable, a restrictive covenant must be reasonable in geographic scope and in duration, must protect a legitimate business interest (such as a company's goodwill), and must be tied to a contract for the sale of an existing business (i.e., no "free standing" restrictive covenants that restrain trade).

due-on-sale clause
loan contract provision that prohibits a seller from assigning a loan arrangement to the buyer. Instead, the buyer is required to finance the remaining loan balance at prevailing interest rates.

covenant not to compete (or restrictive covenants)
an agreement between a buyer and a seller in which the seller agrees not to compete with the buyer within a specific time and geographic area.

Gurbaksh Chahal, known as "G" to his friends, launched an online advertising network, ClickAgent when he was just 16 years old. Two years later, he sold the company to ValueClick for $40 million and signed a restrictive covenant that prevented him from competing in the online advertising business for one year. When the restrictive covenant expired, G started BlueLithum, a global advertising network that uses analytics to target customers based on their online behavior. Within three years, BlueLithium had grown to nine offices around the world with 175 employees. In 2007, G sold BlueLithium to Yahoo! for $300 million. A serial entrepreneur, G, who at 25 has a net worth of $100 million, is working on several new projects, including a reality television show, a charitable foundation, and, of course, another company, gWallet, a company that helps online shoppers find the best deals.[13]

Gurbaksh Chahal

ENTREPRENEURIAL PROFILE

Gurbaksh Chahal: ValueClick

Ongoing Legal Liabilities. Finally, a potential buyer must look for any potential legal liabilities the purchase might expose. These typically arise from three sources: (1) physical premises, (2) product liability claims, and (3) labor relations. First, the buyer must examine the physical premises for safety. Are employees at risk because of asbestos or some other hazardous material? If the business is a manufacturing operation, does it meet Occupational Safety and Health Administration (OSHA) and other regulatory agency requirements? One entrepreneur who purchased a retail business located in a building that once housed a gas station was quite surprised when the Environmental Protection Agency informed him that he would have to pay for cleaning up the results of an old, leaking gas tank that still sat beneath the property. Even though he had no part in running the old gas station and did not know the leaking tank was there, he was responsible for the cost of the cleanup! Removing the tank and cleaning up the site cost him several thousand dollars that he had not budgeted.

Second, the buyer must consider whether existing products contain defects that could result in **product liability lawsuits,** which claim that a company is liable for damages and injuries caused by the products or services they make or sell. Existing lawsuits might be an omen of more to follow. In addition, the buyer must explore products that the company has discontinued because he or she might be liable for them if they prove to be defective. The final bargain between the parties should require the seller to guarantee that the company is not involved in any product liability lawsuits.

Third, what is the relationship between management to employees? Does a union contract exist? The time to discover sour management-labor relations is before the purchase, not after.

If the buyer's investigation reveals potential legal liabilities, it does not necessarily eliminate the business from consideration. Insurance coverage can shift such risks from the potential buyer, but the buyer should check to see whether the insurance will cover lawsuits resulting from actions predating the purchase.

product liability lawsuits
lawsuits that claim a company is liable for damages and injuries caused by the products it makes or sells.

Financial Soundness of the Business

IS THE BUSINESS FINANCIALLY SOUND? A prospective buyer must analyze the financial records of a target business to determine its condition. He or she shouldn't be afraid to ask an accountant for help. Accounting systems and methods can vary tremendously from one type of business to another and can be quite confusing to a novice. Current profits can be inflated by changes in the accounting procedure or in the method for recording sales. For the buyer, the most dependable financial records are audited statements, those prepared by a CPA firm in accordance with generally accepted accounting principles (GAAP). Audited records do not exist in many small companies that are for sale. In some cases, a potential buyer has to hire an accountant to construct reliable financial statements because the owner's accounting and recordkeeping is so sloppy.

ENTREPRENEURIAL PROFILE

Charles Carroll: Integrated Biometric Technology

When Charles Carroll decided to sell his business, Integrated Biometric Technology (IBT), a company that allows employers to conduct criminal background checks in just minutes, he attracted more attention from potential buyers by switching to audited financial statements from reviewed statements. Meeting the more stringent standards increased his accounting costs from $10,000 to $35,000, but Carroll received offers that were higher than he expected from multiple prospects. Ultimately, he sold IBT to a larger company, Viisage, for $35 million in cash, $25 million in Viisage stock, and the prospect of another $10 million if IBT hits specific performance targets.[14]

When evaluating the financial status of any business prospect, buyers must remember that any investment in a company should produce a reasonable salary for themselves, an attractive return on the money they invest, and enough to cover the amount they must borrow to make the purchase. Otherwise, it makes no sense to purchase the business. Because most investors know that they can earn at least 6 to 8 percent per year by investing wisely in the stock market, they expect any business they buy to earn at least that amount plus an extra return that reflects the additional risk of buying a business. Many owners expect to earn a return of at least 15 percent to 30 percent on the amount invested in their businesses.

Buyers also must remember that they are purchasing the future profit potential of an existing business. To evaluate the firm's profit potential, they should review past sales, operating expenses, and profits as well as the assets used to generate those profits. They must compare current balance sheets, income statements, and statements of cash flow with previous ones and then develop a set of projected statements for the next two or three years. Sales tax records, income tax returns, and financial statements are valuable sources of information.

Are profits consistent over the years, or are they erratic? Is this pattern typical in the industry, or is it a result of unique circumstances or poor management? Can the business survive with serious fluctuations in revenues, costs, and profits? If these fluctuations are the result of poor management, can a new owner turn the business around?

Some of the financial records that a potential buyer should examine include the following:

Income statements and balance sheets for the last three to five years. It is important to review data from several years because creative accounting techniques can distort financial data in any single year. Even though buyers are purchasing the future profits of a business, they must remember that many businesses intentionally keep net income low to minimize the owners' tax bills. Low earnings should prompt a buyer to investigate their causes.

Income tax returns for the past three to five years. Comparing basic financial statements with tax returns can reveal discrepancies of which the buyer should be aware. Some small business owners engage in **"skimming"** from their businesses—taking money from sales without reporting it as income. Owners who skim will claim their businesses are more profitable than their tax returns show. Although such underreporting is illegal and unethical, it is surprisingly common. Buyers should *not* pay for undocumented, "phantom" earnings a seller claims exist. In fact, buyers should consider whether they want to buy a business from someone who admits to doing business unethically.

skimming
taking money from sales without reporting it as income.

Owner's compensation (and that of relatives). The owner's compensation is especially important in small companies; and the smaller the company is, the more important it will be. Although many companies do not pay their owners what they are worth, others compensate their owners lavishly. The buyer must consider the impact of benefits—company cars, insurance contracts, country club memberships, and the like. It is important to adjust the company's income statements for the salary and benefits that the seller has paid himself or herself and others.

Cash Flow. Most buyers understand the importance of evaluating a company's profitability, but fewer recognize the necessity of analyzing its cash flow. They assume that if earnings are adequate, there will be sufficient cash to pay all of the bills and to fund an attractive salary for themselves. *That is not necessarily the case!* Before agreeing to a deal, prospective buyers should sit down with an accountant and convert the target company's financial statements into a cash flow forecast. This forecast must take into account not only existing debts and obligations, but also any modifications the buyer would make in the business, including necessary capital expenditures. It must also reflect the repayment of any financing the buyer arranges to purchase the company, whether it is through the seller or a traditional lender. Will the company generate enough cash to be self-supporting? How much cash will it generate for you?

A potential buyer must look for suspicious deviations from normal (in either direction) for sales, expenses, profits, cash flow, assets, and liabilities. Have sales been increasing or decreasing? Is the equipment really as valuable as it is listed on the balance sheet? Are advertising expenses unusually high or low? How is depreciation reflected in the financial statements?

This financial information gives a buyer the opportunity to verify the seller's claims about a company's performance. Sometimes, however, an owner will take short-term actions that produce a healthy financial statement but weaken the company's long-term health and profit potential. For example, a seller might lower expenses and increase earnings by gradually eliminating equipment maintenance or boost sales by selling to marginal businesses that will never pay their bills. Techniques such as these artificially inflate earnings, but a well-prepared buyer should be able to see through them.

Finally, a potential buyer should walk away from a deal—no matter how good it may appear on the surface—if the present owner refuses to disclose the company's financial records—or any other operating information the buyer needs to make an informed decision. If that is the case, says Marc Kramer, author of *Small Business Turnaround*, "don't walk—run—away." [15]

Buying an existing business is a process filled with potential missteps along the way. The expression "Let the buyer beware" should be the prospective buyer's mantra throughout the entire process. However, by following the due diligence procedure described in this section, buyers can lower dramatically the probability of "getting burned" with a business that does not suit their personalities or one that is in on the verge of failure. Figure 7.2 illustrates the sequence of events leading up to a successful negotiation with a seller.

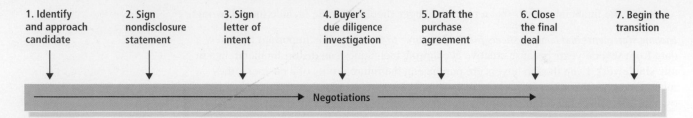

| 1. Identify and approach candidate | 2. Sign nondisclosure statement | 3. Sign letter of intent | 4. Buyer's due diligence investigation | 5. Draft the purchase agreement | 6. Close the final deal | 7. Begin the transition |

→ Negotiations →

1. Approach the candidate. If a business is advertised for sale, the proper approach is through the channel defined in the ad. Sometimes buyers will contact business brokers to help them locate potential target companies. If you have targeted a company in the "hidden market," an introduction from a banker, accountant, or lawyer often is the best approach. During this phase, the seller checks out the buyer's qualifications, and the buyer begins to judge the quality of the company.

2. Sign a nondisclosure document. If the buyer and the seller are satisfied with the results of their preliminary research, they are ready to begin serious negotiations. Throughout the negotiation process, the seller expects the buyer to maintain strict confidentiality of all of the records, documents, and information he or she receives during the investigation and negotiation process. The nondisclosure document is a legally binding contract that ensures the secrecy of the parties' negotiations.

3. Sign a letter of intent. Before a buyer makes a legal offer to buy the company, he or she typically will ask the seller to sign a letter of intent. The letter of intent is a nonbinding document that says that the buyer and the seller have reached a sufficient "meeting of the minds" to justify the time and expense of negotiating a final agreement. The letter should state clearly that it is nonbinding, giving either party the right to walk away from the deal. It should also contain a clause calling for "good faith negotiations" between the parties. A typical letter of intent addresses terms such as price, payment terms, categories of assets to be sold, and a deadline for closing the final deal.

4. Buyer's due diligence. While negotiations are continuing, the buyer is busy studying the business and evaluating its strengths and weaknesses. In short, the buyer must "do his or her homework" to make sure that the business is a good value.

5. Draft the purchase agreement. The purchase agreement spells out the parties' final deal! It sets forth all of the details of the agreement and is the final product of the negotiation process.

6. Close the final deal. Once the parties have drafted the purchase agreement, all that remains to making the deal "official" is the closing. Both buyer and seller sign the necessary documents to make the sale final. The buyer delivers the required money, and the seller turns the company over to the buyer.

7. Begin the transition. For the buyer, the real challenge now begins: making the transition to a successful business owner!

FIGURE 7.2

The Acquisition Process

Source: Adapted from Price Waterhouse, *Buying and Selling: A Company Handbook* (New York: Author, 1993), pp. 38–42; Charles F. Claeys, "The Intent to Buy," *Small Business Reports*, May 1994, pp. 44–47.

YOU BE THE CONSULTANT

The Saga of Selling My Business: Part 2

Once Norm Brodsky and Chris Debbas decided to explore the possibility of Debbas's company, CD Ventures, purchasing Brodsky's business, they embarked on the due diligence process in which the potential buyer investigates the quality of the company, its financial performance, its relationships with customers, and a million other details. "What would you think about having a team of outside accountants, lawyers, and operations people descend on your business to go through your records, question your employees, dissect everything you do, and judge how good your company is and how truthful you really are?" says Brodsky, describing the due diligence process.

On the financial front, Brodsky knew that his company was ready for due diligence. Several years before, he had begun having an accounting firm provide audited financial statements for CitiStorage. The move had increased the company's accounting expenses significantly, but Sam Kaplan, Brodsky's partner in the business, had convinced him that doing so would make raising capital or selling the business much easier. He was right. "The audited statements made the financial part of the due diligence process a walk in the park," says Brodsky. The goal was to adjust the company's income statement to reflect the revenues and expenses that CD Ventures could expect, thus arriving at an earnings value on which both parties could agree. (Recall that the deal was to apply Brodsky's multiplier to the company's earnings; therefore, coming up with the right number was a major part of the deal.)

Throughout the process, everyone at CitiStorage followed what Brodsky calls a "warts and all" policy, refusing to hide the company's problems and giving the due diligence team full access to the records they wanted. "In this kind of transaction, you should tell people on the other side everything that is bad, that might be bad, or has a one-in-a-million chance of going bad," he says.

In the end, CD Ventures settled on an earnings value that was $600,000 less than the one that Brodsky had come up with—not a huge gap considering the size of the deal. "When we got together to discuss our different numbers, I told [Debbas] that he should just accept mine," says Brodsky. "For every dollar that your accountants find, I'm going to find a dollar fifty the other way. You might as well just go with our number." Debbas refused, but eventually he and Brodsky were able to agree on an earnings value for CitiStorage.

While the CD Ventures team was completing its due diligence, Brodsky had time to reflect on what it meant to sell the company that he had launched 16 years before and nurtured into a successful business. "Once I put my emotions aside, I realized it was now or never," he says. "The decision wasn't about selling to this particular group or even about getting the right price. It came down to whether I was ever going to sell." Brodsky knew that his company was financially sound and well managed and that the document storage industry was "hot," with many players looking to buy businesses in that sector. "If I'm ever going to sell [my company], now is the time," he says. For Brodsky, two issues dominated the decision: He wanted the right price for the company, and he wanted his employees to be treated well by the buyer.

Brodsky set a deadline for closing the sale of his business, but it passed with no deal done. As time dragged on, he began to wonder whether CD Ventures and Nova Records Management, the company they planned to fold CitiStorage into, were still interested in doing a deal. The dealmakers assured Brodsky that they were committed to buying his business. Then Debbas called and told Brodsky that the "equity guys" (the people who were providing the equity capital to purchase CitiStorage) had backed out

"What now?" Brodsky asked.

Debbas told him about "plan B," in which investment banker Goldman Sachs would provide all of the financing to complete the deal. After hearing the details, Brodsky agreed that it was a better plan, but it also meant more delays in closing the sale of the business.

The delays were creating another problem. CitiStorage was having its best year ever, which meant that its value had gone up. Yet the sales price that Brodsky had agreed to was based on the previous year's earnings. "It would be very tough for me to sell my company for substantially less than it is worth," says Brodsky.

In an attempt to move the process forward, Brodsky called a meeting with key members from Nova's board and attorneys for both sides with the goal of putting on the table unresolved issues. The group discussed four matters ranging from the company's 401(k) program to the lease agreements and was able to resolve them all. "When can you have this done?" Brodsky asked the attorneys. After some discussion, the parties agreed that the closing would take place on April 5. A year had passed since Brodsky had talked with Debbas about selling his company. "I don't know whether I'm more amazed at how far we've come or how long it's taken," says Brodsky. "I just hope the suspense is over soon and I can finally start focusing on the future."

5. Why is it important for business buyers to be thorough when conducting their due diligence of a company they are considering purchasing?
6. Brodsky followed a "warts and all" policy with CD Ventures and Nova Records Management during due diligence. How typical is his approach among business sellers? Explain your reasoning.
7. Often deals such as the one Brodsky is involved in fall through at the end and are never completed. Do you see any potential deal breakers in the sale of CitiStorage?

Source: Adapted from Norm Brodsky, "The Offer, Part Four," *Inc.*, February 2007, pp. 63–65; Norm Brodsky, "It's All About Trust," *Inc.*, March 2007, pp. 116–119; Norm Brodsky, "The Offer, Part Six," *Inc.*, April 2007, pp. 67–68; Norm Brodsky, "The Offer: Part Seven," *Inc.*, May 2007, pp. 73–74.

Methods for Determining the Value of a Business

LO 4

Describe the various techniques for determining the value of a business.

Business valuation is partly an art and partly a science. Part of what makes establishing a reasonable price for a privately-held business so difficult is the wide variety of factors that influence its value: the nature of the business itself, its position in the market or industry, the outlook for the market or industry, the company's financial status, its earning capacity, any intangible assets it may own (e.g., patents, trademarks, or copyrights), the value of other similar companies, and many other factors.

Computing the value of the company's tangible assets normally poses no major problem, but assigning a price to the intangibles, such as goodwill, almost always creates controversy. **Goodwill** represents the difference in the value of an established business and one that has not yet built a solid reputation for itself. A buyer is willing to pay extra only for those intangible assets that produce additional income. A seller, however, believes that goodwill is a measure of the hard work, sacrifice, and long hours invested in building the business, something for which he or she expects to be paid—often quite handsomely.

goodwill

the difference in the value of an established business and one that has not yet built a solid reputation for itself.

Potential buyers also must recognize the role that the seller's ego can play in the business valuation process. Norm Brodsky, who recently sold his successful document storage business to a larger company, explains:

As a group, we [entrepreneurs] tend to have fairly large egos, which isn't entirely bad. You need one to make a business grow... But our egos can get us into trouble when it comes to putting a dollar value on something we've created. We generally take the highest valuation we've heard for a company somewhat like ours—and multiply it.[16]

So how can the buyer and the seller arrive at a fair price? There are few "hard and fast" rules in establishing the value of a business, but the following guidelines are helpful:

- The wisest approach is to compute a company's value using several techniques and then to choose the one that makes the most sense.
- The deal must be financially feasible for both parties. The seller must be satisfied with the price received for the business, but the buyer cannot pay an excessively high price that would require heavy borrowing and would strain his or her cash flows from the outset.
- The potential buyer must have access to the business records.
- Valuations should be based on facts, not fiction.
- No surprise is the best surprise. Both parties should commit to dealing with one another honestly and in good faith.

The main reason that buyers purchase existing businesses is to get their future earning potential. The second most common reason is to obtain an established asset base; it is much easier to buy assets than to build them. Although some valuation methods take these goals into consideration, many business sellers and buyers simplify the process by relying on rules of thumb that use multiples of a company's net earnings or sales to estimate the value of a business. Although the multipliers vary by industry, most small companies sell for 2 to 12 times their earnings before interest and taxes (EBIT), with an average selling price of between 6 and 7 times EBIT. For instance, a study by Business Valuation Resources of 3,838 business sales over a recent three-year period shows that the median selling price of a lawn and garden service is 2.93 times EBIT, the median price of a grocery store is 6.00 times EBIT, and the median price of business consulting service is 11.39 times EBIT.[17] Factors that increase the value of the multiplier include proprietary products and patents; a strong, diversified customer base; above-average growth rate; a strong, balanced management team; and dominant market share. Factors that decrease the value of the multiplier include generic, "me-too" products; dependence on a single customer or a small group of customers for a significant portion of sales; reliance on the skills of a single manager (e.g., the founder); declining market share; and dependence on a single product for generating sales.[18]

The next section describes three basic techniques and several variations on them for determining the value of a hypothetical business, Lewis Electronics.

Balance Sheet Techniques: Net Worth = Total Assets − Total Liabilities

balance sheet technique
a method of valuing a business based on the value of the company's net worth (net worth = total assets − total liabilities).

BALANCE SHEET TECHNIQUE The **balance sheet technique** is one of the most commonly used methods of evaluating a business although it is not highly recommended because it oversimplifies the valuation process. This method computes the company's net worth or owner's equity (Net worth = Total assets − Total liabilities) and uses this figure as the value. The problem with this technique is that it fails to recognize reality: Most small businesses have market values that exceed their reported book values.

The first step is to determine which assets are included in the sale. In most cases, the owner has some personal assets that he or she does not want to sell. Professional business brokers can help the buyer and the seller arrive at a reasonable value for the collection of assets included in the deal. Remember that net worth reported on a financial statement will differ, sometimes significantly, from actual net worth determined in the marketplace. Figure 7.3 shows the balance sheet for Lewis Electronics. Based on this balance sheet, the company's net worth is $266,091 − $114,325 = $151,766.

adjusted balance sheet technique
a method of valuing a business based on the *market value* of the company's net worth (net worth = total assets − total liabilities).

VARIATION: ADJUSTED BALANCE SHEET TECHNIQUE A more realistic method for determining a company's value is to adjust the book value of net worth to reflect *actual* market value—the so-called **adjusted balance sheet technique.** The values reported on a company's books may either overstate or understate the true value of assets and liabilities. Typical assets in a business sale include notes and accounts receivable, inventories, supplies, and fixtures. If a buyer purchases accounts receivable, he or she should estimate the likelihood of their collection and adjust their value accordingly (refer to Table 7.1). In manufacturing, wholesale, and retail businesses, inventory is usually the largest single asset in the sale. Taking a physical inventory count is the best way to determine accurately the quantity of goods to be included in the sale. The sale may include three types of inventory, each having its own method of valuation: raw materials, work in process, and finished goods. The buyer and the seller must arrive at a method for evaluating the inventory.

FIGURE 7.3

Balance Sheet for Lewis Electronics

Lewis Electronics
Balance Sheet
June 30, 200X

Assets

Current Assets:

Cash	$ 11,655	
Accounts Receivable	15,876	
Inventory	56,523	
Supplies	8,574	
Prepaid Insurance	5,587	
Total Current Assets		$ 98,215

Fixed Assets:

Land		$ 24,000	
Buildings	$ 141,000		
Less Accumulated Depreciation	51,500	89,500	
Office Equipment	$ 12,760		
Less Accumulated Depreciation	7,159	5,601	
Factory Equipment	$ 59,085		
Less Accumulated Depreciation	27,850	31,235	
Trucks and Autos	$ 28,730		
Less Accumulated Depreciation	11,190	17,540	
Total Fixed Assets			$ 167,876
Total Assets:			$ 266,091

Liabilities

Current Liabilities:

Accounts Payable	$ 19,497	
Mortgage Payable (current portion)	5,215	
Salaries Payable	3,671	
Note Payable	10,000	
Total Current Liabilities		$ 38,383

Long-Term Liabilities:

Mortgage Payable	$ 54,542	
Note Payable	21,400	
Total Long-Term Liabilities		$ 75,942
Total Liabilities		$ 114,325

Owners' Equity

Owners' Equity		$ 151,766
Total Liabilities and Owners' Equity		$ 266,091

First-in-first-out (FIFO), last-in-first-out (LIFO), and average costing are three frequently used techniques, but the most common methods use the cost of last purchase and the replacement value of the inventory. Before accepting any inventory value, the buyer should evaluate the condition of the goods. One young couple purchased a lumberyard without sufficiently examining the inventory. After completing the sale, they discovered that most of the lumber in a warehouse they had neglected to inspect was warped and was of little value as building material. The bargain price they paid for the business turned out not to be the good deal they had expected.

To avoid problems, some buyers insist on having a knowledgeable representative on an inventory team to count the inventory and check its condition. Nearly every sale involves merchandise that cannot be sold, but by taking this precaution, a buyer minimizes the chance of being stuck with worthless inventory. Fixed assets transferred in a sale might include land, buildings, equipment, and fixtures. Business owners frequently carry real estate and buildings at values well below their actual market value. Equipment and fixtures, depending on their condition and usefulness, may increase or decrease the true value of the business. Appraisals of these assets on insurance policies are helpful guidelines for establishing market value. In addition, business brokers can be useful in determining the current market value of fixed assets. Some brokers use an estimate of what it would cost to replace a company's physical assets (less a reasonable allowance for depreciation) to determine value. For Lewis Electronics, the adjusted net worth is $274,638 − $114,325 = $160,313 (see the adjusted balance sheet in Figure 7.4), indicating that some of the entries in its books did not accurately reflect true market value.

Business valuations based on balance sheet methods suffer one major drawback: they do not consider the future earning potential of the business. These techniques value assets at current prices and do not consider them as tools for creating future profits. The next method for computing the value of a business is based on its expected future earnings.

earnings approach

a method of valuing a business that recognizes that a buyer is purchasing the future income (earnings) potential of a business.

EARNINGS APPROACH The buyer of an existing business is essentially purchasing its future income. The **earnings approach** focuses on the future income potential of a business and assumes that a company's value depends on its ability to generate consistent earnings over time. In other words, the earnings approach recognizes that assets derive their *real* value from the income they produce in the future. There are three variations of the earnings approach.

VARIATION 1: EXCESS EARNINGS METHOD This method combines both the value of a business's existing assets (minus its liabilities) and an estimate of its future earnings potential to determine its selling price. One advantage of this technique is that it offers an estimate of goodwill. Goodwill is an intangible asset that often creates problems in a business sale. In fact, a common method of valuing a business is to compute its tangible net worth and then to add an often arbitrary adjustment for goodwill. In essence, goodwill is the difference between an established, successful business and one that has yet to prove itself. It is based on a company's reputation and its ability to attract customers. A buyer should not accept blindly the seller's arbitrary adjustment for goodwill because it is likely to be inflated. The *real* value of a company's goodwill lies in its financial value to the buyer, not in its emotional value to the seller.

The excess earnings method provides a consistent and realistic approach for determining the value of goodwill. It measures goodwill by the amount of profit the business earns above that of the average firm in the same industry (its "extra earning power"). It also assumes that the owner is entitled to a reasonable return on the company's adjusted tangible net worth.

Step 1: Compute adjusted tangible net worth. Using the adjusted balance sheet method of valuation, the buyer should compute the firm's adjusted tangible net worth. Total tangible assets (adjusted for market value) minus total liabilities yields adjusted tangible net worth. In the Lewis Electronics example, adjusted tangible net worth is $274,638 − $114,325 = $160,313 (refer to Figure 7.4).

opportunity cost

the cost of the next best alternative choice; the cost of giving up one alternative to get another.

Step 2: Calculate the opportunity costs of investing in the business. **Opportunity** cost represents the cost of forgoing a choice. If a buyer chooses to purchase the assets of a business, he or she cannot invest that money elsewhere. Therefore, the opportunity cost of the purchase would be the amount that the buyer could earn by investing the same amount *in a similar risk investment.*

There are three components in the rate of return used to value a business: (1) the basic, risk-free return, (2) an inflation premium, and (3) the risk allowance for investing in the particular business. The basic, risk-free return and the inflation premium are reflected in investments such as U.S. Treasury bonds. To determine the appropriate rate of return for investing in a business, a buyer must add to this base rate a factor reflecting the risk of purchasing the company. The greater the risk, the higher will be the rate of return. A normal-risk business typically translates into a rate of return in the 20 percent to 25 percent range.

FIGURE 7.4

Balance Sheet for Lewis Electronics, Adjusted to Reflect Market Value

Lewis Electronics
Adjusted Balance Sheet
June 30, 200X

Assets

Current Assets:

Cash	$ 11,655	
Accounts Receivable	10,051	
Inventory	39,261	
Supplies	7,492	
Prepaid Insurance	5,587	
Total Current Assets		$ 74,046

Fixed Assets:

Land		$ 36,900	
Buildings	$ 177,000		
Less Accumulated Depreciation	51,500	125,500	
Office Equipment	$ 11,645		
Less Accumulated Depreciation	7,159	4,486	
Factory Equipment	$ 50,196		
Less Accumulated Depreciation	27,850	22,346	
Trucks and Autos	$ 22,550		
Less Accumulated Depreciation	11,190	11,360	
Total Fixed Assets			$ 200,592
Total Assets			$ 274,638

Liabilities

Current Liabilities:

Accounts Payable	$ 19,497	
Mortgage Payable (current portion)	5,215	
Salaries Payable	3,671	
Note Payable	10,000	
Total Current Liabilities		$ 38,383

Long-Term Liabilities:

Mortgage Payable	$ 54,542	
Note Payable	21,400	
Total Long-Term Liabilities		$ 75,942
Total Liabilities		$ 114,325

Owners' Equity

Owners' Equity	$ 160,313
Total Liabilities and Owners' Equity	$ 274,638

Because Lewis Electronics is a normal risk business, the opportunity cost of an investment in it is $160,313 \times 25\% = \$40,078$.

The second part of the buyer's opportunity cost is the salary that he or she could earn working for someone else. For the Lewis Electronics example, if the buyer purchases the business, she must forgo a modest $25,000 salary that he or she could earn working elsewhere. Adding these amounts together yields a total opportunity cost of $65,078.

Step 3: Project net earnings. The buyer must estimate the company's net earnings for the upcoming year before subtracting the owner's salary. Averages can be misleading; therefore, the buyer must be sure to investigate the trend of net earnings. Have they risen steadily over the last five years, dropped significantly, remained relatively constant, or fluctuated wildly? As you learned earlier in this chapter, past income statements provide useful guidelines for estimating earnings. However, business sellers often "recast" their companies' earnings to create a more realistic picture of them because their goal is to minimize their tax bills by keeping earnings low. One experienced business broker suggests using the following process for recasting a small company's earnings:[19]

- Add back any direct payments to the owner(s), including salary and bonuses. Add a reasonable salary for a manager to take the owner's place.
- Add all other expenses the company pays for the owner(s), such as auto leases, insurance, memberships, retirement benefits, profit-sharing, and others.
- Add the cost of any leases the company has with the owner or his or her family members.
- Add any extraordinary expenses such as the costs of hiring a business broker to sell the company, an accounting firm to audit the company's financial statements, and others.

In the Lewis Electronics example, the prospective buyer and his accountant project net earnings for the upcoming year to be $74,000.

Step 4: Compute extra earning power. A company's extra earning power is the difference between forecasted earnings (Step 3) and total opportunity costs (Step 2). Many small businesses that are for sale do not have extra earning power (i.e., excess earnings), and they show marginal or no profits. The extra earning power of Lewis Electronics is $74,000 - $65,000 = $8,922.

Step 5: Estimate the value of intangibles. The owner can use the business's extra earning power of the business to estimate the value of its intangible assets—that is, its goodwill. Multiplying the extra earning power by a years-of-profit figure yields an estimate of the intangible assets' value. The years-of-profit figure for a normal-risk business ranges from three to four. A very high-risk business may have a years-of-profit figure of just one, whereas a well-established firm might warrant a years-of-profit figure of seven. For Lewis Electronics, the value of intangibles (assuming normal risk) would be $8,922 \times 3 = $26,766.

Step 6: Determine the value of the business. To determine the value of the business, the buyer simply adds together the adjusted tangible net worth (Step 1) and the value of the intangibles (Step 5). Using this method, we find that the value of Lewis Electronics is $160,313 + $26,766 = $187,079.

The buyer and the seller should consider the tax implications of including in the purchase the value of goodwill and the value of a covenant not to compete. Because the *buyer* can amortize both the cost of goodwill and a restrictive covenant over 15 years, the tax treatment of either would be the same for him or her. However, the *seller* would prefer to have the amount of the purchase price in excess of the value of the assets allocated to goodwill, which is a capital asset. The gain on the capital asset would be taxed at the lower capital gains rates. If that same amount were allocated to a restrictive covenant (which is negotiated with the seller personally, not the business), the seller must treat it as ordinary income, which would be taxed at regular rates that are higher than the capital gains rates.

VARIATION 2: CAPITALIZED EARNINGS APPROACH A variation of the earnings approach capitalizes expected net earnings to determine the value of a business. As you learned earlier in this chapter, buyers should prepare their own projected income statements and should ask the seller to prepare them also. Many appraisers use a five-year weighted average of past sales (with the greatest weights assigned to the most recent years) to estimate sales for the upcoming year.

Once again, a buyer must evaluate the risk of purchasing the business to determine the appropriate rate of return on the investment. The greater the perceived risk, the higher is the return that the buyer requires. Risk determination is always somewhat subjective, but it is necessary for proper evaluation.

The **capitalized earnings approach** divides estimated net earnings (*after* subtracting the owner's reasonable salary) by the rate of return that reflects the risk level. For Lewis Electronics, the capitalized value (assuming a reasonable salary of $25,000) is:

$$\frac{\text{Net earnings (after deducting owner's salary)}}{\text{Rate of return}} = \frac{\$74,000 - \$25,000}{25\%} = \$196,000$$

capitalized earnings approach
a method of valuing a business that divides estimated earnings by the rate of return the buyer could earn on a similar risk investment.

Firms with lower risk factors are more valuable (a 10 percent rate of return would yield a value of $499,000 for Lewis Electronics) than are those with higher risk factors (a 50 percent rate of return would yield a value of $99,800). Most normal-risk businesses use a rate-of-return factor ranging from 20 to 25 percent. The lowest risk factor that most buyers will accept for any business is around 15 percent.

VARIATION 3: DISCOUNTED FUTURE EARNINGS APPROACH This variation of the earnings approach assumes that a dollar earned in the future is worth less than that same dollar today. Therefore, using this approach, the buyer estimates the company's net income for several years into the future and then discounts these future earnings back to their present value. The resulting present value is an estimate of the company's worth because it reflects the company's future earning potential stated in today's dollars.

The reduced value of future dollars represents the cost of the buyers' giving up the opportunity to earn a reasonable rate of return by receiving income in the future instead of today, a concept known as the time value of money. To illustrate the importance of the time value of money, consider two $1 million sweepstake winners. Rob wins $1 million in a sweepstakes, but he receives it in $50,000 installments over 20 years. If Rob invested every installment at 8 percent interest, he would have accumulated $2,288,098 at the end of twenty years. Lisa wins $1 million in another sweepstakes, but she collects her winnings in one lump sum. If Lisa invested her $1 million today at 8 percent, she would have accumulated $4,660,957 at the end of twenty years. The difference in their wealth is the result of the time value of money.

DISCOUNTED FUTURE EARNINGS APPROACH The **discounted future earnings approach** includes five steps:

discounted future earnings approach
a method of valuing a business that forecasts a company's earnings several years into the future and then discounts them back to their present value.

Step 1: Project future earnings for five years into the future. One way is to assume that earnings will grow by a constant amount over the next five years. Perhaps a better method is to develop three forecasts—an optimistic, a pessimistic, and a most likely—for each year and then find a weighted average using the following formula, which weights the most likely forecast four times as heavily as either the optimistic or pessimistic forecasts:

$$\frac{\text{Forecasted earnings}}{\text{for year i}} = \frac{\text{(Optimistic earnings for year i)} + \text{Most likely forecast for year i} \times 4 +}{6}$$
$$\frac{\text{(Pessimistic forecast for year i)}}{6}$$

For Lewis Electronics, the buyer's forecasts are as follows:

Year	Pessimistic	Most Likely	Optimistic	Weighted Average
XXX1	65,000	74,000	92,000	75,500
XXX2	74,000	90,000	101,000	89,167
XXX3	82,000	100,000	112,000	99,000
XXX4	88,000	109,000	120,000	107,333
XXX5	88,000	115,000	122,000	111,667

Buyers must remember that the farther into the future they forecast, the less reliable their estimates will be.

Step 2: Discount these future earnings at the appropriate present value rate. The rate that the buyer selects should reflect the rate he or she could earn on a similar risk investment. Because Lewis Electronics is a normal-risk business, the buyer chooses a present value rate of 25 percent.

Year	Income Forecast (Weighted Average)	Present Value Factor (at 25%)*	Net Present Value
XXX1	75,500	0.8000	60,400
XXX2	89,167	0.6400	57,067
XXX3	99,000	0.5120	50,688
XXX4	107,333	0.4096	43,964
XXX5	111,667	0.3277	36,593
		Total	248,712

*The appropriate present value factor can be found by looking in published present value tables, by using modern calculators or computers, or by solving this formula:

$$\text{Present value factor} = \frac{1}{(1 + k)^t}$$

where k = rate of return
t = year ($t = 1, 2, 3 \ldots n$)

Step 3: Estimate the income stream beyond five years. One technique suggests multiplying the fifth year income by 1 ÷ rate of return. For Lewis Electronics, the estimate is:

$$\text{Income beyond year 5} = \$111,667 \times \frac{1}{25\%} = \$446,668$$

Step 4: Discount the income estimate beyond five years using the present value factor for the sixth year. For Lewis Electronics:

Present value of income beyond year 5 = \$446,668 × 0.2622 = \$117,116

Step 5: Compute the total value of the business. Add the present value of the company's estimated earnings for years one through five (Step 2) and the present value of its earnings from years six on (Step 4):

Total value = \$248,712 + \$117,116 = \$365,828

The primary advantage of this technique is that it values a business solely on the basis of its future earning potential, but its reliability depends on making forecasts of future earnings and on choosing a realistic present value rate. In other words, a company's present value is tied to its future performance, which is not always easy to project. The discounted cash flow technique is especially well-suited for valuing service businesses (whose asset bases are often very thin) and for companies experiencing high growth rates.

market approach
a method of valuing a business that uses the price/earnings (P/E) ratio of similar, publicly held companies to determine value.

MARKET APPROACH The **market (or price/earnings) approach** uses the price/earnings (P/E) ratios of similar businesses listed on a stock exchange to establish the value of a company. A buyer must use businesses in the same industry whose stocks are publicly traded to get a meaningful comparison. A company's price/earnings ratio is the price of one share of its common stock in the market divided by its earnings per share (after deducting preferred stock dividends). To get a representative P/E ratio, a buyer should average the P/Es of as many similar businesses as possible.

To compute the company's value, the buyer multiplies the average price/earnings ratio by the private company's estimated earnings. For example, suppose that the buyer found four companies comparable to Lewis Electronics, but whose stock is publicly traded. Their price/earnings ratios are:

Company 1	3.3
Company 2	3.8
Company 3	4.7
Company 4	4.1
Average P/E ratio	3.975

Using this average P/E ratio produces a value of \$294,150:

Value = Average P/E ratio × Estimated net earnings = 3.975 × \$74,000 = \$294,150

The biggest advantage of the market approach is its simplicity. However, this method does have several disadvantages, including the following:

Necessary comparisons between publicly traded and privately owned companies. Because the stock of privately owned companies is not as liquid as that of publicly held companies, the P/E ratio used is often subjective and lower than that of publicly held companies.

Unrepresentative earnings estimates. A private company's net earnings may not realistically reflect its true earning potential. To minimize taxes, owners usually attempt to keep earnings low and rely on fringe benefits and bonuses to make up the difference.

Finding similar companies for comparison. Often, it is extremely difficult for a buyer to find comparable publicly held companies when estimating the appropriate P/E ratio.

Applying the after-tax earnings of a private company to determine its value. If a prospective buyer is using an after-tax P/E ratio from a public company, he or she also must use the after-tax earnings from the private company.

Despite its drawbacks, the market approach is useful as a general guideline for establishing a company's value.

Which of these methods is best for determining the value of a small business? Simply stated, there is no single best method. Valuing a business is partly an art and partly a science. Use of these techniques will yield a range of values. Buyers should look for values that might cluster together and then use their best judgment to determine a reasonable offering price.

Understanding the Seller's Side

A study by DAK Group and Columbia University's Eugene M. Lang Center for Entrepreneurship reports that 64 percent of the owners of closely-held companies expect to sell their businesses within three years.[20] For entrepreneurs, few events are more anticipated—and more emotional—than selling their businesses. Selling their companies often produces vast personal wealth and a completely new lifestyle, and this newly gained wealth offers freedom and the opportunity to catch up on all the things the owners missed out on while building their businesses. Yet many entrepreneurs who sell out experience a tremendous void in their lives, a "separation anxiety" that results from having their lives revolve around the businesses they created and nurtured for so many years. Will Schroter, a serial entrepreneur and CEO of Go Big Network, explains:

Selling your company is a lot like selling your kid. This is something that you've created, nurtured since inception and watched grow up into something beautiful. Now someone else has come along and taken that little baby away from you, and they're not going to give it back. The hardest thing about selling your company is realizing that it's not yours. The big decisions are ultimately made by someone else.[21]

For many business owners, their companies are the focal point of their lives in their communities and are an essential part of their identities. When they sell their companies, a primary concern for many entrepreneurs is preserving the reputation, culture, and principles on which they built and operated the company. Will the new owner display the same values in managing the business? Can the company founder cope with the inevitable changes the new owner will make to the business?

Seven years after founding the California Pizza Kitchen, Rick Rosenfield and Larry Flax were surprised when Pepsico offered to buy a majority stake in their company for $100 million. The soft drink giant kept Rosenfield and Flax on as co-chairmen but relieved them of any daily operating and decision-making duties and replaced them with a more experienced CEO, Fred Hipp. Hipp's strategy for the company was quite different from that of the founders, who had built the company on the basics: quality ingredients, upscale locations, and steady growth. When Hipp's decisions pushed the company toward financial ruin, Pepsico brought Rosenfield and Flax back in to save the company. They closed underperforming outlets, upgraded the remaining ones, and introduced interesting new menu items designed to appeal to California Pizza Kitchen's core customers.[22]

ENTREPRENEURIAL PROFILE

Rick Rosenfield & Larry Flax: California Pizza Kitchen

Some business brokers differentiate between *financial buyers* and *strategic buyers*. Financial buyers, usually individuals, see buying a business as a way to generate income for themselves and their families. They look for businesses in which they can make an initial down payment and finance the remaining 50 to 80 percent of the purchase price. Because they often borrow the money to purchase a business, their primary concern is the company's ability to generate profits and positive cash flow in the future. Strategic buyers, often other businesses or even competitors, view buying a company as part of a larger picture, a piece in a strategic puzzle that gives them an advantage such as access to a new, fast-growing market, a unique product, or a new technological innovation. They are looking for companies that fit strategically with their existing business. "Financial buyers typically will pay a lower price because they have a 'fire sale' mentality," says Andy Agrawal, a partner in an investment banking firm. "You need to find strategic buyers and paint a picture for them," he advises. "Show the strategic buyer how one plus one equals three."[23]

ENTREPRENEURIAL PROFILE___

Darius Bickoff: Glacéau

In 1996, Darius Bickoff launched Glacéau, a beverage company that markets Vitaminwater and Smartwater, after his Manhattan neighborhood was hit with a water contamination scare. Later, while looking for an energy boost on his way to a yoga session, he chewed a vitamin C wafer and chased it with plain water; the combination gave him the idea for Vitaminwater, which became one of the company's best-selling products. In 2007, Bikoff found the right strategic buyer when he sold Glacéau to the Coca-Cola Company for $4.1 billion.[24]

Selling a business involves developing a plan that maximizes the value of the business. Before selling his or her business, an entrepreneur must ask himself or herself some important questions: Do you want to walk away from the business completely, or do you plan to stay on after the sale? If you decide to stay on, how involved do you want to be in running the company? How much can you realistically expect to get for the business? Is this amount of money sufficient to maintain your desired lifestyle? Rather than sell the business to an outsider, should you be transferring ownership to your children or to your employees? Who are the professionals—business brokers, accountants, attorneys, tax advisers—you will need to help you close the sale successfully? How do you expect the buyer to pay for the company? Are you willing to finance at least some of the purchase price?

Sellers who have answered these fundamental questions are prepared to move forward with the sale of their companies.

Structuring the Deal

Next to picking the right buyer, planning the structure of the deal is one of the most important decisions a seller can make. Entrepreneurs who sell their companies without considering the tax implications of the deal may wind up paying the IRS as much as 70 percent of the proceeds in the form of capital gains and other taxes! A skilled tax adviser or financial planner can help business sellers to legally minimize the bite various taxes take out of the proceeds of the sale. When it comes to exit strategies, entrepreneurs have the following options available to them.

Exit Strategies

STRAIGHT BUSINESS SALE A straight business sale often is best for those entrepreneurs who want to step down and turn over the reins of the company to someone else right away.

ENTREPRENEURIAL PROFILE___

Alyssa Torey: Magnolia Bakery

In 1996, Alyssa Torey cofounded the Magnolia Bakery with Jennifer Appel (who left the company in 2000 to open the Buttercup Bake Shop) in New York's West Village, and the bakery soon became famous for its homemade cupcakes. After being featured on the popular television shows *Sex and the City* and *Saturday Night Live*, Magnolia Bakery became a hot spot not only for New Yorkers but also for tourists. In 2007, Torey sold the bakery to friend Steven Abrams, a restaurateur and construction company owner, for a fraction of its value so that she could spend time writing more cookbooks. "She could have sold it for 10 times what I gave her," Abrams says incredulously.[25]

In straight business sales, owners must decide whether to sell the assets of the business or transfer ownership to the buyer through a sale of company stock. Which choice is best for the seller and the buyer depends on the form of ownership. Sole proprietors and partners must sell the assets of their companies because there is no stock. In an S corporation, the seller does not care whether the transaction is through stock or assets because the tax considerations are the same. Owners of C corporations, however, are far better off selling stock rather than selling assets because they pay only capital gains tax on the increased value of their stock. Buyers generally prefer to acquire the "hard" assets of the business, thus, avoiding any potential hidden liabilities. More than 90 percent of business sales involve a sale of shares of stock.[26]

BUSINESS SALE WITH AN AGREEMENT FROM THE FOUNDER TO STAY ON Sometimes business owners want to sell their companies but stay on to operate them. In many deals, the founder sells the company outright, but the buyer pays the founder to stay on as a manager or a consultant for a short time. This strategy allows an entrepreneur to avoid concentrating his or her personal wealth in a single asset—the business—and to stay involved in managing the company he or she founded. Mitchell Schlimer, founder of the Let's Talk Business Network, a support community for entrepreneurs, says that about 90 percent of small business owners who sell their companies to larger businesses remain with the acquiring company—at least for a little while. "They often don't stay long," says Schlimer, "because entrepreneurs are not good soldiers."[27]

Peter Kramer/STAR MAX/ Newscom

In 1977, Tova Borgnine started Tova Corporation as a mail-order fragrance company with a single product, a perfume called Tova Signature. By 1987, her company employed 80 workers and had a line of 65 cosmetics and fragrance products. In 1990, Borgnine began selling Tova products on the shopping network QVC, which purchased her company in 2002 for a seven-figure sum and signed Borgnine to an executive contract. Borgnine, who has sold more than 10 million bottles of Tova Signature, splits her time between a home in California and one in Malvern, Pennsylvania, near QVC's headquarters, where she has had to make the difficult transition from entrepreneur to employee. "All of the products are the same as when I created my company," she says. "I'm in on every strategy meeting, but now there's a collective voice. You have to be able to let go."[28]

Although this exit strategy sounds like the ideal solution for entrepreneurs who are seeking more free time without stepping away entirely from the companies they built, it does not always prove to be. Accustomed to being in control, making the key decisions, and calling all of the shots, entrepreneurs who sell out with an agreement to stay on often have great difficulty relinquishing control of the company to the new owner, especially when the new owner takes the company in a new direction. The situation is particularly grueling when the new owner makes decisions that jeopardize the company's future, forcing the founder to stand by and watch the business spiral slowly downward.

That's exactly what happened to Christopher Asterino, founder of Asterino Associates, a medical billing management company in Albany, New York. Asterino sold his 10-year-old company to National Medical Financial Services (NMFS) and moved to Scottsdale, Arizona, to take an executive position with NMFS. The situation was rocky from the start because Asterino's new boss was the man with whom he had negotiated the sale of his business. "It was very difficult," he recalls. Asterino became disillusioned when he saw how NMFS failed to provide the level of customer service to his former clients that his company had and, five years after selling, Asterino left NMFS to start another medical billing management company. This time, Asterino says that he has no intention of selling his company until he is ready to retire.[29]

A variation on this strategy is an **earn-out,** in which the entrepreneur can increase his or her payout by staying on and making sure that the company hits specific performance targets. When Rich and Sheri Schmelzer sold Jibbitz LLC, the business they started in their basement that

earn-out
an exit strategy in which an entrepreneur can increase his or her payout by staying on and making sure that the company hits specific performance targets.

Rich and Sheri Schmelzer,
co-founders of Jibbitz LLC.

markets ornaments that fit into the holes of Crocs clogs, to Crocs Inc., the company that makes the popular shoes, they received a $10 million payout. The sales agreement says that if Jibbitz reaches certain earnings targets, the Schmelzers, who stayed with the company as president and chief design officer, will receive an additional $10 million in earn-outs.[30]

FORM A FAMILY LIMITED PARTNERSHIP Entrepreneurs also can transfer their businesses to their children but still maintain control over the business by forming a family limited partnership. The entrepreneur takes the role of the general partner, and the children become limited partners in the business. The general partner keeps just 1 percent of the company, but the partnership agreement gives him or her total control over the business. The children own 99 percent of the company but have little or no say over how to run the business. Until the founder decides to step down and turn over the reins of the company to the next generation, he or she continues to run the business and, with proper planning, can set up significant tax savings when the ultimate transfer of power takes place.

SELL A CONTROLLING INTEREST Sometimes business owners sell a majority interest in their companies to investors, competitors, suppliers, or large companies; retain a portion of the ownership themselves; and agree to stay on after the sale as managers or consultants. Since its founding in 1994 by Stanford University students Jerry Yang and David Filo, Internet giant Yahoo has purchased more than 50 small companies, acquiring everything from online games and stock and sports toolbars to auction sites and music players.[31] In some of the deals, the company founders agreed to stay on after Yahoo's acquisition.

Racing legend Richard Petty became part of the wave of NASCAR team owners selling parts of their companies to outside investors when he agreed to sell to private equity firm Boston Ventures a controlling interest in Petty Enterprises, which Petty's family had run since his father founded it in 1949. Petty Enterprises, which has more wins and championships than any NASCAR team, had fallen behind its competitors, not having won a race since 1998, and was in need of a capital infusion. Announcing the sale (which includes the Richard Petty Driving Experience), Petty, who with the sale became chairman emeritus of the company, said, "The time has come for Petty Enterprises to take the steps necessary to get back to Victory Lane. Boston Ventures will provide us with the capital necessary to compete." Petty's son, Kyle, who is a driver for Petty Enterprises, lost his job as president of the family business in the sale. "This is an emotional decision for our family," says Kyle, "but it's absolutely the right decision."[32]

FIGURE 7.5

Restructuring a Business for Sale

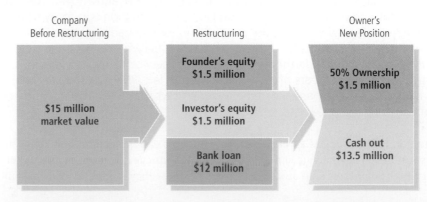

Company Before Restructuring	Restructuring	Owner's New Position
	Founder's equity $1.5 million	50% Ownership $1.5 million
$15 million market value	Investor's equity $1.5 million	
	Bank loan $12 million	Cash out $13.5 million

RESTRUCTURE THE COMPANY Another way for business owners to cash out gradually is to replace the existing corporation with a new one formed with other investors. The owner essentially is performing a leveraged buyout of his or her own company. For example, assume that you own a company worth $15 million. You form a new corporation with $12 million borrowed from a bank and $3 million in equity: $1.5 million of your own equity and $1.5 million in equity from an investor who wants you to stay on with the business. The new company buys your company for $15 million. You net $13.5 in cash ($15 million − your $1.5 million equity investment) and still own 50 percent of the new leveraged business (see Figure 7.5).[33]

SELL TO AN INTERNATIONAL BUYER In an increasingly global marketplace, small U.S. businesses have become attractive buyout targets for foreign companies. Companies from Canada and Great Britain lead the world in acquiring U.S. companies, but China is moving up the list.

> Robert Parker, owner of Adams Pressed Metals, a small, family owned company in Galesburg, Illinois, that makes stamped metal parts, saw his company struggle when John Deere, his largest customer, began buying parts from Tri-Star International, a Chinese manufacturer. Transforming a significant threat into a substantial opportunity, Parker negotiated a deal with Tri-Star to sell a majority interest in the family-run business for $1 million. Tri-Star recognized that Adams Pressed Metals had a solid reputation among its customer base, access to important distribution channels, and a skilled workforce. "Adams will provide Tri-Star with a U.S. platform to expand its global operations," says Parker. "We saved 40 jobs, and [Tri-Star] got American know-how in sales."[34]

As Robert Parker's experience shows, it is not unusual in today's global economy to find companies across the globe with substantial financial resources looking to acquire small businesses in the United States. In many instances, foreign companies buy U.S.–based companies to gain access to a lucrative, growing market. They look for a team of capable managers, whom they typically retain for a given time period. They also want companies that are profitable, stable, and growing. Selling to foreign buyers can have disadvantages, however. They typically purchase 100 percent of a company, thereby making the founder merely an employee. Relationships with foreign owners also can be difficult to manage due to cultural and philosophical differences.

USE A TWO-STEP SALE For owners wanting the security of a sales contract now but not wanting to step down from the company's helm for several years, a two-step sale may be ideal. The buyer purchases the business in two phases—getting 20 to 70 percent today and agreeing to buy the remainder within a specific time period. Until the final transaction takes place, the entrepreneur retains at least partial control of the company.

ESTABLISH AN EMPLOYEE STOCK OWNERSHIP PLAN (ESOP) Some owners who want to sell their businesses but keep them intact cash out by selling to their employees through an **employee stock ownership plan (ESOP).** An ESOP is a form of employee benefit plan in which a trust that is created for employees purchases their employer's stock. Here's how an ESOP works: The company transfers shares of its stock to the ESOP trust, and the trust uses the stock as collateral to borrow enough money to purchase the shares from the company. The company guarantees payment of the loan principal and interest and makes tax deductible contributions to the trust to repay the loan (see Figure 7.6). As the company repays the loan, it distributes the stock to employees' accounts using a predetermined formula. Because of their flexibility, ESOPs permit owners to transfer all or part of a company to employees as gradually or as quickly as they want.

ENTREPRENEURIAL PROFILE

Robert Parker: Adams Pressed Metals

employee stock ownership plan (ESOP)

an employee benefit plan in which a trust created for employees purchases stock in their employers' company.

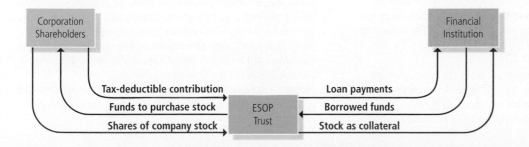

FIGURE 7.6

A Typical Employee Stock Ownership Plan (ESOP)

Source: Corey Rosen, "Sharing Ownership with Employees," *Small Business Reports,* December 1990, p. 63. © 1990 Corey Rosen. Used with permission.

To use an ESOP successfully, a small business should have annual sales of at least $1 million, be profitable (with pre-tax profits exceeding $100,000), and have a payroll of at least $500,000 a year. Generally, companies with fewer than fifteen to twenty employees do not find ESOPs beneficial because the cost to set up an ESOP is $50,000 to $60,000. The ESOP Association, an industry trade association, reports that the typical annual sales for its members range from $20 million to $50 million.[35] For companies that prepare properly, ESOPs offer significant financial and managerial benefits. Owners get tax benefits as well as great flexibility in determining their retirement schedules. An ESOP allows all parties involved to benefit, and the transfer of ownership can be timed to meet the entrepreneur's personal and financial goals.

ENTREPRENEURIAL PROFILE

Tom Krazan: Krazan Associates

Tom Krazan started a site-development engineering business, Krazan Associates (KA), in 1982 in Clovis, California, and the company has grown into a highly respected company with a national reputation. KA now has 13 offices in the western United States, 350 employees, and annual sales of more than $35 million. In 1999, Krazan began implementing a management succession plan and created an ESOP to which he contributed 6.5 percent of the company's stock. In 2007, Krazan decided to step down from actively managing the company and begin the transition to retirement. The ESOP borrowed enough money to purchase more of Krazan's shares, bringing its ownership in the company to 54 percent. Krazan continues to serve on the company's board of directors and devotes his time to public relations and business development, a role he intends to fulfill for the next five years as the ESOP purchases the remainder of his stock. Krazan admits that transferring control to the ESOP has been emotionally challenging. "It was like transitioning from being a dad to being a granddad with really smart grandkids," he says, gesturing to his employees. Yet he says that the ESOP has allowed KA to "transition from being a nice little service company to a junior powerhouse with new ideas and new energy."[36]

The accompanying "Hands On...How To" feature offers tips to help business sellers prepare their companies for sale to get maximum value from them.

HANDS ON... HOW TO

Preparing Your Company for Sale: How to Maximize Its Value

A study by the Alliance of Merger and Acquisition Advisors reports that 70 percent of the owners of small and midsize companies will either sell or transfer ownership of their businesses within the next decade. However, the study estimates that at least 90 percent of these owners are ill-prepared for the transaction. Buyers have become more demanding and often scrutinize the details of a company's operations. "To do a $5 million transaction requires due diligence similar to larger public companies," says Michael Hoesley, who is selling his business brokerage company. "It's the same questions; they're just stripped down to a simpler level."

David Lobel, managing partner in a private equity firm that has purchased dozens of small companies, says that getting a company into shape for to sell "can't be done overnight, but it can be done." What steps can a business seller take to prepare their companies for sale so that they can get maximum value from them? The following tips will help.

1. *Clean up the company's financial records.* Too many business owners are careless about keeping their books in pristine condition. A common excuse is "I'm too busy running my business to worry about keeping up with all of those financial

records." However, a company's financial records are the raw materials from which potential buyers will establish the price they are willing to pay for a company. Make your company's financial records as tidy and as transparent as possible.

2. *Catch up on basic housekeeping.* People who are selling their houses know that cleaning and organizing their homes and eliminating clutter can add to the curb appeal—and to the price—of their houses. The same is true for businesses. Clean up all of the clutter that tends to build up over time, spruce up the physical appearance of the place, and put things in their proper places.

3. *Stop running personal expenses through the company.* Some business owners seek to minimize their company's tax bills by running personal expenses—for instance, gas for the family car—through the company. Tricks such as these make buyers nervous.

4. *Prepare a customer list for prospective buyers.* Buyers want to know that a company's sales will continue after they close the deal. Providing a list of important customers, including details such as how long each one has been buying from the company, how much each one has spent, key contacts (if business customers are involved), and the quality of the relationship will add value to your business.

5. *Prepare a list of your company's key suppliers.* Which ones are most reliable? What kinds of contracts does your company have with them at the present?

6. *Be prepared to show prospective buyers how much it costs to deliver your product or service to a customer.* Buyers want to know that the company's cost estimates are realistic.

7. *Prepare an employee policy manual.* The manual should include a job analysis for each position in the company, complete with a job description and job specifications. What rules of expected behavior does the company have?

8. *Prepare a document that describes how all of the machinery and equipment in the business works.* A list of service and repair contacts also is important.

9. *Consider removing from the payroll family members who are not essential to the operation of the business.* Many small businesses include family members whose contributions to the company are minimal.

10. *Take the time to conduct a business valuation at least every two years.* In many cases, when prospective buyers approach business owners with unsolicited offers for their companies, the entrepreneurs have no basis for making a deal because they have never taken the time to determine the value of their businesses. Seeing what makes up the real value in your business might enable you to operate it more effectively.

11. *Be prepared to stay on after the sale to help the new owner through the transition period.* In many instances, the business founder and his or her knowledge is the most important asset a company has.

12. *Start early.* Take the steps listed here at least three years before you plan to sell your company. Remember: It takes time to prepare a company for sale. "I wanted to retire when I was 60, and now I'm 66," says Norb Kaiser, who recently sold his company, Kamco Plastics, after several years of preparation.

Sources: Adapted from Arden Dale, "Want to Sell a Business? You May Not Be Ready," *Wall Street Journal*, January 8, 2008, p. B6; Jim Melloan, "Sales Tips," *Inc.*, August 2004, p. 72; Laura Rich, "Seller's Market," *Inc.*, May 2005, pp. 39–42.

The Saga of Selling My Business: Part 3

As Norm Brodsky was preparing for the April 5 closing on the sale of his company CitiStorage, a deal he had been negotiating for the last year, a snag popped up and threatened to undo the entire project. Frank, a member of board of directors of Nova Records Management, the company into which CitiStorage would be folded, wanted to cut the sale price by $2.5 million based on a complex calculation that he had developed concerning the land leases that the CitiStorage held. Brodsky was furious. "Two-and-a-half-million dollars is a relatively small amount, less than 3 percent of the total deal," he says. "We had an understanding, however, that the price was set and we weren't going to reopen the issue." Brodsky told Frank that he refused to negotiate because the price had already been established and that the four other members of Nova's board were in favor of closing the deal at that price. Then Frank dropped a bomb on the deal: "Those votes are meaningless. I have veto power."

Brodsky was stunned and immediately called Debbas. "You might have told me before now. I've been negotiating with the wrong guy."

A few telephone calls to other entrepreneurs who had sold their companies to Nova revealed that this was a common tactic that Frank used to buy companies at reduced prices. "He'd drag out the negotiations and then come up with new demands at the end when the other party had committed so much time and money to the sale that it had no choice but to go along," says Brodsky. "I had a choice. I could give in to Frank's demands, or I could call off the sale." For Brodsky, it boiled down to trust, and apparently, he could not trust Nova.

Brodsky insisted that Frank give up his veto power on the deal or there would be no deal. "This deal is off as long as he insists on retaining his veto," he told Debbas.

Brodsky blamed himself. "I hadn't known about [Frank's veto power], but I should have," he says. "I had clearly failed in my due diligence. I would have known if I had asked enough questions in the beginning. Shame on me for not doing it." Brodsky called meetings, first with his managers and then with all of his employees, to tell them that the sale of CitiStorage had fallen through. None of them was shocked or upset. It was April 5, the target date for closing the deal.

Word spread quickly across the industry that CitiStorage's deal with Nova had failed, and almost immediately, Brodsky began receiving calls from others interested in buying the company. Once again, Brodsky and his partner were faced with a decision: what to do with the company. They decided that it was time to sell CitiStorage and that two factors were paramount in any deal: CitiStorage employees and company culture would not be at risk, and they would work only with private equity firms that had the resources to finance a deal themselves.

Brodsky and his partner locked themselves in a room and came up with five criteria for screening potential buyers, one of whom was Allied Capital, a private equity company founded in 1958 from which CitiStorage had received financing six times over the last 35 years. "Over that time, we had formed strong bonds with Allied Capital's people," says Brodsky. When they ranked the top six prospects on the five criteria, Allied capital came out on top. "Why didn't we think to approach Allied much sooner?" Brodsky wondered.

Brodsky and Allied Capital representatives signed a letter of intent, and Allied began its due diligence process. The process moved much faster than it had during negotiations with Nova. "At every step, I couldn't help noticing the enormous difference between negotiating with Allied and negotiating with Nova," says Brodsky. "I can sum up that difference in one word: trust. With Allied, we had it to begin with, and it got stronger as we went along. With Nova, there had never been any trust, and any hints that it might have been developing were an illusion."

On December 21, after four months of due diligence and negotiations, Brodsky signed a deal to sell CitiStorage to Allied Capital, a deal that included Brodsky staying on for a time with the company as a consultant. "Allied Capital clearly wanted us to wind up with a deal we felt good about," he says. "Looking back, we could thank our lucky stars that the Nova deal hadn't happened. My fiasco wasn't such a fiasco after all. It opened my eyes to possibilities I had never considered."

Brodsky admits that selling his company has required him to make some big adjustments, something he is still in the process of doing. "On December 21, I no longer had a job at CitiStorage," he says. "My wife, Elaine, and I are still shareholders. I still have my office. I'm still getting paid, but the money is a consulting fee, not a salary. My work for CitiStorage doesn't get my juices flowing the way starting a business does. There's a bit of a hole in my life at the moment, and I don't know yet how I'm going to fill it. While I loved chasing the rainbow, I have to say that I have mixed feelings about having caught it."

7. How important is the ability to trust the other party in a business sale? Why?

8. One negotiating expert advises, "Never try to extract the last drop of blood in a negotiation. Do not leave the other person feeling as if they have been cheated." Did Nova violate this negotiating principle? If so, what repercussions did doing so have on the final deal?

9. What emotional issues do entrepreneurs face after they sell the companies they founded? What advice would you give Brodsky to fill the hole in his life after selling his company?

Source: Adapted from Norm Brodsky, "The Offer, Part Eight," *Inc.*, June 2007, pp. 61–64; Norm Brodsky, The Offer: Part Nine," *Inc.*, July 2007, pp. 59–61; Norm Brodsky, "The Offer, Part Ten," *Inc.*, April 2008, pp. 65–68; Norm Brodsky, "The Offer: Part Eleven," *Inc.*, May 2008, pp. 73–74.

LO 6

Understand how the negotiation process works and identify the factors that affect it.

Negotiating the Deal

Although determining the value of a business for sale is an important step in the process of buying a business, it is not the final one. The buyer must sit down with the seller to negotiate the actual selling price for the business and, more important, the terms of the deal. The final deal the buyer strikes depends, in large part, on his or her negotiating skills. The first "rule" of negotiating a deal is to avoid confusing price with value. *Value* is what the business is actually worth; *price* is what the buyer agrees to pay. In a business sale, the party who is the better bargainer usually comes out on top. Buyers seek to:

● Get the business at the lowest possible price.
● Negotiate favorable payment terms, preferably over time.
● Get assurances that they are buying the businesses they think they are getting.
● Avoid putting the seller in a position to open a competing business.
● Minimize the amount of cash paid up front.

Sellers are looking to:

● Get the highest price possible for the business.
● Sever all responsibility for the company's liabilities.
● Avoid unreasonable contract terms that might limit their future opportunities.
● Maximize the cash they get from the deal.
● Minimize the tax burden from the sale.
● Make sure the buyer will be able to make all future payments.

One factor that makes the process of negotiating the purchase of a business challenging is that many business founders overestimate the value of their companies because of all of the "sweat equity" they have poured into their businesses over the years. One entrepreneur recalls a negotiation he was involved in for the potential purchase of a rival's business. The company had $4 million in sales but had incurred losses of more than $1 million in the previous two years, owed more than $2.5 million in unpaid bills, and had no machinery that was less than 30 years old. Much to the prospective buyer's amazement, the owner was asking $4 million for the business! [37] To deal with this reality, buyers must understand the negotiation process.

THE NEGOTIATION PROCESS On the surface, the negotiation process appears to be strictly adversarial. Although each party may be trying to accomplish objectives that are at odds with those of the opposing party, the negotiation process does not have to turn into a nasty battle of wits with overtones of "If you win, then I lose." The negotiation process will go much more smoothly and much faster if both parties work to establish a cooperative relationship based on honesty and trust from the outset. A successful deal requires both parties to examine and articulate their respective positions while trying to understand the other party's position.

Corbis RF

Recognizing that neither of them will benefit without a deal, both parties must work to achieve their objectives while making certain concessions to keep the negotiations alive.

To avoid a stalled deal, a buyer should go into the negotiation with a list of objectives ranked in order of priority. Once he or she has developed a list of priorities, it is useful to develop what he or she perceives to be the seller's list of priorities. That requires learning as much as possible about the seller. Knowing which terms are most important (and which are least important) to him or her and to the seller enables a buyer to make concessions without "giving away the farm" and without getting bogged down in "nit-picking," which often leads to a stalemate. If, for instance, the seller insists on a term that the buyer cannot agree to, he or she can explain why and then offer to give up something in exchange. The buyer also should identify the one concrete objective that sits at the top of that list, the one thing he or she absolutely must come away from the negotiations with. The final stage of preparing for the actual negotiation is to study the list and the one he or she has developed based on her perceptions of the seller to determine where the two mesh and where they conflict. The key to a successful negotiation is to use this analysis to look for areas of mutual benefit and to use them as the foundation for the negotiation.

Chapter Summary

1. **Understand the advantages and disadvantages of buying an existing business.**

   The *advantages* of buying an existing business include: A successful business may continue to be successful; the business may already have the best location; employees and suppliers are already established; equipment is installed and its productive capacity known; inventory is in place and trade credit established; the owner hits the ground running; the buyer can use the expertise of the previous owner; and, the business may be a bargain.

   The disadvantages of buying an existing business include: An existing business may be for sale because it is deteriorating; the previous owner may have created ill will; employees inherited with the business may not be suitable; its location may have become unsuitable; equipment and facilities may be obsolete; change and innovation are hard to implement; inventory may be outdated; accounts receivable may be worth less than face value; and the business may be overpriced.

2. **Define the steps involved in the right way to buy a business.**

   Buying a business can be a treacherous experience unless the buyer is well-prepared. The right way to buy a business is to analyze your skills, abilities, and interests to determine the ideal business for you; prepare a list of potential candidates, including those that might be in the "hidden market"; investigate and evaluate candidate businesses and evaluate the best one; explore financing options before you actually need the money; and, finally, ensure a smooth transition.

3. **Explain the process of evaluating an existing business.**

Rushing into a deal can be the biggest mistake a business buyer can make. Before closing a deal, every business buyer should investigate five critical areas: 1. Why does the owner wish to sell? Look for the *real* reason. 2. Determine the physical condition of the business. Consider both the building and its location. 3. Conduct a thorough analysis of the market for your products or services. Who are the present and potential customers? Conduct an equally thorough analysis of competitors, both direct and indirect. How do they operate and why do customers prefer them? 4. Consider all of the legal aspects that might constrain the expansion and growth of the business: Did you comply with the provisions of a bulk transfer? Negotiate a restrictive covenant? Consider ongoing legal liabilities? 5. Analyze the financial condition of the business, looking at financial statements, income tax returns, and especially cash flow.

4. **Describe the various techniques for determining the value of a business.**

Placing a value on a business is partly an art and partly a science. There is no single "best" method for determining the value of a business. The following techniques (with several variations) are useful: the balance sheet technique (adjusted balance sheet technique); the earnings approach (excess earnings method, capitalized earnings approach, and discounted future savings approach); and the market approach.

5. **Understand the seller's side of the buyout decision and how to structure the deal.**

Selling a business takes time, patience, and preparation to locate a suitable buyer, strike a deal, and make the transition. Sellers must always structure the deal with tax consequences in mind. Common exit strategies include: a straight business sale, a business sale with an agreement for the founder to stay on, forming a family limited partnership, selling a controlling interest in the business, restructuring the company, selling to an international buyer, using a two-step sale, and establishing an employee stock ownership plan (ESOP).

6. **Understand how the negotiation process works and identify the factors that affect it.**

The first rule of negotiating is to never confuse price with value. In a business sale, the party who is the better negotiator usually comes out on top. Before beginning negotiations, a buyer should identify the factors that are affecting the negotiations and then develop a negotiating strategy. The best deals are the result of a cooperative relationship between the parties based on trust.

Discussion Questions

1. What advantages can an entrepreneur who buys a business gain over one who starts a business "from scratch"?
2. How would you go about determining the value of the assets of a business if you were unfamiliar with them?
3. Why do so many entrepreneurs run into trouble when they buy an existing business? Outline the steps involved in the *right* way to buy a business.
4. When evaluating an existing business that is for sale, what areas should an entrepreneur consider? Briefly summarize the key elements of each area.
5. What is goodwill? How should a buyer evaluate a business's goodwill?
6. What is a restrictive covenant? Is it fair to ask the seller of a travel agency located in a small town to sign a restrictive covenant for one year covering a twenty-square-mile area? Explain.

7. How much negative information can you expect the seller to give you about the business? How can a prospective buyer find out such information?
8. Why is it so difficult for buyers and sellers to agree on a price for a business?
9. Which method of valuing a business is best? Why? What advice would you offer someone who is negotiating to buy a business about determining its value?
10. Outline the different exit strategy options available to a seller.
11. What tips would you offer someone about to enter into negotiations to buy a business?
12. One entrepreneur who recently purchased a business advises buyers to expect some surprises in the deal no matter how well-prepared they may be. He says that potential buyers must build some "wiggle room" into their plans to buy a company. What steps can a buyer take to ensure that he has sufficient "wiggle room"?

Business PlanPro™ This chapter addresses the process of acquiring an existing business. If this is your situation, determine whether the company has a business plan. If so, how recent is that plan? Does it accurately represent the current state of the organization? Do you have access to other historical information including the financial statements including profit and loss, balance sheet, and cash flow statements? These documents may be a valuable resource to help you to evaluate the business you may purchase.

Business Plan Exercises

A business plan can act as an effective investigative tool to evaluate the attractiveness of acquiring an existing business.

On the Web

If the business has a Web site, review the site. Assess the "online personality" of the business and gather as much information as you can about the business. Does it match what you have learned about the business through the owner and other documents you have reviewed? Do a search for the business name and the owners' names on the Web. Note what you find and determine whether this information correlates with information from other sources.

Sample Plans

Review the executive summaries of these ongoing business plans through the Sample Plan Browser in *Business Plan Pro*™:

- Machine Tooling
- Take Five Sports Bar
- Web Solutions, Inc.

Scan the table of contents and find the section of the plan with information on the company's past performance. What might this historical information tell you about the future of the venture? Which of these businesses would you expect to present the greatest profit potential based on their past performance? Which business represents the greatest risk based on these same criteria? How might this impact its purchase price?

In the Software

If the company that you are considering to acquire has a business plan, enter information into *Business Plan Pro*™. Begin by selecting the "Existing" business plan option in the opening window. Go the Company Summary section and include the results of the due diligence process. The financial statements of the business, including the balance sheet, profit and loss, and cash flow statements for the last three years, will be valuable historical data. This will set a baseline for you as you enter sales and expense scenarios into this plan. This process may help you to better assess the business's future earning potential and its current value.

Building Your Business Plan

One of advantages of using *Business Plan Pro*™ is the ease of creating different financial scenarios for your business. This can be an excellent way to explore multiple "what if" scenarios. Once your business is up and running, updating the plan is a quick and easy process. This will be an efficient way to keep your plan current and, by dating each of these files, offer an excellent historical perspective of your business.

Beyond the Classroom...

1. Ask several new owners who purchased existing businesses the following questions:
   a. How did you determine the value of the business?
   b. How close was the price paid for the business to the value assessed prior to purchase?
   c. What percentage of the accounts receivable was collectible?
   d. How accurate were their projections been concerning customers (sales volume and number of customers, especially)?

2. Visit a business broker and ask him how he brings a buyer and seller together. What does he do to facilitate the sale? What methods does he use to determine the value of a business?

3. Invite an attorney to speak to your class about the legal aspects of buying a business. How does he recommend a business buyer protect himself or herself legally in a business purchase?

Blendtec

CHAPTER 8

Building a Powerful Marketing Plan

No sale is really complete until the product is worn out, and the customer is satisfied.
—*L.L. Bean*

This fishing lure manufacturer I know had all these flashy green and purple lures. I asked, "Do fish take these?" "Charlie," he said, "I don't sell these lures to fish."
—*Charles Munger*

Learning Objectives

On completion of this chapter, you will be able to:

1. Describe the principles of building a guerrilla marketing plan and explain the benefits of preparing one.

2. Explain how small businesses can pinpoint their target markets.

3. Discuss the role of market research in building a guerrilla marketing plan and outline the market research process.

4. Describe how a small business can build a competitive edge in the marketplace using guerrilla marketing strategies: customer focus, quality, convenience, innovation, service, and speed.

5. Discuss the "four *P*s" of marketing—product, place, price, and promotion—and their role in building a successful marketing strategy.

As you learned in Chapter 4, creating a solid business plan improves an entrepreneur's odds of building a successful company. A business plan is a valuable document that defines *what* an entrepreneur plans to accomplish in both quantitative and qualitative terms and *how* he or she plans to accomplish it. The plan consolidates many of the topics we have discussed in preceding chapters with those in this section to produce a concise statement of how an entrepreneur plans to achieve success in the marketplace. This section focuses on building two major components of every business plan: the marketing plan and the financial plan.

Too often, business plans describe in great detail what the entrepreneur intends to accomplish (e.g., "the financials") and pay little, if any, attention to the strategies to achieve those targets. Too many entrepreneurs put too much time and effort into pulling together capital, people, and other resources to sell their products and services but fail to determine what it will take to attract and keep a profitable customer base. Sometimes they fail to determine whether a profitable customer base even exists! "A marketing plan is a road map for doing marketing right," says Lucille Wesnofske, director of a Small Business Development Center in New York.[1] To be effective, a solid business plan must contain both a financial plan *and* a marketing plan. Like the financial plan, an effective marketing plan projects numbers and analyzes them, but from a different perspective. Rather than focusing on cash flow, net income, and owner's equity, a marketing plan concentrates on the *customer*.

This chapter is devoted to creating an effective marketing plan, which is a subset of a total business plan. Before producing reams of computer-generated spreadsheets of financial projections, an entrepreneur must determine what to sell, to whom and how, on what terms and at what price, and how to get the product or service to the customer. In short, a marketing plan identifies a company's target customers and describes how the business will attract and keep them. Its primary focus is capturing and maintaining a competitive edge for a small business. Table 8.1 explains how to build a seven-sentence guerrilla marketing strategy.

Building a Guerrilla Marketing Plan

LO 1

Describe the principles of building a guerrilla marketing plan and explain the benefits of preparing one.

marketing
the process of creating and delivering desired goods and services to customers; involves all of the activities associated with winning and retaining loyal customers.

Marketing is the process of creating and delivering desired goods and services to customers and involves all of the activities associated with winning and retaining loyal customers. The "secret" to successful marketing is to understand your target customers' needs, demands, and wants before your competitors can; offer customers the products and services that will satisfy those needs, demands, and wants; and, provide customers with service, convenience, and value so that they will keep coming back. Unfortunately, there appears to be a sizable gap between sound marketing principles and actual marketing practices among small businesses. A study of small company marketing practices by the National Federation of Independent Businesses reveals many serious weaknesses. For instance, the study reports that 55 percent of small business owners say that their companies do not need marketing because their products and services sell themselves.[2] The unfortunate result is that most business owners devote little time, energy, or resources to marketing their companies. No product or service "sells itself," and insufficient marketing efforts are a common cause of small business failure.

The marketing function cuts across the entire company, affecting every aspect of its operation—from finance and production to hiring and purchasing—as well as the company's ultimate success. As competition for customers becomes more intense, entrepreneurs must understand the importance of developing creative marketing strategies; their success and survival depend on it. A marketing plan is *not* just for mega-corporations competing in international markets. Although they may be small and cannot match their larger rivals' marketing budgets, entrepreneurial companies are not powerless when it comes to developing effective marketing strategies. By using **guerrilla marketing strategies**—unconventional, low-cost, creative techniques—small companies can wring as much or more "bang" from their marketing bucks.

guerrilla marketing strategies
unconventional, low-cost, creative techniques designed to give small companies an edge over their larger, richer, more powerful rivals.

An effective marketing campaign does *not* require an entrepreneur to spend large amounts of money, but it does demand creativity, ingenuity, and an understanding of customers' buying habits. Guerrilla marketing expert J. Conrad Levinson estimates that guerrilla marketers spend between 4 percent and 8 percent of sales on marketing, but they put their money into clever, creative marketing efforts that reach their target customers and raise the profile of their products, services, and companies.[3]

TABLE 8.1 A Seven-Sentence Guerrilla Marketing Strategy

Building a successful guerrilla marketing plan does not have to be complex. Guerrilla marketing expert J. Conrad Levinson says that entrepreneurs can create a guerrilla marketing plan by answering just seven sentences:

1. **What is the purpose of your marketing?** In other words, what action do you want customers or prospective customers to take as a result of your marketing efforts? Should they visit your store? Go to your company's Web site? Call a toll-free number for more information?

2. **What primary benefit can you offer customers?** In other words, what is your company's competitive advantage and what does it do for customers? Guerrilla marketers express their company's competitive advantage as a solution to a customer's problem, which is easier to market than just a positive benefit. Successful guerrilla marketing requires an entrepreneur to have a clear understanding of a company's unique selling proposition (USP), a key customer benefit of a product or service that sets it apart from its competition.

3. **Who is your target market?** At whom are you aiming your marketing efforts? Answering this question often requires some basic research about your target customers, their characteristics, their habits, and their preferences. Guerrilla marketers know that broadcasting is old school; they realize that "narrowcasting"—focusing their marketing efforts on those people who are most interested in and are likely to purchase their goods and services—is much more efficient and effective. Most small companies have more than one target market; be sure to identify all of them.

4. **Which marketing tools will you use to reach your target audience?** This list should include only those tools that your company understands, knows how to use effectively, and can afford. The good news is that marketing tools do not have to be costly to be effective. In fact, guerrilla marketers are experts at using low-cost methods to market their companies.

5. **What is your company's niche in the marketplace?** In other words, how do you intend to position your company against your competition? Guerrilla marketers understand that their markets are crowded with competitors, some of them much larger with gigantic marketing budgets that dwarf their own, and that finding a profitable niche to occupy can be highly profitable. Recall from Chapter 3 that many successful entrepreneurs position their companies in profitable niches. One insurance agent markets his agency as one that "specializes in serving the needs of small businesses." SweetskinZ, launched in 1999, is a company that specializes in high-quality bicycle tires that feature full-color graphics and patterns that are also reflective. The key is to carve out a position that allows your company to differentiate itself from all of its competitors.

6. **What is your company's identity in the marketplace?** A company's identity is a reflection of its personality, its DNA. Small companies often have an advantage over large businesses when it comes to communicating their identities because of the interesting, unique stories behind their creation and the enthusiasm and passion of their founders. Customers enjoy doing business with small companies that have a clear, meaningful, and compelling identity in the marketplace. Southwest Airlines built its business by attracting customers who were drawn to its fun-loving, somewhat irreverent culture and its reputation for taking care of its customers.

7. **How much money will you spend on your marketing; in other words, what is your marketing budget?** Entrepreneurs should decide how much they intend to invest in their marketing efforts, an amount that they usually express as a percentage of sales. The average company in the United States devotes four percent of its sales to marketing. Small companies should allocate a portion of their budgets to marketing; after all, it drives sales. The good news is that many of the guerrilla marketing techniques that small companies can use (and that are described in this chapter) are either low-cost or no-cost. When allocating their budgets, guerrilla marketers recognize the importance of putting their money where they will get the greatest "bang."

Answering these seven questions will give you an outline of your company's marketing plan. *Implementing* a guerrilla marketing plan boils down to two essentials:

1. Having a thorough understanding of your target market, including what customers want and expect from your company and its products and services.

2. Identifying the obstacles that stand in your way of satisfying customers (competitors, barriers to entry, processes, outside influences, budgets, knowledge, and others) and eliminating them.

Source: Adapted from Jay Conrad Levinson and Jeannie Levinson, "Here's the Plan," *Entrepreneur*, February 2008, pp. 92–97; Alan Lautenslager, "Write a Creative Marketing Plan in Seven Sentences," *Entrepreneur*, April 24, 2006, http://www.entrepreneur.com/marketing/marketingideas/guerrillamarketingcolumnistallautenslager/article159486.html.

ENTREPRENEURIAL PROFILE

Emily Powell: Powell's Books

Emily Powell, second-generation owner of Powell's Books, the largest independent bookstore in the United States, which is based in Portland, Oregon, produced *Out of the Book,* a series of 25-minute author films to promote writers and, of course, Powell's Books. She launched the videos at red-carpet events in New York City, at Powell's, and in 50 other independent bookstores around the United States and uploaded them to YouTube as well. "One hundred thousand readers visit Powells.com on a typical day, and many of them come for the content— interviews, original essays, daily book reviews, and a blog," says Dave Weich, the videos' creator. "These films are simply an extension of what Powell's has been doing online for years. The difference is that instead of waiting for people to visit the site, we're taking authors directly to their audience." Powell also markets the company using e-mail newsletters, in-store events such as author signings and book readings, a company blog, and a section on its Web site called "Staff Picks" in which employees recommend books that they have enjoyed reading recently.[4]

A sound guerrilla marketing plan reflects a company's understanding of its customers and recognizes that satisfying them is the foundation of every business. Its purpose is to build a strategy of success for a business—but *from the customer's point of view.* Indeed, the customer is the central player in the cast of every business venture. According to marketing expert Ted Levitt, the primary purpose of a business is not to earn a profit; instead, it is "to create and keep a customer. The rest, given reasonable good sense, will take care of itself."[5]

A guerrilla marketing plan should accomplish four objectives:

1. It should pinpoint the specific target markets the small company will serve.
2. It should determine customer needs and wants through market research.
3. It should analyze the firm's competitive advantages and build a guerrilla marketing strategy around them.
4. It should help create a marketing mix that meets customer needs and wants.

The rest of this chapter focuses on building a customer orientation into these four objectives of the small company's marketing plan.

If Only Sales Were as High as Our Jerky Is!

In 1995, Gregory Nimitz began making beef jerky using his own recipe and giving it to friends and associates. While working on a NASA Mars rover project for an engineering company, Nimitz decided to send samples of his jerky to the food manager for NASA's shuttle program, which eventually led to his beef jerky going into outer space with several astronauts who were flying on the space shuttle and living on the international space station. Nimitz soon registered the URL Beefjerky.com and began selling online four varieties of beef jerky, one of which he named Final Frontier Jerky. The other three varieties that he sells bear the brand name of the company that actually produces Nimitz's jerky, Anderson Valley Ranch, using his recipe.

Working from his home in Twin Falls, Idaho, Nimitz ships all four varieties across the globe, generating annual sales of $150,000 and a profit of $50,000. Nimitz is frustrated because he believes sales of his unique jerky could be much better. Even though Beefjerky.com appears at or near the top of online search engines, Nimitz processes only eight or nine orders per day. "I should be selling 10 times as much," he says. He recognizes that customers often buy beef jerky as an impulse purchase when they are standing at a cash register. Because his products currently are not sold through retail outlets, Beefjerky.com is missing out on those impulse purchases.

In addition, Nimitz notes that only one out of 100 visitors to his Web site actually makes a purchase. He estimates that Beefjerky.com currently has a base of 4,500 customers and says that some of his company's most loyal customers are soldiers who are stationed overseas. He wonders what he can do to increase that number and how he can improve the company's online conversion rate, the ratio of the number of visitors who actually make a purchase divided by the number of visitors to the site.

Nimitz explains that his beef jerky is fresher than his competitors' products. "The jerky I ship is only about two weeks old and has a sell-by date six months from production," he says. "Some other brands have expiration dates that keep them on store shelves for two years." Beefjerky.com's products also are healthier than most jerky products, containing almost no preservatives and no sugar. They also are 96 percent fat-free and deliver a powerful 17 grams of protein per ounce.

Nimitz realizes that he has a unique marketing opportunity because NASA's astronauts chose his company's beef jerky to take into space with them, but he has not used this fact to his company's advantage. Visitors to the company's Web site have to search for Beefjerky.com's connection to NASA. Even though the phrase "Selected by astronauts for space flight" appears on the Final Frontier Jerky package, it is not prominent. Nimitz is learning about guerrilla marketing but has not yet implemented any guerrilla marketing tactics. He is considering sponsoring a jerky-eating contest to raise the visibility of his products.

If Beefjerky.com is going to expand its channel of distribution to include retail stores, Nimitz recognizes that he will have to upgrade its product packaging. Currently, the packages look "homemade" —simple plastic shrink-wrapped packages with a "World Famous Beefjerky.com" label stuck on them. Nimitz would like to emphasize that his jerky is fresh and all natural and wants the packaging to reflect those concepts. He wonders whether customers are confused by the fact that some of his jerky products carry the Beefjerky.com label and others are sold under the Anderson Valley Ranch label. Should he market all of his company's jerky under one brand name? Would doing so increase customer loyalty? How can he get his products into retail stores?

Work with a group of your classmates in brainstorming sessions to accomplish the following:

1. Develop a seven sentence marketing strategy for Beefjerky.com. Refer to Table 8.1.
2. Make recommendations to Nimitz using the questions that he has posed in this story. Explain your reasoning for each recommendation.
3. Identify at least eight guerrilla marketing tactics that Nimitz can use to increase the visibility and the sales of Beefjerky.com's products.
4. Visit the company's Web site (www.beefjerky.com). What recommendations can you make to improve it and to increase the company's conversion rate?

Sources: Based on Brian O'Reilly, "Space Jerky," *FSB*, March 2008, pp. 31–35.

Pinpointing the Target Market

One of the first steps in building a guerrilla marketing plan is to identify a small company's **target market**—the specific group of customers at whom the company aims its goods or services. The more a business knows about its local markets, its customers, and their buying habits and preferences, the more precisely it can focus its marketing efforts on the group(s) of prospective and existing customers who are most likely to buy its products or services. In an effort to increase their sales, many quick-service and fast-casual restaurants are targeting late-night customers, most of whom are in their teens and twenties.

For example, Denny's recently launched its All Nighter menu, which is served only from 10 p.m. to 5 a.m. and is aimed squarely at members of Generation Y, 89 percent of whom are "entertainment seekers" who go out in groups to eat. To appeal to its target audience, the 1,500-store restaurant chain invited independent rock bands to contribute items to the All Nighter menu. The Plain White T's contribution to the menu is Plain White Shake, a cheesecake and ice cream combination topped with whipped cream and white chocolate chips, and the Eagles of Death Metal's creation is heart-shaped pancakes with raspberry sauce, chocolate, and other toppings. Employees who work the late-night shift trade their traditional uniforms for jeans and black T-shirts that sport the slogan "Get your crave on." Denny's markets its All Nighter menu with the help of a "Vote for Bands" page on its All Nighter Web site and a blog written by band members. Within three weeks of launching the site, nearly 1 million people visited it. "We can't be all things to all people," says Michael Polydoroff, director of sales promotion for Denny's. "We have to focus our efforts."[6]

Most marketing experts contend that the greatest marketing mistake small businesses make is failing to define clearly the target market to be served. These entrepreneurs develop new products that do not sell because they are not targeted at a specific audience's needs; they broadcast ads that attempt to reach everyone and end up reaching no one; they spend precious time and money trying to reach customers who are not the most profitable; and many of the customers they attract leave because they do not know what the company stands for. Why, then, do so many small

LO 2
Explain how small businesses can pinpoint their target markets.

target market
the specific group of customers at whom a company aims its goods or services.

ENTREPRENEURIAL PROFILE

Michael Polydoroff: Denny's

companies make this mistake? Because it is easy and does not require market research or a marketing plan! The problem is that this is a sales-driven approach rather than a customer-driven strategy. Smart entrepreneurs know that they do not have the luxury of wasting resources; they must follow a more focused, laser-like approach to marketing. "The real investment is in the time and sweat spent understanding the needs of your customers and coming up with creative ways of communicating your value proposition," says J. Conrad Levinson. "Broadening your search isn't as important as aiming your message at the right people."[7]

To be customer-driven, an effective marketing strategy must be based on a clear, comprehensive understanding of a company's target customers and their needs. Failing to pinpoint their target markets is especially ironic because small firms are far better suited to reach small, often more concentrated market segments that their larger rivals overlook or consider too small to be profitable. A customer-driven marketing strategy is a powerful strategic weapon for any company that lacks the financial and physical resources of its competitors. Customers respond when companies take the time to learn about their unique needs and offer products and services designed to satisfy them.

ENTREPRENEURIAL PROFILE

Arlene Harris: GreatCall

When Arlene Harris noticed that her 80-year-old mother kept the cell phone that she had purchased for her turned off most of the time because she could not see the tiny screen or punch the small keys, Harris spotted a business opportunity. Her research showed that people age 65 and older make up 12.4 percent of the U.S. population and will grow to more than 20 percent of the population by 2030. Harris raised $36.6 million in venture capital to launch GreatCall, a company that makes the Jitterbug cell phone aimed at senior citizens. The phone, with its large screen with jumbo-sized text, oversized buttons, and an ergonomic ear cushion that produces high sound quality, has been a hit with its target audience. "Jitterbug provides advanced technology delivered in an uncomplicated way—everything safety- and simplicity-minded customers want and nothing they don't want," says company co-founder Martin Cooper, Harris's husband. The Jitterbug is just one of many products that companies have created to serve the needs of senior citizens, products that have been dubbed "nana technology."[8]

Like GreatCall, the most successful businesses have well-defined portraits of the customers they are seeking to attract. From market research, they know their customers' income levels, lifestyles, buying patterns, likes and dislikes, and even their psychological profiles—why they buy. These companies offer prices that are appropriate to their target customers' buying power, product lines that appeal to their tastes, and service they expect. The payoff comes in the form of higher sales, profits, and customer loyalty.

For entrepreneurs, pinpointing target customers has become more important than ever before as markets in the United States have become increasingly fragmented and diverse. Mass marketing techniques no longer reach customers the way they did 30 years ago because of the influence now exerted on the nation's purchasing patterns by what were once minority groups such as Hispanic-, Asian-, and African-Americans. Companies using Chinese-born basketball players as spokesmen, television commercials spoken entirely in Spanish (some with no English subtitles), Hip-Hop clothing and music appearing in mainstream stores, and college cafés offering sushi and other specialty dishes are symbols of the tremendous multicultural shift that continues to take place in the United States.

When companies follow a customer-driven marketing strategy, they ensure that their target customers permeate the entire business—from the merchandise sold and the music played on the sound system to the location, layout, and decor of the store. These entrepreneurs have an advantage over their larger rivals because the buying experience they have created resonates with their target customers, and that's why they prosper.

ENTREPRENEURIAL PROFILE

Mike Jackson: Lexus of Palm Beach

The owner of the Lexus dealership in West Palm Beach, Florida, recently invested $35 million to build a new, customer-friendly super-luxury dealership designed with the company's target customers (whom they call "guests") in mind. Taking cues from some of the world's grand hotels and from the interior of Lexus automobiles, the showroom's designer created a space that is unmistakably upscale with a polished porcelain tile floor and walls made of cherry and bird's-eye maple wood. When guests arrive, they leave their cars with a valet, and a personal concierge escorts them to a European-style coffee bar that offers complimentary espresso, cappuccino, and pastries prepared by a chef who trained in Europe, which they can enjoy while seated in luxurious massage chairs. "We have customers who stay in world-class hotels and shop on Fifth Avenue. They expect a certain kind of experience," says CEO Mike Jackson. Since Lexus of Palm Beach opened its new showroom, sales have increased significantly, moving the dealership from twenty-fifth in sales in the nation to fifth in just a matter of months.[9]

Determining Customer Needs and Wants Through Market Research

The changing nature of the U.S. population is a potent force altering the landscape of business. Shifting patterns in age, income, education, race, and other population characteristics (which are the subject of **demographics**) will have a major impact on companies, their customers, and the way companies do business with those customers. Businesses that ignore demographic trends and fail to adjust their strategies accordingly run the risk of becoming competitively obsolete. Small companies that spot demographic trends early and act on them can gain a distinctive edge in the market.

LO 3

Discuss the role of market research in building a guerrilla marketing plan and outline the market research process.

demographics
the study of important population characteristics such as age, income, education, race, and others.

Aaron Petzer created Mint, an easy-to-use personal financial management package that is targeted at young people between the ages of 18 and 29, after he observed alarming trends in the debt load that young people are accumulating. For instance, the average student loan debt for college graduates is $21,100, and the typical college senior has a credit card debt of $2,700. Studies also reveal that many young people do not understand the importance of financial planning and that they have difficulty managing their money. Mint, which is available for free, competes with established financial management software such as Microsoft Money and Intuit's® Quicken®, both of which sell for $30 to $100. In addition to its "price" advantage, Mint also offers an important performance advantage: It automatically downloads, categorizes, and graphs users' financial information, whereas its competitors have much steeper learning curves and require users to spend an hour or two each week entering their financial transactions, something that members of Generation Y are loathe to do. "You set [Mint] up in two minutes, and that's the only work you ever have to do," says Petzer. "It's so easy to use, people will actually use it."[10]

ENTREPRENEURIAL PROFILE _____
Aaron Petzer: Mint

The Value of Market Research

By performing some basic market research, small business owners can detect key demographic and market trends. Indeed, *every* business can benefit from a better understanding of its market, customers, and competitors. "Market information is just as much a business asset and just as important as your inventory or the machine you have in the back room," says one marketing consultant.[11] **Market research** is the vehicle for gathering the information that serves as the foundation for the marketing plan. It involves systematically collecting, analyzing, and interpreting data pertaining to a company's market, customers, and competitors. The objective of market research is to learn how to improve the level of satisfaction for existing customers and to find ways to attract new customers.

Small companies cannot afford to make marketing mistakes because there is little margin for error when funds are scarce and budgets are tight. Small businesses simply cannot afford to miss their target markets, and market research can help them zero in on the bull's-eye.

market research
the vehicle for gathering the information that serves as the foundation for the marketing plan; it involves systematically collecting, analyzing, and interpreting data pertaining to a company's market, customers, and competitors.

Quick-service restaurant Burger King's market research on its target customer, known inside the company as the Super Fan, allows the company to create products, prices, and promotions that are successful at reaching its core customers. The Super Fan is between 18 and 34 years old and, surprisingly, is almost as likely to be a female as a male, according to CEO John Chidsey. Super Fans visit Burger King stores between 9 and 16 times each month. Even though they make up just 18 percent of the chain's total customer base, they account for 50 percent of total store visits. Understanding these core customers allows the company to focus its marketing efforts where they will generate

ENTREPRENEURIAL PROFILE _____
John Chidsey: Burger King

the greatest benefit. For instance, market research guided Burger King's launch of its Stacker sandwiches (double, triple, and even quadruple burgers) and its promotional tie-ins to movies such as *The Simpsons* and *Indiana Jones and the Crystal Skull.* Because 65 percent of Burger King's sales originate at the drive-through window, the company introduced Hold 'Ems, wraps that are served in "holsters" designed to fit into cars' cup holders. Even the company's eerie mascot, The King, has an almost cult following among Burger King's Super Fans. Super Fans are so important to Burger King that the company provided to all of its executives a book called *Food for Thought* that chronicles the company's extensive research on Super Fans. Hector Munoz, the company's director of merchandising, says that Burger King's marketing department conducts research on 90 percent of every marketing effort the company uses.[12]

Market research does *not* have to be time consuming, complex, or expensive to be useful. By applying the same type of creativity to market research that they display when creating their businesses, entrepreneurs can perform effective market research "on the cheap."

ENTREPRENEURIAL PROFILE

Richard Reed, Adam Balon, & Jon Wright: Innocent Drinks

Cambridge graduates Richard Reed, Adam Balon, and Jon Wright were hesitant to dive into entrepreneurship even though they had spent six months testing their smoothie recipes on approving friends when they decided to conduct some inexpensive market research. The reluctant entrepreneurs purchased £500 worth of fresh fruit and used it to make smoothies that they sold at a small music festival in London. They put up a big sign that said, "Do you think we should give up our jobs to make these smoothies?" and put out a bin marked "yes" and another marked "no" and asked people to vote by putting the empty smoothie container in the appropriate bin. "By the end of the weekend, the 'yes' bin was so full we went in the next day and resigned," recalls Reed. Today Innocent Drinks, which makes all-natural, healthy smoothies, thickies (yogurt-based drinks), and juices, employs 275 people and sells its fruity concoctions in more than 10,000 retail outlets around the world.[13]

Many entrepreneurs are discovering the power, the speed, the convenience, and the low cost of conducting market research over the Web. Online surveys, customer opinion polls, and other research projects are easy to conduct, cost virtually nothing, and help companies to connect with their customers. With Web-based surveys, businesses can get real-time feedback from customers, often using surveys they have designed themselves. Many companies such as online shoe company Zappos and food retailer Whole Foods are using as a market research tool Twitter, the social network service that asks members to answer the question "What are you doing?" "In the past companies would hire market research firms to understand their [target customers]," says Mike Hudack, CEO of Blip.tv, a New York City—based video Web site. "We use Twitter to get the fastest, most honest research any company ever heard—good, bad, and ugly—and it doesn't cost a cent." Using Twitter, Hudack monitors everything other Twitterers say about Blip.tv and gets feedback on new ideas that the company is considering. By sharing information about Blip.tv on Twitter, Hudack also is raising the profile of his company among potential customers. Zappos recently tested a new version of the company's Web site on Twitter, "and we were able to make some improvements based on the comments" the company received from Twitterers, says CEO Tony Hsieh.[14]

Faith Popcorn, a marketing consultant, encourages small business owners to be their own "trend-tracking sleuths." Merely by observing their customers' attitudes and actions, small business owners can shift their product lines and services to meet changing tastes in the market. To spot significant trends, entrepreneurs can use the following techniques:

- Read as many current publications as possible, especially ones you normally would not read. Look for specific information about your industry but also watch for references to general trends that influence your business.
- Monitor blogs and newsgroups about your industry. What forces are shaping your business and influencing your customers?
- Watch the top ten TV shows because they are reflections of customers' attitudes and values and indicators of what they are going to buy.

- See the top 10 movies. They also influence consumer behavior, from language to fashions. In the 1930s, Hollywood star Clark Gable took off his shirt in *It Happened One Night* and revealed a bare chest; undershirt sales soon took a dive. After Will Smith and Tommy Lee Jones donned Ray-Ban® sunglasses in *Men in Black*, sales of the sunglasses tripled![15]
- Talk to at least 150 customers a year about what they are buying and why. Make a conscious effort to spend time with some of your target customers, preferably in an informal setting, to find out what they are thinking.
- Talk with the 10 smartest people you know. They can offer valuable insights and fresh perspectives that you may not have considered.
- Listen to your children. ("They can be tremendous guides for you," says Popcorn.)[16]

Next, entrepreneurs should make a list of the major trends they spot and should briefly describe how well their products or services match these trends. Companies whose products or services are diverging from major social, demographic, and economic trends rather than converging with them must change their course or run the risk of failing because their markets can evaporate before their eyes. How can entrepreneurs find the right match among trends, their products or services, and the appropriate target markets? Market research!

How to Conduct Market Research

The goal of market research is to reduce the risks associated with making business decisions. It can replace misinformation and assumptions with facts. Opinion and hearsay are not viable foundations on which to build a solid marketing strategy. Successful market research consists of four steps: define the objective, collect the data, analyze and interpret the data, and draw conclusions.

Step 1. Define the Objective. The first, and most crucial, step in market research is to define the research objective clearly and concisely. A common error at this stage is to confuse a symptom with the true problem. For example, dwindling sales is not a problem; it is a symptom. To get to the heart of the matter, entrepreneurs must list all the possible factors that could have caused it. Do we face new competition? Are our sales representatives impolite or unknowledgeable? Have customer tastes changed? Is our product line too narrow? Do customers have trouble finding what they want? Is our Web site giving customers what they want? Is it easy to navigate?

Step 2. Collect the Data. The marketing approach that dominates today is **individualized (or one-to-one) marketing,** which involves gathering data on individual customers and then developing a marketing program designed specifically to appeal to their needs, tastes, and preferences. In a society in which people feel so isolated and interactions are so impersonal, one-to-one marketing gives a business a competitive edge. Companies following this approach know their customers, understand how to give them the value they want, and, perhaps most important, know how to make them feel special and important. The idea is to treat each customer as an individual, and the goal is to transform a company's best and most profitable customers into loyal, lifetime customers.

individualized (one-to-one) marketing
a system based on gathering data on individual customers and developing a marketing program designed to appeal specifically to their needs, tastes, and preferences.

Individualized marketing requires business owners to gather and assimilate detailed information about their customers. Fortunately, owners of even the smallest companies now have access to affordable technology that creates and manages computerized databases, allowing them to develop close, one-to-one relationships with their customers. Much like gold nuggets waiting to be discovered, significant amounts of valuable information about customers and their buying habits are hidden *inside* many small businesses, tucked away in computerized databases. For most business owners, collecting useful information about their customers and potential new products and markets is simply a matter of sorting and organizing data that are already floating around somewhere in their companies. One marketing research expert explains the situation this way:

> You know a lot about your customers. You know who they are, where they live, what their buying habits are. And if you're like most companies, you've done absolutely nothing with that pile of market intelligence. It just sits there, earning you no money and creating zero shareholder value.[17]

The key is to mine the data that most companies have at their disposal and turn them into useful information that allows the company to "court" its customers with special products, services, ads, and offers that appeal most to them.

How can entrepreneurs collect such valuable market and customer information? Two basic methods are available: conducting *primary research,* data you collect and analyze yourself, and gathering *secondary research,* data that have already been compiled and are available, often at a very reasonable cost (even free). Chapter 4, Conducting a Feasibility Analysis and Crafting a Winning Business Plan, describes many useful sources of secondary research. Primary research techniques include the following:

Customer surveys and questionnaires. Keep them short. Word your questions carefully so that you do not bias the results and use a simple ranking system (e.g., a 1-to-5 scale, with 1 representing "unacceptable" and 5 representing "excellent"). Test your survey for problems on a small number of people before putting it to use. Web surveys conducted on SurveyMonkey or Zoomerang are inexpensive, easy to conduct, and provide feedback fast. Alyssa Rapp, co-founder of Bottlenotes Inc, an upscale wine club in Palo Alto, California, regularly uses customer surveys on her company's Web site to conduct quick market research. "I get real-time, statistically significant customer feedback," says Rapp, who has used the research to formulate special promotions and to create new products.[18]

Focus groups. Enlist a small number of customers to give you feedback on specific issues in your business—quality, convenience, hours of operation, service, and so on. Listen carefully for new marketing opportunities as customers or potential customers tell you what is on their minds. Once again, consider using the Web; one small bicycle company conducts 10 online focus groups each year at virtually no cost and gains valuable marketing information from them.

Daily transactions. Sift as much data as possible from existing company records and daily transactions—customer warranty cards, personal checks, frequent-buyer clubs, credit applications, and others.

Other ideas. Set up a suggestion system (for customers and employees) and use it. Establish a customer advisory panel to determine how well your company is meeting needs. Talk with suppliers about trends they have spotted in the industry. Contact customers who have not bought anything in a long time and find out why. Contact people who are not customers and find out why. Teach employees to be good listeners and then ask them what they hear.

Radio Shack, the consumer electronics chain, has partnered with Sweat Equity Enterprises (SEE), a student-oriented nonprofit organization, in an arrangement in which student members serve on marketing advisory panels. One top manager credits the students for creative ideas in "product design, store display, and creative marketing tactics that we never would have considered in the past" and says that the company's relationship with the student advisors is paying "huge dividends."[19]

Thanks to advances in computer hardware and software, data mining, once available only to large companies with vast computer power and large market research budgets, is now possible for even very small businesses. **Data mining** is a process in which computer software that uses statistical analysis, database technology, and artificial intelligence finds hidden patterns, trends, and connections in data so that business owners can make better marketing decisions and predictions about customers' behavior. By finding relationships among the many components of a data set, identifying clusters of customers with similar buying habits, and predicting customers' buying patterns, data mining gives entrepreneurs incredible marketing power.

data mining
a process in which computer software that uses statistical analysis, database technology, and artificial intelligence finds hidden patterns, trends, and connections in data so that business owners can make better marketing decisions and predictions about customers' behavior.

Step 3. Analyze and Interpret the Data. The results of market research alone do not provide a solution to the problem; business owners must attach some meaning to them. What do the facts mean? Is there a common thread running through the responses? Do the results suggest any changes needed in the way the business operates? Are there new opportunities the owner can take advantage of? There are no hard-and-fast rules for interpreting market research results; entrepreneurs must use judgment and common sense to determine what the results of their research mean.

Step 4. Draw Conclusions and Act. The market research process is not complete until the business owner acts upon the information collected. In many cases, the conclusion is obvious once a small business owner interprets the results of the market research. Based on an understanding of what the facts really mean, the owner must then decide how to use the information in the business. For example, the owner of a retail shop discovered from a survey that her customers preferred evening shopping hours over early morning hours. She made the schedule adjustment, and sales began to climb.

ETHICS AND ENTREPRENEURSHIP

Saving Lives One Straw at a Time

When Mikkel Vestergaard Frandsen was 19, he dropped out of school and moved to Nigeria to sell trucks, but a political coup forced him to leave Africa in 1992 and return to his native Denmark, where he joined the family textile business, Vestergaard Frandsen, on the condition that he focus his work on developing relief-aid products such as blankets and tents. With Mikkel's help, the family-owned company, which was founded by his father Torben in 1957 as a maker of fabric for work clothing, soon began producing disease-control textiles such as Permanet, a widely used, insecticide-treated mosquito net that remains effective for up to four years.

Mikkel's experience in Africa and with the Carter Center, an Atlanta-based human rights organization founded by former President Jimmy Carter and his wife, Rosalynn, awakened him to the plight of people in the developing world who are suffering from illnesses and even death from bacteria they acquire by drinking dirty water. Worldwide, more than one billion people do not have access to safe drinking water, and many young people are robbed of the opportunity for an education because they must spend much of their days hiking to and from contaminated water supplies to fetch enough water to survive. "We started thinking, with 6,000 children dying a day from waterborne diseases, what could we do?" he says. Mikkel and his father, Torben, set out to design a filter that could be used at the water source to reduce the impact of water-borne diseases. They knew that to be effective, the device had to be portable, inexpensive, reliable, and operate without batteries or electricity.

Initially, the Vestergaard Frandsens worked with their company's engineers on a textile-only filter but soon realized that the design would not work and began experimenting with a combination of textile, iodine, and carbon filters. This design proved to be effective, and the result was the LifeStraw,® a 10-inch device that weighs just 4.3 ounces and is comprised of two filtering chambers. The first chamber contains textiles and iodine, which trap and kill bacteria and viruses in the water that passes through it; the second chamber consists of granulated active carbon, which absorbs any residual iodine and improves the taste of the resulting clean water. Tests show that one LifeStraw® is capable of purifying at least 182 gallons of water, removing 99.9999 percent of bacteria, 99.99 percent of water-borne viruses, and 99 percent of parasites, all of which significantly lowers the risk of illness to its users. The LifeStraw® sells for just $3 and has won many awards, including the Saatchi & Saatchi Award for World Changing Ideas. International aid groups have purchased LifeStraws® to help people in Myanmar and in China where towns, homes, and water supplies were devastated by hurricanes and earthquakes.

A year later, Vestergaard Frendsen introduced the LifeStraw® Family, a $15 water purifier that an entire family can use at home. LifeStraw Family®–a larger version of the LifeStraw®—purifies larger quantities of water for families of up to six people and remains effective for up to two years. "LifeStraw Family® will meet a critically important need in the developing world, where 1.8 million people, mostly children, die each year from water-borne diseases," says Mikkel.

Vestergaard Frendsen factories are working around the clock to produce enough LifeStraws® to meet the demand for them. "There is no conflict between doing good and doing business," says Mikkel.

1. What role should business play in solving social problems such as ready access to clean, safe water supplies?
2. Should businesses be able to earn a profit when they help to solve complex social problems?
3. Mikkel Vestergaard Frendsen says, "There is no conflict between doing good and doing business." Do you agree? Explain.

Sources: Adapted from Jilian Mincer, "Water, Water Everywhere…" *Wall Street Journal*, June 23, 2008, p. R7; "LifeStraw Family: A Fresh Approach to a Dirty Problem," *Vestergaard Frendsen Quarterly*, Volume VII, July 2008, p.1.

Plotting a Guerrilla Marketing Strategy: How to Build a Competitive Edge

LO 4

Describe how a small business can build a competitive edge in the marketplace using guerrilla marketing strategies.

To be successful guerrilla marketers, entrepreneurs must be as innovative in creating their marketing strategies as they are in developing new product and service ideas. Table 8.2 describes several low-cost, creative, and highly effective guerrilla marketing tactics small businesses have used to outperform their larger rivals.

TABLE 8.2 Guerrilla Marketing Tactics

- Help organize and sponsor a service- or community-oriented project.
- Sponsor offbeat, memorable events. Build a giant banana split; rent a theater for a morning and invite kids for a free viewing.
- Always be on the lookout for new niches to enter. Try to develop multiple niches.
- Offer to speak about your business, industry, product, or service to local organizations.

(continued)

TABLE 8.2 Guerrilla Marketing Tactics (*continued*)

- Launch a loyalty program that gives customers a reason to return. Be sure to provide loyalty program members with benefits, such as special offers, discounts, shopping previews, and others.
- Reward existing customers for referring new customers to your company. When customers refer business to Choice Translating, a language translation company in Charlotte, North Carolina, they receive a special gift.
- Sell at every opportunity. One brewery includes a mini-catalog advertising T-shirts and mugs in every six-pack it sells. Orders for catalog items are climbing fast.
- Develop a sales "script" that asks customers a series of questions to hone in on what they are looking for and that will lead them to the conclusion that your product or service is IT!!
- Sell gift certificates. They really boost your cash flow.
- Create samples of your product and give them to customers. You'll increase sales later.
- Offer a 100 percent, money-back, no-hassles guarantee. By removing the customer's risk of buying, you increase your product's attractiveness.
- Create a "Frequent Buyer" Program. Remember how valuable existing customers are. Work hard to keep the customers you have! One coffee shop kept its customers coming back with a punch-card promotion that gave a free pound of coffee after a customer purchased nine pounds.
- Clip articles that feature your business and send reprints to customers and potential customers. Keep reminding them of who you are and why you're valuable to them.
- Test how well your ads "pull" with coded coupons that customers bring in. Focus your ad expenditures on those media that produce the best results for you.
- Create "tip sheets" to pass out to customers and potential customers - e.g., landscape tips on lawn maintenance.
- Find ways to make your product or service irresistible to your customers. One furniture company e-mails a digital photo of big-ticket items customers are considering, and sales closing rates have climbed 25 percent.
- Create an award for your community—e.g., a landscape company presented a "best yard" award each season.
- Create a big event of your own: "January is Customer Appreciation Month. Buy one suit and get a second one at 50 percent off."
- Conduct a contest in the community—e.g., a photographer sponsored a juried photo contest for different age groups. One restaurant that targeted the business crowd for lunch encouraged customers to leave their business cards (which gave the restaurateur the ability to e-mail them daily lunch specials) to enter a drawing for a free $50 iTunes gift card.
- Collect testimonials from satisfied customers and use them in ads, brochures, etc. Testimonials are one of the most effective forms of advertising!
- Purchase customized postage stamps that feature your company's logo (see PhotoStamps at http://photo.stamps.com) and use them on business correspondence.
- Get a former journalist to help you write a story "pitch" for local media.
- Show an interest in your customers' needs. If you spot a seminar that would be of interest to them, tell them! Become a valuable resource for them.
- Find unique ways to thank customers (especially first-time buyers) for their business—a note, a lunch, a gift basket....
- Give loyal customers a "freebie" occasionally. You might be surprised at how long they will remember it.
- Create a newsletter that features your customers or clients and their businesses—e.g., a photo of client using your product in his business.
- Cooperate with other businesses selling complementary products and services in marketing efforts and campaigns, a process called fusion marketing. Share mailing lists and advertising time or space, or work together on a special promotion.
- Use major competitors' coupons against them. The owner of an independent sandwich shop routinely pulled business from a nearby national chain by advertising that he would accept its coupons.

- Market your company's uniqueness. Many customers enjoy buying from small companies that are different and unique. The owners of the only tea plantation in the United States used that fact to their advantage in establishing a customer base.

Sources: Adapted from Mickey Meece, "How to Keep Momentum Going for Customers and Employees," *New York Times*, January 3, 2008, http://www.nytimes.com/2008/01/03/business/smallbusiness/03tips.html; Jay Conrad Levinson, "Attention Getters," *Entrepreneur*, March 1998, p.88; Lynn Beresford, Janean Chun, Cynthia E. Griffin, Heather Page, and Debra Phillips, "Marketing 101," *Entrepreneur*, May 1996, pp. 104–114; Guen Sublette, "Marketing 101," *Entrepreneur*, May 1995, pp. 86–98; Denise Osburn, "Bringing Them Back for More," *Nation's Business*, August 1995, p.31R; Jay Conrad Levinson, "Survival Tactics," *Entrepreneur*, March 1996, p. 84; Tom Stein, "Outselling the Giants," *Success*, May 1996, pp. 38–41; Gwen Moran, "Get Noticed," *Entrepreneur*, October 2008, pp. 58–61.

Source: www.cartoonstock.com

Guerrilla Marketing Principles

The following twelve principles can help business owners to create powerful, effective guerrilla marketing strategies.

FIND A NICHE AND FILL IT As you learned in Chapter 3, Strategic Management and the Entrepreneur, many successful small companies choose their niches carefully and defend them fiercely rather than compete head-to-head with larger rivals. A niche strategy allows a small company to maximize the advantages of its size and to compete effectively even in industries dominated by giants by serving its target customers better than its competitors. Focusing on niches that are too small to be attractive to large companies is a common recipe for success among thriving small companies. "Finding unserved niches is an excellent way to begin 'whupping' the big guys, if not in their own back yard, at least on the same street," says one marketing expert.[20]

In 1982, John McKenzie was operating a part-time screen printing business when Richard Childress Racing asked him to create the vinyl sponsors' decals for one of its race cars for an upcoming NASCAR race. By the end of the year, McKenzie was creating the graphics, which cover 85 to 95 percent of a race car, for more than half of the cars on the NASCAR circuit, and a new business, Motorsports Designs was born. Today, the company produces customized eight-panel vinyl wraps that envelope each car and that employees can apply with squeegees in less than six hours. "We do Indy car, drag racing, and sports car racing, but NASCAR is our primary market," says McKenzie, whose company employs 55 people in High Point, North Carolina.[21]

USE THE POWER OF PUBLICITY **Publicity** is any commercial news covered by the media that boosts sales but for which a small company does not pay. Publicity has power; because it is from an unbiased source, a news feature about a company or a product that appears in a newspaper or magazine has more impact on people's buying decisions than an advertisement does. Exposure in any medium raises a company's visibility and boosts sales, and, best of all, publicity is free! It does require some creativity and effort, however.

The following tactics can help entrepreneurs stimulate publicity for their companies.

Write an article that will interest your customers or potential customers. One investment advisor writes a monthly column for the local newspaper on timely topics such as "Retirement Planning," "Minimizing Your Tax Bill," and "How to Pay for College." Not only do the articles help build her credibility as an expert, but they also have attracted new customers to her business.

Sponsor an event designed to attract attention. In 1982, Bob Bisbee, owner of a small fuel dock and fishing store in Newport Beach, California, created a fishing tournament, Bisbee's Black and Blue Tournament (the focus was on black marlin and blue marlin), in an attempt to boost sales for his business. Before long, the event was picked up by major media outlets. The public relations strategy was so successful that the fishing tournament, now one of the world's richest and best-known fishing events, has replaced Bisbee's original business![22]

Involve celebrities "on the cheap." Few small businesses can afford to hire celebrities as spokespersons for their companies. Some companies have discovered other ways to get celebrities to promote their products, however. For instance, when Karen Neuburger, owner of Karen Neuburger's Sleepwear, learned that Oprah Winfrey is a "pajama connoisseur," she sent the talk show host a pair of her pajamas. The move paid off; Neuburger has appeared on Oprah's popular television show on three separate occasions.[23]

Contact local TV and radio stations and offer to be interviewed. Many local news or talk shows are looking for guests to talk about topics of interest to their audiences (especially in January and February). Even local shows can reach new customers.

Publish a newsletter. With a personal computer and desktop publishing software, any entrepreneur can publish a professional-looking newsletter. Freelancers can offer design and editing advice. Use the newsletter to reach present and potential customers.

Contact local business and civic organizations and offer to speak to them. A powerful, informative presentation can win new business. (Be sure your public speaking skills are up to par first! If not, consider joining Toastmasters.)

Offer or sponsor a seminar. Teaching people about a subject you know a great deal about builds confidence and goodwill among potential customers. The owner of a landscaping service and nursery offers a short course in landscape architecture and always sees sales climb afterwards!

Write news releases and fax or e-mail them to the media. The key to having a news release picked up and printed is finding a unique angle on your business or industry that would interest an editor. Keep it short, simple, and interesting. E-mail press releases should be shorter than printed ones—typically four or five paragraphs rather than one or two pages–and they should include a link to the company's Web site.

Volunteer to serve on community and industry boards and committees. You can make your town a better place to live and work and raise your company's visibility at the same time.

Sponsor a community project or support a nonprofit organization or charity. Not only will you be giving something back to the community, but you will also gain recognition, goodwill, and,

ENTREPRENEURIAL PROFILE

Barbara Butler: Barbara Butler Artist Builder Inc.

Barbara Butler, owner of Barbara Butler Artist Builder Inc., a San Francisco-based maker of custom-made wooden play houses and structures for children, generates publicity for her company by donating $55,000 worth of products each year to charitable causes in lieu of spending money on advertisements. Butler chooses charities that are closely connected to her company's mission, such as the Bay Area Discovery Museum, and the publicity that results from the donations attracts customers, including celebrities such as Will Smith. "We'd rather spend money on donation programs than on advertising," says Butler. "We get a lot of publicity, and we try to raise the most money possible [for the charities].[24]

Barbara Butler Artist Builder Inc.

perhaps, customers for your business. The key is to partner with charities that match the company's values and mission.

Promote a cause. According to the Cone Cause Evolution and Environmental Survey, 87 percent of customers say that, other things being equal, they are likely to switch from one brand to another if the other brand is associated with a good cause.[25] By engaging in cause marketing, entrepreneurs can support a worthy cause that is important to them and generate publicity for their companies at the same time. The key is choosing a cause that is important to your customers. One marketing expert offers the following formula for selecting the right cause: Mission statement + personal passion + customer demographics = ideal cause.[26] Gold's Gym International recently joined forces with the American Diabetes Association (ADA) to offer information and exercise programs for diabetes management and prevention and to raise money for the nonprofit organization. Not only did Gold's Gym help raise $600,000 for the ADA, but it also generated new customer inquiries and enrollments for its gyms.[27]

DON'T JUST SELL; ENTERTAIN Numerous surveys have shown that consumers are bored with shopping and that they are less inclined to spend their scarce leisure time shopping than ever before. Winning customers today requires more than low prices and wide merchandise selection; increasingly, businesses are adopting strategies based on **entertailing,** the notion of drawing customers into a store by creating a kaleidoscope of sights, sounds, smells, and activities, all designed to entertain—and, of course, sell (think Disney). The primary goal of entertailing is to catch customers' attention and engage them in some kind of entertaining experience so that they shop longer and buy more goods or services. Entertailing involves "making [shopping] more fun, more educational, more interactive," says one retail consultant.[28] For instance, at the Corvallis, Washington, location of the Book Bin, a small chain of bookstores, customers can read books as they sip lattes and relax on a comfortable couch with one of the store cats, Tess or Eloise, lounging nearby as they wait for either a lecture and book signing by the author or a live musical concert.[29]

Research supports the benefits of entertailing's hands-on, interactive, educational, approach to selling; one study found that, when making a purchase, 34 percent of consumers are driven more by emotional factors such as fun and excitement than by logical factors such as price and convenience.[30] Entertailing's goal, of course, is not only to entertain but also to boost sales.

entertailing
a marketing concept designed to draw customers into a store by creating a kaleidoscope of sights, sounds, smells, and activities, all designed to entertain—and, of course, sell.

ENTREPRENEURIAL PROFILE

Jim & Dick Cabela: Cabela's

Few retailers practice entertailing as well as Cabela's, an innovative company that sells a wide selection of outdoor gear, mostly to hunters and fishermen. The company generates impressive sales through its catalog operations, its Web site, and its 22 stores, all of which are located in small towns in rural America. What is even more amazing is that Cabela's has achieved its position as one of the hottest retailers in the industry by targeting an unusual customer: men who typically hate to shop! Men (and often their families) routinely drive hundreds of miles to visit a Cabela's store, where they spend hours shopping for everything from guns and decoys to fishing rods and tents. Brothers Jim and Dick Cabela know that entertaining customers encourages them to shop longer and spend more. They spend lavishly on each store they build, including glass ceilings that let in natural light and aquariums containing 8,000 gallons of freshwater and game fish in natural settings. A major component of their entertailing strategy is the 45 percent of the floor space taken up by nature scenes situated throughout the stores. One store contains 237,000 square feet of space, the equivalent of five football fields, and another features a waterfall spilling into a stream stocked with trout. Others show off museum-quality taxidermy work. Shoppers stop to marvel at a mountain populated by a grizzly bear, caribou, and big-horn sheep or a display of an African savannah with two lions attacking a zebra. Each store contains about 400 displays, some of which cost more than $10,000. Cabela's may be the only company in the world to have an executive whose title is taxidermy purchasing specialist! Obviously a hit with its prime target audience—men who enjoy the outdoors—Cabela's also is popular with their wives and children because of the expanded line of gifts and clothing it offers.[31]

Successful entertailers rely on the following principles:

- *Sponsor events that will attract your target customers.* One goal of entertailing is to get potential customers into the store. An upscale men's clothing store could offer a workshop on personal finance and investing or how to pull off "business casual" dress appropriately.

- *Give customers the opportunity to interact with your products.* One golf store has an indoor putting green where customers can try out new putters before buying them. A sporting goods retailer has a 20-foot rock wall that allows climbing enthusiasts to test climbing gear.

- *Use technology creatively.* One golf retailer has invested in a golf course simulator that allows customers to "play" some of the world's most famous courses. A landscape architect uses computer software that allows him to landscape digital photographs of his customers' homes so that they can see exactly how different designs look.

- *Remember that the ultimate goal is to sell.* No matter which entertailing techniques you decide to use, remember to design them with the goal of increasing sales.[32]

STRIVE TO BE UNIQUE   One of the most effective guerrilla marketing tactics is to create an image of uniqueness for your business. As you learned in Chapter 3, Strategic Management and the Entrepreneur, entrepreneurs can achieve a unique place in the market in a variety of ways, including through the products and services they offer, the marketing and promotional campaigns they use, the store layouts they design, and the business strategies they employ. The goal is to stand out from the crowd; few things are as uninspiring to customers as a "me-too" business that offers nothing unique.

ENTREPRENEURIAL PROFILE

Bridget Hobson: Quiplip Inc.

In an industry dominated by giant companies such as Hallmark and Gibson, entrepreneur Bridget Hobson, founder of Quiplip Inc., has found a way to stand out in the greeting card business. Rather than create the standard sentimental cards decorated with flowers or pictures of serene mountain streams, Hobson sells a line of cards with sharp, sometimes caustic, but always funny messages. Quiplip's Graphitude series uses charts and graphs to convey messages. One card shows a pie chart with "food," "sleep," "shelter," and "you" sectors; the biggest wedge, of course, is "you." A birthday card from Quiplip's Blunt line asks, "Did I at least get the month right? Happy Birthday." The message on a get well card is, "Can I try some of your painkillers? Get well soon." Hobson decided to launch Quiplip after experiencing difficulty finding cards that suited her personality; sales, which are growing rapidly, have surpassed $400,000. "There are so many warm and fuzzy cards out there," she says. "I [thought] there had to be a niche for these drier sarcastic cards."[33]

CONNECT WITH CUSTOMERS ON AN EMOTIONAL LEVEL   Closely linked to creating a business identity that resonates with customers is the strategy of creating an emotional attachment with customers. Companies that establish a deeper relationship with their customers than one based merely on making a sale have the capacity to be exceptional guerrilla marketers. These businesses win because customers receive an emotional boost every time they buy these companies' products or services. They connect with their customers emotionally by supporting causes that are important to their customer base, taking exceptional care of their customers, surpassing customers' expectations in quality and service, or making doing business with them a fun and enjoyable experience. Building and nurturing an ongoing relationship with customers establishes a relationship of trust, a vital component of every marketing effort. The Cone Cause Evolution and Environmental Survey reports that 69 percent of Americans consider a company's business practices when making purchase decisions.[34]

The goal is to transform customers into "fansumers," people who not only purchase a company's products or services but also promote them to friends, family members, and others. Innocent Drinks, the London-based company that makes smoothies and other fruit-based drinks, created thousands of fansumers with a promotion that involved asking customers to knit tiny hats, which it placed on its drink bottles. The company donated 50 pence to a charity that provides warm clothes for senior citizens for each "hatted" drink it sold. After customers posted photos of their drink hats on photo-sharing site Flickr, Innocent Drinks received more than

400,000 hats in one year![35] Companies such as Innocent Drinks that connect emotionally with their customers turn them into fans who promote the company extensively—and at no cost.

One important aspect of connecting with customers is defining the company's **unique selling proposition (USP)**, a key customer benefit of a product or service that sets it apart from its competition. To be effective, a USP must actually *be* unique—something the competition does not (or cannot) provide, as well as compelling enough to encourage customers to buy. Unfortunately, many business owners never define their companies' USP, and the result is an uninspiring "me-too" message that cries out "buy from us" without offering customers any compelling reason to do so.

A successful USP answers the critical question every customer asks: "What's in it for me?" A successful USP should express in no more than 10 words what a business can do for its customers. Can your product or service save your customers time or money, make their lives easier or more convenient, improve their self-esteem, or make them feel better? If so, you have the foundation for building a USP. For instance, the owner of a quaint New England bed and breakfast came up with a four-word USP that captures the essence of the escape her business offers guests from their busy lives: "Delicious beds, delicious breakfasts." Shmuel Gniwisch, CEO of Ice.com, an online jewelry store, expresses his company's USP quite simply: "We are a candy store for women." Sheila Paterson, co-founder of Marco International, a marketing consulting firm, says her company's USP is "Creative solutions for impossible marketing problems."[36]

The best way to identify a meaningful USP that connects a company to its target customers is to describe the primary benefit(s) its product or service offers customers and then to list other, secondary benefits it provides. A business is unlikely to have more than three top benefits. When describing the top benefits the company offers its customers, entrepreneurs must look beyond just the physical characteristics of the product or service. Sometimes the most powerful USP is the *intangible or psychological* benefit a product or service offers customers—for example, safety, security, acceptance, status, among others. Entrepreneurs must be careful, however, to avoid stressing minuscule differences that are irrelevant to customers. It is also important to develop a brief list of the facts that support your company's USP—for example, 24-hour service, a fully trained staff, awards won, and so on. By focusing the message on these top benefits and the facts supporting them, business owners can communicate their USPs to their target audiences in meaningful, attention-getting ways. Building a firm's marketing message around its core USP spells out for customers the specific benefit they get if they buy that product or service and why they should do business with your company rather than with the competition. Finally, once a small company begins communicating its USP to customers, it has to fulfill the promise! Nothing erodes a company's credibility as quickly as promising customers a benefit and then failing to deliver on that promise.

Many small companies are finding common ground with their customers on an issue that is becoming increasingly important to many people: the environment. Small companies selling everything from jeans to toothpicks are emphasizing their "green" products and are making an emotional connection with their customers in the process. Customers feel good about doing business with companies that manufacture products according to "green" principles, support environmental causes, donate a portion of their pre-tax earnings to philanthropic organizations, and operate with a clear sense of fulfilling their social responsibility.

Kevin Schwartz, owner of BabyGanics, an 11-employee company in Oceanside, New York, that makes safe, environmentally friendly household cleaning products, has watched his company grow at triple-digit rates with annual sales surpassing $1 million. In a powerful demonstration of his company's USP, Schwartz often fills a glass with one of the company's products and drinks it to prove how safe BabyGanics cleaning products are. "It definitely makes the point," he says. "My cleaners taste bad, like soap really, but they're safe to drink." Schwartz, whose products are available in 2,000 retail stores nationwide, has found a way to tap into the $250 billion "green" market, which experts estimate is growing at an impressive 10 percent per year, and to connect with his customers on an emotional level.

CREATE AN IDENTITY FOR YOUR BUSINESS THROUGH BRANDING One of the most effective ways for entrepreneurs to differentiate their businesses from the competition is to create a unique identity for it through branding. Although they may not have the resources to build

unique selling proposition (USP)
a key customer benefit of a product or service that sets it apart from the competition; it answers the critical question every customer asks: "What's in it for me?"

ENTREPRENEURIAL PROFILE

Kevin Schwartz: BabyGanics

a brand name as well known as Coca-Cola, entrepreneurs can be successful in building a brand identity for their companies on a smaller scale in the markets they serve. "Every element that you use to interact with the customer is part of your brand and your story," says Seth Godin, entrepreneur and author of numerous marketing books. "If you build your brand right, you won't need to allocate more funds for marketing."[37]

branding

communicating a company's unique selling proposition (USP) to its target customers in a consistent and integrated manner.

Branding involves communicating a company's unique selling proposition to its target customers in a consistent and integrated manner. A brand is a company's "face" in the marketplace, and it is built on a company's promise of providing quality goods or services to satisfy multiple customer needs. A brand sends an important message to customers; it signals that the benefits a company offers (which may be intangible) are worth more than those its competitors can offer. Companies that build brands successfully benefit from increased customer loyalty, the ability to command higher prices, greater visibility, and increased name recognition. Small companies that attempt to lure customers with discounts or constant sales often dilute their brands and cheapen them in the customers' eyes. "A brand is the most valuable piece of real estate in the world," says one marketing expert, "[It is] a corner of the customer's mind."[38]

ENTREPRENEURIAL PROFILE

David Oreck: Oreck Corporation

David Oreck, founder of the vacuum cleaner manufacturer that bears his name, has spent 45 years building his company's brand by emphasizing the power, durability, and light weight of its vacuum cleaners. "We don't sell the cheapest product on the market," says Oreck, acknowledging that Oreck vacuum cleaners sell at prices that are 33 percent higher than many competitors' models. "But price is only one component of value. Customers want value. If they have confidence in your brand, they'll pay a premium for it."[39]

Figure 8.1 shows the connection between a company's brand and its unique selling proposition.

EMBRACE SOCIAL NETWORKING. Online technology allows companies and their customers to engage in ways that were not possible before, and smart entrepreneurs are using that technology to their advantage. Although sites such as Facebook and MySpace (both of which are among the 10 most popular Web site in the United States) are better known for their personal applications, they also have the potential as marketing tools. Facebook remains a popular site among college students, but more than half of its 53 million users are over the age of 25.[40] That changing demographic has prompted the company to add several business-oriented features, including a survey tool that allows business users to conduct market research and an advertising function that lets businesses create Facebook pages, connect with potential customers, and promote their products and services. In addition to reaching Web-savvy customers, social networking sites allow entrepreneurs to market their companies at little or no cost.

FIGURE 8.1

The Connection between Branding and a USP

Source: Based on Brandsavvy, Highlands Ranch, Colorado.

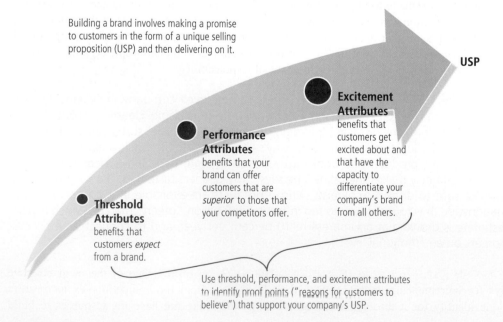

Building a brand involves making a promise to customers in the form of a unique selling proposition (USP) and then delivering on it.

USP

Excitement Attributes
benefits that customers get excited about and that have the capacity to differentiate your company's brand from all others.

Performance Attributes
benefits that your brand can offer customers that are *superior* to those that your competitors offer.

Threshold Attributes
benefits that customers *expect* from a brand.

Use threshold, performance, and excitement attributes to identify proof points ("reasons for customers to believe") that support your company's USP.

YOU Be the CONSULTANT

A Business Makeover

Kundan Sabarwal started her family-run beauty salon, Ziba (which means "beautiful" in Persian), in 1986 in a converted storage area in a building in the Little India section of Artesia, California. What the small company lacked in image, it made up for in service. Sabarwal and her staff specialize in the Eastern art of threading, an ancient form of hair removal that involves rolling a cotton thread over unwanted hairs and gently pulling them out one row at a time. Ziba also creates intricate henna tattoos known as *mehndi* (temporary tattoos made from a reddish-brown paste derived from the henna plant that have been popular with Asian women for centuries) and makeovers, both common practices for brides and their bridal parties. On a typical Saturday morning, Ziba had a line of customers, mostly Asian women, stretching out the door and onto the sidewalk.

As the company's customer base grew, so did its sales, reaching $2.5 million in 2001. Sabarwal's daughter, Sumita Batra, had a grander vision for Ziba. She realized that threading was on the verge of extending beyond the Asian subcultures of the United States and entering mainstream culture. In addition, celebrities such as Madonna, Gwen Stefani, Naomi Campbell (all of whom are Ziba customers), and others were popularizing henna tattoos. "We had all the markers of success," says Batra. "We had long waits and a very loyal group of customers who kept asking us to open in their city." Her goal was to open Ziba stores in upscale shopping malls, but mall managers balked. Batra eventually opened four Ziba stores but had to settle for locations in strip shopping centers near the mall locations she really wanted.

The new locations were successful in raising the small company's visibility and attracting a broader array of customers. By 2005, annual sales had reached $5 million, but Batra realized that Ziba was not reaching its full potential. The stores lacked a uniform look and did not have the "polished" appearance that she wanted. She eventually convinced her reluctant family members to borrow $2.8 million to transform Ziba from a less than polished business relegated to strip mall locations into a slick, mall-worthy upscale threading business with a meaningful brand.

One key factor that works in Ziba's favor is its unique concept, particularly threading, an area in which the company had developed a solid reputation over nearly 20 years and faces very little competition. Batra has discovered only one other upscale threading company, Shobha, which has three locations in New York City. "It was almost as if [Batra] was branding threading itself," says Mario Ciampi, a retail consultant whom Batra hired to help with the Ziba's metamorphosis.

Batra wonders whether the significant amount of floor space that hair and makeovers take up in its existing stores would be better spent on threading, which accounts for 90 percent of the company's total sales. Existing stores naturally have an Indian look both inside and outside, but Batra wants the Ziba brand to emphasize the company's focus on beauty rather than on the founding family's national heritage. New stores, which Batra insists be located in upscale malls, are to be a tangible expression of the company's new brand. Her goal is to open 51 Ziba stores by 2012.

Batra also wants to change Ziba's pricing structure to reflect its more upscale image. As a result, she is considering raising the price of a basic threading treatment from $9 to $11 but worries that her customers will complain, or worse, leave. Transforming a business is

Ziba Beauty

no easy task and carries with it many risks, but Batra is undeterred. "I really believe in this concept," she says.

1. What steps can Batra take to enhance the Ziba brand and build customer recognition of it? Refer to Figure 8.2, connection between branding and a unique selling proposition (USP), and use the table below to:
   a. List threshold, performance, and excitement attributes for Ziba.
   b. Identify "proof points," reasons for customers to believe in the brand, that support each of the attributes you list.
   c. Use the attributes and their proof points to develop a unique selling proposition (USP) for Ziba.

Threshold Attributes	Performance Attributes	Excitement Attributes
Threshold Proof Points	**Performance Proof Points**	**Excitement Proof Points**

USP:

2. Visit the company's Web site at www.zibabeauty.com to learn more about Ziba, the services it offers, and its culture. Work with a team of your classmates to develop a list of guerrilla marketing techniques that the company can use to promote its services and its brand. What physical attributes can the company incorporate into the design of its new stores to reinforce its brand?
3. What recommendations can you offer Batra about raising Ziba's prices?

Source: Adapted from Nitasha Tiku, "Trading Up: How a Shop in Little India Became a Sleek Brand," *Inc.*, August 2008, pp. 27–28; Sumita Batra, "The Power of 11," *Ziba Magazine*, Spring 2008, p.7.

ENTREPRENEURIAL PROFILE_____

Sabena Puri: Junnoon

When Sabena Puri, owner of Junnoon, an upscale Indian restaurant in Palo Alto, California, realized that most of her customers socialized with one another on Facebook, she created a profile page for the restaurant on the popular site. Puri included photos, reviews by food critics, and a link to Amazon.com, where customers can purchase a cookbook written by Junnoon's executive chef. Within months, nearly 100 people signed up to be "fans" of Junnoon, and they began posting comments about their meals at the restaurant and making reservations. Creating the page cost Puri nothing, and she plans to promote the Junnoon Facebook page with e-mails to 5,000 existing customers.[41]

START A BLOG A Web log ("blog") is a frequently updated online personal journal that contains a writer's ideas on a multitude of topics and links to related sites. The proliferation of blogs has been stupendous; everyone from teenagers to giant corporations has created a blog. Technorati, a company that tracks blogs, estimates that 113 million blogs exist online (5,000 of them from businesses) in 81 languages with 120,000 more being added daily.[42] Business blogging can be an effective part of a guerrilla marketing strategy, enabling an entrepreneur to communicate with large numbers of customers very economically. Blogs give small companies the ability to establish a personal connection with their customers at virtually no cost. They also attract the attention of existing and potential customers and boost a company's visibility and its sales. Companies post their blogs, promote them on their Web sites and on other blogs, and then watch as the viral nature of the Web takes over with visitors posting comments and e-mailing their friends about the blog. In fact, many small companies allow customers to contribute to their blogs, offering the potential for one of the most valuable marketing tools: unsolicited endorsements from satisfied users. Blogging's informal dialogue is an ideal match for small companies whose culture and style also are casual. Despite the guerrilla marketing benefits of blogging, only 11 percent of small business owners actively use blogs to connect with their customers, and 45 percent of business owners never use blogs.[43]

The following tips can help entrepreneurs implement a successful blogging strategy:

- *Be honest, balanced, and interesting when writing a blog.* High-pressure sales pitches do not work in the blogger's world. Telling an interesting "inside story" about the company, its products or services, or some aspect of the business attracts readers.
- *Post blog entries consistently so that readers have a reason to return.*
- *Ask customers for feedback.* Blogs are powerful tools for collecting real-time market research inexpensively.
- *Strive to cultivate the image of an expert or a trusted friend on a topic that is important to your customers.* In his blog, the owner of a company that installs water gardens posts tips for maintaining a healthy water garden and answers questions that his readers post.
- *Use services such as Google Alerts that scan the Web for a company's name and send e-mail alerts when it finds posts about a company.* Technorati also provides a search engine that scours blogs for company names. Entrepreneurs must monitor the online "buzz" about their companies; if they discover negative comments, they can address the issues in their blogs. Web analyst and author Pete Blackshaw says, "About 60 percent of Americans are putting content on the Web, and it can affect how your product or service is perceived in the marketplace."[44]
- *Promote the blog via e-mail and promotional Web sites.* When entrepreneur and venture capitalist Guy Kawasaki launched his blog, he sent out 10,000 e-mail announcements about it to the people who had contacted his company in the previous nine years. He also promoted his blog through Feedburner, a Web site that publicizes blogs, podcasts, and other content.[45]

ENTREPRENEURIAL PROFILE_____

Robb Duncan: Dolcezza

Robb Duncan, owner of Dolcezza, a small company that sells fresh hand-made gelato in the Washington, D.C., suburb of Georgetown, created a blog to promote his business. "We've never done any ads or promoting because we can't afford it," says Duncan. "It's guerrilla marketing, and it's free." When Duncan blogged about the gelato giveaway at the grand opening of his second location, more than 1,000 customers showed up! In a recent blog, Duncan described his weekly trip to the Perrydell Farm Dairy and the fresh ingredients that make the company's gelato so delicious.[46]

Blendtec

CREATE ONLINE VIDEOS Video hosting sites such as YouTube give innovative entrepreneurs the opportunity to promote their businesses at no cost by creating videos that feature their company's products and services in action. Unlike television ads, uploading a video to YouTube costs nothing, and, in some cases, the videos reach millions of potential customers. The Pew Internet and American Life Project reports that 19 percent of Internet users watch videos online every day.[47]

To market their companies successfully on YouTube, entrepreneurs should:

- *Think "edutainment."* Some of the most successful online videos combine both educational content and entertainment. Michael Harrosh, founder of Sierra Snowboard in Sacramento, California, created a nine-minute video about how to wax a snowboard properly that was downloaded 23,000 times and resulted in increased traffic on Sierra's Web site.[48]
- *Be funny.* A common denominator among many successful online videos is humor. For businesses, the key is to link the humor in the video to the company's product or service and its customer benefits. Tom Dickson, CEO of Blendtec, a maker of commercial blenders in Orem, Utah, created a series of videos called "Will It Blend?" that have catapulted his company into the spotlight. In the short videos, Dickson, outfitted in a white lab coat and safety goggles, has blended a multitude of objects ranging from light bulbs, marbles, a golf club—even an iPhone! At the end of the videos appears the tag line "Yes, it blends." The videos have drawn more than 60 million downloads, and Blendtec's sales have increased 700 percent, from $5 million to $40 million.[49]
- *Connect with current events.* Tying videos to current events keeps them timely, interesting, and relevant to potential customers.
- *Involve their customers.* Some small businesses have delegated the task of creating videos that promote their companies to their customers. Doing so not only allows them to sidestep the cost and technical issues of creating a video, but it also engages their customers and connects them with the company in unique ways. Moe's Southwest Grill, a chain of quick-serve Mexican restaurants in Atlanta, launched a "Burrito in Every Hand" campaign that encouraged customers to submit short videos designed to promote the company's products among its primary target audience of 18- to 25-year-olds. More than 200,000 customers went online to vote for their favorite videos, and the contest's winners, four rappers "Notorious M.O.E. and Nacho Daddy," won a burrito a week for the next 55 years.[50]
- *Keep it short.* For a video to produce maximum benefit, it should be between one and three minutes long. Short videos are more viral than long ones.

FOCUS ON THE CUSTOMER Too many businesses have lost sight of the important component of every business: the customer. Wooing disillusioned customers back will require businesses to focus on them as never before. Businesses must realize that everything in the business—even the business itself—depends on creating a satisfied customer. One entrepreneur says, "If you're not taking care of your customers and nurturing that relationship, you can bet there's someone else out there who will."[51]

Businesses are discovering the true cost of poor customer relations. *The Retail Customer Dissatisfaction Study 2006*, conducted by the Jay H. Baker Retailing Initiative at the University of Pennsylvania and consulting firm Verde Group, reports that:

- Only six percent of shoppers who experience a problem contact the company to complain. Most customers do not take the time to complain; they simply go away and never come back.

- Thirty-one percent tell family members, friends, and colleagues about their negative experience.
- Six percent of those people tell their "horror stories" to six or more people.
- For every 100 customers who have a negative experience with a business, the company stands to lose 32 to 36 current customers or potential customers.[52]

Paula Courtney, president of the Verde Group, says that this negative word-of-mouth advertising has exponential power. "As people tell the story, the negativity is embellished and grows. Storytelling hurts retailers and entertains customers."[53]

Because about 20 percent of a typical company's customers account for about 80 percent of its sales, it makes more sense to focus resources on keeping the best (and most profitable) customers than to spend them chasing "fair weather" customers who will defect to any better deal that comes along. Suppose that a company increases its customer base by 20 percent each year, but it retains only 85 percent of its existing customers. Its effective growth rate is just 5 percent per year [20% − (100% − 85%) = 5%]. If this same company can raise its customer retention rate to 95 percent, its net growth rate *triples* to 15 percent [20% − (100% − 95%) = 15%].[54]

Although winning new customers keeps a company growing, keeping existing ones is essential to success. Research shows that repeat customers spend 67 percent more than new customers. In addition, attracting a new customer actually costs the typical business *seven to nine times* as much as keeping an existing one.[55] Therefore, small business owners would be better off asking "How can we improve customer value and service to encourage our existing customers to do more business with us?" than "How can we increase our market share by 10 percent?" The *real* key to marketing success lies in a company's existing customer base!

ENTREPRENEURIAL PROFILE

Chico's

At Chico's, a clothing store targeting women of the baby-boomer generation (the average age is 52) in middle- to upper-income brackets, customers who purchase at least $500 in merchandise become members of Chico's Passport Club, which gives them a variety of perks, including a five percent discount on all purchases. The Club has more than 1.9 million members, who account for a whopping 83 percent of the company's sales. Chico's management is well aware of the benefits of retaining these loyal customers. Passport Club members spend, on average, $111 per visit, which is 40 percent more than nonmembers, and come in three to six times as often.[56]

customer experience management (CEM)
the process systematically creating the optimum experience for the customers every time they interact with the company.

The most successful small businesses have developed a customer focus and have instilled a customer satisfaction attitude *throughout* the company. They understand that winning customers for life requires practicing **customer experience management (CEM),** systematically creating the optimum experience for their customers every time they interact with the company. Small companies cannot always be leaders in creating product or technology innovations. However, because their size allows them to have more personal contact with their customers than large companies, small companies can develop *experience* innovations that keep customers coming back and create a competitive advantage. The goal is to create a total customer experience that is so positive that customers keep coming back and tell their friends about it.

Companies with world-class CEM attitudes set themselves apart by paying attention to "little things" such as responding to questions or complaints promptly, remembering a customer's unique product or service preferences, or sending a customer a copy of an article of interest to him or her. Taking care of every small interaction a company has with its customers over time adds up to a positive service experience and can create a strong bond with them. For example, after Dr. Peter Polack, an opthamologist in Ocala, Florida, performs corrective LASIK surgery on his patients, he sends each one a $25 gift certificate to Barnes & Noble with a card that says "Enjoy your new eyesight!" The unexpected surprise reinforces customers' positive service experience with the doctor's practice and enhances its brand awareness.[57] How do these companies manage their customer relationships and stay focused so intently on their customers? They constantly ask customers four basic questions and then act on what they hear:

1. What are we doing right?
2. How can we do that even better?
3. What have we done wrong?
4. What can we do in the future?

Table 8.3 offers some basic strategies for developing and retaining loyal customers.

TABLE 8.3 Strategies for Developing and Retaining Loyal Customers

- Identify your best customers and give them incentives to return. Focus resources on the 20 percent of customers who account for 80 percent of sales.

- When you create a dissatisfied customer, fix the problem *fast*. One study found that, given the chance to complain, 95 percent of customers will buy again *if* a business handles their complaints promptly and effectively. The worst way to handle a complaint is to ignore it, to pass it off to a subordinate, or to let a lot of time slip by before dealing with it. Shortly after luxury car maker Lexus introduced the new ES 350 model, managers discovered that about 700 cars had a small transmission problem that was the result of a factory error. Lexus contacted the affected owners and asked them to take their cars to their local dealers, where they received brand new Lexus 350s—no questions asked. Surveys of these customers that were conducted later showed that they were *more* loyal to Lexus than buyers whose cars did not have the problem in the first place.

- Make sure your business system makes it easy for customers to buy from you. Eliminate unnecessary procedures that challenge customers' patience.

- *Encourage* customer complaints. You can't fix something if you don't know it's broken. Find out what solution the customer wants and try to come as close to that as possible. Smart companies learn from customer complaints and use the feedback to make improvements in their products, services, and processes.

- Contact lost customers to find out why they left. You may uncover a problem you never knew existed.

- Ask employees for feedback on improving customer service. A study by Technical Assistance Research Programs (TARP), a customer service research firm, found that front-line service workers can predict nearly 90 percent of the cases which produce customer complaints. Emphasize that *everyone* is part of the customer satisfaction team.

- Get total commitment to superior customer service from top managers—and allocate resources appropriately.

- Allow managers to wait on customers occasionally. It's a great dose of reality. Ron Shaich, founder of Panera Bread, a chain of bakery cafes with 1,185 locations in 40 states, still visits stores regularly, where he works the cash registers and serves customers so that he can listen to their ideas and concerns.

- Carefully select and train *everyone* who will deal with customers. Never let rude employees work with customers.

- Develop a service theme that communicates your attitude toward customers. Customers want to feel they are getting something special.

- Reward employees "caught" providing exceptional service to the customer.

- Get in the habit of calling customers by name. It's one of the most meaningful ways of connecting with your customers.

- *Remember*: The customer pays the bills. Special treatment wins customers and keeps them coming back.

Sources: Adapted from: Brandi Stewart, "Able Baker," *FSB*, December 2007/January 2008, pp. 53–58; Jerry Fisher, "The Secret's Out," *Entrepreneur*, May 1998, pp 112–119; Laura M. Litvan, "Increasing Revenue With Repeat Sales," *Nation's Business*, January 1996, pp. 36–37. "Encourage Customers To Complain," *Small Business Reports*, June 1990, p. 7; Dave Zielinski, "Improving Service Doesn't Require A Big Investment," *Small Business Reports*, February 1991, p. 20; John H. Sheridan, "Out of the Isolation Booth," *Industry Week*, June 19, 1989, pp. 18–19; Lin Grensing-Pophal, "At Your Service," *Business Start-Ups*, May 1995, pp. 72–74; Bill Taylor, "Lessons from Lexus: Why It Pays to Do the Right Thing," *Mavericks at Work*, December 12, 2007, http://www.mavericksatwork.com/?p=102.

DEVOTION TO QUALITY In this intensely competitive global business environment, quality goods and services are a prerequisite for success—and even survival. According to one marketing axiom, the worst of all marketing catastrophes is to have great advertising and a poor quality product. Customers have come to expect and demand quality goods and services, and those businesses that provide them consistently have a distinct competitive advantage. Research by Josh Gordon, author of *Selling 2.0*, shows that almost 60 percent of customers who change suppliers say they switched because of problems with a company's products or services.[58]

total quality management (TQM)
the philosophy of producing a high quality product or service and achieving quality in every aspect of the business and its relationship with the customer; the focus is on continuous improvement in the quality delivered to customers.

Today, quality is more than just a slogan posted on the company bulletin board; world-class companies treat quality as a strategic objective—an integral part of a company's strategy and culture. This philosophy is called **total quality management (TQM)**—quality not just in the product or service itself, but also in *every* aspect of the business and its relationship with the customer and *continuous improvement* in the quality delivered to customers.

Companies on the cutting edge of the quality movement are developing new ways to measure quality. Manufacturers were the first to apply TQM techniques, but retail, wholesale, and service organizations have seen the benefits of becoming champions of quality. They are tracking customer complaints, contacting "lost" customers, and finding new ways to track the cost of quality (COQ) and their return on quality (ROQ). ROQ recognizes that, although any improvement in quality may improve a company's competitive ability, only those improvements that produce a reasonable rate of return are worthwhile. In essence, ROQ requires managers to ensure that the quality improvements they implement will more than pay for themselves.

The key to developing a successful TQM philosophy is seeing the world from the customer's point of view. In other words, quality must reflect the needs and wants of the customer. How do customers define quality? According to one survey, Americans rank the quality of a product in this order: reliability (average time between failures), durability (how long it lasts), ease of use, a known or trusted brand name, and, last, low price.[59] When buying services, customers look for similar characteristics: tangibles (equipment, facilities, and people), reliability (doing what you say you will do), responsiveness (promptness in helping customers and in solving problems), and assurance and empathy (conveying a caring attitude). For example, the owner of a very successful pest-control company offers his customers a unique, unconditional guarantee: If the company fails to eliminate all insect and rodent breeding and nesting areas on a client's premises, it will refund the customer's last 12 monthly payments and will pay for one year's service by another exterminator. The company has had to honor its guarantee only once in 17 years.

Companies that excel at providing quality products and services discover tangible benefits in the form of increased sales, more repeat customers, higher customer retention, and lower costs. Small businesses that have succeeded in building a reputation for top quality products and services rely on the following guidelines to "get it right the first time":

- Build quality into the process; don't rely on inspection to obtain quality.
- Foster teamwork and dismantle the barriers that divide departments.
- Establish long-term ties with select suppliers; don't award contracts on low price alone.
- Provide managers and employees the training needed to participate fully in the quality improvement program.
- Empower workers at all levels of the organization; give them authority and responsibility for making decisions that determine quality.
- Get managers' commitment to the quality philosophy. Otherwise, the program is doomed. Describing his leadership role in his company's TQM philosophy, one CEO says, "People look to see if you just talk about it or actually do it."[60]
- Be willing to make changes in processes wherever they may be necessary.
- Pay attention to the little things. A study by the Chinese University of Hong Kong reports that when customers do not know how to evaluate the quality of a service, they use external cues such as the appearance of the parking lot or the cleanliness of the floors to make inferences about quality.[61] In other words, first impressions of a business really do register with customers.
- Reward employees for quality work. Ideally, workers' compensation is linked clearly and directly to key measures of quality and customer satisfaction.
- Develop a company-wide strategy for constant improvement of product and service quality.
- Back up the company's quality pledge with a guarantee. Jim and Suzanne Faustlin, owners of The Maids Home Service franchise in Tucson, Arizona, have built a successful business by emphasizing the quality of their cleaning services. Their maids clean floors "the old fashioned way"—on their hands and knees, and the company offers a quality guarantee. 100 percent satisfaction or the customer receives a re clean at no charge.[62]

ATTENTION TO CONVENIENCE Ask customers what they want from the businesses they deal with and one of the most common responses is "convenience." The average workweek in the United States has increased to 42.5 hours, up from 37.5 hours in 2003, leaving customers less time to shop.[63] In this busy, fast-paced world of dual-career couples and lengthy commutes to and from work, convenience is a significant criterion for many customers, and companies that provide it have a competitive advantage. Several studies have found that customers rank easy access to goods and services at the top of their purchase criteria, which is one reason that Internet sales continue to grow at impressive rates. Unfortunately, many businesses fail to deliver adequate levels of convenience, and they fail to attract and retain customers. One print and framing shop, for instance, alienated many potential customers with its abbreviated business hours—9 to 5 daily, except for Wednesday afternoons, Saturdays, and Sundays, when the shop was closed! Other companies make it a chore to do business with them. In an effort to defend themselves against unscrupulous customers, these businesses have created elaborate procedures for exchanges, refunds, writing checks, and other basic transactions. One researcher claims, "What they're doing is treating the 98% of honest customers like crooks to catch the 2% who are crooks."[64]

Successful companies go out of their way to make sure that it is easy for customers to do business with them. To provide their customers with more a more convenient way to order, many restaurants are accepting online orders. According to the National Restaurant Association, 11 percent of restaurant customers ordered online in 2005; today, 18 percent of restaurant customers do so. "I see it going well over 50 percent, especially if text-message ordering takes off," says Sheri Daye Scott, editor of *QSR*, a magazine that tracks the restaurant industry.[65] Papa John's, the pizza chain, says that online ordering has generated more than $1 billion in total sales since the company began offering the option in 2001. Today 20 percent of Papa John's franchisees' orders originate either online or as text-messages.[66] Online ordering may encourage customers to spend more. The owner of a small Asian takeout restaurant in Minneapolis, Minnesota, says that her company's average sale has increased 25 percent since she began accepting online orders.[67]

"I don't like the security chain any more than you do. Now, quit complaining and come try this one on."

Source: www.cartoonstock.com

How can entrepreneurs boost the convenience level of their businesses? By conducting a "convenience audit" from the customer's point of view to get an idea of its ETDBW ("Easy-to-Do-Business-With") index:

- Is your business located near your customers? Does it provide easy access?
- Are your business hours suitable to your customers? Should you be open evenings and weekends to serve them better?
- Would customers appreciate pick-up and delivery service? The owner of a restaurant located near a major office complex installed a Web site and a fax machine to receive orders from busy office workers; a crew of employees delivers lunches to the workers at their desks!
- Does your company make it easy for customers to make purchases on credit or with credit cards?
- Are your employees trained to handle business transactions quickly, efficiently, and politely? Waiting while rude, poorly trained employees fumble through routine transactions destroys customer goodwill.
- Does your company offer "extras" that make customers' lives easier? With a phone call to one small gift store, a customer in need of a special gift simply tells how much she wants to spend, and the owner takes care of the rest – selecting the gift, wrapping it, and shipping it. All the customer has to do is pay the invoice when it arrives in the mail.
- Can you "bundle" some of your existing products or services to make it easier for customers to use them? Whether it involves gardening tools or a spa treatment, assembling products and services into ready-made, all-in-one kits appeals to busy customers and can boost sales.
- How can technology enable your company to offer greater convenience? London Elise, owner of Soothe Spa, a skin-care studio and spa in San Francisco, recently implemented a service that allows customers to book appointments on the company's Web site. Elise no longer has to play "telephone tag" with customers over appointment times, says the new system has "fundamentally changed the landscape of my business."[68]
- Can you adapt existing products to make them more convenient for customers? When J. M. Smucker Company began test-marketing a pre-made, frozen peanut butter and jelly sandwich, CEO Tim Smucker was amazed at the results. The sandwiches, called Uncrustables, generated $20 million in sales, and Smucker now sells them nationwide.[69]
- Does your company handle telephone calls quickly and efficiently? Long waits "on hold," transfers from one office to another, and too many rings before answering signal to customers that they are not important. Jerre Stead, CEO of Ingram Micro Inc., a distributor of computer products, expects every telephone call to the company to be answered within three seconds![70]

CONCENTRATION ON INNOVATION Innovation is the key to future success. A survey by the National Federation of Independent Businesses reports that 78 percent of small business owners believe that adding innovative products and services is important to their companies' success.[71] Markets change too quickly and competitors move too fast for a small company to stand still and remain competitive. Because they cannot outspend their larger rivals, small companies often turn to superior innovation as the way to gain a competitive edge. "Never stop innovating or taking risks," says Michael Dell, founder of Dell Computer. "Keep raising the bar, not just for the industry but for yourself."[72]

Innovation is one of the hallmarks of entrepreneurs, and it shows up in the new products, unique techniques, and unusual marketing approaches they introduce. Despite their limited resources, small businesses frequently are leaders in innovation. "How do small businesses manage to maintain their leadership role in innovating new products and services? They use their size to their advantage, maintaining their speed and flexibility much like a martial arts expert does against a larger opponent. Their closeness to their customers enables them to read subtle shifts in the market and to anticipate trends as they unfold. Their ability to concentrate their efforts and attention in one area also gives small businesses an edge in innovation. One venture capitalist explains, "Small companies have an advantage: a dedicated management team totally focused on a new product or market."[73]

Rawlings Sporting Goods, founded in 1887 by George and Alfred Rawlings, began supplying baseball gloves to the major leagues in 1919, when it introduced the first modern glove, one which separated the thumb and forefinger with laces and formed a deep pocket. (Prior baseball mitts were no more than padded work gloves.) Nearly 90 years later, two Rawlings product managers were discussing the properties of double-walled aluminum baseball bats, which can flex more than single-walled bats to create a burst of energy when striking a ball. One of the managers asked, "Why not multiple walls for a glove?" an idea that led Rawlings to develop its latest innovation in baseball gloves, the Primo. The Primo adds a third layer of leather inside the glove that has shapes and channels cut into it that form a pocket that can be customized for both a particular position (shortstop, first base, etc.) and for an individual player. The innovative glove, which is made of supple Italian leather and requires no breaking in, takes two days to produce and sells for $400. "To stay on top, we continually have to come up with better gloves," says Ted Sizemore, the company's chief liaison with major league players.[74]

DEDICATION TO SERVICE AND CUSTOMER SATISFACTION Customer service has become a lost art in our society, and the penalties associated with providing poor customer service can be severe. A recent survey by America's Research Group reports that 25 percent of shoppers say that they have walked out of a store because of poor customer service.[75] A recent Harris Poll reports that 80 percent of customers say that they will never return to a business after a negative customer service experience.[76] Lost sales are only the beginning of a company's woes, however. Unhappy customers are likely to tell their poor service stories to family members and friends. A study by the Jay H. Baker Retailing Initiative at the University of Pennsylvania reports that 48 percent of shoppers say that they will not patronize stores where they know that other customers have had bad service experiences.[77] Most of these customers never complain; in fact, for every complaint that a company receives, there are 17 other complaints that go unspoken.[78] These disgruntled customers exact revenge over their poor treatment, however. These days, a company that provides poor service may find itself being panned on a YouTube video, a blog, a chat room, or a Web site. "Sales starts a customer relationship," says one customer service expert. "Service turns it into a profitable or unprofitable relationship."[79]

Successful businesses recognize that superior customer service is only an intermediate step toward the goal of customer _satisfaction_. These companies seek to go beyond customer satisfaction, striving for _customer astonishment_! They concentrate on providing customers with quality, convenience, and service as their customers define those terms.

Tom Button, John Gear, and Larry Polster, owners of Kadey-Krogen Yachts, a company whose boats sell for between $800,000 and $2.3 million, decided that providing stellar customer service is the pathway to increased sales and profitability. "Most companies increase revenue by building more or cutting costs," says Polster. "We're taking a different approach." The owners capped the number of yachts they produce annually at 15 so that the staff of 15 employees could stay very close to their customers. When customers' yachts are delivered, a Kady-Krogen captain spends as much time as necessary teaching the owners how to handle and care for them. Everyone in the company pampers customers, including the owners. For instance, Button recently drove 300 miles from the company's headquarters in Stuart, Florida, to install a new battery in a customer's yacht. Because Kady-Krogen treats its customers like members of the family, the company sponsors periodic "Trawler Fests," where happy customers gather to cruise, socialize, and learn about the company's latest innovations. Kady-Krogen also offers courses on navigation and boat handling for owners (some designed specifically for women), and a newsletter called _WayPoints_ profiles both new and existing customers and their yachts. Polster acknowledges that providing extra customer service costs more, but the increased customer loyalty that Kady-Krogen has created with superior service has enabled the company to sell its boats at higher prices, which has resulted in total revenue growth of 20 percent per year.[80]

Certainly the least expensive—and the most effective—way to achieve customer satisfaction is through friendly, personal service. Numerous surveys of customers in a wide diversity of industries—from manufacturing and services to banking and high tech—conclude that the most important element of service is "the personal touch." Calling customers by name; making attentive, friendly contact; and truly caring about their needs and wants is much more essential than any other factor—even convenience, quality, and speed! In our society, business transactions have become so automated that the typical customer is starved for personal attention. *The Retail Customer Dissatisfaction Study* by the Jay H. Baker Retail Initiative at the University of Pennsylvania and consulting firm Verde Group reports that 33 percent of shoppers say that they were unable to find a salesperson to help them. Many of those customers also say that they would not return to the store.[81] Genuine customer service requires that a business bridge that service gap, treat each customer as an individual, and transform "high-tech" applications into a "high-touch" attitude.

Smart entrepreneurs see customer service as an *investment* that builds long-term value for their companies. How can a company achieve stellar customer service and satisfaction?

Listen to customers. The best companies constantly listen to their customers and act on what they hear. This allows them to keep up with customers' changing needs and expectations. The best way to find out what customers really want and value is to ask them. Businesses rely on a number of techniques including surveys, focus groups, telephone interviews, comment cards, suggestion boxes, toll-free hotlines, and regular one-on-one conversations (perhaps the best technique). Cirrus Design, a maker of small airplanes, relies on the input of the 2,500 members of its Cirrus Owners and Pilots Association for advice on how to improve the design and quality of its airplanes. Cirrus airplanes feature many ideas that originated with its customers, which fuels the company's continuous improvement efforts.[82] The Internet is another useful tool for getting feedback from customers; many companies solicit complaints, suggestions, and ideas very inexpensively through their Web sites.

It is important for entrepreneurs to keep customer feedback in its proper perspective, however. Although listening to customers does produce valuable feedback for business owners in many areas, it is *not* a substitute for an innovative company culture, solid market research, and a well-devised marketing plan. Companies that rely solely on their customers to guide their marketing efforts often find themselves lagging the competition. Customers rarely have the foresight to anticipate market trends and do not always have a clear view of how new products or services could satisfy their needs.

Define superior service. Based on what customers say, managers and employees must decide exactly what "superior service" means in the company. Such a statement should: 1) be a strong statement of intent, 2) differentiate the company from others, and 3) have value to customers. Deluxe Corporation, a printer of personal checks, defines superior service quite simply: "Forty-eight hour turnaround; zero defects."[83]

Set standards and measure performance. To be able to deliver on its promise of superior service, a business must establish specific standards and measure overall performance against them. Satisfied customers should exhibit at least one of three behaviors: loyalty (increased customer retention rate), increased purchases (climbing sales and sales per customer), and resistance to rivals' attempts to lure them away with lower prices (market share and price tolerance).[84] Companies must track their performance on these and other service standards and reward employees accordingly.

Examine your company's service cycle. What steps must a customer go through to get your product or service? Business owners often are surprised at the complexity that has seeped into their customer service systems as they have evolved over time. One of the most effective techniques is to work with employees to flowchart each component in the company's service cycle, including *everything* a customer has to do to get your product or service. The goal is to look for steps, policies, and procedures that are unnecessary, redundant, or unreasonable and eliminate them.

Hire the right employees. The key ingredient in the superior service equation is *people*. There is no substitute for friendly, courteous sales/service representatives. "You can't create world-class customer care if you hire run-of-the-mill employees," says customer service expert Ron Zemke.[85] Business owners must always be on the lookout for employees who are empathetic, flexible, articulate, creative, and able to think for themselves.

Train employees to deliver superior service. Successful businesses train *every* employee who deals directly with customers; they don't leave customer service to chance. Superior service

service companies devote 1 to 5 percent of their employees' work hours to training, concentrating on how to meet, greet, and serve customers. David Friedfeld, president of ClearVision Optical, an eyewear distributor in Hauppauge, New York, established an on-site training university for his employees that provides 100 hours of training annually, much of it in customer service. "Every employee is responsible for customer service," says Friedfeld. ClearVision Optical also invests in measuring its customer service ratings by sending surveys to customers every 60 days.[86]

Empower employees to offer superior service. One of the most important variables that determines whether employees deliver superior service is the degree to which they perceive they have permission to do so. The goal is to push decision making down the organization to the employees who have contact with customers. This includes giving them the latitude to circumvent "company policy" if it means improving customer satisfaction. If frontline workers don't have this power to solve disgruntled customers' problems, they fear being punished for overstepping their boundaries and become frustrated—and the superior service cycle breaks down. To be empowered, employees need knowledge and information, adequate resources, and managerial support.

Treat employees with respect and show them how valuable they are. Satisfied employees tend to create satisfied customers. "There's a definite proven connection between employee happiness and customer happiness," says JoAnna Brandi, a customer service consultant. In fact, one study reports that a one percent change in employee morale results in a two percent change in customer satisfaction.[87]

ENTREPRENEURIAL PROFILE

Don Slivensky: MicroTek Computer Labs

Don Slivensky, CEO of MicroTek Computer Labs, a computer training company, understands the connection well and works hard to keep his employees happy. In the past, Slivensky has paid for employees' honeymoons, provided down payments for employees to purchase homes, and sent $500 gift cards to workers expecting babies. "If people are happy," he says, "they enjoy taking care of customers."[88]

Use technology to provide improved service. The role of technology is not to create a rigid bureaucracy but to free employees from routine clerical tasks, giving them more time and better tools to serve customers more effectively. Ideally, technology gives workers the information they need to help their customers and the time to serve them.

Caravan, a woman's clothing boutique in New York City, assembles "wish lists" for its customers and then sends e-mail notices to boyfriends and husbands before significant events such as birthdays, Christmas, or anniversaries. The e-mails include photographs of the items and brief descriptions and suggestions such as, "Perhaps your mother-in-law could buy her the matching necklace and earrings."[89]

Use mystery shoppers to measure customer service. Mystery shoppers are people whom a company pays to pose as regular customers but are trained to observe and later report on the quality of the customer service employees provided. They report on the time their transaction took to complete, how attentive and knowledgeable employees were, whether employees greeted them, whether the salesperson suggested items related to the one purchased, and many other behaviors.

Reward superior service. What gets rewarded gets done. Companies that want employees to provide stellar service must offer rewards for doing so. A study by the National Science Foundation concluded that when pay is linked to performance, employees' motivation and productivity climb by as much as 63 percent.[90]

Get top managers' support. The drive toward superior customer service will fall far short of its target unless top managers support it fully. Success requires more than just a verbal commitment; it calls for managers' involvement and dedication to making service a core company value. Achieving customer satisfaction must become part of the strategic planning process and work its way into every nook and cranny of the organization. Once it does, employees will be able to provide stellar customer service with or without a checklist of "do's and don'ts."

View customer service as an investment, not an expense. The companies that lead the way when it comes to retaining customers view the money they spend on customer service as an investment rather than an expense. One of the most effective ways for entrepreneurs to learn this lesson is to calculate the cost of poor customer service to their companies. Once they calculate it, the cost of lost customers due to poor service is so astonishing to most business owners that they quickly become customer service zealots. For instance, the owner of a small restaurant calculated that if every day he lost to poor service one customer who spent just $5 per week, his business was losing $94,900 in revenue per year! The restaurateur immediately changed his approach to customer service.

EMPHASIS ON SPEED Technology, particularly the Internet, has changed the pace of business so dramatically that speed has become a major competitive weapon. Today's customers expect businesses to serve them at the speed of light! Providing a quality product at a reasonable price once

HANDS ON... HOW TO

Ask the Ultimate Question

Although Tony Hartl's Dallas-based chain of 13 tanning salons and spas generates $10 million in revenue each year and is profitable, the 40-year-old entrepreneur knew that his company, Planet Tan, was facing an important challenge: customer service. "The success of tanning salons is heavily based on the customer experience," he says. "That's the differentiator." Hartl attempted to measure Planet Tan's customer satisfaction level with a lengthy survey that took 30 minutes to complete. The response rate was a paltry 3 percent, and the results were of little value. Then Hartl discovered a simple tool for measuring a company's customer service level called the Net Promoter Score (NPS). Developed by Fred Reichheld, a consultant for Bain and Company, the NPS asks customers just two questions:

1. How likely are you to recommend our company to friends and colleagues?
2. If you would not recommend us, why not?

On question 1, the NPS uses a 1 (not at all likely) to 10 (highly likely) scale. Customers who respond with nines and tens are considered "promoters," those who are so delighted with a company's service that they readily tell others about it. Customers who score a company with sevens and eights are "passives." Any customer who rates a company below a seven is considered to be a "detractor." To calculate its NPS, a company subtracts the percentage of detractors from the percentage of promoters. Reichheld says that the NPS is a nearly ideal measure of a company's reputation in the marketplace and its ability to attract new customers and to retain existing ones. Most companies have NPS values between 10 and 20; in fact, the average NPS score for companies in the United States is 15. Companies with scores above 50 tend to be known for providing superior customer service, but the best businesses score a commanding 80 to 90. Bain and Company's research shows that a company's promoters are responsible for 80 percent of new customer referrals, which makes them a driver of a typical small company's revenue. "Our research reveals that in most industries, the firms with the highest NPS scores have the strongest profits and healthiest growth," explains Reichheld. According to Reichheld, when companies increase their NPS scores, their revenues also increase.

According to research by Bain, 80 percent of managers believe that their companies provide superior customer service, but only 8 percent of their customers agree. "Most customers of the average firm—more than two-thirds—are either passive about the company or are downright detractors," Reichheld explains. "Once you find out who they are and why they're ticked off, you can take [corrective] action." NPS is an effective measure because it

forces everyone in the company to focus on creating satisfied customers. "If customers are willing to promote you, that's the clearest indication of loyalty," says Reichheld. "If they're not going to promote you, follow up with more questions to determine why. Build a dialogue that turns them into promoters."

NPS surveys are ideal for small businesses. They are easy and inexpensive to administer by telephone, mail, e-mail, or in person. Response rates also tend to be high—20 to 30 percent compared to 10 percent or less for traditional surveys—because, unlike most customer satisfaction surveys, the NPS survey takes only moments to complete. The results are easy to tally, and entrepreneurs can communicate them to everyone in the company in an easy-to-understand way. Then they can identify improvements they can make in customer service to improve their companies' scores.

When Hartl sent the NPS to 11,695 of Planet Tan's customers via e-mail, 11 percent of them responded. The company's NPS was a stellar 66. Hartl was pleased with Planet Tan's score but knew that there was plenty of room for improvement. He assigned the task of contacting all of the company's detractors among himself and his managers, and the feedback they received from customers has transformed the way Planet Tan does business. For instance, in response to complaints about the complexity of the company's pricing structure, Hartl moved to a simple monthly membership. Detractors also complained about the lack of attention from staff as they left a tanning session, which prompted Hartl to introduce a new policy that he calls "post-tan affirmation." As customers leave, employees now say things such as, "You got some good color today" or "Can I offer you some moisturizer?" Hartl's goal is to push Planet Tan's NPS score to 70. "Sure, it takes some time," he says, "but the benefits outweigh the time spent."

1. Is the Net Promoter Score an effective way to measure customer satisfaction? What are the advantages and the disadvantages of using the NPS to measure customer satisfaction?
2. Select two companies in your area, one that you consider to offer superior customer service and one that does not. Select a (preferably random) sample of customers of each company and ask them to answer the NPS survey's questions. Tally the results. What conclusions can you draw from your analysis? What recommendations would you make to the business's owner?

Sources: Adapted from Justin Martin, "Get Customers to Sell for You," *FSB*, June 2008, pp. 74–80; Darren Dahl, "Would You Recommend Us?" *Inc.*, September 2006, pp. 40–42; Russ Banham, "Angry and Bored? You Must Be a Customer," *CFO*, July 2006, pp. 62–67; Scott Thurm, "One Question, and Plenty of Debate," *Wall Street Journal*, December 4, 2006, p. B3.

was sufficient to keep customers happy, but that is not enough for modern customers who can find dozens of comparable products with a just few mouse clicks. Customers become disgruntled when companies fail to show respect for their busy schedules and corresponding lack of time. At world-class companies, speed reigns. They recognize that reducing the time it takes to develop, design, manufacture, and deliver a product reduces costs, increases quality, improves customer satisfaction, and boosts market share. A study by McKinsey and Company found that high-tech products that come to market on budget but six months late earn 33 percent less profit over five years. Bringing the product out on time but 50 percent over budget cuts profits just 4 percent![91] Service companies also know that they must build spend into their business system if they are to satisfy their impatient, time-pressured customers. Business is moving so rapidly today that companies "need to accomplish in 90 days what traditionally took a year," explains one entrepreneur.[92]

This philosophy of speed is based on **time compression management (TCM),** which involves three principles: (1) speeding new products to market; (2) shortening customer response time in manufacturing and delivery; and (3) reducing the administrative time required to fill an order. Studies show plenty of room for improvement; most businesses waste 85 to 99 percent of the time it takes to produce products or services without ever realizing it![93] Victory in this time-obsessed economy goes to the company that can deliver goods and services the fastest, not necessarily those that are the biggest and most powerful. Because small companies operate more flexibly than their larger rivals, speed can be the source of a sustainable competitive advantage for them.

time compression management
a marketing strategy that relies on three principles: 1. speeding products to market, 2. shortening customer response time in manufacturing and delivery, and 3. reducing the administrative time required to fill an order.

ENTREPRENEURIAL PROFILE _____

Kara Clayton & Joe Kortsch: Central Texas Express Metalwork

When Kara Clayton and her husband, Joe Kortsch, purchased Central Texas Express Metalwork (CTEM) in San Antonio, Texas, they decided to make speed the foundation of the company's competitive advantage. They began taking orders with quick turnaround times that larger competitors refused, and within just two years, annual sales had grown from $670,000 to $1.7 million. After completing a $45,000 rush job for a local zoo, the company later received a $500,000 contract from the zoo for another job.[94]

Although speeding up the manufacturing process is a common goal, companies using TCM have learned that manufacturing takes only 5 to 10 percent of the total time between an order and getting the product into the customer's hands. The rest is consumed by clerical and administrative tasks. "The primary opportunity for TCM lies in its application to the administrative process," says one manager. Companies relying on TCM to help them turn speed into a competitive edge should:

- "Re-engineer" the entire process rather than attempt to do the same things in the same way—only faster. Peter Schultz, founder of Symyx, a small technology company in Santa Clara, California, applied the principles of rapid drug development used in the pharmaceutical industry to the field of materials science and changed the way new chemical compounds are created. Symyx's technology allows its employees to test small amounts of chemicals and metals in parallel—up to 1,000 combinations per day—to create new materials. Processes that not so long ago required two years of intense work now produce marketable results in less time. "If you have speed advantage, you win," explains a manager at Dow Chemical Company, one of Symyx's customers.[95]
- Create cross-functional teams of workers and give them the power to attack and solve problems. In world-class companies, product teams include engineers, manufacturing workers, sales people, quality experts—even customers.
- Set aggressive goals for time reduction and stick to the schedule. Some companies using TCM have been able to reduce cycle time from several weeks to just a few hours!
- Rethink the supply chain. Can you electronically link with your suppliers or your customers to speed up orders and deliveries?
- Instill speed in the culture. At Domino's Pizza, kitchen workers watch videos of the fastest pizza makers in the country.
- Use technology to find shortcuts wherever possible. Properly integrated into a company's strategy for speed, technology can restructure a company's operating timetable. Rather than build costly, time-consuming prototypes, many time-sensitive businesses use computer aided design and computer assisted manufacturing (CAD/CAM) to speed product design and testing.
- Put the Internet to work for you. Perhaps nothing symbolizes speed better than the Internet, and companies that harness its lightning-fast power can become leaders in TCM.

The Marketing Mix

The major elements of a marketing strategy are the four Ps of marketing—**p**roduct, **p**lace, **p**rice, and **p**romotion. These four elements are interconnected, and, when properly coordinated with a solid marketing plan, increase the sales appeal of a product or service. Small business managers must integrate these elements to maximize the impact of their product or service on the consumer. All four Ps must reinforce the image of the product or service the company presents to the potential customer. One long-time retailer claims, "None of the modern marvels of computerized inventory control and point-of-sale telecommunications have replaced the need for the entrepreneur who understands the customer and can translate that into the appropriate merchandise mix."[96]

Product

The product itself is an essential element in marketing. As you learned in Chapter 1, throughout history small companies have been an important source of innovative products, a trend that continues today. For instance, many small companies are on the leading edge of wearable technology, clothing that is embedded with computer technology and performs a variety of useful and sometimes entertaining functions. Motion Response Sportswear, founded by Kerri Wallace, makes clothing that takes readings from an athlete's body and changes colors to show the intensity of his or her workout.[97]

ENTREPRENEURIAL PROFILE

Richard Helmer: Air Guitar Shirt

Richard Helmer, a research engineer for Australia's Commonwealth Scientific and Industrial Research Organization, has invented an air guitar shirt. The shirt incorporates textile motion sensors that recognize and interpret the "player's" arm positions and movements and relay it wirelessly to a computer that plays the appropriate chords. "It's an easy-to-use virtual instrument that allows real-time music making, even by players without significant musical or computing skills," says Helmer. "It allows you to jump around, and the sound generated is just like an original MP3."[98]

product life cycle

describes the stages of development, growth, and decline in a product's life.

Figure 8.2 shows the five characteristics of a great product.

Products travel through various stages of development. The **product life cycle** (see Figure 8.3) describe these stages of growth. Knowing which stage of the life cycle a product is in allows managers to make decisions about whether to continue selling the product, when to introduce new follow-up

FIGURE 8.2

Five Characteristics of a Great Product

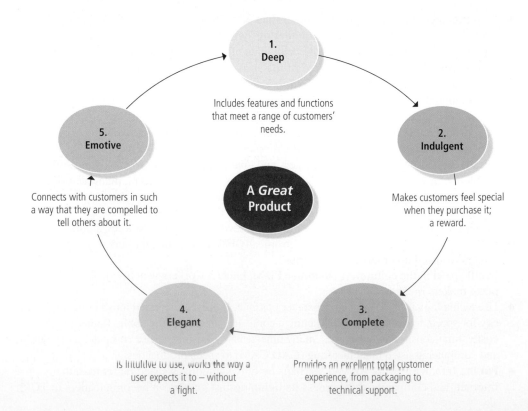

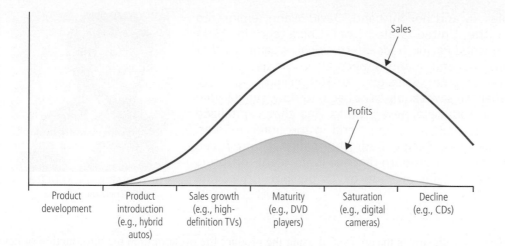

FIGURE 8.3
The Product Life Cycle

products, and when to introduce changes to an existing product. The length of a product's life cycle depends on many variables, including the type of product. Fashion clothing may have a life cycle of just a few weeks, but a video game console's life cycle typically lasts about four years.[99] The typical product's life cycle is growing shorter, however. Apple's popular iPod, which has sold a total of 140 million units in its various forms, has a life cycle of 1.5 years, down from two years just a few years ago.[100]

In the **introductory stage,** marketers present their product to potential consumers. Initial high levels of acceptance are rare. Generally, new products must break into existing markets and compete with established products. Advertising and promotion help the new product become recognized more quickly. Potential customers must get information about the product, how to use it, and the needs it can satisfy. The cost of marketing a product at this level of the life cycle is usually high because a company must overcome customer resistance and inertia. Thus, profits generally are low, or even negative, in the introductory stage.

After the introductory stage, the product enters the **growth and acceptance stage.** In the growth stage, customers begin to purchase the product in large enough numbers for sales to rise and profits to materialize. Products that reach this stage, however, do not necessarily become successful. If in the introductory or the growth stage the product fails to meet consumer needs, it does not sell and eventually disappears from the marketplace. For successful products, sales and profit margins continue to rise through the growth stage. For a video game console, the growth and acceptance stage typically takes place in the second and third year after its introduction, when economies of scale allow the maker to lower prices and when third-party developers release "must-have" games.

In the **maturity and competition stage,** sales volume continues to rise, but profit margins peak and then begin to fall as competitors enter the market. Normally, this causes reduction in the product's selling price to meet competition and to hold its share of the market. For a video game console, this stage normally takes place in the third and fourth years after the product's introduction.

Sales peak in the **market saturation stage** of the product life cycle and give the marketer fair warning that it is time to introduce the next generation product. For a video game console maker, this occurs in year five as "buzz" begins to build about the upcoming version of the product.

The final stage of the product life cycle is the **product decline stage.** Sales continue to drop, and profit margins fall drastically. However, when a product reaches this stage of the cycle, it does not mean that it is doomed to failure. Products that have remained popular are always being revised. No firm can maintain its sales position without product innovation and change. Apple's marketing strategy is to introduce iPod innovations, which so far include the Classic, the Mini, the Nano, the Shuffle, and the Touch, to make previous models "obsolete" before its competitors can. By adding enhanced features that are so appealing to users, Apple encourages them to purchase upgrades. The company's successful marketing strategy has given it a commanding 70 percent share of the MP3 player market.[101]

Some companies wait too late into the life cycle of one product to introduce another. The result is that they are totally unprepared when a competitor produces "a better mousetrap" and their sales decline. "If you are not developing something new early in the current product's life cycle, you're living on borrowed time," says Thomas Venable, owner of Spectrum Control, Inc., a maker of control systems for the electronics industry. "If you wait until your line is mature, you're dead. The whole idea behind the process is to avoid crises. You want to be ready to go with the second product just as the first one is about to die off."[102]

introductory stage
the stage in which a product or service must break into the market and overcome customer inertia.

growth and acceptance stage
the stage in which customers begin to purchase a product in large enough numbers for sales to rise and profits to materialize.

maturity and competition stage
the stage in which sales rise, but profits peak and then fall as competitors enter the market.

market saturation stage
stage in which sales peak, indicating the time to introduce the next generation product.

product decline stage
the stage in which sales continue to fall and profit margins decline drastically.

Mei Xu and her husband, David Wang, emigrated to the United States from China and in 1994 launched Pacific Trade International, a company that designs and markets decorative candles for the home market. Sales grew to $60 million a year, but when Xu saw candle sales begin to slow, she decided to introduce a new product line that capitalized on the next emerging trend in the home market: fragrances. Pacific Trade International introduced a line of potpourri and plug-in scent diffusers and saw sales increase by 15 percent in just one year.[103]

CHESAPEAK BAY CANDLE ®
— Pacific Trade International

Figure 8.4 illustrates the concept of using the product life cycle to time the introduction of new products.

Place

Place (or method of distribution) has grown in importance as customers expect greater service and more convenience from businesses. This trend is one of the forces driving the rapid growth of the Web as a shopping tool; customers simply place their orders with a few mouse clicks, and within a few days, the merchandise appears on their doorsteps! Entrepreneurs have come up with other clever ways to distribute their products and services and offer their customers more convenience. For instance, many traditionally stationary businesses have added wheels, becoming mobile animal clinics, computer shops, dentist offices, and windshield repair services. Others build on the model popularized by Tupperware in the 1950s, distributing their products through home-based parties. For instance, Susan Handley, who started Beijo Bags LLC in 2002, uses home-based parties as the primary distribution method for the stylish, functional handbags her company produces. Handley, who started in business by selling her first 300 handbags at a holiday fair, says that the company's home-based "showcase parties" generate annual sales of $10 million.[104]

Some companies intentionally limit the distribution network for their products to enhance their brands.

Deckers Outdoors, the company that makes Uggs, the sheepskin boots that have been popular with celebrities ranging from Miley Cyrus to Reese Witherspoon, who pair them with everything from jeans and shorts to skirts and bathing suits, has limited distribution to its Ugg stores and a handful of department stores and specialty shops. By making their brands scarce, companies such as Deckers Outdoors make them more desirable, increase their popularity, and extend their product life cycle. Recognizing that the rugged boot look eventually will run its course, Deckers Outdoors also has introduced casual shoes, slippers, outerwear, and accessories to capitalize on the popularity of the Ugg brand.[105]

FIGURE 8.4

**Time between
Introduction of Products**

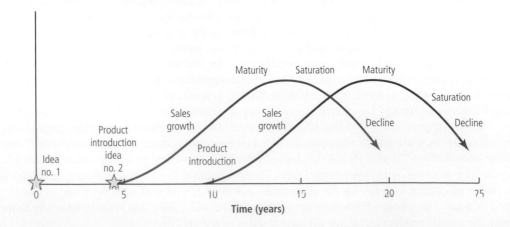

Price

Almost everyone agrees that the price of the product or service is a key factor in the decision to buy. Price affects both sales volume and profits, and without the right price, both sales and profits will suffer. For small businesses, non-price competition—focusing on factors other than price—often is a more effective strategy than trying to beat larger competitors in a price war. Non-price competition, such as free trial offers, free delivery, lengthy warranties, and money back guarantees, intends to play down the product's price and stress its durability, quality, reputation, or special features. We will discuss pricing in more detail in Chapter 10.

Promotion

The goal of promotion is to inform and persuade consumers. Advertising communicates to potential customers through some mass medium the benefits of a good or service. In addition to using traditional advertising media, small companies are turning to innovative advertising techniques that connect with customers where ever they are. For instance, in a clever guerrilla marketing campaign, White Castle, the first fast-food hamburger chain and home of the famous Slyder, partnered with Got Game Entertainment to cross-promote the action-packed "Artic Stud Poker Run" video game, in which White Castle restaurants appear. At various points in the game, players can eat White Castle Slyders to boost their strength and stamina. A demo version of the game links to Whitecastle's Web site, and the company, which has 412 outlets, placed coupons for free burgers in the game's retail boxes.[106]

A small company's promotional program can play a significant role in creating a specific image in its customers' minds—whether it is upscale, discount, or somewhere in between. "Marketing is not a battle of products; it's a battle of perceptions," says one marketing expert.[107]

Chapter Summary

1. **Describe the principles of building a guerrilla marketing plan and explain the benefits of preparing one.**

   A major part of the entrepreneur's business plan is the marketing plan, which focuses on a company's target customers and how best to satisfy their needs and wants. A solid marketing plan should:

   - Determine customer needs and wants through market research.
   - Pinpoint the specific target markets the company will serve.
   - Analyze the firm's competitive advantages and build a marketing strategy around them.
   - Create a marketing mix that meets customer needs and wants.

2. **Explain how small businesses can pinpoint their target markets.**

   Sound market research helps the owner pinpoint his target market. The most successful businesses have well-defined portraits of the customers they are seeking to attract.

3. **Discuss the role of market research and outline the market research process.**

   Market research is the vehicle for gathering the information that serves as the foundation of the marketing plan. Good research does *not* have to be complex and expensive to be useful. The steps in conducting market research include:

   - Defining the objective: "What do you want to know?"
   - Collecting the data from either primary or secondary sources.
   - Analyzing and interpreting the data.
   - Drawing conclusions and acting on them.

4. **Describe the factors on which a small business can build a competitive edge in the marketplace: customer focus, quality, convenience, innovation, service, and speed.**

   When plotting a marketing strategy, owners must strive to achieve a competitive advantage—some way to make their companies different from and better than the competition. Successful small businesses rely on eleven sources to develop a competitive edge:

   - Find a niche and fill it.
   - Use the power of publicity.
   - Don't just sell; entertain.
   - Strive to be unique.
   - Connect customers on an emotional level.
   - Create an identity for your business through branding.
   - Embrace social networking.
   - Start a blog.
   - Create online videos.

- Focus on the customer.
- Be devoted to quality.
- Pay attention to convenience.
- Concentrate on innovation.
- Be dedicated to service.
- Emphasize speed

5. Discuss the "four *P*s" of marketing—product, place, price, and promotion—and their role in building a successful marketing strategy.

The marketing mix consists of the "4 *P*s":

- Product. Entrepreneurs should understand where in the product life cycle their products are.

- Place. The focus here is on choosing the appropriate channel of distribution and using it most efficiently.
- Price. Setting the right price for a product or service is partly an art and partly a science.
- Promotion. Promotion involves both informing and persuading customers.

Discussion Questions

1. Define the marketing plan. What lies at its center?
2. What objectives should a marketing plan accomplish?
3. How can market research benefit a small business owner? List some possible sources of market information.
4. Does market research have to be expensive and sophisticated to be valuable? Explain.
5. Describe several market trends that are driving markets into the next millennium and their impact on small businesses.
6. Why is it important for small business owners to define their target markets as part of their marketing strategies?
7. What is a competitive advantage? Why is it important for a small business owner to create a plan for establishing one?
8. Describe how a small business owner could use the following sources of a competitive advantage:

   - Find a niche and fill it.
   - Use the power of publicity.
   - Don't just sell; entertain.
   - Strive to be unique.
   - Create an identity for the business.
   - Connect with customers on an emotional level.
   - Create an identity for your business through branding.
   - Embrace social networking.
   - Start a blog.
   - Create online videos.
   - Focus on the customer.
   - Be devoted to quality.
   - Give attention to convenience.
   - Concentrate on innovation.
   - Be dedicated to service.
   - Emphasize speed.

9. One manager says, "When a company provides great service, its reputation benefits from a stronger emotional connection with its customers, as well as from increased confidence that it will stand behind its products." Do you agree? Explain. If so, describe a positive service experience you have had with a company and your impressions of that business. What are the implications of a company providing poor customer service? Once again, describe a negative service experience you have had with a company and your impressions of that business. How likely are you to do business with that company again?
10. a. Consumer behavior expert and retail consultant Paco Underhill says, "A [retail] store is a 3-D brand. Everything that's there has to be there for a reason." Do you agree? Explain.

    b. Find two retail stores in the local area—one that offers a good example of a 3-D brand and one that does not. Prepare a one-page summary explaining you reasoning for selecting these two stores.
11. Explain the concept of the marketing mix. What are the four Ps?
12. List and explain the stages in the product life cycle. How can a small firm extend its product's life?
13. With a 70 percent customer retention rate (average for most U.S. firms, according to the American Management Association) every $1 million of business will grow to more than $4 million in 10 years. If a company retains 80 percent of your customers, the $1 million will grow to a little over $6 million. If a company can keep 90 percent of its customers, that $1 million will grow to more than $9.5 million. What can the typical small business do to increase its customer retention rate?

Business PlanPro™ The marketing plan section of the business plan will tell the story of the "4 *Ps*" as it supports the mission and objectives of the business.

On the Web

The Internet is an efficient tool for conducting market research. The Web can help you to determine what form of market research is going to work best for your plan. Your market research should provide specific information about your target market and the key factors that influence their buying decisions. Market research is often associated with elaborate processes conducted by third parties that demand a tremendous amount of time and money. However, casual and efficient market research can be valuable. Your business plan will benefit from even the most elementary market research, and, if it does not provide new information, that research will validate what you already know. You investment in market research may be based on the quality, cost, or the amount of time to acquire the information. Make that determination based on the value you will receive versus the time and other resources you need to invest to gain access to that information.

The Internet can help you to identify relevant industry associations. Assess what information is on the association's Web site. Does the association have publications available? What benefits do they provide to their members? What does it cost to join the association? Industry associations may be a valuable source of market research.

Excellent data are also available through U.S. Government resources and is available on the Web in the following areas:

- Small Business Administration (SBA): http://www.sba.gov
- Small Business Development Center (SBDC): http://www.sba.gov/sbdc
- U.S. Census Bureau: http://www.census.gov/
- U.S. Department of Commerce: http://www.trade.gov
- U.S. Chamber of Commerce: http://www.uschamber.com

For example, the information through the U.S. Census Bureau at http://www.census.gov provides a menu of available demographic reports that include reports on various manufacturing industries, county-specific economic surveys, business patterns for a specific zip code, and others. Additional online information is available through educational resources on community college, college, and university Web sites.

Private market research sources are plentiful on the Web. Although most provide this information for a fee, many sites offer preliminary information at no cost. One example is geocluster data called PRIZM, an acronym for "Potential Rating Index by Zip Markets." This information, available through Claritas Inc., offers descriptions of consumers by zip code and 62 distinct lifestyle groups based on education, affluence, family life cycle, urbanization, mobility, race, and ethnicity. You can look up PRIZM information by going to http://www.claritas.com/MyBestSegments and click on the "Zip Code Look-Up" tab at the top. Enter your zip code into the search window for your results. This information may be very useful—available at no cost. Other market research information is available through sites such as Zap Data at http://www.zapdata.com. Here you will find industry data reports with preliminary information, also at no charge. This information, sorted by Standard Industrial Classification code, tracks how many companies are in the industry, their average sales, the number of employees, the company size, and their locations.

The Web can also be helpful in finding publications that focus on your geographic business area. Reviewing online magazine, newspaper, and other publications may be an efficient way to search for related articles and other information. Many industry-specific magazines publish statistical editions and market reviews at regular intervals. Search the indexes to identify published information that might help the marketing section of your business plan. You may find an index listing for an article that forecasts your industry or addresses industry economics or trends. You can also contact their editorial departments for additional information.

Sample Plans

Review the marketing sections of a sample plan that you found to be helpful. Note the information regarding market segmentation, the target market, the industry, and the competitors. Notice the use of tables and graphics in these sections that illustrate this marketing information. This type of marketing information is essential to establish a solid understanding of the market your business will serve. It will establish a basis for developing and validating your marketing strategy.

In the Software

With this information in mind, review each of the following sections in your business plan.

Your Company. Does this section capture a viable marketing focus? Does this section place the necessary emphasis on valuing the customer relationship? Add to and edit your work to reflect this critical perspective.

What You Are Selling. Make certain this section presents what you are selling to your customer. It must concisely communicate this in a way that represents your customers and the value they will realize from choosing to do business with you and benefit from your products and services.

Service Summary. Think about the unique nature of the services your business provides. How will your services offer greater benefit than those of your competitors? How will your services be superior and provide meaningful value to your customers in a way that will enhance their loyalty? Address these questions in this section of your plan.

Your Market. Add new information that you have gleaned from your marketing research to describe your market in as much detail as possible.

Target Market Segment. Review the concepts in "Pinpointing the Target Market" on pages 231–233. Use those concepts to help you to develop a clear picture of your target customers. Consider writing a profile of those customers. You may want to incorporate these profiles into this section to describe your target market segment.

Competition. A thorough discussion and analysis of each of the current and potential competitor is critical. There is no substitute for this depth of analysis. The business plan must demonstrate that you have evaluated this critical factor and can identify, in realistic and practical terms, how your business will successfully compete. Demonstrate your knowledge of why customers make purchasing decisions and how your proposed venture can gain their business. Be honest and objective as you describe your competitors' strengths and weaknesses. Discuss the customer appeal, pricing strategies, advertising campaigns, and the products and services that competitors offer.

Competitive Edge. What unique attributes does your business offer that will provide real or perceived benefits for your customers? Make sure that you capture those thoughts in this section. Be as detailed as possible, and specifically explain your strategies for creating this advantage. Incorporate material from your marketing and sales plan that will show how these strategic advantages will support your sales forecast.

The Sales Forecast. Does the sales forecast appear to be realistic? Does the cost of goods sold seem accurate? Go to the narrative section of the sales forecast and explain the numbers in the sales forecast. Include any assumptions on which you have developed your sales forecast. Explain why your sales volume will change over time. Include any key events that may affect your sales and how and why they will influence the sales forecast. Developing financial forecasts using published statistics from sources such as RMA Annual Statement Studies (http://www.rmahq.org), market research, industry studies, and other sources lends credibility to you plan. Once again, you will find information and links at http://www.prenhall/scarborough.com that may be helpful.

Marketing Plan Summary. A marketing strategy should present a clear link to generate sales revenue. Use a detailed analysis and explanation of all assumptions on which the analysis rests. Your company's pricing, product distribution, and promotion plans combined should produce a unified marketing strategy.

Building Your Business Plan. Continue to build your business plan with the new information you have acquired. Step back to assess whether you have a solid understanding of your market and whether your business plan effectively communicates that knowledge.

Beyond the Classroom...

1. Interview the owner of a local restaurant about its marketing strategy. From how large a geographic region does the restaurant draw its clientele? What is the firm's target market? What are its characteristics? Does the restaurant have a competitive edge?

2. Select a local small manufacturing operation and evaluate its primary product. What stage of the product life cycle is it in? What channels of distribution does the product follow after leaving the manufacturer?

3. Visit the Web site for the Small Business Administration's "Marketing Mall" at: http://www.sba.gov/smallbusinessplanner/manage/marketandprice/index.html
   Interview a local business owner, using the resources there as a guide. What sources for developing a competitive edge did you find? What weaknesses do you see? How do you recommend overcoming them? What recommendations can you make to help the owner make better use of its marketing techniques? Evaluate the business's approach to the 4 *P*s of marketing. What guerrilla marketing strategies can you suggest to enhance current marketing efforts?

4. Contact three local small business owners and ask them about their marketing strategies. How have they achieved a competitive edge? Develop a series of questions to judge the sources of their competitive edge—a focus on the customer; using the power of publicity; devotion to quality; attention to convenience; creating an identity through branding; embracing social networking; starting a blog; creating online videos; concentration on innovation; dedication to service; and emphasis on speed. How do the businesses compare?

5. Select three local businesses (one large and two small) and play the role of "mystery shopper." How easy was it to do business with each company? How would you rate their service, quality, and convenience? Were sales people helpful and friendly? Did they handle transactions professionally and courteously? How would rate the business's appearance? How would you describe each company's competitive advantage? What future would you predict for each company? Prepare a brief report for your class on your findings and conclusions.

David Burges/Newscom

CHAPTER 9

E-Commerce and the Entrepreneur

> The Internet remains a place where you can start with nothing and
> soon challenge the gods.
> —*Mark DiMassimo*

> A good Web site gives you a competitive advantage. It is a powerful marketing tool.
> A good Web site can dramatically increase sales while a poorly executed site can
> cast your business in a negative light.
> —*Frank Farris*

Learning Objectives

On completion of this chapter, you will be able to:

1. Understand the factors an entrepreneur should consider before launching into e-commerce.

2. Explain the ten myths of e-commerce and how to avoid falling victim to them.

3. Explain the basic strategies entrepreneurs should follow to achieve success in their e-commerce efforts.

4. Learn the techniques of designing a killer Web site.

5. Explain how companies track the results from their Web sites.

6. Describe how e-businesses ensure the privacy and security of the information they collect and store from the Web.

E-commerce is creating a new way of doing business, one that is connecting producers, sellers, and customers via technology in ways that have never been possible before. The result is a new set of companies built on business models that are turning traditional methods of commerce and industry on their heads. Companies that ignore the impact of the Internet on their markets run the risk of becoming as relevant to customers as a rotary-dial telephone. The most successful companies are embracing the Internet, not as merely another advertising medium or marketing tool but as a mechanism for transforming their companies and changing *everything* about the way they do business. As these companies discover new, innovative ways to use the Internet, computers, and communications technology to connect with their suppliers and to serve their customers better, they are creating a new industrial order. In short, e-commerce has launched a revolution. Just as in previous revolutions in the business world, some old established players are being ousted, and new leaders are emerging. The winners are discovering new business opportunities, improved ways of designing work, and better ways of organizing and operating their businesses. Yet one lesson that entrepreneurs engaged in e-commerce have learned is that business basics still apply, whether a company is on the Web or not. Companies engaging in e-commerce still have to take care of their customers and earn a profit to stay in business.

In the world of e-commerce, the new business models recognize the power the Internet gives customers, whether they buy online or offline. By 2011, Web-based activity will influence more than $1 billion in offline sales.[1] Pricing, for example, has become more transparent than ever before because of the Web. The Web's global reach means that entrepreneurs can no longer be content to take into account only local competitors when setting their prices. With a few mouse clicks, customers can compare the prices of the same or similar products and services from companies across the globe. In the new wired and connected economy, the balance of power is shifting to customers, and new business models recognize this fact. Whatever products they may sell—from digital cameras and high definition televisions to cars and flowers—retailers are dealing with customers who are more informed and aware of the price and feature comparisons of the items for which they are shopping. A study by the Pew Internet and American Life Project reports that 60 percent of Americans research products and services online before buying them, up from 35 percent in 2000.[2] These informed shoppers are taking price out of the buying equation, causing retailers to emphasize other factors such as service or convenience to build long-term relationships. The connection between online and offline business runs both ways. A study by iProspect and Jupiter Research reports that 67 percent of online shoppers conduct Web searches as a result of offline exposure to a company's advertisement.[3] These trends point to the need for retailers to market their products and services by taking a multi-channel selling approach that includes the Web as one option.

A Nielsen study of global e-commerce trends reports that 86 percent of the world's online population has used the Internet to make a purchase, up from 40 percent in 2006.[4] The items purchased most often online are computer hardware and software, tickets for entertainment events, books, music (which is shifting rapidly away from CDs to digital

FIGURE 9.1

Online Retail Sales in the U.S.

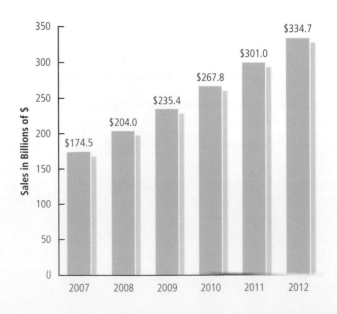

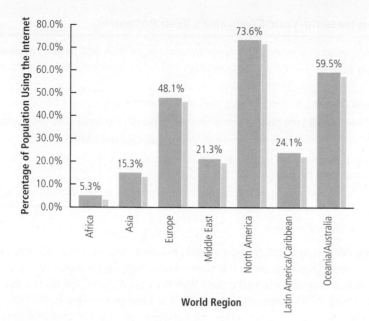

FIGURE 9.2
**World Internet
Penetration by Region**

downloads of songs), DVDs, gift cards, toys and video games, and baby products.[5] However, companies can—and do—sell practically anything over the Web, from antiques and pharmaceuticals to groceries and drug-free urine. Forrester Research estimates that 10.7 percent of total retail sales in the United States will occur online in 2012, totaling nearly $335 billion (see Figure 9.1).[6]

Companies of all sizes are busy establishing a presence on the Web because that's where their customers are. The number of Internet users worldwide now stands at nearly 1.5 billion, up from 147 million in 1998 (see Figure 9.2).[7] Consumers have adopted the Internet much more quickly than any other major innovation in the past. It reached 50 percent penetration in the United States in just seven years, compared to 30 years for the computer, 40 years for electricity, and more than 100 years for steam power.[8]

Factors to Consider before Launching into E-Commerce

The first e-commerce transaction took place on August 11, 1994, when NetMarket, a small company founded by recent college graduate Daniel Kohn, sold a CD by Sting, *Ten Summoner's Tales*, to a student at Swarthmore College for $12.48 plus shipping.[9] From these humble beginnings grew a distribution channel that now accounts for $235 billion in annual retail sales. Not every small business owner is ready to embrace e-commerce, however. According to a study by the Small Business Research Board, 57.3 percent of small business owners in the United States have Web sites, nearly double the percentage that were operating online in 1997. However, of those small business owners who have Web sites, only 56.1 percent actually engage in e-commerce.[10] Why are owners of small companies hesitant to embrace the Web as a business tool? For many entrepreneurs, the key barrier is not knowing where or how to start an e-commerce effort, while for others cost and time concerns are major issues. Other roadblocks include the fear that customers will not use the Web site and the problems associated with ensuring online security.

In the fast-paced world of e-commerce, size no longer matters as much as speed and flexibility, which tips the balance in favor of small companies. However, before launching an e-commerce effort, business owners should consider the following important issues:

- The way a company exploits the Web's interconnectivity and the opportunities it creates to transform relationships with its suppliers and vendors, its customers, and other external stakeholders are crucial to its success.
- Web success requires a company to develop a plan for integrating the Web into its overall strategy. The plan should address issues such as site design and maintenance, creating and managing a brand name, marketing and promotional strategies, sales, and customer service.

LO 1

Discuss the relationships among pricing, image, competition, and value.

TABLE 9.1 Assessing Your Company's Web Potential

Considering launching an online company or transforming a brick-and-mortar business into one with an online presence? The following questions will help you assess your company's Web potential.

1. Does your product have broad appeal to customers everywhere?
2. Do you want to sell your product to customers outside of your immediate geographical area?
3. Can the product you sell be delivered conveniently and economically?
4. Can your company realize significant cost advantages, such as lower rent, labor, inventory, and printing expenses, by going online?
5. Can you draw customers to your company's Web site with a reasonable investment?

- Developing deep, lasting relationships with customers takes on even greater importance on the Web. Attracting customers on the Web costs money, and companies must be able to retain their online customers to make their Web sites profitable. That means that online companies must give their customers good reasons to keep coming back.
- Creating a meaningful presence on the Web requires an ongoing investment of resources—time, money, energy, and talent. Establishing an attractive Web site brimming with catchy photographs and descriptions of products is only the beginning.
- Measuring the success of its Web-based sales effort is essential if a company is to remain relevant to customers whose tastes, needs, and preferences are always changing.

Table 9.1 provides a set of questions designed to help entrepreneurs assess their companies' potential to become an online success.

LO 2

Explain the twelve myths of
e-commerce and how to avoid
falling victim to them.

Ten Myths of E-Commerce

Although many entrepreneurs have made their fortunes through e-commerce, setting up shop on the Web is no guarantee of success. Scores of entrepreneurs have plunged unprepared into the world of e-commerce only to discover that there is more to it than merely setting up a Web site and waiting for orders to start pouring in. Make sure that you do not fall victim to one of the following e-commerce myths.

Myth 1. Online customers are easy to please. Customers who shop online today tend to be experienced Internet users whose expectations of their online shopping experiences are high and continue to rise. A recent survey by Forrester Research shows that 32 percent of online shoppers have been buying on the Web for seven years or more, up from 18 percent in 2003. The percentage of online shoppers who have been buying on the Web for less than one year declined to 9 percent from 16 percent between 2007 and 2008.[11] Experienced online shoppers tend to be unforgiving, quickly clicking to another site if their shopping experience is subpar or they cannot find the products and information they want. Because Web shoppers are becoming more discriminating, companies are finding that they must improve their Web sites to attract and keep their customers.

To be successful online marketers, small companies must create Web sites with the features that appeal to experienced Web shoppers, such as simple navigation, customer reviews, rock-solid security, and quick access to product information, videos, and blogs. Many small businesses outsource most (sometimes all) of the activities associated with conducting business online to companies that specialize in e-commerce services. These companies prefer to focus on their core competencies—product design, marketing, extending a brand, manufacturing, and others—and hire other companies whose core competencies reside in e-commerce to handle Web site design, hosting, order processing, and order fulfillment ("pick, pack, and ship"). Rather than make constant investments in technology that may not produce a reasonable return, these small companies preserve their capital and their energy and focus them on the aspects of business that they do best.

Having worked in the cosmetics industry for nine years, including a stint as a marketing and trends expert for a global cosmetics company, Maggie Vasilyadis was in the perfect place to spot the trend toward natural beauty products and decided to launch a part-time business to capitalize on the trend. She located vendors of natural cosmetics products, used a Web site building tool from a popular Web hosting site, registered the name Essenceology, and launched her online business within one month. Vasilyadis quickly recognized the limitations that the low-cost Web site imposed and began working with online business consulting firm ProStores on a more sophisticated site that included not only more photographs and more detailed product descriptions but also offered convenient checkout and captured information about sales patterns and customers' shopping behavior. Although Vasilyadis still has complete control over the Essenceology Web site, she has outsourced its management to ProStores. "My expertise is in the beauty industry, not in building and designing a [Web] site, she says."[12]

Other entrepreneurs prefer to keep the design and operation of their Web sites in-house.

When Jerrel Klaver decided to quit his corporate job and launch Salus, an online organic bath and body store, with his wife, Elissa, the copreneurs wanted to keep their business lean with minimal overhead expenses. The Klavers used a Web site-building package that offers full-blown e-commerce capability to launch their Web site, www.shopsalus.com. Because the package meshes with the Klavers accounting software (Quickbooks), the major credit card processing companies, and leading shipping services, it gives them seamless control over their business. To promote Salus's Web site, the Klavers also maintain a natural body care blog that is powered by WordPress, and post to the popular social networking site Twitter. Although the Klavers have been in business for little more than a year, their do-it-yourself approach to e-commerce produces annual sales that exceed $160,000.[13]

Companies that decide to operate their own e-commerce businesses quickly learn that setting up a site is only the first investment required. Sooner or later, most companies encounter follow-up investments, including updating and revising the Web site, buying more hardware to support the site, automating or expanding their supply chain to meet customer demand, integrating their inventory control system into the Web site, and increasing customer service capacity. When it comes to e-commerce, the lesson for entrepreneurs is this: Focus your efforts on the core competencies that your company has developed, whether they reside in "traditional" business practices or online, and outsource all of the other aspects of doing business online to companies that have the expertise to make your e-commerce business successful.

Myth 2. If I Launch a Site, Customers Will Flock to It. Some entrepreneurs think that once they set up their Web sites, their expenses end there. Not true! Without promotional support, no Web site will draw enough traffic to support a business. With more than 185 million Web sites in existence and the number growing daily, getting a site noticed in the crowd has become increasingly difficult.[14] Even listing a site with popular Web search engines cannot guarantee that customers surfing the Web will find your company's site. Just like traditional retail stores seeking to attract customers, virtual companies have discovered that drawing sufficient traffic to a Web site requires constant promotion—and lots of it! Setting up a Web site and then failing to drive customers to it with adequate promotional support is like setting up a physical store in a back alley; you may be in business, but nobody knows you're there!

Entrepreneurs with both physical and virtual stores must promote their Web sites at every opportunity by printing their URLs on everything related to their physical stores–on signs, in print and broadcast ads, on shopping bags, on merchandise labels, and anywhere else their customers will see. Issuing a press release that announces a company's new or revised Web site drives traffic to the site. Virtual shop owners should consider buying ads in traditional advertising media as well as using banner ads, banner exchange programs, and cross-marketing arrangements with companies selling complementary products on their Web sites. The key to promoting a Web site is *networking*, building relationships with other companies, customers, trade associations, online directories, and other Web sites your company's customers visit. Convincing other online sites to establish links to a company's site boosts its Web site's rankings among major search engines. Some entrepreneurs have increased traffic to their Web sites by selling their products on eBay and then drawing those customers to their companies' Web sites. Other techniques for promoting a site include creating some type of interactivity with customers such as e-mailing newsletters, writing articles that link to the company's site, creating podcasts, hosting a chat room that allows customers to interact with one another and with company personnel, sponsoring an online contest, or establishing a blog, a regularly updated online journal.

ENTREPRENEURIAL PROFILE

Lolita Carrico: Modern Mom

Lolita Carrico, founder of Modern Mom, a Web site and online magazine aimed at sophisticated, upscale, mostly urban mothers, has established her company as an expert in its field by garnering loads of publicity for it and promoting it everywhere where her target audience is most likely to be, including like-minded companies such as Liz Lange Maternity and Stroller Strides. Carrico says that "partnering with [not only] other online companies but also brands that are offline to reach our target audience" has proved to be "extremely successful" for Modern Mom. Carrico's *Modern Mom* newsletter goes to more than 115,000 subscribers. The site (www.modernmom.com), which includes useful articles on a multitude of topics, news, message boards, blogs, an "ask the expert" section, a retail store (of course!), and other features, attracts more than 500,000 visitors each month! "To create a Web site that resonates and attracts repeat traffic, you have to have a connection with your audience," says Carrico. Because of Carrico's highly successful promotion strategy, Modern Mom, with annual sales of $2.4 million, has experienced an impressive growth rate of 200 percent per year since its founding in 2002.[15]

As more Web users gain online access from mobile devices, entrepreneurs are making their Web sites easily accessible from cell phones and PDAs by creating dot-mobi versions of their sites. Internet research firm IDC reports that more than 1 billion people around the world access the Internet from a mobile device at least once a month.[16] However, according to mTLD Top Level Domain Ltd., the company that serves as the official global registry for mobile domain names, fewer than one percent of existing Web sites are mobile-friendly.[17] A site that carries the ".mobi" extension tells customers that it is compatible with mobile devices such as smart phones and PDAs. Entrepreneurs who want to create a Web site that is compatible with mobile devices simply register for one in the same way that they register for any other Web site. The real key, however, is formatting the mobile site so that it will appear appropriately on the small screens of mobile devices and requires navigation with only up and down keys. That typically means stripping a site down to its bare bones. (mTLD offers a free tool that allows companies to determine how well their Web sites meet dot-mobi standards.) Companies that have added mobile Web sites have seen the traffic on their sites increase by 13 percent.[18]

Myth 3. Making Money on the Web Is Easy. Promoters who hawk "get-rich-quick" schemes on the Web lure many entrepreneurs with the promise that making money on the Web is easy. It isn't. More than 80 percent of online companies say that their Web sites are profitable, but making money online requires an investment of time, energy, and a solid plan. Success online requires a sound business strategy that is aimed at the appropriate target audience and that an entrepreneur must implement effectively and efficiently—in other words, the same elements that are required for success offline. Many entrepreneurs are earning healthy profits from their Web-based businesses, but doing so takes hard work!

As thousands of new sites spring up every day, getting a company's site noticed requires more effort and marketing muscle than ever before. Attracting customers to a Web site is really no different from attracting customers to a brick-and-mortar store; entrepreneurs must define their target customers, devise a marketing plan to reach them, and offer them good value and superior customer service to keep them coming back. Successful e-tailers have discovered that comprehensive FAQ (frequently asked questions) pages, e-mail order confirmations and shipment notices, and highly visible telephone and e-mail contact information followed by quick responses enhance their reputations for online customer service.

Myth 4. Privacy Is Not an Important Issue on the Web. The Web allows companies to gain access to almost unbelievable amounts of information about their customers' online behavior. Tracking tools monitor customers' behavior while they are on a site, giving Web-based businesses the information they need to make their Web sites and their online marketing efforts more effective. Another common tool that many sites use is offering visitors "freebies" in exchange for information about themselves. Businesses that collect information from their online customers have the responsibility of keeping it secure, however. Protecting online customers' privacy has become a topic of debate among many interested parties, including government agencies, consumer watchdog groups, customers, and industry trade associations. Shoppers' privacy concerns are a limiting factor on e-commerce. *The Pew Internet & American Life Project* reports that if Internet users had more confidence in revealing their credit card numbers and other personal information online, the percentage of online buyers would increase from 66 percent to 73 percent.[19]

Companies that collect information from their online customers must safeguard their customers' privacy, protect the information they collect from unauthorized use, and use it responsibly. That means that businesses should post a privacy policy on their Web sites, explaining to customers how they intend to use the information they collect. Then they must be sure to follow it! One of the surest ways to alienate online customers is to abuse the information collected from them by selling it to third parties or by spamming customers with unwanted solicitations. BBBOnLine offers a useful resource center designed to help small business owners wanting to establish or upgrade their Web site's privacy policies (http://www.bbbonline.org/UnderstandingPrivacy/PMRC/).

Many online customers don't trust the Web sites they visit. The Digital Trust Barometer, a survey conducted by TNS Sofres, a large research company, reports that just 22 percent of U.S. adults are confident in the security of the digital technology they use.[20] One key to a successful e-commerce effort, especially for small companies that tend to be less well known, is building trust among customers. Businesses that create meaningful privacy policies and then adhere to them build that trust. Privacy *does* matter on the Web, and businesses that respect and protect their customers' privacy will win their customers' trust. Trust is the foundation on which the long-term customer relationships that are so crucial to Web success are built. Table 9.2 provides a privacy assessment tool from BBB OnLine that helps business owners determine their companies' privacy quotient.

TABLE 9.2 What's Your Company's Privacy Quotient?

Rate your company's privacy quotient on a scale of 0 (definitely not) to 10 (definitely) using the following ten questions.

1. Do you have a privacy policy posted prominently on your Web site? If so, does it meet industry guidelines?

2. Do you have internal privacy policies and procedures for securely managing customer data that you collect online?

3. Do you have established security procedures that meet or exceed industry standards?

4. Do you have a system for managing customer inquiries and complaints about privacy? Can your customers contact you easily? Do you take adequate steps to comply with customers' requests when they ask you not to contact them?

5. Have you reviewed the processes by which you collect, store, use, and transfer customers' information so that it is not misused or put at risk? Do you conduct regular privacy training for employees so that they understand your privacy policy and how to implement it?

6. Do you monitor your privacy program regularly to determine how well it works? Is someone in your company assigned responsibility for privacy enforcement?

7. Are you in compliance with the European Union Directive on Data Protection?

8. Is your Web site targeted at children? If so, do you comply with the Children's Online Privacy Protection Act?

9. Do you have a privacy policy in place for managing employee data?

10. Is someone in your company responsible for monitoring compliance with federal, state, and foreign laws that govern privacy?

Total Score

(continued)

TABLE 9.2 What's Your Company's Privacy Quotient? (*continued*)

Scoring:

Score	Grade	Comments
90–100	A	Great job! You have already done a lot of work to implement excellent privacy practices. Focus on keeping your systems and policies current.
80–89	B	Your company has made a good start on privacy. You have some work to do to get to the next level.
70–79	C	You company has taken some basic steps toward ensuring your customers' privacy, but gaps exist. You have a good bit of work to do to implement excellent privacy policies.
60–69	D	Your company is at risk. It is time to get started down the road to managing your customers' privacy properly. Study the basic steps involved in protecting your customers' privacy and start implementing them immediately.
59 and below	I	Your company is at high risk. Your privacy quotient is incomplete. Start learning about the basics of privacy management immediately to avoid potentially serious problems ahead.

Source: BizRate.com, 2000. Cited in Bronwyn Fryer and Lee Smith, ".Com or Bust," *Forbes Small Business*, December 1999/January 2000, pp. 38–49.

Myth 5. The Most Important Part of Any E-Commerce Effort is Technology. Although understanding the technology of e-commerce is an important part of the formula for success, it is *not* the most crucial ingredient. What matters most is the ability to understand the underlying business and to develop a workable business model that offers customers something of value at a reasonable price while producing a reasonable return for the company. The entrepreneurs who are proving to be most successful in e-commerce are those who know how their industries work inside and out and then build an e-business around their expertise. They know that they can hire Webmasters, database experts, and fulfillment companies to design the technical aspects of their businesses, but that nothing can substitute for a solid understanding of their industry, their target market, and the strategy needed to pull the various parts together. The key is seeing the Web for what it really is: a way to transform in a positive fashion the way they do business by serving their customers more efficiently and effectively through another channel.

Myth 6. "Strategy? I Don't Need a Strategy to Sell on the Web! Just Give Me a Web Site, and the Rest Will Take Care of Itself." Building a successful e-business is no different than building a successful brick-and-mortar business, and that requires a well-thought-out strategy. Building a strategy means that an entrepreneur must first develop a clear definition of the company's target audience and a thorough understanding of those customers' needs, wants, likes, and dislikes. To be successful, a Web site must be appealing to the customers it seeks to attract just as a traditional store's design and décor must draw foot traffic. If a Web site is to become the foundation for a successful e-business, an entrepreneur must create it with the target audience in mind.

Recall from Chapter 3 that one goal of developing a strategy is to set a business apart from its competitors. The same is true for creating a strategy for conducting business online. It is just as important, if not more important, for an online business to differentiate itself from the competition if it is to be successful. Unlike customers in a retail store, who must exert the effort to go to a competitor's store if they cannot find what they want, online customers only have to make a mouse click or two to go to a rival Web site. Therefore, competition online is fierce, and to succeed, a company must have a sound strategy.

ENTREPRENEURIAL
PROFILE

Naresh Mansukhani:
SuitYourSelf.com

In 1989, Naresh Mansukhani moved from Spain to Bridgeport, Connecticut, where he opened a retail store called In Style that sold moderately priced men's clothing. After several years, Mansukhani saw an opportunity to take his business upscale and relocated and changed the name of his shop to the Fairfield Clothiers. In 1993, he decided to utilize the newly emerging Web as a sales tool and launched a Web site, "the first one in the industry where you could buy products online," says Mansukhani. In 2002,

Mansukhani re-launched the company's Web site as SuitYourSelf.com to increase sales and extend the brand beyond the borders of Bridgeport. "The Web is important to us [because] we have access to the whole world," he says, "while retail is limited to the area you're in." Mansukhani's e-commerce strategy involves extending to online customers the same caliber of customer service that in-store customers receive. The site lists the company's full range of upscale product lines, which include Gitman and Ike Behar (shirts), Alden and Allen Edmonds (shoes), Ermenegildo Zegna and Belvest (suits), and others and features an easy-to-use search engine that attracts customers from all over the world. Mansukhani also devotes a significant portion of the site to educating customers about making wise clothing purchases. For instance, visitors can find articles on the proper care of wool garments, deciphering international shoes sizes, finding the perfect fit in a garment, and assembling a classic business wardrobe using eight building blocks. Mansukhani, who likens himself to a university professor when it comes to educating people about putting together a wardrobe, says that the SuitYourSelf.com Web site allows us "to share our philosophy with the rest of the world."[21]

Myth 7. On the Web, Customer Service Is Not as Important as It Is in a Traditional Retail Store. Many Web sites treat customer service as an afterthought, and it shows. Sites that are difficult to navigate, slow to load, or confusing will turn customers away quickly, never to return. The fact is that customer service is just as important (if not more so) on the Web as it is in traditional brick-and-mortar stores. As shoppers become more accustomed to shopping online, they have higher expectations of the sites on which they shop. One recent study by Harris Interactive reports that more than 22 percent of online shoppers said that they expect higher levels of customer service than they do in offline, traditional stores.[22]

There is plenty of room for improvement in customer service on the Web. The Harris Interactive survey cited above reveals that nearly 90 percent of Web shoppers say that they have had problems completing an online transaction. Forty-one percent of those who experienced problems either went to another site or abandoned their purchase altogether. (Another alarming result is that 84 percent of these shoppers say that they would share their negative online shopping experience with others!)[23] Shoppers' unmet expectations of superior customer service translate into a high shopping cart abandonment rate. E-commerce research company MarketLive estimates that 58 percent of Web shoppers who fill their online shopping carts abandon them without checking out.[24] Figure 9.3 shows the leading causes of shopping cart abandonment.

Perhaps the most significant actions online companies can take to bolster their customer service efforts are to create a well-staffed and well-trained customer response team, offer a simple return process, provide an easy order-tracking process so customers can check the status of their orders at any time, and offer the opportunity to chat live with a customer service representative. Currently, 27 percent of e-tailers offer live chat, which serves as a cyberspace version of a call center, where representatives answer customers' questions that go beyond the scope of the typical "FAQ" section.[25] Even small companies that lack the manpower to staff a live chat center still can provide customer-responsive chat options on

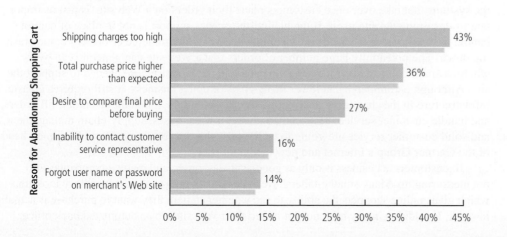

FIGURE 9.3

Reasons for Abandoning Online Shopping Carts

their Web sites by using virtual chat agents. Loaded onto a company's site, these virtual employees can step in at the appropriate time to interact with one customer or millions of customers, answering their questions or giving them the extra nudge they need—an offer of free shipping or a discount or details on how buyers can create customized assortments of nuts, for example—to close the deal.

ENTREPRENEURIAL PROFILE

Zach Bobker: Nuts on the Net

Zach Bobker, head of e-commerce at Nuts on the Net, a family-owned online retailer of gourmet nuts, says that adding a customizable virtual chat agent to the company's Web site increased sales by 10 percent. Bobker decided to add the chat agent when the company's Web site metrics showed that many customers "were coming to the site and just leaving, not giving us any information." Not only was the company losing sales, but its owners also were troubled by the poor customer service those online shoppers were experiencing. The third-generation family business has a proud heritage of staying connected to its customers. "During the holiday season, we experience an especially large flow online traffic," says Bobker. "There's no way that the family can personally connect with every buyer and remain efficient. That's where the [virtual chat] agent comes in." If a customer appears to be about to leave the company's Web site without making a purchase, the agent steps in with a special offer. "We customized what the agent says, including literature about our products and company history, and have things [such as] shipping information in there. [Everything] is consistent with what we'd say if a customer contacted us directly."[26]

Myth 8. Flashy Web Sites Are Better Than Simple Ones. Businesses that fall into this trap pour significant amounts of money into designing flashy Web sites with all of the "bells and whistles." The logic is that to stand out on the Web, a site really has to sparkle. That logic leads to a "more is better" mentality when designing a site. On the Web, however, "more" does *not* necessarily equate to "better." Keep the design of your site simple. Although fancy graphics, photographs, videos, playful music, and spinning icons may attract attention, they also can be quite distracting and very slow to download. The time required to download a Web page is one of the most important determinants of its effectiveness at selling. In fact, slow download time is the leading reason that Web users abandon sites.

To Web users, whose expectations concerning online speed continue to escalate, a good online shopping experience is a fast, uncomplicated one. For years, many e-tailers set their sights on meeting the eight-second rule, which says that if a Web page does not download within eight seconds, the user is likely to abandon the site. Today that time limit is just *four* seconds. "Customers have high expectations," says Rod Ketchum, who is in charge of the e-commerce division at outdoor equipment retailer REI. "They don't want to have to wait on the Internet, and they shouldn't have to."[27] Proper content, formatting, and design are important ingredients in determining a site's performance. Smart e-tailers periodically test their sites' performance on speed and reliability measures using a variety of online tools.

Myth 9. It's What's Up Front That Counts. Designing an attractive Web site and driving traffic to it are important to building a successful e-business. However, designing the back office, the systems that take over once customers place their orders on a Web site, is just as important as designing the site itself. If the behind-the-scenes support is not in place or cannot handle the traffic from the Web site, a company's entire e-commerce effort will come crashing down. The potentially large number of orders that a Web site can generate can overwhelm a small company that has failed to establish the infrastructure needed to support the site. Although e-commerce can lower many costs of doing business, it still requires a basic infrastructure in the channel of distribution to process orders, maintain inventory, fill orders, and handle customer service. "The companies with warehouses, supply-chain management, and solid customer service are going to be the ones that survive," says Daryl Plummer, head of the Gartner Group's Internet and new media division.[28]

To customers, a business is only as good as its last order, and many e-companies are not measuring up. Many small e-tailers' Web sites do not offer real-time inventory look-up, which gives online shoppers the ability to see whether an item they want to purchase is actually in stock. In addition, many have not yet linked their Web sites to an automated back office, which means that processing orders takes longer and that errors are more likely. As software to integrate Web sites with the back office becomes easier to use and more affordable, more small businesses will offer these features, but in the meantime these companies' reputations and sales will suffer from late shipments, incorrect orders, and poor service.

Web-based entrepreneurs often discover that the greatest challenge their businesses face is not necessarily attracting customers on the Web but creating a workable order fulfillment strategy. Order fulfillment involves everything required to get goods from a warehouse into a customer's hands and includes order processing, warehousing, picking and packing, shipping, and billing. In a study of the connection between online companies' order fulfillment processes and their ultimate success or failure, researchers Sergui Netessine, Taylor Randall, and Nels Rudi found an important link. They concluded, "If an Internet company chooses its supply chain type logically—if it's aligned with its strategy, products, and operating environment—it's highly correlated with success."[29]

Cyber Monday, touted as the busiest online shopping day of the year (actually it is not; Cyber Monday typically ranks outside the top ten in online sales volume), takes place on the Monday after Thanksgiving, when workers return to their jobs and begin their online Christmas shopping.

ENTREPRENEURIAL PROFILE

John & Kira Doyle: John & Kira's Chocolates

John and Kira Doyle's company, John & Kira's Chocolates, a Philadelphia-based maker of premium, handmade, preservative-free confections, experiences its peak sales at Christmas and again at Valentines' Day. The copreneurs use ingredients from local farms to create their exotic chocolate concoctions, such as bergamot orange, lavender honey, Glenn's raspberry, and saffron rosewater. "Our cream comes from a family farm and our honey from a part-time beekeeper," says John. The small company handled its order volume easily until John and Kira's was featured on the cover of *Gourmet* Magazine, after which orders began pouring in from across the country. Because the Doyles had built their company's Web site with growth in mind, they had the foresight to launch it using software that allowed them to integrate the vital back office operations into the site. Although the company experienced some minor growing pains, the Doyles were able to scale up their Web site to meet surging demand, much of it from large corporations ordering gifts for customers and employees. "We were able to handle the influx of orders thanks to [our integrated e-commerce software]," says John.[30]

Some entrepreneurs choose to handle order fulfillment in-house with their own employees, but others find it more economical to hire specialized fulfillment houses to handle these functions. Virtual order fulfillment (or drop-shipping) suits many e-tailers perfectly. When a customer orders a product from its Web site, the company forwards the order to its wholesaler or distributor, who then ships the product to the customer with the online merchant's label on it. This strategy allows a small business to avoid the cost and the risk of carrying inventory. Ty Simpson, founder of Ty's Toy Box, an online retailer of character-licensed toys, including Barney, Bob the Builder, Thomas and Friends, Strawberry Shortcake, Diego, The Wiggles, and many others, recently selected CommerceHub as his company's virtual order fulfillment partner.[31]

Myth 10. It's Too Late to Get on the Web. A common myth, especially among small companies, is that those businesses that have not yet moved onto the Web have missed a golden opportunity. E-commerce is still in its childhood. Companies are still figuring out how to succeed on the Web, learning which techniques work and which ones don't. One fact of e-commerce that has emerged is the importance of speed. Companies doing business on the Web have discovered that those who reach customers first often have a significant advantage over their slower rivals. "The lesson of the Web is not how the big eat the small, but how the fast eat the slow," says a manager at a venture capital firm specializing in Web-based companies.[32]

Succumbing to this myth often leads entrepreneurs to make a fundamental mistake once they finally decide to go online: They believe they have to have a "perfect" site before they can launch it. Few businesses get their sites "right" the first time. In fact, the most successful e-commerce sites are constantly changing, removing what does not work and adding new features to see what does. Successful Web sites are much like a well-designed flower garden, constantly growing and improving, yet changing to reflect the climate of each season. Their creators worry less about creating the perfect site at the outset than about getting a site online and then fixing it, tweaking it, and updating it to meet changing customer demands. "The person trying to create the perfect (online) store will fail," says Gerry Goldsholle, founder of two Web sites aimed at small companies. "Part of the Internet process is 'try it, learn from it, and fix it.' Delay is your biggest enemy. If you delay, someone else will do it."[33]

Landing Online Customers and Keeping Them

Trunkt

In 2004, Husband and wife entrepreneurs Dev Tandon and Ayasha Ahmad launched Trunkt, a design loft located in New York City's funky Tribeca district that features clothing, accessories, jewelry, gourmet food, and art from an array of independent, up-and-coming designers, to provide shoppers with unique, one-of-a-kind items that they could not find in more traditional stores. "People who are passionate about design and craftsmanship are naturally curious, much like designers are," says Ahmad. "That philosophy is a lifestyle, and the Trunkt store is a place where like-minded people can gather."

In 2005, Tandon and Ahmad launched the Trunkt Web site to complement their physical location. With their diverse array of products and designers, the copreneurs knew that their Web site had to be well organized and easy for online shoppers to use. The site allows buyers to display the collection of products based on personal preferences, such as product category, type of artisan, or designer. The results have been impressive. Tandon and Ahmad also have established groups in Twitter, created a company presence on Facebook, posted videos on YouTube, and built a popular library of blogs in their online "Reading Room." In addition, they have added widgets that are designed to help the designers and the artists whose work they sell promote their creations. With the addition of the Web site and the copreneurs' social networking efforts, Trunkt's sales reached $1 million just three years after start-up. The company is growing so fast that Tandon and Ahmad say that sales have since doubled.

GourmetStation

In 1997, Donna Lynes-Miller and her husband were trying to manage their corporate careers, restore their home that was built in 1905, and care for their pack of Russian Wolfhounds, all of which left very little time for the couple to shop and cook. Lynes-Miller hired a personal chef, who delivered to their home a variety of exquisitely prepared appetizers, soups, and entrees. In 2000, that experience inspired her to launch GourmetStation, a company that delivers gourmet dinners to busy customers in need of a dinner for a special occasion such as a birthday or anniversary or three- and four-course meals as part of a five-day meal plan. In 2002, Lynes-Miller expanded her target customers to include businesses that want to give unique gifts, incentives, and rewards.

Lynes-Miller was frustrated by the number of visitors to her Web site who either left without buying anything or who began filling a shopping cart and then abandoned it. To combat the problem, she added to her site a virtual sales agent named Jenny, who greets visitors, engages them in a "conversation" in an instant messaging window, and offers them a special incentive, such as a reduced shipping fee, in an attempt to make a sale. Using a combination of artificial intelligence and Web analytics, Jenny monitors a shopper's movements within the Web site, which allows her to provide the proper incentive to make a purchase. For example, a recent conversation with Jenny went like this:

Jenny: Hey wait! Please don't go. Just this once, we'd like to offer you an instant $10 savings discount on shipping. That's 50 percent off the regular cost of shipping if you order today. Click Here and enter "Saveship7" in the promo code box.

Customer: I'm not sure.

Jenny: GourmetStation is the premier spot for Web fine dining delivered, and we are willing to take $10 off the cost of shipping for today only! Would you like me to provide you the link back to the order page to take advantage of this amazing limited time offer?

Since Lynes-Miller added the virtual sales agent feature, which she purchased from UpSellit.com, a small Internet start-up that specializes in a niche known as chat marketing, sales have increased by more than 10 percent to $1.2 million. Lynes-Miller says that her company's shopping cart abandonment rate has decreased sharply and attributes about 12 percent of GourmetStation's sales to Jenny. In addition, by analyzing chat logs that the virtual agent software provides, Lynes-Miller has been able to identify new product lines that customers want to purchase. For instance, many customers asked Jenny about purchasing whole desserts rather than just individual servings. GourmetStation now offers whole-dessert options, and sales are growing.

1. Trunkt and GourmetStation have discovered several keys to designing effective Web sites. Use the Web to research tips on creating an effective Web site.
2. Use the Web to research mistakes that small business owners typically make when designing Web sites for their companies.
3. Visit the Web sites for these two companies and note the design elements and online marketing strategies they employ. Then go to the Web site for a business with which you are familiar and, in a brainstorming session with several of your classmates, develop a set of strategies for improving the site using what you have learned in questions 1 and 2.

Sources: Adapted from: Heather Clancy, "Do You See What I See?" *Entrepreneur*, October 2007, p. 58; Kristopher Dukes, "Trunkt Tribeca Store Opening," Fashion Wire Daily, October 14, 2005, http://www.kristopherdukes.com/2005/10/14/fashion-wire-daily-trunkt-tribeca-store-opening; Heather Clancy, "Reel 'Em In," *Entrepreneur*, July 2008, p. 48; "About Us," Gourmet Station, http://www.gourmetstation.com/cgi-bin/gourmet/aboutus.html?id=nvttAeyd; Wendy Bounds, "A Chat with Jenny—The Automated Saleswoman," *Wall Street Journal*, December 18, 2007, http://blogs.wsj.com/independentstreet/2007/12/18/a-chat-with-jenny-the-automated-web-saleswoman/?mod=WSJBlog.

Strategies for E-Success

Twenty-five percent of Americans have never known a world without Internet access.[34] For these 76.5 million people, going online is as natural as turning on the television or the microwave oven. In fact, the average person spends each 183 hours per year online, more than he or she spends reading newspapers, magazines, or books, listening to recorded music, playing videogames, or watching home videos.[35] In other words, people now spend more time online than ever before. However, converting these Web surfers into online customers requires a business to do more than merely set up a Web site and wait for the hits to start rolling up. Building sufficient volume for a site takes energy, time, money, creativity, and, perhaps most important, a well-defined marketing and promotional strategy.

Although the Web is a unique medium for creating a company, launching an e-business is not much different from launching a traditional offline company. The basic drivers of a successful business remain in place on the Web as well as on Main Street. To be successful, both offline and online companies require solid planning and a well-formulated strategy that emphasizes customer service. The goals of e-commerce are no different from traditional offline businesses—to increase sales, improve efficiency, and boost profits by serving customers better. How a company integrates the Web into its overall business strategy determines how successful it ultimately will be. Following are some guidelines for building a successful e-commerce strategy for a small company.

FOCUS ON A NICHE IN THE MARKET Rather than try to compete head-to-head with the dominant players on the Web who have the resources and the recognition to squash smaller competitors, many entrepreneurs find success serving market niches. Smaller companies' limited resources usually are better spent focusing on niche markets than trying to be everything to everyone (recall the discussion of the focus strategy in Chapter 3). The idea is to concentrate on serving a small corner of the market that the giants have overlooked. Niches exist in every industry and can be highly profitable, given the right strategy for serving them. A niche can be defined in many ways, including by geography, customer profile, product, product usage, and many others.

Because of its pervasive reach and ability to tap large numbers of customers with a common interest, the Web provides an ideal mechanism for implementing a focus strategy.

ENTREPRENEURIAL PROFILE _____

Lynn & Richard Yoss: PuzzlesUSA

PuzzlesUSA reaches around the globe to find customers who love jigsaw puzzles. The company, founded in 1999 by copreneurs Lynn and Richard Yoss, offers a full line of puzzles that range from the simplest (fewer than 100 pieces) to the extremely challenging (24,000 pieces) as well as rare, collectible puzzles. The Yosses launched PuzzlesUSA with $500,000 that came from various sources, including their own pockets, friends and family members, and a bank; annual sales are approaching $4 million. Their Web site allows customers to shop for puzzles by brand, by theme, by piece count, or by their own search criteria with a popular "quick find" option. "We were an early adapter to e-commerce and online retailing," says Lynn. "We focused on niche products that were overlooked by the big guys."[36]

DEVELOP A COMMUNITY On the Web, competitors are just a mouse click away. To attract customers and keep them coming back, e-companies have discovered the need to offer more than just quality products and excellent customer service. Many seek to develop a community of customers with similar interests, the nucleus of which is their Web site. Capitalizing on the intent of Web 2.0, these business owners are adding a social component to their Web sites, with the goal of increasing customers' loyalty by giving them the ability to interact with other like-minded visitors or with experts to discuss and learn more about topics about which they are passionate.

E-mail lists, chat rooms, customer polls ("What is your favorite sports drink?"), product ratings and reviews, blogs, guest books, and message boards are powerful tools for building a community of visitors at a site because they give visitors the opportunity to have conversations about products, services, and topics that interest them. Internet users frequent sites that embrace the social aspects of Web 2.0 and give them the opportunity to interact as part of a community with other customers and company employees.

ENTREPRENEURIAL PROFILE_____

Joey Shamah: Eyes, Lips, Face Cosmetics

Joey Shamah, founder of Eyes, Lips, Face Cosmetics (or e.l.f.), sells an array of beauty and makeup items at modest prices, some as low as $1, through his company's Web site. He knew that his small company could not afford celebrity endorsements that large cosmetics companies use but knew that his company needed to create "buzz" to succeed. He offers gift certificates to current customers who refer new customers to the e.l.f. Web site, and he created a gossip-filled blog called Ask Achelle that offers beauty tips, makes product suggestions, and invites customers to weigh in with their comments. In another section of the site, shoppers can enter information about their complexions and skin type and receive specific product recommendations. Since adding the intereactive features, e.l.f.'s e-commerce sales have increased by 50 percent, and the average time customers spend on the site has increased from four minutes to 13 minutes. "When we saw what [adding] a blog meant in terms of customer interaction, we said, 'Let's take it up a notch,' " Shamah explains.[37]

Like e.l.f, companies that successfully create a community around their Web sites turn mere customers into loyal fans who keep coming back and, better yet, invite others to join them.

Someday you be household name, Blog.

Source: Wall Street Journal,
September 8–9, 2007, p.A12.

ATTRACT VISITORS BY GIVING AWAY "FREEBIES" One of the most important words on the Internet is "free." Many successful e-merchants have discovered the ability to attract visitors to their sites by giving away something free and then selling them something else. One e-commerce consultant calls this cycle of giving something away and then selling something "the rhythm of the Web."[38] The "freebie" must be something customers value, but it does *not* have to be expensive nor does it have to be a product. In fact, one of the most common giveaways on the Web is *information.* (After all, that's what most people on the Web are after!) Creating a free online or e-mail newsletter with links to your company's site, of course, and to others of interest is one of the most effective ways of driving potential customers to a site. Meaningful content presented in a clear, professional fashion is a must. Experts advise keeping online newsletters short—no more than about 600 words. *Poor Richard's E-Mail Publishing* by Chris Pirillo (Top Floor Publishing) offers much useful advice on creating online newsletters.

ENTREPRENEURIAL PROFILE_____

Lonely Planet

To attract customers to its travel Web site, Lonely Planet, a publisher of travel books sold in more than 200 countries, offers customers travel tips and advice, articles filled with useful information, travel blogs by the authors of the books it publishes, and a free newsletter. The site's main section is "Worldguide," a handy hub that allows visitors to select a country and access an exhaustive compendium of information about it—from how to get there and the currency used to its history and culture. The "Postcard" section provides travel updates and travel warnings as well as actual messages from postcards sent in by Lonely Planet travelers. Lonely Planet recognizes that offering customers a great deal of useful travel information for free on its Web site increases the likelihood that they will purchase the company's travel books. The Lonely Planet Web site, which recently won a Webby Award (the Web equivalent of an Emmy Award, which recognizes excellence in Web design, creativity, usability, and functionality), has been a key reason that the company sells more than 6.5 million books a year.[39]

MAKE CREATIVE USE OF E-MAIL, BUT AVOID BECOMING A "SPAMMER" Used properly and creatively, e-mail can be an effective, low-cost way to build traffic on a Web site, and small business owners recognize this. According to the *The State of Retailing Online*, sending e-mail messages to existing customers is the most prevalent marketing tactic that e-commerce companies use; 91 percent of online businesses send marketing e-mails. The study confirms the reason for e-mail's popularity: The average cost per order of e-mails is $6.53, and the average customer order that e-mail marketing generates is an impressive $111.27. The average order conversion rate for e-mails is 6 percent, well above the average conversion rate of 3.15 percent for Web sites as a whole.[40] Unfortunately, spam, those unsolicited and universally despised e-mail messages (which rank below postal "junk mail" and telemarketing calls as the worst form of junk advertising), limits the effectiveness of companies' e-mail legitimate marketing efforts. Spam is a fast-growing problem on the Internet; Barracuda Networks, a company that specializes in Web and e-mail security, estimates that 90 to 95 percent of e-mails sent are spam, up from just 5 percent in 2001![41]

To avoid having their marketing messages become part of that electronic clutter, companies should rely on permission e-mails, collecting customers' and visitors' e-mail addresses (and their permission to send them e-mail messages) when they register on a site to receive a "freebie." To be successful at collecting a sufficient number of e-mail addresses, a company must make clear to customers that they will receive messages that are meaningful to them and that the company will not sell e-mail addresses to others (which should be part of its posted privacy policy). Once a business has a customer's permission to send information in additional e-mail messages, it has a meaningful marketing opportunity to create a long-term customer relationship and to build customer loyalty.

Just as with a newsletter, an e-mail's content should offer something of value to recipients. Supported by online newsletters or chat rooms, customers welcome well-constructed permission e-mail that directs them to a company's site for information or special deals. The typical company sends its customers 64 e-mails per year, an average of slightly more than one e-mail a week.[42] Junonia, a company started by Anne Kelly that sells plus-size clothing for women, relies on permission e-mail more heavily than it has in the past. "We were doing four to five e-mailings a month," says Tom Lindmeier, Junonia's e-commerce director. "Now we do two a week." As its success with e-mail grows, the company hopes to be able to reduce the number of catalogs it sends customers—currently eighteen 56-page catalogs each year. "Catalogs are very expensive to send out, but e-mail costs almost nothing," says Lindmeier.[43]

Figure 9.4 shows e-mail read and click-through rates by day of the week.

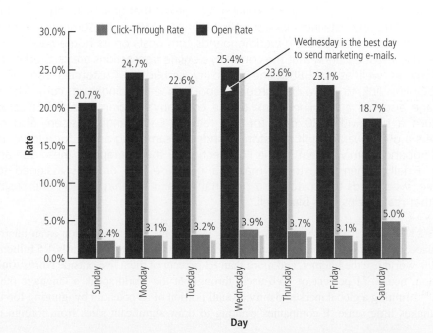

FIGURE 9.4

E-Mail Open and Click-Through Rates by the Day of the Week

MAKE SURE YOUR WEB SITE SAYS "CREDIBILITY" Online shoppers are wary, and with the prevalence of online fraud, they have every right to be. In essence, many shoppers simply do not trust Web sites. Unless a company can build visitors' trust in its Web site, selling to them is virtually impossible. Visitors begin to evaluate the credibility of a site as soon as they arrive. Does the site look professional? Are there misspelled words and typographical errors? If the site provides information, does it note the sources of that information? If so, are those sources legitimate? Are they trustworthy? Is the presentation of the information fair and objective, or is it biased? Are there dead links on the site? Does the company have its privacy and merchandise return policies posted in a prominent place?

One of the simplest ways to establish credibility with customers is to use brand names they know and trust. Whether a company sells nationally-recognized brands or its own well-known private brand, using those names on its site creates a sense of legitimacy. People buy brand names they trust, and online companies can use that to their advantage. Businesses selling lesser-known brands should use customer testimonials and endorsements (with their permission, of course) about a product or service.

Another effective way to build customer confidence is by joining an online seal program such as TRUSTe or BBBOnLine. The online equivalent of the Underwriter Laboratories stamp or the Good Housekeeping Seal of Approval, these seals mean that a company meets certain standards concerning the privacy of customers' information and the resolution of customer complaints. TopBulb.com, the company that sells every kind of light bulb imaginable, has won the BBBOnline reliability seal of approval and displays it prominently on its Web site. Providing a street address, an e-mail address, and a toll-free telephone number also sends a subtle message to shoppers that a legitimate business is behind a Web site. Another effective technique is to include an "about us" page on the Web site so that customers can read about the company's "story"—its founders, how they started the business, the challenges they have overcome, and other details. Customers enjoy supporting small businesses with which they feel a connection, and this is a perfect opportunity for a small company to establish that connection. Many small companies include photographs of their brick-and-mortar stores and of their employees to combat the Web's anonymity and to give shoppers the feeling that they are supporting a friendly small business. One small online retailer includes on his Web site short anecdotes about his dog, Cody, the official company mascot, and Cody's "views" on featured products. The response to the technique has been so strong that Cody has become a celebrity among the company's customers and even has her own e-mail address.

ENTREPRENEURIAL PROFILE

Steve Blackwell: e-weddingbands.com

Steve Blackwell, who in 1997 co-founded e-weddingbands.com, an online company that sells all types of wedding bands, loose diamonds, and bridal gifts, knew that to be successful he had to design a Web site that communicated to customers a message of trust, confidence, and credibility. Blackwell has achieved that goal by using several techniques. The company's site includes a prominent link to customer testimonials—currently 10 pages of them. In addition, e-weddingbands.com posts on its home page a certificate from GeoTrust ensuring that the company's online transactions are secured with SSL technology as well as its BBBOnline reliability certificate. Customers can click on the BBBOnline link to get a background report on e-weddingbands.com. The site's front page also has a prominent link to the company's guarantee policy: Customers can return a ring within 30 days for any reason. E-weddingbands.com also offers customers a price guarantee: If a customer finds the same ring online for a lower price, e-weddingbands.com will beat it. The FAQ section of the site repeats these guarantees as well. Finally, when a customer makes a purchase, the order is assigned to an employee, who sends the customer a personal e-mail. "It's that one-on-one customer service that really helps, says Blackwell."[44]

MAKE THE MOST OF THE WEB'S GLOBAL REACH Despite the Web's reputation as an international marketplace, many Web entrepreneurs fail to utilize fully its global reach. Nearly 1.5 billion people around the world use the Internet, and more than 83 percent of them live outside North America![45] In addition, nearly 71 percent of Web users throughout the world speak a language other than English.[46] Limiting a global market to only a small portion of its potential by ignoring foreign customers makes little sense. E-companies wanting to draw significant sales from foreign markets must design their sites with these foreign customers in mind. A common mechanism is to include several "language buttons" on the opening page of a site that take customers to pages in the language of their choice. Experienced e-commerce companies have learned that offering a localized page for every country or region they target pays off in increased sales. Doing so allows entrepreneurs to adapt the terminology they use on their sites and in their search engines to local dialects. For instance, an e-commerce company based in the United States might think it is selling diapers, but its customers in the United Kingdom are looking for "nappies."

When translating the content of their Web pages into other languages, e-companies must use extreme caution. This is *not* the time to pull out their notes from an introductory Spanish course and begin their own translations. Hiring professional translation and localization services to convert a company's Web content into other languages minimizes the likelihood of a company unintentionally offending foreign customers.

USE THE TOOLS OF WEB 2.0 TO ATTRACT AND RETAIN CUSTOMERS The social aspects of the Internet that are evident in sites such as MySpace and Facebook have become part of companies' e-commerce efforts. Known as Enterprise 2.0, these online selling techniques recognize that shoppers, especially young ones, expect to take a proactive role in their shopping experience by writing (and reading) product reviews, asking questions, posting comments to blogs, and engaging in other interactive behavior. "The number one trend impacting e-commerce is social networking," says Ken Burke, founder of e-commerce technology company MarketLive. "Consumers today are more connected to other consumers."[47] According to the Pew Internet & American Life Project, 48 percent of Internet users watch online videos, 39 percent read blogs, 30 percent post online reviews of products and services, and 16 percent participate in social networking sites.[48] Simply inviting customers to post product reviews on a site can boost sales. A study by retail consulting company J. C. Williams Group Ltd. reports that 92 percent of online shoppers in the United States say that customer reviews are very or extremely useful when making a purchase decision.[49]

Small businesses are responding to the opportunity to connect with their customers online by adding the following social media to their e-commerce strategies (See Figure 9.5):

- *Mashups.* A **mashup** is a Web site or an application that combines content from multiple sources into a single Web service. For example, Twitzu is a mashup that allows users to manage invitations and responses to events. They invite their Twitter followers to an event—the grand opening of a new location, for example—and then receive responses from guests on Twitter.
- *Really Simple Syndication (RSS).* **Really Simple Syndication** is an application that allows subscribers to aggregate content from their favorite Web sites into a single feed that is delivered automatically whenever the content is updated. RSS is ideal for companies whose customers are information junkies. "[RSS] is a must-have for any company Web site or blog because it allows people to track current news via their RSS feeds," says Louis Columbus, an expert on using social media.[50]

mashup
a Web site or an application that combines content from multiple sources.

Really Simple Syndication (RSS)
an application that allows subscribers to aggregate content from their favorite Web sites into a single feed that is delivered automatically whenever the content is updated.

FIGURE 9.5

Web 2.0 Tools

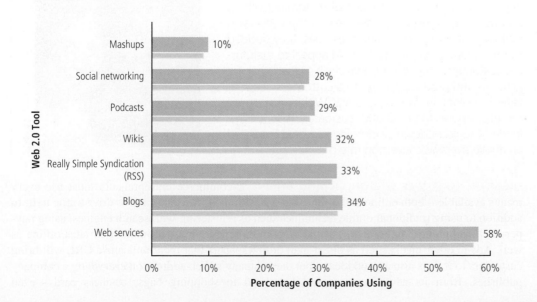

- *Social Networking.* Many small businesses attract potential customers to their Web sites by adding a social networking component that allows visitors to engage in "conversation" with one another through bulletin boards and blog.

Michelle Breyer and Gretchen Heber, co-founders of Naturallycurly.com, an online company that sells products aimed at women with curly hair, added a "CurlTalk" section to their Web site, where more than 25,000 visitors regularly engage in discussions about topics ranging from how to care for curly hair and recommendations on local hair stylists to cute nicknames for people with curly hair and their favorite celebrities. Breyer and Heber say that the cost of setting up CurlTalk was minimal but the benefits have been big; annual sales have increased to more than $1.8 million.[51]

NaturallyCurly.com, Inc.

Companies also are using existing social networking sites such as Twitter, the service that asks members to post their answers to the question "What are you doing?," to make contacts with their customers. Tony Hsieh, CEO of online shoe retailer Zappos, uses his Twitter account to update more than 14,000 followers on news about the company and its products.[52] Other companies are finding that enabling customers to post their favorite products to their MySpace and Facebook profiles can increase sales.

wiki
a dynamic collection of Web pages that allows users to add to or edit their content.

- *Wikis.* A **wiki** is a dynamic collection of Web pages that allows users to add to or edit their content. The most popular wiki is Wikipedia, the user-created online encyclopedia for which users provide the content. Some companies use wikis to encourage customers to participate in the design of their products, a process called co-creation.

widget
a low-cost application that appears like a small television screen on a Web site, a blog, or a computer desktop and performs a specific function.

- *Widgets.* Another tool that small companies use to attract attention on the Web is **widgets** (also known as gadgets), low-cost applications that appear like small television screens on Web sites, blogs, or computer desktops and perform specific functions. Entrepreneurs can create their own widgets or purchase them from developers and customize them, adding their own names, brands, and logos. Customers and visitors can download the widget to their desktops or, perhaps, post it to their own blogs or Facebook pages, where other Web users see it, and the social nature of the Web exposes the company to thousands of potential customers. A popular widget not only drives customers to a site but it also can improve a company's ranking on major search engines. "It's a great way to continually remind people that you exist," says Ivan Pope, CEO of widget developer Snipperoo.[53]

When Albert and Shannon DiPadova, the copreneurs behind Due Maternity, a retailer of maternity clothing and accessories, noticed a decrease in the conversion rate of their e-mail marketing messages, they decided to try creating a widget that would appeal to their target customers. Their countdown clock suggests helpful activities and products related to a customer's needs at various points in her pregnancy. Within just seven months, more than 30,000 customers had downloaded the countdown clock widget, which produced an above-average conversion rate of 5 percent.[54]

Due Maternity

PROMOTE YOUR WEB SITE ONLINE AND OFFLINE E-commerce entrepreneurs must use every means available—both online and offline—to promote their Web sites and to drive traffic to it. In addition to using traditional online techniques such as registering with search engines, using pay-per-click techniques, and creating blogs, Web entrepreneurs must promote their sites offline as well. Ads in other media such as direct mail or newspapers that mention a site's URL will bring customers to it. It is also a good idea to put the company's Web address on *everything* a company publishes, from its advertisements and letterhead to shopping bags, business cards—even employees' uniforms! The techniques for generating publicity for an offline business described in Chapter 8 can be just as effective for online businesses needing to make their domain names better known without breaking their budgets. A passive approach to generating Web site traffic is a recipe for failure; entrepreneurs who are as innovative at promoting their e-businesses as they are at creating them can attract impressive numbers of visitors to their sites.

DEVELOP AN EFFECTIVE SEARCH ENGINE OPTIMIZATION (SEO) STRATEGY Because of the popularity of search engines among Internet shoppers, Web search strategies have become an essential part of online companies' promotion strategies. According to *The State of Retailing Online* study, retailers say that search engine marketing continues to be the most effective way to reach new customers.[55] Given that the sheer volume of Web pages, which number well into the billions, is overwhelming, it is no surprise that Internet shoppers' first stop usually is a search engine. For a company engaged in e-commerce, a well-defined search marketing strategy is a vital part of its overall marketing strategy.

One of the biggest challenges facing e-commerce entrepreneurs is maintaining the effectiveness of their search engine marketing strategies. Because the most popular search engines are constantly updating and refining their algorithms, the secretive formulas and methodology search engines use to find and rank the results of Web searches, Web entrepreneurs also must evaluate and constantly refine their search strategies. A company's Web search strategy must recognize the three basic types of search engine results: natural or organic listings, paid or sponsored listings, and paid inclusion. Paid or sponsored listings are the most popular strategy, accounting for 87.4 percent of total search engine marketing expenditures.[56]

Natural (or organic) listings arise as a result of "spiders," powerful programs that search engines use to crawl around the Web and analyze sites for keywords, links, and other data. Based on what they find, spiders use complex algorithms to index Web sites so that a search engine can display a listing of relevant Web sites when a person enters a keyword in the engine to start a search. Some search engines use people-powered searches rather than spider-powered ones to assemble their indexes. With natural listings, landing a spot at or near the top of a search engine's results, a technique known as search engine optimization, list is important; 92 percent of search engine users click a result that appears within the first three pages of search results before conducting a different search.[57]

natural (organic) listings search engine listings that are the result of "spiders," powerful programs that crawl around the Web and analyze sites for keywords, links, and other data.

Paid or sponsored listings are short text advertisements with links to the sponsoring company's Web site that appear on the results pages of a search engine when a user types in a keyword or phrase. Entrepreneurs use paid search listings to accomplish what natural listings cannot. In fact, 90 percent of online retailers use pay-for-performance search placement.[58] Because organic listings can take months to materialize, many e-commerce companies rely on paid listings, which give them an immediate presence in search engines. Fortunately, just five search engines—Google, Yahoo, MSN/Windows Live, AOL, and Ask.com—account for about 96 percent of the searches conducted in the United States.[59] Google, the most popular search engine, displays paid listings (which companies purchase through Google Adwords) as "sponsored links" at the top and down the side of each results page, and Yahoo! shows "sponsored results" (which companies purchase through Yahoo Search Marketing) at the top and the bottom of its results pages. With this pay-for-placement method, advertisers bid on keywords to determine their placement on a search engine's results page. The highest bidder for a keyword gets the most prominent placement (at the top) on the search engine's results page when a user types in that keyword on the search engine. The advertiser pays only when a shopper clicks through to its Web site from the search engine. For this reason, paid listings also are called pay-for-placement, pay-per-click, and pay-for-performance ads. The average cost per click for keywords is 92 cents, but some words can bring as little as five cents or as much as $100![60]* Although it can be expensive, one advantage of paid listings is the ability of the advertiser to evaluate the effectiveness of the each listing. "You can track down to the individual keyword exactly what it's worth all the way to the conversion rate," says Brad Fallon of MyWeddingFavors.com, who uses paid listings to supplement his natural search listings efforts. "It's crazy not to do it."[61]

Selecting the right key words at the right price is the key to a successful pay-per-click marketing effort.

---

*An online merchant's cost per sale = cost per click ÷ merchant's conversion rate. For example, a merchant with a two percent conversion rate who submits a keyword bid of 10 cents per click is paying $5 per sale ($0.10 ÷ 0.02 = $5.00).

ENTREPRENEURIAL PROFILE

Gerri Gussin: Bluefly.com

Gerri Gussin, vice-president of marketing for online fashion retailer Bluefly.com, bids on the names of hundreds of clothing labels that the company carries on the major search engines. Gussin also pays Reprise, a search engine optimization company, to manage several thousand non-branded terms and phrases such as "cocktail dress" and "designer handbags" (including variations of words that are commonly misspelled) that customers are most likely to enter into search engines. The result is literally millions of terms on which Bluefly.com bids, but Gussin and Reprise track their search engine results in real time and make adjustments as necessary. Over time, Bluefly has built a library of key terms that produce results by keeping those that exceed the company's cost per sale and dropping the ones that do not.* Bluefly's search strategy produces $8 in sales for every $1 spent on search engine marketing.[62]

The accompanying "Hands On: How To…" feature explains how to determine the value of a keyword using a diagnostic known as the cost of acquisition.

HANDS ON... HOW TO

Determine How Much You Can Afford to Bid on That Keyword

Creating a Web site for a company without a strategy for driving traffic to it is fruitless and an incredible waste of resources. A strategy to maximize your e-company's natural listing on search engines is important, but even the best search engine strategy cannot produce top search engine rankings every time. That's why it is imperative for entrepreneurs to supplement their companies' natural listings with paid listings. With paid listings, companies pay for top-tier search results by bidding on keywords and paying for them on a per-click basis. The highest bidder for a keyword gets the most prominent placement (at the top) on the search engine's results page when a user types in that keyword on the search engine. The company pays only when a shopper clicks through to its Web site from the search engine. The cost of this technique can add up quickly, and search engines allow entrepreneurs to set spending caps on their accounts so they don't overspend.

So how much should you bid on a keyword? You have to do the math to see how much you can afford to spend. It all begins with calculating your e-company's conversion rate, the percentage of visitors to your company's Web site who actually make a purchase. Conversion rates vary from one online industry to another, but the average conversion rate is about 3.2 percent. That means that for every 1,000 visitors to a company's site, 32 of them actually make a purchase. For this example, let's assume that your company's conversion rate is 3.2 percent.

The next step is to calculate your company's profit per online sale. Like conversion rates, the profit a company earns per sale varies dramatically from one industry to another. A company that sells upscale jewelry online may generate a profit per sale of several hundreds of dollars, but a company that sells books or DVDs may make a profit of a just few dollars—or just a few pennies–per sale. For our example, let's assume that your company's profit per sale is $9.00.

To calculate the maximum amount your company could afford [to bi]d on a keyword, you use the following formula:

[Ma]ximum Keyword Bid = Conversion rate × Profit per sale

For your company, the results are:

Maximum keyword bid = 3.2% × $9.00 = $0.288 or 28.8 cents per click

This is the *maximum* amount you should be willing to bid for a keyword search term.

Suppose you bid 18 cents per click for a keyword on a popular search engine. If 1,000 shoppers click through to your Web site, your total cost of the paid listing would be $180 (1,000 shoppers clicking through × $0.18 per click = $180). With a conversion rate of 3.2 percent, you can expect 32 sales (1,000 shoppers × 3.2% conversion rate = 32 customers). If your normal profit is $9.00 per sale, these 32 sales will generate $288 in profit. Subtracting the $180 cost of acquiring these customers leaves your company with a net profit of $108. As long as your company's profit per sale is greater than its cost of acquisition, you will make money on its paid listing. Notice that the maximum bid you can afford on a keyword is sensitive to your company's conversion rate. In this example, if the company's conversion rate were 4.5 percent (rather than 3.2 percent), the maximum bid for a keyword would be 40.5 cents (4.5% × $9.00 = $0.405) rather than 28.8 cents. Similarly, if a company's profit per sale increases, the amount it can afford to bid on a keyword also goes up. In this example, a company with a 4.5 percent conversion rate and a profit per sale of $20 would have a maximum bid of 90 cents (4.5% × $20 = $0.90).

The next issue, of course, is which keywords to bid on. One way to determine the words that are most likely to drive customers to your company's Web site is to use the keyword tool on the major search engines. Simply enter a keyword, and the tool produces a report showing how many times shoppers typed in that keyword as well as other keywords related to it. For instance, a recent search for "wedding ring" on Overture's Keyword Tool revealed that shoppers typed in the phrase "wedding ring" 165,277 times. Other related terms included "titanium wedding ring," (65,992 times), "platinum wedding ring" (30,469 times), and even "cheap diamond wedding ring" (254 times). The most popular terms in the resulting lists offer clues about the ones you will want to consider bidding on. You also will want to build these words into the meta tags, text, and titles of the pages of your company's Web site to boost its ranking in natural and organic sites.

Bidding on general keywords such as "clothing" not only can cost a small company lots of money, but it also tends to bring to a Web site shoppers who are not the company's best prospects for becoming paying customers. (Imagine a small company bidding $0.18 per click on the phrase "wedding ring" and getting the 165,277 "hits" mentioned in the previous example. If all 165,277 shoppers clicked through to its site, the cost to the company would be $29,750!) A better keyword strategy is to use more specific terms such as "Western clothing" or "baby clothes" that are far less expensive per click and are more likely to attract the particular customers a company is targeting.

A common mistake entrepreneurs make is failing to bid on a sufficient number of keywords. "A lot of people bid on just the basic terms," says Brad Fallon, a search engine optimization specialist and owner of a successful e-commerce business. "They don't drill down far enough to words that might get only one search a day. If you have lots of keywords that have only a few searches

[each] and add them all together, they can produce a significant amount of business." In addition, these less popular keywords cost almost nothing but still generate sales. "You want to bid on thousands of terms," advises Fallon.

Finally, you must use Web analytics software to track the results of your paid listing campaign. Which search engines are customers using most often to enter your company's Web site? Which keywords are most successful at driving customers to your site? What impact are paid listings having on your company's conversion rate? Learning the answers to these and other related questions will help you to get the greatest return for the least investment in a paid listings strategy.

Sources: Adapted from James Maguire, "Starting Your Own E-Business, Part 4: Marketing on a Shoestring," *E-Commerce Guide*, October 24, 2005, www.ecommerce-guide.com/solutions/advertising/article.php/3558651; James Maguire, "MyWeddingFavors Shares Search Success Secrets," *E-Commerce Guide*, October 8, 2004, www.ecommerce-guide.com/solutions/advertising/article.php/3419121; Catherine Seda, "In the Click," *Entrepreneur*, August 2004, pp. 61–63.

One problem facing companies that rely on paid listings to generate Web traffic is **click fraud,** which occurs when a company pays for clicks that are generated by someone with no interest in or intent to purchase its products or services. "Clickbots," programs that can generate thousands of phony clicks on a Web site, are a common source of click fraud. The pay-per-click fraud rate is 16 percent.[63] Web analytics software can help online merchants detect click fraud, which can add significant costs to a company's search engine marketing effort. Large numbers of visitors who leave within seconds of arriving at a site, computer IP addresses that appear from all over the world, and pay-per-click costs that rise without any corresponding increase in sales are clues that a company is a victim of click fraud.

Another popular alternative to paid listings for increasing a site's visibility is a tool known as paid inclusion. In **paid inclusion,** a company pays a search engine for the right to submit either selected pages or the content of its entire Web site. (Google does not offer paid inclusion.) To keep their natural listings current, search engines regularly crawl through the Internet in the hunt for new and updated Web sites and material to include in their databases, but searching through the huge volume of pages on the Web means that it may take weeks or even months to locate a company's Web site. Because a company pays to submit its Web content into the search engine's database, a paid inclusion eliminates the necessity of waiting for a search engine to find its site. Not every search engine accepts paid inclusions, however.

click fraud
a situation that occurs when a company pays for clicks that are generated by someone with no interest in or intent to purchase its products or services.

paid inclusion
when a company pays a search engine for the right to submit either selected pages or the entire content of the Web site.

Designing a Killer Web Site

LO 4
Learn the techniques of designing a killer Web site.

Many small business owners pay little attention to the look, feel, and navigability of their Web sites, and the impression that their sites create with shoppers. "Your Web site isn't 'about' your company," says one writer. "It's an extension of your company. If it's unprofessional, you're unprofessional. If it's cluttered, you're cluttered. If it's hard to work with, you're hard to work with. By contrast, if it's well put together, smart, and easy to use, so is your company. At least that's what people will perceive. Most small business Web sites don't do their companies justice."[64]

With 185 million Web sites online and thousands more added each day, how can entrepreneurs design a Web site that will capture and hold potential customers' attention long enough to make a sale? What can they do to keep customers coming back on a regular basis? There is no sure-fire formula for stopping surfers in their tracks, but the following suggestions will help:

UNDERSTAND YOUR TARGET CUSTOMER Before launching into the design of their Web sites, entrepreneurs must develop a clear picture of their target customers. Only then will they be ready to design a site that will appeal to their customers. The goal is create a design in which customers see themselves when they visit. Creating a site in which customers find a comfortable fit requires a careful blend of market research, sales know-how, and aesthetics. The challenge for a business on the Web is to create the same image, style, and ambiance in its online presence as in its offline stores. For example, a Web site that sells discount baby clothing will have an entirely different look and feel than one that sells upscale outdoor gear.

GIVE CUSTOMERS WHAT THEY WANT Although Web shoppers are price-conscious, they rank fast delivery as the most important criteria in their purchase decisions. Studies show that online shoppers also look for a large selection of merchandise available to them immediately. Remember that the essence of the selling on the Web is providing *convenience* to customers. Sites that allow them to shop at any time of day, choose from a wide selection of products, find what they are looking for quickly and easily, and pay for it conveniently and securely keep customers coming back. Figure 9.6 shows a comparison of the online shopping features that merchants believe are important to shoppers and those that shoppers identify as most important.

SELECT AN INTUITIVE DOMAIN NAME Decide on a domain name that is consistent with the image you want to create for your company and register it. Entrepreneurs should never underestimate the power of the right domain name or universal resource locator (URL), which is a company's address on the Internet. It not only tells Web surfers where to find a company, but it also should suggest something about the company and what it does. Even the casual Web surfer could guess that the "toys.com" name belongs to a company selling children's toys. (It does; it belongs to eToys Inc., which also owns "etoys.com," "e-toys.com," and several other variations of its name.) Entrepreneurs must recognize that a domain name is part of the brand they are creating and should create the proper image for the company.

The ideal domain name should be:

- *Short.* Short names are easy for people to remember, so the shorter a company's URL is, the more likely it is that potential customers will recall it.
- *Memorable.* Not every short domain name is necessarily memorable. Some business owners use their companies' initials as their domain name (for example, www.sbfo.com for Stanley Brothers Furniture Outlet). The problem with using initials for a domain name is that customers rarely associate the two, which makes a company virtually invisible on the Web.

FIGURE 9.6

The Importance of Online Shopping Features

- *Indicative of a company's business or business name.* Perhaps the best domain name for a company is one that customers can guess easily if they know the company's name. For instance, New Pig, a maker of absorbent materials for a variety of industrial applications, uses http://www.newpig.com as its domain name. (The company carries this concept over to its toll-free number, which is 1-800-HOT-HOGS.)
- *Easy to spell.* Even though a company's domain name may be easy to spell, it is usually wise to buy several variations of the correct spelling simply because it is likely that some customers are not good spellers!

Just because you come up with the perfect URL for your company's Web site does not necessarily mean that you can use it. According to the American Registry for Internet Numbers, only 19 percent of Internet addresses available under the current IPv4 system remain available. (The IPv6 system will offer 16 billion-billion possible Internet addresses.)[65] Domain names are given on a first-come, first-serve basis. Before business owners can use a domain name, they must ensure that someone else has not already taken it. The simplest way to do that is to go to a domain name registration service such as Network Solutions' Internic at http://www.networksolutions.com/ or Netnames at http://www.netnames.com to conduct a name search. Entrepreneurs who find the domain name they have selected already registered to someone else have two choices: they can select another name, or they can try to buy the name from the original registrant or a domain name broker. When Diane Strickland, a realtor in Savannah, Georgia, discovered that the ideal domain name for her company, www.savannahmls.com, was already registered, she worked through a broker to purchase it for $2,400. Strickland was convinced that having an intuitive domain name for her company's Web site would allow her to spend less on advertising, "and it has," she says. Web analytics show that many customers who visit her site arrive by typing the URL directly into the address bar.[66]

Once entrepreneurs find an unused name that is suitable, they should register it (plus any variations of it)—and the sooner, the better! Registering is quite easy: simply use one of the registration services cited previously to fill out a form and pay the necessary fees. The next step is to register the domain name with the U.S. Patent and Trademark Office (USPTO) at a cost of $275. The USPTO's Web site (http://www.uspto.gov/) not only allows users to register a trademark online, but it also offers useful information on trademarks and the protection they offer.

MAKE YOUR WEB SITE EASY TO NAVIGATE Research shows that the leading factor in convincing online shoppers to make a purchase from a Web site is its ease of navigation. The starting point for evaluating a site's navigability is to conduct a user test. Find several willing shoppers, sit them down in front of a computer, and watch them as they cruise through the company's Web site to make a purchase. It is one of the best ways to get meaningful, immediate feedback on the navigability of a site. Watching these test customers as they navigate the site also is useful. Where do they pause? Do they get lost in the site? Are they confused by the choices the site gives them? Is the checkout process too complex? Are the navigation buttons from one page of the site to another clearly marked, and do they make sense? (One popular Web site critic says that sites with vague navigation tools are guilty of "mystery meat navigation.") Web analytics tools (more about these later in this chapter) also offer insight into how long visitors spend on a company's Web site, where they abandon the site, how they arrived, and much other valuable feedback for improving the navigability of a site.

The starting point for easy navigability involves creating the right **landing pages,** the pages on which visitors land after they click on a sponsored link in a search engine, e-mail ad, or online ad. Ideally, a landing page should have the same marketing message as the link that led to it; otherwise, customers are likely to abandon the site immediately (an occurrence that is measured by a site's "bounce rate," the percentage of visits in which customers leave a site from the landing page). A good landing page also allows customers to search or to dig deeper into the company's Web site to the products or services that they are seeking. After Joy Gendusa, owner of PostcardMania, an online postcard marketing company, customized her site's landing pages based on how the potential customer arrived at the site, she saw sales increase. Gendusa says that the site's improved landing pages have resulted in sales of nearly $500,000 in just two years.[67]

Successful Web sites recognize that shoppers employ different strategies to make a purchase. Some shoppers want to use a search tool, others want to browse through product categories, and

landing page
the page on which a visitor lands after clicking on a sponsored link in a search engine, e-mail ad, or online ad.

still others prefer a company to make product recommendations. Effective sites accommodate all three strategies in their design. Two important Web site design features that online companies often get wrong involve the mechanisms by which customers locate products and then get information about them.

Locating Products. Customers won't buy what they cannot find! Products should be easy for customers to find, no matter how many pages a Web site includes. Too often, online companies do a poor job of product categorization, listing their product lines in ways that may make sense to them but that befuddle the typical shopper. User tests can be extremely helpful in revealing product categorization problems. In addition to establishing simple product categories that reflect the way customers actually shop (for example, including categories such as business dress, business casual, sportswear, outerwear, formal wear, shoes, and accessories for a clothing store), one simple solution is to use an internal search tool. An easy-to-use internal search tool can pay for itself many times over in increased sales and higher conversion rates. In addition, an internal search tool will reveal volumes of information about which items shoppers are looking for and how they search for them, information online merchants can use in their keyword strategies for paid listings. Rather than build their own internal search engines, many online companies use Google's Site Search, which can cost as little as $100 a year, to power customer searches on their sites.

ENTREPRENEURIAL PROFILE

Jamin Arvig: Waterfilters.com

Waterfilters.net, a leading distributor of many different types of water filters, ranging from simple shower filters and ultraviolet filters to commercial and residential filters and whole-house systems made by dozens of manufacturers, began receiving complaints from customers about their inability to find the right water filter to fit their needs. "There was no doubt that many customers left our site after not finding the filters they were searching for," says Jamin Arvig, the company's director of business development. After creating an internal search engine called the Water Filter Finder using Google Site Search, Waterfilters.net saw its sales increase and its conversion rate go up by 11 percent.[68]

Getting Product Information. Once a site is designed to enable shoppers to find products easily, the next task online merchants face is to provide enough product information to convince shoppers to buy. One survey reports that 72 percent of online shoppers say that they have abandoned a Web site in favor of a competitor's site (even if the competitor's prices were higher) if they encounter incomplete product information.[69] Unlike at brick-and-mortar stores, customers cannot pick up an item, try it on, or engage a sales person in a face-to-face conversation about its features and merits. Online merchants must walk a fine line because providing too little information may fail to answer the questions customers have, causing them to abandon their shopping carts. On the other hand, providing too much information can overwhelm customers, who aren't willing to wade through reams of text just to find the answer to some basic questions. The solution is to provide basic product information in easy-to-understand terms (always including a picture of the item) and also to provide a link to more detailed information (which should be only one click away) that customers can click to if they choose. Where appropriate, photos that provide a 360-degree product view can boost conversion rates as well. Giving customers the option of enlarging a photo also helps, but the enlarged photo must be much bigger. Many Web sites make the mistake of enlarging photos by only 20 percent; a better choice is to fill the screen with a *much* bigger photo!

ADD WISH LIST CAPABILITY Giving customers the ability to create wish lists of products and services they want and then connecting other people to those lists not only boosts a company's sales but also increases its visibility.

USE ONLINE VIDEOS A study by the Pew Internet & American Life Project reports that 57 percent of online adults have either watched or downloaded a video.[70] Adding video to a Web site not only can increase customer traffic but also can increase its conversion rate.

ENTREPRENEURIAL
PROFILE _____

James Laird: Restaurant
Serenade

James Laird, owner and chef of Restaurant Serenade, an upscale restaurant in Chatham, New Jersey, sensed that the company's Web site could do more to generate sales. Initially, the site was nothing more than an online brochure, and Laird later added a "make reservations" option. Laird decided to try creating four five-minute cooking videos to add to the site, a project that cost just $1,500 and less than three hours of his time. After posting the videos on the Restaurant Serenade Web site, Laird saw the number of visitors climb to more than 3,000 per month, and online dinner reservations have gone from just two per month to more than 150![71]

Posting a video that includes a link to the company's site on YouTube, the most popular video Web site, also drives traffic to a company's site. YouTube's Insight tools offer business owners the ability to determine how effective the videos they post are at reaching potential customers. These tools show entrepreneurs how many times their videos have been viewed over a period of time, how popular their videos are compared to other YouTube videos, how viewers discovered their videos, and basic demographic profiles of their viewers.

CREATE A GIFT IDEA CENTER Online retailers have discovered that one of the most successful tools for improving their conversion rates is to offer a gift idea center. A gift idea center is a section of a Web site that includes a variety of gift ideas that shoppers can browse through for ideas based on price, gender, or category. Gift centers can provide a huge boost for e-tailers, particularly around holidays, because they offer creative suggestions for shoppers looking for the perfect gift.

ENTREPRENEURIAL
PROFILE _____

Francoise & John Shirley:
Sleepyheads.com

Francoise and John Shirley, who in 1999 co-founded Sleepyheads.com, an online company that sells a variety of sleepwear and accessories, recently added a gift idea center to their company's Web site and found that their average order size increased from $75 to $125. Shoppers can access the gift center easily from a link on the home page and can find gift suggestions organized into creative categories such as "Good Luck," "New Mom and Mom-to-Be," "Boyfriend Breakup," and "Gifts for Me." Every month, the Shirleys update the gift selection and rotate some of the categories, depending upon the season.[72]

Other variations of this approach that have proved to be successful for e-commerce entrepreneurs include suggested items pages, bargain basement pages, and featured sale pages.

BUILD LOYALTY BY GIVING ONLINE CUSTOMERS A REASON TO RETURN TO YOUR WEB SITE Just as with brick-and-mortar retailers, e-tailers that constantly have to incur the expense of attracting new customers find it difficult to remain profitable because of the extra cost required to acquire customers. One of the most effective ways to encourage customers to return to a site is to establish an incentive program that rewards them for repeat purchases. "Frequent-buyer" programs that offer discounts or points toward future purchases, give-aways such as T-shirts emblazoned with a company's logo, or special services are common components of incentive programs. Incentive programs that are properly designed with a company's target customer in mind really work. A study by market research firm NFO Interactive found that 53 percent of online customers say they would return to a particular site to shop if it offered an incentive program.[73]

ESTABLISH HYPERLINKS WITH OTHER BUSINESSES, PREFERABLY THOSE SELLING PRODUCTS OR SERVICES THAT COMPLEMENT YOURS Listing the Web addresses of complementary businesses on a company's site and having them list your company's address on their sites offers customers more value and can bring traffic to your site that you otherwise would have missed. For instance, the owner of a site selling upscale kitchen gadgets should consider a cross-listing arrangement with sites that feature gourmet recipes, wines, and kitchen appliances.

INCLUDE AN E-MAIL OPTION AND A TELEPHONE NUMBER ON YOUR SITE Customers will appreciate the opportunity to communicate with your company. When you include e-mail access on your site, be sure to respond to it promptly. Nothing alienates cyber-customers faster than a company that is slow to respond or fails to respond to their e-mail messages. Also, be sure to include a toll-free telephone number for customers who prefer to call with their questions. Unfortunately, many companies either fail to include their telephone numbers on their sites or bury them so deeply within the site's pages that customers never find them. Smart web entrepreneurs put a toll-free number on every page of their Web sites.

GIVE SHOPPERS THE ABILITY TO TRACK THEIR ORDERS ONLINE Many customers who order items online want to track the progress of their orders. One of the most effective ways to keep a customer happy is to send an e-mail confirmation that your company received the order and another e-mail notification when you ship the order. The shipment notice should include the shipper's tracking number and instructions on how to track the order from the shipper's site. Order and shipping confirmations instill confidence in even the most Web-wary shoppers.

OFFER WEB SHOPPERS A SPECIAL ALL THEIR OWN Give Web customers a special deal that you don't offer in any other advertising piece. Change your specials often (weekly, if possible) and use clever "teasers" to draw attention to the offer. Regular special offers available only on the Web give customers an incentive to keep visiting a company's site.

FOLLOW A SIMPLE DESIGN Catchy graphics and photographs are important to snaring customers, but designers must choose them carefully. Designs that are overly complex take a long time to download, and customers are likely to move on before they appear.

Following are some specific design tips:

- Avoid clutter. The best designs are simple and elegant with a balance of text and graphics.
- Avoid huge graphic headers that must download first, prohibiting customers from seeing anything else on your site as they wait (or more likely, *don't* wait). Use graphics judiciously so that the site loads quickly. Many studies show that customers abandon Web sites that load slowly. The average retail Web site downloads in 3.8 seconds, but 33 percent of retailers' sites require more than 5 seconds to download.[74] For impatient online shoppers, faster is better.
- Include a menu bar at the top of the page that makes it easy for customers to find their way around the site.
- Make the site easy to navigate by including navigation buttons at the bottom of pages that enable customers to return to the top of the page or to the menu bar. This avoids what one expert calls "the pogo effect," by which visitors bounce from page to page in a Web site looking for what they need. Without navigation buttons or a site map page, a company runs the risk of customers getting lost in its site and leaving.
- Regularly look for broken links on your site and purge them.
- Incorporate meaningful content in the site that is useful to visitors, well-organized, easy to read, and current. The content should be consistent with the message a company sends in the other advertising media it uses. Although a Web site should be designed to sell, providing useful, current information attracts visitors, keeps them coming back and establishes a company's reputation as an expert in the field.
- Include a "frequently asked questions" (FAQ) section. Adding this section to a page can reduce dramatically the number of telephone calls and e-mails customer service representatives must handle. FAQ sections typically span a wide range of issues—from how to place an order to how to return merchandise—and cover whatever topics customers most often want to know about.
- Be sure to post prominently privacy and return policies as well as product guarantees the company offers.
- If your site is heavy on content, say, 100 or more pages, or has more than 100 products for sale, include a search tool that allows visitors to find the product or information they want. Smaller, simpler sites can get by without a search tool if they are organized properly. Setting up a search tool is easy with either a remote search service (available for a monthly fee) or off-the-shelf software.
- Avoid fancy typefaces and small fonts because they are too hard to read. Limit font and color choices to two or three to avoid a circus look.
- Be vigilant for misspelled words, typographical errors, and formatting mistakes; they destroy a site's credibility in no time.
- Avoid using small fonts on "busy" backgrounds; no one will read them!
- Use contrasting colors of text and graphics. For instance, blue text on a green background is nearly impossible to read.

- Be careful with frames. Using frames that are so thick that they crowd out text makes for a poor design.
- Test your site on different Web browsers and on different-size monitors. A Web site may look exactly the way it was designed to look on one Web browser and be a garbled mess on another. Sites designed to display correctly on large monitors may not view well on small ones.
- Use your Web site to collect information from visitors, but don't tie up visitors immediately with a tedious registration process. Most will simply leave the site never to return. Offers for a free e-mail newsletter or a contest giveaway can give visitors enough incentive to register with a site.
- Avoid automated music that plays continuously and cannot be cut off.
- Make sure the overall look of the page is appealing. "When a site is poorly designed, lacks information, or cannot support customer needs, that [company's] reputation is seriously jeopardized," says one expert.[75]
- Remember: Simpler usually is better.

CREATE A FAST, SIMPLE CHECKOUT PROCESS   One sure-fire way to destroy an online company's conversion rate is to impose a lengthy, convoluted checkout process that requires customers to wade through pages of forms to fill out just to complete a purchase. When faced with a lengthy checkout process, customers simply abandon a site and make their purchases elsewhere. One recent study of online retailers by the E-Tailing Group reports that the average number of clicks required from product selection to final checkout is 5.2. E-commerce experts suggest that the top performing sites require a maximum of five clicks to check out, but the fewer the steps required for customers to check out, the more successful is a site at generating sales.[76]

Once customers put items into a shopping cart, they should be able to see a complete list and photographs of the products they have selected and should be able to access more information about them with one click. The cart should allow customers to change product quantities (and, believe it or not, to remove items from the cart). Every cart should have a "return to shopping" link in it as well.

ASSURE CUSTOMERS THAT THEIR ONLINE TRANSACTIONS ARE SECURE   If you are serious about doing business on the Web, make sure that your site includes the proper security software and encryption devices. The average amount of an online order is $148, and missing a sale because your site lacks proper security makes no sense![77] Web-savvy customers are not willing to divulge their credit card information on sites that are not secure.

ESTABLISH REASONABLE SHIPPING AND HANDLING CHARGES AND POST THEM UP FRONT   The number one reason that shoppers do not buy more goods online is high shipping costs. A closely related gripe among online shoppers is that some e-tailers reveal their shipping and handling charges too late in the checkout process. Responsible online merchants keep shipping and handling charges reasonable and display them early on in the buying process. Merchants have discovered that free shipping (often with a minimum purchase amount) is a powerful tool for boosting online sales. As shipping costs have risen quickly in recent years, online merchants must balance the desire to convert browsers into buyers with free or low-cost shipping and keeping their costs under control.

ENTREPRENEURIAL PROFILE

Tony Hsieh: Zappos.com

Zappos, an online shoe retailer that boasts an inventory of 4 million shoes in 200,000 styles from 1,200 makers, offers free shipping—and free return shipping—to its customers, tangible evidence of CEO Tony Hsieh's commitment to superior customer service. Zappos, which recently crossed the $1 billion mark in annual sales, pays more than $100 million in shipping costs each year. It's a cost Hsieh is willing to incur, however, because "it creates a 'wow' experience and generates positive word of mouth."[78]

CONFIRM TRANSACTIONS   Order-confirmation e-mails, which a company can generate automatically, let a customer know that the company received the online order and can be an important first line of defense against online fraud. If the customer claims not to have placed the order, the company can cancel it and report the credit card information as suspicious.

KEEP YOUR SITE UPDATED   Customers want to see something new when they visit stores, and they expect the same when they visit virtual stores as well. Delete any hyperlinks that have disappeared, and keep the information on your Web site current. One sure way to run off customers on the Web is to continue to advertise your company's "Christmas Special" in August! On the other hand, fresh information and new specials keep customers coming back.

TEST YOUR SITE OFTEN Smart e-commerce entrepreneurs check their sites frequently to make sure they are running smoothly and are not causing customers unexpected problems. A good rule of thumb is to check your site at least monthly – or weekly if its content changes frequently.

CONSIDER HIRING A PROFESSIONAL TO DESIGN YOUR SITE Pros can do it a lot faster and better than you can. However, don't give designers free rein to do whatever they want to with your site. Make sure it meets your criteria for an effective site that can sell.

Entrepreneurs must remember that on the World Wide Web every company, no matter how big or small it is, has the exact same screen size for its site. What matters most is not the size of your company but how you put that screen size to use.

YOU BE THE CONSULTANT

Using Web 2.0 Technology to Become a Global Player

David Burges/Newscom

In 1991, when Heather Gorringe started a small environmentally-friendly garden supply company on the centuries-old farm where her husband tends 150 acres of grains, sunflowers, and other crops, she had no idea that one day her company would win the British Small Business Champions Award (which is given only to the "brightest stars in the small business firmament") and be recognized by Dell as a recipient of the Global Small Business Excellence Award. Gorringe operates Wiggly Wigglers, a company that sells a variety of organic garden supplies ranging from composters and apple peelers to seeds and earthworms (great little composters!) online and through a catalog, from a rustic farm house on the Lower Blakemere Farm in rural Herefordshire, UK. From the outside, the business looks more like it should sell organic milk to local villagers (population 63) than a company that embraces the latest Web 2.0 technology to sell garden supplies all over the globe.

Gorringe and her 20 employees, including the company's two chocolate labs, Toast and Jam, and company cat, Noah, run the fast-growing company from the converted barns located just behind the farm house. For years, Gorringe earned a decent profit by selling garden products through catalogs. Eventually, she worked up the courage to create a Web site, and sales began to increase as customers discovered the charming little garden supply store with its quirky mix of products. Gorringe, who says that she is no technol-

ogy wizard, began searching for ways to stay closely connected to her growing customer base, something that she saw as essential to maintaining Wiggly Wiggler's character. "We are a direct business–mail order, Web site, phone," she says. It's a question of trying to communicate directly with customers." Gorringe heard about podcasts and wondered whether they might be the solution for customer connectivity that she was seeking. She and Michael Maloney, Wiggly Wigglers' graphics designer and IT consultant, decided to attend a United Kingdom PodcastCon conference to find out. What they learned at the conference ultimately would transform the small company located in the gorgeous British countryside into a global player. "The idea of being able to listen to something wherever and whenever you like from someone who was free to say whatever they wanted was amazing," says Gorringe. "I wanted to be able to lead people around our garden and to explain how to do worm composting and other things." Soon Wiggly Wigglers would become the first U.K. gardening company to create a podcast.

Gorringe and Maloney created the company's first podcast in the farmhouse living room using simple software that they downloaded for about £50. Gorringe, some of her employees, and, often, an invited guest, spend about two hours recording a podcast from what is now known as "the Wiggly Sofa" and another two hours editing to produce a half-hour podcast. Maloney uploads the finished product to the iTunes, AOL, and Yahoo podcast services, and customers who have subscribed to the company's podcasts automatically receive the update through RSS (Really Simple Syndication) 2.0. She estimates that the entire process cost Wiggly Wigglers about £250. Today the company produces weekly podcasts on an array of topics, ranging from growing heritage potatoes and exploring the rare species of apple trees growing on the Lower Blakemere Farm to sharing goat facts and the results of a professional archeological exploration taking place on the farm. One of the company's most popular podcasts was a "Gardeners' Question Time" that was held before a packed house in the Village Hall at nearby Preston-on-Wye. Gorringe says that the podcasts reach thousands of listeners each week.

To support the company's social networking strategy, Gorringe uses other Web 2.0 tools, including blogs, a company FaceBook page, videocasts, and a traditional mail order catalogue with a Wiki twist: customers make suggestions for the catalog via a Wiki page in FaceBook. Wiggly Wiggler's FaceBook page has more than 1,000 fans

Use of Social Media Tools among Small Businesses

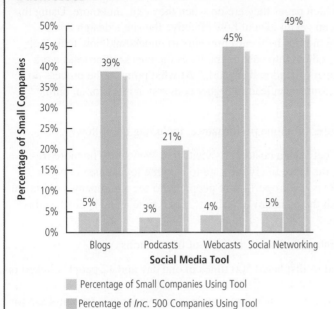

and more than 170 discussion topics. Wiggly Wigglers is on the leading edge of using social networking as a marketing tool; research by Access Markets International (AMI) Partners shows that just 5 percent of small businesses use social networking tools (see accompanying figure). The company's multi-pronged Web 2.0 strategy has resulted in a customer base of 90,000 people worldwide. Not only has Wiggly Wiggler's social networking strategy been successful at attracting thousands of customers, but it also has allowed Gorringe to reduce the company's advertising budget by more than 80 percent! When presenting Gorringe with the Global Small Business Excellence Award,

Dave Marmonti, president of Dell Europe, said, "The fact that Wiggly Wigglers is growing while cutting their operating expenses so dramatically because of their use of technology is a key reason they earned this recognition. Small businesses everywhere can learn from what they are doing and implement similar strategies in their companies."

1. Describe the benefits that Wiggly' Wigglers' social networking strategy has produced for the company.
2. Do you think that Wiggly Wigglers would have been able to build a customer base of 90,000 customers around the world as fast by using traditional marketing methods? Explain.
3. Use the accompanying figure to compare the percentage of all small businesses that use various Web 2.0 tools to the percentage of small companies that have made *Inc.* magazine's list of the 500 fastest small companies in the United States. What lessons can you draw from your comparison?

Sources: Adapted from Madeleine Acey, Peas in a Podcast," *TimesOnline*, January 10, 2008, http://www.timesonline.co.uk/tol/life_and_style/commercial/article787015.ece; "Wiggly Wigglers: 2008 Dell Global Award Winner," International Council for Small Business, November 8, 2008, http://www.icsb.org/article.asp?messageID=90; "Welcome to the Wiggly Podcast Archive," Wiggly Wigglers, http://www.wigglywigglers.com/podcasts/index.html?-session=shopper:4104A3901b8a82322EwnN14B4E7B; Amy Stewart, "Wiggly Wigglers Podcasts Dish the Dirt on Gardening," *San Francisco Chronicle*, September 23, 2006, http://www.sfgate.com/cgi-bin/article.cgi?f=/c/a/2006/09/23/HOGS6LA3GR1.DTL; "2008 Small Business Excellence Award Finalists," Dell Inc., May 6, 2008, http://www1.euro.dell.com/content/topics/reftopic.aspx/bsd/sbaward/en/sbe_award?c=uk&cs=&l=en&s=bsd; "Rural England Natural Gardening Company Worms Its Way to Global Dell Small Business Excellece Award," November 6, 2008, http://www.dell.com/content/topics/global.aspx/corp/pressoffice/en/2008/2008_11_06_rr_001?c=us&cs=ABA&l=en&s=bsd; "U.K. Small Business Winner: Wiggly Wigglers," International Council for Small Business, October 8, 2008, http://www.icsb.org/article.asp?messageID=71; Laurie McCabe, "Dell Launches a New Social Media On-ramp for Small Businesses, AMI Partners, September 24, 2008, pp.1–3.

Tracking Web Results

Software Solutions

LO 5

Explain how companies track the results from their Web sites.

As they develop their Web sites, entrepreneurs seek to create sites that generate sales by converting visitors into customers, improve customer relationships, or lower costs. How can entrepreneurs determine the effectiveness of their sites? **Web analytics,** tools that measure a Web site's ability to attract customers, generate sales, and keep customers coming back, help entrepreneurs to know what works—and what doesn't—on their sites. Unfortunately, only about 40 percent of e-businesses use Web analytics strategically to refashion their Web sites and improve their performance.[79] Online companies that use Web analytics have an advantage over those that do not. Their owners can review the data collected from their customers' Web site activity, analyze them, make adjustments to the Web site, and then start the monitoring process over again to see whether the changes improve the site's performance. In other words, Web analytics give entrepreneurs the ability to apply the principles of continuous improvement to their sites. In addition, the changes these e-business owners make are based on facts (the data from the Web analytics) rather than on mere guesses about how customers interact with a site. There are many Web analytics software packages, but effective ones offer the following types of information:

Web analytics

tools that measure a Web site's ability to attract customers, generate sales, and keep customers coming back.

- *Commerce metrics.* These are basic analytics such as sales revenue generated, number of items sold, which products are selling best (and which are not), and others.
- *Visitor segmentation measurements.* These measurements provide entrepreneurs valuable information about online shoppers and customers, including whether they are return customers or new customers, how they arrived at the site (for example, via a search engine or a pay-per-click ad), which search terms they used (if they used a search engine), and others.

- *Content reports.* This information tells entrepreneurs which products customers are looking for and which pages they view most often (and least often), how they navigate through the site, how long they stay, which pages they are on when they exit, and more. Using this information, an entrepreneur can get an idea of how effective the site's design is.
- *Process measurements.* These metrics help entrepreneurs to understand how their Web sites attract visitors and convert them into customers. Does the checkout process work smoothly? How often do shoppers abandon their carts? At what point in the process do they abandon them? These measures can lead to higher conversion rates for an online business.

E-businesses rely on several measures of online performance, including the following:

recency
the length of time between a customer's visit to a Web site

click-through rate
measures the proportion of people who see a small company's online ad and actually click on it to reach the company's Web site.

cost per acquisition (CPA)
measures the cost a company incurs to generate each purchase (or customer registration).

conversion (or browse-to-buy) ratio
measures the proportion of visitors to a site who actually make a purchase.

- **Recency** is the length of time between a customer's visits to a Web site. The more frequently customers visit a site, the more likely they are to become loyal customers.
- The **click-through rate (CTR)** is the proportion of people who see a company's online ad and actually click on it to reach the company's Web site. Each time an ad is displayed is called an impression; therefore:

$$CTR = \text{number of clicks} \div \text{number of impressions}$$

For instance, if a company's ad us displayed 500 times in one day and 12 people clicked on it, the CTR is $12 \div 500 = .024 = 2.4\%$

- The **cost per acquistion (CPA)** is the cost a company incurs to generate each purchase (or customer registration):

$$CPA = \text{Total cost of acquiring a new customer} \div \text{number of new customers}$$

For example, if a company purchases an advertisement in an e-magazine for $200, and it yields 15 new customers, then the cost of acquistion is $200 \div 15 = $13.33.

- The **conversion (or browse-to-buy) rate** is the proportion of visitors to a site who actually make a purchase. It is one of the most important measures of Web success and is calculated as follows:

$$\text{Conversion rate} = \text{number of customers who male a purchase} \div \text{number of visitors to the site}$$

Although conversion rates vary dramatically across industries, the average conversion rate is 3.15 percent.[80] In other words, out of every 1,000 people who visit a Web site, about 32 of them actually make a purchase. Table 9.3 offers practical advice to entrepreneurs who are looking to boost their conversion rates.

TABLE 9.3 Tips for Boosting Your Conversion Rate

Looking for ways to boost your online company's conversion rate? Try these techniques:
- Include an on-site search tool that makes it easy for shoppers to find the items they are seeking. Any shopper's search should turn up the requested item as well as sales "boosters" such as special offers and cross-sells (products that complement the requested item).
- Streamline the checkout process. Making checkout as simple and fast as possible increases the probability of closing an online sale.
- Organize your site so that navigating it is as simple and as intuitive as possible. Online shoppers are frustrated easily by confusing sites. "Eighty percent of shopper will leave after three pages" if they cannot find what they want, says one conversion rate expert.
- Offer an attractive display of products for customers. The most successful online retailers engage in visual merchandising just like their brick-and-mortar counterparts. Set the stage properly to encourage shoppers to buy.
- Offer something free. Whether it is a "buy two, get one free" deal or an offer for free shipping, the word "free" gets attention online.
- Do everything you can to win shoppers' trust. Anything that causes shoppers to doubt the legitimacy of your Web site or your business will lower your company's conversion rate.
- Encourage repeat customers to keep repeating. One of the easiest ways to increase conversion rates is to romance your existing customers. The possibilities are endless but might include timely e-mails and special offers or discounts just for existing customers.

- Let customers know whether or not the items they have selected are in stock and when they will be shipped. Lack of information about product availability and delivery dates can destroy a company's conversion rate.

- Include a prominently displayed "Buy" button at every opportunity. A study by Jakob Nielsen, a Web design expert, found that six percent of all online "sales catastrophes" (a failure to make a sale) were the result of customers who had already decided to make a purchase but had difficulty getting the item into a shopping cart! Locating at the top of Web pages a "Buy" button that is set off in a different color makes it easy for customers to find their way to a shopping cart.

Sources: Jennifer Schiff, "Getting More Out of Your Web Site," *E-Commerce Guide*, November 29, 2005, www.ecommerce-guide.com/solutions/building/article.php/3567091; James Maguire, "E-Commerce Design: The Product Page Is King," *Small Business Computing*, February 3, 2006, www.smallbusinesscomputing.com/emarketing/article.php/3582696; James Maguire, "E-Commerce Design: Category Pages," *E-Commerce Guide*, January 30, 2006, www.ecommerce-guide.com/solutions/design/article.php/3581446; James Maguire, "Merchant Secrets for Driving Conversion: Part 1," *Small Business Computing*, November 22, 1005, www.smallbusinesscomputing.com/emarketing/article.php/3566026; James Maguire, "Merchant Secrets for Driving Conversion: Part 2," *Small Business Computing*, November 14, 1005, www.smallbusinesscomputing.com/emarketing/article.php/3563956. Christopher Saunders, "How Do I: Attract and Keep Customers?" *E-Commerce*, June 8, 2004, www.ecommerce.internet.com/how/customers/article/0.10363_3365551.00.html.

Ensuring Web Privacy and Security

Privacy

The Web's ability to track customers' every move naturally raises concerns over the privacy of the information companies collect. E-commerce gives businesses access to tremendous volumes of information about their customers, creating a responsibility to protect that information and to use it wisely. According to the *Pew Internet & American Life Project*, 75 percent of Internet users have concerns about providing credit card and other personal information online.[81] To make sure they are using the information they collect from visitors to their Web sites legally and ethically, companies should take the following steps:

LO 6

Describe how e-businesses ensure the privacy and security of the information they collect and store from the Web.

TAKE AN INVENTORY OF THE CUSTOMER DATA COLLECTED The first step to ensuring proper data handling is to assess exactly the type of data the company is collecting and storing. How are you collecting them? Why are you collecting them? How are you using them? Do visitors know how you are using the data? Do you need to get their permission to use them in this way? Do you use all of the data you are collecting?

DEVELOP A COMPANY PRIVACY POLICY FOR THE INFORMATION YOU COLLECT A **privacy policy** is a statement explaining the nature of the information a company collects online, what it does with that information, and the recourse customers have if they believe the company is misusing the information. Several online privacy firms, such as TRUSTe (http://www.truste.org), BBBOnline (http://www.bbbonline.com), and BetterWeb (http://www.betterweb.com) offer Web "seal programs," the equivalent of the Good Housekeeping seal of privacy approval. To earn a privacy seal of approval, a company must adopt a privacy policy, implement it, and monitor its effectiveness. Many of these privacy sites also provide online policy wizards, automated questionnaires that help e-business owners create comprehensive privacy statements.

privacy policy
a statement explaining the nature of the information a company collects online, what it does with that information, and the recourse customers have if they believe the company is misusing the information.

POST YOUR COMPANY'S PRIVACY POLICY PROMINENTLY ON YOUR WEB SITE AND FOLLOW IT Creating a privacy policy is not sufficient; posting it in a prominent place on the Web site (It should be accessible from *every* page on the Web site) and then abiding by it make a policy meaningful. One of the worst mistakes a company can make is to publish its privacy policy online and then to fail to follow it. Not only is this unethical, but it also can lead to serious damage awards if customers take legal action against the company.

Security

For online merchants, the result of shoppers' privacy and security concerns is lost sales. A recent study by research firm TNS reports that 70 percent of online shoppers have abandoned a purchase because of security concerns.[82] Every company doing business on the Web faces two conflicting goals: (1) to establish a presence on the Web so that customers from across the globe can have access to its site, and (2) to maintain a high level of security so that the business, its site, and the information it collects is safe from hackers and intruders intent on doing harm. Companies have a number of safeguards available to them, but hackers with enough time, talent, and determination usually can beat even the most sophisticated safety measures. If hackers manage to break into a system, they can do irreparable damage, stealing programs and sensitive customer data, modifying or deleting valuable information, changing the look and content of sites, or crashing sites altogether.

No company, no matter how small it is, is immune to online security breaches. The Identity Theft Resource Center lists large corporations, government agencies, cities, universities, and small companies as victims of data breaches. The costs associated with a security breach include not only the actual cost of the lost data and the lawsuits that inevitably result from customers but also the long-term impact of the lost trust that customers have for a business whose security has been breached. To minimize the likelihood of invasion by hackers, e-companies rely on a several tools, including virus detection software, intrusion detection software, and firewalls. At the most basic level of protection is **virus detection software,** which scans computer drives for viruses, nasty programs written by devious hackers and designed to harm computers and the information they contain. *Internet Security Trends,* a study by Cisco and Ironport, reports that both the frequency and the cost of virus attacks on business continue to climb.[83] The severity of viruses ranges widely, from relatively harmless programs that put humorous messages on a user's screen to those that erase a computer's hard drive or cause the entire system to crash. Because hackers are *always* writing new viruses to attack computer systems, entrepreneurs must keep their virus detection software up-to-date and must run it often. An attack by one virus can bring a company's entire e-commerce platform to a screeching halt in no time!

Intrusion detection software is essential for any company doing business on the Web. These packages constantly monitor the activity on a company's network server and sound an alert if they detect someone breaking into the company's computer system or if they detect unusual network activity. Intrusion detection software not only can detect attempts by unauthorized users to break into a computer system while they are happening, but it also can trace the hacker's location. Most packages also have the ability to preserve a record of the attempted break-in that will stand up in court so that companies can take legal action against cyber-intruders.

A **firewall** is a combination of hardware and software operating between the Internet and a company's computer network that allows employees to have access to the Internet but keeps unauthorized users from entering a company's network and the programs and data it contains. Establishing a firewall is essential to operating a company on the Web, but entrepreneurs must make sure that their firewalls are set up properly. Otherwise, they are useless! Even with all of these security measures in place, it is best for a company to run its Web site on a separate server from the network that runs the business. If hackers break into the site, they still do not have access to the company's sensitive data and programs.

In e-commerce just as in traditional retailing, sales do not matter unless a company gets paid! On the Web customers demand transactions they can complete with ease and convenience, and the simplest way to allow customers to pay for e-commerce transactions is with credit cards. From a Web customer's perspective, however, one of the most important security issues is the security of his or her credit card information. To ensure the security of their customers' credit card information, online retailers typically use **secure sockets layer (SSL) technology** to encrypt customers' transaction information as it travels across the Internet. By using secure shopping cart features from storefront-building services or Internet service providers, even the smallest e-commerce stores can offer their customers secure on-line transactions.

Processing credit card transactions requires a company to obtain an Internet merchant account from a bank or financial intermediary. Setup fees for an Internet merchant account typically range from $500 to $1,000, but companies also pay monthly access and statement fees of between $40 and $80 plus a transaction fee of 10 to 60 cents per transaction. Once an online company has a merchant account, it can accept credit cards from online customers. To ensure the security of their customers' credit card numbers, online retailers typically use secure sockets layer (SSL) technology to encrypt customers' transaction information as it travels across the Internet. By using secure shopping cart features from storefront-building services or Internet service providers, even the smallest e-commerce stores can offer their customers secure online transactions.

virus detection software
programs that scan computer drives for viruses, nasty programs written by devious hackers and designed to harm computers and the information they contain.

intrusion detection software
programs that constantly monitor the activity on a company's network server and sound an alert if they detect someone breaking into the system or if they detect unusual network activity.

firewall
a combination of hardware and software that allows employees to have access to the Internet but keeps unauthorized users from entering a company's network and the programs and data it contains.

Online credit card transactions also pose a risk for merchants; online fraud cost companies an estimated $3.6 billion in annual revenues.[84] The most common problem is **chargebacks,** online transactions that customers dispute. Unlike credit card transactions in a retail store, those made online involve no signatures, and Internet merchants incur the loss when a customer disputes an online credit card transaction. One way to prevent fraud is to ask customers for their card verification value (CVV or CVV2), the three-digit number above the signature panel on the back of the credit card, as well as their card number and expiration date. Online merchants also can subscribe to a real-time credit card processing service that authorizes credit card transactions, but the fees can be high. In addition, using a shipper that provides the ability to track shipments enables online merchants to prove that the customer actually received the merchandise can help minimize the threat of payment fraud.

chargebacks

online transactions that customers dispute.

Chapter Summary

E-commerce is creating a new economy, one that is connecting producers, sellers, and customers via technology in ways that have never been possible before. In this fast-paced world of e-commerce, size no longer matters as much as speed and flexibility do. The Internet is creating a new industrial order, and companies that fail to adapt to it will soon become extinct.

1. **Understand the factors an entrepreneur should consider before launching into e-commerce.**

   Before launching an e-commerce effort, business owners should consider the following important issues:

   - How a company exploits the Web's interconnectivity and the opportunities it creates to transform relationships with its suppliers and vendors, its customers, and other external stakeholders is crucial to its success.
   - Web success requires a company to develop a plan for integrating the Web into its overall strategy. The plan should address issues such as site design and maintenance, creating and managing a brand name, marketing and promotional strategies, sales, and customer service.
   - Developing deep, lasting relationships with customers takes on even greater importance on the Web. Attracting customers on the Web costs money, and companies must be able to retain their online customers to make their Web sites profitable.
   - Creating a meaningful presence on the Web requires an ongoing investment of resources–time, money, energy, and talent. Establishing an attractive Web site brimming with catchy photographs of products is only the beginning.
   - Measuring the success of its Web-based sales effort is essential to remaining relevant to customers whose tastes, needs, and preferences are always changing.

2. **Explain the ten myths of e-commerce and how to avoid falling victim to them.**

   The twelve myths of e-commerce are:

   Myth 1. Online customers are easy to please.
   Myth 2. If I launch a site, customers will flock to it.

   Myth 3. Making money on the Web is easy.
   Myth 4. Privacy is not an important issue on the Web.
   Myth 5. The most important part of any e-commerce effort is technology.
   Myth 6. "Strategy? I don't need a strategy to sell on the Web! Just give me a Web site, and the rest will take care of itself."
   Myth 7. On the Web, customer service is not as important as it is in a traditional retail store.
   Myth 8. Flashy Web sites are better than simple ones.
   Myth 9. It's what's up front that counts.
   Myth 10. It's too late to get on the Web.

3. **Explain the basic strategies entrepreneurs should follow to achieve success in their e-commerce efforts.**

   Following are some guidelines for building a successful Web strategy for a small e-company:

   - Focus on a niche in the market.
   - Develop a community of online customers.
   - Attract visitors by giving away "freebies."
   - Make creative use of e-mail, but avoid becoming a "spammer."
   - Make sure your Web site says "credibility."
   - Make the most of the Web's global reach.
   - Use the tools of Web 2.0 to attract and retain customers.
   - Promote your Web site online and offline.
   - Develop an effective search engine optimization strategy.

4. **Learn the techniques of designing a killer Web site.**

   There is no sure-fire formula for stopping Web shoppers in their tracks, but the following suggestions will help:

   - Understand your target customer.
   - Give customers want they want.
   - Select a domain name that is consistent with the image you want to create for your company and register it.
   - Make your Web site easy to navigate.

- Create a gift idea center.
- Build loyalty by giving online customers a reason to return to your Web site.
- Establish hyperlinks with other businesses, preferably those selling products or services that complement yours.
- Include an e-mail option and a telephone number in your site.
- Give shoppers the ability to track their orders online.
- Offer Web shoppers a special all their own.
- Follow a simple design for your Web page.
- Create a fast, simple checkout process.
- Assure customers that their online transactions are secure.
- Post shipping and handling charges up front.
- Confirm transactions.
- Keep your site updated.
- Test your site often.
- Consider hiring a professional to design your site.

5. Explain how companies track the results from their Web sites.

One option for tracking Web activity is through log-analysis software. Server logs record every page,

graphic, audio clip, or photograph that visitors to a site access, and log-analysis software analyzes these logs and generates reports describing how visitors behave when they get to a site. Key metrics for measuring the effectiveness of a site's performance include the click-through rate, the cost per acquisition, and the conversion rate.

6. Describe how e-businesses ensure the privacy and security of the information they collect and store from the Web.

To make sure they are using the information they collect from visitors to their Web sites legally and ethically, companies should take the following steps:

- Take an inventory of the customer data collected.
- Develop a company privacy policy for the information collected.
- Post the company's privacy policy prominently on the Web site and follow it.

To ensure the security of the information they collect and store from Web transactions, companies should rely on virus and intrusion detection software and firewalls to ward off attacks from hackers.

Discussion Questions

1. In what ways have the Internet and e-commerce changed the ways companies do business?
2. Discuss the factors entrepreneurs should consider before launching an e-commerce site.
3. What are the 10 myths of e-commerce? What can an entrepreneur do to avoid them?
4. Explain the five basic approaches available to entrepreneurs for launching an e-commerce effort. What are the advantages, the disadvantages, and the costs associated with each one?
5. What strategic advice would you offer an entrepreneur about to start an e-company?
6. What design characteristics make for a successful Web page?
7. Explain the characteristics of an ideal domain name.
8. Describe the techniques that are available to e-companies for tracking results from their Web sites. What advantages does each offer?
9. What steps should e-businesses take to ensure the privacy of the information they collect and store from the Web?
10. What techniques can e-companies use to protect their banks of information and their customers' transaction data from hackers?
11. In what ways does evaluating the effectiveness of a Web site pose a problem for online entrepreneurs?

Business PlanPro™ One question in the *Business Plan Pro*™ wizard relates to your business Web site. Think about the presence you would like your business to have on the Web. Will your Web site be an "information-only" site or do you plan to have an online store? As you look through the list of the 10 myths mentioned in this chapter, ask yourself whether you have fallen prey to any of these myths.

Business Plan Exercises

Creating an effective Web presence may be a critical piece of business planning and your overall strategy.

On the Web

If you plan to host an information-only Web site, visit sites that accomplish that goal. Note the layout and navigation of the site and how it presents this information. If you plan to have a dynamic online store, visit sites that do that best. What aspects of the site make it simple and efficient for new and returning buyers? Next, select three Web sites that you find to have attractive parallels with the look and feel of your future Web site. These sites may be from entirely different industries but possess appealing attributes you want to incorporate into your Web site. Identify those qualities and explore how your site might also benefit from those attributes.

Sample Plans

Find the PrintingSoutions.com sample plan in *Business Plan Pro.*™ Review the Executive Summary and then go to the Web Plan Summary in section 6.0. The Web will play a critical role in this online business. What role will the Web play in yours?

In the Software

Open your business plan in *Business Plan Pro*™ and go to the Web Summary section. If you have changed your mind about having a Web site, click on View and Wizard and change that decision. The outline of your business plan will then reflect that change and bring the Web Summary section into your outline. Read the instructions within the software and click on the sample plan link in the upper right-hand section of the instructions. If beneficial, add content to this section. These questions may help you to consider the following:

- Do you have a URL registered for your business? If not, how will you begin that process to secure and register that Web address?
- Describe your target market's expected use of the Web site.
- List the objectives you hope to realize through the site.

- Is the site going to have an online store? If so, explore how to implement credit card and other online payment options.
- Who will design and launch the site? Will you do this work, someone in your organization, or will you outsource that work?
- How will you measure, track, and assess the performance of your site? How often that will occur?
- Are you going to incorporate Web analytics tools and resources that may help you to measure your Web site's performance?
- Does your business plan demonstrate that you have you planned and budgeted for your Web site based on the required resources to design, launch, and maintain your site?

Building Your Business Plan

Step back and review what you have captured in your plan to date. With these additions, does your plan continue to tell a consistent and coherent story about your business? Review and edit other sections that interact with the additions to the Web section. Some of those sections may include areas that relate to marketing promotions, communications, expenses, and revenues.

Beyond the Classroom...

1. Work with a team of your classmates to come up with an Internet business you would be interested in launching. Come up with several suitable domain names for your hypothetical e-company. Once you have chosen a few names, go to a domain name registration service such as Network Solutions' Internic at http://www.networksolutions.com/ or Netnames at http://www.netnames.com to conduct a name search. How many of the names your team came up with were already registered to someone? If an entrepreneur's top choice for a domain name is already registered to someone else, what options does he or she have?

2. Select several online companies with which you are familiar and visit their Web sites. What percentage of them have privacy policies posted on their sites? How comprehensive are these policies? What percentage of the sites you visited belonged to a privacy watchdog agency such as TRUSTe or BBBOnLine? How

important is a posted privacy policy for e-companies? Explain.

3. Visit five e-commerce sites on the Web and evaluate them on the basis of the Web site design principles described in this chapter. How well do they measure up? What suggestions can you offer for improving the design of each site? If you were a customer trying to make a purchase from each site, how would you respond to the design?

4. Visit the "Understanding Privacy" Web site at BBBOnLine (http://www.bbbonline.org/understandingprivacy/). Contact the owner of a Web-based business in your town and use the assessment tool "How's Your Privacy Quotient" from the BBBOnLine Web site to evaluate the company's privacy policy. How does the company score on the PQ assessment tool? Use the resources on this site and others to develop a list of suggestions for improving the company's score.

David Johnson/Calico Coatings/Anyway
Artists, Inc.

CHAPTER 10

Pricing Strategies

There is hardly anything in the world that someone cannot make a little worse
and sell a little cheaper, and he who considers price only is this man's lawful prey.
—John Ruskin

The price is what you pay; the value is what you receive.
—Anonymous

Learning Objectives

On completion of this chapter, you will be able to:

1. Discuss the relationships among pricing, image, competition, and value.

2. Describe effective pricing techniques for introducing new products or services and for existing ones.

3. Explain the pricing methods and strategies for retailers, manufacturers, and service firms.

4. Describe the impact of credit on pricing.

Setting prices is a business decision governed by both art and science—with a measure of instinct thrown in for good measure. Setting prices for their products and services requires entrepreneurs to balance a multitude of complex forces, many of them working in opposite directions. Entrepreneurs must determine prices for their goods and services that will draw customers and produce a profit. Unfortunately, many small business owners set prices without enough information about their cost of operations and their customers. Price is an important factor in building long-term relationships with customers, and haphazard pricing techniques can confuse and alienate customers and endanger a small company's profitability. Setting prices is not only one of the toughest decisions small business owners face, but it also is one of the most important. Research by the consulting firm McKinsey and Company shows that proper pricing strategies have far greater impact on a company's profits than corresponding reductions in fixed or variable costs.[1] For instance, when a company that earns a 10 percent net profit margin raises its prices by one percent, its profits increase by 10 percent (assuming its unit sales remain the same).

Improper pricing has destroyed countless businesses whose owners mistakenly thought their prices were high enough to generate a profit when, in fact, they were not.

After working with a consultant, Jeff Trott, founder of Timeless Message, a company that sells bottles with greeting messages inside them, raised its prices from an average of $30 per bottle to $60 per bottle. The company had underestimated both its costs and the market value of its products. The price increase resulted in a brief sales dip, but, according to Trott, "We started making a profit for the first time in four years. It was like we had been shipping a ten-dollar bill out the door with each order."[2]

ENTREPRENEURIAL PROFILE

Jeff Trott: Timeless Message

Pricing decisions cut across every aspect of a small company, influencing everything from its marketing and sales efforts to its operations and strategy. Price is the monetary value of a product or service in the marketplace; it is a measure of what the customer must give up to obtain various goods and services. Price also is a signal of a product's or service's value to an individual, and different customers assign different values to the same goods and services. From an entrepreneur's viewpoint, price must be compatible with customers' perceptions of value. "Pricing is not just a math problem," says one business writer. "It's a psychology test."[3] The psychology of pricing is an art much more than it is a science. It focuses on creating value in the customer's mind but recognizes that value is what the customer perceives it to be. Shoppers can buy jeans at most discounters for $25 or less, but Kuyichi, a maker of fashionable jeans, commands prices upwards of $160 for its jeans, which are made from organic, fair trade cotton and include a code that allows buyers to go online to see the people who picked the cotton from which the jeans are made and who actually sewed them. Kuyichi customers see value in the company's upscale jeans because of their style and their eco-friendly manufacturing process.[4]

Customers often look to a product's or service's price for clues about value. Consider the following examples, which illustrate the sometimes puzzling connection between price and perceived value.

- In 1891, Gennaro Sferra launched a company that made luxury bed linens, including sheets, duvets, quilts, pillows, and shams. The company that bears his name continues its proud tradition of premium bed sheets with its top-of-the line sheets that are made from Giza 45, a silky yarn known as "the queen of Egyptian cotton" that previously had been used exclusively by an Italian luxury shirt-maker. Sferra sells a queen-size set of sheets in either ivory or white for $2,895.[5]
- No longer limited to use on the range, cowboy boots have become a personalized fashion statement for urban cowboys, and few companies boast a list of celebrity customers as long as Tres Outlaws. The company counts among its loyal customers more than 600 celebrities such as Arnold Schwarzenegger (who owns more than 30 pairs), the late Johnny Cash, Tom Hanks, Dustin Hoffman, Madonna, Nicole Kidman, and many others. The company's boots are handmade by skilled artisans in a process that requires between 200 and 400 steps, the first of which involves creating a pattern from the customer's feet. Co-founders Scott Emmerich, Jerry Black, and Carlos Salazar (who has left the company) work with their customers to create designs that range from simple and understated to brightly-colored, elaborate patterns and artwork that may take hundreds of hours of hand labor.

"The Autry" Cowboy boots
designed and created by Scott
Wayne Emmerich.

The Tres Outlaws Boots Company, El Paso TX. *The Autry* Cowboy boots designed and created by Scott Wayne Emmerich

Customers who want a pair of Tres Outlaws boots must be patient and prepared to pony up between $900 and $50,000 per pair, prices that generate more than $1 million in annual revenue for the 17-person company.[6]

As you can see, setting higher prices sometimes can *increase* the appeal of a product or service ("If you charge more, you must be worth it"). Value for these products is not found solely in their superior technical performance but in their scarcity and uniqueness and the resulting image they create for the buyer. Although entrepreneurs must recognize the shallow depth of the market for ultra-luxury items such as these, the ego-satisfying ownership of limited-edition watches, pens, cars, jewelry, and other items is the psychological force supporting a premium price strategy.

Three Potent Forces: Image, Competition, and Value

LO 1

Discuss the relationships among pricing, image, competition, and value.

Because pricing decisions have such a pervasive influence on all aspects of a small company, one of the most important considerations for entrepreneurs is to take a strategic rather than a piecemeal approach to pricing their companies' products and services. Research by the University of Pennsylvania's Wharton School shows that companies that take a strategic approach to pricing and monitor the results can raise their sales revenue between 1 percent and 8 percent. After analyzing its existing pricing techniques using price management software, New York City drugstore chain Duane Reade discovered that parents of newborns are less price sensitive than are parents of toddlers. Managers decided to make diaper pricing a function of the child's age, cutting prices to meet those of competitors on toddlers' diapers and raising them on diapers for newborns. A year later, the company's new pricing strategy had produced a 27 percent increase in its baby care revenue.[7]

A company's pricing strategy is a major determinant of its image in the marketplace, is influenced by the pricing strategies of its competitors, and is an important element in the value that customers perceive its products or services provide.

Price Conveys Image

A company's pricing policies communicate important information about its overall image to customers. "Pricing tells a story," says Per Sjofors, a pricing consultant. For example, the prices charged by a posh men's clothing store reflect a completely different image from those charged by a factory outlet.[8] Customers look at prices to determine the type of store they are dealing with. High prices frequently convey the idea of quality, prestige, and uniqueness to customers. "People bring a whole set of equations with them when they make a purchase, and one of the values for most people is that high price equals quality," says Rob Docters, a pricing expert.[9]

Accordingly, when developing a marketing approach to pricing, entrepreneurs must establish prices that are compatible with what customers expect and are willing to pay. Too often, small business owners *underprice* their goods and services, believing that low prices are the only way they can achieve a competitive advantage. A study by the Copernicus consulting firm found that only 15 to 35 percent of customers consider price to be the chief criterion when selecting a product or service.[10]

Chris Carmon, co-founder of the Carmon Group, a Cleveland, Ohio, recruiting firm, estimates that over the first three years that he was in business, he missed out on $1 million in revenue by establishing prices that were too low for the fast, highly specialized search services that he provides his clients. Carmon's original pricing strategy, which was simply to match what other recruiting company's charged, 25 percent of an employee's first year's salary, failed to reflect the extra value he offered by taking on difficult or fast-track searches. Today Carmon sets prices for searches based on the client's demands. He recently found a veteran bridge designer for a company and charged 35 percent of the first year's salary. Carmon says that the 24-employee company's new pricing strategy has increased both sales and profits.[11]

Like Chris Carmon, many entrepreneurs make the common pricing mistake of failing to recognize the extra value, convenience, service, and quality they give their customers—all things that many customers are willing to pay for. These companies fall into the trap of trying to compete solely on the basis of price when they lack the sales volume—and, hence, the lower cost structures–of their larger rivals. It is a recipe for failure. "People want quality," says one merchant selling upscale goods at upscale prices. "They want value. But if you lower prices, they think that you are lowering the value and lowering the quality."[12] It is a dangerous cycle that can destroy a business. A study of businesses in multiple industries by Rafi Mohammed, author of *The Art of Pricing*, found that those companies that raised prices by 1 percent saw their profits increase 11 percent. Those that raised their prices by 10 percent realized profit increases of 100 percent![13] The study does not imply that businesses have free rein to raise prices to any level, but it does suggest that many companies could raise their prices enough to improve their financial results significantly if they could convince customers that their products offer superior value.

A key ingredient to setting prices properly is to understand a company's target market, the customer groups at which the small company is aiming its goods or services. Rather than ask "How much should I charge for my product or service?" entrepreneurs should ask "How much are my target customers willing to pay?" Target market, business image, and pricing strategy are closely related.

When Tamara Donaghy-Bates launched Sway & Cake, a Seattle, Washington, retail store selling women's clothing, her target audience was young professional women in their late twenties to late thirties who are looking for something other than traditional styles. Donaghy-Bates describes the clothing she sells in Sway & Cake as "funky" and "flirty"—trendy, fashion-forward styles that are common in metropolitan areas such as New York or Los Angeles but are hard to find in smaller cities such as Seattle. Her upscale pricing strategy is geared toward her target audience, and it works; her company's first year sales exceeded $800,000. Working with customers every day in the shop provided Donaghy-Bates with clear insight into her customers' fashion preferences, and she soon saw an opportunity to tap into another target audience with a different pricing strategy: students and young women in their early to mid-twenties. To reach this group of customers, Donaghy-Bates opened TBC (To Be Continued) in Seattle as a lower-cost outlet for similar styles of clothing that she sells in Sway & Cake. In fact, nearly half of the merchandise sold in TBC is clothing that did not sell in Sway & Cake and has been marked down at a significant discount, sometimes as much as 50 or 60 percent off the normal retail price. TBC's remaining merchandise is new, lower-priced, and aimed at a younger audience. Customers have responded to both stores' pricing strategies and merchandise mix, and combined sales for the two stores have grown well beyond the $1 million mark.[14]

Competition and Prices

Small businesses face competition from local, foreign, and Web-based businesses. When setting prices, entrepreneurs should take into account their competitors' prices, but they should *not* automatically match or beat them. However, unless a small company can differentiate itself by creating a distinctive image in customers' minds or by offering superior service, quality, design, convenience, or speed, it must match its competitors' prices or risk losing sales. Before matching any competitor's prices, however, small business owners should consider a rival's motives. A competitor may establish its price structure on a unique set of criteria and a totally different strategy. Blindly matching competitors' prices can lead a company to financial ruin, and companies that set their prices this way typically do so because they perceive themselves in a position of strategic weakness. Recall from Chapter 3, Strategic Management and the Entrepreneur, that companies that execute a successful differentiation strategy can charge prices higher than those of their competitors.

**ENTREPRENEURIAL
PROFILE**_____

Anthony Shurman:
Yosha Enterprises

When Anthony Shurman launched Yosha Enterprises in 2002, a company that markets liquid breath mints, he established a price of $1.99 for a 36-mint package. Later, in response to competitors' prices, he lowered the price to $1.79 and then to $1.69 per pack. Momints contained more mints than any of the competing brands, but customers failed to recognize that benefit and based their purchase decisions on the package price. When Shurman recently rolled out Momints at a regional chain of grocery stores, he cut the size of the pack to the industry standard 28 mints and set a price of 99 cents. "Our sales went up 350 percent," he says. Yosha generates $3 million in annual revenue, and Shurman believes that he can sell even more mints at the lower 99-cent price.[15]

Generally, entrepreneurs should avoid head-to-head price competition with other firms that can more easily achieve lower prices through lower cost structures. For instance, most locally owned drugstores cannot compete with the prices of large national drug chains that buy in large quantities and negotiate significant discounts. However, many local drugstores operate successfully by using non-price competition; these stores offer more personal service, free delivery, credit sales, and other extras that the chains have eliminated. Non-price competition can be an effective strategy for a small business in the face of larger, more powerful companies because experimenting with price changes can be dangerous for small companies. Price changes cause fluctuations in sales volume that a small company may not be able to tolerate. In addition, frequent price changes may muddle a company's image and damage customer relations.

Attempting to undercut competitors' prices may lead to a price war, one of the most deadly games a small business can play. Price wars can eradicate companies' profit margins and scar an entire industry for years. Price wars usually begin when one competitor thinks he or she can achieve higher volume instantaneously by lowering prices. Rather than sticking to their strategic guns, competitors believe they must follow suit. For instance, as sales of personal computers slowed recently in an economic downturn, Hewlett-Packard and Dell, the industry's market share leaders, resorted to price cuts, even on their most popular models, in attempt to prop up sales. The resulting price war wiped out almost all of the industry's profit margin, which typically averages 6 percent of sales. Rather than engage in the price war, industry rebel Apple Inc. added more features to its computers and held the line on prices across its product lines, even though prices for its most basic MacBook notebook computers already were more than $450 higher than the average selling price of all notebook computers. The strategy allowed Apple to maintain its brand's premium reputation and its industry-leading profit margins, which average nearly 20 percent of sales, while watching sales increase by double-digits.[16]

Entrepreneurs usually overestimate the power of price cuts. In reality, sales volume rarely rises enough to offset the lower profit margins of a lower price. A business with a 25 percent gross profit margin that cuts its price by 10 percent would have to *triple* its sales volume just to break even. In a price war, a company may cut its prices so severely that it is impossible to achieve the volume necessary to offset the lower profit margins. Even when price cuts work, their effects often are temporary. Customers lured by the lowest price usually have almost no loyalty to a business. The lesson: The best way to survive a price war is to stay out of it by emphasizing the unique features, benefits, and value your company offers its customers!

Focus on Value

Ultimately, the "right" price for a product or service depends on one factor: the value that it provides for a customer. There are two aspects of value, however. Entrepreneurs may recognize the *objective* value of their products and services, which is the price customers would be willing to pay if they understood perfectly the benefits that a product or service delivers for them. Unfortunately, few, if any, customers can see a product's or a service's true objective value; instead, they see only its *perceived* value, which determines the price they are willing to pay for it. Research into purchasing decisions has revealed a fundamental problem that adds to the complexity of a business owner's pricing decision: People faced with pricing decisions often act irrationally. In one classic study, researchers asked shoppers if they would travel an additional 20 minutes to save $5 on a calculator that costs $15; most said they would. When asked the same question about a $125 jacket, most of the shoppers said no, even though they would be saving the exact same amount of money! "People make [purchasing] decisions piecemeal, influenced by the context of the choice," says Richard Thaler, who won a Nobel Prize for his work in behavioral economics.[17]

Note that value does not necessarily always equate to low price. Businesses that underprice their products and services or run special discount price promotions may be short circuiting the value proposition they are trying to build and communicate to their customers.

ENTREPRENEURIAL PROFILE

Lyn & Jenny Gaylord: Lyn Gaylord Accessories

In 1992, Lyn Gaylord and her daughter Jenny launched Lyn Gaylord Accessories, a small company that sells belts with sterling silver buckles that feature unique designs of horses, dogs, butterflies, and other characters that are drawn from the European antiques that have fascinated the Gaylords for years. At one point when the company's sales were slipping, Gaylord cut the prices of her unique belts and buckles to less

Lyn Gaylord Accessories/Anyway Artists, Inc.

Lyn Gaylord Accessories/Anyway Artists, Inc.

than $100 because she thought she had to match rivals' prices. Sales continued to fall, and Gaylord realized her mistake. "I priced too cheaply," she says, and people weren't sure my belts were special." With silver prices skyrocketing, Gaylord raised her prices by 75 percent to an average price of $350, and the company's sales and profits increased. "Price doesn't matter if customers want what they can't get elsewhere," Gaylord says.[18]

Customers may respond to price cuts, but companies that rely on them to boost sales risk undermining the perceived value of their products and services. In addition, once customers grow accustomed to buying products and services during special promotions, the habit can be difficult to break. They simply wait for the next sale. Some companies in the auto industry have faced this problem as customers accustomed to buying autos with large rebates postpone buying new cars until automakers offer them special incentives. The result has been fluctuating sales and a diminished value of those automotive brands.

One of the most important determinants of customers' response to a price is whether they perceive the price to be a fair exchange for the value they receive from the product or service. For most shoppers, three reference points define a fair price: the price they have paid for the product or service in the past, the prices competitors charge for the same or similar product or service, and the costs a company incurs to provide the product or service. The price that customers have paid in the past for an item serves as a baseline reference point, but people often forget that inflation causes a company's costs to rise from year to year. Therefore, it is important for business owners to remind customers periodically that they must raise prices to offset the increased cost of doing business. "Over time, costs always go up," says Norm Brodsky, owner of a successful document storage company. "I'd rather raise prices a little every year or with every new contract than be forced to demand a big increase down the road."[19]

As we have seen already, companies often find it necessary to match competitors' prices on the same or similar items unless they can establish a distinctive image in customers' minds. One

Source: ZITS © ZITS PARTNERSHIP, King Features Syndicate

of the most successful strategies for companies facing direct competition is to differentiate their products or services by adding value for customers and then charging for it. For instance, a company might offer faster delivery, a longer product warranty, extra service, or something else that adds value to an item for its customers and allows the business to charge a higher price.

Perhaps the least understood of the three reference points is a company's cost structure. Customers often underestimate the costs businesses incur to provide products and services, whether it is a simple cotton T-shirt on a shelf in a beach-front shop or a life-saving drug that may have cost hundreds of millions of dollars and many years to develop. For instance, in a study on pricing conducted by the University of Pennsylvania's Wharton School, shoppers estimated the average grocery store's net profit margin to be 27 percent when, in reality, it is less than 2 percent.[20] Customers forget that business owners must make or buy the products they sell, market them, pay their employees, and cover a host of other operating expenses, ranging from health care to legal fees.

ENTREPRENEURIAL PROFILE

Tracy Trotter: Calico Coatings

Tracy Trotter, CEO of Calico Coatings, a 22-employee company in Denver, North Carolina, that makes dry film lubricants that are used to keep the engines in race cars and monster trucks running smoothly, had not raised prices in three years even though his operating costs had gone up significantly in that time. "I worried that we'd lose customers," he says, even though his profit margin was shrinking fast— 5 percentage points each year. Faced with the inevitability of incurring losses, Trotter reluctantly raised the prices on his

David Johnson/Calico Coatings/ Anyway Artists, Inc.

company's lubricants by an average of 18 percent and hoped that his customers would not disappear. None did, and Calico Coatings sales revenue and profits immediately rebounded. "I was surprised by how much leeway we have on what we charge," admits Trotter.[21]

Entrepreneurs facing rapidly rising costs in their businesses should consider the following strategies:

- Pass along rising costs to customers. Customers expect prices to increase over time, but companies must exercise caution in how they implement increases. Some airlines angered many customers by eliminating their free beverage and snack services and offering to sell customers in-flight beverages and snacks for $3. "You wouldn't give a second thought to a $603 plane ticket that included refreshments," says one business writer, "but if you pay $600 for a ticket and they want $3 for a soft drink, you're going to roll your eyes at the price gouging."[22]
- Communicate with customers about the reasons behind price increases. Rather than hide bad news from customers, let them know what is happening. When the owner of a wholesale coffee business saw coffee bean prices escalate because of bad weather in key coffee-producing countries, he included copies of news articles in a letter he sent to customers explaining his company's price increases.
- Focus on improving efficiency in the company. One way to lessen the impact of rising costs in one area of a business is to look for ways to cut costs in other areas. Improving operating efficiency may not offset totally the increased costs of doing business, but it will help to dampen their effects.
- Consider absorbing the cost increases. When Norm Brodsky, owner of the document storage company mentioned earlier, saw his competitors add a fuel surcharge to their customers' bills to offset steep increases in gas prices, he decided *not* to add a fuel surcharge. Then he used the

pricing decision to attract new accounts, telling them, "We have found other ways besides a surcharge to deal with the problem. When we say the price [of our contract] is fixed for five years, we mean it, and you can count on it." Brodsky also used the fuel surcharge issue to build loyalty among his existing customers, something he is certain will pay off in the future.[23]

- Modify the product or service to lower its cost. Launched in 2003, McDonald's Dollar Menu has been a driving force behind the company's sales, particularly during economic downturns. The eight-item menu accounts for 14 percent of McDonald's sales in the United States, but rapidly rising food and energy costs have squeezed franchisees' profits on these items, particularly the double cheeseburger. The company had raised prices on the other items it sells to compensate for higher costs, but prices on its dollar menu remained the same for six years. After months of testing, McDonald's removed the popular sandwich from the dollar menu, raised its price to $1.19, and replaced it with a McDouble burger that has two meat patties but only one slice of cheese rather than two, a change that will save the company six cents per sandwich. Faced with the same dilemma with its Value Menu, Burger King shaved two ounces from each of the beef patties on its popular Whopper Junior sandwich and held the price at $1.[24] Companies using this strategy must exercise caution, taking care not to reduce the quality of their products and services and damage their reputations.
- Diversify your product line. Some small businesses can combat rising raw materials cost by adding new products to their lines.

In 1988, brothers Dan and Jon Levy started selling roasted almonds from a tiny kiosk in a mall in Grand Rapids, Michigan. Before long, their company, Nuts Are Good!, became the largest wholesaler of cinnamon-roasted almonds in the United States. When raw almond prices doubled in less than two years, however, the Levys were concerned that their sales "would come to a screeching halt." The brothers decided to add less costly snack items such as cashew nuts, flavored peanuts (including apple cinnamon, piña colada, and a popular spicy Buffalo flavor), and organic granola mix to their product line, a move that added more than $3 million to the company's sales.[25]

ENTREPRENEURIAL PROFILE

Dan & Jon Levy: Nuts Are Good!

- Anticipate rising costs and try to lock in prices of raw materials early. By tracking coffee and tea prices on commodities exchanges every day, the owner of a small coffee and tea shop was able to anticipate price increases for her raw materials and committed early on to purchase 125,000 pounds of coffee at a fixed price for one year. When coffee prices doubled, she saved more than $80,000.
- Emphasize the value your company's product or service delivers to customers. Customers have a tendency to forget the benefits and value a business provides unless an entrepreneur periodically reminds them.

Setting prices with an emphasis on value is more important than trying to choose the ideal price for a product. In fact, for most products there is an acceptable price range, not a single ideal price. This price range is the area between the price ceiling defined by customers in the market and the price floor established by the company's cost structure. An entrepreneur's goal is to position the company's prices within this acceptable price range. The final price that business owners set depends on the desired image they want to create for the business in their customers' minds—discount, middle-of-the-road, or prestige (see Figure 10.1).

In an attempt to appeal to a broad range of customers, some companies, particularly quick-service restaurants, have had success using a barbell pricing strategy that emphasizes both premium, higher-priced items and value-oriented, lower-priced items. Quick-serve chains such as Hardees, Burger King, and Taco Bell say that this two-tiered pricing strategy attracts both customers who are looking for inexpensive items as well as those who are willing to pay more for premium fare. At Taco Bell, most items on the menu are priced at $2 or less, but the company has added items such as the Triple Steak Burrito that sell at twice that price.[26] One danger of a barbell pricing strategy is creating confusion about a company's image among customers.

For many businesses, the pricing decision has become more challenging because the Web gives customers access to incredible amounts of information about the prices of products ranging from cars to computers. E-commerce also gives companies significant pricing power.

FIGURE 10.1

What Determines Price?

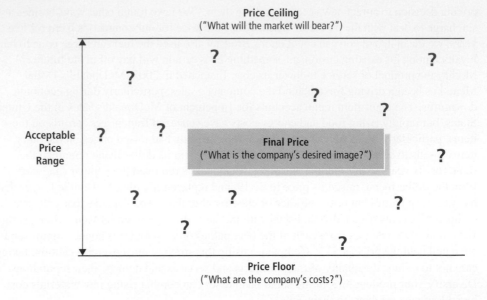

Price Ceiling
("What will the market will bear?")

Acceptable
Price
Range

Final Price
("What is the company's desired image?")

Price Floor
("What are the company's costs?")

customized (dynamic) pricing
a pricing strategy in which companies set different prices for their products or services for different customers using the information they have collected about their customers.

Because they can collect and analyze so much information so quickly about their customers' online buying habits, e-commerce companies have the ability to use this information to customize their pricing strategies to individual customers using **customized** or **dynamic pricing,** in which they set different prices on the same products and services for different customers using the information they have collected about their customers. Dynamic pricing allows both online and traditional companies to set the prices of goods and services for different customers based on their customers' ability and willingness to pay. For instance, a first-time customer making a purchase at an online store may pay a higher price for an item than a regular customer who shops there frequently pays for that same item. AllState Insurance Company relies on a huge database of statistical research that includes information ranging from customers' driving records and their age to their credit scores and whether they pay their bills on time to determine the prices it charges for insurance coverage. AllState's credit-derived premiums have enabled the company to go from a system that established prices using three broad-based categories to one that divides customers into nearly 400 categories, each with its own price point. Since implementing the dynamic pricing strategy, AllState's sales and profitability have climbed significantly.[27]

The Ethics of Dynamic Pricing

In *Casblanca*, the classic romance drama film from 1942, Ilsa, the character played by Ingrid Bergman, is looking at a set of lace napkins in a shopping bazaar when she mentions that she is a friend of Rick, the film's lead character played by Humphrey Bogart. The merchant quickly replaces the replaces the original 700-franc price tag with one bearing a 100-franc price. "For special friends of Rick's, we have special discounts," he explains to Ilsa. The message was clear: Different prices apply to different customers.

Companies now have access to more data on their customers than at any other point in business history, and many of these businesses use that information to serve their customers better, providing them with the goods and services they need just when they need them. One offshoot of this wealth of information is dynamic or customized pricing, a system in which companies charge different prices for the same products and services for different customers using the information they have collected about their customers. The principle is the same as that in *Casablanca*:

Different prices apply to different customers. Movie theaters have used a simple version of dynamic pricing for years. Buy a ticket for an afternoon showing, traditionally a slower time for sales of movie tickets, and you get a lower price. Online digital music store AmieStreet.com, a company in which e-commerce giant Amazon has invested, offers ringtones using dynamic pricing. The company initially prices all ringtones at zero cents; as demand for a ringtone increases, so does its price until it reaches the company's maximum price of $1.99.

The practice of dynamic pricing has created controversy, however. Is it ethical for companies to charge different customers different prices for the same goods and services? A study by the Annenberg Public Policy Center of the University of Pennsylvania reports that 87 percent of people surveyed say that customized pricing is *not* an acceptable business practice. However, empirical evidence shows that customized pricing not only benefits the companies using it but it also can benefit customers. For instance, a study by the Texas Department of Insurance reports that a credit-based dynamic pricing approach in the insurance industry has *reduced* premiums for 70 percent of customers. Managers at AllState Insurance, one of the leading users of dynamic pricing, say that they have been able to use their massive databases of customer information to understand the actual risk levels potential customers represent and to price their insurance products more appropriately. "Now we can offer coverage to many more people and at far more competitive prices," explains Fred Cripe, vice-president for product operations. However, 40 states now have laws in place to limit the use of credit-based pricing for insurance premiums on the grounds that doing so discriminates against people with bad credit.

Dynamic pricing has stood successfully against several legal challenges. Denise Katzman filed a class action lawsuit against retailer Victoria's Secret when she discovered that a catalogue that she received offered higher prices than a nearly identical catalog the company sent to a male co-worker. She alleged that the company had engaged in illegal price discrimination by charging different prices for identical items to different categories of customers. Because Victoria's Secret had sent the catalogs through the U.S. mail, Katzman claimed that the company's discriminatory pricing structure constituted mail fraud. U.S. District Court judge Robert W. Sweet upheld the validity of Victoria's Secret's dynamic pricing policies, ruling that "offering different discounts to different catalogue customers does not constitute mail fraud under any reading of the law." On appeal, the U.S. Court of Appeals for the Second Circuit upheld Judge Sweet's decision. This case suggests that businesses can charge different customers different prices as long as the price differences are based on reasonable business practices such as rewarding loyal customers and do not discriminate against customers for race, gender, national origin, or some other illegal category.

Dynamic pricing has emerged as a marketing strategy out of necessity. Entrepreneurs say that the Internet has lowered the transaction costs of doing business and moves business along at such a fast pace that the fixed pricing strategies of the past no longer work. To keep up with fluid, fast-changing markets, companies must change their prices quickly. They must be able to adapt the prices they charge their customers on a real-time basis and to charge higher prices to those customers who cost their companies more to serve.

1. Work with a team of your classmates to define the ethical issues involved in dynamic pricing.
2. What are the advantages and the disadvantages of dynamic pricing to the companies that use it? To the customers of the companies that use it?
3. According to an old proverb, "The value of a thing is what it will bring." Do you agree? Explain. Should companies be allowed to engage in dynamic pricing?
4. If you owned your own business and had the information required to engage in dynamic pricing, would you do so? Explain.

Sources: Adapted from "AmieStreet.com and Myxer Partner to Bring Demand-Based Pricing to the Mobile Ringtone Marketplace," *Business Wire*, September 17, 2007, http://findarticles.com/p/articles/mi_m0EIN/is_/ai_n19521604; Robert M. Weiss and Ajay K. Mehrotra, "Online Dynamic Pricing: Efficiency, Equity, and the Future of E-Commerce," *Virginia Journal of Law and Technology*, Summer 2001, University of Virginia, Issue No.2. Volume 6, p. 7; Matthew Maier, "Finding Riches in a Mine of Credit Data," *Business 2.0*, October 2005, pp. 72–74; Peter Coffee, "More 'Dynamic Pricing' Is on the Way," *eWeek*, September 2002, http://www.eweek.com/article2/0,1759,1011178,00.asp.

Pricing Strategies and Tactics

LO 2

Describe effective pricing techniques for introducing new products or services and for existing ones.

There is no limit to the number of variations in pricing strategies and tactics. This wide variety of options is exactly what allows the small business manager to be so creative. This section examines some of the more commonly used tactics under a variety of conditions. Pricing always plays a critical role in a firm's overall strategy; pricing policies must be compatible with a company's total marketing plan and the image it plans to create in the marketplace.

Introducing a New Product

Most entrepreneurs approach setting the price of a new product with a great deal of apprehension because they have no precedent on which to base their decisions. If the new product's price is excessively high, it is in danger of failing because of low sales volume. However, if its price is too low, the product's sales revenue might not cover costs. In addition, the company runs the risk of establishing the product's value at a low level. Management consulting firm McKinsey and Company claims that 80 to 90 percent of the pricing problems on new products are the result of companies setting prices that are too low.[28] When pricing any new product, the owner should try to satisfy three objectives:

1. *Getting the product accepted.* No matter how unusual a product is, its price must be acceptable to a company's potential customers. The acceptable price range for a new product depends, in part, on the product's position:
   • **Revolutionary products** are so new and unique that they transform existing markets. The acceptable price range for revolutionary products tends to be rather wide, but the businesses introducing them must be prepared to make an investment in educating customers about them.

revolutionary products

products that are so new and unique that they transform existing markets.

evolutionary products
products that offer upgrades and enhancements to existing products.

me-too products
products that offer the same basic features as existing products on the market.

- **Evolutionary products** offer upgrades and enhancements to existing products. The acceptable price range for evolutionary products is not a wide as it is for revolutionary products. Companies that introduce evolutionary products with many new features at prices that are too low may initiate a price war.
- **Me-too products,** as the name suggests, offer the same basic features as existing products on the market. The acceptable price range for these products is quite narrow, and many companies introducing them find themselves left with me-too pricing strategies that are the same or similar to those of their competitors.

2. *Maintaining market share as competition grows.* If a new product is successful, competitors will enter the market, and the small company must work to expand or at least maintain its market share. Continuously reappraising the product's price in conjunction with special advertising and promotion techniques helps to retain a satisfactory market share.

3. *Earning a profit.* A small business must establish a price for a new product that is higher than its cost. Entrepreneurs should not introduce a new product at a price below cost because it is much easier to lower a price than to increase it once the product is on the market. Pricing their products too low is a common and often fatal mistake for new businesses; entrepreneurs are tempted to underprice their products and services when they enter a new market to ensure their acceptance or to gain market share quickly. Doing so, however, sets customers' value expectations at low levels as well, and that can be a difficult perception to overcome. Steve McKee, president of McKee Wallwork Cleveland Advertising, an advertising agency that targets small companies, says, "It can be odd to feel good about losing customers because of price, but if you're not, you may be backing yourself into a low-margin corner. Don't kid yourself; other than Wal-Mart, very few companies can sustain a low-price position."[29]

Entrepreneurs have three basic strategies to choose from when establishing a new product's price: a penetration pricing strategy, a skimming pricing strategy, and a life cycle pricing strategy.

MARKET PENETRATION   If a small business introduces a product into a highly competitive market in which a large number of similar products are competing for acceptance, the product must penetrate the market to be successful. To gain quick acceptance and extensive distribution in the mass market, entrepreneurs should consider introducing the product at a low price. In other words, it should set the price just above total unit cost to develop a wedge in the market and quickly achieve a high volume of sales. The resulting low profit margins tend to discourage competitors from entering the market with similar products.

In most cases, a penetration pricing strategy is used to introduce relatively low-priced goods into a market where no elite segment and little opportunity for differentiation exists. The introduction is usually accompanied by heavy advertising and promotional techniques, special sales, and discounts. Entrepreneurs must recognize that penetration pricing is a long-range strategy; until customers accept the product, profits are likely to be small. If the strategy works and the product achieves mass market penetration, sales volume will increase, and the company will earn adequate profits. The objectives of the penetration strategy are to break into the market quickly, generate a high sales volume as soon as possible, and build market share. Many consumer products, such as soap, shampoo, and light bulbs, are introduced with penetration pricing strategies.

SKIMMING   A skimming pricing strategy often is used when a company introduces a new product into a market with little or no competition or to establish the company and its products or services as unique and superior to those of its competitors. Sometimes a business employs this tactic when introducing a product into a competitive market that contains an elite group that is able to pay a higher price. Here an entrepreneur uses a higher-than-normal price in an effort to quickly recover the initial developmental and promotional costs of the product. The idea is to set a price well above the total unit cost and to promote the product heavily to appeal to the segment of the market that is not sensitive to price. This pricing tactic often reinforces the unique, prestigious image of a store and projects a quality picture of the product. Another advantage of this technique is that entrepreneurs can correct pricing mistakes quickly and easily. If a product's price proves to be too low under a penetration strategy, raising the price can be very difficult. If a company using a skimming strategy sets a price too high to generate sufficient volume, it can always lower the price. Successful skimming strategies require a company to differentiate its products or services from those of the competition, justifying the above-average price.

ENTREPRENEURIAL PROFILE_____

Todd Barrato: Brioni

> Brioni, an Italian luxury clothing company, makes some of the finest men's suits in the world at prices that range from $5,000 for an off-the-rack model to $25,000 for the finest-quality bespoke garment. Each Brioni suit requires between 18 and 25 hours of hand-sewing in addition to the time that the fabric must "rest" between each process. "There are more than 5,000 hand stitches per jacket," explains Todd Barrato, a Brioni executive vice president. "Each suit goes through 42 pressings." Brioni, which has tailored all of the suits for the stars of the James Bond films since 1995, recently took orders for custom-made suits made from 78 rare fabrics, including Brioni's Super 230s 12-micron wool, the most luxurious in the world and so scarce that the company made only 12 suits from it.[30]

LIFE CYCLE PRICING One variation of the skimming price strategy is called life cycle pricing. Using this tactic, the small company introduces a product at a high price. Then, technological advances enable the firm to lower its costs quickly and to reduce the product's price before its competition can. By beating other businesses in a price decline, the small company discourages competitors and gradually, over time, becomes a high-volume producer. High-definition television sets are a prime example of a product introduced at a high price that quickly cascaded downward as companies forged important technological advances and took advantage of economies of scale. When they were first introduced in 1999, high-definition TVs sold for $19,000; today, they are priced at $500 or less.

Life cycle pricing is a short-term strategy that assumes that competition will eventually emerge. Even if no competition arises, however, the small business almost always lowers the product's price to attract a larger segment of the market. Nonetheless, the initial high price contributes to a rapid return of startup costs and generates a pool of funds to finance expansion and technological advances. Ten weeks after introducing its popular iPhone, (during which time it sold 1 million units), Apple reduced the price of the multi-function phone by one-third, opening the market for less price-sensitive customers heading into the all-important holiday season and pumping up the company's sales volume dramatically. Customers who purchased the iPhone when it was first released howled in protest, prompting CEO Steve Jobs to apologize and offer them a partial rebate.[31]

Pricing Established Goods and Services

Each of the following pricing tactics or techniques can become part of the toolbox of pricing tactics entrepreneurs can use to set prices of established goods and services.

ODD PRICING Although studies of consumer reactions to prices are mixed and generally inconclusive, many small business managers use the technique known as **odd pricing.** These managers prefer to establish prices that end in odd numbers such as 5, 7, or 9 because they believe that merchandise selling for $12.69 appears to be much cheaper than the item priced at $13.00. Psychological techniques such as odd pricing are designed to appeal to certain customer interests, but research on their effectiveness is mixed. Some studies show no benefits from using odd pricing, but others have concluded that the technique can produce significant increases in sales. Omitting the "$" symbol from prices may help, too. Researchers at Cornell University have discovered that restaurants that list menu prices without the "$" symbol achieved $5.55 more in sales on average than those whose menu prices were written in script or included a "$" symbol.[32]

odd pricing
a pricing technique that sets prices that end in odd numbers to create the psychological impression of low prices.

PRICE LINING **Price lining** is a technique that greatly simplifies the pricing function by pricing different products in a product line at different price points, depending on their quality, features, and cost. Under this system, entrepreneurs stock merchandise in several different price ranges, or price lines. Each category of merchandise contains items that are similar in appearance but that differ in quality, cost, performance, or other features. Many lined products appear in sets of three—good, better, and best—at prices designed to satisfy different market segment needs and incomes. Price lining can boost a store's sales because it makes goods available to a wide range of shoppers, simplifies the purchase decision for customers, and allows them to keep their purchases within their budgets.

price lining
a technique that greatly simplifies the pricing function by pricing different products in a product line at different price points, depending on their quality, features, and cost.

leader pricing
a technique that involves marking down the normal price of a popular item in an attempt to attract more customers who make incidental purchases of other items at regular prices.

LEADER PRICING **Leader pricing** is a technique in which a retailer marks down the customary price (i.e., the price consumers are accustomed to paying) of a popular item in an attempt to attract more customers. The company earns a much smaller profit on each unit because the markup is lower, but purchases of other merchandise by customers seeking the leader item often boost sales and profits. In other words, the incidental purchases that consumers make when shopping for the leader item boost sales revenue enough to offset a lower profit margin on the leader. Grocery chains frequently use leader pricing. For instance, during the holiday season, stores often use turkeys as a price leader, knowing that they will earn higher margins on the other items shoppers purchase with their turkeys. Many discount warehouses such as Costco and supermarket chains such as Albertsons, Kroger, and Ingles sell gasoline as a price leader to encourage customers to make more frequent visits to their retail stores.[33]

discounts (markdowns)
reductions from normal list prices.

DISCOUNTS Many small business managers use **discounts or markdowns**—reductions from normal list prices–to move stale, outdated, damaged, or slow-moving merchandise. A seasonal discount is a price reduction designed to encourage shoppers to purchase merchandise before an upcoming season. For instance, many retailers offer after-Christmas discounts to make room for their spring merchandise. Some firms grant purchase discounts to special groups of customers, such as senior citizens or students, to establish a faithful clientele and to generate repeat business.

Small businesses that use a differentiation strategy to create an upscale image must approach discounting carefully because excessive discounting can ruin their reputation for exclusivity and superior quality and service. One less visible way for these small businesses to offer discounts is by enrolling customers in a loyalty program that entitles them to "free" benefits. For instance, the Omni Berkshire Place Hotel in Manhattan, which caters to upscale business travelers, waives the $10 per day wireless Internet access fee for loyal customers who enroll in its Select Guest program.[34] Researchers at Southern Methodist University have discovered another tool that companies can use to avoid diluting customers' perceptions of their products and services: the time-limited discount ("$150 regular price; $120 sale price *for three days only*").[35]

multiple unit pricing
a technique offering customers discounts if they purchase in quantity.

Multiple unit pricing is a promotional technique that offers customers discounts if they purchase in quantity. Many products, especially those with relatively low unit value, are sold using multiple pricing. For example, instead of selling an item for 50 cents, a small company might offer 5 for $2.

bundling
a pricing method that involves grouping together several products or services, or both, into a package that offers customers extra value at a special price.

BUNDLING Many small businesses have discovered the marketing benefits of **bundling,** grouping together several products or services, or both, into a package that offers customers extra value at a special price. Bundling is another way for companies to offer customers discounts without damaging their reputations. For instance, many software manufacturers bundle several computer programs (such as a word processor, spreadsheet, database, presentation graphics, and Web browser) into "suites" that offer customers a discount over purchasing the same packages separately. Fast-food outlets often bundle items into "meal deals" that customers can purchase at lower prices than if they bought the items separately.

optional-product pricing
a technique that involves selling the base product for one price but selling the options or accessories for it at a much higher markup.

OPTIONAL-PRODUCT PRICING Optional-product pricing involves selling the base product for one price but selling the options or accessories for it at a much higher markup. Automobiles are often sold at a base price with each option priced separately. In some cases, the car is sold with some of the options "bundled" together, as explained previously.

ENTREPRENEURIAL
PROFILE _____

Campbell Gower: Phil & Teds

Phil & Teds, a New Zealand company founded by Campbell Gower, uses an optional-product pricing strategy that more closely mimics BMW than Babies "R" Us. The company's upscale baby strollers offer tiny occupants ergonomically designed seats and their parents sturdy, lightweight aluminum frames that fold flat, and the added safety of a one-touch hand brake. One of the company's most popular models, the Vibe, sells for just under $700, but a variety of options that range from an optional second seat ($110) and a rolling travel bag ($100) to a storm cover ($60) and a travel system ($34.99) quickly pushes the price to $1,000 or more, far

Phil & Teds USA, Inc.

above the price of an average stroller. Despite Phil & Ted's premium prices, parents who want only the best for their children, including celebrities Gwyneth Paltrow and Jennifer Garner, are snapping up the company's high-quality strollers fast enough that its sales now exceed $150 million annually.[36]

CAPTIVE-PRODUCT PRICING Captive-product pricing is a pricing strategy in which the base product is not functional without the appropriate accessory. King Gillette, the founder of Gillette, taught the business world that the real money is not in selling the razor (the product) but in selling the blades (the accessory)! Most companies in the desktop printer business use this technique. They introduce a printer at a low initial price and then price replacement cartridges so that they earn high margins on them. Manufacturers of electronic games also rely on captive-product pricing, earning lower margins on the game consoles and substantially higher margins on the game cartridges.

captive-product pricing
a technique that involves selling a product for a low price and charging a higher price for the accessories that accompany it.

BYPRODUCT PRICING Byproduct pricing is a technique in which the revenues from the sale of byproducts allow a company to be more competitive in its pricing of the main product. For years, sawmills thought that the bark from the trees they processed was a nuisance. Now it is packaged and sold to gardeners who use the bark chips for ground cover. Zoos across the globe offer one of the most creative examples of byproduct pricing, packaging once-worthless exotic animal droppings and marketing it as fertilizer under the clever name "Zoo Doo."

byproduct pricing
a technique in which a company uses the revenues from the sale of byproducts to be more competitive in pricing the main product.

SUGGESTED RETAIL PRICES Many manufacturers print suggested retail prices on their products or include them on invoices or in wholesale catalogs. Small business owners frequently follow these suggested retail prices because this eliminates the need to make a pricing decision. Nonetheless, following prices established by a distant manufacturer may create problems for a small firm. For example, a haberdasher may try to create a high-quality, exclusive image through a prestige pricing policy, but manufacturers may suggest discount outlet prices that are incompatible with the small company's image. Another danger of accepting the manufacturer's suggested price is that it does not take into consideration a small company's cost structure or competitive situation. A recent U.S. Supreme Court decision overturned a nearly 100-year-old ruling and allows manufacturers to set and enforce minimum prices that retailers can charge for the manufacturer's produces as long as doing so does not reduce competition.

Is the Price Right?

To increase sales of a particular product or service, business owners often resort to lowering its price. After all, doing so is consistent with the law of demand, which says that as price decreases, quantity demanded increases. However, there are exceptions to every rule, including the law of demand. A product's or service's price tag says a great deal about it. Shoppers often have difficulty judging the quality of the goods and services they purchase and look to their prices for clues. The prices that entrepreneurs set for the products and services they sell are a significant factor in the image they create for their companies in their customers' minds, whether that image is one of a discount store or one of an upscale, exclusive shop. These two entrepreneurs are faced with a pricing decision that will influence the image and ultimately the success of their companies:

Sweetriot

Sarah Endline, founder of Sweetriot, a candy manufacturer in New York City, has traveled, lived, and worked in more than 50 countries, but grew up on a farm in a small town in Michigan. Her company is the embodiment of her life and travel experiences, selling roasted cacao beans covered in all-natural dark chocolate that she purchases from a supplier in Latin America that engages in fair trade practices. Endline, whose title is Mastermind and Chief Rioter, wants shoppers to perceive her products as high quality and fun. She has studied the prices of other premium chocolates and has discovered that they range from $2.99 to $7.99. She must decide how to price the one-ounce tins of chocolate covered cacao beans that are adorned with the artwork of up-and-coming artists. Endline says that at the original price of $4.99, "we kept hearing people say, 'Wow, I'll buy this for a special occasion or as a gift' Part of the philosophy of Sweetriot is to be accessible; we don't want to charge a price that's unapproachable."

Kriser's Pet Supplies

Jeff Kalish is cofounder of this start-up chain of pet supplies and dog grooming services in Chicago and has plans to expand the business rapidly. Dog grooming services are a key part of the company's sales equation because they drive customer traffic to the company's three stores. In an attempt to generate more customer traffic, Kriser's Pet Supplies set its dog grooming prices at an average of $46, which is noticeably lower than those of other pet groomers. Feedback from potential customers makes Kalish wonder whether Kriser's pricing strategy is creating the wrong impression of the chain in customers' eyes. "When they heard our price, people would start asking questions," says Kalish. "Did we do full service? Were our groomers experienced?"

What steps can entrepreneurs take when it comes to setting prices the right way? The following tips will help:

- Know your costs, including the direct and the indirect costs, of providing your product or service.
- Don't set your price below your costs. "We lose money on every unit we sell, but we make up for it in volume" is a business philosophy that never works.
- Price increases are easier to accomplish when a company faces fewer competitors. The more intense the competition, the more difficult it is to raise prices.
- If you must raise prices shortly after launching your business, try to soften the blow by bundling products and services to create more value for customers.
- Assign someone in your company to track competitors' prices regularly (at least monthly) and to present the results on a timely basis.

- Do not simply follow your competitors' pricing strategies.
- Base your pricing on the value that your product or service offers customers. Remember that sometimes the most valuable components of a product or service are intangible.
- Define the image you want to create for your business and use your pricing strategy to communicate that image to your customers and to position your company in the market.

1. Why do many entrepreneurs underprice their goods and services, especially when they first get into business? Discuss the connection between the prices a company establishes for its goods and services and the image it creates for the company.
2. What advice on pricing can you offer Sarah Endline and Jeff Kalish? Work with a group of your classmates to brainstorm various pricing strategies and the impact that they might have on these companies. How do you recommend that they implement your pricing suggestions?

Sources: Stephanie Clifford, "How Low Can You Go?" *Inc.*, August 2007, pp. 42–43; Bridget McCrea, "When Is the Price Right? Effective Pricing Is Crucial to Remain Competitive and Move Product, *Black Enterprise*, July 2004, pp. 78–79.

LO 3

Explain the pricing methods and strategies for retailers.

Pricing Strategies and Methods for Retailers

As customers have become more price-conscious, retailers have changed their pricing strategies to emphasize value. This value/price relationship allows for a wide variety of highly creative pricing and marketing practices. As discussed previously, delivering high levels of recognized value in products and services is one key to retail customer loyalty.

Markup

markup (or markon)
the difference between the cost of a product or service and its selling price.

The basic premise of a successful business operation is selling a good or service for more than it costs. The difference between the cost of a product or service and its selling price is called **markup (or markon).** Markup can be expressed in dollars or as a percentage of either cost or selling price:

$$\text{Dollar markup} = \text{Retail price} - \text{Cost of the merchandise}$$

$$\text{Percentage (of retail price) markup} = \frac{\text{Dollar markup}}{\text{Retail price}}$$

$$\text{Percentage (of cost) markup} = \frac{\text{Dollar markup}}{\text{Cost of unit}}$$

For example, if a man's shirt costs $14, and a retailer plans to sell it for $25, the markup would be as follows:

$$\text{Dollar markup} = \$25 - \$14 = \$11$$

$$\text{Percentage (of retail price) markup} = \frac{\$11}{\$25} = 44.0\%$$

$$\text{Percentage (of cost) markup} = \frac{\$11}{\$14} = 78.6\%$$

Notice that the percentage of retail price markup is always less than the percentage of cost markup for any item. The cost of merchandise used in computing markup includes not only the wholesale price of the merchandise but also any incidental costs (e.g., selling or transportation charges) that the retailer incurs and a profit minus any discounts (quantity, cash) that the wholesaler offers.

Once a business owner has a financial plan, including sales estimates and anticipated expenses, he or she can compute the company's initial markup. The initial markup is the *average* markup required on all merchandise to cover the cost of the items, all incidental expenses, and a reasonable profit:

$$\text{Initial dollar markup} = \frac{\text{operating expenses} + \text{reductions} + \text{profits}}{\text{net sales} + \text{reductions}}$$

where operating expenses include the cost of doing business, such as rent, utilities, and depreciation, and reductions include employee and customer discounts, markdowns, special sales, and the cost of stockouts.

For example, if a small retailer forecasts sales of $380,000, expenses of $177,000, and $24,000 in reductions, and he or she establishes a target profit of $42,000, the initial markup (of retail price) percentage is calculated as follows:

$$\text{Initial markup percentage} = \frac{177,000 + 24,000 + 42,000}{380,000 + 24,000} = 60.1\%$$

This retailer knows that an average percentage (of retail price) markup of 60.1 percent is required to cover costs and generate an adequate profit.

Some businesses employ a standard markup on all of their merchandise. This technique, which is usually used in retail stores carrying related products, applies a standard percentage markup to all merchandise. Most stores find it much more practical to use a flexible markup, which assigns various markup percentages to different types of products. Because of the wide range of prices and types of merchandise they sell, department stores frequently rely on a flexible markup. It would be impractical for them to use a standard markup on all items because they have such a divergent cost and volume range. For instance, the markup percentage for socks is not likely to be suitable as a markup for washing machines.

Once an entrepreneur determines a suitable initial percentage markup, he or she can compute the appropriate retail price using the following formula:

$$\text{Retail price} = \frac{\text{Dollar cost}}{(1 - \text{Percentage of retail price markup})}$$

For instance, taking the markup of a particular item represents 60 percent of the retail price calculated in the previous example and applying it to an item that cost the retailer $18 gives the following result:

$$\text{Retail price} = \frac{\$18.00}{(1 - .60)} = \$45.00$$

The owner will set a retail price of $45 for this item using a 60 percent (of retail price) markup.

Finally, retailers must verify that the retail price they have calculated is consistent with their planned initial markup percentage. Will it generate the desired profit? Is it congruent with the firm's overall price image? Is the final price in line with the company's strategy? Is it within an acceptable price range? How does it compare to the prices charged by competitors? And, perhaps most important, are the customers willing and able to pay this price? Figure 10.2 explains the mathematics of markups—and markdowns—at the retail level.

Follow-the-Leader Pricing

Some small companies make no effort to be price leaders in their immediate geographic areas and simply follow the prices that their competitors establish. Entrepreneurs wisely monitor their competitors' pricing policies and individual prices by reviewing their advertisements or by hiring part-time or full-time comparison shoppers. However, some retailers use this information to establish "me too" pricing policies, which eradicate any opportunity to create a special price image for their businesses. Although many retailers must match competitors' prices on identical items, maintaining a follow-the-leader pricing policy may not be healthy for a small business because it robs the company of the opportunity to create a distinctive image in its customers' eyes.

FIGURE 10.2

The Mathematics of Markups and Markdowns

The Sale Rack Shuffle

Have you ever purchased an item of clothing at a significant discount from the sale rack and then wondered if the store actually made any profit on the item? Here is how the markdown process typically works:

1. Clothing company makes dress at a cost of $50.
2. Sells dress to retailer at a wholesale cost of $80.
3. Retailer marks dress up to $200.
4. If unsold after eight to twelve weeks, dress is marked down by 25 percent to $150.
5. If dress still does not sell, it is marked down further until it does. Clothing company and retailer negotiate on how to share the cost of the markdown.

Below-Market Pricing

Some small businesses choose to create a discount image in the market by offering goods at below-market prices. By setting prices below those of their competitors, these businesses hope to attract a sufficient level of volume to offset the lower profit margins. Many retailers using a below-market pricing strategy eliminate most of the extra services that their above-market-pricing competitors offer. For instance, these businesses trim operating costs by cutting out services like delivery, installation, credit granting, and sales assistance. Below-market pricing strategies can be risky for small companies because they require them to constantly achieve high sales volume to remain competitive.

LO 4

Explain the pricing methods and strategies for manufacturers.

Pricing Concepts for Manufacturers

For manufacturers, the pricing decision requires the support of accurate, timely accounting records. The most commonly used pricing technique for manufacturers is cost-plus pricing. Using this method, a manufacturer establishes a price that is composed of direct materials, direct labor, factory overhead, selling and administrative costs, plus the desired profit margin. Figure 10.3 illustrates the cost-plus pricing components.

The main advantage of the cost-plus pricing method is its simplicity. Given the proper cost accounting data, computing a product's final selling price is relatively easy. In addition, because they add a profit onto the top of their companies' costs, manufacturers are guaranteed the desired profit margin. This process, however, does not encourage manufacturers to use their resources efficiently. Even if the company fails to employ its resources in the most effective manner, it will still earn a reasonable profit, and thus there is no motivation to conserve resources in the manufacturing process. Finally, because manufacturers' cost structures vary so greatly, cost-plus pricing fails to consider the competition (and market forces) sufficiently. Despite its drawbacks, the cost-plus method of establishing prices remains prominent in many industries such as construction and printing.

FIGURE 10.3

Cost-Plus Pricing Components

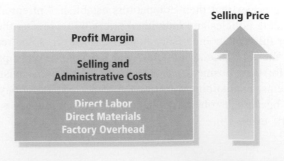

Direct Costing and Pricing

One requisite for a successful pricing policy in manufacturing is a reliable cost accounting system that can generate timely reports to determine the costs of processing raw materials into finished goods. The traditional method of product costing is called **absorption costing** because all manufacturing and overhead costs are absorbed into a finished product's total cost. Absorption costing includes direct materials, direct labor, plus a portion of fixed and variable factory overhead in each unit manufactured. Full absorption financial statements are used in published annual reports and in tax reports and are very useful in performing financial analysis. However, full absorption statements are of little help to manufacturers when determining prices or the impact of price changes.

A more useful technique for managerial decision making is **variable (or direct) costing,** in which the cost of the products manufactured includes only those costs that vary directly with the quantity produced. In other words, variable costing encompasses direct materials, direct labor, and factory overhead costs that vary with the level of the company's output of finished goods. Factory overhead costs that are fixed (rent, depreciation, insurance) are *not* included in the costs of finished items. Instead, they are considered to be expenses of the period.

A manufacturer's goal when establishing prices is to discover the combination of selling price and sales volume that covers the variable costs of producing a product and contributes toward covering fixed costs and earning a profit. Full-absorption costing clouds the true relationships among price, volume, and costs by including fixed expenses in unit cost. Direct costing, however, yields a constant unit cost for the product no matter what volume of production. The result is a clearer picture of the price/volume/costs relationship.

The starting point for establishing product prices is the direct cost income statement. As Table 10.1 indicates, the direct cost statement yields the same net income as does the

absorption costing
the traditional method of product costing in which all manufacturing and overhead costs are absorbed into the product's total cost.

variable (direct) costing
a method of product costing that includes in the product's cost only those costs that vary directly with the quantity produced.

TABLE 10.1 Full-Absorption versus Direct-Cost Income Statement

Full-Absorption Income Statement

Sales Revenue		$790,000
Cost of Goods Sold		
Materials	250,500	
Direct Labor	190,200	
Factory Overhead	120,200	560,900
Gross Profit		$229,100
Operating Expenses		
General & Administrative	66,100	
Selling	112,000	
Other	11,000	
Total Operating Expenses		189,100
Net Income (before taxes)		$ 40,000

Direct-Cost Income Statement

Sales Revenue (100%)		$790,000
Variable Costs		
Materials	250,500	
Direct Labor	190,200	
Variable Factory Overhead	13,200	
Variable Selling Expenses	48,100	
Total Variable Costs (63.5%)		502,000
Contribution Margin (36.5%)		288,000
Fixed Costs		
Fixed Factory Overhead	107,000	
Fixed Selling Expenses	63,900	
General and Administrative	66,100	
Other Fixed Expenses	11,000	
Total Fixed Expenses (31.4%)		248,000
Net Income (before taxes)(5.1%)		$ 40,000

full-absorption income statement. The only difference between the two statements is the format. The full-absorption statement allocates costs such as advertising, rent, and utilities according to the activity that caused them, but the direct cost income statement separates expenses into their fixed and variable components. Fixed expenses remain constant regardless of the production level, but variable expenses fluctuate according to production volume.

When variable costs are subtracted from total revenues, the result is the manufacturer's **contribution margin**—the amount remaining that contributes to covering fixed expenses and earning a profit. Expressing this contribution margin as a percentage of total revenue yields the company's contribution percentage. Computing the contribution percentage is a critical step in establishing prices through the direct costing method. This manufacturer's contribution margin percentage is 36.5 percent, which is calculated as follows:

contribution margin
the amount left over out of a dollar of sales after variable expenses are paid that contributes to covering fixed expenses and earning a profit.

$$\text{Contribution percentage} = 1 - \frac{\text{Variable expenses}}{\text{Sales Revenue}}$$

$$= 1 - \frac{\$502,000}{\$790,000} = 36.5\%$$

Computing the Break-Even Selling Price

The manufacturer's contribution percentage tells what portion of total revenues remains after covering variable costs to contribute toward meeting fixed expenses and earning a profit. This manufacturer's contribution percentage is 36.5 percent, which means that variable costs absorb 63.5 percent of total revenue. In other words, variable costs make up 63.5 percent $(1.00 - 0.365 = 0.635)$ of the product's selling price. Suppose that this manufacturer's variable costs include the following:

Material	$2.08/unit
Direct labor	$4.12/unit
Variable factory overhead	$0.78/unit
Total variable cost	$6.98/unit

The minimum price at which the manufacturer would sell the item for is $6.98. Any price below this would not cover variable costs. To compute the break-even selling price for this product, we find the selling price using the following equation:

$$\text{Break-even selling price} =$$
$$\frac{\text{profit} + (\text{variable cost per unit} \times \text{quantity produced}) + \text{total fixed cost}}{\text{quantity produced}}$$

To break even, the manufacturer assumes $0 profit. Suppose that his plans are to produce 50,000 units of the product and that fixed costs will be $110,000. The break-even selling price is as follows:

$$\text{Break-even selling price} = \frac{\$0 + (\$6.98 \times 50,000\,\text{units}) + \$110,000}{50,000\,\text{units}}$$

$$= \frac{\$459,000}{50,000\,\text{units}}$$

$$= \$9.18/\text{unit}$$

Thus, $2.20 ($9.18/unit − $6.98/unit) of the $9.18 break-even price contributes to meeting fixed production costs. But suppose the manufacturer wants to earn a $50,000 profit. Then the selling price is calculated as follows:

$$\text{Selling price} = \frac{\$50,000 + (\$6.98/\text{unit} \times 50,000\,\text{units}) + \$110,000}{50,000\,\text{units}}$$

$$= \frac{\$509,000}{50,000\,\text{units}}$$

$$= \$10.18/\text{unit}$$

Now the manufacturer must decide whether customers will purchase 50,000 units at $10.18. If not, he or she must decide either to produce a different, more profitable product or to lower the selling price. Any price above $9.18 will generate some profit, although less than that desired. In the short run, the manufacturer could sell the product for less than $9.18 if competitive factors so dictated, but not below $6.98 because this would not cover the variable cost of production.

Because the manufacturer's capacity in the short run is fixed, pricing decisions should be aimed at employing these resources most efficiently. The fixed costs of operating the plant cannot be avoided, and the variable costs can be eliminated only if the firm ceases offering the product. Therefore, the selling price must be at least equal to the variable costs (per unit) of making the product. Any price above this amount contributes to covering fixed costs and providing a reasonable profit.

Of course, over the long run, a manufacturer cannot sell below total costs and continue to survive. The final selling price must cover total product cost—both fixed and variable—and generate a reasonable profit.

HANDS ON...
HOW TO

Calculate Your Company's Pocket Price Band

When entrepreneurs make pricing decisions, they usually look at the retail price or the invoice price they charge. Doing so, however, may be misleading if the company offers significant "off-invoice" discounts such as cash discounts for paying early, quantity discounts for large purchases, special promotional discounts, and others. These invoice leakages mean that a business is getting less, sometimes far less, than the retail or invoice price listed. In some cases, a company's pocket price, the price it receives for a product or a service after deducting all discounts and purchase incentives, is far below the listed retail or invoice price. The impact of these discounts can be significant. Research by the consulting firm McKinsey and Company shows that a decrease of one percent in a typical company's average prices reduces its operating profits by eight percent if all other factors remain constant.

How are discounts affecting your business? To find out, you must estimate your company's pocket price waterfall and its pocket price band. The pocket price waterfall starts with a company's invoice or retail price on the far left of the diagram and then shows how much every discount or incentive the company offers its customers reduces that price. In the example in Figure 1, this small manufacturer offers a cash discount for early payment that shaves 2.0 percent off of the retail price, a 3.5 percent discount for companies whose purchases exceed a particular volume, a cooperative advertising program (in which it splits the cost of advertising its products with retailers) that amounts to 4.4 percent, and periodic promotional discounts to move products that average 10.8 percent. Other discounts the company offered customers further reduced its pocket price. In the end, the company's average pocket price is 77.2 percent of the listed invoice price.

Not every customer qualifies for every discount, however. The type and the amount of the discount vary from one customer to another; the pocket prices they pay can vary a good deal. Therefore, it is important to estimate the width of the company's pocket price band, which shows the percentage of sales each pocket price (shown as a percentage of the listed invoice or retail price) accounts for (see Figure 2). In this example, pocket prices that are 90 percent or more of the company's invoice price account for just 28.3 percent

Pocket Price Waterfall

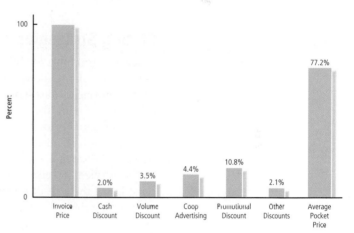

of its total revenue. Conversely, pocket prices that are 80 percent or less of its invoice price make up 46.2 percent of its total revenue. The final step in the process is to identify the individual customers that make up each segment of the company's pocket price band. When one manufacturer analyzed its pocket price band, managers discovered that sales to 20 percent of its customers had slipped below its breakeven point, which caused the company to lose money on those customers. To restore profitability, managers raised prices selectively and lowered their costs by reducing the frequency of deliveries and encouraging customers to place orders online.

A wide pocket price band is not necessarily bad. It simply shows that some customers generate much higher pocket prices than others. When a band is wide, small changes in its shape can produce big results for a company. If an entrepreneur can increase sales at the upper end of the band while reducing or even dropping those at the lower end of the band, both the company's revenues and profits will climb. If a company's price band is narrow, an entrepreneur has less room to maneuver prices, changing the shape of the band is more difficult, and any changes the entrepreneur can make tend to have less impact on the company's sales and revenues.

Sample Pocket Price Band

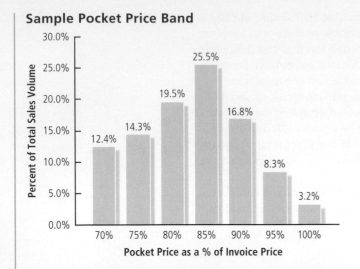

Pocket Price as a % of Invoice Price

When one lighting company calculated its pocket price band, managers were surprised at its width. Once managers realized how big a dent discounts were putting in its revenues and profits, they worked with the sales force to realign the company's discount structure. Some of the company's smallest accounts had been getting the largest discounts, despite their small volume of purchases. Managers also focused on boosting sales to those accounts that were producing the highest pocket prices. These changes resulted in the company's average pocket price rising by 3.8 percent and its profits climbing 51 percent!

Discounts tend to work their way into a company's pricing structure gradually over time, often one transaction at a time, especially if an entrepreneur gives sales representatives latitude to negotiate prices with customers. Few companies make the effort to track these discounts, and, as a result, few companies realize the impact that discounts have on their profitability. By monitoring their companies' pocket price waterfall and the resulting pocket price band, entrepreneurs can improve significantly the revenue and the profits they generate.

Sources: Michael V. Marn, Eric V. Roegner, and Craig C. Zawada, "The Power of Pricing," *The McKinsey Quarterly*, Number 1, 2003, www.mckinseyquarterly.com; Cheri N. Eyink, Michael V. Marn, and Stephen C. Moss, "Pricing in an Inflationary Downturn," *The McKinsey Quarterly*, September 2008, http://www.mckinseyquarterly.com/Pricing_in_a_downturn_2189.

Pricing Strategies and Methods for Service Firms

LO 5

Explain the pricing methods and strategies for service firms.

A service firm must establish a price based on the materials used to provide the service, the labor employed, an allowance for overhead, and a profit. As in the manufacturing operation, a service business must have a reliable, accurate accounting system to keep a tally of the total costs of providing the service. Most service firms base their prices on an hourly rate, usually the actual number of hours required to perform the service. Some companies, however, base their fees on a standard number of hours, determined by the average number of hours needed to perform the service. For most firms, labor and materials comprise the largest portion of the cost of the service. To establish a reasonable, profitable price for service, small business owners must know the cost of materials, direct labor, and overhead for each unit of service they provide. Using these basic cost data and a desired profit margin, an owner of a small service firm can determine the appropriate price for the service.

Consider a simple example for pricing a common service—television repair. Ned's T.V. Repair Shop uses the direct costing method to prepare an income statement for exercising managerial control (see Table 10.2). Ned estimates that he and his employees spent about 9,250 hours in the

TABLE 10.2 Direct-Cost Income Statement, Ned's T.V. Repair Shop

Sales Revenue		$199,000
Variable Expenses		
Labor	52,000	
Materials	40,500	
Variable Factory Overhead	11,500	
Total Variable Expenses		104,000
Fixed Expenses		
Rent	2,500	
Salaries	38,500	
Fixed Overhead	27,000	
Total Fixed Expenses		68,000
Net Income		$27,000

actual production of television service. Therefore, total cost ($104,000 + $68,000 = $172,000) per productive hour for Ned's T.V. Repair Shop comes to the following:

$$\frac{\$172,000}{9,250 \, \text{hours}} = \$18.59/\text{hour}$$

Now Ned must add in an amount for his desired profit. He expects a net operating profit of 18 percent on sales. To compute the final price he uses the following equation:

Price per hour = total cost per productive hour ÷ (1 − net profit target as % of sales)

$$= \$18.59 \div (1 - .18)$$

$$= \$22.68/\text{hour}$$

A price of $22.68 per hour will cover Ned's costs and generate the desired profit. The wise service shop owner computes his cost per production hour at regular intervals throughout the year. Rapidly rising labor costs and material prices dictate that the service firm's price per hour be computed even more frequently. As in the case of the retailer and the manufacturer, Ned must evaluate the pricing policies of competitors and decide whether his price is consistent with his firm's image.

Of course, the price of $22.68 per hour assumes that each job requires the same amount of materials. If this is not a valid assumption, Ned must recalculate the price per hour *without* including the cost of materials:

$$\text{Cost per productive hour} = \frac{\$172,000 - \$40,500}{9,250 \, \text{hours}}$$

$$= \$14.22/\text{hour}$$

Factoring in the desired 18 percent net operating profit on sales gives:

Price per hour = $14.22/hour ÷ (1.00 − 0.18)

$$= \$17.34/\text{hour}$$

Under these conditions Ned would charge $17.34 per hour plus the actual cost of materials used and any markup on the cost of material. A repair job that takes four hours to complete would have the following price:

Cost of service (4 hours × $17.34/hour)	$ 69.36
Cost of materials	$ 41.00
Markup on material (40%)	$ 16.40
Total price	$126.76

Finding the right price for his business and event planning service was a problem facing Joshua Estrin, founder of Concepts in Success. Initially, Estrin established a reasonable annual salary for himself and then set the price for each project as a percentage of that salary. Because that system required him to spend excessive amounts of time documenting details of every expense for his clients, Estrin soon switched to an hourly rate that exceeded $100 per hour. Now that he has more experience, Estrin charges for the services that Concepts in Success offers using set price points that depend on the services his clients choose. Estrin's pricing policy is working. His company now generates $1 million in annual revenue and counts several major corporations, including American Express, Hertz, and PepsiCo, among its clients.[37]

ENTREPRENEURIAL PROFILE _____

Joshua Estrin: Concepts in Success

The Impact of Credit on Pricing

Consumers crave convenience when they shop, and one of the most common conveniences they demand is the ability to purchase goods and services on credit. Small businesses that fail to offer credit to their customers lose sales to competitors who do. However, companies that do sell on credit incur additional expenses for offering this convenience. Small companies have three options for selling to customers on credit: credit cards, installment credit, and trade credit.

LO 6

Describe the impact of credit on pricing.

Pricing Web Services

Kerry Pinella, a recent business graduate of a small private college, started her career working for a large multinational computer software maker as a sales representative. After two years in sales, Kerry applied for a position on a development team that was working on Web-based software applications. Kerry thrived on the team atmosphere and learned the technical aspects of the new assignment very quickly. Not only did her team bring their project in on budget, but it also completed it slightly ahead of schedule. Team members give much of the credit for the project's success to Kerry's unofficial role as team leader. Her work ethic and relentless pursuit of quality inspired other team members.

After Kerry's team completed their project, however, Kerry had a hard time recapturing the thrill and excitement of developing the Web-based software. Subsequent projects simply could not measure up to the "magic" of that first assignment. After talking with several of the members of that software team, Kerry discovered that they felt the same way. Before long, Kerry and two of her former team members left the company to launch their own computer consulting company, Web Consultants. Having worked on the forefront of the Web's commercialization, Kerry and her partners saw the potential it had for revolutionizing business. Their company would specialize in developing, designing, and maintaining Web sites for clients. In their first year of business, Web Consultants accepted jobs from virtually anybody who wanted a Web site. Although they experienced some "growing pains," Web Consultants quickly earned a reputation for producing quality work on time and became more selective in the jobs it bid on.

Halfway into their second year of operation, the partners planned a weekend retreat at a nearby resort so they could get away, review their progress, and plan for the future. As they reviewed their latest financial statements, one of the questions that kept popping up dealt with pricing. Were Web Consultant's pricing policies appropriate? Its sales were growing twice as fast as the industry average, and the company's bid-winning ratio was well above that of practically all of its competitors. For the current year, sales were up, but Web Consultants' net profits were virtually the same as they had been in their first year.

Pulling the records from a computer database for each job they had completed since founding the company, they found that the partners and their employees had spent 22,450 hours developing projects for their clients at a total cost of $951,207. "We were shooting for a net profit of 25 percent on sales," Kerry reminded her partners, "but we so far, our net profit margin is just 7.7 percent, only one-third of our target."

"Maybe we could increase our profits if we increased our sales," offered one partner.

The partners began to wonder whether their price of $45 per hour was appropriate. Admittedly, they had been so busy completing projects for clients that they had not kept up with what their competitors were charging. Nor had they been as diligent in analyzing their financial statements as they should have been.

As Kerry closed the cover on her laptop computer, she looked at her partners and asked, "What should Web Consultant's hourly price be?"

1. Help Kerry answer the question she has posed.
2. What factors should Kerry and her partners consider when determining Web Consultant's final price?
3. Is the company's current price too low? If so, what signals could have alerted Kerry and her partners?

Credit Cards

Approximately 176 million people in the United States own credit cards; in fact, the typical consumer in the United States has four credit cards. Nearly 51 percent of adults in the United States have at least two credit cards, and 14 percent of them have 10 or more credit cards.[38] Shoppers charge more than $2 trillion worth of goods and services annually.[39] The message is clear: Customers expect to make purchases with credit cards, and small companies that fail to accept credit cards run the risk of losing sales to competitors who do. Research shows that customers who use credit cards make purchases that are 12 percent higher than if they had used cash.[40] In addition, surveys show that customers rate businesses offering credit options higher on key performance measures such as reputation, reliability, and service.[41] In short, accepting credit cards broadens a small company's customer base and closes sales that it would normally lose if customers had to pay in cash.

The convenience of credit cards is not free to business owners, however. Businesses must pay to use the system, typically one to six percent of the total credit card charge, which they must factor into the prices of their products or services. They also pay a transaction fee of 5 to 25 cents per charge. (The average fee is 10 cents per transaction.) Given customer expectations, small businesses cannot drop major cards, even when credit card companies raise the fees that merchants must pay. Fees operate on a multi-step process (see Figure 10.4). On a typical $100 credit card purchase that a customer makes at a retailer, the bank that issued the customer's card receives $1.89, an amount that consists of a 1.79 percent processing fee called the **interchange fee,** the fee that banks collect from retailers whenever customers use a

interchange fee
the fee that banks collect from retailers whenever customers use a credit or a debit card to pay for a purchase.

credit or a debit card to pay for a purchase, and a 10-cent flat transaction fee. The retailer's bank, called the processing bank, receives a processing fee of 0.4 percent of the purchase amount (or 40 cents in this example), which leaves the retailer with $97.71. Before it can accept credit cards, a business must obtain merchant status from either a bank or an independent sales organization (ISO).

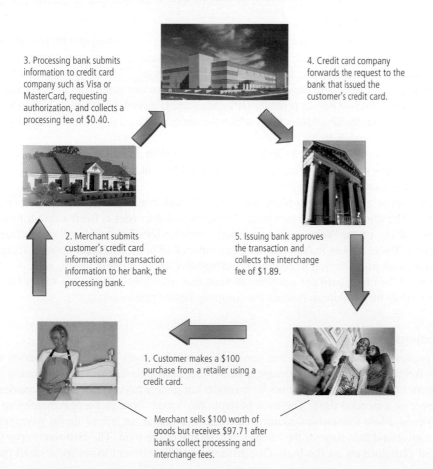

FIGURE 10.4

How a Typical Credit Card Transaction Works

Source: Adapted from "Credit cards," United States Government Accounting Office, September 2006, pp. 73–74.

3. Processing bank submits information to credit card company such as Visa or MasterCard, requesting authorization, and collects a processing fee of $0.40.

4. Credit card company forwards the request to the bank that issued the customer's credit card.

2. Merchant submits customer's credit card information and transaction information to her bank, the processing bank.

5. Issuing bank approves the transaction and collects the interchange fee of $1.89.

1. Customer makes a $100 purchase from a retailer using a credit card.

Merchant sells $100 worth of goods but receives $97.71 after banks collect processing and interchange fees.

In 2003, for the first time in history, shoppers used credit and debit cards more often than cash or checks to make retail purchases.[42] (Debit cards are particularly popular among college students, who make 37 percent of their purchases with debit cards and 36 percent with cash. Only 8 percent of student spending is done with credit cards.[43]) As debit cards have become more widely used, many small businesses are equipping their stores to handle debit card transactions, which act as electronic checks, automatically deducting the purchase amount immediately from a customer's checking account. The equipment is easy to install and to set up, and the cost to the company is negligible. The payoff can be big, however, in the form of increased sales and decreased losses from bad checks. "How can you possibly lose when you're offering customers another avenue for purchasing merchandise?" says Mark Knauff, who recently installed a debit card terminal in his guitar shop.[44]

E-COMMERCE AND CREDIT CARDS   When it comes to online business transactions, the most common method of payment is the credit card. Internet vendors are constantly challenged by the need to provide secure methods of transacting business in a safe environment. As you learned in Chapter 9, E-Commerce and Entrepreneurship, many shoppers are suspicious of online transactions for reasons of security and privacy. Therefore, online merchants must ensure their customers' privacy and the security of their credit card transactions by using computer encryption software.

Online merchants also face another obstacle: credit card fraud. Because they lack the face-to-face contact with their customers, online merchants face special challenges to avoid credit card fraud. Identity and credit card theft results in customers denying the authenticity of certain purchases and disputing the charges that appear on their bills. Unless merchants are vigilant, they will end up shouldering most of the burden for these chargebacks. According to consulting firm Celent Communications, about 2 percent of online credit card transactions are fraudulent, costing merchants more than $3.2 billion a year![45] Brian Mortensen, whose company NJPhones is an authorized reseller of telephone equipment, says that fraudulent online charges nearly cost him his business. Fraudulent charges and transaction fees sucked $20,000 out of his small company in just one year.[46]

The following steps can help online merchants reduce the probability that they will become victims of credit card fraud:

- Use an address verification system (AVS) to compare every customer's billing information on the order form with the billing information in the bank or credit card company's records.
- Require customers to provide the CVV2 number from the back of the credit card. Although crooks can get access to this number, it can help screen out some fraudulent orders.
- Check customers' internet protocol (IP) addresses. If an order contains a billing address in California, but the IP address from which the order is placed is in China, chances are that the order is fraudulent.
- Monitor activity on the Web site with the help of a Web analytics software package. There are many packages available, and analyzing log files can help online entrepreneurs to pinpoint the sources of fraud.
- Verify large orders. Large orders are a cause for celebration but only if they are legitimate. Check the authenticity of large orders, especially if the order is from a first-time customer.
- Post notices on the Web site that your company uses anti-fraud technology to screen orders. These notices make legitimate customers feel more confident about placing their orders and crooks trying to commit fraud tentative about running their scams.
- Contact the credit card company or the bank that issued the card. If you suspect that an order may be fraudulent, contact the company *before* processing it. [47]

Installment Credit

Small companies that sell big-ticket consumer durables—such as major appliances, cars, and boats—frequently rely on installment credit to support their sales efforts. Because very few customers can purchase such items in a single lump-sum payment, small businesses finance them over an extended time. The time horizon may range from just a few months up to 30 or more years. Most companies require customers to make an initial down payment for the merchandise and then finance the balance for the life of the loan. The customer repays the loan principal plus interest on the loan. One advantage of installment loans for a small business is that the owner retains a security interest as collateral on the loan. If a customer defaults on the loan, the owner still holds the title to the merchandise. Because installment credit absorbs a small company's cash, many rely on financial institutions such as banks and credit unions to provide installment credit. When a company has the financial strength to "carry its own paper," the interest income from the installment loan contract often yields more than the initial profit on the sale of the product. For some businesses, such as furniture stores, this traditionally has been a major source of income.

Trade Credit

Companies that sell small-ticket items frequently offer their customers trade credit—that is, they create customer charge accounts. The typical small business bills its credit customers each month. To speed collections, some offer cash discounts if customers pay their balances early; others impose penalties on late payers. Before deciding to use trade credit as a competitive weapon, the small business owner must make sure that the company's cash position is strong enough to support the additional pressure.

Chapter Summary

1. **Describe effective pricing techniques for introducing new goods or services and for existing ones.**

   - Pricing a new product is often difficult for the small business manager, but it should accomplish three objectives: getting the product accepted; maintaining market share as the competition grows; and earning a profit. Generally, there are three major pricing strategies used to introduce new products into the market: penetration, skimming, and life cycle.
   - Pricing techniques for existing products and services include odd pricing, price lining, leader pricing, geographic pricing, discounts, multiple unit pricing, bundling, optional-product pricing, captive-product pricing, byproduct pricing, and suggested retail pricing.

2. **Explain the pricing methods and strategies for retailers, manufacturers, and service firms.**

   - Pricing for the retailer means pricing to move merchandise. Markup is the difference between the cost of a product or service and its selling price. Most retailers compute their markup as a percentage of retail price, but some retailers put a standard markup on all their merchandise; more frequently, they use a flexible markup.

   - A manufacturer's pricing decision depends on the support of accurate cost accounting records. The most common technique is cost-plus pricing, in which the manufacturer charges a price that covers the cost of producing a product plus a reasonable profit. Every manufacturer should calculate a product's break-even price, the price which produces neither a profit nor a loss.
   - Service firms often suffer from the effects of vague, unfounded pricing procedures, and frequently charge the going rate without any idea of their costs. A service firm must set a price based on the cost of materials used, labor involved, overhead, and a profit. The proper price reflects the total cost of providing a unit of service.

3. **Describe the impact of credit on pricing.**

   - Offering consumer credit enhances a small company's reputation and increases the probability, speed, and magnitude of customers' purchases. Small firms offer three types of consumer credit: credit cards, installment credit, and trade credit (charge accounts).

Discussion Questions

1. How does pricing affect a small firm's image?
2. What competitive factors must the small firm consider when establishing prices?
3. Describe the strategies a small business could use in setting the price of a new product. What objectives should the strategy seek to achieve?
4. Define the following pricing techniques: odd pricing, price lining, leader pricing, geographic pricing, multiple unit pricing, bundling, optional-product pricing, captive-product pricing, byproduct pricing, and discounts.
5. Why do many small businesses use the manufacturer's suggested retail price? What are the disadvantages of this technique?
6. What is a markup? How is it used to determine individual price?
7. What is a standard markup? A flexible markup?

8. What is cost-plus pricing? Why do so many manufacturers use it? What are the disadvantages of using it?

9. Explain the difference between full-absorption costing and direct costing. How does absorption costing help a manufacturer determine a reasonable price?

10. Explain the technique for a small service firm setting an hourly price.

11. What benefits does a small business get by offering customers credit? What costs does it incur?

Business PlanPro™

Setting the price of your products and services and understanding your break-even point are major elements of your business plan. Resources and information in *Business Plan Pro*™ may help you to gain a perspective regarding the impact that pricing will have on your business.

Business Plan Exercises

Business Plan Pro™ will guide you through the steps of documenting your fixed cost, variable cost, and an average price. Once you enter this information, the software automatically creates a break-even chart for your plan.

Sample Plans

Review the break-even information in your favorite sample plans. Note how the plans use the fixed and variable costs with an average price to determine the break-even point. Look at the break-even graph and find the break-even point for each sample plan.

On the Web

Perform competitive pricing research on the Web. Search for products and services that are similar to what you are offering. Confirm that you are making parallel comparisons of these products. For example, are you considering the entire price, which may include shipping, handling, complementary products, and other attributes that will influence the final price to the customer? Do you consider these businesses to be direct competitors? If not, why? What does this information tell you about your price point? Does your price coincide with your stated business strategy?

In the Software

Open your business plan and locate the Break-even Analysis section under the Financial Plan. Follow the instructions and enter the information that will enable to you to determine your break-even point. This will require you to have estimated figures for your fixed costs, variable costs, and price. Once you have entered that information, look at the break-even point shown in units and revenue. Based on what you find, is this break-even point realistic? How many months will it take to reach the break-even point? Is this time period acceptable? Now, increase your price by 10%. What does this do to your break-even point? You may want to experiment with your break-even point by entering different price points and costs to see the impact price will have on the break-even point when you will begin making a profit.

Building Your Business Plan

Go to the Sales Forecast table under the Sales Strategy section. You may use the wizard or enter information directly into the worksheet. If you have not done so yet, enter your pricing information in that section. Work through the table and estimate your direct unit costs. The instructions and examples will assist you through the process.

Beyond the Classroom...

1. Apple Inc. dominates the market for media players with its line of iPods, which currently includes the Shuffle, the Nano, the Classic, and the Touch. Because the company constantly introduces new models and features, it also adjusts prices on these popular players. Use the Web to research the history of the iPod and write a brief summary of Apple's pricing strategy on its popular media player. Which products compete with the iPod? How do the prices of similar models compare to the iPod? Is Apple able to command a premium for its brand? If so, what factors allow the company to do so?

2. Interview the owner of a successful small retailer and ask the following questions: Does he or she seek a specific image through the company's prices? What role do competitors play in the business owner's pricing? Does the owner use specific pricing techniques such as odd pricing, price lining, leader pricing, or geographic pricing? How are discounts calculated? What markup percentage does the firm use? How are prices derived? What are their cost structures?

3. Select an industry that has several competing small firms in your area. Contact these firms and compare their approaches to determining prices. Do prices on identical or similar items differ? Why?

Snap Fitness

CHAPTER **11**

Creating a Successful Financial Plan

Volume is vanity; profitability is sanity.
—*Brad Skelton*

There cannot be a crisis today; my schedule is already full.
—*Henry Kissinger*

Learning Objectives

On completion of this chapter, you will be able to:

1. Understand the importance of preparing a financial plan.

2. Describe how to prepare the basic financial statements and use them to manage a small business.

3. Create projected (pro forma) financial statements.

4. Understand the basic financial statements through ratio analysis.

5. Interpret financial ratios.

6. Conduct a break-even analysis for a small company.

LO 1

Understand the importance of preparing a financial plan.

financial management

a process that provides entrepreneurs with relevant financial information in an easy-to-read format on a timely basis; it allows entrepreneurs to know not only how their businesses are doing financially but also why they are performing that way.

The Importance of a Financial Plan

Fashioning a well-designed, logical financial plan as part of a comprehensive business plan is one of the most important steps to launching a new business venture. Entrepreneurs who fail to develop workable strategies for earning a profit from the outset eventually will suffer the ultimate business penalty: failure. Potential lenders and investors demand a realistic financial plan before putting their money into a start-up company. More important, a financial plan is a vital tool that helps entrepreneurs to manage their businesses more effectively, steering their way around the pitfalls that cause failures. Proper **financial management** requires putting in place a system that provides entrepreneurs with relevant financial information in an easy-to-read format on a timely basis; it allows entrepreneurs to know not only *how* their businesses are doing financially, but also *why* their companies are performing that way. The information in a small company's financial records is one resource to which competitors have no access. Smart entrepreneurs recognize this and put their companies' numbers to work for them so that they can make their businesses more successful. "Salted away in your accounting records are financial alerts, ways to trim costs, and tips on where profit is hiding," explains one business writer.[1]

Unfortunately, failure to collect and analyze basic financial data is a common mistake among entrepreneurs. Both research and anecdotal evidence suggest that a significant percentage of entrepreneurs run their companies without any kind of financial plan. One classic study found that only 11 percent of small business owners analyzed their financial statements as part of the managerial planning and decision-making process.[2] To reach profit objectives, entrepreneurs must be aware of their companies' overall financial position and the changes in financial status that occur over time. Most accounting experts advise entrepreneurs to use one of the popular computerized small business accounting programs such as Quickbooks, Peachtree Accounting, and others to manage routine recordkeeping tasks. Working with an accountant to set up the system at the outset and then having an employee or a bookkeeping service enter the transactions is most efficient for most businesses. These programs make analyzing a company's financial statements, preparing reports, and summarizing data a snap.

This chapter focuses on some very practical tools that will help entrepreneurs develop a workable financial plan, keep them aware of their company's financial plan, and enable them to plan for profit. They can use these tools to help them anticipate changes and plot an appropriate profit strategy to meet them head on. These profit planning techniques are not difficult to master, nor are they overly time consuming. We will discuss the techniques involved in preparing projected (pro forma) financial statements, conducting ratio analysis, and performing break-even analysis.

Luca Pacioli, a monk and a friend of Leonardo Da Vinci, created double-entry accounting and the balance sheet in the late fifteenth century.

Erich Lessing/Art Resource, N.Y.

FIGURE 11.1

Balance Sheet, Sam's Appliance Shop

Assets		
Current Assets		
Cash		$49,855
Accounts Receivable	$179,225	
Less Allowance for Doubtful Accounts	$6,000	$173,225
Inventory		$455,455
Prepaid Expenses		$8,450
Total Current Assets		$686,985
Fixed Assets		
Land		$59,150
Buildings	$74,650	
Less Accumulated Depreciation	$7,050	$67,600
Equipment	$22,375	
Less Accumulated Depreciation	$1,250	$21,125
Furniture and Fixtures	$10,295	
Less Accumulated Depreciation	$1,000	$9,295
Total Fixed Assets		$157,170
Intangibles (Goodwill)		$3,500
Total Assets		$847,655
Liabilities		
Current Liabilities		
Accounts Payable		$152,580
Notes Payable		$83,920
Accrued Wages/Salaries Payable		$38,150
Accrued Interest Payable		$42,380
Accrued Taxes Payable		$50,820
Total Current Liabilities		$367,850
Long-Term Liabilities		
Mortgage		$127,150
Note Payable		$85,000
Total Long-Term Liabilities		$212,150
Owner's Equity		
Sam Lloyd, Capital		$267,655
Total Liabilities and Owner's Equity		$847,655

Basic Financial Statements

Before we begin building projected financial statements, it would be helpful to review the basic financial reports that measure a company's financial position: the balance sheet, the income statement, and the statement of cash flows. The level of financial sophistication among small business owners may not be high, but the extent of financial reporting among small businesses is. Most small businesses regularly produce summary financial information, almost all of it in the form of these traditional financial statements.

The Balance Sheet

The **balance sheet** takes a "snapshot" of a business's financial position, providing owners with an estimate of its worth on a given date. Its two major sections show the assets the business owns and the claims creditors and owners have against those assets. The balance sheet is usually prepared on the last day of the month. Figure 11.1 shows the balance sheet for Sam's Appliance Shop for the year ended December 31, 201X.

LO 2

Describe how to prepare basic financial statements and use them to manage a small business.

balance sheet

a financial statement that provides a snapshot of a business's financial position, estimating its worth on a given date; it is built on the fundamental accounting equation: Assets = Liabilities + Owner's Equity.

current assets

assets such as cash and other items to be converted into cash within one year, or within a company's normal operating cycle.

fixed assets

assets acquired for long-term use in a business.

liabilities

creditors' claims against a company's assets.

current liabilities

those debts that must be paid within one year or within the normal operating cycle of a company

long-term liabilities

liabilities that come due after one year.

owner's equity

the value of the owner's investment in a business.

income statement (profit and loss statement or "P&L")

a financial statement that represents a moving picture of a business, comparing its expenses against its revenue over a period of time to show its net profit (or loss).

cost of goods sold

the total cost, including shipping, of the merchandise sold during an accounting period.

gross profit margin

gross profit divided by net sales revenue.

The balance sheet is built on the fundamental accounting equation: Assets = Liabilities + Owner's Equity. Any increase or decrease on one side of the equation must be offset by an increase or decrease on the other side; hence the name *balance sheet*. It provides a baseline from which to measure future changes in assets, liabilities, and equity. The first section of the balance sheet lists the company's assets (valued at cost, not actual market value) and shows the total value of everything the business owns. **Current assets** consist of cash and items to be converted into cash within one year or within the normal operating cycle of the company, whichever is longer, such as accounts receivable and inventory, and **fixed assets** are those acquired for long-term use in the business. Intangible assets include items such as goodwill, copyrights, and patents that, although valuable, are not tangible.

The second section shows the business's **liabilities**—the creditors' claims against the company's assets. **Current liabilities** are those debts that must be paid within one year or within the normal operating cycle of the company, whichever is longer, and **long-term liabilities** are those that come due after one year. This section of the balance sheet also shows the **owner's equity**, the value of the owner's investment in the business. It is the balancing factor on the balance sheet, representing all of the owner's capital contributions to the business plus all accumulated (or retained) earnings not distributed to the owner(s).

The Income Statement

The **income statement (profit and loss statement or "P&L")** compares expenses against revenue over a certain period of time to show the firm's net profit (or loss). The income statement is a "moving picture" of a firm's profitability over time. The annual P&L statement reports the bottom line of the business over the fiscal/calendar year. Figure 11.2 shows the income statement for Sam's Appliance Shop for the year ended December 31, 201X.

To calculate net profit or loss, an entrepreneur records sales revenues for the year, which includes all income that flows into the business from sales of goods and services. Income from other sources (rent, investments, interest) also must be included in the revenue section of the income statement. To determine net sales revenue, owners subtract the value of returned items and refunds from gross revenue. **Cost of goods sold** represents the total cost, including shipping, of the merchandise sold during the accounting period. Manufacturers, wholesalers, and retailers calculate cost of goods sold by adding purchases to beginning inventory and subtracting ending inventory. Service-providing companies typically have no cost of goods sold because they do not carry inventory.

Net sales revenue minus cost of goods sold results in a company's gross profit. Dividing gross profit by net sales revenue produces the **gross profit margin**, a ratio that every small business owner should watch closely. If a company's gross profit margin slips too low, it is likely that it will operate at a loss (negative net income) because a company must pay all of its operating expenses out of its gross profit. A business that operates at a gross profit margin of 50 percent must generate $2.00 in sales for every $1 of operating expenses just to break even. However, a company with a 10 percent gross profit margin must generate $10 in sales for every $1 of operating expenses to reach its break-even point.

Many business owners whose companies are losing money mistakenly believe that the problem is inadequate sales volume; therefore, they focus on pumping up sales at any cost. In many cases, however, the losses their companies are incurring are the result of an inadequate gross profit margin, and pumping up sales only deepens their losses! Repairing a poor gross profit margin requires a company to raise prices, cut manufacturing or purchasing costs, refuse orders with low profit margins, "fire" unprofitable customers, or add new products with more attractive profit margins. *Increasing sales will not resolve the problem.* Monitoring the gross profit margin over time and comparing it to those of other companies in the same industry are important steps to maintaining a company's long-term profitability.

ENTREPRENEURIAL PROFILE

Todd & Jan Haedrich:
My Flat in London

After watching sales double every year for several years, copreneurs Todd and Jan Haedrich decided to apply the brakes to sales growth and focus on improving the profitability of their small handbag-making business, My Flat in London. Initially, the Haedriches sold their handbags to both small boutique retailers and to large department stores, which demanded generous return policies, long payment terms, and price concessions. "What I've learned is that [selling to] a large vendor has hidden costs," says

Net Sales Revenue		$1,870,841
Credit Sales	$1,309,589	
Cash Sales	$561,252	
Cost of Goods Sold		
Beginning Inventory, 1/1/xx	$805,745	
+ Purchases	$939,827	
Goods Available for Sale	$1,745,572	
− Ending Inventory, 12/31/xx	$455,455	
Cost of Goods Sold		$1,290,117
Gross Profit		$580,724
Operating Expenses		
Advertising	$139,670	
Insurance	$46,125	
Depreciation		
Building	$18,700	
Equipment	$9,000	
Salaries	$224,500	
Travel	$4,000	
Entertainment	$2,500	
Total Operating Expenses		$444,495
General Expenses		
Utilities	$5,300	
Telephone	$2,500	
Postage	$1,200	
Payroll Taxes	$25,000	
Total General Expenses		$34,000
Other Expenses		
Interest Expense	$39,850	
Bad Check Expense	$1,750	
Total Other Expenses		$41,600
Total Expenses		$520,095
Net Income		$60,629

FIGURE 11.2

Income Statement, Sam's Appliance Shop

Todd. Eliminating unprofitable large customers meant slowing the company's growth in sales to just 15 percent, but the Haedriches saw their profits increase by 40 percent! "We're not twice as big as we were, but we're a lot more profitable," says Todd.[3]

Operating expenses include those costs that contribute directly to the manufacture and distribution of goods. General expenses are indirect costs incurred in operating the business. "Other expenses" is a catch-all category covering all other expenses that don't fit into the other two categories. Total revenue minus total expenses gives the net income (or loss) for the accounting period. Reducing expenses increases a company's net income, and even small reductions in expenses can add up to big savings.

Eric McCallum, owner of Arctic Wire Rope and Supply Inc., a maker of tow ropes, slings, nets, and other items based in Anchorage, Alaska, recently invested $15,000 to replace all of the light fixtures in the company's 22,000-square-foot warehouse with more efficient ones that also provide a better quality of light. The new bulbs use 58 percent less electricity, which has reduced the company's annual light bill from $14,000 to $10,000, savings that will allow McCallum to recoup his investment in three-and-a-half years.[4]

operating expenses

those costs that contribute directly to the manufacture and distribution of goods.

ENTREPRENEURIAL PROFILE

Eric McCallum: Arctic Wire Rope and Supply Company

Comparing a company's current income statement to those of prior accounting periods often reveals valuable information about key trends and a company's progress toward its financial goals.

The Statement of Cash Flows

statement of cash flows
a financial statement showing the changes in a company's working capital from the beginning of the year by listing both the sources and the uses of those funds.

The **statement of cash flows** show the changes in the firm's working capital from the beginning of the year by listing both the sources of funds and the uses of those funds. Many small businesses never need to prepare such a statement, but in some cases creditors, investors, new owners, or the IRS may require this information.

To prepare the statement, the owner must assemble the balance sheets and the income statements summarizing the present year's operations. She begins with the company's net income for the period (from the income statement). Then she adds the sources of the company's funds—borrowed funds, owner contributions, decreases in accounts receivable, increases in accounts payable, decreases in inventory, depreciation, and any others. Depreciation is listed as a source of funds because it is a non-cash expense that has already been deducted as a cost of doing business. Because the owner has already paid for the item being depreciated, however, its depreciation is a source of funds. Next the owner subtracts the uses of these funds–plant and equipment purchases, dividends to owners, repayment of debt, increases in accounts receivable, decreases in accounts payable, increases in inventory, and so on. The difference between the total sources and the total uses is the increase or decrease in working capital. By investigating the changes in their companies' working capital and the reasons for them, owners can create a more practical financial action plan for the future of the enterprise.

These financial statements are more than just complex documents used only by accountants and financial officers. When used in conjunction with the analytical tools described in the following sections, they can help entrepreneurs to map a firm's financial future and actively plan for profit. Merely preparing these statement is not enough, however; owners and employees must *understand and use* the information contained in them to make the business more effective and efficient.

Creating Projected Financial Statements

LO 3

Create projected (pro forma) financial statements.

Creating projected financial statements helps a small business owner transform business goals into reality. This section focuses on creating projected income statements and balance sheets for a small start-up. These projected (or pro forma) statements are a crucial component of every business plan because they estimate the profitability and the overall financial condition of a company in the future. They are an integral part of convincing potential lenders and investors to provide the financing needed to get the company off the ground (the topic of chapter 13). In addition, because these statements project a company's financial position through the end of the forecasted period, they help entrepreneurs to plan the route to improved financial strength and healthy business growth. To be useful, however, these forecasts must be *realistic*! "A business plan is not complete until it contains a set of financial projections that are not only inspiring but also logical and defensible," says one business writer.[5]

Because an established business has a history of operating data from which to construct pro forma financial statements, the task is not nearly as difficult as it is for the beginning business. When creating pro forma financial statements for a brand new business, an entrepreneur typically relies on published statistics summarizing the operation of similar-size companies in the same industry. These statistics are available from a number of sources (described later), but this section draws on information found in *RMA Annual Statement Studies*, a compilation of financial data collected from 150,000 companies across more than 750 industries organized by Standard Industrial Classification (SIC) Code and North American Industry Classification System (NAICS). Because conditions and markets change so rapidly, entrepreneurs developing financial forecasts for start-ups should focus on creating projections for two years into the future. Investors want to see that entrepreneurs have realistic expectations about their companies' income and expenses and when they expect to start earning a profit.

Projected Financial Statements for a Small Business

One of the most important tasks confronting the entrepreneur launching a new enterprise is to determine the amount of funding required to begin operation as well as the amount required to keep the company going through its initial growth period until it can generate positive cash flow. The amount of money needed to begin a business depends on the type of operation, its location, inventory requirements, sales volume, and many other factors. However, every new firm must have enough capital to cover all start-up costs, including funds to rent or buy plant, equipment, and tools, as well as pay for advertising, wages, licenses, utilities, and other expenses. In addition, entrepreneurs must maintain a reserve of capital to carry the company until it begins to generate positive cash flow. Too often entrepreneurs are overly optimistic in their financial plans and fail to recognize that expenses initially exceed income (and cash outflow exceeds cash inflow) for most small firms. This period of net losses (and negative cash flow) is normal and may last from just a few months to several years. During this time, entrepreneurs must be able to pay the company's regular bills, meet payroll, purchase inventory, take advantage of cash discounts, grant customers credit, and meet their personal financial obligations.

THE PROJECTED INCOME STATEMENT   Although they are projections, financial forecasts must be based in reality; otherwise the resulting financial plan is nothing more than a hopeless dream. When creating a projected income statement, an entrepreneur has two options: to develop a sales forecast and work down or set a profit target and work up. Developing a realistic sales forecast for a business start-up is not always easy, but with creativity and research it is possible. Talking with owners of existing businesses in the industry (outside of the local trading area, of course) can provide meaningful insight into the sales levels a company can expect to generate during its early years. For a reasonable fee, entrepreneurs can access published aggregated financial statistics that industry trade associations collect on the companies in their industries. Other organizations, such as the Risk Management Association and Dun & Bradstreet, publish useful financial information for a wide range of industries. Web searches and trips to the local library will produce the necessary information. Interviews with potential customers and test marketing an actual product or service also can reveal the number of customers a company can expect to attract. One method for checking the accuracy of a sales estimate is to calculate the revenue other companies in the same industry generate per employee and compare it to your own projected revenue per employee. A value that is out of line with industry standards is not likely to be realistic.

Many entrepreneurs prefer the other method of creating a projected income statement, targeting a profit figure and then "working up" to determine the sales level they must achieve to reach it. Of course, it is important to compare this sales target against the results of the marketing plan to determine whether it is realistic. The next step is to estimate the expenses the business will incur in securing those sales. In any small business, the profit generated must be large enough to produce a reasonable return on time the owners spend operating the business and a return on their investment in the business.

An entrepreneur who earns less in his own business than he could earn working for someone else must weigh carefully the advantages and disadvantages of choosing the path of entrepreneurship. Why be exposed to all of the risks, sacrifices, and hard work of beginning and operating a small business if the rewards are less than those of remaining in the secure employment of another? Although there are many non-financial benefits of owning a business, the net profit after taxes a company generates should be at least as much as an entrepreneur could earn by working for someone else.

An adequate profit must also include a reasonable return on the owner's total investment in the business. (The owner's total investment is the amount contributed to the company at its inception plus any retained earnings, profits from previous years that were funneled back into the business.) In other words, an entrepreneur's target income is the sum of a reasonable salary for the time spent running the business and a normal return on the amount invested in the company. Determining this amount is the first step in creating the projected income statement.

An entrepreneur then must translate this target profit into a net sales figure for the forecasted period. To calculate net sales from a target profit, the entrepreneur can use published industry statistics. Suppose an entrepreneur wants to launch a small bookstore and has determined that his target net income is $30,000. Statistics gathered from *RMA's Annual Statement Studies* show that the typical bookstore's net profit margin (net profit ÷ net sales) is 7.3 percent. Using this information, he can compute the sales level required to produce a net profit of $30,000:

$$\text{Net profit margin} = \frac{\text{net profit}}{\text{net sales (annual)}}$$

$$7.3\% = \frac{\$30,000}{\text{net sales (annual)}}$$

$$\text{Net sales} = \frac{\$30,000}{0.073} = \$410,959$$

Now this entrepreneur knows that to make a net profit of $30,000 (before taxes), he must achieve annual sales of $410,959. To complete the projected income statement, the owner simply applies the appropriate statistics from *Annual Statement Studies* to the annual sales figure. Because the statistics for each income statement item are expressed as percentages of net sales, he merely multiplies the proper percentage by the annual sales figure to obtain the desired value. For example, cost of goods sold usually comprises 61.4 percent of net sales for the typical small bookstore; therefore, the owner of this new bookstore expects his cost of goods sold to be the following:

Cost of goods sold = $410,959 × 0.614 = $252,329

The bookstore's complete projected income statement is shown as follows:

Net sales	(100%)	$410,959
− Cost of goods sold	(61.4%)	$252,329
Gross profit margin	(38.6%)	$158,630
− Operating expenses	(31.3%)	$128,630
Net profit (before taxes)	(7.3%)	$30,000

At this point, the business appears to be a lucrative venture. But remember: this income statement represents a sales *goal* that the owner may not be able to reach. The next step is to determine whether this required sales volume is reasonable. One useful technique is to break down the required annual sales volume into *daily* sales figures. Assuming the store will be open six days per week for 50 weeks (300 days), we see that the owner must average $1,370 per day in sales:

$$\text{Average daily sales} = \frac{\$410,959}{300\,\text{days}} = \$1,370/\text{day}$$

This calculation gives the owner a better perspective of the sales required to yield an annual profit of $30,000.

To determine whether the profit expected from the business will meet or exceed the target income, the entrepreneur also should use this same process to create income statements that are built on pessimistic, most likely, and optimistic sales estimates. The previous analysis shows an entrepreneur the sales level needed to reach a desired profit. But what happens if sales are lower? Higher? Making these projections requires a reliable sales forecast using the market research techniques described in Chapter 8, Building a Powerful Marketing Plan.

Suppose, for example, that after conducting research on the industry, a marketing survey of local customers, and talking with owners of bookstores in other markets, the prospective bookstore operator projects annual sales for the proposed business's first year of operation to be only $385,000. The entrepreneur can take this sales estimate and develop a projected income statement.

Net Sales	(100%)	$385,000
− Cost of Goods Sold	(61.4%)	$236,390
Gross Profit Margin	(38.6%)	$148,610
− Operating Expenses	(31.3%)	$83,505
Net Profit (before taxes)	(7.3%)	$28,105

Based on sales of $385,000, this entrepreneur should expect a net income (before taxes) of $28,105. If this amount is acceptable as a return on the investment of time and money in the business, he should proceed with his planning.

At this stage in developing the financial plan, the owner should create a more detailed picture of the venture's expected operating expenses. In addition to gathering information from industry trade associations about typical operating expenses, an entrepreneur can contact potential vendors, suppliers, and providers to get estimates of the expenses he or she can expect to incur in his or her area of operation. One entrepreneur who was preparing a business plan for the launch of an upscale women's clothing store contacted local utility companies, insurance agencies, radio and television stations, newspapers, and other vendors to get estimates of her utility, insurance, advertising, and other general expenses.

To ensure that they have not overlooked any business expenses in preparing the business plan, entrepreneurs should list all of the expenses they will incur and have an accountant review the list. Sometimes in their estimates of expenses entrepreneurs neglect to include salaries for themselves, which immediately raises a red flag among lenders and investors. Without drawing a salary, how will an entrepreneur pay her own bills? At the other extreme, lenders and investors frown on exorbitantly high salaries for owners of business start-ups. Typically, salaries are not the best use of cash in a start-up; one guideline is to draw a salary that is about 25 to 30 percent below the market rate for a similar position (and to make adjustments from there if conditions warrant). In addition, as the company grows, executive salaries should be among the *last* expenses to be increased. Reinvesting the extra money back into the company for essentials will accelerate its growth rate even more.

ENTREPRENEURIAL PROFILE____

Stephen Culp: Smart Furniture

Stephen Culp, who in 2001 started Smart Furniture, a Chattanooga, Tennessee-based modular furniture company, drew no salary at all for his first three years in business, choosing instead to live very frugally off of his personal savings. Culp planned his company this way from the outset, using the money he could have drawn as his salary to hire two employees who played key roles in tripling the company's sales in just three years. "It's a prioritization of cash flow," explains Culp. "If I can survive on cereal and take all that cash that I would have spent on a more extravagant lifestyle and put it back into the company, it increases my chances of success." Culp's plan called for attracting venture capital to accelerate his company's growth, and he knew that he would have to include a salary for himself before approaching venture capital firms. Culp researched the industry and talked with colleagues to determine a reasonable salary, discounted that number by 30 percent, and came up with a salary of less than $100,000. "I'm still trying to show investors that I'm in this for the long haul," he says.[6]

Figures 11.3 and 11.4 show two useful forms designed to help entrepreneurs estimate both monthly and start-up expenses. Totals derived from this list of expenses should approximate the total expense figures calculated from published statistics. Naturally, an entrepreneur should be more confident in his or her own list of expenses because it reflects his or her company's particular set of circumstances.

THE PROJECTED BALANCE SHEET In addition to projecting a small company's net profit or loss, an entrepreneur must develop a pro forma balance sheet outlining the fledgling firm's assets and liabilities. Most entrepreneurs' primary concern is profitability because, on the surface, the importance of a business's assets is less obvious. In many cases, small companies begin their lives on weak financial footing because entrepreneurs fail to determine their firms' total asset requirements. To prevent this major oversight, entrepreneurs should prepare a projected balance sheet listing every asset their businesses will need and all the claims against these assets.

ASSETS Cash is one of the most useful assets the business owns; it is highly liquid and can quickly be converted into other tangible assets. But how much cash should a small business have at its inception? Obviously, there is no single dollar figure that fits the needs of every small firm. One practical rule of thumb, however, suggests that a company's cash balance should cover its

FIGURE 11.3

Anticipated Expenses

Source: U.S. Small Business
Administration, *Checklist for Going into
Business.* (Small Marketers Aid No. 71)
(Washington, DC,1982), pp. 6–7.

Worksheet No. 2
Estimated Monthly Expenses

Item	Your estimate of monthly expenses based on sales of $ _____ per year	Your estimate of how much cash you need to start your business (see column 3)	Guidelines for minimum amount to enter in column 2
	Column 1	**Column 2**	**Column 3**
Salary of owner-manager	$	$	2 times column 1
All other salaries and wages			3 times column 1
Rent			3 times column 1
Advertising			3 times column 1
Delivery expense			3 times column 1
Supplies			3 times column 1
Telephone and Internet			3 times column 1
Other utilities			3 times column 1
Insurance			Payment required by insurance company
Taxes, including Social Security			4 times column 1
Interest			3 times column 1
Maintenance			3 times column 1
Legal and other professional fees			3 times column 1
Miscellaneous			3 times column 1
Starting Costs You Have to Pay Only Once			
Fixtures and equipment			Fill in worksheet 3 and put the total here
Decorating and remodeling			Talk with a contractor
Installation of fixtures and equipment			Talk to suppliers from whom you buy these
Starting inventory			Suppliers can help you estimate this
Deposits with public utilities			Find out from utility companies
Legal and other professional fees			Lawyer, accountant, and so on
Licenses and permits			Find out from city offices what you have to have
Advertising and promotion of opening			Estimate what you'll use
Accounts receivable			What you need to buy more stock until tredi customers pay
Cash			For unexpected expenses or losses, special purchases, etc.
Other			Make a separate lis and enter total
Total Estimated Cash You Need to Start		$	Add up all the numbers in column 2

FIGURE 11.4

Anticipated Expenditures for Fixtures and Equipment

Worksheet No. 3
List of Furniture, Fixtures, and Equipment

Leave out or add items to suit your business. Use separate sheets to list exactly what you need for each of the items below.	If you plan to pay cash in full, enter the full amount below and in the last column.	If you are going to pay by installments, fill out the columns below. Enter in the last column your down payment plus at least one installment.			Estimate of the cash you need for furniture, fixtures, and equipment.
		Price	Down payment	Amount of each installment	
Counters	$	$	$	$	$
Storage shelves, cabinets					
Display stands, shelves, tables					
Cash register					
Safe					
Window display fixtures					
Special lighting					
Outside sign					
Delivery equipment if needed					
Total furniture, fixtures, and equipment (Enter this figure also in worksheet 2 under "Starting Costs You Have to Pay Only Once.")				$	

operating expenses (less depreciation, a non-cash expense) for at least one inventory turnover period. Using this guideline, the cash balance for the small bookstore is calculated as follows:

Operating expenses = $128,630 (from projected income statement)
Less: depreciation (1.4% of annual sales[*]) of $5,753

Equals: cash expenses (annual) = $122,877

Annual inventory turnover ratio[*] = 3.6 times per year

$$\text{Cash requirement} = \frac{\text{cash expenses}}{\text{average inventory turnover}}$$

$$= \frac{\$122,877}{3.6}$$

$$= \$34,132$$

[*] from *RMA Annual Statement Studies.*

Notice the inverse relationship between the small firm's average turnover ratio and its cash requirement. The smaller the number of inventory turns a company generates, the higher is its cash requirement.

Another decision facing the entrepreneur is how much inventory the business should carry. A rough estimate of the inventory requirement can be calculated from the information found on the projected income statement and from published statistics:

Cost of goods sold = $252,329 (from projected income statement)

$$\text{Average inventory turnover} = \frac{\text{cost of goods sold}}{\text{inventory level}} = 3.6\,\text{times/year}$$

Substituting, we obtain:

$$3.6\,\text{times/year} = \frac{\$252,329}{\text{inventory level}}$$

FIGURE 11.5

Projected Balance Sheet for a Small Bookstore

Assets		Liabilities	
Current Assets		**Current Liabilities**	
Cash	$ 34,132	Accounts Payable	$ 48,796
Inventory	70,091	Note Payable	3,750
Miscellaneous	1,800		
Total Current Assets	$106,024	Total Current Liabilities	$ 52,546
Fixed Assets		**Long-Term Liabilities**	
Fixtures	$ 27,500	Note Payable	$ 40,000
Office Equipment	4,850		
Computer/Cash Register	5,125	Total Liabilities	$ 92,546
Signs	6,200		
Miscellaneous	1,500		
Total Fixed Assets	$ 45,175	**Owner's Equity**	$ 58,653
Total Assets	$151,199	**Total Liabilities and Owner's Equity**	$151,199

Solving for the inventory level gives:

$$\text{Inventory level} = \$70,091$$

Entrepreneurs can use the planning forms shown in Figures 11.3 and 11.4 to estimate fixed assets (land, building, equipment, and fixtures). Suppose the estimate of fixed assets is as follows:

Fixtures	$27,500
Office equipment	4,850
Computers/cash register	5,125
Signs	6,200
Miscellaneous	1,500
Total	$45,175

LIABILITIES To complete the projected balance sheet, the owner must record all of the small firm's liabilities, the claims against its assets. The bookstore owner was able to finance 50 percent of the inventory and fixtures ($48,796) through suppliers and has a short-term note payable in the amount of $3,750. The only other major claim against the firm's assets is a note payable to the entrepreneur's father-in-law for $40,000. The difference between the company's assets ($151,199) and its total liabilities ($92,546) represents the owner's investment in the business (owner's equity) of $58,653.

The final step is to compile all of these items into a projected balance sheet, as shown in Figure 11.5.

LO 4

Understand the basic financial statements through ratio analysis.

Ratio Analysis

"How is my company doing?" is a question that constantly nags entrepreneurs. It is an important question to ask but is particularly important during an economic recession. John Pearce II, a business professor at Villanova University, estimates that during each of the last three U.S. recessions, 500,000 small businesses closed or went bankrupt. Unfortunately, many of these entrepreneurs never realized that their companies were in trouble until it was too late to do anything about it. To avoid becoming another failure statistic, entrepreneurs must understand the numbers that drive their businesses. Norm Brodsky, a successful entrepreneur who recently sold two of his businesses for $110 million, explains:

To be successful in any business, you need to develop a feel for the numbers. You need to get a sense of the relationships between them, see the connections, figure out which ones are critical and have to be monitored. Why? Because these numbers run businesses. They tell you how you can make the most money in the least time and with the least effort. You can give it all away if you want to, but first you have to earn it, and the numbers can tell you how to do that as efficiently as possible, provided [that] you understand their language. When the numbers change, those changes can be significant. They may herald new competition arriving or indicate a shift in your customers' preferences or reflect unseen problems with your products or services. But you'll see [the reasons for the changes]–and be able to respond quickly–only if you get into the habit early on of looking for them and trying to understand what they mean.[7]

Smart entrepreneurs know that once they have their businesses up and running with the help of a solid financial plan, the next step is to keep their companies moving in the right direction with the help of proper financial controls. Establishing these controls–and using them consistently–is one of the keys to keeping a business vibrant and healthy. A sound system of financial controls serves as an early warning device for underlying problems that could destroy a young business. The key is hearing and focusing on the signals.

YOU BE THE CONSULTANT

The Question: To Grow or Not to Grow

It's a common trap that catches many entrepreneurs: the pursuit of growth at all costs. Rather than see the many contributions their businesses make to the local community and the accomplishments they have achieved, entrepreneurs often have a nagging sense of inadequacy. No matter how successful they may appear to be, it's never quite enough. Focusing on growing the top line (revenue) can cause small companies to make sacrifices on the bottom line (profits). "Bigger is better–that's the old Holy Grail," says Paul Schaye, a principal at an investment banking firm. "It gets you bragging rights at the bar, but those bragging rights are what drives people to do crazy things." Perhaps that is why many small business owners eschew growth and choose to stay small. A recent survey by Discover Financial Services reports that 69 percent of small business owners prefer to keep their companies small.

Jim Christy, founder of Incredible Foods, a dessert delivery service in Gibsonia, Pennsylvania, fell into the "growth is good" trap before he finally realized that more sales do not necessarily equate to a better business. Christy started Incredible Foods after he tasted a cheesecake from a San Diego bakery on a trip to the west coast and ordered 30 cheesecakes from the bakery to sell to food vendors in Pennsylvania, his home state. Christy soon expanded his product line to include a variety of desserts and added colleges, hotels, and restaurants to his customer base.

Four years after starting Incredible Foods, Christy landed its biggest customer: Starbucks. The coffee giant was adding new stores rapidly and wanted Incredible Foods to distribute a single product, crumb cake, to its stores in Ohio and Pennsylvania. Incredible Foods's sales reached $3.4 million, but those sales came at a price. "The cost of fuel, employee benefits, insurance, and workers' compensation made the whole thing completely unprofitable," says Christy. "I had two employees who did nothing but write reports for Starbucks."

Although Starbucks accounted for 48 percent of Incredible Foods's sales, Christy decided to end the relationship with his largest customer because he believed that his business would be stronger and more profitable *without* Starbucks. He closed one of his two offices, reduced office staff from 13 employees to six, and began focusing on smaller accounts. Christy's courageous decision

Jim Christy, founder of Incredible Foods.

Pete Taunton, founder of Snap Fitness.

paid off. Within one year, the company had rebounded; although sales had fallen to $2.2 million, Incredible Foods earned a healthy profit. "I can do half the business, make twice the money, and have a tenth of the headaches," says Christy.

Entrepreneur Pete Taunton learned a similar lesson from the "big box" gyms that he operated. Taunton began managing a big gym for a group of owners when he was just 21 years old. Before long he bought the gym from the owners and used the building as collateral on a loan to open five other gyms, all of them successful—and huge, including everything from child care and steam rooms to climbing walls and pools.

The success was exacting a toll on Taunton, however. "The gyms had huge overhead [costs]," he says. "It cost more than $1.5 million to buy the building, [which required] me to take out significant loans. I also had to supervise 200 employees and drive to each location daily to meet with managers, tour facilities, and monitor programs." Taunton's intense schedule was affecting his family life, and he decided to sell his business.

Six months later, he and a group of his former employees decided to launch a new gym business, but this time things would be different. "I was finished with 75-hour workweeks, and I didn't want to make a massive investment," he says. Taunton recalled how many of his former customers asked if they could pay a lower monthly fee to use only the basic equipment in his gyms and decided to launch a smaller, more efficient gym, Snap Fitness. Because the operating costs were much lower than for his earlier mega-gyms, Snap Fitness offered the benefit of a lower break-even point. Taunton's research also showed that a more basic gym would draw on a larger base of customers who were willing and able to pay monthly fees of no more than $35, compared to $50 to $80 per month at big box gyms. "My old fitness centers were 40,000 square feet; a Snap Fitness gym is less than 3,000," he says. "The buildings, which I lease instead of own, cost $150,000 to open. The big gyms cost 12 times as much. Operating the [small gyms] is a breeze: low maintenance, little insurance, and just one person to run the entire gym. Now I'm out the door by 6 p.m."

Taunton has built Snap Fitness into a franchised chain of gyms with more than 160,000 members and annual sales that exceed $16 million. "It's a better, leaner business model, and it makes my life easier too," he says.

Fast growth is not an enticement to Christy, Taunton, and other entrepreneurs of their ilk. These visionary entrepreneurs prefer to grow steadily at their own manageable pace and to define their success in terms of satisfied customers, dedicated employees, and profitable companies.

1. Why is it so easy for entrepreneurs to fall into the high-growth trap, even when growing fast may have negative repercussions on their companies?
2. What benefits do entrepreneurs such as Jim Christy and Pete Taunton experience by choosing to pursue profitability over sales growth? What are the costs of such a strategy?
3. Research the companies listed on the *Inc.* 500 list of the fastest growing companies in the United States from five years ago. Find the most recent listing of the *Inc.* 500 list. How many of the companies from the past appear on the current list? Use *Inc.* magazine and the resources of the Web to research some of the companies that appeared on the earlier list but that are missing from the current list. What happened to them? What lessons can entrepreneurs learn from their stories?

Source: Adapted from; Ellyn Spragins and Verne Harnish, "Size Doesn't Matter—Profits Do," *FSB*, March 2004, pp. 37–42; Pete Taunton, "Trimming the Fat, *FSB*, February, 2008, p. 81; Mina Kimes, "When Less Means More," FSB, November 2008, pp. 81–90.[8]

ratio analysis
a method of expressing the relationships between any two accounting elements that allows business owners to analyze their companies' financial performances.

What are these signals, and how does an entrepreneur go about hearing and focusing on them? One extremely helpful tool is ratio analysis. **Ratio analysis,** a method of expressing the relationships between any two elements on financial statements, provides a convenient technique for performing financial analysis. When analyzed properly, ratios serve as barometers of a company's financial health. "You owe it to yourself to understand each ratio and what it means to your business," says one accountant. "Ratios point out potential trouble areas so you can correct them before they multiply."[9] Ratio analysis allows entrepreneurs to determine whether their companies are carrying excessive inventory, experiencing heavy operating expenses, overextending credit, taking on too much debt, and managing to pay their bills on time and to answer other questions relating to the efficient and effective operation of the overall business. Unfortunately, studies show that few business owners actually compute financial ratios and use them to manage their businesses.

Smart business owners use financial ratio analysis to identify problems in their businesses while they are still problems and not business threatening crises. Tracking these ratios over time permits an owner to spot a variety of "red flags" that are indications of these problem areas. This is critical to business success because business owners cannot solve problems they do not know exist! Business owners also can use ratio analysis to increase the likelihood of obtaining loans. By analyzing their financial statements with ratios, business owners can anticipate potential problems and identify important strengths in advance. And loan officers *do* use ratios to analyze the financial statements of companies applying for loans, comparing them against industry averages and looking for trends over time.

How many ratios should a small business owner monitor to maintain adequate financial control over the firm? The number of ratios that an owner could calculate is limited only by the number of accounts on a firm's financial statements. However, tracking too many ratios only creates confusion and saps the meaning from an entrepreneur's financial analysis. The secret to successful ratio analysis is *simplicity*, focusing on just enough ratios to provide a clear picture of a company's financial standing.

Twelve Key Ratios

In keeping with the idea of simplicity, we will describe twelve key ratios that enable most business owners to monitor their companies' financial positions without becoming bogged down in financial details. This chapter presents explanations of these ratios and examples based on the balance sheet and the income statement for Sam's Appliance Shop shown in Figures 11.1 and 11.2. We will group them into four categories: liquidity ratios, leverage ratios, operating ratios, and profitability ratios.

LIQUIDITY RATIOS **Liquidity ratios** tell whether a small business will be able to meet its short-term financial obligations as they come due. These ratios can forewarn a business owner of impending cash flow problems. A small company with solid liquidity not only is able to pay its bills on time, but it also has enough cash to take advantage of attractive business opportunities as they arise. Liquidity ratios measure a company's ability to convert its assets to cash quickly and without a loss of value to pay its short-term liabilities. The primary measures of liquidity are the current ratio and the quick ratio.

liquidity ratios
tell whether a small business will be able to meet its short-term obligations as they come due.

1. *Current Ratio.* The **current ratio** measures a small firm's solvency by indicating its ability to pay current liabilities (debts) from current assets. It is calculated in the following manner:

$$\text{Current ratio} = \frac{\text{current assets}}{\text{current liabilities}}$$

$$= \frac{\$686,985}{\$367,850}$$

$$= 1.87:1$$

current ratio
measures a small firm's solvency by indicating its ability to pay current liabilities out of current assets.

Sam's Appliance Shop has $1.87 in current assets for every $1 it has in current liabilities.

Current assets are those that an owner expects to convert into cash in the ordinary business cycle, and normally include cash, notes/accounts receivable, inventory, and any other short-term marketable securities. Current liabilities are those short-term obligations that come due within one year, and include notes/accounts payable, taxes payable, and accruals.

The current ratio is sometimes called the *working capital ratio* and is the most commonly used measure of short-term solvency. Typically, financial analysts suggest that a small business maintain a current ratio of at least 2:1 (i.e., two dollars of current assets for every one dollar of current liabilities) to maintain a comfortable cushion of working capital. Generally, the higher a company's current ratio, the stronger is its financial position; however, a high current ratio does not guarantee that a company is using its assets in the most profitable manner. For example, a business may be have an abundance of accounts receivable (many of which may not even be collectible) or may be overinvesting in inventory.

With its current ratio of 1.87, Sam's Appliance Shop could liquidate its current assets at 53.5% (1 ÷ 1.87 = 0.535) of its book value and still manage to pay its current creditors in full.

2. *Quick Ratio.* The current ratio sometimes can be misleading because it does not reflect the *quality* of a company's current assets. As we have already seen, a company with a large number of past-due receivables and stale inventory could boast an impressive current ratio and still be on the verge of financial collapse. The **quick ratio** (**acid test ratio**) is a more conservative measure of a company's liquidity because it shows the extent to which its most liquid assets cover its current liabilities. This ratio includes only a company's "quick assets," excluding the most illiquid asset of all—inventory. It is calculated as follows:

quick ratio
a conservative measure of a firm's liquidity, measuring the extent to which its most liquid assets cover its current liabilities.

$$\text{Quick ratio} = \frac{\text{quick assets}}{\text{current liabilities}}$$

$$= \frac{\$686,985 - \$455,455}{\$367,850}$$

$$= 0.63:1$$

Sam's Appliance Shop has 63 cents in quick assets for every $1 of current liabilities.

Quick assets include cash, readily marketable securities, and notes/accounts receivables, assets that can be converted into cash immediately if needed. Most small firms determine quick assets by subtracting inventory from current assets because they cannot convert

SuperStock, Inc.

leverage ratios

measure the financing supplied by a firm's owners against that supplied by its creditors; they are a gauge of the depth of a company's debt.

inventory into cash quickly. Moreover, inventory is the asset on which losses are most likely to occur in case of liquidation.

The quick ratio is a more specific measure of a firm's ability to meet its short-term obligations and is a more rigorous test of its liquidity. It expresses capacity to pay current debts if all sales income ceased immediately. Generally, a quick ratio of 1:1 is considered satisfactory. A ratio of less than 1:1 indicates that the small firm is overly dependent on inventory and on future sales to satisfy short-term debt. A quick ratio of greater than 1:1 indicates a greater degree of financial security.

Leverage Ratios. **Leverage ratios** measure the financing supplied by a firm's owners against that supplied by its creditors; they are a gauge of the depth of a company's debt. These ratios show the extent to which an entrepreneur relies on debt capital (rather than equity capital) to finance operating expenses, capital expenditures, and expansion costs. As such, it is a measure of the degree of financial risk in a company. Generally, small businesses with low leverage ratios are less affected by economic downturns, but the returns for these firms are lower during economic booms. Conversely, small companies with high leverage ratios are more vulnerable to economic slides because their debt loads demolish cash flow; however, they have greater potential for large profits.

Debt is a powerful financial tool, but companies must handle it carefully–just as a demolitionist handles dynamite. And, like dynamite, too much debt can be deadly. Over the last decade, many businesses in the United States have relied increasingly on debt financing to fuel their growth and expansion. Unfortunately, some companies have pushed their debt loads beyond the safety barrier (see Figure 11.6) and are struggling to survive. Heavy debt loads can be deadly, particularly when a company's sales and earnings falter.

ENTREPRENEURIAL PROFILE

Bill Heard: Bill Heard Enterprises

Bill Heard Enterprises (BHE), the largest Chevrolet dealer in the world with 14 dealerships in seven southern states, declared bankruptcy when its sales slowed and the company could no longer make payments on the significant level of debt it had accumulated. The company started as a single dealership founded by Heard's father in Columbus, Georgia, in 1919 and grew rapidly after the younger Heard, who called himself "Mr. Big Volume," took over. However, when the economy faltered, credit tightened, and car sales plummeted, BHE's dealerships began losing from $2 million to $5 million per month, putting the company in a cash bind and a downward financial spiral. BHE's Chapter 11 bankruptcy filing showed that the company owed nearly 5,000 creditors, ranging from GMAC and banks to employees and state tax authorities, between $500 million and $1 billion.[10]

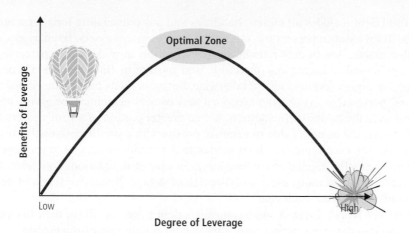

FIGURE 11.6

The Right Amount of Debt Is a Balancing Act

Managed carefully, however, debt can boost a company's performance and improve its productivity. Table 11.1 describes how lenders view liquidity and leverage.

3. *Debt Ratio.* A small company's **debt ratio** measures the percentage of total assets financed by its creditors compared to its owners. The debt ratio is calculated as follows:

$$\text{Debt ratio} = \frac{\text{total debt (or liabilities)}}{\text{total assets}}$$

$$= \frac{\$367,850 + \$212,150}{\$847,655}$$

$$= 0.68{:}1$$

debt ratio

measures the percentage of total assets financed by a company's creditors compared to its owners.

Creditors have claims of 68 cents against every $1 of assets that Sam's Appliance Shop owns.

TABLE 11.1 How Lenders View Liquidity and Leverage

	Liquidity	Leverage
Low	If chronic, this is often evidence of mismanagement. It is a sign that the owner has not planned for the company's working capital needs. In most businesses characterized by low liquidity, there is usually no financial plan. This situation is often associated with last minute or "Friday night" financing.	This is a very conservative position. With this kind of leverage, lenders are likely to lend money to satisfy a company's capital needs. Owners in this position should have no trouble borrowing money.
Average	This is an indication of good management. The company is using its current assets wisely and productively. Although they may not be impressed, lenders feel comfortable making loans to companies with adequate liquidity.	If a company's leverage is comparable to that of other businesses of similar size in the same industry, lenders are comfortable making loans. The company is not overburdened with debt and is demonstrating its ability to use its resources to grow.
High	Some lenders look for this because it indicates a most conservative company. However, companies that constantly operate this way usually are forgoing growth opportunities because they are not making the most of their assets.	Businesses that carry excessive levels of debt scare most lenders off. Companies in this position normally have difficulty borrowing money unless they can show lenders good reasons for making loans. Owners of these companies must be prepared to sell lenders on their ability to repay.

Source: Adapted from David H. Bangs, Jr., *Financial Troubleshooting,* Upstart Publishing Company, (Dover, New Hampshire, 1992), p. 124.

Total debt includes all current liabilities and any outstanding long-term notes and bonds. Total assets represent the sum of the firm's current assets, fixed assets, and intangible assets. A high debt ratio means that creditors provide a large percentage of a company's total financing and, therefore, bear most of its financial risk. Owners generally prefer higher leverage ratios; otherwise, business funds must come either from the owners' personal assets or from taking on new owners, which means giving up more control over the business. In addition, with a greater portion of a firm's assets financed by creditors, the owner is able to generate profits with a smaller personal investment. Creditors, however, typically prefer moderate debt ratios because a lower debt ratio indicates a smaller chance of creditor losses in case of liquidation. To lenders and creditors, high debt ratios mean a higher risk of default. Excessive levels of debt sink thousands of business each year.

debt to net worth (or debt to equity) ratio

the relationship between the capital contributions from creditors and those from owners. It measures how highly leveraged a company is.

4. *Debt to Net Worth Ratio.* A small company's **debt to net worth** (or **debt to equity**) **ratio** also expresses the relationship between the capital contributions from creditors and those from owners and measures how highly leveraged a company is. This ratio reveals a company's capital structure by comparing what the business "owes" to "what it is worth." It is a measure of the small firm's ability to meet both its creditor and owner obligations in case of liquidation. The debt to net worth ratio is calculated as follows:

$$\text{Debt-to-net worth-ratio} = \frac{\text{total debt (or liabilities)}}{\text{tangible net worth}}$$

$$= \frac{\$367{,}850 + \$212{,}150}{\$267{,}655 - \$3{,}500}$$

$$= 2.20{:}1$$

Sam's Appliance Shop owes creditors $2.20 for every $1 of equity that Sam owns.

Total debt is the sum of current liabilities and long-term liabilities, and tangible net worth represents the owners' investment in the business (capital + capital stock + earned surplus + retained earnings) less any intangible assets (e.g., goodwill) the firm owns.

The higher this ratio, the more leverage a business is using and the lower the degree of protection afforded creditors if the business should fail. A higher debt to net worth ratio also means that the firm has less capacity to borrow; lenders and creditors see the firm as being "borrowed up." Conversely, a low ratio typically is associated with a higher level of financial security, giving the business greater borrowing potential.

ENTREPRENEURIAL PROFILE____

Vicorp Restaurants Inc.: Village Inn & Bakers Square

Founded in 1958, Vicorp Restaurants Inc., the parent company of Village Inn and Bakers Square restaurant chains, began incurring losses when sales declined and food and operating costs increased. The company's 250 restaurants were serving 1.1 million eggs each week, but when egg prices tripled over a two year period, its earnings were squeezed even though the company raised menu prices. Increases in the minimum wage and energy costs pushed the company's operating expenses even higher. Vicorp increased its debt load to cover the higher costs and to remodel its stores, actions that pushed its debt to net worth ratio from 4.0 to 10.0, just months before the company filed for Chapter 11 bankruptcy protection.[11]

As a company's debt-to-net worth ratio approaches 1:1, the creditors' interest in the business approaches that of the owners'. If the ratio is greater than 1:1, creditors' claims exceed those of the owners', and the business may be undercapitalized. In other words, the owner has not supplied an adequate amount of capital, forcing the business to be overextended in terms of debt. Lenders become nervous when a company's debt to equity ratio reaches 3:1 or more.

times interest earned ratio

measures a small firm's ability to make the interest payments on its debt.

5. *Times Interest Earned.* The **times interest earned ratio** is a measure of a small firm's ability to make the interest payments on its debt. It tells how many times a company's earnings cover the interest payments on the debt it is carrying. This ratio measures the size of

the cushion a company has in covering the interest cost of its debt load. The times interest earned ratio is calculated as follows:

$$\text{Times interest earned} = \frac{\text{earnings before interest and taxes (or EBIT)}}{\text{total interest expense}}$$

$$= \frac{\$60,629 + \$39,850}{\$39,850}$$

$$= 2.52{:}1$$

Sam's Appliance Shop's earnings are 2.5 times greater than its interest expense.

EBIT is the firm's profit *before* deducting interest expense and taxes; the denominator measures the amount the business paid in interest over the accounting period.

A high ratio suggests that the company would have little difficulty meeting the interest payments on its loans; creditors see this as a sign of safety for future loans. Conversely, a low ratio is an indication that the company is overextended in its debts; earnings will not be able to cover its debt service if this ratio is less than one. "I look for a [times interest earned] ratio of higher than three-to-one," says one financial analyst, "which indicates that management has considerable breathing room to make its debt payments. When the ratio drops below one-to-one, it clearly indicates management is under tremendous pressure to raise cash. The risk of default or bankruptcy is very high."[12] Many creditors look for a times interest earned ratio of at least 4:1 to 6:1 before pronouncing a company a good credit risk. Before Vicorp Restaurants Inc., the owner of Village Inn and Bakers Square restaurant chains, filed for bankruptcy, its times interest earned ratio had slipped from nearly 3:1 to just 1.85:1.[13]

Although low to moderate levels of debt can boost a company's financial performance, trouble looms on the horizon for businesses whose debt loads are so heavy that they must starve critical operations, research and development, customer service, and others just to pay interest on the debt. Because their interest payments are so large, highly leveraged companies find that they are restricted when it comes to spending cash, whether on an acquisition, normal operations, or capital spending. Charter Communications, a cable television and broadband communications company in which Microsoft co-founder Paul Allen has majority ownership, has struggled under a heavy debt burden that has grown to $21.3 billion. Charter does not generate enough cash to pay its debt, a situation that has forced the company to negotiate extended maturity dates on its debt every year since 2004. Charter declared bankruptcy in 2009 and developed a plan to restructure its balance sheet and survive.[14]

Operating Ratios. **Operating ratios** help an entrepreneur evaluate a small company's overall performance and indicate how effectively the business employs its resources. The more effectively its resources are used, the less capital a small business will require. These five operating ratios are designed to help an entrepreneur spot those areas she must improve if her business is to remain competitive.

6. *Average Inventory Turnover.* A small firm's **average inventory turnover ratio** measures the number of times its average inventory is sold out, or turned over, during the accounting period. This ratio tells whether an entrepreneur is managing inventory properly. It indicates whether a business's inventory is understocked, overstocked, or obsolete. The average inventory turnover ratio is calculated as follows:

> **operating ratios**
> help an entrepreneur evaluate a small company's overall performance and indicate how effectively the business employs its resources.

> **average inventory turnover ratio**
> measures the number of times its average inventory is sold out, or turned over, during an accounting period.

$$\text{Average inventory turnover ratio} = \frac{\text{cost of goods sold}}{\text{average inventory}}$$

$$= \frac{\$1,290,117}{(\$805,745 + \$455,455) \div 2}$$

$$= 2.05 \, \text{times/year}$$

Sam's Appliance Shop turns its inventory about two times a year, or once every 178 days.

Average inventory is the sum of the value of the firm's inventory at the beginning of the accounting period and its value at the end of the accounting period, divided by 2.

Andersen Ross/Brand X/Corbis RF

This ratio tells an entrepreneur how fast merchandise is moving through the business and helps him or her to balance the company's inventory on the fine line between oversupply and undersupply. To determine the average number of days that units remain in inventory, the owner can divide the average inventory turnover ratio into the number of days in the accounting period (e.g., 365 days ÷ average inventory turnover ratio). The result is called *days' inventory (or average age of inventory)*.

YOU BE THE CONSULTANT

The Perils of Debt

Chuck Bidwell, a serial entrepreneur, and Jennifer Guarino, a former handbag designer, agreed that if they ever found the right business to purchase, they would do so together. Over the course of several years, the entrepreneurs passed on many businesses, but when the opportunity arose to purchase J. W. Hulme Company, a St. Paul, Minnesota-based small maker of hunting bags and fishing rod cases, Bidwell and Guarino bought the company for $600,000. Founded in 1905, Hulme made military tents during World War I, canvas awnings in the post-war era, and travel bags for upscale retailers such as Orvis. When Bidwell and Guarino purchased the company, it employed three people who made outdoor gear.

Their vision for Hulme was to ramp up the company's growth rate by focusing on luxury markets with a broader line of products that included briefcases, backpacks, and handbags that they would market through catalogs and a Web site. Doing so, however, would require the entrepreneurs to borrow heavily. Their business plan called for increasing the company's mailing list from just 1,000 customers to more than 10,000 and expanding its product line from just 100 items to 250 products. If their strategy worked, their forecast showed annual sales of $2 million and positive cash flow.

To fund their expansion plans, Bidwell took a $130,000 second mortgage on his house, and he and Guarino presented their business plan to Fizal Kassim, head of Maple Bank in nearby Champlin, Minnesota. Maple Bank granted the entrepreneurs a

$70,000 loan and a $200,000 line of credit, the first in a series of ever-larger loans to the small company with big growth plans. Within three years, the plans that Bidwell and Guarino seemed to be coming to fruition; Hulme's sales had increased by 89 percent to $1.4 million, and the company earned a profit (before interest, depreciation, and taxes) of $325,000.

Bidwell and Guarino approached another local lender, St. Stephen Bank, for a $700,000 loan that would be guaranteed by the Small Business Administration (SBA). Expecting the loan to be processed quickly, the company hired employees and raw materials and began cranking up production. They also began planning an all-important catalog mailing for the upcoming season. Management changes at St. Stephen Bank slowed delayed the loan for six months, which meant that Bidwell and Guarino had to borrow more money—and fast. They turned to family members, friends, and business associates for loans totaling $500,000, but piecing together that much money took longer than expected, and Hulme missed several important catalog mailing deadlines, which handicapped the company's ability to generate sales. By the end of the year, the small company, now laden with debt, had generated only $1.5 million in sales, well below the $2 million target that Bidwell and Guarino had established.

The SBA-backed loan from St. Stephen Bank finally came through, which helped the entrepreneurs pay for new equipment, inventory, catalogs, and other expenses associated with their growth plans. Unfortunately, the loans from the banks, friends, and relatives pushed Hulme's debt-to-equity ratio from 2.94:1 to 5.53:1 in just one year. Because lenders prefer to see companies keep this ratio below 3:1, Hulme's creditors began to get nervous. When Bidwell approached Maple Bank for another $250,000 loan to print and mail the next round of catalogs, Kassim explained that a looming credit crisis (which would later sweep through the banking industry) made it difficult for Maple Bank to lend any more money to Hulme. Kassim also expressed concern that an economic recession could slow demand for the company's upscale product line, which included $500 garment bags and $1,200 leather duffle bags. Kassim also had concerns about the company's building inventory. Kassim told Bidwell that Maple Bank preferred to see inventory levels that were no more than 50 percent of sales, but Hulme's inventory represented 67 percent of sales.

Bidwell and Guarino stopped drawing their modest $40,000 salaries from the company and laid off 6 of their 14 employees. One seamstress who was laid off says, "They had been running out of supplies, like the hardware that goes on the bags, because they didn't have the money." The entrepreneurs went back to Maple Bank and told Kassim that if they could not get a $250,000 loan, they would have to shut down the company, which meant that the bank and all the company's other creditors would lose all of their money. Meanwhile, Hulme's catalog printer became aware of the company's cash problems and demanded advance payment for the upcoming round of catalogs. Caught in a bind, Bidwell convinced some friends to guarantee a $125,000 loan from Maple Bank. The money allowed Hulme to get its catalogs in customers' hands, although the mailing was more than a month late. The company's sales shrank because it could send out only 175,000 catalogs, down from 600,000 the previous year. "If we'd had the proper financing in place and had been able to mail our catalogs on time, we would have had a very successful year," says Bidwell. Instead, he and Guarino are battling to save their company. Guarino has drained her savings, lost all of her credit cards, and constantly fields calls from creditors wondering when—and if—they will be paid. Bidwell lost his house and has been forced to sell his collection of vintage Buicks. The entrepreneurs have had to lay off employees and renegotiate payments with their suppliers as well as with the banks that extended them loans. They know that there is no guarantee that J. W. Hulme will survive.

1. What are the benefits to entrepreneurs who use debt capital (leverage) to finance their companies' growth?
2. What are the risks associated with debt financing?
3. Assume the role of a small business banker. Suppose that Bidwell and Guarino had approached you for a bank loan when they were buying J. W. Hulme. Which financial ratios would you be most interested in? Why? What advice would you offer them?

Source: Based on Julie Jargon, "On Front Lines of Debt Crisis, Luggage Maker Fights for Life," *Wall Street Journal*, January 9, 2009, pp. A1, A8.

Auto dealerships often use the average age of inventory as a measure of their performance and consider 50 to 60 days' worth of stock to be an adequate inventory.

As cars from the Detroit Three lost their luster among consumers, John Zapp, owner of an Oklahoma City dealership that sells Buck, Pontiac, GMC, Dodge, and Chrysler brands, saw his dealership's days' inventory edge upward. Having spent four decades in the car business, Zapp knew that turning inventory quickly was a key to success. He decided to shift the focus of his dealerships to used cars, which allowed him to make important changes in his business model. Rather than carry an inventory of 200 new cars that turns, on average every 72 days, Zapp keeps 100 used cars on his lot that turn in an average of 27 days. In addition to tying up less cash in inventory, Zapp earns profit margins on used cars that are seven times higher than those on new cars. The strategy is working; used cars now contribute 96 percent of the dealership's gross profit.[15]

ENTREPRENEURIAL PROFILE

John Zapp: Bob Howard Chrysler-Jeep-Dodge

An above-average inventory turnover indicates that the small business has a healthy, salable, and liquid inventory that is supported by sound pricing policies. A below-average inventory turnover suggests an illiquid inventory characterized by obsolescence, overstocking, stale merchandise, and poor purchasing and pricing procedures. Businesses that turn their inventories more rapidly require a smaller inventory investment to produce a particular sales volume. That means that these companies tie up less cash in inventory that idly sits on shelves. For instance, if Sam's could turn its inventory *four* times each year instead of just *two*, the company would require an average inventory of just $322,529 instead of the current level of $630,600 to generate sales of $1,870,841. Increasing the number of inventory turns would free up more than $308,000 in cash currently tied up in excess inventory! Sam's would benefit from improved cash flow and higher profits.

The inventory turnover ratio can be misleading, however. For example, an excessively high ratio could mean that a company does not have enough inventory on hand and may be losing sales due to stockouts. Similarly, a low ratio could be the result of planned inventory stockpiling to meet seasonal peak demand. Another problem is that the ratio is based on an inventory balance calculated from two days out of the entire accounting period. Thus, inventory fluctuations due to seasonal demand patterns are ignored, which may bias the resulting ratio. There is no universal, ideal inventory turnover ratio. Financial analysts suggest that a favorable turnover ratio depends on the type of business, its size, its profitability, its method of inventory valuation, and other relevant factors. For instance, the typical supermarket turns its inventory on average about 16 times a year, but a jewelry store averages just 1.5 to 2 inventory turns a year.

average collection period ratio
measures the number of days it takes to collect accounts receivable.

7. *Average Collection Period Ratio.* A small firm's **average collection period ratio** (or **days sales outstanding, DSO)** tells the average number of days it takes to collect accounts receivable. To compute the average collection period ratio, you must first calculate the firm's receivables turnover. Given that Sam's *credit* sales for the year were $1,309,589 (out of the total sales of $1,870,841), then the company's receivables turnover ratio is as follows:

$$\text{Receivables turnover ratio} = \frac{\text{credit sales}}{\text{accounts receivable}}$$

$$= \frac{\$1,309,589}{\$179,225}$$

$$= 7.31 \, \text{times/year}$$

Sam's Appliance Shop turns over its receivables 7.31 times per year. This ratio measures the number of times the firm's accounts receivable turn over during the accounting period. The higher the firm's receivables turnover ratio, the shorter the time lag is between the sale and the cash collection.

Use the following to calculate the firm's average collection period ratio:

$$\text{Average collection period ratio} = \frac{\text{days in accounting period}}{\text{receivables turnover ratio}}$$

$$= \frac{365 \, \text{days}}{7.31 \, \text{times/year}}$$

$$= 50.0 \, \text{days}$$

The lower a company's average collection period, the faster it is collecting its receivables. Sam's Appliance Shop's accounts receivable are outstanding for an average of 50 days. Typically, the higher a firm's average collection period ratio, the greater is its chance of incurring bad debt losses.

One of the most useful applications of the collection period ratio is to compare it to the industry average and to the firm's credit terms. This comparison indicates the degree of the small company's control over its credit sales and collection techniques. A healthy collection period ratio depends on the industry in which a company operates. For instance, the average collection period for companies that manufacture laboratory instruments is 51 days; for tire retailers, it is just 20 days.[16] Perhaps the most meaningful analysis is comparing the collection period ratio to a company's credit terms. One rule of thumb suggests that a company's collection period ratio should be no more than one-third greater than its credit terms. For example, if a small company's credit terms are net 30 (payment due within 30 days), its average collection period ratio should be no more than 40 days (30 + 30 × 1/3). For this company, a ratio greater than 40 days indicates poor collection procedures.

Slow payers represent a great risk to many small businesses. Many entrepreneurs proudly point to rapidly rising sales only to find that they must borrow money to keep their companies going because their credit customers are paying their bills in 45, 60, or even 90 days instead of the desired 30. Slow receivables are a real danger because they usually lead to a cash crisis that threatens a company's survival.

During an economic slowdown, Gregg Moore, president of Workplace Integra, a 13-employee company in Greensboro, North Carolina, that helps manufacturers comply with government-mandated workplace noise restrictions, saw his company's average collection period increase from 39 to 56 days. Slower receivables put intense pressure on Workplace Integra's cash flow, forcing Moore to tap the company's line of credit, a move that he had never had to make before. Cash flow woes have slowed the company's growth because Moore is hesitant to expand and to add employees. "Right now we're hunkering down and weathering the storm," he says.[17]

ENTREPRENEURIAL PROFILE _____

Gregg Moore:
Workplace Integra

Table 11.2 shows how to calculate the savings associated with lowering a company's average collection period ratio.

8. *Average Payable Period Ratio.* The converse of the average collection period, the **average payable period ratio** (or **days payables outstanding, DPO),** tells the average number of days it takes a company to pay its accounts payable. Like the average collection period, it is measured in days. To compute this ratio, we first calculate the payables turnover ratio. Sam's payables turnover ratio is as follows:

average payable period ratio measures the number of days it takes a company to pay its accounts payable.

$$\text{Payables turnover} = \frac{\text{purchases}}{\text{accounts payable}}$$

$$= \frac{\$939,827}{\$152,580}$$

$$= 6.16 \text{ times/year}$$

TABLE 11.2 How Lowering Your Average Collection Period Can Save You Money

Too often, entrepreneurs fail to recognize the importance of collecting their accounts receivable on time. After all, collecting accounts is not as glamorous or as much fun as generating sales. Lowering a company's average collection period ratio, however, *can* produce tangible—and often significant—savings. The following formula shows how to convert an improvement in a company's average collection period ratio into dollar savings:

Annual Savings

$$= \frac{(\text{Credit sales} \times \text{annual interest rate} \times \text{number of days average collection period is lowered})}{365}$$

where,

credit sales = company's annual credit sales in $.

annual interest rate = the interest rate at which the company borrows money.

number of days average collection period is lowered = the difference between the previous year's average collection period ratio and the current one.

Example:

Sam's Appliance Shop's average collection period ratio is 50 days. Suppose that the previous year's average collection period ratio was 58 days, an eight-day improvement. The company's credit sales for the most recent year were $1,309,589. If Sam borrows money at 8.75%, this six-day improvement has generated savings for Sam's Appliance Shop of:

$$\text{Savings} = \frac{\$1,309,589 \times 8.75\% \times 8 \text{ days}}{365 \text{ days}} = \$2,512$$

By collecting his accounts receivable just six days faster on the average, Sam has saved his business more than $2,512! Of course, if a company's average collection period ratio rises, the same calculation will tell the owner how much that costs.

Source: Adapted from "Days Saved, Thousands Earned," *Inc.*, November 1995, p. 98.

To find the average payable period, we use the following computation:

$$\text{Average payable period} = \frac{\text{days in accounting period}}{\text{payables turnover ratio}}$$

$$= \frac{365\,\text{days}}{6.16\,\text{times per year}}$$

$$= 59.3\,\text{days}$$

Sam's Appliance Shop takes an average of 59 days to pay its accounts with suppliers. An excessively high average payables period ratio indicates the presence of a significant amount of past-due accounts payable. Although sound cash management calls for a business owner to keep his or her cash as long as possible, slowing payables too drastically can severely damage the company's credit rating. Ideally, the average payable period would match (or exceed) the time it takes to convert inventory into sales and ultimately into cash. In this case, the company's vendors would be financing its inventory and its credit sales. Online retailer Amazon reaps the benefits of this situation; it does not pay its vendors until after it collects from its customers.[18]

One of the most meaningful comparisons for this ratio is against the credit terms suppliers offer (or an average of the credit terms offered). If the average payable ratio slips beyond vendors' credit terms, it is an indication that the company is suffering from a sloppy accounts payable procedure or from cash shortages, and its credit rating is in danger. If this ratio is significantly lower than vendors' credit terms, it may be a sign that a company is not using its cash most effectively.

Comparing a company's average collection period ratio (days sales outstanding, DSO) to its average payable period ratio (days payables outstanding, DPO) gives owners meaningful insight into their companies' cash position. Subtracting DSO from DPO yields a company's float, the net number of days of cash that flow into or out of a company. Sam's Appliance Shop's float is:

$$\text{Float} = \text{DPO} - \text{DSO} = 59.3\,\text{days} - 50.0\,\text{days} = 9.3\,\text{days}$$

A positive value for float means that cash will accumulate in a company over time, but a negative number means that the company's cash balance will diminish over time. Multiplying float by the company's average daily cash balance sales tells Sam how much the company's cash balance will change over the course of the year as a result of its collection and payable processes. For Sam's Appliance Shop:

$$\text{Change in cash position} = \$1{,}870{,}841 \div 365\,\text{days} \times 9.3\,\text{days} = \$47{,}668$$

We will see the impact that these three operating ratios—inventory turnover, accounts receivable, and accounts payable—have on a small company's cash flow in the next chapter.

net sales to total assets (total asset turnover) ratio
measures a company's ability to generate sales in relation to its asset base.

9. *Net Sales to Total Assets.* A small company's **net sales to total assets ratio** (also called the **total asset turnover ratio**) is a general measure of its ability to generate sales in relation to its assets. It describes how productively the firm employs its assets to produce sales revenue. The total assets turnover ratio is calculated as follows:

$$\text{Total assets turnover ratio} = \frac{\text{net sales}}{\text{total assets}}$$

$$= \frac{\$1{,}870{,}841}{\$847{,}655}$$

$$= 2.21{:}1$$

Sam's Appliance Shop is generating $2.21 in sales for every dollar of assets.

The denominator of this ratio, net total assets, is the sum of all of a company's assets (cash, inventory, land, buildings, equipment, tools, and everything it owns) less depreciation. This ratio is meaningful only when compared to that of similar size firms in the same industry category. Monitoring it over time is very helpful for maintaining a sufficient asset base as a small business grows. A total assets turnover ratio below the industry average indicates that a small company is not generating an adequate sales volume for its asset size.

Amanda Friedman, Inc.

Ram Katalan, president of NorthStar Moving and Storage in Los Angeles, California, noticed that his company's total asset turnover ratio was below the industry average; sales at the moving company had slowed significantly among middle market customers. To remedy the problem, Katalan began emphasizing the company's premium services and launched new ones that range from home electronics installations to pet sitting and are aimed at upscale customers who are less price sensitive. NorthStar's Photo Perfect Packing, a service in which movers take photographs of every object before loading it onto a truck and arrange them in the new location as closely as possible to the previous layout, has proved to be especially popular. Within just four months, NorthStar's premium services accounted for 50 percent of all moving jobs, up from 20 percent, and the company's total asset turnover ratio is above the industry average.[19]

Profitability Ratios. **Profitability ratios** indicate how efficiently a small company is being managed. They provide the owner with information about a company's bottom line; in other words, they describe how successfully the firm is using its available resources to generate a profit.

10. *Net Profit on Sales.* **The net profit on sales ratio** (also called the **profit margin on sales** or **net profit margin**) measures a company's profit per dollar of sales. The computed percentage shows the portion of each sales dollar remaining after deducting all expenses. The profit margin on sales is calculated as follows:

$$\text{Net profit on sales ratio} = \frac{\text{net profit}}{\text{net sales}}$$

$$= \frac{\$60,629}{\$1,870,841}$$

$$= 3.24\%$$

For every dollar in sales Sam's Appliance Shop generates, Sam keeps 3.24 cents in profit.

Many small business owners believe that a high profit margin on sales is necessary for a successful business operation, but this is a myth. To evaluate this ratio properly, an entrepreneur must consider a firm's asset value, its inventory and receivables turnover ratios, and its

profitability ratios
indicate how efficiently a small company is being managed.

net profit on sales ratio
measures a company's profit per dollar of sales.

"And this is where we had to start selling the furniture."

total capitalization. For example, the typical small supermarket earns an average net profit of only one or two cents on each dollar of sales, but, as we have seen, its inventory turnover ratio is 16 times a year. If a company's profit margin on sales is below the industry average, it may be a sign that its prices are too low, that its costs are excessively high, or both.

<table>
<tr><td>

ENTREPRENEURIAL PROFILE _____

Stephen Hanson: B. R. Guest

</td><td>

Stephen Hanson, founder of B.R. Guest, a company that owns 17 fine dining restaurants in New York City, Chicago, and Las Vegas, knows that personal involvement in every aspect of managing a restaurant is the key to profitability. "There are 20,000 working parts in a restaurant," he says. "You have to watch them all." In addition to using software to coordinate volume purchases for the 17 restaurants that increases the company's buying efficiency, Hanson also employs a Guest Recognition System that tracks guests' e-mail addresses, telephone numbers, spending patterns, and personal preferences such as favorite dishes and table locations. The result is a profit margin of 10.4 percent, which is well above the industry average of 5.5 percent.[20]

</td></tr>
</table>

A natural reaction to low profitability ratios is to embark on a cost-cutting effort. Although minimizing costs does improve profitability, entrepreneurs must be judicious in their cost-cutting, taking a strategic approach rather than imposing across-the-board cuts. The key is to reduce costs without diminishing customer service and damaging employee morale. Cutting costs in areas that are vital to operating success—such as a retail jeweler eliminating its advertising expenditures or a restaurant reducing the quality of its ingredients—can inhibit a company's ability to compete and can lead to failure. For instance, choosing to lay off workers, a common reaction at many companies facing financial challenges, often backfires. Not only does a company risk losing talented workers and the knowledge they have built up over time, but research also shows that repeated rounds of layoffs destroy the morale and the productivity of the remaining workers.[21]

In other cases, entrepreneurs on cost-cutting vendettas alienate employees and sap worker morale by eliminating nitpicking costs that affect employees adversely and really don't save much money. The owner of one company thought he would save money by eliminating the free coffee the company provided for its workers. Employee productivity took a hit, however, when workers began taking trips several times a day to a nearby coffee shop. "What a wonderful productivity enhancer!" says one former employee sarcastically.[22]

If a company's net profit on sales ratio is excessively low, the owner first should check the gross profit margin (net sales minus cost of goods sold expressed as a percentage of net sales). Of course, a reasonable gross profit margin varies from industry to industry. For instance, a service company may have a gross profit margin of 75 percent, while a manufacturer's may be 35 percent. The key is to know what a reasonable gross profit margin is for your particular business. If this margin slips too low, it puts a company's future in immediate jeopardy. An inadequate gross profit margin cannot cover all of a company's business expenses and still be able to generate a profit.

<table>
<tr><td>

net profit to assets (or the return on assets, ROA)

a ratio that tells how much profit a company generates for each dollar of assets that it owns.

</td><td>

11. *Net Profit to Assets.* The **net profit to assets** (or **the return on assets, ROA**), ratio tells how much profit a company generates for each dollar of assets that it owns. This ratio describes how efficiently a business is putting to work all of the assets it owns to generate a profit. It tells how much net income an entrepreneur is squeezing from each dollar's worth of the company's assets. It is calculated as follows:

$$\text{Net profit to assets ratio} = \frac{\text{net profit}}{\text{total assets}}$$

$$= \frac{\$60,629}{\$847,655}$$

$$= 7.15\%$$

</td></tr>
</table>

All Is Not Paradise in Eden's Garden: Part 1

Joe and Kaitlin Eden, co-owners of Eden's Garden, a small nursery, lawn, and garden supply business, have just received their year-end financial statements from their accountant. At their last meeting

Balance Sheet, Eden's Garden

Assets

Current Assets

Cash		$6,457
Accounts Receivable	$29,152	
Less Allowance for		
Doubtful Accounts	$3,200	$25,952
Inventory		$88,157
Supplies		$7,514
Prepaid Expenses		$1,856
Total Current Assets		$129,936

Fixed Assets

Land		$59,150
Buildings	$51,027	
Less Accumulated Depreciation	$2,061	$48,966
Autos	$24,671	
Less Accumulated		
Depreciation	$12,300	$12,371
Equipment	$22,375	
Less Accumulated Depreciation	$1,250	$21,125
Furniture and fixtures	$10,295	
Less Accumulated Depreciation	$1,000	$9,295
Total Fixed Assets		$150,907
Intangibles (Goodwill)		$0
Total Assets		$280,843

Liabilities

Current Liabilities

Accounts Payable	$54,258
Notes Payable	$20,150
Credit Line Payable	$8,118
Accrued Wages/Salaries Payable	$1,344
Accrued Interest Payable	$1,785
Accrued Taxes Payable	$1,967
Total Current Liabilities	$87,622

Long-Term Liabilities

Mortgage	$72,846
Note Payable	$47,000
Total Long-term Liabilities	$119,846

Owner's Equity

Sam Lloyd, Capital	$73,375
Total Liabilities and Owner's Equity	$280,843

Income Statement, Eden's Garden

Net Sales Revenue*		$689,247

Cost of Goods Sold

Beginning Inventory, 1/1/xx	$78,271	
+ Purchases	$403,569	
Goods available for Sale	$481,840	
− Ending Inventory, 12,31/xx	$86,157	
Cost of Goods Sold		$395,683
Gross Profit		$293,564

Operating Expenses

Advertising	$22,150	
Insurance	$9,187	
Depreciation		
Building	$26,705	
Autos	$7,895	
Equipment	$11,200	
Salaries	$116,541	
Uniforms	$4,018	
Repairs and Maintenance	$9,097	
Travel	$2,658	
Entertainment	$2,798	
Total Operating Expenses		$212,249

General Expenses

Utilities	$7,987	
Telephone	$2,753	
Professional Fees	$3,000	
Postage	$1,892	
Payroll Taxes	$11,589	
Total General Expenses		$27,221

Other Expenses

Interest Expense	$21,978	
Bad check Expense	$679	
Miscellaneous expense	$1,248	
Total Other Expenses		$23,905
Total Expenses		$263,375
Net Income		$30,189

*Credit sales represented $289,484 of this total.

with their accountant, Shelley Edison, three months ago, the Edens had mentioned that they seemed to be having trouble paying their bills on time. "Some of our suppliers have threatened to put us on 'credit-hold,'" said Joe.

"I think you need to sit down with me very soon and let me show you how to analyze your financial statements so you can see what's happening in your business," Edison told them at that meeting. Unfortunately, that was the beginning of Eden's Garden's busy season, and the Edens were so busy running the company that they never got around to setting a time to meet with Shelley.

"Now that business has slowed down a little, perhaps we should call Shelley and see what she can do to help us understand what our financial statements are trying to tell us," said Kaitlin.

"Right. Before it's too late to do anything about it...." said Joe, pulling out the following financial statements.

1. Assume the role of Shelley Edison. Using the financial statements for Eden's Garden, calculate the 12 ratios covered in this chapter.
2. Do you see any ratios that, on the surface, look suspicious? Explain.

Sam's Appliance shop earns a return of 7.15 percent on its asset base. This ratio provides clues about the asset intensity of an industry. Return on assets ratios that are below 5 percent are indicative of asset-intense industries that require heavy investments in assets to stay in business (e.g., manufacturing and railroads). Return on assets ratios that exceed 20 percent tend to occur in asset-light industries such as business or personal services—for example, advertising agencies and computer services. A net profit to assets ratio that is below the industry average suggests that a company is not using its assets very efficiently to produce a profit. Another common application of this ratio is to compare it to the company's cost of borrowed capital. Ideally, a company's ROA should exceed the cost of borrowing money to purchase those assets. Companies that experience significant swings in the value of their assets over the course of a year often use an average value of the asset base over the accounting period to get a more realistic estimate of this ratio.

net profit to equity ratio
measures the owners' rate of return on investment.

12. *Net Profit to Equity.* The **net profit to equity ratio** (or **return on net worth ratio**) measures the owners' rate of return on investment (ROI). Because it reports the percentage of the owners' investment in the business that is being returned through profits annually, it is one of the most important indicators of a firm's profitability or a management's efficiency. The net profit to equity ratio is computed as follows:

$$\text{Net profit to equity} = \frac{\text{net profit}}{\text{owners' equity (or net worth)}}$$

$$= \frac{\$60,629}{\$267,655}$$

$$= 22.65\%$$

Sam is earning 22.65 percent on the money he has invested in this business.

This ratio compares profits earned during the accounting period with the amount the owner has invested in the business during that time. If this interest rate on the owners' investment is excessively low, some of this capital might be better employed elsewhere.

Interpreting Business Ratios

LO 5

Explain how to interpret financial ratios.

Ratios are useful yardsticks when measuring a small firm's performance and can point out potential problems before they develop into serious crises. But calculating these ratios is not enough to ensure proper financial control. In addition to knowing how to calculate these ratios, entrepreneurs must understand how to interpret them and apply them to the managing their businesses more effectively and efficiently.

ENTREPRENEURIAL PROFILE

Linda Nespole: Hi-Shear Technology

For instance, with the help of financial ratios, Linda Nespole, a top manager at Hi-Shear Technology, an aerospace subcontracting company in Torrance, California, noticed the company's performance beginning to slip. Given the signals her analysis revealed, she immediately devised a strategy to restore Hi-Shear's financial position, focusing first on cost-cutting measures. Simply charting the company's major costs led Nespole to discover leaking water pipes and inefficient lighting that were driving up costs unnecessarily.

Some basic repairs lowered utility costs significantly, and a new, more efficient lighting system paid for itself in just six months. Nespole's cost-saving attitude took hold throughout the entire company, and soon all 125 employees were finding ways to keep costs down—from switching long-distance carriers to cutting the cost of its 401(k) retirement plan by 30 percent.[23]

Not every business measures its success with the same ratios. In fact, key performance ratios vary dramatically across industries and even within different segments of the same industry. Entrepreneurs must know and understand which ratios are most crucial to their companies' success and focus on monitoring and controlling those. Sometimes business owners develop ratios and measures that are unique to their own operations to help them achieve success. Known as **critical numbers,** these indicators measure key financial and operational aspects of a company's performance. When these critical numbers are headed in the right direction, a business is on track to achieve its objectives. Norm Brodsky, who owned a document storage and delivery business for more than 30 years before selling it for $110 million, breaks his business into four categories and tracks critical numbers for each one. Every Monday morning, he receives a report comparing the previous week's critical numbers to those of the previous 28 weeks and the same week for the previous three years. "In 30 seconds, I can see what's going on in every part of my delivery business," he says. "I get another sheet for my storage business because I need to track a different set of numbers there, but the idea is the same."[24] Examples of critical numbers at other companies include the following:

critical numbers
indicators that measure key financial and operational aspects of a company's performance; when these numbers are moving in the right direction, a business is on track to reach its objectives.

- A bank's "happy-to-grumpy" ratio, which measures the level of satisfaction of its employees. Studies show that employees at the bank who score high on this index are more productive and receive higher customer satisfaction ratings.[25]
- Sales per labor hour at a supermarket.
- The number of new boxes put into storage each week in a records storage business. "Tell me how many new boxes came in during [a particular week]," says Norm Brodsky, owner of CitiStorage, a successful records storage company in New York City, "and I can tell you our overall sales figure for [that week] within one or two percent of the actual figure."[26]
- Food costs as a percentage of sales for a restaurant. When rapidly rising flour and cheese prices pushed food costs as a percentage of sales from the normal 34 percent to 40 percent at Mark Parry's pizza restaurant, he was forced to raise prices. "We're not set to [earn] a profit when we're [operating] at 40 percent food costs," says Parry.[27] At Dos Caminos, a Mexican restaurant in New York City, chef Ivy Stark's goal is to keep the restaurant's food cost at or below 26 percent of sales. Stark relies on a five-page spreadsheet generated each morning to keep food costs under control.[28]

Critical numbers may be different for two companies who compete in the same industry. The key is knowing what *your* company's critical numbers are, monitoring them, and then driving them in the right direction. That requires communicating the importance of these critical numbers to employees and giving them feedback on how well the business is achieving them. For instance, one California retail chain established the daily customer count and the average sale per customer as its critical numbers. The company organized a monthly contest with prizes and posted charts tracking each store's performance. Soon employees were working hard to improve their stores' performances over the previous year and to outdo other stores in the chain. The healthy rivalry among stores boosted the company's performance significantly.[29]

Another valuable way to use ratios is to compare them with those of similar businesses in the same industry. By comparing the company's financial statistics to industry averages, an entrepreneur is able to locate problem areas and maintain adequate financial controls. "Knowing your own numbers is only half the story," says Brian Hamilton, founder of

TABLE 11.3 Putting Your Ratios to the Test

When comparing your company's ratios to your industry's standards, ask the following questions:

1. Is there a significant difference in my company's ratio and the industry average?
2. If so, is this a *meaningful* difference?
3. Is the difference good or bad?
4. What are the possible causes of this difference? What is the most likely cause?
5. Does this cause require that I take action?
6. What action should I take to correct the problem?

Source: Based on George M. Dawson, "Divided We Stand," *Business Start-Ups*, May 2000, p. 34.

Sageworks, a company that tracks financial data for thousands of private companies. "When you look at how you compare to your peers, you can see where you are strong and what you need to work on."[30]

The principle behind calculating these ratios and comparing them to industry norms is the same as that of most medical tests in the healthcare profession. Just as a healthy person's blood pressure and cholesterol levels should fall within a range of normal values, so should a financially healthy company's ratios. A company cannot deviate too far from these normal values and remain successful for long. When deviations from "normal" do occur (and they will), a business owner should focus on determining the cause of the deviations (see Table 11.3). In some cases, such deviations are the result of sound business decisions, such as taking on inventory in preparation for the busy season, investing heavily in new technology, and others. In other instances, however, ratios that are out of the normal range for a particular type of business are indicators of what could become serious problems for a company. Properly used, ratio analysis can help owners to identify potential problem areas in their businesses early on—*before* they become crises that threaten their very survival.

Several organizations regularly compile and publish operating statistics, including key ratios, that summarize the financial performance of many businesses across a wide range of industries. The local library should subscribe to most of these publications:

Risk Management Association. Founded in 1914, the Risk Management Association publishes its *Annual Statement Studies*, showing ratios and other financial data for more than 750 different industrial, wholesale, retail, and service categories that are organized by North American Industry Classification System (NAICS) and Standard Industrial Classification (SIC) code.

Dun & Bradstreet, Inc. Since 1932, Dun & Bradstreet has published *Industry Norms and Key Business Ratios*, which covers more than 800 business categories. Dun & Bradstreet also publishes Cost of Doing Business, a series of operating ratios compiled from the IRS's Statistics of Income reports.

Almanac of Business and Financial Ratios. Published by CCH, this almanac reports comparative financial data and ratios for nearly 200 industries by company size.

Financial Studies of the Small Business. Financial Research Associates publishes this book that lists 16 ratios for small companies that have total capitalization of less than $1 million in 70 industries.

Vest Pocket Guide to Financial Ratios. This handy guide, published by Prentice Hall, gives key ratios and financial data for a wide variety of industries.

Standard & Poor's Industry Surveys. In addition to providing information on financial ratios and comparative financial analysis, these surveys also contain useful details on how the industry operates, current industry trends, key terms in the industry, and others.

Industry Spotlight. Published by Schonfeld & Associates, this publication, which can be customized for any one of 250 industries, contains financial statement data and key ratios gleaned from IRS tax returns. *Industry Spotlight* also provides detailed financial information for both profitable companies and those with losses. Schonfeld and Associates also publishes *IRS Corporate Financial Ratios*, a comprehensive reference book that features 76 financial ratios for more than 250 industries using NAICS codes.

Online Resources. Many companies publish comparative financial resources online. Some require subscriptions, but others are free:

- Bizstats publishes common-size financial statements and ratios for 95 business categories for sole proprietorships, S corporations, and corporations.
- Reuters provides an overview of many industries that includes industry trends and news as well as financial ratios.
- A subscription to Lexis/Nexis allows users to view detailed company profiles, including financial reports and analysis, for publicly-held companies.

Trade Associations. Virtually every type of business is represented by a national trade association, which publishes detailed financial data compiled from its membership. For example, owners of small supermarkets could contact the National Association of Retail Grocers or check the *Progressive Grocer,* its trade publication, for financial statistics relevant to their operations.

Government Agencies. Several government agencies, including the Internal Revenue Service, Federal Trade Commission, Department of Commerce, Census Bureau, Department of Agriculture, and Securities and Exchange Commission, periodically publish reports that provide financial operating data on a variety of industries, although the categories are more general. For instance, the IRS publishes *Statistics of Income,* which includes income statement and balance sheet statistics that are compiled from income tax returns and are arranged by industry, asset size, and annual sales. Every five years (years ending in 2 and 7), the U.S. Census Bureau publishes the *Economic Census* (http://www.census.gov/econ/census/), which provides general industry statistics and ratios.

What Do All of These Numbers Mean?

Learning to interpret financial ratios just takes a little practice! This section will show you how it's done by comparing the ratios from the operating data already computed for Sam's to those taken from *RMA's Annual Statement Studies.* (The industry median is the ratio falling exactly in the middle when sample elements are arranged in ascending or descending order.)

Sam's Appliance Shop	**Industry Median**

Liquidity Ratios—tell whether or not a small business will be able to meet its maturing obligations as they come due.

1. Current Ratio = 1.87:1   1.50:1

    Sam's Appliance Shop falls short of the rule of thumb of 2:1, but its current ratio is above the industry median by a significant amount. Sam's should have no problem meeting its short-term debts as they come due. By this measure, the company's liquidity is solid.

2. Quick Ratio = 0.63:1   0.50:1

    Again, Sam's is below the rule of thumb of 1:1, but the company passes this test of liquidity when measured against industry standards. Sam's relies on selling inventory to satisfy short-term debt (as do most appliance shops). If sales slump, the result could be liquidity problems for Sam's. Sam's should begin building a cash reserve as a precautionary measure.

Leverage Ratios—measure the financing supplied by a firm's owners against that supplied by its creditors and serve as a gauge of the depth of a company's debt.

3. Debt-Ratio = 0.68:1   0.64:1

    Creditors provide 68 percent of Sam's total assets, very close to the industry median of 64 percent. Although Sam's does not appear to be overburdened with debt, the company might have difficulty borrowing additional money, especially from conservative lenders.

4. Debt to Net Worth Ratio = 2.20:1   1.90:1

Sam's Appliance Shop owes creditors $2.20 for every $1.00 the owner has invested in the business (compared to $1.90 in debt to every $1.00 in equity for the typical business). Although this is not an exorbitant amount of debt, many lenders and creditors will see Sam's as "borrowed up." The company's borrowing capacity is limited because creditors' claims against the business are more than twice those of the owners. Sam should consider increasing his owner's equity in the business through retained earnings or by paying down some of the company's debt.

5. Times Interest Earned = 2.52:1   2.0:1

Sam's earnings are high enough to cover the interest payments on its debt by a factor of 2.52, slightly better than the typical firm in the industry, whose earnings cover its interest payments just two times. Sam's Appliance Shop has a cushion (although a small one) in meeting its interest payments.

Operating Ratios—evaluate the firm's overall performance and show how effectively it is putting its resources to work.

6. Average Inventory Turnover Ratio = 2.05 times/year   4.0 times/year

Inventory is moving through Sam's at a very slow pace, *half* that of the industry median. The company has a problem with slow-moving items in its inventory and, perhaps, too much inventory. Which items are they, and why are they slow-moving? Does Sam need to drop some product lines? Sam must analyze his company's inventory and reevaluate his inventory control procedures.

7. Average Collection Period Ratio = 50.0 days   19.3 days

Sam's Appliance Shop collects the average account receivable after 50 days (compared with the industry median of 19 days), more than two-and-one-half times longer. A more meaningful comparison is against Sam's credit terms; if credit terms are net 30 (or anywhere close to that), Sam's has a dangerous collection problem, one that drains cash and profits and demands *immediate* attention! Sam's must implement the cash management procedures you will learn about in Chapter 12.

8. Average Payable Period Ratio = 59.3 days   43 days

Sam's payables are nearly 40 percent slower than those of the typical firm in the industry. Stretching payables too far could seriously damage the company's credit rating, causing suppliers to cut off future trade credit. This could be a sign of cash flow problems or a sloppy accounts payable procedure. This problem also demands *immediate* attention. Once again, Sam must implement proper cash management procedures to resolve this problem.

9. Net Sales to Total Assets Ratio = 2.21:1   2.7:1

Sam's Appliance Shop is not generating enough sales, given the size of its asset base. This could be the result of a number of factors—improper inventory, inappropriate pricing, poor location, intense competition, poorly trained sales personnel, and many others. The key is to find the cause... *Fast!*

Profitability Ratios—measure how efficiently a firm is operating and offer information about its bottom line.

10. Net Profit on Sales Ratio = 3.24%   7.6%

After deducting all expenses, 3.24 cents of each sales dollar remains as profit for Sam's—less than half the industry median. Sam's should check the company's gross profit margin and investigate its operating expenses, checking them against industry standards and looking for those that are out of balance.

11. Net Profit to Assets Ratio = 7.15%   5.5%

Sam's generates a return of 7.15% for every $1 in assets, which is 30 percent *above* the industry average. Given the company's asset base, Sam's is squeezing an above-average return out of the company. This could be an indication that Sam's is highly profitable; however, given the previous ratio, this is unlikely. It is more likely that Sam's asset base is thinner than the industry average.

12. Net Profit to Equity Ratio = 22.65%   12.6%

Sam's Appliance Shop's owners are earning 22.65 percent on the money they have invested in the business. This yield is nearly twice that of the industry median, and, given the previous two ratios, is more likely the result of the owners' relatively low investment in the business than an indication of its superior profitability. Sam's is using OPM (Other People's Money) to generate a profit in his business.

When comparing ratios for their individual businesses to published statistics, entrepreneurs must remember that the comparison is made against averages. An entrepreneur should strive to achieve ratios that are at least as good as these average figures. The goal should be to manage the business so that its financial performance is above average. As entrpreneurs compare their company's financial performance to those covered in the published statistics, they inevitably will discern differences between them. They should note those items that are substantially out of line from the industry average. However, a ratio that varies from the average does not *necessarily* mean that the small business is in financial jeopardy. Instead of making drastic changes in financial policy, entrepreneurs must explore *why* the figures are out of line.

Greg Smith, CEO of Petra Group, a systems integrator with $1.5 million in annual sales, once gave little thought to comparing his company's financial performance against industry standards. Then, Petra Group's sales flattened and Smith's company faced the prospect of losing money for the first time. Smith worked with an accounting firm, using information from Risk Management Association and a nonprofit organization that provides similar studies, to analyze his company's financial position. Comparing his numbers to industry statistics, Smith quickly saw that his payroll expenses for his 15-person company were too high to allow the company to generate a profit. He also discovered that Petra Group's debt ratio was too high. To restore his company's financial strength, Smith reduced his staff by two and began relying more on temporary employees and independent contractors. He realigned Petra Group's financing, reducing the company's line of credit from $100,000 to just $35,000. The analysis also revealed several strengths for the company. For instance, the company's average collection period was 36.5 days, compared to an industry average of 73 days! Smith continues to use ratio comparisons to make key decisions for his company, and he credits the initial financial analysis with getting his company back on the track to profitability.[31]

In addition to comparing ratios to industry averages, owners should analyze their firms' financial ratios over time. By themselves, these ratios are "snapshots" of a company's financial position at a single instant; but by examining these trends over time, an entrepreneur can detect gradual shifts that otherwise might go unnoticed until a financial crisis is looming (see Figure 11.7).

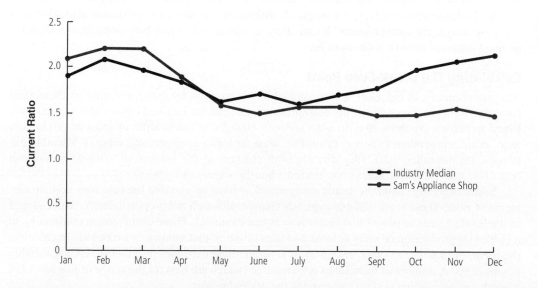

FIGURE 11.7
Trend Analysis of Ratios

All Is Not Paradise in Eden's Garden: Part 2

Remember Joe and Kaitlin Eden, co-owners of Eden's Garden? Assume the role of Shelley Edison, their accountant. Tomorrow, you have scheduled a meeting with them to review their company's financial statements and to make recommendations about how they can improve their company's financial position. Use the worksheet below to summarize the ratios you calculated earlier in this

Ratio Comparison

Ratio	Eden's Garden	Garden Supply Industry Median[*]
Liquidity Ratios		
Current ratio		1.4
Quick ratio		0.5
Leverage Ratios		
Debt ratio		0.6
Debt to net worth ratio		1.8
Times interest earned ratio		2.6

Operating Ratios	
Average inventory turnover ratio	5.6
Average collection period ratio	9 days
Average payable period ratio	17 days
Net sales to total assets ratio	3.0
Profitability Ratios	
Net profit on sales ratio	7.5%
Net profit to asset ratio	9.1%
Net profit to equity ratio	15.0%

*Risk Management Association's *Annual Statement Studies.*

chapter. Then compare them against the industry averages from Risk Management Association *Annual Statement Studies.*

1. Analyze the comparisons you have made of Eden's Garden's ratios with those from the Risk Management Association. What "red flags" do you see?
2. What might be causing the deviations you have observed?
3. What recommendations can you make to the Edens to improve their company's financial performance in the future?

LO 6

Conduct a break-even analysis for a small company.

break-even point

the level of operation (sales dollars or production quantity) at which a company neither earns a profit nor incurs a loss.

Break-Even Analysis

Another key component of every sound financial plan is a breakeven analysis. A small company's **break-even point** is the level of operation (typically expressed as sales dollars or production quantity) at which it neither earns a profit nor incurs a loss. At this level of activity, sales revenue equals expenses—that is, the firm "breaks even." By analyzing costs and expenses, an entrepreneur can calculate the minimum level of activity required to keep a company in operation. These techniques can then be refined to project the sales necessary to generate a desired profit. Most potential lenders and investors expect entrepreneurs to prepare a breakeven analysis to assist them in evaluating the earning potential of the new business. In addition to its being a simple, useful screening device for financial institutions, breakeven analysis can also serve as a planning device for entrepreneurs. It can show an entrepreneur just how unprofitable a poorly planned business venture is likely to be.

Calculating the Break-Even Point

An entrepreneur can calculate a company's breakeven point by using a simple mathematical formula. To begin the analysis, the entrepreneur must determine fixed costs and variable costs. **Fixed expenses** are those that do not vary with changes in the volume of sales or production (e.g., rent, depreciation expense, insurance, lease or loan payments, and others). **Variable expenses,** on the other hand, vary directly with changes in the volume of sales or production (e.g., raw material costs, sales commissions, hourly wages, and others).

Some expenses cannot be neatly categorized as fixed or variable because they contain elements of both. These semi-variable expenses change, although not proportionately, with changes in the level of sales or production (electricity is one example). These costs remain constant up to a particular production or sales volume and then climb as that volume is exceeded. To calculate the break-even point, an entrepreneur must separate these expenses into their fixed and variable components. A number of techniques are available (which are beyond the scope of this text), but a good cost accounting system can provide the desired results.

fixed expenses

expenses that do not vary with changes in the volume of sales or production.

variable expenses

expenses that vary directly with changes in the volume of sales or production.

Here are the steps an entrepreneur must take to compute the break-even point using an example of a typical small business, the Magic Shop:

Step 1. Forecast the expenses the business can expect to incur. With the help of a budget, an entrepreneur can develop estimates of sales revenue, cost of goods sold, and expenses for the upcoming accounting period. The Magic Shop expects net sales of $950,000 in the upcoming year, with a cost of goods sold of $646,000 and total expenses of $236,500.

Step 2. Categorize the expenses estimated in Step 1 into fixed expenses and variable expenses. Separate semi-variable expenses into their component parts. From the budget, the owner anticipates variable expenses (including the cost of goods sold) of $705,125 and fixed expenses of $177,375.

Step 3. Calculate the ratio of variable expenses to net sales. For the Magic Shop, this percentage is $705,125 ÷ $950,000 = 74 percent. The Magic Shop uses $0.74 out of every sales dollar to cover variable expenses, which leaves $0.26 ($1.00 − 0.74) of each sales dollar as a contribution margin to cover fixed costs and make a profit.

Step 4. Compute the break-even point by inserting this information into the following formula:

$$\text{Break-even sales}(\$) = \frac{\text{total fixed cost}}{\text{contribution margin expressed as a percentage of sales}}$$

For the Magic Shop,

$$\text{Break-even sales} = \frac{\$177,375}{0.26}$$

$$= \$682,212$$

Thus, the Magic Shop will break even with sales of $682,212. At this point, sales revenue generated will just cover total fixed and variable expense. The Magic Shop will earn no profit and will incur no loss. We can verify this with the following calculations:

Sales at break-even point	$ 682,212
− Variable expenses (74% of sales)	−504,837
Contribution margin	177,375
− Fixed expenses	− 177,375
Net profit (or net loss)	$ 0

Some entrepreneurs find it more meaningful to break down their companies' annual break-even point into a daily sales figure. If the Magic Shop will be open 312 days per year, the average daily sales it must generate just to break even is $682,212 ÷ 312 days = $2,187 per day.

Adding a Profit

What if the Magic Shop's owner wants to do *better* than just break even? His analysis can be adjusted to consider such a possibility. Suppose the owner expects a reasonable profit (before taxes) of $80,000. What level of sales must the Magic Shop achieve to generate this? He can calculate this by treating the desired profit as if it were a fixed cost. In other words, he modifies the formula to include the desired net income:

$$\text{Sales}(\$) = \frac{\text{total fixed expenses} + \text{desired net income}}{\text{contribution margin expressed as a percentage of sales}}$$

$$= \frac{\$177,375 + \$80\,000}{0.26}$$

$$= \$989,904$$

To achieve a net profit of $80,000 (before taxes), the Magic Shop must generate net sales of $989,904.

Break-Even Point in Units

Some small businesses may prefer to express the breakeven point in units produced or sold instead of in dollars. Manufacturers often find this approach particularly useful. The following formula computes the break-even point in units:

$$\text{Break-even volume} = \frac{\text{total fixed costs}}{\text{sales price per unit} - \text{variable cost per unit}}$$

For example, suppose that Trilex Manufacturing Company estimates its fixed costs for producing its line of small appliances at $390,000. The variable costs (including materials, direct labor, and factory overhead) amount to $12.10 per unit, and the selling price per unit is $17.50. So, Trilex computes its contribution margin this way:

$$\text{Contribution margin} = \text{price per unit} - \text{variable cost per unit}$$

$$= \$17.50 \text{ per unit} - \$12.10 \text{ per unit}$$

$$= \$5.40 \text{ per unit}$$

So, Trilex's break-even volume is as follows:

$$\text{Break-even volume (units)} = \frac{\text{total fixed costs}}{\text{per unit contribution margin}}$$

$$= \frac{\$390,000}{\$5.40 \text{ per unit}}$$

$$= 72,222 \text{ units}$$

To convert this number of units to break-even sales dollars, Trilex simply multiplies it by the selling price per unit:

$$\text{Breakeven sales} = 72,222 \text{ units} \times \$17.50 \text{ per unit} = \$1,263,889$$

Trilex could compute the sales required to produce a desired profit by treating the profit as if it were a fixed cost:

$$\text{Sales (units)} = \frac{\text{total fixed costs} + \text{desired net income}}{\text{per unit contribution margin}}$$

For example, if Trilex wanted to earn a $60,000 profit, its required sales would be:

$$\text{Sales (units)} = \frac{390,000 + 60,000}{5.40} = 83,333 \text{ units}$$

which would require 83,333 units × $17.50 per unit = $1,458,328 in sales.

Constructing a Break-Even Chart

The following steps outline the procedure for constructing a graph that visually portrays the firm's break-even point (that point where revenues equal expenses):

Step 1. On the horizontal axis, mark a scale measuring sales volume in dollars (or in units sold or some other measure of volume). The break-even chart for the Magic Shop shown in Figure 11.8 uses sales volume in dollars because it applies to all types of businesses, departments, and products.

Step 2. On the vertical axis, mark a scale measuring income and expenses in dollars.

Step 3. Draw a fixed expense line intersecting the vertical axis at the proper dollar level parallel to the horizontal axis. The area between this line and the horizontal axis represents the firm's fixed expenses. On the break-even chart for the Magic Shop shown in Figure 11.8, the fixed expense line is drawn horizontally beginning at $177,375 (point A). Because this line is parallel to the horizontal axis, it indicates that fixed expenses remain constant at all levels of activity.

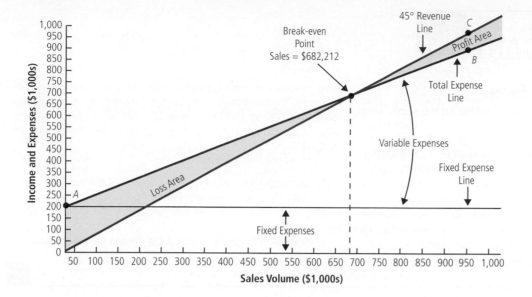

FIGURE 11.8

Break-Even Chart for the Magic Shop

Step 4. Draw a total expense line that slopes upward beginning at the point where the fixed cost line intersects the vertical axis. The precise location of the total expense line is determined by plotting the total cost incurred at a particular sales volume. The total cost for a given sales level is found by using the following formula:

Total expenses = Fixed expenses + Variable expenses expressed as a % of sales × Sales level

Arbitrarily choosing a sales level of $950,000, the Magic Shop's total costs would be as follows:

$$\text{Total expenses} = \$177{,}375 + (0.74 \times \$950{,}000)$$

$$= \$880{,}375$$

Thus, the Magic Shop's total cost is $880,375 at a net sales level of $950,000 (point B). The variable cost line is drawn by connecting points A and B. The area between the total cost line and the horizontal axis measures the total costs the Magic Shop incurs at various levels of sales. For example, if the Magic Shop's sales are $850,000, its total costs will be $806,375.

Step 5. Beginning at the graph's origin, draw a 45-degree revenue line showing where total sales volume equals total income. For the Magic Shop, point C shows that sales = income = $950,000.

Step 6. Locate the break-even point by finding the intersection of the total expense line and the revenue line. If the Magic Shop operates at a sales volume to the left of the break-even point, it will incur a loss because the expense line is higher than the revenue line over this range. This is shown by the triangular section labeled "Loss Area." On the other hand, if the firm operates at a sales volume to the right of the break-even point, it will earn a profit because the revenue line lies above the expense line over this range. This is shown by the triangular section labeled "Profit Area."

Using Break-Even Analysis

Break-even analysis is a useful planning tool for the potential small business owner, especially when approaching potential lenders and investors for funds. It provides an opportunity for integrated analysis of sales volume, expenses, income, and other relevant factors. Break-even analysis is a simple, preliminary screening device for the entrepreneur faced with the business start-up decision. It is easy to understand and use. With just a few calculations, a small business owner can determine the effects of various financial strategies on the business operation. It is a helpful tool for evaluating the impact of changes in investments and expenditures. Greg Smith, for instance,

YOU BE THE CONSULTANT

Where Do We Break Even?

Anita Dawson is doing some financial planning for her music store. Based on her budget for the upcoming year, Anita is expecting net sales of $495,000. She estimates that cost of goods sold will be $337,000 and that other variable expenses will total $42,750. Using the previous year as a guide, Anita anticipates fixed expenses of $78,100.

Anita recalls an earlier meeting with her accountant, who mentioned that her store had already passed the break-even point $8^1/_2$ months into the year. She was pleased, but really didn't know how the accountant had come up with that calculation. Now, Anita is considering expanding her store into a vacant building

next store to her existing location and taking on three new product lines. The company's cost structure would change, adding another $66,000 to fixed costs and $22,400 to variable expenses. Anita believes the expansion could generate additional sales of $102,000.

She wonders what she should do.

1. Calculate Anita's break-even point without the expansion plans. Draw a break-even chart.
2. Compute the break-even point assuming that Anita decides to expand.
3. Would you recommend that Anita expand her business? Explain.

---

knows that Petra Group's breakeven point is $23,000 per week, and he compares sales to that figure every week.[32]

Calculating the break-even point for a start-up business is important because it tells an entrepreneur the minimum volume of sales required to stay in business in the long run.

ENTREPRENEURIAL PROFILE

Silverjet

The founders of Silverjet, a British airline company that sold only business-class seats on transatlantic flights from London to New York and Dubai, knew that they had to operate their jets at 65 percent capacity to break even. In its first month of operation, the company's flights averaged just 45 percent of capacity, but within six months its planes were 76 percent full. Unfortunately, jet fuel prices reached record highs just a few months later, causing Silverjet's operating costs to spiral out of control, and the company began operating below its breakeven point. Just 18 months after start-up, Silverjet joined Eos Airlines and MAXjet, both business-class-only airlines, in bankruptcy. Although the founders of all three airlines had visions of changing the flight experience for transatlantic business travelers, they failed to operate consistently above their companies' breakeven points.[33]

Break-even analysis does have certain limitations. It is too simple to use as a final screening device because it ignores the importance of cash flows. In addition, the accuracy of the analysis depends on the accuracy of the revenue and expense estimates. Finally, the assumptions pertaining to break-even analysis may not be realistic for some businesses. Break-even calculations assume the following: fixed expenses remain constant for all levels of sales volume; variable expenses change in direct proportion to changes in sales volume; and changes in sales volume have no effect on unit sales price. Relaxing these assumptions does not render this tool useless, however. For example, the owner could employ nonlinear break-even analysis to determine a company's break-even point.

Chapter Summary

1. **Understand the importance of preparing a financial plan.**
   - Launching a successful business requires an entrepreneur to create a solid financial plan. Not only is such a plan an important tool in raising the capital needed to get a company off the ground, but it also is an essential ingredient in managing a growing business.
   - Earning a profit does not occur by accident; it takes planning.

2. **Describe how to prepare the basic financial statements and use them to manage a small business.**
   1. Entrepreneurs rely on three basic financial statements to understand the financial conditions of their companies:
   The balance sheet—Built on the accounting equation: Assets = Liabilities + Owner's Equity (Net Worth), it provides an estimate of the company's value on a particular date.

2. *The income statement*—This statement compares the firm's revenues against its expenses to determine its net profit (or loss). It provides information about the company's bottom line.
3. *The statement of cash flows*—This statement shows the change in the company's working capital over the accounting period by listing the sources and the uses of funds.

3. Create projected (pro forma) financial statements.

- Projected financial statements are a basic component of a sound financial plan. They help the manager plot the company's financial future by setting operating objectives and by analyzing the reasons for variations from targeted results. In addition, the small business in search of startup funds will need these pro forma statements to present to prospective lenders and investors. They also assist in determining the amount of cash, inventory, fixtures, and other assets the business will need to begin operation.

4. Understand the basic financial statements through ratio analysis.

- The twelve key ratios described in this chapter are divided into four major categories: *liquidity ratios,* which show the small firm's ability to meet its current obligations; *leverage ratios,* which tell how much of the company's financing is provided by owners and how much by creditors; *operating ratios,* which show how effectively the firm uses its resources; and *profitability ratios,* which disclose the company's profitability.
- Many agencies and organizations regularly publish such statistics. If there is a discrepancy between the small firm's ratios and those of the typical business, the owner should investigate the reason for the difference. A below average ratio does not necessarily mean that the business is in trouble.

5. Explain how to interpret financial ratios.

- To benefit from ratio analysis, the small company should compare its ratios to those of other companies in the same line of business and look for trends over time.
- When business owners detect deviations in their companies' ratios from industry standards, they should determine the cause of the deviations. In some cases, such deviations are the result of sound business decisions; in other instances, however, ratios that are out of the normal range for a particular type of business are indicators of what could become serious problems for a company.

6. Conduct a break-even analysis for a small company.

- Business owners should know their firm's break-even point, the level of operations at which total revenues equal total costs; it is the point at which companies neither earn a profit nor incur a loss. Although just a simple screening device, break-even analysis is a useful planning and decision-making tool.

Discussion Questions

1. Why is developing a financial plan so important to an entrepreneur about to launch a business?
2. How should a small business manager use the 12 ratios discussed in this chapter?
3. Outline the key points of the twelve ratios discussed in this chapter. What signals does each give a business owner?
4. Describe the method for building a projected income statement and a projected balance sheet for a beginning business.
5. Why are pro forma financial statements important to the financial planning process?
6. How can breakeven analysis help an entrepreneur planning to launch a business?

Business PlanPro™

One of the advantages *Business Plan Pro*™ offers is the efficient creation of pro forma financial statements including the balance sheet, profit and loss statement, and cash flow statement. Once you enter the revenues, expenses, and other relevant figures, your financial statements are complete. This can save time and produces a format that is recognized and respected by bankers and investors. This process also enables you to create "what if" scenarios applying various revenues and expenses simply by saving versions of your business plan under unique file names.

Business Plan Exercises

Clear and accurate financial statements are an essential part of an effective business plan. These statements are only as good as the information that you provide.

On the Web

Go to http://www.bplans.com or use the link at http://www.pearsonhighered.com/scarborough/ under the Business Plan Resource tab. Find the Finance and Business Calculators tab. Here you will see a collection of online tools including the Break Even Calculator. Open this tool and enter the information it requests including the average per unit revenue, the average per unit cost, and the estimated monthly fixed costs you anticipate. This tool will calculate your break-even point in units and revenue. Change the data and observe the difference in your break-even point. What does this tell you about the level of risk that you may experience based on the most realistic projections you can make?

Sample Plans

Review a sample plan and note the format and organization of the financial section. Note how the plan presents the breakeven information along with the balance sheet, profit and loss statement, and cash flow statement.

In the Software

Provide the month-to-month detail for the first year with annual totals for subsequent years. In addition, note the tables and graphics that appear within the financial plan. Graphics can be excellent communication tools, particularly when you are communicating information about financial trends and relationships.

Building Your Business Plan

Review all information within the Financial Plan section of your business plan. Add any important assumptions to this section. This is a good place to make notes and comments to test or further research any of these assumptions. If you are in the start-up stage, capture the costs that you expect will be incurred to launch your business. The Investment Offering may appear, based on your choice in the Plan Wizard, and this may be a good opportunity to add that information. Review your break-even analysis and the financial statements including your profit and loss, cash flow, and balance sheet statements. What does this tell you about the financial opportunity and health of your business?

This chapter identifies 12 key business ratios. Once you enter your projections, review each ratio and compare them to industry standard ratios. If there are significant differences in these comparisons, determine why those variances exist. Might this tell you something about the reality of your projections, or is this just due to the stage and differences of your business compared to the larger industry? These ratios can be excellent tools for helping question, test, and validate assumptions and projections. Good business planning, solid financial projections, and a thorough analysis of these ratios can help you to launch a more viable business with greater certainty of the outcome.

Beyond the Classroom . . .

1. Ask the owner of a small business to provide your class with copies of his or her company's financial statements (current or past).
   - Using these statements, compute the twelve key ratios described in this chapter.
   - Compare the company's ratios with those of the typical firm in this line of business.
   - Interpret the ratios and make suggestions for operating improvements.
   - Prepare a break-even analysis for the owner.

2. Find a publicly-held company of interest to you that provides its financial statements on the Web. You can conduct a Web search using the company's name or you can find lists of companies at the Securities and Exchange Commission's EDGAR database at: http://www.sec.gov/edgar/searchedgar/webusers.htm or visit AnnualReports.com at: http://www.annualreports.com/ to download the annual report of a company that interests you. Analyze the company's financial statements by calculating the twelve ratios covered in this chapter and compare these ratios to industry averages found in RMA's *Annual Statement Studies* or one of the other financial analysis resources found in your library. Do you spot any problem areas? Strengths? What recommendations can you make to improve the company's financial position? What do you project the company's future to be? Do you recommend investing in the company? Explain.

Corbis RF

CHAPTER 12

Managing Cash Flow

A deficit is what you have when you haven't got as much as when you had nothing.
—*Gerald F. Lieberman*

If it appreciates, buy it. If it depreciates, lease it.
—*J. Paul Getty*

Learning Objectives

On completion of this chapter, you will be able to:

1. Explain the importance of cash management to a small company's success.

2. Differentiate between cash and profits.

3. Understand the five steps in creating a cash budget and use them to create one.

4. Describe fundamental principles involved in managing the "big three" of cash management: accounts receivable, accounts payable, and inventory.

5. Explain the techniques for avoiding a cash crunch in a small company.

Cash—a four-letter word that has become a curse for many small businesses. Lack of this valuable asset has driven countless small companies into bankruptcy. Unfortunately, many more firms will become failure statistics because their owners have neglected the principles of cash management that can spell the difference between success and failure. "Everything is about cash," says entrepreneur-turned-venture-capitalist Guy Kawasaki, "raising it, conserving it, collecting it."[1] Indeed, developing a cash forecast is essential for new businesses because start-up companies usually do not generate positive cash flow right away. A common cause of business failures, especially in start-up and fast-growth companies, is overemphasis on increasing sales with little concern for collecting the receivables those sales generate. "Your sales figures may be great, but it's cash flow that determines whether you can keep the doors open," says one business writer.[2] Another problem is that owners neglect to forecast how much cash their companies will need until they reach the point of generating positive cash flow. The result is always the same: a cash crisis.

ENTREPRENEURIAL PROFILE ___

**Cookie Driscoll:
C. Cookie Driscoll Inc.**

Cookie Driscoll, owner of C. Cookie Driscoll Inc. (CCDI), a small business in Fairfield, Pennsylvania, that sells animal-themed gifts and promotional products, is struggling to keep her 20-year-old company going because of cash flow problems. Rising costs for everything from energy and shipping to raw materials and insurance have squeezed the company's cash flow. In addition, at least nine of her small retail customers have closed their doors, many of them without paying their outstanding invoices. About 12 percent of her customers' accounts are 30 days past due, more than double the usual amount. CCDI's sales have slipped from $230,000 just a few years ago to just $60,000. When credit markets tightened, Driscoll's bank converted her company's $16,000 line of credit to a regular loan. Because of cash flow woes, Driscoll draws only a miniscule salary from the business and has been forced to pay company bills from her personal retirement account. Driscoll is conserving cash wherever she can; she has stopped heating her office, choosing instead to wear a coat to work during winter. "I'm as close to a panic as I've ever been," she says.[3]

As you learned in the previous chapter, controlling the financial aspects of a business using the traditional analysis of basic financial statements with ratios is immensely important; however, by themselves, these techniques are insufficient for achieving business success. Entrepreneurs are prone to focus on their companies' income statements–particularly sales and profits. The income statement, of course, shows only part of a company's financial picture. It is entirely possible for a business to earn a profit and still go out of business *by running out of cash*. In other words, managing a company's total financial performance effectively requires an entrepreneur to look beyond the "bottom line" and focus on what it takes to keep a company going—cash.

Cash Management

A survey by American Express OPEN Small Business Monitor reports that 59 percent of small business owners say they experience problems managing cash flow and that their biggest cash flow concern is the ability to paying their bills on time.[4] Figure 12.1 shows the techniques that small business owners rely on most often to improve their cash flow.

The best way to avoid a potentially business-crushing cash crisis is to use the principles of cash management. **Cash management** involves forecasting, collecting, disbursing, investing, and planning for the cash a company needs to operate smoothly. Cash management is a vital task because cash is the most important yet least productive asset that a small business owns. A business must have enough cash to meet its obligations or it will be declared bankrupt. Creditors, employees, and lenders expect to be paid on time, and cash is the required medium of exchange. But some firms retain an excessive amount of cash to meet any unexpected circumstances that might arise. These dormant dollars have an income-earning potential that owners are ignoring, and this restricts a firm's growth and lowers its profitability. Investing this cash, even for a short time, can add to a company's earnings. Proper cash management permits the owner to adequately meet the cash demands of the business, avoid retaining unnecessarily large cash balances, and stretch the profit-generating power of each dollar the business owns.

cash management
the process of forecasting, collecting, disbursing, investing, and planning for the cash a company needs to operate smoothly.

Although cash flow difficulties afflict companies of all sizes and ages, young companies, especially, are cash sponges, soaking up every available dollar and always hungry for more. The reason usually is that their cash generating "engines" are not operating at full speed yet and cannot provide enough power to generate the cash necessary to cover rapidly climbing operating expenses. Entrepreneurs must manage cash flow from the day they launch their businesses.

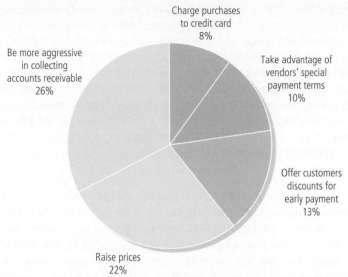

Charge purchases
to credit card
8%

Be more aggressive
in collecting
accounts receivable
26%

Take advantage of
vendors' special
payment terms
10%

Offer customers
discounts for
early payment
13%

Raise prices
22%

Source: American Express OPEN Small Business Monitor, 2008.

FIGURE 12.1

Small Business Owners' Strategies for Improving Cash Flow

Shortly after he launched his new company on June 16, 1903, entrepreneur Henry Ford ran headlong into a cash crisis that nearly wiped out the Ford Motor Company. Start-up expenses (including $10,000 to the Dodge brothers for engines and other parts and $640 to the Hartford Rubber Works for 64 tires) quickly soaked up Ford's $28,000 in start-up capital he and eleven associates invested, and by July 10, the company's cash balance had fallen to a mere $223.65. Another payroll and more parts orders were just around the corner, and the 25-day-old company was already on the brink of a financial collapse. On July 11, an investor saved the day with a $5,000 contribution. Four days later the Ford Motor Company sold its first car to Dr. E. Pfennig of Chicago, pushing the company's cash balance to $6,486.44. From this shaky financial beginning grew one of the largest automakers in the world![5]

ENTREPRENEURIAL PROFILE

Henry Ford: Ford Motor Company

   Managing cash flow is also an acute problem for rapidly growing businesses. In fact, fast-track companies are most likely to suffer cash shortages. Many successful, growing, and profitable businesses fail because they become insolvent; they do not have adequate cash to meet the needs of a growing business with a booming sales volume. If a company's sales are increasing, its owner also must hire more employees, expand plant capacity, increase the sales force, build inventory, and incur other drains on the firm's cash supply. During rapid growth, cash collections typically fall behind, compounding the problem. Cash flows out of these high-growth companies much faster than it comes in. The head of the National Federation of Independent Businesses says that many small business owners "wake up one day to find that the price of success is no cash on hand. They don't understand that if they're successful, inventory and receivables will increase faster than profits can fund them."[6] The resulting cash crisis may force the owner to lose equity control of the business or, ultimately, declare bankruptcy and close.

Corbis RF

ENTREPRENEURIAL PROFILE

Steve Shore & Barry Prevor: Steve and Barry's

Discount clothing retailer Steve and Barry's grew rapidly over its 23-year history only to succumb to the perils of a cash crisis. Co-founders Steve Shore and Barry Prevor opened new stores at a breakneck pace and attracted endorsements for their clothing, all of which sold for no more than $10, from celebrities such as Sarah Jessica Parker, Venus Williams, Amanda Bynes, and Laird Hamilton. Unfortunately Steve and Barry's cash flow could not support its fast-paced growth, and the company's payments to its vendors and suppliers began falling behind. As the company's supply of cash dwindled, more vendors and suppliers, ranging from small contractors to the University of Michigan student newspaper, went unpaid. Within months, Steve and Barry's filed for bankruptcy, citing a cash crisis as the cause of the company's liquidation.[7]

cash flow cycle
the time lag between paying suppliers for merchandise or materials and receiving payment from customers.

Table 12.1 shows how to calculate the additional cash required to support an increase in sales.

The first step in managing cash more effectively is to understand the company's **cash flow cycle**–the time lag between paying suppliers for merchandise or materials and receiving payment from customers for the product or service (see Figure 12.2). The longer this cash flow cycle, the more likely it is that the business owner will encounter a cash crisis. Preparing a cash forecast that recognizes this cycle, however, will help to avoid a crisis. Understanding the cash flow patterns of a business over the course of a year is essential to creating a successful cash management strategy. Business owners should calculate their cash flow cycles whenever they prepare their financial statements (or at least quarterly). On a *daily* basis, business owners should generate a report showing the following items: total cash on hand, bank balance, a summary of the day's sales, a summary of the day's cash receipts, a summary of the day's cash disbursements, and a summary of accounts receivable collections. Compiling these reports into monthly summaries provides the basis for making reliable cash forecasts.

The next step in effective cash management is to analyze the cash flow cycle, looking for ways to reduce its length. Reducing the cycle from 240 days to, say, 150 days would free up

TABLE 12.1 How Much Cash is Required to Support an Increase in Sales?

Too often, entrepreneurs believe that increasing sales is the ideal solution to a cash crunch only to discover (often after it is too late) that it takes extra cash to support extra sales. The following worksheet demonstrates how to calculate the amount of additional cash required to support an increase in sales.

To make the calculation, a business owner needs the following information:

- the increase in sales planned ($)
- the time frame for adding new sales (days)
- the company's gross profit margin, gross profit ÷ net sales (%)
- the estimated additional expenses required to generate additional sales ($)
- the company's average collection period (days)

To calculate the amount of additional cash needed, use the following formula:

Extra cash required = ((New sales − Gross profit + Extra overhead) × (Average collection period × 1.20[*])) ÷ (Time frame in days for adding new sales)

Consider the following example:

The owner of Ardent Company wants to increase sales by $75,000 over the next year. The company's gross profit margin is 30 percent of sales (so its gross profit on these additional sales would be $75,000 × 30% = $22,500), its average collection period is 47 days, and managers estimate that generating the additional sales will require an increase in expenses of $21,300. The additional cash that Ardent will need to support this higher level of sales is:

Extra cash required = (($75,000 - $22,500 + 21,300) × (47 × 1.2)) ÷ 365 = $11,404

Ardent will need $11,404 in extra cash to support the additional sales of $75,000 it plans to bring in over the next year.

[*] The extra 20 percent is added as a cushion.
Source: Adapted from Norm Brodsky, "Paying for Growth: How Much Cash You Need to Carry New Sales," *Inc. Online Tools & Apps: Worksheet,* http://www.inc.com/tools/details/0,6152,CNT61_HOM1_LOC0_NAVhome_TOL11648,00.html

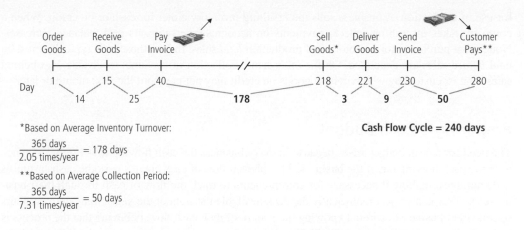

FIGURE 12.2
The Cash Flow Cycle

incredible amounts of cash that this company could use to finance growth and dramatically reduce its borrowing costs. What steps would you suggest the owner of the business whose cash flow cycle is illustrated in Figure 12.2 take to reduce its length?

Cash and Profits Are Not the Same

When analyzing cash flow, entrepreneurs must understand that cash and profits are not the same. Attempting to discern the status of a small company's cash position by analyzing its profitability is futile; profitability is not necessarily highly correlated with cash flow. "Entrepreneurs think, 'If I'm selling products and I've got revenue, then I'm going to have cash,'" says one small business consultant. "That's not necessarily so."[8] In fact, a company can be growing and earning a profit and still be forced to close its doors because it runs out of cash. Profit (or net income) is the difference between a company's total revenue and its total expenses. It measures how efficiently a business is operating. Cash is the money that is free and readily available to use in a business. **Cash flow** measures a company's liquidity and its ability to pay its bills and other financial obligations on time by tracking the flow of cash into and out of the business over a period of time. Many small business owners soon discover that profitability does not guarantee liquidity. As important as earning a profit is, no business owner can pay suppliers, creditors, employees, the government, and lenders in profits; that requires *cash*! Although profits are tied up in many forms, such as inventory, computers, or machinery, cash is the money that flows through a business in a continuous cycle without being tied up in any other asset. "Businesses fail not because they are making or losing money," warns one financial expert, "but because they simply run out of cash."[9]

Figure 12.3 shows the flow of cash through a typical small business. Cash flow is the volume of actual cash that comes into and goes out of the business during an accounting period. Decreases in cash occur when the business purchases, on credit or for cash, goods for inventory or materials

cash flow
a method of tracking a company's liquidity and its ability to pay its bills and other financial obligations on time by tracking the flow of cash into and out of the business over a period of time.

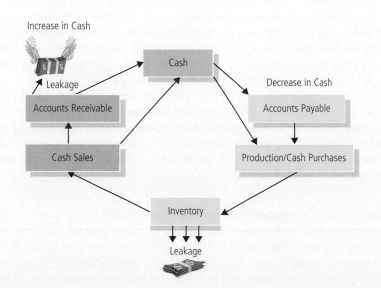

FIGURE 12.3
Cash Flow

for use in production. A business sells the resulting inventory either for cash or on credit. When a company takes in cash or collects payments on accounts receivable, its cash balance increases. Notice that purchases for inventory and production *lead* sales; that is, these bills typically must be paid *before* sales are generated. On the other hand, collection of accounts receivable *lags* behind sales; that is, customers who purchase goods on credit may not pay until the next month or later.

LO 2

Understand the five steps in creating a cash budget and use them to create one.

Preparing a Cash Budget

The need for a cash budget arises because in every business the cash flowing in is rarely "in sync" with the cash flowing out of the business. This uneven flow of cash creates periodic cash surpluses and shortages, making it necessary for entrepreneurs to track the flow of cash through their businesses so they can project realistically the cash available throughout the year. Many entrepreneurs operate their businesses without knowing the pattern of their cash flow, believing that the process is too complex or time consuming. In reality, entrepreneurs simply cannot afford to disregard the process of cash management. They must ensure that their businesses have on hand an adequate, but not excessive, supply of cash to meet their operating needs. The goal of cash management is to have enough cash available to meet the company's cash needs at a given time.

How much cash is enough? What is suitable for one business may be totally inadequate for another, depending on each firm's size, nature, seasonal pattern of sales, and particular situation. The small business manager should prepare a **cash budget,** which is nothing more than a "cash map," showing the amount and the timing of the cash receipts and the cash disbursements day-by-day, week-by-week, or month-by-month. It is used to predict the amount of cash a company will need to operate smoothly over a specific period of time, and it is a valuable tool in managing a company successfully. A cash budget can illuminate a host of approaching problems, giving entrepreneurs adequate time to handle, or better yet, avoid them. A cash budget reveals important clues about how well a company balances its accounts payable and accounts receivable, controls inventory, finances its growth, and makes use of the cash it has.

cash budget

a "cash map," showing the amount and the timing of cash receipts and cash disbursements on a daily, weekly, or monthly basis.

Typically, small business owners should prepare a projected monthly cash budget for at least one year into the future and quarterly estimates for another. The forecast must cover all seasonal sales fluctuations. The more variable a firm's sales pattern, the shorter should be its planning horizon. For example, a company whose sales fluctuate widely over a relatively short time frame might require a weekly cash budget. The key is to track cash flow over time. The timing of a company's cash flow is as important as the amounts. "An alert cash flow manager keeps an eye not on cash receipts or on cash demands as average quantities but on cash as a function of the *calendar*," says one business owner.[10]

Creating a written cash plan is not an excessively time-consuming task and can help the owner to avoid unexpected cash shortages, a situation that can cause a business to fail. Preparing a cash budget helps business owners avoid adverse cash surprises. Computer spreadsheets such as Microsoft Excel and others make the job fast and easy to complete and allow entrepreneurs to update their cash flow forecasts with very little time and effort.

A cash budget is based on the cash method of accounting, which means that cash receipts and cash disbursements are recorded in the forecast *only when the cash transaction is expected to take place*. For example, credit sales to customers are not reported until the company expects to receive the cash from them. Similarly, purchases made on credit are not recorded until the owner expects to pay them. Because depreciation, bad debt expense, and other non-cash items involve no cash transfers, they are omitted entirely from the cash budget.

A cash budget is nothing more than a forecast of the firm's cash inflows and outflows for a specific time period, and it will never be completely accurate. However, it does give an entrepreneur a clear picture of a company's estimated cash balance for the period, pointing out where external cash infusions may be required or where surplus cash balances may be available to invest. Also, by comparing actual cash flows with projections, an owner can revise the forecast so that future cash budgets will be more accurate.

ENTREPRENEURIAL PROFILE _____

Joseph Popper: Computer Gallery

Joseph Popper, CEO of Computer Gallery, knows how deadly running out of cash can be for a small company and does everything he can to make sure his business avoids that trap. Popper uses a spreadsheet to extract key sales, collection, and disbursement totals and to generate the resulting cash balance each day. Even when he is traveling, Popper keeps up with his company's daily cash balance. He has the spreadsheet results sent to an Internet service, which e-mails them to his alphanumeric pager every day he is out of the office. "We've been paranoid about cash from day one," Popper says. But his system keeps accounts receivable in control, ensures that the company's available cash working hard, and improves his relationship with the company's banker.[11]

Formats for preparing a cash budget vary depending on the pattern of a company's cash flow. Table 12.2 shows a most likely monthly cash budget for a small department store over a six-month period. (Creating pessimistic and optimistic cash forecasts is a snap once the most likely cash budget is in place.) Each monthly column should be divided into two sections—estimated and actual (not shown)–so that each succeeding cash forecast can be updated to reflect actual cash flows. (The Service Corps of Retired Executives, SCORE, provides a handy set of templates, including one for forecasting cash flow, on its Web site, http://www.score.org/template_gallery.html.)

TABLE 12.2 Cash Budget for Small Department Store

Assumptions:

Cash balance on December 31 = $12,000

Minimum cash balance = $10,000

Sales are 75% credit and 25% cash

Credit sales are collected in the following manner:

* 60% collected in the first month after the sale

* 30% collected in the second month after the sale

* 5% collected in the third month after the sale

* 5% are never collected

Sales forecasts are as follows:	Pessimistic	Most Likely	Optimistic
October (actual)	–	$ 300,000	–
November (actual)	–	350,000	–
December (actual)	–	400,000	–
January	120,000	150,000	175,000
February	160,000	200,000	250,000
March	160,000	200,000	250,000
April	250,000	300,000	340,000
May	260,000	315,000	360,000
June	265,000	320,000	375,000

Rent is $3,000 per month

Interest payments of $664 and $817 are due in April and May, respectively

A tax prepayment of $18,000 is due in March

A capital addition payment of $130,000 is due in February

A bank note payment of $7,500 is due in March

Insurance premiums are $475 per month

Other expense estimates include:	Purchases	Wages and Salaries	Utilities	Advertising	Miscellaneous
January	$ 140,000	$ 30,000	$ 1,450	$ 1,600	$ 500
February	140,000	38,000	1,400	1,600	$ 500
March	210,000	40,000	1,250	1,500	$ 500
April	185,000	42,000	1,250	2,000	$ 550
May	190,000	44,000	1,250	2,000	$ 550
June	180,000	44,000	1,400	2,200	$ 550

(continued)

TABLE 12.2 Cash Budget - Most Likely Sales Forecast

	Oct	Nov	Dec	Jan	Feb	Mar	Apr	May	Jun
Cash Receipts									
Sales	$ 300,000	$ 350,000	$ 400,000	$ 150,000	$ 200,000	$ 200,000	$ 300,000	$ 315,000	$ 320,000
Credit Sales	225,000	262,500	300,000	112,500	150,000	150,000	225,000	236,250	240,000
Collections									
60% - First month after sale				180,000	67,500	90,000	90,000	135,000	141,750
30% - Second month after sale				78,750	90,000	33,750	45,000	45,000	67,500
5% - Third month after sale				11,250	13,125	15,000	5,625	7,500	7,500
Cash Sales				37,500	50,000	50,000	75,000	78,750	80,000
Other cash receipts				25	35	50	60	60	65
Total Cash Receipts				307,525	220,660	188,800	215,685	266,310	296,815
Cash Disbursements									
Purchases				140,000	140,000	210,000	185,000	190,000	180,000
Rent				3,000	3,000	3,000	3,000	3,000	3,000
Utilities				1,450	1,400	1,250	1,250	1,250	1,400
Bank Note				–	–	7,500	–	–	–
Tax Prepayment				–	–	18,000	–	–	–
Capital Additions				–	130,000	–	–	–	–
Wages and Salaries				30,000	38,000	40,000	42,000	44,000	44,000
Insurance				475	475	475	475	475	475
Advertising				1,600	1,600	1,500	2,000	2,000	2,200
Interest				–	–	–	664	817	–
Miscellaneous				500	500	500	550	550	550
Total Cash Disbursements				177,025	314,975	282,225	234,939	242,092	231,625
End-of-Month Balance									
Beginning cash balance				12,000	142,500	48,185	10,000	10,000	14,218
+ Cash receipts				307,525	220,660	188,800	215,685	266,310	296,815
- Cash disbursements				177,025	314,975	282,225	234,939	242,092	231,625
Cash (end-of-month)				142,500	48,185	(45,240)	(9,254)	34,218	79,408
Borrowing				–	–	55,240	19,254	–	–
Repayment				–	–	–	–	20,000	53,830
Final Cash Balance				$ 142,500	$ 48,185	$ 10,000	$ 10,000	$ 14,218	$ 25,578
Monthly Surplus/(Deficit)				130,500	(94,315)	(93,425)	(19,254)	24,218	65,190

Comparing forecasted amounts to actual cash flows and learning the causes of any significant discrepancies allows entrepreneurs to improve the accuracy of future cash budgets.

Creating a cash budget requires five basic steps:

1. Determining an adequate minimum cash balance.
2. Forecasting sales.
3. Forecasting cash receipts.
4. Forecasting cash disbursements.
5. Determining the end-of-month cash balance.

Step 1. Determining an Adequate Minimum Cash Balance

What is considered an excessive cash balance for one small business may be inadequate for another, even though the two companies are in the same industry. Some suggest that a firm's cash balance should equal at least one-fourth of its current liabilities, but this general rule clearly will not work for all small businesses. The most reliable method of deciding the right minimum cash balance is based on past experience. Past operating records will indicate the cash cushion an entrepreneur needs to cover any unexpected expenses after all normal cash outlays are deducted from the month's cash receipts. For example, past records may indicate that it is desirable to maintain a cash balance equal to five days' sales. Seasonal fluctuations may cause a firm's minimum cash balance to change. For example, the desired cash balance for a retailer may be greater in June than in December.

Step 2. Forecasting Sales

The heart of the cash budget is the sales forecast. It is the central factor in creating an accurate picture of the firm's cash position because sales ultimately are transformed into cash receipts and cash disbursements. For most businesses, sales constitute the major source of the cash flowing into the business. Similarly, sales of merchandise require that cash to be used to replenish inventory. As a result, the cash budget is only as accurate as the sales forecast from which it is derived.

For an established business, a sales forecast is based on past sales, but owners must be careful not to be excessively optimistic in projecting sales. Economic swings, increased competition, fluctuations in demand, normal seasonal variations, and other factors can drastically affect sales patterns and, therefore, a company's cash flow. Most businesses, from retailers and hotels to accounting firms and builders, have sales patterns that are "lumpy" and not evenly distributed throughout the year. Although the Shallow Shaft Restaurant, an upscale restaurant perched at an altitude of 9,000 feet in the ski resort town of Alta, Utah, is open for most of the year, it generates 80 percent to 90 percent of its annual sales during the few months of the area's busy snow skiing season.[12]

Many small retailers generate most of their sales and as much as one-third of their profits in the months of November and December. For instance, 40 percent of all toy sales take place in the last six weeks of the year, and companies that make fruitcakes typically generate 50 percent to 90 percent of their sales during the holiday season.[13] The typical wine and spirits shop makes 15 to 18 percent of its total sales volume for the entire year between December 15 and December 31.[14] Companies that sell television sets and recliners see sales surge in the weeks before the Super Bowl, and Super Bowl Sunday is one of the busiest days of the year for pizza makers, producing revenues that are five times that of the typical Sunday.[15] For fireworks companies, the three weeks before July 4 account for the majority of annual sales with another smaller peak occurring before New Year's Eve.[16] For companies with highly seasonal sales patterns, proper cash management is an essential activity.

Several quantitative techniques, which are beyond the scope of this text (linear regression, multiple regression, time series analysis, exponential smoothing), are available to owners of existing

Super Bowl Sunday is one of the busiest days of the year for pizzerias.

Bob Daemmrich/The Image Works

businesses with an established sales pattern for forecasting sales. These methods enable a small business owner to extrapolate past and present sales trends to arrive at a fairly accurate sales forecast.

The task of forecasting sales for a new firm is more difficult but not impossible. For example, the new owner might conduct research on similar firms and their sales patterns in the first year of operation to come up with a forecast. The local chamber of commerce and trade associations in the various industries also collect such information. Publications such as "Risk Management Association's (RMA)" *Annual Statement Studies*, which profiles financial statements for companies of all sizes in hundreds of industries, is also a useful tool. Market research is another source of information that may be used to estimate annual sales for a fledgling firm. Other potential sources that may help to predict sales include census reports, newspapers, radio and television customer profiles, polls and surveys, and local government statistics. Talking with owners of similar businesses (outside the local trading area, of course) can provide entrepreneurs with realistic estimates of start-up sales. Table 12.3 provides an example of how one entrepreneur used such marketing information to derive a sales forecast for his first year of operation.

No matter what techniques entrepreneurs employ, they must recognize that even the best sales estimates will be wrong. Many financial analysts suggest that the owner create *three* estimates–an optimistic, a pessimistic, and a most likely sales estimate–and then make a separate cash budget for each forecast (a very simple task with a spreadsheet). This dynamic forecast enables the owner to determine the range within which his or her sales will likely be as the year progresses.

Step 3. Forecasting Cash Receipts

As you learned earlier, sales constitute the primary source of cash receipts. When a company sells goods and services on credit, the cash budget must account for the delay between the sale and the actual collection of the proceeds. Remember: You cannot spend cash you haven't collected yet! For instance, an appliance store might not collect the cash from a refrigerator sold in February until April or May, and the cash budget must reflect this delay. To project accurately cash receipts, an entrepreneur must analyze accounts receivable to determine the company's collection pattern. For example, past records may indicate that 20 percent of sales are for cash, 50 percent are paid in the month following the sale, 20 percent are paid two months after the sale, 5 percent are paid after three months, and 5 percent are never collected. In addition to cash and credit sales, a small business may receive cash in a number of forms–interest income, rental income, dividends, and others.

TABLE 12.3 Forecasting Sales for a Business Start-up

Robert Adler wants to open a repair shop for imported cars. The trade association for automotive garages estimates that the owner of an imported car spends an average of $485 per year on repairs and maintenance. The typical garage attracts its clientele from a trading zone (the area from which a business draws its customers) with a 20-mile radius. Census reports show that the families within a 20-mile radius of Robert's proposed location own 84,000 cars, of which 24 are imports. Based on a local consultant's market research, Robert believes he can capture 9.9 percent of the market this year. Robert's estimate of his company's first year's sales are as follows:

Number of cars in trading zone	84,0000 autos
$\times$ Percent of imports	$\times$ 24 %
= Number of imported cars in trading zone	20, 160 imports
Number of imports in trading zone	20,160 imports
$\times$ Average expenditure on repairs and maintenance	$\times$ $485
= Total import repair sales potential	$9,777,600
Total import repair sales potential	$9,777,600
$\times$ Estimated share of the market	$\times$ 9.9%
= Sales estimate	$967,982

Now Robert Adler can convert this annual sales estimate of $967,982 into monthly sales estimates for use in his company's cash budget.

A Short Season

Dennis and Steve Vourderis, owners of Deno's Wonder Wheel Amusement Park on the boardwalk at New York's famous Coney Island, know that their business has to make the most of its revenue generating potential when the time is right. The company, started by their parents and home to the Wonder Wheel, a famous Ferris wheel built in 1920, generates all of its sales in the six month stretch from April to October. Years of experience have taught them that the business must be operating profitably by the July 4 holiday, or the company will struggle. Operating a highly seasonal business is a challenge in many ways. "You have to budget carefully to make sure you don't overspend," says Dennis. "Maintenance, taxes, and equipment financing are based on a 12-month year. You need to know that you'll have enough funding to cover those expenses during the time you have no cash flow." During the winter months, the Vourderis brothers are busy preparing for the next season. They and their staff disassemble the seats and other parts of the rides, inspect and refurbish them, and store them until the spring. Every year, they also repaint the Wonder Wheel, which stands 150 feet tall and weighs 400,000 pounds.

"A seasonal business is infinitely more difficult to manage than most other businesses," says Les Charm, who teaches entrepreneurship at Babson College. How can business owners whose companies face highly seasonal sales patterns manage the uneven cash flow?

- *Be financially disciplined.* Seasonal business owners must establish a realistic budget, stick to it, and avoid the temptation to spend lavishly when cash flow is plentiful. Teevan McManus, owner of the Coronado Surfing Academy in San Diego, failed to heed this advice in his first year of business. "I burned through everything I made in the summer and was living off of my business line of credit before the next season came around," he recalls. "I barely made it to the next June."

- *Manage your time and your employees' time carefully.* During the busy season, employees may be working overtime to serve the rush of customers; during the off season, a business owner may cut back to 20-hour work weeks or operate with a skeleton crew.

- *Use permanent employees sparingly.* Many owners of seasonal businesses use a small core of permanent employees and then hire part-time workers or student interns during their busy season. Planning for the right number of seasonal employees and recruiting them early ensures that a business will be able to serve its customers properly.

- *Put aside cash in a separate account that you use only for the lean months of your seasonal business.*

- *Maximize your productivity in the off season.* Use the slow season to conduct market research, perform routine maintenance and repairs, revise your Web site, and stay in touch with customers. Steve Kopelman's company, HauntedHouse.com, earns all of its $2.6 million in annual revenue in a six-week period leading up to Halloween. Starting in November, Kopelman surveys his customers so that he can

Jeffrey Greenberg/Photo Researchers, Inc.

refine his marketing efforts for the next season and solicit suggestions for improvement. He visits trade shows to look for the latest technology and gadgets to keep his haunted houses fresh and exciting for his customers. Kopelman also negotiates leases on properties for the next season and studies his competition by visiting every haunted house Web site that he can find.

- *Keep inventory at minimal levels during the off season.* As you learned in this chapter, holding inventory unnecessarily merely ties up valuable cash uselessly.

- *Offer off-peak discounts.* Doing so may generate some revenue during slow periods.

- *Consider starting a complementary seasonal business.* Jan Axel, founder of Delphinium Design Landscaping in South Salem, New York, sees her business slow down considerably during the winter and decided to launch a holiday decorating service that generates cash flow when landscape sales evaporate.

- *Create a cash flow forecast.* Perhaps one of the most important steps that seasonal business owners can take is to develop a forecast of their companies' cash flow. Doing so allows them to spot patterns and trends and to make plans for covering inevitable cash shortages. Make sure that you include a pessimistic or worst-case scenario in your cash forecast.

- *Establish a bank line of credit.* The line of credit should be large enough to cover at least three months' worth of expenses. Use your cash flow forecast to show the banker how and when your company will be able to repay the loan. "[A good cash forecast] shows the banker that you know exactly where the peaks and valleys are and what your cash needs are," says one banker.

1. What impact do highly seasonal sales have on a small company's cash flow?
2. What other advice can you offer owners of seasonal businesses about coping with the effects of their companies' highly irregular sales patterns? About managing cash flow in general?

Source: Adapted from Rich Mintzer, "Running a Seasonal Business," *Entrepreneur*, March 16, 2007, http://www.entrepreneur.com/management/

operations/article175954.html; Sarah Pierce, "Surviving a Seasonal Business," *Entrepreneur*, July 15, 2008, http://www.entrepreneur.com/startingabusiness/businessideas/article195680.html; Dan Kehrer, "10 Steps to Seasonal Success," Business.com, May 2006, http://www.business.com/directory/advice/sales-and-marketing/sales/10-steps-to-seasonal-success/; Amy Barrett, "Basics for Seasonal Business Owners," *Business Week*, April 16, 2008, http://www.businessweek.com/magazine/content/08_64/s0804058908582.htm?chan=smallbiz_smallbiz+index+page_best+of+smallbiz+magazine.

Collecting accounts receivable promptly poses problems for many small companies; in fact, difficulty in collecting accounts receivable is the primary cause of cash flow problems cited by small business owners.[17] Figure 12.4 demonstrates the importance of acting promptly once an account becomes past due. Notice how the probability of collecting an outstanding account diminishes the longer the account is delinquent. Table 12.4 illustrates the high cost of failing to collect accounts receivable on time.

ENTREPRENEURIAL PROFILE

Jeremy Brandt: 1-800-CashOffer

Jeremy Brandt, owner of 1-800-CashOffer, a company that connects home sellers with reputable investors, traditionally extended credit terms of 15 to 30 days. However, when he saw a housing crisis looming on the horizon, Brandt knew that his company could be headed for a cash crisis if his customers began stretching out their payments to 45 to 60 days or longer. Many of the company's customers already had started paying more slowly, which pushed Brandt to make the decision to require payment up front. "We decided to take the hard-line approach that everything is paid in advance for services," he explains. "That way we don't get stuck holding the bag." Brandt and his employees are careful to explain CashOffer's new policy and the reasons behind it to customers, most of whom have accepted it without any problem.[18]

Step 4. Forecasting Cash Disbursements

Most owners of established businesses have a clear picture of the firm's pattern of cash disbursements. In fact, many cash payments, such as rent, loan repayments, and interest, are fixed amounts due on specified dates. The key factor when forecasting disbursements for a cash budget is to record them in *the month in which they will be paid*, *not when the obligation is incurred*. Of course, the number of cash disbursements varies with each particular business, but the following disbursement categories are standard: purchases of inventory or raw materials; wages and salaries, rent, utilities, taxes, loan payments, interest, advertising, fixed-asset purchases, overhead expenses, and miscellaneous expenses.

Usually, an owner's tendency is to underestimate cash disbursements, which can result in a cash crisis. To prevent this, wise entrepreneurs cushion their cash disbursement estimates, assuming they will be higher than expected. This is particularly important for entrepreneurs

FIGURE 12.4

Collecting Delinquent Accounts

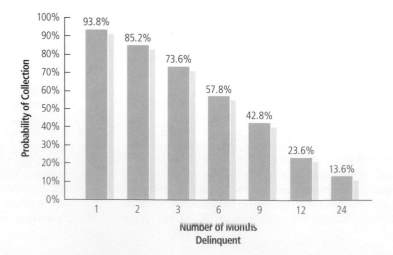

TABLE 12.4 Managing Accounts Receivable

Are your customers who purchase on credit paying late? If so, these outstanding accounts receivable represent a significant leak in your company's cash flow. Slow paying customers, in effect, are borrowing money from your business interest-free. One experienced business owner says, "Whether you realize it or not you're sort of a banker, and you need to start thinking like one...to assess the quality of your [customers' accounts]." Slow-paying customers are using your money without paying you interest while you forgo opportunities to place it in interest-earning investments or pay interest on money that you must borrow to replace the missing funds. Exactly how much is poor credit control costing your company? The answer may surprise you.

The first step is to calculate your company's average collection period ratio (See "Operating Ratios" section in Chapter 9). The second step is to age your accounts receivable to determine how many accounts are current and how many are overdue. The following example shows how to use these numbers to calculate the cost of past due accounts for a company whose credit terms are "net 30":

Average collection period	65 days
− credit terms	−30 days
Excess in accounts receivable	35 days
Average daily sales of $21,500* × 35 days	$752,500
× Normal rate of return	× 8%
Annual cost of excess	$60,200

Slow-paying customers are costing this company more than $60,000 a year! If your business is highly seasonal, quarterly or monthly figures may be more meaningful than annual ones.

*Average daily sales = Annual sales ÷ 365 days = $7,847,500 ÷ 365 = $21,500 per day

Source: Adapted from Norm Brodsky, "What Are You, a Bank?" *Inc.,* November 2007, pp. 81--82; "Financial Control," *Inc.,* Reprinted with permission of the publisher.

opening new businesses. In fact, some financial analysts recommend that new owners estimate cash disbursements as best they can and then add another 10 to 25 percent of the total! Whatever forecasting technique is used, entrepreneurs must avoid underestimating cash disbursements, which may lead to severe cash shortages and possible bankruptcy.

Sometimes business owners have difficulty developing initial forecasts of cash receipts and cash disbursements. One of the most effective techniques for overcoming the "I don't know where to begin" hurdle is to make a *daily* list of the items that generated cash (receipts) and those that consumed it (disbursements).

ENTREPRENEURIAL PROFILE

Susan Bowen:
Champion Awards

For example, Susan Bowen, CEO of Champion Awards, a $9 million T-shirt screen printer, monitors cash flow by tracking the cash that flows into and out of her company every day. Focusing on keeping the process simple, Bowen sets aside a few minutes each morning to track updates from the previous day on four key numbers:

Accounts receivable:
1. What did we bill yesterday?
2. How much did we actually collect?

Accounts payable:
3. What invoices did we receive yesterday?
4. How much in total did we pay out?

If Bowen observes the wrong trend—more new bills than new sales or more money going out than coming in—she makes immediate adjustments to protect her cash flow. The benefits produced (not the least of which is the peace of mind in knowing that no cash crisis is looming) more than outweigh the ten minutes she invests in the process every day. "I've tried to balance my books every single day since I started my company in 1970," says Bowen.[19]

Step 5. Estimating the End-of-Month Cash Balance

To estimate a company's cash balance for each month, a business owner first must determine the cash balance at the beginning of each month. The beginning cash balance includes cash-on-hand as well as cash in checking and savings accounts. As development of the cash budget progresses, the cash balance at the end of a month becomes the beginning balance for the following month. Next the owner simply adds total cash receipts and subtracts total cash disbursements to obtain the end-of-month balance before any borrowing takes place. A positive amount indicates that the firm has a cash surplus for the month, but a negative amount shows a cash shortage will occur unless the owner is able to collect or borrow additional funds.

Normally, a company's cash balance fluctuates from month to month, reflecting seasonal sales patterns in the business. These fluctuations are normal, but business owners must watch closely for *trends* in the cash balance over time. A trend of increases indicates that a company is solvent; on the other hand, a pattern of cash decreases should alert the owner that the business is approaching a cash crisis. One easy but effective tracking technique is to calculate the company's monthly cash surplus or deficit (cash receipts – cash disbursements) at the bottom of the cash budget (refer to Table 12.2). Strings of deficits (and the declining cash balance that results from them) should set off alarms that a company is headed for a cash crisis.

A cash budget not only illustrates the flow of cash into and out of the small business, but it also allows the owner to *anticipate* cash shortages and cash surpluses. By planning cash needs ahead of time, a small business is able to achieve the following benefits:

- Increase the amount and the speed of cash flowing into the company.
- Reduce the amount and the speed of cash flowing out of the company.
- Make the most efficient use of available cash.
- Take advantage of money-saving opportunities, such as quantity and cash discounts.
- Finance seasonal business needs.
- Develop a sound borrowing program.
- Develop a workable program of debt repayment.
- Impress lenders and investors with its ability to plan and repay financing.
- Provide funds for expansion.
- Plan for investing surplus cash.

"Cash flow spells survival for every business," claims one expert. "Manage cash flow effectively, and your business works. If your cash flow is not well managed, then sooner or later your business goes under. It's that simple."[20] Unfortunately, most small business owners forego these benefits because they fail to track their company's cash flow consistently. Because cash flow problems usually sneak up on a business over time, improper cash management often proves to be a costly – and fatal – mistake. One way to avoid this pitfall is to establish a *daily* report that shows the amount of cash on hand, the cash received, and the cash spent.

In Search of a Cash Flow Forecast

"I'll never make that mistake again," Douglas Martinez said to himself as he got into his car. Martinez had just left a meeting with his banker, who had not been optimistic about the chances of Martinez's plumbing supply company getting the loan it needed. "I should have been better prepared for the meeting," he muttered, knowing that he could be angry only at himself. "That consultant at the Small Business Development Center was right. Bankers' primary concern when making loans is cash flow."

"At least I salvaged the meeting by telling him I wasn't ready to officially apply for a loan yet," Martinez thought. "But I've got a lot of work to do. I've got a week to figure out how to put together a cash budget to supplement my loan application. Maybe that consultant can help me."

When he returned to his office, Martinez gathered up the file folders containing all of his fast-growing company's financial reports and printed his projected revenues and expenses using his computer spreadsheet. Then he called the SBDC consultant he had worked with when he was launching his company and explained the situation. When he arrived at the consultant's office that after-noon, they started organizing the information. Here is what they came up with:

Current cash balance	$8,750
Sales pattern	71% on credit and 29% in cash
Collections of credit sales	68% in the same month as the sale;
	19% in the first month after the sale;
	7% in the second month after the sale;
	6% never collected (bad debts).

Sales forecasts:

	Pessimistic	Most Likely	Optimistic
July (actual)	–	$18,750	–
August (actual)	–	$19,200	–
September (actual)	–	$17,840	–
October	$15,000	$17,500	$19,750
November	$14,000	$16,500	$18,500
December	$11,200	$13,000	$14,000
January	$ 9,900	$12,500	$14,900
February	$10,500	$13,800	$15,800
March	$13,500	$17,500	$19,900

Utilities expenses	$800 per month
Rent	$1,200 per month
Truck loan	$317 per month

The company's wages and salaries (including payroll taxes) estimates are:

October	$2,050
November	$1,825
December	$1,725
January	$1,725
February	$1,950
March	$2,425

The company pays 63 percent of the sales price for the inventory it purchases, an amount that it actually pays in the following month. (Martinez has negotiated "net 30" credit terms with his suppliers.)

Other expenses include:

Insurance premiums	$1,200, payable in August and February.
Office supplies	$ 95 per month
Maintenance	$ 75 per month
Computer supplies	$ 75 per month
Advertising	$ 550 per month
Legal and accounting fees	$ 250 per month
Miscellaneous expenses	$ 60 per month

A tax payment of $1,400 is due in December.

Martinez has established a minimum cash balance of $2,000 and can borrow money at an interest rate of 8.75 percent.

"Well, what do you think?" Douglas asked the consultant.

1. Assume the role of the SBDC consultant and help Douglas put together a cash budget for the six months beginning in October.

2. What conclusions can you draw about Douglas's business from this cash budget?

3. What suggestions can you make to help Douglas improve his company's cash flow?

The "Big Three" of Cash Management

It is unrealistic for business owners to expect to trace the flow of every dollar through their businesses. However, by concentrating on the three primary causes of cash flow problems, they can dramatically lower the likelihood of experiencing a devastating cash crisis. The "big three" of cash management are accounts receivable, accounts payable, and inventory. These three variables are leading indicators of a company's cash flow. If a company's accounts receivable balance is increasing, its cash balance may be declining. Similarly, accounts payable and inventory balances that are increasing faster than sales are signs of mounting pressure on a company's cash flow. A good cash management "recipe" involves accelerating a company's receivables to collect cash as quickly as possible, economizing to keep operating costs low, and paying out cash as slowly as possible (without damaging the company's credit rating). Business owners also must monitor inventory levels carefully to avoid tying up valuable cash in an excessive supply of goods.

Accounts Receivable

Selling merchandise and services on credit is a necessary evil for most small businesses. Many customers expect to buy on credit, and business owners extend it to avoid losing customers to competitors. However, selling to customers on credit is expensive; it requires more paperwork, more staff, and more cash to service accounts receivable. In addition, because extending credit is, in essence, lending money, the risk involved is higher. Every business owner who sells on credit will encounter customers who pay late or, worst of all, who never pay at all. Most small companies operate with very thin cash reserves; therefore, a late payment from a major customer can spell create a cash crisis. Figure 12.5 depicts the results of a study by American Express of small business owners who have cash flow concerns; note that the greatest cash flow problem these entrepreneurs cite is collecting accounts receivable.

Selling on credit is a common practice in business. Experts estimate that 90 percent of industrial and wholesale sales are on credit and that 40 percent of retail sales are on account.[21] One survey of small businesses across a variety of industries reported that 77 percent extend credit to their customers.[22] Because credit sales are so prevalent, an assertive collection program is essential to managing a company's cash flow. A credit policy that is too lenient can destroy a business's cash flow, attracting nothing but slow-paying or "deadbeat" customers who never pay. On the other hand, a carefully designed policy can be a powerful selling tool, attracting customers and boosting cash flow. Entrepreneurs must remember that a sale does not count until they collect the cash from it!

Transforming accounts receivable into cash is essential to staying in business.

FIGURE 12.5

Cash Flow Concerns

Source: Based on American Express Corporation, 2005.

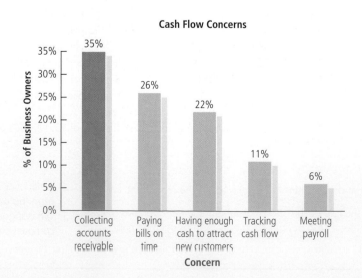

Cash Flow Concerns

Jefferson Jewell, cofounder of Blackfin Technology, a software development and consulting company in Boise, Idaho, learned a valuable cash management lesson when one of the company's major customers failed to pay its invoices, which forced the founders to forgo their salaries for three months to avoid a cash crisis. Four years later, Jewell, who had begun tracking cash closely after the first crisis, saw the company's average collection period ratio increase, a precursor to potential cash flow problems. This time, however, Blackfin was much better prepared and was able to avoid a cash crunch. Jewell had established a line of credit with a local bank, revamped the company's collection policy (including sending invoices by e-mail to speed up collections), and established a mechanism for tracking accounts receivable and accounts payable. He also began asking customers to pay at least a portion of the cost of a job up front.[23]

ENTREPRENEURIAL PROFILE

Jefferson Jewell:
Blackfin Technology

How to Establish a Credit and Collection Policy. The first step in establishing a workable credit policy is to screen customers carefully *before* granting them credit. Unfortunately, few small businesses conduct any kind of credit investigation before selling to a new customer. Many entrepreneurs that sell on credit sell to *anyone* who wants to buy; most have no credit-checking procedure. The first line of defense against bad debt losses is a detailed credit application. Before selling to any customer on credit, a business owner should have the customer fill out a customized application designed to provide the information needed to judge the potential customer's creditworthiness. At a minimum, this credit profile should include the following information about customers:

- Name, address, social security number, and telephone number.
- Form of ownership (proprietorship, S corporation, LLC, corporation, etc.) and number of years in business.
- Credit references (e.g., other suppliers), including contact names, addresses, and telephone numbers.
- Bank and credit card references.

After collecting this information, a business owner should use it by checking the potential customer's credit references! The savings from lower bad debt expenses can more than offset the cost of using a credit reporting service. Companies such as Dun & Bradstreet (www.dnb.com), Experian (www.experian.com), Equifax (www.equifax.com), TransUnion (www.transunion.com), and KnowX (www.knowx.com) enable entrepreneurs to gather credit information on potential customers. For entrepreneurs who sell to other business, D & B offers many useful services, including a Small Business Risk New Account Score, a tool for evaluating the credit risk of new businesses. The National Association of Credit Management (http://www.nacm.org) is another important source of credit information because it collects information on many small businesses that other reporting services ignore. The cost to check a potential customer's credit at reporting services such as these ranges from $15 to $85, a small price to pay when a small business is considering selling thousands of dollars worth of goods or services to a new customer. Unfortunately, few small businesses take the time to conduct a credit check.

The next step involves establishing a firm written credit policy and letting every customer know in advance the company's credit terms. Industry practices often dictate credit terms, but a business does not have to abide by industry standards. A credit agreement must state clearly all of the terms the business will enforce if the account goes bad—including interest, late charges, attorney's fees, and others. Failure to specify these terms in the contract means they *cannot* be added later after problems arise. When will you invoice? How soon is payment due: immediately, after 30 days, after 60 days? (According to a survey by the National Federation of Independent Businesses (NFIB), the most common term for small companies selling on credit is "net 30"—payment is due within 30 days of receiving the invoice.[24]) Will you add a late charge? If so, how much? (The NFIB poll reports that 65 percent of small business owners do *not* add late fees or charge interest on overdue balances.[25]) To maximize its cash flow, a small company's credit policies should be as tight as possible and within federal and state credit laws. According to the American Collectors Association, if a business is writing off more than five percent of sales as bad debts, the owner should tighten its credit and collection policy.[26]

cycle billing
a method in which a company bills a portion of its credit customers each day of the month in order to smooth out uneven cash receipts.

The third step in an effective credit policy is to send invoices promptly because customers rarely pay *before* they receive their bills. The cornerstone of collecting accounts receivable on time is making sure you invoice your customers or send them their periodic billing statements promptly. "The sooner you mail your invoice, the sooner the check will be in the mail," says one entrepreneur. "In the manufacturing environment, get the invoice en route to the customer as soon as the shipment goes out the door," he advises. "Likewise, service industries with billable hours should keep track of hours daily or weekly and bill as often as the contract or agreement with the client permits."[27] Some businesses use **cycle billing,** in which a company bills a portion of its credit customers each day of the month, to smooth out uneven cash receipts.

Small business owners can take several steps to encourage prompt payment of invoices:

- Ensure that all invoices are clear, accurate, and timely.
- State clearly a description of the goods or services purchased and an account number.
- Make sure that the prices and the language on invoices agree with the price quotations on purchase orders or contracts.
- Highlight the balance due and the terms of sale (e.g., "net 30") on all invoices. A study by Xerox Corporation found that highlighting with color the balance due section of invoices increased the speed of collection by 30 percent.[28]
- Include a telephone number and a contact person in your organization in case the customer has a question or a dispute.

When an account becomes overdue, a small business owner must take *immediate* action. The longer an account is past due, the lower is the probability of collecting it. One of the most effective techniques is to have someone in the company who already has a relationship with the customer, perhaps a salesperson or a customer service representative, contact him or her about the past-due account. When contacting a delinquent customer, the goal is to get a commitment to pay the full amount of the bill by a specific date (*not* "soon" or "next week"). Following up the personal contact with an e-mail or a letter that summarizes the verbal commitment also helps. If the customer still refuses to pay the bill, collection experts recommend the following:

- Send a letter from the company's attorney.
- Turn the account over to a collection attorney.
- As a last resort, hire a collection agency. (The Commercial Law League of America (http://www.clla.org/) can provide a list of reputable agencies.)

Although collection agencies and attorneys typically take 25 to 30 percent of any accounts they collect, they are often worth the price. Collection agencies collect $40.4 billion annually for businesses.[29] According to the American Collectors Association, only five percent of accounts more than 90 days delinquent will be paid voluntarily. Business owners must be sure to abide by the provisions of the federal Fair Debt Collection Practices Act, which prohibits any kind of harassment when collecting debts (e.g., telephoning repeatedly, issuing threats of violence, telling third parties about the debt, or using abusive language). The primary rule when collecting past-due accounts is "*Never* lose your cool." Establishing a friendly but firm attitude that treats customers with respect is more likely to produce payment than hostile threats Table 12.5 describes ten collection blunders that small business owners typically make and how to avoid them.

security agreement
a contract in which a business selling an asset on credit gets a security interest in that asset (the collateral), protecting its legal rights in case the buyer fails to pay.

Another strategy that small companies, particularly those selling high-priced items, can use to protect the cash they have tied up in receivables is to couple a security agreement with a financing statement. This strategy falls under Article 9 of the Uniform Commercial Code (UCC), which governs a wide variety of business transactions, from the sale of goods to security interests. A **security agreement** is a contract in which a business selling an asset on credit gets a security interest in that asset (the collateral), protecting its legal rights in case the buyer fails to pay. To get the protection it seeks in the security agreement, the seller must file a financing statement called a UCC-1 form with the proper state or county office (a process the UCC calls "perfection"). The UCC-1 form gives notice to other creditors and to the general public that the seller holds a secured interest in the collateral named in the security agreement. The UCC-1 form must include the name, address, and signature of the

TABLE 12.5 Ten Collection Blunders and How to Avoid Them

Business owners often make mistakes when trying to collect the money their customers owe. Checking potential credit customers' credit records and creating a thorough sales contract that spells out exactly what happens if the account becomes past due can help minimize collection problems. Sooner or later, however, even the best system will encounter late payers. What happens then? Business owners should avoid these collection blunders.

Blunder 1: Delaying collection phone calls. Many entrepreneurs waste valuable time and resources sending four or five "past due" letters to delinquent customers, usually with limited effectiveness.

Instead: Once a bill becomes past due, call the customer within a week to verify that he received the bill and that it is accurate. Ask for payment.

Blunder 2: Failing to ask for payment in clear terms. To avoid angering a customer, some entrepreneurs ask meekly, "Do you think you could take care of this bill soon?"

Instead: Firmly, but professionally, ask for payment (the full amount) by a specific date.

Blunder 3: Sounding desperate. Some entrepreneurs show weakness by saying that they must have payment or they "can't meet payroll" or "can't pay bills." That gives the customer more leverage to negotiate additional discounts or time.

Instead: Ask for payment simply because the invoice is past due—without any other explanation. Don't apologize for your request; it's *your* money.

Blunder 4: Talking tough. Getting nasty with delinquent customers does not make them pay any faster and may be a violation of the Fair Debt Collections Practices Act.

Instead: Remain polite and professional when dealing with past-due customers, even if you think they don't deserve it. *Never* lose your temper. Don't ruin your reputation by being rude.

Blunder 5: Trying to find out the customer's problem. Some entrepreneurs think it is necessary to find out why a delinquent customer has not paid a bill.

Instead: Don't waste time playing private investigator. Focus on the "business at hand," collecting your money.

Blunder 6: Asking customers how much they can pay. When customers claim that they cannot pay the bill in full, inexperienced entrepreneurs ask, "Well, how much can you pay?" They don't realize that they have just turned control of the situation over to the delinquent customer.

Instead: Take charge of negotiations from the outset. Let the customer know that you expect full payment. If you cannot get full payment immediately, suggest a new deadline. Only as a last resort should you offer an extended payment plan.

Blunder 7: Continuing to talk after you get a promise to pay. Some entrepreneurs "blow the deal" by not knowing when to stop talking. They keep interrogating a customer after they have a promise to pay.

Instead: Wrap up the conversation as soon as you have a commitment. Summarize the agreement, thank the customer, and end the conversation on a positive note.

Blunder 8: Calling without being prepared. Some entrepreneurs call customers without knowing exactly which invoices are past due and what amounts are involved. The effort is usually fruitless.

Instead: Have all account details in front of you when you call and be specific in your requests.

Blunder 9: Trusting your memory. Some entrepreneurs think they can remember previous collection calls, conversations, and agreements.

Instead: Keep accurate records of all calls and conversations. Take notes about each customer contact and resulting agreements.

Blunder 10: Letting your computer control your collection efforts. Inexperienced entrepreneurs tend to think that their computers can manage debt collection for them.

Instead: Recognize that a computer is a valuable tool in collecting accounts but that you are in control. "Past due" notices from a computer may collect some accounts, but your efforts will produce more results. Getting to know the people who handle the invoices at your customers' businesses can be a major advantage when collecting accounts.

Sources: Adapted from "Tips for Collecting Cash," *FSB*, May 2002, p. 72; Janine Latus Musick, "Collecting Payments Due," *Nation's Business*, January 1999, pp. 44-46; Bob Weinstein, "Collect Calls," *Entrepreneur*, August 1995, pp. 66-69; Elaine Pofeldt, "Collect Calls," *Success*, March 1998, pp. 22-24.

buyer; a description of the collateral; and the name and address of the seller. If the buyer declares bankruptcy, the small business that sells the asset is not guaranteed payment, but the filing puts its claim to the asset ahead of those of unsecured creditors.

Suppose that Lanford Mechanical sells a piece of manufacturing machinery to Abbott Chemical Company for $64,000, accepting $12,000 in cash and retaining the $52,000 balance on account, payable over 24 months. As part of the sales contract (which also is governed by Article 2 of the UCC), Lanford gets Abbott to sign a security agreement, giving Lanford a security interest in the machine. If Lanford files the financing statement (the UCC-1 form) with the secretary of state for a small fee, it has perfected its security interest in the machine. If Abbott fails to pay the account balance in full, Lanford can repossess the machine and sell it to satisfy the remaining balance. If Abbott were to declare bankruptcy, Lanford is not guaranteed payment, but its filing puts its claim to the machinery ahead of those of unsecured creditors. Lanford's degree of safety on this large credit sale is much higher with a security agreement and a properly filed financing statement.

HANDS ON...
HOW TO

Control Your Company's Accounts Receivable

Dann Battina, CEO of Beltmann Group, a moving company in Roseville, Minnesota, was pleased that his business was on track to match the previous year's sales of $100 million because he knew that the economy was slowing. He also knew that to weather the coming economic storm his company would require a larger minimum cash balance. The problem he faced, however, involved Beltmann's average collection period ratio, which stood at 61 days. Just five percent of the company's customers paid on delivery, which meant that at any given time, approximately $16.7 million in cash was in Battina's customers' accounts rather than in his company's bank account. Battina frequently had to tap into Beltmann's line of credit to pay his vendors on time, usually within 30 days. "I knew it was time to figure out how to get our hands on more money before the situation became really extreme," he says.

With the help of a financial consultant, Battina began to examine his company's collection and payable procedures and its cash flow. To move customers' furnishings, Beltmann uses 300 independent contractors, who submit the job's details to one of the company's 13 nationwide branches. The analysis revealed that 40 percent of the documents were filled out or handled incorrectly, which lengthened the company's cash flow cycle. Battina also discovered that the documents followed a convoluted path inside the company, bouncing from one department to another, which meant that sending an invoice to a customer required 10 days. "It was embarrassing how severe the problem was," says Battina.

Bettina redesigned his company's billing and collection procedures and included a quality control checklist that the independent contractors must complete for each job. He also began tracking the time that each branch takes to send invoices. Already the changes have allowed Beltmann to reduce the time required to send invoices to six days, which freed up $1.1 million in cash.

Small businesses report that their customers, particularly large companies, are stretching their accounts payable longer, paying invoices more slowly now than they were just a few years ago. When faced with 30-day credit terms, it is not uncommon for large companies to delay their payments to 45 or even 60 days. The Small Business Network Monitor, a study of small businesses by American Express, confirms the challenge this presents for entrepreneurs. More than half of the small business owners surveyed say their companies experience cash flow problems, and their primary concern is collecting accounts receivable (Refer to Figure 12.5). The average small business incurs $1,500 in past due payments from its customers each month.

"If the money is coming in the front door at 100 miles per hour," explains Brian Hamilton, CEO of Sageworks, a financial consulting firm, "and going out the back door at 110 miles per hour, that's not a good thing. Businesses don't fail because they are unprofitable; they fail because they get crushed on the accounts receivable side." What steps can entrepreneurs take to avoid a cash crisis caused by accounts receivable that turn slowly? The following steps can help:

- *Evaluate your company's collection process.* How many people are involved in generating an invoice? (Fewer is better.) Where do bottlenecks in the billing process occur? (Setting a time limit on processing paperwork helps.) What percentage of your company's invoices are erroneous? (The higher the percentage of errors, the slower the company's collections will be.)
- *Increase your company's cash reserves.* Smart business owners keep at least three months' worth of expenses on hand so that they aren't caught cash-short if receivables slow down more than expected or if sales suddenly drop.
- *Boost your company's line of credit.* Business owners can increase their lines of credit with their banks, but the key is to do so *before* they need the money. Be prepared to use your company's financial statements to prove to your banker why you need – and deserve – an increased line of credit.
- *Monitor accounts receivable closely.* Some small business owners generate daily summaries of their company's accounts receivable, always on the lookout for disturbing trends. Doing so enables them to spot slow payers who might become non-payers unless the company takes immediate action.
- *Get to know the people responsible for paying invoices at your biggest customers' or clients' companies.* Collections are easier if you know the right person to call.

- *Take immediate action when an account becomes past due.* Resist the tendency to simply sit back and wait for the customer to pay. If a customer has not paid by the invoice due date, contact him or her immediately and ask for payment.
- *Watch for signs that customers may be about to declare bankruptcy.* When a customer declares bankruptcy, the probability that a company can collect the cash it is owed is miniscule. Terri Oyarzun, founder of Goats R Us, a company that owns a herd of goats that provide fire mitigation services by eating shrubs and brush that could fuel blazes, realized that when Lehman Brothers declared bankruptcy, she would never be able to collect the $53,000 the financial company owed her company. Oyarzun says that she had to postpone purchasing a new truck for the farm and hiring new goat herders.
- *Stick to your credit terms.* Define the credit terms with every client up front. If clients balk when it comes time for payment, remind them that they have a commitment to live up to the terms of the sales contract.
- *Raise prices to cover the extra cost of late payments.* If clients refuse to pay on time, determine how much their slower payments cost your company, and raise your rates or your prices enough to cover the cost.
- *Require customers to pay at least part of total price of a contract up front.* Because the jobs that one small film production company performs require the owner to incur some rather sizeable expenses before they are completed, the owner implemented a policy that requires customers to pay one-third of the cost up front, another one-third at mid-project, and the balance on completion.
- *Offer discounts to encourage early payment.* Cash discounts (such as "2/10, net 30," which means that you offer the client a two percent discount if he or she pays within 10 days; otherwise, the full invoice amount is due in 30 days) can reduce a small company's profit margin, but they also provide an incentive for clients to pay early. Remember: More companies fail for lack of cash than for lack of profit.

Source: Based on Shivani Vora, "Need Cash? Try Looking Inward," *Inc.*, May 2008, pp. 43-44; Amy Feldman, "The Cash-Flow Crunch," *Inc.*, December 2005, pp. 50-52; Michael Corkery and Alex Frangos, "Far Away from Wall Street, a Herd Gets Gored," *Wall Street Journal*, January 24-25, 2009, pp. A1, A12.

Accounts Payable

The second element of the "big three" of cash management is accounts payable. The timing of payables is just as crucial to proper cash management as the timing of receivables, but the objective is exactly the opposite. Entrepreneurs should strive to stretch out payables as long as possible *without damaging their companies' credit rating.* Otherwise, suppliers may begin demanding prepayment or cash-on-delivery (C.O.D.) terms, which severely impair a company's cash flow, or they may stop doing business with it altogether. When one computer manufacturer ran into cash flow problems, it deferred payments to its suppliers for as long as 100 days (compared to an industry average of about 40 days). Because of the company's slow payments, many suppliers simply stopped selling to the computer maker.[30] One cash management consultant says, "Some companies pay too early and wind up forgoing the interest they could have earned on their cash. Others pay too late and either wind up with late penalties or being forced to buy on a C.O.D. basis, which really kills them."[31] It is perfectly acceptable for small business owners to regulate payments to their companies' advantage. Efficient cash managers set up a payment calendar each month that allows them to pay their bills on time and to take advantage of cash discounts for early payment.

Nancy Dunis, CEO of Dunis & Associates, a Portland, Oregon, marketing firm, recognizes the importance of controlling accounts payable. "Our payables must be functioning just right to keep our cash flow running smoothly," says Dunis. She has set up a simple five-point accounts payable system:[32]

1. *Set scheduling goals.* Dunis strives to pay her company's bills 45 days after receiving them and to collect all her receivables within 30 days. Even though "it doesn't always work that way," her goal is to make the most of her cash flow.
2. *Keep paperwork organized.* Dunis dates every invoice she receives and carefully files it according to her payment plan. "This helps us remember when to cut the check" she says, and, "it helps us stagger our payments, over days or weeks," significantly improving the company's cash flow.
3. *Prioritize.* Dunis cannot stretch out all of her company's creditors for 45 days; some demand payment sooner. Those suppliers are at the top of the accounts payable list.

ENTREPRENEURIAL PROFILE

Nancy Dunis: Dunis & Associates

4. *Be consistent.* "Companies want consistent customers," says Dunis. "With a few exceptions," she explains, "most businesses will be happy to accept 45-day payments, so long as they know you'll always pay your full obligation at that point."

5. *Look for warning signs.* Dunis sees her accounts payable as an early warning system for cash flow problems. "The first indication I get that cash flow is in trouble is when I see I'm getting low on cash and could have trouble paying my bills according to my staggered filing system," she says. Other signs that a business is heading for cash flow problems include difficulty making principal and interest payments on loans and incurring penalties for late payment of routine bills.

Business owners should verify all invoices before paying them. Some unscrupulous vendors send out invoices for goods they never shipped or services they never rendered, knowing that many business owners will simply pay the bill without checking its authenticity. Two common scams aimed at small business owners involve bogus operators sending invoices for office supplies or ads in nonexistent printed or online "yellow pages" directories. To avoid falling victim to such scams, someone in the company–for instance, the accounts payable clerk–should have the responsibility of verifying *every* invoice received.

A clever cash manager also negotiates the best possible credit terms with his or her suppliers. Almost all vendors grant their customers trade credit, and small business owners should take advantage of it. However, because trade credit can be so easy to get, entrepreneurs must be careful not to overuse and abuse it, putting their businesses in a precarious financial position.

Favorable credit terms can make a tremendous difference in a company's cash flow. Table 12.6 shows the same most likely cash budget from Table 12.2 with one exception: instead of purchasing on cash-on-delivery (C.O.D.) terms as shown in Table 12.2, the owner has negotiated "net 30" payment terms (Table 12.6). Notice the drastic improvement in the company's cash flow that results from improved credit terms.

If owners do find themselves financially strapped when payment to a vendor is due, they should avoid making empty promises that "the check is in the mail." Instead, they should discuss the situation honestly with the vendor. Most vendors will work out payment terms for extended credit.

Small business owners also can improve their firms' cash flow by scheduling controllable cash disbursements so that they do not come due at the same time. For example, paying employees every two weeks (or every month) rather than every week reduces administrative costs and gives the business more time to use its cash. Owners of fledgling businesses may be able to conserve cash by hiring part-time employees or by using freelance workers rather than full-time, permanent workers. Scheduling insurance premiums monthly or quarterly rather than annually also can improve cash flow.

Wise use of business credit cards is another way to stretch the firm's cash balance. However, entrepreneurs should avoid cards that charge transaction fees. Credit cards differ in their interest-charging policies; many begin charging interest from the date of purchase, but some charge interest only from the invoice date. Increasingly, entrepreneurs are using low-interest credit cards to finance their business start-up costs. Although it is a risky practice (the low interest rates don't last forever), many entrepreneurs say that they cannot get startup financing any other way.

TABLE 12.6 Cash Budget - Most Likely Sales Forecast After Negotiating "Net 30" Trade Credit Terms

	Oct	Nov	Dec	Jan	Feb	Mar	Apr	May	Jun
Cash Receipts									
Sales	$ 300,000	$ 350,000	$ 400,000	$ 150,000	$ 200,000	$ 200,000	$ 300,000	$ 315,000	$ 320,000
Credit Sales	225,000	262,500	300,000	112,500	150,000	150,000	225,000	236,250	240,000
Collections									
60% - First month after sale				180,000	67,500	90,000	90,000	135,000	141,750
30% - Second month after sale				78,750	90,000	33,750	45,000	45,000	67,500
5% - Third month after sale				11,250	13,125	15,000	5,625	7,500	7,500
Cash Sales				37,500	50,000	50,000	75,000	78,750	80,000
Other cash receipts				25	35	50	60	60	65
Total Cash Receipts				307,525	220,660	188,800	215,685	266,310	296,815
Cash Disbursements									
Purchases*				105,000	140,000	140,000	210,000	185,000	190,000
Rent				3,000	3,000	3,000	3,000	3,000	3,000
Utilities				1,450	1,400	1,250	1,250	1,250	1,400
Bank Note				–	–	7,500	–	–	–
Tax Prepayment				–	–	18,000	–	–	–
Capital Additions				–	130,000	–	–	–	–
Wages and Salaries				30,000	38,000	40,000	42,000	44,000	44,000
Insurance				475	475	475	475	475	475
Advertising				1,600	1,600	1,500	2,000	2,000	2,200
Interest				–	–	–	249	–	–
Miscellaneous				500	500	500	550	550	550
Total Cash Disbursements				142,025	314,975	212,225	259,524	236,275	241,625
End-of-Month Balance									
Beginning cash balance				12,000	177,500	83,185	59,760	15,921	45,956
+ Cash receipts				307,525	220,660	188,800	215,685	266,310	296,815
- Cash disbursements				142,025	314,975	212,225	259,524	236,275	241,625
Cash (end-of-month)				177,500	83,185	59,760	15,921	45,956	101,146
Borrowing				–	–	–	–	–	–
Repayment				–	–	–	–	–	–
Final Cash Balance				$ 177,500	$ 83,185	$ 59,760	$ 15,921	$ 45,956	$ 101,146
Monthly Surplus/(Deficit)				165,500	(94,315)	(23,425)	(43,839)	30,035	55,190

*After negotiating "net 30" trade credit terms

Inventory

Inventory is a significant investment for many small businesses and can create a severe strain on cash flow. The typical grocery store now stocks more than 46,000 items, three times as many as it did 20 years ago, and many other types of businesses are following this pattern.[33] Offering customers a wider variety of products is one way a business can outshine its competitors, but product proliferation increases the need for tight inventory control to avoid a cash crisis. Although inventory represents the largest capital investment for most small businesses, few owners use any formal methods for managing it. As a result, the typical small business not only has too much inventory but also too much of the *wrong* kind of inventory! Because inventory is illiquid, it can quickly siphon off a company's pool of available cash. "Small companies need cash to grow," says one consultant. "They've got to be able to turn [cash] over quickly. That's difficult to do if a lot of money is tied up in excess inventory."[34]

Surplus inventory yields a zero rate of return and unnecessarily ties up a company's cash. "Carrying inventory is expensive," says one small business consultant. "A typical manufacturing company pays 25 percent to 30 percent of the value of the inventory for the cost of borrowed money, warehouse space, materials handling, staff, lift-truck expenses, and fixed costs. This shocks a lot of people. Once they realize it, they look at inventory differently."[35] Even though volume discounts lower inventory costs, large purchases may tie up the company's valuable cash. Wise business owners avoid overbuying inventory, recognizing that excess inventory ties up cash unproductively. In fact, only 20 percent of a typical business' inventory turns over quickly; therefore, owners must watch constantly for stale items.[36] If a small business must pay its suppliers within 30 days of receiving an inventory shipment and the merchandise sits on the shelf for another 30 to 60 days (or more!), the pressure on its cash flow intensifies. Increasing a company's inventory turnover ratio frees surprising amounts of cash. For instance, if a company with $2 million in annual sales that turns its inventory twice each year improves its inventory turnover ratio by just two weeks, it will improve its cash flow by nearly $18,900.

Carrying too little inventory is not the ideal solution to cash flow challenges because companies with excessive "stockouts" lose sales (and eventually customers if the problem persists). However, carrying too much inventory usually results in slow-moving inventory and a low inventory turnover ratio. Experienced business owners understand the importance of shedding slow-moving inventory during end-of-season sales, even if they must resort to markdowns. Businesses must be "proactive with their markdowns," says a retail merchandising expert. "Cash flow and [inventory] turnover are the name of the game."[37]

ENTREPRENEURIAL PROFILE

Channeled Resources

Recognizing the high cost of holding inventory, managers at Channeled Resources, a company that sells recycled paper and film products, give the sales force the power to sell slow-moving items at any price that is not below the company's cost. The company also lists slow-moving items on its Web site. "We just want to move the stuff and get cash for it," says one manager. "Even if they sell it at cost, it's better than letting it sit here."[38]

Carrying too much inventory increases the chances that a business will run out of cash. An entrepreneur's goal is to minimize the company's investment in inventory without sacrificing sales, selection, and customer satisfaction. "The cash that pays for goods is channeled into inventory," says one business writer, "where its flow is dead-ended until the inventory is sold and the cash is set free again. The cash flow trick is to commit just enough cash to inventory to meet demand."[39] Scheduling inventory deliveries at the latest possible date prevents premature payment of invoices. Finally, given goods of comparable quality and price, an entrepreneur should purchase goods from the fastest supplier to keep inventory levels as low as possible. All of these tactics require entrepreneurs to manage their supply chains carefully and to treat their suppliers as partners in their businesses. To keep inventory churning rapidly through a small business requires creating a nimble, adaptive supply chain that responds to a company's changing needs.

ENTREPRENEURIAL PROFILE

Zara

Zara, a chain of retail stores that sells inexpensive, stylish clothing to young fashion-conscious people, manages its supply chain so efficiently that its inventory turnover ratio is much higher than the industry average, which means that the company ties up less cash in inventory than its competition. Zara's fast-fashion approach also keeps customers coming back by keeping stores' inventory fresh, adding new items constantly at a rate that leaves most of its competitors in awe. In fact, Zara can take a garment from design to store shelf in just two to three weeks instead of the five to twelve months that most clothing retailers require. The company tracks the latest fashion trends and manufactures small runs of items, which allows it to avoid being stuck with large quantities of unpopular garments that it must mark down. Zara has created an irresistible image of scarcity that appeals to its faithful customers, who know that when they find something they like, they had better buy it, or it may be gone for good. The result is that Zara's stores, which are located in Europe and the United States, sell 85 percent of their inventory at full price, compared to the industry average of 50 percent to 70 percent. Another benefit is a minimal investment in inventory that ties up little cash but yields above average sales and profits.[40]

Business owners also should take advantage of quantity discounts and cash discounts that their suppliers offer. **Quantity discounts** give businesses a price break when they order large quantities of merchandise and supplies and exist in two forms: non-cumulative and cumulative. Non-cumulative quantity discounts are granted only if a certain volume of merchandise is purchased in a single order. For example, a wholesaler may offer small retailers a 3 percent discount only if they purchase 10 gross of Halloween masks in a single order. Cumulative quantity discounts are offered if a firm's purchases from a particular vendor exceed a specified quantity or dollar value over a predetermined time period. The time frame varies, but a yearly basis is most common. For example, a manufacturer of appliances may offer a small business a 3 percent discount on subsequent orders if its purchases exceed $10,000 per year.

Cash discounts are offered to customers as an incentive to pay for merchandise promptly. Many vendors grant cash discounts to avoid being used as an interest-free bank by customers who purchase merchandise and then fail to pay by the invoice due date. To encourage prompt payment of invoices, many vendors allow customers to deduct a percentage of the purchase amount if payment is remitted within a specified time. Cash discount terms "2/10, net 30" are common in many industries. This notation means that the total amount of the invoice is due 30 days after its date, but if the bill is paid within 10 days, the buyer may deduct 2 percent from the total. A discount offering "2/10, EOM" (EOM means "end of month") indicates that the buyer may deduct 2 percent if the bill is paid by the tenth of the month after purchase.

In general, it is sound business practice to take advantage of cash discounts because a company incurs an implicit (opportunity) cost by forgoing a cash discount. By failing to take advantage of a cash discount, a business owner is, in effect, paying an annual interest rate to retain the use of the discounted amount for the remainder of the credit period. For example, suppose the Print Shop receives an invoice for $1,000 from a vendor offering a cash discount of 2/10, net 30. Figure 12.6 illustrates this situation and shows how to compute the cost of forgoing the cash discount. Notice that the cost of forgoing this cash discount is 37.25%. Table 12.7 summarizes the cost of forgoing cash discounts with different terms.

Monitoring the big three of cash management can help every business owner avoid a cash crisis while making the best use of available cash. According to one expert, maximizing cash flow involves "getting money from customers sooner; paying bills at the last moment

quantity discounts

discounts that give businesses a price break when they order large quantities of merchandise and supplies. They exist in two forms: non-cumulative and cumulative.

cash discounts

discounts offered to customers as an incentive to pay for merchandise promptly.

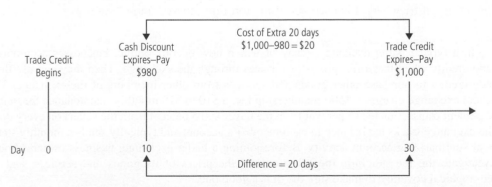

FIGURE 12.6

A Cash Discount

Annual Cost of Foregoing a 2/10, net 30 Cash Discount:

Rate = Interest/Principle × Time

$$\text{Rate} = \frac{\$20}{\$980 \times 20 \text{ days/365 days}}$$

Rate = 37.25%

TABLE 12.7 Cost of Forgoing Cash Discounts

Cash Discount Terms	Cost of Forgoing the Cash Discount (Annually)
2/10, net 30	37.25%
2/10, net 40	24.83%
3/10, net 30	56.44%
3/10, net 40	37.63%

possible; consolidating money in a single bank account; managing accounts payable, accounts receivable, and inventory more effectively; and squeezing every penny out of your daily business."[41]

LO 4

Explain the techniques for avoiding a cash crunch in a small company.

Avoiding the Cash Crunch

Nearly every small business has the potential to improve its cash position with little or no investment. The key is to make an objective evaluation of the company's financial policies, searching for inefficiency in its cash flow. Young firms cannot afford to waste resources, especially one as vital as cash. By utilizing the following techniques, entrepreneurs can get maximum benefit from their companies' pool of available cash.

Barter

bartering

the exchange of goods and services for other goods and services rather than for cash.

Bartering, the exchange of goods and services for other goods and services rather than for cash, is an effective way to conserve cash. An ancient concept, bartering has regained popularity in recent years. Today more than 500 barter exchanges operate across the United States, and they cater primarily to small- and medium-sized businesses looking to conserve cash. More than 350,000 companies—most of them small—engage in more than $4.4 billion worth of barter each year.[42] Every day, entrepreneurs across the nation use bartering to buy much needed materials, services, equipment, and supplies—*without* using precious cash.

ENTREPRENEURIAL PROFILE

Paul Fitzsimmons: Print Now

Paul Fitzsimmons, owner of Print Now, a small printing company in Pensacola, Florida, is a member of Gulf Coast Trade Exchange, a barter exchange through which he actively trades printing work for a variety of products and services his business needs. Fitzsimmons regularly uses printing work to barter for Print Now's routine operating expenses as well as repair work and renovations. In addition to conserving precious cash, bartering also attracts new customers for the company, which has $1 million in annual sales. Fitzsimmons estimates that six percent of his company's sales come from customers that he met through the barter exchange. "I probably would never have had [these additional sales] if they hadn't known about me through the exchange," he says.[43]

In a typical barter exchange, many of which now operate online, businesses accumulate trade credits when they offer goods or services through the exchange. Then they can use their trade credits to purchase other goods and services from other members of the exchange. The typical exchange charges a $500 membership fee, a $10 to $15 monthly maintenance fee, and a 10 percent transaction fee (5 percent from the buyer and 5 percent from the seller) on every deal. The exchange tracks the balance in each member's account and typically sends a monthly statement summarizing account activity. Before joining a barter exchange, business owners should investigate the fee structure, the selection and the prices of its goods and services, and its geographical coverage to make sure the fit is a good one.

Trim Overhead Costs

High overhead expenses can strain a small firm's cash supply to the breaking point; simple cost-cutting measures can save big money. Frugal small business owners can trim their overhead in a number of ways.

Ask for discounts and "freebies." Another way entrepreneurs can conserve cash is to negotiate discounts on the purchases they make and to make the use of free services whenever possible. For instance, rather than pay a high-priced consultant to assist him with his business plan, one entrepreneur opted instead to use the free services of his local Small Business Development Center (SBDC). The move not only improved the quality of his business plan, which enabled him to get the financing he needed to launch his business, but it also conserved valuable cash for the startup.

ENTREPRENEURIAL PROFILE _____

Sid Jaridly: The Original Mr. Cabinet Care

Sid Jaridly, CEO of the Original Mr. Cabinet Care, a kitchen remodeling business in Anaheim, California, saw his company's profit margins being squeezed from an industry downturn and approached his top 50 vendors and asked for price reductions of 10 to 15 percent. Nearly 30 of his suppliers agreed to his request for price concessions, a move that saved his company almost $500,000 in just one year![44]

Periodically evaluate expenses. Business owners not only should attempt to keep their operating costs low, but they also should evaluate them periodically to make sure they have not gotten out of line. Comparing current expenses with past levels is helpful and so is comparing a company's expenses against industry standards. Useful resources for determining typical expenses in an industry include RMA's *Annual Statement Studies*, Dun & Bradstreet's *Industry Norms and Key Business Ratios*, and Prentice *Hall's Almanac of Business and Industrial Financial Ratios*.

When practical, lease instead of buy. By leasing automobiles, computers, office equipment, machinery, and many other types of assets rather than buying them, an entrepreneur can conserve valuable cash. The value of these assets is not in *owning* them but in *using* them. Businesses can lease practically any kind of equipment—from office furniture and computers to construction equipment and manufacturing machinery. Leasing is a popular cash management strategy; according to a recent survey by the Equipment Leasing Association, eight out of ten companies lease some or all of their equipment.[45] "These companies are long on ideas, short on capital, and in need of flexibility as they grow and change," says Suzanne Jackson of the Equipment Leasing Association of America. "They lease for efficiency and convenience."[46] For instance, to minimize its investment in technology that requires frequent updates, Forever 21, a clothing store that targets young people, leases the point-of-sale system that helps drive its fast-turning inventory strategy.[47]

Although total lease payments typically are greater than those for a conventional loan, most leases offer 100 percent financing, which means that the owner avoids the large capital outlays required as down payments on most loans. (Sometimes a lease requires the first and last months' payments to be made up front.) Furthermore, leasing is an "off-the-balance-sheet" method of financing and requires no collateral. The equipment a company leases does not have to be depreciated because the small business does not actually own it. A lease is considered an operating expense on the income statement, not a liability on the balance sheet. Thus, leasing conserves a company's borrowing capacity. Because lease payments are fixed amounts paid over a particular time period, leasing allows business owners to forecast more accurately their cash flows. Lease agreements also are flexible. Leasing companies typically offer a variety of terms and allow businesses to stretch payments over a longer time period than those of a conventional loan. "There are so many ways to tailor a lease agreement to a company's individual equipment and financial needs that you might call it a personalized rental agreement," says the owner of a small construction firm.[48]

Avoid nonessential outlays. By forgoing costly ego indulgences like ostentatious office equipment, first-class travel, and flashy company cars, entrepreneurs can make the most efficient use of a company's cash. Before putting scarce cash into an asset, every business owner should put the decision to the acid test: "What will this purchase add to my company's ability to compete and to become more successful?" Making across-the-board spending cuts to conserve cash is dangerous, however, because the owner runs the risk of cutting expenditures that literally drive the business. One common mistake during business slowdowns is cutting marketing and advertising expenditures. Economic slowdowns present a prime opportunity for smart business owners to bring increased attention to their products and services and to gain market share if they hold the line on their marketing and advertising budgets as their competitors cut back. The secret to successful cost-saving is cutting *nonessential* expenditures. "If the lifeblood of your company is marketing, cut it less," advises one advertising executive. "If it is customer service, that is the last thing you want to cut back on. Cut from areas that are not essential to business growth."[49]

When rising costs began straining their company's cash flow and cutting into its profit margins, Mike Weinstein and Brian O'Byrne, co-founders of Hydrive Energy LLC, a small company that makes energy drinks, began looking for ways to cut operating costs. Prices for the company's raw materials, including the plastic bottles that Hydrive Energy uses, increased by 20 percent in just one year. To offset the impact of those increases, the company cut its travel budget and began conducting some of its market research in-house. Using online survey tools such as Survey Monkey kept employees in touch with their customers and saved the company $12,000 in one year.[50]

Negotiate fixed loan payments to coincide with your company's cash flow cycle. Many banks allow businesses to structure loans so that they can skip specific payments when their cash flow ebbs to its lowest point. Negotiating such terms gives businesses the opportunity to customize their loan repayments to their cash flow cycles.

For example, Ted Zoli, president of Torrington Industries, a construction-materials supplier and contracting business, consistently uses "skipped payment loans" in his highly seasonal business. "Every time we buy a piece of construction machinery," he says, "we set it up so that we're making payments for eight or nine months, and then skipping three or four months during the winter."[51]

Buy used or reconditioned equipment, especially if it is "behind-the-scenes" machinery. One restaurateur saved thousands of dollars in the start-up phase of his business by buying used equipment from a restaurant equipment broker.

Hire part-time employees and freelance specialists whenever possible. Hiring part-time workers and freelancers rather than full-time employees saves on the cost of both salaries and benefits.

Outsource. One way that many entrepreneurs conserve valuable cash is to outsource certain activities to businesses that specialize in performing them rather than hiring someone to do them in-house (or doing the activities themselves). In addition to saving cash, outsourcing enables entrepreneurs to focus on the most important aspects of running their businesses. "Stick to what you are good at and outsource everything else," advises one entrepreneur.[52]

Tessa Luu was operating Inside Avenue, a successful furniture showroom that featured luxury home furnishings and accessories with a contemporary flair, but was concerned because her business's operating costs increased each year. Five years after she started the business, Luu decided to move it online and outsource almost all of its operations. Finding the right contractors to handle the work took six months and some trial-and-error, but Luu was able to cut the company's operating expenses by 75 percent. "I would be bankrupt now had I not changed my [business] model," she says. Although Inside Avenue's headquarters is in Oak Park, California, Luu's contractors are spread across the map. Programming for the company's Web site takes place in Wisconsin, customer service is housed in Iowa, data entry is done in the Philippines, and orders are filled and shipped from North Carolina. "I used to have to pay salaries, insurance, and worker's compensation, even when there was no work, but now I pay only when there is a project," says Luu.[53]

Control employee advances and loans. An entrepreneur should grant only those advances and loans that are necessary and should keep accurate records on payments and balances.

Establish an internal security and control system. Too many owners encourage employee theft by failing to establish a system of controls. Reconciling the bank statement monthly and requiring special approval for checks over a specific amount, say $1,000, will help to minimize losses. Separating recordkeeping and check-writing responsibilities, rather than assigning them to a single employee, offers more protection.

Develop a system to battle check fraud. Bad checks and check fraud can wreak havoc on a small company's cash flow. On a typical day in the United States, consumers and businesses write two million checks that will be returned because of insufficient funds, a closed account, or some other problem. On average, customers write an estimated 2 million checks each day that "bounce," and nearly 1.4 million checks are forged. About 70 percent of all "bounced" checks occur because nine out of ten customers fail to keep their checkbooks balanced; the remaining 30 percent of bad checks are the result of fraud.[54] Simple techniques for minimizing losses from bad checks include requesting proper identification (preferably with a photograph) from customers, recording customers' telephone numbers, and training cashiers to watch for forged or counterfeit checks. Perhaps the most effective way to battle bad checks is to subscribe to an electronic check approval service. The service works at the cash register, and approval takes only a minute or less. The fee a small business pays to use the service depends on the volume of checks. For most small companies, charges amount to one to two percent of the cleared checks' value.

Change your shipping terms. Changing a company's shipping terms from "F.O.B (free on board) buyer," in which the *seller* pays the cost of freight, to "F.O.B seller," in which the *buyer* absorbs all shipping costs, improves its cash flow.

Start Selling Gift Cards

Prepaid gift cards can be a real boost to a small company's cash flow. Customers pay for the cards up front, but the typical recipient does not redeem the gift card until later, sometimes much later, giving the company the use of the cash during that time. Selling gift cards also can increase a company's revenue because studies show that the typical card recipient spends an average of $29 over the value of the card.[55]

Colleen Stone, owner of Inspa Corporation, a fast-growing Seattle, Washington–based chain of day spas, uses gift cards to stretch her company's cash flow. Gift cards account for 25 percent of her company's sales, and Stone has discovered that many of the gift cards she sells are not redeemed for a year, giving her a source of interest-free cash in the interim. "We plow all that cash flow right back into opening new stores," says Stone.[56]

Switch to Zero-Based Budgeting

Zero-based budgeting (ZBB) primarily is a shift in the philosophy of budgeting. Rather than build the current year budget on *increases* from the previous year's budget, ZBB starts from a budget of zero and evaluates the necessity of every item. "Start with zero and review all expenses, asking yourself whether each one is necessary," says one business consultant.[57]

Be on the Lookout for Shoplifting and Employee Theft

Companies lose billions of dollars each year to shoplifting and employee theft. Shoplifting is the most common business crime, costing retailers an estimated $13.5 billion each year.[58] Shoplifting takes an especially heavy toll on small businesses because they usually have the weakest lines of defense against shoplifters. If a shoplifter steals just one item that sells for $100 from a small business with a 8 percent net profit margin, the company must sell an additional $1,250 worth of goods to make up for the loss.

Even though shoplifting occurs more frequently than employee theft, businesses lose more money each year to employee theft. Experts estimate that employee theft cost small

YOU Be the CONSULTANT

The Trusted Employee

Dr. Thomas Brunner, a dentist in Fort Wayne, Indiana, was surprised to learn that Cindy Allen, the woman whom he had trusted to manage his dental office for several years, had been stealing from him. The theft involved far more than just some office supplies and money for lunch from petty cash. Allen had used the company's credit cards to make personal purchases, including clothing, music, food, and dog treats, that totaled more than $130,000. She also used the credit cards to withdraw more than $51,000 in cash advances, which she used to support a lavish lifestyle. When Brunner called to cancel his company's accounts, he learned that the same card carried a $38,000 balance and that Allen had been charging purchases on another credit card, which had a $24,000 balance. Brunner says that although his practice's accounting records for the last four years are missing, he estimates that his highly competent and highly trusted office manager stole nearly $268,000.

The owner of an interior design company and her bookkeeper had worked together for five years. More like sisters than co-workers, they shared a close friendship, often socializing together and meeting outside of work so that their children could play together. The entrepreneur was in the office one weekend when she noticed a bank statement, something she always delegated to her bookkeeping friend, lying open on her friend's desk. She picked it up and noticed a large check that she did not remember signing. (The bookkeeper always wrote the company's checks and then presented them to the owner to sign.) She searched through stacks of canceled checks but could not find the suspicious check. Later, the bank supplied a copy of the check, complete with her perfectly forged signature. She was devastated that her longtime friend had been stealing from her. "Many times I have [business owners] in my office crying because it was their trusted bookkeeper," says Isabel Cumming, an attorney who leads a state white-collar crime division.

Because small businesses often lack the control procedures that large companies impose, they are more likely to be victims of employee theft. One workplace crime prevention expert says that small companies are common targets of employee theft because employees "know their systems, controls, and weaknesses, and can bide their time waiting for the right opportunity." A survey by Auditors Inc. reports that 40 percent of small companies are victims of employee theft or embezzlement but only two percent of victimized small companies report the crimes. The median theft at small businesses is $98,000, an amount significant enough to threaten the existence of the businesses themselves.

One accountant says that in most cases the perpetrator is the person one would least expect, "the long-term, very trusted, very valued employee who never committed fraud before," says one accountant. A recent study of employee theft by PriceWaterhouseCoopers reveals that 85 percent of thieves are male, 44 percent are between the ages of 31 and 40, and 38 percent have at least a bachelor's degree. Approximately 25 percent of all employee theft is discovered by accident, and a tip from another employee reveals another 39 percent of thefts.

1. Identify the factors that led these companies to become victims of employee theft and embezzlement. What impact does this crime have on a company's cash flow?
2. Use the resources of the Web to develop a list of steps that entrepreneurs should take to prevent their businesses from becoming victims of employee theft and embezzlement.

Source: Adapted from Sarah E. Needleman, "Businesses Say Employee Theft Is Up," *Wall Street Journal*, December 11, 2008, http://online.wsj.com/article/SB122896381748896999.html; John Grossmann, "A Thief Within," *Inc.*, May 2003, pp. 42—44; Kathleen Johnston Jarboe, "Employee Theft at Small Business High and Hard to Detect," *The Daily Record*, October 14, 2005, http://findarticles.com/p/articles/mi_qn4183/is_20051014/ai_n15712876; Rebecca S. Green, "Dentist Sues Over Theft by Employee," *The Journal Gazette*, December 23, 2008, http://www.journalgazette.net/apps/pbcs.dll/article?AID=/20081223/LOCAL03/812230379/1002/LOCAL.

businesses more than $40 billion a year and that as much as 75 percent of all employee theft goes unnoticed![59] Because small business owners often rely on informal procedures for managing cash (or no procedures at all) and often lack proper control procedures, they are most likely to become victims of employee theft, embezzlement, and fraud by their employees. Although any business can be a victim of employee theft, retailers are particularly vulnerable. Retailers lose 1.4 percent of the value of their sales to employee theft and shoplifting each year.[60] One source of the problem is the entrepreneur's attitude that "we're all family here; no one would steal from family." Although establishing a totalitarian police state and trusting no one is not conducive to a positive work environment, putting in place adequate financial control systems is essential. Separating key cash management duties—such as writing checks, handling bank statements, and conducting regular financial audits—among at least two employees can be an effective deterrent to employee theft.

Keep Your Business Plan Current

Before approaching any potential lender or investor, a business owner must prepare a solid business plan. Smart owners keep their plans up to date in case an unexpected cash crisis forces them

Getty Images, Inc.-Stockbyte Royalty Free.

Employee theft cost small businesses more than $40 billion per year.

to seek emergency financing. Revising the plan annually also forces the owner to focus on managing the business more effectively.

Invest Surplus Cash

Because of the uneven flow of receipts and disbursements, a company will often temporarily have more cash than it needs—for a week, month, quarter, or even longer. When this happens, most small business owners simply ignore the surplus because they are not sure how soon they will need it. They believe that relatively small amounts of cash sitting around for just a few days or weeks are not worth investing. However, this is not the case. Small business owners who put surplus cash to work *immediately* rather than allowing it to sit idle soon discover that the yield adds up to a significant amount over time. This money can help ease the daily cash crunch during business troughs. "Your goal... should be to identify every dollar you don't need to pay today's bills and to keep that money invested to improve your cash flow," explains a consultant.[61]

However, when investing surplus cash, an entrepreneur's primary objective should *not* be to earn the highest yield (which usually carries with it high levels of risk); instead, the focus should be on the safety and the liquidity of the investments. Making high-risk investments with a company's cash cushion makes no sense and could jeopardize its future. The need to minimize risk and to have ready access to the cash restricts an entrepreneur's investment options to just a few such as money market accounts, zero balance accounts, and sweep accounts. A **money market account** is an interest-bearing account offered by a variety of financial institutions ranging from banks to mutual funds. Money market accounts pay interest while allowing depositors to write checks (most have minimum check amounts) without tying their money up for a specific period of time. After surviving a cash crisis shortly after launching their branding and communications company, Jaye Donaldson and her partner Chester Makoski now keep enough cash invested in a money market account to cover at least three to six months' of expenses.[62]

A **zero balance account** is a checking account that technically never has any funds in it but is tied to a master account. The company keeps its money in the master account where it earns interest, but it writes checks on the ZBA. At the end of the day, the bank pays all of the checks drawn on the ZBA; then it withdraws enough money from the master account to cover them. ZBAs allow a company to keep more cash working during the float period, the time between a check being issued and its being cashed. A **sweep account**

money market account
an interest-bearing account that allows depositors to write checks without tying up their money for a specific period of time.

zero balance account (ZBA)
a checking account that never has any funds in it. A company keeps its money in an interest-bearing master account tied to the ZBA; when a check is drawn on the ZBA, the bank withdraws enough money from the master account to cover it.

sweep account
a checking account that automatically sweeps all funds in a company's checking account above a predetermined minimum into an interest-bearing account.

automatically "sweeps" all funds in a company's checking account above a predetermined minimum into an interest-bearing account, enabling it to keep otherwise idle cash invested until it is needed to cover checks.

Conclusion

Successful owners run their businesses "lean and mean." Trimming wasteful expenditures, investing surplus funds, and carefully planning and managing the company's cash flow enable them to compete effectively. The simple but effective techniques covered in this chapter can improve every small company's cash position. One business writer says, "In the day-to-day course of running a company, other people's capital flows past an imaginative CEO as opportunity. By looking forward and keeping an analytical eye on your cash account as events unfold (remembering that if there's no real cash there when you need it, you're history), you can generate leverage as surely as if that capital were yours to keep."[63]

Chapter Summary

1. **Explain the importance of cash management to a small company's success.**

   - Cash is the most important but least productive asset the small business has. The manager must maintain enough cash to meet the firm's normal requirements (plus a reserve for emergencies) without retaining excessively large, unproductive cash balances.
   - Without adequate cash, a small business will fail.

2. **Differentiate between cash and profits.**

   - Cash and profits are *not* the same. More businesses fail for lack of cash than for lack of profits.
   - Profits, the difference between total revenue and total expenses, are an accounting concept. Cash flow represents the flow of actual cash (the only thing businesses can use to pay bills) through a business in a continuous cycle. A business can be earning a profit and be forced out of business because it runs out of cash.

3. **Understand the five steps in creating a cash budget and use them to create a cash budget.**

   - The cash budgeting procedure outlined in this chapter tracks the flow of cash through the business and enables the owner to project cash surpluses and cash deficits at specific intervals.
   - The five steps in creating a cash budget are as follows: determining a minimum cash balance, forecasting sales, forecasting cash receipts, forecasting cash disbursements, and determining the end-of-month cash balance.

4. **Describe fundamental principles involved in managing the "big three" of cash management: accounts receivable, accounts payable, and inventory.**

   - Controlling accounts receivable requires business owners to establish clear, firm credit and collection policies and to screen customers *before* granting them credit. Sending invoices promptly and acting on past-due accounts quickly also improve cash flow. The goal is to collect cash from receivables as quickly as possible.
   - When managing accounts payable, a manager's goal is to stretch out payables as long a possible without damaging the company's credit rating. Other techniques include: verifying invoices before paying them, taking advantage of cash discounts, and negotiating the best possible credit terms.
   - Inventory frequently causes cash headaches for small business managers. Excess inventory earns a zero rate of return and ties up a company's cash unnecessarily. Owners must watch for stale merchandise.

5. **Explain the techniques for avoiding a cash crunch in a small company.**

   - Trimming overhead costs by bartering, leasing assets, avoiding nonessential outlays, using zero-based budgeting, and implementing an internal control system boost a firm's cash flow position.
   - In addition, investing surplus cash maximizes the firm's earning power. The primary criteria for investing surplus cash are security and liquidity.

Discussion Questions

1. Why must entrepreneurs concentrate on effective cash flow management?
2. Explain the difference between cash and profit.
3. Outline the steps involved in developing a cash budget.
4. How can an entrepreneur launching a new business forecast sales?
5. What are the "big three" of cash management? What effect do they have on a company's cash flow?
6. Outline the basic principles of managing a small firm's receivables, payables, and inventory.
7. How can bartering improve a company's cash position?
8. What steps can entrepreneurs take to conserve the cash within their companies?
9. What should be a small business owner's primary concern when investing surplus cash?

Business PlanPro™

In addition to being a valuable planning tool, the cash flow statement can assess the future health and potential of your venture. As the chapter states, cash and profit are not the same. There are aspects of cash flow that are nonintuitive, and the cash flow statement provides a realistic view of the availability of cash for the business.

Business Plan Exercises

Review the cash flow statement that is in your plan, determine what you can learn from that statement, and assess the financial health of your plan based on the current information.

On the Web

Go to http://http://www.pearsonhighered.com/scarborough and look at the links associated with Chapter 12. These online resources offer additional information regarding the cash flow statement and the role it will play in your business plan.

Sample Plans

Review one or more of the sample plans to get a sense of how the cash flow statement predicts the availability of cash. Find the lowest point of cash flow. This is the point where cash is limited.

In the Software

Review the sales forecast and the expense information. Change any figures that look unrealistic. Review the proforma profit and loss statement. How do you feel about the status of those statements? Now, go to the Financial Statement section and look at your Projected Cash Flow Statement. Do any of these months show a negative cash flow? If this is the case, your projections indicate you do not have an adequate cash cushion. The lowest amount indicates the minimal amount of additional cash your business needs. Make sure that your projections are realistic and that you have adequate cash to make it through this negative period by bringing in additional cash. Advanced planning is your best opportunity to avoid bankruptcy. Conversely, if there are months where your projections indicate an excess amount of cash, explore options to use this cash to its best ability when that time comes.

Save the changes you have made in your plan. Assume this version of your plan represents your "most likely" outcome based on realistic expense and revenue projections. We are now going to do two "what-if" scenarios. For example, save this same file with the words "worst case" after the file name, or use a file name that will enable you to save all your work from before and create another version of your business plan. This will enable you to make changes in your plan, and assess what that does to your cash flow. Reduce revenues by 25 percent. What does that do to you cash flow? Now, increase expenses by 25 percent. What impact does that have regarding the amount of cash you will need to get through the lowest cash flow months? If you are extending credit for 30 days, increase that to 45 days. What does your cash flow statement look like now? Make pessimistic changes to paint a negative picture and save the plan under the "worst case" file name. Save and close that plan. Next, open your original so we can start with your "most likely" scenario again. Save your original under a "best case" file name. If you are planning to extend credit, decrease the number of collection days by seven. What does that do to your cash flow? Increase your revenues by 15 percent. Decrease your projected expenses by 15 percent. Working through these scenarios can help you to test and validate your numbers and prepare your for contingencies and options as your plan becomes a reality.

Building Your Business Plan

Review the data that affect your cash flow statement. Are there revisions you need to make based on your pro forma cash flow statement? What are some of the most significant cash demands of your business? Is excessive cash tied up in inventory? Do payroll expenses demand substantial amounts of cash? Are rent or lease expenditures disproportionately high based on your projected revenues? Can you take steps to reduce or better control these expenditures as you build your revenue stream? Once you have answered these questions, determine whether you have adequate cash for your venture, allowing for potential cost overruns or revenues below your projections.

Beyond the Classroom...

1. Interview several local small business owners about their cash management policies. Do they know how much cash their businesses have during the month? How do they track their cash flows? Do they use some type of cash budget? If not, ask if you can help the owner develop one. Does the owner invest surplus cash? If so, where?

2. Volunteer to help a small business owner develop a cash budget for his or her company. What patterns do you detect? What recommendations can you make for improving the company's cash management system?

3. Contact the International Reciprocal Trade Association (http://www.irta.net/) and get a list of the barter exchanges in your state. Interview the manager of one of the exchanges and prepare a report on how barter exchanges work and how they benefit small businesses. Ask the manager to refer you to a small business owner who benefits from the barter exchange and interview him or her. How does the owner use the exchange? How much cash has bartering saved? What other benefits has the owner discovered?

4. Use the resources of the Web to research leasing options for small companies. The Equipment Leasing and Financing Association of America (http://www.elfaonline .org/) is a good place to start. What advantages does leasing offer? Disadvantages? Identify and explain the various types of leases.

5. Contact a local small business owner who sells on credit. Is collecting accounts receivable on time a problem? What steps does the owner take to manage the company's accounts receivable? Do late payers strain the company's cash flow? How does the owner deal with customers who pay late?

6. Conduct an online search for the National Retail Security Survey that the University of Florida Department of Criminology, Law, and Society conducts annually. Summarize the key findings of the survey concerning losses that businesses incur from shoplifting, employee theft, and fraud. What steps can small businesses take to minimize their losses to these problems?

Graphic Mechanic Design Studio

CHAPTER 13

Sources of Financing: Debt and Equity

Get the facts straight. Don't lie. Leave nothing out. Take the money as soon as it is offered.
—*Venture capital legend Eugene Kleiner's four rules for entrepreneurs raising money*

If you don't know who the fool is in a deal, it's you.
—*Michael Wolff*

Learning Objectives

On completion of this chapter, you will be able to:

1. Explain the importance of planning for a company's capital requirements.

2. Describe the differences between equity capital and debt capital and the advantages and disadvantages of each.

3. Discuss the various sources of equity capital available to entrepreneurs, including personal savings, friends and relatives, angels, partners, corporations, venture capital, public stock offerings, and simplified registrations and exemptions.

4. Describe the process of "going public," as well as its advantages and disadvantages and the various simplified registrations and exemptions from registration available to small businesses wanting to sell securities to investors.

5. Describe the various sources of debt capital and the advantages and disadvantages of each: banks, asset-based

lenders, vendors (trade credit), equipment suppliers, commercial finance companies, savings and loan associations, stock brokers, insurance companies, credit unions, bonds, private placements, Small Business Investment Companies (SBICs), and Small Business Lending Companies (SBLCs).

6. Identify the various federal loan programs aimed at small businesses.

7. Describe the various loan programs available from the Small Business Administration.

8. Explain the state and local economic development programs available to entrepreneurs.

9. Discuss valuable methods of financing growth and expansion internally.

Capital is a crucial element in the process of creating new ventures. Yet, raising the money to launch a new business venture has always been a challenge for entrepreneurs. Capital markets rise and fall with the stock market, overall economic conditions, and investors' fortunes. These swells and troughs in the availability of capital make the search for financing look like a wild roller coaster ride. Most entrepreneurs, especially those in less glamorous industries or those just starting out, face difficulty finding outside sources of financing. Many banks shy away from making loans to start-ups, and venture capitalists have become more risk averse, shifting their investments away from start-up companies to more established businesses. Private investors have grown cautious, and making a public stock offering remains a viable option for only a handful of promising companies with good track records and fast-growth futures. The result has been a credit crunch for entrepreneurs looking for small to moderate amounts of start-up capital. Entrepreneurs and business owners who need between $100,000 and $3 million are especially hard-hit because of the vacuum that exists at that level of financing.

In the face of this capital crunch, business's need for capital has never been greater. Lenders and investors pump hundreds of millions of dollars into small businesses every year; yet, entrepreneurs are left clamoring for more capital. In a recent survey by Capital One, 56 percent of small business owners say that their companies' growth rates would be higher if they had more capital.[1] When searching for the capital to launch their companies, entrepreneurs must remember the following "secrets" to successful financing:

- *Choosing the right sources of capital for a business can be just as important as choosing the right form of ownership or the right location.* It is a decision that will influence a company for a lifetime, so entrepreneurs must weigh their options carefully before committing to a particular funding source. "It is important that companies in need of capital align themselves with sources that best fit their needs," says one financial consultant. "The success of a company often depends on the success of that relationship."[2]
- *The money is out there; the key is knowing where to look.* Entrepreneurs must do their homework *before* they set out to raise money for their ventures. Understanding which sources of funding are best-suited for the various stages of a company's growth and then taking the time to learn how those sources work is essential to success.
- *Raising money takes time and effort.* Sometimes entrepreneurs are surprised at the energy and the time required to raise the capital needed to feed their cash-hungry, growing businesses. The process usually includes lots of promising leads, most of which turn out to be dead-ends. Meetings with and presentations to lots of potential investors and lenders can crowd out the time required to manage a growing company. Entrepreneurs also discover that raising capital is an ongoing job. "The fund-raising game is a marathon, not a sprint," says Jerusha Stewart, founder of iSpiritus Soul Spa, a store selling personal growth and well-being products.[3]
- *Creativity counts.* Although some traditional sources of funds now play a lesser role in small business finance than in the past, other sources—from large corporations and customers to international venture capitalists and state or local programs—are taking up the slack. To find the financing their businesses demand, entrepreneurs must use as much creativity in attracting financing as they did in generating the ideas for their products and services. For instance, after striking out with traditional sources of funding, EZConserve, a company that makes software that provides energy management tools for large PC networks, turned to the non-profit group Northwest Energy Efficiency Alliance and received a sizeable grant as well as marketing assistance that fueled its growth.[4]
- *The Web puts at entrepreneurs' fingertips vast resources of information that can lead to financing; use it.* The Web often offers entrepreneurs, especially those looking for relatively small amounts of money, the opportunity to discover sources of funds that they otherwise might miss. The Web site created for this book (www.prenhall.com/scarborough) provides links to many useful sites related to raising both start-up and growth capital. The Web also provides a low-cost, convenient way for entrepreneurs to get their business plans into potential investors' hands anywhere in the world. When searching for sources of capital, entrepreneurs must not overlook this valuable tool!
- *Be thoroughly prepared before approaching potential lenders and investors.* In the hunt for capital, tracking down leads is tough enough; don't blow a potential deal by failing to be

ready to present your business idea to potential lenders and investors in a clear, concise, convincing way. That, of course, requires a solid business plan and a well-rehearsed elevator pitch, one or two minutes on the nature of your business and the source of its competitive edge, a pitch that is capable of winning over potential investors and lenders. "Entrepreneurs who come across with unsubstantiated market assessments, no competitive analysis, and flimsy marketing and sales plans will be the losers in the race to money," says venture capitalist John May.[5]

- *Entrepreneurs cannot overestimate the importance of making sure that the "chemistry" among themselves, their companies, and their funding sources is a good one.* Too many entrepreneurs get into financial deals because they needed the money to keep their businesses growing, only to discover that their plans do not match those of their financial partners.

Rather than rely primarily on a single source of funds as they have in the past, entrepreneurs must piece together capital from multiple sources, a method known as **layered financing.** Entrepreneurs have discovered that raising capital successfully requires them to cast a wide net to capture the financing they need to launch their businesses.

layered financing
the technique of raising capital from multiple sources.

Kirsten Tobey and Kristin Groos Richmond, co-founders of Revolution Foods, a company based in Alameda, California, that sells 20,000 nutritious meals a day for students in 150 California schools, met while they were students at the Haas School of Business at the University of California at Berkeley. Building on the experience they gained in careers in education, Tobey and Richmond launched Revolution Foods in 2006 with their own funds. The business grew quickly, and Tobey and Richmond were able to secure $4.5 million in growth capital from a group of private investors and several venture capital firms. Revolution Foods also received a $75,000 low-interest loan from one of its suppliers, Whole Foods, which also helps the company keep its cost of goods sold low by providing access to its network of suppliers. Tobey and Richmond recently secured $6.5 million in second round of financing ("Round B" financing) from its venture capital partners, an investment that the founders say will allow them to double the company's annual sales to $20 million by expanding into other markets.[6]

ENTREPRENEURIAL PROFILE _____

Kirsten Tobey and Kristin Groos Richmond: Revolution Foods

This chapter will guide you through the myriad financing options available to entrepreneurs, focusing on both sources of equity (ownership) and debt (borrowed) financing.

Planning for Capital Requirements

Becoming a successful entrepreneur requires one to become a skilled fund-raiser, a job that usually requires more time and energy than most business founders realize. In start-up companies, raising capital can easily consume as much as one-half of the entrepreneur's time and can take many months to complete. In addition, many entrepreneurs find it necessary to raise capital constantly to fuel the hefty capital appetites of their young, fast-growing companies. Very few entrepreneurs need more than $1 million to launch their companies. Indeed, most need less than $100,000. (One study of the fastest-growing companies in the United States reports that 73 percent of them were started with less than $100,000 in capital.[7]) However, these "small" amounts of capital can be some of the most difficult to secure.

Capital is any form of wealth employed to produce more wealth. It exists in many forms in a typical business, including cash, inventory, plant, and equipment. Entrepreneurs have access to two different types of capital, equity and debt.

LO 1
Explain the importance of planning for a company's capital requirements.

capital
any form of wealth employed to produce more wealth.

Equity Capital vs. Debt Capital

Equity capital represents the personal investment of the owner (or owners) in a business and is sometimes called *risk capital* because these investors assume the primary risk of losing their funds if the business fails.

equity capital
capital that represents the personal investment of the owner (or owners) of a company; sometimes called risk capital.

ENTREPRENEURIAL PROFILE

Vern Raburn: Eclipse Aviation

In 1999, Vern Raburn launched Eclipse Aviation Corporation, a company that manufactured small, low-cost, personal jets, with the vision of transforming the air transportation industry. Production and cash flow problems plagued the company, however, and in 2008, Eclipse filed for bankruptcy, which meant that investors lost all of the money they had put into the company. In addition to Raburn, Eclipse investors included Microsoft founder Bill Gates (Raburn's former boss), the state of New Mexico (which invested $19 million), and billionaire Alfred Mann, who invested $139 million in the company. As part of the bankruptcy filing, Eclipse's largest stockholder, Luxembourg-based ETIRC Aviation, agreed to acquire the company's remaining assets.[8]

If a venture succeeds, however, founders and investors share in the benefits, which can be quite substantial. The founders of and early investors in Yahoo, Sun Microsystems, Federal Express, Intel, and Microsoft became multimillionaires when the companies went public and their equity investments finally paid off. Michael Moritz, a partner in the venture capital firm Sequoia Capital, recalls a meeting in 1999 that took place around a ping-pong table that doubled as a conference table for Sergey Brin and Larry Page, the founders of a start-up company that had developed a search engine called Google. The young company had just changed its name from Backrub and had only 12 employees when Moritz agreed to invest $25 million in exchange for 16 percent of the company's stock. When Google made an initial public offering five years later, Moritz's original investment was worth $3 billion![9]

To entrepreneurs, the primary advantage of equity capital is that it does not have to be repaid like a loan does. Equity investors are entitled to share in the company's earnings (if there are any) and usually to have a voice in the company's future direction. The primary disadvantage of equity capital is that the entrepreneur must give up some—sometimes even *most*—of the ownership in the business to outsiders. Although 50 percent of something is better than 100 percent of nothing, giving up control of a company can be disconcerting and dangerous. Entrepreneurs are most likely to give up significant amounts of equity in their businesses in the start-up phase than in any other. To avoid having to give up control of their companies early on, entrepreneurs should strive to launch their companies with the least amount of money possible.

Debt capital is the financing that a small business owner has borrowed and must repay with interest. Very few entrepreneurs have adequate personal savings needed to finance the complete start-up costs of a small business; many of them must rely on some form of debt capital to launch their companies. Lenders of capital are more numerous than investors, but small business loans can be just as difficult (if not more difficult) to obtain. Although borrowed capital allows entrepreneurs to maintain complete ownership of their businesses, it must be carried as a liability on the balance sheet as well as be repaid with interest in the future. In addition, because lenders consider small businesses to be greater risks than bigger corporate customers, they require higher interest rates on loans to small companies because of the risk-return tradeoff—the higher the risk, the greater the return demanded. Most small firms pay the prime rate—the interest rate banks charge their most creditworthy customers—*plus* a few percentage points. Unlike equity financing, however, debt financing does not require entrepreneurs to dilute their ownership interest in their companies. We now turn our attention to eight common sources of equity capital.

debt capital
the financing that a small business owner has borrowed and must repay with interest.

Sources of Equity Financing

Personal Savings

The *first* place entrepreneurs should look for start-up money is in their own pockets. It's the least expensive source of funds available! "The sooner you take outside money, the more ownership in your company you'll have to surrender," warns one small business expert.[10] Entrepreneurs apparently see the benefits of self-sufficiency; the most common source of equity funds used to start a small business is the entrepreneur's pool of personal savings. The Global Entrepreneurship Monitor (GEM) study of entrepreneurship across the globe reports that the average cost to start a business is $65,000 and that the typical entrepreneur provides 62 percent of the initial capital requirement.[11]

Paul Williams started Grey Hat Research, an information security consulting company, with just $4,000 of his own money. Williams looked for ways to keep his start-up costs low. He used an online service to incorporate the business, conducted a contest that produced the company's name and logo, and relied on a friend to host Grey Hat's Web site and e-mail for free. Williams purchased inexpensive furniture for $600, paid $25 for business cards, and decided to operate the business from his home. Grey Hat's annual sales have surpassed $4 million, and because he financed the company with his own money, Williams owns 100 percent of the business.[12]

ENTREPRENEURIAL PROFILE_____

Paul Williams: Grey Hat Research

Lenders and investors *expect* entrepreneurs to put their own money into a business start-up. If an entrepreneur is not willing to risk his or her own money, potential investors are not likely to risk their money in the business either. Furthermore, failing to put up sufficient capital of their own means that entrepreneurs must either borrow an excessive amount of capital or give up a significant portion of ownership to outsiders to fund the business properly. Excessive borrowing in the early days of a business puts intense pressure on its cash flow, and becoming a minority shareholder may dampen a founder's enthusiasm for making a business successful.

Friends and Family Members

Although most entrepreneurs look to their own bank accounts first to finance a business, few have sufficient resources to launch their businesses alone. After emptying their own pockets, where should entrepreneurs should turn for capital? The second place most entrepreneurs look is to friends and family members who might be willing to invest in (or lend to) a business venture. Because of their relationships with the founder, these people are most likely to invest. Often they are more patient than other outside investors and are less meddlesome (but not always!) in a business's affairs than many other types of investors.

The Global Entrepreneurship Monitor, a study of entrepreneurial trends across the globe, reports that family members and friends are the biggest source of external capital used to launch new businesses. Investments from family and friends are an important source of capital for entrepreneurs, but the amounts invested typically are small, often no more than just a few thousand dollars. Across the globe, the average amount that family members and friends invest in start-up businesses averages just $3,000.[13] In the United States alone, family members and friends invest an average of $27,715 in a typical small business start-up for an astonishing total of $100 billion per year, far greater than the investments of either angels or venture capital firms![14]

Investments (or loans) from family and friends are an excellent source of seed capital and can get a start-up far enough along to attract money from private investors or venture capital companies. Inherent dangers lurk in family business investments and loans, however. A recent study reports a default rate of 14 percent on business loans from family and friends, compared to a default rate of 1 percent for bank loans.[15] Unrealistic expectations or misunderstood risks have destroyed many friendships and have ruined many family reunions. To avoid problems, an entrepreneur must honestly present the investment opportunity and the nature of the risks involved to avoid alienating friends and family members if the business fails. Smart entrepreneurs treat family members and friends who invest in their companies in the same way they would treat business partners. Some investments in start-up companies return more than friends and family members ever could have imagined. In 1995, Mike and Jackie Bezos invested $300,000 into their son Jeff's

HANDS ON... HOW TO

Structure Family and Friendship Financing Deals

Tapping family members and friends for start-up capital, whether in the form of equity or debt financing, is a popular method of financing business ideas. In a typical year, some 6 million individuals in the United States invest about $100 billion in entrepreneurial ventures. Unfortunately, not all of these deals work to the satisfaction of both parties. The following suggestions can help entrepreneurs avoid needlessly destroying family relationships and friendships:

- *Consider the impact of the investment on everyone involved.* Will the investment be a hardship for anyone? Is the investor putting up the money because he wants to or because he feels obligated to? Can all parties afford the loan if the business folds? Lynn McPhee used $250,000 from family members to launch Xuny, a Web-based clothing store. "Our basic rule of thumb was, if [the investment is] going to strap someone, we won't take it," she says.
- *Keep the arrangement strictly business.* The parties should treat all loans and investments in a business-like manner, no matter how close the friendship or family relationship, to avoid problems down the line. If the transaction is a loan exceeding $10,000, it must carry a rate of interest at least as high as the market rate; otherwise the IRS may consider the loan a gift and penalize the lender.
- *Prepare a business plan.* When Anastasia Lomonova began at age 23 designing a clothing line under her own name and selling it to independent boutiques from her apartment in Montreal, Canada, she financed her entrepreneurial venture with her own money, a few grants, and a $4,000 loan from her mother. Even though the loan came from her mother, Lomonova prepared a 150-page business plan that explained her business idea and included financial projections. "You have to give [relatives and friends] a sense of confidence," she says. "They can't bet on a dream."
- *Settle the details up front.* Before any money changes hands, both parties must agree on the details of the deal. How much money is involved? Is it a loan or an investment? How will the investor cash out? How will the loan be paid off? What happens if the business fails?

- *Never accept more than investors can afford to lose.* No matter how much capital you may need, accepting more than family members or friends can afford to lose is a recipe for disaster—and perhaps bankruptcy for the investors.
- *Create a written contract.* Don't make the mistake of closing a financial deal with just a handshake. The probability of misunderstandings skyrockets! Putting an agreement in writing demonstrates the parties' commitment to the deal and minimizes the chances of disputes from faulty memories and misunderstandings.
- *Treat the money as "bridge financing."* Although family and friends can help you launch your business, it is unlikely that they can provide enough capital to sustain it over the long term. Sooner or later, you will need to establish a relationship with other sources of credit if your company is to survive and thrive. Consider money from family and friends as a bridge to take your company to the next level of financing.
- *Develop a payment schedule that suits both the entrepreneur and the lender or investor.* Although lenders and investors may want to get their money back as quickly as possible, a rapid repayment or cash-out schedule can jeopardize a fledgling company's survival. Establish a realistic repayment plan that works for the parties without putting excessive strain on the young company's cash flow.
- *Have an exit plan.* Every deal should define exactly how investors will "cash out" their investments.

Source: Adapted from Sarah Dougherty, "'Love Money' Seeds Many Budding Ventures," *Financial Post*, January 30, 2008, http://www.financialpost.com/small-business/business-solutions/story.html?id=269859; Paulette Thomas, "It's All Relative," *Wall Street Journal*, November 29, 2004, pp. RR4, R8; Andrea Coombes, "Retirees as Venture Capitalists," CBS.MarketWatch.com, November 2, 2003, http://netscape.marketwatch.com/news/story.asp?dist=feed&siteid=netscape&guid={1E1267CD-32A4-4558-9F7E-40E4B7892D01}; Paul Kvinta, "Frogskins, Shekels, Bucks, Moolah, Cash, Simoleans, Dough, Dinero: Everybody Wants It. Your Business Needs It. Here's How to Get It," *Smart Business*, August 2000, pp. 74–89; Alex Markels, "A Little Help from Their Friends," *Wall Street Journal*, May 22, 1995, p. R10.

start-up business, Amazon.com. Today, Mike and Jackie own six percent of Amazon.com's stock, and their shares are worth billions of dollars![16] The accompanying "Hands On: How To" feature offers suggestions for structuring successful family or friendship financing deals.

Angels

After dipping into their own pockets and convincing friends and relatives to invest in their business ventures, many entrepreneurs still find themselves short of the seed capital they need. Frequently, the next stop on the road to business financing is private investors. These **private investors (or "angels")** are wealthy individuals, often entrepreneurs themselves, who invest in business start-ups in exchange for equity stakes in the companies. Angel investors have provided much-needed capital to entrepreneurs for many years. In 1938, when World War I flying ace

angels
wealthy individuals, often entrepreneurs themselves, who invest in business start-ups in exchange for equity stakes in the companies.

Eddie Rickenbacker needed money to launch Eastern Airlines, millionaire Laurance Rockefeller provided it.[17] Alexander Graham Bell, inventor of the telephone, used angel capital to start Bell Telephone in 1877. More recently, companies such as Google, Apple, Starbucks, Kinko's, and the Body Shop relied on angel financing in their early years to finance growth.

In many cases, angels are willing to put money into companies in the earliest stages, long before venture capital firms and institutional investors jump in. Angel financing, the fastest growing segment of the small business capital market, is ideal for companies that have outgrown the capacity of investments from friends and family but are still too small to attract the interest of venture capital companies. Angel financing is vital to the nation's small business sector because it fills this capital gap in which small companies need investments ranging from $100,000 or less to perhaps $5 million. For instance, after raising the money to launch Amazon.com from family and friends, Jeff Bezos turned to angels for capital because venture capital firms were not interested in investing in a business start-up. Bezos attracted $1.2 million from a dozen angels before landing $8 million from venture capital firms a year later.[18]

Angels are a primary source of start-up capital for companies in the embryonic stage through the growth stage, and their role in financing small businesses is significant. Research at the University of New Hampshire shows that more than 258,000 angels and angel groups invest $26 billion a year in 57,000 small companies, most of them in the start-up phase.[19] Because the angel market is so fragmented and, in many cases, built on anonymity, it is difficult to get a completely accurate estimate of its investment in business start-ups. Although they may disagree on the exact amount of angel investments, experts concur on one fact: angels are one of the largest and most important sources of external equity capital for small businesses. Their investments in young companies nearly match those of professional venture capitalists, providing more capital to 15 times as many small companies (See Figure 13.1).

Michael O'Brien grew up in southern California, but when he moved to the Midwest, he quickly grew tired of the cycle of putting on and removing snow chains from his car's tires. One day, an idea struck him: Why not make a tire that has retractable metal studs that grip the road and provide traction in snow or ice? O'Brien developed a prototype tire and in 2006 launched Q Tires, a company that makes the tires that allow drivers to flip a switch inside the car to extend gripping metal cleats when roads are covered in snow or ice. When the snow or ice melts, the driver flips the switch, the cleats retract, and the tires become normal again, which reduces the wear on highways. (The company's name was inspired by Q, the genius behind the gadgets in the James Bond films, whose creations included studded tires that gave Bond's Aston Martin extra traction in *Die Another Day.*) O'Brien raised $10 million from angel investors, set up headquarters in Greenville, South Carolina, and began equipping a factory in China to manufacture the tires.[20]

Angels fill a significant gap in the seed capital market. They are most likely to finance start-ups with capital requirements in the $10,000 to $2,000,000 range, well below the $3 million to $10 million minimum investments most professional venture capitalists prefer. (Because angels tend to invest in the earliest stages of a business, they incur the highest levels of risk. In fact, 52 percent of angels' investments lose money, returning less than the angels' original investment. The potential for investing in big winners exists as well; 7 percent of angels' investments produce a return of more than 10 times their original investments.[21]

Lewis Gersh, an experienced angel investor, says that out of 10 companies that an angel invests in, five will fail, two will break even, and two will return two to three times the original investment. Just one company out of ten will produce a significant return, "which means that every one of them has to have the potential of being a home run," says Gersh. Most angels consider a "home run" investment to be one that results in a return of 10 to 30 times the original investment in five to seven years, somewhat lower than the returns that venture capital firms expect.[22] Because of the inherent risks in start-up companies, many venture capitalists have shifted their investment portfolios away from start-ups toward more established firms. That's why angel financing is so important: Angels often finance deals that no venture capitalist will consider.

FIGURE 13.1

Angel Financing

Source: Center for Venture Financing, Whittemore School of Business, University of New Hampshire, www.unh.edu/cvr.

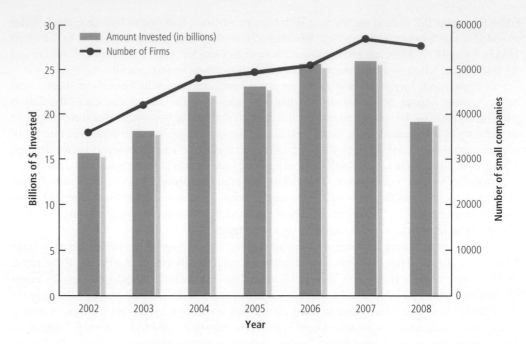

The typical angel invests an average of $50,000 in a company that is at the seed or growth stages. Most angels are seasoned entrepreneurs themselves; on average, angel investors have founded 2.7 companies and have 14.5 years of entrepreneurial experience. They also are well educated; 99 percent have college degrees. The typical angel invests in one company per year, and the average time required to close an angel financing deal is 67 days.[23] When evaluating a proposal, angels look for a qualified management team and a business with a clearly defined niche, market potential, and a competitive advantage. They also want to see market research that proves the existence of a sizeable customer base and a viable exit strategy, the avenue by which they get their investments back, ideally with a handsome return. "It's a good deal only if there's an exit option that offers us the return we want," says one angel investor.[24]

ENTREPRENEURIAL PROFILE

Joe Whinney: Theo Chocolate

Joe Whinney, founder of Theo Chocolate, a Seattle-based company that sells organic, gourmet chocolate from its own retail store and through more than 2,500 retailers nationwide, presented his business plan to a dozen groups of angel investors with little initial success. When Whinney discovered that potential investors were concerned about his willingness to sell the company down the road (which provides them with a viable exit strategy), he changed his presentation to address their concerns and angels began investing. Before long, Whinney was able to raise more than $1 million in capital from 30 angel investors to expand its production capacity and its distribution network.[25]

Entrepreneurs in search of capital quickly learn that the real challenge lies in *finding* angels. Most angels have substantial business and financial experience, and many of them are entrepreneurs or former entrepreneurs. Because most angels frown on "cold calls" from entrepreneurs they don't know, locating them boils down to making the right contacts. Networking is the key. Asking friends, attorneys, bankers, stockbrokers, accountants, other business owners, and consultants for suggestions and introductions is a good way to start. Angels almost always invest their money locally, so entrepreneurs should look close to home for them—typically within a 50- to 100-mile radius. In fact, seven out of ten angels invest in companies that are within 50 miles of their homes or offices.[26] Angels also look for businesses they know something about, and most expect to invest their knowledge, experience, and energy as well as their money in a company. In fact, the advice and the network of contacts that angels bring to a deal can sometimes be as valuable as their money!

Angels tend to invest in clusters as well. In fact, a significant trend in angel investing is the growth of angel networks, organized groups of angels who pool their capital and make investment decisions much like venture capital companies do. According to the Angel Capital Association, 265 angel groups now operate in the United States, up from fewer than 100 in 1999.[27] Taking a more sophisticated and formal approach than informal angel clusters, angel networks are more visible and make the task of locating angels much easier for entrepreneurs in search of capital.

ENTREPRENEURIAL PROFILE _____

Hans Severiens: the Band of Angels

In 1994, Hans Severiens, a professional investor, created the Band of Angels, a group of about 130 angels (mostly Silicon Valley millionaires, many of whom are retired entrepreneurs) who meet monthly in Portola Valley, California, to listen to entrepreneurs pitch their business plans. The Band of Angels reviews about 30 proposals each month before inviting three entrepreneurs to make brief presentations at their monthly meeting. Interested members often team up with one another to invest in the businesses they consider most promising. Over the years, the Band of Angels has invested a total of more than $186 million in 209 promising young companies (45 of which have been acquired at a gain to investors and 9 of which have made initial public offerings). The average investment is $890,000, which usually nets the angels between 15 percent and 25 percent of a company's stock. At one meeting, Howard Field and Kevin McCurdy, cofounders of Picaboo, a company that allows customers to create and share digital photo albums easily, had 10 minutes to make their elevator pitch to the members of the Band of Angels. Within weeks of the presentation, several members of the Band of Angels decided to invest, giving Picaboo the capital it needed to fuel its growth. Since launching their company in 2002, Field and McCurdy have conducted three rounds of fundraising that have generated $5.1 million in capital, some of it from angels and the rest from venture capital firms.[28]

The Internet has expanded greatly the ability of entrepreneurs in search of capital and angels in search of businesses to find one another. Dozens of angel networks have set up shop on the Web, many of which are members of the Angel Capital Association (ACA, www.angelcapitalassociation.org). The association reports that its average member group has 42 investors and makes investments in four small companies each year.[29] Entrepreneurs can expand the scope of their hunt for financing by including online angel groups and the ACA's membership list in their searches.

Angels are an excellent source of "patient money," often willing to wait seven years or longer to cash out their investments. They earn their returns through the increased value of the business, not through dividends and interest. For example, more than 1,000 early investors in Microsoft Inc. are now multimillionaires. A study by the Kauffman Foundation reports that the average return on angels' investments in small companies is 2.6 times the original investment in 3.5 years, which is the equivalent of a 27 percent internal rate of return.[30] Angel investors typically purchase 15 to 30 percent ownership in a small company, leaving the majority ownership to the company founder(s). They look for the same exit strategies that venture capital firms look for: either an initial public offering or a buyout by a larger company. The lesson: If an entrepreneur needs relatively small amounts of money to launch or to grow a company, angels are an excellent source.

Partners

As we saw in Chapter 4, entrepreneurs can take on partners to expand the capital foundation of a business. Before entering into any partnership arrangement, however, entrepreneurs must consider the impact of giving up some personal control over operations and of sharing profits with others. Whenever entrepreneurs give up equity in their businesses (through whatever mechanism), they run the risk of losing control over it. As the founder's ownership in a company becomes increasingly diluted, the probability of losing control of its future direction and the entire decision-making process increases. "It's tough to keep control," says an entrepreneur who was pushed out of the company that he had started. "For every penny you get in the door, you have to give something up."[31]

Venture Capital Companies

venture capital companies
private, for-profit companies that assemble pools of capital and then use them to purchase equity positions in young businesses they believe have high-growth and high-profit potential.

Venture capital companies are private, for-profit organizations that assemble pools of capital and then use them to purchase equity positions in young businesses they believe have high-growth and high-profit potential, producing annual returns of 300 to 500 percent within five to seven years. More than 740 venture capital firms operate across the United States today, investing billions of dollars (see Figure 13.2) in promising small companies in a wide variety of industries. The high-tech hubs in Silicon Valley and Boston account for about half of all venture capital investments,.[32]

Venture capital firms, which provide about seven percent of all funding for private companies, have invested billions of dollars in high potential small companies over the years, including such notable businesses as Google, Apple, FedEx, Netscape, Home Depot, Microsoft., Intel, Starbucks, Whole Foods Market, and Genentech.[33] In many of these deals, several venture capital companies invested money, experience, and advice across several stages of growth, a common practice in the industry.

ENTREPRENEURIAL PROFILE

Robert Rizika: Blackwave Inc.

Robert Rizika, CEO of Blackwave Inc., a company that provides storage and delivery systems for online video that are seven to ten times more efficient—and less expensive—than its competitors, recently raised $16 million in just two months from three venture capital companies. Blackwave needed the money to gear up production of its hardware and software, hire sales representatives, and market its unique products and services, which combine a variety of network elements into a single package. Rizika already had received $5 million in first-round financing from two venture capital firms, both of which participated in the company's round B funding.[34]

POLICIES AND INVESTMENT STRATEGIES Venture capital firms usually establish stringent policies to implement their overall investment strategies.

Investment Size and Screening. Most venture capital firms seek investments in the $3 million to $10 million range to justify the cost of investigating the large number of proposals they receive. The venture capital screening process is *extremely* rigorous. According to the Global

FIGURE 13.2

Venture Capital Funding

Source: Based on PriceWaterhouse Coopers http://www.pwcmoney tree.com

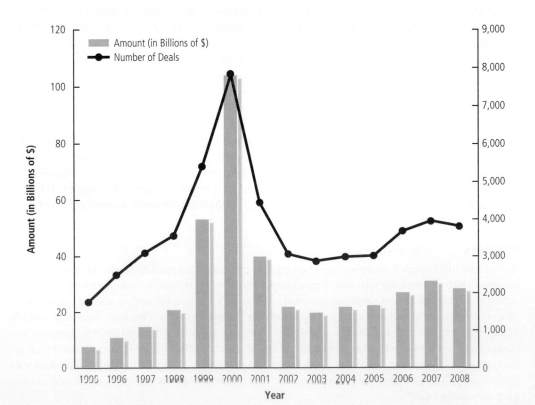

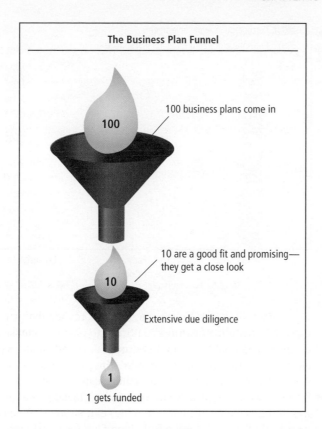

The Business Plan Funnel

100 business plans come in

10 are a good fit and promising—
they get a close look

Extensive due diligence

1 gets funded

FIGURE 13.3

The Business Plan Funnel

Source: Venture Impact: The Economic Importance of Venture Backed Companies to the U.S. Economy, Fourth edition, National Venture Capital Association, 2007, p.10.

Entrepreneurship Monitor, only about one in 1,000 businesses in the United States receives venture capital during its existence.[35] The typical venture capital firm receives about 1,100 business plans each year. For every 100 business plans that the average venture capital firm receives, 90 of them are rejected immediately because they do not match the firm's investment criteria or requirements. The firm conducts a thorough due diligence investigation of the remaining 10 companies and typically invests in only one of them (see Figure 13.3). The average time required to close a venture capital deal is 80 days, slightly longer than the time required to complete angel financing.[36]

Ownership and Control. Most venture capitalists prefer to purchase ownership in a small business through common stock or convertible preferred stock. Typically, a venture capital company seeks to purchase 20 percent to 40 percent of a business, but in some cases, a venture capitalist may buy 70 percent or more of a company's stock, leaving its founders with a minority share of ownership.

Stage of Investment. Most venture capital firms invest in companies that are either in the early stages of development (called early-stage investing) or in the rapid-growth phase (called expansion-stage investing); very few invest in small companies that are in the start-up phase. About 96 to 98 percent of all venture capital goes to businesses in these stages, although a few venture capital firms are showing more interest in companies in the start-up phase because of the tremendous returns that are possible by investing then.[37] According to the Global Entrepreneurship Monitor, only one in 10,000 entrepreneurs worldwide receives venture capital funding at start-up.[38]

Investment Preferences. The venture capital industry has undergone important changes over the last decade. Venture capital funds now are larger and more specialized. As the industry matures, venture capital funds increasingly are focusing their investments in niches—everything from low-calorie custards to the latest Web technology. Some will invest in almost any industry, but most prefer companies in later stages. Traditionally, only two to four percent of the companies receiving venture capital financing are in the start-up or seed stage, when entrepreneurs are forming a company or developing a product or service and when angels are most likely to invest (see Figure 13.4). Most of the start-up businesses that attract venture capital are technology companies—software, biotechnology, energy, medical devices, and telecommunications.[39]

FIGURE 13.4

Angel Investing and Venture Capital Investing

Source: Robert Wiltbank and Warren Boeker, *Returns to Angel Investors in Groups,* Angel Capital Education Foundation, *ttp://www.kauffinan.org/ Details.aspx?id=1032,* and PWC Moneytree Report, Pricewaterhouse Coopers, *https://www.pwcmoneytree .com/MTPublic/ns/index.jsp.*

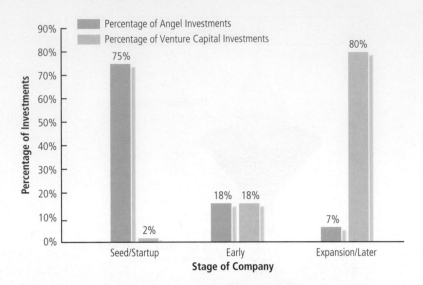

WHAT VENTURE CAPITALISTS LOOK FOR   Entrepreneurs must realize that it is very difficult for any small business, especially fledgling or struggling firms, to pass the intense screening process of a venture capital company and qualify for an investment. A sound business plan is essential to convincing venture capital firms to invest in a company. "Investors want to see proof that a concept works," says Geeta Vemuri, a principal in a venture capital firm.[40] Venture capital firms finance only about 3,500 deals in a typical year. Two factors make a deal attractive to venture capitalists: high returns and a convenient (and profitable) exit strategy. When evaluating potential investments, venture capitalists look for the following features (see Figure 13.5):

Competent Management. The most important ingredient in the success of any business is the ability of the management team, and venture capitalists recognize this. To venture capitalists, the ideal management team has experience, managerial skills, commitment, and the ability to build teams. "If you don't have good management [in place], it's going to bite you," says Phil Soran, CEO of Compellent Technologies, a data storage company that has attracted venture capital successfully.[41]

FIGURE 13.5

Which Factors Are Most Important to Venture Capitalists

Source: Dee Powers and Brian E. Hill, Venture Capital Survey, The Capital Connection, http://www.capital-connection.com/survey-value.html.

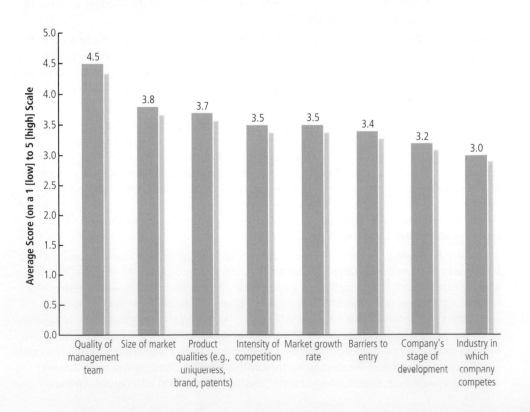

Competitive Edge. Investors are searching for some factor that will enable a small business to set itself apart from its competitors. This distinctive competence may range from an innovative product or service that satisfies unmet customer needs to a unique marketing or R&D approach. It must be something with the potential to create a sustainable competitive edge, making the company a leader in its industry. "I look for transformational ideas," says Bill Turner, founder of venture capital firm Signature Capital, explaining his investments in a variety of businesses, including an online music service, a hearing-aid maker, and an HIV-therapy company.[42]

Growth Industry. Hot industries attract profits—and venture capital. Most venture capital funds focus their searches for prospects in rapidly expanding fields because they believe the profit potential is greater in these areas. Venture capital firms are most interested in young companies that have enough growth potential to become at least $100 million businesses within three to five years. Venture capitalists know that most of the businesses they invest in will flop, so their winners have to be *big* winners.

Some venture capitalists' investments *are* big winners. In 1976, Kleiner Perkins, one of the most successful venture capital firms in history, invested $250,000 in exchange for 33 percent of a young company called Genentech. Today, Kleiner Perkins's shares are worth an impressive $26 billion![43] The economic impact of successful venture-backed companies such as Genentech is significant. The National Venture Capital Association estimates that the total revenue of venture-backed companies in the United States accounts for 17.6 percent of GDP and that employment at these companies comprises 9.1 percent of private sector employment in the United States.[44]

Viable Exit Strategy. Venture capitalists not only look for promising companies with the ability to dominate a market, but they also want to see a plan for a feasible exit strategy, typically to be executed within three to five years. Venture capital firms realize the return on their investments when the companies they invest in either make an initial public offering or are acquired by or merged into another business. As the market for initial public offerings has softened, venture capitalists have had to be more patient in their exit strategies. Venture-backed companies that go public now take an average of 5.5 years from the time of their first venture capital investment to their stock offering, up from an average of less than three years in 1998.[45]

The venture capital firms that have invested in LinkedIn, the business networking Web site with more than 23 million users, hope to see the company make an initial public offering, something that would produce a handsome return on their investments. Founder Reid Hoffman has guided LinkedIn through four rounds of venture financing from firms including Bain Capital, Sequoia Capital, Greylock Partners, and Bessemer Venture Partners. In its latest round, LinkedIn received a $53 million capital infusion to fund its growth, including expanding into Europe and perhaps acquiring small companies that can help the company achieve its strategic objectives.[46]

Intangible Factors. Some other important factors considered in the screening process are not easily measured; they are the intuitive, intangible factors the venture capitalist detects by gut feeling. This feeling might be the result of the small firm's solid sense of direction, its strategic planning process, the chemistry of its management team, or a number of other factors.

Despite its many benefits, venture capital is not suited for every entrepreneur. "VC money comes at a price," warns one entrepreneur. "Before boarding a one-way money train, ask yourself if this is the best route for your business and personal desires, because investors are like department stores the day after Christmas—they expect a lot of returns in a short period of time."[47]

Corporate Venture Capital

Large corporations have gotten into the business of financing small companies and invest in small companies for both strategic and financial reasons. Today, about 300 large corporations across the globe, including Google, Comcast, Amazon, Qualcomm, Intel, General Electric, Dow Chemical, Cisco Systems, UPS, Wal-Mart, Unilever, and Johnson & Johnson, invest in small companies, usually companies that are in the later stage of growth and, because of their maturity, are less risky. Approximately 6 to 8 percent of all venture capital invested comes from corporations.[48] Young companies not only get a boost from the capital injections large companies give them, but they also stand to gain many other benefits from the relationship. The right corporate partner may share technical expertise, distribution channels, and marketing know-how and provide introductions to important customers and suppliers. Another intangible yet highly important advantage an investment from a large corporate partner gives a small company is credibility. Doors that otherwise would be closed to a small company magically open when the right corporation becomes a strategic partner.

Public Stock Sale ("Going Public")

In some cases, entrepreneurs can "go public" by selling shares of stock in their corporations to outside investors. In an **initial public offering (IPO),** a company raises capital by selling shares of its stock to the general public for the first time. A public offering is an effective method of raising large amounts of capital, but it can be an expensive and time-consuming process filled with regulatory nightmares. Once a company makes an initial public offering, *nothing* will ever be the same again. Managers must consider the impact of their decisions not only on the company and its employees but also on its shareholders and the value of their stock.

Going public isn't for every business. In fact, most small companies do not meet the criteria for making a successful public stock offering. Since 2000, the average number of companies that make initial public offerings each year is 173, and only about 20,000 companies in the United States—less than one percent of the total—are publicly held (see Figure 13.6). Few companies with less than $25 million in annual sales manage to go public successfully. It is extremely difficult for a start-up company with no track record of success to raise money with a public offering. Instead, the investment bankers who underwrite public stock offerings typically look for established companies with the following characteristics:

- Consistently high growth rates.
- A strong record of earnings. Strangely enough, profitability at the time of the IPO is not essential; from 2001 to 2008, 47 percent of companies making IPOs had negative earnings.[49]
- Three to five years of audited financial statements that meet or exceed SEC standards. After the Enron and WorldCom scandals, investors are demanding impeccable financial statements.

LO 3

Describe the process of "going public" as well as its advantages and disadvantages and the various simplified registrations and exemptions from registration available to small businesses.

initial public offering

a method of raising equity capital in which a company sells shares of its stock to the general public for the first time.

FIGURE 13.6

Initial Public Offerings (IPOs)

Source: Thomson Financial Securities Data.

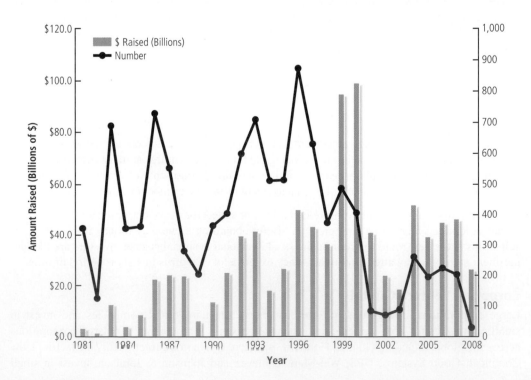

- A solid position in a rapidly-growing industry. In 2000, the median age of companies making IPOs was three years; today, it is 14 years.[50]
- A sound management team with experience and a strong board of directors.

THE REGISTRATION PROCESS Taking a company public is a complicated, bureaucratic process that usually takes several months to complete. Many experts compare the IPO process to running a corporate marathon, and both the company and its management team must be in shape and up to the grueling task. The typical entrepreneur *cannot* take his or her company public alone. It requires a coordinated effort from a team of professionals, including company executives, an accountant, a securities attorney, a financial printer, and at least one underwriter. Table 13.1 shows a typical timetable for an IPO. The key steps in taking a company public include the following:

Choose the Underwriter. The single most important ingredient in making a successful IPO is selecting a capable **underwriter (or investment banker).** The underwriter serves two primary roles: helping to prepare the registration statement for the issue and promoting the company's stock to potential investors. The underwriter works with company managers as an advisor to prepare the registration statement that must be filed with the SEC, promotes the issue, prices the stock, and provides after-market support. Once the registration statement is finished, the underwriter's primary job is selling the company's stock through an underwriting syndicate of other investment bankers it develops. According to a study by Notre Dame professors Shane Corwin and Paul Schultz, the larger the syndicate that supports an IPO, the more likely it is that the company will obtain more favorable pricing and overall results from the offering.[51]

underwriter (or investment banker)
a financial company that serves two important roles: helping to prepare the registration statement for an issue and promoting the company's stock to potential investors.

Sourcefire, a company founded in 2001 by Martin Roesch that makes intrusion detection software designed to monitor computer systems for attacks by hackers, recently completed an initial public offering. Investment bankers Morgan Stanley, UBS Investment Bank, and Jeffries managed the offering of 5.8 million shares that generated $87 million to fuel the growth of Sourcefire, whose shares trade on the Nasdaq Global Market under the symbol "FIRE."[52]

ENTREPRENEURIAL PROFILE

Martin Roesch: Sourcefire

TABLE 13.1 Timetable for an initial public offering.

Time	Action
Week 1	Conduct "all hands" organizational meeting with IPO team, including underwriter, attorneys, accountants, and others. Begin drafting registration statement.
Week 5	Distribute first draft of registration statement to IPO team and make revisions.
Week 6	Distribute second draft of registration statement and make revisions.
Week 7	Distribute third draft of registration statement and make revisions.
Week 8	File registration statement with the SEC. Begin preparing presentations for road show to attract other investment bankers to the underwriting syndicate. Comply with Blue Sky laws in states where offering will be sold. "Quiet period" officially begins and runs until 25 days after the company's stock begins trading.
Week 13	Receive comment letter on registration statement from SEC* and state authorities. Amend registration statement to satisfy SEC and other regulatory agencies.
Week 14	File amended registration statement with SEC. Prepare and distribute preliminary offering prospectus (called a "red herring") to members of underwriting syndicate. Begin road show meetings.
Week 16	Receive approval for offering from SEC (unless further amendments are required). Issuing company and lead underwriter agree on final offering price. Prepare, file, and distribute final offering prospectus.
Week 17	Company and underwriter sign the final agreement. Underwriter issues stock, collects the proceeds from the sale, and delivers proceeds (less commission) to company.

* SEC's response may require more than five weeks, which will cause all remaining events to be pushed back.
Sources: Adapted from "Initial Public Offering," Entrepreneur, June 14, 2002, http://www.entrepreneur.com/article/0,4621,300892,00.html; "IPO Basics: IPO ABCs," MSN Money, http://moneycentral.hoovers.com/business-information/—pageid__1960—/global-msn-index.xhtml.

letter of intent
an agreement between the underwriter and the company about to go public that outlines the details of the deal.

Negotiate a Letter of Intent. To begin an offering, the entrepreneur and the underwriter must negotiate a **letter of intent,** which outlines the details of the deal. The letter of intent covers a variety of important issues, including the type of underwriting, its size and price range, the underwriter's commission, and any warrants and options included. It almost always states that the underwriter is not bound to the offering until it is executed—usually the day before or the day of the offering. However, the letter usually creates a binding obligation for the company to pay any direct expenses the underwriter incurs relating to the offer.

The company and the underwriter must decide on the size of the offering and the price of the shares. To keep the stock active in the aftermarket, most underwriters prefer to offer a *minimum* of 400,000 to 500,000 shares. A smaller number of shares inhibits sufficiently broad distribution. Most underwriters recommend selling 25 percent to 40 percent of the company in the IPO. They also strive to price the issue so that the total value of the offering is at least $8 to $15 million. (Although there are exceptions, some underwriters, especially regional ones, are interested in IPOs in the $2 to $5 million range.) To meet these criteria and to keep interest in the issue high, the underwriter usually recommends an initial price between $10 and $20 per share. The underwriter establishes an estimated price range for the company's IPO in the underwriting agreement, but it does not establish the final price until the day before the offering takes place. Depending on anticipated demand for the company's shares, the condition of the CEO market, and other factors, the actual price may be outside the estimated range. For instance, in Sourcefire's IPO, lead underwriter Morgan Stanley estimated the stock price to be $12 to $14 per share, but because of strong demand for the issue, the final offering price was $15 per share.[53]

registration statement
the document a company must file with the SEC that describes both the company and its stock offering and discloses information about the risk of investing.

Prepare the Registration Statement. After a company signs the letter of intent, the next task is to prepare the **registration statement** to be filed with the Securities and Exchange Commission (SEC). This document describes both the company and the stock offering and discloses information about the risks of investing. It includes information on the use of the proceeds, the company's history, its financial position, its capital structure, the risks it faces, its managers' experience, and *many* other details. The statement is extremely comprehensive and may take months to develop. To prepare the statement, entrepreneurs must rely on their team of professionals.

File with the SEC. When the statement is finished (with the exception of pricing the shares, proceeds, and commissions, which cannot be determined until just before the issue goes to market), the company officially files the statement with the SEC and awaits the review of the Division of Corporate Finance, a process that takes 30 to 45 days (or more). The Division sends notice of any deficiencies in the registration statement to the company's attorney in a comment letter. The company and its team of professionals must cure all of the deficiencies in the statement noted in the comment letter. Finally, the company files the revised registration statement, along with a pricing amendment (giving the price of the shares, the proceeds, and the commissions).

Wait to Go Effective. While waiting for the SEC's approval, the managers and the underwriters are busy. The underwriters are building a syndicate of other underwriters who will market the company's stock. (No stock sales can be made prior to the effective date of the offering, however.) The SEC also limits the publicity and information a company may release during this quiet period (which officially starts when the company reaches a preliminary agreement with the managing underwriter and ends 90 days after the effective date).

road show
a gathering of potential syndicate members sponsored by the managing underwriter for the purpose of promoting a company's initial public offering.

Securities laws do permit a **road show,** a gathering of potential syndicate members sponsored by the managing underwriter. Its purpose is to promote interest among potential underwriters in the IPO by featuring the company, its management, and the proposed deal. The managing underwriter and key company officials barnstorm major financial centers at a grueling pace.

ENTREPRENEURIAL PROFILE

Walter Allessandrini:
Ometric Corporation

During the road show for Ometric Corporation, a South Carolina-based company that has developed the technology to provide real-time spectroscopy in a variety of industrial applications, CEO Walter Allessandrini made 140 presentations to potential syndicate members in both Europe and the United States in just two and a half weeks!

On the last day before the registration statement becomes effective, the company signs the formal underwriting agreement. The final settlement, or closing, takes place a few days after the effective date for the issue. At this meeting the underwriters receive their shares to sell and the company receives the proceeds of the offering.

Typically, the entire process of going public takes from 120 to 180 days, but it can take much longer if the issuing company is not properly prepared for the process.

Simplified Registrations and Exemptions

The IPO process just described (called an S-1 filing) requires maximum disclosure in the initial filing and discourages most small businesses from using it. Fortunately, the SEC allows several exemptions from this full-disclosure process for small businesses. Many small businesses that go public choose one of these simplified options the SEC has designed for small companies. The SEC has established the following simplified registration statements and exemptions from the registration process:

REGULATION S-B Regulation S-B is a simplified registration process for small companies seeking to make initial or subsequent public offerings. Not only does this regulation simplify the initial filing requirements with the SEC, but it also reduces the ongoing disclosure and filings required of companies. Its primary goals are to open the doors to capital markets to smaller companies by cutting the paperwork and the costs of raising capital. Companies using the simplified registration process have two options: Form SB-1, a "transitional" registration statement for companies issuing less than $10 million worth of securities over a 12-month period, and Form SB-2, reserved for small companies seeking more than $10 million in a 12-month period.

To be eligible for the simplified registration process under simplified registration process under Regulation S-B, a company must meet the following criteria:

- Must be based in the United States or Canada.
- Must have revenues of less than $25 million.
- Must have outstanding publicly held stock worth no more than $25 million.
- Must not be an investment company.
- Must provide audited financial statements for two fiscal years.

REGULATION D (RULE 504): SMALL COMPANY OFFERING REGISTRATION Created in the late 1980s, the Small Company Offering Registration (SCOR) is designed to make it easier and less expensive for small companies to sell their stock to the public by eliminating the requirement for registering the offering with the SEC. The whole process typically costs less than half of what a traditional public offering costs. Entrepreneurs using SCOR need audited financial statements, an experienced attorney, and an accountant to help them with the issue, but some can get by without a securities lawyer, which can save tens of thousands of dollars. Some entrepreneurs even choose to market their companies' securities themselves (for example, to customers), saving the expense of hiring a broker. However, selling an issue is both time- and energy-consuming, and most SCOR experts recommend hiring a professional securities or brokerage firm to sell the company's shares. The SEC's objective in creating SCOR was to give small companies the same access to equity financing that large companies have via the stock market while bypassing many of the same costs and filing requirements.

The capital ceiling on a SCOR issue is $1 million (except in Texas, where there is no limit), and the price of a share must be at least $1 (although some states require a higher minimum price). Most SCOR offerings are priced between $2 and $5 per share. To complete a SCOR offering, a company must file a standardized disclosure statement, the U-7, which is a question-and-answer registration form. The U-7, which asks for information such as how much money the company needs, how the money will be used, what investors receive, how investors can sell their investments, and other pertinent questions, closely resembles a business plan but also serves as a state securities offering registration, a disclosure document, and a prospectus. Entrepreneurs using SCOR may advertise their companies' offerings and can sell them directly to any investor with no restrictions and no minimums. An entrepreneur can sell practically any kind of security through a SCOR, including common stock, preferred stock, convertible preferred stock, stock options, stock warrants, and others.

REGULATION D (RULES 505 AND 506): PRIVATE PLACEMENTS Rules 505 and 506 of Regulation D, also known as the Private Placement Memorandum (PPM), are exemptions from federal registration requirements that give emerging companies the opportunity to sell stock through private placements without actually going public. In a private placement, a company sells its shares directly to private investors without having to register them with the SEC or incur the expenses of an IPO. Instead, a knowledgeable attorney simply draws up an investment agreement that meets state and federal requirements between the company and its private investors. Most companies offer private investors "book deals," proposals with terms that the company determines and makes on a take-it-or-leave-it basis.

A *Rule 505* offering has a higher capital ceiling than a SCOR offering ($5 million) in a 12-month period but imposes more restrictions (no more than 35 non-accredited investors, no advertising of the offer, and more stringent disclosure requirements).

Rule 506 imposes no ceiling on the amount that can be raised, but, like a Rule 505 offering, it limits the issue to 35 non-accredited investors and prohibits advertising the offer to the public. There is no limit on the number of accredited investors, however. Rule 506 also requires detailed disclosure of relative information, but the extent depends on the dollar size of the offering.

These Regulation D rules minimize the expense and the time required to raise equity capital for small businesses. Fees for private placements typically range from one to five percent rather than the seven to 13 percent underwriters normally charge for managing a public offering. Offerings made under Regulation D do impose limitations and demand certain disclosures, but they require a company to file a simple form (Form D) with the SEC within 15 days of the first sale of stock. One drawback of private placements is that the SEC does not allow a company to advertise its stock offering, which means that entrepreneurs must develop a network of wealthy contacts if the placement is to succeed.

SECTION 4(6)   Section 4(6) covers private placements and is similar to Regulation D, Rules 505 and 506. It does not require registration on offerings up to $5 million if they are made only to accredited investors.

INTRASTATE OFFERINGS (RULE 147)   Rule 147 governs intrastate offerings, those sold only to investors in a single state by a company doing business in that state. To qualify, a company must be incorporated in the state, maintain its executive offices there, have 50 percent of its assets there, derive 50 percent of its revenues from the state, and use 50 percent of the offering proceeds for business in the state. There is no ceiling on the amount of the offering, but only residents of the state in which the issuing company operates can invest. The maximum number of shareholders is 500, and a company's asset base cannot exceed $10 million.

ENTREPRENEURIAL PROFILE ————

Ben Cohen & Jerry Greenfield: Ben & Jerry's Homemade

Years ago, Ben Cohen and Jerry Greenfield founded a small ice cream manufacturing business named after themselves that struck a chord with customers. Ben & Jerry's Homemade grew rapidly, and the founders needed $600,000 to build a new manufacturing plant in Vermont, where the company was based. They decided to "give the opportunity to our neighbors to grow with our company" by making an intrastate offering under Rule 147. Cohen and Greenfield registered their offering of 73,500 shares of stock with the Vermont Division of Banking and Insurance. Ben & Jerry's Homemade sold the entire offering (mostly to loyal customers) by placing ads in newspapers and stickers on ice cream containers that touted "Get a Scoop of the Action."[54]

REGULATION A   Regulation A, although currently not used often, allows an exemption for offerings up to $5 million over a 12-month period. Regulation A imposes few restrictions, but it is more costly than the other types of exempted offerings, usually running between $80,000 and $120,000. The primary difference between a SCOR offering and a Regulation A offering is that a company must register its SCOR offering only in the states where it will sell its stock; in a Regulation A offering, the company also must file an offering statement with the SEC. Under Regulation A, a company's financial statements do not have to be audited. Like a SCOR offering, a Regulation A offering requires only a simplified question-and-answer SEC filing and allows a company to sell its shares directly to investors.

Table 13.2 provides a summary of the major types of exemptions and simplified offerings. Of these, the limited offerings and private placements are most commonly used.

TABLE 13.2 Simplified Registrations and Exemptions

Feature	Regulation D Rule 504 (SCOR)	Regulation D Rule 505	Regulation D Rule 506	Private Placements Section 4(6)	Intrastate Offerings	Regulation A	Form SB-1	Form SB-2
Ceiling on amount raised	$1 million in any 12-month period	$5 million in any 12-month period	None	$5 million	None	$5 million in any 12-month period	$10 million in any 12-month period	None
Limit on number of purchasers	No	No, if selling to accredited investors; maximum of 35 non-accredited investors	No, if selling to accredited investors; maximum of 35 non-accredited investors	No	No	No	No	No
Limitation on types of purchasers	Depends	Yes	Yes	Yes. All must be accredited	Yes. Must be residents of the state in which the company is incorporated	No	No	No
General solicitation and advertising allowed	Yes, if the company sells to accredited investors; otherwise, no	No	No	No	Yes	Yes	Yes	Yes
Resale restrictions	Yes	Yes	Yes	Yes	Yes	No	No	No

Sources: Adapted from "IPO Alternatives: SEC Registration Exemptions," *Inc.*, November 1999, http://www.inc.com/articles/1999/11/15743.html; "Q&A: Small Business and the SEC," U.S. Securities and Exchange Commission, http://www.sec.gov/info/smallbus/qasbsec.htm; *Small Business: Efforts to Facilitate Equity Capital Formation, A Report to the Chariman, Committee on Small Business, U.S. Senate,* Government Accounting Office, Washington, DC, 2000, http://www.gao.gov/archive/2000/gg00190.pdf#search=%22Simplified%20registrations%20exemptions%20SB%22.

YOU BE THE CONSULTANT

Busted Knuckles and Capital Needs

The idea for the Busted Knuckle Garage (BKG) came to Warren Tracy while he was at the bottom of the Grand Canyon, where he spent 11 years as the manager of the Phantom Ranch, a hospitable little lodge that can be reached only by mule, by foot, or by rafting the Colorado River. The catchy name came to Tracy one night while he was sleeping, and he stumbled out of bed to write it down and sketch out the logo, a hand with a bandaged finger grasping a wrench. A year later, Tracy, who earned plenty of busted knuckles while tinkering with cars as a teenager, established the Busted Knuckle Garage "for no other reason than to help us all celebrate the fun we have tinkering, puttering, and playing around with our favorite car, truck, or motorcycle." The company motto is "Repair and despair under one roof."

Tracy filed a trademark for the Busted Knuckle Garage name even though he had no products to sell until he commissioned a sign maker to create a few signs bearing the name and logo. "We sold 100 [signs] the first month," he recalls. He soon struck a deal with one of his customers from the Phantom Ranch, a woman who made a soothing herbal salve that all of the Grand Canyon guides swore by. Tracy began marketing the salve under the BKG brand, and "it just took off," he recalls. "We knew we were on to something."

Tracy resigned from the Phantom Ranch, took out a home equity loan and maxed out several credit cards and made BKG a full-time career. Soon, the company was selling more than 250 different products ranging from clothing and car-care products to collectibles and home décor all aimed at fellow wrench-twisters. Tracy says that 70 percent of BKG retail sales are from women buying gifts for men. In 2007, Tracy negotiated a deal in which automotive tools giant Mac Tools would distribute BKG products through its catalog and Web site. Sales exploded. Orders were eight times the optimistic sales forecast that Tracy had developed. The small company hired six additional employees just to handle the additional orders and began increasing its inventory purchases. Because Mac Tools had 90-day credit terms and BKG had only 30-day credit terms from its vendors, cash flow became a problem. Tracy approached several banks, but all of them refused to extend BKG loans because the company lacked collateral, had a limited track record, and was facing cash

The Busted Knuckle Garage

flow shortages. Tracy believes that an injection of capital will fuel his company's growth and earn it a spot in the winner's circle. The question is: Where will the capital come from?

1. Describe the advantages and the disadvantages of both equity capital and debt capital for Warren Tracy.
2. Explain why the following funding sources would or would not be appropriate for Tracy: family and friends, angel investors, an initial public offering, a traditional bank loan, asset-based borrowing, or one of the many federal or SBA loans.
3. Assume the role of consultant to Tracy. Work with a team of your classmates to brainstorm ways that BKG could attract the growth capital it needs. What steps would you recommend he take before approaching the potential sources of funding you have identified?

Sources: Adapted from "CFG: Going Where Banks Simply Don't Go," Commercial Finance Group, May 2008, http://www.cfgroup.net/files/email/cfg_newsletter_05-08.html; T. Foster Jones, "Garage Brand," *Costco Connection*, March 2009, p. 19; "Head Wrench," Busted Knuckle Garage, http://www.bustedknucklegarage.com/servlet/the-template/about/Page; Brandy Shaffels, "Father's Day Gift Ideas from the Busted Knuckle Garage," *Automotive Traveler*, June 6, 2008, http://www.automotivetraveler.com/index.php?option=com_content&task=view&id=278&Itemid=129.

LO 4

Describe the various sources of debt capital and the advantages and disadvantages of each.

The Nature of Debt Financing

Debt financing is a popular tool that many entrepreneurs use to acquire capital; outstanding small business loans total nearly $685 billion. Debt financing involves the funds that the small business owner borrows and must repay with interest. Lenders of capital are more numerous than investors, although small business loans can be just as difficult (if not more difficult) to obtain. The National Small Business Association reports that its members consistently identify access to capital as one of the top ten challenges their businesses face.[55] Amy Rhodes, owner of A-2-Z Scuba, a small scuba shop in Puyallup, Washington, says that her company is struggling to survive in the midst of an economic downturn and a national credit crisis. "We can't expand, and we can't buy inventory," says the frustrated entrepreneur. "We've had to do everything on credit cards because the banks won't even look at us. Every dime of our $40,000 profit last year went right back into the business. Now sales are down, and we're having to make ends meet out of our own pockets."[56]

Although borrowed capital allows entrepreneurs to maintain complete ownership of their businesses, it must be carried as a liability on the balance sheet as well as be repaid with interest at some point in the future. In addition, because small businesses are considered to be greater risks than bigger corporate customers, they must pay higher interest rates because of the risk-return tradeoff—the higher the risk, the greater is the return demanded. Most small firms pay well above the **prime rate,** the interest rate banks charge their most creditworthy customers. A study by David Walker, a professor at Georgetown University, reports that small businesses pay two to three times the prime rate, primarily because they rely heavily on high-cost credit cards for debt financing.[57] Entrepreneurs seeking debt capital are quickly confronted with an astounding range of credit options varying greatly in complexity, availability, and flexibility. Not all of these sources of debt capital are equally favorable, however. By understanding the various sources of debt capital and their characteristics, entrepreneurs can greatly increase the chances of obtaining a loan.

We now turn to the various sources of debt capital.

prime rate
the interest rate banks charge their most creditworthy customers.

Sources of Debt Capital

COMMERCIAL BANKS Commercial banks are the very heart of the financial market for small businesses, providing the greatest number and variety of loans to small companies. A study by the Small Business Administration found that commercial banks provide 64.7 percent of all traditional debt to small businesses, compared to 12.3 percent supplied by commercial finance companies, the next most prominent source of small business lending.[58] For small business owners, banks are lenders of *first* resort. The average micro business loan (those less than $100,000) is $7,400, and the average small business loan (those between $100,000 and $1 million) is $181,000.

Banks tend to be conservative in their lending practices and prefer to make loans to established small businesses rather than to high-risk start-ups. A study by Wells Fargo/Gallup Small Business Index reports that 12 percent of entrepreneurs receive bank loans to start their businesses.[59] Unfortunately for entrepreneurs, the meltdown in the financial markets has caused banks to tighten their lending standards, which has made it more difficult for small businesses, even established ones, to qualify for loans.

Kenneth Barnett, founder of Aqua Lights, a four-year-old manufacturer of underwater lights for boats that is based in Alpharetta, Georgia, is frustrated by his inability to secure a $500,000 loan to fund his company's growth. Although Aqua Lights is profitable and its sales are growing, Barnett's pitches to bankers have been unsuccessful, despite his presentation of a highly polished business plan. "We were hopeful in the beginning," he says, "but we've been turned down three times, even from the bank I've had a relationship with for nearly eight years."[60]

ENTREPRENEURIAL PROFILE

Kenneth Barnett: Aqua Lights

Because start-up companies are so risky, bankers prefer to make loans to existing businesses with successful track records. They are concerned with a firm's operating past and will scrutinize its financial reports to project its position in the future. They also want proof of the stability of the company's sales and its ability to generate adequate cash flow to repay the loan. If they do make loans to a start-up venture, banks like to see sufficient cash flow to repay the loan, ample collateral to secure it, or a Small Business Administration (SBA) guarantee to insure it. Although large banks account for the majority of small business loans, entrepreneurs should not overlook small community banks (those with less than $300 million in assets) for business loans. These small banks, which make up 98 percent of U.S. banking institutions, account for 35 percent of the dollar volume of all small business loans.[61] They also tend to be "small business friendly" and are more likely than their larger counterparts to customize the terms of their loans to the particular needs of small businesses, offering, for example, flexible payment terms to match the seasonal pattern of a company's cash flow or interest-only payments until a piece of equipment begins generating revenue.

When evaluating a loan application, especially for a business start-up, banks focus on a company's capacity to create positive cash flow because they know that is where the money to repay their loans will come from. The first question in most bankers' minds when reviewing an entrepreneur's business plan is, "Can this business generate sufficient cash to repay the loan?" Even though they rely on collateral to secure their loans, the last thing banks want is for a borrower to default, forcing them to sell the collateral (often at "fire sale" prices) and use the proceeds to pay off the loan. *That's* why bankers stress cash flow when analyzing a loan request, especially for a business start-up. "Cash is more important than your mother," jokes one experienced borrower.[62]

Banks and other lenders also require entrepreneurs to sign personal guarantees for any loan they make to small businesses. By making a personal loan guarantee, an entrepreneur is pledging that he or she will be liable *personally* for repaying the loan in the event that the business itself cannot repay the loan. (It is as if these individuals have "cosigned" the loan with the business.)

Short-Term Loans

Short-term loans, extended for less than one year, are the most common type of commercial loan banks make to small companies. These funds typically are used to replenish the working capital account to finance the purchase of inventory, boost output, finance credit sales to customers, or take advantage of cash discounts. As a result, an entrepreneur repays the loan after converting inventory and receivables into cash. There are several types of short-term loans.

HOME EQUITY LOANS Many entrepreneurs use the equity that they have built in their homes to finance their business start-ups. Entrepreneurs are borrowing from themselves by pledging their homes as collateral for the loans they receive. Jennifer Behar, founder of Jennifer's Homemade, a Miami-based bakery that sells gourmet biscotti and flatbread through upscale grocers and her own Web site, launched her business in 2005 with a home equity loan and a credit card. A year later, she was able to establish a $50,000 line of credit with a local bank.[63]

COMMERCIAL LOANS (OR "TRADITIONAL BANK LOANS") A basic short-term loan is the commercial bank's specialty. Business owners use commercial loans for a specific expenditure—to buy a particular piece of equipment or to make a specific purchase, and terms usually require repayment as a lump sum within three to six months. Two types of commercial loans exist: secured and unsecured. A secured loan is one in which the borrower's promise to repay is secured by giving the bank an interest in some asset (collateral). Although secured loans give banks a safety cushion in case the borrower defaults on the loan, they are much more expensive to administer and maintain. With an unsecured loan, the bank grants a loan to a business owner without requiring him or her to pledge any specific collateral to support the loan in case of default.

Jennifer Behar, founder of Jennifer's Homemade.

Until business owners can prove their companies' creditworthiness to the bank's satisfaction, they are not likely to qualify for unsecured commercial loans.

LINES OF CREDIT   One of the most common requests entrepreneurs make of banks and commercial finance companies is to establish a commercial **line of credit,** a short-term loan with a preset limit that provides much-needed cash flow for day-to-day operations. A line of credit is ideal for helping business owners smooth out the uneven flow of cash that results from seasonal sales, slow-moving inventory, rapid growth, extending trade credit, and other causes. Like commercial loans, lines of credit can be secured or unsecured. A business typically pays a small handling fee (1 to 2 percent of the maximum amount of credit) plus interest on the amount borrowed—usually prime-plus-three-points or more. Mark Snyder, co-founder of Superior Medical Supply, a Denver-based company whose customers include physicians' offices, surgical centers, and nursing homes, needed a line of credit to bridge the gap in his growing company's cash flow. Superior's customers normally take 60 days to pay for the medical supplies they purchase, but Snyder must pay his vendors within 30 days. To avoid a cash crisis, Snyder convinced a community bank to grant Superior a $100,000 line of credit, which subsequently has increased to $175,000.[64]

FLOOR PLANNING   Floor planning is a form of financing frequently employed by retailers of "big ticket items" that are easily distinguishable from one another (usually by serial number), such as automobiles, boats, and major appliances. For example, a commercial bank finances Auto City's purchase of its inventory of automobiles and maintains a security interest in each car in the order by holding its title as collateral. Auto City pays interest on the loan monthly and repays the principal as it sells the cars. The longer a floor-planned item sits in inventory, the more it costs the business owner in interest expense. Banks and other floor-planners often discourage retailers from using their money without authorization by performing spot checks to verify prompt repayment of the principal as items are sold.

Intermediate and Long-Term Loans

Banks primarily are lenders of short-term capital to small businesses, although they will make intermediate and long-term loans. Intermediate and long-term loans, which are normally secured by collateral, are extended for one year or longer and are normally used to increase fixed- and growth-capital balances. Commercial banks grant these loans for constructing a plant, purchasing real estate and equipment, expanding a business, and other long-term investments. Matching the amount and the purpose of a loan to the appropriate type and length of loan is important. Loan repayments are normally made monthly or quarterly.

INSTALLMENT LOANS   One of the most common types of intermediate-term loans is an installment loan, which banks make to small firms for purchasing equipment, facilities, real estate, and other fixed assets. When financing equipment, a bank usually lends the small business from 60 to 80 percent of the equipment's value in return for a security interest in the equipment. The loan's amortization schedule, which is based on a set number of monthly payments, typically coincides with the length of the equipment's usable life. In financing real estate (commercial mortgages), banks typically lend up to 75 to 80 percent of the property's value and allow a lengthier repayment schedule of 10 to 30 years.

TERM LOANS   Another common type of loan banks make to small businesses is a **term loan.** Typically unsecured, banks grant these loans to businesses whose past operating history suggests a high probability of repayment. Some banks make only secured term loans, however. Term loans impose restrictions (called covenants) on the business decisions an entrepreneur makes concerning the company's operations. For instance, a term loan may set limits on owners' salaries, prohibit further borrowing without the bank's approval, or maintain certain financial ratios (recall the discussion of ratio analysis in Chapter 11).

The accompanying "Hands On: How To" feature describes the six most common reasons bankers reject small business loan applications and how to avoid them.

Although they usually are the first stop for entrepreneurs in search of debt capital, banks are not the only lending game in town. We now turn our attention to other sources of debt capital that entrepreneurs can tap to feed their cash-hungry companies.

line of credit
a short-term bank loan with a preset limit that provides working capital for day-to-day operations

term loan
a bank loan that imposes restrictions (covenants) on the business decisions an entrepreneur makes concerning the company's operations.

HANDS ON...
HOW TO

Get a Bank to Say "Yes" to Your Loan Application

Entrepreneurs often complain that bankers don't understand the financial needs they face when starting and operating their businesses. In many instances, however, business owners fail to help themselves when they apply for bank loans. Following are the six most common reasons bankers reject small business loan applications (and how you can avoid them).

Reason 1. "Our bank doesn't make small business loans."

Cure: Before applying for a bank loan, research banks to find out which ones actively seek the type of loan you need. Some banks don't emphasize loans under $500,000, whereas others focus almost exclusively on small company loans. The Small Business Administration's reports *Micro-Business-Friendly Banks in the United States* and *Small Business Lending in the United States* are valuable resources for locating the banks in your area that are most likely to make small business loans. Small local banks tend to be most receptive to small business loan requests. Other factors that determine the types of loans banks make include the industry in which the company competes and the company's geographic location.

Reason 2. "I don't know enough about you or your business."

Cure: Develop a detailed business plan that explains what your company does (or will do) and describes how you will gain a competitive edge over your rivals. The plan should address your company's major competition, what it will take to succeed in the market, and how your business will gain a competitive advantage in the market. Also, be prepared to supply business credit references and a personal credit history. Finally, make sure you have your "elevator pitch" honed; you should be able to describe your business, what it does, sells, or makes, and the source of its competitive edge in just one or two minutes.

Reason 3. "You haven't told me why you need the money."

Cure: A solid business plan will explain how much money you need and how you plan to use it. Make sure your request is specific; avoid requests for loans "for working capital." Don't make the mistake of answering the question, "How much money do you need?" with "How much will you lend me?" "A lot of business owners do themselves a disservice by pulling a number out and saying, 'I think I need $400,000,'" says one lending expert. Know how much money you need and present a sound business plan that includes realistic financial forecasts that support your loan request. Remember: bankers want to make loans (after all, that's how they generate a profit), but they want to make loans only to those people they believe will repay them. Make sure your plan clearly shows how your company will be able to repay the bank loan.

Renee Wood, founder of The Comfort Company.

Reason 4. "Your numbers don't support your loan request."

Cure: Include a cash flow forecast in your business plan. Bankers analyze a company's balance sheet and income statement to judge the quality of its assets and its profitability, but they lend primarily on the basis of cash flow. They know that's how you'll repay the loan. If adequate cash flow isn't available, don't expect a loan. Prove to the banker that you know what your company's cash flow is and how to manage it.

Reason 5. "You don't have enough collateral."

Cure: Be prepared to pledge your company's assets—and perhaps your personal assets—as collateral for the loan. Bankers like to have the security of collateral before they make a loan. They also expect more than $1 in collateral for every $1 of money they lend. Banks typically lend 80 to 90 percent of the value of real estate, 70 to 80 percent of the value of accounts receivable, and just 10 to 50 percent of the value of inventory pledged as collateral.

Reason 6. "Your business does not support the loan on its own."

Cure: Be prepared to provide a personal guarantee on the loan. By doing so, you're telling the banker that if your business cannot repay the loan, you will. Many bankers see their small business clients and their companies as one and the same. Even if you choose a form of ownership that provides you with limited personal liability, most bankers will ask you to override that protection by personally guaranteeing the loan.

When Renee Wood, founder of The Comfort Company, an Geneva, Illinois-based online business that sells sympathy and memorial gifts, approached her bank for a $180,000 loan to purchase a new warehouse for her growing company, she was well prepared. She took a polished business plan with realistic financial projections to support her pitch. Not only did the bank approve her loan, but her banker also suggested that she open a $50,000 line of credit to help finance the company's growth. Wood had an established relationship with her bank, having been a customer for 10 years. "They know my business, and they know me," she says. "They could look at the business checking account and see the growth trends."

The Comfort Company

There's no magic to getting a bank to approve your loan request. The secret is proper preparation and building a solid business plan that enhances your credibility as a business owner with your banker. Use your plan to prove that you have what it takes to survive and thrive. "If you have a good business plan and you've already worked with your bank, there's money to be had," says the head of the Independent Community Bankers of America.

Sources: Adapted from Emily Maltby, "How to Land a Bank Loan," *CNNMoney*, September 17, 2008, http://money.cnn.com/2008/09/16/smallbusiness/land_a_bank_loan.smb/index.htm; Jim Melloan, "Do Not Say 'I Just Want the Money,'" *Inc.*, July 2005, p. 96; Anne Field, "Getting the Bank to Yes," *Success*, May 1999, pp. 67–71; J. Tol Broome, Jr., "How to Get a 'Yes' From Your Banker," *Nation's Business*, April 1996, p. 37; "Five Red Flags to Avoid When Applying for a Bank Loan," National Federation of Independent Businesses, June 18, 2002, www.nfib.com/object/3387621; "How a Start-up Small Business Can Maximize Chances for a Bank Loan," December 9, 2004, National Federation of Independent Businesses, www.nfib.com/object/IO_19179; Crystal Detamore-Rodman, "Just Your Size," *Entrepreneur*, April 2005, pp. 59–61; Crystal Detamore-Rodman, "Raising Money: Loan Packaging Help," *Entrepreneur*, October 2008, p. 56; C.J. Prince, "Something to Bank on," *Entrepreneur*, August 2008, p. 57.

Asset-Based Lenders

Asset-based lenders, which are usually smaller commercial banks, commercial finance companies, or specialty lenders, allow small businesses to borrow money by pledging otherwise idle assets such as accounts receivable, inventory, or purchase orders as collateral. This form of financing works especially well for manufacturers, wholesalers, distributors, and other companies that have significant stocks of inventory or accounts receivable. Even unprofitable companies whose financial statements could not convince loan officers to make traditional loans can get asset-based loans. These cash-poor but asset-rich companies can use normally unproductive assets—accounts receivable, inventory, fixtures, and purchase orders—to finance rapid growth and the cash crises that often accompany it.

ENTREPRENEURIAL PROFILE

Katalin Posztos: Borneo Fitness International

Katalin Posztos, founder of Borneo Fitness International, a company that sells sporty, stylish activewear, faced a dilemma that confronts many entrepreneurs: Orders were pouring into her company, but she lacked the capital and the cash flow to fill them. Posztos tried to land a bank loan to finance the growth, but the four-year-old company's track record was not strong enough to convince bankers to lend any money. "We had a bunch of big orders and nowhere to go," recalls Posztos. That's when she turned to an asset-based lender, Capstone Business Credit. Using customer orders as collateral, Posztos borrowed enough capital to pay fabric suppliers and manufacturers to produce the garments she had designed. When she sold the clothing, Posztos took the accounts receivable that they generated and used them as collateral to borrow the money to launch a new upscale clothing line to complement the existing mass market line. Posztos's asset-based borrowing, which to date has cost $100,000 in interest and fees, has been "invaluable" she says; Borneo's sales have increased three-fold to more than $8 million annually.[65]

Like banks, asset-based lenders consider in a company's cash flow, but they are more interested in the quality of the assets pledged as collateral. The amount a small business can borrow through asset-based lending depends on the **advance rate,** the percentage of an asset's value that a lender will lend. For example, a company pledging $100,000 of accounts receivable might negotiate a 70 percent advance rate and qualify for a $70,000 asset-based loan. Advance rates can vary dramatically depending upon the quality of the assets pledged and the lender. Because inventory is an illiquid asset (i.e., hard to sell), the advance rate on inventory-based loans is quite low, usually 10 percent to 60 percent. A business pledging high-quality accounts receivable as collateral, however, may be able to negotiate up to an 85 percent advance rate. The most common types of asset-based financing are discounting accounts receivable and inventory financing.

advance rate
the percentage of an asset's value that a lender will lend.

DISCOUNTING ACCOUNTS RECEIVABLE The most common form of secured credit is accounts receivable financing. Under this arrangement, a small business pledges its accounts receivable as collateral; in return, the lender advances a loan against the value of approved accounts receivable.

The amount of the loan tendered is not equal to the face value of the accounts receivable, however. Even though the bank screens a company's accounts and accepts only qualified receivables, it makes an allowance for the risk involved because some will be written off as uncollectible. A small business usually can borrow an amount equal to 55 to 85 percent of its receivables, depending on their quality. Generally, lenders do not accept receivables that are past due.

INVENTORY FINANCING Here, a small business loan is secured by its inventory of raw materials, work in process, and finished goods. If an owner defaults on the loan, the lender can claim the pledged inventory, sell it, and use the proceeds to satisfy the loan (assuming the bank's claim is superior to the claims of other creditors). Because inventory usually is not a highly liquid asset and its value can be difficult to determine, lenders are willing to lend only a portion of its worth, usually no more than 60 percent of the inventory's value. Most asset-based lenders avoid inventory-only deals; they prefer to make loans backed by inventory *and* more secure accounts receivable. The key to qualifying for inventory financing is proving that a company has a plan or a process in place to ensure that the inventory securing the loan sells quickly.

ENTREPRENEURIAL PROFILE

Philip Asherian: E & S International Enterprises

Philip Asherian, CEO of E & S International Enterprises, a maker of electronics in Van Nuys, California, knew that the company's $150 million unsecured line of credit from a consortium of five banks was in jeopardy because of a crisis sweeping the financial industry. E & S relied on its line of credit to smooth out the swings in its cash flow that are the result of having to pay its suppliers well before it receives payment from its retail customers. The gap in the company's cash flow cycle can be as long as four months. Asherian turned to Siemens First Capital Commercial Finance Company for an asset-based line of credit that is secured by E & S's inventory and accounts receivable. Although the interest rate on the company's new line of credit is somewhat higher than the rate on its previous one, Asherian knows that the credit that E & S counts on for its success will be there when the company needs it.[66]

Asset-based financing is a powerful tool, particularly for small companies that have significant sales opportunities but lack the track record to qualify for traditional bank loans. A small business that could obtain a $1 million line of credit with a bank would be able to borrow as much as $3 million by using accounts receivable as collateral. Asset-based borrowing is also an efficient method of borrowing because a small business owner has the money she needs when she needs it. In other words, the business pays only for the capital it actually needs and uses.

Asset-based loans are more expensive than traditional bank loans because of the cost of originating and maintaining them and the higher risk involved. Rates usually run from two to seven percentage points (or more) above the prime rate. Because of this rate differential, small business owners should not use asset-based loans for long-term financing; their goal should be to establish their credit through asset-based financing and then to move up to a line of credit.

Vendor Financing

Many small companies borrow money from their vendors and suppliers in the form of trade credit. Because of its ready availability, trade credit is an extremely important source of financing to most entrepreneurs. When banks refuse to lend money to a start-up business because they see it as a high credit risk, an entrepreneur may be able to turn to trade credit for capital. Getting vendors to extend credit in the form of delayed payments (e.g., "net 30" credit terms) usually is much easier for small businesses than obtaining bank financing. Essentially, a company receiving trade credit from a supplier is getting a short-term, interest-free loan for the amount of the goods purchased.

It is no surprise that businesses receive $1.50 of credit from suppliers for every $1 they receive from banks as loans.[67] Vendors and suppliers often are willing to finance a small business's purchases of goods from 30 to 60 days (sometimes longer), interest free. Some entrepreneurs have convinced their suppliers to become investors in their start-up companies.

Ted Farnsworth, founder of the Purple Beverage Company, which sells a healthy drink made from seven of the world's most antioxidant-rich berries, persuaded suppliers, including the company's advertising agency, to provide services in exchange for shares of stock. Doing so allowed Farnsworth to conserve his company's precious cash during the turbulent start-up period and to avoid taking on excessive levels of debt. "I'd rather have partners than vendors because they've got their own interests aligned with ours," says Farnsworth.[68]

Photo by Jared Lazarus/Miami Herald staff.
Photo courtesy of Miamia Hearld, 2008.

ENTREPRENEURIAL
PROFILE _____

Ted Farnsworth: Purple Beverage Company

Equipment Suppliers

Most equipment vendors encourage business owners to purchase their equipment by offering to finance the purchase. This method of financing is similar to trade credit but with slightly different terms. Equipment vendors offer reasonable credit terms with only a modest down payment, with the balance financed over the life of the equipment (often several years). In some cases, the vendor will repurchase equipment for salvage value at the end of its useful life and offer the business owner another credit agreement on new equipment. Start-up companies often use trade credit from equipment suppliers to purchase equipment and fixtures such as counters, display cases, refrigeration units, and machinery. It pays to scrutinize vendors' credit terms, however; they may be less attractive than those of other lenders.

Commercial Finance Companies

When denied bank loans, small business owners often look to commercial finance companies for the same types of loans. Commercial finance companies are second only to banks in making loans to small businesses, and, unlike their conservative counterparts, they are willing to tolerate more risk in their loan portfolios. Of course, their primary consideration is collecting their loans, but finance companies tend to rely more on obtaining a security interest in some type of collateral, given the higher risk loans that make up their portfolios. Because commercial finance companies depend on collateral to recover most of their losses, they are able to make loans to small companies with very irregular cash flows or to those that are not yet profitable.

Approximately 150 large commercial finance companies such as AT&T Small Business Lending, GE Capital Small Business Finance, and others make a variety of loans to small companies, ranging from asset-based loans and business leases to construction and Small Business Administration loans. Dubbed "the Wal-Marts of finance," commercial finance companies usually offer many of the same credit options as commercial banks do. Because their loans are subject to more risks, finance companies charge a higher interest rate than commercial banks. Their most common methods of providing credit to small businesses are asset-based, secured by accounts receivable financing and inventory loans. Rates on these loans vary but can be as high as 15 to 30 percent (including fees), depending on the risk a particular business presents and the quality of the assets involved.

Mark Snyder, co-founder of Superior Medical Supply, the Denver-based company whose customers include physicians' offices, surgical centers, and nursing homes, recently applied for a loan from his bank for capital to fuel his company's fast growth but was turned down because his young company had scant collateral and lacked a proven track record. Snyder then turned to a commercial finance company and received a loan. Although the interest rate that Superior is paying (30 percent) is higher than that on a bank loan, Snyder is glad to have the capital. "We desperately need more capital to grow our sales," he explains.[69]

ENTREPRENEURIAL
PROFILE _____

Mark Snyder: Superior Medical Supply

Savings and Loan Associations

Savings and loan associations (S&Ls) specialize in loans for real property. In addition to their traditional role of providing mortgages for personal residences, savings and loan associations offer financing on commercial and industrial property. In the typical commercial or industrial loan, the S&L will lend up to 80 percent of the property's value with a repayment schedule of up to 30 years. Most S&Ls hesitate to lend money for buildings specially designed for a particular customer's needs. S&Ls expect the mortgage to be repaid from the company's future profits.

Stock Brokers

Stockbrokers also make loans, and many of the loans they make to their customers carry lower interest rates than those from banks. These **margin loans** carry lower rates because the collateral supporting them—the stocks and bonds in the customer's portfolio—is of high quality and is highly liquid. Moreover, brokerage firms make it easy to borrow. Brokers often set up a line of credit for their customers when they open a brokerage account. To tap that line of credit, the customer simply writes a check or uses a debit card. Typically, there is no fixed repayment schedule for a margin loan; the debt can remain outstanding indefinitely as long as the market value of the borrower's portfolio of collateral meets minimum requirements. Aspiring entrepreneurs can borrow up to 50 percent of the value of their stock portfolios, up to 70 percent of their bond portfolios, and up to 90 percent of the value of their government securities.

There is risk involved in using stocks and bonds as collateral on a loan. Brokers typically require a 30 percent cushion on margin loans. If the value of the borrower's portfolio drops, the broker can make a **margin** (or **maintenance**) **call**—that is, the broker can call the loan and require the borrower to provide more cash and securities as collateral. Recent swings in the stock market have translated into margin calls for many entrepreneurs, requiring them to repay a significant portion of their loan balances within a matter of days—or hours. If an account lacks adequate collateral, the broker can sell off the customer's portfolio to pay off the loan.

Credit Unions

Credit unions, nonprofit financial cooperatives that promote saving and provide loans to their members, are best known for making consumer and car loans. However, many are also willing to lend money to their members to launch businesses. Nearly 8,000 state- and federally-chartered credit unions with some 90 million members operate in the United States, and they make loans to their members totaling more than $575 billion a year. About 18 percent of credit union loans, an estimated $104 billion, are for business start-up and expansion.[70]

Not every credit union makes business loans (about 25 percent of credit unions do), and credit unions don't make loans to just anyone. To qualify for a loan, an entrepreneur must be a member. Lending practices at credit unions are very much like those at banks, but credit unions usually are willing to make smaller loans.

margin loans
loans from a stockbroker that use the stocks and bonds in the borrower's portfolio as collateral.

margin (or maintenance) call
occurs when the value of a borrower's portfolio drops and the broker calls the loan in, requiring the borrower to put up more cash and securities as collateral.

credit union
a nonprofit financial cooperative that promotes saving and provides loans to its members.

ENTREPRENEURIAL PROFILE

Amy Loera: Tio's Mexican

Amy Loera, CEO of her family's Mexican restaurant, Tio's Mexican, in San Bernardino, California, presented a polished business plan to support her request for a loan to add another location. Despite Tio's having no debt on its balance sheet, a strong performance history, and a set of realistic financial forecasts for the new location, nine banks refused Loera's loan request. Frustrated, Loera turned to Arrowhead Credit Union, a local credit union that makes business loans, and within weeks received approval for a $643,000 loan. "[Arrowhead] is local and could see that we are a family-owned restaurant and had a very good formula for keeping our overhead [costs] low and prices reasonable," says Loera.[71]

Private Placements

Earlier in this chapter, we saw how companies can raise capital by making private placements of their stock (equity). Private placements are also available for debt instruments. A private placement involves selling debt to one or a small number of investors, usually insurance companies or pension funds. Private placement debt is a hybrid between a conventional loan and a bond. At its heart, it is a bond, but its terms are tailored to the borrower's individual needs, as a loan would be.

In addition to making equity investments in small companies, venture capital firms also provide venture debt financing, often in private placements. Interest rates on venture debt typically vary from prime-plus-one-percent to prime-plus-five-percent, and the loan terms range from

24 to 48 months. Venture debt deals often include warrants, which gives the venture capital firm the right to purchase shares of stock in a company at a fixed price. Venture debt financing is a hybrid between a loan and venture capital. Most venture loans come with covenants, requirements that a company must meet (such as meeting profit targets or maintaining certain financial ratios) or incur a penalty such as a paying higher interest rate or giving up more stock.

Small Business Investment Companies

Small Business Investment Companies (SBICs), created in 1958 when Congress passed the Small Business Investment Act, are privately owned financial institutions that are licensed and regulated by the SBA. The 418 SBICs operating in the United States use a combination of private capital and federally guaranteed debt to provide long-term venture capital to small businesses. Most SBICs prefer later round financing over funding start-ups. Because of changes in their financial structure made a few years ago, however, SBICs now are better equipped to invest in start-up companies. In fact, more than 58 percent of initial SBIC investments go to companies that are no more than three years old.[72] Funding from SBICs helped launch companies such as Apple, Gymboree, Cutter and Buck, Build-a-Bear Workshop, Federal Express, Staples, Sun Microsystems, and Callaway Golf.

> **Small Business Investment Companies (SBICs)**
> privately owned financial institutions that are licensed by the SBA and use a combination of private capital and federally guaranteed debt to provide long-term venture capital to small businesses.

Since 1958, SBICs have provided more than $556 billion in long-term debt and equity financing to some 106,000 small businesses, adding many thousands of jobs to the American economy.[73] SBICs must be capitalized privately with a minimum of $5 million, at which point they qualify for up to three dollars in long-term SBA loans for every dollar of private capital invested in small businesses up to a maximum of $150 million. As a general rule, SBICs may provide financial assistance only to small businesses with a net worth of less than $18 million and average after-tax earnings of $6 million during its last two years. However, employment and total annual sales standards vary from industry to industry. SBICs are limited to a maximum investment or loan amount of 20 percent of their private capital to a single client.

SBICs provide both debt and equity financing to small businesses. Because of SBA regulations affecting the financing arrangements an SBIC can offer, most SBICs extend their investments as loans with an option to convert the debt instrument into an equity interest later. Most SBIC loans are in the much-needed range of $100,000 to $5 million, and the loan term is longer than most banks allow. The average SBIC loan is $719,856.[74] When they make equity investments, SBICs are prohibited from obtaining a controlling interest in the companies in which they invest (no more than 49 percent ownership). The average SBIC equity investment is $868,400, far below the average equity investment by venture capital firms of $7.4 million. The most common forms of SBIC financing (in order of their frequency) are: a loan with an option to buy stock, a convertible debenture, a straight loan, and preferred stock.

Outback Steakhouse, a restaurant chain with an Australian theme founded by Chris Sullivan, Robert Basham, Tim Gannon, and Trudy Cooper, received financing early on from an SBIC, Kitty Hawk Capital I, that allowed it to grow. In 1990, Outback had been in business less than three years when the SBIC decided to invest $151,000 to boost the company's working capital balance. That capital infusion gave Outback the financing it needed to grow. The company made an initial public offering in 1991 and today generates sales of more than $2.5 billion a year![75]

ENTREPRENEURIAL PROFILE

Chris Sullivan, Robert Basham, Tim Gannon, & Trudy Cooper: Outback Steakhouse

Small Business Lending Companies

Small business lending companies (SBLCs) make only intermediate and long-term SBA-guaranteed loans. They specialize in loans that many banks would not consider and operate on a nationwide basis. Most SBLC loans have terms extending for at least 10 years. The maximum interest rate for loans of seven years or longer is 2.75 percent above the prime rate; for shorter-term loans, the ceiling is 2.25 percent above prime. Another feature of SBLC loans is the expertise the SBLC offers borrowing companies in critical areas. Corporations own most of the nation's SBLCs, giving them a solid capital base.

LO 5

Identify the various federal loan programs aimed at small companies.

Federally Sponsored Programs

Federally sponsored lending programs have suffered from budget reductions in the last several years. Current trends suggest that the federal government is reducing its involvement in the lending business, but many programs are still quite active and some are actually growing.

Economic Development Administration

The Economic Development Administration (EDA), a branch of the Commerce Department, offers loan guarantees to create new business and to expand existing businesses in areas with below average incomes and high unemployment rates. Focusing on economically distressed communities, the EDA often works with local governments to finance long-term investment projects needed to stimulate economic growth and to create jobs by making loan guarantees. The EDA guarantees loans up to 80 percent of business loans between $750,000 and $10 million. Entrepreneurs apply for loans through private lenders, for whom an EDA loan guarantee significantly reduces the risk of lending. Start-up companies must supply 15 percent of the guaranteed amount in the form of equity, and established businesses must make equity investments of at least 15 percent of the guaranteed amount. Small businesses can use the loan proceeds for a variety of ways, from supplementing working capital and purchasing equipment to buying land and renovating buildings.

ENTREPRENEURIAL PROFILE

Ed Miller & Pro Tape: Specialties

The New Jersey Economic Development Authority recently used funds from the EDA to partner with a local bank to provide more than $2 million in financing to Pro Tape & Specialties, a small manufacturer of specialty tapes. "With the EDA's assistance, we were able to fund our production expansion plan," says president Ed Miller. "The EDA not only stepped in and provided the additional financing but did so at a rate and with a payment schedule that allowed us to operate with little cash-flow disruption." Pro Tape & Specialty used the loan to triple its production capacity over a five year period, allowing the company to add 60 jobs and double its revenue.[76]

Department of Housing and Urban Development

Although the Department of Housing and Urban Development (HUD) does not extend loans or grants directly to entrepreneurs for launching businesses, it does sponsor several programs that can help qualified entrepreneurs to raise the capital they need. Community Development Block Grants (CDBGs) are extended to cities and counties that, in turn, lend or grant money to entrepreneurs to start small businesses that will strengthen the local economy. Grants are aimed at cities and towns in need of revitalization and economic stimulation. Some grants are used to construct buildings and plants to be leased to entrepreneurs, sometimes with an option to buy. Others are earmarked for revitalizing a crime-ridden area or making start-up loans to entrepreneurs or expansion loans to existing business owners. No ceilings or geographic limitations are placed on CDBG loans and grants, but projects must benefit low- and moderate-income families. In tiny Stratton, Nebraska, HUD provided a Community Development Block Grant to the Nebraska Department of Economic Development that allowed Timber Creek Homes, a maker of modular homes, to build a new factory. The expansion allowed the company to increase its workforce from 17 to 80, broaden its customer base, and boost its sales.[77]

U.S. Department of Agriculture's Rural Business-Cooperative Service

The U.S. Department of Agriculture (USDA) provides financial assistance to certain small businesses through its Rural Business-Cooperative Service (RBS). The RBS program is open to all types of businesses (not just farms) and is designed to create nonfarm employment opportunities in rural areas—those with populations below 50,000 and not adjacent to a city where densities exceed 100 people per square mile. Entrepreneurs in many small towns, especially those with populations below 25,000, are eligible to apply for loans through the RBS program, which makes almost $900 million in loan guarantees each year.

The RBS does make a limited number of direct loans to small businesses, but the majority of its activity is in loan guarantees. Through its Business and Industry Guaranteed Loan Program, the RBS will guarantee as much as 80 percent of a commercial lender's loan up to $25 million (although actual guarantee amounts are almost always far less, usually between $200,000 and $1 million) for qualified applicants.[78] Entrepreneurs apply for loans through private lenders, who view applicants with loan guarantees much more favorably than those without such guarantees. The RBS guarantee reduces a lender's risk dramatically because the guarantee means that the government agency would pay off the loan balance (up to the ceiling) if the entrepreneur defaults on the loan.

Aero Flite Inc., a small company in Kingman, Arizona, that provides aerial firefighting services, is an important part of the state's battle against devastating forest fires. With a guarantee from the USDA's Business and Industry Guaranteed Loan Program, Aero Flite received a $2.5 million loan to purchase two Bombardier Superscooper™ aircraft that are designed for aerial firefighting. (The airplanes have the ability to scoop water from nearby lakes to deposit on forest fires or to drop chemical retardant on fires if no water supply is available.) Not only does the loan guarantee protect rural communities from raging forest fires, but it also saved 26 high-paying jobs that would have disappeared.[79]

ENTREPRENEURIAL PROFILE_____

Aero Flite Inc.

Small Business Innovation Research Program

Started as a pilot program by the National Science Foundation in the 1970s, the Small Business Innovation Research (SBIR) program has expanded to eleven federal agencies, ranging from NASA to the Department of Defense. These agencies award cash grants or long-term contracts totaling $2 billion annually to small companies that want to initiate or to expand their research and development (R&D) efforts. SBIR grants give innovative small companies the opportunity to attract early-stage capital investments *without* having to give up significant equity stakes or taking on burdensome levels of debt. The SBIR process involves three phases. Phase I ("proof of concept") grants, which determine the feasibility and commercial potential of a technology or product, last for up to six months and have a ceiling of $100,000. Phase II ("prototype development") grants, designed to develop the concept into a specific technology or product, run for up to 24 months and have a ceiling of $750,000. Approximately 40 percent of all Phase II applicants receive funding. Phase III is the commercialization phase, in which the company pursues commercial applications of the research and development conducted in phases I and II and must use private or non-SBIR federal funding to bring a product to market.

Competition for SBIR funding is intense; only 17 percent of the small companies that apply receive funding. So far, nearly 108,400 SBIR awards totaling more than $25.2 billion (26 percent in Phase I and 74 percent in Phase II) have gone to more than 16,000 small companies, which traditionally have had difficulty competing with big corporations for federal R&D dollars. The government's dollars have been well invested. Nearly 45 percent of small businesses receiving second-phase SBIR awards have achieved commercial success with their products.[80]

Drs. Daniel Arick and Shlomo Silman received both Phase I and Phase II SBIR grants of $1,024,123 from the National Institutes of Health to develop and test the EarPopper, a hand-held, battery-powered device that relieves the discomfort of inner ear pressure. Middle-ear fluid is the second most common reason (the common cold is the most common reason) for children's visits to doctors, which adds $4 billion each year to the nation's health care costs. The EarPopper pumps a steady, controlled stream of air into the Eustachian tube to relieve the pressure imbalance in the inner ear and can be used on children and adults. Clinical trials, for which the SBIR grants helped pay, showed that the EarPopper provides relief for 85 percent of patients. After developing and testing the device, Arick and Silman licensed it to Micromedics, a privately-owned medical supply company based in St. Paul, Minnesota, which brought the product to market.[81]

ENTREPRENEURIAL PROFILE_____

Daniel Arick & Shlomo Silman: EarPopper

The Small Business Technology Transfer Program

The Small Business Technology Transfer Program (STTR) program complements the Small Business Innovation Research Program. Whereas the SBIR focuses on commercially promising ideas that originate in small businesses, the STTR uses companies to exploit the vast reservoir of

The Hunt for Money

Mobo Systems.

In 2006, 26-year-old Noah Glass launched Mobo Systems, a New York City—based company that lets customers order coffee and takeout food via text messages from their cell phones. Mobo Systems charges the order to the customer's credit card and collects a 10 percent transaction fee from the restaurant. Glass says that the average text-message order is $9.69. Not only does the service offer customers the convenience of ordering by text message wherever they may be, but it also allows them to avoid waiting in lines and to pick up their orders when they arrive at the restaurant. "We've signed up 60 restaurants in the metropolitan area [of New York City]," says Glass, "and now we're opening the service to any restaurant in the country." Restaurants can sign up online for Mobo Systems' service, which already has several thousand diners placing orders in New York restaurants and generates $3 million in annual sales.

"We're hoping that this concept will spread virally across college campuses the way Facebook did," says Glass, who predicts rapid growth in the use of mobile text orders. "The only question is which app is going to be the killer app. We think ours is the best thing out there." Glass is seeking $5 million in capital to allow Mobo Systems to expand and build a brand name, allowing the company to become the dominant player in the budding mobile orders.

Sing-2-School.

As school teachers in New York City, Shawn Chandler and Ronald Speed-Bey, Jr., discovered a Hip-Hop CD that taught multiplication to young children. They liked the idea, but "the Hip-Hop wasn't authentic, and the kids couldn't relate to it," says Chandler. "We thought we could do it better." Chandler and Speed-Bey recorded their own Hip-Hop educational CD with Chandler (a.k.a. "Ah-Choo") performing. They began selling it to parents of the children

in their school and launched a Web site to promote Sing-2-School, their educational entertainment company whose mission is to use Hip-Hop culture in a positive way to reach children. So far, Sing-2-School has sold 16,000 copies of their educational CD, and Chandler and Speed-Bey are seeking $250,000 for branding and product development. "We've recorded a few more albums, we're working on a children's book, and we'd like to make animated videos," explains Chandler. "Eventually we'd like to license our brand for clothing and toys." The entrepreneurs also are trying to increase sales, which currently are less than $10,000 per year, by signing a distribution agreement with a major retail outlet such as Target, K-Mart, or QVC.

1. Explain why the following funding sources would or would not be appropriate for Noah Glass, Shawn Chandler, and Ronald Speed-Bey, Jr.: family and friends, angel investors, venture capital, an initial public offering, a traditional bank loan, asset-based borrowing, or one of the many federal or SBA loans.
2. Angels who invest in companies are looking to "cash out" their investments in five to seven years. Suppose that these entrepreneurs are able to convince private investors to invest in their companies. Discuss the exit strategies that are available to them. What are the advantages and disadvantages of each one?
3. Work with a team of your classmates to brainstorm ways that these entrepreneurs could attract the capital they need for their businesses. What steps would you recommend they take before they approach the potential sources of funding you have identified?

Sources: Adapted from Max Chafkin, "Elevator Pitch: Mobo Systems," *Entrepreneur,* September 2007, pp. 40–41; Jenalia Moreno and Brad Hem, "Small Businesses Stymied as Credit Gets Scarce," *Houston Chronicle,* October 3, 2008, http://apps.chron.com/disp/story.mpl/business/6039412.html; Dalia Fahmy, "Elevator Pitch: Sing-2-School," *Inc.,* August 2007, pp. 36–37.

commercially promising ideas that originate in universities, federally funded R&D centers, and nonprofit research institutions. Researchers at these institutions can join forces with small businesses and can spin off commercially promising ideas while remaining employed at their research institutions. Five federal agencies award grants of up to $750,000 in three phases to these research partnerships.

Small Business Administration (SBA)

LO 6

Describe the various loan programs available from the Small Business Administration.

The Small Business Administration (SBA) has several programs designed to help finance both start-up and existing small companies that cannot qualify for traditional loans because of their thin asset base and their high risk of failure. In its more than 50 years of operation, the SBA has helped nearly 20 million small businesses through a multitude of programs, enabling many of them to get the financing they need for start-up or for growth. The SBA's $85 billion portfolio of loans makes it the largest single financial backer of small businesses in the nation.[82] To be eligible for SBA funds, a business must meet the SBA's criteria that define a small business. In addition, some types of businesses, such as those engaged in gambling, pyramid sales schemes, or real estate speculation, among others, are ineligible for SBA loans.

The loan application process can take from between three days to several months, depending on how well prepared the entrepreneur is and which bank is involved. To reduce the paperwork requirements and processing time involved in its loans, the SBA created the **SBA***Express* **Program**, in which participating lenders use their own loan procedures and applications to make loans of up to $350,000 to small businesses. Because the SBA guarantees up to 50 percent of the loan, banks often are willing to make smaller loans to entrepreneurs who might otherwise have difficulty meeting lenders' standards. Loan maturities on SBA*Express* loans typically are between five and ten years, but loan maturities for fixed assets can be up to 25 years. The average SBA*Express* loan is $50,000.[83]

Patriot Express Program

In 2007, the SBA launched the **Patriot Express Program,** which is designed to assist some of the nation's 25 million veterans and their spouses who want to become entrepreneurs. The loan ceiling is $500,000, and the SBA guarantees up to 85 percent of the loan amount in case the borrower defaults. Like SBA*Express* loans, the turnaround time on loan applications is just 36 hours. Patriot Express loans carry interest rates that range from 2.25 percent to 4.75 percent above the prime interest rate. The average Patriot Express loan is $98,000.[84]

SBA*Express* **Program**
an SBA program that allows participating lenders to use their own loan procedures to make SBA-guaranteed loans of up to $350,000.

Patriot Express Program
an SBA program that is designed to assist some of the nation's 25 million veterans and their spouses who want to become entrepreneurs.

As an Air Force fighter pilot for 20 years, Dave Brackett flew hundreds of missions, but when he retired from the military and wanted to launch a pizza restaurant in his hometown of Colorado Springs, Colorado, he faced another challenging mission: finding the necessary financing. Brackett, who has an MBA, envisioned a small, Italian-style trattoria like the ones he frequented while stationed in Italy, but the only way he could get bank financing was to open a franchised pizza restaurant. "No way was I doing a franchise," he says. "I was going to open an independent restaurant or not do it at all." Fortunately, Brackett learned about the Patriot Express program and applied for a loan. Within weeks, he had secured a $52,000 loan and began remodeling a vintage brick building to accommodate wood-fired brick ovens and up to 40 diners. Within months, customers were lining up to eat at Pizzeria Rustica, which recently earned a five-star rating from the Colorado Springs daily newspaper. "The [Patriot Express] loan allowed me to do it the right way," says Brackett.[85]

Pizzeria Rustica LLC

ENTREPRENEURIAL PROFILE _____

Dave Brackett:
Pizzeria Rustica

Community*Express* Program

In 1999, working with the National Community Reinvestment Coalition, the SBA created the **Community***Express* **program,** which provides loans to entrepreneurs in communities that have experienced economic distress (and who are viewed as high-risk borrowers. The maximum loan amount is $250,000 with an SBA guarantee of 85 percent, and turnaround times on loan requests can be as fast as 24 to 36 hours. Community Express loans account for 9 percent of all SBA loans, up from just 1 percent in 2002.[86] Approximately 70 percent of Community*Express* loans go to minority entrepreneurs. Like Patriot Express loans, Community*Express* loans carry interest rates that range from 2.25 percent to 4.75 percent above the prime interest rate. The average Community*Express* loan is $27,000.[87]

Community*Express* **Program**
an SBA loan program that provides loans to entrepreneurs in communities that have experienced economic distress and who are viewed as high-risk borrowers.

Other SBA Loan Programs

7(A) LOAN GUARANTY PROGRAM The SBA works with local lenders (both bank and non-bank) to offer many other loan programs that are designed to help entrepreneurs who cannot get capital from traditional sources gain access to the financing they need to launch and grow their businesses. When they were just small companies, Callaway Golf, Outback Steakhouse, and Intel Corporation borrowed through the SBA's loan programs. The most popular SBA loan program is the **7(a) loan guaranty program** (see Figure 13.7). Nearly 2,700 private lenders extend these loans to small businesses, but the SBA guarantees them (85 percent of loans up to $150,000; 75 percent of loans

7(a) loan guaranty program
an SBA program in which loans made by private lenders to small businesses are guaranteed up to a ceiling by the SBA.

FIGURE 13.7

SBA 7(A) Guaranteed Loans

Source: U.S. Small Business Administration.

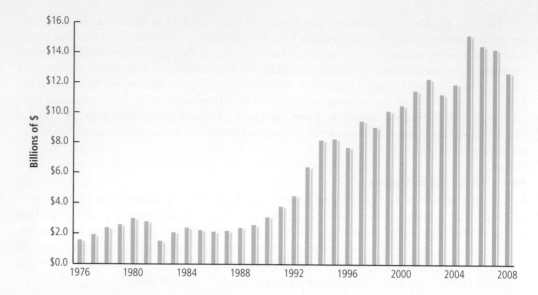

that range from $150,001 up to the loan cap of $ 2 million). The average 7(a) loan is $183,000, and more than 5,000 lenders currently have 7(a) loans outstanding.[88] Note that the SBA does not actually lend any money; it merely acts as an insurer, guaranteeing the lender this much repayment in case the small business borrower defaults on the loan. Because SBA-guaranteed loans are riskier, their default rate is higher than that of standard bank loans. A recent study reports that the default rate on SBA loans has increased from 2.4 percent in 2004 to 11.9 percent today.[89]

Because the SBA assumes most of the credit risk, lenders are more willing to consider riskier deals that they normally would refuse. With the SBA's guarantee, borrowers also have to come up with less collateral than with a traditional bank loan.

ENTREPRENEURIAL PROFILE

Mike & Kim Schmidt: Bella's Fat cat

Milwaukee, Wisconsin, natives Mike and Kim Schmidt had both entrepreneurial experience and restaurant experience, but their business plan for a hamburger and custard eatery fell into the "high risk" category at the local banks they approached. The copreneurs had money of their own to invest in their business idea but needed additional capital to make it a reality. Carol Mick, vice-president of SBA lending at Stearns Bank in St. Cloud, Minnesota, worked with the Schmidts to make an initial $75,000 loan under the SBA's 7(a) program to enable them to launch Bella's Fat Cat (named after their beloved and somewhat chunky pet), which was originally located in Milwaukee's Brady Street shopping district. The Schmidts received a second loan, this one with a 15-year maturity, of $285,000 to purchase, remodel, and equip a second restaurant in an old pharmacy building. The Schmidts have since repaid their original SBA-backed loan and have taken out a third loan for $225,000 to continue their company's expansion.[90]

Qualifying for an SBA loan guarantee requires cooperation among the entrepreneur, the participating lender, and the SBA. The participating lender determines the loan's terms and sets the interest rate within SBA limits. Contrary to popular belief, SBA-guaranteed loans do *not* carry special deals on interest rates. Typically, rates are negotiated with the participating lender, with a ceiling of prime-plus-2.25 percent on loans of less than seven years and prime-plus-2.75 percent on loans of seven to 25 years. Interest rates on loans of less than $25,000 can run up to prime-plus-4.75 percent. The average interest rate on SBA-guaranteed loans is prime-plus-2 percent (compared to prime-plus-1 percent on conventional bank loans). The SBA also assesses a one-time guaranty fee of 1 to 3.75 percent for all loan guarantees. The maximum loan available through the 7(a) guaranty program is $2,000,000.

The average duration of an SBA loan is 12 years—far longer than the average commercial small business loan. In fact, longer loan terms are a distinct advantage of SBA loans. At least half of all bank business loans are for less than one year. By contrast, SBA real estate loans can extend for up to 25 years (compared to just 10 to 15 years for a conventional loan), and working capital loans have maturities of seven years (compared with two to five years at most banks). These longer terms translate into lower loan payments, which are better suited for young, fast-growing, cash-strapped companies.

SECTION 504 CERTIFIED DEVELOPMENT COMPANY PROGRAM The second most popular SBA loan program is the Section 504 program, which is designed to encourage small businesses to expand their facilities and to create jobs. Section 504 loans provide long-term, fixed asset financing to small companies to purchase land, buildings, or equipment—"brick-and-mortar" loans. Three lenders play a role in every 504 loan: a bank, the SBA, and a **certified development company (CDC).** A CDC is a nonprofit organization licensed by the SBA and designed to promote economic growth in local communities. Some 270 CDCs operate across the United States. The entrepreneur is required to make a down payment of just 10 percent of the total project cost rather than the typical 20 to 30 percent traditional bank loans require. The CDC provides 40 percent at a long-term fixed rate, supported by an SBA loan guarantee in case the entrepreneur defaults. The bank provides long-term financing for the remaining 50 percent, also supported by an SBA guarantee. The major advantages of Section 504 loans are their fixed rates and terms, their 10- and 20-year maturities, and the low down payment required. The maximum loan amount that the SBA will guarantee is $4 million, and the average CDC loan is $597,000.

> After emigrating from his native Vietnam, 18-year-old John Le, who spoke no English, landed in San Jose, California, where he enrolled in a local community college to learn English and took jobs washing dishes and driving delivery trucks. The owner of a company that imported meat from Australia wanted to begin importing seafood and asked Le to create and manage the new division. "I made a lot of connections and started thinking about doing it on my own," says Le. In 2001, Le struck out on his own and launched Seafood Connection with 500-square-feet of freezer space he rented from a customer. The business grew quickly, prompting Le to move three times in search of more space. When a friend suggested that he buy a building to house his fast-growing company, Le raised $600,000 from family members and friends but needed much more capital. He worked with a CDC, Bay Area Development Company, Comerica Bank, and the SBA to get a $4.4 million loan to purchase a 30,000 square foot building in San Jose. Seafood Connection's annual sales now exceed $43 million, and Le believes that the company can surpass $100 million in revenue within the next few years.[91]

MICROLOAN PROGRAM About three-fourths of all entrepreneurs need less than $100,000 to launch their businesses. Indeed, most entrepreneurs require less than $50,000 to start their companies. Unfortunately, loans of that amount can be the most difficult to get. Lending these relatively small amounts to entrepreneurs starting businesses is the purpose of the SBA's Microloan Program. Called **microloans** because they range from just $100 to as much as $35,000, these loans have helped thousands of people take their first steps toward entrepreneurship. Banks typically shun loans in such small amounts because they consider them to be risky and unprofitable. In an attempt to fill the void in small loans to start-up companies, the SBA launched the microloan program in 1992, and it has gone on to become the single largest source of funding for microenterprises. Today, more than 150 authorized lenders make SBA-backed microloans. The average size of a microloan is $13,000, with a maturity of three years (the maximum term is six years), and lenders' standards are less demanding than those on conventional loans. Nearly 40 percent of all microloans go to business start-ups, and more than half of all microloans go to women and minority-owned businesses.[92] All microloans are made through nonprofit intermediaries that are approved by the SBA and operate in 46 states.

certified development company (CDC)
a nonprofit organization licensed by the SBA and designed to promote growth in local communities by working with commercial banks and the SBA to make long-term loans to small businesses.

ENTREPRENEURIAL PROFILE ____

John Le: Seafood Connection

microloan Program
an SBA program that makes small loans, some as small as $100, to entrepreneurs.

Joey Johnson, founder of Graphic Mechanic Design Studio.

Graphic Mechanic Design Studio

For nearly ten years, Joey Johnson ran her graphic design business, Graphic Mechanic Design Studio, part-time from her home while working full-time for Electronic Data Systems in Atlanta. She had built a solid clientele, many of them repeat customers, but lacked the capital to upgrade to the equipment she would need to operate her businessfull time. She also wanted help preparing a business plan and advice on managing a company. Johnson turned to the SBA's microloan program that was administered locally by the Women's Economic Development Agency (WEDA). She enrolled in a WEDA course on starting and managing a business, developed a business plan, and landed a $15,000 microloan, which she used to transform Graphic Mechanic Design Studio into a full-time business. In just one year, sales doubled to $50,000.[93]

CAPLine Program

an SBA program that makes short-term capital loans to growing companies needing to finance seasonal buildups in inventory or accounts receivable.

THE CAPLINE PROGRAM In addition to its basic 7(a) loan guarantee program (through which the SBA makes about 80 percent of its loans), the SBA provides guarantees on small business loans for start-up, real estate, machinery and equipment, fixtures, working capital, exporting, and re-structuring debt through several other methods. About two-thirds of all SBA loan guarantees are for machinery and equipment or working capital. The **CAPLine Program** offers short-term capital to growing companies needing to finance seasonal buildups in inventory or accounts receivable under five separate programs, each with maturities up to five years: seasonal line of credit (provides advances against inventory and accounts receivable to help businesses weather seasonal sales fluctuations), contract line of credit (finances the cost of direct labor and materials costs associated with performing contracts), builder's line of credit (helps small contractors and builders finance labor and materials costs), standard asset-based line of credit (an asset-based revolving line of credit for financing short-term needs), and small asset-based line of credit (an asset-based revolving line of credit up to $200,000). CAPLine is aimed at helping cash-hungry small businesses by giving them a credit line to draw on when they need it. These loans built around lines of credit are what small companies need most because they are so flexible, efficient, and, unfortunately, so hard for small businesses to get from traditional lenders.

Export Working Capital (EWC) Program

an SBA loan program that provides working capital to small exporters.

LOANS INVOLVING INTERNATIONAL TRADE For small businesses going global, the SBA has the *Export Working Capital (EWC) Program,* which is designed to provide working capital to small exporters. The SBA works in conjunction with the Export-Import Bank to administer this loan guarantee program. Applicants file a one-page loan application, and the response time normally is 10 days or less. The maximum loan is $2 million, and proceeds must be used to finance small business exports.

Stephen Fantone started Optikos Corporation as a part-time business in the basement of his home and has built the maker of equipment that measures optical image quality into a global business with 40 employees and annual sales of more than $10 million. Optikos's products are used in a variety of industries, and the company counts among its customers many major corporations. Optikos's foray into global markets began in 1999 when Fantone decided to purchase the assets of a British company, which opened the door to customers in Europe and Asia. Because purchasing cycles in these regions are longer than in the United States, Optikos needed a line of credit to finance its growing export business. Most banks are hesitant to extend credit on foreign sales, but Fantone's banker was an experienced SBA lender and helped Optikos qualify for a $750,000 loan through the SBA's Export Working Capital program. The line of credit allowed Optikos to increase exports to 30 percent of the company's total sales. Fantone credits the EWC line of credit with allowing Optkos to "establish a global market for the company and its products."[94]

International Trade Program

an SBA loan program for small businesses that are engaging in international trade or are adversely affected by competition from imports.

The **International Trade Program** is for small businesses that are engaging in international trade or are adversely affected by competition from imports. The SBA allows global entrepreneurs to combine loans from the Export Working Capital Program with those from International Trade Program for up to $2 million with a maximum guarantee of $1.75 million. Loan maturities range from one to 25 years. Only about 3 percent of SBA loans originate in these two international programs.[95]

disaster loans

an SBA loan program that makes loans to small businesses devastated by some kind of financial or physical loss.

DISASTER LOANS As their name implies, **disaster loans** are made to small businesses devastated by some kind of financial or physical loss. The maximum disaster loan usually is $1.5 million, but

TABLE 13.3 SBA Loan Program Overview.

Program	Maximum Loan Amount	Guaranty Percentage	Use of Proceeds	Loan Maturity	Maximum Interest Rates
Standard 7(a)	$2 million	85%* on loans up to $150,000; 75 percent on loans between $151,000 and $2 million	Purchase land or buildings; expand or renovate existing buildings; acquire equipment and fixtures; make leasehold improvements; refinance existing debt; purchase inventory; establish seasonal line of credit	Working capital – up to 7 years; equipment – up to 10 years; real estate – up to 25 years	Loans of 7 years or less: prime + 2.25%; loans longer than 7 years: prime + 2.75%; for loans of less than $50,000, rates can be up to prime + 4.25%
SBA*Express*	$350,000	50%	Same as Standard 7(a) loan purposes and revolving line of credit	Up to 7 years	Loans of $50,000 or less: prime + 6.5%; Loans of $50,001 to $350,000: prime + 4.5%
Community*Express*	$250,000	Same as Standard 7(a)	Same as SBA*Express*	Up to 7 years	Same as SBA*Express*
Patriot Express	$500,000	Same as Standard 7(a)	Same as Standard 7(a)	Same as Standard 7(a)	Same as Standard 7(a)
CAPLines	$2 million	Same as Standard 7(a)	Working capital needs that are associated with specific contracts	Up to 5 years	Same as Standard 7(a)
International Trade	$2 million	Same as Standard 7(a)	Acquire fixed assets	Up to 25 years	Same as Standard 7(a)
Export Working Capital	$2 million (may be combined with International Trade loan)	90% up to $1.5 million maximum	Short-term working capital for exporting	Generally 1 year or a single transaction cycle	No cap
Section 504 Community Development Corporation	$10 million	40% up to $2 million maximum	Fixed asset projects such as constructing new buildings, purchasing and renovating existing buildings, and purchasing equipment and machinery	Equipment – up to 10 years; real estate – up to 20 years	Loans of less than 7 years: prime + 3.25%; loans of 7 years or more: prime + 3.75%
Microloan	$35,000	N/A	Same as Standard 7(a)	Up to 6 years	Variable; generally between 8% and 13%

*Proposed to increase to 90%.

Source: Small Business Administration and "The SBA's 7(a) Loan Program: A Flexible Tool for Commercial Lenders," *Community Development Insights*, Washington, D.C.: U.S. Department of the Treasury, September 2008, http://www.occ.treas.gov/cdd/Insights-SBAs7(a).pdf, p. 4.

Congress often raises that ceiling when circumstances warrant. Disaster loans carry below-market interest rates as low as four percent and terms as long as 30 years. Loans for physical damage above $10,000 and financial damage of more than $5,000 require an entrepreneur to pledge some kind of collateral, usually a lien on the business property. The SBA has helped entrepreneurs whose businesses have been disrupted by a variety of disasters, ranging from hurricanes on the Southeastern coast and earthquakes on the West coast to floods and tornadoes in the Midwest and the terrorist attacks of September 11, 2001. In the aftermath of floods in the Midwest and hurricanes along the Gulf Coast, the SBA approved 20,100 disaster loans for a total of $1 billion.[96]

Table 13.3 summarizes the features of the major SBA loan programs.

State and Local Economic Development Programs

LO 7

Explain the state and local economic development programs that are available to entrepreneurs.

Many states have created economic development programs to provide funds for business start-ups and expansions. They have decided that their funds are better spent encouraging small business growth rather than "chasing smokestacks"—trying to entice large businesses to locate within their boundaries. These programs come in a wide variety of forms, but they all tend to focus on developing small businesses that create the greatest number of jobs and economic benefits. Although each state's approach to economic development is unique, one common element is some kind of small business financing program: loans, loan guarantees, development grants, venture capital pools, and others. One approach many states have had success with is **Capital Access Programs (CAPs).** First introduced in Michigan in 1986, many states now offer CAPs that are designed to encourage lending institutions to make loans to businesses that do not qualify for traditional financing because of their higher risk. Under a CAP, a bank and a borrower each pay an upfront fee (a portion of the loan amount) into a loan-loss reserve fund at the participating bank, and the state matches this amount. The reserve fund, which normally ranges from 6 to 14 percent of the loan amount, acts as an insurance policy against the potential loss a bank might experience on a loan and frees the bank to make loans that it otherwise might refuse. One study of CAPs found that 55 percent of the entrepreneurs who received loans under a CAP would not have been granted loans without the backing of the program.[97]

Capital Access Programs
a state lending program that encourages lending institutions to make loans to businesses that do not qualify for traditional financing because of their higher risk.

Even cities and small towns have joined in the effort to develop small businesses and help them grow. Many communities across the United States operate **revolving loan funds** (RLFs) that combine private and public funds to make loans to small businesses, often at favorable interest rates, for the purpose of starting or expanding businesses that create jobs and contribute to economic development. As money is repaid into the funds, it is loaned back out to other entrepreneurs.

revolving loan fund
a program offered by communities that combine private and public funds to make loans to small businesses, often at favorable interest rates.

ENTREPRENEURIAL PROFILE

Larry & Karen Royal: Earthworm Soil Factory

California's Recycling Market Development Zone (RMDZ) Loan Program, a revolving loan program that is part of the state's Capital Access Program (CalCAP), provides loans to businesses that sell recycled products or use them in their production processes. Copreneurs Larry and Karen Royal recently received a loan from RMDZ to transform 42 acres of land that is unsuitable for farming into a vermiculture (earthworm breeding) and vermicomposting (using earthworms to process waste products into nutrient-rich soil) operation aptly named the Earthworm Soil Factory. "Thanks to a low-interest loan from [RMDZ], we were able to purchase the equipment needed for our business," says Larry. By collecting yard debris and food and agricultural waste, the Royals prevent tons of material from going into landfills. They sell their product, naturally enriched soil, to nurseries, landscape companies, homeowners, and organic farmers.[98]

Internal Methods of Financing

LO 8

Discuss valuable methods of financing growth and expansion internally.

Small business owners do not have to rely solely on financial institutions and government agencies for capital; their businesses have the capacity to generate capital. This type of financing, called **bootstrap financing,** is available to virtually every small business and encompasses factoring, leasing rather than purchasing equipment, using credit cards, and managing the business frugally.

bootstrap financing
internal methods of financing a company's need for capital.

Factoring Accounts Receivable

Instead of carrying credit sales on its own books (some of which may never be collected), a small business can sell outright its accounts receivable to a factor. A **factor** buys a company's accounts receivable and pays for them in two parts. The first payment, which the factor makes immediately, is for 50 to 80 percent of the accounts' agreed-upon (and usually discounted) value. The factor makes the second payment of 15 to 18 percent, which makes up the balance less the factor's service fees, when the original customer pays the invoice. Factoring is a more expensive type of financing than loans from either banks or commercial finance companies, but for businesses that cannot qualify for those loans, it may be the only choice!

Factoring deals are either with recourse or without recourse. Under deals arranged with recourse, a small business owner retains the responsibility for customers who fail to pay their accounts. The business owner must take back these uncollectible invoices. Under deals arranged without recourse, however, the owner is relieved of the responsibility for collecting them. If customers fail to pay their accounts, the factor bears the loss. Because the factoring company assumes the risk of collecting the accounts, it normally screens the firm's credit customers, accepts those judged to be creditworthy, and advances the small business owner a portion of the value of the accounts receivable. Factors discount anywhere from 2 to 40 percent of the face value of a company's accounts receivable, depending on a small company's:

- Customers' financial strength and credit ratings.
- Industry and its customers' industries because some industries have a reputation for slow payments.
- History and financial strength, especially in deals arranged with recourse.
- Credit policies.[99]

factor
a financial institution that buys business's accounts receivable at a discount.

Leasing

Leasing is another common bootstrap financing technique. Today, small businesses can lease virtually any kind of asset-from office space and telephones to computers and heavy equipment. By leasing expensive assets, the small business owner is able to use them without locking in valuable capital for an extended period of time. In other words, entrepreneurs can reduce the long-term capital requirements of the business by leasing equipment and facilities, and they are not investing their capital in depreciating assets. In addition, because no down payment is required and because the cost of the asset is spread over a longer time (lowering monthly payments), a company's cash flow improves.

Credit Cards

Unable to find financing elsewhere, many entrepreneurs launch their companies using the fastest and most convenient source of debt capital available: credit cards! In 1998, Google cofounders Larry Page and Sergey Brin used three credit cards to purchase the $15,000 worth of hardware that they needed to launch their budding search engine.[100] A survey by National Small Business United found that 44 percent of the owners of small and medium-sized businesses used credit cards as a source of funds, making it the most common form of business financing (see Figure 13.8).[101] Putting business start-up costs on credit cards charging 21 percent or more in annual interest is expensive and risky, especially if sales fail to materialize as quickly as planned, but some entrepreneurs have no other choice.

Chris Mauzy applied for a bank loan to start Zip Express Installation, a home electronics installation service, but banks rejected his business plan because he had no collateral with which to secure the loan. Mauzy believed in his business plan and launched the Zip Express by charging $30,000 in start-up expenses to two credit cards. Fortunately, sales were brisk, and Mauzy was able to pay off the balance on the cards each month. Zip Express recently landed a contract for installations with Target and generated sales of $5.5 million in its first year of operation.[102]

ENTREPRENEURIAL PROFILE

Chris Mauzy: Zip Express Installation

FIGURE 13.8

Where Do Small Businesses Get Their Financing?

Source: Based on 2008 Survey of Small and Mid-Sized Businesses, *National Small Business Association, Washington, DC, 2009.*

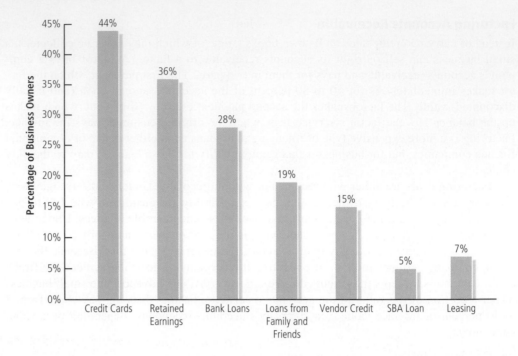

Chapter Summary

1. Explain the importance of planning for a company's capital requirements.

- Capital is any form of wealth employed to produce more wealth.

2. Describe the differences between equity capital and debt capital and the advantages and disadvantages of each.

- Equity financing represents the personal investment of the owner (or owners), and it offers the advantage of not having to be repaid with interest.
- Debt capital is the financing that a small business owner has borrowed and must repay with interest. It does not require entrepreneurs to give up ownership in their companies.

3. Describe the various sources of equity capital available to entrepreneurs, including personal savings, friends and relatives, "angels," partners, corporations, venture capital, public stock offerings, and simplified registrations and exemptions.

- The most common source of financing a business is the owner's personal savings. After emptying their own pockets, the next place entrepreneurs turn for capital is family members and friends. Angels are private investors who not only invest their money in small companies, but they also offer valuable advice and counsel to them. Some business owners have success financing their companies by taking on limited partners as investors or by forming an alliance with a corporation, often a customer or a supplier.

Venture capital companies are for-profit, professional investors looking for fast-growing companies in "hot" industries. When screening prospects, venture capital firms look for competent management, a competitive edge, a growth industry, and important intangibles that will make a business successful. Some owners choose to attract capital by taking their companies public, which requires registering the public offering with the SEC.

4. Describe the process of "going public" and the various simplified registrations and exemptions from registration available to small businesses wanting to sell securities to investors.

- Going public involves: (1) choosing the underwriter, (2) negotiating a letter of intent, (3) preparing the registration statement, (4) filing with the SEC, and (5) meeting state requirements.
- Rather than go through the complete registration process, some companies use one of the simplified registration options and exemptions available to small companies: Regulation S-B, Regulation D (Rule 504) Small Company Offering Registration (SCOR), Regulation D (Rule 505 and Rule 506) Private Placements, Section 4(6), Rule 147, Regulation A, direct stock offerings, and foreign stock markets.

5. Describe the various sources of debt capital and the advantages and disadvantages of each: banks, asset-based lenders, vendors (trade credit), equipment suppliers, commercial finance

companies, savings and loan associations, stock brokers, insurance companies, credit unions, bonds, private placements, Small business investment companies (SBICs), and Small business lending companies (SBLCs).

- Commercial banks offer the greatest variety of loans, although they are conservative lenders. Typical short-term bank loans include commercial loans, lines of credit, discounting accounts receivable, inventory financing, and floor planning.
- Trade credit is used extensively by small businesses as a source of financing. Vendors and suppliers commonly finance sales to businesses for 30, 60, or even 90 days.
- Equipment suppliers offer small businesses financing similar to trade credit, but with slightly different terms.
- Commercial finance companies offer many of the same types of loans that banks do, but they are more risk oriented in their lending practices. They emphasize accounts receivable financing and inventory loans.
- Savings and loan associations specialize in loans to purchase real property - commercial and industrial mortgages—for up to 30 years.
- Stock-brokerage houses offer loans to prospective entrepreneurs at lower interest rates than banks because they have high quality, liquid collateral - stocks and bonds in the borrower's portfolio.
- Small business investment companies are privately owned companies licensed and regulated by the SBA that qualify for SBA loans to be invested in or loaned to small businesses.
- Small business lending companies make only intermediate and long-term loans that are guaranteed by the SBA.

6. Identify the various federal loan programs aimed at small businesses.

- The Economic Development Administration, a branch of the Commerce Department, makes loan guarantees to create and expand small businesses in economically depressed areas.

- The Department of Housing and Urban Development extends grants (such as Community Development Block Grants) to cities that, in turn, lend and grant money to small businesses in an attempt to strengthen the local economy.
- The Department of Agriculture's Rural Business-Cooperative Service loan program is designed to create nonfarm employment opportunities in rural areas through loans and loan guarantees.
- The Small Business Innovation Research Program involves 11 federal agencies that award cash grants or long-term contracts to small companies wanting to initiate or to expand their research and development (R&D) efforts.
- The Small Business Technology Transfer Program allows researchers at universities, federally funded R&D centers, and nonprofit research institutions to join forces with small businesses and develop commercially promising ideas.

7. Describe the various loan programs available from the Small Business Administration.

- Almost all SBA loan activity is in the form of loan guarantees rather than direct loans. Popular SBA programs include: the SBA*Express* program, the 7(A) loan guaranty program, the CAPLine program, the Export Working Capital program, the Section 504 Certified Development Company program, the Microloan program, the Prequalification Loan Program, and the Disaster Loan program.
- Many state and local loan and development programs such as Capital Access Programs and Revolving Loan Funds complement those sponsored by federal agencies.

8. Discuss valuable methods of financing growth and expansion internally.

- Small business owners may also look inside their firms for capital. By factoring accounts receivable, leasing equipment instead of buying it, and by minimizing costs, owners can stretch their supplies of capital.

Discussion Questions

1. Why is it so difficult for most small business owners to raise the capital needed to start, operate, or expand their ventures?
2. Define equity financing. What advantage does it offer over debt financing?
3. What is the most common source of equity funds in a typical small business? If an owner lacks sufficient equity capital to invest in the firm, what options are available for raising it?
4. What guidelines should an entrepreneur follow if friends and relatives choose to invest in her business?
5. What is an "angel"? Assemble a brief profile of the typical private investor. How can entrepreneurs locate potential angels to invest in their businesses?
6. What advice would you offer an entrepreneur about to strike a deal with a private investor to avoid problems?
7. What types of businesses are most likely to attract venture capital? What investment criteria do venture capitalists use when screening potential businesses? How do these compare to the typical angel's criteria?
8. How do venture capital firms operate? Describe their procedure for screening investment proposals?

9. Summarize the major exemptions and simplified registrations available to small companies wanting to make public offerings of their stock.

10. What role do commercial banks play in providing debt financing to small businesses? Outline and briefly describe the major types of short-term, intermediate, and long-term loans commercial banks offer.

11. What is trade credit? How important is it as a source of debt financing to small firms?

12. What function do SBICs serve? How does an SBIC operate? What methods of financing do SBICs rely on most heavily?

13. Briefly describe the loan programs offered by the following:
    a. the Economic Development Administration.
    b. the Department of Housing and Urban Development.
    c. the Department of Agriculture.
    d. local development companies.

14. Explain the purpose and the methods of operation of the Small Business Innovation Research Program and the Small Business Technology Transfer Program.

15. How can a firm employ bootstrap financing to stretch its current capital supply?

16. What is a factor? How does the typical factor operate? Explain the advantages and the disadvantages of using factors as a source of funding.

Business PlanPro™

One reason for creating a business plan is to secure funding. Your business plan can be an excellent communication tool for convincing lenders and investors that your company is an attractive investment with a bright future.

Business Plan Exercises

Consider the financial needs of your company. Do you need start-up funding to purchase equipment, make space improvements, or for other reasons? Is your business going to need working capital based on your cash flow projections and needs? Does your business need additional financing for growth? If there is a need to raise capital, your business plan can help clarify those needs and formulate a strategy for raising capital.

On the Web

If you need start-up or growth capital for your venture, visit http://www.pearsonhighered.com/scarborough, click on Chapter 13 and review these financing options. Determine whether these sources may be of use as you explore financing opportunities. You will also find information regarding bootstrap and nontraditional funding.

Sample Plans

Review your favorite sample plans and note the capital needs in the financial section. If you are creating a start-up plan, you may also want to review these sample plans:

- Elsewares Promotional
- Westbury Storage, Inc.

If you will be searching for financing for an ongoing business, these plans may be of interest:

- Coach House Bed & Breakfast
- Bioring SA (second-round financing)

These plans present financial information that may give you ideas on how to best communicate your financial needs. Use approaches that your audience will find enticing. Your lender will want to confirm that you are going to be able to make your payments on time. Investors will want to learn more about the growth and earning potential of your business. Leverage each aspect of the financial section—the break-even analysis, projected profit and loss, projected cash flow, projected balance sheet and business ratios—that you deem valuable for your financial audience.

In the Software

Open your business plan in *Business Plan Pro* and go to the Financial Plan section. You may want to begin by providing an overview of your financial situation and needs. State assumptions about your financial environment. These assumptions will help to identify general facts about your plan, such as anticipated economic conditions, current short-term and long-term interest rates, expected tax rates, personnel expenses, cash expenses, sales on credit, or any areas that you hope to develop and confirm through further research. Let the software lead you through this section. Next, assess the type and the amount of funding that you will need. Do you anticipate the business will need short-term or long-term financing? Are you going to bring in capital through a loan or through investors? If you are adding investors, what will be their percentage of the total ownership? How does this effect your ownership position? What role will the investors playin the business? These questions will be important to address in this section of your business plan. Make certain this section clearly tells your financial story. It is critical to provide relevant information that will be meaningful to others who will review your plan for investment or loan purposes.

Building Your Business Plan

One of the most valuable aspects of developing the financial section of your business plan is to assess the financial needs, describe the use of these funds, and make certain that you can live with the consequences of these decisions. Keep in mind that potential lenders and investors will also assess the qualifications of your management team, the growth rate of the industry, your proposed exit strategy, and other factors as they judge the financial stability and potential of your venture. Your business plan may serve as a "financial road map" to analyze your funding alternatives and determine the most attractive options available. Test each alternative against your plan to assess its viability and fit with your venture's financial needs.

Beyond the Classroom....

1. Interview several local business owners about how they financed their businesses. Where did their initial capital come from? Ask the following questions:

   a. How did you raise your starting capital? What percentage did you supply on your own?
   b. What percentage was debt capital and what percentage was equity capital?
   c. Which of the sources of funds described in this chapter do you use? Are they used to finance fixed, working, or growth capital needs?
   d. How much money did you need to launch your businesses? Where did subsequent capital come from? What advice do you offer others seeking capital?

2. Contact a local private investor and ask him or her to address your class. (You may have to search to locate one!). What kinds of businesses does this angel prefer to invest in? What screening criteria does he or she use? How are the deals typically structured?

3. Contact a local venture capitalist and ask him or her to address your class. What kinds of businesses does his or her company invest in? What screening criteria does the company use? How are deals typically structured?

4. Invite an investment banker or a financing expert from a local accounting firm to address your class about the process of taking a company public. What do these individuals look for in a potential IPO candidate? What is the process, and how long does it usually take?

5. Interview the administrator of a financial institution program offering a method of financing with which you are unfamiliar, and prepare a short report on its method of operation.

6. Contact your state's economic development board and prepare a report on the financial assistance programs it offers small businesses.

8. Go to the IPO home section of the Web site for Renaissance Capital (www.renaissancecapital.com) and explore the details of a company that is involved in making an initial public offering. View some of the documents the company has filed with the SEC, especially the initial public offering filing. Prepare a brief report on the company. What is its business? Who are its major competitors? How fast is the industry growing? What risk factors has the company identified? How much money does it plan to raise in the IPO? What is the anticipated IPO stock price? How many shares of stock will the company sell in the IPO? Would you buy this company's stock? Explain.

808 Bounce LLC

CHAPTER 14

Choosing the Right Location and Layout

The more alternatives, the more difficult the choice.
—Abbe' D'Allanival

Good order is the foundation of all things.
—Edmund Burke

Learning Objectives

On completion of this chapter, you will be able to:

1. Explain the stages in the location decision: choosing the region, the state, the city, and the specific site.

2. Describe the location criteria for retail and service businesses.

3. Outline the location options for retail and service businesses: central business districts (CBDs), neighborhoods, shopping centers and malls, near competitors, outlying areas, and at home.

4. Explain the site selection process for manufacturers.

5. Describe the criteria used to analyze the layout and design considerations of a building, including the Americans with Disabilities Act.

6. Explain the principles of effective layouts for retailers, service businesses, and manufacturers.

Location: A Source of Competitive Advantage

LO 1

Explain the stages in the location decision: choosing the region, the state, the city, and then the specific site.

Much like choosing a form of ownership and selecting particular sources of financing, the location decision has far-reaching and often long-lasting effects on a small company's future. Entrepreneurs who choose their locations wisely—with their customers' preferences and their companies' needs in mind—can establish an important competitive advantage over rivals who choose their locations haphazardly. Because the availability of qualified workers, tax rates, quality of infrastructure, traffic patterns, quality of life, and many other factors vary from one site to another, the location decision is an important one that can influence the growth rate and the ultimate success of a company. Thanks to widespread digital connectivity, mobile computing, extensive cellular coverage, and affordable air travel, entrepreneurs have more flexibility when choosing a business location than ever before.

The location selection process is like an interactive computer game in which each decision opens the way to make another decision on the way to solving the puzzle. The answer to the puzzle, of course, is the best location for a business. At each step in the decision process entrepreneurs must analyze how well the characteristics of a particular location match the unique requirements of their businesses. Because of their significant impact on a company, location decisions can be difficult; however, as with the interactive computer game, there are lots of clues that guide entrepreneurs to the best decision.

The location decision process resembles an inverted pyramid. The first level of the decision is the broadest, requiring an entrepreneur to select a particular region of the country. (We will address locating a business in a foreign country in Chapter 15, Global Aspects of Entrepreneurship.) Then an entrepreneur must select the right state, then the right city, and finally, the right site within the city. The secret to selecting the ideal location lies in knowing the factors that are most important to a company's success and then finding a location that satisfies as many of them as possible, particularly those that are most critical. For instance, one of the most important location factors for high-tech companies is the availability of a skilled labor force, and their choice of location reflects this. If physically locating near customers is vital to a company's success, then an entrepreneur's goal is to find a site that makes it most convenient for his or her target customers to do business with the company!

ENTREPRENEURIAL PROFILE

Tony & John Calamunci: Johnny's Lunch

When Tony and John Calamunci began selling franchises based on the family-owned diner that their grandfather, Johnny Colera, started in Jamestown, New York, in 1936 (and that their parents still operate), they realized that opening outlets in areas in which large concentrations of their target customers lived was essential to their success. They hired an experienced franchise veteran, George Goulson, and worked with Pitney-Bowes MapInfo to use the latest geospatial technology to determine the ideal locations for their restaurants, which sell budget-priced meals such as hot dogs, hamburgers, onion rings, and milkshakes. The Calamuncis started by defining their target customers, which they discovered include people in the lower-middle to upper-middle income bracket who fall between the ages of 16 and 24 or over 60. Using the software, they identified 72 types of neighborhoods that best match the demographic and psychographic profile of Johnny's Lunch customers. The next step was to find locations that matched the 72 prototype neighborhoods. Managers identified 4,500 areas across the United States that held large concentrations of potential Johnny's Lunch customers (most of whom lived within one mile of the proposed location) and would be good locations for restaurants. "These models increase our ability to pick 'home-run' locations and avoid the site mistakes that can cripple a budding franchise," says Goulson. Johnny's Lunch is launching its franchising effort in and around Toldeo, Ohio, which Goulson says is a microcosm of the United States. "Small restaurant owners like us can use location intelligence to prevent mistakes that could cripple franchising plans from the start. They can't afford not to invest in location intelligence."[1]

Johnny's Lunch Franchise, LLC

Johnny's Lunch Franchise, LLC

The characteristics that make for an ideal location often vary dramatically from one company to another due to the nature of their business. In the early twentieth century, companies looked for ready supplies of water, raw materials, or access to railroads; today, they are more likely to look for sites that are close to universities and offer high-speed Internet access and accessible airports. In fact, one study concluded that the factors that made an area most suitable for starting and growing small companies included access to dynamic universities, an ample supply of skilled workers, a nearby airport, a temperate climate, and a high quality of life.[2] The key to finding a suitable location is identifying the characteristics that can give a company a competitive edge and then searching out potential sites that meet those criteria.

Choosing the Region

The first step in selecting the best location is to focus on selecting the right region. This requires entrepreneurs to look at the location decision from the "30,000-foot level," as if he or she were in an airplane looking down. In fact, in the early days of their companies, Sam Walton, founder of retail giant Wal-Mart, and Ray Kroc, who built McDonald's into a fast-food giant, actually used private planes to survey the countryside for prime locations for their stores.

ENTREPRENEURIAL PROFILE

Walt Disney: Disney World

Walt Disney first spotted the location for Disney World while flying over central Florida in a private plane (which is now on display at Disney World). Because Disney lacked sufficient space to expand Disneyland in California, he and a group of top managers established several criteria, including a place with good weather throughout most of the year, plenty of land at bargain prices, a location near a major city, and access to major highways and infrastructure for the company's second theme park (dubbed "Project X"). When Disney flew over the intersection of I-4 and Route 192 near Orlando, he knew that he had found the ideal location for Disney World, which encompasses 30,000 acres, an area that is about the size of San Francisco![3]

Which region of the country has the characteristics necessary for a new business to succeed? Above all, entrepreneurs must place their customers first when considering a location. As the experience of Johnny's Lunch suggests, facts and statistics, not speculation, lead entrepreneurs to the best locations for their businesses. Common requirements may include rapid growth in the population of a certain age group, rising disposable incomes, the existence of necessary infrastructure, a nonunion environment, and low costs. At the broadest level of the location decision, entrepreneurs prefer to locate in regions of the country that are experiencing substantial growth. Every year many popular business publications prepare reports on the various regions of the nation—which ones are growing, which are stagnant, and which are declining. Studying shifts in population and industrial growth will give entrepreneurs an idea of where the action is—and isn't. Questions to consider include: How large is the population? How fast is it growing? What is the makeup of overall population? Which segments are growing fastest? Slowest? What is the trend in the population's income? Is it increasing or decreasing? Are other businesses moving into the region? If so, what kind of businesses? Generally, entrepreneurs want to avoid dying regions; they simply cannot support a broad base of potential customers.

One of the first stops entrepreneurs should make when conducting a regional evaluation is the U.S. Census Bureau. Excellent sources of basic demographic and population data include the *U.S. Statistical Abstract* and the *County and City Data Book*. The *U.S. Statistical Abstract* provides entrepreneurs looking for the right location with a multitude of helpful information, ranging from basic population characteristics and projections to poverty rates and energy consumption. Every state also publishes its own statistical abstract, which provides the same type of data for its own population. The *County and City Data Book* contains useful statistics on the populations of all of the nation's 3,141 counties and 12,175 cities with populations of 25,000 or more (and even more data for cities with populations that exceed 100,000). *Counties USA* provides similar information and focuses only on the nation's counties. The *State and Metropolitan Area Data Book* includes more than 1,500 data items for individual states, counties, and metropolitan areas. In addition to the printed versions of the publications it offers, the Census Bureau makes most of the information contained in its vast and valuable data banks available to entrepreneurs researching potential sites through its easy-to-use Web site (http://www.census.gov/). There entrepreneurs can access for specific locations vital demographic information such as age, income, educational level, employment level, occupation, ancestry, commuting times, housing data (house value, number of rooms, mortgage or rent status, number of vehicles owned, and so on), and many other characteristics. With a little practice, entrepreneurs can prepare customized reports on the potential sites they are considering. These Web-based resources give entrepreneurs instant access to important site-location information that only a few years ago would have taken many hours of intense research to compile!

The Census Bureau's American FactFinder site (http://factfinder.census.gov) provides easily accessible demographic fact sheets and maps on nearly every community in the United States, including small towns. The Census Bureau's American Community Survey provides detailed information on the demographic and economic characteristics of areas with populations of at least 250,000 and of other selected areas with populations of at least 65,000. Both the American FactFinder and the American Community Survey allow entrepreneurs to produce easy-to-read, customizable maps of the information they generate in their searches.

> When Scott Fiore was looking for a location for his natural pharmacy, The Herbal Remedy, he turned first to the demographic data from the U.S. Census Bureau. Not only did his analysis provide him with a picture of the potential customers in each area, but it also pointed him to Douglas County, Colorado, one of the fastest-growing counties in the nation. The profile that emerged from the demographic data for the county was one of young, affluent, well-educated residents, a perfect fit with Fiore's definition of his target customer. As he drove around the area, Fiore noticed that Douglas County and neighboring Arapaho County were "very sports-oriented, athletic places," which was also consistent with his target audience. More research led Fiore to the town of Littleton, which is conveniently located for customers in both counties but offers relatively low rental rates.[4]

ZoomProspector is a useful Web site that allows entrepreneurs to search for the ideal location using a multitude of factors including population size, job growth rate, number of patents issued, venture capital invested, education level, household incomes, and proximity to interstate highways, railroads, and airports. Once entrepreneurs locate a city that matches their customer profiles, they find other cities across the United States that have similar profiles with a single mouse click! Entrepreneurs who are considering a particular region can display "heat maps" that visually display the areas that have the highest concentrations of people that have a particular characteristic, such as a bachelor's degree or the highest household incomes.

> Jamin Arn, founder of OfficePro, a retailer of office furniture and supplies based in Janesville, Wisconsin, recently used ZoomProspector to find the ideal location for his third store. ZoomProspector led him to a community that he otherwise would have overlooked: Normal, Illinois, a city with a population of 50,000 people situated about two hours from Chicago. Arn was able to determine that Normal's population, job growth rates, and income and education levels are very similar to Janesville, which has proved to be a successful location for his first two stores.[5]

The Population Reference Bureau (http://www.prb.org) provides a detailed breakdown of the most relevant data collected from the most recent census reports. The DataFinder is a database that includes 244 variables for the United States and 132 variables for 210 other nations. The site also includes helpful articles that discuss the implications of the changing demographic and economic profile of the nation's (and the world's) population, such as the impact of aging baby boomers on business and the composition of the U.S. workforce. STAT-USA (www.statusa.gov) is a service of the United States Department of Commerce that offers financial, employment, and economic data about the United States as well as trade data for the United States and for Europe. Here entrepreneurs can locate everything from the latest consumer price index and the number of housing starts to leads for global trading partners and tips on conducting business in practically any country in the world.

Other helpful resources merit mention as well. *Demographics USA* is a publication that covers the United States, its counties, and zip code areas. This useful publication provides market surveys on various segments of U.S. demographics, including purchasing power, retail sales by type of merchandise, employment and payroll data, and forecasts of economic conditions at both the zip code and the county level. The buying power indices in *Demographics USA* indicate an area's purchasing potential for economy products, mid-priced products, and premium products. This publication also indicates consumers' spending on particular types of products and services such as apparel, entertainment, and appliances. Entrepreneurs can use *Demographics USA* to analyze the level of competition in a particular area, assess the sales potential of a particular location, compare consumers' buying power across a dozen categories, and more.

Lifestyle Market Analyst, a four-part annual publication, matches population demographics with lifestyle interests. Section 1 provides demographics and lifestyle information for 210 "Designated Market Areas" across the United States. Section 2 gives demographic and geographic profiles of 77 lifestyle interests that range from avid readers and dieters to wine aficionados and pet owners. Section 3 describes the dominant lifestyle interests for each of the 210 market areas. Section 4 provides comparisons of other activities that correspond with each lifestyle interest. Entrepreneurs can use *Lifestyle Market Analyst* to determine, for example, how likely members of a particular market segment are to own a dog, collect antiques, play golf, own a vacation home, engage in extreme sports, invest in stocks or bonds, or participate in a host of other activities.

Other sources of demographic data include the *Survey of Buying Power, Editor and Publisher Market Guide, The American Marketplace: Demographics and Spending Patterns, Rand McNally's Commercial Atlas and Marketing Guide,* and *Zip Code Atlas and Market Planner.* The *Survey of Buying Power*, having recently undergone the most extensive overhaul in its 80-year history, provides statistics, rankings, and projections for every county and media market in the United States with demographics segmented by age, race, city, county, and state. This publication, now available only online, also includes current information on retail spending and forecasts for each spending category. The data are divided into 323 metro markets as defined by the Census Bureau and 210 media markets, which are television or broadcast markets defined by Nielsen Media Research. The *Survey* also includes several unique statistics. Effective buying income (EBI) is a measure of disposable income, and the buying power index (BPI), for which the *Survey* is best known, is a unique measure of spending power that takes population, EBI, and retail sales into account to determine a market's ability to buy goods and services.

The *Editor and Publisher Market Guide* is similar to the *Survey of Buying Power* but provides additional information on markets. The *Guide* includes detailed economic and demographic information, ranging from population and income statistics to information on climate and transportation networks for all 3,096 counties in the United States and more than 1,600 key cities in both the United States and Canada.

The American Marketplace: Demographics and Spending Patterns provides useful demographic information in eight areas: education, health, income, labor force, living arrangements, population, race and ethnicity, and spending and wealth. Most of the tables in the book are derived from government statistics, but *The American Marketplace* also includes a discussion of the data in each table as well as a forecast of future trends. Many users say the primary advantage of *The American Marketplace* is its ease of use.

The *Commercial Atlas and Marketing Guide* reports on more than 120,000 places in the United States, many of which are not available through Census reports. This guide, which includes two volumes, one an index and the other the actual guide, covers 11 economic indicators for every major geographic market; tables showing population trends, income, buying power, trade, and manufacturing activity; and large, cross-reference maps. The U.S. Census Bureau also offers the Zip Code Tabulation Areas (ZCTA) Web site (http://www.census.gov/geo/ZCTA/zcta.html), which organizes the wealth of census data by zip code. The database of 33,178 ZCTAs across the United States allows users to create tables and plot maps of census data by zip code.

The task of analyzing various potential locations—gathering and synthesizing data on a wide variety of demographic and geographic variables—is one ideally suited for a computer. In fact, a growing number of entrepreneurs are relying on geographic information systems (GIS), powerful software programs that combine map drawing with database management capability, to pinpoint the ideal location for their businesses. GIS packages allow users to search through virtually any database containing a wealth of information and plot the results on a map of the country, an individual state, a specific city, or even a single city block. The visual display highlights what otherwise would be indiscernible business trends. For instance, using GIS programs, entrepreneurs can plot their existing customer base on a map with various colors representing the different population densities. Then they can zoom in on those areas with the greatest concentration of customers, mapping a detailed view of zip code borders or even city streets. GIS street files originate in the U.S. Census Department's TIGER (Topographically Integrated Geographic Encoding Referencing) file, which contains map information broken down for every square foot of Metropolitan Statistical Areas (MSAs). In essence, TIGER is a massive database of geographic features such as roads, railways, and political boundaries across the entire United States that, when linked with mapping programs and demographic databases, gives entrepreneurs incredible power to pinpoint existing and potential customers on easy-to-read digital maps. Many states and counties across the United States now provide GIS files online that allow entrepreneurs to identify sites that meet certain location criteria for their businesses.

Once an entrepreneur has identified the best region of the country, the next step is to evaluate the individual states in that region.

Choosing the State

Every state has an economic development office working to recruit new businesses. Even though the publications produced by these offices will be biased in favor of locating in that state, they are an excellent source of information and can help entrepreneurs assess the business climate in each state. Some of the key issues to explore include the laws, regulations, and taxes that govern businesses and any incentives or investment credits the state may offer to businesses that locate there.

For instance, the founders of MedcoTek, a small company that provides software that allows hospitals and physicians offices to transmit radiological images across the Internet in a highly secure fashion, recently decided to relocate the company's headquarters from its Charlotte, North Carolina, birthplace to the New York State Center of Excellence in Bioinformatics and Life Sciences in downtown Buffalo, New York, a city with an emerging biotechnology focus. The relocation decision was made to ensure that the small company has access to the capital, strategic partners, and resources necessary to solidify its position in a fast-growing market. "[This] is a strategic move designed to leverage Buffalo's research assets and to take advantage of the professional services the region provides to biotech companies," says CEO Fredric Ziegler. "The region's quality of life, spirit of scientific collaboration, and community friendliness also were factors in our decision." It did not take long for MedcoTek to realize the benefits of its new location. The company recently signed a licensing agreement to use technology developed by researchers at the University of Buffalo Medical Center that improves the quality of the radiological images transmitted over the Internet.[6]

ENTREPRENEURIAL PROFILE _____

Fredric Ziegler: MedcoTek

Movin' On

Rancho Santa Margarita, California, had been the home of Industrial Motion (IM), an industrial parts distributor, since Eric Kozlowski and Brian Pfeifer launched the company in 1998. However, Kozlowski and Pfeifer became concerned as they watched spiraling operating costs cause IM's profits to evaporate. Every year, property taxes, insurance rates, and wages increased significantly. In California, the average wage for customer service and warehouse employees was about $60,000 annually, and workers' compensation cost for a warehouse employee was $740 per month. "The cost was pretty extraordinary, but we didn't know any better," says Kozlowski. Long commutes necessitated by high housing costs resulted in a high employee turnover rate.

Kozlowski and Pfeifer realized that their company might drown in a pool of rising costs and decided to relocate it. They initially considered moving to Reno, Nevada, or Phoenix, Arizona, to capitalize

on the lower operating costs those cities offered but were turned off by the desert climate. When one of Kozlowski's neighbors moved across the country to Charlotte, North Carolina, the business partners began considering a wider range of locations for IM, including those on the East Coast. A few minutes online convinced Kozlowski and Pfeifer that the Charlotte area deserved a closer look as a potential home for IM. Housing prices were two-thirds lower than those in Southern California, and office and warehouse space would cost half of the amount the company was paying for its current location. "That was the first real awakening," says Kozlowski.

One trip to North Carolina confirmed everything the entrepreneurs had discovered online, and they decided to move to Mooresville, North Carolina, a small city just outside of Charlotte. When they returned to California, they developed a relocation plan and set the first week in February, a slow time in their business, as the target date to make the move, which would take place over a three-day weekend. They told their 17 employees about their plans to relocate the company and offered to pay moving expenses for those who wanted to stay with the company; only one employee, the logistics manager, accepted their offer. On Friday of the target weekend, a moving company packed four tractor-trailers with the contents of the warehouse, and Kozlowski and Pfeifer boarded a plane with the company's server, in its own ticketed seat, between them. When they arrived in their new Mooresville office, they set up the server and started working on folding tables and chairs.

Staffing the company in their new location took longer than the entrepreneurs thought it would. They hired three employees right away but had trouble filling orders while the new workers learned their jobs. Kozlowski contacted a former account manager and offered to fly her to North Carolina for a few weeks to help IM get back on track. She accepted the offer, and after spending a few weeks in Mooresville, decided that she liked the area so much that she stayed.

The decision to relocate their company provided everything that Kozlowski and Pfeifer thought it would—and more. The wages that IM pays typically are between $35,000 and $45,000 per year, 25 percent to 42 percent lower than the wages the company paid

in California. Property taxes are half of what they were in Rancho Santa Margarita, and the company's workers' compensation insurance costs just 10 percent of the rate in California. Even the cost of the company's security system is lower—$25 per month, down from $280 per month. In addition, the entrepreneurs say that their workforce is better educated and more mature. IM, now with 42 employees, has seen its employee turnover rate plummet. In addition, Kozlowski, Pfeifer, and their families are enjoying a lifestyle that includes quality schools for their children, reasonable housing costs, and amenities such as nearby outdoor activities and a host of entertainment options.

1. What lessons does Industrial Motion's story offer about the importance of an entrepreneur's location decision?
2. What issues should entrepreneurs such as Kozlowski and Pfeifer consider when deciding where to locate their businesses?

Source: Based on Simona Covel, "Moving Across the Country to Cut Costs," *Wall Street Journal*, January 10, 2008, p. B4.

Other factors entrepreneurs should consider when choosing a location include proximity to markets, proximity to raw materials, wage rates, quantity and quality of the labor supply, general business climate, tax rates, Internet access, and total operating costs.

PROXIMITY TO MARKETS Locating close to markets they plan to serve is extremely critical to manufacturers, especially when the cost of transporting finished goods is high relative to their value. Locating near customers is necessary to remain competitive. For instance, with its location in the center of the country and its ready access to a variety of transportation systems, St. Louis, Missouri, has become home to many companies' distribution centers. Not only do businesses in St. Louis benefit from a well-educated workforce, but they also can ship to customers anywhere in the country quickly and efficiently.

ENTREPRENEURIAL PROFILE

John Jansheski: DenTek Oral Care

John Jansheski launched DenTek Oral Care, a company that makes oral care supplies, in Petaluma, California. However, he soon realized that that more than 80 percent of the company's shipments were going east of the Mississippi and that shipping products across the Rocky Mountains added three percentage points to the cost of DenTek's products. In 2001, Jansheski decided to relocate the company to Maryville, Tennessee. Although he has had to hire nearly all new workers (very few of the company's employees chose to make the move from California), Jansheski is confident the move has made his company more competitive. "It was the most important financial decision we've ever made," he says. "We're putting all of that money back into the company, and as a result, sales are twice what they were."[7]

PROXIMITY TO NEEDED RAW MATERIALS If a business requires raw materials that are difficult or expensive to transport, it may require a location near the source of those raw materials. For instance, one producer of kitty litter chose a location on a major vein of kaolin, the highly absorbent clay from which kitty litter is made. Transporting the heavy, low-value material over long distances would impractical—and unprofitable. In other situations in which bulk or weight is not a factor, locating manufacturing in close proximity to the suppliers can facilitate quick deliveries and reduce holding costs for inventories. The value of products and materials, their cost of transportation, and their unique function all interact to determine how close a business must be to its source of supplies.

WAGE RATES Existing and anticipated wage rates provide another measure for comparison among states. Wages can sometimes vary from one state or region to another, significantly affecting a company's cost of doing business. For instance, according to the Bureau of Labor

Statistics, the average hourly compensation for workers (including wages and benefits) ranges from a low of $24.23 in the South to a high of $31.77 in the Northeast.[8] Wage rate differentials within geographic regions can be even more drastic. When reviewing wage rates, entrepreneurs must be sure to measure the wage rates for jobs that relate to their particular industries or companies. In addition to surveys by the Bureau of Labor Statistics (www.bls.gov), local newspaper ads can give entrepreneurs an idea of the pay scale in an area. Entrepreneurs should study not only prevailing wage rates but also *trends* in rates. How does the rate of increase in wage rates compare to those in other states? Another factor influencing wage rates is the level of union activity in a state. How much union organizing activity has the state seen within the last two years? Is it increasing or decreasing?

LABOR SUPPLY NEEDS For many businesses, especially technology-driven companies, one of the most important characteristics of a potential location is the composition of the local workforce. Entrepreneurs must consider two factors when analyzing the labor supply in a potential location: the number of workers available in the area and their levels of education, training, adaptability, and experience. For example, the small town of Castelfidardo, Italy, is known as the international center of accordion production because it is the home to dozens of small manufacturers of these unique musical instruments. Brothers Paolo, Silvio, and Settimio Soprani established the first commercial accordion factory in 1872 in Castelfidardo just as the instrument's popularity began to grow. Although the accordion is not as popular as it was in the late nineteenth century, Castelfidardo remains the center of accordion production because of the high concentration of skilled accordion workers who remain to this day in the area.[9]

Of course, an entrepreneur wants to know how many qualified people are available in the area to do the work required in the business. However, unemployment and labor cost statistics can be misleading if a company needs people with particular qualifications. Some states have attempted to attract industry with the promise of cheap labor. Unfortunately, businesses locating there found exactly what the term implied—unskilled, low-wage labor that is ill-suited for performing the work the companies needed.

BUSINESS CLIMATE What is the state's overall attitude toward your kind of business? Has it passed laws that impose restrictions on the way a company can operate? Are there "blue laws" that prohibit certain business activity on Sundays? Does the state offer small business support programs or financial assistance to entrepreneurs?

ENTREPRENEURIAL PROFILE ──────

Riza Berken & Pentti Kouri: Hakia

Riza Berken and Pentti Kouri, founders of Hakia, a semantics-based search engine that offers more focused results than traditional search engines, relocated from Washington, D.C., to New York City for the superior business climate it offered their technology start-up. New York offered greater venture capital funding opportunities, a rich pool of talented high-tech workers, and a business climate that offered plenty of business-to-business sales potential for Hakia. Although New York City is one of cities with the highest cost of doing business, Berken and Kouri say that it offers the ideal location for their company.[10]

Some states and cities are more "small business friendly" than others. For instance, *FSB* magazine recently named Manchester, New Hampshire, one of the best locations for small businesses, citing its well-educated workforce and receptivity of small companies as major assets. Many factors, including a diversified economic base of both large and small companies, access to a significant population of private investors interested in investing in promising small companies, and several state and local government support systems such as the New Hampshire Business Resource Center that offer entrepreneurial assistance and advice, make Manchester, once a crumbling factory town, a desirable location for entrepreneurs. Although property taxes are higher in Manchester than in surrounding areas, their impact is offset by no sales or income taxes and reasonable real estate prices. Accessible highways and an expanded airport provide important pieces of business infrastructure. Small companies such as Oasys Technology, a business that makes enhanced vision systems for aircraft pilots, have discovered that Manchester's quality of life, small town charm with big city amenities, and easy access to the area's natural beauty make it easy to attract skilled workers.[11]

TAX RATES   Another important factor that entrepreneurs must consider when screening states for potential locations is the tax burden they impose on businesses and individuals. Does the state impose a corporate income tax? How heavy are the state's property, income, and sales taxes? Income taxes may be the most obvious tax that states impose on both business and individuals, but entrepreneurs also must evaluate the impact of payroll taxes, sales taxes, property taxes, inventory taxes, and specialized taxes on the cost of their operations. Currently, seven states impose no income tax on their residents, but state governments always impose taxes of some sort on businesses and individuals. In some cases, states offer special tax rates or are willing to negotiate fees in lieu of taxes for companies that will create jobs and stimulate the local economy.

ENTREPRENEURIAL PROFILE ___

Bruce Cowan: Acclaim Electronics

After graduating from UCLA, Bruce Cowan, a native Californian, started Acclaim Electronics, an electronic chip and computer products distribution business in Carlsbad, California. Cowan decided to relocate his company to Las Vegas, Nevada, where taxes and regulatory costs are far lower. In fact, Nevada imposes no corporate, franchise, capital gains, or inventory taxes. Cowan says the move to Nevada has lowered Acclaim's annual operating costs by 40 percent![12]

INTERNET ACCESS   Speedy and reliable Internet access is an increasingly important factor in the location decision. Fast Internet access is essential for high-tech companies and those that engage in e-commerce. Even those companies that may not do business over the Web currently are finding it nearly certain that they will use the Web as a business tool. Companies that fall behind in high-tech communication find themselves at a severe competitive disadvantage.

TOTAL OPERATING COSTS   When scouting a state in which to locate a company, an entrepreneur must consider the total cost of operating a business. For instance, a state may offer low utility rates, but its labor costs and tax rates may be among the highest in the nation. To select the ideal location, entrepreneurs must consider the impact of a state's total cost of operation on their business ventures. The state evaluation matrix in Table 14.1 provides a handy tool designed to help

TABLE 14.1 State Evaluation Matrix

Location Criterion	Weight	Score (Low = 1, High = 5)	State Weighted Score (Weight × Score)		
			State 1	State 2	State 3
Quality of labor force					
Wage rates					
Union activity					
Property/building costs					
Utility costs					
Transportation costs					
Tax burden					
Educational/training assistance					
Start-up incentives					
Raw material availability					
Quality of life					
Other:					
Other:					
		Total Score			

Assign to each location criterion a weight that reflects its relative importance to your company. Then score each state on a scale of 1 (low) to 5 (high). Calculate the weighted score (weight × score) for each state. Finally, add up the total weighted score for each state. The state with the highest total score is the best location for your business.

entrepreneurs determine which states best suit the most important location criteria for their companies. This same matrix can be adapted to analyze individual cities as well. Claremont McKenna College's Kosmont-Rose Institute Cost of Doing Business Survey reports that Cheyenne (WY), Eugene (OR), Fort Worth (TX), Reno (NV), and Vancouver (WA) are among the cities that offer the lowest cost of doing business, and New York City (NY), Los Angeles (CA), San Francisco (CA), Philadelphia (PA), and Newark (NJ) are those with the highest costs of doing business.[13]

Dell Inc., a manufacturer of personal computers based in Round Rock, Texas, recently closed its manufacturing plant in Limerick, Ireland, and relocated it to Poland as part of a company-wide cost-cutting strategy designed to allow the company to maintain its position in the hotly competitive global PC business. Although Ireland still offers a low corporate tax rate (just 12.5 percent compared to 39.5 percent in the United States), labor costs are much higher there than in Poland, which also offers companies a low corporate tax rate. Other key considerations for Dell managers are Poland's central location in Europe, which allows the company to distribute its PCs inexpensively to the important European market, and the ability to avoid European import tariffs.[14]

Table 14.2 shows the cost of doing business index for the states with the highest and the lowest cost of doing business.

TABLE 14.2 Cost of Doing Business Index

Ten *most* expensive states in which to do business…*

State	Wage Cost Index	Tax Burden Index	Electricity Cost Index	Industrial Rent Cost Index	Office Rent Cost Index	Cost of Doing Business Index
Hawaii	91.9	162.1	260.7	269.5	140.4	**151.5**
New York	128.5	102.5	141.5	154.4	189.4	**130.9**
Alaska	100.3	153.0	150.3	232.7	84.5	**130.8**
Massachusetts	122.1	101.0	187.8	129.0	165.2	**130.6**
Connecticut	128.9	106.8	163.8	113.5	116.1	**127.5**
California	114.8	120.6	134.7	141.4	141.4	**122.9**
New Jersey	121.2	94.5	129.7	161.0	117.3	**120.9**
Vermont	83.9	173.1	134.0	91.9	87.3	**110.2**
Delaware	110.5	132.1	87.8	96.3	112.3	**110.1**
Rhode Island	94.6	105.6	174.9	74.0	118.7	**108.0**

Ten *least* expensive states in which to do business…

State	Wage Cost Index	Tax Burden Index	Electricity Cost Index	Industrial Rent Cost Index	Office Rent Cost Index	Cost of Doing Business Index
Arkansas	75.9	136.3	74.1	56.1	69.2	**85.4**
Tennessee	87.7	83.9	85.6	72.3	89.9	**85.2**
Missouri	87.5	81.9	63.2	103.5	92.7	**84.6**
Montana	73.3	112.8	85.0	81.7	78.4	**84.1**
South Carolina	81.0	93.6	80.1	71.3	92.1	**82.9**
Idaho	76.2	110.0	60.7	97.5	77.7	**82.8**
Nebraska	80.5	100.1	68.5	68.9	96.5	**82.3**
North Dakota	73.7	120.5	68.9	61.2	76.9	**81.3**
Iowa	80.4	94.9	80.2	51.0	68.0	**79.7**
South Dakota	71.8	68.5	73.7	61.2	69.0	**70.2**

* An index score of 100 means that a state is equal to the national average. A score of 120 means that a state's cost of doing business is 20 percent higher than the national average. Similarly, a score of 80 means that a state's cost of doing business is 20 percent lower than the national average.
Source: Milliken Institute, February 2009.

Choosing the City

POPULATION TRENDS Analyzing over time the lists of "best cities for business" compiled annually by many magazines reveals one consistent trend: Successful small companies in a city tend to track the city's population growth. In other words, more potential customers mean that a small business has a better chance of success. The Census Bureau recently named Raleigh–Cary, North Carolina, Austin–Round Rock, Texas, and Kennewick–Pasco-Richland, Washington, the fastest-growing cities in the United States.

ENTREPRENEURIAL PROFILE

Jaime & Elvira Picos:
Fiesta Tortillas

Jaime and Elvira Picos started Fiesta Tortillas in Del Rio, Texas, as a home-based business and sold their corn and flour tortillas, which they made from an old-fashioned recipe handed down from Jaime's grandmother, Mama Tomasita, to local meat markets. As the company's reputation and sales grew, the Picos moved into a small factory. After 14 years in Del Rio, the Picos noticed the rapid growth that the city of Austin, which had become a magnet for high-tech companies, was experiencing and decided to move their business there, opening a tortilla factory with used equipment in an old shopping center. After they produced a batch of tortillas, the Picos would close their factory and take their products around town to prospective customers. Fiesta Tortillas grew quickly and now operates from a state-of-the-art bakery that turns out thousands of tortillas each day, many of them for businesses in the fast-growing Austin area. The company's customer base still includes many of the local, family-owned restaurants that have been with Fiesta Tortillas for more than 20 years, as well as large food service companies and five-star hotels located in the area.[15]

Entrepreneurs should know more about the cities in which their businesses are located than do the people who live there. By analyzing population and other demographic data, an entrepreneur can examine a city in detail, and the location decision becomes more than just an educated guess, or, worse, a shot in the dark. Studying the trends and the demographics of a city, including population size and density, growth trends, family size, age breakdowns, education, income levels, job categories, gender, religion, race, and nationality, gives an entrepreneur the facts she needs to make an informed location decision. In fact, using only basic census data, entrepreneurs can determine the value of the homes in an area, how many rooms the homes contain, how many bedrooms they include, what percentage of the population own their homes, and the amount of the residents' monthly rental or mortgage payments. Imagine how useful that information would be to someone about to launch a bed and bath shop!

The amount of available data on the population of any city or town is staggering. These statistics allow entrepreneurs to compare a wide variety of cities or towns and to narrow the choices to those few that warrant further investigation. Analyzing this data makes it possible to screen out undesirable locations and to narrow the list of suitable locations to a few, but it does not make the final location decision for an entrepreneur. Entrepreneurs must see the potential locations on their "short list" *firsthand*. Only by seeing a potential location can an entrepreneur add the intangible factor of intuition into the decision-making process. Spending time at a potential location tells an entrepreneur not only how many people frequent it but also what they are like, how long they stay, and what they buy. Walking or driving around the area will give an entrepreneur clues about the people who live and work there. What are their houses like? What kinds of cars do they drive? What stage of life are they in? Do they have children? Is the area on the rise, or is it past its prime?

ENTREPRENEURIAL PROFILE

Tony Hard: Planet Tan

When Tony Hard, owner of Planet Tan, a Dallas-based chain of tanning salons, scouts a new location for one of his company's outlets, he starts with basic demographic data, looking only at sites with at least 100,000 residents living within a three- to five-mile radius. Once he narrows the choices using census data, Hard then visits the potential locations, where he looks at the conditions of the houses and nearby buildings, talks with the owners of existing businesses, looks for businesses that would complement his, and interviews local residents to judge their interest in patronizing his salons. If at least 30 percent of the potential customers he interviews say they would become customers, the site is a "go."[16]

Other factors that entrepreneurs should consider when evaluating cities as possible business locations include the following:

COMPETITION For some retailers, it makes sense to locate near competitors because similar businesses located near one another may serve to increase traffic flow to all. This location strategy works well for products for which customers are most likely to comparison shop. For instance, in many cities, auto dealers locate next to one another in a "motor mile," trying to create a shopping magnet for customers. The convenience of being able to shop for dozens of brands of cars all within a few hundred yards of one another draws customers from a sizable trading area. Locating near competitors is a common strategy for restaurants as well.

> When George Stathakis opened his sixth restaurant, Stax Omega, in Greenville, South Carolina, he chose a site at the intersection of an interstate highway and a busy road where several other popular restaurants were already operating. With years of experience in the restaurant business, Stathakis knows that a cluster of restaurants create business for one another. "I always liked the idea of locating my restaurants near competitors," he says.[17]

ENTREPRENEURIAL PROFILE_____

George Stathakis: Stax Omega

Of course, this strategy has limits. Overcrowding of businesses of the same type in an area can create an undesirable impact on the profitability of all competing firms.

Studying the size of the market for a product or service and the number of existing competitors helps an entrepreneur determine whether she can capture a sufficiently large market share to earn a profit. Again, census reports can be a valuable source of information. *County Business Patterns* gives a breakdown, by county, of businesses in manufacturing, wholesale, retail, and service categories and estimates companies' annual payrolls and number of employees. *Zip Code Business Patterns* provides the same data as County Business Patterns except it organizes the data by zip code. The *Economic Census*, which is produced for years that end in "2" and "7," gives an overview of the businesses in an area–their sales (or other measure of output), employment, payroll, and form of organization. It covers eight industry categories—including retail, wholesale, service, manufacturing, construction, and others—and gives statistics at not only the national level, but also by state, metropolitan statistical area, county, places with 2,500 or more inhabitants, and zip code. The *Economic Census* is a useful tool for helping entrepreneurs determine whether the areas they are considering as a location are already saturated with competitors.

CLUSTERING Some cities have characteristics that attract certain industries, and, as a result, companies tend to cluster there. **Clusters** are geographic concentrations of interconnected companies, specialized suppliers, distribution networks, and service providers that are present in a region.[18] According to Harvard professor Michael Porter, clusters are important because they allow companies in them to increase their productivity and to gain a competitive edge. For instance, with its highly trained, well-educated, and technologically literate workforce, Austin, Texas, has become a Mecca for high-tech companies. Home to Dell Inc. and Hewlett-Packard, Austin offers many small technology companies exactly what they need to succeed.

clusters
geographic concentrations of interconnected companies, specialized suppliers, and service providers that are present in a region.

Once a concentration of companies takes root in a city, other businesses in those industries tend to spring up there as well. California's Napa Valley is home to more than 300 wineries, many of them small, family-owned operations that are among the best in the United States. The region's climate and soil, both of which are ideal for growing grapes, led entrepreneurs to establish wineries as early as 1861. As in most clusters, over time these vintners shared both knowledge and best practices, which led to the formation of more wineries, increased productivity and innovation, and the resulting competitive advantages.

> When Mike Grgich emigrated from Yugoslavia in 1958 with a cardboard suitcase that contained everything he owned (mostly textbooks on wine and wine making), he was drawn to Napa Valley, where he began working for vintners in the area and learned about the science and the art of winemaking. In 1977, after helping the Napa Valley vineyard where he worked gain international acclaim, Grgich launched his own vineyard, Grgich Hills Estate. Today, Grgich, now 85, and his daughter Violet, are recognized throughout the world for producing some of the finest wines anywhere.[19]

ENTREPRENEURIAL PROFILE_____

Mike Grgich: Grgich Hills Estate

COMPATIBILITY WITH THE COMMUNITY One of the intangibles that can be determined only by a visit to an area is the degree of compatibility a business has with the surrounding community. In other words, a small company's image must fit in with the character of a town and the needs and wants of its residents. For example, Beverly Hills' ritzy Rodeo Drive or Palm Beach's Worth Avenue are home to shops that match the characteristics of the area's wealthy residents. Shops such as Cartier, Versace, Louis Vuitton, Tiffany & Company, and other exclusive stores abound, catering to the area's rich and famous residents.

LOCAL LAWS AND REGULATIONS Before settling on a city, an entrepreneur must consider the regulatory burden local government might impose. Government regulations affect many aspects of small business's operation, from acquiring business licenses and building permits to erecting business signs and dumping trash. Some cities are regulatory activists, creating so many rules that they discourage business creation; others take a more laissez-faire approach, imposing few restrictions on businesses.

zoning
a system that divides a city or county into small cells or districts to control the use of land, buildings, and sites.

Zoning laws can have a major impact on an entrepreneur's location decision. **Zoning** is a system that divides a city or county into small cells or districts to control the use of land, buildings, and sites. Its purpose is to contain similar activities in suitable locations. For instance, one section of a city may be zoned residential, whereas the primary retail district is zoned commercial and another is zoned industrial to house manufacturing operations. Before selecting a particular site within a city, entrepreneurs must explore local zoning laws to determine whether there are any ordinances that would place restrictions on business activity or that would prohibit establishing a business altogether. Zoning regulations may make a particular location out of bounds. In some cases, an entrepreneur may appeal to the local zoning commission to rezone a site or to grant a **variance** (a special exception to a zoning ordinance), but this is risky and could be devastating if the board disallows the variance. As the number of home-based businesses has increased in the last several years, more entrepreneurs have found themselves at odds with zoning commissions.

variance
a special exemption to a zoning ordinance.

APPROPRIATE INFRASTRUCTURE Business owners must consider the quality of the infrastructure in a potential location. Is an airport located nearby? Are flights available to the necessary cities and are the schedules convenient? If a company needs access to a railroad spur, is one available in the city? How convenient is the area's access to major highways? What about travel distances to major customers? How long will it take to deliver shipments to them? Are the transportation rates reasonable? How far away is the nearest seaport? In some situations, double-or triple-handling of merchandise and inventory causes transportation costs to skyrocket. For many businesses, the availability of loading and unloading zones is an important feature of a suitable location. Some downtown locations suffer from a lack of sufficient space for carriers to unload deliveries of merchandise.

ENTREPRENEURIAL PROFILE

Aaron Gross: Streit's

Streit's, a fifth-generation maker of matzo, a mixture of unleavened flour and water, founded by Aaron and Nettie Streit in 1915, recently moved production from its antiquated factory (which is the last remaining matzo factory in the United States) in New York City's Lower East Side to a new facility in New Jersey. Aaron Gross, a descendent of the founder and a manager at the family-owned company, cites a number of factors that prompted the move, including the city's highly congested streets, which complicated deliveries by large tractor-trailers, and complaints from residential and commercial neighbors about the loud machines (some of which date to the 1930s) that mix, roll, and cut the dough before it is baked in 72-foot long ovens.[20]

COST OF UTILITIES AND PUBLIC SERVICES A location should be served by a governmental unit that provides water and sewer services, trash and garage collection, and other necessary utilities at a reasonable cost. The streets should be in good repair with adequate drainage. If the location is not within the jurisdiction of a municipality that provides these services, they will become a continuing cost to the business.

INCENTIVES Some cities and counties offer financial and other incentives to encourage businesses that will create jobs to locate within their borders. These incentives range from job training for workers and reduced tax rates to financial grants and loans.

After working in the Hollywood film industry for several years, Stephen Jennings launched Grasshorse Technologies, an animation and special-effects film production company whose clients include Warner Brothers Studios and the Cartoon Network. A few years later, on a visit to his native Iowa, Jennings noticed the juxtaposition between the frenetic pace of life in California and the slower, more pleasurable pace in Iowa. During his visit, Jennings learned about the Iowa Film, Television, and Video Project, which provides tax incentives to companies that film in Iowa. One incentive included in the project is a tax abatement for all film, video, or movie companies that operate in the state. "These incentives really sealed the deal," says Jennings, whose research of Iowa revealed other benefits, including the University of Iowa, a major research institution, a highly-trained workforce, and an emerging high-tech industry with a focus on computer simulation. Jennings recently relocated his company from Hollywood to Iowa City.[21]

QUALITY OF LIFE   A final consideration when selecting a city is the quality of life it offers. For many entrepreneurs, quality of life is one of the key determinants of their choice of locale. Cities that offer comfortable weather, cultural events, colleges and universities, museums, outdoor activities, concerts, unique restaurants, and an interesting nightlife have become magnets for entrepreneurs looking to start companies. Over the last two decades, cities such as Austin, Boston, Seattle, San Francisco, Washington, Dallas, Minneapolis, and others have become incubators for creativity and entrepreneurship as educated young people drawn by the cities' quality of life have moved in.

Not only can a location in a city offering a high quality of life be attractive to an entrepreneur, but it can also make recruiting employees much easier. According to a study of the importance of location on recruiting employees conducted by the Human Capital Institute, the three most important factors in attracting talent are job opportunities, a clean and safe community, and an affordable cost of living.[22]

Earl Overstreet, founder of General Microsystems Inc., a Bellevue, Washington, computer system supply company, has discovered that the area's high quality of life allows his company to attract the highly qualified employees that his company counts on for success. It is not unusual to see Overstreet and many of his employees walking through Mercer Slough Nature Park, which is located across the street from the company's headquarters. Many of the company's employees spend their free time taking advantage of the outdoor activities that the nearby Cascade Mountains, lakes, streams, and bike trails offer. Bellevue, with a population of 117,000, boasts 90 parks and 50 miles of trails.[23]

Source: www.cartoonstock.com

Choosing the Site

The final step in the location selection process is choosing the actual site for the business. Again, facts will guide an entrepreneur to the best location decision. Every business has its own unique set of criteria for an ideal location. A manufacturer's prime consideration may be access to raw materials, suppliers, labor, transportation, and customers. Service firms need access to customers but can generally survive in lower-rent properties. A retailer's prime consideration is sufficient customer traffic. For example, an entrepreneur who is planning to launch a convenience store should know that generating a sufficient volume of sales requires a population of at least 500 to 1,000 people who live within a one-mile radius of the outlet; he or she should choose the location accordingly.[24] The one element common to all three types of businesses is the need to locate where customers want to do business.

The site location decision draws on the most precise information available on the makeup of the area. Using the source of published statistics described earlier in this chapter, an entrepreneur can develop valuable insights regarding the characteristics of people and businesses in the immediate community. Franchisors are noted for their ability to hone in on the best locations for their outlets by combining their extensive knowledge of their target customers with demographic profiles of potential locations. For instance, one auto repair franchise helps franchisees screen potential locations for new stores and forecast their sales by using customer sophisticated analytics software that evaluates the composition of surrounding households and their typical purchasing patterns. The software also uses geospatial technology to estimate how far customers will drive to reach a particular location. The analysis allows franchisees to pinpoint the best location for their outlets.[25]

Rental or lease rates are an important factor when choosing a site. Of course, entrepreneurs must be sure that the rent or lease payments for a particular location fit comfortably into their financial forecasts. Although "cheap" rental rates can be indicative of a second-class location (and the resulting poor revenues they generate), entrepreneurs should not agree to exorbitant rental rates that jeopardize their ability to surpass their breakeven points.

ENTREPRENEURIAL PROFILE

Cipriani family: the Rainbow Room

The Cipriani family, owners of New York's famous Rainbow Room since 1998, recently closed the landmark restaurant, which opened in 1934 and was located on the 65th floor of Rockefeller Center ("30 Rock"), because the annual rent had more than doubled from $4 million in 1998 to $8.7 million! A lawsuit filed by the Ciprianis against landlord Tishman Speyer Properties claims that sales at the Rainbow Room, where dinner for two easily topped $600, "could not possibly support" rent that high.[26]

Many businesses are downsizing their outlets to lower their start-up and operating costs and to allow for a greater number of location options that are not available to full-sized stores. Franchises such as Cinnabon and Burger King are finding success by placing smaller, less expensive outlets in locations that cannot support a full-sized store. Burger King recently opened its first Whopper Bar in Universal Studio's CityWalk in Orlando, Florida. At just 700 square feet, the Whopper Bar is one-fifth the size of a traditional Burger King outlet and is ideal for locations in theme parks, airports, museums, casinos, cruise ships, and shopping malls. "It's really [ideal] for any limited-space venue," says Chuck Fallon, president of Burger King North America, "especially where there is a captive audience and the potential for high impact volumes." A Whopper Bar, which offers several versions of the franchise's signature sandwich and a "Whopper topper area," in which customers customize their orders with 22 different toppings, cost between $600,000 and $800,000 to build, which is 30 percent less than the smallest Burger King restaurant. Despite its size, the Whopper Bar's sales per square foot exceed those of traditional franchise outlets.[27]

Finally, an entrepreneur must be careful to select a site that creates the right impression for a business in the customers' eyes. A company's location speaks volumes about a company's "personality."

ENTREPRENEURIAL PROFILE

Charlene Dupray & Pascal Siegler: South'n France

When copreneurs Charlene Dupray and Pascal Siegler saw an old diner in downtown Wilmington, North Carolina, with its salmon pink concrete exterior, 13-foot ceilings, and diner stools, they knew that they had found the perfect building to house their chocolate bonbon business, South'n France. In addition to its unique character, the building came equipped with freezers capable of holding 20,000 bonbons, provided sufficient space for Dupray and Siegler to manufacture their chocolate delicacies, and included rooms that they could convert into a retail storefront. Even though their business is on the verge of outgrowing the space, Dupray says, "We love it so much that we're considering adding another story or buying nearby residences because this old luncheonette really is a workhorse for us."

LO 2

Describe the location criteria for retail and service businesses.

Location Criteria for Retail and Service Businesses

Few decisions are as important for retailers and service firms as the choice of a location. Because their success depends on a steady flow of customers, these businesses must locate their businesses with their target customers' convenience and preferences in mind. The following are important considerations:

Trade Area Size

Every retail and service business should determine the extent of its **trading area,** the region from which a business can expect to draw customers over a reasonable time span. The primary variables that influence the scope of the trading area are the type and the size of the business. If a retail store specializes in a particular product line and offers a wide selection and knowledgeable sales people, it may draw customers from a great distance. In contrast, a convenience store with a general line of merchandise has a small trading area because it is unlikely that customers will drive across town to purchase items that are available within blocks of their homes or businesses. As a rule, the larger the store, the greater its selection, and the better its service, the broader is its trading area. Businesses that offer a narrow selection of products and services tend to have smaller trading areas. For instance, the majority of a massage therapist's clients live within three to five miles of the location with a secondary tier of clients who live within five to ten miles. Clients who are willing to travel more than 15 minutes for a session are rare.[28]

The following environmental factors also influence trading area size:

trading area
the region from which a business can expect to draw customers over a reasonable time span.

Retail Compatibility

Shoppers tend to be drawn to clusters of related businesses. That's one reason shopping malls and outlet shopping centers are popular destinations for shoppers and are attractive locations for retailers. The concentration of businesses pulls customers from a larger trading area than a single free-standing business does. **Retail compatibility** describes the benefits a company receives by locating near other businesses that sell complementary products and services or generate high volumes of foot traffic. Clever business owners choose their locations with an eye on the surrounding mix of businesses. For instance, grocery store operators prefer not to locate in shopping centers with movie theaters, offices, and fitness centers, all businesses whose customers occupy parking spaces for extended time periods. Drugstores, nail salons, and ice cream parlors have proved to be much better shopping center neighbors for grocers.

retail compatibility
the benefits a company receives by locating near other businesses that sell complementary products and services or generate high volumes of traffic.

Degree of Competition

The size, location, and activity of competing businesses also influence the size of a company's trading area. If a business will be the first of its kind in a location, its trading area might be quite extensive. However, if the area already has eight or ten nearby stores that directly compete with a business, its trading area might be very small because the market is saturated with competitors. Market saturation is a problem for businesses in many industries, ranging from fast-food restaurants to convenience stores. Red Mango, an upscale yogurt chain based in Los Angeles, recently saw four of its franchises in Los Angeles close due to poor location choices. The company is continuing with its expansion plans but will focus them on other cities that are less saturated with frozen yogurt shops.[29]

The Index of Retail Saturation

One of the best measures of the level of saturation in an area is the index of retail saturation (IRS), which takes into account both the number of customers and the intensity of competition in a trading area. The **index of retail saturation** is a measure of the potential sales per square foot of store space for a given product within a specific trading area. It is the ratio of a trading area's sales potential for a particular product or service to its sales capacity:

index of retail saturation
a measure of the potential sales per square foot of store space for a given product within a specific trading area; it is the ratio of a trading area's sales potential for a product or service to its sales capacity.

$$\text{IRS} = \frac{C \times \text{RE}}{\text{RF}}$$

where

C = Number of customers in the trading area

RE = Retail expenditures = Average expenditure per person ($) for the product in the trading area

RF = Retail facilities = Total square feet of selling space allocated to the product in the trading area

This computation is an important one for every retailer to make. Locating in an area already saturated with competitors results in dismal sales volume and often leads to failure.

To illustrate the index of retail saturation, suppose that an entrepreneur looking at two sites for a shoe store finds that he needs sales of $175 per square foot to be profitable. Site 1 has a trading area with 25,875 potential customers who spend an average of $42 on shoes annually; the only competitor in the trading area has 6,000 square feet of selling space. Site 2 has 27,750 potential customers spending an average of $43.50 on shoes annually; two competitors occupy 8,400 square feet of space.

Site 1

$$IRS = \frac{25,875 \times 42}{6,000}$$

$$= \$181.12 \text{ sales potential per square foot}$$

Site 2

$$IRS = \frac{27,750 \times 43.50}{8,400}$$

$$= \$143.71 \text{ sales potential per square foot}$$

Although site 2 appears to be more favorable on the surface, the index shows that site 1 is preferable; site 2 fails to meet the minimum standard of $175 per square foot.

Reilly's Law of Retail Gravitation

Reilly's Law of Retail Gravitation, a classic work in market analysis published in 1931 by William J. Reilly, uses the analogy of gravity to estimate the attractiveness of a particular business to potential customers. A business's ability to draw customers is directly related to the extent to which customers see it as a "destination" and is inversely related to the distance customers must travel to reach it. Reilly's model also provides a way to estimate the trade boundary between two market areas by calculating the "break point" between them. The break point between two primary market areas is the boundary between the two where customers become indifferent about shopping at one or the other. The key factor in determining this point of indifference is the size of the communities. If two nearby cities have the same population sizes, then the break point lies halfway between them. The following is the equation for Reilly's Law: [30]

$$BP = \frac{d}{1 + \sqrt{\frac{P_b}{P_a}}}$$

where:

BP = Distance in miles from location A to the break point

d   = Distance in miles between locations A and B

P_a = Population surrounding location A

P_b = Population surrounding location B

For example, if city A and city B are 22 miles apart, and city A has a population of 25,500 and city B has a population of 42,900, the break point according to Reilly's law is:

$$BP = \frac{22}{1 + \sqrt{\frac{42,900}{22,500}}} = 9.2 \text{ miles}$$

The outer edge of city A's trading area lies about 9 miles between city A and city B. Although only a rough estimate, this simple calculation using readily available data can be useful for screening potential locations.

Transportation Network

The transportation networks are the highways, roads, and public service routes that presently exist or are planned. If customers find it inconvenient to get to a location, the store's trading area is reduced. Entrepreneurs should verify that the transportation system works smoothly and is free of barriers that might prevent customers from reaching their shopping destinations. Is it easy for customers traveling in the opposite direction to cross traffic? Do signs and traffic lights allow traffic to flow smoothly? When traffic flow is critical to the success of a business venture, entrepreneurs should contact city government officials about future road construction projects that may be planned or are under consideration. The key is to determine whether their impact on a particular location is beneficial or disastrous.

Physical and Psychological Barriers

Trading area shape and size also are influenced by physical and psychological barriers that may exist. Physical barriers may be parks, rivers, lakes, or any other natural or man-made obstruction that hinders customers' access to the area. Locating on one side of a large park may reduce the number of customers who will drive around it to get to a store. Psychological barriers include areas that have a reputation for crime and illegal activities. If high crime areas exist near a site, potential customers will not travel through them to reach a business.

Other factors retailers should consider when evaluating potential sites include:

Customer Traffic

Perhaps the most important screening criterion for a potential retail (and often for a service) location is the number of potential customers passing by the site during business hours. To be successful, a business must be able to generate sufficient sales to surpass its break-even point, and that requires an ample volume of customer traffic going past its doors. The key success factor for many retail stores is a high-volume location with easy accessibility. Entrepreneurs should use traffic counts (pedestrian and/or auto) and traffic pattern studies to confirm that the sites they are considering as potential locations are capable of generating sufficient sales volume.

ENTREPRENEURIAL
PROFILE _____

Seth Smart & Jefferey
Agee: Brewed
Awakenings

Seth Smart and Jefferey Agee, co-owners of Brewed Awakenings, a drive-through coffee kiosk in Tigard, Oregon, selected a location for their business that offers the benefit of high traffic volume. The entrepreneurs credit their location for much of their business's success. Brewed Awakenings is in a highly visible location in a busy shopping complex that sits at the intersection of two major roads, one of which funnels traffic from downtown Portland and the other leads to an upscale mall. "[Finding the ideal location] is all about traffic counts, visual exposure, and means of access," says Ed Arvidson, a consultant to coffee retailers.[31]

Adequate Parking

If customers cannot find convenient and safe parking, they are not likely to stop in the area. Many downtown areas have lost customers because of inadequate parking. Although shopping malls average five parking spaces per 1,000 square feet of shopping space, many central business districts get by with 3.5 spaces per 1,000 square feet. Customers generally will not pay to park if parking is free at shopping centers or in front of competitive stores. Even when free parking is provided, some potential customers may not feel safe on the streets, especially after dark. Some large city downtown business districts become virtual ghost towns at the end of the business day. A location where traffic vanishes after 6 p.m. may not be as valuable as mall or shopping center locations that mark the beginning of the prime sales time at 6 p.m.

Reputation

Like people, a site can have a bad reputation. In some cases the reputation of the previous business lowers the value of the location. Sites where businesses have failed repeatedly create negative impressions in customers' minds; many people view the business as just another one that soon will be gone. Sometimes previous failures are indicative of a fundamental problem with the location itself, but, in other cases, the cause of the previous failure was not the choice of a poor location but a poorly managed business. When entrepreneurs decide to conduct business in a location that has housed previous failures, it is essential that they make many highly visible changes to the site so that customers perceive the company as a "fresh start."

Visibility

A final characteristic of a good location is visibility. Highly visible locations simply make it easy for customers to find a business and make purchases. A site that lacks visibility puts a company at a major disadvantage before it ever opens its doors for business.

LO 3

Outline the location options for retail and service businesses.

Location Options for Retail and Service Businesses

There are seven basic areas where retail and service business owners can locate: the central business district (CBD); neighborhoods; shopping centers and malls; near competitors; inside large retail stores; outlying areas; and at home. According to the International Council of Shopping Centers, the average cost to lease space in a shopping center is about $17 per square foot. At regional malls, lifestyle centers, and power centers, rental rates typically range from $20 to $25 per square foot. In central business locations, the average cost is between $35 and $45 per square foot (although rental rates can vary significantly in either direction of that average, depending upon the city).[32] Of course, cost is just one factor a business owner must consider when choosing a location.

Central Business District

The central business district (CBD) is the traditional center of town—the downtown concentration of businesses established early in the development of most towns and cities. Entrepreneurs derive several advantages from a downtown location. Because the business is centrally located, it attracts customers from the entire trading area of the city. In addition, a small business usually benefits from the customer traffic generated by the other stores in the district. Many cities have undertaken revitalization efforts in their CBDs and have transformed these areas into thriving, vigorous hubs of economic activity that are proving to be ideal locations for small businesses. However, locating in some CBDs does have certain disadvantages. Many CBDs are characterized by intense competition, high rental rates, traffic congestion, and inadequate parking facilities.

ENTREPRENEURIAL PROFILE

Thomas Nauls, Kenneth Baugh, & Dace Graham: The Tipping Point

Entrepreneurs Thomas Nauls, Kenneth Baugh, and Dace Graham recently opened The Tipping Point, a store that sells unique styles of sneakers in a rainbow of colors in an atmosphere that is a combination of a retail store, a museum, and an art gallery, in the heart of downtown Houston, a city that is working to revitalize its CBD. Even though the store sells brands ranging from Nike and Puma to classics such as Converse and PF Flyer, customer traffic in the downtown area has been slow, and parking is a problem. "Right now, it's just us and Macy's," says Nauls, referring to the limited number of stores downtown.[33]

Beginning in the 1950s, many cities saw their older downtown business districts begin to decay as residents moved to the suburbs and began shopping at newer, more convenient malls. Today, however, many of these CBDs are experiencing rebirth as cities restore them to their former splendor and shoppers return. Many customers find irresistible the charming atmosphere that traditional downtown districts offer with their rich mix of stores, their unique architecture and streetscapes, and their historic character. Cities have begun to reverse the urban decay of their downtown business districts through proactive revitalization programs designed to attract visitors and residents alike to cultural events by locating major theaters and museums in the downtown area. In addition, many cities are providing economic incentives to real estate developers to build apartment and condominium complexes in the heart of the downtown area. Vitality is returning as residents live and shop in the once nearly abandoned downtown areas. The "ghost-town" image is being replaced by both younger and older residents who love the convenience and excitement of life at the center of the city.

Neighborhood Locations

Small businesses that locate near residential areas rely heavily on the local trading areas for business. Businesses that provide convenience as a major attraction for customers find that locating on a street or road just outside major residential areas provides the needed traffic counts essential for success. Gas stations and convenience stores seem to thrive in these high traffic areas. One study of food stores found that the majority of the typical grocer's customers live within a five-mile radius. The primary advantages of a neighborhood location include relatively low operating costs and rents and close contact with customers.

Shopping Centers and Malls

Until the early twentieth century, central business districts were the primary shopping venues in the United States. As cars and transportation networks became more popular in the 1920s, shopping centers began popping up outside cities' central business districts. Then in October 1956, the nation's first shopping mall, Southdale, opened in the Minneapolis, Minnesota, suburb of Edina. Designed by Victor Gruen, the fully-enclosed mall featured 72 shops anchored by two competing department stores (a radical concept at the time), a garden courtyard with a goldfish pond, an aviary, hanging plants, and artificial trees. With its multilevel layout and parking garage, Southdale was a huge success and forever changed the way Americans would shop.[34] Today shopping centers and malls have become a mainstay of the American landscape. Since 1970, the number of shopping malls and centers in the United States has climbed from 11,000 to 48,700, and they occupy 6.85 billion square feet of retail space (or about 245 square miles). Because many different types of stores operate under one roof, shopping malls give meaning to the term "one-stop shopping." In a typical month, nearly 191 million adults visit malls or shopping centers, which generate $2.25 trillion in annual sales.[35] There are eight types of shopping centers (See Table 14.3):

- *Neighborhood shopping centers.* The typical neighborhood shopping center is relatively small, containing from three to 12 stores and serving a population of up to 40,000 people who live within a 10-minute drive. The anchor store in these centers is usually a supermarket or a drugstore. Neighborhood shopping centers typically are straight-line strip malls with parking available in front and primarily serve the daily shopping needs of customers in the surrounding area.
- *Community shopping centers.* A community shopping center contains from 12 to fifty stores and serves a population ranging from 40,000 to 150,000 people. The leading tenant often is a large department or variety store, a super drug store, or a supermarket. Community shopping centers sell more clothing and other soft goods than do neighborhood shopping centers. Of the eight types of shopping centers, community shopping centers take on the greatest variety of shapes, designs, and tenants.
- *Power centers.* A power center combines the drawing strength of a large regional mall with the convenience of a neighborhood shopping center. Anchored by several large specialty retailers such as warehouse clubs, discount department stores, or large specialty stores, these centers target older, wealthier baby boomers, who want selection and convenience. Anchor stores usually account for 80 percent of power center space, compared with 50 percent in the typical community shopping center. Just as in a shopping mall, small businesses can benefit from the traffic generated by anchor stores, but they must choose their locations carefully so that they are not overshadowed by their larger neighbors.
- *Theme or festival centers.* Festival shopping centers employ a unifying theme that individual stores display in their décor and sometimes in the merchandise they sell. Entertainment is a common theme for these shopping centers, which often target tourists. Many festival shopping centers are located in urban areas and are housed in older, sometimes historic, buildings that have been renovated to serve as shopping centers.
- *Outlet centers.* As their name suggests, outlet centers feature manufacturers' and retailers' outlet stores selling name-brand goods at a discount. Unlike most other types of shopping centers, outlet centers typically have no anchor stores; the discounted merchandise they offer draws sufficient traffic. Most outlet centers are open-air and are laid out in strips or in clusters, creating small "villages" of shops.

TABLE 14.3 Types of Shopping Centers

Type of Shopping Center	Concept	Square Footage (including anchors)	Acreage	Typical Anchor		Anchor Ratio (%)[a]	Primary Trade Area (miles)[b]
				Number	Type		
Malls							
Regional Center	General and fashion merchandise; mall (typically enclosed)	480,000 – 800,000	40 – 100	2 or more	Full-line department store; junior department store; mass merchant; discount department store; fashion apparel	50 – 70	5 – 15
Super-regional Center	Similar to regional center but offers more variety	>800,000	60 – 120	3 or more	Full-line department store; junior department store; mass merchant; fashion apparel	50 – 70	5 – 25
Open-Air Centers							
Neighborhood Center	Convenience	30,000 – 150,000	3 – 15	1 or more	Supermarket	30 – 50	3
Community Center	General merchandise; convenience	100,000 – 350,000	10 – 40	2 or more	Discount department store; supermarket; drug; home improvement; large specialty or discount apparel	40 – 60	3 – 6
Lifestyle Center	Upscale national chain specialty stores, dining, and entertainment in an outdoor setting	150,000 – 500,000 but can be larger or smaller	10 – 40	0 – 2	Not usually anchored in the traditional sense but may include book store; large specialty retailers; multiplex cinema; small department store	0 – 50	8 – 12
Power Center	Category-dominant anchors; few small business tenants	250,000 – 600,000	25 – 80	3 or more	Category killer; home improvement; discount; department store; warehouse club; off-price	75 – 90	5 – 10
Theme/Festival Center	Leisure; tourist oriented; retail and service	80,000 – 250,000	5 – 20	Unspecified	Restaurants; entertainment	N/A	25 – 75
Outlet Center	Manufacturers' outlet stores	50,000 – 400,000	10 – 50	N/A	Manufacturers' outlet stores	N/A	25 – 75

[a] The share of a center's total square footage that is occupied by its anchors.
[b] The area from which 60% to 80% of the center's sales originate.
Source: International Council of Shopping Centers, New York.

- *Lifestyle centers.* Typically located near affluent residential neighborhoods where their target customers live, lifestyle centers are designed to look less like shopping centers and malls and more like the busy streets in the central business districts that existed in towns and cities in their heyday. Occupied by many upscale national chain specialty stores such as Talbots, Coach, Sharper Image, and many others, these centers combine shopping convenience and entertainment ranging from movie theaters and open-air concerts to art galleries and people-watching. "Lifestyle centers create a shopping-leisure destination that's an extension of customers' personal lifestyles," says one industry expert. The typical lifestyle center generates between $400 and $500 in sales per square foot compared to $330 in sales per square foot in a traditional mall. The first lifestyle center, The Shops of Saddle Creek, opened in Germantown, Tennessee, in 1987. Today, lifestyle centers are among the most popular types of shopping centers being built, and 140 lifestyle centers operate across the United States.[36]

- *Regional shopping malls.* The regional shopping mall serves a large trading area, usually from five to 15 miles or more in all directions. These enclosed malls contain from 50 to 100 stores and serve a population of 150,000 or more living within a 20- to 40-minute drive. The anchor is typically one or more major department stores with smaller specialty stores occupying the spaces between the anchors. Clothing is one of the popular items sold in regional shopping malls.

- *Super-regional shopping malls.* A super-regional mall is similar to a regional mall but is bigger, containing more anchor stores and a greater variety of shops selling deeper lines of merchandise. Its trade area stretches up to 25 or more miles out. Canada's West Edmonton Mall, the largest mall in North America, with more than 800 stores and 100 restaurants, is one of the most famous super-regional malls in the world. In addition to its abundance of retail shops, the mall contains an ice skating rink, a water park, an amusement park, miniature golf courses, and a 21-screen movie complex.

Major department or mass merchandising stores serve as anchors and attract a significant volume of customer traffic to malls and shopping centers, which allows small businesses with their unique, sometimes quirky, product offerings, boutique atmospheres, and marketing approaches to thrive in their shadows.

In 2007, Paul Sailor, a former Marine who lives in Honolulu, saw an entrepreneurial opportunity in entertaining children and launched 808 Bounce, a company that rents large inflatable bouncers for special events and parties. Less than two years after launching 808 Bounce, Sailor opened a store in Honolulu's Windward Mall, where children can play on six of the company's bouncers by buying an all-day pass or host their birthday parties. Sailor says that the high traffic mall location has increased the company's rental income by providing increased exposure to mall shoppers, some of whom become 808 Bounce customers.[37]

ENTREPRENEURIAL PROFILE

Paul Sailor: 808 Bounce

When evaluating a mall or shopping center location, an entrepreneur should consider the following questions:

- Is there a good fit with other products and brands sold in the mall or center?
- Who are the other tenants? Which stores are the anchors that will bring people into the mall or center?
- Demographically, is the center a good fit for your products or services? What are its customer demographics? (See Figure 14.1)
- How much foot traffic does the mall or center generate? How much traffic passes the specific site you are considering?
- How much vehicle traffic does the mall or center generate? Check its proximity to major population centers, the volume of tourists it draws, and the volume of drive-by freeway traffic. A mall or center that scores well on all three is more likely to be a winner.
- What is the mall's vacancy rate? What is the turnover rate of its tenants?
- How much is the rent and how is it calculated? Most mall tenants pay a base amount of rent plus a small percentage of their sales above a specified level.
- Is the mall or center successful? How many dollars in sales does it generate per square foot? Compare its record against industry averages. (The International Council of Shopping Centers in New York (http://www.icsc.org/) is a good source of industry information.)

Near Competitors

Although some business owners avoid locations near direct competitors, others see locating near rivals as an advantage. For instance, restaurateurs know that successful restaurants attract other restaurants, which, in turn, attract more customers. Many cities have at least one

FIGURE 14.1

Source: International Council of Shoping Centers.

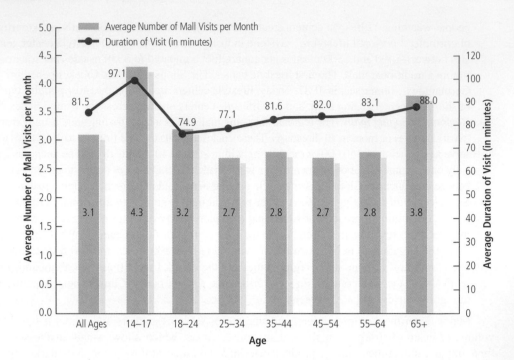

"restaurant row," where restaurants cluster together; each restaurant feeds customers to the others.

Locating near competitors has its limits, however. Clustering too many businesses of a single type into a small area ultimately will erode their sales once the market reaches the saturation point. When an area becomes saturated with competitors, the shops cannibalize sales from one another, making it difficult for any of them to be successful.

Inside Large Retail Stores

Rather than compete against giant retailers, some small business owners are cooperating with them, locating their businesses inside the larger company's stores. These small companies offer products that the large retailers do not and benefit from the large volume of customer traffic the large stores attract. The world's largest retailer, Wal-Mart, is a host to several small businesses, including national fast-food chains Subway and McDonald's and The Taco Maker, a small chain of 185 quick-service Mexican restaurants that offer fresh ingredients. "Taking our menu to a broader audience via America's largest retailer brings us closer to our goal of becoming the premier Mexican quick-service restaurant brand to customers nationwide," says CEO Thomas Torres.[38]

Outlying Areas

An entrepreneur should consider the cost of a location (its rental or lease expense) in light of its visibility to potential customers. Generally, it is not advisable for a small business to locate in a remote area because accessibility and traffic flow are vital to retail and service success, but there are exceptions. If a less expensive location is difficult for customers to find and has a low traffic count, a business located there will have to spend a disproportionate amount of money on promotion. Consequently, a superior, highly visible location may offer lower total operating costs because of the traffic it generates. Many customers do not want to go exploring to find a business and, consequently, never bother to try.

Home-based Businesses

For millions of entrepreneurs, home is where the business is, and the number of home-based businesses is swelling. One recent study from the SBA reports that 52 percent of all small companies are home-based.[39] Although a home-based retail business usually is not a good idea, locating a service business at home is quite popular. Many service companies do not have customers come to their places of business, so an expensive office location is unnecessary. For instance, customers typically contact plumbers or exterminators by telephone, and the work is performed in customers' homes.

Entrepreneurs locating their businesses at home reap several benefits. Perhaps the biggest benefit is the low cost of setting up the business. Most often, home-based entrepreneurs set up shop in a spare bedroom or basement, avoiding the cost of renting, leasing, or buying a building. With a few basic pieces of office equipment—a computer, printer, fax machine, copier, and Internet-capable cell phone—a lone entrepreneur can perform just like a major corporation.

ENTREPRENEURIAL PROFILE

Andrew Aussie & Mark Oliver: Honest Foods

In 2006, Andrew Aussie, who worked in marketing for Kashi Company for 11 years, and Mark Oliver launched Honest Foods, a natural food company, from Aussie's Del Mar, California, home so that they could put their start-up capital into research and development. Aussie and Oliver furnished the home office with hand-me-down furniture from Aussie's father but invested in a top-quality computer, copiers, and telephone system. Rather than hire employees, Honest Foods relies on several independent contractors, who also work from their homes. Aussie and Oliver's home-based business now generates annual sales of $1 million.[40]

Choosing a home location has certain disadvantages, however. Interruptions are more frequent, the refrigerator is all too handy, work is always just a few steps away, and isolation can be a problem. Another difficulty facing some home-based entrepreneurs involves zoning laws. As their businesses grow and become more successful, entrepreneurs' neighbors often begin to complain about the increased traffic, noise, and disruptions from deliveries, employees, and customers who drive through their residential neighborhoods to conduct business. Many communities now face the challenge of passing updated zoning laws that reflect the reality of today's home-based businesses while protecting the interests of residential homeowners.

The Location Decision for Manufacturers

The criteria for the location decision for manufacturers are very different from those of retailers and service businesses; however, the decision can have just as much impact on the company's success. In some cases, a manufacturer has special needs that influence the choice of a location. For instance when one manufacturer of photographic plates and film was searching for a location for a new plant, it had to limit its search to those sites with a large supply of available fresh water, a necessary part of its process. In other cases, the location decision is controlled by zoning ordinances. If a manufacturer's process creates offensive odors or excessive noise, it may be even further restricted in its choices.

LO 4
Explain the site selection process for manufacturers.

Zoning maps show potential manufacturers the areas of the city or county set aside for industrial development. Most cities have developed industrial parks in cooperation with private industry. These industrial parks typically are equipped with sewage and electrical power sufficient for manufacturing. Many locations are not so equipped, and it can be extremely expensive for a small manufacturer to have such utilities brought to an existing site.

The type of transportation facilities required dictates location of a plant in some cases. Some manufacturers may need to locate on a railroad siding, whereas others may only need reliable trucking service. If raw materials are purchased by the carload for economies of scale, the location must be convenient to a railroad siding. Bulk materials are sometimes shipped by barge and consequently require a facility convenient to a navigable river or lake. The added cost of using multiple shipping methods (e.g., rail-to-truck or barge-to-truck) can significantly increase shipping costs and make a location unfeasible for a manufacturer. Northstar Wind Towers recently built a wind turbine tower manufacturing factory in Blair, Nebraska, a small town north of Omaha. "The main driver was logistics," says senior VP Peder Hansen, who calls Blair, "the perfect location" because it allowed Northstar Wind Towers to bring raw materials in "at the least possible cost." The area's skilled labor force, nonunion environment, and reasonable wage rates also made Blair an ideal location for the company.[41]

As fuel costs escalate, the cost of shipping finished products to customers also influences the location decision for many manufacturers, forcing them to open factories or warehouses in locations that are close to their primary markets to reduce transportation costs. Nebraska also proved to be the ideal location for Novozymes, a Denmark-based company with factories in

FIGURE 14.2

How a Foreign Trade Zone (FTZ) Works

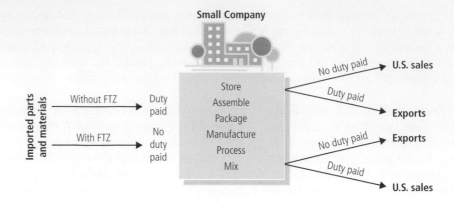

Sweden, China, Brazil, and the United States, that manufactures enzymes that are used in the production of biofuels. Mark Paige, VP of Production, says that the site selection team literally started with a map of the world but eventually focused on the Midwestern United States because it offered the closest proximity to the company's major customers. Other factors that led Novozymes to Nebraska included affordable energy costs, sound transportation networks, and access to a water supply.[42]

Foreign Trade Zones

foreign trade zone
a specially designated area in or near a United States customs port of entry that allows resident companies to import materials and components from foreign countries; assemble, process, manufacture, or package them; and then ship the finished product back out while either reducing or eliminating tariffs and duties.

Foreign trade zones can be an attractive location for small manufacturers that engage in global trade and are looking to reduce or eliminate the tariffs, duties, and excise taxes they pay on the materials and parts they import and the goods they export. A **foreign trade zone** (see Figure 14.2) is a specially designated area in or near a United States customs port of entry that allows resident companies to import materials and components from foreign countries; assemble, process, manufacture, or package them; and then ship the finished product back out while either reducing or eliminating completely tariffs and duties. As far as tariffs and duties are concerned, a company located in a foreign trade zone is treated as if it is located outside the United States. For instance, a maker of speakers can import components from around the world and assemble them at its plant located in a foreign trade zone. The company would pay no duties on the components it imports or on the speakers it exports to other foreign markets. The only duties the manufacturer would pay are on the speakers it sells in the United States. There are 256 foreign trade zones and 498 subzones, which are special foreign trade zones that are established for limited purposes, operating in the United States.

Empowerment Zones

empowerment zone
an area designated as economically disadvantaged in which businesses receive tax breaks on the investments they make within zone boundaries.

Originally created to encourage companies to locate in economically blighted areas, **empowerment zones** offer businesses tax breaks on the investments they make within zone boundaries. Companies can get federal tax credits, grants, and loans for hiring workers living in empowerment zones and for investments they make in plant and equipment in the zones. Empowerment zones operate in both urban and rural areas, ranging from Los Angeles, California, to Sumter, South Carolina. Boston, Massachusetts, has a technology-oriented business incubator located within a federal empowerment zone called TechSpace, which provides high potential start-up businesses with a full-service facility featuring completely integrated information technology and business services.

Business Incubators

business incubator
an organization that combines low-cost, flexible rental space with a multitude of support services for its small business residents.

For many start-up companies, a business incubator may make the ideal initial location. A **business incubator** is an organization that combines low-cost, flexible rental space with a multitude of support services for its small business residents. The overwhelming reason for establishing an incubator is to enhance economic development by attracting new business ventures to an area, as well as to diversify the local economy. An incubator's goal is to nurture young companies during the volatile start-up period and to help them survive until they

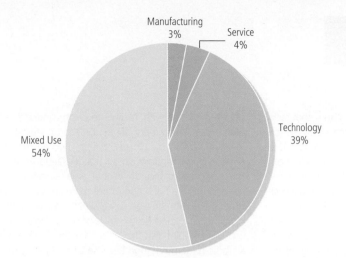

Manufacturing
3%

Service
4%

Technology
39%

Mixed Use
54%

FIGURE 14.3

**Business Incubator
Tenants by Industry**

Source: National Business Incubation
Association.

are strong enough to go out on their own. Common sponsors of incubators include economic development organizations (31 percent), government entities (21 percent), colleges or universities (20 percent), economic development organizations (15 percent), and others. Most incubators (54 percent) are "mixed-use," hosting a variety of start-up companies, followed by incubators that focus on technology companies (see Figure 14.3).[43]

The shared resources incubators typically provide their tenants include secretarial services, a telephone system, computers and software, fax machines, meeting facilities and, sometimes, management consulting services and financing. Not only do these services save young companies money, but they also save them valuable time. Instead of searching for the resources they need to build their companies, entrepreneurs can focus on getting their products and services to market faster than their competitors can. The typical incubator has entry requirements that prospective residents must meet. Incubators also have criteria that establish the conditions a business must maintain to remain in the facility as well as the expectations for "graduation" into the business community.

More than 1,100 incubators operate across the United States, up from just 12 in 1980. Perhaps the greatest advantage of choosing to locate a start-up company in an incubator is a greater chance for success; according to the National Business Incubation Association, graduates from incubators have a success rate of 87 percent, and 84 percent of the companies that graduate stay in the local community. Each year, business incubators help an estimated 27,000 start-up companies that provide full-time employment for more than 100,000 workers.[44]

Ari Presler started Silicon Imaging, a company that makes compact, high-definition digital video cameras, in the RPI Incubator located at Rensselaer Polytechnic Institute in Troy, New York, in 2000. Silicon Imaging, now with 10 employees, has since graduated from the RPI Incubator, and generates more than $2 million in annual revenue from sales to both industrial and commercial customers for applications ranging from surveillance and crash testing to medical applications and entertainment. The company's greatest claim to fame to date is that the director of the Academy Award-winning film *Slumdog Millionaire* used Silicon Imaging cameras (which were still in the prototype phase) to shoot 60 percent of the movie's scenes. The hand-held, lightweight cameras, which were equipped with gyroscopes to eliminate jerkiness, take 24 to 30 frames per second, making them ideal for shooting scenes in the hot, crowded slums of Mumbai because they allowed the director to review footage immediately and reshoot scenes when necessary.[45]

CELADOR FILMS/Picture Desk Inc./
Kobal Collection

**ENTREPRENEURIAL
PROFILE**

Ari Presler: Silicon
Imaging

Many scenes from *Slumdog
Millionaire* were filmed with
Silicon Imaging cameras.

Small Really Is Beautiful

Like many franchises, Cinnabon, the Atlanta-based chain that sells a delectable blend of gooey cinnamon rolls and pecan buns, is introducing smaller versions of its stores called Cinnabon Express. The miniscule outlets, which occupy just 5 feet of counter space and offer a pared-down version of the chain's menu, are ideal for locations that have been beyond the reach of full-sized outlets, such as museums, sports stadiums and arenas, and mall kiosks. Because they offer lower building and operating costs, Cinnabon Express outlets do not require the foot traffic that a full-size store does. Their small stature makes the outlets ideal for piggybacking inside other full-size franchises. In fact, Cinnabon has set up express outlets in 30 Schlotzsky's sandwich restaurants and is negotiating with other franchises for similar deals.

Other retail outlets are opening temporary stores during peak traffic times in prime locations. Victoria's Secret uses "pop-up" stores on a dozen college campuses, some open for only one day, to market its Pink brand of clothing to young women as they return for the beginning of a school term. Employees hand out free promotional materials and accept clothing donations for charity. Flip-flop maker Havaianas also has opened temporary stores on college campuses and generates "buzz" by sponsoring contests, some of which include all-expense-paid trips to Brazil. Both Victoria Secret and Havaianas use their pop-up stores to reach the members of their primary target market, whose purchasing power has grown markedly since 2005. Discretionary spending among 18- to 30-year-old students is estimated to exceed $53 billion annually. The pop-up locations work. A Pink pop-up store at Penn State University recently rang up sales of $20,000 in a single day! By choosing these temporary locations, companies not only generate impressive sales, but they also seek to create brand loyalty among their core target audience.

City Brew Coffee, a franchise based in Billings, Montana, began with traditional brick-and-mortar stores in 1998 but soon saw the benefit of opening small drive-through kiosks. The kiosks, which are less than 100 square-feet in size, contain all of the coffee-making equipment required to satisfy customers' needs and require only a fraction of the capital to build that a full-size coffee shop requires. Mike Blanchard, co-owner of a City Brew kiosk in Webster, New York,

says that a kiosk, with its drive-through windows, is ideal for meeting the needs of customers' always-on-the-go lifestyles. The typical kiosk measures 8 feet by 12 feet, houses two employees, and features a drive-through window on each side. Design efficiency has enabled the company to include in that small space everything employees need to make a full range of premium coffees and teas, including refrigeration units, storage space, sinks, and, of course, coffee brewing machinery. Not only do the costs of operating a kiosk produce a lower break-even point, but they also offer the added benefit of portability. If traffic patterns change because of a highway rerouting, for example, a City Brew franchise can pick up and move to a better location at a relatively low cost. "The goal is to expand the business using kiosks in areas that wouldn't support a [full-size store]," says Michael Taylor, director of kiosk operations at City Brew, "for example, near major transportation corridors or manufacturing areas."

1. What advantages and disadvantages do small outlets such as the ones described here offer entrepreneurs?
2. What types of businesses would be successful opening pop-up stores temporarily on your campus or on a nearby campus? What advice would you offer them about the store? When should they open and for how long?
3. Would a kiosk store (perhaps selling something other than coffee) such as the ones that City Brew uses be successful in your community? Explain. Work with a team of your classmates to identify three products or product lines that would be successful in your community if they were sold from a kiosk or express outlet.

Source: Based on Joe Guy Collier, "Cinnabon Warms Up to Smaller Sweet Spots," *Atlanta Journal Constitution*, September 19, 2008, http://www.ajc.com/business/content/business/stories/2008/09/19/cinnabon_stores.html; Jennifer Saranow, "Retailers Give It the Old College Try," *Wall Street Journal*, August 28, 2008, p. B8; Francis B. Allgood, "Drive-Thru Coffee Shops Seek Hot Corners," *GSA Business*, November 26, 2007, p. 28; Jason Schultz, "City Brew Coffee Cooks Up New Business Model," *Webster Herald*, January 23, 2008, p. C1; Joan Reis Nielsen, "SMART Carts," Tea and Coffee, October/November 2005, http://www.teaandcoffee.net/1005/special.htm.

LO 5

Describe the criteria used to analyze the layout and design considerations of a building, including the Americans with Disabilities Act.

layout

the logical arrangement of the physical facilities in a business that contributes to efficient operations, increased productivity, and higher sales.

Layout and Design Considerations

Once an entrepreneur chooses the best location for his or her business, the next issue to address is designing the proper layout for the space to maximize sales (retail) or productivity (manufacturing or service). **Layout** is the logical arrangement of the physical facilities in a business that contributes to efficient operations, increased productivity, and higher sales. Planning for the most effective and efficient layout in a business environment can produce dramatic improvements in a company's operating effectiveness and efficiency. An attractive, effective layout can help a company's recruiting efforts, reduce absenteeism, and improve employee productivity and satisfaction. A recent *U.S. Workplace Survey* by global design firm Gensler reports that employees believe that the quality and the quantity of their work would increase by an average of 25 percent with better workplace design.[46] The changing nature of work demands that workspace design also changes. Although many jobs require workers to focus on "heads down," individual tasks, collaboration with co-workers is becoming a more significant component of work. An effective workspace must be flexible enough to accommodate and encourage both types of work. Increasingly, work is becoming more complex, team-based, technology dependent, and mobile, and workspaces must change to accommodate these characteristics. The study by Gensler concludes that top performing companies have workspaces that are more effective than those of average companies, particularly for collaboration. Gensler also reports that employees at top performing companies spend 23 percent more time collaborating with their co-workers than do employees at average companies.[47]

At Gravitytank, a strategy consulting firm in Chicago, a layout that encourages collaboration is essential because employees often work together on project teams for several months. Designers came up with a flexible layout that includes work bays that can be reconfigured quickly and easily by moving lightweight dividers made from cardboard that hang from an overhead grid. Cork bulletin boards (which also serve as dividers) allow employees to share ideas easily, and the pieces of furniture in each bay have built-in power outlets, Ethernet cables, and trays of office supplies, giving employees easy access to all of the tools they need to work. Employees have the flexibility they need in an office space, and Gravitytank created the entire space for just $20,000.[48]

When creating a layout, managers must consider its impact on space itself (comfort, flexibility, size, and ergonomics), the people who occupy it (type of work, special requirements, need for interaction, tasks performed), and the technology they use (communication, Internet access, and equipment).[49] The following factors have a significant impact on a space's layout and design.

Size

A building must be large enough to accommodate a business's daily operations comfortably. If it is too small at the outset of operations, efficiency will suffer. A space must have enough room for customers' movement, inventory, displays, storage, work areas, offices, and restrooms. Haphazard layouts undermine employee productivity and create organizational chaos. Too many small business owners start their operations in locations that are already overcrowded or lack the capacity for expansion. The result is that an owner is forced to make a costly move to a new location within the first few years of operation.

Construction and External Appearance

Is the construction of the building sound? It pays to have an expert look it over before buying and leasing the property. Is the building's appearance consistent with the entrepreneur's desired image for the business? Many retailers, such as franchised quick-service

"It'll take a little getting used to, but we're saving a bundle on cubicles, and you'll find you are scratching a lot less."

Source: From *The Wall Street Journal,* permission Cartoon Features Syndicate

restaurants and hotels, reinforce their brands with a consistent architecture when they add new outlets.

Retailers and service providers, in particular, must recognize the importance of creating the proper image for their stores and how their shops' layouts and physical facilities influence this image. A store's external appearance contributes significantly to establishing its identity among its target customers. In many ways a building's appearance sets the tone for what the customer expects in the way of quality and service. A building's appearance should reflect a company's "personality." Should the building project an exclusive image or an economical one? Is the atmosphere informal and relaxed or formal and businesslike? Physical facilities send important messages to customers.

Communicating the right signals through layout and physical facilities is an important step in attracting a steady stream of customers. Retail consultant Paco Underhill advises merchants to "seduce" passersby with their storefronts. "The seduction process should start a minimum of 10 paces away," he says.[50]

ENTREPRENEURIAL PROFILE

Pacific Sunwear

For instance, when Pacific Sunwear, a surfing-oriented clothing company, redesigned its mall stores, managers opted for a unique curved entryway designed to remind shoppers of the "curl"—the tunnel that surfers see when they are inside a wave. Looking into the store, shoppers' eyes are drawn straight to the illuminated back wall, where shoes are displayed in a creative design.[51]

For many businesses, a drive-through window adds another dimension to the concept of customer convenience and is a relatively inexpensive way to increase sales. In the quick-service restaurant business, drive-through windows are an essential design component, accounting for 70 percent of sales, an increase from 60 percent in 2002.[52] Although drive-through windows are staples at fast-food restaurants and banks, they can add value for customers in other businesses as well, including drugstores, hardware stores, and even wedding chapels.

Entrances

Entrances to a business should *invite* customers into a store. Wide entry ways and attractive merchandise displays that are set back from the doorway can draw customers into a business. A store's entrance should catch passing customers' attention and draw them inside. "That's where you want somebody to slam on the brakes and realize they're going someplace new," says retail consultant Paco Underhill.[53] Retailers with heavy traffic flows such as supermarkets or drugstores often install automatic doors to ensure a smooth traffic flow into and out of their stores. Retailers should remove any barriers that interfere with customers' easy access to the storefront. Broken sidewalks, sagging steps, mud puddles, and sticking or heavy doors not only create obstacles that might discourage potential customers but they also create legal hazards for a business if they cause customers to be injured. The goal is to overcome anything that creates what one expert calls "threshold resistance."[54]

The Americans With Disabilities Act

Americans with Disabilities Act
a law that requires practically all businesses to make their facilities available to physically challenged customers and employees.

The **Americans with Disabilities Act (ADA),** passed in July 1990, requires practically all businesses to make their facilities available to physically challenged customers and employees. In addition, the law requires businesses with 15 or more employees to accommodate physically challenged candidates in their hiring practices. Most states have similar laws, many of them more stringent than the ADA, that apply to smaller companies as well. The rules of the these state laws and the ADA's Title III are designed to ensure that mentally and physically challenged customers have equal access to a firm's goods or services. For instance the act requires business owners to remove architectural and communication barriers when "readily achievable." The ADA allows flexibility in how a business achieves this equal access, however. For example, a restaurant could either provide menus in Braille or could offer to have a staff member read the menu to blind customers. A small dry cleaner might not be able to add a wheelchair ramp to its storefront without incurring significant expense, but the owner could comply with the ADA by offering curbside pick-up and delivery services at no extra charge for disabled customers.

Although the law allows a good deal of flexibility in retrofitting existing structures, buildings that were occupied after January 25, 1993, must be designed to comply with all aspects of the law. For example, buildings with three stories or more must have elevators; an access ramp must be in place anywhere the floor level changes by more than one-half inch. In retail stores, checkouts aisles must be wide enough—at least 36 inches—to accommodate wheelchairs. Restaurants must have five percent of their tables accessible to wheelchair-bound patrons.

Complying with the ADA does not necessarily require businesses to spend large amounts of money. The Justice Department estimates that more than 20 percent of the cases customers have filed under Title III involved changes the business owners could have made at no cost, and another 60 percent would have cost less than $1,000![55] In addition, companies with $1 million or less in annual sales or with 30 or fewer full-time employees that invest in making their locations more accessible to all qualify for a tax credit. The credit is 50 percent of their expenses between $250 and $10,500. Businesses that remove physical, structural, and transportation barriers for disabled employees and customers also qualify for a tax deduction of up to $15,000.

Signs

One of the lowest-cost and most effective methods of communicating with customers is a business sign. Signs tell potential customers what a business does, where it is, and what it is selling. The United States is a very mobile society, and a well-designed, well-placed sign can be a powerful tool for reaching potential customers. The Viva McDonald's restaurant on Las Vegas Boulevard (or "the Strip") includes an oversized sign and four jumbo display screens – all with video playback ability – mounted on the front of the store. Designers recognized that a restaurant located in a city known for gaudy neon light displays required a sign that would stand out to attract customers.[56]

A sign should be large enough for passersby to read it from a distance, taking into consideration the location and speed of surrounding traffic arteries. To be most effective, the message should be short, simple, and clear. A sign should be legible in both daylight and at night; proper illumination is a must. Contrasting colors and simple typefaces are best. The most common problems with business signs are that they are illegible, poorly designed, improperly located, poorly maintained, and have color schemes that are unattractive or are hard to read.

Before investing in a sign, an entrepreneur should investigate the local community's sign ordinance. In some cities and towns, local regulations impose restrictions on the size, location, height, and construction materials used in business signs.

Building Interiors

Designing a functional, efficient interior layout demands research, planning, and attention to detail. Retailers in particular have known for a long time that their stores' layouts influence their customers' buying behavior. Retailers such as Cabela's, Barnes and Noble, and Starbucks use layouts that encourage customers to linger and spend time (and money). Others such as Lowe's, Aldi, and Wal-Mart reinforce their discount images with layouts that communicate a warehouse environment, often complete with pallets, to shoppers. Luxury retailers such as Tiffany and Company, Coach, and Nordstrom create opulent layouts in which their upscale customers feel comfortable.

Piecing together an effective layout is not a haphazard process. **Ergonomics,** the science of adapting work and the work environment to complement employees' strengths and to suit customers' needs, is an integral part of a successful design. For example, chairs, desks, and table heights that allow people to work comfortably can help employees perform their jobs faster and more easily. Design experts claim that improved lighting, better acoustics, and proper climate control benefit the company as well as employees. An ergonomically designed workplace can improve workers' productivity significantly and lower days lost due to injuries and accidents. A study for the Commission of Architecture and the Built Environment and the British Council for Offices reports that simple features such as proper lighting reduce absenteeism by 15 percent and increase productivity between 2.8 percent and 20 percent.[57]

Unfortunately, many businesses fail to incorporate ergonomic design principles into their layouts, and the result is costly. Every year, 1.8 million workers experience injuries related to repetitive motion or overexertion. The most frequent and most expensive workplace injuries are

ergonomics
the science of adapting work and the work environment to complement employees' strengths and to suit customers' needs.

musculoskeletal disorders (MSDs), which cost U.S. businesses $20 billion in workers' compensation claims each year. According to the Occupational Safety and Health Administration (OSHA), MSDs account for 34 percent of all lost-work injuries and illnesses and one-third of all workers compensation claims.[58] Workers who spend their days staring at computer monitors (a significant and growing proportion of the workforce) often are victims of MSDs. The good news for employers, however, is that preventing injuries, accidents, and lost days does *not* require spending thousands of dollars on ergonomically correct solutions. Most of the solutions to MSDs are actually quite simple and inexpensive, ranging from installing equipment that eliminates workers' repetitive motions to introducing breaks during which workers engage in exercises designed by occupational therapists to combat MSDs.

Lighting, Sound, and Scent

Retailers can increase sales by engaging all of customers' senses. Retail behavioral expert Paco Underhill, founder of Envirosell, a market research company, says that most of customers' unplanned purchases come after they touch, taste, smell, or hear something in a store. For example, stores that sell fresh food will see sales increase if they offer free samples to customers. "If somebody doesn't try 'em, they're not going to buy 'em," quips Underhill.[59] Lighting, sound, and scent are particularly important.

LIGHTING Good lighting allows employees to work at maximum efficiency. Proper lighting is measured by the amount of light required to do a job properly with the greatest lighting efficiency. Efficiency is essential because lighting consumes 24 percent of the total energy used in the typical commercial building.[60] Technological advances are increasing the popularity of light emitting diode (LED) lighting. LEDs use just 20 percent of the electricity of incandescent lights and 50 percent of compact fluorescent lights. LEDs also generate less heat, which reduces business's cooling costs.

Lighting provides a good return on investment given its overall impact on a business. Few people seek out businesses that are dimly lit because they convey an image of untrustworthiness. The use of natural light gives a business an open and cheerful look and actually can boost sales. Saladworks, a chain of fast-casual restaurants based in Conshohocken, Pennsylvania, recently redesigned its stores to minimize the use of fluorescent lights and to include a glass front and skylights that allow in more natural light.[61] A series of studies by energy research firm Heschong Mahone Group found that stores using natural light experience sales that are 40 percent higher than those of similar stores using fluorescent lighting.[62]

SOUND In an attempt to engage all of their customers' senses, companies are focusing on sound and scent as key marketing ingredients in their layouts. Research shows that a business's "soundscape" can have an impact on the length of time and the amount of money that customers spend. Background music that appeals to a company's target customers (called "audio architecture") can be an effective marketing tool, subtly communicating important messages about its brand to customers. "Music is an extension of a brand, something you can reinforce without the customer looking at it or touching it," says Greg Sapier, vice-president of Melody, a company that provides customized music to businesses. At Emeril's, the South Beach, Florida, Cajun-themed restaurant owned by celebrity chef Emeril Agassi, diners hear an eclectic mix of rhythm and blues and Cajun music dubbed "Gumbo."[63] One rule is clear for retail soundscapes: slow is good. People's biorhythms reflect the sounds around them, and soothing classical music encourages shoppers to relax and slow down, which means they will shop longer and be likely to spend more. Classical music also makes shoppers feel more affluent and increases sales more than any other type of music.[64]

SCENT Research shows that scents can have a powerful effect in retail stores. The Sense of Smell Institute reports that the average human being can recognize 10,000 different odors and can recall scents with 65 percent accuracy after one year, a much higher recall rate than visual stimuli produce. In one experiment, when Eric Spangenberg of Washington State University diffused a subtle scent of vanilla into the women's department of a store and rose maroc into the men's department, he discovered that sales nearly doubled. (He also discovered that if he switched the scents, sales in both departments fell well below their normal average.)[65] Many companies—from casinos to convenience stores—are beginning to understand the power of using scent as a marketing tool. Bakeries use fans to push the smell of fresh-baked breads and sweets into pedestrian traffic lanes, tempting them to sample some of their delectable goodies. A chain of gas stations in California installed a device that emits the aroma of brewing coffee to customers at its gas pumps to increase coffee sales. Appliance retailer H. H. Gregg has discovered that the faint smell of home cooking, such as apple pie or sugar cookies, boosted its in-store sales by 33 percent![66]

Environmentally-Friendly Design

Businesses are designing their buildings in more environmentally-friendly ways not only because it is the right thing to do but also because it saves money. Companies are using recycled materials, installing high efficiency lighting, fixtures, appliances, and LEED (Leadership in Energy and Environmental Design) principles in construction and renovation. McDonald's recently renovated one of its restaurants in Chicago to meet LEED standards. It contains high efficiency appliances, furnishings made from recycled materials, water-conserving plumbing fixtures, permeable pavement that minimizes the runoff of rainwater into city waterways, and a cistern that collects rainwater that is used to irrigate landscaping. The restaurant is lit by skylights and energy-saving LED lighting that adjusts automatically to complement the level of natural light. A garden on the roof not only is attractive but also insulates the building naturally. McDonald's even used paints that do not emit chemical odors. The company plans to build more "green" restaurants in the future.[67]

A Campus Bookstore Makeover

The bookstore on the Vancouver campus of Simon Fraser University in British Columbia, Canada, faced a challenge. Located in the heart of Vancouver's downtown financial district in a combination shopping mall and office complex, the store occupies a partially subterranean site that had once been the stockroom of a department store. Fluctuating ceiling levels and ductwork for the entire complex create a maze-like appearance. The store has two entrances at opposite ends, one for the general public that is at street level and one that is less visible and adjoins the university. "The location is unconventional," says Michael Dzuba, the bookstore's manager. The store caters to SFU students but also attracts a broader range of customers. "SFU Vancouver bookstore customers are of all ages and include a solid segment of mid-career professionals and older adults who attend conferences, lectures, meetings, exhibits, and performances on campus." Urban professionals, tourists, and visiting international students round out the bookstore's customer base.

To capitalize on the opportunity that the bookstore offered for reaching this diverse set of potential customers, SFU Vancouver embarked on a renovation of the entire space that was designed to make it more appealing and more comfortable, a place where customers would enjoy shopping and spending time. SFU hired GHA design studios, a Montreal-based design firm, to create the new bookstore. The guiding principle was to create a series of zones within the store to give the impression of an upscale residence with different rooms.

GHA design studios used woods that reflected the forests that are prevalent in British Columbia and a sleek, simple layout that draws on Japanese design principles that would appeal to the large Asian population that inhabits the city and to the university's inter-

Roger Books Photography

national student population. According to project designer Joni Vallon, Japanese architecture reflects "an ordered geometry," which is visible in the store's sleek display tables, modular fixtures, and use of natural woods, charcoal colored metal fixtures, and accents of cream and apple green.

The goal is to create a calm respite from the hectic pace of the downtown street and the campus. When students enter from the campus, they are greeted with a magazine lounge that includes upholstered bench seating that invites them to linger, concealed shelf lighting, and suspended light shades covered with Japanese-inspired grass cloth. Wooden grids and acoustic panels overhead conceal heating and air conditioning ducts and create a cozy atmosphere. The student entrance also features movable displays of school supplies and SFU-themed clothing. Much like the yellow brick road in *The Wizard of Oz*, a center aisle paved with bamboo draws customers farther into the store. "The flooring serves to direct students to their required course books, which are purposely situated at the back of the store," says Dzuba.

Different ceiling treatments define the various "rooms" that exist within the store. For instance, the textbook area is identified by multiple 4-foot circular acoustic panels that create a playful setting in what otherwise might be a "mundane department," says Fallon. Oversized grass cloth lampshades define the store's core, where gifts and stationery are displayed.

To draw customers from the busy city street entrance, designers at GHA design studios knew that they had to attract attention. They created a large cedar totem pole, another reflection of the rich cultural heritage and history of the British Columbia region, that features a carved owl (what better symbol than a wise owl for a bookstore?). "Visitors often come in to snap a shot of him," says Dzuba. "We merchandised his roost with local interest books and tourist items."

The street entrance also features large windows, simple displays of books, and eye-catching graphics. The store uses a system of interchangeable signs and graphics that allow employees to change displays for various events, sales, and seasons. Employees regularly change the displays and the inventory so that regular customers do not see the same look every time they come in.

The bookstore's new layout and design have made a huge difference in the store's performance. "After the renovation, we measured a surge of first-time shoppers," says Dzuba. "The subsequent 25 percent increase in general giftware sales and steadily growing book sales area clear indications that we succeeded in capturing a greater share of customers."

1. What impact does the layout and design of a retail store have on its customers and its sales?
2. Michael Dzuba says that the textbooks that students purchase for their courses at SFU are purposely located at the back of the store. Why?
3. Work with a team of your classmates to brainstorm recommendations for giving your campus bookstore a makeover. For each recommendation that you make, include your reasoning for it.

Source: Based on Janet Groeber, "An Open Book," *DDI Magazine*, June 1, 2007, http://www.ddimagazine.com/displayanddesignideas/search/article_display.jsp?vnu_content_id=1003592425.

LO 6

Explain the principles of effective layouts for retailers, service businesses, and manufacturers.

Layout: Maximizing Revenues, Increasing Efficiency, or Reducing Costs

The ideal layout for a building depends on the type of business it houses and on the entrepreneur's strategy for gaining a competitive edge. An effective layout can reinforce a brand and contribute to a company's desired image.

ENTREPRENEURIAL PROFILE

John Lavey: Hammock Publishing

John Lavey, CEO of Hammock Publishing, a small custom publisher in Nashville, Tennessee, realized that his company's lobby and offices needed a makeover. "The space was very gray and beige and nondescript," he says. Lavey hired a local marketing company, Advent, to transform the company's image. "We made their lobby over from boring to branded," says Advent CEO John Roberson. Brightly colored walls are visually appealing, artistic panels that feature the company's projects adorn the space, and the company's tagline, "Your story starts here," is painted on a wall that greets visitors when they enter. "[Clients] have been impressed with how we've branded our space," says Lavey.[68]

Retailers design their layouts with the goal of maximizing sales revenue and reinforcing the brand; manufacturers see layout as an opportunity to increase efficiency and productivity and to lower costs.

Layout for Retailers

Retail layout is the arrangement of merchandise in a store and its method of display. A retailer's success depends, in part, on a well-designed floor display. Retail expert Paco Underhill says "a store's interior architecture is fundamental to the customers' experience—the stage upon which a retail company functions."[69] A retail layout should pull customers into the store and make it easy for them to locate merchandise, compare price, quality, and features, and ultimately make a purchase. This is another area in which small stores may have an advantage over their larger rivals. Small stores allow customers to find the products that they want to purchase quickly and easily. (One study reports that the average shopper in a cavernous Wal-Mart Supercenter spends 21 minutes in the store but finds only 7 out of 10 items on his or her shopping list![70])

In addition, a floor plan should take customers past displays of other items that they may buy on impulse. Customers make a significant percentage of their buying decisions once they enter a store, which means that the right layout can boost sales significantly. One of the most comprehensive studies of impulse purchases found that one-third of shoppers made impulse purchases. The median impulse purchase amount was $30 but varied by product category, ranging from $6 for food items to $60 for jewelry and sporting goods. Although the urge to take advantage of discounts was the most common driver of unplanned buying decisions, the location and attractiveness of the display also were important factors.[71]

Retailers have always recognized that some locations within a store are superior to others. Customer traffic patterns give the owner a clue to the best location for the highest gross margin items. Merchandise purchased on impulse and convenience goods should be located near the front of the store. Items people shop around for before buying and specialty goods attract their own customers and should not be placed in prime space. Generally, prime selling space should be reserved for products that carry the highest markups.

Layout in a retail store evolves from a clear understanding of customers' buying habits. If customers come into the store for specific products and have a tendency to walk directly to those items, placing complementary products in their path boosts sales. Observing customer behavior can help the owner identify the "hot spots" where merchandise sells briskly and "cold spots" where it may sit indefinitely. By experimenting with factors such as traffic flow, lighting, aisle size, music type and audio levels, signs, and colors, an owner can discover the most productive store layout. For instance, one of the hot spots in a Barnes & Noble bookstore during the busy holiday season is the "Christmas table" at the front of the children's department. The table, which holds between 75 and 125 titles, draws lots of traffic, making it the most desired spot for a book aimed at children.[72]

Business owners should display merchandise as attractively as their budgets allow. Customers' eyes focus on displays, which tell them the type of merchandise the business sells. It is easier for customers to relate to one display than to a rack or shelf of merchandise. Open displays of merchandise can surround the focus display, creating an attractive selling area. Spacious aisles provide shoppers an open view of merchandise and reduce the likelihood of shoplifting. One study found that shoppers, especially women, are reluctant to enter narrow aisles in a store. Narrow aisles force customers to jostle past one another (experts call this the "butt-brush factor"), which makes them extremely nervous. The same study also found that placing shopping baskets in several areas around a store can increase sales. Seventy-five percent of shoppers who pick up a basket buy something, compared to just 34 percent of customers who do not pick up a basket.[73]

Retailers can also boost sales by displaying together items that complement each other. For example, displaying ties near dress shirts or handbags next to shoes often leads to multiple sales. Placement of items on store shelves is important, too, and storeowners must keep their target customers in mind when stocking shelves. For example, putting hearing aid batteries on bottom shelves where the elderly have trouble getting to them or placing popular children's toys on top shelves where little ones cannot reach them hurt sales. Retailers must remember to separate the selling and nonselling areas of a store. One fundamental rule: Do not waste prime selling space on nonselling functions (storage, office, dressing rooms, and others). Although nonselling activities are necessary for a successful retail operation, they should not occupy a store's most valuable selling space. Many retailers place their nonselling departments in the rear of the building, recognizing the value of each foot of space in a retail store and locating their most profitable items in the best-selling areas. The checkout process is a particularly important ingredient in customer satisfaction. Research shows that shoppers tend to be impatient, willing to wait only about four minutes in a checkout line before becoming exasperated. One study reports that 43 percent of customers say that long checkout lines make them less likely to shop at a store.[74]

Not every portion of a small store's interior space is of equal value in generating sales revenue. Certain areas contribute more to revenue than others. The value of store space depends on floor location in a multistory building, location with respect to aisles and walkways, and proximity to entrances. Space values decrease as distance from the main entry-level floor increases. Selling areas on the main level contribute a greater portion to sales than those on other floors in the building because they offer greater exposure to customers than either

FIGURE 14.4

Space Values for a Small Store

Source: Retailing, 6e, 1997 Prentice Hall © Dale M. Lewison.

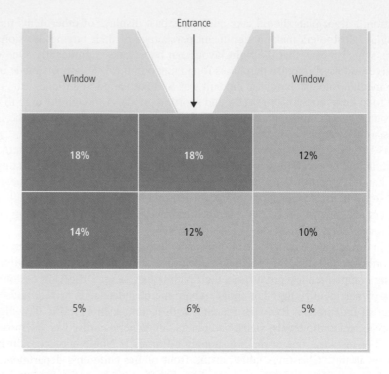

basement or higher-level locations. Therefore, main-level locations carry a greater share of rent than other levels.

Space values also depend on their position relative to the store entrance. Typically, the farther away an area is from the entrance, the lower is its value. Another consideration is that in North America, most shoppers turn to the right entering a store and move around it counterclockwise. (This apparently is culturally determined; studies of shoppers in Australia and Great Britain find that they turn *left* on entering a store.) Finally, only about one-fourth of a store's customers will go more than halfway into the store. Based on these characteristics, Figure 14.4 illustrates space values for a typical small store.

Understanding the value of store space ensures proper placement of merchandise. The items placed in the high-rent areas of the store should generate adequate sales and contribute enough to profit to justify their high-value locations. The decline in value of store space from front to back of the shop is expressed in the 40-30-20-10 rule. This rule assigns 40 percent of a store's rental cost to the front quarter of the shop, 30 percent to the second quarter, 20 percent to the third quarter, and 10 percent to the final quarter. Similarly, each quarter of the store should contribute the same percentage of sales revenue.

For example, suppose that a small store anticipates $720,000 in sales this year. Each quarter of the store should generate the following sales volume:

Front quarter	$720,000 × 0.40 = $288,000
Second quarter	$720,000 × 0.30 = $216,000
Third quarter	$720,000 × 0.20 = $144,000
Fourth quarter	$720,000 × 0.10 = $72,000
Total	= $720,000

Layout for Manufacturers

Manufacturing layout decisions take into consideration the arrangement of departments, workstations, machines, and stock-holding points within a production facility. The general objective is to arrange these elements to ensure a smooth, efficient workflow. Manufacturing facilities have come under increasing scrutiny as firms attempt to improve quality, decrease inventories, and increase productivity through facilities that are integrated, flexible, and efficient. Facility layout has a dramatic effect on product processing, material handling, storage, production volume, and quality.

HANDS ON...
HOW TO

Create the Ideal Layout

As the world shifts to a knowledge-based economy, more workers are engaging in office work, in which measuring productivity sometimes proves difficult. Research shows that a well-designed office is one of the simplest and most cost-effective ways to increase workers' productivity and satisfaction. For instance, if a company builds and operates an office building, the cost of initial construction accounts for just 2 percent of the building's total cost over 30 years. Operating expenses account for 6 percent. The remaining 92 percent of the total cost of operating the building over 30 years goes to paying the salaries and benefits of the people who occupy the space! Top performing companies recognize that their employees account for the largest portion of the total cost of a work environment and make adequate investments to ensure that the work space maximizes their efficiency, satisfaction, and productivity. Unfortunately, many other companies remain stuck in the antiquated cubicle culture that provides the fodder for so many Dilbert cartoon strips and that squelches individual expression, collaboration with colleagues, and creativity.

What principles make for a good office design and allow a company to get the most out of its investment in designing a workspace?

Observe how employees use the existing space

The nature of employees' work changes over time and so do their workspace needs. A design that was suitable a few years ago may be inappropriate today. Entrepreneurs should take the time to observe employees at work. When do workers use office space? Which spaces are at maximum capacity, and which ones are underutilized? Why? Does the existing design support employees' ability to do their jobs or hinder it? Red flags include the following:

- People whose work requires collaboration do not naturally interact with their colleagues during the course of a day.
- Employees waste a lot of time in transit to meeting rooms, printers, copiers, and other office equipment.
- Workers are competing for the use of certain pieces of office equipment.
- An area is either typically overcrowded or empty.
- Employees schedule meetings at nearby coffee shops or restaurants because these places provide better common space for collaboration.

At Cisco Systems, studies showed that employees' cubicles sat vacant 35 percent of the time; workers came to the office mainly for meetings and to socialize. The company removed the cubicles and converted the office into a flexible, multifunctional "Connected Workspace" where employees can pick almost any spot to do their work. Desks, chairs, and dividers on wheels give employees the flexibility to rearrange the work space to fit their needs. An IP telephone system allows them to transfer their calls to any telephone in the office. Cisco says that the redesign allows 140 employees to work in a space that formerly housed only 88 workers and that both productivity and employee satisfaction have increased.

Involve employees in the redesign

One of the worst mistakes designers make is creating a new layout without the input of the people who will be working in the space. Asking employees up front for ideas and suggestions is essential to producing an effective layout. What barriers to their work does the existing design create? How can you eliminate them? One sure-fire way to alienate employees is to fail to involve them in the redesign of their workspace.

Plan the new design

Redesigning a workspace can be a major undertaking. The process goes much more smoothly and the end result is superior for companies that invest in significant planning than for those companies that do not. Successful designs usually result when entrepreneurs and their employees define two to five priorities such as increased collaboration, enhanced productivity, reduced absenteeism and turnover, or improved energy efficiency for design professionals to achieve.

An extensive report, *Innovative Workplace Strategies*, from the General Services Administration lists the following hallmarks of the productive workplace:

- *Spatial equity*. Do workers have adequate space to accomplish their tasks and have access to privacy, natural light, and aesthetics?
- *Healthfulness*. Is the workspace a healthy environment with access to air, light, and water? Is it free of harmful contaminants and excess noise?
- *Flexibility*. Can workers adjust their work environment to respond to important functional changes?
- *Comfort*. Can workers adjust light, temperature, acoustic levels, and furnishings to their individual preferences?
- *Technological Connectivity*. Can on-site and off-site workers stay connected with one another and gain access to the information they need? Does technology enhance their ability to collaborate on projects?
- *Reliability*. Does the workplace have dependable mechanical and technological systems that receive proper support?
- *Sense of place*. Does the workplace décor and atmosphere reflect the company's mission and brand? Does the space create a culture that is appropriate for accomplishing the tasks at hand?

Rely on continuous improvement

A redesign project is not finished just because the work is complete. Smart entrepreneurs resist the temptation to sit back and admire the finished product and think about how happy they are to be "done." Instead, they recognize that no redesign, however well planned, is perfect. They are willing to tweak the project and to make necessary adjustments to meet employees' changing needs.

Sources: Based on Jane Hodges, "How to Build a Better Office," *BNET*, 2007, http://www.bnet.com/2403-13056_23-190221.html; Julie Schlosser, "The Great Escape," *Fortune*, March 20, 2006, pp. 107–110; Michael Lev-Ram, "How to Make Your Workspace Better," *Business 2.0*, November 2006, pp. 58–60; Jeffrey Pfeffer, "Thinking Outside the Cube," *Business 2.0*, April 2007, p. 60; *Innovative Workplace Strategies*, General Services Administration, Office of Governmentwide Policy, Office of Real Property, Washington, DC: 2003, p. 70.

FACTORS IN MANUFACTURING LAYOUT The ideal layout for a manufacturing operation depends on a number of factors, including the following:

- *Type of product.* Product design and quality standards; whether the product is produced for inventory or for order; and the physical properties such as the size of materials and products, special handling requirements, susceptibility to damage, and perishability.
- *Type of production process.* Technology used; types of materials handled; means of providing a service; and processing requirements in terms of number of operations involved and amount of interaction between departments and work centers.
- *Ergonomic considerations.* Worker safety; avoiding injuries and accidents; increasing productivity.
- *Economic considerations.* Volume of production; costs of materials, machines, workstations, and labor; pattern and variability of demand; minimizing cycle time, the amount of time between receiving a customer's order and delivering the finished product.
- *Space availability within the facility itself.*

DESIGNING LAYOUTS The starting point in layout design is determining how and in what sequence product parts or service tasks flow together. One of the most effective techniques is to create an overall picture of the manufacturing process using assembly charts and process flowcharts. Given the tasks and their sequence, plus knowledge of the volume of products to be produced or of customers to be served, an entrepreneur can analyze space and equipment needs to get an idea of the facility's capacity. When using a product or line layout, these demands take precedent, and manufacturers must arrange equipment and workstations to fit the production tasks and their sequence. With a process or functional layout, different products or customers with different needs place demands on the facility. Rather than having a single best flow, there may be one flow for each product or customer, and compromises in efficiency may be necessary. As a result, the layout for any one product or customer may not be optimal but is flexible enough to serve the specific situation.

ANALYZING PRODUCTION LAYOUTS Although there is no standard procedure for analyzing the numerous interdependent factors that enter into layout design, specific layout problems lend themselves to detailed analysis. Two important criteria for selecting and designing a layout are workers' productivity and material handling costs. An effective layout allows workers to maximize their productivity by providing them the tools and a system for doing their jobs properly. For example, a layout that requires a production worker to step away from the work area in search of the proper tool is inefficient. An effective manufacturing layout avoids what lean manufacturing principles identify as the seven forms of waste:

- *Transportation.* Unnecessary movement of inventory, materials, and information
- *Inventory.* Carrying unnecessary inventory
- *Motion.* Engaging in motion that does not add value to the product or process
- *Waiting.* Periods of inactivity when people, materials, or information are idle
- *Overproduction.* Producing more than customer demand dictates
- *Processing.* Using tools and procedures that are inappropriate for the job
- *Defects.* Producing poor quality products, which requires scrapping or reworking material

Manufacturers can lower materials handling costs by using the following principles that are hallmarks of a lean, efficient manufacturing layout:

- Planned materials flow pattern
- Straight-line layout where possible
- Straight, clearly-marked aisles
- "Backtracking" of products kept to a minimum
- Related operations located close together
- Minimum amount of in-process inventory on hand
- Easy adjustment to changing conditions
- Minimum materials handling distances
- Minimum of manual handling of materials and products

- Ergonomically designed work centers
- Minimum distances between work stations and processes
- No unnecessary re-handling of material
- Minimum handling between operations
- Minimum storage
- Materials delivered to production employees just in time
- Materials efficiently removed from the work area
- Maximum visibility; maintain clear lines of site to spot problems and improve safety
- Orderly materials handling and storage
- Good housekeeping; minimize clutter
- Maximum flexibility
- Maximum communication

Using the principles of lean manufacturing can improve efficiency, quality, and productivity and lower costs.

Boride Engineered Abrasives, a Traverse City, Michigan, company that makes abrasive products for industrial and consumer use, applied the "5S" principles (Sort, Shine, Simplify, Standardize, and Sustain) that world-class auto maker Toyota uses in its lean manufacturing process. As employees throughout the company began to buy into the process, improvements became apparent. Productivity increased by 70 percent, back orders declined from 50 percent to between 5 and 10 percent, and time required to fill customer order decreased from 3 weeks to 5 days. Boride also saw its sales increase by 44 percent.[75]

Chapter Summary

1. **Explain the stages in the location decision—choosing the region, the state, the city, and the final site.**

   - The location decision is one of the most important decisions an entrepreneur will make, given its long-term effects on the company. An entrepreneur should look at the choice as a series of increasingly narrow decisions: Which region of the country? Which state? Which city? Which site? Choosing the right location requires an entrepreneur to evaluate potential sites with her target customers in mind. Demographic statistics are available from a wide variety of sources, but government agencies such as the Census Bureau have a wealth of detailed data that can guide an entrepreneur in her location decision.

2. **Describe the location criteria for retail and service businesses.**

   - For retailers, the location decision is especially crucial. Retailers must consider the size of the trade area, the volume of customer traffic, number of parking spots, availability of room for expansion, and the visibility of a site.

3. **Outline the basic location options for retail and service businesses.**

   - Retail and service businesses have six basic location options: central business districts (CBDs); neighborhoods; shopping centers and malls; near competitors; inside large retail stores; outlying areas; and at home.

4. **Explain the site selection process for manufacturers.**

   - A manufacturer's location decision is strongly influenced by local zoning ordinances. Some areas offer industrial parks designed specifically to attract manufacturers. Two crucial factors for most manufacturers are the reliability (and the cost of transporting) raw materials and the quality and quantity of available labor.
   - A foreign trade zone is a specially designated area in or near a U.S. customs port of entry that allows resident companies to import materials and components from foreign countries; assemble, process, manufacture, or package them; and then ship the finished product while either reducing or eliminating tariffs and duties.
   - Empowerment zones offer businesses tax breaks on the investments they make within zone boundaries.
   - Business incubators are locations that offer flexible, low-cost rental space to their tenants as well as business and consulting services. Their goal is to nurture small companies until they are ready to "graduate" into the business community. Many government agencies and universities offer incubator locations.

5. **Describe the criteria used to analyze the layout and design considerations of a building, including the Americans with Disabilities Act.**

   - When evaluating the suitability of a particular building, an entrepreneur should consider several factors: size (Is it large enough to accommodate the business with some room for growth?); construction and external appearance (Is the building structurally sound and does it create the right impression for the business?); entrances (Are they inviting?); legal issues (Does the building comply with the Americans with Disabilities Act? If not, how much will it cost to bring it up to standard?); signs (Are they legible, well-located, and easy to see?); interior (Does the interior design contribute to our ability to make sales? Is it ergonomically designed?); and lights and fixtures (Is the lighting adequate for the tasks workers will be performing? What is the estimated cost of lighting?).

6. **Explain the principles of effective layouts for retailers, service businesses, and manufacturers.**

- Layout for retail stores and service businesses depends on the owner's understanding of her customers' buying habits. Retailers have three basic layout options from which to choose: grid, free-form, and boutique. Some areas of a retail store generate more sales per square foot and therefore are more valuable.
- The goal of a manufacturer's layout is to create a smooth, efficient work flow. Three basic options exist: product layout, process layout, and fixed position layout. Two key considerations are worker productivity and materials handling costs.

Discussion Questions

1. How do most small business owners choose a location? Is this wise?
2. What factors should a manager consider when evaluating a region in which to locate a business? Where are such data available?
3. Outline the factors important when selecting a state in which to locate a business.
4. What factors should a seafood processing plant, a beauty shop, and an exclusive jewelry store consider in choosing a location? List factors for each type of business.
5. What intangible factors might enter into the entrepreneur's location decision?
6. What are zoning laws? How do they affect the location decision?
7. What is the trade area? What determines a small retailer's trade area?
8. Why is it important to discover more than just the number of passersby in a traffic count?
9. What types of information can the entrepreneur collect from census data?
10. Why may a "cheap location" not be the "best location"?
11. What is a foreign trade zone? An empowerment zone? A business incubator? What advantages and

disadvantages does each one of these offer a small business locating there?
12. Why is it costly for a small firm to choose a location that is too small?
13. What function does a small company's sign serve? What are the characteristics of an effective business sign?
14. Explain the Americans with Disabilities Act. Which businesses does it affect? What is its purpose?
15. What is ergonomics? Why should entrepreneurs utilize the principles of ergonomics in the design of their facilities?
16. Explain the statement, "Not every portion of a small store's interior space is of equal value in generating sales revenue." What areas are most valuable?
17. According to market research firm NPD Group, in 1985, women purchased 70 percent of all men's clothing; today, women buy just 34 percent of men's apparel. What implications does this have for modern store layouts?
18. What are some of the key features that are determine a good manufacturing layout?

Business PlanPro™

Analyzing the value of potential business site is critical. A retail or service-based company will benefit from a high-traffic location with optimal exposure. A manufacturing, repair, or storage business must to meet the demands of shipping and receiving logistics. Selecting the wrong location places the business must at a disadvantage before the other challenges of a managing a profitable business come into play.

Business Plan Exercises

This chapter emphasizes that selecting the right location is critical to a retail venture or any business venture in which customers

will benefit from face-to-face contact and the ability to view, touch, try, and ultimately purchase their products.

On the Web

The Web offers valuable information regarding location information. One resource mentioned earlier in the marketing chapter of the text is the PRIZM information from Claritas, Inc. (http://www.claritas.com/MyBestSegments). This information identifies the most common market segments in your zip code and may be a way to validate whether you location is in proximity to your target markets. PRIZM categorizes U.S. consumer markets based on demographic and customer segmentation profiling research data by zip code. A retail business, for example, will find that locating close to its target customers is a critical success factor. Additional information, such as traffic counts and other location attributes, will also be important to include in your business plan.

Sample Plans

Identify a sample plan with a business concept that demands a high traffic location. Now, find a sample plan that has specific location needs for other reasons. Note how each plan presents the needs and importance of the location and the facility.

In the Software

Open your business plan and go to the Your Company section. Describe your ideal, potential, or existing location. If you already have selected a location for your business, you may want to assess whether it is a strength or a weaknesses in your SWOT analysis. If your location possesses some of the positive attributes mentioned in the chapter, identify your location as strength. If your location has negative characteristics, recognize it as a weakness and have your plan address how you will overcome the challenges your location presents. The location may be so important to the business that you will also list it under the Keys to Success section. Remember to include the expense for your location—rent, lease, or mortgage payments—into the financial section of your plan.

Building Your Business Plan

Selecting your location is an important strategic business decision for most business ventures. Your business plan can help you to profile, describe, and ultimately decide on the most attractive business location available. Once you determine a location, your plan can leverage that location's strongest attributes to optimize customer exposure, sales, and profits.

Beyond the Classroom...

1. Select a specific type of business you would like to go into one day and use census data and other reports from the Web or the local library to choose a specific site for the business in the local region. What location factors are critical to the success of this business? Would it be likely to succeed in your hometown?

2. Interview a sample of local small business owners. How did they decide on their particular locations? What are the positive and negative features of their existing locations

3. Locate the most recent issue of either *Entrepreneur* or *Fortune* describing the "best cities for (small) business." (For *Entrepreneur*, it is usually the October issue, and for *Fortune*, it is normally an issue in November.) Which cities are in the top 10? What factors did the magazine use to select these cities? Pick a city and explain what makes it an attractive destination for locating a business there.

4. Select a manufacturing operation, a wholesale business, or a retail store, and evaluate their layouts using the guidelines presented in this chapter. What changes would you recommend? Why? Does the layout contribute to a more effective operation?

5. Choose one of the businesses you studied in Exercise #4 and design an improved layout for the operation. How expensive would these alterations be?

6. Every year, *Site Selection* magazine selects the states with the Top Business Climate. Use the Web to locate the latest state rankings. Which states top the list? Which states are at the bottom of the list? What factors affect a state's ranking? Why are these factors important to entrepreneurs' location decisions?

7. Visit the Web site for the Census Bureau at:
   http://www.census.gov/
   Go to the Census data for your town and use it to discuss its suitability as a location for the following types of businesses:
   - A new motel with 25 units
   - A bookstore
   - An exclusive women's clothing shop
   - A Mexican restaurant
   - A residential plumber
   - A day-care center
   - A high-quality stereo shop
   - A family hair care center

8. Visit the Census Bureau's Web site and use the American FactFinder section to prepare a demographic profile of your hometown or city or of the town or city in which you attend college. Using the demographic profile as an analytical tool, what kinds of businesses do you think would be successful there? Unsuccessful? Explain.

The Great American Hanger Company

CHAPTER 15

Global Aspects
of Entrepreneurship

Arguing against globalization is like arguing against the laws of gravity.
—*Kofi Annan*

*If we ignore the opportunities to go internationally, generally the option
is to go out of business.*
—*Matthew Calvage*

Learning Objectives

On completion of this chapter, you will be able to:

1. Explain why "going global" has become an integral part of the marketing strategies of many small companies.

2. Describe the principal strategies small businesses have for going global.

3. Explain how to build a thriving export program.

4. Discuss the major barriers to international trade and their impact on the global community.

5. Describe the trade agreements that will have the greatest influence on foreign trade in the twenty-first century—WTO, NAFTA, and CAFTA.

Until recently, the world of international business was much like astronomy before Copernicus, who revolutionized the study of the planets and the stars with his theory of planetary motion. In the sixteenth century, the Copernican system replaced the Ptolemaic system, which held that the earth was the center of the universe with the sun and all the other planets revolving around it. The Copernican system, however, placed the sun at the center of the solar system with all of the planets revolving around it. Astronomy would never be the same.

In the same sense, business owners across the globe have been guilty of having Ptolemaic tunnel vision when it came to viewing international business opportunities. Like their pre-Copernican counterparts, owners saw an economy that revolved around the nations that served as their home bases. Market opportunities stopped at their homelands' borders. Global trade was only for giant corporations that had the money and the management talent to tap foreign markets and enough resources to survive if the venture flopped. This scenario no longer holds true in the twenty-first century.

Today the global marketplace is as much the territory of small upstart companies as it is that of giant multinational corporations. Powerful, affordable technology, the Internet, increased access to information on conducting global business, and the growing interdependence of the world's economies have made it easier for companies of all sizes to engage in international trade. A study of the future of small business by Intuit predicts that nearly half of U.S. small businesses will engage in some kind of global trade by 2018.[1]

ENTREPRENEURIAL PROFILE

Andy Ory & Patrick MeLampy: Acme Packet

Acme Packet, a maker of telecommunications equipment in Burlington, Massachusetts, began selling in international markets shortly after co-founders Andy Ory and Patrick MeLampy launched it in 2000. The move paid off. By 2003, the company had nearly 50 employees and generated 75 percent of its $3.3 million in annual sales in Italy and Japan, the two markets in which managers decided to focus initially. Today, Acme Packet has 300 employees (20 percent of whom are located in 22 countries), generates nearly $130 million in annual revenue, and sells to customers in 95 countries across the globe.[2]

As globalization transforms entire industries, even experienced business owners and managers must rethink the rules of competition on which they have relied for years. To thrive, they know they must develop new business models and new sources of competitive advantages. One survey by management consulting firm Bain and Company reports that 75 percent of global executives believe that they will have to revamp their core businesses to remain competitive, and 80 percent say that the speed of global business has made maintaining a competitive edge more difficult.[3]

Entrepreneurs are discovering that the tools of global business are within their reach, the costs of going global are decreasing, and the benefits of conducting global business can be substantial. In fact, more than 75 percent of the world's purchasing power lies *outside* of the borders of the United States! "The timing has never been better for small businesses to get out of their backyards and become "global players," says Laurel Delaney, founder of GlobeTrade.com, a consulting company.[4]

Why Go Global?

LO 1

Explain why "going global" has become an integral part of many small companies' marketing strategies.

Failure to cultivate global markets can be a lethal mistake for modern businesses, whatever their size. A few decades ago, small companies needed to concern themselves mainly with competitors who were perhaps six blocks away; today, small companies face fierce competition from companies that may be six *time zones* away! As a result, entrepreneurs find themselves under greater pressure to expand into international markets and to build businesses without borders. Today, it is not uncommon for entrepreneurs to purchase goods from overseas suppliers or to have the components they use in their products made in foreign countries and assembled in another country, and then to sell the finished products to customers in many countries.

Build a Successful Global Company

When Mia Abbruzzese worked for athletic global shoe makers New Balance, Fila Sports, and Stride Rite, she became accustomed to traveling to Asia to visit the factories that turned out shoes. For ten years, she traveled in business class and rode in limousines. Then she launched her own shoe company, Morgan & Milo, and although many of her destinations were the same, her style of travel changed dramatically. Now she buys coach airfare tickets on Orbitz.com and takes public buses and taxis to reach the Asian factories that make the line of children's shoes her company sells.

Abbruzzese used her experience at some of the world's largest shoe companies to realize her dream of owning her own international shoe business. With just three executives working from three different locations, an office loft in Boston that serves loosely as company headquarters, and connections to a Chinese shoe factory, Abbruzzese operates her small company on a global scale. Morgan & Milo creates children's shoe designs, has them manufactured to specifications in China, and sells them to retailers in the United States and Europe. Following are some of the lessons she has learned about operating a global small business.

Hit 'em where they ain't

When asked about the secret to his batting titles, Hall of Fame baseball player Wee Willy Keeler, known as baseball's greatest place hitter, answered, "I hit 'em where they ain't." Abbruzzese took the same approach when building her international shoe company. She chose a niche—children's shoes—that she knew was being underserved by the major players in the shoe industry. "It's a great market no one is paying attention to," she says. Abbruzzese learned the benefits of pursuing "undiscovered" markets when she was at New Balance working on the walking shoe product line, which became the company's third biggest line

Success in international markets depends on a network of connections

Because she had launched several shoe lines during her days in corporate America, Abbruzzese knew that success in the shoe business requires an extensive network of connections in all corners of the globe. Using her industry contacts, Abbruzzese found a Taiwanese investor who provided $595,000 in start-up capital for Morgan & Milo as well as enough working capital to cover the company's operating expenses until cash flow turned positive. The investor also introduced Abbruzzese to the owner of the factory in southern China that makes many of the shoes that Morgan & Milo designs. Abbruzzese also relies on two industry veterans who have an extensive network of contacts in the shoe industry and have proved to be extremely valuable to her young company.

Do not assume that your international partners do business the same way that you do in the United States

Business dealings are a reflection of a country's culture, and entrepreneurs must educate themselves about the nuances of doing business in the host country before they set out. In the United States, businesspeople are transaction oriented. They want to set up an appointment, negotiate a deal quickly and efficiently, sign a contract, and leave. In many other countries, landing a deal takes much longer because businesspeople expect to get to know their potential partners first. In China, businesspeople tend to be relationship oriented, doing business only with people they know, like, and respect. Developing relationships can take time, which makes a network of connections all the more important. Abbruzze had to learn that formal contracts, which are the foundation of business deals in the United States, are not as important in China. She also had to adjust the speed at which she expects to close deals and take more time to build relationships with suppliers.

Organize for speed

When she worked for the major shoe companies, Abbruzzese could not help but notice that the time it took from designing a shoe to getting it into retailer's stores was quite lengthy. One of the key competitive advantages of her small, faster, and more nimble company is *speed*. Morgan & Milo can go from shoe design to a finished product in just three or four months, compared to at least six months for a big shoe company, and retailers appreciate that. Manufacturing shoes in China and getting them into retail stores quickly, however, requires careful coordination across international borders, something that Morgan & Milo's organization is designed to do.

Invest in technology

Operating a global company efficiently requires an investment in technology, and Abbruzzese has made that investment in both basics such as smart phones and e-mail and in sophisticated systems that track inventory, orders, and shipping schedules anywhere the world. With their investment in technology (which the company constantly updates), Abbruzzese and her team can track results and communicate with manufacturers in China or customers in Europe.

Look bigger than you are

To build a successful global company, Abbruzzese understands that Morgan & Milo has to look bigger than it actually is. One way to accomplish that is to build a successful brand. "I couldn't just create shoes," she says. "I had to position them and create a story and feeling behind them." The logo and the polished, professional sales literature that Abbruzze designed for Morgan & Milo go a long way toward creating the image of a big, successful company. "When competing in a global marketplace of shoe giants, you have to do all of the things that people don't expect from [a small company] operating out of a 1,000-square-foot office," she says.

Sources: Based on Allessandra Bianchi, "Small & Global: The World As a Factory," *FSB*, June 2004, pp. 40–42; Sheri Qualters, "Operating on a Shoestring," *Boston Business Journal*, June 10, 2005, http://boston.bizjournals.com/boston/stories/2005/06/13/smallb1.html; Emily Maltby, "Rising Yuan Crunches Outsourcers' Bottom Line," *FSB*, April 3, 2008, http://money.cnn.com/2008/04/02/smbusiness/rising_yuan.fsb/index.htm; Janet Carmosky, "7 Deadly Perceptions About Doing Business with China," *Business Pundit*, August 21, 2008, http://www.businesspundit.com/7-deadly-perceptions-about-doing-business-with-china/.

For instance, Gayle Warwick, founder of Gayle Warwick Fine Linen, a maker of luxury bed and table linen, lives in London and purchases the organic, extra long-staple pima cotton that goes into her company's luxury linens in the American Southwest, Peru, and Egypt. She has the raw cotton spun and woven in Switzerland, finished in Italy, and embroidered in Vietnam. "I didn't set out to create a global business," Warwick admits. "I just tried to find the best suppliers. It takes patience and persistence, but it is possible even for a small business to achieve this type of network."[5]

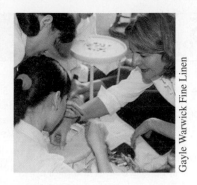

Gayle Warwick Fine Linen

ENTREPRENEURIAL PROFILE

Gayle Warwick: Gayle Warwick Fine Linen

As Gayle Warwick Fine Linen demonstrates, operating a successful business increasingly requires entrepreneurs to see their companies as global citizens rather than as companies based in a particular geographic region. For small companies around the world, going global is a matter of survival, not preference. To be successful, small companies must take their place in the world market. Success in a global economy requires constant innovation; staying nimble enough to use speed as a competitive weapon; maintaining a high level of quality and constantly improving it; being sensitive to foreign customers' unique requirements; adopting a more respectful attitude toward foreign habits and customs; hiring motivated, multilingual employees; and retaining a desire to learn constantly about global markets. In short, business owners must strive to become "insiders" rather than just "exporters."

Becoming a global entrepreneur does require a different mindset. To be successful, entrepreneurs must see their companies from a global perspective and must instill a global culture throughout their companies that permeates everything the business does. To these entrepreneurs and their companies, national boundaries are irrelevant; they see the world as a market opportunity. Indeed, learning to *think globally* may be the first—and most challenging—obstacle an entrepreneur must overcome on the way to creating a truly global business. Global thinking is the ability to appreciate, understand, and respect the different beliefs, values, behavior, and business practices of companies and people in different cultures and countries. This requires entrepreneurs to "do their homework" to learn about the people, places, business techniques, potential customers, and culture of the countries in which they intend to do business. Several U.S. government agencies, including the Department of

"I try to think globally, but I can't get past New Jersey."

Source: From *The Wall Street Journal*, permission Cartoon Features Syndicate.

ETHICS AND ENTREPRENEURSHIP

Cool Phone, But Is It Real?

Many U.S.–based companies engaged in international business face a threat from counterfeit goods produced by illicit manufacturers, many of whom operate in foreign lands. Counterfeit goods seized in raids have ranged from helicopter components and DVDs to auto parts and birth control pills. China poses one of the greatest challenges for companies that invest in developing and marketing proprietary products that become best sellers. Experts estimate that two-thirds of all counterfeit goods sold globally originate in China. Chinese companies have been making and selling knockoffs of up-scale handbags, watches, clothing, and other consumer goods for years. Some counterfeit items are produced on a "night shift" in the same factories to which "genuine" companies have outsourced production to lower their costs. It is not uncommon for counterfeit DVDs of popular movies to be on sale in the streets in China even *before* the genuine film hits the theaters. Western visitors to China often are accosted by Chinese street salesmen offering to sell them "Rolex" watches—for just $2 each. Although China's admission to the World Trade Organization in 2001 was contingent on the nation passing laws to protect intellectual property, enforcement of those laws is proving to be difficult, in part because modern technology makes counterfeiting goods much easier.

Near Shenzhen, hundreds of companies, most of them small, rely on local suppliers, some of whom supply components to the makers of genuine products, then turn out *shanzhai*, or black market, cell phones and sell them for as little as $20 each. "It's just as good," says a sales clerk as he shows a potential customer a sleek, touch-screen phone called the Hi-Phone manufactured by Organe (perhaps a misspelling of "Orange" and a direct affront to Apple's Iphone). Nearby, other vendors sell knockoffs of Nokia, Samsung, and other phones. The "brand" names printed on the phones are "Nckia" and "Sumsung." Late-night television infomercials make no effort to disguise the legitimacy of the fakes they are hawking as they tout the same function and look as the original but at one-fifth the price. "Buy *shanzhai* to show the love of our country," exclaims one ad.

The damage to the companies that legitimately own the intellectual property rights is very real. Experts estimate that U.S. companies alone lose $250 million in sales to counterfeit goods manufactured around the globe. Large cities such as Beijing and Shanghai host high concentrations of companies that make counterfeit consumer products, and industrialized areas such as

Shenzhen are home to companies that make high-tech knockoffs. China represents one of the largest cell phone markets in the world, and experts estimate that 30 percent of the cell phones sold annually in China are *shanzhai* knockoffs. An estimated 60 million of them are exported to other countries. Not only are many of the knockoffs unreliable, but they also are unsafe. China's Ministry of Industry and Information technology recently warned that the radiation levels in *shanzai* cell phones exceed allowable safety limits. One man was burned severely when his cell phone exploded in his shirt pocket. Some of the cheap knockoff items are so cleverly packaged that distributors have difficulty spotting them, which makes combating the problem extremely difficult.

Counterfeiting in China appears to be unfettered by ethical considerations. Many of the counterfeiters take pride in their ability to react faster to changing market trends than the companies that make the genuine products, and often view themselves as innovators. Chinese customers justify their counterfeit purchases by pointing to the low prices they pay for phony goods. "I saw iPhone pictures on the Web," says one customer. "It's so cool, but it costs over $500—too expensive. I decided to buy a *shanzhai* phone. It looked exactly like the iPhone."

1. What are the implications for companies whose products are the targets of counterfeiters? Their customers?
2. Use the Internet to research the problem of counterfeit goods and the problems it poses. Write a one-page report on a company's battle with fake goods and the steps it took to combat the problem.
3. What steps can companies take to battle companies that manufacture knockoffs of their products?

Sources: Based on David Barboza, "In China, Knockoff Cell Phones Are a Hit," *New York Times*, April 28, 2009, http://www.nytimes.com/2009/04/28/technology/28cell.html; Suzanne Deffree, "Countering China's Counterfeit Components," *Electronics Design, Strategy, News*, July 16, 2008, http://www.edn.com/blog/690000269/post/860030086.html; Michael Backman, "China's Counterfeit Culture Is Quite an Education," *The Age*, March 28, 2007, http://www.theage.com.au/news/business/chinas-counterfeit-culture-is-quite-an-education/2007/03/27/1174761469475.html#; S. L. Shen, "China's Amazing Knockoffs," *UPI Asia*, December 9, 2008, http://www.upiasia.com/Society_Culture/2008/12/09/chinas_amazing_knockoffs/7656/; Daniel Allen, "Knocking Out China's Knockoffs," *Asia Times*, February 15, 2007, http://www.atimes.com/atimes/China_Business/IB15Cb08.html.

Commerce, offer vast amounts of information about all nations, including economic data that can be useful to entrepreneurs searching for market opportunities. Doing business globally presents extraordinary opportunities only to those who are prepared. "With a little know-how, creativity, and confidence, even the smallest business can find opportunities around the globe," says Donna Sharp, director of the World Trade Institute at Pace University.[6]

LO 2

Describe the principal strategies small businesses have for going global.

Strategies for Going Global

Small companies pursuing a global presence have nine principal strategies from which to choose: creating a presence on the Web, relying on trade intermediaries, outsourcing production, establishing joint ventures, engaging in foreign licensing arrangements, franchising, using countertrading and bartering, exporting products or services, and the establishing international locations (see Figure 15.1).

FIGURE 15.1

Nine Strategies for Going Global

Creating a Presence on the Web

Perhaps in our technology-rich global environment, the fastest, least expensive, and lowest cost strategic option to developing a global business presence is to create a Web site. As you saw in Chapter 9 on e-commerce, the Web gives even the smallest business the ability to sell its goods and services all over the globe. By establishing a presence online, a local candy maker or a home-based luxury boat broker gains immediate access to customers around the world. With a well-designed Web site, an entrepreneur can extend its reach to customers anywhere in the world—and without breaking the budget! A company's Web site is available to anyone anywhere in the world and provides exposure 24 hours a day to its products or services seven days a week. For many small companies, the Web has become a tool that is as essential to doing business as the telephone and the fax machine.

Establishing a presence on the Web has become an important part of a company's strategy for reaching customers outside the United States. A study by Internet World Stats estimates the number of World Wide Web users to be 1.60 billion worldwide. Approximately 220 million of them live in the United States, leaving nearly 1.4 *billion* potential Web customers outside this country's borders![7] Internet World Stats reports that customers who live outside the United States account for more than 50 percent of all online sales by U.S. companies.[8] Figure 15.2 shows global Internet usage by world region. eBay, another popular online channel for entrepreneurs, provides access to international shoppers; 54 percent of all eBay transactions take place outside the United States.[9]

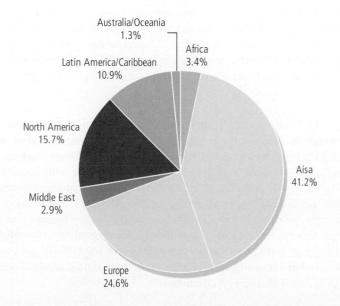

FIGURE 15.2

Internet Users by World Region

Source: Internet World Status: Usage and Population Statistics, http://www/internetworldstats.com/stats.htm.

Before the advent of the Internet, small businesses usually took incremental steps toward becoming global businesses. They began selling locally, and, then, after establishing a reputation, expanded regionally and perhaps nationally. Only after establishing themselves domestically did small businesses begin to think about selling their products or services internationally. The Web makes that business model obsolete because it provides small companies with a low-cost global distribution channel that they can utilize from the day they are launched.

ENTREPRENEURIAL PROFILE

Joe Gebbia: CritBuns

When Joe Gebbia was a student at the Rhode Island School of Design, he noticed how uncomfortable he and his classmates were sitting on hard seats, sometimes for hours on end, during professors' critiques ("crits") of their work. Spotting an opportunity, 26-year-old Gebbia designed a comfortable portable cushion that sported a unique, fashionable look and after graduating built a company and a Web site to sell it. Dozens of retailers rejected Gebbia's patented CritBuns until he convinced the New York Museum of Modern Art to purchase 200 units. Publicity from a

Tokyo design show and a feature in a design magazine called *I.D.* spurred CritBuns's sales. The foam material from which CritBuns is made makes it lightweight and easy to clean; Gebbia's design incorporates a handle for portability, which explains why users have taken the product beyond the art studio to stadiums, gardens, concerts, and yoga studios. Today, 25 percent of the San Francisco–based company's sales are made to international customers in Canada, Europe, Japan, and other countries. "People found the Web site, and I started getting orders from all over the world," says Gebbia, who is now marketing SportsBuns to fans of athletic events around the world.[10]

Trade Intermediaries

trade intermediaries
domestic agencies that serve as distributors in foreign countries for domestic companies of all sizes.

Another alternative for low cost and low risk entry into international markets is to use a trade intermediary. **Trade intermediaries** are domestic agencies that serve as distributors in foreign countries for domestic companies of all sizes. They rely on their networks of contacts, their extensive knowledge of local customs and markets, and their experience in international trade to market products effectively and efficiently all across the globe. These trade intermediaries serve as the export departments for small businesses, enabling small companies to focus on what they do best and delegate the responsibility for coordinating foreign sales efforts to the intermediaries. They are especially valuable to small companies that are getting started in the global arena, often producing benefits that far outweigh their costs. Lawrence Harding, president of High Street Partners, a trade intermediary that manages foreign sales for small companies, points to the example of a company that imported telecommunications equipment into the United Kingdom to sell to its customers there. The deal triggered a hefty 17.5 percent duty that Harding says the company could have avoided paying if it had imported the equipment in a different way.[11]

Although a broad array of trade intermediaries is available, the following are ideally suited for small businesses.

export management companies
merchant intermediaries that provide small businesses with a low-cost, efficient, off-site international marketing department.

EXPORT MANAGEMENT COMPANIES **Export management companies (EMCs)** are an important channel of foreign distribution for small companies just getting started in international trade or for those lacking the resources to assign their own people to foreign markets. Most EMCs are merchant intermediaries, working on a buy-and-sell arrangement with domestic small companies, taking title to the goods and then reselling them in foreign markets; others work on commission. More than 1,000 EMCs operate across the United States, and many of them specialize in particular industries, products, or product lines as well as in the foreign countries they target. For instance, Neal Asbury, founder of export management company Greenfield World Trade, specializes in selling and servicing food service equipment for U.S.–based companies in more than 130 countries. Asbury recently received the National Small Business Exporter of the Year Award from the U.S. Small Business Administration.[12]

EMCs provide small businesses with a low-cost, efficient, independent international marketing and export department, offering services that range from conducting market research and giving advice on patent protection to arranging financing and handling shipping.

> William Johnson's Mequon, Wisconsin-based tool company, Johnson Level and Tool, already was selling its tools in four foreign markets when a representative from M&P Export Management, an export management company, approached Johnson about representing the company in other foreign markets where the EMC had a presence. With the EMC's help, Johnson Level and Tool now sells its products in 40 international markets. After working with the EMC, company managers gained more experience in conducting international business and capitalized on other global opportunities. The company now has two manufacturing joint ventures with similar companies in Canada and Mexico.[13]

ENTREPRENEURIAL PROFILE ____

William Johnson: Johnson Level & Tool

The greatest benefits EMCs offer small companies are ready access to global markets and an extensive knowledge base on foreign trade, both of which are vital for entrepreneurs who are inexperienced in conducting global business. In return for their services, EMCs usually earn an extra discount on the goods they buy from their clients or, if they operate on a commission rate, a higher commission than domestic distributors earn on what they sell. EMCs charge commission rates of about 10 percent on consumer goods and 15 percent on industrial products. Although EMCs rarely advertise their services, finding one is not difficult. The Federation of International Trade Associations (FITA) provides useful information for small companies about global business and trade intermediaries on its Web site (http://fita.org), including a *Directory of Export Management Companies*. Industry trade associations and publications and the U.S. Department of Commerce's Export Assistance Centers* also can help entrepreneurs to locate EMCs and other trade intermediaries.

EXPORT TRADING COMPANIES Another tactic for getting into international markets with a minimum of cost and effort is through export trading companies (ETCs). **Export trading companies** are businesses that buy and sell products in a number of countries, and they typically offer a wide range of services to their clients, such as exporting, importing, shipping, storing, distributing, and others. Unlike EMCs, which tend to focus on exporting, ETCs usually perform both import and export trades across many countries' borders. Although EMCs usually create exclusive contracts with companies for a particular product line, ETCs often represent several companies selling the same product line. However, like EMCs, ETCs lower the risk of exporting for small businesses. Some of the largest ETCs in the world are based in the United States and Japan. In fact, many businesses that have successfully navigated Japan's complex system of distribution have done so with the help of ETCs.

In 1982, Congress passed the Export Trading Company Act to allow producers of similar products to form ETC cooperatives without the fear of violating antitrust laws. The goal was to encourage U.S. companies to export more goods by allowing businesses in the same industry to band together to form ETCs.

MANUFACTURER'S EXPORT AGENTS **Manufacturer's export agents (MEAs)** act as international sales representatives in a limited number of markets for various noncompeting domestic companies. Unlike the close, partnering relationship formed with most EMCs, the relationship between the MEA and a small company is a short-term one, and the MEA typically operates on a commission basis.

EXPORT MERCHANTS **Export merchants** are domestic wholesalers who do business in foreign markets. They buy goods from many domestic manufacturers and then market them in foreign markets. Unlike MEAs, export merchants often carry competing lines, which means they have little loyalty to suppliers. Most export merchants specialize in particular industries such as office equipment, computers, industrial supplies, and others.

RESIDENT BUYING OFFICES Another approach to exporting is to sell to a **resident buying office,** a government-owned or privately owned operation of one country established in another country

export trading companies (ETCs)
businesses that buy and sell products in a number of countries and offer a wide variety of services to their clients.

manufacturer's export agents (MEAs)
businesses that act as international sales representatives in a limited number of markets for noncompeting domestic companies.

export merchants
domestic wholesalers who do business in foreign markets.

resident buying offices
government- or privately-owned operations of one country established in another country for the purpose of buying goods made there.

---

*A searchable list of the Export Assistance Centers is available at the Export.gov Web site http://www.export.gov/eac/.

for the purpose of buying goods made there. Many foreign governments and businesses have set up buying offices in the United States. Selling to them is just like selling to domestic customers because the buying office handles all the details of exporting.

FOREIGN DISTRIBUTORS Some small businesses work through foreign distributors to reach international markets. Domestic small companies export their products to these distributors, who handle all of the marketing, distribution, support, and service functions in the foreign country.

ENTREPRENEURIAL PROFILE

Hans Fredman: Polymer Technology Systems

Founded in 1992, Polymer Technology Systems (PTS), a small Indianapolis, Indiana-based company that manufactures a small cholesterol-checking device called the CardioCheck, focused on the domestic market until Boots, the largest drugstore chain in the United Kingdom, expressed an interest in using CardioCheck meters for promotional cholesterol screenings at 1,400 of its stores. PTS's relationship with Boots led to partnerships with European pharmaceutical companies that wanted to use the meter to promote their cholesterol-lowering drugs and with distributors in the United Kingdom. To find the right distributors, PTS used a matching service provided by the U.S. Department of Commerce. Hans Fredman, the company's vice-president of international sales, makes frequent contact with PTS's distributors in the U.K. by e-mail and phone to avoid problems. PTS managers value their relationship with their foreign distributors because their local partners make it easier for the company to navigate the many rules, regulations, and customs that exist in each nation.[14]

THE VALUE OF USING TRADE INTERMEDIARIES Trade intermediaries such as these are becoming increasingly popular among businesses attempting to branch out into world markets because they make that transition much faster and easier. Most small business owners simply do not have the knowledge, resources, or confidence to go global alone. Intermediaries' global networks of buyers and sellers allow their small business customers to build their international sales much faster and with fewer hassles and mistakes. Entrepreneurs who are inexperienced in global sales and attempt to crack certain foreign markets quickly discover just how difficult the challenge can be. However, with their know-how, experience, and contacts, trade intermediaries can get small companies' products into foreign markets quickly and efficiently. The primary disadvantage of using trade intermediaries is that doing so requires entrepreneurs to surrender control over their foreign sales. Maintaining close contact with intermediaries and evaluating their performance regularly help to avoid major problems, however.

Table 15.1. describes various resources that can help entrepreneurs located trade intermediaries.

Joint Ventures

Joint ventures, both domestic and foreign, lower the risk of entering global markets for small businesses. They also give small companies more clout in foreign lands. In a **domestic joint venture,** two or more U.S. small businesses form an alliance for the purpose of exporting their goods and services. For export ventures, participating companies get antitrust immunity, allowing them to cooperate freely. The businesses share the responsibility and the costs of getting export licenses and permits, and they split the venture's profits. Establishing a joint venture with the right partner has become an essential part of maintaining a competitive position in global markets for a growing number of industries.

In a **foreign joint venture,** a domestic small business forms an alliance with a company in the target nation. The host partner brings to the joint venture valuable knowledge of the local market and its method of operation as well as of the customs and the tastes of local customers, making it much easier to conduct business in the foreign country. Sometimes foreign countries place certain limitations on joint ventures, for example, requiring host companies to hold a majority stake in the venture.

domestic joint venture
an alliance of two or more U.S. small companies for the purpose of exporting their goods and services abroad.

foreign joint venture
an alliance between a U.S. small business and a company in the target nation.

ENTREPRENEURIAL PROFILE

Brown Shoe Company: Hongquo Holdings Limited

The Brown Shoe Company, a manufacturer of many shoe brands including Naturalizer and Franco Sarto and operator of the Famous Footwear chain of retail stores, recently entered into a foreign joint venture with Hongguo Holdings Limited, one of China's leading footwear companies, to market shoes. The joint venture will operate in Dongguan, Guangdong Province, where one of Brown Shoe's Chinese suppliers operates a factory. The joint venture ultimately will operate more than 500 stores in China by 2012. Brown Shoe will own 51 percent of the joint venture, and Hongguo Holdings will hold the remaining 49 percent.[15]

TABLE 15.1 Resources for Locating a Trade Intermediary

Trade intermediaries make doing business around the world much easier for small companies, but finding the right one can be a challenge. Fortunately, several government agencies offer a wealth of information to businesses interested in reaching global markets with the help of trade intermediaries. Entrepreneurs looking for help in breaking into global markets should contact the International Trade Administration, the U.S. Commerce Department, and the Small Business Administration first to take advantage of the following services:

- **Agent/Distributor Service (ADS).** Provides customized searches to locate interested and qualified foreign distributors for a product or service (Search cost, $250 per country).
- **Commercial Service International Contacts (CSIC) List.** Provides contact and product information for more than 82,000 foreign agents, distributors, and importers interested in doing business with U.S. companies.
- **Country Directories of International Contacts (CDIC) List.** Provides the same kind of information as the CSIC List but is organized by country.
- **Industry Sector Analyses (ISAs).** Offer in-depth reports on industries in foreign countries, including information on distribution practices, end-users, and top sales prospects.
- **International Market Insights (IMIs).** Include reports on specific foreign market conditions, upcoming opportunities for U.S. companies, trade contacts, trade show schedules, and other information.
- **Trade Opportunity Program (TOP).** Provides up-to-the-minute, prescreened sales leads around the world for U.S. businesses, including joint venture and licensing partners, direct sales leads, and representation offers.
- **International Company Profiles (ICPs).** Commercial specialists who will investigate potential partners, agents, distributors, or customers for U.S. companies and will issue profiles on them.
- *Commercial News USA.* A government-published magazine that promotes U.S. companies' products and services to 259,000 business readers in 152 countries at a fraction of the cost of commercial advertising. Small companies can use *Commercial News USA* to reach new customers around the world for as little as $395.
- **Gold Key Service.** A service provided by the Department of Commerce. For a small fee, business owners wanting to target a specific country can use the Gold Key Service, in which experienced trade professionals arrange meetings with prescreened contacts whose interests match their own.
- **Matchmaker Trade Delegations Program.** Helps small U.S. companies establish business relationships in major markets abroad by introducing them to the right contacts.
- **Multi-State/Catalog Exhibition Program.** A service provided by the Department of Commerce in conjunction with state economic development offices to present companies' product and sales literature to hundreds of interested business prospects in foreign countries.
- **International Fair Certification Program.** Promotes U.S. companies' participation in foreign trade shows that represent the best marketing opportunities for them.
- **National Trade Data Bank (NTDB).** The U.S. government's most comprehensive database of world trade data, containing most of the information listed above. With the NTDB, small companies have access to information that only *Fortune* 500 companies could afford.
- **Economic Bulletin Board (EBB).** Provides online trade leads and valuable market research on foreign countries compiled from a variety of federal agencies.
- **U.S. Export Assistance Centers.** A service provided by the Department of Commerce, which has established 18 export centers around the country to serve as one-stop shops for entrepreneurs needing export help (http://www.sba.gov/aboutsba/sbaprograms/internationaltrade/useac/index.html).
- **Trade Information Center.** Helps locate federal export assistance, provides export assistance, and offers a 24-hour automated fax retrieval system that gives entrepreneurs free information on export promotion programs, regional market information, and international trade agreements. Call USA-TRADE.
- *Office of International Trade.* A service by the Small Business Administration that provides a variety of export development assistance, how-to publications, and information on foreign markets.
- *Export Hotline.* Provides no-cost trade information on more than 50 industries in 80 countries. Call (800) 872-9767.
- *Export Opportunity Hotline.* A hotline giving trade specialists access to online databases and reports from government and private agencies concerning foreign markets. Call (202) 628-8389.

Where Do We Start?

Specialty Building Supplies is a small company with $6.4 million in annual sales that manufactures and sells a line of building supply products such as foundation vents, innovative insulation materials, and fireplace blowers to building supply stores in the northeastern United States. The eight-year-old company, founded by Tad Meyers, has won several awards for its unique and innovative products and has earned a solid reputation among its supply store customers and the builders and homeowners who ultimately buy its products. Before launching the company, Meyers had been a home-builder. As he watched the price of home heating fuels climb dramatically over time, Meyers began to incorporate into the houses he built simple, inexpensive ways to help homeowners save energy. He began tinkering with existing products, looking for ways to improve them. The first product he designed (and the product that ultimately led him to launch Specialty Building Supplies) was an automatic foundation vent that was thermostatically controlled (no electricity needed). The vent would automatically open and close depending on the outside temperature, keeping cold drafts from blowing under a house. Simple and inexpensive in its design, the Autovent was a big hit in newly constructed homes in the Northeast because it not only saved energy but it also avoided a major headache for homeowners in cold climates: water pipes that would freeze and burst. Before long, Meyers stopped building houses and focused on selling the Autovent. Its success prompted him to add other products to the company's line.

Specialty's sales have been lackluster for more than a year now, primarily due to a slump in new home construction in its primary market. Tad Meyers recently met with the company's top marketing managers and salespeople to talk about their options for getting

Specialty's sales and profit growth back on track. "What about selling our products in international markets?" asked Dee Rada, the company's marketing manager. "I read an article just last week about small companies doing good business in other countries, and many of them were smaller than we are."

"Interesting idea," Meyers said, pondering the concept. "I've never really thought about selling anything overseas. In fact, other than my years in the military, I've never traveled overseas and don't know anything about doing business there."

"It's a big world out there. Where should we sell our products?" said Hal Milam, Specialty's sales manager. "How do we find out what the building codes are in foreign countries? Would we have to modify our designs to meet foreign standards?"

"I don't know," shrugged Meyers. "Those are some good questions..."

"How would we distribute our products?" asked Rada. "We have an established network of distributors here in the U.S., but how do we find foreign distributors?"

"I wonder if exporting is our only option," said Meyers. "There must be other ways to get into the global market besides exporting. What do you think? Where do we start?"

1. What advice would you offer Meyers and the other managers at Specialty Building Supplies about their prospects of "going global"?
2. How would you suggest these managers go about finding the answers to the questions they have posed? What other questions would you advise them to answer?
3. Outline the steps these managers should take to assemble an international marketing plan.

The most important ingredient in the recipe for a successful joint venture is choosing the right partner. Taking the following steps will help avoid problems:

- Select a partner that shares their company's values and standards of conduct.
- Define at the outset important issues such as each party's contributions and responsibilities, the distribution of earnings, the expected life of the relationship, and the circumstances under which the parties can terminate the relationship.
- Understand their partner's reasons and objectives for joining the venture.
- Spell out in writing exactly how the venture will work and where decision-making authority lies.
- Select a partner whose skills are different from but compatible with those of their own company's.
- Prepare a "prenuptial agreement" that spells out what will happen in case of a business "divorce."

Foreign Licensing

Rather than sell their products or services directly to customers overseas, some small companies enter foreign markets by licensing businesses in other nations to use their patents, trademarks, copyrights, technology, processes, or products. In return for licensing these assets, a small company collects royalties from the sales of its foreign licenses. Licensing is a relatively simple way for even the most inexperienced business owner to extend his reach into global markets. Licensing is ideal for a company whose value lies in its intellectual property, unique products or services, recognized name, or proprietary technology. Although many businesses consider licensing only their products to foreign companies, the licensing potential for intangibles such as processes technology, copyrights, and trademarks often is greater. Some entrepreneurs earn more money from licensing their know-how for product design, manufacturing, or quality control than they do from actually selling their finished goods in a highly competitive foreign market with which they are not familiar. Foreign licensing enables a small business to enter foreign markets quickly, easily, and with virtually no capital investment. Risks to the company include the potential loss of control over its manufacturing and marketing processes and creating a competitor if the licensee gains too much knowledge and control. Securing proper patent, trademark, and copyright protection beforehand can minimize those risks, however.

International Franchising

Over the last several decades, a growing number of franchises have been attracted to international markets to boost sales and profits as the domestic market has become increasingly saturated with outlets and much tougher to wring growth from. Although international expansion is not a good idea for a new franchiser, it is an appropriate strategy for experienced franchisers. Both the cost and the complexity of franchising increase as the distance between the franchiser and its franchisees increases. In addition, complex legal and regulatory requirements and cultural differences make international franchising challenging for inexperienced franchisers. Franchisers should consider expanding into global markets when foreign markets present an important growth opportunity for the franchise and when they meet the following criteria:

- Sufficient resources to devote to globalization.
- A solid track record of success in the United States.
- Adequate trademark protection for the franchise's brand.
- Time-tested training, support, and reporting procedures that help franchisees succeed.[16]

Franchisers that decide to expand internationally should take these steps:

1. *Identify the country or countries that are best suited to the franchiser's business concept.* Factors to consider include a country's business climate, demographic profile, level of economic development, rate of economic growth, degree of legal protection, language and cultural barriers, and market potential. Franchisers making their first forays into global markets should consider focusing on a single nation or a small group of similar nations. The International Franchise Association (IFA) recently ranked nations on their attractiveness for franchises using the results of many global studies. Figure 15.3 shows the IFA's country rankings (a rating of 1 is most attractive and a rating of 4 is least attractive).

2. *Generate leads for potential franchisees.* Franchisers looking for prospective franchisees in foreign markets have many tools available to them, including international franchise trade shows, their own Web sites, trade missions, and brokers. Many franchisers have had success with trade missions such as those sponsored by trade groups such as the International Franchise Association or the U.S. Department of Commerce's Gold Key Program. These trade missions are designed to introduce franchisers to qualified franchise candidates in target countries. Others rely on brokers who have extensive business contacts in specific countries.

3. *Select quality candidates.* Just as in any franchise relationship, the real key to success is choosing the right franchisee. Because of the complexity and cost of international franchising, selecting quality franchisees is essential to success. Establishing an intranet allows franchisers to stay in contact with their international franchisees no matter which time zones they are in.

4. *Structure the franchise deal.* Franchisers can structure international franchise arrangements in a variety of ways, but three techniques are most popular: direct franchising, area development, and master franchising.

FIGURE 15.3

Which Countries Rate Best for Franchising?

Source: Data from Edwards, W., "International Expansion: Do Opportunities Outweigh Challenges." From *Franchise World*, February 1, 2008.

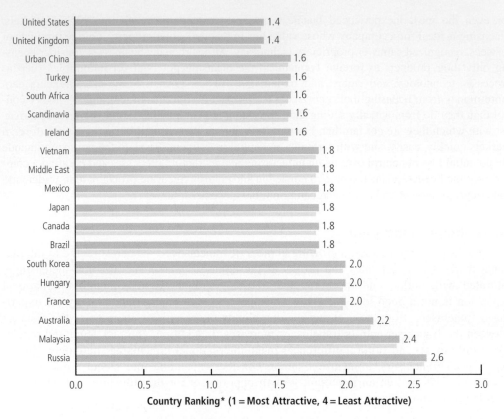

* An overall score that reflects the following factors: East of entry, openness to new concepts, legal protection, market size, and government regulation.

- Direct franchising, so common in domestic franchise deals, involves selling single-unit franchises to individual operators in foreign countries. Although dealing with individual franchisees makes it easier for the franchiser to maintain control, it also requires more of the franchiser's time and resources.
- Area development is similar to direct franchising except that the franchiser allows the franchisee to develop multiple units in a particular territory, perhaps a province, a county, or even an entire nation. A successful area development strategy depends on a franchiser selecting and supporting quality franchisees. Subway recently entered into an area development agreement with Raphael Chan to expand the sandwich chain's presence in Singapore. Chan, who is the head of Subway Singapore Development Pte Ltd, plans to open 125 new Subway outlets in Singapore by 2015.[17]
- Master franchising is the most popular strategy for companies entering international markets. Here, a franchiser grants an experienced master franchisee the right to sell outlets to sub-franchisees in a broad geographic area or an entire nation. Although master franchising simplifies a franchiser's expansion into global markets, it gives franchisers the least amount of control over their international franchisees. Atlanta, Georgia-based fast-food chain Church's Chicken recently expanded its presence in Russia, Ukraine, Belarus, and Kazakhstan when it granted a master franchise to European Active Corporation. Yuri Tetrov, CEO of European Active, plans to open 100 new restaurants under the name "Texas Chicken" by 2013. Church's also is looking to expand in China with the help of master franchisees.[18]

Just as they do in the United States, franchisers in international markets sell virtually every kind of product or service imaginable—from fast food to child daycare. In some cases, the products and services sold in international markets are identical to those sold in the United States. However, most franchisers have learned that adaptation is the key to making sure that their goods and services suit local tastes and customs. Traveling the world, one discovers that American fast-food giants such as Domino's, KFC, and McDonald's make significant modifications in their menu to remain attractive to local customers.

For instance, in addition to its 5,050 domestic outlets, Domino's Pizza operates more than 3,700 restaurants in 55 foreign countries, where local franchises offer pizza toppings that are quite different from traditional ones used in the United States, including squid (Japan), pickled ginger (India), tuna and sweet corn (England), green peas (Brazil), and reindeer sausage (Iceland) to cater to customers' palates. In Taiwan, the best-selling pizza is a seafood delight, made with onions, peas, squid, shrimp, and crab toppings. Although the toppings used vary widely around the world, the dough, the sauce, and the cheese are standard in every Domino's location.[19]

WU HONG/epa/CORBIS All Rights Reserved

Countertrading and Bartering

A **countertrade** is a transaction in which a company selling goods in a foreign country agrees to promote investment and trade in that country. The goal of the transaction is to help offset the capital drain from the foreign country's purchases. As entrepreneurs enter more and more developing countries, they will need to develop skills at implementing this strategy. In some cases, small and medium-sized businesses find it advantageous to work together with large corporations that have experience in the implementation of this marketing strategy.

Countertrading does suffer numerous drawbacks. Countertrade transactions can be complicated, cumbersome, and time-consuming. They also increase the chances that a company will get stuck with merchandise that it cannot move. They can lead to unpleasant surprises concerning the quantity and quality of products required in the countertrade. Still, countertrading offers one major advantage: Sometimes it's the only way to make a sale!

Entrepreneurs must weigh the advantages against the disadvantages for their company before committing to a countertrade deal. Because of its complexity and the risks involved, countertrading is not the best choice for a novice entrepreneur looking to break into the global marketplace.

Bartering, the exchange of goods and services for other goods and services, is another way of trading with countries lacking convertible currency. In a barter exchange, a company that manufactures electronics components might trade its products for the coffee that a business in a foreign country processes, which it then sells to a third company for cash. Barter transactions require finding a business with complementary needs, but they are much simpler than countertrade transactions.

Exporting

For many years, small businesses in the United States focused solely on the domestic market, never venturing beyond its borders. As global competition exerts pressure on domestic markets, as transportation becomes more affordable and easier to coordinate, and as trade agreements continue to open foreign markets, growing numbers of small companies are looking to exporting as a way of gaining or maintaining a competitive edge. Large companies continue to dominate export sales, however. Although small companies with fewer than 100 employees account for 90.7 percent of the 266,500 U.S. businesses that export goods and services, they generate only 21.0 percent of the nation's export sales.[20] Their impact is significant, however; small companies generate $1.1 billion each day in export sales.[21]

The biggest barrier facing companies that have never exported is not knowing where or how to start. The U.S. Chamber of Commerce's Trade Roots initiative, an international trade leadership program that networks more than 3,000 local U.S. chambers of commerce, is a useful resource for entrepreneurs looking to launch into global business. The program provides information on the benefits and methods for its members' who want to engage in international trade but aren't sure where to start. The U.S. Commercial Service's *Export Programs Guide* provides entrepreneurs with a comprehensive list of federal programs designed to help U.S. exporters. The U.S. Commercial Service Web site (www.buyusa.gov) is an excellent starting point for entrepreneurs who are looking for international business partners to help their companies expand into global markets.

countertrade
a transaction in which a company selling goods in a foreign country agrees to promote investment and trade in that country.

bartering
the exchange of goods and services for other goods and services.

LO 3
Explain how to build a thriving export program.

U.S. Export Assistance Centers are another valuable source of information (http://www
.sba.gov/aboutsba/sbaprograms/internationaltrade/useac/index.html). These centers serve as single contact points for information on the multitude of federal export programs that are designed to help entrepreneurs who want to start exporting. Entrepreneurs who want to learn more about exporting should investigate *A Basic Guide to Exporting* (http://www.unzco.com/basicguide/), which is published by the Department of Commerce and Unz and Company. The U.S. government export portal, www.export.gov, gives entrepreneurs access to valuable information about exporting in general (finance, shipping, documentation, and others) as well as details on individual nations (market research, trade agreements, statistics, and more). Learning more about exporting and realizing that it is within the realm of possibility for small companies—even *very* small companies—is the first, and often most difficult, step in breaking the psychological barrier to exporting. The next challenge is to create a sound export strategy:

Step 1. Recognize that even the tiniest companies and least experienced entrepreneurs have the potential to export. A business's size has nothing to do with the global potential of its products. In fact, 32.0 percent of the small companies that are exporters have no employees![22] If a company's products meet the needs of global customers, it has the potential to export. Studies suggest that small companies that export grow markedly faster than those that do not.

ENTREPRENEURIAL PROFILE

Jim Giermanski & Ed Harrison: Powers International

In 2002, Jim Giermanski and Ed Harrison, both former FBI agents with extensive experience in logistics, terrorism, and counterintelligence, launched Powers International, a Greenville, South Carolina, company selling a patented system designed to provide a satellite-based system that ensures the security of shipping containers from point-to-point. Because of concern about terrorist attacks, the two-person company is attracting interest from companies around the globe. The Powers Secured® Satellite System (PSSS) not only provides security for containers but also gives companies real-time control over their shipments and reduces shipping costs. Powers International recently signed contracts with companies in China and Europe for the use of its innovative system.[23]

Step 2. Analyze your product or service. Is it special? New? Unique? High quality? Priced favorably because of lower costs or favorable exchange rates? Does it fit well with the culture and traditions of a country or region? Southland Log Homes, a small business located in Irmo, South Carolina, that manufactures log homes, has been able to sell its homes in Asia. "Log homes are a natural product, and that makes them a good fit with the culture and values of those countries," says Tim Bradley, the company's CFO. Southland now has a foreign distributor in Japan and has discovered that, because of its proximity to the port of Charleston, shipping a log home to Japan costs less than shipping one to Texas![24]

In many foreign countries, products from the United States are in demand because they have an air of mystery about them! In some cases, entrepreneurs find that they must make slight modifications to their products to accommodate local tastes, customs, and preferences. For instance, when Joseph Zaritski, owner of an Australian juice company, began marketing his company's products in Russia, he met with limited success until he realized that package size was the problem. Willing customers simply could not afford to purchase the two-liter bottles in which the juice was packaged. Zaritski switched to one-liter bottles and saw sales climb by 80 percent within six months![25]

Step 3. Analyze your commitment. Are you willing to devote the time and energy to develop export markets? Does your company have the necessary resources? Patience is essential. An exporting initiative can take from six to eight months (or longer) to get off the ground, but entering foreign markets isn't as tough as most entrepreneurs think.

Step 4. Research markets and pick your target. One-third of small business exporters sell to just one or two countries (see Figure 15.4). Before investing in a costly sales trip abroad, however, entrepreneurs should search the Web or make a trip to the local library or the nearest branch of the Department of Commerce.

Armed with research, entrepreneurs can avoid wasting a lot of time and money on markets with limited potential for their products and can concentrate on those with the greatest

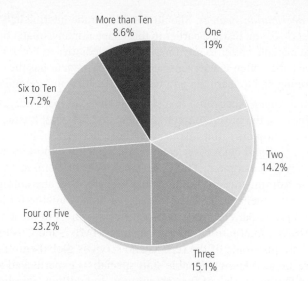

FIGURE 15.4

Small Business Exports: Number of Countries to Which Small Companies Export

promise. The nations that account for the greatest export volume for U.S. businesses are Canada, Mexico, China, Japan, and the United Kingdom.[26] Some of the most helpful tools for researching foreign markets are the Country and Industry Market Reports available at the U.S. government's export Web portal (http://www.export.gov/marketresearch.html), which provides detailed information on the economic, political, regulatory, and investment environment for countries ranging from Afghanistan to Zimbabwe. The research in these reports shows export entrepreneurs whether they need to modify their existing products and services to suit the tastes and preferences of their foreign target customers. Sometimes foreign customers' lifestyles, housing needs, body size, and cultures require exporters to make alterations in their product lines. Making just slight modifications to adapt products and services to local tastes can sometimes spell the difference between success and failure in the global market. Table 15.2 offers questions to guide entrepreneurs conducting export research.

TABLE 15.2 Questions to Guide International Market Research

- Is there an overseas market for your company's products or services?
- Are there specific target markets that look most promising?
- Which new markets abroad are most likely to open up or expand?
- How big is the market your company is targeting, and how fast is it growing?
- What are the major economic, political, legal, social, technological, and other environmental factors affecting this market?
- What are the demographic and cultural factors affecting this market (e.g., disposable income, occupation, age, gender, opinions, activities, interests, tastes, and values)?
- Who are your company's present and potential customers abroad?
- What are their needs and desires? What factors influence their buying decisions: price, credit terms, delivery terms, quality, brand name, and the like?
- How would they use your company's produce or service? What modifications, if any, would be necessary to sell to your target customers?
- Who are your primary competitors in the foreign market?
- How do competitors distribute, sell, and promote their products? What are their prices?
- What are the best channels of distribution for your product?
- What is the best way for your company to gain exposure in this market?
- Are there any barriers such as tariffs, quotas duties, or regulations to selling your product in this market? Are there any incentives?
- Are there any potential licensing or joint venture partners already in this market?

Source: Adapted from *A Basic Guide to Exporting*, Washington, DC: Department of Commerce, 1986, p. 11.

Step 5. Develop a distribution strategy. Should you use a trade intermediary or sell directly to foreign customers? As you learned earlier in this chapter, many small companies just entering international markets prefer to rely on trade intermediaries to break new ground. Relying on intermediaries often makes sense until an entrepreneur has the chance to gain experience in exporting and to learn the ground rules of selling in foreign lands.

Step 6. Find your customer. According to a study by the National Federation of Independent Businesses, the most common problem among small business exporters is finding prospective customers (after all, establishing a network of business contacts takes time and resources).[27] Small businesses can rely on a host of export specialists to help them track down foreign customers. The U.S. Department of Commerce and the International Trade Administration should be the first stops on any entrepreneur's agenda for going global. These agencies have the market research available for locating the best target markets for a particular company and specific customers in those markets. Industry Sector Analyses (ISAs), International Market Insights (IMIs), and Customized Market Analyses (CMAs) are just some of the reports and services global entrepreneurs find most useful. There are also knowledgeable staff specialists experienced in the details of global trade and in the intricacies of foreign cultures. In addition, for about $500, the U.S. Commercial Service will provide entrepreneurs who want to take their companies global with a list of screened distributors and potential customers and will arrange face-to-face meetings as well.

One of the most efficient and least expensive ways for entrepreneurs to locate potential customers for their companies' products and services is to participate in a trade mission. These missions usually are sponsored by either a federal or a state economic development agency or an industry trade association for the purpose of cultivating international trade by connecting domestic companies with potential trading partners overseas. A trade mission may focus on a particular industry or may cover several industries but target a particular country. "Trade missions are a great way to find quality buyers, partners, and agents in international markets," says Maria Cino, who has led many trade mission trips for the U.S. and Foreign Commercial Service.[28]

ENTREPRENEURIAL PROFILE

Alan Bostick: Sunshine Pet Foods

Alan Bostick, CEO of Sunshine Pet Foods, a family-owned business in Red Bay, Alabama, that produces and markets healthy pet foods, began attending trade shows in the United States, where he received inquiries from potential customers in other countries. Those inquiries prompted Bostick to work with the Small Business Administration and the Alabama International Trade Center to identify potential international customers. Bostick traveled to a trade show in Japan, where he was able to establish a relationship with a pet food distributor in that country that allowed the company to increase its sales by more than $500,000 in just one year.[29]

Step 7. Find financing. One of the biggest barriers to small business exports is lack of financing. Access to adequate financing is a crucial ingredient in a successful export program because the cost of generating foreign sales often is higher and collection cycles are longer than in domestic markets. The trouble is that bankers and other sources of capital don't always understand the intricacies of international sales and view financing them as excessively risky. In addition, among major industrialized nations, the U.S. government spends the least per capita to promote exports.

Several federal, state, and private programs are operating to fill this export financing void, however. Loan programs from the Small Business Administration include its Export Working Capital program (90 percent loan guarantees up to $1,500,000), International Trade Loan program (75 percent loan guarantees up to $1,250,000), and Export Express program (75 percent loan guarantees up to $250,000). In addition, the Export-Import Bank (www.exim.gov), the Overseas Private Investment Corporation, and a variety of state-sponsored programs offer export-minded entrepreneurs both direct loans and loan guarantees. (Recall that the *Export Programs Guide* provides a list of the 20 government agencies that help companies to develop their export potential.)

The Export-Import Bank (Ex-Im Bank), which has been financing the sale of U.S. exports for more than 70 years, provides small exporters with export credit insurance and loans through its working capital line of credit and a variety of pre-export loan programs. The Bankers Association for Foreign Trade (http://www.baft.org/jsps/) is an association of 150 banks around the world that matches exporters needing foreign trade financing with interested banks.

ENTREPRENEURIAL PROFILE

Hans Fredman: Polymer Technology Systems

With the help of Ex-Im Bank guarantees on loans from Chase Bank, Polymer Technology Systems (PTS), the Indianapolis, Indiana, maker of the hand-held CardioCheck meter that monitors cholesterol levels, was able to finance its export sales to the United Kingdom. PTS had to endure a 90 to 120 delay in collecting cash from its sales to international customers, which put a strain on its cash flow. "Typically, banks don't lend on international receivables," explains Mandy Parris, an executive with Chase Bank. However, with the Ex-Im Bank loan guarantees, Chase Bank provided PTS with a $1 million line of credit to finance its international sales.[30]

Step 8. Ship your goods. Export novices usually rely on international freight forwarders and custom-house agents—experienced specialists in overseas shipping—for help in navigating the bureaucratic morass of packaging requirements and paperwork demanded by customs. These specialists, also known as transport architects, are to exporters what travel agents are to travelers and normally charge relatively small fees for a valuable service. They move shipments of all sizes to destinations all over the world efficiently, saving entrepreneurs many headaches. Mia Abruzzese, who left her job as an executive at a major shoe company to start Morgan & Milo, a children's shoe company, advises entrepreneurs to use experienced international freight forwarders. Abruzzese relies on a forwarder that specializes in shoes and has valuable connections at several shipping companies and at several ports.[31]

Shipping terms, always important for determining which party in a transaction pays the cost of shipping and bears the risk of loss or damage to the goods while they are in transit, take on heightened importance in international transactions. Table 15.3 explains the implications of some of the most common shipping terms used in international transactions.

Step 9. Collect your money. A study by the Export-Import Bank reports that the top concern of companies that export is collecting payment for the goods and services they sell.[32] Collecting foreign accounts can be more complex than collecting domestic ones, but by picking their customers carefully and checking their credit references closely, entrepreneurs can minimize bad-debt losses. Businesses that engage in international sales use four primary payment methods (ranked from least risky to most risky): cash in advance, a letter of credit, a bank (or documentary) draft, and an open account. The safest method of selling to foreign customers is to collect cash in advance of the sale because it eliminates the risk of collection problems and provides immediate cash flow. However, requiring cash payments up front may limit severely a small company's base of foreign customers.

A **letter of credit** is an agreement between an exporter's bank and the foreign buyer's bank that guarantees payment to the exporter for a specific shipment of goods. In essence, a letter of credit reduces the financial risk for the exporter by substituting a bank's creditworthiness for that of the purchaser (see Figure 15.5). A **bank draft** is a document the seller draws on the buyer, requiring the buyer to pay the face amount (the purchase price of the goods) either on sight (a sight draft) or on a specified date (a time draft) once the goods have been shipped. With either letters of credit or bank drafts, small exporters must be sure that all of the required documentation is present and accurate; otherwise, they may experience delays in the payments due to them from the buyer or the participating banks. Rather than use letters of credit or drafts, some exporters simply sell to foreign customers on open account. In other words, they ship the goods to a foreign customer without any guarantee of payment. This method is riskiest because collecting a delinquent account from a foreign customer is even more difficult than collecting past-due payments from a domestic customer. The parties involved in an international deal should agree in advance on an acceptable method of payment.

letter of credit
an agreement between an exporter's bank and the foreign buyer's bank that guarantees payment to the exporter for a specific shipment of goods.

bank draft
a document the seller draws on the buyer, requiring the buyer to pay the face amount either on sight or on a specified date.

TABLE 15.3 Common International Shipping Terms and Their Meaning

Shipping Term	Seller's Responsibility	Buyer's Responsibility	Shipping Methods Used
FOB ("Free on Board") (Seller)	Deliver goods to carrier and provide export license and clean on-board receipt. Bear risk of loss until goods are delivered to carrier.	Pay shipping, freight, and insurance charges. Bear risk of loss while goods are in transit.	All
FOB ("Free on Board") Buyer	Deliver goods to the buyer's place of business and provide export license and clean on-board receipt. Pay shipping, freight, and insurance charges.	Accept delivery of goods after documents are tendered.	All
FAS ("Free Along Side")	Deliver goods alongside ship. Provides an "alongside" receipt.	Provide export license and proof of delivery of the goods to the carrier. Bear risk of loss once goods are delivered to the carrier.	Ship
CFR ("Cost and Freight")	Deliver goods to carrier, obtain export licenses, and pay export taxes. Provide buyer with clean bill of lading. Pay freight and shipping charges. Bear risk of loss until goods are delivered to buyer.	Pay insurance charges. Accept delivery of goods after documents are tendered.	Ship
CIF ("Cost, Insurance, and Freight")	Same as CFR plus pay insurance charges and provide buyer with insurance policy.	Accept delivery of goods after documents are tendered.	Ship
CPT ("Carriage Paid to…")	Deliver goods to carrier, obtain export licenses, and pay export taxes. Provide buyer with clean transportation documents. Pay shipping and freight charges.	Pay insurance charges. Accept delivery of goods after documents are tendered.	All
CIP ("Carriage and Insurance Paid to…")	Same as CPT plus pay insurance charges and provide buyer with insurance policy.	Accept delivery of good after documents are tendered.	All
DDU ("Delivered Duty Unpaid")	Obtain export license, pay insurance charges, and provide buyer documents for taking delivery.	Take delivery of goods and pay import duties.	All
DDP ("Delivered Duty Paid")	Obtain export license and pay import duty, pay insurance charges, and provide buyer documents for taking delivery.	Take delivery of goods.	All

Source: Adapted from Guide to the Finance of International Trade, edited by Gordon Platt (HBSC Trade Services, Marine Midland Bank, and the Journal of Commerce), infoserv2.ita.doc.gov/efm/efm.nsf/503d177e3c6f0b48525675900112e24/6218a8703573b329852567590004c41f3/$FILE/Finance_.pdf/, pp. 6–10.

FIGURE 15.5

How a Letter of Credit Works

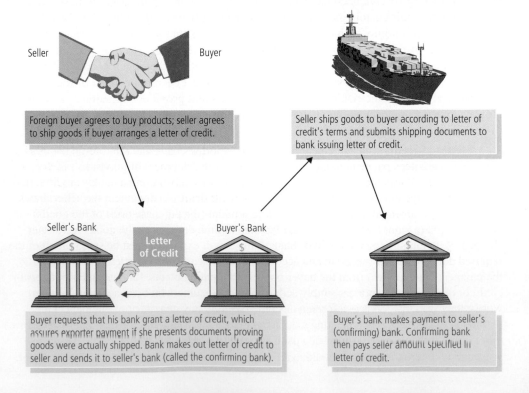

Seller   Buyer

Foreign buyer agrees to buy products; seller agrees to ship goods if buyer arranges a letter of credit.

Seller ships goods to buyer according to letter of credit's terms and submits shipping documents to bank issuing letter of credit.

Seller's Bank   Letter of Credit   Buyer's Bank

Buyer requests that his bank grant a letter of credit, which assures exporter payment if she presents documents proving goods were actually shipped. Bank makes out letter of credit to seller and sends it to seller's bank (called the confirming bank).

Buyer's bank makes payment to seller's (confirming) bank. Confirming bank then pays seller amount specified in letter of credit.

On to Japan...

"It's hard to believe how far we've come in just 14 months," said Tad Meyers, president of Specialty Building Supplies.

"That's true," chimed in Dee Rada, the company's marketing manager. "When we started this whole international business idea, we had no notion of how complicated and time-consuming it would be. We were total rookies! Which one of us would have thought we'd be trying to sell our products in Japan?"

"True. But now it looks like the big payoff is just around the corner," said Hal Milam, the company's sales manager.

As the three celebrated their success to date in taking their company into the exciting world of international business, each was proud of what they had accomplished and how much they had learned in just a short time. Yet, their excitement was tinged with anxiety because Meyers and Rada were about to travel abroad to meet with several potential distributors for the company's building supplies. In one week, they would be in Japan, negotiating deals with business people they had never met before and whose native language neither spoke.

"I do know how to say 'Thank you' in Japanese," said Rada. "It's pronounced "Du-omo ah-ree-gha-toe."

"You should probably find out how to say, 'Where's the bathroom?' and 'We're lost. Will you take us home?' in Japanese too," joked Milam.

"You know, we probably should find out as much as possible about how the Japanese do business," said Meyers. "I understand their way is very different from what we're used to."

"Such as...?" said Milam.

"You know...little things," said Rada. "I do know that they make a big deal out of exchanging business cards. They call it *meishi*. In fact, I've had cards printed for Tad and me with English on one side and Japanese on the other. When you take their cards, don't just stick them in your pocket or scribble notes on the backs of them. That's an insult."

"No kidding?" said Meyers. "I didn't know that..."

"I thought we'd take some gifts along to give to our guests," said Rada. "I've had them wrapped in pure white paper with these big red ribbons."

"What are you going to give them?" asked Milam.

"I had some nice golf shirts printed up with our logo, and then I had them add the U.S. and Japanese flags crossing one another."

"Cool! They ought to love that."

"We're taking along some brochures detailing our product line, emphasizing its unique nature and superb quality," said Rada. "I had them printed in Japanese just for this trip. Full color, lots of pictures. They cost a few bucks, but I thought it would be a wise investment."

"We will be on a tight schedule while we're there," said Meyers. "We'll have to get right down to business, close the deal, and then get on to the next appointment. There won't be a lot of time for sightseeing or small talk. I hope we can have these deals done by the time we are back on the plane for home."

"I just hope they don't try to impress us with authentic Japanese meals while we're there," said Meyers. "I'm pretty much a 'meat-and-potatoes' kind of guy. I don't do sushi. But I hear that McDonald's has restaurants in Japan. I just hope there's one nearby!"

"Where's your sense of adventure?" teased Rada. "Remember: We can't afford to offend our guests. We need to be sensitive to their culture, habits, and tastes. I just hope we don't do something unintentional that upsets somebody...."

1. Evaluate the preparations the Meyers and Rada have made for their upcoming trip to Japan.
2. Using the library and the World Wide Web as resources*, read about Japanese culture and Japanese business practices. Based on what you learn, would you advise them to change any of their plans? Explain.

*The Do's and Taboos of International Trade, Gestures; The Do's and Taboos of Body Language Around the World; and Do's and Taboos Around the World: A Guide to International Behavior, all by Roger Axtell, are excellent resources.

Establishing International Locations

Once established in international markets, some small businesses set up permanent locations there. Establishing an office or a factory in a foreign land can require a substantial investment reaching beyond the budgets of many small companies. In addition, setting up an international office can be an incredibly frustrating experience in some countries where business infrastructure is in disrepair or is nonexistent. Hayden Hamilton, founder of GreenPrint Technologies, a company that sells software that reduces printing costs by eliminating unnecessary pages, opened an office in India, where he can get bargain rates on quality software programming. He was frustrated when it took three hours to apply for a telephone line—and one month to get it installed. Because power outages in India are common, GreenPrint also had to purchase expensive backup generators.[33]

In some countries, securing necessary licenses and permits from bureaucrats often takes more time than filing the necessary paperwork; in some nations, bureaucrats expect payments to "grease the wheels" of commerce. U.S. entrepreneurs consider payments to reduce the amount of red tape involved in an international transaction to be bribery, and many simply avoid doing business in countries where "grease payments" are standard procedure. In fact, the Foreign Corrupt Practice Act, passed in 1977, considers bribing foreign officials to be a criminal act. One study by the World Bank of "grease payments," made for the purpose of minimizing the red tape imposed by foreign regulations, concludes that the payments do not work; in fact, companies that actually used them experienced greater government scrutiny and red tape in their international transactions.[34] Finally, finding the right person to manage an international office is crucial to success; it also is a major challenge, especially for small businesses. Small companies usually have lean management staffs and cannot afford to send key people abroad without running the risk of losing their focus.

Importing and Outsourcing

In addition to selling their goods in foreign markets, small companies also buy goods from distributors and manufacturers in foreign markets. In the United States alone, companies import more than $2.5 trillion worth of goods and services each year.[35] The intensity of price competition in many industries—from textiles and handbags to industrial machinery and computers—means that more companies now shop the world market, looking for the lowest prices they can find. Because labor costs in countries such as China and India are far below those in other nations, businesses there offer goods and services at very low prices. For instance, a computer programmer in the United States might earn $100,000 a year, but in India, a computer programmer doing the same work earns $20,000 a year or less. As a result, many companies either import goods or outsource work directly to manufacturers in countries where costs are far lower than they would be domestically.

The Great American Hanger Company

ENTREPRENEURIAL PROFILE

Devon Rifkin: Great American Hanger Company

Devon Rifkin, founder of the Great American Hanger Company, a small company that sells clothes hangers of all types—from inexpensive wire hangers to customized wooden ones—started his search for a low-cost, reliable supplier of hangers from his office computer. A quick search on Alibaba.com, a leading business-to-business e-commerce site that connects businesses with suppliers around the world, led Rifkin to Wooden Enterprises and Trading Cooperative (WETC), a manufacturer of metal and wood products that is based in India. After checking WETC's references and getting samples of the company's work, Rifkin visited the factory in person. "Although technology can save a lot of time and money, there is nothing like putting a name with a face and seeing the factory with your own eyes," he says. WETC is now one of Rifkin's most reliable suppliers.[36]

Entrepreneurs who are considering importing goods and service or outsourcing their manufacturing to foreign countries should follow these steps:

- *Make sure that importing or outsourcing is right for your business.* Even though foreign manufacturers often can provide items at significant cost savings, using them may not always be the best business decision. Some foreign manufacturers require sizeable minimum orders, sometimes hundreds of thousands of dollars' worth, before they will produce a product. Entrepreneurs sometimes discover that achieving the lowest price may require a tradeoff of other important factors such as quality and speed of delivery.

ENTREPRENEURIAL PROFILE

Amber McCrocklin: Paws Aboard

Amber McCrocklin started Paws Aboard, a small company that makes supplies such as boat ladders, life jackets, and waterproof leashes for pet owners who want to take their dogs on their boats. As the volume of orders increased, McCrocklin decided to outsource production to a factory in China, a move that would cut her production cost in half and allow her to focus on designing new products to add to the company's line. An engineer in Shenzen located a factory to produce the items, but McCrocklin quickly realized that quality and reliable delivery were problems. McCrocklin feared that her company's reputation would suffer irreparable damage and quickly switched to another factory that One World Sourcing, a strategic sourcing company in Brooklyn Heights, Ohio, helped her locate. Quality is no longer a problem, and Paws Aboard's profits have rebounded.[37]

- *Establish a target cost for your product.* Before setting off on a global shopping spree, entrepreneurs first should determine exactly what they can afford to spend on manufacturing a product to be able to make a profit on it. Given the low labor costs of many foreign manufacturers, products that are the most labor intensive make good candidates for outsourcing.
- *Do your research before you leave home.* As Devon Rifkin discovered, investing time in basic research about the industry and potential suppliers in other countries is essential before setting foot on foreign soil. Useful resources are plentiful, and entrepreneurs should use them, including the Web, the Federation of International Trade Associations, industry trade associations, government agencies (for example, the U.S. Commercial Service's Gold Key Matching Service), and consultants.

At a dinner party, Dieter Kondek learned about Moonlight, a German company that makes unique polyethylene, globe-shaped lights that can illuminate a pathway, cast an enchanting glow while floating in a pool, or simply light a room. Kondek researched the company and learned that the globes, which range from 13 to 30 inches in diameter and can withstand temperatures from -40° F to 140°F, were popular in upscale homes and businesses in Europe, Asia, and the Middle East but had not yet reached the United States. Within months, Kondek negotiated a deal to become the exclusive U.S. distributor for Moonlight and established Moonlight U.S.A., which the parent company says soon will account for half of its annual sales.[38]

- *Be sensitive to cultural differences.* When making contacts, setting up business appointments, or calling on prospective manufacturers in foreign lands, make sure you understand what is accepted business behavior and what is not. This is where your research pays off; be sure to study the cultural nuances of doing business in the countries you will visit.
- *Do your groundwork.* Once you locate potential manufacturers, contact them to set up appointments, and go visit them. Preliminary research is essential to finding reliable sources of supply, but "face time" with representatives from various companies allows entrepreneurs to judge the intangible factors that can make or break a relationship. Entrepreneurs who visit foreign suppliers often find that they receive better service because their suppliers know them personally.
- *Protect your company's intellectual property.* A common problem that many entrepreneurs have encountered with outsourcing is "knockoffs." Some foreign manufacturers see nothing wrong with agreeing to manufacture a product for a company and then selling their own knockoff version of it that they manufacture in a "ghost shift." Securing a nondisclosure agreement and a contract that prohibits such behavior helps, but experts say that securing a patent for the item in the source country itself (not just the United States) is a good idea.
- *Select a manufacturer.* Using quality, speed of delivery, level of trust, degree of legal protection, cost, and other factors, select the manufacturer that can do the job for your company.
- *Provide an exact model of the product you want manufactured.* Providing a manufacturer with an actual model of the item to be manufactured will save lots of time, mistakes, and problems. "It's always better to [determine] cost from an actual item rather than an idea of an item," says Jennifer Adams, owner of a consulting firm that helps entrepreneurs to locate foreign manufacturers.[39]
- *Stay in constant contact with the manufacturer and try to build a long-term relationship.* Communication is a key to building and maintaining a successful relationship with a foreign manufacturer. Weekly teleconferences, e-mails, and periodic visits are essential to making sure that your company gets the performance you expect from a foreign manufacturer.

Barriers to International Trade

LO 4

Discuss the major barriers to international trade and their impact on the global economy.

Governments traditionally have used a variety of barriers to block free trade among nations in an attempt to protect businesses within their own borders. The benefit of protecting their own companies, however, comes at the expense of foreign businesses, which face limited access to global markets. Numerous trade barriers domestic and international restrict the freedom of businesses in global trading. Even with these barriers, global trade of goods and services has grown to more than $16.9 trillion.[40]

Domestic Barriers

Sometimes the biggest barriers potential exporters face are those right here at home. Three major domestic roadblocks are common: attitude, information, and financing. Perhaps the biggest barrier to small businesses exporting is the attitude that "My company is too small to export. That's just for big corporations." The first lesson of exporting is "Take nothing for granted about who can export and what you can and cannot export." The first step to building an export program is recognizing that the opportunity to export exists. Another reason entrepreneurs neglect international markets is a lack of information about how to get started. The keys to success in international markets are choosing the correct target market and designing the appropriate strategy to reach it. That requires access to information and research. A successful global marketing strategy recognizes that not all international markets are the same. Companies must be flexible, willing to make adjustments to their products and services, promotional campaigns, packaging, and sales techniques.

International Barriers

Domestic barriers aren't the only ones export-minded entrepreneurs must overcome. Trading nations also erect obstacles to free trade. Two types of international barriers are common: tariff and nontariff.

tariff
a tax, or duty, that a government imposes on goods and services imported into that country.

TARIFF BARRIERS A **tariff** is a tax, or duty, that a government imposes on goods and services imported into that country. Imposing tariffs raises the price of the imported goods—making them less attractive to consumers—and protects the domestic makers of comparable product and services. Currently, the *Harmonized Tariff Schedule,* which sets tariffs for products imported into the United States, includes 37,000 categories of goods. About one-third of all products imported into the United States are subject to tariffs, and the average U.S. tariff is 1.3 percent (compared to the global average of 8.8 percent).[41] U.S. tariffs vary greatly and depend on the particular type of good. For instance, inexpensive acrylic sweaters carry a 32 percent tariff, but the tariff on cashmere sweaters is 4 percent; cheap sneakers are taxed at 48 percent, but leather dress shoes have an 8.5 percent tariff.[42] Tariff rates also vary among nations. Singapore and Hong Kong impose no tariffs at all on imported goods, but India's average tariff rate is 19.2 percent. The Bahamas have the highest average tariff rate in the world at 30.2 percent.[43]

NONTARIFF BARRIERS Many nations have lowered the tariffs they impose on products and services brought into their borders, but they rely on other nontariff structures as protectionist trade barriers.

quota
a limit on the amount of a product imported into a country.

QUOTAS Rather than impose a direct tariff on certain imported products, nations often use quotas to protect their industries. A **quota** is a limit on the amount of a product imported into a country. Those who favor quotas argue that they protect domestic industries and the jobs they create. Thos who oppose quotas say that they artificially raise prices on the restricted goods, imposing a hidden tax on customers who purchase them. Korea recently brought a

case against Japan to the World Trade Organization over a 50-year-old quota on imported lavar, edible seaweed, claiming that the quotas should be eliminated in favor of reasonable tariffs. Japan also has quotas on the amount of other seafood products that companies can import.[44] On January 1, 2009, the United States eliminated long-standing quotas on the amount of clothing and textile products that could be imported from countries such as China, India, and Vietnam.[45]

EMBARGOES An **embargo** is a total ban on imports of certain products. The motivation for embargoes is not always economic but also can involve political differences, environmental disputes, war, terrorism, and other issues. For instance, the United States imposes embargoes on products from nations it considers to be adversarial, including Cuba, Iran, Iraq, and North Korea, among others. In 1994, the United States lifted a total trade embargo on Vietnam that had stood since 1975, when Saigon fell into communist hands at the end of the Vietnam War. Today the United States imports $12.9 billion worth of goods from Vietnam and exports goods worth $2.8 billion.[46]

embargo
a total ban on imports of certain products into a country.

DUMPING In an effort to grab market share quickly, some companies have been guilty of **dumping** products: selling large quantities of them at prices that are below cost in foreign countries. The United States has been a dumping ground for steel, televisions, shoes, and computer chips from other nations in the past. Under the U.S. Antidumping Act, a company must prove that the foreign company's prices are lower here than in the home country and that U.S. companies are directly harmed. Disputes over dumping at the World Trade Organization have increased significantly over the last five years, and China has been the target of most of the complaints from WTO member nations. The U.S. International Trade Commission, without the involvement of the WTO, recently ruled that government-subsidized makers of wire clothes hangers in China were guilty of dumping their product in the United States for as much as 187 percent below "fair value." Alabama-based M&B Metal Products, one of a handful of remaining U.S.-based wire hanger manufacturers initiated the charge, which resulted in punitive anti-dumping duties of up to 187 percent on the Chinese companies. Domestic manufacturers produce just 9 percent of the 3.3 billion metal hangers sold in the United States each year.[47]

dumping
selling large quantities of goods at prices that are below cost in foreign countries in an effort to grab market share quickly.

Political Barriers

Entrepreneurs who go global quickly discover a labyrinth of political tangles. Although many U.S. business owners complain of excessive government regulation in the United States, they are often astounded by the onerous web of governmental and legal regulations and barriers they encounter in foreign countries. One entrepreneur who established a business location in Russia says that he had to visit more than two dozen agencies to complete the necessary paperwork and get 90 different documents signed.[48]

Companies doing business in politically risky lands face the very real dangers of government takeovers of private property; coups to overthrow ruling parties; kidnapping, bombings, and other violent acts against businesses and their employees; and other threatening events. Their investments of millions of dollars may evaporate overnight in the wake of a government coup or the passage of a law nationalizing an industry (giving control of an entire industry to the government).

Business Barriers

American companies doing business internationally quickly learn that business practices and regulations in foreign lands can be quite different from those in the United States. Simply duplicating the practices they have adopted (and have used successfully) in the domestic market and using them in foreign markets is not always a good idea. Business owners new to international business sometimes are shocked at the wide range of labor costs they encounter and the accompanying wide range of skilled labor available. In some countries, what appear to be "bargain" labor rates turn out to be excessively high after accounting for the quality of the labor force and the benefits their governments mandate: from company-sponsored housing, meals, and clothing to profit-sharing and extended vacations. Hefty taxes, ineffective legal systems, corruption, and shady business associates can make doing business in foreign countries difficult.

Cultural Barriers

culture
the beliefs, values, views, and mores that a nation's inhabitants share.

Even though travel and communications technology has increased the ease and the frequency with which entrepreneurs engage in global transactions, the potential for cultural blunders has increased. The **culture** of a nation includes the beliefs, values, views, and mores that its inhabitants share. Differences in cultures among nations create another barrier to international trade. The diversity of languages, business philosophies, practices, and traditions make international trade more complex than selling to the business down the street. Consider the following examples:

- A U.S. entrepreneur, eager to expand into the European Union, arrives at the headquarters of his company's potential business partner in France. Confidently, he strides into the meeting room, enthusiastically pumps his host's hand, slaps him on the back, and says, "Tony, I've heard a great deal about you; please, call me Bill." Eager to explain the benefits of his product, he opens his briefcase and gets right down to business. The French executive politely excuses himself and leaves the room before negotiations ever begin, shocked by the American's rudeness and ill manners. Rudeness and ill manners? Yes—from the French executive's perspective.

- Another American business owner flies to Tokyo to close a deal with a Japanese executive. He is pleased when his host invites him to play a round of golf shortly after he arrives. He plays well and manages to win by a few strokes. The Japanese executive invites him to play again the next day, and again he wins by a few strokes. Invited to play another round the following day, the American asks, "But when are we going to start doing business?" His host, surprised by the question, says, "But we *have* been doing business."

- An American businesswoman in London is invited to a party hosted by an advertising agency. Unsure of her ability to navigate the streets and subways of London alone, she approaches a British colleague who is driving to the party and asks him, "Could I get a ride with you?" After he turns bright red from embarrassment, he regains his composure and politely says, "Lucky for you I know what you meant." Unknowingly, the young woman had requested a sexual encounter with her colleague, not a lift to the party![49]

- One pharmaceutical company was about to market a weight-loss pill under the name Tegro, which sounds harmless enough in English. However, phonetically, the word sounds identical to the French phrase *t'es gros,* which translates "You are fat." Another global company attempted to market a technology training system whose name sounded exactly like the Korean phrase for "porn movie."[50]

When American businesspeople enter international markets for the first time, they often are amazed at the differences in foreign cultures' habits and customs. In the first scenario above, for instance, had the entrepreneur done his homework, he would have known that the French are very formal (backslapping is *definitely* taboo!) and do not typically use first names in business relationships (even among long-time colleagues). In the second scenario, a global manager would have known that the Japanese place a tremendous importance on developing personal relationships before committing to any business deals. Thus, he would have seen the golf games for what they really were: an integral part of building a business relationship.

Understanding and heeding these often subtle cultural differences is one of the most important keys to international business success. Conducting a business meeting with a foreign executive in the same manner as one with an American businessperson could doom the deal from the outset. Business customs and behaviors that are acceptable, even expected, in the United States may be taboo in others.

Culture, customs, and the norms of behavior differ greatly among nations, and making the correct impression is extremely critical to building a long-term business relationship. Consider the following examples:

- In Europe and China, just as in the United States, punctuality for business meetings is important. In Latin America, Africa, and many Middle Eastern countries, however, business meetings rarely start at the scheduled time, which does not seem to bother locals.

- In Great Britain, businesspeople consider it extremely important to conduct business "properly"—with formality and reserve. Boisterous behavior such as backslapping or overindulging in alcohol and ostentatious displays of wealth are considered ill-mannered. The British do not respond to hard-sell tactics but do appreciate well-mannered executives. Politeness and impeccable manners are useful tools for conducting business successfully.

- Japanese executives conduct business much like the British with an emphasis on formality, thoughtfulness, and respect. Don't expect to hear Japanese executives say "no," even during a negotiation; they don't want to offend or to appear confrontational. Instead of "no" the Japanese negotiator will say, "It is very difficult," "Let us think about that," or "Let us get back to you on that." Similarly, "yes" from a Japanese executive doesn't necessarily mean that. It could mean, "I understand" "I hear you," or "I don't understand what you mean, but I don't want to embarrass you."

- In India, a limp handshake and avoiding eye contact are not signs of weakness or dislike; they convey respect.[51]

- When doing business in Greece, U.S. executives must be thoughtful of their hand gestures; the hand-waving gesture that means "goodbye" in the United States is considered an insult in Greece.[52]

- In Japan and South Korea, exchanging business cards, known in Japan as *meishi,* is an important business function (unlike Great Britain, where exchanging business cards is less popular). A Western executive who accepts a Japanese companion's card and then slips it into his pocket or scribbles notes on it has committed a major blunder. Tradition there says a business card must be treated just as its owner would be—with respect. Travelers should present their own cards using both hands with the card positioned so the recipient can read it. (The flip side should be printed in Japanese, an expected courtesy.)

- Greeting a Japanese executive properly includes a bow and a handshake—showing respect for both cultures. In many traditional Japanese businesses, exchanging gifts at the first meeting is appropriate. In addition, a love of golf (the Japanese are fanatics about the game) is a real plus for winning business in Japan.

- Exercise caution when giving gifts. Although gift-giving is standard practice in Japan, businesspeople in other countries, such as Malaysia, may see a gift as a bribe. In many countries, gifts of flowers are considered inappropriate because they connote romantic attention. In South Korea, giving a clock as a gift is considered good luck, but in China, it is considered a bad omen.[53] Avoid giving gifts to business associates that are traditional symbols of their own cultures, such as chocolates to the Swiss or tea to the Chinese.

- In China, entrepreneurs will need an ample dose of the "three *P*s": patience, patience, patience. Nothing in China—especially business—happens fast, and entrepreneurs wanting to do business there must be persistent! In conversation and negotiations, periods of silence are common; they are a sign of politeness and contemplation. The Chinese view personal space much differently than Americans; in normal conversation, they will stand much closer to their partners. At a business meal, sampling every dish, no matter how exotic, is considered polite. In addition, do not expect to conduct business the week before or after the Chinese New Year ("Yuandan"), whose dates vary from year to year, because many businesses are closed.

- American entrepreneurs doing business in the Pacific Rim should avoid hard-sell techniques, which are an immediate turnoff to Asian businesspeople. Harmony, patience, and consensus make good business companions in this region. It is also a good idea to minimize the importance of legal documents in negotiations. Although getting deals and trade agreements down in writing always is advisable, attempting to negotiate detailed contracts (as most American businesses tend to do) would insult most Asians, who base their deals on mutual trust and benefits.

YOU BE THE **CONSULTANT**

A Chocolate Oasis

When Allison Nelson launched Chocolate Bar, a restaurant and retro-style candy store, in New York City, she planned to expand later into other urban areas such as Chicago, Miami, and Los Angeles. Although she believed that London one day might be a good location for a Chocolate Bar, she had not considered international locations too seriously, believing that she had to establish her business in the United States first. She opened the original Chocolate Bar (which she bills as "a candy store for grown-ups") in New York's Greenwich Village in

2002 but recently relocated the store to New York's trendy East Village after her landlord converted the retail shop to residential space. In 2006, Nelson expanded her business by opening a location in Beach Haven, New Jersey, a seaside community where her parents live. (Nelson's mother, Meg, bakes cookies and brownies for the Chocolate Bar.) In 2007, Nelson opened a Chocolate Bar café in the upscale Henri Bendel store on Fifth Avenue. Although each location carries the same basic product line, Nelson has modified the menu to accommodate local preferences. For instance, because the Beach Haven location caters more to families than the New York City locations, its menu includes more kid-friendly items, such as chocolate-covered Oreos and unique candy bars, and more iced drinks. Nelson never suspected that her next location would be in Dubai in the United Arab Emirates.

Mary Ghorbial, a resident of Dubai, realized that the Middle East in general and Dubai in particular would be an ideal location for an upscale chocolate company. An Internet search led her to the Chocolate Bar and to Nelson. Ghorbial contacted Nelson and suggested a partnership for a location in Dubai. She saw that the region's growing wealth and appetite for high-end goods of all types would provide a perfect fit with the company's target customer. "The Arabic customer is becoming more globalized," says Ghorbial.

Nelson balked at first, telling Ghorbial, "I'm not interested. I haven't opened a store in Los Angeles [yet]. How am I going to open [one] clear across the globe?" However, she was intrigued by the idea and began researching Dubai and the surrounding region. She discovered that the residents of Dubai are among the wealthiest in the world and that the population is young, with significant numbers of people between the ages of 25 and 39, and growing. Nelson learned that products made in the United States have a certain cachet with many customers in the Middle East. Arabs also eat lots of chocolate and eat it as part of celebrations, including holidays, engagements, birthdays, and other events. "It might work," she realized. Nelson knew chocolate, and Ghorbial knew the Middle East and how to conduct business there.

Nelson and Ghorbial negotiated a deal in which Ghorbial and her husband created Gourmet Company, which will operate as a Chocolate Bar licensee. The Gourmet Company will pay an upfront fee and a percentage of each store's sales to the Chocolate Bar. The plan is to open 30 stores across the Middle East over 10 years, starting with locations in Dubai and Qatar.

Nelson has been busy preparing for the expansion into the Middle East. The menus in the new stores will reflect the fact that Middle Easterners prefer milk chocolate to dark chocolate. Nelson even added more milk to her recipes for the products that these stores will sell and is offering an extensive line of white chocolates, something that accounts for a very small percentage of sales in her New York locations. After visiting Dubai, Nelson learned that residents enjoy figs and dates. "It's the quick snack there," she says. In another move to adapt her stores' menu to local tastes, Nelson is adding chocolate-dipped versions of figs and dates as well as a fruit-and-nut bar to the menu. The highly Muslim residents of the region do not eat pork, which prompted Nelson to remove prosciutto from the company's signature salad. She also is adding more feta and olive ingredients to salads and sandwiches.

Even the layout of the new stores reflects cultural differences. Because Arabs prefer not to sit close to strangers, Nelson redesigned the store layouts, which she had originally planned to be identical to those in New York. Chairs are upholstered in gold leather, and the stores boast lavish chandeliers that fit Dubai's preference for opulence.

Nelson has learned that going global presents challenges that she has never had to face in the United States. Problems that she normally is able to solve via e-mail or a brief telephone call require face-to-face meetings or hours of telephone calls. Business transactions in the Middle East require a slower pace than Nelson is accustomed to. A meeting with a supplier about refrigerators and chef's tables took four hours, far longer than Nelson is accustomed to back home. "It's customary that you sit and have tea and talk," Nelson says of business meetings. Despite the risks and challenges of going global, Nelson believes that it is the right move for Chocolate Bar. "I think it'll be a great American story—a little company that didn't make it big in America but made it in the global marketplace."

1. Identify the risks and the benefits that Chocolate Bar faces by expanding globally.
2. Why are steps such as adapting menus, business practices, expectations, and store designs important to success in global markets? What other changes might Nelson have to make to adapt Chocolate Bar to local customers' tastes?
3. What steps do you recommend that entrepreneurs such as Alison Nelson take before they make the decision to take their companies global?

Source: Based on Simona Covel, "New York Eatery Looks for the Sweet Spot Overseas," *Wall Street Journal*, September 4, 2008, p. B4; Billy Jam, "Choc Graf," *New York Press*, March 28–April 3, 2007, p. 7; Eric Lenvin, "The Chocolate Bar Steps Up in Size," *New Jersey Monthly*, June 2007, p. 25; Chris Shott, "Death by Chocolate," *New York Observer*, April 14, 2008, pp. 12, 25; Kevin Whitelaw, Dubai Rides the Oil Boom," *U.S. News & World Report*, June 5, 2008.

Brian Kennedy/Chocolate Bar Press

International Trade Agreements

LO 5

Discuss the trade agreements that will have the greatest influence on foreign trade in the twenty-first century.

With the fundamental assumption that free trade among nations results in enhanced economic prosperity for all parties involved, the last 50 years have witnessed a gradual opening of trade among nations. Hundreds of agreements have been negotiated among nations in this period, with each contributing to free trade across the globe. Although completely free trade across international borders remains elusive, the following trade agreements have reduced some of the barriers to free trade that had stood for many years.

The World Trade Organization (WTO)

The World Trade Organization (WTO) was established in January 1995 and replaced the General Agreement of Tariffs and Trade (GATT), the first global tariff agreement, which was created in 1947 and designed to reduce tariffs among member nations. The WTO, currently with 153 member countries, is the only international organization that establishes rules for trade among nations. Its member countries represent more than 97 percent of all world trade. The rules and agreements of the WTO, called the multilateral trading system, are the result of negotiations among its members. The WTO actively implements the rules established by the Uruguay Round negotiations of GATT from 1986 to 1994 and continues to negotiate additional trade agreements. Through the agreements of the WTO, members commit themselves to nondiscriminatory trade practices. These agreements spell out the rights and obligations of each member country. Each member country receives guarantees that its exports will be treated fairly and consistently in other member countries' markets. The WTO's General Agreement on Trade in Services (GATS) addresses specific industries, including banking, insurance, telecommunications, and tourism. In addition, the WTO's intellectual property agreement, which covers patents, copyrights, and trademarks, defines rules for protecting ideas and creativity across borders.

In addition to the development of agreements among members, the WTO is involved in the resolution of trade disputes among members. The WTO system is designed to encourage dispute resolutions through consultation. If this approach fails, the WTO has a stage-by-stage procedure that can culminate in a ruling by a panel of experts.

NAFTA

The North American Free Trade Agreement (NAFTA) created a free-trade area among Canada, Mexico, and the United States. A **free trade area** is an association of countries that have agreed to eliminate trade barriers, both tariff and nontariff, among partner nations. Under the provision of NAFTA, these barriers were eliminated for trade among the three countries, but each remained free to set its own tariffs on imports from nonmember nations.

NAFTA forged the world's largest free trade area, a unified United States-Canada-Mexico market of 442.4 million people with a total annual output of more than $15.4 trillion dollars in goods and services.[54] This important trade agreement binds together the three nations on the North American continent into a single trading unit stretching from the Yukon to the Yucatan. NAFTA's provisions called for the reduction of tariffs to zero on most goods traded among these three nations and have enhanced trade among the United States, Canada, and Mexico. NAFTA also has made that trade more profitable and less cumbersome for companies of all sizes and has opened new opportunities many businesses. Since NAFTA's passage, trade among the three nations has tripled; these countries now conduct nearly $2.5 billion in trilateral trade each day![55]

free trade area
an association of countries that have agreed to eliminate trade barriers, both tariff and nontariff, among partner nations.

Curt Rone, executive vice-president of Loxcreen Company, a Columbia, South Carolina, manufacturer of aluminum- and plastic-extruded products used in the construction industry, says that international sales, which account for 20 percent of the company's total revenue, "are an important growth area for us." NAFTA has been instrumental in the company's ability to increase sales in Canada and Mexico. "We are working to expand our presence in Canada and Mexico in addition to developing new trade opportunities in Europe and Asia," Rone says. "We must gain access to those markets if we are to gain the economies of scale and compete in the global economy."[56]

ENTREPRENEURIAL
PROFILE —————

Curt Rone: Loxcreen
Company

Dominican Republic-Central America Free Trade Agreement (CAFTA-DR)

The Dominican Republic-Central America Free Trade Agreement (CAFTA-DR) is to Central America what NAFTA is to North America. The agreement, which was implemented in stages between 2006 and 2008, is designed to promote free trade among the United States and six Central American countries: Costa Rica, El Salvador, Guatemala, Honduras, Dominican Republic, and Nicaragua. U.S. exports to these six nations exceed $22 billion a year.[57] In addition to reducing tariffs among these nations, CAFTA-DR protects U.S. companies' investments and intellectual property in the region, simplifies the export process for U.S. companies, and provides easier access to Central American markets.

BKI, a small manufacturer of food service equipment for retail and convenience stores and restaurants located in Simpsonville, South Carolina, started exporting its products in 1958 and recently entered markets in Central America as a result of CAFTA-DR. "Lower [trade] duties make our equipment more affordable" to customers in the region, says Jose Tapia, BKI's international sales manager. "CAFTA-DR has had a positive impact because we are better able to compete with manufacturers from other countries."[58]

Conclusion

To remain competitive, small businesses must assume a global posture. Global effectiveness requires entrepreneurs to be able to leverage workers' skills and company resources and know-how across borders and throughout cultures across the world. They also must concentrate on maintaining competitive cost structures and a focus on the core of every business—the *customer!* Although there are no surefire rules for going global, small businesses that want to become successful international competitors should observe these guidelines.

- Take the time to learn about doing business globally before jumping in. Avoiding mistakes is easier and less expensive than cleaning up the results of mistakes later.
- If you have never conducted international business, consider hiring a trade intermediary or finding a local partner to help you.
- Make yourself at home in all three of the world's key markets: North America, Europe, and Asia. This triad of regions is forging a new world order in trade that will dominate global markets for years to come.
- Appeal to the similarities within the various regions in which you operate but recognize the differences in their specific cultures. Although the European Union is a single trading bloc composed of 27 countries, smart entrepreneurs know that each country has its own cultural uniqueness and do not treat the nearly half-billion people in them as a unified market.
- Develop new products for the world market. Make sure your products and services measure up to world-class quality standards.
- Familiarize yourself with foreign customs and languages; constantly scan, clip, and build a file on other cultures: their lifestyles, values, customs, and business practices.
- Learn to understand your customers from the perspective of *their* culture, not your own. Bridge cultural gaps by adapting your business practices to suit their preferences and customs.
- "Glocalize." Make global decisions about products, markets, and management but allow local employees to make tactical decisions about packaging, advertising, and service.
- Recruit and retain multicultural workers who can give your company meaningful insight into the intricacies of global markets.
- Train employees to think globally, send them on international trips, and equip them with state-of-the-art communications technology.
- Hire local managers to staff foreign offices and branches.
- Do whatever seems best wherever it seems best, even if people at home lose jobs or responsibilities.
- Consider using partners and joint ventures to break into foreign markets you cannot penetrate on your own.

By its very nature, going global can be a frightening experience. Most entrepreneurs who have already made the jump, however, have found that the benefits outweigh the risks and that their companies are much stronger because of it.

Chapter Summary

1. **Explain why "going global" has become an integral part of many small companies' marketing strategies.**
   - Companies that move into international business can reap many benefits, including offsetting sales declines in the domestic market; increasing sales and profits; extending their products' life cycles;

lowering manufacturing costs; improving competitive position; raising quality levels; and becoming more customer oriented.

2. **Describe the principal strategies for going global.**
   - Perhaps the simplest and least expensive way for a small business to begin conducting business

globally is to establish a site on the World Wide Web. Companies wanting to sell goods on the Web should establish a secure ordering and payment system for online customers.

- Trade intermediaries such as export management companies, export trading companies, manufacturer's export agents, export merchants, resident buying offices, and foreign distributors can serve as a small company's "export department."

- In a domestic joint venture, two or more U.S. small companies form an alliance for the purpose of exporting their goods and services abroad. In a foreign joint venture, a domestic small business forms an alliance with a company in the target area.

- Some small businesses enter foreign markets by licensing businesses in other nations to use their patents, trademarks, copyrights, technology, processes, or products.

- Franchising has become a major industry for the United States. Successful franchisers have learned to adapt their products and services to suit local customers' tastes.

- Some countries lack a hard currency that is convertible into other currencies, so companies doing business there must rely on countertrading or bartering. A countertrade is a transaction in which a business selling goods in a foreign country agrees to promote investment and trade in that country. Bartering involves trading goods and services for other goods and services.

- Although small companies account for 90.7 percent of the companies involved in exporting, they generate only 21.0 percent of the dollar value of the nation's exports. However, small companies, realizing the incredible profit potential it offers, are making exporting an ever-expanding part of their marketing plans.

- Once established in international markets, some small businesses set up permanent locations there. Although they can be very expensive to establish and maintain, international locations give businesses the opportunity to stay in close contact with their international customers.

3. Explain how to build a thriving export business.

- Building a successful export program takes patience and research. Steps include: Realize that even the tiniest firms have the potential to export; analyze your product or service; analyze your commitment to exporting; research markets and pick your target; develop a distribution strategy; find your customer; find financing; ship your goods; and collect your money.

4. Discuss the major barriers to international trade and their impact on the global economy.

- Three domestic barriers to international trade are common: the attitude that "we're too small to export," lack of information on how to get started in global trade, and a lack of available financing.

- International barriers include tariffs, quotas, embargoes, dumping, and political, business, and cultural barriers.

5. Describe the trade agreements that will have the greatest influence on foreign trade into the twenty-first century.

- The World Trade Organization (WTO) was established in 1995 to implement the rules established by the Uruguay Round negotiations of GATT from 1986 to 1994, and it continues to negotiate additional trade agreements. The WTO has 153 member nations and represents more than 97 percent of all global trade. The WTO is the governing body that resolves trade disputes among members.

- The North American Free Trade Agreement (NAFTA) created a free trade area among Canada, Mexico, and the United States. The agreement created an association that knocked down trade barriers, both tariff and nontariff, among the partner nations.

- The Dominican Republic-Central America Free Trade Agreement (CAFTA-DR) created a free trade area among the United States and six nations in Central America: Costa Rica, El Salvador, Guatemala, Honduras, Dominican Republic, and Nicaragua. In addition to reducing tariffs among these nations, CAFTA protects U.S. companies' investments and intellectual property in the region, simplifies the export process for U.S. companies, and provides easier access to Central American markets.

Discussion Questions

1. Why must entrepreneurs learn to think globally?
2. What forces are driving small businesses into international markets?
3. What advantages does going global offer a small business owner? Risks?
4. Outline the nine strategies that small businesses can use to go global.
5. Describe the various types of trade intermediaries small business owners can use. What functions do they perform?
6. What is a domestic joint venture? A foreign joint venture? What advantages does taking on an international partner through a joint venture offer? Disadvantages?

7. What mistake are first-time exporters most likely to make? Outline the steps a small company should take to establish a successful export program.

8. What are the benefits of establishing international locations? Disadvantages?

9. Describe the barriers businesses face when trying to conduct business internationally. How can a small business owner overcome these obstacles?

10. What is a tariff? A quota? What impact do they have on international trade?

11. What impact have the WTO, NAFTA, and CAFTA-DR trade agreements had on small companies that want to go global? What provisions are included in these trade agreements?

12. What advice would you offer an entrepreneur interested in launching a global business effort?

Business PlanPro™ Are there global opportunities for your business concept? If so, include those as an "opportunity" in your SWOT analysis. Review the other sections that will benefit from incorporating these global plans into your business strategy. For example, you may need to address your global strategy in the marketing strategy and the Web site sections of your business plan. You may need to include additional expenses into the financial section of your business plan supporting to your global strategy. If your global strategy increases risk, this is another factor to capture in your business plan.

Business Plan Exercises

A business plan can help to define and clarify global opportunities, resources and challenges.

On the Web

You will find links to Web resources that address global strategies at http://www.pearsonhighered.com/scarborough associated with Chapter 15. In addition, a site that may also be helpful is a management portal for global strategy at http://www.themanager.org/Knowledgebase/Strategy/Global.

Sample Plans

Review the executive summary for the sample plan called Grutzen Watches. Note the information that relates to their global strategy and the additional complexities this introduces to the business plan.

In the Software

If you plan to employ a global strategy, make certain that you have addressed that aspect of your strategy in your business plan. International activity of any kind may have implications for multiple sections of your business plan, including the product and services, market analysis, strategy, implementation, Web plans, management, and financial sections.

This is also an excellent time to review your entire plan, paying specific attention to the summary sections at the beginning of each major section. You may have used these areas for notes, but, at this time, review what you have written in the initial stage of each of these sections. Those sections include the following:

- Company
- Product and Services
- Market Analysis
- Strategy and Implementation
- Web Plan
- Management Plan
- Financial Plan

These initial introductory statements will add flow to your plan. You may also want to review each section to avoid redundancy and optimize the efficiency of your overall plan.

Building Your Business Plan

As you near the final stages of creating your business plan, have others review the plan and ask these questions:

- Does the plan tell a complete story about the business including potential global opportunities?
- Do they have questions that the plan does not address?
- Is the plan compelling?
- Would they find this to be an attractive business investment?

Based on their comments, assess whether the plan was successful at communicating your message and make any necessary changes.

Beyond the Classroom...

1. Go to lunch with a student from a foreign country. Discuss the products and services that are most needed in that country. How does the business system there differ from ours? How much government regulation affects business? What cultural differences exist? What trade barriers has the government erected?

2. Review several current business publications and prepare a brief report on which nations seem to be the most promising for U.S. entrepreneurs. What steps should a small business owner take to break into those markets? Which nations are the least promising? Why?

3. Select a nation that interests you and prepare a report on its business customs and practices. How are they different from those in the United States? How are they similar?

CHAPTER 16

Building a New Venture Team and Planning for the Next Generation

Leadership: The art of getting someone else to do what you want done because he wants to do it.
—*Dwight D. Eisenhower*

Big businesses can afford to hire managers and employees. Entrepreneurs need to hire missionaries.
—*Robert Kiyosaki*

Learning Objectives

On completion of this chapter, you will be able to:

1. Explain the challenges involved in the entrepreneur's role as leader and what it takes to be a successful leader.

2. Describe the importance of hiring the right employees and how to avoid making hiring mistakes.

3. Explain how to create a company culture that encourages employee retention.

4. Describe the steps in developing a management succession plan for a growing business that will allow a smooth transition of leadership to the next generation.

5. Explain the exit strategies available to entrepreneurs.

Leadership in the New Economy

leadership
the process of influencing and inspiring others to work to achieve a common goal and then giving them the power and the freedom to achieve it.

LO 1

Explain the challenges involved in the entrepreneur's role as leader and what it takes to be a successful leader.

To be successful, an entrepreneur must assume a wide range of roles, tasks, and responsibilities, but none is more important than the role of leader. Some entrepreneurs are uncomfortable assuming this role, but they must learn to be effective leaders if their companies are to grow and reach their potential. **Leadership** is the process of influencing and inspiring others to work to achieve a common goal and then giving them the power and the freedom to achieve it. Without leadership ability, entrepreneurs—and their companies—never rise above mediocrity. Entrepreneurs can learn to be effective leaders, but the task requires dedication, discipline, and hard work. In the past, business owners often relied on an autocratic management style, one built on command and control. Today's workforce is more knowledgeable, has more options, and is more skilled, and, as a result, expects a different, more sophisticated style of leadership. Companies that fail to provide that leadership are at risk of losing their best employees.

The rapid pace of change in the new economy also is placing new demands on leaders. Technology is changing the ways in which people work, the ways in which the various parts of an organization operate and interconnect, and the ways in which competitors strive for market dominance. To remain in the game, companies must operate at this new speed of business, and that requires a new style of leadership. Leaders of small companies must gather information and make decisions with lightning-fast speed, and they must give workers the resources and the freedom to solve problems and exploit opportunities as they arise. Effective leaders empower employees to act in the best interest of the business. Until recently, experts compared a leader's job to that of a symphony orchestra conductor. Like the symphony leader, an entrepreneur made sure that everyone in the company was playing the same score, coordinated individual efforts to produce a harmonious sound, and directed the orchestra members as they played. The conductor (entrepreneur) retained virtually all of the power and made all of the decisions about how the orchestra would play the music without any input from the musicians themselves. Today's successful entrepreneur, however, is more like the leader of a jazz band, which is known for its improvisation, innovation, creativity, and free-wheeling style. "The success of a small [jazz band] rests on the ability to be agile and flexible, skills that are equally central to today's business world," says Michael Gold, founder of Jazz Impact, a company that teaches management skills through jazz.[1] Business leaders, like the leaders of jazz bands, should exhibit the following characteristics:

> *Innovative.* Leaders must step out of their own comfort zones to embrace new ideas; they should avoid the comfort of complacency.
>
> *Passionate.* One of entrepreneurs' greatest strengths is their passion for their businesses. Members of their team feed off of that passion and draw inspiration from it.
>
> *Willing to take risks.* "[Taking] risk is not an option in jazz or for any company that wants to be solvent 10 years from now," says Gold.[2]
>
> *Adaptable.* Although leaders must stand on a bedrock of resolute values, like jazz band leaders, they must adapt their leadership styles to fit the situation and the people involved.

Management and leadership are not the same; yet, both are essential to a company's success. Leadership without management is unbridled; management without leadership is uninspired. Leadership gets a small business going; management keeps it going. In other words, leaders are the architects of small businesses; managers are the builders. Some entrepreneurs are good managers yet are poor leaders; others are powerful leaders but are weak managers. The best bet for the latter is to hire people with solid management skills to help them to execute the vision they have for their companies. Stephen Covey, author of *Principle-Centered Leadership*, explains the difference between management and leadership in this way:

> Leadership deals with people; management deals with things. You manage things; you lead people. Leadership deals with vision; management deals with logistics toward that vision. Leadership deals with doing the right things; management focuses on doing things right. Leadership deals with examining the paradigms on which you are operating; management operates within those paradigms. Leadership comes first, then management, but both are necessary.[3]

Effective leaders exhibit certain behaviors. They:

- *Create a set of values and beliefs for employees and passionately pursue them.* Values are the foundation on which a company's vision is built. Leaders should be like beacons in the night, constantly shining light on the principles, values, and beliefs on which they founded their companies.
- *Establish a culture of ethics.* One of the most important tasks facing leaders is to mold a highly ethical culture for their companies. They also must demonstrate the character and the courage necessary to stick to the ethical standards that they create—especially in the face of difficulty.
- *Define and then constantly reinforce the vision they have for the company.* Effective leaders have a clear vision of where they want their companies to go, and they concentrate on communicating that vision to those around them. Clarity of purpose is essential to a successful organization because people want to be a part of something that is bigger than they are; however, the purpose must be more than merely achieving continuous quarterly profits.
- *Respect and support their employees.* To gain the respect of their employees, leaders must first respect those who work for them. They know that a loyal, dedicated work force is a company's most valuable resource, and they treat their employees that way.
- *Set the example for their employees.* Leaders' words ring hollow if they fail to "practice what you preach." Few signals are transmitted to workers faster than a leader who sells employees on one set of values and principles and then acts according to a different set. That is why integrity is perhaps the most important determinant of a leader's effectiveness.
- *Create a climate of trust in the organization.* Leaders who demonstrate integrity soon win the trust of their employees, an essential ingredient in the success of any organization. Honest, open communication and a consistent pattern of leaders doing what they say they will do serve to build trust in a business. Research suggests that building trust among employees is one of the most important tasks of leaders, wherever they may work. One extensive study across 62 nations found that trustworthy leaders were highly valued by employees in every culture studied.[4] Table 16.1 shows the results of a study that identified the top five "trust-building" and "trust-busting" actions leaders can take.
- *Build credibility with their employees.* To be effective, leaders must have credibility with their employees, a sometimes challenging task for entrepreneurs, especially as their companies grow and they become insulated from the daily activities of their businesses. To combat the problem of losing touch with the problems their employees face as they do their jobs, many managers periodically return to the front line to serve customers. For instance, at Southwest Airlines, top managers spend one day each quarter loading baggage onto planes, checking passengers onto flights, serving as flight attendants, and other performing other front-line jobs. The CEO of a major hotel chain requires his executives to staff front-line jobs at least once a year.[5]

TABLE 16.1 Trust-Building and Trust-Busting Behavior by Leaders

Top Five Trust-Building Behaviors Among Leaders

1. Communicate openly and honestly without distorting any information.
2. Show confidence in staff abilities by treating them as skilled, competent associates.
3. Listen to and value what others say, even though you may not agree with it.
4. Keep promises and commitments.
5. Practice what you preach.

Top Five Trust-Busting Behaviors Among Leaders

1. Send mixed messages, making it impossible for employees to know where you stand.
2. Act more concerned about your own welfare.
3. Avoid taking responsibility for your actions.
4. Jump to conclusions without checking the facts first.
5. Hide information or lie.

Source: "A Managers Guide to Trust," *CFO*, June 2006, p. 32. Copyright © 2006 CFO, Inc. Used with permission.

- *Focus employees' efforts on challenging goals and keep them driving toward those goals.* When asked by a student intern to define leadership, one entrepreneur said, "Leadership is the ability to convince people to follow a path they have never taken before to a place they have never been—and upon finding it to be successful, to do it over and over again."[6]
- *Provide the resources employees need to achieve their goals.* Effective leaders know that workers cannot do their jobs well unless they have the tools they need. They provide workers not only with the physical resources they need to excel, but also the necessary intangible resources such as training, coaching, and mentoring.
- *Listen to their employees.* Leaders know that communication is a two-way street. Open communication takes on even greater importance when a company faces a difficult or uncertain future.
- *Value the diversity of their workers.* Smart business leaders recognize the value of their workers' varied skills, abilities, backgrounds, and interests. Good leaders get to know their workers and to understand the diversity of their strengths.
- *Celebrate their workers' successes.* Effective leaders recognize that workers want to be winners, and they do everything they can to encourage top performance among their people. The rewards they give are not always financial; in many cases, it may be as simple as a handwritten congratulatory note.
- *Are willing to take risks.* Entrepreneurs know better than most that launching a business requires taking risks. They also understand that to remain competitive, they must constantly encourage risk taking in their companies.
- *Encourage creativity among their workers.* Rather than punish workers who take risks and fail, effective leaders are willing to accept failure as a natural part of innovation and creativity. They know that innovative behavior is the key to future success and do everything they can to encourage it among workers.
- *Maintain a sense of humor.* One of the most important tools a leader can have is a sense of humor. Without it, work can become dull and unexciting for everyone.

ENTREPRENEURIAL PROFILE

Richard Branson: Virgin Group

Sir Richard Branson, founder of Virgin Group, a diversified company whose businesses range from airlines and bridal gowns to cosmetics and consumer electronics, is famous for creating a work environment of fun for himself and his employees. "Some 80% of your life is spent working," he says. "Why shouldn't you have fun at work?" Branson has put on a wedding dress, bungee-jumped, and hosted off-site events designed strictly to allow employees to have fun. The culture of fun at Virgin Group has built an ésprit de corps that gives the company a unique advantage that competitors find difficult to match, and crown prince Richard Branson is its architect.[7]

- *Create an environment in which people have the motivation, the training, and the freedom to achieve the goals they have set.* Leaders know that *their* success is determined by the success of their followers.
- *Create a work climate that encourages maximum performance.* Leaders understand that they play a significant role in shaping a company culture that sets high standards of performance.
- *Become a catalyst for change.* With market and competitive climates changing so rapidly, entrepreneurs must reinvent their companies constantly. Although leaders must cling to the values and principles that form the bedrock of their companies, they must be willing to change, sometimes radically, the policies, procedures, and processes within their businesses.
- *Develop leadership talent.* Effective leaders look beyond themselves to spot tomorrow's leaders and take the time to help them grow into their leadership potential.
- *Keep their eyes on the horizon.* Effective leaders are never satisfied with what they and their employees accomplished yesterday. They know that yesterday's successes are not enough to sustain their companies indefinitely. "A leader's job is to rally people toward a better future," says Marcus Buckingham, who has spent nearly two decades studying effective leaders.[8]

Leading an organization, whatever its size, is one of the biggest challenges any entrepreneur faces. Yet, for an entrepreneur, leadership success is one of the key determinants of a company's success. Research suggests that there is no single "best" style of leadership; the style a leader uses depends, in part, on the situation at hand. Some situations are best suited for a participative leadership style, but in others, an authoritarian style actually may be best. Research by Daniel Goleman and others suggests that today's workers tend to respond more to adaptive, humble leaders who are results-oriented and who take the time to cultivate other leaders in the organization.[9] The practice is known as **servant leadership,** a phrase coined by Robert Greenleaf in 1970. Servant leaders are servants *first* and leaders second, putting their employees and their employees' needs ahead of their own. They are more concerned about empowering others in the organization than they are at enhancing their own power bases.

servant leadership
a leadership style in which a leader takes on the role of servant first and leader second.

ENTREPRENEURIAL PROFILE _____

Jeremy Brandt: FastHomeOffers.com

Jeremy Brandt, founder of FastHomeOffers.com, a $1.35 million company that generates leads for real estate investors, learned the principles of servant leadership when the pastor at his Grapevine, Texas, church asked him to lead 25 volunteer mission groups. Brandt went in with a "we'll-do-it-this-way" approach, which failed miserably. "It's very natural to let your ego get in the way," says Brandt. "It's illuminating to manage volunteers because if you act that way, no one listens to you." Brandt shifted to a servant leader approach, asking question such as "What problems do you have?" and "How can I help you," and the volunteers responded. Brandt applied the lessons he learned from his volunteer experience when he launched his company, and doing so has made all the difference. "I solve people's problems," he explains. "I give them what they need so they can blossom."[10]

One business writer explains servant leadership this way:

Real leadership is grounded in a higher level of self-interest that's tied to the interests of those who trust and follow their leader. It [creates] an atmosphere of confidence and light of clarity that flows from and surrounds the leader and that fills the room with the exhilaration of possibility.[11]

To tap into that exhilaration of possibility, an entrepreneurial leader must perform many important tasks, including the following:

- Add the right employees to the entrepreneurial team and constantly improve their skills.
- Create a culture for motivating and retaining employees.
- Plan for "passing the torch" to the next generation of leadership.

Building an Entrepreneurial Team: Hiring the Right Employees

The decision to hire a new employee is an important one for every business, but its impact is magnified many times in a small company. Every new hire a business owner makes determines the heights to which the company can climb—or the depths to which it will plunge. "Bad hires" can poison a small company's culture. Unfortunately, hiring mistakes in business are all too common: Hiring managers say that they regret 50 percent of their hiring decisions.[12] A study by Leadership IQ reports that 46 percent of newly hired employees fail in their new jobs within 18 months and that only 19 percent achieve unequivocal success. The study also reveals that the most common cause of failure was not a lack of technical skills for the job at hand but rather a lack of interpersonal skills.[13] The culprit in most cases? The company's selection and hiring process.

Even the best training program cannot overcome a flawed hiring decision. One study reported in the *Harvard Business Review* concludes that 80 percent of employee turnover is caused by bad hiring decisions.[14] The most common causes of a company's poor hiring decisions include:

- Managers who rely on candidates' descriptions of themselves rather than requiring candidates to demonstrate their abilities.

LO 2
Describe the importance of hiring the right employees and how to avoid making hiring mistakes.

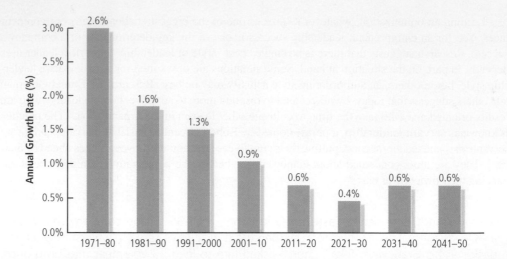

- Managers who fail to follow a consistent, evidence-based selection process. Forty seven percent of managers admit that they make hiring decisions in 30 minutes or less, and 44 percent of managers say that they rely on their intuition to make hiring decisions.
- Managers who fail to provide candidates with sufficient information about what the jobs for which they are hiring actually entail.[15]

As crucial as finding good employees is to a small company's future, it is no easy task because entrepreneurs face a labor shortage, particularly among knowledge-based workers. The severity of this shortage will worsen as baby boomers retire in increasing numbers and the growth rate of the U.S. labor force slows (see Figure 16.1). According to the National Commission for Employment Policy, the impact of these demographic changes will be a "skilled worker gap" (in which the demand for skilled workers outstrips the supply) of 14 million in 2020.[16] The result is that businesses of all sizes find themselves pursuing the best talent not just across the United States but across the globe.

As a result of the intense competition for quality workers among businesses, employers often feel pressured to hire someone, even if that person is not a good fit for the job. A study by Development Dimensions International (DDI) reports that 34 percent of hiring managers admit to making bad hiring decisions because they were under pressure to fill a job.[17] The result is the same: An expensive hiring mistake for the company.

Hiring mistakes are incredibly expensive, and no organization, especially small ones, can afford too many of them. A study by career consulting firm Right Management reports that the average cost to a company to replace a new employee who does not succeed is 2.5 times the potential employee's first-year salary. Companies say that in addition to the amount that they must spend on recruiting, selecting, and training for the employee's replacement, the cost of lower employee morale, reduced productivity, the cost of lost customers, and the negative impact a bad hire can have on a company are the most significant.[18]

How to Hire Winners

Even though the importance of hiring decisions is magnified in small companies, small businesses are most likely to make hiring mistakes because they lack the human resources experts and the disciplined hiring procedures large companies have. In many small businesses, the hiring process is informal, and the results often are unpredictable. In the early days of a company, entrepreneurs rarely take the time to create job descriptions and specifications; instead, they usually hire people because they know or trust them rather than for their job or interpersonal skills. As the company grows, business owners hire people to fit in around these existing employees, often creating a very unusual, inefficient organization structure built around jobs that are poorly planned and designed.

The following guidelines can help entrepreneurs to hire winners and avoid making costly hiring mistakes as they build their team of employees.

COMMIT TO HIRING THE BEST TALENT Smart entrepreneurs follow the old adage, "A players hire A players; B players hire C players." They are not threatened by hiring people who may be smarter and more talented than they are. In fact, they recognize that doing so is the best way to build a quality team.

ELEVATE RECRUITING TO A STRATEGIC POSITION IN THE COMPANY Assembling a quality work-force begins with a sound recruiting effort. By investing time and money at this crucial phase of the staffing process, entrepreneurs can generate spectacular savings down the road by hiring the best talent. The recruiting process is the starting point for building quality into a company. Recruiting is so important that many entrepreneurs choose to become actively involved in the process themselves. Visionary entrepreneurs are *always* recruiting because top quality talent is hard to find and is extremely valuable. Tom Bonney, founder of CMF Associates, a fast-growing financial consulting firm in Philadelphia, knows that finding superior talent is essential to the success of his service business. "I never stop recruiting," he says. "Even if I don't have a need, I am always looking."[19]

Attracting a pool of qualified job candidates requires not only constant attention but also creativity, especially among smaller companies that often find it difficult to match the more generous offers large companies make. With a sound recruiting strategy and a willingness to look in new places, however, smaller companies *can* hire and retain high caliber employees. The following techniques will help.

Look inside the company first. One of the best sources for top prospects is right inside the company itself. A promotion-from-within policy serves as an incentive for existing workers to upgrade their skills and to produce results. In addition, an entrepreneur already knows the employee's work habits, and the employee already understands the company's culture.

Encourage employee referrals. To cope with the shortage of available talent, many companies are offering their employees (and others) bonuses for referring candidates who come to work and prove to be valuable employees. Employees serve as reliable screens because they do not want to jeopardize their reputations with their employer. At Automated Concepts, a systems integration company, referral bonuses range from $2,000 to $4,000 (for especially hard-to-fill positions) and include drawings for big-screen TVs and vacations in England.[20]

Make employment advertisements stand out. Getting employment ads noticed in traditional media is becoming more difficult because they get lost in the swarm of ads from other companies.

Roger Mody, founder and former CEO of Signal Corporation, an information technology services provider, uses humor to make his employment ads stand out and to communicate the sense of fun in the company's culture. One ad ran a photo of Mody after a company pie-eating contest with the tag line "And you should see us on casual day."[21]

Use multiple channels to recruit talent. Although newspaper ads still top employers' list of job postings, many businesses are successfully attracting candidates through other media, particularly the Internet. Posting job listings on career-oriented sites such as Monster.com, Hotjobs.com, and others not only expands a small company's reach far beyond an ad in a local newspaper but also is very inexpensive. Employers also are connecting with potential employees (not all of whom are actively seeking new jobs) through their employees' network of contacts, company blogs, career sites such as LinkedIn and Jobirn, and social media sites such as Facebook, MySpace, and Twitter.

Ben Swartz, co-founder of Marcel Media, an interactive marketing company in Chicago, says that he has hired about 75 percent of his 21-person staff using Web 2.0 tools. Swartz routinely uses LinkedIn and Facebook to delve into candidates' backgrounds. Doing so "gives us more dimensions than a static résumé can offer," he says.[22]

Recruit on campus. For many employers, college and university campuses remain an excellent source of workers, especially for entry-level positions. After screening résumés, a recruiter can interview a dozen or more high-potential students in just one day.

Get involved in a college internship program. As colleges and universities begin to offer students more internship opportunities, a small business can gain greatly by hosting one or more students for a semester or for the summer. The company has an opportunity to observe the student's work habits and, if positive, sell the student on a permanent position on graduation.

Recruit "retired" workers. Older employees also can be a valuable asset to small firms. With a lifetime of work experience and time on their hands and a strong work ethic, retired workers can be the ideal solution to many entrepreneurs' labor problems. One survey by WorldatWork, an international association of human resource professionals, reports that just 49.4 percent of employers proactively pursue older workers in their recruiting efforts.[23]

Consider using offbeat recruiting techniques. To attract the workers they need to support their growing businesses, some entrepreneurs have resorted to creative recruiting techniques such as the following:

- Sending young recruiters to mingle with college students on spring break.
- Using social networking media such as Facebook, MySpace, blogs, and podcasts to reach potential employees, especially younger ones.
- Sponsoring a "job shadowing" program that gives students and other prospects the opportunity to observe firsthand the nature of the work and the work environment.
- Inviting college seniors to a company tailgating party at a sports event.
- Posting "what it's like to work here" videos created by current employees on YouTube and other video sites.
- Keeping a file of all of the workers mentioned in the "People on the Move" column in the business section of the local newspaper and then contacting them a year later to see whether they are happy in their jobs.[24]

Offer what workers want. Adequate compensation and benefits are important considerations for job candidates, but other, less tangible factors also weigh heavily in a prospect's decision to accept a job. To recruit effectively, entrepreneurs must consider what a McKinsey and Company study calls the "employee value proposition," the factors that would make the ideal employee want to work for their businesses. Flexible work schedules and telecommuting that allow employees to balance the demands of work and life can attract quality workers to small companies. In fact, a study by staffing firm Robert Half International reports that after salary and benefits, flexible work schedules and telecommuting were the most important incentives in attracting employees.[25]

Many of the companies listed on *Fortune's* "100 Best Companies to Work For" offer low-cost but valuable (from their employees' perspectives) perks such as take-home meals, personal concierge services that coordinate everything from dry cleaning to auto maintenance for employees, exercise facilities, and company movie outings.[26]

ENTREPRENEURIAL PROFILE

Teri Rogers: Take Two LLC

Teri Rogers, president of Take Two LLC, a film and video production company in Kansas City, Missouri, says her company's "family-first policy" that allows employees to adjust their work schedule to accommodate family obligations enables her to attract and retain quality employees. Rogers also periodically hires massage therapists, provides a daily breakfast and an afternoon snack, and gives a "spa day" to staffers who have worked hard to complete a special project.[27]

job analysis
the process by which a firm determines the duties and nature of the jobs to be filled and the skills and experience required of the people who are to fill them.

job description
a written statement of the duties, responsibilities, reporting relationships, working conditions, and methods and techniques, as well as materials and equipment used in a job.

CREATE PRACTICAL JOB DESCRIPTIONS AND JOB SPECIFICATIONS Business owners must recognize that what they do *before* they ever start interviewing candidates for a position determines to a great extent how successful they will be at hiring winners. The first step is to perform a **job analysis,** the process by which a firm determines the duties and nature of the jobs to be filled and the skills and experience required of the people who are to fill them. Without a proper job analysis, a hiring decision is, at best, a coin toss. The first step in conducting a job analysis is to develop a **job description,** a written statement of the duties, responsibilities, reporting relationships, working conditions, and methods and techniques, as well as materials and equipment used in a job. A results-oriented job description explains what a job entails and the duties the person filling it is expected to perform. A detailed job description includes a job title, job summary, duties to be performed, nature of supervision, job's

TABLE 16.2 A Sample Job Description from the *Dictionary of Occupational Titles*

Worm Picker—gathers worms to be used as fish bait; walks about grassy areas, such as gardens, parks, and golf courses and picks up earthworms (commonly called dew worms and nightcrawlers). Sprinkles chlorinated water on lawn to cause worms to come to the surface and locates worms by use of lantern or flashlight. Counts worms, sorts them, and packs them into containers for shipment. (# 413.687–014 in D.O.T)

relationship to others in the company, working conditions, definitions of job-specific terms, and general comments needed to clarify any of the above.

Without the blueprint that a job description provides, a manager tends to hire the person with experience whom they like the best. Useful sources of information for writing job descriptions include the manager's knowledge of the job, the worker(s) currently holding the job, and the *Dictionary of Occupational Titles (D.O.T)*, available at most libraries. *The Dictionary of Occupational* Titles, published by the Department of Labor, lists more than 20,000 job titles and descriptions and serves as a useful tool for getting a small business owner started when writing job descriptions. Internet searches also are a valuable tool for finding templates for writing job descriptions. Table 16.2 provides an example of the description drawn from the D.O.T. for an unusual job.

The second objective of a job analysis is to create a **job specification,** a written statement of the qualifications and characteristics needed for a job stated in terms such as, education, skills, and experience. A job specification shows a small business manager what kind of person to recruit and establishes the standards an applicant must meet to be hired. In essence, it is a written "success profile" of the ideal employee. Does the person have to be a good listener, empathetic, well-organized, decisive, a "self-starter"? Should he or she have experience in Java or C++ programming? One of the best ways to develop this success profile is to study the top performers currently working for the company and to identify the characteristics that make them successful. Before hiring new sales representatives, sales managers at Blackboard, Inc., a Washington, D.C., company that sells software for the educational market, study their top sales producers to identify the characteristics they demonstrate in four areas—skills, experience, knowledge, and personality traits. Table 16.3 provides an example that links the tasks for a sales representative's job (drawn from a job description) to the traits or characteristics an entrepreneur identified as necessary to succeed in that job. These traits become the foundation for writing the job specification.

job specification
a written statement of the qualifications and characteristics needed for a job stated in terms such as education, skills, and experience.

PLAN AN EFFECTIVE INTERVIEW Once an entrepreneur knows what to look for in a job candidate, he or she can develop a plan for conducting an informative job interview. Too often, business owners go into an interview unprepared, and as a result, they fail to get the information they need to judge the candidate's qualifications, qualities, and suitability for the job. A common symptom of failing to prepare for an interview is that the interviewer rather than the candidate does most of the talking. "It's the most common mistake made by interviewers," says one human resource manager.[28]

The following guidelines will help entrepreneurs develop interview questions that will give them meaningful insight into an applicant's qualifications, personality, and character:

Involve others in the interview process. Solo interviews are prone to errors. A better process is to involve other employees, particularly employees with whom the prospect would be working, in the interview process either individually or as part of a panel.

TABLE 16.3 Linking Tasks from a Job Description to the Traits Necessary to Perform a Job Successfully

Job Task	Trait or Characteristic
Generate and close new sales	"Outgoing"; persuasive; friendly
Make 15 "cold calls" per week	"Self-starter"; determined; optimistic; independent; confident
Analyze customers' needs and recommend proper equipment	Good listener; patient; empathetic
Counsel customers about options and features needed	Organized; polished speaker; "other oriented"
Prepare and explain financing methods	Honest; "numbers oriented"; comfortable with computers and spreadsheets
Retain existing customers	Customer oriented; relationship builder

ETHICS AND ENTREPRENEURSHIP

Honesty in Job Descriptions

> our time unless thorough..., qualified. M. L. Barker, 1408 Chapman Bldg.
>
> ### MEN WANTED
>
> for hazardous journey, small wages, bitter cold, long months of complete darkness, constant danger, safe return doubtful, honor and recognition in case of success.
>
> Ernest Shackleton 4 Burlington st.
>
> MEN—Neat-appearing young men of pleasing personality, between ages of 01 and 40 to work

Explorer Ernest Shackleton reportedly placed this advertisement in a British newspaper to recruit the crew for his 1914 expedition with the goal of "crossing the South Polar continent from sea to sea," a distance of 1,800 miles in the face of some of the most grueling and dangerous conditions possible. Nearly 5,000 men applied, from which Shackleton selected 28 of the most capable men, carefully matching their skills and abilities to the challenges that the journey would present. On August 1, 1914, Shackleton and his crew left London on their ship, the *Endurance*, to document the largely unexplored Antarctic. On October 27, 1915, after watching the *Endurance* splintered after being stuck in pack ice for 10 months, Shackleton and his crew began a harrowing journey of survival that would not end until August 20, 1916, 22 months after their expedition began. Even though Shackleton's ad stated "safe return doubtful," Shackleton and his entire crew returned safely to London after an amazing adventure.

Like Shackleton, smart entrepreneurs know writing job descriptions that make jobs sound more interesting, glamorous, and exciting than they really are is not only misleading but also leads to problems for their businesses. To avoid high turnover rates, low morale, and abysmal productivity rates among their employees, entrepreneurs must paint realistic pictures of the jobs when they create job descriptions. Recruiters at Lindblad Expeditions, a company that takes guests on adventure cruises to exciting destinations around the globe, makes sure that job applicants get a unvarnished picture of what their jobs would entail—warts and all. Prospective employees receive a DVD that shows crew members performing their daily tasks—from serving meals to guests and seeing wildlife on the Galapagos Islands to washing windows and swabbing toilets. "The

things you see and the places that you go are amazing, but you're still doing this incredibly hard work," says one employee. "You're going to put in 10- to 12-hour days," adds another. The video discourages most applicants, but those who do apply tend to be just the kind of young people Lindblad is looking for to take on a six-month assignment of taking care of guests' safety and comfort. "If they get on board and say, 'This is not what I expected,' then shame on us," says Kris Thompson, vice-president of human resources.

Tony Hseih, CEO of Zappos, the online shoe retailer whose ten core values include "deliver WOW through service" and "create fun and a little weirdness," relies on an unusual policy to make sure that his company hires only those employees who are most committed to fulfilling the company's mission. After the first week of the company's four-week training program, during which employees earn a full salary, Zappos presents them with "The Offer:" Stay with the company or take a $1,000 payout to leave, no strings attached. Only about 10 percent of new employees take the money and leave. Hseih says that those who remain are more likely to believe in Zappo's values and to commit themselves to upholding the company's commitment to customer service. Every year, Zappos publishes the Zappos Culture Book, in which employees have the opportunity to write anything they want about Zappos core values and its culture, what the values and culture mean to them, and what they do to uphold them. In the foreword of a recent edition of the Zappos Culture Book, Hseih wrote, "...for us to succeed as a service company, we need to create, maintain, and grow a culture where employees want to play a part in providing great service....As we grow as a company and hire new people, we need to make sure that they understand and become a part of our culture."

1. Why is it important for entrepreneurs to create honest job descriptions to potential employees? What are the implications for entrepreneurs who fail to do so?
2. Is it ethical for small companies to present to potential employees only the "fun" aspects of a job and to gloss over its less appealing components?
3. Lindblad Expeditions and Zappos sometimes receive criticism for being too extreme in the honesty of their recruiting approaches. Do you agree? Explain.

Source: Based on *Shackleton's Expedition*, NOVA, http://www.pbs.org/wgbh/nova/shackleton/1914/; Boost Retention with Honest Job Previews," *Manager's e-Bulletin*, July 24, 2008, pp. 1–2; "Would You Give an Employee $1,000 to Quit?" *Marketing Profs*, June 2, 2008, pp. 1–2; Lisa Everitt, "Zappos Tells New Employees: Please Go Away," *BNet*, May 21, 2008, http://industry.bnet.com/retail/100066/zappos-tells-new-employees-please-go-away/; Bud Bilanich, "Zappos and Employee Engagement and Commitment," Common Sense Solutions to Tough Business Problems, November 20, 1007, http://bbilanich.typepad.com/blog/2007/11/last-week-i-blo.html.

ENTREPRENEURIAL PROFILE_____

Paula Labian: Whole Foods Market

After Whole Foods Market experienced a growth spurt, says human resources vice-president Paula Labian, "we saw a lot of turnover within the first six months on the job. We realized we needed a better way to assess people before we hired them." The company revamped its hiring process, one that involved an employment test and two solo interviews, into one that includes an intensive series of panel interviews that involve anywhere from 4 to 14 employees who would be the candidate's prospective peers. Although the manager has the final say, the employees' input is a significant part of the final decision. The result: Whole Foods' employee turnover rate fell to 26 percent, less than half the industry average of 61 percent.[29]

Develop a series of core questions and ask them of every candidate. To give the screening process more consistency, smart business owners rely on a set of relevant questions they ask in every interview. Of course, they also customize each interview using impromptu questions based on an individual candidate's responses.

Ask open-ended questions (including on-the-job "scenarios") rather than questions calling for "yes or no" answers. These types of questions are most effective because they encourage candidates to talk about their work experience in a way that discloses the presence or the absence of the traits and characteristics the business owner is seeking. Peter Bregman, CEO of Bregman Partners, a company that helps businesses implement change, says that one of the most revealing questions that an interviewer can ask candidates is "What do you do in your spare time?" The answer to this question offers unique insight that helps interviewers differentiate between those who are merely competent and those who are stars. "Understand a person's obsessions and you will understand his or her natural motivation," says Bregman, pointing to the example of Captain C. B. "Sully" Sullenberger, the pilot who safely landed a disabled jet with 155 passengers on the Hudson River using skills that he learned from his hobby, flying gliders.[30]

Create hypothetical situations candidates would be likely to encounter on the job and ask how they would handle them. Building the interview around these kinds of questions gives the owner a preview of the candidate's actual work habits and attitudes. Some companies take this idea a step farther and put candidates into a simulated work environment to see how they prioritize activities and handle mail, e-mail, and a host of "real world" problems they are likely to encounter on the job, ranging from complaining customers to problematic employees. Known as **situational interviews,** their goal is to give interviewers keener insight into how candidates would perform in the work environment.

situational interview
an interview in which the interviewer gives candidates a typical job-related situation (e.g., a job simulation) to see how they respond to it.

Robert Manella/Corbis RF

Probe for specific examples in the candidate's past work experience that demonstrate the necessary traits and characteristics. A common mistake interviewers make is failing to get candidates to provide the detail they need to make an informed decision.

Ask candidates to describe a recent success and a recent failure and how they dealt with them. Smart entrepreneurs look for candidates who describe their successes and their failures with equal enthusiasm because they know that peak performers put as much into their failures as they do their successes and usually learn something valuable from their failures.

Arrange a "non-interview" setting that allows several employees to observe the candidate in an informal setting. Taking candidates on a plant tour, setting up a coffee break, or taking them to lunch gives more people a chance to judge a candidate's interpersonal skills and personality outside the formal interview process. These informal settings can be very revealing.

ENTREPRENEURIAL PROFILE

Jeffrey Swartz:
Timberland

Before Jeffrey Swartz, CEO of Timberland, the popular shoe and boot maker, makes an offer to a candidate for a management position, he invites the candidate to participate in one of the company's community service projects. "In an interview, I'm sure you're more clever than I am," he says. "But on a service site, you will reveal who you [really] are."[31]

Table 16.4 shows an example of some interview questions one business owner uses to uncover the traits and characteristics he was seeking in a top-performing sales representative.

CONDUCT THE INTERVIEW An effective interview contains three phases: breaking the ice, asking questions, and selling the candidate on the company.

Breaking the ice. In the opening phase of the interview, the manager's primary job is to diffuse the tension that exists because of the nervousness of both parties. Many skilled interviewers use the job description to explain the nature of the job and the company's culture to the applicant. Then they use "ice-breakers," questions about a hobby or special interest, to get the candidate to relax and begin talking.

Asking questions. During the second phase of the interview, the employer asks the questions from the question bank to determine the applicant's suitability for the job. The interviewer's primary job at this point is to listen. Effective interviewers spend about 25 percent of the interview talking and about 75 percent listening. They also take notes during the interview to help them ask follow-up questions based on a candidate's comments and to evaluate a candidate after the interview is over. Experienced interviewers also pay close attention to a candidate's nonverbal clues, or body language, during the interview. They know that candidates may be able to say exactly what they want with their words, but that their body language does not lie!

Some of the most valuable interview questions are designed to gain insight into a candidate's creativity and capacity for abstract thinking. Known as **puzzle interviews,** their goal is to determine how candidates think by asking them offbeat questions such as, "How would you weigh a plane without using scales?", "How would you design Bill Gates's bathroom?" (a favorite at Microsoft), or "How do they make M&Ms?" The logic and creativity candidates use to derive an answer is much more important than the answer itself.

puzzle interview
an interview that includes offbeat questions to determine how job candidates think and reason and to judge their capacity for creativity.

TABLE 16.4 Interview Questions for Candidates for a Sales Representative Position

Trait or Characteristic	Question
"Outgoing"; persuasive; friendly; "self-starter"; determined' optimistic; independent; confident.	How do you persuade reluctant prospects to buy?
Good listener; patient; empathetic; organized; polished speaker; "other oriented."	What would you say to a fellow salesperson who was getting more than his share of rejections and was having difficulty getting appointments?
Honest; customer oriented, relationship builder.	How do you feel when someone questions the truth of what you say? What do you do in such situations/
Other questions:	If you owned a company, why would you hire yourself?
	If you were head of your department, what would you do differently?
	How do you recognize the contributions of others in your department?
	If you weren't in sales, what other job would you be in?

Selling the candidate on the company. In the final phase of the interview, the employer tries to sell desirable candidates on the company. This phase begins by allowing the candidate to ask questions about the company, the job, or other issues. Again, experienced interviewers note the nature of these questions and the insights they give into the candidate's personality. This part of the interview offers the employer a prime opportunity to explain to the candidate why the company is an attractive place to work. Remember: The best candidates will have other offers, and it's up to you to make sure they leave the interview wanting to work for your company. Finally, before closing the interview, the employer should thank the candidate and tell him what happens next (for example, "We'll be contacting you about our decision within two weeks.")

Table 16.5 provides a quiz that tests your knowledge of the legality of certain interview questions.

CONTACT REFERENCES AND CONDUCT A BACKGROUND CHECK Business owners should take the time to conduct a background check and contact a candidate's references. Background checks are inexpensive to perform, typically costing between $25 and $100, and identify "red flags" that allow a company to avoid making an expensive hiring mistake. By performing a basic background check, employers can steer clear of candidates with criminal or other high-risk backgrounds. Andy Bell, founder of Handyman Matters Franchising, a company that has more than 100 home repair franchises in 37 states, knows that performing background checks on applicants is essential in his business because his franchisees' workers go into customers' homes. "We took a random sample of 100 applicants, and [after a background check] only 30 of them were qualified to work in someone's home," he says, pointing out that some applicants had serious criminal offenses on their records.[32]

TABLE 16.5 Is It Legal?

Some interview questions can lead an employer into legal problems. Test your knowledge concerning which questions are legal to ask in an interview using the following quiz.

Legal	Illegal	*Interview Question*
☐	☐	1. Are you currently using illegal drugs?
☐	☐	2. Have you ever been arrested?
☐	☐	3. Do you have any children or do you plan to have children?
☐	☐	4. When and where were you born?
☐	☐	5. Is there any limit on your ability to work overtime or travel?
☐	☐	6. How tall are you? How much do you weigh?
☐	☐	7. Do you drink alcohol?
☐	☐	8. How much alcohol do you drink each week?
☐	☐	9. Would your religious beliefs interfere with your ability to do the job?
☐	☐	10. What contraceptive practices do you use?
☐	☐	11. Are you HIV positive?
☐	☐	12. Have you ever filed a lawsuit or worker's compensation claim against a former employer?
☐	☐	13. Do you have physical/mental disabilities that would interfere with doing your job?
☐	☐	14. Are you a US citizen?

Answers: 1. Legal. 2. Illegal. Employers cannot ask about an applicant's arrest record, but they can ask whether a candidate has ever been *convicted* of a crime. 3. Illegal. Employers cannot ask questions that could lead to discrimination against a particular group [e.g., women, physically challenged, etc]. 4. Illegal. The Civil Rights Act of 1964 bans discrimination on the basis of race, color, sex, religion, or national origin. 5. Legal. 6. Illegal. Unless a person's physical characteristics are necessary for job performance [e.g., lifting 100-pound sacks of mulch], employers cannot ask candidates such questions. 7. Legal. 8. Illegal. Notice the fine line between question 7 and question 8; this is what makes interviewing so challenging. 9. Illegal. This question violates the Civil Rights Act of 1964. 10. Illegal. What relevance would this have to an employee's job performance? 11. Illegal. Under the Americans with Disabilities Act, which prohibits discrimination against people with disabilities, people that are HIV positive or have AIDS are considered "disabled." 12. Illegal. Workers who file workers' compensation suits are protected from retribution by a variety of federal and state laws. 13. Illegal. This question also violates the Americans with Disabilities Act. 14. Illegal. This question violates the Civil Rights Act of 1964.

Checking potential employees' social networking pages such as FaceBook and MySpace also can provide a revealing look at their character. A study by CareerBuilder reports that 22 percent of employers investigate job candidates' FaceBook and MySpace pages and that one-third have discovered something there that caused them to reject a candidate.[33]

Although many business owners see checking references as a formality and pay little attention to it, others realize the need to protect themselves (and their customers) from hiring unscrupulous workers. Is it really necessary? Yes! According to a survey of hiring managers by CareerBuilder, 49 percent of candidates either exaggerate or falsify information about their previous employment on their résumés.[34] Checking references thoroughly can help employers uncover false or exaggerated information. Rather than contacting only the references listed, experienced employers call applicants' previous employers and talk to their immediate supervisors to get a clear picture of the applicant's job performance, character, and work habits.

Many employers implement a probationary "trial" period for new hires that may range from two weeks to several months. Doing so increases the probability that the company has found the right person for the job. After two weeks on the job at Whole Foods Market, team members of new hires vote on whether to keep the new employees or to let them go.[35]

Experienced entrepreneurs know that hiring an employee is not a single event but the beginning of a long-term relationship. Table 16.6 features some strange but true incidents that employers have encountered during the selection process.

TABLE 16.6 Strange but True!

If you read enough resumes, conduct enough interviews, and check enough references, sooner or later you will encounter something bizarre. Consider the following examples (all true).

- After having lunch with a job candidate, a business owner took the applicant to her office for more discussion. The discussion ended, however, when the applicant dozed off and began snoring.
- When asked to provide a writing sample, one candidate said that she could not because all of her previous writing had been for the CIA and was "classified."
- When asked what person, living or dead, he would most like to meet, one candidate replied, "The living one."
- One candidate answered his cell phone during the interview and asked the interviewer to leave her own office because it was a personal call.
- When asked about his personal interests, one candidate proudly replied, "Donating blood. Fourteen gallons so far!"
- At the end of an interview, the interviewer asked the candidate if he had any questions. His only question: "Is the office close enough so I can run home three times a day to Water Pik my teeth?"
- One candidate asked if he could bring his rabbit to work with him, adding that the rabbit was focused and reliable but that he himself had been fired before.
- One man who forgot to wear socks to his interview remedied the problem by coloring his ankles with a black felt-tip marker.

Recommendations from previous employers can sometimes be quite entertaining too. The following are statements from managers about workers.

- "Works well when under constant supervision and cornered like a rat in a trap."
- "This young lady has delusions of adequacy."
- "A photographic memory but with the lens cover glued on."
- "If you were to give him a penny for his thoughts, you'd get change."
- "If you stand close enough to him, you can hear the ocean."
- "He's so dense that light bends around him."

Sources: Based on "Survey Reveals Wackiest Job Interview Mistakes," *SmartPros*, March 13, 2008, http://accounting.smartpros.com/x61115.xml ; "Hiring Horrors," *Your Company*, April 1999, p. 14, Mike B. Hall, "From Job Applicants," Joke-of-the-Day, http://wwwjokeoftheday.com, December 8, 2000; Karen Axelton, "L L L Losers!" *Business Start Ups*, April 2000, p. 13; "Great Places to Work: Interview Horror Stories," *Washingtonian*, November 1, 2005, http://www.washingtonian.com/articles/businesscareers/2159.html.

HANDS ON... HOW TO

Make Your Small Business a Great Place to Work

Smart entrepreneurs know that although they may be the driving force behind their businesses, their highly committed and engaged employees are the *real* keys to their companies' success. As a result, these entrepreneurs carefully select their employees, develop their talents through training and education, and create a culture that reflects the central role that their employees. Following are 11 lessons for creating a great workplace drawn from small companies that have been recognized by Winning Workplaces, *The Wall Street Journal*, and the Families Work Institute.

Lesson 1. Take a long-term view of your business

Owners of small, privately held companies have a distinct advantage over managers in large, publicly held firms in that they can make decisions that are in the best interest of their companies over the long haul rather than managing to meet quarterly financial expectations. These companies are willing to sacrifice short-term results for long-term stability and success. At Phenomenex, a company in Torrance, California, that provides chromatography products, founder Fasha Mahjoor provides employee benefits that many companies would dismiss as too expensive. Employees who are first-time home buyers receive a $2,000 stipend, and Phenomenex provides an on-site concierge to help employees handle errands. A profit-sharing plan, which recently paid out $475,000, gives employees a sense of ownership.

Lesson 2. Recognize your company's responsibility to society

These leading small companies strive for more than profitability; they aim to make a difference in the world, both locally and globally, and they get their employees involved in their efforts. At Redwoods Group, a Morrisville, North Carolina, company that specializes in providing insurance to YMCAs and Jewish community centers, employees are required to donate at least 40 hours of volunteer time annually for a nonprofit organization of their choice—on company time. The company also donates up to $300 annually to any nonprofit in which employees volunteer their own time and matches up to $1,000 per year charitable donations that employees make.

Lesson 3. Honest, open, two-way communication helps your company in good times and bad times

Managers at these small companies recognize that good communication is a key to building trust with employees and to encouraging them to participate in making decisions that make the workplace better. At Decagon Instruments, a family-owned maker of scientific instruments in Pullman, Washington, the company's 72 employees eat lunch together, which provides managers and employees with an opportunity to share news about the company, learn about new projects, and learn about a variety of topics, including how to read the company's financial statements.

Lesson 4. Teamwork counts

Managers at leading small companies understand that a genuine team spirit leads to innovation, unparalleled productivity, and a fun atmosphere of camaraderie. They rely on team-based awards and recognition to encourage a team spirit and help employees understand how their jobs fit into the "big picture." At Jump Associates, an innovation consulting company in San Mateo, California, employees gather every morning for a "scrum," a short meeting in which they learn about company news, do quick yoga exercises, and engage in a short, creativity-stimulating game to get them energized for the day.

Lesson 5. Investing in your employees is one of the best investments you can make

At Paducah Bank & Trust (PB&T), a community bank in Paducah, Kentucky, employees can earn spots in a leadership development program that meets monthly for 18 months. The course not only teaches banking fundamentals but also helps employees learn how to become more effective leaders. The bank also pays for employees to attend the Kentucky Banking School. "The most significant thing we've accomplished is not just the development of the knowledge," says CEO Joe Frampton, "but the intrinsic value among employees of, 'Oh, I'm important.'" Not surprisingly, 80 percent of PB&T's managers are promoted from within the company.

Lesson 6. Workspace design affects teamwork, collaboration, and productivity

The layout of the offices at Jump Associates is designed to encourage teamwork and collaboration, both of which are essential to customer satisfaction and, ultimately, the company's success. All employees, including senior managers, work in open "neighborhoods" that contain five or six workers and make it easy for them to collaborate or brainstorm ideas.

Lesson 7. Give your employees a real sense of ownership

Every employer's dream is to have employees who act like owners of the company. The best way to achieve that is to make them owners of the company! Kim Jordan and Jeff Lebesch, a husband-and-wife team who launched the New Belgium Brewing Company in 1991, believed that allowing their employees to own part of the company would increase their level of engagement. The copreneurs created an employee stock ownership plan (ESOP), and employees now own 32 percent of the company. Jordan and Lebesch also practice open book management and teach employees how to read the company's financial statements. The result is an ownership mentality and a workforce that is dedicated to making the company successful.

Lesson 8. Encourage your employees to stay healthy

With health care costs rising rapidly, smart business owners know that anything they can do to help their employees stay healthy not only will lower costs but will also help their employees to lead better personal and work lives. Many of these leading small companies pay 100 percent of the cost of their employees' health insurance. Others provide incentives for employees to improve their health by quitting smoking, reaching and maintaining an ideal weight, or exercising regularly. Some companies provide on-site exercise facilities or pay for employees memberships at local gyms.

Lesson 9. Recognize your employees' stellar performances publicly and privately—and often

At J. A. Frate, a regional trucking company in Crystal Lake, Illinois, a Driver Recognition Committee names Drivers of the Month, using criteria such as undamaged freight, on-time deliveries, and accurate log books. The winners are recognized publicly and receive a variety of gifts and a chance to be selected Driver of the Year, which qualifies them for a larger award. Recently, Joe Rhamey, was named Driver of the Year in consecutive years. The company purchased a new truck for him equipped with $4,000 worth of embellishments, such as satellite radio, power windows, and chrome wheels.

Lesson 10. Let your employees have fun

Just because you are at work does not mean that you cannot have fun. Nancy Kramer, CEO of Resource Interactive, a digital marketing company in Columbus, Ohio, periodically throws a "jungle breakfast," where she hides boxes of cereal and doughnuts around the office for employees to find. Every year, employees nominate colleagues whom they believe best embody the company's seven core values for the company's "Orbie Awards." The company recognizes the winners at an annual banquet with trophies and prizes such as iPods and Wii game systems.

Lesson 11. Give your employees the flexibility they need for work-life balance

Small companies that offer flextime, job sharing, telecommuting, and other flexible work arrangements have an edge when it comes to hiring the best workers. At Henry and Horne, an accounting firm in Chandler, Arizona, employees have the freedom to set their own work schedules, shift between full-time and part-time positions, come back to work gradually after a major life event, and even retire gradually.

Resource Interactive

Nancy Kramer, CEO of Resource Interactive

Sources: Based on Kelly K. Spors, "Top Small Workplaces 2008," *Wall Street Journal*, February 22, 2009, http://online.wsj.com/article/SB122347733961315417.html; "Top Small Workplaces 2008: Executive Summary," Winning Workplaces, pp. 2–5; *2008 Guide to Bold New Ideas for Making Work Work*, Families and Work Institute, New York: 2008, pp. 3–6, 42.

LO 3

Explain how to create a company culture that encourages employee retention.

culture
the distinctive, unwritten, informal code of conduct that governs an organization's behavior, attitudes, relationships, and style.

Creating an Organizational Culture That Encourages Employee Motivation and Retention

Culture

A company's **culture** is the distinctive, unwritten, informal code of conduct that governs its behavior, attitudes, relationships, and style. It is the essence of "the way we do things around here." In many small companies, culture plays as important a part in gaining a competitive edge as strategy does. Culture has a powerful impact on the way people work together in a business, how they do their jobs, and how they treat their customers. Company culture manifests itself in many ways—from how workers dress and act to the language they use. For instance, at some companies, the unspoken dress code requires workers to wear suits and ties, but at others employees routinely come to work in jeans and T-shirts.

Although it is an intangible characteristic, a company's culture has a powerful influence on everyone the company touches, especially its employees.

ENTREPRENEURIAL PROFILE

Mary Cheddie: Burton Snowboards

At Burton Snowboards, about one-fourth of employees bring their dogs to work on any given day. One employee says that some of his best ideas come to him when he is away from his desk, walking or playing with his dog. When associates at Orvis, a retailer of fine sporting equipment whose headquarters is in Manchester, Vermont, take their breaks, they can fly fish using free equipment on a 377-acre company-owned pond stocked with fish. "It helps align the associates with what we do and why we do it," says vice-president of human resources Mary Cheddie.[36]

Sustaining a company's culture begins with the hiring process. Beyond the normal requirements of competitive pay and working conditions, the hiring process must focus on finding employees who share the values of the organization. The process is continuous.

ENTREPRENEURIAL PROFILE

Ari Weinzeig:
Zingerman's
Delicatessen

Ari Weinzeig, co-founder of Zingerman's Delicatessen in Ann Arbor, Michigan, and seven other businesses, relies on an eight-page document, Zingerman's Vision for the Year 2020, to communicate his company's culture to prospective employees and looks for candidates whose values are aligned with those of the company. "We want to hire people who are passionate about food, who will serve their fellow employees (not just customers), who can handle roles that aren't defined in black-and-white, and who have a drive for greatness," he says. Weinzeig conducts job interviews on the floor of the delicatessen to see how candidates react to the bedlam, watching carefully for nonverbal clues. He also uses panel interviews that involve eight to 10 employees whose opinions weigh heavily in the hiring decision.[37]

Zingerman's Delicatessen

Creating a culture that supports a company's strategy is no easy task, but entrepreneurs who have been most successful at it believe that having a set of overarching beliefs serves as a powerful guide for everyday action. Culture arises from an entrepreneur's consistent and relentless pursuit of a set of core values that everyone in the company can believe in. "Values outlive business models," says management guru Gary Hamel.[38]

As a new generation of employees enters the workforce, companies are discovering that more relaxed, open cultures have an edge in attracting the best workers. These companies embrace nontraditional, fun cultures that incorporate concepts such as casual dress, team-based assignments, telecommuting, flexible work schedules, free meals, company outings, and many other unique options. Modern organizational culture relies on several principles that are fundamental to creating a productive, fun workplace.

Respect for Work and Life Balance. Successful companies recognize that their employees have lives away from work. One study of Generation *X* workers found that those companies that people most wanted to work for erased the traditional barriers between home life and work life

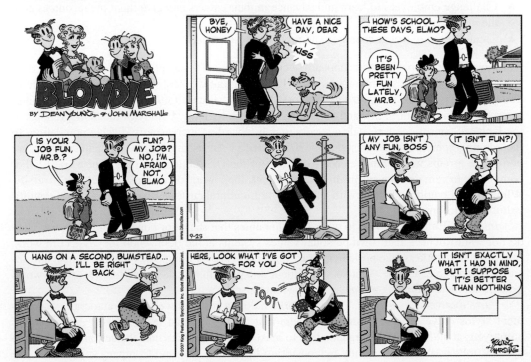

Source: © King Features Syndicate

by making it easier for employees to deal with the pressures they face away from their jobs. These businesses offer flexible work schedules, part-time jobs, job sharing, telecommuting, sabbaticals, and services such as on-site day care and dry cleaning.

ENTREPRENEURIAL PROFILE

Tess Coody: Guerra DeBerry Coody

Guerra DeBerry Coody (GDC), an advertising agency based in San Antonio, Texas, not only attracts top-quality talent but also reaps the benefits of high productivity and employee retention by emphasizing work-life balance. The company provides its employees with flexible work schedules, three one-hour exercise sessions with a personal trainer (on company time) each week, and on-site daycare center, benefits that allow employees to more easily balance their work-life demands.[39]

A Sense of Purpose. As you learned in Chapter 3, Strategic Management and the Entrepreneur, one of the most important jobs an entrepreneur faces is defining the company's vision and then communicating it effectively to everyone the company touches. Effective companies use a strong sense of purpose to make employees feel connected to the company's mission. At motorcycle legend Harley-Davidson, employees are so in tune with the company's mission that some of them have tattooed the company's name on their bodies.

A Sense of Fun. For some companies, the lines between work and play are blurred. The founders of these businesses see no reason for work and fun to be mutually exclusive. In fact, they believe that a work place that creates a sense of fun makes it easier to recruit quality workers and encourages them to be more productive and more customer-oriented. "Healthy and sustainable organizations focus on the fundamentals: quality, service, fiscal responsibility, leadership—but they didn't forget to add fun to that formula," says Leslie Yerkes, a consultant and author.[40] At Interface Software, an Oak Brook, Illinois provider of CRM software, the company's Ambassador of Fun, Jodi Wasserman, recently coordinated a "Trading Workspaces" event based on the television show *Trading Spaces* in which employees redecorated each other's workspaces.[41]

Engagement. Employees who are fully engaged in their work take pride in making valuable contributions to the organization's success and derive personal satisfaction from doing so. Although engaged employees are a key ingredient in superior business performance, just 29 percent of employees in North America are fully engaged in their work. Nearly 20 percent of them actually are disengaged.[42] What can managers do to improve employee engagement?

- Constantly communicate the purpose and vision of the organization and why it matters.
- Challenge employees to learn and advance in their careers and give them the resources and the incentives to do so.
- Create a culture that encourages and rewards engagement.

Diversity. Companies with appealing cultures not only accept cultural diversity in their workforces, but they also embrace it, actively seeking out workers with different backgrounds. Today businesses must recognize that a workforce that has a rich mix of cultural diversity gives a company more talent, skills, and abilities from which to draw. A study of the demographics of the United States quickly reveals a steady march toward an increasingly diverse population. In fact, demographic trends suggest that by 2050, African-Americans, Asians, Hispanics, and other non-white groups will comprise nearly one-half of the U.S. population (see Figure 16.2).[43] For companies to remain relevant in this environment, their workforces must reflect this diversity. Who is better equipped to deal with a diverse, multicultural customer base than a diverse, multicultural work force?

Integrity. Employees want to work for companies that stand for honesty and integrity. They do not want to check their own personal values systems at the door when they report to work. Indeed, many workers take pride in the fact that they work for companies that are ethical and socially responsible. People want to work for a company that makes a difference in the world rather than merely making a product or providing a service.

Participative Management. Today's workers do not respond well to the autocratic management styles of yesteryear. Company owners and managers must learn to trust and empower employees at all levels of the organization to make decisions and to take the actions they need to do their jobs well. A recent study by consulting firm McKinsey and Company reports a strong

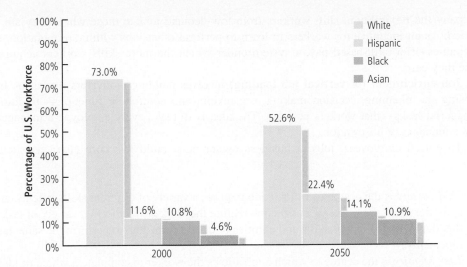

FIGURE 16.2

Composition of U.S. Workforce

Source: Jennifer Cheeseman Day, "Population Profile of the United States," U. S. Census Bureau, July 8, 2008, http://www.census.gov/population/www/popprofile/natproj.html.

correlation among the quality of a decision, clarity concerning the person responsible for implementing the decision, and that person's involvement in the decision-making process.[44]

Learning Environment. Progressive companies encourage and support lifelong learning among their employees. They are willing to invest in their employees, improving their skills and helping them to reach their full potential. These companies are magnets for the best and the brightest young workers, who know that to stay at the top of their fields, they must always be learning.

> Ron Huston, CEO of Advanced Circuits, an Aurora, Colorado company that makes printed circuit boards, understands the importance of training in the journey toward continuous improvement. In addition to their certification training, every employee receives two hours of training each month on topics that range from technical topics to management skills. The company also encourages employees to cross-train, learning job skills in other departments. "We want the best employees here, and the only way to do that is to give your employees the tools to be the best," says human resource manager Julie Olson.[45]

ENTREPRENEURIAL PROFILE

Ron Huston: Advanced Circuits

Job Design

Managers have learned that the job itself and the way it is designed is an important factor in a company's ability to attract and retain quality workers. In some companies, work is organized on the principle of **job simplification,** breaking the work down into its simplest form and standardizing each task, as in an assembly line operation. The scope of jobs organized in such a way is extremely narrow, resulting in impersonal, monotonous, and boring work that creates little challenge or motivation for workers. Job simplification invites workers to "check their brains at the door" and offers them little opportunity for excitement, enthusiasm, or pride in their work. The result can be apathetic, unmotivated workers who don't care about quality, customers, or costs.

To break this destructive cycle, some companies have redesigned workers' jobs. The following strategies are common: job enlargement, job rotation, job enrichment, flextime, job sharing, and flexplace.

Job enlargement (or **horizontal job loading**) adds more tasks to a job to broaden its scope. For instance, rather than an employee simply mounting four screws in computers coming down an assembly line, a worker might assemble, install and test the entire motherboard (perhaps as part of a team). The idea is to make the job more varied and to allow employees to perform a more complete unit of work.

Job rotation involves cross-training employees so they can move from one job in the company to others, giving them a greater number and variety of tasks to perform. As employees learn other jobs within an organization, both their skills and their understanding of the company's purpose and processes rise. Cross-trained workers are more valuable because they give a

job simplification

the type of job design that breaks work down into its simplest form and standardizes each task.

job enlargement (or horizontal job loading)

the type of job design that adds more tasks to a job to broaden its scope.

job rotation

the type of job design that involves cross-training employees so they can move from one job in the company to others, giving them a greater number and variety of tasks to perform.

company the flexibility to shift workers from low-demand jobs to those where they are most needed. As an incentive for workers to learn to perform other jobs within an operation, some companies offer skill-based pay, a system under which the more skills workers acquire, the more they earn.

job enrichment (or vertical job loading)
the type of job design that involves building motivators into a job by increasing the planning, decision making, organizing, and controlling functions workers perform.

Job enrichment (or vertical job loading) involves building motivators into a job by increasing the planning, decision making, organizing, and controlling functions—traditionally managerial tasks—that workers perform. The idea is to make every employee a manager—at least a manager of his own job.

To enrich employees' jobs, a business owner must build five core characteristics into them:

- *Skill variety* is the degree to which a job requires a variety of different skills, talents, and activities from the worker. Does the job require the worker to perform a variety of tasks that demand a variety of skills and abilities or does it force him to perform the same task repeatedly?
- *Task identity* is the degree to which a job allows the worker to complete a whole or identifiable piece of work. Does the employee build an entire piece of furniture (perhaps as part of a team) or does he merely attach four screws?
- *Task significance* is the degree to which a job substantially influences the lives or work of others—employees or final customers. Does the employee get to deal with customers, either internal or external? One effective way to establish task significance is to put employees in touch with customers so they can see how customers use the product or service they make.
- *Autonomy* is the degree to which a job gives a worker the freedom, independence, and discretion in planning and performing tasks. Does the employee make decisions affecting his work or must he rely on someone else to "call the shots"?
- *Feedback* is the degree to which a job gives the worker direct, timely information about the quality of his performance. Does the job give employees feedback about the quality of their work or does the product (and all information about it) simply disappear after it leaves the worker's station?

A study conducted by researchers at the University of New Hampshire and the Bureau of Labor Statistics concludes that employees of companies that use job enrichment principles are more satisfied than those who work in jobs designed using principles of simplification.[46]

flextime
an arrangement under which employees work a normal number of hours but have flexibility about when they start and stop work.

Flextime is an arrangement under which employees work a normal number of hours but have flexibility about when they start and stop work. Most flextime arrangements require employees to build their work schedules around a set of "core hours"—such as 10 a.m. to 2 p.m., but give them the freedom to set their schedules outside of those core hours. For instance, one worker might choose to come in at 7 a.m. and leave at 3 p.m. to attend her son's soccer game, and another may work from 11 a.m. to 7 p.m. Flextime not only raises worker morale, but it also makes it easier for companies to attract high-quality young workers who want rewarding careers without sacrificing their lifestyles. In addition, companies using flextime schedules often experience lower levels of tardiness, turnover, and absenteeism.

ENTREPRENEURIAL PROFILE

Sarah Novotny: Blue Gecko

Blue Gecko, a Seattle-based company that provides database services, uses technology to give its employees the flexibility to set their work schedules and locations. "Most of our work requires only an Internet connection and focus," says co-founder Sarah Novotny. Offering flextime helps her employees keep their work and their lives in balance and gives her company access to a larger pool of more qualified applicants.[47]

Flextime is becoming an increasingly popular job design strategy. A recent survey by Families and Work Institute found that 79 percent of the nation's workers have flexible schedules, up from 68 percent in 1998.[48] The number of companies using flextime is likely to continue to grow as companies find recruiting capable, qualified full-time workers more difficult and as technology makes working from a dedicated office space less important. Research shows that when considering job offers, candidates, particularly members of Generation Y, weigh heavily the flexibility of the work schedule companies offer.

Job sharing is a work arrangement in which two or more people share a single full-time job. For instance, two college students might share the same 40-hour-a-week job, one working mornings and the other working afternoons. Salary and benefits are prorated between the workers sharing a job. Because job sharing is a simple solution to the growing challenge of life-and-work balance, it is becoming more popular. Companies already using it are finding it easier to recruit and retain qualified workers. "Employers get the combined strengths of two people, but they only have to pay for one," says one hotel sales manager, herself a job sharer.[49]

Flexplace is a work arrangement in which employees work at a place other than the traditional office, such as a satellite branch closer to their homes or, in many cases, at home. Flexplace is an easy job design strategy for companies to use because of **telecommuting.** Using modern communication technology such as Wi-Fi, smart phones, texting, e-mail, and portable computers, employees have more flexibility in choosing where they work. Today, it is quite simple for workers to connect electronically to their workplaces (and to all of the people and the information there) from practically anywhere on the planet. According to a study by information technology provider CDW-G, 36 percent of private sector companies allow telecommuting, and 14 percent of private sector employees are telecommuters.[50] Telecommuting employees get the flexibility they seek, and companies reap many benefits as well, including improved employee morale, less absenteeism, lower turnover, higher productivity, and more satisfied, more loyal employees. Studies show that telecommuting can reduce employee turnover by 20 percent and increase productivity between 15 percent and 20 percent.[51]

job sharing
a work arrangement in which two or more people share a single full-time job.

flexplace
a work arrangement in which employees work at a place other than the traditional office, such as a satellite branch closer to their homes or at home.

telecommuting
an arrangement in which employees working remotely use modern communications equipment to connect electronically to their workplaces.

Fourteen of 23 employees at MindWave Research, a market research company in Austin, Texas, telecommute either all or most of the time. For a total cost of $30,000, the company installed in their home offices fast computers, reliable, high-speed Internet connections to the company's central computer, and Web cameras for video conferencing. Because of telecommuting, Jonathan Hilland, CEO of the $5 million company, was able to move MindWave's office to a smaller space, saving $7,000 per month in rent.[52]

ENTREPRENEURIAL PROFILE

Jonathan Hilland:
MindWave Research

Rewards and Compensation

Another important aspect of creating a culture that attracts and retains quality workers is establishing a robust system of rewards and compensation. The rewards an employee gets from the job itself are intrinsic rewards, but managers have at their disposal a wide variety of extrinsic rewards (those outside the job itself) to attract, retain, and motivate workers. The keys to using rewards to motivate are linking them to performance and tailoring them to the needs and characteristics of the workers. Entrepreneurs must base rewards and compensation on what is really important to their employees. For instance, to a technician making $25,000 a chance to earn a $3,000 performance bonus would most likely be a powerful motivator. To an executive earning $175,000 a year, it may not be.

Getty Images Inc. RF

Telecommuting reduces employee turnover and increases productivity.

One of the most popular rewards is money. Cash is an effective motivator—up to a point. Simple performance bonuses are a common reward at many companies. The closer the bonus payment is to the action that prompted it, the more effective it will be.

ENTREPRENEURIAL PROFILE

Robert Verdun: Computer Facility Integration

pay-for-performance compensation system
a compensation system in which employees' pay depends on how well they perform their jobs.

profit-sharing plan
a reward system in which employees receive a portion of the company's profits.

open book management
a system in which entrepreneurs share openly their companies' financial results with employees.

At Computer Facility Integration (CFI), a technology installation company in Southfield, Michigan, CEO Robert Verdun pays his 75 employees bonuses at the end of every month in which they meet specific performance targets. "We clearly state what everyone should be achieving, and we reward people accordingly," he says. CFI's sales are growing at 30 percent per year, and its employee turnover rate is just 4 percent per year, compared to the industry average of 30 percent.[53]

Other companies have moved to **pay-for-performance compensation systems,** in which employees' pay depends on how well they perform their jobs. In other words, extra productivity equals extra pay. By linking employees' compensation directly to the company's financial performance, a business owner increases the likelihood that workers will achieve performance targets that are in their best interest and in the company's best interest. Pay-for-performance systems work only when employees see a clear connection between their performance and their pay, however. That's where small businesses have an advantage over large businesses. Because they work for small companies, employees can see more clearly the impact their performances have on the company's profitability and ultimate success than their counterparts at large corporations.

Some companies offer their employees financial rewards in the form of **profit-sharing plans** in which employees receive a portion of the company's profits. A few companies have gone even farther, coupling profit sharing plans with **open book management,** a system in which entrepreneurs share openly their companies' financial results with employees. The goal is teach employees how their job performances have a direct impact on profits and to give them an incentive for improving the company's bottom line. "Open book [management] gives everyone the chance to see what we need to do to succeed," says Jack Stack, CEO of SRC Holdings, a holding company of 26 employee-owned businesses, and a long-time advocate of open book management.[54]

ENTREPRENEURIAL PROFILE

Trish Karter: Dancing Deer Baking Company

Dancing Deer Baking Company, a Boston-based bakery that sells baked goods made from all-natural ingredients, uses open book management and distributes 15 percent of the company's after-tax net income to all of the company's 35 employees on a pro rata basis. Managers regularly present the details of the Dancing Deer's financial performance to employees. "We all rise and fall together," says Trish Karter, CEO and cofounder. Employees know that "if they're more productive and efficient, they see it at the end of the year in the profits and in their salaries."[55]

Dancing Deer Baking Company

Money isn't the only motivator business owners have at their disposal, of course. In fact, money tends to be only a short-term motivator. In addition to the financial compensation they provide, most companies offer their employees a wide array of benefits. In an economy in which they must compete aggressively for employees, entrepreneurs must recognize that compensation and benefits no longer follow a "one-size-fits-all" pattern. The diversity of today's workforce requires employers to be highly flexible and innovative with the compensation and benefits they provide. To attract and retain quality workers, creative entrepreneurs offer employees benefits designed to appeal to their employees' particular needs. This diversity has led to the popularity of **cafeteria benefit plans,** in which employers provide certain base benefits and then allocate a specific dollar amount for employees to select the benefits that suit their needs best. Beyond flexible benefits plans, many small companies are setting themselves apart from others by offering unique benefits, including the following:[56]

caferia benefit plan
a plan under which employers provide certain base benefits and then allocate a specific dollar amount for employees to select the benefits that suit their needs best.

- At its San Jose, California, headquarters, Cisco Systems Inc. operates a child care center for its employees' children, complete with Internet cameras so parents can connect to the Internet and check on their kids from work.
- Employees at eBay get a four-week paid sabbatical leave every five years to pursue some topic of interest to them.
- Google, the search engine company based in Mountain View, California, offers free organic food, laundry machines, a gym, massages, volleyball court, bike repairs and medical care—all onsite. "We provide many unusual benefits to our employees, but we are careful to consider the long-term advantages to the company of these benefits," explain cofounders Sergey Brin and Larry Page.

Many small business owners whose companies may not be able to afford benefits such as these find other ways to reward their employees, including vacation days on their birthdays, an occasional catered lunch (especially after completing a big project successfully), and free tickets to a local game, movie, or performance.

June Wilcox, founder of Adec Group, a Greenville, South Carolina-based company that provides customized software implementation services, recently celebrated the successful completion of a large project by giving her staff an afternoon off and treating them to a local baseball game. In addition, every quarter, employees take one day off to work together on a community service project.

ENTREPRENEURIAL PROFILE

June Wilcox: Adec Group

Besides the wages, salaries, and attractive benefits they use as motivators, creative entrepreneurs have discovered that intangible incentives can be more important sources of employee motivation. After an initial boost, money loses its impact as a motivator; it does not have a lasting motivational effect (which for small businesses, with their limited resources, is a plus). For many workers the most meaningful motivational factors are the simplest ones—praise, recognition, feedback, job security, promotions, and others—things that any small business, no matter how limited its budget, can do. When the economy is in a downturn, a business that can display its commitment to employees through a record of job security has a powerful tool to recruit good employees.

Praise is another simple yet powerful motivational tool. People enjoy getting praise, especially from a manager or business owner; it's just human nature. As Mark Twain said, "I can live for two months on a good compliment." Praise is an easy and inexpensive reward for employees producing extraordinary work. A short note to an employee for a job well done costs practically nothing, yet it can be a potent source of motivation. The owner of one company who wrote short notes of appreciation on Post-Its to each of his employees was amazed at how much his simple gesture meant to them. How often have you had an employer say "thank you" for a job you performed well?

Because they lack the financial resources of bigger companies, small business owners must be more creative when it comes to giving rewards that motivate workers. In many cases, however, using rewards other than money gives small businesses an advantage because they usually have more impact on employee performance over time. Rewards do not have to be expensive to be effective, and managers are not the only ones who can give them. At Interface Software, the

Managing a Multigenerational Workforce

The workforce in the United States is undergoing a significant transformation as a wave of Baby Boomers retires and members of Generations X and Y take their places. In fact, Generation Y now outnumber Baby Boomers, a major change from 2000 (see Figure 3). The new generation of workers offers many advantages to the entrepreneurs who employ them, but they also pose many challenges for entrepreneurs who are not prepared to manage them properly. What factors and expectations set Generation Y apart from those from Generation X and the Baby Boomers who entered the workforce before them?

- Gen Y workers have more opportunities to switch careers, and they take advantage of those opportunities often. Employers who expect this generation of workers to stay with one company for decades will be disappointed; this generation of workers simply does not have the job loyalty that Baby Boomers demonstrated.
- They expect to have input at work and want to change the companies at which they work for the better. Gen Y workers know that they have a great deal of knowledge to bring to their employers, and they expect to apply it. Smart employers give them plenty of chances to have input into decisions at work.
- Gen Y workers do not respond to traditional command-and-control style of management. They expect an environment built on participative management.
- They are very comfortable with technology and social networking. This generation of workers has grown up with technology, which they expect to use on the job. Texting, posting tweets, writing blogs, and checking their FaceBook pages are part of their normal routine. "They're quick learners and are quick to put together information," says one Generation Y expert.

- They do not expect to be chained to their desks. With laptops, wireless Internet, and Smart phones, they are accustomed to accomplishing tasks remotely from almost anywhere.
- Generation Y workers expect not only financial rewards from their work but also personal and social rewards as well. They want to know that what they do makes a difference.
- They expect companies to provide flexible work arrangements to allow them to achieve work-life balance. They prefer to work for companies that offer flextime, telecommuting, job sharing, and other flexible work arrangements.
- They decide where they want to live *first* and then focus on finding a job there. A recent survey of Gen Y'ers reports the most important work considerations are: salary, benefits, opportunities for career growth, and company location.
- They expect instant communication and feedback on their performance. For Generation Y, e-mail often is too slow. They are accustomed to instant messaging and texting.
- They expect to contribute to the company, but they expect the company to help them grow and learn. Companies that expose new hires to various assignments, work situations, and job content have an advantage in keeping them and keeping them motivated. After Ken Sawka, owner of Outward Insights, a small consulting firm in Burlington, Massachusetts, hired a Generation Y MBA graduate, he created a six-month training program that included attendance at professional conferences and one-on-one mentoring sessions with Sawka. He took the time to learn the types of assignments that interested his new hire, assigned him to them, and over time increased the complexity and the responsibility of each one. "It's worked well," says Sawka. "His impact and performance project to project are improving steadily."
- Gen Y workers prefer casual dress over business attire. Only 4 percent of Generation Y workers say that they prefer traditional business attire. To avoid problems, business owners should set some basic ground rules about the types of dress that are appropriate for work.

FIGURE 16.3

U.S. Workforce by Generation

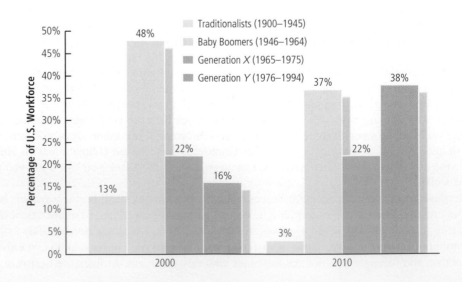

The table below provides some helpful insight into managing this multigenerational workforce.

1. Does the summary provided here reflect accurately the expectations that you have for your career? Explain.
2. What other insights can you provide about members of Generation Y in the workforce and how they compare to Baby Boomers and members of Generation X?
3. Work with a team of your classmates to develop a list of suggestions to help current business owners attract, retain, and motivate members of Generation Y. Why is doing so important to business owners?

Source: Based on Andrew Tilin, "What Is a Millennial?" *BNET Briefing*, http://www.bnet.com/2403-13059_23-201716.html; "Innovating Human Resources," BrainReactions, Janaury 16, 2007, pp. 4–7; Don Tapscott, "How to Hire the Net Generation," *Business Week*, November 22, 2008, http://www.businessweek.com/technology/content/nov2008/tc20081121_82 8725.htm; Stephanie Armour, "Generation Y: They've Arrived at Work with a New Attitude," *USA Today*, November 6, 2005, http://www.usatoday.com/money/workplace/2005-11-06-gen-y_x.htm; Chris Pentilla, "Talent Scout," *Entrepreneur*, July 2008, pp. 19–20.

Workplace Issue	Baby Boomers (1946-1964)	Generation X (1965-1975)	Generation Y (1976-1994)
Compensation	Long-term view because of long-term focus and loyalty to company	Impatient for rewards. Question job security and want rewards now	Salary is important, but so are flexible work arrangements. Expect performance-based pay
Technology	Do not trust technology. Somewhat resistance to the latest technology	Techno-savvy. Want to know and use the latest technology	Extremely comfortable with technology. Expect to use the latest gadgets on the job and are accustomed to interactivity
View of job hopping	Leads to loss of seniority and status. Harmful to future opportunities	Essential to building an impressive résumé	Expected. Key to pursuing multiple careers at the same time
Preferred management structure	Accepting of hierarchical structure. Comfortable with the chain of command	Prefer nonhierarchical, participatory, and democratic structure	Resistant to hierarchy. Team-oriented. Expect to be involved in decisions. Willing to skirt chain of command to be heard
Learning orientation	Not essential to job satisfaction	Prefer learning and developing new skills	Learning and developing new skills are essential. Hungry for information
Job loyalty	Loyal to company. Accustomed to putting in long hours and subordinating personal lives for career	Loyal to themselves. More loyal to their work team than to the company	Loyal to themselves, family, friends, and community. Expect to change companies and careers repeatedly
Attitude toward change	Resistant. Less flexible	Change is good.	Embrace change enthusiastically. Highly adaptable and flexible
Core Values	Optimism, hard work, involvement, loyalty	Diversity, fun, self reliance, pragmatism	Optimism, social responsibility, diversity, confidence

LO 4

Describe the steps in developing a management succession plan for a growing business that will allow a smooth transition of leadership to the next generation.

CRM software development company, employees hand out STAR (Special Thanks and Recognition) cards that are redeemable for free merchandise to coworkers who go above and beyond the call of duty in their jobs. An employee team selects a weekly winner from the nominees, and every Monday morning that person receives a special glass trophy and a blue ribbon at his or her workspace.[57]

Management Succession: Passing the Torch of Leadership

More than 90 percent of all companies in the United States are family-owned, and their contributions to the U.S. economy are significant. They create 64 percent of the nation's gross domestic product (GDP) and employ 62 percent of the private sector workforce. Not all family-owned businesses are small, however; 37 percent of *Fortune 500* companies are family businesses. Family-owned companies such as Wal-Mart, Ford, Mars, and Gap employ thousands of people and generate billions of dollars in annual revenue. Family firms also have created 80 percent of the U.S. economy's net new jobs over the last two decades.[58]

Unfortunately, the stumbling block for most family businesses is management succession. Just when they are ready to make the transition from one generation of leaders to the next, family businesses are most vulnerable. Nearly 70 percent of first-generation businesses fail to survive into the second generation; of those that do survive, only 12 percent make it to the third generation, and just 3 percent make it to the fourth generation and beyond.[59] As a result, the average life expectancy of a family business is 24 years, although some last *much* longer.[60] For instance, the oldest family business in the world is Houshi Onsen, an inn and spa that was founded in Komatsu, Japan in 718 by Gengoro Sasakiri. The forty-sixth generation of Sasakiri's descendants operate the business today.[61]

The primary causes of family businesses' lack of continuity are inadequate estate planning, failure to create a management succession plan, and lack of funds to pay estate taxes.[62] In addition, sibling rivalries, fights over control of the business, and personality conflicts often lead to nasty battles that can tear families apart and destroy once-thriving businesses. The best way to avoid deadly turf battles and conflicts is to develop a succession plan for the company. Numerous studies have found the existence of a positive relationship between the existence of a management succession plan and the longevity of family businesses.

ENTREPRENEURIAL PROFILE

Mark Gunlogson: Moutain Madness

Mountain Madness, a Seattle-based mountain guide service, nearly went out of business because there was no succession plan in place after its founder Scott Fischer died in a climbing accident on Mount Everest. Christine Boskoff, a corporate dropout and enthusiastic climber, purchased the business in 1997, revived it, and created a succession plan that named long-time employee Mark Gunlogson as her successor. When Boskoff was killed in an avalanche while climbing in China in 2006, Gunlogson assumed leadership of the company and continues its legacy as one of the premier guide services in the world.[63]

Although business founders inevitably want their businesses to survive them and almost 81 percent intend to pass them on to family members, they seldom support their intentions with a plan to accomplish that goal. Just 29 percent of family business owners have prepared written management succession plans.[64] Often, the reason for failing to develop a succession plan is that the entrepreneur is unwilling to make tough, and potentially disruptive, family-oriented decisions that require selecting the successor. Family feuds often erupt over who is (and is not) selected as the successor in the family business.

Most of the family businesses in existence today were started after World War II, and their founders are ready to pass the torch of leadership on to the next generation. Experts estimate that by 2055, $41 trillion in wealth will be transferred from one generation to the next, much of it through family businesses.[65] For these companies to have a smooth transition from one generation to the next, they must develop management succession plans. Succession planning reduces the tension and stress created by these conflicts by gradually "changing the guard." A well-developed succession plan is like the smooth, graceful exchange of a baton between runners in a relay race. The new runner still has maximum energy; the concluding runner has already spent her energy by running at maximum speed. The athletes never come to a stop to exchange the baton; instead, the handoff takes place on the move. The race is a skillful blend of the talents of all team members; the exchange of leadership is so smooth and powerful that the business never falters but accelerates, fueled by a new source of energy at each leg of the race.

HOW TO DEVELOP A MANAGEMENT SUCCESSION PLAN   Creating a succession plan involves the following steps:

Step 1. Select the successor. There comes a time for even the most dedicated company founder to step down from the helm of the business and hand the reins over to the next generation. Between 2008 and 2018, 12 million business owners will retire from their companies, looking either to sell them or hand them over to the next generation.[66] Unfortunately, only 41 percent of family business owners have identified their successors.[67]

Entrepreneurs should never assume that their children want to take control of the family business, however. It is critical to remember at this juncture in the life of a business that children do not necessarily inherit their parents' entrepreneurial skills and interests. By leveling with the children about the business and their options regarding a family succession, the owner will know which heirs, if any, are willing to assume leadership of the business.

When naming a successor, merit is a better standard to use than birth order. When considering a successor, an entrepreneur should consider taking the following actions:

- Make it clear to every family member involved that he or she is not required to join the business on a full-time basis. Family members' goals, ambitions, and talents should be foremost in their career decisions.
- Do not assume that a successor must always come from within the family. Simply being born into a family does *not* guarantee that a person will make a good business leader.
- Give family members the opportunity to work outside the business first to learn firsthand how others conduct business. Working for others allows them to develop knowledge, confidence, and credibility before stepping back into the family business. Seventy percent of the successors who have been identified have full-time work experience outside the family business.[68]

One of the worst mistakes entrepreneurs can make is to postpone naming a successor until just before they are ready to step down. The problem is especially acute when more than one family member works for the company and is interested in assuming leadership of it. Sometimes founders avoid naming successors because they don't want to hurt the family members who are not chosen to succeed them. However, both the business and the family will be better off if, after observing the family members as they work in the business, the founder picks a successor based on that person's skills and abilities.

ENTREPRENEURIAL PROFILE_____

Irwin & Paul Jacobs: Qualcomm

Qualcomm co-founder Irwin Jacobs made it clear that his oldest son, Paul, would be his successor as CEO of the highly successful wireless communications company when he stepped down. Even though Paul took over the CEO slot at just 42, he already had earned a PhD in electrical engineering and had logged 18 years in the family business. Before assuming the role of CEO, the younger Jacobs had managed several divisions in the company and had played a key role in developing some of Qualcomm's key technologies. "Growing up in the company...allowed me to get into very significant positions at a relatively young age," says Paul. "I have a lot of experience even though I'm not very old."[69]

Step 2. Create a survival kit for the successor. Once she identifies a successor, an entrepreneur should prepare a survival kit and then brief the future leader on its contents, which should include all of the company's critical documents (wills, trusts, insurance policies, financial statements, bank accounts, key contracts, corporate bylaws, and so forth). The founder should be sure that the successor reads and understands all the relevant documents in the kit. Other important steps the owner should take to prepare the successor to take over leadership of the business include:

- Create a strategic analysis for the future. Working with the successor, entrepreneurs should identify the primary opportunities and the challenges facing the company and the requirements for meeting them. The goal is to help the successor understand the company's history and traditions while viewing it through the lens of the current and future business environment.
- Explain the strategies of the business and its key success factors.
- Discuss the values and philosophy of the business and how they have inspired and influenced past actions.
- Discuss the people in the business and their strengths and weaknesses.
- Make a list of the firm's most important customers and its key suppliers or vendors and review the history of all dealings with the parties on both lists.
- Develop a job description by taking an inventory of the activities involved in leading the company. This analysis can show successors those activities on which they should be spending most of their time.
- Document as much process knowledge—"how we do things and why"—as possible. After many years in their jobs, business owners are not even aware of their vast reservoirs of knowledge. For them, making decisions is a natural part of their business lives. They do it effortlessly because they have so much knowledge and experience. It is easy to forget that a successor will not have the benefit of those years of experience unless the founder communicates it.

Step 3. Groom the successor. Typically, founders transfer their knowledge to their successors gradually over time. The discussions that set the stage for the transition of leadership are time consuming and require openness by both parties. In fact, grooming a successor is the founder's greatest teaching and development responsibility, and it takes time and deliberate effort. To create ability and confidence in a successor, a founder must be:

- Patient, realizing that the transfer of power is gradual and evolutionary and that the successor should earn responsibility and authority one step at a time until the final transfer of power takes place.
- Willing to accept that the successor will make mistakes.
- Skillful at using the successor's mistakes as a teaching tool.
- An effective communicator and an especially tolerant listener.
- Capable of establishing reasonable expectations for the successor's performance.
- Able to articulate the keys to the successor's successful performance.

Grooming a successor can begin at an early age simply by involving children in the family business and observing which ones have the greatest ability and interest in the company.

ENTREPRENEURIAL PROFILE

Jay Alexander: Alexander Machinery

At age nine, Jay Alexander started going to work with his father at the family business, Alexander Machinery, a maker of textile and road construction equipment. At 11, Jay approached his father and asked for a job in the company, beginning a long succession of jobs over the next 12 years. "I've worked practically every job in the company," says Jay. "I've never worked anywhere else." When Jay's father, Bill, decided to step away from the business he founded, Jay was the natural choice as his successor, although Jay's sister also works for the company. "This business has come naturally to him," says Bill.[70]

Step 4: Promote an environment of trust and respect. Another priceless gift a founder can leave a successor is an environment of trust and respect. Trust and respect on the part of the founder and others fuel the successor's desire to learn and excel and build the successor's confidence in making decisions. Developing a competent successor over a five-to-ten-year period is realistic. Empowering the successor by gradually delegating responsibilities creates an environment in which all parties can objectively view the growth and development of the successor. Customers, creditors, suppliers, and staff members can gradually develop confidence in the successor. The final transfer of power is not a dramatic, wrenching change but a smooth, coordinated passage. Founders must be careful at this stage to avoid the "meddling retiree syndrome" in which they continue to report for work after they have officially step down and take control of matters that are no longer their responsibility. Doing so undermines a successor's authority and credibility among workers quickly.

Step 5: Cope with the financial realities of estate and gift taxes. The final step in developing a workable management succession plan is structuring the transition to minimize the impact of estate, gift, and inheritance taxes on family members and the business. Entrepreneurs who fail to consider the impact of these taxes may force their heirs to sell a successful business just to pay the estate's tax bill. Currently, without proper estate planning, an entrepreneur's family members will incur a painful tax bite that can be as high as 45 percent when they inherit the business (see Table 16.7). Entrepreneurs should be actively engaged in estate planning no later than age 45; those who start businesses early in their lives or whose businesses grow rapidly may need to begin as early as age 30. A variety of options exist that may prove to be helpful in reducing the estate tax liability. Each operates in a different fashion, but their objective remains the same: to remove a portion of business owners' assets out of their estates so that when they die, those assets will not be subject to estate taxes. Many of these estate planning tools need time to work their magic, so the key is to put them in place early on in the life of the business.

buy-sell agreement
a contract among co-owners of a business stating that each agrees to buy out the others in case of the death or disability of one.

BUY-SELL AGREEMENT One of the most popular estate planning techniques is the buy-sell agreement. A **buy-sell agreement** is a contract that co-owners often rely on to ensure the continuity of a business. In a typical arrangement, the co-owners create a contract stating that each agrees to buy the others out in case of the death or disability of one. That way, the heirs of the deceased or disabled

TABLE 16.7 Changes in the Estate and Gift Taxes

After years of complaints from family business owners, Congress finally overhauled the often punishing structures of estate and gift taxes. The federal estate tax is actually interwoven with the gift tax, the impact of the two taxes began differing in 2004. The estate tax originally was scheduled to be repealed in 2010, but under current proposals, it will remain in place. The following table shows the exemptions and the minimum tax rates for the estate and gift taxes as they currently stand:

Year	Estate Tax Exemption	Gift Tax Exemption	Maximum Tax Rate
2001	$675,000	$675,000	55%
2002	$1 million	$1 million	50%
2003	$1 million	$1 million	49%
2004	$1.5 million	$1 million	48%
2005	$1.5 million	$1 million	47%
2006	$2 million	$1 million	46%
2007	$2 million	$1 million	45%
2008	$2 million	$1 million	45%
2009	$3.5 million	$1 million	45%
2010	Tax repealed*	$1 million	35% (gifts only)
2011	$1 million*	$1 million	55%
2012 and after	$3.5 million	$1 million	45%

However the federal laws governing estate taxes may change over the next few years, entrepreneurs whose businesses have been successful must not neglect estate planning. Even though the federal estate tax burden has eased somewhat, many states have *increased* their estate tax rates.

*Current proposals would retain the estate tax in 2010 and establish an estate tax exemption of $3.5 million, a gift tax exemption of $1 million, and a maximum tax rate of 35 percent. These exemptions and rates would apply in 2011 and beyond.

owner can "cash out" of the business while leaving control of the business in the hands of the remaining owners. The buy-sell agreement specifies a formula for determining the value of the business at the time the agreement is to be executed. One problem with buy-sell agreements is that the remaining co-owners may not have the cash available to buy out the disabled or deceased owner. To resolve this issue, many businesses purchase life and disability insurance for each of the owners in amounts large enough to cover the purchase price of their respective shares of the business.

Larry Jaffe and Bob Gross, co-owners of Jaffe and Gross, a successful jewelry store in Dayton, Ohio, failed to create a buy-sell agreement backed by insurance for their business. When Gross died suddenly of a heart attack, Jaffe did not have enough cash to purchase Gross's share of ownership in the business. "Bob just assumed that I'd be Larry's partner and the business would go on," says Gross's widow. However, Gross's heirs, who inherited his shares of the business, had no interest in operating the jewelry store, and without a buy-sell agreement or a succession plan in place, the 27-year-old company folded. Jaffe has since launched his own jewelry store, Jaffe's Jewelers, but admits that things would have been much easier had he and Gross taken the time to create a succession plan.[71]

LIFETIME GIFTING The owner of a successful business may transfer money or stock to his or her children from the estate throughout his or her life. Current federal tax regulations allow individuals to make gifts of $13,000 per year, per parent, per recipient that are exempt from federal gift taxes. Each child is required to pay income taxes on the $13,000 gift he or she receives, but the children are usually in lower tax brackets than the giver. For instance, husband-and-wife business owners could give $1,560,000 worth of company stock to their three children and their spouses over a period of 10 years without incurring any estate or gift taxes at all. To be an effective estate planning strategy, lifetime gifting requires time to work, which means that business owners must create a plan for using it early on.

trust

a contract between a grantor (the company founder) and a trustee in which the grantor gives the trustee assets (e.g., company stock), which the trustee holds for the trust's beneficiaries (e.g., the grantor's heirs).

revocable trust

a trust that a grantor can change or revoke during his or her lifetime.

irrevocable trust

a trust in which a grantor cannot require the trustee to return the assets held in trust.

SETTING UP A TRUST A **trust** is a contract between a grantor (the company founder) and a trustee (generally a bank officer or an attorney) in which the grantor gives to the trustee legal title to assets (e.g., stock in the company), which the trustee agrees to hold for the beneficiaries (the founder's children). The beneficiaries can receive income from the trust, or they can receive the property in the trust, or both, at some specified time. Trusts can take a wide variety of forms, but two broad categories of trusts are available: revocable trusts and irrevocable trusts. A **revocable trust** is one that a grantor can change or revoke during his lifetime. Under present tax laws, however, the only trust that provides a tax benefit is an **irrevocable trust,** in which the grantor cannot require the trustee to return the assets held in trust. The value of the grantor's estate is lowered because the assets in an irrevocable trust are excluded from the value of the estate. However, an irrevocable trust places severe restrictions on the grantor's control of the property placed in the trust. Business owners use several types of irrevocable trusts to lower their estate tax liabilities:

- *Bypass trust.* The most basic type of trust is the bypass trust, which allows business owners to put assets worth up to $3,500,000 into a trust and to name their spouse as beneficiary of the trust on their death. The spouse receives the income from the trust throughout his or her life, but the principal in the trust goes to the couple's heirs free of estate taxes on the spouse's death. A bypass trust is particularly useful for couples who plan their estates together. By leaving assets to one another in bypass trusts, they can make sure that their assets are taxed only once between them. However, entrepreneurs should work with experienced attorneys to create bypass trusts because the IRS requires that they contain certain precise language to be valid.

  Many business owners combine a bypass trust with a qualified terminal interest property (QTIP) trust to minimize estate taxes. For instance, a business owner can set up a bypass trust for $3.5 million, establish a QTIP trust for the remainder of the estate, and name his children as beneficiaries of both trusts. When he dies, the assets of the QTIP trust go into his *spouse's* estate rather than his own estate, which can save thousands of dollars in estate taxes and generate income for the spouse during her lifetime. When the spouse dies, the value of the assets of the QTIP trust are include in her estate, but the assets themselves go to the children just as the business owner directed.

- *Irrevocable life insurance trust (ILIT).* This type of trust allows business owners to keep the proceeds of a life insurance policy out of their estates and away from estate taxes, freeing up that money to pay the taxes on the remainder of their estates. To get the tax benefit, business owners must be sure that the business or the trust (rather than the individuals themselves) owns the insurance policy. The primary disadvantage of an irrevocable life insurance trust is that if the owner dies within three years of establishing it, the insurance proceeds *do* become part of the estate and *are* subject to estate taxes. Because the trust is irrevocable, it cannot be amended or rescinded once it is established. Like most trusts, ILITs must meet stringent requirements to be valid, and entrepreneurs should use experienced attorneys to create them.

- *Irrevocable asset trust.* An irrevocable asset trust is similar to a life insurance trust except that it is designed to pass the assets (such as stock in a family business) in the parents' estate on to their children. The children do not have control of the assets while the parents are living, but they do receive the income from those assets. On the parents' death, the assets in the trust go to the children without being subjected to the estate tax.

- *Grantor retained annuity trust (GRAT).* A grantor retained annuity trust (GRAT) is a special type of irrevocable trust and has become one of the most popular tools for entrepreneurs to transfer ownership of a business while maintaining control over it and minimizing estate taxes. Under a GRAT, an owner can put property (such as company stock) in an irrevocable trust for a maximum of 10 years. While the trust is in effect, the grantor (owner) retains the voting power and receives the interest income from the property in the trust. At the end of the trust (not to exceed 10 years), the property passes to the beneficiaries (heirs). The beneficiaries are required to pay a gift tax on the value of the assets placed in the GRAT. However, the IRS taxes GRAT gifts only according to their discounted present value because the heirs did not receive use of the property while it was in trust. The primary disadvantage of using a GRAT in estate planning is that if the grantor dies during the life of the GRAT, its assets pass back into the grantor's estate. These assets then become subject to the full estate tax.

Establishing a trust requires meeting many specific legal requirements and is not something business owners should do on their own. It is much better to work with experienced attorneys, accountants, and financial advisors to create them. Although the cost of establishing a trust can be high, the tax savings they generate are well worth the expense.

ESTATE FREEZE An **estate freeze** minimizes estate taxes by having family members create two classes of stock for the business: (1) preferred voting stock for the parents and (2) nonvoting common stock for the children. The value of the preferred stock is frozen whereas the common stock reflects the anticipated increased market value of the business. Any appreciation in the value of the business after the transfer is not subject to estate taxes. However, the parent must pay gift taxes on the value of the common stock given to the children. The value of the common stock is the total value of the business less the value of the voting preferred stock retained by the parent. The parents also must accept taxable dividends at the market rate on the preferred stock they own.

estate freeze
a strategy that minimizes estate taxes by creating two classes of stock for a business: preferred voting stock for the parents and nonvoting common stock for the children.

FAMILY LIMITED PARTNERSHIP Creating a **family limited partnership (FLP)** allows business-owning parents to transfer their company to their children (and lower their estate taxes) while still retaining control over it for themselves. To create a family limited partnership, the parents (or parent) set up a partnership among themselves and their children. The parents retain the general partnership interest, which can be as low as 1 percent, and the children become the limited partners. As general partners, the parents control both the limited partnership and the family business. In other words, nothing in the way the company operates has to change. Over time, the parents transfer company stock into the limited partnership, ultimately passing ownership of the company to their children. One of the principal tax benefits of an FLP is that it allows discounts on the value of the shares of company stock the parents transfer into the limited partnership. Because a family business is closely held, shares of ownership in it, especially minority shares, are not as marketable as those of a publicly-held company. As a result, company shares transferred into the limited partnership are discounted at 20 to 50 percent of their full market value, producing a large tax savings for everyone involved. The average discount is 40 percent, but that amount varies based on the industry and the individual company involved. Because of their ability to reduce estate and gift taxes, family limited partnerships became one of the most popular estate planning tools in recent years.

family limited partnership
a strategy that allows business-owning parents to transfer their company to their children (lowering their estate taxes) while still retaining control over it for themselves.

Developing a succession plan and preparing a successor require a wide variety of skills, some of which the business founder will not have. That's why it is important to bring into the process experts when necessary. Entrepreneurs often call on their attorneys, accountants, insurance agents, and financial planners to help them build a succession plan that works best for their particular situations. Because the issues involved can be highly complex and charged with emotion, bringing in trusted advisors to help improves the quality of the process and provides an objective perspective.

Who's the (Next) Boss?

Red Rocket is a $150 million company that manufactures toy vehicles and is located on the outskirts of a large American city. The company, now in its second generation of family ownership, has been in existence since 1955 and has a workforce of 175 people, including a 25-members sales team that covers North America, Europe, and Australia. The managers are proud that the company is still family-owned and has always been profitable. They have dismissed numerous suggestions to take the company public and have worked hard to develop and maintain a strong management team with little employee turnover.

Sean Leeds, the patriarch and founder of Red Rocket, died in 1982 following a long bout with cancer. He founded the company having had a life-long, joyous relationship with toy cars and maintained that the enthusiasm in his role as chair of the research and development team in the company until his death. Sean and his wife, Mary, who still lives near company headquarters, had two children, Patrick and Anne.

Patrick, 57, is the current president and CEO of Red Rocket. Patrick took over the business in 1980 and has been managing it ever since. Patrick has an MBA in finance and also has an accounting degree from a prominent Midwestern university. He had four years of experience working in Europe prior to joining Red Rocket. Patrick holds 100% of Red Rocket's voting stock, which gives him complete control over the company.

Patrick is married to Kelly, who is Red Rocket's chief information officer. They have five children: Sheila (31), Robert (29), twins Courtney and James (27), and Ted (23). Only Robert and James, both of whom have worked at Red Rocket for several years, are being groomed as future leaders of the business.

Both Robert and James are single and have been involved in the company since they were children. Robert is quiet and reserved, thoughtful, and well-respected; his background is in the management and accounting side of the business. Currently, he is in charge of the accounting and distribution departments. James is more outgoing with the quintessential sales personality and lots of energy. He leads the sales team and has been a member of the research and development team. Throughout their childhood, Robert and James were playful and competitive. They went to separate universities and had separate groups of friends. They rarely socialize together and don't have much in common other than the family business.

Patrick was caught off guard recently when Robert requested a breakfast meeting with him, during which he inquired about his father's management succession plans. During their conversation, Robert told Patrick that if he was not made president of the company within one year, he would leave and pursue his own

entrepreneurial venture. Patrick was not only completely surprised by his son's statement but also was shocked at the tone in which Robert delivered it.

A week later, James took his father aside during a family gathering and told him that if Robert became president of Red Rocket, he would leave the company. James went on to say that *he* should be made president and gave his father the same ultimatum as Robert: that if he were not made president within a year, he would leave the company. Patrick was shocked. He saw himself as too young to slow down or relinquish control of the company at age 57. He had always thought that his sons would run the company one day but not for another 10 to 15 years. Patrick did not know what to say to either of his sons because he never saw this dilemma coming.

1. How common is the problem that Patrick faces in other family businesses?
2. What do you think is the cause of the problem facing Patrick and Red Rocket?
3. What steps should Patrick and his family take to address the issue of management succession at Red Rocket? What do you predict will happen if they do not address the problem?

Source: Fredde Herz Brown, "Engines at the Ready," Family Firm Institute, http://www.ffi.org/default.asp?id=327&c002_ui=sa&c002_id=187. Reprinted with permission from The Family Firm Institute, Inc. All Rights Reserved.

Exit Strategies

LO 5

Explain the exit strategies available to entrepreneurs.

Most family business founders want their companies to stay within their families, but in some cases, maintaining family control is not practical. Sometimes no one in the next generation of family members has an interest in managing the company or has the necessary skills and experience to handle the job. In fact, 25 percent of business owners say that the next generation of family members lacks the competence to manage the family business successfully.[72] Under these circumstances, the founder must look outside the family for leadership if the company is to survive. Entrepreneurs who are planning to retire often use two strategies: sell to outsiders or sell to (non-family) insiders. We turn now to these two exit strategies.

Selling to Outsiders

As you learned in Chapter 5, selling a business to an outsider is no simple task. Done properly, it takes time, patience, and preparation to locate a suitable buyer, strike a deal, and make the transition. Advance preparation, maintaining accurate financial records, and timing are the keys to a successful sale. A straight sale may be best for those entrepreneurs who want to step down and turn the reins of the company over to someone else. However, selling a business outright is not an attractive exit strategy for those who want to stay on with the company or for those who want to surrender control of the company gradually rather than all at once.

ENTREPRENEURIAL PROFILE

Doris Christopher: The Pampered Chef

Doris Christopher launched The Pampered Chef, a company that sells quality kitchen tools through in-home demonstrations called cooking shows, from the basement of her suburban Chicago home in 1980 with a $3,000 loan. The Pampered Chef grew rapidly into a business with more than 12 million customers served by tens of thousands of independent Kitchen Consultants. In 2004, Christopher decided to retire and sold the company to Warren Buffet's Berkshire Hathaway for $700 million.[73]

Selling to Insiders

When entrepreneurs have no family members to whom they can transfer ownership or who want to assume the responsibilities of running a company, selling the business to employees is often the preferred option. In most situations, the options available to owners are a leveraged buyout and an employee stock ownership plan (ESOP).

LEVERAGED BUYOUTS In a **leveraged buyout (LBO),** managers and/or employees borrow money from a financial institution and pay the owner the total agreed-on price at closing; then they use the cash generated from the company's operations to pay off the debt. The drawback of this technique is that it creates a highly leveraged business. Because of the high levels of debt they take on, the new management has very little room for error. Too many management mistakes or a slowing economy has led many highly leveraged businesses into bankruptcy.

If properly structured, LBOs can be an attractive to both buyers and sellers. Because sellers get their money up-front, they do not incur the risk of loss if the buyers cannot keep the business operating successfully. The managers and employees who buy the company have a strong incentive to make sure the business succeeds because they own a piece of the action and some of their capital is at risk in the business. The result can be a highly motivated workforce that works hard and makes sure that the company operates efficiently.

EMPLOYEE STOCK OWNERSHIP PLANS (ESOPs) Unlike LBOs, **employee stock ownership plans (ESOPs)** allow employees and managers (that is, the future owners) to purchase the business gradually, which frees up enough cash to finance the venture's future growth. With an ESOP, employees contribute a portion of their salaries and wages over time toward purchasing shares of the company's stock from the founder until they own the company outright. (In leveraged ESOPs, the ESOP borrows the money to buy the owner's stock up front. Then, using employees' contributions, the ESOP repays the loan over time. Another advantage of a leveraged ESOP is that the principal and the interest the ESOP borrows to buy the business are tax deductible, which can save thousands or even millions of dollars in taxes.) Transferring ownership to employees through an ESOP is a long-term exit strategy that benefits everyone involved. The owner sells the business to the people he or she can trust the most—his or her managers and employees. The managers and employees buy a business they already know how to run successfully. In addition, because they own the company, the managers and employees have a huge incentive to see that it operates effectively and efficiently. One study of employee stock ownership plans in privately held companies found that the ESOPs increased sales, employment, and sales per employee by 2.4 percent a year.[74]

In 1951, Henry Carris founded Carris Reels, a company that manufactures reels for cable, wiring, and other products, in Rutland, Vermont, with two employees. The company was successful and grew rapidly in the post-war boom. In 1980, Henry's son, Bill, purchased the company from his father, who was retiring. In 1995, Bill began executing the succession plan that he had created and set up an ESOP that over the course of 10 to 15 years would purchase the growing company. He also shared his vision for the company's future with its future owners in a document that he created called The Long Term Plan. Carris Reels, which became 100 percent employee-owned in 2008, recently was named the ESOP Company of the Year by the ESOP Association. "Carris Reels is an example of the value and potential that employee ownership can bring to a company," says Michael Keeling, president of the ESOP Association. "The employee owners of Carris Reels strive to make their company stronger each day, and it shows in the work they do and the value they place on the people who make up their company."[75]

leveraged buyout (LBO)

a situation in which managers and/or employees borrow money from a financial institution to purchase a business; then they use the money from the company's operations to pay off the debt.

employee stock ownership plan (ESOP)

an arrangement in which employees and/or managers contribute a portion of their salaries and wages over time toward purchasing shares of a company's stock from the founder until they own the company outright.

ENTREPRENEURIAL PROFILE _____

Bill Carris: Carris Reels

Chapter Summary

1. **Explain the challenges involved in the entrepreneur's role as leader and what it takes to be a successful leader.**

   - Leadership is the process of influencing and inspiring others to work to achieve a common goal and then giving them the power and the freedom to achieve it.
   - Management and leadership are not the same, yet both are essential to a small company's success. Leadership without management is unbridled;

   management without leadership is uninspired. Leadership gets a small business going; management keeps it going.

2. **Describe the importance of hiring the right employees and how to avoid making hiring mistakes.**

   - The decision to hire a new employee is an important one for every business, but its impact is magnified many times in a small company. Every new hire a business owner makes determines the heights to which the company can climb—or the depths to which it will plunge.

- To avoid making hiring mistakes, entrepreneurs should: develop meaningful job descriptions and job specifications, plan and conduct an effective interview, and check references before hiring any employee.

3. Explain how to create a company culture and that encourages employee retention.

- Company culture is the distinctive, unwritten code of conduct that governs the behavior, attitudes, relationships, and style of an organization. Culture arises from an entrepreneur's consistent and relentless pursuit of a set of core values that everyone in the company can believe in. Small companies' flexible structures can be a major competitive weapon.
- Job design techniques for enhancing employee motivation include job enlargement, job rotation, job enrichment, flextime, job sharing, and flex-place (which includes telecommuting).
- Money is an important motivator for many workers, but not the only one. The key to using rewards such as recognition and praise and to motivate involves tailoring them to the needs and characteristics of the workers.

- Giving employees timely, relevant feedback about their job performances through a performance appraisal system can also be a powerful motivator.

4. Describe the steps in developing a management succession plan for a growing business that will allow a smooth transition of leadership to the next generation.

- As their companies grow, entrepreneurs must begin to plan for passing the leadership baton to the next generation well in advance. A succession plan is a crucial element in successfully transferring a company to the next generation. Preparing a succession plan involves five steps: (1) select the successor; (2) create a survival kit for the successor; (3) groom the successor; (4) promote an environment of trust and respect; and (5) cope with the financial realities of estate taxes.

5. Explain the exit strategies available to entrepreneurs.

- Family business owners wanting to step down from their companies can sell to outsiders or to insiders. Common tools for selling to insiders (employees or managers) include leveraged buyouts (LBOs) and employee stock ownership plans (ESOPs).

Discussion Questions

1. What is leadership? What is the difference between leadership and management?
2. What behaviors do effective leaders exhibit?
3. Why is it so important for small companies to hire the right employees? What can small business owners do to avoid making hiring mistakes?
4. What is a job description? A job specification? What functions do they serve in the hiring process?
5. Outline the procedure for conducting an effective interview.
6. What is company culture? What role does it play in a small company's success? What threats does rapid growth pose for a company's culture?
7. Explain the differences among job simplification, job enlargement, job rotation, and job enrichment. What impact do these different job designs have on workers?

8. Is money the "best" motivator? How do pay-for-performance compensation systems work? What other rewards are available to small business managers to use as motivators? How effective are they?
9. Why is it so important for a small business owner to develop a management succession plan? Why is it so difficult for most business owners to develop such a plan? What are the steps that are involved in creating a succession plan?
10. Briefly describe the options a small business owner wanting to pass the family business on to the next generation can take to minimize the impact of estate taxes.

Business PlanPro™   This chapter discusses the importance of people, their roles, and how they influence an organization. The Management section is where these issues are most often addressed in the business plan. This section of the plan captures the key information about your Management team, both its strengths and weaknesses. The Management section of the business plan also addresses other key personnel issues for the venture.

Business Plan Exercises

Review the Management section of your business plan and make certain that it addresses the important management and personnel issues for your venture. Check to see that your plan includes the relevant concepts presented in this chapter and captures those thoughts. Think about the business culture your are hoping to build. Assess the leadership abilities of your current management team. Are additional managers or other positions needed? Have you accounted for those new hires and the anticipated expenses associated with these additional employees? Does your plan address factors that will encourage retention of existing employees? Your plan may also benefit from succession planning or an exit strategy. Remember, you can add or modify topics of your choice within *Business Plan Pro*™ by right-clicking on the outline in the left-hand navigation of the page.

On the Web

Visit http://www.pearsonhighered.com/scarborough and review the links that are presented under the Web Destinations tab. You will find resources that address leadership issues, interviewing techniques, employee incentive programs, succession planning, exit strategies, and other topics that you may find of value. These areas may offer additional insight for the human resource and managerial aspects of your business that you may choose to incorporate into your business plan.

Sample Plans

Review an executive summary from a sample plan that you have found beneficial. You may also want to consider these options:

- Pegasus Sports
- Sagebrush Sam's
- Salvador's Inc.

Next, review the Management sections of these plans. Note how these plans present informaiton about their owners and their personnel. Incorporate relevant management and personnel informaiton into your plan.

In the Software

The chapters in this book address all key aspects of creating a business plan. The final section you will complete, and one that many consider to be the most important, is the executive summary. The executive summary is the first section presented, and your plan may be judged on its value and impact alone. Your executive summary should be no more than two pages—one is even better—and its intent is to capture the highlights of your plan. In addition to communicating important concepts and ideas about your plan, the executive summary should also include key financial forecasts along with brief summaries of key sections. A concise executive summary enables the reader to quickly grasp the essence of the plan for your business. This section should be compelling, allowing the reader to see your vision for the venture and motivate him or her to want to read the entire plan.

Building Your Business Plan

Write your executive summary in *Business Plan Pro*™. Remember, this section incorporates key highlights of information in the plan ahead. Show this executive summary to others and test its effectiveness in describing the most important ideas of your business plan. Remember, the executive summary should be the most powerful and convincing pages of your business plan—a written version of your elevator pitch. Does your executive summary accomplish that goal?

Beyond the Classroom....

1. Visit a local business that has experienced rapid growth in the past three years and ask the owner about the specific problems he or she had to face due to the organization's growth. How did the owner handle these problems? Looking back, what would he or she do differently?

2. Contact a local small business with at least 20 employees. Does the company have job descriptions and job specifications? What process does the owner use to hire a new employee? What questions does the owner typically ask candidates in an interview?

3. Ask the owner of a small manufacturing operation to give you a tour of his or her operation. During your tour, observe the way jobs are organized. To what extent does the company use the following job design concepts: job simplification? Job enlargement? Job rotation? Job enrichment? Flextime? Job sharing? Based on your observations, what recommendations would you make to the owner about the company's job design?

4. Find *Fortune*'s "100 Best Companies to Work For" issue. Read the profiles of the companies included on the list and develop a list of at least five ideas that you would like to incorporate into the company that you plan to launch.

5. Contact five small business owners about their plans for passing their businesses on to the next generation. Do they intend to pass the business along to a family member? Do they have a management succession plan? When do they plan to name a successor? Have they developed a plan for minimizing the effects of estate taxes? How many more years do they plan to work before retiring?

6. Entrepreneurs say that they have learned much about leadership from the movies! "Films beg to be interpreted and discussed," says one leadership consultant, "and from those discussions businesspeople come up with principles for their own jobs." A recent survey of small company CEOs by *Inc.* magazine* resulted in the following list of the best movies for leadership lessons: *Apollo 13* (1995), *The Bridge on the River Kwai* (1957), *Dead Poets Society* (1989), *Elizabeth* (1998), *Glengarry Glen Ross* (1992), *It's a Wonderful Life* (1946), *Norma Rae* (1979), *One Flew Over the Cuckoo's Nest* (1975), *Twelve Angry Men* (1957), and *Twelve O'Clock High* (1949). Rent one of these films and watch it with a group of your classmates. After viewing the movie, discuss the leadership lessons you learned from it and report the results to the other members of your class.

---

*Leigh Buchanan and Mike Hofman, "Everything I Know About Leadership, I Learned from the Movies," *Inc.*, March 2000, pp. 58–70.

Appendix

Think Archimedes
Business Plan

By Michelle Carl and
Andrew Turner

1.0 Executive Summary

The college planning industry became prominent in the early 1990s as competition among students intensified and tuition costs began skyrocketing. *Entrepreneur* recently rated the college planning industry as one of the top five most attractive market sectors for the next decade. Why? The U.S. education system is not serving its customers when "a third of students are leaving high school without a diploma,"[1] when "only 6.4% of [17-year-olds] can perform simple multistep problems such as calculating total repayment (principal plus interest) on a loan,"[2] and when "only about 1 in 17-year-olds can read and gain information from specialized text, for example the science section in the local newspaper."[3] These problems are not likely to be solved anytime soon by the system itself because the politics, bureaucracy, and unions involved in the decision-making process make it nearly impossible to implement the radical changes required to prepare students for the future. Furthermore, the long-standing giants in the private education industry fail to address the issue because they operate using the same assumptions as the school system. Although they claim to have much to offer—SAT prep, ACT prep, GMAT prep, LSAT prep—it's all the same thing: test preparation. Even if students' test scores improve as a result of these classes, they don't actually become more intelligent because learning test-taking strategies does *not* increase aptitude. Children don't need mental Band-aids; they need the ability to quickly learn on their own.

Charleston, South Carolina-based Think Archimedes fills the gaps of the incomplete curriculum in America by restoring the foundations of what a classic education once gave students: logic, rhetoric, and the ability to discuss mathematics in plain English. The future of our nation depends on the competency of its citizens, and Think Archimedes has the right people with the right solution at the right time to begin this transformative process.

Now is the ideal time for private education to capture a significant percentage of the market. Historically, tough economic cycles have been the best environments in which to introduce new business models because people are open to solutions that are outside the norm in a way they wouldn't be otherwise. We estimate the number of people nationally who are willing to pay for specialized education to be 7.25 million, of which 1.5 million are considered prime prospects. South Carolina's share of this market represents 116,000 and 24,000 respectively, providing plenty of opportunity to grow profitably from a grassroots, state level. Our goal is to garner 10% of the private education market share in South Carolina over the next three years.

About Us

First, a quick overview of four key terms:

College Advisor. A financial planner who specializes in funding a college education for a family. This person provides value-added services to his or her clients to help the family make wise choices about college.

College Advisor Pro. A proprietary sales-assistant software program that we created for college advisors. It has been independently rated the best college planning software program on the market by industry leaders.

Think Archimedes. A company that uses classic teaching methods such as the Socratic method, parables, history, and demonstration to teach students the math skills they must have for success in college and in their careers.

College Planning U. A niche-market social networking Web site and the parent company of Think Archimedes.

College Planning U (CPU) has two primary target markets: college advisors and prospective college students. CPU will market College Advisor Pro to college advisors who advise prospective college students and their families and guide them through the college admissions process. Think Archimedes is aimed at helping high school and other students prepare academically to excel on college admissions tests such as the SAT and ACT and to teach them the math skills that they must have for success in college and in their careers. Unlike test preparation services, Think Archimedes's focus is on teaching high school students to speed read, perform mental math, think logically, and *then* apply these techniques on standardized tests.

By fusing both proprietary and existing open source technologies, we have created an innovative concept in the college planning industry. Because our products are largely information-based and deliverable on the Web, our overhead expenses are minimal. We can immediately react to market trends, adopt and integrate new technologies as they become available, and thrive even in the worst economic conditions. While other companies become burdened with many physical locations, bloated staffs, and monthly debt services, we have none of those problems. To create name recognition in the market, we are introducing the SAT 1050 Project, which is designed to raise students' combined SAT math/verbal score to 1050 at no cost. The goal is to prove to students that we can help them become better students and that the value-added resources we make available beyond test preparation are worth the investment. Currently, we broadcast the College Prep Course live from our Mt. Pleasant location to the Web. Each session is recorded and posted in the video archive and available 24/7 in the Student Resource Center on our Web site, www.thinkarchimedes.com. All training, information, and resources are in electronic format on the Web.

Our growth strategy is simple: Generate massive publicity through articles and community projects to gain clout and recognition, use that exposure to gain strategic alliances, and promote our products in other niche markets. We already have established media relationships with most local outlets. Our affiliate and Education Relief Initiative programs also are underway. Potential affiliate companies are looking for ways to generate revenue, and Think Archimedes's low-cost structure allows us to share revenues with them, giving them an incentive to promote our program.

Our initial focus is in building local market share first before expanding throughout the rest of South Carolina, the Southeast, and the United States. Eventually, our goal is to take our company global because our program is a College Prep Course and is not exclusively related to the SAT and ACT, which are not administered abroad.

Management Team

Our current management team consists of President and VP of Marketing, Andrew Turner; VP of Sales, Steve Turner; VP of Business Development, J. R. Getches; and VP of Development, Scott Turner.

In his dual role as President and VP of Marketing, Andrew brings his extensive experience of mathematics, entrepreneurship, systemization, and web development. He has coded two software programs, devised College Advisor Pro's encryption methodology, and is responsible for the educational content on the Web site.

VP of Sales, Steve Turner, has spent more than a decade in the College Planning arena and brings his experience of starting two successful college planning practices. His insight, decade-deep network, and recognized expertise are valuable to Think Archimedes' ability to compete effectively.

Our VP of Development, Scott Turner, has been in charge of overseeing, testing, debugging, and delivering the technical components of Think Archimedes. He is responsible for all of the video content on Think Archimedes and the recent launch of College Planning U's BETA community site platform.

VP of Business Development, J. R. Getches, has spent his 20-year career in the technology industry building large-scale transaction, database, Internet, and telephony systems for some of America's largest corporations, including McDonald's, Dow Jones, Public Service Electric and Gas, The Voyager Company, and The Recovery Network.

Financial Results

Think Archimedes projects rapid growth as its social networking, online marketing, affiliate, and incentive programs drive a growing volume of traffic to our Web site. We expect our profits to increase from $100,000 in year 1 to $325,000 in year 2 and $875,000 in year 3 (See Figure 1).

FIGURE 1

Sales and Net Income Forecast

Financing

Think Archimedes anticipates one round of funding to optimize its Web site to serve high traffic volume. We seek $250,000 from investors to complete the necessary programming and Web applications, hire and train a sales staff, and launch our marketing campaign.

1.1 Objectives

- Generate massive exposure and media attention by submitting attention-grabbing articles and essays to existing local, state, and national media. By addressing the major flaws in the public education system with common sense solutions, we will become increasingly known to a larger and wider audience. Not only will this generate free publicity, but it also demonstrates our relevance on a deeper level than paid marketing campaigns.
- Create a more standardized, user-friendly online learning system to teach students the same specialized principles, lessons, and techniques demonstrated in live classes.
- Complete all areas of the site and adapt our material to service other niche markets.
- Institute a sales & marketing system to reach our revenue targets.

1.2 Mission

Think Archimedes seeks to restore integrity to the academic institutions of America by starting with the home. As the world becomes increasingly globalized and technologically advanced, it is becoming more important than ever to ensure that future generations understand that they must possess the ability to learn on their own pace—faster than schools can teach. We teach the importance of responsible citizenship through self-reliance and self-education.

1.3 Keys to Success

- *Effective Sales System:* Hiring and training a passionate sales force to achieve company goals and generate consistent cash flow.
- *Marketing:* Building brand recognition, goodwill in the community, and awareness of our services through creative campaigns, promotions, and publicity.
- *Lesson Production:* Consistently creating engaging, original lessons that produce quantifiable, measurable results immediately to our existing client base.
- *Strategic Partnerships:* Finding relevant third-party companies with whom we share a common target audience and negotiating marketing agreements.
- *Product Convenience:* Ensuring that our services are available online with 24/7 tech support and experience no downtime outside of scheduled Web site maintenance. Additionally, the site must be bug-free, cross-browser compatible, and user-friendly.
- *Focus Strategy:* Continuing to identify niche markets to which we can profitably market our services and to create customized products specific to each group's needs, wants, and interests.
- *Intellectual Property Security:* Securing necessary copyrights and trademarks to protect our company from infringement. This includes having a constant data backup of all materials and a full time Web security team highly competent in guarding against malicious acts or data theft.

2.0 Company Summary

Think Archimedes, which is named after the ancient Greek mathematician, brands itself as The Student Development Company and is the only company of its kind on the Web. The company's founder, Andrew Turner, spent the last decade working with students to create a unique themed mathematics curriculum, and in 2006 launched Think Archimedes to serve South Carolina students. Our headquarters are located at 613 Longpoint Road in Mt. Pleasant, SC, and we are currently a four-person company that operates as a limited liability company that is 100% owned by Andrew Turner.

From the company's inception, our goal was to create an online presence so that Think Archimedes could serve millions of potential customers while keeping our overhead as low as possible at all times. Our site's URL is www.thinkarchimedes.com. Students who have benefitted from utilizing Think Archimedes are high school students who:

- Experience math or test anxiety.
- Believe they are not good at math.
- Have difficulty teaching themselves conceptual content.

- Find themselves rereading the same pages multiple times just to understand the content.
- Write at a subpar level or have a difficult time analyzing and improving sentence structure.
- Have had little or no formal training in logic.
- Earn decent grades but do not perform well on standardized tests.
- Know that they must become better students to remain competitive.

Our goal is to expand our definition of a "student" by including adults who are returning to college to upgrade their skills, those who are pursuing GEDs, and military personnel who require remedial work.

2.1 Company History

Think Archimedes began with the goal of finding and teaching more creative ways to think about mathematics. After four years of working with students at every level—from third grade math to Calculus II—it became apparent that schools were teaching mathematics almost exclusively in a mechanical way, skipping the philosophical aspects that allow students to achieve higher levels of skill, such as the development of logic and rhetoric. Students simply could not engage in an intelligent conversation about mathematics, and this deficiency naturally fostered a lack of rigor in other subjects as well. This realization inspired Think Archimedes founder Andrew Turner to transform his mathematics tutoring business into a comprehensive student development company.

In 2005, parents began asking Andrew to help with prepare their children for the SAT. After compiling research from the Educational Testing Service and other sources, he bought the College Board's Official SAT Study Guide. Not only did he get a perfect score on every math section, he finished very quickly, recognizing that little about the test had changed since he scored 790 on the math section in high school. Andrew set out to create a program that would guarantee a minimum of a 100 point increase in the SAT Math section alone. He compiled a comprehensive manual on the correct methods for solving every math question on the College Board's SAT and constructed a matrix that that allowed him to weave his unique approach into a complete math curriculum.

After several years of success, Andrew decided to develop the Think Archimedes brand into a business that provided far more than simple test preparation and higher test scores. Think Archimedes would change students' entire outlook on life, teaching them a unique set of tools that enabled them to use their brains differently. Think Archimedes would be a technology company that focused on total student development, personal development that prepares students for success in college and in their professional lives.

Sales started slowly (see Figure 2), but in 2008, Scott Turner joined Andrew and began building the company's Web site, handling video production, and overseeing business development, which allowed Andrew to teach and improve the course content and to work with Steve Turner to create CollegePlanningU and College Advisor Pro, Web sites that guide students and their parents through the maze of college selection and admissions. Andrew raised nearly $100,000 from a private investor to finance CollegePlanningU, CollegeAdvisorPro, and Think

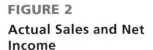

FIGURE 2

Actual Sales and Net Income

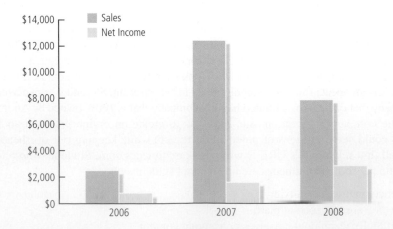

Archimedes. J. R. Getches joined the Think Archimedes team in 2009, bringing his expertise in business systems, database management, and strategic marketing to the company.

3.0 Services

Think Archimedes primary offers students a 10-step college prep course designed to enrich the mind by teaching students that there are easier, more efficient ways to think about language, mathematics, and education than are presented in schools. Four times a year, we target a specific SAT/ACT test date and offer a 10-week test preparation course for high school students. The course includes three weekly sessions:

Monday Night Coaching Call to Action is a 30-minute streaming video session that gives students their assignments for the week and explains how to prepare for class on Thursday night.

Thursday Night Student Development Program is a two-hour class in live streaming video broadcast over the Internet. Each week the class covers a new topic and demonstrates its applications to the SAT and ACT.

Saturday Morning Weekend Review is a one-and-a-half hour live streaming video session with a video book review, guest speaker, and a wrap-up of the week's lessons, including live questions from students.

With these three sessions, Think Archimedes blends an exceptional math class with lessons that teach students the skills of speed reading, logic, rhetoric, and writing analysis in 10 easy steps:

Step 1: Belief & Goal Setting. Think Archimedes always begins with an orientation demonstrating the results, benefits, and effectiveness of the course. The first barrier to overcome is students' lack of self confidence. Our goal is to enable them to believe that they can become better, more successful students.

Step 2: Reading Competency. Few students have been taught advanced reading or speed-reading techniques. We demonstrate the power and relevance of active reading, show students how to dig deep into the information contained within text and apply to these techniques in class.

Step 3: NLP & Observation. We teach students how to use Neurolingustic Programming (NLP), the art of modeling success by observing the philosophies, habits, and language patterns of the highest achievers and applying the same success traits to one's own life.

Step 4: Vocabulary & Semantics. Logic, mathematics, and rhetoric each have their own set of vocabulary that students must understand. With these foundational concepts, most of which appear on standardized tests, students learn to dissect text for meaning.

Step 5: Logic Analysis. Few high schools teach logic analysis. We teach students to dissect the structure of logical arguments, assess the validity of those statements, and apply these techniques to test questions.

Step 6: Writing & Language. Having a solid understanding of good grammar, sentence structure, and language patterns helps students improve their writing. Teaching students a few simple rules enables them to enhance their writing styles with a more intelligent voice.

Step 7: Number Theory. Very few high schools teach number theory to students, yet this concept appears regularly on standardized tests. These concepts help students to perform mental arithmetic easily and to think of numbers abstractly.

Step 8: Algebra. Our courses give students a solid foundation in the basics of algebra, ranging from observing number patterns to solving for unknown values.

Step 9: Geometry. Because standardized exams are timed, test writers almost always give students an easy way out by using predictable, special-case shapes. By showing students how to identify these shapes, we demonstrate the speed and accuracy with which students can move through geometry test questions.

Step 10: Test Preparation. Only after students have mastered the basics in steps 1 through 9 do we teach them test-taking strategies that are designed to improve their scores. Students soon see that the test-taking and timing strategies are the simplest concepts to learn when preparing for a standardized test.

Think Archimedes offers three convenient ways for students to learn these 10 steps in our College Prep Course:

- *On Location:* Students have the opportunity to learn from a teacher in a classroom. This option provides a hands-on experience with personalized attention and is recommended for students who learn best from live Q&A opportunities.
- *In Real-Time:* Students who participate in the live streaming video session see the same course content as those students who sit in the classroom. They have the opportunity to ask live questions and can be called on by name. This option is ideal for students who cannot attend the live class.
- *On Your Time:* Students have full access to all the same resources as every student going through the live and streaming video classes. This option appeals to students who prefer self-study courses and are self-motivated.

Unlike test preparation services, Think Archimedes does not give students practice tests. Our class is taught using the Socratic method, asking students questions from the material they have studied and their homework assignments.

Think Archimedes offers a "Can't Lose, Must Succeed, Or I Will FORCE You To" Guarantee for on-site students. Because our system has helped students raise their SAT scores by an average of 150 points (or a 3 point gain on the ACT), we offer a money-back guarantee with an option to retake the course. We also have a relationship with Rocket Reader, a company that provides software that enhances reading speed and comprehension, that allows us to purchase their artificial intelligence-based speed-reading product for $20 (retail = $129). Rocket Reader's product is included in each College Prep Course, and we sell it a la carte for $99.

4.0 Market Analysis Summary

Total Market

"The $6 billion online education market is growing by 25% to 30% annually, and there is room for new players," says Eric Bassett, director of research at Boston-based Eduventures, a research firm. "To establish a revenue stream in this market is very possible."[4] Our goal is to capture 14,000 customers in this growing market over the next three years to generate $3.5 million in annual sales.

Three Year Market Acquisition Goal

Market Size	$6,000,000,000
Target Gross Revenues	$3,500,000
Average Customer Receipts	$250.00
Number of Customers	14,000

Homeschooling Market

The number of students in the United States who are home schooled is 1.5 million[5], and the average amount spent annually for each child's education is $546.[6] The market potential in this sector, whose needs align perfectly with Think Archimedes' offerings, is $655 million. Furthermore, our expected average customer receipt of $250 is well within the existing budgets of families in this market segment, especially during test prep years when they are more likely to pay for supplemental services.

South Carolina's Market

Think Archimedes's "home" market in South Carolina generates 1.45% of the $6 billion spent in online education annually, accounting for $87 million in potential sales. We believe that Think Archimedes can capture 5 percent of this market segment over the next three years and 10 percent of it over the subsequent five years.

4.1 Market Segmentation

Think Archimedes identifies the following eight market segments:

Homeschoolers. This segment is the easiest to tap into because these are families that already understand that the public schools face significant challenges in their attempts to prepare students for college and the real world and have unplugged from the system.

Adult Continuing Education. Although we have dealt only with high school students in the past, we plan to expand into several other market segments by modifying the College Prep Course to create a Continuing Education Prep Course for adults going back to school. Many adults who have been downsized are returning to school so that they can be more competitive and earn a better wage. Most of them have not been to school in a long time and need a refresher course on effective study habits, general mathematics, and advanced reading techniques.

Families in Private Schools. Parents who can afford a private education understand the value of paying for a quality education. They are more likely to see the value in a specialized education that most people typically do not have access to, and can generally afford an extracurricular class if they find enough value in it.

GED-Seeking Students. Although this sector is largely made up of dropouts, many adults are now motivated to go back to college and need to earn their GED before they can attend. A comprehensive course that addresses all the basics is what many are looking for.

SAT/ACT Prep. Obviously, this is an easy market to identify. Students who score higher on exams tend to accumulate more scholarship money, and for many, taking the preparation course pays off in scholarships down the road.

Spanish-Speaking Populations. This sector is worth looking into because it is becoming increasingly large and represents a growing trend in service opportunities. Furthermore, as we become ready to expand into Spanish speaking countries, we will already have most of the course translated, documented, deployed online.

Military Remediation for New Recruits. The military has traditionally accepted recruits who need to address educational deficiencies before being put through regular training. This represents a huge potential market for us to tap into, especially since most of what we teach is acquired rapidly and easy to remember.

K–12 Students in South Carolina and across the United States. With 462,000 K–12 students in South Carolina, there is a significant market opportunity for Think Archimedes in our home state. At least 25% of these students' families are paying for educational support, and we estimate that the families of at least 24,000 of these students are motivated to find professional educational help. In the United States, 15.85 million students are enrolled in grades K–12, and their numbers are expected to increase to 16.4 million by 2019 (see Figure 3).

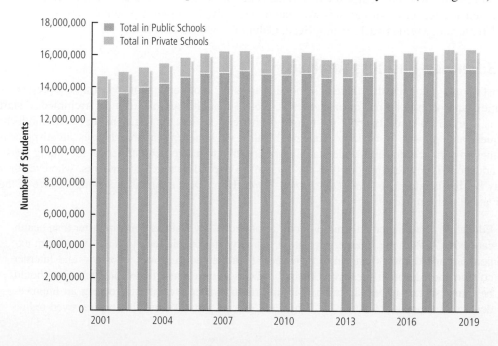

FIGURE 3

Public and Private High School Enrollments in the United States

Parents are important to Think Archimedes because they are the ones who pay for their children to take test preparation courses. Several studies have shown that parents who pay for their children to take test preparation courses tend to be highly educated themselves and typically earn a higher income than the parents of students who do not participate in these test prep classes. These parents are also more deeply involved in their children's studies and well-being in school.[7]

4.2 Target Market Segment Strategies

Homeschoolers. Most home-school families are tied into a local organization for support, field trips, and social life. They also hear about new ideas from the media, press, private publication magazines, and word-of-mouth and are looking for the latest new ideas and programs. We will reach them by submitting articles to specialized journals, newspapers, and media outlets. We also will connect with this audience by tapping into the online blogging community and contacting the heads of home-school organizations.

Adult continuing education. We will use search engine optimization (SEO) techniques, existing relationships with families through students we have served, and article submission to media outlets to reach this group. We also intend to forge third party strategic marketing relationships to gain access to large lists of continuing education students and approach corporations to offer employee upgrading services for their staff.

Families in private schools. We will rely on media exposure by submitting articles, stories, and research to newspapers, radio, and television media to reach this target audience.

GED-seeking students. We will use SEO techniques and articles in local media to reach GED students.

SAT/ACT prep. We already have discovered many effective keywords for online search engines in our industry, and we will use them to extend these results into other markets. Our marketing campaigns for this audience use humor to catch people's attention and are innocently controversial enough to get people talking.

Spanish-speaking populations. To reach this fast-growing segment of the population, we will hire a consultant to help us put together an effective marketing campaign.

Military remediation for new recruits. We are in the process of learning how to reach this unique but promising market. There is a real opportunity to tap into this market, and we already have existing relationships within the military hierarchy who are responsible for training, educating, and recruiting in several armed services branches.

K–12 Students in South Carolina and across the United States. Through the South Carolina Education Relief Initiative and word-of-mouth advertising from our successful students, we will be able to get our name out across the state. In the Charleston area, we are well recognized as a leader in our industry. We plan to target five key cities in South Carolina: Charleston, Myrtle Beach, Hilton Head, Columbia, and Greenville.

4.3 Service Business Analysis

Most people recognize that there is something missing in our education system. Test-prep companies' approach is far narrower and less effective than the approach Think Archimedes' staff uses. They teach students about the format of the tests, review the basics using traditional techniques, and provide test-taking strategies. Think Archimedes's approach uses creative techniques to enhance students' understanding rather than to teach them strategies for taking a test. In addition, Think Archimedes uses the Internet to expand its reach to students, wherever they may be. In his book *The Great Depression Ahead*, Harry Dent explains the changing face of the private education market:

> Education costs are the only major sector of our economy that has gone up faster than health care costs…With the Internet revolution today, young people tend to learn more from experts around the world and from their peers than they do in school anyway – and Internet college and education sites are booming!…Does it make sense that education costs should be rising so fast when education is an information-intensive industry during an unprecedented information revolution?…Why can't greater parts of education be conveyed online

with greater access to experts and peers around the world? Why do we need sprawling campuses with elaborate landscaping, buildings, libraries, etc., in an Internet world? Why should students be restricted to teachers and experts in a local area when they can have video and interactive feedback from around the world from the best experts, peers, and blogs?

The Think Archimedes team saw this trend early on and began building a strategy that capitalizes on the extensive reach and low cost of the Web to transform the private education market.

4.3.1 Competition and Buying Patterns

Think Archimedes's main competitors are Kaplan, Princeton Review, College Board, and PrepMe. Kaplan and Princeton Review have offices in or near Charleston and target a similar market to Think Archimedes. College Board is the only competitor that does not offer live classes or private tutoring to students who prefer to have one-on-one time with an expert in the field of test preparation.

A few new players have entered the market recently, demonstrating that it is possible to acquire sizeable market share in short periods of time. The Internet has completely challenged the domination that large established companies enjoyed for decades. Companies such as PrepMe and Veritas Prep have been able to enter the market and become profitable. The founders of these two companies took first place in national business plan competitions. These companies serve different market segments, and they have been successful at differentiating themselves from their larger, more powerful competitors.

PrepMe's approach is really no different from that of Kaplan and the others. This company teaches exactly the same information as Kaplan and Princeton Review but offers a few unique approaches to some of the standardized test questions.

All of Think Archimedes's competitors offer students and parents the convenience of online services, and as the trend continues toward the online education industry, the most telling factors in who wins the online race will be those who deliver the best results in the most time efficient way at the best price with a user-friendly, bug-free interface. In March 2009, *Time* reported, "One of the biggest low-cost growth areas is in online tutoring, a relatively new addition to the $4 billion test prep industry... Many [Chappaqua, N.Y., residents] are choosing to fill in the gaps through the online program [WilsonDailyPrep] launched in October and already boasts 470 students."[8] With the proper differentiation strategy, start-up companies can gain substantial market share in this business in just a matter of months. The online education market is the Louisiana Purchase of the education industry. As the market continues to grow at double-digit rates of over 20%, small companies can challenge the established giants successfully with new strategies, programs, and ideas.

Think Archimedes offers affordable prices; our prices are "in the middle of the pack." Think Archimedes offers the option of money back or retaking the test in the event a score does not improve satisfactorily; most competitors allow the student to retake the course at no charge or have established difficult criteria to qualify for a money-back guarantee.

5.0 Technology Plan Summary

Think Archimedes registered the domain name www.ThinkArchimedes.com in December 2006 and created a Web development plan for 2007. We began a three-phase Web development process in January 2008 which we continued to update in 2009. We see great opportunity to capture market share as a recession has taken a toll on school budgets and families looking for low cost, private education solutions.

Think Archimedes plans to trademark and patent its own line of Web applications and games to test for subject competency rather than use traditional diagnostic tests and quizzes, which students find boring.

5.1 Game & Web Application Development

Game and Web application development are the most revolutionary parts of our educational approach. Rather than using games to test students' ability merely to find the correct answer like every other company on the market, Think Archimedes uses games that test students' understanding of concepts in plain English so that they can actually apply their knowledge to standardized test questions. It is a complete 180-degree shift from traditional testing and preparation methodology and accomplishes through fun, interactive games what a live teacher does to build understanding in students. Think Archimedes has built or is developing the following games:

Plato's Punchout. A spoof on Mike Tyson's *Punchout* in which students box Ancient philosophers and mathematicians by answering simple arithmetic questions that increase in difficulty as they go up against stronger opponents, this game wires students' minds to compute arithmetic mentally, faster than a calculator. It also drills students on fraction operations by giving students two fractions that they either have to add, subtract, multiply, or divide, picking the correct answer from one of four options below.

Boogey Man Boxing (Teaches Fractions, Decimals, and Percents). This comedy boxing game has a boogey man under the bed with a fraction on his forehead. The player, who "sits" on a virtual bed, must select the proper hand (each hand contains a decimal or percentage that corresponds to the fraction on the boogey man's head) with which to punch the boogey man. The difficulty of the questions increases as students' skill level increases.

Factoring. This game asks students to select the value from four choices that equals a given polynomial.

Shape Identifier. This game gives students a random special-case shape. They must identify the type of right triangle or calculate the length of a particular side or area.

Number Congruence (and Number Patterns). This game helps students recognize number patterns.

Math & Logic Vocabulary. This game presents students with a word and requires them to select the proper definition from a list of options.

Phonetic Numbers. An advanced version of a speed math trainer, this game helps advanced students learn to convert numbers into words for making complex mental arithmetic operations and then convert the words back into numbers.

Algebra to English/English to Algebra. This game presents students with a math equation or sentence, and they pick the correct conversion from a list of four options.

Functions. This game trains students to master mathematical functions using a format that is similar to the speed math trainer.

Absolute Values. Students select the correct English translation for an absolute value mathematical statement.

Trigonometry. This game uses the Socratic method to teach trigonometry and includes translating and defining the language of trigonometry, calculations, graphing, and proofs.

Limits. This visual reference game teaches students the concept of functions and limits as values approach infinity and zero.

Base Numbers. This game helps students understand that numbers are flexible and can be written in an infinite number of different ways.

5.2 Information Delivery Systems

Because different students learn best through different media, Think Archimedes offers several types of delivery vehicles for our programs:

Interactive DVDs. We will transfer the entire video series for our College Prep Course onto an interactive DVD and integrate into it an initial diagnostic test, quizzes, and games that are infused with artificial intelligence. The ultimate goal is to distribute these DVDs through major retailers and video rental outlets.

Podcasts/Videocasts. iPods are ubiquitous, especially among Think Archimedes' primary target customers. Therefore, we will create a version of our program for these devices, offering it through iTunes or a syndicated feed from our Web site.

Mobile and Handheld Devices. Smart phones are becoming increasingly popular, replacing traditional cell phones. Smart phones now can handle sophisticated flash games and applications, and we intend to use them as another delivery method.

SMS Text Messaging. Students can interact with the Think Archimedes server, which texts them test, language, and concept questions randomly throughout the day.

6.0 SWOT Analysis

The following SWOT analysis captures the key strengths and weaknesses within Think Archimedes and allows us to examine the strengths, weaknesses, opportunities, and threats that lie before Think Archimedes.

6.0.1 Strengths

Minimal Expenses. Because Think Archimedes provides a service rather than products to its customers, the company is able to keep expenses to a minimum. Think Archimedes has the advantage of low overhead costs and labor expenses. The owners teach the lessons once and record the classes for distribution online, DVD, and other media. The technological expertise of the founder also enables the company to maintain a streamlined workforce by automating administration tasks and creating auto-response systems. The company does not carry inventory, which simplifies its operation and lowers its cash flow demands.

Small, Knowledgeable Staff. Each member of Think Archimedes's small staff brings a diverse range of ideas and expertise to the company, which enables us to serve our customers better than our larger rivals.

Automated Business. Automation is one of the great advantages of any technology platform. Labor is traditionally the largest expense in a company, but through automation and programming, we can create servers that handle most of the work for us. Automatic computer processing methods, such as autoresponse e-mail systems and automatic server back-up saves thousands of dollars in labor each year.

Information Technology. Inexpensive to create, easy to modify, and highly lucrative: These are the hallmarks of working with information technology. The greatest challenge is finding a niche market and developing with solutions that solve customers' problems in that niche. Think Archimedes has found a growing niche market, and by leveraging multimedia capabilities online, we are able to shrink significantly the learning curve for millions of people and add intellectual value to their lives.

Cheaper Marketing. Think Archimedes relies mostly on publicity and word-of-mouth advertising by the students who have already gone through the course. Currently the company incurs very modest marketing expenses; however, the owners are planning significant new guerrilla marketing strategies for the coming year.

No Geographic Limitations. The Internet transcends any geographic location, which gives Think Archimedes a potential client base of millions of parents and students.

Clear Vision of the Market Need. The Think Archimedes team knows what it takes to build a student development company that does more than teach students how to take standardized tests. Our company differentiates itself by teaching our customers the skills they need for success in college and in the real world.

6.0.2 Weaknesses

Name Recognition. Think Archimedes has relied on word-of-mouth advertising only for the last three years, and many potential customers are not aware of our services. Furthermore, although our name is academic and implies a thoughtful pursuit of mathematics, it doesn't explicitly say, "Preparing for higher education." Therefore, our marketing campaigns must be very effective in conveying what we do and the results we get for our students.

Limited Capital Investment. Think Archimedes has been underfunded from its start. The founders have paid for expenses out of our own pockets. Currently, the company has no line of credit. Like most entrepreneurs in the start-up phase, we have had to be creative in the way we market the business, generate sales, and build our Web site. The process has taken longer than we would have liked, but the company is moving forward. We are now at a point at which acquiring adequate capital will accelerate Think Archimedes's growth.

6.0.3 Opportunities

Deficient Math Skills. Math skills of high school students in the United States have fallen far behind those of students in other developed countries. The Program for International Student Assessment reports that the average math score for teenagers in the United States lags behind those of students in 23 other developed countries. The test is designed to gauge the ability to apply math in a real-world context.[9] There is a tremendous need for Think Archimedes' line of services.

State Budget Cuts. An economic recession has forced policymakers in many states to cut education budgets. At least 22 states are cutting budgets in K-12 and early education. Arizona, Florida, and South Carolina have cut school funding by an estimated $95 or more per student.[10] In many states, class sizes are growing, and parents are concerned that their children are not getting the individual attention they need in the classroom. In short, the timing is ideal for Think Archimedes's reasonably priced private education to fill the gap in the quality of public and private education.

Growing Population of High School Graduates. According to *Knocking at the College Door*, a study of high school graduates, the population of high school graduates in the United States will increase by 13.7 percent from 2001 to 2019.[11] These students represent Think Archimedes's primary target audience.

Niche Market. Think Archimedes has a strong team of staff members and teachers who have the diverse skills necessary to target the market of students who need help with math preparation.

Availability of a Highly Skilled Workforce. Downsizing at large companies has made available to small companies such as Think Archimedes a pool of highly skilled, experienced managers and workers. The ability hire high quality individuals in this market is greater than in times of economic plenty, which provides us with an amazing selection of talent to add to our team both in software development and sales.

6.0.4 Threats

Competition. Think Archimedes faces stiff competition in the market, and some competitors, such as Kaplan and Princeton Review, are well established. Some of Think Archimedes' competitors offer similar products at lower prices than we do. However, our focus on math skills and our live classes are unique points of differentiation.

Market and Concept Infringement. Intellectual property is the life blood of Think Archimedes; yet, intellectual property protection can be fragile. As the company's success becomes apparent, other companies may attempt to copy our ideas. We intend to guard and defend our intellectual property, educational processes, and educational system by securing necessary patents, trademarks, and copyrights.

6.1 Competitive Edge

Think Archimedes' major advantage is its creative use of the arts of logic, rhetoric, and the Socratic method to teach students the math skills they need for success in college and life beyond college. By teaching students how to understand abstract concepts—not merely how to take tests—we instill the oral tradition of understanding and demonstrate the power of explanation in learning. We also leverage artificial intelligence-based Web activities, live streaming video multimedia presentations, and interactive games to make learning fun and interesting. *Results* are another source of competitive advantage. Because the curriculum fuses philosophy, history, and psychology into each lesson, the College Prep Courses' greatest strength is in the high concept retention rate, which we estimate to be approximately 70%. Concept retention rates exceed 90% with the interactive games that Think Archimedes is devising.

Other competitive advantages include low costs and speed. Switching to a Web-based technology platform gives Think Archimedes an advantage because graphic design, multimedia production, marketing, development, and sales are done in-house, which lowers cost and increases the speed and flexibility of the company.

Think Archimedes teaches students about logical living, the importance of having a strong work ethic and character, and how to adapt to the technologically advanced culture in which we live. Students who complete the College Prep Course will be able to:

- Use the most effective methods to absorb information quickly
- Put the knowledge they gain into practice immediately
- Double their reading speeds with increased comprehension
- Understand and explain mathematics in plain English
- Use advanced logic techniques to discern the validity of statements
- Write effectively using sophisticated language patterns
- Perform mental arithmetic faster than a calculator for standard operations
- Develop high degrees of self-confidence and conquer test and math anxiety

Think Archimedes's holistic approach to education sets it apart from the competition.

6.2 Marketing Strategy

We have many different guerrilla marketing strategies in Think Archimedes's marketing arsenal that are designed to increase brand recognition. Some are already underway, and others will begin when we acquire the necessary growth capital.

Educational Relief Initiative (ERI):

We started by contacting the heads of fund-raising organizations such as athletic booster clubs, band departments, and the PTSOs at every local high school in the Charleston area with phone calls, e-mails, and direct mail explaining the Education Relief Initiative (ERI) program. Families save 20% on our services, we donate 20% to schools, and an additional 5% goes into the Think Archimedes Scholarship Endowment Fund. Each organization is given a specific tracking code, and each time someone uses that code, the affiliated organization receives a donation. We also sent local newspapers and radio and TV stations information on the ERI and how it helps the community, students, and school organizations. Several newspapers in the Charleston area have included articles about the ERI.

Niche Market Advertising

Our marketing campaigns are meant to be attention grabbing, playfully controversial, and somewhat irreverent.

POTENTIAL ADVERTISING MEDIA

- High school newspapers. Student newspapers are an excellent tool for reaching our primary target audience.
- Niche market trade magazines. These include education journals, homeschooling magazines, and pop culture titles targeting teens such as *Seventeen*.
- Guerrilla research projects. This would be a telemarketing campaign for "survey purposes only."
- Trade shows. Colleges sponsor events all around the country. By setting up a booth at these events, we can spread the word about our services to both colleges and the students they seek to attract.
- Guidance Offices. We are allowed to place our promotional materials next to any other competitor in high school guidance offices. We also will use permission e-mail to send

informative monthly newsletters that contain useful information to teachers and guidance counselors.

- Newspaper Ads & Articles. By submitting op ed pieces and placing strategic ads in newspapers, we can increase Think Archimedes' name recognition.

Sample Marketing Messages and Themes

- "Archimedes knows how to school some suckas" is a play on words that portrays traditional schooling as out of touch. Imagery may be dunking a book into a basketball hoop over students.
- "Tale of two students" is a cartoon that depicts two students, one who learns mere test taking strategies and the other who takes the Think Archimedes College Prep Course and invests time to become a better, more knowledgeable person.
- "Bathroom Wall" is a postcard that looks like the front and back of a bathroom wall. On one side it says "For a good ~~time~~ score, call Think Archimedes." Our contact info is on the back.
- "Secret" is a campaign that is already in use. Its theme is the secrecy and exclusivity of how students are earning large scholarships to college.
- "PC/Mac Videos" builds on the well-established PC/Mac advertisements. On the left is a stodgy old man who represents tradition and encourages students to buy into the current system. On the right is a young, hip guy whose response is "Why can't I just go get a book and learn that in like…3 days?" or "Why would I spend $10,000 and a whole semester on that when I can learn it at Think Archimedes in five weeks?"

Publicity

Because publicity is one of the most effective ways of promoting a company, we intend to maximize coverage of Think Archimedes in the media by submitting high quality, thought-provoking articles to get interviews, stories, and media time.

SAT 1050 Project

The SAT 1050 Project is an educational experiment designed to empower students by handing them the reigns to their own education. The goal is to increase the average SAT scores to 1050 by giving students access to the resources, expertise, and coaching they need to raise their SAT scores to 1050. The only catch is that after students reach the 1050 mark, they pass on their success by committing to help another student achieve the same result. Students and parents sign a contract that says parents will hold their children accountable at home, and students commit to helping a fellow student to reach the 1050 level in return for this free service. It's the old fashioned "pay-it-forward" approach. The greatest advantage of this strategy is that is puts into practice the adage, "People learn best by teaching others."

Search Engine Optimization

Currently, the Think Archimedes Web site receives about 20 visits per day and earns the following organic search rankings in Google for the keywords "test preparation" and its variations.

We plan to target additional keywords in the coming months to drive more traffic to the Think Archimedes Web site. As part of our search engine optimization (SEO) strategy, we also will use a variety of Web analytics to discover other key words on which we can bid at reasonable prices on the main search engines, Google, Yahoo, MSN/Windows Live, AOL, and Ask.

Social Networking

Social networking is one of the most powerful ways in to reach our primary target customers. We will establish a presence on popular sites such as FaceBook, MySpace, YouTube, and Twitter. We will encourage some of our successful graduates to post comments on their Facebook and MySpace pages and to post tweets about taking Think Archimedes courses. We will offer a prize for the best YouTube video about Think Archimedes

Strategic Alliances

We plan to cultivate strategic alliances with companies in many different industries whose product or services complement those of Think Archimedes. Some of these companies include the following:

Verizon Communications. This wireless telephone service has a large subscriber base across the United States and can send out coupons with printed bills to clients who can afford premium services.

Comcast. By partnering with this Internet provider, we can secure bandwidth for deploying the SAT 1050 Project and provide an avenue for both companies to build goodwill.

Adobe Software. Adobe is a natural partner because we currently use many of this company's products to deliver our educational system. Adobe also can reap the benefits of goodwill by partnering with us to deliver the SAT 1050 Project.

Movie Theaters and Producers. Producers are looking for creative ways to promote their films, and we can help them reach the prime movie-going audience: teens. We will partner with producers of positive, high quality films to give away free educational DVDs to students.

Magazine & Book Publishers. One of our goals is to encourage students to read; therefore, strategic alliances with publishers of magazines and books is a logical step for Think Archimedes.

College Planning U (CPU): The Three-Step Marketing Dynamic

College Planning U focuses on a different target market: college advisors who help families navigate the college admissions maze. We will reach these advisors by using the following process:

- Step 1: College Advisors are looking for a way to enhance revenues with value-added services. CPU gives them a sales and marketing program that helps them gain access to students in their areas. Our goal is to enable them to reach 400 families a year, the maximum number that a single advisor can handle at a time.
- Step 2: With the help of CPU, college advisors offer a free consultation to the 400 potential clients in their local areas. Experience shows that about 250 will accept the invitation.
- Step 3: Out of the 250 families that an advisor meets with, Think Archimedes will be a fit for a sale with about 150 families. Our goal is to sign on 100 college advisors, which will generate $2.62 million in revenue per year.

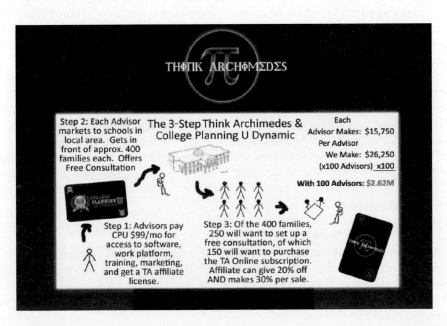

FIGURE 4

The 3 Step Think Archimedes & College Planning U Dynamic

6.3 Sales Strategy

In the local market, Steve and Scott are responsible for sales of Think Archimedes's services. Steve is responsible for calling on high schools in the local market, setting up affiliate programs around the country, and establishing relationships with existing college advisors, college admissions specialists, and other companies that serve high school students and parents. He already has established relationships with AAA of New England, AAA of the Carolinas, 911 Driving Schools, and several companies that sell products aimed at high school students.

All sales are automated, which sets paid clients up with a login name and a password in an e-mail that gives them step-by-step directions on what to do next. Each product sale will trigger a supportive, service-oriented e-mail campaign that strategically directs customers to other useful tools and services, both proprietary and affiliate.

7.0 Management Summary

We have four key executive members on staff:

President, VP of Marketing: Andrew Turner

Andrew Turner has spent nearly a decade privately tutoring mathematics. He has created his own proprietary methods, lessons, and style for conveying complex ideas in easy-to-understand contexts. Andrew created and systematically pieced together nearly all of the content on the Think Archimedes site and has written two software programs, one for the college planning market—College Advisor Pro (CAP)—and the other a home equity management piece (not released to the public domain).

He co-founded a Web development company, Arcimedia, and created the founding specs for CollegePlanningU.com, detailing how CAP could be integrated into the framework and establishing a sales-driven marketing dynamic between Think Archimedes and CPU.

VP of Business Development: J. R. Getches

Mr. Getches has spent his 20-year career in the technology industry building large-scale transaction, database, Internet, and telephony systems for some of America's largest corporations.

Mr. Getches received a Bachelor of Arts degree in Theater from the University of Virginia.

VP of Sales: Steve Turner

Steve Turner has been an entrepreneur for the last two decades. Early in his business career he founded a restaurant design and equipment supply firm serving the fast growing Las Vegas, Nevada market. Wanting to move from the Vegas area to a slower lifestyle, he closed his business and moved to Kentucky, where he pursued new career opportunities. Steve began working part-time as a registered financial representative, and is now an Registered Investment Advisor Representative. Steve has continued to build his practice and is now serving the Charleston, South Carolina area.

Steve is a founding member of the American College Planning Foundation, a national non-profit educational organization. He serves the local community by providing free seminars to promote the issue of college affordability and financial aid assistance opportunities. Steve has specialized in the area of college admissions and college funding for more than 12 years.

Recently Steve has spearheaded a new business model for college planning at CollegePlanningU.com. This new venture will reach more families using social networking on the Internet to deliver a no nonsense approach to college planning. This platform will also teach other financial professionals how to properly assist their clients in college admissions and college-funding strategies.

VP of Production: Scott Turner

Scott Turner began his career as a marketer for a small financial company based in South Carolina. His work for that firm led him into Web site development and online business systems. After two years of Web development for Arcimedia, Scott turned his focus to project management. His personal knowledge of Web design provides a strong foundation for accurate estimates and project delivery times.

7.1 Personnel Plan

Currently, Think Archimedes will maintain the four people whom it currently employs. Because we are maintaining a small personnel staff, we are allowed a great deal of flexibility and we can communicate information smoothly, quickly, and directly between each member when the need arises.

Personnel	
President/CEO	**$50,000**
VP - Biz Dev	**$50,000**
VP - Production	**$50,000**
VP - Sales	**$50,000**
Total Personnel	**$200,000**

In the future, we will hire up to seven other employees:

Secretary	**$36,000**
Marketing	**$60,000**
Programmer	**$60,000**
Graphic Designer	**$36,000**
Videographer	**$48,000**
Database/Network Admin	**$60,000**
Bookkeeper	**$36,000**
Total	**$336,000**

8.0 Financial Plan

Our forecasts recognize Think Archimedes's potential to grow rapidly. Once we implement our marketing plan, our customer base will increase quickly. Sales, net income, and cash flow also increase accordingly (see page 568).

8.1 Assumptions

Sales occur entirely online; therefore, we collect no sales tax. We project sales to increase from $600,000 in year 1 to $3.5 million in year 3. We assume that completing the remainder of the programming and game development will require six months. We also assume that we will receive a capital injection of $250,000 from an investor in February of year 1.

8.2 Sales Forecast

Table: Sales Forecast

Sales Forecast	Year 1	Year 2	Year 3
Sales			
SAT Online	$132,620	$ 431,015	$ 950,000
Education Relief Initiative	$ 74,750	$ 209,300	$ 600,000
Affiliate Program	$150,995	$ 373,750	$ 900,000
Live SAT Classes	$ 35,750	$ 50,000	$ 50,000
Live Webinar Classes	$146,185	$ 316,535	$ 625,000
In School Classes	$ 59,700	$ 119,400	$ 375,000
Total Sales	$558,315	$1,500,000	$3,500,000
Direct Cost of Sales			
Marketing	$ 50,000	$ 150,000	$ 200,000
Taxes, Fees, Office, and Computer Budget	$ 30,000	$ 50,000	$ 75,000
Website Programming	$ 50,000	$ 50,000	$ 50,000
Subtotal Direct Cost of Sales	$130,000	$ 250,000	$ 325,000

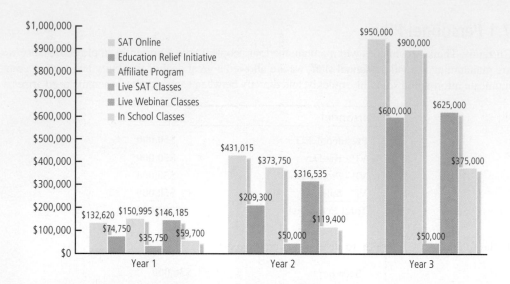

FIGURE 5
Sales by Revenue Source

8.3 Break-even Analysis

A review of our cost estimates produces monthly fixed expenses of $52,424 and break-even point of $68,083 per month, which is well within the scope of our sales forecast.

Break-even Analysis

Monthly Revenue to Break-even	$68,083
Assumptions:	
Average Percent Variable Cost	23%
Estimated Monthly Fixed Cost	$52,424

8.4 Projected Profit and Loss

This appendix contains forecasted income statements for year 1 for Think Archimedes. We expect sales to increase from $600,000 in year 1 to $3.5 million in year 3. Because of Think Archimedes's ability to capitalize on operating efficiency, we are forecasting profits to increase faster than sales.

8.5 Projected Cash Flow

As Think Archimedes grows, our cash balance greatly increases each year. Like most small companies, Think Archimedes will not experience smooth cash flows throughout the year. During the summer months we expect sales to be lower because school is not in session; however, we will promote summer programs to maintain sales and increase market awareness. Although we expect cash outflow to exceed cash inflow during the summer (because of the seasonality of our sales), we forecast that monthly cash flow will average $42,000 in year 1 and remain positive from that point forward.

Projected Income Statement Year 1

	Jan	Feb	Mar	Apr	May	Jun	Jul	Aug	Sep	Oct	Nov	Dec	Total
Sales	$15,750	$50,000	$60,250	$62,500	$17,500	$3,500	$3,500	$48,000	$80,000	$99,000	$103,000	$57,000	$600,000
Direct Cost of Sales	$10,834	$10,832	$10,834	$10,832	$10,834	$10,834	$10,834	$10,834	$10,834	$10,832	$10,834	$10,832	$130,000
Total Cost of Sales	$10,834	$10,832	$10,834	$10,832	$10,834	$10,834	$10,834	$10,834	$10,834	$10,832	$10,834	$10,832	$130,000
Gross Margin	($99)	$40,023	$44,266	$47,258	$4,616	($7,344)	($10,834)	$31,326	$61,506	$82,938	$89,416	$45,243	$428,315
Gross Margin %	−0.63%	80.05%	73.47%	75.61%	26.38%	−209.83%	−309.54%	65.26%	76.88%	83.78%	86.81%	79.37%	71.39%
Expenses													
Payroll	$16,667	$16,667	$16,667	$16,667	$16,667	$16,667	$16,667	$16,667	$16,667	$16,667	$16,667	$16,667	$200,004
Marketing/Promotion	$8,000	$8,000	$8,000	$8,000	$6,000	$6,000	$6,000	$6,000	$8,000	$8,000	$8,000	$8,000	$88,000
Depreciation	$59	$59	$59	$59	$59	$59	$59	$59	$59	$59	$60	$60	$710
Domain Registration Fee	$1	$1	$1	$1	$1	$1	$1	$1	$1	$1	$1	$1	$12
Hosting Fee	$2,000	$2,000	$2,000	$2,000	$2,000	$2,000	$2,000	$2,000	$2,000	$2,000	$2,000	$2,000	$24,000
Affiliate Fees	$504	$1,600	$1,928	$2,000	$560	$112	$112	$1,536	$2,560	$3,168	$3,296	$1,824	$19,200
Supplies	$8	$8	$8	$8	$8	$8	$8	$8	$8	$8	$8	$8	$96
Total Operating Expenses	$27,239	$28,335	$28,663	$28,735	$25,295	$24,847	$24,847	$26,271	$29,295	$29,903	$30,032	$28,560	$332,022
Profit Before Interest and Taxes	($27,338)	$11,688	$15,603	$18,523	($20,679)	($32,191)	($35,681)	$5,055	$32,211	$53,035	$59,384	$16,683	$96,293
Interest Expense	$0	$0	$0	$0	$0	$0	$0	$0	$0	$0	$0	$0	$0
Taxes Incurred	$0	$5,316	$6,588	$7,487	$0	$0	$0	$2,706	$11,760	$18,189	$20,132	$6,881	$79,059
Net Income	($27,338)	$6,372	$9,015	$11,036	($20,679)	($32,191)	($35,681)	$2,349	$20,451	$34,846	$39,252	$9,802	$17,234
Net Income/Sales	−173.57%	12.74%	14.96%	17.66%	−118.17%	−919.74%	−1019.46%	4.89%	25.56%	35.20%	38.11%	17.20%	2.87%

Projected Cash Flow Year 1

	Jan	Feb	Mar	Apr	May	Jun	Jul	Aug	Sep	Oct	Nov	Dec
Cash Receipts												
Cash from Operations												
Cash Sales	$15,750	$50,000	$60,250	$62,500	$17,500	$3,500	$3,500	$48,000	$80,000	$99,000	$103,000	$57,000
Subtotal Cash from Operations	$15,750	$50,000	$60,250	$62,500	$17,500	$3,500	$3,500	$48,000	$80,000	$99,000	$103,000	$57,000
Additional Cash Received												
Sales Tax, VAT, HST/GST Received	$0	$0	$0	$0	$0	$0	$0	$0	$0	$0	$0	$0
New Current Borrowing	$0	$0	$0	$0	$0	$0	$0	$0	$0	$0	$0	$0
New Other Liabilities	$0	$0	$0	$0	$0	$0	$0	$0	$0	$0	$0	$0
New Long-term Liabilities	$0	$0	$0	$0	$0	$0	$0	$0	$0	$0	$0	$0
Sales of Other Current Assets	$0	$0	$0	$0	$0	$0	$0	$0	$0	$0	$0	$0
Sales of Long-term Assets	$0	$0	$0	$0	$0	$0	$0	$0	$0	$0	$0	$0
New Investment Received	$0	$250,000	$0	$0	$0	$0	$0	$0	$0	$0	$0	$0
Subtotal Cash Received	$15,750	$300,000	$60,250	$62,500	$17,500	$3,500	$3,500	$48,000	$80,000	$99,000	$103,000	$57,000
Expenditures from Operations												
Cash Spending	$27,239	$28,335	$28,663	$28,735	$25,295	$24,847	$24,847	$26,271	$29,295	$29,903	$30,032	$28,560
Subtotal Spent on Operations	$27,239	$28,335	$28,663	$28,735	$25,295	$24,847	$24,847	$26,271	$29,295	$29,903	$30,032	$28,560
Additional Cash Spent												
Sales Tax/VAT/HST/GST Paid	$0	$0	$0	$0	$0	$0	$0	$0	$0	$0	$0	$0
Principal Repayment of Current Borrowing	$0	$0	$0	$0	$0	$0	$0	$0	$0	$0	$0	$0
Other Liabilities Principal Repayment	$0	$0	$0	$0	$0	$0	$0	$0	$0	$0	$0	$0
Long-term Liabilities Principal Repayment	$0	$0	$0	$0	$0	$0	$0	$0	$0	$0	$0	$0
Purchase Other Current Assets	$0	$0	$0	$0	$0	$0	$0	$0	$0	$0	$0	$0
Purchase Long-term Assets	$0	$0	$0	$0	$0	$0	$0	$0	$10,000	$1,500	$0	$0
Dividends	$0	$0	$0	$0	$0	$0	$0	$0	$0	$0	$0	$0
Subtotal Cash Spent	$27,239	$28,335	$28,663	$28,735	$25,295	$24,847	$24,847	$26,271	$39,295	$31,403	$30,032	$28,560
Net Cash Flow	($11,489)	$271,665	$31,587	$33,765	($7,795)	($21,347)	($21,347)	$21,729	$40,705	$67,597	$72,968	$28,440
Cash Balance	($11,489)	$260,176	$291,763	$325,528	$317,733	$296,386	$275,039	$296,768	$337,473	$405,070	$478,038	$506,478

Case 1

Division 9 Flooring

Growth is Good, Right?

In 2002, Chuck Young started Division 9 Flooring, a carpet, tile, and hardwood floor installation company, in Woodinville, Washington, and a year later sold 40 percent of the company to his uncle, Mike Quinton, in a move to manage the company's rapid growth. "I don't have the experience to run a multimillion-dollar business," says Young, who started in the industry as an installer. Four years later, Young and Quinton sold 20 percent of the company to Melissa Boggan, who is the company's chief financial officer and handles office duties such as budgets and billing. Despite a slowdown in its residential business, Division 9's growth has been propelled by strong sales among commercial accounts, primarily through large contractors, and the company's reputation for honesty and customer service.

The company's fast growth track has created a common problem: cash flow. "Growth is good," says Young, "but we need to balance it with cash flow." The company's residential customers typically pay 50 percent of both material and labor costs up front, but commercial clients do not pay for the materials for their jobs until several weeks after Division 9 has already paid for them, forcing the small company to use bank loans to finance its materials purchases. Constant borrowing has pushed the company's debt-to-equity ratio to 2.2:1, well above the industry standard of no more than 1.2:1. Young, Quinton, and Boggan want to lower the debt-to-equity ratio but are not sure where they can find the money to finance their purchases of inventory and materials.

At times, the partners also struggle to maintain open lines of communication among themselves and their employees and to distribute their managerial duties so that they remain focused on the tasks that are most important to the company's success. The partners schedule regular meetings but often find themselves discussing the same topics repeatedly. "We need to be accountable to each other," says Young. Boggan agrees and says that she is frustrated by the partners' vague meeting agendas. "Usually, the subject is 'How should we totally reorganize our business this week?'" As the newest addition to the company's ownership, Boggan's role is least defined. Her job title is chief financial officer, but last week she processed the company's payroll. Young and Quinton handle sales and manage the 15 to 25 contract installers who work for Division 9 on any given day.

Young created a business plan when he started the company. One of the goals stated in the plan was to achieve $15 million in sales, which Division 9 has accomplished. The partners admit that they have not revised the original business plan, however. "We focus on doing business as best we can," says Young.

Like many small companies experiencing rapid growth, managing people is a constant challenge. Boggan is concerned about the confusion among staff members over the role of the company's latest hire. The partners are impressed with the new employee's intelligence and experience and see her personality as a good fit with Division 9's culture, but they hired her without a job description or specific title. "No one [on the staff] knows what she's doing or why she's here," admits Boggan sheepishly.

Questions

1. What steps should Division 9 Flooring take to remedy its cash flow problems?
2. What recommendations can you make to the partners to make their regular meetings more effective?
3. What should the partners do to manage Division 9's growth more effectively?
4. What recommendations can you make for managing the company's employees?

Source: Based on Phaedra Hise, "Floored by Growth," *FSB*, July/August 2008, pp. 35–40.

Case 2

Successories

Catalog Costs are Increasing, But is a Move to the Web the Answer?

Few people would fault Jack Miller for retiring and taking it easy. The 79-year-old direct-mail entrepreneur launched Quill Corporation in 1956 in a corner of his father's poultry store and built it into a giant office products catalog business before selling it to Staples 42 years later for $700 million. Miller wasn't done yet, however. Shortly after selling Quill, he invested in Successories, a small company that sells motivational posters, awards, cards, and desktop items through catalogs from its Aurora, Illinois, offices, and also joined its board of directors. In 2003, when he was 74, Miller purchased a controlling interest in the company, which had been publicly traded, because he believed that it had plenty of potential but had veered away from its original mission.

Miller applied his vast experience in business and in the catalog business in particular to turn around the struggling company. In 1990, inspired by a passion for motivational quotations and writings, Mac Anderson, founded Successories, whose products appear on the walls of companies of all sizes, from small operations to *Fortune* 500 businesses. In a tribute to the company's success, Successories's products have been parodied in the cartoon strip "Dilbert" and the television show *The Office*. To stop the company's losses, Miller reduced costs by cutting back on the amount of color in catalogs, discontinuing unprofitable product lines, and operating more efficiently. By 2007, Successories was once again profitable (for the first time in seven years) on sales of $20 million.

An economic recession threatened to undo all of the progress that Miller and Successories had made, however. In 2008, sales declined 15 percent, and costs were rising even faster. "Ours is not a need-to-have product," Miller says. To make matters worse, Miller had run out of cost-cutting options. He considered the company's 100 employees to be a "bare-bones" staff. Rent was the company's largest expense, but its office space was locked up in a long-term lease. The next biggest expenses were catalog costs: paper and postage. Successories mailed 24 to 30 fat catalogs each year to tens of thousands of prospective customers. The cost of producing a Successories catalog had increased by 55 percent in the five years since Miller had purchased the company, and postage was going up every year. Miller was hesitant to reduce the number of catalog mailings because he had learned long ago that the more frequent the mailings, the larger the sales they generate. He wondered whether this "rule" that he had learned over nearly 50 years in the catalog business still applied in the age of e-commerce.

Miller called a meeting with his executive team and asked them for ideas about how to solve the serious problem facing Successories. John Carroll, the company's president, suggested significantly scaling back the catalog mailings and moving the company online. It was a strategy that Miller and the executive team had considered before. In fact, Carroll had commissioned Shay Digital, a small Web consulting firm, to analyze Successories's Web site, which at the time was nothing more than an online version of its catalogs. The original plan was to make the transformation to the Web gradually over time; now Carroll was suggesting a quick transition to a fully-functional e-commerce site and to pay for most of cost of upgrading the site by cutting catalog mailings by two-thirds. It is a risky strategy, but the company's very existence is on the line, and the management team knows it.

The cost of upgrading the Web site is $400,000, and the company's cash balance already is tight. One manager suggests selling overstocked merchandise at steep discounts to raise the remaining cash. Another recommends allocating almost all of the company's marketing budget to the e-commerce effort. If the e-commerce strategy fails, the company would most likely have to close its doors. Miller, whose entire career had been built around catalogs, naturally was hesitant to completely transform the company in one fell swoop. Carroll, however, points to a study of the company's customers that shows that they tend to purchase about the same amount whether the company mails its catalog frequently or not. Financial forecasts showed that a successful e-commerce strategy could increase sales by 20 percent and reduce production costs from 25 percent of sales to less than 15 percent of sales.

Questions

1. Should Successories's executive team transform the company from a catalog business to an online business? Explain your reasoning.
2. If the management team decides to make the shift from catalogs to the Web, what recommendations can you make concerning Successories's e-commerce strategy?
3. Which social networking tools should Successories use to market its product line? What specific recommendations can you make for using these tools?
4. Which guerrilla marketing strategies should Successories use to increase sales and attract new customers?

Source: Adapted from Brendan Coffey, "Case Study: Will a Move to the Web Save the Day?" *Inc.*, July 2008, pp. 57–59; "A Brief History," Successories, http://www.successories.com/category/company+info/our+history.do.

Case 3

Texas Best Barbecue Sauce

Sales are Not Smokin'...Yet

In 1933, Ruby and George Smith noticed the wonderful aroma from the barbecue that their handyman Fred brought for his lunch. One day, "Aunt Ruby" asked Fred for a taste of his barbecue and was impressed with its rich flavor. "It's in the sauce," Fred explained. "Whatever I put it on comes out good." When Aunt Ruby asked what was in the sauce, Fred replied, "some of this, some of that." Aunt Ruby finally convinced Fred to show her how to make his special sauce, and she and Uncle George began adding a bit more of "this and that" of their own before Uncle George finally pronounced their concoction, "the best barbeque sauce in Texas."

In 1955, Aunt Ruby shared the secret recipe with her 13-year-old nephew, Alen Smith, but only after he promised never to reveal its ingredients. When he grew up, Smith began using the recipe for his backyard barbecues, and the sauce soon became the talk of the neighborhood. His next-door neighbor suggested that he bottle it and sell it. Before doing so, however, Fred called Aunt Ruby to get her blessing. "That's fine," she said, "but only if you keep the recipe a secret."

Smith bought a used bottling machine for $250 and hired a food broker to help him sell the sauce, now proudly labeled "Texas Best Barbecue Sauce." They invited a buyer for the Winn-Dixie grocery chain for a round of golf and afterward offered him some barbecue seasoned with Smith's sauce. The buyer was impressed, and the next day, Winn-Dixie ordered 135 cases of Texas Best. Soon Smith's company was selling thousands of bottles of Texas Best to customers from Texas to Massachusetts. In 1978, Romanoff International, a food conglomerate, offered Smith a seven-figure price for the company, and he accepted. As soon as he signed the contract, however, Smith knew that he had made a mistake. "I was a fool," he says.

Romanoff changed the recipe for Texas Best, and sales plummeted from a high of $1.7 million annually to just $254,000. By 2006, T. Marzetti, the company that had acquired Romanoff, took Texas Best off the market, much to the dismay of a core of loyal customers. At age 66, Smith, dismayed over what the corporate giant had done to his company, bought it back with his son, Reed. They began planning a national re-launch of Texas Best in supermarkets and specialty stores. Their first task was to find a company that had the resources to produce the sauce, which requires an extended, slow-cooking process.

Alen and Reed then turned their attention to promoting the return of Texas Best Barbecue Sauce. Their first stop was the World Championship of Barbecue in Memphis, Tennessee, where they handed out 10 cases of sauce to barbecue aficionados to announce that the best sauce in Texas was back. Within one month, they were selling the sauce online from their Web site, www.texasbestbarbecuesauce.com. Sales soon reached 1,200 bottles per month, but the challenges that face the company are daunting. Neither Alen nor Reed has extensive experience in the retail food business, and competition among sauces is intense. Many of the products that Texas Best competes against are owned by large companies with deep pockets and large marketing budgets. The Smiths wonder where they should start their marketing efforts—at large national chains, club store chains (such as Costco, Sam's and BJ's), or smaller regional chains and specialty stores. Their limited marketing budget forces them to make some difficult choices.

The Smiths have positioned Texas Best as a premium product that retails at $3.99 per bottle, more than double the price of the best-selling supermarket brands. Texas Best sells a case (12 bottles) of sauce, which costs the company $19.02 to make, to a retailer for $23. The Smiths hope to lower their cost of production in the future by purchasing ingredients at lower costs once their sales volume increases sufficiently. Overhead costs are very low at this point because the Smiths are running the business from home and neither Alen nor Reed currently is drawing a salary. "If you are serious about growing this business," says one advisor, "you must plan ahead for costs, including salaries for yourself and for others."

The Smiths believe that one of the best ways to pump up sales is by allowing potential customers to taste Texas Best. Reed recalls that his father originally marketed Texas Best by using in-store demonstrations, handing out free samples of barbecue topped with the sauce. A company advisor says that food-safety laws have made in-store demonstrations more expensive, about $200 per store. However, they can increase sales immediately by 300 to 500 percent.

The Smiths recognize the importance of an effective e-commerce strategy for Texas Best but recognize that they have a long way to go. "We know our Web site needs work," says Reed, who plans to add a section for customers to post recipes using Texas Best and photos of their Texas Best barbecues. Reed is unsure about the best strategy for moving Texas Best into the top 10 results on search engines such as Google and Yahoo. "Will adding one recipe each week to the site attract the attention of the search engines?" he wonders.

Questions

1. Evaluate Reed's plans to revise the company's existing Web site. What guerrilla marketing strategies should the Smiths use to market and promote Texas Best Barbecue Sauce?
2. Develop at least five recommendations for the Smiths concerning an e-commerce strategy for Texas Best Barbecue Sauce. How should the company use social networking tools to market their sauce?
3. Calculate Texas Best's markup (as a percentage of cost and as a percentage of retail price) for a bottle of sauce. What conclusions can you draw about the company's markup? What steps can the Smiths take to improve the company's markup—and its profitability?
4. What should the Smiths do to differentiate Texas Best from other barbecue sauces, most of which sell for lower prices?

Source: Based on Patricia B. Gray, "Spicing Up Sales," *FSB*, December 2008/January 2009, pp. 45–50; "History," Texas Best Barbecue Sauce, http://www.texasbestbarbequesauce.com/; Addie Broyles, "Texas Best Barbecue Sauce Is Back on Shelves," *Austin 360,* May 20, 2009, http://www.austin360.com/blogs/content/shared-gen/blogs/austin/food2/entries/2009/05/20/texas_best_barbeque_sauce_is_b.html.

Case 4

AllHipHop.com

Averting a Cash Flow Crisis

Greg "Grouchy" Watkins and Chuck "Jigsaw" Creekmur grew up as childhood buddies in Newark, Delaware, and were drawn together by their common interests, one of which was rap music. In 1997, Watkins purchased the rights to the domain name AllHipHop.com to promote Oblique Records, the small record label that he had founded. Creekmur, a freelance journalist, was planning the launch of a rap music magazine. In 1998, the two decided to join forces in New York City and launch AllHipHop.com, billing it as "the world's most dangerous site." The site featured daily news, interviews with artists and producers, previews of upcoming music, and multimedia content focused on the world of Hip-Hop music. *Essence* magazine dubbed their site "the CNN of hip-hop." AllHipHop.com also delivers news feeds to subscribers' smart phones and wireless devices.

The number of visitors to the site grew steadily, and by 2003, AllHipHop.com was generating enough revenue for Watkins to quit his regular job and work for the company full time. Creekmur began working for the company full-time the following year. Initially, the partners focused their attention on the site's content, updating it daily, but paid little attention to selling advertising despite the fast-growing volume of traffic to the AllHipHop.com. Their dream was to transform their company into a global brand that promoted live concerts and other events, sold CDs and music downloads through the Web site, and produced music on their own record label. Watkins and Creekmur still own 100 percent of the company but recognize that soon they will need access to capital to fuel AllHipHop.com's rapid growth.

Their first step toward that vision came in 2002, when AllHipHop.com hosted a barbecue in New York City that attracted about 100 people. Over the next several years, as their brand's recognition grew, the barbecue became a weeklong series of events that they named AllHipHop Week. Although the promotion drew several hundred people, it produced no real financial boost to the company that was now generating $2 million in annual revenue and attracting 5 million visitors to its Web site each month. However, most of the pages on the Web site lacked revenue-generating advertisements because Watkins and Creekmur were too busy updating content to sell ads.

In 2006, Watkins and Creekmur decided to step things up, hosting a series of high-profile live events during AllHipHop Week that would publicize their brand name around the world. They would include an art show, a showcase for new talent, a fashion show, a panel discussion with rap artists, and a culminating concert featuring Busta Rhymes, Lloyd Banks, Clipse, and Remy Ma at New York's Hammerstein Ballroom. They estimated that the grand event would cost $150,000, a ten-fold increase over the cost previous year's less ambitious event.

Watkins and Creekmur quickly learned that their cost estimate was low. The fashion show alone cost $25,000. Even though the concert performers agreed to perform for no fee, they expected to be wined and dined in New York's finest venues. The grand finale concert cost $90,000, and Watkins and Creekmur ended up giving away lots of free tickets to make sure that the 2,500-seat auditorium was filled. Watkins and Creekmur were concerned about the impact that running over budget—way over budget—would have on their company's future. To compound the problem, several of the advertisers on the AllHipHop.com Web site were late with their payments that totaled $500,000, which plunged the company into a cash crisis. "[In the past,], if someone was late with a payment, we didn't worry about it," says Creekmur. "We got the money when we got the money." Now they *were* worried about getting timely payments because the future of their company depended on it. From a marketing and publicity perspective, AllHipHop Week was a success, but when Watkins and Creekmur finally tallied the cost of the event, they were shocked to see that they had spent $300,000, twice the amount that they had budgeted. Could their promising company survive this financial crisis?

Questions

1. What steps should Watkins and Creekmur take to gain control of their company's cash flow?
2. What should Watkins and Creekmur do to collect the cash from the companies that advertise on their Web site faster and more efficiently?
3. Visit the company's new Web site at www.allhiphop.com. Develop at least five recommendations for an e-commerce strategy for AllHipHop.com. How should the company use social networking tools to promote their business?
4. Would Watkins and Creekmur be better off spending $300,000 to upgrade and promote their Web site rather than to promote live events during AllHipHop Week? Explain your reasoning.
5. To fuel their company's growth, Watkins and Creekmur will need access to capital. Where should they look for capital? What advice can you offer them as they begin their search for capital?

Source: Based on Kermit Pattison, "Case Study: AllHipHop.com," *Inc.*, February 2008, pp. 48–51; "About HipHop.com," AllHipHop.com, http://www.allhiphop.com/languages/en-US/docs/about.aspx; Chuck Creekmur and Greg Watkins, "Staying Power," *Remix*, March 1, 2008, http://remixmag.com/production/music_business/remix_staying_power/; "AllHipHop.com Relaunches New Urban Lifestyle Web Site," *Free Library*, September 1, 2007, http://www.thefreelibrary.com/ALLHIPHOP.COM+RELAUNCHES+NEW+URBAN+LIFESTYLE+WEBSITE.-a0167751579.

Case 5

Peter Pap Oriental Rugs

On a Magic Carpet Ride

Peter Pap has been dealing in antique Oriental rugs for more than three decades and is recognized not only as an expert but also as a celebrity in the world of fine rugs, some of which sell for as much as $250,000. Pap's celebrity status is owed, in part, to his frequent appearances as an appraiser on the popular PBS series, *Antiques Roadshow*. Despite growing customer interest in oriental rugs and an extensive inventory of more than 1,000 rugs worth several million dollars, Peter Pap Oriental Rugs's (PPOR) sales are stuck at $3.5 million a year. "I do best buying and selling [rugs]," says Pap, "but I'm spending 80 percent of my time doing what others should do." He is one of just a handful of Oriental rug dealers in the United States who have the knowledge, experience, and skill to buy and sell the highest quality rugs. Most of PPOR's customers are wealthy art and furniture collectors who are seeking the finest Oriental rugs available.

Pap's first job after high school was as a stock boy at a rug store in Boston. He quickly developed an appreciation and a keen eye for the high-quality antique rugs that the store's customers traded in for the new rugs that his employer sold. Within two years, Pap struck out on his own, buying rugs across New England and reselling them primarily in Europe, where customers were more interested in collecting antique Oriental rugs. Today, his company is profitable, but Pap knows that he is not maximizing its potential. Pap is no techno-wizard and admits that his company's Web site needs improvement, but he simply does not have the time or the background to make the necessary changes. "It takes forever for someone to download an image from my Web site," he laments. His goal for the site is for buyers to be able to enter descriptions of the types of rugs they want and get photos of them quickly. Doing so requires creating a database of information and multiple photographs for more than 1,000 rugs. He recognizes that few customers may purchase a fine rug online without seeing it first but that many of them are likely to begin their search for a rug online.

Pap enjoys teaching others about the beauty, durability, and investment value of fine Oriental rugs, but his business allows him little time to do so. He uses no customer relations management software and admits that he has mismanaged one of his company's most valuable assets: its loyal following of wealthy customers, who are among the nation's most discriminating collectors of antique Oriental rugs. He rarely has time to call them and because he has never collected their e-mail addresses, he has no way to send them e-mails or electronic newsletters.

Pap would like to borrow several million dollars from a bank to expand his inventory. (As Baby Boomers retire and downsize their homes, many valuable antique Oriental rugs are coming up for sale, many of them at bargain prices.) He has other plans for the proceeds of a loan as well. "I want to ramp up the business with new employees, more advertising, more PR," he says. He intends to use his extensive inventory of rugs as collateral for a loan but has not yet talked to any loan officers about a loan. Preparing financial reports is a challenge because his showrooms in San Francisco (where Pap lives) and in Dublin, New Hampshire, use different accounting programs.

Pap is frustrated that he spends most of his time on administrative tasks rather than buying and selling rugs and marketing and promoting his business.

Questions

1. What advice can you offer Pap for managing the administrative tasks of his company?
2. What guerrilla marketing techniques should Pap employ to promote his business?
3. What steps should Pap take to capitalize on his reputation and celebrity status in the world of antique Oriental rugs? What recommendations can you give him for connecting with the company's customers?
4. Visit the company's new Web site at www.peterpap.com. Develop at least five recommendations for an e-commerce strategy for Peter Pap Oriental Rugs.
5. What advice can you offer Pap about pursuing a bank loan of several millions of dollars? What are his chances of qualifying for a loan of this magnitude? What other sources of financing do you recommend that he explore?

Source: Adapted from Brian O'Reilly, "Rugs to Riches," *FSB*, May 2007, pp. 51–54; Brian O'Reilly, "Rolling Up Profits," *FSB*, May 2008, p. 33; "About Peter Pap," Shoebone Productions, http://shoebone.com/peter/about.html.

Case 6

James Confectioners

Squeezed by Rising Costs, a Confectioner Struggles to Cope

Telford James and his wife, Ivey, are the second generation owners of James Confectioners, a family-owned manufacturer of premium chocolates that was started by Telford's father, Frank, in 1964 in Eau Claire, Wisconsin. In its nearly 50 years, James Confectioners has grown from its roots in a converted hardware store into a large, modern factory with sophisticated production and quality-control equipment. In the early days, all of Frank's customers were local shops and stores, but the company now supplies customers across the United States and a few in Canada. Telford and Ivey have built on the company's reputation as an honest, reliable supplier of chocolates. The prices they charge for their chocolates are above the industry average but are not anywhere near the highest prices in the industry even though the company is known for producing quality products.

Annual sales for the company have grown to $3.9 million, and its purchases of the base chocolate used as the raw materials for their products have increased from 25,000 pounds 20 years ago to 150,000 pounds. The Jameses are concerned about the impact of the rapidly rising cost of the base chocolate, however. Bad weather in South America and Africa, where most of the world's cocoa is grown, and a workers' strike disrupted the global supply of chocolate, sending prices upward. There appears to be no relief from high chocolate prices in the near future. The International Cocoa Organization, an industry trade association, forecasts world production of cocoa, from which chocolate is made, to decline by 7.2 percent this year.[1] Escalating milk and sugar prices are squeezing the company's profit margins as well. Much to Telford and Ivey's dismay, James Confectioners' long-term contracts with its chocolate suppliers have run out, and the company is purchasing its raw materials under short-term, variable-price contracts. They are concerned about the impact that these increases in cost will have on the company's financial statements and on its long-term health.

Ivey, who has the primary responsibility for managing James Confectioners's finances, has compiled the balance sheet and the income statement for the fiscal year that just ended. The two financial statements appear below.

---

[1] "Cocoa Forecasts," International Cocoa Organization, May 27, 2009, http://www.icco.org/about/press2.aspx?Id=0ji12056.

Balance Sheet, James Confectioners
December 31, 20XX

	Assets
Current Assets	
Cash	$ 161,254
Accounts Receivable	$ 507,951
Inventory	$ 568,421
Supplies	$ 84,658
Prepaid Expenses	$ 32,251
Total Current Assets	$1,354,535
Fixed Assets	
Land	$ 104,815
Buildings, net	$ 203,583
Autos, net	$ 64,502
Equipment, net	$ 247,928
Furniture and Fixtures, net	$ 40,314
Total Fixed Assets	$ 661,142
Total Assets	$2,015,677

	Liabilities
Current Liabilities	
Accounts Payable	$ 241,881
Notes Payable	$ 221,725
Line of Credit Payable	$ 141,097
Accrued Wages/Salaries Payable	$ 40,314
Accrued Interest Payable	$ 20,157
Accrued Taxes Payable	$ 10,078
Total Current Liabilities	$ 675,252
Long-term Liabilities	
Mortgage	$ 346,697
Loan	$ 217,693
Total Long-term Liabilities	$ 564,390
	Owner's Equity
James, Capital	$ 776,036
Total Liabilities and Owner's Equity	$2,015,678

Income Statement, James Confectioners

Net Sales Revenue		$3,897,564
Cost of Goods Sold		
Beginning Inventory, 1/1/xx	$ 627,853	
+ Purchases	$2,565,908	
Goods Available for Sale	$3,193,761	
− Ending Inventory, 12/31/xx	$ 568,421	
Cost of Goods Sold		$2,625,340
Gross Profit		$1,272,224
Operating Expenses		
Utilities	$163,698	
Advertising	$155,903	
Insurance	$ 74,054	
Depreciation	$ 74,054	
Salaries and Benefits	$381,961	
E-commerce	$ 38,976	
Repairs and Maintenance	$ 58,463	
Travel	$ 23,385	
Supplies	$ 15,590	
Total Operating Expenses		$ 986,084
Other Expenses		
Interest Expense	$119,658	
Miscellaneous Expense	$ 1,248	
Total Other Expenses		$ 120,906
Total Expenses		$1,106,990
Net Income		$ 165,234

Ratio Comparison

Ratio	James Confectioners Current Year	Last Year	Confectionery Industry Median*	
Liquidity Ratios				
Current ratio		1.86	1.7	
Quick ratio		1.07	0.8	
Leverage Ratios				
Debt ratio		0.64	0.7	
Debt-to-Net-Worth ratio		1.71	1.0	
Times Interest earned ratio		2.49	2.3	
Operating Ratios				
Average Inventory Turnover ratio		4.75	4.9	
Average Collection Period ratio		34.6	23.0	days
Average Payable Period ratio		31.1	33.5	days
Net Sales to Total Assets ratio		2.17	2.1	
Profitability Ratios				
Net Profit on Sales ratio		7.40%	7.1%	
Net Profit to Assets ratio		9.20%	5.6%	
Net Profit to Equity ratio		29.21%	16.5%	

*from Risk Management Associates Annual Statement Studies.

To see how the company's financial position changes over time, Ivey calculates twelve ratios. She also compares James Confectioners's ratios to those of the typical firm in the industry. The table below shows the value of each of the twelve ratios from last year.

"How does the financial analysis look for this year, Hon?" Telford asks.

"I'm about to crunch the numbers now," says Ivey. "I'm sure that rising chocolate prices have cut into our profit margins. The question is 'how much?'"

"I think we're going to have to consider raising prices, but I'm not sure how our customers will respond if we do," says Telford. "What other options do we have?"

Questions

1. Calculate the twelve ratios for James Confectioners for this year.

2. How do the ratios you calculated for this year compare to those Ivey calculated for the company last year? What factors are most likely to account for those changes?

3. How do the ratios you calculated for this year compare to those of the typical company in the industry? Do you spot any areas that could cause the company problems in the future? Explain.

4. Develop a set of recommendations for improving the financial performance of James Confectioners using the analysis you conducted in questions 1–3.

5. What pricing recommendations can you make to Telford and Ivey James?

Case 7

Medina Bakery

Is it Past Time to Pass the Leadership Baton to the Next Generation?

At age 66, Josia Medina was not ready to hand the management of the family business over to the third generation of owners. Josia had begun working at age 8 in the bakery that his father, Eduardo, started when he emigrated to the United States in 1940. Josia helped make the cake doughnuts that would make the Medina Bakery famous, and his father paid his "salary" in doughnuts. Josia grew up in the business, and it was only natural that he take over the business when Eduardo retired at the age of 79. Under Josia's leadership, the company grew steadily, expanding from serving local customers in Lubbock, Texas, to retail shops across the United States. In addition to doughnuts, Medina Bakery bakes a line of muffins, bagels, croissants, cakes, and other sweet goods. The family-owned business also produces a line of baked goods aimed at the Hispanic market. Sales of these goods have grown exceptionally fast, reflecting the rapid growth in the Hispanic population in the United States.

The bakery industry is dominated by large companies; the 50 largest commercial bakers control more than 80 percent of the market.[1] However, Medina Bakery has managed to carve out a niche by offering high-quality baked goods at reasonable prices and delivering them quickly and on time. Two of Josia's children, Elena, 40, and Gaspar, 36, are members of the bakery's management team. Both have worked in a variety of jobs since graduating from college, but currently, Gaspar is in charge of production, and Elena handles the company's marketing and e-commerce functions. Everyone in the company, however, knows that Josia is the "boss." Josia, Gaspar, Elena, and three long-time outside advisors form the company's board of directors, but Josia continues to make most of the major decisions in the company himself. With Josia at the helm, the board serves only in an advisory capacity.

For several years, Gaspar, Elena, and the members of the board have been trying to convince Josia to name his successor and begin the management succession process. So far, however, Josia has resisted their suggestions, which now have become pleas, to start the succession process. "I intend to run this company for several more years," he says. "My father stayed on the

[1] "Bakeries: Industry Profile Excerpt," First Research, http://www.firstresearch.com/Industry-Research/Bakeries.html.

job until he was 79. Why should I have to start thinking about turning over the reins of my company before I am ready?"

Josia's estate plan consists only of a will. At the urging of Lamar Butterfield, his accountant, he has given 15 percent of Medina Bakery's stock to Gaspar and Elena through lifetime gifting. Butterfield recently tried to explain the consequences of failing to create a management succession plan, but Josia showed little interest in the conversation. His passion is baking, and he has dedicated much of his life to building the family business, which, with a sweep of his hand, he says that he will continue to manage "until Gaspar and Elena are ready to handle all of this responsibility."

Both Gaspar and Elena have talked with their father about the future of the family business but have not been able to convince him to start the management succession process. Neither of them knows whom their father plans to name as CEO when he does step down. Gaspar and Elena have had a close relationship since they were children, and they and their spouses often socialize after work. Both of them want to work in the family business, and they assume that one of them will become CEO when their father does retire. They have positive working and personal relationships, and no serious family squabbles have erupted as a result of their father's unwillingness to develop and implement a management succession plan—yet. Gaspar and Elena sometimes are frustrated because their father fails to delegate to them decisions that they believe they are ready to make. At other times, they express concern that Josia makes so many decisions based on his extensive knowledge and experience in the industry but often fails to share that knowledge with his own children. When Gaspar and Elena ask for details, Josia sometimes responds impatiently, "If you knew what I know, you'd make the same decision, too."

Questions

1. Why do some entrepreneurs in family owned businesses put off management succession planning?
2. Is it time for Josia to name a successor and develop a management succession plan for Medina Bakery? Explain.
3. What are the consequences for Josia, his estate, his family, and Medina Bakery if he fails to engage in succession and estate planning?
4. Outline the process that you recommend that Josia engage in to develop and implement a succession plan.
5. Which estate planning tools should Josia use to minimize the impact of taxes on his estate, the bakery, and his heirs?

Case 8

Saranne Rothberg, MS and ComedyCures Foundation

Arm Yourself with a Punch Line: Develop Your Comic Perspective

I fractured my funny bone in February 1999. I heard "malignant tumor, surgery, radiation, chemo" and felt as if I'd forgotten how to breathe. The Cancer Team had gone home and I was told to come back Monday. Suddenly, an old magazine article about a man who had "laughed himself well" hijacked my thoughts.

If laughing helped Norman Cousins beat his rare nerve disease decades ago, why couldn't I bemuse my breast cancer? Treatment wouldn't start until Monday. I yanked off my hospital gown and ran to the video store in search of comedy.

I returned home armed with stacks of comedy performances. Barely holding back an eroding dam of tears, I squeaked out bedtime prayers with my 5-year-old daughter, Lauriel. Torturous questions bombarded my mind as Lauriel fell asleep. "How many more bedtime stories will I read to her?" "Will I be strong enough to bathe her after chemo starts?"

Sobbing, I ran to the television in another room and fumbled to insert the first videotape. Could the comedy cavalry rescue me? Sitting in front of the TV, I prayed for a miracle.

A young Eddie Murphy appeared on the screen. He set up his first joke, delivered the punch line, and the audience's laughter filled my room. I demanded that my mind listen to Eddie, even though it was more interested in my self-chatter about my own mortality.

Another Eddie joke, I cried, and blew my nose. Another joke, and I laughed from my soul. I could still laugh!

Watching Jackie Mason, I discovered that each laugh delivered a deeper breath and a sense of calm. Robin Williams's relentless antics caused me to laugh without pause, jiggling all those stomach knots caused by the cancer diagnosis. Laughing at Jerry Seinfeld's "Lost Socks in the Dryer" monologue, it hit me, "I lose socks too. I am not alone. Millions of people are on this cancer journey with me tonight."

A myriad of comics taught me a crash course in comic perspective, turning stress and disease on its head. When Lauriel arose in the morning I excitedly enlisted her to become my "Humor Buddy." We watched and laughed at Bill Cosby's "Chocolate Cake" routine. We made our list of all the things that bring us joy, and we pledged to make an "Appointment to Laugh" every day.

During my first chemotherapy treatment, we organized a "Chemo Comedy Party," including friends, family, sparkling cider, dessert, party favors, and six hours of stand-up. I spontaneously invited the doctors, nurses, fellow outpatients, and their family members to join us. The "ComedyCures Epiphany" happened as Adriamycin coursed through my veins: I would launch a nonprofit organization to bring joy, hope and comedy into the trenches of treatment.

What had appeared to be three decades of scattered "random events" were actually constellations of my life experiences; everything I needed to launch these ComedyCures patient programs and beat cancer had already been provided. I was born a fighter at only 28 weeks, weighing in at a mere 2-plus pounds. I was raised by a single dad who taught me to ask, "Says who?" I started relentlessly knocking on doors for "Jerry's Kids' Telethon" in elementary school. Amazing opportunities presented themselves, and I seized them, becoming one of the youngest news anchors in the country, scouting comics for Dick Clark, working on the first Anti-Apartheid movie in South Africa, teaching ill and physically challenged kids, and then becoming CEO of ComedyCures.

It's been almost ten years, three surgeries, 44 radiation treatments, and too many chemo cocktails since my all-night comedy marathon. My biggest personal challenge became my greatest professional accomplishment. Since the launch of our ComedyCures Foundation, we have entertained more than 400,000 people worldwide at live ComedyCures events. My ComedyCures co-founder, Lauriel, is now 16, and we have shared our programs, strategies, and comedians with the United Nations, Marines, orphanages, women's shelters, schools, hospitals on several continents, and families impacted by the September 11 attacks. The punch line is that I am cancer-free, and my funny bone healed.

Now it's 11:20 a.m. on a crisp Big Apple day and my Cabbie is wrestling our way across town to my next ComedyCures patient program. I catch a glimpse of my unexpected new red hair in the pane and smile, remembering the perks of chemo-triggered baldness: no shaving, plucking, tweezing, threading, waxing, shampooing, conditioning, curling, straightening, drying, dyeing, perming, or highlighting. The years that I had cancer, I saved thousands of dollars in coiffing, reclaimed hours each month from the beauty parlor, and I actually ran on time.

My vibrating cell phone immediately refocuses me on my nine-page call sheet, bursting out of my briefcase as yet two more callers catapult into voicemail.

"Sorry, lady," interrupts my Taxi Man from the front seat, "There's a demonstration on 5th Avenue. I think we should just wait it out."

I nod into his rear view mirror and surrender into his back vinyl seat as the demonstrators march by. I do believe you are exactly where you are supposed to be, whether in a chemo chair at New York Hospital, or a gridlocked taxi in Manhattan.

As a CEO you'd think I would have already mastered all those "Highly Effective Habits" but I just continue to use every pause to reduce the sea of requests bombarding our entrepreneurial 501(c)3 organization. The daily dialing ritual begins:

"Hi, this is Saranne Rothberg from The ComedyCures Foundation returning your call regarding our therapeutic comedy programs. Patients and caregivers attend for free, please visit: www.ComedyCures.org to confirm. Looking forward to meeting and laughing with you."

"Hi, this is Saranne from The ComedyCures Foundation. Just confirming my Keynote. Call 888-300-3990 or info@ComedyCures.org to arrange travel. We are honored to serve your staff."

"Mr. Rock's manager please. I'm the stage four cancer survivor with no visible disease who did the event for the families of September 11th on Broadway. Yes, Oprah. Thanks. Would Mr. & Mrs. Rock be available to appear on our ComedyCures LaughTalk Radio Show. Thanks!"

"Hello, this is Saranne returning Mr. Paul's call, could you tell him that I'm sorry I never used his energy drink. ComedyCures cannot endorse it. Thanks."

"Hi Betty, this is Saranne. Please tell Jeff that the program sponsorship check arrived. Thanks."

"Principal, this is Saranne from ComedyCures. We are confirming our participation in your Mind Body Symposium. We can bring LIVE LOVE LAUGH bands. We're excited!"

"Nancy, I wanted to express my deepest sympathy. Your dad loved to laugh at our LaughingLunch program. Many generous donations arrived in his memory. Thank you and my sincerest condolences."

My cabbie turned around to me in the backseat and burst out before I could dial Frankie (one of my performers), "Lady, I drive a lot of people. You are lucky." He continued before I could acknowledge him. "I'm serious. You got purpose. Not many people got purpose. I'm sorry you had cancer, but you know exactly why you are here." The truck behind us beeped to tell him that traffic was moving. I smiled back at my Taxi Man through his mirror, thanking him.

"I got purpose." I am also blessed to have an amazing daughter and my health. I dodged the cancer bullet and get to run this awesome charity that I founded from my chemo chair with a cell phone and a laptop.

But more and more program demand, patients, caregivers, donors, sponsors, celebrities, media, and staff! Personally, can I continue to balance it all while always keeping my daughter the priority? With all the media exposure, "fans" already show up at our house and office unexpectedly. Many e-mailers are demanding immediate responses. As we expand, will the privacy boundaries fully deteriorate?

Questions

1. If you were told you had less than five years to live what would be your top three priorities? Passions? What dream would you want to realize? What people would you allow near or want to learn from? How would you want to spend your time? How would it differ from the way you structure your goals and day now?

2. What was Saranne's "Aha" moment? Do you think you've had yours yet? What is it? How can you parlay that strength in your life? List three situations where you already use that strength and three where you could use it.

3. How does one start a service project? What steps do you need to take to create a one page executive summary of your plan? Develop a one-page executive summary for a service project or business idea that you have.

4. What role has the media played in the success of ComedyCures? How could it help your venture or idea developed in question #2? What would your "storyline" be?

Case 9

Brenda Galilee Rhodes, SugarBeets Productions THE HOT MOMMAS PROJECT

CEO, Actress, Producer, and Mom

Good Grief! Where is he?

Of course they didn't say it exactly like that. They asked "*Is he here yet?*" "*What time does class start?*" or "*Do you know where he is?*"

Yes, I knew where he was! My father was in his crappy little apartment undoubtedly sleeping off last night's drunk, counting on me to wake him, even though I'd already called him at least a dozen times. It must have been a doozy of a night because he hadn't responded, and I headed over to drag him out of bed.

He didn't answer the door. When I finally was able to gain entry with the help of the landlord's son, I saw why my father was late, and it wasn't because he was hung-over. It was because he was dead. On the bathroom floor.

A substantial piece of my heart died that day with my much beloved alcoholic father. In the aftermath of the trauma, I came to realize that my goal of maintaining a home for myself and my two little girls also evaporated because every cent I'd had (which was very little as a college dropout and single mother) had been poured into the business I shared with my dad, who was also my best friend. My dad was the "meat" of the business, and it just wasn't going to survive without him.

Within months, I was facing bankruptcy and foreclosure and trying to raise two little girls on my own. Although my mother was still living and I had seven brothers and sisters, there was no hope that they could help me out financially. I was broke, scared, and feeling pretty beaten down by life. At 27, I was ready to cry "uncle" and give up.

But in all honesty, what did giving up mean? Give up what? I'd already lost everything. There wasn't really much left—except for those two little girls who needed a mother to care for them. Pushing all thoughts of giving up from my mind, I went into overdrive.

It was 1981, and I lived in the middle of Silicon Valley, surrounded by technology entrepreneurs who were literally inventing the future. If they were successful, surely their companies would need tech-savvy engineers to design and build their products. I was always good at bringing people together. If someone would invest a bit of training in me, I could be a technical recruiter! All I had to do was convince someone to take a chance on me....

In August of 1981, I did convince a brilliant entrepreneur to hire me as a technical recruiter, and over the next seven years, I made my way out of the hole I was in, finding a love for my work, the engineers with whom I dealt, and the energy and excitement of Silicon Valley. I was making a terrific income, loved my job, and loved my life. I was never going to leave it. That is until I was fired!

In July 1987, my boss told me that I had done a good job until now managing his $3 million recruiting company, but he needed a different type of leader now to take it to the big time. His sights were set on developing a $10 million business, and he was sure that Brenda Rhodes was a talented manager of a *small* business.

"Go open your own agency," he said. "But keep it small. That's really where you are best at managing!"

So began my second attempt at entrepreneurship. My little start-up of 1987, Hall Kinion and Associates, grew into a mid-sized regional company by 1994, and a public NASDAQ company (HaKi) by 1997. My company eventually reached $300 million in revenue, employed 3,000 workers, and operated on three continents. And yes, my former boss eventually reached his "big" goal of $10 million.

The ten-year stretch from start up to IPO involved three years at Harvard's OPM program, where I learned the language of finance. My family life grew to include four daughters. I became a competent CEO capable of wowing Wall Street with a successful IPO and a secondary offering before eventually selling Hall Kinion in 2004 to a large corporation.

In 2004, I found myself single again, independent, and ready to look for my "next big thing." Reaching back into my dreams as a young girl I set out to try my skills as an actress. "You're kidding, right?" exclaimed by 14 year old daughter. "You can't be in a movie—you've never done that, and you're 50 years old! This is embarrassing!"

She wasn't so embarrassed when, after completing the esteemed acting program at ACT in San Francisco, I landed my first "gig" as the teacher in an MTV video, *California* by Hawk Nelson (http://www.youtube.com/watch?v=kub0BiruPsM)! More than a few independent productions later, I find myself in 2009 anxiously awaiting the release (direct to DVD) of my first full-length comedies, *Knight To F4* (http://www.knighttof4.com, co-starring Brenda Galilee Rhodes), and, in theaters, *Bart Got a Room* (http://www.imdb.com/title/tt0472050/), starring William Macy and Alia Shawkat!

I am excited to be balancing my life with a position as the CEO of a terrific little start-up, InTouch Corporation (https://www.iwillbeintouch.com/), an educational and consulting company for sales professionals, and some acting and producing as I send my last daughter off to college to pursue her dreams of being a photojournalist. The same daughter who had little faith in her mother at 14 is a young woman of great confidence at 17!

Pursuing dreams, walking thru fear, being nimble in the face of obstacles: These are all traits that I hope that my five daughters have absorbed from me. They are the strengths that I believe have enabled me to live a full and abundant life. A friend and I jointly constructed this sentiment, which I keep on my desk: "*When I am gone I will long for even the worst day of my life. Such has been the joy in my life.*" signed....*Brenda Galilee Rhodes.*

Wherever my dad is, I think he's smiling, watching me, and saying, "I knew you could do it angel!" That feels really, really good.

Questions

1. What characteristics of the typical entrepreneur does Brenda Galilee Rhodes exhibit?
2. What traits enable entrepreneurs to start companies when their lives are at a low point?
3. Would you describe Rhodes as a success? Why?
4. Develop at least three lessons about entrepreneurship (and life) that you can glean from Rhodes' experiences.

Case 10

LeSara Firefox, The Ecstatic Presence Project & Gratitude Games

Finding Balance in the Extreme

According to the National Institute of Mental Health, approximately 5.7 million adults in the United States suffer bipolar disorder. I'm one of them.

Although I try not to over-identify with my diagnosis, the truth is that my diagnosis is one of the main reasons that I am driven to make the entrepreneurial life work for me. At first glance this may seem paradoxical, especially for those who don't know much about bipolar disorder. With a deeper look at the disorder—and how it manifested in me—it actually makes sense. Consider me an entrepreneur by necessity.

I was diagnosed with bipolar disorder at 29. However, I'd had my suspicions for many years that bipolar disorder could have been at the heart of my wildly tumultuous youth. I'd been both driven, and scattered. My first career was activism (activism rarely pays) and odd jobs. This didn't exactly lead to the development of a solid career path.

After years of "fighting the good fight," I decided I was done fighting and transitioned my desire to create change to another format—healing from the inside out. But that's another story. I moved around physically a lot, too. In my early 20s, I lived out of my truck for more than a year. Although that may seem to be an irresponsible choice, it was the most responsible choice I could have made given my circumstances.

Bipolar Disorder is a Serious Consideration

I knew—with no small amount of shame—that I was unable to hold any job for longer than three months although I didn't know why. Three months was all I could take before the pressure of external expectations broke me down. The requirement to show up at the same place, at the same time, and do the same thing—regardless of mood, ability, or desire—was too much for me. Therefore, rent and bills were an albatross I couldn't abide by.

Sometimes bipolar disorder shows up on an emotional level, and sometimes it shows up as physical symptoms. Along with the mood swings, periods of deep depression, and the recurrent inability to sit still, I also suffered migraines, skeletal problems, stress disorders, and chronic pain. For me, none of this led to an easy relationship with employers. I simply wasn't a good candidate to work for anyone—but myself.

I work hard—if you're an entrepreneur you know the routine: long hours and sometimes less return than you would hope for. Yet it's still the best choice for me. The upsides are many, but the downsides are too.

Thinking of Becoming an Entrepreneur by Necessity?

On most days, if you were to ask for my recommendations on building a career, I'd say this: If at all possible...work for someone else, someone who will be helping you build toward retirement, paying a portion your health care, and guaranteeing you a regular paycheck. The stability and predictability of that life is something I yearn for often but will never be able to have. Kind of like a diabetic kid, nose up against the candy-store window.

For those of you who cannot or will not heed that sage piece of advice (from someone who didn't/couldn't/wouldn't heed it herself), here are some benefits to the entrepreneurial endeavor, some cautionary comments, and some strategies that will help you make working for yourself work for you!

Benefits:

Working for myself allows me to:
- Build a career at my own pace.
- Focus on the tasks I am up to on any given day (or week, or month, or season) and to put the ones I can't master at the moment off until I am capable.
- Create my schedule according to how I feel and to take care of myself by staying within my limits.
- Have something left for my kids when they come home, not having used up all my "good hours" in a day at the office.
- Stop working and go for a run, do yoga, or sit outside in the sun. If it's a really rough day and I just can't shut down the inner cacophony, watch TV.

Cautionary Comments for the Bipolar Set

- As a bipolar entrepreneur, sometimes it's hard to tell the difference between good planning and an optimistic outlook, and mania or hypomania.
- Trusted advisers, allies, and friends-in-the-know are a must for keeping feet on the ground, while reaching for the stars.
- Sometimes hypomania manifests as the insistent and driving need to *get it done NOW!* The stress I put myself under with writing and project deadlines can lead to a serious intensification of my symptoms, and in the past on more than one occasion, has lead to a full-on breakdown, which then necessitated a long period of recovery.
- Say "yes" to a project only after you've truly weighed its merit; say "no" as often as you need to to stay healthy.
- If you experience bipolar disorder or any other mood disorder, thought disorder, or disability, discuss it thoroughly with those close to you. Help them to help you. Create language that is safe for you and your loved ones so they can let you know when you're symptomatic.
- Disclose your condition to anyone who is offering business advice and tell them how they can best help you. Do you need to be assisted in staying focused on immediate goals? Do you need regular reality checks when making plans and setting goals? Do you need help figuring out the steps between where you are now, and where you want to be?

The Answers I Rely On

The tried and true answers that allow me to live a more or less balanced life are:

1. knowing my limits
2. enacting my rituals:

- Eating at the right time—even when I don't want to. Mania can arrest the appetite, and so can depression, and going without food will intensify either of those states.

- Exercising daily, or semi-daily. In some cases, exercise is as effective as medication in the treatment of depression and anxiety.
- Being dedicated and disciplined in caring for myself.
- Making time to spend with my husband and with my kids, where a "no work" rule is in effect. My husband and I have a weekly date night that we hold to religiously, and our family has a family night as well.
- Practicing and celebrating gratitude, especially when it's a stretch to feel grateful.
- Saying "no" when I know I have reached my limit.
- Knowing when to be on medication, knowing when it's safe to be off, and learning more about what helps me to maintain my balance all the time.
- When I get confused, to come back to my center through meditation, prayer, touch (hugging, cuddling, massage, sex), and yoga.

In Closing

As I've grown into it, my "fatal flaw" has become my greatest strength. Living with a potentially progressive, occasionally debilitating disorder has led me to a life that is honest, clear, and directed. My so-called disorder has taken me to strange heights and stranger valleys. It's carried me into amazing moments, and arduous ones. It has caused me to make lifestyle choices that keep me safe and sane. Made it possible to make peace with childhood memories of my father, who also suffers bipolar disorder. When it gets hard to be grateful for the personal cross I bear, I remember the heroes that "*crazy*" has brought us. Without a bit of craziness in the world, Einstein may never have discovered the theory of relativity. Beethoven's Ninth Symphony would never have been composed. My book would never have been written, either.

There's always something to be grateful for. Right now, I'm grateful for the choices I have made.

Questions

1. What does LeSara Firefox mean when she says that she is a necessity entrepreneur?
2. Firefox offers this advice: "If at all possible . . . work for someone else." Does it seem strange that an entrepreneur would offer this advice? How does she explain her reasoning?
3. Are the advantages and disadvantages of entrepreneurship any different for people with disorders than for those who do not have disorders? Is entrepreneurship a good career choice for people who suffer from disorders such as bipolar disorder? Explain.

Endnotes

Chapter 1

1. Niels Bosma, Kent Jones, Erkko Autio, and Jonathan Levie, *Global Entrepreneurship Monitor 2007 Executive Report*, Babson College, London School of Business, and Global Entrepreneurship Research Consortium, 2008, p. 16.

2. Robert W. Farlie, *Kauffman Index of Entrepreneurial Activity*, Ewing Marion Kauffman Foundation (St. Louis, MO: 2005), p.1.

3. *Small Business Profile: United States*, Small Business Administration, Office of Advocacy (Washington, DC: 2007), p. 2.

4. Howard H. Stevens, "We Create Entrepreneurs," *Success*, September 1995, p. 51.

5. Niels Bosma, Kent Jones, Erkko Autio, and Jonathan Levie, *Global Entrepreneurship Monitor 2007 Executive Report*, Babson College, London School of Business, and Global Entrepreneurship Research Consortium, 2008, pp. 6, 23; Erkko Autio, *2007 Global Report on High-Growth Entrepreneurship*, Babson College, London School of Business, and Global Entrepreneurship Research Consortium, 2008, p. 31; William D. Bygrave and Mark Quill, *2006 Financing Report*, Babson College, London School of Business, and Global Entrepreneurship Research Consortium, 2008, p. 4.

6. "Entrepreneurship Is Going Global," Babson College Newsroom, January 18, 2008, http://www3.babson.edu/Newsroom/Releases/GEM-2007-Global-Report.cfm.

7. Sara Wilson, "Biz U: The Global Arena," *Entrepreneur*, February 2008, pp. 128–129; David Lister, "Teenager's Homemade Jam to Earn Him Pots of Money," *TimesOnline*, http://www.timesonline.co.uk/tol/news/article1415473.ece.

8. Thomas K. McCraw, "Mapping the Entrepreneurial Psyche," *Inc.*, August 2007, pp. 73–74.

9. David McClelland, "*The Achieving Society*, (Princeton, NJ: Van Nostrand, 1961), p. 16.

10. Rod Kurtz, "What It Takes," *Inc. 500*, Fall 2004, p. 120.

11. Evan T. Robbins, "E Is for Entrepreneurship," *Syllabus*, November 2002, p. 24.

12. "First Major Study on Gen Y and Boomer Entrepreneurs Shows Business Confidence and Different Appetites for Risk," American Express, April 26, 2007, http://home3.americanexpress.com/corp/pc/2007/geny.asp.

13. Gayle Sato Stodder, "Goodbye Mom & Pop," *Entrepreneur*, May 1999, p. 112.

14. "First Major Study on Gen Y and Boomer Entrepreneurs Shows Business Confidence and Different Appetites for Risk," American Express, April 26, 2007, http://home3.americanexpress.com/corp/pc/2007/geny.asp.

15. Niels Bosma, Kent Jones, Erkko Autio, and Jonathan Levie, *Global Entrepreneurship Monitor 2007 Executive Report*, Babson College, London School of Business, and Global Entrepreneurship Research Consortium, 2008, p. 19.

16. Andrea Cooper, "Serial Starter," *Entrepreneur*, April 2008, pp. 17–18; "About Jen Groover," http://www.jengroover.com/aboutme.htm.

17. Stephanie Clifford, "They Just Can't Stop Themselves," *Inc.*, March 2005, p. 104.

18. Thomas K. McCraw, "Mapping the Entrepreneurial Psyche," *Inc.*, August 2007, p. 73.

19. George Gendron, "The Origin of the Entrepreneurial Species," *Inc.*, February 2000, p. 107.

20. "The History of Soaps and Detergents," *Inventors*, http://www.inventors.about.com/library/inventors/blsoap.htm.

21. "History: Milton S. Hershey," Hershey Entertainment and Resorts, http://www.hersheypa.com/town_of_hershey/history/index.html.

22. Dan Goodgame, "Our Roving Editor," *FSB*, April 2008, p. 10.

23. John Case, "The Origins of Entrepreneurship," *Inc.*, June 1989, p. 52.

24. Priya Jain, "Master of His Own Destiny," *Express Computer*, March 12, 2007, http://www.expresscomputeronline.com/20070312/technologylife03.shtml.

25. Nichole L. Torres, Sara Wilson, Amanda C. Kooser, James Park, Lindsay Holloway, Jessica Chen, and Kim Orr, "Young Millionaires," *Entrepreneur*, October 2007, http://www.entrepreneur.com/youngmillionaires.

26. Matthew Miller, "The Forbes 400," *Forbes*, September 20, 2007, http://www.forbes.com/lists/2007/54/richlist07_The-400-Richest-Americans_Rank.html.

27. "Most Middle Class Millionaires Are Entrepreneurs," *Small Business Labs*, May 13, 2008, http://genylabs.typepad.com/small_biz_labs/2008/05/most-middle-cla.html; Thomas Kostigen, "The 'Middle Class Millionaire,'" *MarketWatch*, March 5, 2008, http://www.marketwatch.com/news/story/rise-middle-class-millionaire-reshaping-us/story.aspx?guid=%7B6CF2AF9B-7A4C-487E-8AD1-8B49A6A87104%7D.

28. Nichole L. Torres, Sara Wilson, Amanda C. Kooser, James Park, Lindsay Holloway, Jessica Chen, and Kim Orr, "Young Millionaires," *Entrepreneur*, October 2007, http://www.entrepreneur.com/youngmillionaires; Jan Ellen Spiegel, "Faith in Granola Earned Its Makers Millions," *New York Times*, January 27, 2008, pp. 1,6; Jessica Harris, "Bear Naked Ambition: The Inside Start-Up Story," *FSB*, February 6, 2008, http://money.cnn.com/2008/02/05/smbusiness/bear_naked.fsb/index.htm.

29. Renuka Rayasam, "Small Business Tops Poll on Trust," *U.S. News & World Report*, March 6, 2007, http://www.usnews.com/blogs/small-biz-scene/2007/3/6/small-business-tops-poll-on-trust.html.

30. April Y. Pennington, "On the Rise," *Entrepreneur*, July 2005, p. 30.

31. Martin, "Slump? What Slump?" *FSB*, December 2002/January 2003, p. 67.

32. John Knox, "Hot Rod Tractors," *FSB*, December 2007/January 2008, p. 41.

33. NFIB Small Business Policy Guide, National Federation of Independent Businesses (Washington, DC), 2003, p. 16.

34. "Survey: Small Business Discovers the Six-Day Work Week," *Central Valley Business Times*, August 9, 2005, http://www.accountingweb.com/cgi-bin/item.cgi?id=101254; David Cooke, "New Hours and Earning Series for Labor Market Information Fans," Oregon Employment Department, March 21, 2008, http://www.qualityinfo.org/olmisj/ArticleReader?itemid=00005833.

35. Rosa Alphonso, "Small Business Owners Vacation Plans Remain Steady, But More Entrepreneurs Take Time Off to

Relieve Stress, According to American Express Open Survey," *American Express*, May 19, 2008, http://home3 .americanexpress.com/corp/pc/2008/sbvp.asp.

36. Chantelle Ludski, "A Day in the Life: Entrepreneurship," mba.com, http://www.mba.com/NR/exeres/4ECE6033-C16C-4DC4-816E-B04DEAA021A3,frameless.htm

37. Rosa Alphonso, "Small Business Optimism Is on an Upswing, According to the OPEN from American Express Small Business Monitor," *American Express*, May 24, 2007, http://home3.americanexpress.com/corp/pc/2007/monitor.asp.

38. William J. Dennis, *National Small Business Poll: Advice and Advisers*, Volume 2, Issue 5, National Federation of Independent Businesses: Washington, DC, 2002, p. 1.

39. "Small Business Owners Work Long Hours But Manage Work/Life Balance," *Accounting Web*, August 31, 2005, http://www.accountingweb.com/cgi-bin/item.cgi?id=101254.

40. "Poll: Small in Business Is Beautiful," United Press International, March 11, 2008, http://www.upi.com/NewsTrack/Business/2008/03/11/poll_small_in_business_is_beautiful/2374/.

41. Brian Dumaine and Elaine Pofeldt, "Best Colleges for Aspiring Entrepreneurs," *FSB*, September 2007, p. 61; "Entrepreneurship Unleashed in Universities Across the Country," Kauffman Foundation, June 2006, http://www.kauffman.org/items.cfm?itemID=712.

42. "Services Trade Fuels Growth of U.S. Economy," Office of the United States Trade Representative, January 2007, http://www.ustr.gov/assets/Trade_Sectors/Services/How_does_trade_in_services_benefit_your_state/asset_upload_file425_10868.pdf, p. 1; Mary Yanni, "Business 101: ISM Service Sector Index," *New Jersey Business News*, April 3, 2008, http://www.nj.com/business/index.ssf/2008/04/business_101_ism_servicesector.html.

43. Celeste Hoang, "Smart Ideas: Quick Fix," *Entrepreneur*, May 2008, pp. 118–120.

44. Jimbo Wales, "The Knowledge Maestro," *Fortune*, September 17, 2007, p. 36.

45. "Unusual Business News," May 2008, http://unusualbusinessnews.blogspot.com/search?updated-min=2008-01-01T00%3A00%3A00-08%3A00&updated-max=2009-01-01T00%3A00%3A00-08%3A00&max-results=32.

46. *2007 NSBA Survey of Small and Mid-Sized Businesses*, National Small Business Association, Washington, DC, 2007, p. 25.

47. Pallavi Gogoi, "No Business Like Tour Business," *Business Week*, October 6, 2005, http://www.businessweek.com/smallbiz/content/oct2005/sb20051006_352042.htm.

48. "Opportunities in Exporting," Office of International Trade, U.S. Small Business Administration, http://www.sba.gov/OIT/txt/export/whyexport.html.

49. Andrea Poe, "Snapshot: Sweet Success," *Entrepreneur*, February 2008, p. 73; "Raising the Bar: Chocolate Has Always Been Decadent and Delicious; Now It's Really, Really Rich," *The Sun*, February 7, 2007, p. 12.

50. Donna Fenn, "The Making of an Entrepreneurial Generation," *Inc.*, July 2007, http://www.inc.com/30under30/2007/the-entrepreneurial-generation.html.

51. Sharon Jayson, "Gen Y Makes a Mark, and Their Imprint Is Entrepreneurship," *USA Today*, December 8, 2006,

http://www.usatoday.com/news/nation/2006-12-06-gen-next-entrepreneurs_x.htm; Donna Fenn, "30 Under 30: Ben Kaufman," *Inc.*, July 2007, http://www.inc.com/30under30/2007/1-kaufman.html.

52. "2006 Industry Distribution of 51% or More Women-Owned Firms," Center for Women's Business Research, 2007, http://www.cfwbr.org/assets/347_2006factsheetchart3.gif; "Industry Growth of 51% or More Women-Owned Firms, 1997–2006" Center for Women's Business Research, 2007, http://www.cfwbr.org/assets/348_2006factsheetchart4.gif.

53. Key Facts About Women-Owned Businesses," Center for Women's Business Research, 2008, http://www.nfwbo.org/facts/index.php.

54. Francine Russo, "Jumping for Joy —and Profit," *Business 2.0*, October 2007, p. 46; "Inc. 500: Pump It Up," *Inc.*, September 2007, http://www.inc.com/inc5000/2007/company-profile.html?id=200702310.

55. "Minorities in Business: A Demographic Review of Minority Business Ownership," *Small Business Research Summary*, Small Business Administration Office of Advocacy, April 2007, p. 1.

56. "Minorities in Business: A Demographic Review of Minority Business Ownership," *Small Business Research Summary*, Small Business Administration Office of Advocacy, April 2007, p. 1.

57. Liz Welch, "Things I Can't Live Without," *Inc.*, February 2008, p. 72; "Using Grassroots Marketing: Lavetta's Key Move," *Startup Nation*, http://www.startupnation.com/pages/keymoves/KM_LavettaWillis.asp.

58. "Minorities in Business: A Demographic Review of Minority Business Ownership," *Small Business Research Summary*, Small Business Administration Office of Advocacy, April 2007, p. 1.

59. *Minorities in Business: A Demographic Review of Minority Business Ownership*, Small Business Administration Office of Advocacy, Washington, DC: April 10, 2007, p. 27.

60. Sara Wilson, "Midas Touch," *Entrepreneur*, April 2008, p. 160; "The Designer," Lana Jewelry, http://www.lanajewelry.com/about_lana.aspx.

61. Mark Henricks, "Perfect Timing," *Entrepreneur*, September 2007, http://www.entrepreneur.com/ebusiness/ebaycenter/article183926.html.

62. Kameliia Petrova, "Part-Time Entrepreneurship and Wealth Effects: New Evidence from the Panel Study of Entrepreneurial Dynamics," Boston College, November 2005, http://129.3.20.41/eps/mic/papers/0510/0510006.pdf.

63. "Home-Based Business Facts," National Black Business Trade Association, http://www.inc.com/articles/2007/12/home.html.

64. Tamara Schweitzer, "Escape from Cubicle Hell," *Inc.*, December 2007, http://www.inc.com/articles/2007/12/home.html.

65. "Joanne H. Pratt, "The Impact of Location on Net Income: A Comparison of Homebased and Non-Homebased Sole Proprietors," *Small Business Research Summary*, Small Business Administration, Office of Advocacy, May 2006, p. 1.

66. "Facts and Perspectives on Family Business Around the World: United States," Family Firm Institute, http://www.ffi.org/genTemplate.asp?cid=186#us; "Facts and Figures: Family

Business in the U.S." *Family Business Magazine*, http://www.business.com/ bdcframe.asp?ticker=&src=http%l 3A//rd.business.com/index.asp%3Fbdcz%3Di.l.l.ml.e%26bd cr%3D1%26bdcu%3Dhttp%253A//www.familybusiness- magazine.com/%26bdcs%3D0CD38920-C1E8-4FF8-B724- 77BBCF2BA89F%26bdcf%3D0D92C0F3-4149-444B- 938B-EFABD06FCD31%26bdcp%3D%26partner% 3Dbdc%26title%3DFamily%2520Business% 2520magazine&back=http%3A//www.business.com/ directory/media_and_entertainment/publishing/magazines/ family_business_publishing/family_business_magazine/ index.asp%3Fpartner%3Dinc&path=/directory/media_ and_entertainment/publishing/magazines/family_business_ publishing/family_business_magazine; "Family Business Statistics," American Management Services, http://www .amserv.com/familystatistics.html.

67. Erick Calonius, "Blood and Money," *Newsweek: Special Issue*, p. 82.

68. "Family Business Facts," University of St. Francis, Fort Wayne, Indiana, http://www.sfc.edu/business/fbc_facts.shtml.

69. Adam Bluestein, "The Success Gene: A.E. Schmidt Company," Inc., April 2008, pp. 83–94; Margaret Schroeder, "Customizing Billiard Tables," *American Profile*, February 24, 2008, http://www.americanprofile.com/article/25660.html.

70. Udayan Gupta, "And Business Makes Three: Couples Working Together," *Wall Street Journal*, February 26, 1990, p. B2.

71. Pia Chatterjee, "Making Beautiful Start-Ups Together," *Business 2.0*, September 2007, p. 43.

72. Echo M. Garrett, "And Business Makes Three," *Small Business Reports*, September 1993, pp. 27–31.

73. Pia Chatterjee, "Making Beautiful Start-Ups Together," *Business 2.0*, September 2007, pp. 3442–44.

74. Phaedra Hise, "Everyone Wants to Start a Business," *CNN Money*, February 1, 2007, http://money.cnn.com/ 2007/03/26/magazines/fsb/womenetc.fsb/.

75. Sara Wilson, "The Wide World of Franchisees," *Entrepreneur*, January 2007, http://www.entrepreneur.com/ franchises/buyingafranchise/franchisebasics/article 172032.html.

76. Jeff Bailey, "Anger Can Power the Creation of New Companies," *Wall Street Journal*, June 4, 2002, p. B5.

77. *NFIB Small Business Policy Guide* (Washington, DC: NFIB Education Foundation, 2003), p. 21.

78. J. J. Ramberg, "Waste Not," *Entrepreneur*, April 2008, p.21; "RecycleBank Secures $30 Million in Series B Funding from Top Venture Capital Firms, Investorideas.com, April 16, 2008, http://www.investorideas.com/News/041608b.asp.

79. Tamara Schweitzer, "The Grandmother of Invention," Inc., November 2007, http://www.inc.com/8over80/ 2007/1-lisa-gable-the-grandmother-of-invention.html; Angus Loten, "The Retirement Myth," Inc., October 2007, http://www.inc.com/8over80/2007/the- retirement-myth.html.

80. *"FAQs"*, U.S. Small Business Administration (Washington, DC, 2007), http://app1.sba.gov/ faqs/faqIndexAll.cfm?areaid=24.

81. "Cognetics Corporate Quiz," Cognetics, Inc., http://www.cogonline.com/IndexL.htm; Garry Powers,

"Wanted: More Small, Fast-Growing Firms," *Business & Economic Review*, April-June 1999, pp. 19–22.

82. *"FAQs,"* U.S. Small Business Administration (Washington, DC, 2007), http://app1.sba.gov/ faqs/faqIndexAll.cfm?areaid=24; Kathryn Kobe, "The Small Business Share of GDP," Small Business Research Summary, Small Business Administration, Office of Advocacy, April 2007, http://www.sba.gov/advo/ research/rs299tot.pdf.

83. *"FAQs,"* U.S. Small Business Administration (Washington, DC, 2007), http://app1.sba.gov/faqs/faqIndexAll.cfm? areaid=24.

84. Amy Knaup, "Survival and Longevity in the Business Employment Dynamics Data," *Monthly Labor Review*, Vol. 28, No. 5, May 2005, p. 51.

85. Michael Warsaw, "Great Comebacks," *Success*, July/August, 1995, p. 43.

86. Paige Arnof-Fenn, "Failing Your Way to Success," *Entrepreneur*, November 21, 2005, http://www.entrepreneur .com/worklife/worklifebalanceadvice/theentrepre- neurslifecolumnistpaigearnoffenn/article81130.html.

87. Marc Gunther, "They All Want a Piece of Bill Gross," *Fortune*, November 11, 2002, p. 140.

88. Chuck Salter, "Failure Doesn't Suck," *Fast Company*, May 2007, p. 44.

89. Philip J. Kaplan, "Maybe Next Time," *Entrepreneur*, December 2007, p. 58; John Cook, "Venture Capital: Dot-com Founders Got a Crash Course in Business," *Seattle Post Intelligencer*, July 12, 2002, http://seattlepi.nwsource.com/venture/78258_vc12.shtml.

90. Carol Tice, "Experience Counts," *Entrepreneur*, April 2008, http://www.entrepreneur.com/magazine/ entrepreneur/2008/april/191498.html; Sam Phillips, "Laura Bennett, FSA," Image of the Actuary, http://www.imageoftheactuary.org/Home/TheHeritage/Pio neers/LauraBennettFSA/tabid/236/Default.aspx.

91. "History," TerraCycle, http://www.terracycle.net/history.htm.

92. G. David Doran, Michelle Prather, Elaine Teague, and Laura Tiffany, "Young Guns," *Business Start-Ups*, April 1999, pp. 28–35.

93. Rhonda Abrams, "Building Blocks of Business: Great Faith, Great Doubt, Great Effort," *Business*, March 4, 2001, p. 2.

Chapter 2

1. Christopher John Farley, "How an Amateur Inventor Got Wheeled Footwear Concept Rolling," *Wall Street Journal*, February 14, 2007, p. B11.

2. "U.S. R&D Expenditures Increased 6.0% in 2006 According to NSF Projections," National Science Foundation, April 2007, http://www.nsf.gov/statistics/infbrief/nsf07317/.

3. "Small Business Innovation Spurs Economic Growth," U.S. Small Business Administration Office of Advocacy, March 2009, http://www.sba.gov/advo/research/ factsinnovation09.pdf.

4. "The Power of Innovation," Inc., State of Small Business 2001, p. 103; Leigh Buchanan, "Built to Invent," Inc., August 2002, p. 53.

5. Warren Bennis, "Cultivating Creative Collaboration," *Industry Week*, August 18, 1997, p. 86.

6. Roger von Oech, *A Whack on the Side of the Head* (New York: Warner Books, Inc., 1990), p.108.

7. Amol Sharma, "Floating a New Idea for Going Wireless, Parachute Included," *Wall Street Journal*, February 20, 2008, pp.A1, A9; "Up, Up, and Away," MIT Alumni Association, http://alum.mit.edu/ne/noteworthy/profiles/knoblach.html.

8. Michael Maiello, "They Almost Changed the World," *Forbes*, December 23, 2002, p. 217.

9. Peter Carbonara, "30 Great Small Business Ideas," *Your Company*, August/September 1998, pp. 32–58.

10. Charlie Farrell, "A Penny for Your Thoughts," *Business & Economic Review*, October–December 2006, p. 25.

11. Robert Fulghum, "Time to Sacrifice the Queen," *Reader's Digest*, August 1993, pp. 136–138.

12. Chuck Salter, "Failure Doesn't Suck," *Fast Company*, May 2007, p. 44; James Dyson, "Cleaning Up in His Industry," *Fortune*, January 22, 2007, p. 33.

13. Hillary Wooley, "Agriculture in the Sky," *Business 2.0*, September 2007, p. 32.

14. Roger von Oech, *A Whack on the Side of the Head* (New York: Warner Books, Inc., 1990), pp. 21–167; "Obstacles to Creativity," Creativity Web, http://www.ozemail.com.au/~caveman/Creative/Basics/obstacles.htm.

15. Tiffany Meyers, "Dry Idea," *Entrepreneur*, April 2008, http://www.entrepreneur.com/magazine/entrepreneur/2008/april/191526.html.

16. Dave Powers, "Making a Splash," *Business 2.0*, May 2007, p. 46.

17. Karen Axelton, "Imagine That," *Entrepreneur*, April 1998, p. 96; "Thomas Edison Biography," http://edison-ford-estate.com/ed_bio.htm.

18. Chuck Salter, "Failure Doesn't Suck," *Fast Company*, May 2007, p. 44.

19. Sally Fegley, "Painting the Town," *Entrepreneur*, July 1997, p. 14.

20. Joseph Schumpeter, "The Creative Response in Economic History, " *Journal of Economic History*, November 1947, pp. 149–159.

21. "Harnessing Your Team's Creativity," *BNET*, June 7, 2007, http://www.bnet.com/2403–13059_23–52990.html.

22. "Make Your Company an Idea Factory," *FSB*, May/June 2000, p. 124.

23. Andy Grove, "Think Disruptive," *Condé Nast Portfolio*, December 2007, pp. 170–175.

24. Anya Kamenetz, "The Power of the Prize," *Fast Company*, May 2008, pp. 43–45.

25. Larry Olmstead, "Nonstop Innovation," *Inc.*, July 2005, p. 34.

26. Carol Tice, "Fueling Change," *Entrepreneur*, November 2007, p. 47.

27. Ibid.

28. J. Michael Krivyanski, "Creative Genius," *Entrepreneur*, January 2008, p. 79.

29. Marie Cannizzaro, "Coffee Gets a Color Correction," *Business 2.0*, August 2007, p. 31; "Product and Company Summary," Smart Lid Systems, http://www.smartlidsystems.com/Company_Lid_brief.pdf.

30. Robert Epstein, "How To Get a Great Idea," *Reader's Digest*, December 1992, p. 102.

31. Georgia Flight, "How They Did It: Seven Intrapraneur Success Stories," *BNET*, April 18, 2007, http://www.bnet.com/2403-13070_23-196890.html.

32. Brian Libby, "How to Nurture New Ideas," *BNET*, June 7, 2007, http://www.bnet.com/2403-13068_23-68479.html.

33. Ibid.

34. Nichole L. Torres, "Industrial Revolution," *Entrepreneur*, November 2007, pp. 142–143.

35. Thea Singer and Lea Buchanan, "A Field Guide to Innovation," *Inc.*, August 2002, pp. 63–70.

36. Lucas Conley, "Rise and Repeat," *Fast Company*, July 2005, pp. 76–77.

37. Stephanie Kang, "Fashion Secret: Why Big Designers Haunt Vintage Shops," *Wall Street Journal*, April 2, 2007, pp. A1, A10.

38. Harold Evans, "What Drives America's Great Innovators?" *Fortune*, October 18, 2004, pp. 84–86.

39. Nichole L. Torres, "How Sweet It Is," *Entrepreneur*, May 2008, p. 82; "About Us," Edible Arrangements, http://www.ediblearrangements.com/about/about.aspx.

40. Kip Crosby, "Stumbling Into the Future," *Forbes ASAP*, November 20, 2000, pp. 105–112; John Steele Gordon with Michael Maiello, "Pioneers Die Broke," *Forbes*, December 23, 2002, pp. 258–264.

41. Kim Orr, "Vend a Dog a Bone," *Entrepreneur*, April 2007, http://www.entrepreneur.com/magazine/entrepreneur/2007/april/175924.html; "About Us," Hey Buddy! Pet Supply Vending Company, http://www.heybuddyvending.com/about.html.

42. Don Debelak, "Ideas Unlimited," *Business Start-Ups*, May 1999, pp. 57–58.

43. Anne Fisher, "The Internet Entrepreneur," *Fortune*, September 17, 2007, p. 38.

44. Lucas Conley, "Rise and Repeat," *Fast Company*, July 2005, pp. 76–77.

45. Nina Sovich, "Look, Mom, I'm Rich," *FSB*, April 2004, p. 28;. "The Crayon Holder," By Kids, For Kids, http://kids.patentcafe.com/products/index.asp#2.

46. Julie Sloane, "Inside the Mind of a (Rich) Inventor," *FSB*, November 2007, pp. 90–102.

47. Rosa Alphonso, "Small Business Optimism Is on an Upswing, According to the OPEN from American Express Small Business Monitor," American Express, May 24, 2007, http://home3.americanexpress.com/corp/pc/2007/monitor.asp.

48. Melinda Beck, "If at First You Don't Succeed, You're in Excellent Company," *Wall Street Journal*, April 29, 2008, p. D1; Nancy Gibb, "J.K. Rowling," *Time*, December 19, 2007, http://www.time.com/time/specials/2007/ personoftheyear/article/0,28804,1690753_1695388_1695436,00.html.

49. Roy Rowan, "Those Hunches Are More Than Blind Faith," *Fortune*, April 23, 1979, p. 112.

50. Michael Waldholz, "A Hallucination Inspires a Vision For AIDS Drug," *Wall Street Journal*, September 29, 1993, pp. B1, B5.

51. "A Greener Tire," *Fortune*, March 3, 2008, p.50.

52. Max Chafkin, "Student Teachers: Looking for New Ideas? Hire Some College Kids," *Inc.*, October 2006, pp. 44–46.

53. Siri Schubert, "A Duffer's Dream," *Business 2.0*, November 2006, p. 56.

54. Nick D'Alto, "Think Big," *Business Start-Ups*, January 2000, pp. 61–65.

55. Brian Nadel, "The Art of Innovation," Advertising Insert, *Fortune*, December 13, 2004, pp. S1–S22.

56. Thea Singer, "Your Brain on Innovation," *Inc.*, September 2002, pp. 86–88.

57. Paul Bagne, "When to Follow a Hunch," *Reader's Digest*, May 1994, p. 77.

58. Michael V. Copeland, "Six Leaps of Innovation," *Fortune*, January 21, 2008, pp. 27–30.

59. Waldholz, "A Hallucination Inspires a Vision For AIDS Drug," p. B5.

60. Thea Singer and Leah Buchanan, "Seeing It Fresh," *Inc.*, August 2002, p. 68.

61. Robert Epstein, "How To Get a Great Idea," *Reader's Digest*, December 1992, p. 104.

62. Michael Waldholz, "A Hallucination Inspires a Vision For AIDS Drug," *Wall Street Journal*, September 29, 1993, p. B5.

63. Bridget Finn, "Brainstorming for Better Brainstorming," *Business 2.0*, April 2005, pp. 109–114.

64. Chun, "Theory of Creativity," *Entrepreneur*, pp. 130–131.

65. Amantha Imber, "Finding Inspiration on the Treadmill," *Get to the Point: Small Business* (Marketing Profs), May 12, 2008, pp. 1–2.

66. Bridget Finn, "Brainstorming for Better Brainstorming," *Business 2.0*, April 2005, pp. 109–114.

67. Ed Brown, "A Day at Innovation U," *Fortune*, April 12, 1999, pp. 163–165.

68. The Hall of Science and Exploration, "Academy of Achievement: Linus Pauling, PhD," http://www.achievement.org/autodoc/page/pau0pro-1.

69. Anne Fisher, "Ideas Made Here," *Fortune*, June 11, 2007, pp. 35–41.

70. Andy Raskin, "A Higher Plane of Problem-Solving," *Business 2.0*, June 2003, pp. 54–56; "TRIZ 40," Triz 40 Principles, http://www.triz40.com/aff_Principles.htm.

71. Sloane, "Inside the Mind of a (Rich) Inventor," *FSB*, November 2007, pp. 90–102.

72. Ed Brown, "A Day at Innovation U," *Fortune*, April 12, 1999, p. 165.

73. Ed Brown, "A Day at Innovation U," *Fortune*, April 12, 1999, p. 165.

74. StopFakes.gov/smallbusiness, U.S. Patent and Trademark Office, http://www.uspto.gov/smallbusiness/.

75. "Get Real: The Truth About Counterfeiting," The International Anticounterfeiting Coalition, http://www.iacc.org/counterfeiting/counterfeiting.php.

76. Sara Schaefer Muñoz, "Patent No. 6,004,596: Peanut Butter and Jelly Sandwich," *Wall Street Journal*, April 5, 2005, pp. B1, B9; Malia Rulon, "Smucker Can't Patent PBJ, Court Says," *Greenville News*, April 9, 2005, pp. 18A, 21A.

77. "U.S. Patent Statistics," U.S. Patent and Trademark Office, http://www.uspto.gov/web/offices/ac/ido/oeip/taf/us_stat.pdf

78. Michael S. Malone, "The Smother of Invention," *Forbes ASAP*, June 24, 2002, pp. 32–40.

79. Jeff Wolfson and Russ Emerson, "Preparing for (and Avoiding) the Courtroom," *Nature Biotechnology*, June 19, 2008, http://www.nature.com/bioent/2008/080601/full/bioe.2008.6.html; Kris Frieswick, "License to Steal?" *CFO*, September 2001, pp. 89–91; Megan Barnett, "Patents Pending," *U.S. News & World Report*, June 10, 2002, pp. 33–34; Tomima Edmark, "On Guard," *Entrepreneur*, August 1997, pp. 92–94; Tomima Edmark, "On Guard," *Entrepreneur*, February 1997, pp.109–111.

80. John Liu and Chinmei Sung, "iPhone Knockoffs Steal Market Share as Apple Delays Asia Sales," *Bloomberg*, September 10, 2007, http://www.bloomberg.com/apps/news?pid=20601109&refer=home&sid=aSm8mwwFMr8k.

81. Michael B. Sapherstein, "The Registrability of the Harley-Davidson Roar" A Multimedia Analysis," http://www.bc.edu/bc_org/avp/law/st_org/iptf/articles/content/1998101101.html; Tomima Edmark, "How Much Is Too Much?" *Entrepreneur*, February 1998, pp. 93–95.

82. Peter Lattman, "Best of the Law Blog: Lex and the City," *Wall Street Journal*, October 24, 2007, p. B2; Kati Cornell, "Catfight with 'Sex & City': Feisty Gal's Trademark Battle," *New York Post*, November 15, 2007, http://www.nypost.com/seven/11152007/news/regionalnews/catfight_with_sex___city_819989.htm; Ed Pilkington, "Health and the City Falls Afoul of HBO Lawyers," *The Guardian*, October 27, 2007, http://www.guardian.co.uk/world/2007/oct/27/film.usa; Michael Atkins, "HBO Decides Not to Fight Application to Register Health and the City," *Seattle Trademark Lawyer*, November 29, 2007, http://seattletrademarklawyer.com/blog/2007/11/30/hbo-decides-not-to-fight-application-to-register-health-and.html.

83. Kevin J. O'Brien, "Silver Lining in Report on Software Piracy," *International Herald Tribune*, May 13, 2008, http://www.iht.com/articles/2008/05/13/technology/piracy.php.

84. *"The Cost of Movie Piracy,"* Motion Picture Association of America, 2006, http://www.mpaa.org/leksummaryMPA%20revised.pdf.

Chapter 3

1. "AmEx's Ken Chenault Talks about Leadership, Integrity, and the Credit Card Business," *Leadership and Change*, Knowledge @Wharton, http://knowledge@wharton.upenn.edu/index/cfm?fa=printArticle&ID=1179.

2. Alvin Toffler, "Shocking Truths About the Future," *Journal of Business Strategy*, July/August 1996, p. 6.

3. Thomas A. Stewart, "You Think Your Company's So Smart? Prove It," *Fortune*, April 30, 2001, p. 188.

4. Matthew Boyle, "John Mackey," *Fortune*, July 23, 2007, pp. 72–76; Jeffrey Pfeffer, "Dare to Be Different," *Business 2.0*, September 2004, p. 58; "Company Facts," Whole Foods Market, http://www.wholefoodsmarket.com/company/facts.html.

5. Gail Appleson, "Whole Foods Prepares to Open Town and Country Store," *St. Louis Today*, June 20, 2008, http://www.stltoday.com/stltoday/business/stories.nsf/story/6636B1111341CBE38625746E000A730E?OpenDocument; Matthew Boyle, "John Mackey," *Fortune*, July 23, 2007, pp. 72–76.

6. "Who Are We?" Zoots, http://www.zoots.com/aboutWhoWeAre.aspx.

7. Jeanette Borzo, "Nurses on Demand," *Business 2.0*, May 2007, p. 40; "Why Online Staffing?" ShiftWise, http://www.shift wise.net/whyOnlineStaffing.asp; "Nursing Shortage," American Association of Colleges of Nursing, April 2008, http://www.aacn.nche.edu/media/FactSheets/NursingShortage.htm.

8. "A Conversation with Scott Cook," *Inc.*, September 2007, p. 215.

9. Jeanette Borzo, "Taking on the Recruiting Monster," *FSB*, May 2007, pp. 89–90.

10. Lark Reynolds, "Restaurateurs Hot to See Greer Company's Cookware," *Greenville News*, May 11, 2008, p. 1F; "Advanced Composite Materials (ACM) Annouces New Headquarters, Manufacturing Facility in Greer," Greer Area Development Corporation, August 9, 2007, http://www.greerdevelopment.com/documents/Advanced CompostieMaterialspressreleaseAug9071.pdf.

11. Ken Blanchard, "The New Bottom Line," *Entrepreneur*, February 1998, p. 127.

12. Thomas A. Stewart, "Why Values Statements Don't Work," *Fortune*, June 10, 1996, p. 137.

13. Michael Barrier, "Back From the Brink," *Nation's Business*, September 1995, p. 21.

14. William Cooper, "Chick-Fil-A CEO, S. Truett Cathy," *ChristiaNet News*, http://christiannews.christianet.com/1097585115.htm; Richard Schneider, "Chain Reaction," *Guideposts*, April 2003, pp. 18–19; Chick-Fil-A, http://www.chickfila.com/Company.asp; "Chick-Fil-A Founder Truett Cathy's Grandson to Open Chain's Newest Stand-Alone Restaurant in Durham January 10," *Reuters*, January 9, 2008, http://www.reuters.com/article/pressRelease/idUS130426+09-Jan-2008+MW20080109.

15. "The Secret to Innovation at Method," Method, http://peopleagainstdirty.typepad.com/people_against_dirty/.

16. Ellen Spragins, "Unmasking Your Motivations," FSB, November 2002, p. 86.

17. "Our Philosophy," Google, http://www.google.com/corporate/tenthings.html.

18. "Our Story," Great Harvest Bread Company: Duluth, http://getfreshbread.com/ourStory.htm.

19. "Our Mission," Eileen Fisher Inc., http://www.eileenfisher.com/scripts/ecatalogisapi.dll/group?group=34081&Template=9990000001057050.

20. Anjali Cordero, "Health Food Is Going to the Dogs – Literally," *Wall Street Journal*, April 9, 2008, p. D3; Diane Brady and Christopher Palmeri, "The Pet Economy," *Business Week*, August 6, 2007, http://www.businessweek.com/magazine/content/07_32/b4045001.htm.

21. Peggy Edersheim Kalb, "A Movie Theater as Comfy as Our Sofa," *Wall Street Journal*, April 24, 2008, p. D2; Catherine Donaldson-Evans, "Doomsayers Predict Death of Movie Theater," *Fox News*, January 16, 2006, http://www.foxnews.com/story/0,2933,181722,00.html; Andy Serwer, Corey Hajim, and Susan M. Kaufman, "Movie Theaters: Extreme Makeover," *Fortune*, May 23,2006, http://money.cnn.com/2006/05/19/magazines/fortune/theater_futureof_fortune/index.htm; Paul Donsky, "New Theaters to Offer One-Stop Dinner and a Movie," *Access Atlanta*, April 25, 2008, http://www.accessatlanta.com/movies/content/movies/stories/2008/04/25/movie_0426.html?cxntlid=homepage_tab_newstab.

22. Rachel Dodes, "Master of a Fading Art," *Wall Street Journal,* July 5–6, 2008, p. W3; Michael M. Phillips, "Why Turkish Tailors Seem So Well-Suited to Work in Tennessee," *Wall Street Journal*, April 12, 2005, pp. A1, A7; Kevin Cowan, "Tailors Tee Up to Craft Tiger's Custom Jacket," *Knoxville News Sentinel,* June 19, 2008, http://www.knoxnews.com/news/2008/jun/19/tailors-tee-up-to-craft-tigers-custom-jacket/.

23. William J. Dennis, Jr., *National Small Business Poll: Competition,* National Federation of Independent Businesses (Washington, DC: 2003), Volume 3, Issue 8, p. 1.

24. Erick Schonfeld and Chris Morrison, "The Next Disruptors: Expensr," *Business 2.0*, September 2007, pp. 58–59.

25. Carolyn Z. Lawrence, "Know Your Competition," *Business Start-Ups*, April 1997, p. 51.

26. Beth Kwon, "Toolbox: Staying Competitive," *FSB*, December 2002/January 2003, p. 89.

27. Kevin Coyne and John Horne, "How Companies Respond to Competitors: A McKinsey Global Survey," *The McKinsey Quarterly*, May 2008, http://www.mckinseyquarterly.com/How_companies_respond_to_competitors_2146.

28. Kirsten Osound, "Secret Agent Plan," *Entrepreneur*, June 2005, p. 98.

29. Brian Caulfield, "Know Your Enemy," *Business 2.0*, June 2004, pp. 89–90.

30. Lewis Carroll, *Alice in Wonderland* (Mount Vernon, NY:Peter Pauper Press, 1937), pp.78–79.

31. Rhonda Abrams, "Set Sights on One Big New Goal for '05," *Business*, October 10, 2004, p. 7; Mark Henricks, "In the BHAG," *Entrepreneur*, August 1999, pp. 65–67.

32. Joseph C. Picken and Gregory Dess, "The Seven Traps of Strategic Planning," *Inc.*, November 1996, p. 99.

33. Michael E. Porter, *Competitive Strategy* (New York: Free Press, 1980), Chapter 2.

34. Jennifer Bjorhus, "No-Frills Gyms Take Off," *Pioneer Press*, March 22, 2008, www.twincities.com/ci_8659962?source=most_emailed; Neil Janowitz, "Anytime Fitness Offers Slimmed-Down Gyms," *Shopping Centers Today*, April 2007, http://www.icsc.org/srch/sct/sct0407/Retail_anytime_fitness.php; "The Anytime Fitness Story," Anytime Fitness, http://www.anytimefitness.com/en-us/corporate/about.

35. Ann Zimmerman, "Behind the Dollar-Store Boom: A Nation of Bargain Hunters," *Wall Street Journal*, December 13, 2004, pp. A1, A10; Brendan Coffey, "Every Penny Counts," *Forbes*, September 30, 2002, pp. 68–70; Amber McDowell, "Discount Retailers Prosper Amid Economic Instability," *Greenville News Business*, December 23, 2002, pp. 6, 13.

36. Nicole L. Torres, "Women in Charge: Bold Moves," Entrepreneur, January 2008, pp. 33–36; "Green Chocolate: Conversations with Katrina Markoff," *Beanstockd News*, May 10, 2008, http://www.beanstockd.com/greenstockd/2008/05/10/green-chocolate-conversations-with-katrina-markoff; Patricia Greco, "Katrina Markoff: A Chocolate Success Story," *Good Housekeeping*, January 2007, http://www.goodhousekeeping.com/names/real/chocolate-success-story-jan07.

37. Celia Farber, "Anice Hotel," *Inc.*, June 2002, pp. 88–90; Shelly Branch, "Havin' an Ice Team," *Fortune*, March 1, 1999, pp. 277–278; Eleena De Lisser, "The Hot New Travel Spot Is Freezing Cold," *Wall Street Journal*, October 16, 2002, pp. D1,D4; Ice Hotel, http://www.icehotel.com/.

38. Debra Phillips. "Leaders of the Pack," *Entrepreneur*, September 1996, p.127.

39. J. J. Ramberg, "Fair Fashion," *Entrepreneur*, October 2007, p. 36; Gwendolyn Bounds, "Green Clothing Maker Indigenous Designs Puts Fashion First," *Wall Street Journal*, July 17, 2007, p. B9.

40. "Intuit Study: Next-Gen Artisans Fuel New Entrepreneurial Economy," Intuit and Institute for the Future, February 13, 2008, http://www.intuit.com/about_intuit/press_room/press_release/2008/0213.jsp, p.1.

41. Anthony Trento, "Birds of Play," *FSB*, April 2008, pp. 44–45; "Feather Designer Tickles Fancy of Celebrities, Broadway," *MCLA Beacon*, September 27, 2007, http://media.www.mclabeacon.com/media/storage/paper802/news/2007/09/27/Entertainment/Feather.Designer.Tickles.Fancy.Of.Celebrities.Broadway-2994435.shtml.

42. Norm Brodsky, "How Independents Can Hold On," *Inc.*, August 2007, p. 66.

43. Raymund Flandez, "Nostalgia Helps Put Old Kiddie Rides Back in Play," *Wall Street Journal*, March 25, 2008, p. B6.

44. "Three Reasons Why Good Strategies Fail: Execution, Execution,…" *Strategic Management*, Knowldege @Wharton, University of Pennsylvania, http://knowledge.wharton.edu/index.cfm?fa=printArticle&ID=1252.

45. Joel Kurtzman, "Is Your Company Off Course? Now You Can Find Out Why," *Fortune*, February 17, 1997, p.128.

46. Michelle Bitoun, "Show Them the Data," *Trustee*, September 2002, p. 35.

47. Gene Marks, "The Key to Better Management: A Balanced Scorecard," *Forbes*, April 29, 2008, http://www.forbes.com/2008/04/29/small-business-management-mange-cx_gm_0429genemarksmetric.html.

48. Robert S. Kaplan and David P. Norton, "The Balanced Scorecard—Measures That Drive Performance," *Harvard Business Review*, January–February 1992, pp.71–79.

Chapter 4

1. Kelly K. Spors, "Do Start-Ups Really Need Formal Business Plans?" *Wall Street Journal*, January 9, 2007, p. B9.

2. Charles Fishman, "The Wal-Mart You Don't Know," *Fast Company*, December 2003, http://www.fastcompany.com/magazine/77/walmart.html.

3. Brian O'Reilly, "Profits from Polyester," *FSB*, June 2007, http://money.cnn.com/magazines/fsb/fsb_archive/2007/06/01/100051008/index.htm; Brian O'Reilly, "Bigger Servings," *FSB*, July/August 2008, p. 38.

4. Mark Henricks, "Test Run," *Entrepreneur*, December 2007, pp. 116–120.

5. Karen J. Bannan, "Companies Save Time, Money with Online Surveys," *BtoBOnline.com*, June 6, 2003, http://www.btobonline.com/article.cms?articleId=11115.

6. Don Debelak, "Join Hands," *Entrepreneur*, September 2005, pp. 138–140.

7. Jena McGregor, "The Art of Service: Intuit," *Fast Company*, October 2005, p. 53; Michael S. Hopkins, "America's 25 Most Fascinating Entrepreneurs: Scott Cook, Intuit," *Inc.*, April 2004, http://www.inc.com/magazine/20040401/25cook.html; "How Intuit Found Fame and Fortune and Beat Out Microsoft," *Knowledge @Wharton*, November 5, 2003, http://knowledge.wharton.upenn.edu/index.cfm?fa=viewArticle&id=869.

8. Debelak, "Join Hands," *Entrepreneur*, September 2005, pp. 138–140.

9. Karen E. Klein, "Building a Better Business Plan," *Business Week*, September 12, 2006, http://www.businessweek.com/smallbiz/content/sep2006/sb20060912_981004.htm.

10. Karen E. Klein, "Writing a Living Business Plan," *Business Week*, May 5, 2008, http://www.businessweek.com/smallbiz/content/may2008/sb2008055_225008.htm.

11. Scott A. Shane, *The Illusions of Entrepreneurship*, (New Haven, Connecticut and London: Yale University Press), 2008, p. 74.

12. Steve Marshall Cohen, "Money Rules," *Business Start-Ups*, July 1995, p. 31.

13. Alison Stein Wellner, "You Know What Your Company Does: Can You Explain It in 30 seconds?" *Inc.*, July 2007, pp. 92–97.

14. Adam McCulloch, "Prefab with a View," *Business 2.0*, May 2005, p. 70.

15. *ESRI Trend Analysis: 2008/2013*, ESRI White Paper, (Redlands, California: June 2008), http://esri.com/library/whitepapers/pdfs/trend-analysis-2008-2013.pdf, p. 5; Sharon McLoone, "Booming Hispanic Market Opens Business Opportunities," *Washington Post*, June 27, 2008, http://blog.washingtonpost.com/small-business/2008/06/booming_hispanic_market_opens.html; Steve Strauss, "To Tap the Hispanic Market, You First Have to Understand It," *USA Today*, February 20, 2007, http://www.usatoday.com/money/smallbusiness/columnist/strauss/2007-02-19-hispanic_x.htm.

16. Sharon McLoone, "Booming Hispanic Market Opens Business Opportunities," *Washington Post*, June 27, 2008, http://blog.washingtonpost.com/small-business/2008/06/booming_hispanic_market_opens.html.

17. Steve Fey, "Gotta' Get Some Groceries!" *Living Las Vegas*, July 18, 2008, http://living-las-vegas.com/2008/07/grocery-stores-las-vegas/; Arnold M. Knightly, "Hispanic Groceries Battling for Latino Dollar," *Las Vegas Business Press*, August 21, 2006, http://www.lvbusinesspress.com/articles/2006/08/21/news/news09.txt; "About Us," Mariana's, http://www.marianasmarkets.com/aboutus.aspx.

18. Kerry Miller, "How to Write a Winning Business Plan," *Business Week*, December 3, 2007, http://www.businessweek.com/smallbiz/content/dec2007/sb2007123_109728.htm.

19. Andriana Gardella, "Tickets, Anyone?" *FSB*, May 2008, pp. 61–67.

20. James Maguire, "Veteran E-Commerce Designer Finds Her Mojo," *Small Business Computing*, April 22, 2005, http://www.ecommerce-guide.com/article.php/3499766; James Maguire, "Starting Your Own E-Business: Part 1" *Small Business Computing*, October 3, 2005, www.smallbusinesscomputing.com/emarketing/article.pho/35553126.

21. Nicole L. Torres, "Sowing the Seeds," *Entrepreneur B.Y.O.B.*, May 2004, pp. 118–122.

22. Conversation with Charles Burke, CEO Burke Financial Associates.

23. "Raising Money," *Entrepreneur*, July 2005, p. 58.

24. Michael V. Copeland, "How to Make Your Business Plan the Perfect Pitch," *Business 2.0*, September 2005, p. 88.

25. Conversation with Charles Burke, CEO Burke Financial Associates.

26. Karen Axelton, "Good Plan, Stan," *Business Start-Ups*, March 2000, p. 17.

27. Vivek Wadhwa, "Before You Write a Business Plan," *Business Week*, January 7, 2008, http://www.businessweek.com/smallbiz/content/jan2008/sb2008017_119570.htm?chan=smallbiz_special+report+—+the+abcs+of+business+plans_the+abcs+of+business+plans.

Chapter 5

1. Virginia Munger Kahn, "Room to Grow," *Business Week*, September 3, 2007, http://www.businessweek .com/magazine/content/07_36/b4048436.htm?chan= search.
2. Chris Harrison, "Form Is Everything," *E-Merging Business*, Fall–Winter 2000, pp. 194–199.
3. Jacquelyn Lynn, "Partnership Procedures," *Business Start-Ups*, June 1996, p. 73.
4. Amy Joyce, "Getting It Together," *Washington Post*, June 12, 2005, http://www.washingtonpost.com/wp-dyn/ content/article/2005/06/10/AR2005061001353 .html.
5. Norm Brodsky, "Sam and Me," *Inc.*, June 2006, p. 67.
6. Matthew Bandyk, "Five Things Entrepreneurs Should Know About Business Partners," *U.S. News and World Report*, May 6, 2008, http://www.usnews.com/articles/ business/small-business-entrepreneurs/2008/05/06/ 5-things-entrepreneurs-should-know-about-business- partners.html.
7. Nichole L. Torres, "Teacher's Pet," *Entrepreneur*, May 2008, pp. 128–129.
8. Kelly Spors, "Small Talk," *Wall Street Journal*, April 4, 2006, p. A16.
9. Michael Barrier, "Someone's in the Kitchen with Wolfgang," *Success*, September 2000, pp. 28–33; "Company Info," Wolfgang Puck, http://www .wolfgangpuck.com/company/.
10. Chief Justice John Marshall, cited by Henry R. Cheeseman, *Contemporary Business and Online Commerce Law*, Sixth Edition (Upper Saddle River, New Jersey: Pearson Publishing Co., 2008), p. 750.
11. Max Chafkin, "A Haven for Virtual Companies," *Inc.*, July 2008, p. 27.
12. Virginia Munger Kahn, "Room to Grow," *Business Week*, September 3, 2007, http://www.businessweek.com/ magazine/content/07_36/b4048436.htm?chan=search.
13. Paul J. Lim, "Google: Off and Running, *U.S. News & World Report*, August 19, 2004, http://www.usnews.com/ usnews/biztech/buzz/archive/buzz040819.htm.; Paul Shread, "Google IPO Investors Get a Break," Internet.com, Augist 19, 2004, http://www.internetnews.com/bus-news/article .php/3397571.
14. Matthew Miller, "Gates No Longer World's Richest Man," *Forbes*, March 5, 2008, http://www.forbes.com/2008/03/05/ buffett-worlds-richest-cx_mm_0229buffetrichest.html.
15. Virginia Munger Kahn, "Room to Grow," *Business Week*, September 3, 2007, http://www.businessweek.com/ magazine/content/07_36/b4048436.htm?chan=search.
16. Ibid.
17. Richard Burke, "How I Did It: Pulling Away from the Pack," *Inc.*, July 2005, pp. 110–112.

Chapter 6

1. Sara Wilson, "Biz Kids," *Entrepreneur*, October 2006, pp. 146–47; Nick Nelson, "Youngest Franchisee Loves Company, Product," *Caller Times*, October 4, 2005, http://m.caller.com/news/2005/Oct/04/youngest-franchisee- loves-company-product/; Dale Buss, "Chain Lightning," *Hispanic Business*, May 2005, http://www.hispanicbusiness .com/news/2005/4/29/chain_lightning.htm.

2. *Economic Impact of Franchised Businesses, Volume 2: Executive Summary and Highlights*, International Franchise Association and Price Waterhouse Coopers (Washington, DC: 2007), pp. 4–6.
3. *Economic Impact of Franchised Businesses, Volume 2: Executive Summary and Highlights*, International Franchise Association and Price Waterhouse Coopers (Washington, DC: 2007), p. 8.
4. Megan Barnett, "Size Up a Ready-Made Business," *U.S. News & World Report*, August 2, 2004, p. 70.
5. *Economic Impact of Franchised Businesses, Volume 2: Executive Summary and Highlights*, International Franchise Association and Price Waterhouse Coopers (Washington, DC: 2007), pp. 10, 15.
6. Melana Yanos, "Franchise Opportunities for Young People," *NuWire Investor*, May 13, 2008, http://www.nuwireinvestor.com/articles/franchise- opportunities-for-young-people-51561.aspx.
7. Sara Wilson, "Early to Rise," *Entrepreneur*, August 2008, pp. 90–94.
8. Ibid.
9. Eve Tahmincioglu, "Don't Go West. Young Man. Buy Yourself a Franchise Instead," *New York Times*, July 26, 2007, http://www.nytimes.com/2007/07/26/business/ 26sbiz.html.
10. "FAQ," Ben & Jerry's Homemade, Inc., http://www.benjerry .com/scoop_shops/franchise_info/faqs.cfm.
11. Michele Deluca, "Franchise Owners Pay Price for Success," *Tonawanda News*, April 28, 2008, http://www.tonawanda- news.com/business/ gnnbusiness_story_119141835.html.
12. "Papa John's Receives Highest Customer Satisfaction Rating for Ninth Consecutive Year," *Reuters*, May 20, 2008, http://www.reuters.com/article/pressRelease/idUS139161+ 20-May-2008+BW20080520; Anne Field, "Piping Hot Performance," *Success*, March 1999, pp. 76–80.
13. *The Profile of Franchising 2006*, International Franchise Association (Washington, DC: 2007), p. 67.
14. Ibid.
15. Ibid.
16. April Y. Pennington, "The Right Stuff," *Entrepreneur*, September 2004, pp. 90–100.
17. Darrell Johnson and John Reynolds, "A Study of Franchise Loan Performance in the SBA Guaranty Programs," *Franchising World*," September 2007, pp. 53–56; Richard Gibson, "How to Finance a Franchise," *Wall Street Journal*, March 17, 2008, p. R8.
18. Sara Wilson, "Early to Rise," *Entrepreneur*, August 2008, pp. 90–94.
19. Michele Deluca, "Franchise Owners Pay Price for Success," *Tonawanda News*, April 28, 2008, http:// www.tonawanda-news.com/business/gnnbusiness_story_ 119141835.html.
20. Steven C. Michael and James G. Combs, "Entrepreneurial Failure: The Case of Franchisees," *Journal of Small Business Management*, January 2008, Volume 46, Number 1, pp. 75–90.
21. Jeffrey McCracken and Janet Adamy, "Dining Chains Close Doors," *Wall Street Journal*, July 30, 2008, p. B1.
22. Richard Gibson, "Why Franchisees Fail," *Wall Street Journal*, April 30, 2007, p. R9.
23. Steven C. Michael and James G. Combs, "Entrepreneurial Failure: The Case of Franchisees," *Journal of Small*

Business Management, January 2008, Volume 46, Number 1, pp. 75–90.

24. Iris Taylor, "Franchises Can Be Freedom from Corporate America," *WSLS*, July 9, 2008, http://www.wsls.com/sls/business/consumer/article/franchises_can_be_freedom_from_corporate_america/13747/.

25. *The Profile of Franchising 2006*, International Franchise Association (Washington, DC: 2007), p. 62.

26. *The Profile of Franchising*, (Washington, DC: FRANDATA Corp and the IFA Educational Foundation, 2000), p. 123.

27. *The Profile of Franchising 2006*, International Franchise Association (Washington, DC: 2007), p. 66.

28. *The Profile of Franchising 2006*, International Franchise Association (Washington, DC: 2007), p. 68.

29. Daniel Kruger, "You Want Data with That?" *Forbes*, March 29, 2004, pp. 58–59.

30. Wendy Bounds, "Cold Stone Case Study: Three Warnings for Franchise Buyers," *Wall Street Journal*, June 16, 2008, http://blogs.wsj.com/independentstreet/2008/06/16/cold-stone-case-study-three-warnings-for-franchise-buyers/.

31. Richard Gibson, "McDonald's Franchisees Grumble over Dollar Menu," *Wall Street Journal*, May 21, 2008, p. B3.

32. Richard Gibson, "The Inside Scoop," *Wall Street Journal*, June 16, 2008, http://wsj.com/article/SB121321718319265569.html?mod=Financing_1.

33. "Super-Size What? The Big Mac Turns 40," *USA Today*, August 24, 2007, http://www.usatoday.com/news/nation/2007-08-24-big-mac-at-40_N.htm.

34. *The Profile of Franchising*, (Washington, DC: FRANDATA Corp and the IFA Educational Foundation, 2000), p. 116.

35. Jeannie Ralston, "Before You Bet Your Buns," *Venture*, March 1988, p. 57.

36. *The Profile of Franchising 2006*, International Franchise Association (Washington, DC: 2007), p. 73.

37. Richard Gibson, "Franchise Fever," *Wall Street Journal*, December 15, 2003, p. R1.

38. Kelly K. Spors, "Not So Fast," *Wall Street Journal*, September 19, 2005, p. R11; Joshua Kurlantzick, "Serving Up Success," *Entrepreneur*, November 2003, http://www.entrepreneur.com/article/print/0,2361,311429,00.html; "Subway Restaurant News," Subway, http://www.subway.com/subwayroot/index.aspx.

39. Anne Fisher, "Risk Reward," *FSB*, December 2005/January 2006, p. 58.

40. Gregory Matusky, "What Every Business Can Learn from Franchising," *Inc.*, January 1994, p. 90.

41. Elaine Pofeldt, "Success Franchisee Satisfaction Survey," *Success*, April 1999, p. 59.

42. *The Profile of Franchising 2006*, International Franchise Association (Washington, DC: 2007), p. 77.

43. Douglas MacMillan, "Finding the Perfect Franchise Fit," *Business Week*, July 31, 2006, http://www.businessweek.com/smallbiz/content/jul2006/sb20060728_328561.htm?chan=top+news_top+news.

44. Hilary Maynard, "Sign of the Times," *Business Examiner*, March 17, 2008, http://exchange.franchoice.com/Documents/News/Business%20Examiner%203.17.2008.pdf.

45. Anne Field, "Piping Hot Performance," *Success*, March 1999, pp. 76–80.

46. April Y. Pennington, "Would You Like a Franchise with That?" *Entrepreneur*, January 2005, pp. 120-127.

47. Paula Schleis, "Franchise Freedom," *Ohio.com*, December 17, 2007, http://www.ohio.com/business/12555331.html?page=all&c=y.

48. John Reynolds, "Minorities, Women Have Big Stake in Franchised Businesses," International Franchise Association, October 22, 2007, http://www.franchise.org/Franchise-Industry-News-Detail.aspx?id=35934.

49. Sara Wilson, "Running Start," *Entrepreneur*, January 2008, pp. 144–150.

50. Ibid.

51. Jacy Cochran, "Generation Y: Make Way for the Fresh Faces of Franchising," *All Business*, January 1, 2007, http://www.allbusiness.com/retail-trade/3969190-1.html.

52. "If You Want to Play Big, Then Get the Big Players," *Franchise Research News*, Volume 1, 2007 (Arlington, Virginia: FRANdata), p. 2.

53. Sara Wilson, "Show Me the Way," *Entrepreneur*, September 2006, pp. 116–124.

54. Joseph Wheeler, "The Multi-Unit Franchise Revolution," *Area Developer*, October 10, 2004, http://www.areadeveloper.us/archive.shtml.

55. "Bill Welter Creates Everybody's Favorite Place," *Area Developer*, August 10, 2004, http://www.areadeveloper.us/news_20040810.shtml.

56. David J. Kaufman, "What a Ride!" *Entrepreneur*, May 2007, pp. 108–113.

57. Ibid.

58. "Burger King Projects 80 Percent of Future Growth to Come from International Expansion," *Nation's Restaurant News*, July 11, 2007, www.nrn,com/breakingNews.aspxx?id=342920&menu_id=1368#.

59. *McDonald's Corporation 2007 Annual Report*, p. 24.

60. Udo Schlentrich and Hachemi Aliouche, "Rosenberg Center Confirms Global Franchise Growth," *Franchising World*, August 2006, http://www.franchise.org/Franchise-News-Detail.aspx?id=31120.

61. Dhawal Shah, "India: A Market for the Masses," *Franchising World*, June 2008, http://www.franchise.org/Franchise-News-Detail.aspx?id=40638.

62. Carlye Adler, "How China Eats a Sandwich," *Fortune*, March 21, 2005, pp. 210[B]–210[D].

63. Lawrence Bivens, "U.S. Franchisors Are Making Major Global Inroads," *Wall Street Journal*, April 10, 2008, p. D4; "China Owns the Most Franchise Stores in the World," *People's Daily Online*, April 14, 2005, http://english.peopledaily.com.cn/200504/14/eng20050414_181082.html.

64. *Franchising Industry in China,* Stat-USA, U.S. Foreign Commercial Service (Washington, DC: 2004), http://www.buyusainfo.net/docs/x_5566195.pdf.

65. "Dunkin Donuts Plans Mainland China Expansion," *Boston Business Journal*, January 25, 2008, http://boston.bizjournals.com/boston/stories/2008/01/21/daily67.html; "Dunkin' Donuts Coming to Mainland China," *USA Today*, January 25, 2008, http://www.usatoday.com/money/world/2008-01-25-dunkin-shanghai_N.htm.

66. "New Nontraditional Subways," *CSP Daily News*, August 1, 2007, http://www.cspnet.com/ME2/Audiences/dirmod.asp?sid=&nm=&type=Publishing&mod=Publications%3A%3AArticle&mid=8F3A7027421841978F18BE895F87F791&tier=4&id=3146FE87D5CA4B77BE30868FA2C153F2&AudID=8D2273B133A14EB6903E0EECCBC32777.

67. "Camille's to Open Units in Wal-Marts," *Franchising .com*, January 16, 2008, http://www.franchising.com/ pressreleases/4705/.

68. Richard C. Hoffman and John F. Preble, "Convert to Compete: Competitive Advantage Through Conversion Financing," *Journal of Small Business Management*, Vol. 41, No.2, April 2003, pp.127–140.

69. Julia Boorstin, "Yum Isn't Chicken of China—or Atkins," *Fortune*, March 8, 2004, p. 50.

70. Gabrielle Solomon, "Co-Branding Alliances: Arranged Marriages Made by Marketers," *Fortune*, October 12, 1998, p. 188[N].

71. Lindsay Holloway, James Park, Nichole L. Torres, and Sara Wilson, "This Just In . . ." *Entrepreneur*, January 2008, pp. 100–110; Virginia Sole-Smith, "She Got Rich Doing What?" *More*, July/August 2008, pp. 90–94.

72. Raymund Flandez, "A Look at High-Performing Franchises," *Wall Street Journal*, February 12, 2008, p. B5; Lindsay Holloway, James Park, Nichole L. Torres, and Sara Wilson, "This Just In . . ." *Entrepreneur*, January 2008, pp. 100–110.

73. April Y. Pennington, "An American Icon," *Entrepreneur*, January 2005, http://www.entrepreneur.com/magazine/ entrepreneur/2005/january/74992.html.

Chapter 7

1. Darren Dahl, "The Most Valuable Companies in America," *Inc.*, April 2008, pp. 97–05.

2. Nichole Torres, "Fixer Upper," *Entrepreneur B.Y.O.B.*, November 2001, pp. 120–128; Ian Zack, "On the Rack," *Forbes*, March 5, 2001, http://www.forbes.com/ forbes/2001/0305/152.html.

3. Abigail Tucker, "Artist Brings *Star Wars* Mannequins to Real Life," *Greenville News*, February 27, 2005, p. 6E.

4. Eugenia Levenson, "For Love and Money," *Fortune*, November 27, 2006, pp. 269–274.

5. Sara Harvey, "Legendary Clemson Bar to Get Facelift," *Greenville News*, August 31, 2003, pp. 1B, 7B.

6. Justin Martin," The Time to Sell Is Now!" *FSB*, September 2006, pp. 28–43.

7. Melana Yanos, "Business Listings: The Top Five Online Business Marketplaces," *NuWire Investor*, May 26, 2008, http://www.nuwireinvestor.com/articles/business-listings- the-top-5-online-business-marketplaces-51624.aspx.

8. Dimitra Kessenides, "Buyer Beware," *Inc.*, December 2004, pp. 48–49.

9. Elaine Appleton Grant, "How to Buy a Small Business Without Getting Taken," *U.S. News and World Report*," February 26, 2008, http://www.usnews.com/articles/ business/small-business-entrepreneurs/2008/02/26/how-to- buy-a-small-business-without-getting-taken.html.

10. Crystal Detamore-Rodman, "An Acquired Taste," *Entrepreneur*, October 2004, pp. 62–64.

11. Luisa Kroll, "Gotcha: Pushing the Limits of Due Diligence," *Forbes*, October 30, 2000, pp. 186–187.

12. Richard Breeden, "Small Talk: Selling the Company," *Wall Street Journal*, April 6, 2004, p. B4.

13. "Attention, Please," *Entrepreneur*, April 2008, p. 188; "What's Next," Gurbaksh Chahal, http://www.chahal.com/; Ty McMahan, "BlueLithium Founder Gets Back to Business," *Venture Wire*, May 2, 2008, http://www.chahal.com/venturewire.pdf.

14. Justin Martin, "The Time to Sell Is Now!" *FSB*, September 2006, pp. 28–43.

15. Torres, "Fixer Upper," p. 126.

16. Norm Brodsky, "What's Your Business Really Worth?" *Inc.*, April 2005, p. 55.

17. Darren Dahl, "The Most Valuable Companies in America," *Inc.*, April 2008, pp. 97–105.

18. James Laabs, ""What Is Your Company Worth?" *The Business Sale Center*, http://www .businesssalecenter.com/new_page_3.htm.

19. James Laabs, "Recasting: A Key to Building Value for the Seller," *The Business Sale Center*, http://www.businesssalecenter.com/new_page_3.htm.

20. Richard Breeden, "Outsourcing Affects Owners' Plans to Sell Firms," *Wall Street Journal*, May 24, 2005, p. B7.

21. Will Schroter, "Selling Company to Another Entails Entrepreneur's Hardest, Best Move," *Washington Business Journal*, June 25, 2007, http://washington.bizjournals.com/ extraedge/consultants/go_big/2007/06/25/column6.html? market=washington

22. David Stires, "Founders to the Rescue!" *Fortune*, October 3, 2005, p. 28.

23. David Worrell, "Go for the Gold," *Entrepreneur*, October 2004, p. 70.

24. Ryan McCarthy, "Coke Pays Billions for Vitaminwater," *Inc.*, August 2007, p. 18; "Coke Set to Buy Glacéau for $4.2 Billion," *Reuters*, May 25, 2007, http://www.reuters.com/ article/businessNews/idUSWNAS248120070525.

25. "Jennifer Fermino, "A Fair $hake & Bake," *New York Post*, January 4, 2007, http://www.nypost.com/seven/ 01042007/news/regionalnews/a_fair_hake__bake_ regionalnews_jennifer_fermino.htm; Lee McGrath, "Off the Menu," *New York Times*, January 3, 2007, http://www.nytimes.com/2007/01/03/dining/03off.html?sc p=1&sq=Magnolia+Bakery+Abrams&st=nyt.

26. Jill Andresky Fraser, "Putting Your Company on the Block", *Inc.*, April 2001, pp. 106–107.

27. Abby Ellin, "After Selling the Company, Remorse," *New York Times*, July 10, 2008, http://www.nytimes.com/2008/07/10/ business/smallbusiness/10sbiz.html?partner=rssnyt&emc=rss.

28. "Tova Did It Her Way: Celebrating 25 Years of the Tova Signature Fragrance," *Global Cosmetic Industry*, May 29, 2008, http://www.gcimagazine.com/news/webexclusives/ 19294029.html; Abby Ellin, "After Selling the Company, Remorse," *New York Times*, July 10, 2008, http://www.nytimes.com/2008/07/10/business/smallbusine ss/10sbiz.html?partner=rssnyt&emc=rss.

29. Abby Ellin, "After Selling the Company, Remorse," *New York Times*, July 10, 2008, http://www.nytimes.com/ 2008/07/10/business/smallbusiness/10sbiz.html?partner= rssnyt&emc=rss.

30. Ian Mount, "Clogging for Dollars," *FSB*, December2006/January 2007, p. 18; Zan O'Leary, "Crocs Inc. Enters into Definitive Agreement to Buy Jibbitz LLC," Crocs Newsroom, October 3, 2006, http://www1.jibbitz .com/newsroom/press_100306.php.

31. Stacy McIntyre, "The Yahoo Family Tree," *Portfolio*, June 2008, p. 34.

32. Jenna Fryar, "Pettys Sell Controlling Interest in Company," *In Rich*, June 12, 2008, http://www.inrich.com/cva/ ric/sports.apx_content=articles-RTD-2008-06-12-0091.html; "Pettys Sell Controlling Interest in NASCAR Team,"

Motorsport 100, June 13, 2008, http://www.motorsport100
.co.uk/news/week-9_6_2008#13-06-08_7; "Massachusetts
Equity Firm Takes Control of Richard Petty's NASCAR
Franchise," *Projo Sports Blog*, June 11, 2008, http://www
.beloblog.com/ProJo_Blogs/sportsblog/2008/06/mass-
equity-fir.html.

33. Peter Collins, "Cashing Out and Maintaining Control,"
Small Business Reports, December 1989, p. 28.

34. Paul Kaihla, "Why China Wants to Scoop Up Your Company,"
Business 2.0, June 2005, pp. 29–30; "State Aids Galesburg
Company in Retaining Workers," Illinois Department of
Commerce and Economic Opportunity, June 9, 2003,
http://www.illinoisbiz.biz/dceo/Bureaus/Community_
Development/News/PR_06092003.htm.

35. "ESOP Fact Sheet," ESOP Association, http://www
.esopassociation.org/media/media_factsheet.asp.

36. Emily Meyertholen, "Karzan and Associates: Building a
Company of Owners," Beyer Institute, University of
California at San Diego, Rady School of Management,
February 2008, http://beysterinstitute.org/other_resources/
leading_companies/feb08/lc0208Krazan.html; "Company,"
Krazan Associates, http://www.krazan.com/pages/
company.htm.

37. Kevin Kelly, "Look Under the Hood," *FSB*, October 2004,
p. 35.

Chapter 8

1. Jamie, Herzlich, "Marketing Plan Sets Direction for
Sales," *Chicago Tribune*, December 31, 2007,
http://www.chicagotribune.com/business/chi-mon_small-
biz_1231dec31,1,5198222.story.

2. Claes Hultman and Gerald E. Hills, *NFIB National Small
Business Poll: Marketing Perspectives*, Volume 6, Issue 8,
2006 (NFIB: Washington, D.C.), p. 3.

3. Scott Reeves, "How to Swing with Guerrilla Marketing,"
Forbes, June 8, 2006, http://www.forbes.com/entrepreneurs/
2006/06/08/entrepreneurs-marketing-harley-davidson-cx_
sr_0608askanexpert.html.

4. David Weich, "Powell's to Take Authors Out of the
Book," *Powell's in the Press*, Powell's Books,
http://www.powells.com/news_ootbfilm.html.

5. Howard Dana Shaw, "Customer Care Checklist," *In
Business*, September/October, 1987, p. 28.

6. Gregg Cebrzynski, "Nocturnal Diners Targeted by New
Marketing Tactics," *Nation's Restaurant News*, June 16,
2008, http://www.nrn.com/article.aspx?keyword=&menu
_id=1416&id=355688; Emily Bryson York, "Taco Bell
Enjoys Its Gig as Indie-Rock Promoter," *Advertising Age*,
September 11, 2008, http://adage.com/madisonandvine/
article?article_id=130908; "Denny's All Nighter,"
Denny's, http://www.dennysallnighter.com/index.php.

7. Scott Reeves, "How to Swing with Guerrilla Marketing,"
Forbes, June 8, 2006, http://www.forbes.com/
entrepreneurs/2006/06/08/entrepreneurs-marketing-
harley-davidson-cx_sr_0608askanexpert.html.

8. Phoung Ly, "Nana Technology," *FSB*, November 2007,
pp. 105–106; "GreatCall and Samsung Announce Jitterbug:
First Cell Offering to Provide Simplicity to Boomers and
Their Parents, GreatCall, April 3, 2006, http://www.jitterbug.
com/pdfs/GC_Samsung_Release_4_3_06.pdf.

9. Neal E. Boudette, "Luxury-Car Sellers Put on the Ritz,"
Wall Street Journal, December 18, 2007, p. B1, B2.

10. "Anya Kamenetz, "Easy Money," *Fast Company*,
December 2007/January 2008, pp. 46–48; Adam Uhernick,
"Study Shows Average College Student Owes $2,700 on a
Credit Card," *KTIV*, September 14, 2008,
http://www.ktiv.com/global/story.asp?s=9007416.

11. Roberta Maynard, "New Directions in Marketing"
Nation's Business, July 1995, p.26.

12. Janet Adamy, "Man Behind Burger King Turnaround,"
Wall Street Journal, April 2, 2008, pp. B1,B7; Bruce
Horovitz, "Burger King of Cool?" *USA Today*, February
7, 2007, http://www.usatoday.com/money/industries/
food/2007-02-06-burger-king-usat_x.htm; "A Whopping
Success," In-Store Marketing Institute, http://www
.shoppermarketingmag.com/article.php?nid=43486.

13. "Our Story," Innocent Drinks,
http://www.innocentdrinks.co.uk/us/?Page=our_story.

14. Jefferson Graham, "Twitter and Twitterers: Running
Full Speed Ahead to Keep Up," *E-Commerce Times*,
July 29, 2008, http://www.technewsworld.com/
story/63943.html.

15. Al Cole, "Cinematic Chic," *Modern Maturity*,
March–April 1998, p. 24.

16. Nancy L. Croft, "Smart Selling," *Nation's Business*,
March 1988, pp. 51–52.

17. Larry Selden and Geoffrey Colvin, "A Measure of
Success," *Business 2.0*, November 2001, p. 59.

18. Melissa Campanelli, "Poll Vaulting," *Entrepreneur*, July
2007, pp. 40–42.

19. Phil Patton, "Urban Outfitters," *Fast Company*, February
2008, pp. 53–56.

20. Paul Hughes, "Service Savvy," *Business Start-Ups*,
January 1996, p 48.

21. Patrick J. Sauer, "Behind the Scenes: Companies at the
Heart of Everyday Life," *Inc.*, July 2008, pp. 20–21;
Kacey King, "Motorsports Designs Takes Pole Position,"
Big Picture, May 15, 2006, http://bigpicture.net/index
.php3?channelnum=7&content=3438&displaynow=
yes&openchan=yes.

22. Eilene Zimmerman, "Big Marlin, Big Money," *FSB*,
October 2006, pp. 104–110.

23. Debra Phillips, "Fast Track," *Entrepreneur*, April 1999, p. 42.

24. Francine Kizner, "The Playhousing Market, *Entrepreneur*,
July 2008, p. 69.

25. *2007 Cone Cause Marketing and Environmental Survey*
(Boston, MA: Cone LLC), http://www.coneinc.com/files/
2007ConeSurveyReport.pdf, p.7.

26. Peggy Linial, "Small Business and Cause Related
Marketing: Getting Started," Cause Marketing Forum,
http://www.causemarketingforum.com/framemain.asp?
ID=189.

27. Kim T. Gordon, "Join Forces," *Entrepreneur*, February
2008, p. 78.

28. Dale D. Buss, "Entertailing," *Nation's Business*,
December 1997, pp. 18.

29. Marty Schultz, "Welcome to Entertailing," *Albany Biz
Center*, http://www.bizcenter.org/Article/105/959/1103/;
Book Bin, "About Us: Corvallis," http://www.bookbin.com/.

30. Buss, "Entertailing," pp. 12–18.

31. Michael A. Prospero, "Leading Listener: Cabela's,"
Fast Company, October 2005, p. 53; Mike Schoby,
"Jim and Dick Cabela," *Sports Afield*, April/May 2004,
http://www.findarticles.com/p/articles/mi_qa3775/is_200404/

ai_n9358147; Kevin Helliker, "Rare Retailer Scores by Targeting Men Who Hate to Shop," *Wall Street Journal*, December 17, 2002, pp. A1–A11.

32. Marty Schultz, "Welcome to Entertailing," *Albany Biz Center*, http://www.bizcenter.org/Article/105/959/1103/.

33. Coeli Carr, "Don't Say It with Flowers," *FSB*, November 2005, pp. 93–94; "Quiplip Cards," Quiplip.com, http://www.quiplip.com/index.htm.

34. *2007 Cone Cause Marketing and Environmental Survey* (Boston, MA: Cone LLC), http://www.coneinc.com/files/2007ConeSurveyReport.pdf, p. 12.

35. "Social Marketing: How Companies Are Generating Value from Customer Input," *Knowledge @ Wharton*, December 12, 2007, http://knowledge.wharton.upenn.edu/article.cfm?articleid=1864.

36. James Maguire, "Business Remains Hot at Ice.com," *e-Commerce Guide*," May 23, 2005, www.e-commerceguide.com/solutions/advertising/article.php/3507011; Lin Grensing-Pophal, "Who Are You?" *Business Start-Ups*, September 1997, pp. 38–44.

37. Maureen Farrell, "How to Market Your New Idea," *Forbes*, December 21, 2007, http://www.forbes.com/entrepreneurs/2007/12/21/marketing-branding-identity-ent-cx_mf_1221brand.html.

38. "Marketing Definitions: Brand," BuildingBrands Inc., http://www.buildingbrands.com/definitions/02_brand_definition.shtml.

39. Fawn Fitter, "Selling Clean Machines," *FSB*, July/August 2008, pp. 104–108.

40. Gwen Moran, "Group Dynamics," *Entrepreneur*, February 2008, p. 79.

41. Helen Coster, "Fanbook," *Forbes*, January 28, 2008, p. 62.

42. Sarah Halzack, "Marketing Moves to the Blogosphere," *Washington Post*, August 25, 2008, http://www.washingtonpost.com/wp-dyn/content/article/2008/08/24/AR2008082401517.html.

43. "Small Businesses Not Taking Full Advantage of Opportunities to Connect with Customers on the Web," Capital Access Network, July 9, 2007, http://www.advanceme.com/media_kit/press_release/pdf/canq22007_pressrelease.pdf.

44. John J. Curran, "What Are They Saying About You?" *FSB*, July/August 2008, p. 63.

45. Guy Kawasaki, "Blog-A-Thon," *Entrepreneur*, February 2008, p. 44.

46. Sarah Halzack, "Marketing Moves to the Blogosphere," *Washington Post*, August 25, 2008, http://www.washingtonpost.com/wp-dyn/content/article/2008/08/24/AR2008082401517.html.

47. Leigh Buchanan, Max Chafkin, and Ryan McCarthy, "Get Ready for Your Close-up," *Inc.*, February 2008, p. 88.

48. Gwen Moran, "I Tube, You Tube," *Entrepreneur*, November 2007, p. 101.

49. Leigh Buchanan, Max Chafkin, and Ryan McCarthy, "Get Ready for Your Close-up," *Inc.*, February 2008, p. 88; Raymund Flandez, "Lights! Camera! Sales!" *Wall Street Journal*, November 26, 2007, pp. R1, R3.

50. "That's a Rap: Four Rappers Win Burritos for Life In Moe's Southwest Grill's Video Nation Contest," Moe's Southwest Grill, April 13, 2007, http://www.moes.com/news_static_upload/That%27s%20a%20Rap%20-%20Four%20Rappers%20Win%20Burritos%20for%20Life.pdf; Raymund Flandez, "Lights! Camera! Sales!" *Wall Street Journal*, November 26, 2007, pp. R1, R3.

51. Aimee L. Stern, "How To Build Customer Loyalty," *Your Company*, Spring 1995, p.37.

52. "Beware of Dissatisfied Customers: They Like to Blab," *Knowledge @ Wharton*, March 8, 2006, http://knowledge.wharton.upenn.edu/article.cfm?articleid=1422.

53. Ibid.

54. William A. Sherden, "The Tools of Retention," *Small Business Reports*, November 1994, pp. 43–47.

55. Richard Stone, "Retaining Customers Requires Constant Contact," *Small Business Computing*, January 11, 2005, www.smallbusinesscomputing.com/biztools/print.pho/3457221.

56. Mark Albright, "Black and White," *St. Petersburg Times*, August 13, 2006, http://www.sptimes.com/2006/08/13/Business/Black__white.shtm; Staci Surrock, "Chico's Devotion to Real Women Wins Customer Loyalty," *Miami Herald*, January 16, 2006, http://www.miami.com/mld/miamiherald/business/13622717.htm; Katherine Hobson, "Chic—and Comfortable," *U.S. News & World Report*, May 13, 2002, p. 40.

57. "How Can You give Customers a Little Thrill?" *MarketingProfs: Get to the Point*, April 30, 2008, p. 1.

58. Emily Barker, "You Just Don't Get It," *Inc.*, November 2001, p. 120.

59. Faye Rice, "How to Deal With Tougher Customers," *Fortune*, December 3, 1990, pp. 39–40.

60. Rahul Jacob, "TQM: More Than a Dying Fad," *Fortune*, October 18, 1993, p. 67.

61. "I Trust You Because Your Floor Looks Clean and Shiny," *Get to the Point*, April 16, 2008, pp.1–2.

62. Lee Allen, "From the World of Computers to the Bucket Brigade," *Inside Tucson Business*, January 3, 2008, http://www.azbiz.com/articles/2008/01/03/news/profiles/doc477d887f83d2e289092759.txt.

63. Joe Napsha, "American Workers Are Laboring Longer Hours," *Pittsburgh Tribune-Review*, January 2, 2008, http://www.pittsburghlive.com/x/pittsburghtrib/business/s_545439.html.

64. Dave Zielinski, "Improving Service Doesn't Require a Big Investment," *Small Business Reports*, February 1991, p. 20.

65. David Wethe, "More Skip Lunch Lines to Order Meals on Web," *Seattle Times*, January 28, 2008, http://seattletimes.nwsource.com/html/businesstechnology/2004148754_btfoodorders28.html.

66. "Papa John's Surpasses $1 Billion in Online Sales," *Restaurant News Resource*, May 7, 2008, http://www.restaurantnewsresource.com/article32498.html.

67. Harvey Mackay, "Swimming with Sharks: Technology Needs to be Used Right by Small Business," *Minneapolis-St. Paul Star Tribune*, January 16, 2008, http://www.startribune.com/business/13851576.html.

68. Jennifer Alsever, "No More No-Shows," *FSB*, September 2008, pp. 43–44.

69. Emily Nelson, "Marketers Push Individual Portions and Families Bite," *Wall Street Journal*, July 23, 2002, pp. A1, A6.

70. Lucy McCauley, "Measure What Matters," *Fast Company*, May 1999, p. 100.

71. Claes Hultman and Gerald E. Hills, *National Small Business Poll: Marketing Perspectives*," Washington, DC: National Federation of Independent Businesses, Volume 8, Issue 6, 2006, p. 6.

72. Michael Dell, "Thrive in a Sick Economy," *Business 2.0*, December 2002/January 2003, p. 88.

73. Alan Deutschman, "America's Fastest Risers," *Fortune*, October 7, 1991, p. 58.

74. Matthew Boyle, "A Glove Story," *Fortune*, September 3, 2007, pp. 29–31; "93 Products We Love," *Men's Health: TechGuide 2008*, http://www.menshealth.com/techguide/sports_gear/Rawlings_Primo_Glove.html.

75. Cathryn Creno, "Retailers Use Customer Satisfaction to Create Loyalty," *Arizona Republic*, December 15, 2007, http://www.azcentral.com/business/articles/1215biz-threestores1216.html.

76. "Debbie Kelly, "Poor Customer Service Paralyzes U.S. Companies," *CRM Daily*, February 8, 2008, www.crm-daily.com/story.xhtml?story_id=103001XXU5EQ.

77. Cathryn Creno, "Retailers Use Customer Satisfaction to Create Loyalty," *Arizona Republic*, December 15, 2007, http://www.azcentral.com/business/articles/1215biz-threestores1216.html.

78. "Beware of Dissatisfied Customers: They Like to Blab," *Knowledge @ Wharton*, March 8, 2006, http://knowledge.wharton.upenn.edu/article.cfm?articleid=1422.

79. Mark Henricks, "Satisfaction Guaranteed," *Entrepreneur*, May 1991, p. 122.

80. Ian Mount, "First Mate to the Client," *FSB*, September 2008, pp. 67–69.

81. "Are Your Customers Dissatisfied? Try Checking Out Your Salespeople," *Knowledge @ Wharton*, May 16, 2007, http://knowledge.wharton.upenn.edu/article.cfm?articleid=1735.

82. Rich Karlgaard, "How Fast Can You Learn?" *Forbes*, November 26, 2007, p. 31.

83. Ron Zemke and Dick Schaaf, "The Service Edge," *Small Business Reports*, July 1990, pp. 57–60.

84. Thomas A. Stewart, "After All You've Done for Your Customers, Why Are They Still NOT HAPPY?" *Fortune*, December 11, 1995, pp. 178–182.

85. Mark Henricks, "5 Best Customer Service Ideas," *Entrepreneur*, March 1999, p. 122.

86. Jamie Herzlich, "Small Business: Good Customer Service Is Key," *NewsDay*, September 8, 2008, http://www.newsday.com/business/ny-bzherz5833981sep08,0,7013385.story.

87. Brian Lee, "The 3 Cornerstones of Cultural Change," *CEO's Kickstart Retreat*, September 2005, p. 1–5.

88. Anne Fisher, "A Happy Staff Equals Happy Customers," *Fortune*, July 12, 2004, p. 52.

89. Cheryl Lu-Lien Tan, "Hey, Honey Bunny, Stores Know What Your Wife Wants," *Wall Street Journal*, December 1–2, 2007, pp. A1, A10.

90. Zemke and Schaaf, "The Service Edge," p. 60.

91. Desiree De Meyer, "Get to Market Faster," *Smart Business*, October 2001, pp. 62-65; Brian Dumaine, "How Managers Can Succeed Through Speed," *Fortune*, February 13, 1989, pp. 54–59.

92. Geoff Williams, "Speed Freaks," *Entrepreneur*, September 1999, p. 120.

93. Mark Henricks, "Time Is Money," *Entrepreneur,* February 1993, p. 44.

94. Alec Foege, "We Weld Faster," *FSB*, March 2008, p. 39.

95. Zina Moukheiber, "The World's Fastest Chemicals," *Forbes*, October 17, 2005, p. 63.

96. Stanley J. Winkelman, "Why Big-Name Stores Are Losing Out," *Fortune*, May 8, 1989, pp. 14–15.

97. Ashley Laurel Wilson, "Wearing Tech: Where Fashion Meets Technology," *CIO*, September 9, 2008, http://www.cio.com/article/448437/Wearing_Tech_Where_Fashion_Meets_Technology.

98. "It's Not Rocket Science…It's Rockin' Science," Commonwealth Scientific and Industrial Research Organization, http://www.csiro.au/science/AirGuitar.html.

99. Jeffrey M. O'Brien, ""Wii Will Rock You," *Fortune*, June 4, 2007, http://money.cnn.com/magazines/fortune/fortune_archive/2007/06/11/100083454/index.htm.

100. Katie Marsal, "How Big Can It Get?" *Apple Insider*, May 24, 2006, http://www.appleinsider.com/articles/06/05/24/ipod_how_big_can_it_get.html.

101. Turley Muller, "A Look at Apple's iPod Business," *StraightStocks*, April 23, 2008, http://www.straightstocks.com/stock-watch/a-look-at-apples-aapl-ipod-business/.

102. Paul B. Brown, "The Eternal Second Act," *Inc.*, June 1988, pp. 119–120.

103. Martha C. White," New Year's Resolutions: How Three Companies Came Up with Their 2008 Growth Strategies," *Inc.*, January 2008, pp. 47–49; Jennie L. Ilustre, "For PTI's Mei Xu, Success Is Bliss and Fragrant Too," *Asian Fortune*, November 2007, http://www.asianfortunenews.com/site/article_1107.php?article_id=73.

104. Kimberly L. McCall, "Bags to Riches," *Entrepreneur*, May 2005, p. 85.

105. Suzanne Kapner, "The Shoe That Won't Quit," *Fortune*, June 9, 2008, pp. 25–26.

106. "Got Game Entertainment and White Castle Make a Deal for 'Artic Stud Poker Run,'" *Reuters*, March 25, 2008, http://www.reuters.com/article/pressRelease/idUS112958+25-Mar-2008+PRN20080325; Gregg Cebrzynski, "Chains Tap New Digital Marketing Options to Target Specific Groups," *Nation's Restaurant News*, April 7, 2008, http://www.nrn.com/article.aspx?id=352440&searchWords=Chains%20&%20Tap%20&%20New%20&%20DIgital%20&%20Marketing%20&%20Options%20&%20White%20&%20Castle.

107. Bob Weinstein, "Set in Stone," *Business Start-Ups*, October 1995, p. 27.

Chapter 9

1. John Rizzi, "Four Ways to Grow Your E-mail List: Get Offline Customers to Go Online," *Multichannel Merchant*, March 5, 2007, http://multichannelmerchant.com/crosschannel/lists/rizzi_03052007/.

2. John B. Horrigan, *Online Shopping*, Pew Internet and American Life Project, February 13, 2008, p.iii.

3. *iProspect Offline Channel Influence on Online Search Behavior Study*, iProspect, August 2007, p. 8.

4. *Trends in Online Shopping*, Nielsen Global Online Survey, The Nielsen Company (New York: 2008), p. 1.

5. "Online Retailers Keen to Try Social Networking," *Research Recap*, May 21, 2008, http://www.researchrecap.com/index.php/2008/05/21/online-retailers-keen-to-try-social-network-marketing/.

6. "Online Retailers Keen to Try Social Networking," *Research Recap*, May 21, 2008, http://www.researchrecap .com/index.php/2008/05/21/online-retailers-keen-to-try-social-network-marketing/.

7. "Internet Usage Statistics," Internet World Stats, http://www.internetworldstats.com/stats.htm.

8. Jerry Useem, "Our 10 Principles of the New Economy, Slightly Revised," *Business 2.0*, August/September 2001, p. 85.

9. Susan Kuchinskas, "Where Are We Now? A Decade of E-Commerce," E-Commerce Guide, www.ecommerceguide .com/news/trends/article.php/3426371.

10. "Small Business Research Board E-commerce Study: Nearly 30% of Small Businesses Expect Internet Sales to Increase Next 12–24 Months According to Latest SBRB Study," *Internet Business Law Services News Portal*, September 26, 2007, http://www.ibls.com/internet_law_ news_portal_view_prn.aspx?s=latestnews&id=1861.

11. Don Davis, "Raising the Stakes," *Internet Retailer*, May 2008, http://www.internetretailer.com/article.asp?id=26243.

12. Gwen Moran, "Time for Change," *Entrepreneur*, November 2006, http://www.entrepreneur.com/ ebusiness/article169164.html.

13. Amanda C. Kooser, "Simple Startup," *Entrepreneur*, August 2008, p. 108.

14. "September 2008 Web Server Survey," http://news.netcraft .com/archives/web_server_survey.html.

15. Nichole L. Torres, "Sites Set," *Entrepreneur*, November 2007, p. 122.

16. Melissa Campanelli, "Scale It Down," *Entrepreneur*, January 2008, p. 52.

17. "Why Should I Make My Web Site Mobile?" mTLD Top Level Domain Ltd, 2008, p.1.

18. Ibid.

19. John B. Horrigan, *Online Shopping*, Pew Internet and American Life Project, February 13, 2008, p.ii.

20. "In Online We Don't Trust: Survey Finds U.S. Consumers Wary of Password Security for E-Commerce," *Reuters*, April 7, 2008, http://www.reuters.com/article/ pressRelease/idUS116952+07-Apr-2008+BW20080407.

21. "About Us: A Brief History of Fairfield Clothiers/ SuitYourSelf.com, http://suityourself.com/company-details.asp; Christine Cooney, "'Net Breaks Limitations for Clothier," *Connecticut Post*, February 23, 2004, p. C1; "SuitYourSelf Case Study," GoECart, http://www.goecart .com/Men_Formal_Wear_Store.asp.

22. Kenneth Corbin, "Study Cites Flaw in E-tail Experience," *E-Commerce Guide*, September 19, 2008, http://www .ecommerce-guide.com/news/news/article.php/3772771.

23. Kenneth Corbin, "Study Cites Flaw in E-tail Experience," *E-Commerce Guide*, September 19, 2008, http://www .ecommerce-guide.com/news/news/article.php/3772771.

24. "New Meaning for an Old Metric," *eMarketer*, May 29, 2008, http://www.emarketer.com/Article.aspx?1006338.

25. Jeff Ayres, "Online Chats Are Newest Way to Help," *Clarion Ledger*, December 26, 2007. www.clarionledger .com/apps/pbcs.dll/article?AID=20071226/BIZ/712260339 .html.

26. Michelle Megna, "Customized Chat Adds Seasonal Sales Advantage," *E-Commerce Guide*, September 22, 2008, http://www.ecommerce-guide.com/solutions/customer_ relations/article.php/3773096.

27. "Case Study: REI," Keynote, http://www.keynote.com/ docs/success_stories/REI.pdf.

28. Fred Vogelstein, "A Cold Bath for Dot-Com Fever," *U.S. News & World Report*, September 13, 1999, p. 37.

29. Can E-tailers Find Fulfillment with Drop Shipping?" *Inc.*, July 18, 2002, http://www.inc.com/articles/biz_online/ do_biz_online/sell_online/24433.html.

30. "Success Stories: John & Kira's Chocolates," Netsuite, http://www.netsuite.com/portal/customers/ecommerce.sh tml; "The (Fun) Story Behind John & Kira's," John & Kira's, http://www.johnandkiras.com/site/businfo_2 .html.

31. "Ty's Toy Box Selects CommerceHub Supply-on-Demand Platform for E-Commerce Supply Chain Integration," CommerceHub, June 18, 2007, http://www.commercehub .com/company/news_pr061807.html.

32. Bronwyn Fryer and Lee Smith, ".Com or Bust," *FSB*, December 1999/January 2000, p. 41.

33. Dana Dratch, "These E-Gardening Tips Will Help Your Web Site Grow from Sprout to Giant," *Bankrate.com*, February 29, 2000 http://www.bankrate.com/brm/news/ biz/Ecommerce/20000117.asp.

34. "A Wired World," *Stand Firm*, August 2008, p. 5.

35. "Media Usage and Consumer Spending: 2000 to 2010," *Statistical Abstract of the United States, 2008*, U.S. Census Bureau, p. 703.

36. "Hot 500: TNG Enterprises Inc.," *2007 Entrepreneur Hot 500*, https://www.entrepreneur.com/Hot500/Details/182 .html; "About Us," PuzzlesUSA, http://www.puzzlesusa .com/cgi-bin/category.cgi?category=about.

37. Heather Clancy, "Know How to Hold 'Em," *Entrepreneur*, August 2008, p. 48.

38. Ralph F. Wilson, "The Five Mutable Laws of Web Marketing," *Web Marketing Today* (http://www.wilsonweb.com/wmta/basic-principles.htm), April 1, 1999, pp.1–7.

39. Péter Jascó, "Lonely Planet Online," Gale Reference Reviews, July 2005, http://reviews.gale.com/index.php/ digital-reference-shelf/2005/07/lonely-planet-online/; "Lonely Planet 8th Most Powerful Brand in Asia-Pacific," Scoop Independent News, January 26, 2006, http://www.scoop.co.nz/stories/WO0601/S00363.htm; Lonely Planet, http://www.lonelyplanet.com/.

40. *The State of Retailing Online 2007: Part 2*, Shop.org and Forrester Research, pp. 8–9,11–12.

41. "Barracuda Networks Releases Annual Spam Report," Barracuda Networks, December 12, 2007, http://www .barracudanetworks.com/ns/news_and_events/index.php? nid=232.

42. Tamara Gielen, "State of Retailing Online 2007," *B2B E-mail Marketing*, September 27, 2007, http://www .b2bemailmarketing.com/2007/09/state-of-retail.html.

43. James Maguire, "Smart Marketing Helps Plus-Size Retailer Grow," *Small Business Computing*, September 7, 2005, www.smallbusinesscomputing.com/emarketing/ article.php/3532441.

44. James Maguire, "Strategies in Building Shopper Trust," *E-Commerce Guide*, June 4, 2004, http://www.ecommerce-guide.com/news/news/article.php/3363841.

45. "World Internet Usage and Population Statistics," *Internet World Stats*, 2008, http://www.internetworldstats .com/stats.htm.

46. "The Top Ten Languages Used in the Web," *Internet World Stats*, 2008, http://www.internetworldstats.com/stats7.htm.

47. Don Davis, "Raising the Stakes," *Internet Retailer*, May 2008, http://www.internetretailer.com/article.asp?id=26243.

48. Ibid.

49. Bill Siwicki, "Can Social Networking Sway Shoppers?" *Internet Retailer*, September 2006, http://www.internetretailer.com/internet/marketing-conference/44521-can-social-networking-sway-shoppers.html.

50. Louis Columbus, "Is Social Networking and Asset or a Liability for Your Company?" *CRM Buyer*, September 2, 2008, http://www.crmbuyer.com/story/64352.html.

51. Melissa Campanelli, "Make Your Mark," *Entrepreneur*, September 2007, pp. 52–53.

52. Jessica E. Vascellaro, "Twitter Goes Mainstream," *Wall Street Journal*, October 27, 2008, pp. R1,R8.

53. Dan Briody, "Puppy Power," *Inc.*, November 2007, pp. 55–56.

54. Gwen Moran, "Small Wonders," *Entrepreneur*, August 2008, p. 72.

55. Joan Johnson, "Online Sales Expected to Slow, Still Grow by 17% in 2008," *Colorado Springs Business Journal*, April 11, 2008, http://www.csbj.com/story.cfm?id=19778&searchString=state%20and%20retailing%20and%20online%20and%202008.

56. "Search Engine Marketers Sticking to Basics But Eying Video, According to SEMPRO 2007 State of Market Survey," Search Engine Marketing Professional Organization, June 19, 2008, http://www.sempo.org/news/releases/06-19-08.

57. *iProspect Blended Search Results Study*, April 2008, iProspect, http://www.iprospect.com/premiumPDFs/researchstudy_apr2008_blendedsearchresults.pdf, p. 6.

58. Joan Johnson, "Online Sales Expected to Slow, Still Grow by 17% in 2008," *Colorado Springs Business Journal*, April 11, 2008, http://www.csbj.com/story.cfm?id=19778&searchString=state%20and%20retailing%20and%20online%20and%202008.

59. "Share of Online Searches: August 2008 and September 2008," *Marketing Charts*, September 2008, http://www.marketingcharts.com/interactive/share-of-online-searches-by-engine-september-2008-6580/.

60. *The State of Retailing Online 2007: Part 2*, Shop.org and Forrester Research, p. 10.

61. James Maguire, "MyWeddingFavors Shares Search Success Secrets," *E-Commerce Guide*, October 8, 2004, www.ecommerce-guide.com/solutions/advertising/article.php/3419121.

62. Jonathan Blum, "Search Deeper, Catch More," *FSB*, July/August 2007, pp.51–54.

63. "Industry Click Fraud Rate Hovers at 16 Percent for Third Quarter 2008," ClickForensics, October 23, 2008, http://www.clickforensics.com/newsroom/press-releases/114-industry-click-fraud-rate-hovers-at-16-percent-for-third-quarter-2008-.html.

64. Steve McKee, "Make Your Web Site Work for You," *Business Week*, June 2008, http://www.businessweek.com/smallbiz/content/jun2008/sb2008069_643453.htm.

65. Thomas Claburn, "The Internet's Filling Up," *Information Week*, May 28, 2007, p. 24.

66. Jessica Seld, "A Domain by Any Other Name Is Not the Same," *CNNMoney*, August 2, 2006, http://money.cnn.com/2006/08/02/smbusiness/domains/index.htm/.

67. Gwen Moran, "Stick the Landing Page," *Entrepreneur*, October 2008, p. 89.

68. "Waterfilters.net Increased Their Conversion Rate by 11% with Google Site Search, Google Site Search Case Study, http://www.google.com/sitesearch/.

69. Michelle Magna, "Creating Content That Turns Browsers into Buyers," *E-Commerce Guide*, April 24, 2008, http://www.ecommerce-guide.com/solutions/design/article.php/3742836.

70. Mary Madden, "Online Video," Pew Internet & American Life Project, July 25, 2007, http://www.pewinternet.org/pdfs/PIP_Online_Video_2007.pdf.

71. Steve Coomes, "Restaurants Cook Up New Business with Online 'Chef' Videos," *Nation's Restaurant News,* April 30, 2008, www.nrn.com/id=35314.

72. Melissa Campanelli, "Holiday Bonus, *Entrepreneur*, September 2005, pp. 48–50.

73. Ibid.

74. *The State of Retailing Online 2007: Part 2*, Shop.org and Forrester Research, p. 23.

75. Stavraka, "There's No Stopping E-Business. Are You Ready?" *Forbes*, December 13, 1999, Special Advertising Section.

76. James Maguire, "The 'Mystery Shopping' Report," *E-Commerce Guide*, February 21, 2006, www.e-commerce-guide.com/solutions/customer_relations/article.php/3586441.

77. "Coremetrics Benchmark Industry Report (in United States)," Coremetrics, November 2008, www.coremetrics.com/solutions/benchmarking.php.

78. Helen Coster, "A Step Ahead," *Forbes*, June 2, 2008, http://www.forbes.com/entrepreneurs/forbes/2008/0602/078.html.

79. James Maguire, "Web Analytics: A User's Guide: Part 1," *E-commerce Guide*, October 4, 2004, www.e-commerceguide.com/solutions/customer_relations/article.php/3416791.

80. Ken Burke, Jaye Sullican, and Catherine Thorpe, *MarketLive Performance Index, Volume 5: Focus on Engagement: The Elements of Effective Product Discovery*, MarketLive, September 1, 2008, p.3.

81. John B. Horrigan, *Online Shopping*, Pew Internet and American Life Project, February 13, 2008, p.ii.

82. *Security and Trust: The Backbone of Doing Business over the Internet*, VeriSign, October 2008, p3.

83. *2008 Internet Security Trends*, Cisco and Ironport, 2008, pp. 11–13.

84. *9th Annual Online Fraud Report*, Cybersource, 2008, p. 3.

Chapter 10

1. Amy Cortese, "The Power of Optimal Pricing," *Business 2.0*, September 2002, pp. 68–70.

2. Ron Stodghill, "The Shipping News," *FSB*, December 2005/January 2006, p. 80.

3. Howard Scott, "The Tricky Art of Raising Prices," *Nation's Business*, February 1999, p. 32.

4. Dan Heath and Chip Heath, "The Inevitability of $300 Socks," *Fast Company*, September 2007, pp. 68–70.

5. "An Unlikely Yarn," *Forbes Life*, March 10, 2008, p. 22.

6. "Mark Grischke, "This is Santa's Big Scene," *Forbes Life*, December 2006, pp. 142–155; "Boots Handmade," Tres Outlaws, http://www.falconhead.com/.

7. "The Price Is Right, But Maybe It's Not, and How Do You Know?" *Knowledge @ Wharton*, October 3, 2007, http://knowledge.wharton.upenn.edu/article.cfm?articleid=1813; Victoria Murphy Barret, "What the Market Will Bear," *Forbes*, July 3, 2006, http://www.forbes.com/business/forbes/2006/0703/069.html.

8. Stephanie Clifford, "How Low Can You Go?" *Inc.*, August 2007, p. 42.

9. Geoff Williams, "Name Your Price," *Entrepreneur*, September 2005, p. 112.

10. Robert Shulman and Richard Miniter, "Discounting Is No Bargain," *Wall Street Journal*, December 7, 1998, p. A30.

11. Justin Martin, "Gentlemen (and Ladies), Raise Your Prices!" *FSB*, October 2007, pp. 26–30.

12. William Echilkson, "The Return of Luxury," *Fortune*, October 17, 1994, p. 18.

13. Mark Henricks, "Stop on a Dime," *Entrepreneur*, January 2006, p. 27.

14. Kathy Schultz, "Boutiques on a Budget," *Seattle Weekly*, September 22, 2004, http://www.seattleweekly.com/diversions/0438/040922_fashion_boutiques.php; Eric Engleman, "Fashion Maven: Funky Seattle Retailer Uses Unsold Clothing for Another Store," *Puget Sound Business Journal*, June 18, 2004, http://www.bizjournals.com/seattle/stories/2004/06/21/smallb1.html?page=2; Nichole L. Torres, "Choose Your Path," *Entrepreneur*, March 2005, http://www.entrepreneur.com/article/0,4621,319940,00.html.

15. Geoff Williams, "Name Your Price," *Entrepreneur*, September 2005, pp. 108–115.

16. Justin Scheck and Yukari Iwatani Kane, "PC Makers Scramble as Demand Shrivels," *Wall Street Journal*, November 14, 2008, pp. B1–B5.

17. Alison Stein Wellner, "Boost Your Bottom Line by Taking the Guesswork Out of Pricing," *Inc.*, June 2005, p. 78.

18. Justin Martin, "Gentlemen (and Ladies), Raise Your Prices!" *FSB*, October 2007, pp. 26–30.

19. Norm Brodsky, "Dealing with Cost Hikes," *Inc.*, August 2005, p. 49.

20. "Pricing and Fairness: Do Your Customers Assume You Are Gouging Them?" *Knowledge @ Wharton*, September 11, 2002, http://knowledge.wharton.upenn.edu/article.cfm?articleid=622#.

21. Justin Martin, "Gentlemen (and Ladies), Raise Your Prices!" *FSB*, October 2007, pp. 26–30.

22. Ryan Karpeles, "The Wrong Way to Make a Buck," *Living Light Bulbs*, January 14, 2008, http://ryankarpeles.blogspot.com/2008/01/wrong-way-to-make-buck.html.

23. Norm Brodsky, "Dealing with Cost Hikes," *Inc.*, August 2005, p. 49.

24. Janet Adamy, "McDonald's Tests Changes in $1 Burger as Costs Rise," *Wall Street Journal*, August 4, 2008, p. B1; Janet Adamy, "McDonald's to Raise Burger's Price," *Wall Street Journal*, November 26, 2008, p. B4; David Sterrett, "Changes Coming to McD's Value Menu: CEO," *Chicago Business*, October 22, 2008, http://www.chicagobusiness.com/cgi-bin/news.pl?id=31506&seenIt=1; Janet Adamy and Julie Jargon, "Burger King Fights Cost with Smaller Burger," *Wall Street Journal*, August 22, 2008, p. B1.

25. David Worrell, "For Peanuts Only," *Entrepreneur*, May 2008, p. 59.

26. "Study: Consumers Will Pay More for Premium Items Even in Harsh Times," *Nation's Restaurant News*, October 14, 2008, http://www.nrn.com/landingPage.aspx?menu_id=1368&coll_id=564&id=359374.

27. Matther Maier, "Finding Riches in a Mine of Credit Data," *Business 2.0*, October 2005, pp. 72–74.

28. Michael V. Marn, Eric V. Roegner, and Craig C. Zawada, "Pricing New Products," *The McKinsey Quarterly*, Number 3, 2003, p.1.

29. Steve McKee, "Low Prices Are Not Always Your Friend," *Business Week*, April 2008, http://www.businessweek.com/smallbiz/content/apr2008/sb20080414_027855.htm.

30. "Suits in a Box," *Forbes Life*, September 2007, p. 40; "James Bond Taylor Shares Secrets with Fashionistas," *MI6*, March 19, 2008, http://www.mi6.co.uk/news/index.php?itemid=6016.

31. "The Price Is Right, But Maybe It's Not, and How Do You Know?" *Knowledge @ Wharton*, October 3, 2007, http://knowledge.wharton.upenn.edu/article.cfm?articleid=1813; Rich Karlgaard, "Why Apple Slashed iPhone Prices," *Forbes*, October 29, 2007, p. 33; Charlie Sorrell, "Apple's iPod Strategy: Aggressive Prices, Overwhelming Features," *Wired*, September 6, 2007, http://www.wired.com/gadgets/portablemusic/news/2007/09/ipod_follow.

32. Sarah Schmidt, "Diners Spend More if Menu Avoids $ Sign," *Edmonton Journal*, August 14, 2008, http://www.canada.com/edmontonjournal/news/business/story.html?id=73e86808-da12-4430-acfc-6d64bc3b8efc.

33. Amy Feldman, "The Tiger in Costco's Tank," *Fast Company*, July/August 2007, pp. 38–40.

34. Sarah Nassauer and Andrea Petersen, "Loyalty Plans at Hotels—For Beginners," *Wall Street Journal*, September 25, 2008, http://online.wsj.com/article/SB122229693535873029.html.

35. "On Sale Now, But Time's a' Wastin'," *Marketing Profs*, April 9, 2008, http://www.marketingprofs.com/short-articles/311/on-sale-now-but-times-a-wastin.

36. "News," Phil & Teds, http://philandteds.com/news/; Sarah McDonald, "Baby Boom Drives $300 Million Business Towards Acquisitions," *National Business Review*, December 4, 2008, http://www.nbr.co.nz/article/baby-boom-drives-300m-buggy-business-toward-acquisitions-38606; Lisa Estall, "Star Shopping: Phil & Teds Double Sport Buggy," *Parent Center*, September 15, 2008, http://blogs.parentcenter.babycenter.com/celebrities/2008/09/15/star-shopping-phil-and-teds-sport-buggy/.

37. Geoff Williams, "Name Your Price," *Entrepreneur*, September 2005, pp. 108–115.

38. "Experian Study Shows That 14 Percent of Consumers Have More Than Ten Credit Cards, and One in Seven Consumers Use at Least 50 Percent of Their Available Credit," Experian National Score Index, http://www.nationalscoreindex.com/ScoreNews_Archive_13.aspx.

39. "Credit Cards," United States Government Accountability Office, September 2006, p. 10.

40. "Credit Counseling Statistics," Consumer Credit Counseling Service, http://creditcounselingbiz .com/credit_counseling_statistics.htm.

41. "Top 10 Reasons to Start Accepting Credit Cards Today," *100 Best Merchant Accounts*, http://www.100best-merchant-accounts.com/articles1.html.

42. Robin Sidel, "Banks, Customers Adapt to Paperless Check Processing," *Wall Street Journal*, October 28, 2004, pp. B1, B3.

43. *Annual Financial Services Study*, Student Monitor, Spring 2008, http://www.studentmonitor.com/financial.php.

44. Bob Weinstein, "Getting Carded," *Entrepreneur*, September 1995, p. 76.

45. *Statistics for General and Online Card Fraud*, ePayNews, http://www.epaynews.com/statistics/fraud.html.

46. Jon Swartz and Byron Acohido, "Credit Card Fraud Hits Small Online Merchants Hard," *USA Today*, June 29, 2005, http://www.usatoday.com/money/industries/technology/2005-06-27-merchants-usat_x.htm.

47. Michael Bloch, "Preventing Credit Card Chargebacks—Anti-Fraud Strategies," Taming the Beast, http://www .tamingthebeast.net/articles2/card-fraud-strategies.htm.

Chapter 11

1. Mike Hogan, "Stay in Touch," *Entrepreneur*, September 2005, pp. 44–46.

2. Richard G.P. MaMahon and Scott Holmes, "Small Business Financial Management Practices in North America: A Literature Review," *Journal of Small Business Management*, April 1991, p. 21.

3. David Worrell, "So Long, Big Guys," *Entrepreneur*, September 2007, p. 59.

4. Raymund Flandez and Kelly Spors, "Tackling the Energy Monster," *Wall Street Journal*, June 16, 2008, pp. R1, R3.

5. Paul A. Broni, "Making Your Financials Add Up," *Inc.*, March 2002, http://www.inc.com/articles/2002/03/24019.html.

6. Alison Stein Wellner, "Are You Paying Yourself Enough?" *Inc.*, November 2004, pp. 87–92.

7. Norm Brodsky, "Follow the Numbers," *Inc.*, January 2008, p. 63.

8. Diedrich Von Soosten, "The Roots of Financial Destruction," *Industry Week*, April 5, 1993, pp. 33–34.

9. Richard Maturi, "Take Your Pulse," *Business Start-Ups*, January 1996, p. 72.

10. Alan Judd, "Bill Heard Dealerships Took Risky Road," *Atlanta Journal Constitution*, September 28, 2008, http://www.ajc.com/gwinnett/content/metro/stories/2008/09/28/bill_heard_dealerships.html; Kristi E. Swartz, "Bill Heard Dealerships File for Bankruptcy," *Atlanta Journal Constitution*, September 29, 2008, http://www.ajc.com/news/content/business/stories/2008/09/29/bill_heard_bankruptcy.html?cxntlid=inform_artr; Dawn McCarty, "GM Dealer Group Bill Heard Files for Bankruptcy," *Bloomberg*, September 29, 2008, http://www.bloomberg.com/apps/news?pid=20601087&sid=a4tKxbx1zGu0& refer=home; Kate Linebaugh, "The Trials of the Auto Dealer," *Wall Street Journal*, January 3, 2009, http://www.careerjournal.com/article/SB122969965719421799 .html.

11. Dina Berta, "Village Inn, Bakers Square Parent Files for Bankruptcy," *Nation's Restaurant News*, April 3, 2008, http://www.nrn.com/breakingNews.aspx?id=352348#; Jeffrey McCracken and Janet Adamy, "Restaurants Feel Sting of Surging Costs, Debt," *Wall Street Journal*, April 24, 2008, pp. A1, A10.

12. "Analyzing Creditworthiness," *Inc.*, November 1991, p. 196.

13. Dina Berta, "Village Inn, Bakers Square Parent Files for Bankruptcy," *Nation's Restaurant News*, April 3, 2008, http://www.nrn.com/breakingNews.aspx?id=352348#; Jeffrey McCracken and Janet Adamy, "Restaurants Feel Sting of Surging Costs, Debt," *Wall Street Journal*, April 24, 2008, pp. A1, A10.

14. Peter Grant, "Charter Communications May Restructure," *Wall Street Journal*, August 16, 2007, p. A2; "Charter Communications Bonds Sink on Debt Plans," *Reuters*, December 12, 2008, http://www.reuters.com/article/marketsNews/idUSN1227211220081212; Karen Brettell, "Charter Bankruptcy May Be Option for Debt Refinancing," *Reuters*, December 17, 2008, http://www.reuters.com/article/rbssTechMediaTelecomNews/idUSN1762209820081217.

15. Alex Taylor III, "Survival on Dealer's Row," *Fortune*, March 31, 2008, p. 24.

16. *RMA Annual Statement Studies: Financial Ratio Benchmarks, 2008–2009*, Risk Management Association, Philadelphia, PA: 2008, pp. 662, 674.

17. Simona Covell, "Slump Batters Small Business, Threatening Owners' Dreams," *Wall Street Journal*, December 26, 2008, pp. A1, A8.

18. Kayte Vanscoy, "Dead or Alive?" *Smart Business*, August 2001, p. 32.

19. Ian Mount, "Slump Busters," *FSB*, March 2008, pp. 24–27; Laura Lowenstein, "At Your Service: California Moves," *Robb Report*, November 1, 2008, http://www .robbreportcollection.com/Articles/Home-Products-Design/Residential-Services/Index.asp.

20. Dirk Smillie, "What Recession?" *Forbes*, August 11, 2008, p. 64; "B.R. Guest to Shutter Restaurants in NYC, Chicago," *Nation's Restaurant News A.M.*, January 15, 2009, p. 1.

21. Jon E. Hilsenrath, "Adventures in Cost Cutting," *Wall Street Journal*, May 10, 2004, pp. R1, R3.

22. Audrey Warren, "The Small Stuff," *Wall Street Journal*, May 10, 2004, p. R9.

23. Ilan Mochari, "A Simple Little System," *Inc.*, October 1999, p. 87.

24. Bo Burlingham, "Inc. Query: Number Crunching," *Inc.*, February 1, 2002, http://www.inc.com/articles/finance/fin_manage/basic_fin_manage/23857.html.

25. Scott Leibs, "Measuring Up," *CFO*, June 2007, pp. 63–66.

26. Norm Brodsky, "The Magic Number," *Inc.*, September 2003, pp. 43–46.

27. Al Olson, "Pizza and Beer Now Cost an Arm and a Leg," *MSNBC*, February 29, 2008, http://www.msnbc.msn .com/id/23415510/; Richard Breen, "Margins Melt as Cheese Burns Pizza Industry," *GSA Business*, January 24, 2005, pp. 1, 6.

28. Dirk Smillie, "What Recession?" *Forbes*, August 11, 2008, p. 64.

29. John Case, "Critical Numbers in Action," *Inc.*, January 21, 2000, http://www.inc.com/articles/finance/fin_manage/forecast/15981.html.

30. Hannah Clark Steiman, "Quarterly Financial Report: How Do You Stack Up?" *Inc.*, November 2008, p. 105.
31. Ilan Mochari, "Significant Figures," *Inc.,* July 2000, p. 128.
32. Ibid.
33. Diane Anderson, "Upgrading the Business-Class Jet," *Business 2.0*, October 2007, p. 32; Julia Werdigier, "Silverjet Grounded as Funding Falls Through," *International Herald Tribune*, May 30, 2008, http://www.iht.com/bin/printfriendly.php?id=13344269; Ben Mutzabaugh, "Eos Airlines to Shut Down," *USA Today*, April 27, 2008, http://blogs.usatoday.com/sky/2008/04/eos-airlines-to.html.

Chapter 12

1. Wendy Taylor and Marty Jerome, "Dead Men Talking," *Smart Business*, December 2001/ January 2002, p. 19.
2. Ilana DeBare, "Tips for Small Businesses to Survive Recession," *San Francisco Chronicle*, March 23, 2008, http://www.sfgate.com/cgi-bin/article.cgi?f=/c/a/2008/03/22/BUSQVMKH3.DTL.
3. Simona Covel, "Slump Batters Small Business, Threatening Owner's Dreams," *Wall Street Journal*, December 26, 2008, pp. A1, A8.
4. *National Small Business Poll: The Cash Flow Problem*, National Federation of Independent Businesses (Washington, DC: 2002), p. 2.
5. Jerry Useem, "The Icon That Almost Wasn't," *Inc: The State of Small Business 1998*, p. 142; "History," Ford Motor Company, http://www.ford.com/en/heritage/history/default.htm.
6. Daniel Kehrer, "Big Ideas For Your Small Business," *Changing Times*, November 1989, p. 58.
7. Peter Lattman and Jeffrey McCracken, "Steve and Barry's Faces Cash Crunch," *Wall Street Journal*, June 21–22, 2008, p. A4; Jeffrey McCracken and Peter Lattman, "Steve and Barry's Hits Trouble," *Wall Street Journal*, June 26, 2008, p. B10; Jeffrey McCracken and Peter Lattman, "Steve and Barry's, Short of Cash, May Shut Stores, *Wall Street Journal*, July 1, 2008, p. B3; Kevin Kingsbury, "Steve and Barry's Files for Chapter 11, Cites Liquidity Squeeze, Economy," *Wall Street Journal*, July 10, 2008, http://online.wsj.com/article/SB121562423538939709.html.
8. Nichole L. Torres, "Got Money?" *Entrepreneur*, March 2009, p 88.
9. Douglas Bartholomew, "4 Common Financial Management Mistakes…And How To Avoid Them," *Your Company*, Fall 1991, p. 9.
10. Robert A. Mamis, "Money In, Money Out," *Inc.*, March 1993, p. 98.
11. Phaedra Hise, "Paging for Cash Flow," *Inc.*, December 1995, p.131.
12. Kelly K. Spors, "Handling the Risks of a Seasonal Business," *Wall Street Journal*, July 8, 2007, http://online.wsj.com/article/SB118384926330960140.html; Ted Sheffler, "Just Talkin' 'Bout Shaft," *Salt Lake City Weekly*, June 28, 2007, http://cityweekly.net/index.cfm?do=article.details&id=795AC71A-1372-FCBB-83F0C731219C3A9D.
13. Kortney Stringer, "Neither Anthrax Nor the Economy Stops the Fruitcake," *Wall Street Journal*, December 19,
2001, pp, B1, B4; Dirk Smillie, "Signs of Life," *Forbes*, November 11, 2002, p. 160.
14. Gwendolyn Bounds, "Store's Sales Can Rest on a Moment," *Wall Street Journal*, January 3, 2006, p. A.23.
15. Ashwin Verghese, "Rochester-Area Pizza Shops Prepare for Annual Super Bowl Blitz,' *Democrat Chronicle*, January 26, 2009, http://www.democratandchronicle.com/article/20090126/NEWS01/901260336.
16. Gwendolyn Bounds, "Preparing for the Big Bang," *Wall Street Journal*, June 29, 2004, pp. B1, B7.
17. *National Small Business Poll: The Cash Flow Problem*, National Federation of Independent Businesses (Washington, DC: 2002), p. 1.
18. C. J. Prince, "Currency in a Pinch," *Entrepreneur*, May 2008, p. 62.
19. Jill Andresky Fraser, "Monitoring Daily Cash Trends," *Inc.*, October 1992, p. 49.
20. David H. Bangs, *Financial Troubleshooting: An Action Plan for Money Management in the Small Business*, Dover, New Hampshire: Upstart Publishing Company, 1992, p. 61.
21. "Cash Flow/Cash Flow Management," *Small Business Reporter*, No. 9, p. 5.
22. William Bak, "Make 'Em Pay," *Entrepreneur*, November 1992, p. 64.
23. C. J. Prince, "Time Bomb," *Entrepreneur*, January 2008, p. 66.
24. William J. Dennis, Jr., *National Small Business Poll: Getting Paid*, National Federation of Independent Businesses, Volume 1, Issue #7, July 2001, p. 11.
25. Ibid.
26. American Collectors Association, http://www.collector.com/; Howard Muson, "Collecting Overdue Accounts," *Your Company*, Spring 1993, p.4.
27. Richard J. Maturi, "Collection Dues and Don'ts," *Entrepreneur*, January 1992, p. 326.
28. Elaine Pofeldt, "Collect Calls," *Success*, March 1998, pp. 22–24.
29. *Value of Third Party Debt Collection to the U.S. Economy in 2007: Survey and Analysis*, PriceWaterhouseCooper's National Economic Consulting Group and ACA International, June 12, 2008, p. iii.
30. Jim Carlton, "Tight Squeeze," *Wall Street Journal*, March 26, 1996, pp. A1, A6.
31. Jill Andresky Fraser, "A Confidence Game," *Inc.*, December 1989, p. 178.
32. Jill Andresky Fraser, "How To Get Paid," *Inc.*, March 1992, p. 105.
33. Mark Henricks, "No Long-Term Parking," *Entrepreneur*, January 2002, www.entrepreneur.com/article/0,4621,295660.html.
34. Stephanie Barlow, "Frozen Assets," *Entrepreneur*, September 1993, p. 53.
35. Roberta Maynard, "Can You Benefit from Barter?" *Nation's Business*, July 1994, p.6.
36. "33 Ways to Increase Your Cash Flow and Manage Cash Balances," *The Business Owner*, February 1988, p. 8.
37. R. J. Anderson, "Mark Down and Turn Up," *Inside Outdoor*, Issue #9, April 2004, p. 28.
38. "Specials and News," Channeled Resources, http://www.channeledresources.com/specials.htm; "301 Great Ideas for Selling Smarter," *Inc.*, January 1, 1998, p. 47.

39. Robert A. Mamis, "Money In, Money Out," *Inc.*, March 1993, p. 102.
40. Doug Hardman, Simon Harper, and Ashok Notaney, "Keeping Inventory – and Profits – Off the Discount Rack," Booz, Allen, and Hamilton, http://www.boozallen.com/media/file/Off_the_Discount_Rack.pdf, pp.1—2; Rachel Tiplady, "Zara: Taking the Lead in Fast-Fashion," *Business Week*, April 4, 2006, http://www.boozallen.com/media/file/Off_the_Discount_Rack.pdf.
41. Jeffrey Lant, "Cash Is King," *Small Business Reports*, May 1991, p. 49.
42. "Tom McDowell, "Ask the Experts," *Barter Brief*, National Association of Barter Exchanges, Volume #2, 2008, p. 2.
43. Crystal Detamore-Rodman, "Care to Barter?" *Entrepreneur*, December 2008, p. 54.
44. Raymund Flandez, "Small Businesses Cut Costs by Renegotiation," *Wall Street Journal*, January 20, 2009, http://online.wsj.com/article/SB123241078342495977.html.
45. "Equipment Finance 101," Equipment Leasing and Finance Association, May 9, 2008, http://www.elfaonline.org/pub/abtind/Fin101/basics.cfm.
46. Jill Amadio, "To Lease or Not to Lease?" *Entrepreneur*, February 1998, p. 133.
47. Pia Sarkar, "Disposable Chic," November 8, 2005, SFGate.com, http://www.sfgate.com/cgi-bin/article.cgi?f=/c/a/2005/11/08/BUGSOFKG9F1.DTL; Kimberly Pfaff, "Cheap Chic," *Retailing Today*, March 2002, http://www.icsc.org/srch/sct/sct0302/page35.php?region=; "Forever 21 and IBM Fashion a One-Stop POS Solution with Just the Right Fit," Case Studies: IBM Global Financing, April 26, 2005, http://www-03.ibm.com/financing/pdf/us/igf5-a214.pdf.
48. Jack Wynn, "To Use But Not to Own," *Nation's Business*, January 1991, p. 38.
49. Roger Thompson, "Business Copes With the Recession," *Nation's Business*, January 1991, p. 20.
50. Anjali Cordeiro, "Firms Struggle with Commodities Cost," *Wall Street Journal*, October 14, 2008, p. B8.
51. Bruce G. Posner, "Skipped-Payment Loans," *Inc.*, September 1992, p. 40.
52. Gerry Blackwell," Don't Hire, Outsource," *Small Business Computing*, July 5, 2005, www.smallbusinesscomputing.com/news/article.php/3512451.
53. Emily Maltby, "Overseas Outsourcing Heats Up Again," *CNN Money*, November 11, 2008, http://money.cnn.com/2008/11/10/smallbusiness/outsourcing.smb/index.htm.
54. "Check Fraud," Rutgers University, http://crimeprevention.rutgers.edu/crime/checkfraud/checkfraud.htm.
55. "Insights into the Consumer Appeal of Gift Cards," *Payments News*, May 20, 2008, http://www.paymentsnews.com/2008/05/insights-into-t.html.
56. David Worrell, "It's in the Cards," *Entrepreneur*, April 2005, p. 57.
57. Roger Thompson, "Business Copes With the Recession," *Nation's Business,* January 1991, p. 21.
58. Kathy Grannis, "Retail Losses Hit $41.6 Billion Last Year, According to National Retail Security Survey," National Retail Federation, June 11, 2007, http://www.nrf.com/modules.php?name=News&op=viewlive&sp_id=318.
59. Raymund Flandez, "Stop That Thief," *Wall Street Journal*, June 16, 2008, p. R6.
60. Susan Dickison, "Annual National Retail Security Survey Shows Shoplifting and Retail Loss on the Decline, Organized Retail Crime on the Rise," *Home Accents Today,* June 26, 2008, http://www.homeaccentstoday.com/blog/240000224/post/1440028944.html.
61. Jill Andresky Fraser, "Better Cash Management," *Inc.*, May 1993, p. 42.
62. C. J. Prince, "Money to Burn?" *Entrepreneur*, July 2004, pp. 51—52.
63. Robert A. Mamis, "Money In, Money Out," *Inc.*, March 1993, p. 103.

Chapter 13

1. "What's in Store for Small Business?" Special Advertising Section, *Inc.*, December 2007, p. 72.
2. Dayan Gupta, "The Right Fit," *Wall Street Journal,* May 22, 1995, p. R8.
3. Aliza Pilar Sherman, "The Opposite Sex," *Entrepreneur,* September 2002, p. 36.
4. U.N. Umesh and Patrick Criteser, "Venture Capital's Foul Weather Friends," *Wall Street Journal,* January 14, 2003, p. B13; "Press Releases," Northwest Energy Efficiency Alliance, http://www.nwalliance.org/news/pressreleases.asp.
5. Kasey Wehrum, "Angel Investing 2009," *Inc.*, January/February 2009, p. 85.
6. Nicole Periroth, "Health Nuts," *Forbes,* February 2, 2009, p. 42.
7. Keith McFarland, "Myth of the Fearless Entrepreneur," *Time,* May 22, 2008, http://www.time.com/time/magazine/article/0,9171,1808633,00.html.
8. J. Lynn Lunsford, "Eclipse Ousts Raburn to Win Financing," *Wall Street Journal,* July 29, 2008, p, B3; Eric Anderson, "Sale of Eclipse Aviation's Assets Gets Judge's Approval," *Albany Times Union,* January 20, 2009, http://blogs.timesunion.com/business/?p=7523; Andy Pasztor, "Eclipse Aviation Files for Chapter 11," *Wall Street Journal,* November 26, 2008, http://online.wsj.com/article/SB122765456029258007.html.
9. Douglas McMillan, "Google's Historic IPO Run: Beatable," *Business Week,* August 16, 2007, http://www.businessweek.com/technology/content/aug2007/tc20070816_081016.htm?chan=technology_technology+index+page_top+stories; Robert Andrews, "Google Gamble," *I.T. Wales,* May 17, 2004, http://www.itwales.com/998765.htm.
10. Elizabeth Fenner, "How to Raise the Cash You Need," *Money Guide,* Summer 1991, p. 45.
11. William D. Bygrave with Mark Quill, *Global Entrepreneurship Monitor: 2006 Financing Report,* Global Entrepreneurship Research Association, 2006, p.23.
12. Carol Tice, "Launch for Less," *Entrepreneur,* May 23, 2008, http://www.entrepreneur.com/magazine/entrepreneursstartupsmagazine/2008/may/193402.html.
13. *Global Entrepreneurship Monitor 2006 Financing Report,* Global Entrepreneurship Research Association, 2006, p.8.
14. *Global Entrepreneurship Monitor: National Entrepreneurship Assessment—United States of America, 2004–2005 Executive Report,* Global Entrepreneurship Research Association, 2006, p.22.
15. Stephen L. Rosenstein, "Use Caution with Family Loans for Your Business," *Baltimore Sun,* August 10, 2008,

www.**baltimoresun**.com/business/bal-bz.ml.
biztip10aug10,cs-bears today,6345879.column.

16. Paul Kvinta, "Frogskins, Shekels, Bucks, Moolah, Cash, Simoleans, Dough, Dinero: Everybody Wants It. Your Business Needs It. Here's How to Get It," *Smart Business,* August 2000, pp. 74–89.

17. Joseph R. Bell, Kenneth M. Huggins, and Christine McClatchey, "Profiling the Angel Investor," presented at Small Business Insitute Director's Association Conference, February 7, 2002, San Diego California, p.1; "Biography: Laurance Spelman Rockefeller," InfoPlease.com, http://www.infoplease. com/ipa/A0771997.html.

18. Pamela Sherrid, "Angels of Capitalism," *U.S. News & World Report,* October 13, 1997, pp. 43–45.

19. Jeffrey Sohl, "The Angel Investor Market in 2007," University of New Hampshire Center for Venture Research, www.unh.edu/cvr, 2007, p.1.

20. Francis B. Allgood, "Five Years Later, InnoVenture Hotter Than Ever," *GSA Business*, March 17, 2008, pp. 3, 6; "Company Tests New Retractable-Stud Snow Tires to Offer Safe Driving Without Roadway Damage," *International Herald Tribune,* March 30, 2008, http://www.iht .com/articles/ap/2008/03/30/america/Retractable-Studs.php.

21. Robert Wiltbank and Warren Boeker, "Returns to Angel Investors in Groups," Angel Capital Education Foundation, November 2007, http://www.angelcapitaleducation .org/dir_downloads/resources/RSCH_-_ACEF_-_Returns_to_Angel_Investor_in_Groups.pdf.

22. "Raising Funds," *Inc.*, November 2008, pp. 69–70.

23. "Robert E. Wilbank and Warren Boeker, "Angel Performance Project," Angel Capital Education Foundation, November 2007, http://www.angelcapitalassociation.org/ dir_downloads/resources/RSCH_-_ACEF_-_Returns_to_Angel_Investors_PPT.pdf. What Is the Average Closing Time to Receive Financing?" *Jian Business Power Tools,* http://www.jian.com/library-of-business-information/f252/ venture-capital/what-is-the-average-closing-time-it-takes-between-receiving-a.php.

24. Josh Hyatt, "More Guardian, Less Angel," *CFO,* September 2008, p. 45.

25. "Raising Funds," *Inc.*, June 2008, p. 65.

26. Josh Hyatt, "More Guardian, Less Angel," *CFO,* September 2008, pp. 41–45.

27. Kelly K. Spors, "Angel Groups Spread Their Wings Beyond Tech," *Wall Street Journal,* October 30, 2007, p. B9.

28. "Portfolio," Band of Angels, http://www.bandangels .com/portfolio/index.php; "About Us," Picaboo, http://www.picaboo.com/aboutus/index.html; "Company Summary: Picaboo," Link Silicon Valley, http://www .linksv.com/lsvDev/lsv/companySummary.aspx?co_ idURl=30826&company=Picaboo.

29. "About ACA," Angel Capital Association, http://www .angelcapitalassociation.org/dir_about/overview.aspx.

30. Robert Wiltbank and Warren Boeker, "Returns to Angel Investors in Groups," Angel Capital Education Foundation, November 2007, http://www.angelcapitaleducation .org/dir_downloads/resources/RSCH_-_ACEF_-_Returns_ to_Angel_Investor_in_Groups.pdf.

31. Mark Henricks, "Stand Your Ground," *Entrepreneur*, January 1993, p. 264.

32. Carole Carlson and Prabal Chakrabarti, "Venture Capital Opportunities in Secondary Cities: Issues and Opportunities for Impact," Federal Reserve Bank of Boston, April 2007, p. 3.

33. *Venture Impact: The Economic Importance of Venture Backed Companies to the U.S. Economy,* Fourth edition, National Venture Capital Association, 2007, pp. 8–9.

34. Carol Tice, "It's Go Time," *Entrepreneur*, May 2008, p. 60; Wade Roush, "Blackwave Raises $16 Million for Internet Video Delivery," *Xconomy*, December 3, 2007, http://www.xconomy.com/2007/12/03/blackwave-raises-16-million-for-internet-video-delivery/.

35. William D. Bygrave with Mark Quill, *Global Entrepreneurship Monitor: 2006 Financing Report,* Global Entrepreneurship Research Association, 2006, p.23.

36. Dee Power and Brian E. Hill, "Venture Capital Survey," *The Capital Connection,* 2008, http://www.capital-connection.com/survey-close.html.

37. Singer, "Where the Money Is," pp. 52–55; National Venture Capital Association, http://www.nvca.org; PriceWaterhouseCoopers MoneyTree Survey, http://www.pwcmoneytree.com/moneytree/index.jsp.

38. Mabel Brecrick-Okereke, "Report to U.N. Cautions that Focus on Venture Capital Can Hinder Entrepreneurial Economy," United Nations Association of the United States of America, http://unusa.school.aol.com/newsroom/ NewsReleases/ean_venture.asp ; Cara Cannella, "Where Seed Money Really Comes From," *Inc.*, August 2003, p. 26.

39. "Investments by Industry," PriceWaterhouseCoopers MoneyTree Survey, http://www.pwcmoneytree.com/ MTPublic/ns/nav.jsp?page=industry.

40. Kate O'Sullivan, "Not-So-Easy Money, *CFO*, October 2005, p. 20.

41. Rebecca Buckman, "Baby Sitting for Start-Ups," *Wall Street Journal,* March 13, 2006, p. B3.

42. Andrea Poe, "Venturing Out," *Entrepreneur*, September 2008, p. 31.

43. Roger Lowenstein, "Adventure Capitalist," *Portfolio,* December 2007, p. 152.

44. *Venture Impact: The Economic Importance of Venture Backed Companies to the U.S. Economy*, Fourth edition, National Venture Capital Association, 2007, p. 4.

45. Rebecca Buckman, "BabySitting for Start-Ups," *Wall Street Journal*, March 13, 2006, pp. B1, B3.

46. Rebecca Buckman, "LinkedIn's Venture-Capitalist Connection," *Wall Street Journal*, June 18, 2008, p. B6; "LinkedIn," TradeVibes, http://www.tradevibes.com/ company/profile/linkedin?search=simple.

47. Dave Pell, "What's Old Is New Again," *FSB*, July/August 2000, p. 122.

48. Ian MacMillan, Edward Roberts, Val Livada, and Andrew Wang, *Corporate Venture Capital (CVC): Seeking Innovation and Strategic Growth*, National Institute of Standards and Technology, U.S. Department of Commerce, June 2008, p. 2.

49. Jay R. Ritter, "Some Factoids About the 2008 IPO Market," Working Paper, University of Florida, December 2008, http://bear.cba.ufl.edu/ritter/work_papers/ IPOs2008Factoids.pdf.

50. Ibid.

51. "The More the Merrier," *CFO*, October 2005, p. 18.

52. Robert J. Terry, "Over-Allotment Option Pushes Sourcefire IPO to $86M," *Baltimore Business Journal*, March 23, 2007,

http://baltimore.bizjournals.com/baltimore/stories/2007/03/19/daily44.html?jst=s_cn_hl; "Sourcefire," *IPO Home,* http://www.ipohome.com/ipohome/ipoprofile.aspx?ticker=FIRE.

53. "Security Solutions Provider Sourcefire Announces Terms,"*IPO Home,* February 7, 2007, http://www.ipohome.com/ipohome/news/iponews2.aspx?article=5675.

54. Telephone interview with David Barash, Ben & Jerry's Homemade.

55. Marilyn Landis, "The Impact of the Credit Crunch on Small Business," April 16, 2008, National Small Business Association, p. 1.

56. Stacy Cowley, "Message to Obama: Send Loans Fast," *CNNMoney,* November 16, 2008, http://money.cnn.com/2008/11/14/smallbusiness/loans_needed_asap.smb/index.htm.

57. John Tozzi, "Credit Cards Replace Small Business Loans," *Business Week,* August 20, 2008, http://www.businessweek.com/smallbiz/content/aug2008/sb20080820_288348.htm?chan=smallbiz_smallbiz+index+page_top+small+business+stories.

58. Charles Ou, *Banking and SME Financing in the United States,* SBA Office of Advocacy, June 2006, http://www.sba.gov/advo/research/rs277tot.pdf, p. 7.

59. Jim Hopkins, "Where Do Start-ups Get Their Money?" *USA Today,* October 24, 2006, http://www.usatoday.com/money/smallbusiness/2006-10-18-small-finance-usat_x.htm.

60. Emily Maltby, "How to Land a Bank Loan," *CNNMoney,* September 17, 2008, http://money.cnn.com/2008/09/16/smallbusiness/land_a_bank_loan.smb/index.htm.

61. "Community Banking Facts," Independent Community Bankers of America, June 2008, p.2, http://www.icba.org/files/ICBASites/PDFs/cbfacts.pdf?sn.ItemNumber=1745.

62. Daniel M. Clark, "Banks and Bankability," *Venture,* September 1989, p. 29.

63. J. Alex Tarquinio, "Brother, Can You Spare a Loan?" *New York Times,* October 1, 2008, http://www.nytimes.com/2008/10/01/business/smallbusiness/01CREDIT.html?_r=1&scp=1&sq=Brother%20Can%20You%20spare%20a%20Loan&st=cse.

64. Louis Uchitelle, "Small Businesses Feeling the Chill," *New York Times,* October 2, 2008, http://www.nytimes.com/2008/10/02/business/smallbusiness/02sbiz.html?em.

65. Catherine Curan, "In a Cash Crunch?" *Inc.,* March 2006, pp. 34-36.

66. Kelly K. Spors and Simona Covel, "When a Bank Loan Isn't an Option," *Wall Street Journal,* May 1, 2008, p. B9.

67. "What Is Business Credit?" National Association of Credit Management, http://www.nacm.org/aboutnacm/what.html ; "Financing Small Business," *Small Business Reporter,* c3, p. 9.

68. C. J. Prince, "Shared Effort," *Entrepreneur,* February 2008, p. 62.

69. Louis Uchitelle, "Small Businesses Feeling the Chill," *New York Times,* October 2, 2008, http://www.nytimes.com/2008/10/02/business/smallbusiness/02sbiz.html?em.

70. "U.S. Credit Union Profile," Credit Union National Association, February 25, 2009, http://advice.cuna.org/download/uscu_profile_1q09.pdf.

71. "Anjali Cordeiro, "Small Firms Get Local Loans," *Wall Street Journal,* November 11, 2008, p. B4.

72. *Summary of SBIC Program Financing,* U.S. Small Business Administration (Washington, DC), 2009, http://www.sba.gov/aboutsba/sbaprograms/inv/inv_aboutus_program_financing.html.

73. National Association of Small Business Investment Companies, http://www.nasbic.org/.

74. *Summary of SBIC Program Financing,* U.S. Small Business Administration (Washington, DC), 2009, http://www.sba.gov/aboutsba/sbaprograms/inv/inv_aboutus_program_financing.html.

75. "Success Stories: Outback Steakhouse," National Association of Small Business Investment Companies, http://www.nasbic.com/success/stories/outback.cfm ; "Company Statistics," Outback Steakhouse, http://www.corporate-ir.net/ireye/ir_site.zhtml?ticker=osi&script=950&layout=11&item_id='ps=1*pg=2.

76. "Success Stories: Pro Tape & Specialties," New Jersey Economic Development Authority, http://www.njeda.com/web/Aspx_pg/templates/success_story.aspx?doc_id=971&menuid=1323&levelid=6&midid=1175&topid=718.

77. "CDBG Success Stories," Nebraska Department of Economic Development, http://www.neded.org/files/crd/2008/CDBG/CDBGSuccessStories07.pdf, pp. 9–10.

78. Elizabeth Morrisey, "Small Businesses Get Tips on Raising Capital," *GSA Business,* September 15, 2008, pp. 3,8.

79. "Business Programs: Business and Industry Guaranteed Loan Success Stories," United States Department of Agriculture, Rural Development, http://www.rurdev.usda.gov/rbs/busp/ss/bpbisuccess.htm.

80. Charles Wessner, "An Assessment of the SBIR Program," National Research Council, http://books.nap.edu/openbook.php?record_id=11989&page=12, pp. 91–107.

81. "SBIR and STTR Success Story for ARISIL, Inc.," National Institutes of Health, http://grants1.nih.gov/grants/funding/sbir_successes/1119.htm; "FAQ," EarPopper, http://www.earpopper .com/faqs/index.htm.

82. Gretchen Morgenson, "SBA Lender, Uncensored," *New York Times,* August 3, 2008, http://www.nytimes.com/2008/08/03/business/03gret.html.

83. "The SBA's 7(a) Loan Program: A Flexible Tool for Commercial Lenders," *Community Development Insights,* Washington, D.C.: U.S. Department of the Treasury, September 2008, http://www.occ.treas.gov/cdd/Insights-SBAs7(a).pdf, p. 2.

84. "The SBA's 7(a) Loan Program: A Flexible Tool for Commercial Lenders," *Community Development Insights,* Washington, D.C.: U.S. Department of the Treasury, September 2008, http://www.occ.treas.gov/cdd/Insights-SBAs7(a).pdf, p. 3.

85. David Port, "From Servicemen to Businessmen," *Entrepreneur,* November 21, 2008, http://www.entrepreneur.com/startingabusiness/successstories/article198798.html.

86. Raymund Flandez, "SBA Loan Cap Hits Minority Owners," *Wall Street Journal,* December 9, 2008, pp. B1, B7.

87. "The SBA's 7(a) Loan Program: A Flexible Tool for Commercial Lenders," *Community Development Insights,* Washington, D.C.: U.S. Department of the Treasury, September 2008, http://www.occ.treas.gov/cdd/Insights-SBAs7(a).pdf, p. 3.

88. "The SBA's 7(a) Loan Program: A Flexible Tool for Commercial Lenders," *Community Development Insights*, Washington, D.C.: U.S. Department of the Treasury, September 2008, http://www.occ.treas.gov/cdd/Insights-SBAs7(a).pdf, pp.1–2.

89. Emily Maltby, "Small Biz Loan Failure Rate Hits 12%," *CNNMoney*, February 25, 2009, http://money.cnn.com/2009/02/25/smallbusiness/smallbiz_loan_defaults_soar.smb/index.htm.

90. Rich Kirchen, "SBA Backing Put Expansion Back on the Menu," *BizJournals*, 2008, http://www.bizjournals.com/small_business_administration/sba2008/sba_backing_put_expansion_on_menu.html?s=sbc:1.

91. Mary Duan, "504 Loan Leads to Smoother Sailing," *BizJournals*, 2008, http://www.bizjournals.com/small_business_administration/sba2008/504_loan_leads_to_smoother_sailing.html?s=sbc:1.

92. *SBA Microloan Program: FY 2007*, Women Impacting Public Policy, http://www.wipp.org/news_details.asp?story_id=204&memberonly=False.

93. Lori Johnston, "Artist Draws on Microloan, Training," *BizJournals*, 2008, http://www.bizjournals.com/small_business_administration/sba2008/artist_draws_on_microloan_training.html?s=sbc:1.

94. Keith Regan, "Credit Line Gives Global Sales a Lift," *BizJournals*, 2008, http://www.bizjournals.com/small_business_administration/sba2008/credit_line_gives_global_sales_a_lift.html?s=sbc:1.

95. The SBA's 7(a) Loan Program: A Flexible Tool for Commercial Lenders," *Community Development Insights*, Washington, D.C.: U.S. Department of the Treasury, September 2008, http://www.occ.treas.gov/cdd/Insights-SBAs7(a).pdf, p. 4.

96. Carol Chastang, "SBA Approves More than $1 Billion in Disaster Loans to Midwest Floods and Gulf Coast Hurricane Survivors," SBA Press Office, December 22, 2008, p. 1.

97. Ziona Austrian and Zhongcai Zhang, "An Inventory and Assessment of Pollution Control and Prevention Financing Programs," Great Lakes Environmental Finance Center, Levin College of Urban Affairs, Cleveland State University, http://www.csuohio.edu/glefc/inventor.htm#sba.

98. "Worms, Worms, and More Worms: Earthworms Soil Factory," California Integrated Waste Management Board, http://www.ciwmb.ca.gov/RMDZ/BizProfiles/EarthWorm.htm

99. Roberta Reynes, "A Big Factor in Expansion," *Nation's Business*, January 1999, pp. 31-32; Bruce J. Blechman, "The High Cost of Credit," *Entrepreneur,* January 1993, pp. 22–25.

100. Rich Karlgaard, "Bootstrappers Rule," *Forbes*, January 12, 2009, p. 25; "Larry Page and Sergey Brin Boigraphy," *Encyclopedia of World Biography*, http://www.notablebiographies.com/news/Ow-Sh/Page-Larry-and-Brin-Sergey.html.

101. *2008 Survey of Small and Mid-Sized Businesses*, National Small Business Association, Washington, DC, 2009, p. 19.

102. John Tozzi, "Credit Cards Replace Small Business Loans," *Business Week*, August 20, 2008, http://www.businessweek.com/smallbiz/content/aug2008/sb20080820_288348.htm?chan=smallbiz_smallbiz+index+page_top+small+business+stories.

Chapter 14

1. Karen E. Klein, "Finding the Perfect Location," *Business Week*, March 24, 2008, http://www.businessweek.com/smallbiz/content/mar2008/sb20080324_098559.htm?chan=smallbiz_smallbiz+index+page_top+small+business+stories; Nora Parker, "Johnny's Lunch Plans Franchise Expansion with LI," Directions Magazine, October 8, 2007, http://www.directionsmag.com/article.php?article_id=2569&trv=1; Chris Knape, "New Diner Downtown Is Johnny on the Spot," *Grand Rapids Press*, May 12, 2008, p. B4.

2. Mark Henricks, "Hot Spots," *Entrepreneur*, October 2005, pp. 68–74.

3. Louis Mongello, "Walt Disney World History 101: How to Buy 27,000 Acres of Land and No One Notice," Gather.com, December 18, 2005, http://www.gather.com/viewArticle.jsp?articleId=281474976719796.

4. Michelle Prather, "Hit the Spot," *Business Start-Ups*, April 1999, p. 104.

5. Jason Del Ray, "A New Way to Search for the Right Place to Set Up Shop," *Inc.*, January/February 2009, pp. 102-104.

6. "North Carolina Company to Relocate to UB's Center of Excellence," University of Buffalo, March 15, 2007, http://www.buffalo.edu/news/fast-execute.cgi/article-page.html?article=85040009; John Dellacontrada, "Medcotek Licenses UB Technology," *UB Reporter*, April 17, 2008, http://www.buffalo.edu/ubreporter/archives/vol39/vol39n29/articles/MedcotekUB.html.

7. David Worrell, "Move Over," *Entrepreneur*, September 2005, p. 55.

8. "Employer Costs for Employee Compensation for the Regions," December 2008, Bureau of Labor Statistics, http://www.bls.gov/ro9/ececwest.htm.

9. Nico Matouschek and Frederic Robert Nicoud, "The Role of Human Capital Investments in the Location Decision of Firms," Kellogg School of Business, Northwestern University, http://www.kellogg.northwestern.edu/faculty/matouschek/htm/research/Paper_6_t.pdf, p. 1; "History," Accordions Worldwide, http://www.accordions.com/index/his/his_it.shtml; "The Dawn of the Italian Accordion Industry," The Home for Wayward Accordions, http://www.klezmusic.com/index.html.

10. Sara Wilson, "Tech and the City," *Entrepreneur*, February 2009, p. 19.

11. Victoria Rivers, "100 Best Places to Live and Launch: Manchester, New Hampshire," *FSB*, April 2008, pp. 74–77; "100 Best Places to Live and Launch: Manchester, New Hampshire," *FSB*, April 2008, http://money.cnn.com/galleries/2008/fsb/0803/gallery.best_places_to_launch.fsb/13.html.

12. Chris Penttila, "State Your Case," *Entrepreneur*, March 2005, pp. 17–18.

13. "14 Annual Kosmont-Rose Institute Cost of Doing Business Survey Published by the Rose Institute of Sate and Local Government at McKenna College," *Earth Times*, December 11, 2008, http://www.earthtimes.org/articles/show/14th-annual-kosmont-rose-institute-cost,652402.shtml.

14. Quentin Fottrell and Justin Scheck, "Dell Moving Irish Operations to Poland," *Wall Street Journal*, January 9, 2009, p. B4; Justin Scheck and Joellen Perry, "Dell's Plan to Sell Plants Causes Jitters in Ireland," *Wall Street Journal*, September 15, 2008, p. B3.

15. "From Our Kitchen to Yours: Our History," Fiesta Tortillas, http://www.fiestatortillas.com/history.html.

16. "Ask Inc.," *Inc.*, February 2005, p. 44.

17. Richard Breen, "Stax Omega Joins Pelham Party," *GSA Business*, December 27, 2004, pp. 5, 9.

18. "Clusters and Cluster Development," Institute for Strategy and Competitiveness, Harvard Business School, http://www.isc.hbs.edu/econ-clusters.htm.

19. Douglas Woodward, "Porter's Cluster Strategy Versus Industrial Targeting," International Conference in Information Technology, December 3, 2004, Orlando, Florida, p. 7; *Grgich Hills Estate Newsletter*, Spring 2009, pp. 2,5; "History of Wine Making in Napa Valley," Golden Haven Hot Springs and Resort, http://www.goldenhaven.com/regions/napa_valley/napa_valley_history.html.

20. Verena Dobnik, "An Immigrant Era Ends: Matzo Factory Closing," *Greenville News*, December 29, 2007, p. 16A; Bonnie Rosenstock, "The Streit Family Dynasty," *The Villager*, Volume 73,, Number 38, January 21–27, 2004, http://www.thevillager.com/villager_38/thestreitsfamily.html.

21. Mark Svenvold, "100 Best Places to Live and Launch: Iowa City, Iowa" *FSB*, April 2008, pp. 77–78.

22. "Worker Relocation Worries," *Inside Training Newsletter*, November 29, 2007, p. 1.

23. Eilene Zimmerman, "100 Best Places to Live and Launch: Bellevue, Washington" *FSB*, April 2008, pp. 68–69.

24. "Starting a Convenience Store," Canada Business: Services for Entrepreneurs, November 25, 2008, http://www.canadabusiness.ca/servlet/ContentServer?cid=1099483437618&lang=en&pagename=CBSC_FE%2Fdisplay&c=GuidcHowto.

25. Rich Hollander, "Predicting the Future, One Customer at a Time," *Franchising World*, March 2008, http://www.franchise.org/Franchise-Industry-News-Detail.aspx?id=38390.

26. "Ciprianis Told to Vacate Rainbow Room," *Nation's Restaurant News*, January 11, 2009, http://www.nrn.com/breakingNews.aspx?id=362066&menu_id=1368; "Rainbow Room's Grill to Close as Economy, Lease Dispute Dull Future," *Nation's Restaurant News*, January 5, 2009, http://www.nrn.com/breakingNews.aspx?id=361810; Oshrat Carmiel and Peter S. Green, "Cipriani Dining Empire Loses BlackRock, Rainbow Room," *Bloomberg*, February 5, 2009, http://www.bloomberg.com/apps/news?pid=20601088&sid=abZWspVJXPSA&refer=muse#.

27. Ron Ruggless, "BK Debuts Whopper Bar Concept, Eyes on-site Arena in Plan to Beef up Growth," *Nation's Restaurant News*, http://www.nrn.com/landingPage.aspx?menu_id=1424&coll_id=676&id=364528; "BK to Debut Whopper Bar Next Year," *Nation's Restaurant News*, October 7, 2008, http://www.nrn.com/breakingNews.aspx?id=359160.

28. Shannon Perez, "6 Tips to Finding the Perfect Location for Your Practice," Massage Therapy, http://www.massagetherapy.com/articles/index.php/article_id/1377.

29. Lisa Jennings, "Upscale Brands Positioned as Less Luxury, More Valuable," *Nation's Restaurant News*, March 16, 2009, http://www.nrn.com/landingPage.aspx?coll_id=554&keyword=%20frozen%20yogurt&id=364242#.

30. Matt Rosenberg, About Reilly's Law of Retail Gravitation, About.com, http://geography.about.com/cs/citiesurbangeo/a/aa041403a.htm ; G.I. Thrall and J.C.del Valle, "The Calculation of Retail Market Areas: The Reilly Model," *GeoInfoSystems* Volume 7, No.4, 1997, pp. 46–49.

31. Xylia Buros, "The Improved Grab-and-Go Model," *Fresh Cup*, January 2009, http://www.freshcup.com/featured-article.php?id=84.

32. Sasha M. Pardy, "U.S. Retail Property Market Bracing for a Long Year in 2009," CoStar's Retail News Roundup, January 28, 2009, http://www.costar.com/News/Article.aspx?id=ED7FC8D5E020BB47B80E9E825AEEC62E.

33. Mason Lerner, "Boutique Sneaker Shop Seeks to Become a Downtown Presence, but Biggest Obstacle to Success Is a Lack of Parking, Foot Traffic," *Houston Chronicle*, November 9, 2007, www.chron.com/disp/story.mpl/business/5290563.html

34. Paul Lukas, "Our Malls, Ourselves," *Fortune*, October 18, 2004, pp. 243–256.

35. "Industry Fun Facts," International Council of Shopping Centers, http://www.icsc.org/srch/about/impactofshoppingcenters/Did_You_Know.pdf.

36. "ICSC Shopping Center Definitions," International Council of Shopping Centers, www.icsc.org; Andrew Blum, "The Mall Goes Undercover," *Washington Post*, April 6, 2005, www.slate.com/id/2116246/; Parija Bhatnagar, "It's Not a Mall, It's a Lifestyle Center," *CNN/Money*, January 12, 2005, http://money.cnn.com/2005/01/11news/fortune500/retail_lifestylecenter.

37. Nanea Kalani, "Mall Location Gives Hawaii Business More Bounce," *Pacific Business News*, January 30, 2009, http://pacific.bizjournals.com/pacific/stories/2009/02/02/smallb1.html.

38. "The Taco Maker Inks Wal-Mart Agreement," *Quick Service Restaurant*, May 12, 2008, http://www.qsrmagazine.com/articles/news/story.phtml?id=6543.

39. "Frequently Asked Questions," Small Business Administration, Office of Advocacy, September 2008, p.1.

40. Sara Wilson, "In-House," *Entrepreneur*, November 14, 2007, http://www.entrepreneur.com/homebasedbiz/homebasedbasics/article186854-2.html.

41. Mark Arend, "Think Globally, Hire Locally," *Site Selection*, November 2008, www.siteselection.com/features/2008/nov/Nebraska/

42. Mark Arend, "Think Globally, Hire Locally," *Site Selection*, November 2008, www.siteselection.com/features/2008/nov/Nebraska/

43. "Business Incubation FAQ," National Business Incubation Association, http://www.nbia.org/resource_center/bus_inc_facts/index.php.

44. "Business Incubation FAQ," National Business Incubation Association, http://www.nbia.org/resource_center/bus_inc_facts/index.php.

45. Eric Anderson, "Mumbai by Way of Niskayuna," *Times Union*, February 25, 2009, http://www.timesunion.com/AspStories/story.asp?storyID=773529&category=BUSINESS; "Cinematography Oscar for 'Slumdog' Focuses Attention on Silicon Imaging, a Graduate of RPI Incubator Program," Business Incubator Program of New York State, February 26, 2009, http://bianys.com/node/499.

46. "Workplace design = Job Performance?" *Inside Training*, October 29, 2008, p. 1.

47. Ibid.

48. Michael Lev-Ram, "How to Make Your Workspace Work Better," *Business 2.0*, November 2006, pp. 60.

49. *The Integrated Workplace*, Office of Governmentwide Policy, Office of Real Property, Washington, DC: 2008, pp. 8–9.

50. Laura Tiffany, "The Rules of…Retail," *Business Start-Ups*, December 1999, p. 106.

51. Georgia Flight, "Corporate Identity Through Architecture," *Business 2.0*, November 2005, pp. 58–60.

52. Mike Hughlett, "Drive-Throughs Done Right Ring Up Returns," *Chicago Tribune*, November 28, 2008, http://www.chicagotribune.com/business/chi-fri-drive-throughs-1128-nov28,0,4729183.story.

53. Tiffany, "The Rules of…Retail," p. 106.

54. A. Alfred Taubman, "Getting Over the Threshold," *Inc.*, April 2007, pp. 75–76.

55. "Educational Kit," President's Committee on Employment of People with Disabilities, http://www50.pcepd.gov/pcepd/archives/pubs/ek99/wholedoc.htm#decisions.

56. "McD Unveils One-Off Restaurant in Las Vegas," *Nation's Restaurant News*, December 10, 2008, http://www.nrn.com/breakingNews.aspx?id=361116.

57. Brian Amble, "Poor Workplace Design Damages Productivity," *Management-Issues*, May 23, 2006, http://www.management-issues.com/2006/8/24/research/poor-workplace-design-damages-productivity.asp.

58. "Proposal for an Ergonomics Program Standard," The Occupational Health and Safety Administration, http://www.osha-slc.gov/ergonomics-standard/ergo-faq.html.

59. "Paco Underhill: Shopping Scientist," *CBC News*, November 7, 2000, http://www.cbc.ca/consumers/market/files/home/shopping/index.html.

60. Tiffany Meyers, "Waste Not," *Entrepreneur*, February 2008, p. 75.

61. Julie Sturgeon, "Fast Casuals Light Up," *Fast Casual*, March 10, 2009, www.fastcasual.com/article.php?id=13677.

62. Jennifer Alsever, "Showing Products in a Better Light," *Business 2.0*, September 2005, p. 62.

63. Nicholas Spangler, "The Stores Are Alive with the Sound of Muzak," *Miami Herald*, December 15, 2008, www.miamiherald.com/news/front-page/v-print/story/814552.html.

64. Michael Morain, "Muzak – It Remains Music to Retailers' Ears," *Greenville News*, December 23, 2007, p. 3F; Theunis Bates,"Volume Control," *Time*, August 2, 2007, www.time.com/time/printout/0,8816,1649304,00.html.

65. Linda Tischler, "Smells Like a Brand Spirit," *Fast Company*, August 2005, pp. 52–59.

66. Kara Newman, "How to Sell with Smell," *Business 2.0*, April 2007, p. 36; Linda Tischler, "Smells Like a Brand Spirit," *Fast Company*, August 2005, pp. 52–59.

67. Andrew Martin, "Green Plans in Blueprints of Retailers," *New York Times*, November 8, 2008, http://www.nytimes.com/2008/11/08/business/08build.html?ref=science.

68. Mark Henricks, "Change Can Do You Good," *Entrepreneur*, December 2008, p. 22.

69. Paul Keegan, "The Architect of Happy Customers," *Business 2.0*, August 2002, pp. 85–87.

70. Kris Hudson and Ann Zimmerman, "Big Boxes Aim to Speed Up Shopping," *Wall Street Journal*, June 27, 2007, pp. B1, B8.

71. Annette Elton, "I'll Take That Too: Increasing Impulse Buys," *Gift Shop*, Spring 2008, http://www.giftshopmag.com/2008/spring/unique_giftware/increasing_impulse_buys.

72. Jeffrey A, Trachtenberg, "How a Children's Book Got a Christmas Break," *Wall Street Journal*, December 5, 2005, pp. B1, B5.

73. Kenneth Labich, "This Man Is Watching You," *Fortune*, July 19, 1999, pp. 131–134.

74. Kris Hudson and Ann Zimmerman, "Big Boxes Aim to Speed Up Shopping," *Wall Street Journal*, June 27, 2007, pp. B1, B8; Tom Ryan, "Checkout Time Limit Around Four Minutes," *Retail Wire*, July 8, 2008, http://www.retailwire.com/discussions/Sngl_Discussion.cfm/13077?.

75. "Boride Engineered Abrasives," *Success Story*, Michigan Manufacturing Technology Center, 2007, p.1.

Chapter 15

1. *Intuit Future of Small Business Report, Part Three: The New Artisan Economy*, Institute for the Future, February 2008, p. 24.

2. Phred Dvorak, "Small Firms Hire Guides as They Head Abroad," *Wall Street Journal*, November 5, 2007, p. B3; "Acme Packet Posts Strong Results for First Quarter of 2009," Acme Packet, April 30, 2009, http://www.ir.acmepacket.com/phoenix.zhtml?c=200804&p=irol-newsArticle&ID=1282956&highlight=.

3. "Global Executives Brace for Change," *Sales & Marketing Management's Performance e-Newsletter*, January 10, 2005, p. 1.

4. Edward Iwata, "Small U.S. Firms Make Big Global Sales," *USA Today*, April 7, 2008, http://www.usatoday.com/money/smallbusiness/2008-04-07-small-business-exports_N.htm.

5. "Gayle Warwick Linens," *Forbes FYI*, October 2005, p. 24; Jane L. Levere, "A Small Company, A Global Approach," *New York Times*, January 1, 2004, http://www.nytimes.com/2004/01/01/business/small-business-a-small-company-a-global-approach.html?sec=&spon=&pagewanted=all.

6. Jane L. Levere, "A Small Company, A Global Approach," *New York Times*, January 1, 2004, http://www.nytimes.com/2004/01/01/business/small-business-a-small-company-a-global-approach.html?sec=&spon=&pagewanted=all.

7. "Internet Usage Statistics: The Big Picture," Internet World Stats, http://www.internetworldstats.com/stats.htm.

8. "Expand Your Reach: Open the Door to the World with Global Sales, *Entrepreneur*, October 2008, https://www.entrepreneur.com/tradejournals/article/188788529.html.

9. Rick Aristotle Munarriz, "Lights Out eBay," *The Motley Fool*, January 24, 2008, http://www.fool.com/investing/general/2008/01/24/lights-out-ebay.aspx.

10. Edward Iwata, "Small U.S. Firms Make Big Global Sales," *USA Today*, April 7, 2008, http://www.usatoday.com/money/smallbusiness/2008-04-07-small-business-exports_N.htm; "Form, Foam, and Fun: A Design-trepreneur Brings New Life to an Everyday Product," CritBuns, May 2007, http://www.critbuns.com/press_release_051707.html.

11. Phred Dvorak, "Small Firms Hire Guides as They Head Abroad," *Wall Street Journal*, November 5, 2007, p. B3.

12. "South Florida Businessman Goes Beyond U.S. Shores and Finds Global Success," *Small Business Success Story*, U.S. Small Business Administration, September 2008, p.1.

13. Claudine Williams, "Searching for the Right Connection," Federation of International Trade Associations, www.fita.org/aotm/1000.html; "History," Johnson Level and Tool, http://www.johnsonlevel.com/history.html.

14. Peggy Olive, "The Future Is Now: U.S. Small Businesses Overcome Export Barriers," ProQuest Discovery Guides, August 2008, http://www.csa.com/discoveryguides/entrepreneur/review.php.

15. "Brown Shoe Company Will Launch Naturalizer, Via Spiga in China Through Joint Venture with Hongguo International Holdings Limited," Brown Shoe Company, June 19, 2007, http://www.brownshoe.com/news/index.asp?UNID=6B7A1E777C60072186257300004BF4B0.

16. William Edwards, "International Expansion: Do Opportunities Outweigh Challenges?" *Franchising World,* February 2008, http://www.franchise.org/Franchise-News-Detail.aspx?id=37992.

17. N. Ravindran, "Place Your Savings and Sweat in Sandwiches," *Today's Manager,* June 1, 2007, http://www.entrepreneur.com/tradejournals/article/164872284.html.

18. Leslie Wiggins, "Church's Chicken Plans Big Expansion in Russia," *Atlanta Business Chronicle,* March 17, 2008, http://atlanta.bizjournals.com/atlanta/stories/2008/03/17/newscolumn3.html; "Church's Chicken Chain Unveils Ukraine Plans," *Kyiv Post,* December 19, 2007, http://www.kyivpost.com/nation/28032.

19. "International Specialty Regional Toppings," Domino's, http://www.dominos.com/Public-EN/Site+Content/Secondary/Inside+Dominos/Pizza+Particulars/International+Speciality+Toppings/.

20. *A Profile of U.S. Exporting Companies, 2006–2007,* U.S. Census Bureau, U.S. Department of Commerce, Washington, DC: April 9, 2009, p. 6.

21. "SBA Loans to Business Exporters Surpass $1 Billion," *Inside the New York District Office,* March 2007, p. 2; Rachel Solomon, "Time to Test Foreign Waters," *Entrepreneur,* May 2008, http://www.entrepreneur.com/startingabusiness/smsmallbiz/article194854.html.

22. *The Small Business Economy: A Report to the President,* U.S. Small Business Administration, Office of Advocacy, U.S. Government Printing Office, Washington, DC: 2009, p. 73.

23. Jenny Munro, "World Beats Path to Powers' Door," *Greenville News,* January 18, 2009, p. 1E.

24. "Faces of Trade: Southland Log Homes," *Trade Roots,* U.S. Department of Commerce, April 2009, http://blog.illumen.org/traderoots/docs/2009/04/southland-log-homes-inc.pdf.

25. Joseph Zaritski, "15 Tips to Start Successful Export Business," Australian Export Online: Export 61, http://www.export61.com/export-tutorials.asp?ttl=tips.

26. *The Small Business Economy: A Report to the President,* U.S. Small Business Administration, Office of Advocacy, U.S. Government Printing Office, Washington, DC: 2009, p. 103.

27. *NFIB National Small Business Poll: International Trade,* National Federation of Independent Businesses, (Washington, DC: 2004), Volume 4, Issue 1, p. 4.

28. Butler, "Making the Most of Trade Missions: Advice from Women Who've Been There (and Back)," p. 9.

29. Brian Davis, "Japanese Pets Enjoy Southern Cuisine," Alabama International Trade Center, http://www.aitc.ua.edu/success.html.

30. Peggy Olive, "The Future Is Now: U.S. Small Businesses Overcome Export Barriers," ProQuest Discovery Guides, August 2008, http://www.csa.com/discoveryguides/entrepreneur/review.php.

31. Alessandra Bianchi, "Take Your Business Global," *FSB,* October 18, 2007, http://money.cnn.com/2007/07/12/magazines/fsb/going_global.fsb/.

32. Peggy Olive, "The Future Is Now: U.S. Small Businesses Overcome Export Barriers," ProQuest Discovery Guides, August 2008, http://www.csa.com/discoveryguides/entrepreneur/review.php.

33. Lee Gimpel, "Global Hot Spots," *Entrepreneur,* June 2008, pp. 62–70.

34. Daniel Kaufmann and Shang-Jin Wei, "Does 'Grease Money' Speed Up the Wheels of Commerce?" World Bank, http://www.worldbank.org/wbi/governance/pdf/grease.pdf.

35. "U.S. International Trade in Goods and Services," U.S. Census Bureau, U.S. Bureau of Economic Analysis, May 12, 2009, p. 1.

36. Alessandra Bianchi, "Take Your Business Global," *FSB,* October 18, 2007, http://money.cnn.com/2007/07/12/magazines/fsb/going_global.fsb/.

37. Mina Kimes, "The New China Price," *Fortune,* November 12, 2007, pp. F-1–F-2.

38. Jessica Centers, "Great Balls of Light," *FSB,* April 2008, p. 25; Mark Mavrigian, "An Illuminating Idea," *BizBash,* July/August 2008, p. 19.

39. Joshua Kurlantzick, "On Foreign Soil," *Entrepreneur,* June 2005, p. 92.

40. "International Trade Statistics 2008," World Trade Organization, http://www.wto.org/english/res_e/statis_e/its2008_e/its08_world_trade_dev_e.htm.

41. "The United States Collects More Tariff Money from Cambodia than from Britain," Progressive Policy Institute, February 20, 2008, http://www.ppionline.org/ppi_ci.cfm?contentID=254579&knlgAreaID=108&subsecID=127&FREM=Y&sid=1&mid=26721.

42. "Tariffs Are One Percent of American Tax Revenue, but Once Were Half," Progressive Policy Institute, March 4, 2009, http://www.ppionline.org/ppi_ci.cfm?knlgAreaID=108&subsecID=900003&contentID=254924.

43. *World Tariff Profiles 2008,* World Trade Organization, Secretariat, Switzerland: 2008, pp. 2–6.

44. "Trade Law and Free Trade Agreements," New Zealand Ministry of Foreign Affairs and Trade, May 1, 2009, http://www.mfat.govt.nz/Treaties-and-International-Law/02-Trade-law-and-free-trade-agreements/NZ-involvement-in-trade-disputes.php.

45. Xinhua, "New World for Textile Imports as Quota System Ends," *China Daily,* January 1, 2009, http://www.chinadaily.com.cn/bizchina/2009-01/01/content_7359650.htm.

46. "Trade in Goods (Imports, Exports, and Trade Balance) with Vietnam," *Foreign Trade Statistics,* U.S. Census Bureau, http://www.census.gov/foreign-trade/balance/c5520.html#2009.

47. "Washington Clears Way for Tariffs on Wire Hangers from China," *Wall Street Journal,* September 12, 2008, p. A2; "Fact Sheet: Commerce Finds Unfair Dumping of Steel Wire Hangers from People's Republic of China," International Trade Administration, http://ia.ita.doc.gov/download/factsheets/factsheet-prc-swgh-final-080808.pdf.

48. Gary D. Bruton, David Ahlstrom, Michael N. Young, and Yuri Rubanik, "In Emerging Markets, Know What Your Partners Expect," *Wall Street Journal,* December 15, 2008, p. R5.

49. Lawrence Van Gelder, "It Pays to Watch Words, Gestures While Abroad," *Greenville News*, April 7, 1996, p. 8E.

50. Malika Zouhali-Worrall, "Watch Your Language!" *FSB*, July/August 2008, pp. 71–72.

51. Scott McCartney, "Teaching Americans How to Behave Abroad," *Wall Street Journal*, April 11, 2006, pp. D1, D4.

52. Aliza Pilar Sherman, "Going Global," *Entrepreneur*, December 2004, p. 34.

53. Ibid.

54. *NAFTA: The Road Ahead*, U.S. Trade Representative, Vancouver, 2007, http://www.ustr.gov/assets/Trade_Agreements/Regional/NAFTA/asset_upload_file147_13248.pdf?ht=, p. 1.

55. Ibid.

56. Faces of Trade: Loxcreen Company," *Trade Roots*, U.S. Department of Commerce, April 2009, http://blog.illumen.org/traderoots/docs/2009/04/loxcreen.pdf.

57. "Secretary Gutierrez Leads CAFT-DR Business Development Mission," Department of Commerce, September 29, 2008, http://www.commerce.gov/NewsRoom/PressReleases_FactSheets/PROD01_007306.

58. "Faces of Trade: BKI," *Trade Roots*, U.S. Department of Commerce, April 2009, http://blog.illumen.org/traderoots/docs/2009/04/bki1.pdf.

Chapter 16

1. Michael Gold, "Jazzin' CEO," *Manage Smarter*, January 9, 2008, p. 1.

2. Ibid.

3. Francis Huffman, "Taking the Lead," *Entrepreneur*, November 1993, p. 101.

4. Edward Teach, "Suspicious Minds," *CFO*, June 2006, p. 31.

5. Ryan Underwood, "The CEO Next Door," *Fast Company*, September 2005, pp. 64–66; Jeffrey Pfeffer, "A Field Day for Executives," *Business 2.0*, December 2004, p. 88.

6. John Mariotti, "The Role of a Leader," *Industry Week*, February 1, 1999, p. 75.

7. Dan Schawbel, "A Sense of Humor Is Worth Big Money in the Workplace," Personal Branding Blog, September 17, 2008, http://personalbrandingblog.com/a-sense-of-humor-is-worth-big-money-in-the-workplace/; Evan Carmichael, "Lesson #5: Have Fun," Famous Entrepreneur Advice, http://www.evancarmichael.com/Famous-Entrepreneurs/592/Lesson-5-Have-Fun.html.

8. Bill Breen, "The Clear Leader," *Fast Company*, March 2005, p. 66.

9. Dave Zielinski, "New Ways to Look at Leadership," *Presentations*, June 2005, pp. 26–33.

10. Leigh Buchanan, "In Praise of Selflessness: Why the Best Leaders Are Servants," *Inc.*, May 2007, pp. 33–35.

11. James Lea, "Leadership Is a Choice – One You Should Make Carefully," *Bizjournals*, July 16, 2007, http://sacramento.bizjournals.com/extraedge/consultants/family_business/2007/07/16/column267.html.

12. "Hiring Decisions Miss the Mark 50% of the Time," Corporate Executive Board, October 24, 2008, http://ir.executiveboard.com/phoenix.zhtml?c=113226&p=irol-newsArticle&ID=1205091&highlight=.

13. "Interpersonal Failure," *Inside Training Newsletter*, September 28, 2005, p. 1.

14. David Meyer, "Nine Recruiting and Selection Tips to Ensure Successful Hiring," About.com, http://humanresources.about.com/od/selectemployees/a/staff_selection_p.htm.

15. Hiring Decisions Miss the Mark 50% of the Time," Corporate Executive Board, October 24, 2008, http://ir.executiveboard.com/phoenix.zhtml?c=113226&p=irol-newsArticle&ID=1205091&highlight=; "2 Out of 3 Managers Still Fear a Hiring Decision They'll Regret," DDI, March 16, 2009, http://www.ddiworld.com/about/pr_releases_en.asp?id=211.

16. Mark Foster, "The Global Talent Crisis," *Business Week*, September 19, 2008, http://www.businessweek.com/managing/content/sep2008/ca20080919_403840.htm.

17. Jennifer Gilbert, "Choosing Wisely," *Sales & Marketing Management*, October 2004, p. 9.

18. "Lower Employee Morale and Decreased Productivity Are Biggest Consequences of Bad Hires and Promotions," Right Management, April 11, 2006, p. 1.

19. Chris Pentilla, "Talent Scout," *Entrepreneur*, July 2008,p. 19.

20. "Employee Referral Bonus Jackpots: 15 Companies with Awesome New-Hire Incentives," *HR World*, March 11, 2008, http://www.hrworld.com/features/referral-bonus-jackpot-031108/.

21. Christopher Caggiano, "Recruiting Secrets of the Smartest Companies Around," *Inc.*, October 1998, http://hiring.inc.com/inc/magazine/19981001/1008.html.

22. Mark Henricks, "Recruiting 2.0," *Entrepreneur*, February 2009, pp. 5–57.

23. *The Real Talent Debate: Will Aging Boomers Deplete the Workforce?* WorldatWork, Scottsdale, Arizona, 2007, p.12.

24. "Innovating Human Resources," *BrainReactions*, January 16, 2007, http://www.brainreactions.com/whitepapers/brainreactions_hr_innovation_paper.pdf, pp. 11-14; Christopher Caggiano, "Recruiting Secrets," *Inc.*, October 1998, pp. 30–42.

25. Amy Barrett, "Making Telcommuting Work," *Business Week*, October 17, 2008, http://www.businessweek.com/magazine/content/08_70/s0810048750962.htm?chan=smallbiz_smallbiz+index+page_best+of+small+biz+magazine.

26. Robert Levering and Milton Moskowitz, "The 100 Best Companies to Work For," *Fortune*, January 20, 2008, pp. 67–78.

27. Aliza Pilar Sherman, "Central Perks," *Entrepreneur*, September 2005, http://www.entrepreneur.com/article/print/0,2361,322834,00.html.

28. Ann Marsh, "Babbling Interviewer Disease," *Business 2.0*, March 2005, p. 54.

29. Anne Fisher, "Staying Power: Whole Foods Market," *Fortune* Insert, July 7, 2008. p. 6.

30. Peter Bregman, "The Interview Question You Should Always Ask," *Harvard Business Publishing*, Janaury 27, 2009, http://blogs.harvardbusiness.org/cs/2009/01/the_interview_question_you_sho.html.

31. Kate Bonamici, "The Shoe-In," *Fortune*, January 20, 2006, p. 116.

32. Gwendolyn Bounds, "Handyman Etiquette: Stay Calm, Avert Eyes," *Wall Street Journal*, May 10, 2005, pp. B1, B4.

33. Vasanth Sridharan, "22% of Employers Check Your FaceBook Profile When They Are Looking to Hire You,

That's It?" *Business Insider*, September 11, 2008, http://www.businessinsider.com/2008/9/22-of-employers-check-your-facebook-profile-when-they-re-looking-to-hire-you-that-s-it-.

34. "A Little Resume Fiction Can Lose You a Job," *Greenville News*, August 10, 2008, p. 1E.

35. Anne Fisher, "Staying Power: Whole Foods Market," *Fortune* Insert, July 7, 2008, p.6.

36. Jennifer Saranow, "Anybody Want to Take a Nap?" *Wall Street Journal*, Jamuary 24, 2005, p. R5.

37. Ari Weinzberg, "Ask Ari Weinzberg," *Inc.*, December 2007, p. 84.

38. Damon Darlin, "When Your Start-Up Takes Off," *Business 2.0*, May 2005, p. 127.

39. "Serving the Greater Familial Good," *Winning Workplaces*, http://www.winningworkplaces.org/library/success/serving_greater_familial_good.php.

40. Nichole L. Torres, "Let the Good Times Roll," *Entrepreneur*, November 2004, p. 57.

41. "Winning Workplaces: Building a Fun Work Culture," *Small Business Review*, http://smallbusinessreview.com/human_resources/Building_a_fun_work_culture/.

42. *The State of Employee Engagement 2008*, North American Overview, BlessingWhite North America, Skillman, New Jersey: 2008, pp. 3,7.

43. Jennifer Cheeseman Day, "Population Profile of the United States," U.S. Census Bureau, July 8, 2008, http://www.census.gov/population/www/pop-profile/natproj.html.

44. "How Companies Make Good Decisions" McKinsey Global Survey Results," *McKinsey Quarterly*, January 2009, http://www.mckinseyquarterly.com/How_companies_make_good_decisions_McKinsey_Global_Survey_Results_2282.

45. "A Winning Team," *Winning Workplaces*, http://www.winningworkplaces.org/library/success/a_winning_team.php.

46. Robert D. Mohr and Cindy Zoghi, "Is Job Enrichment Really Enriching?," U.S. Department of Labor, U.S. Bureau of Labor Statistics, Office of Productivity and Technology, Washington, DC: January 2006, pp. 13–15.

47. Ellen Galinsky, Sheila Eby, and Shanny L. Peer, *2008 Guide to Bold New Ideas for Making Work Work*, Families and Work Institute, New York" 2008, p. 23.

48. Ellen Galinsky, James T. Bond, Kelly Sakai, Stacy S. Kim, and Nicole Giuntoli, *2008 National Study of Employers*, Families and Work Institute, New York: May 2008, p. 6.

49. Carol Kleiman, "Job Sharing Working Its Way Into Mainstream," *Greenville News*, August 6, 2000. p. 3G.

50. Gerry Blackwell,"Telecommuting Trend Taking Off for Small Biz," *Small Business Computing*, September 22, 2008, http://www.smallbusinesscomputing.com/news/article.php/3773076.

51. Meredith Levinson, "Survey: Telecommuting Improves Productivity, Lowers Cost," *CIO*, October 7, 2008, http://www.cio.com/article/453289/Telecommuting_Improves_Productivity_Lowers_Costs_New_Survey_Finds; Harriet Hagestad, "New Ways to Work: Telecommuting and Job Sharing," *Career Builder*, June 23, 2006, http://www.careerbuilder.com/JobSeeker/careerbytes/CBArticle.aspx?articleID=369&cbRecursionCnt=1&cbsid=49944662f7b64dc38639d9a3ef87dd18-204624985-R5-4.

52. Amy Barrett, "Making Telcommuting Work," *Business Week*, October 17, 2008, http://www.businessweek.com/magazine/content/08_70/s0810048750962.htm?chan=smallbiz_smallbiz+index+page_best+of+small+biz+magazine.

53. Anne Fisher, "Staying Power: Computerized Facility Integration," *Fortune* Insert, July 7, 2008, p. 4.

54. Darren Dahl, "Open Book Management's Lessons for Detroit," *New York Times*, May 20, 2009, http://www.nytimes.com/2009/05/21/business/smallbusiness/21open.html.

55. "On the Rise," *Winning Workplaces*, http://www.winningworkplaces.org/library/success/on_the_rise.php.

56. "The Best Companies to Work for 2008," *Fortune*, February 4, 2008, p. 90.; Jacquelyn Lynn, "Rub It In," *Entrepreneur*, September 1999, p. 46; Anne Fisher, "The 100 Best Companies to Work For in America," *Fortune*, January 12, 1998, pp. 69–70; Joann S. Lublin, "Climbing the Walls on Company Time," *Wall Street Journal*, December 1, 1998, pp. B1, B16; Quentin Hardy, "Aloft in a Career Without Fetters," *Wall Street Journal*, September 29, 1998, pp. B1, B14; Jerry Useem, "Welcome to the New Company Town," *Fortune*, January 10, 2000, pp. 62–70; Brittany Maling, "Building Company Loyalty with Unusual Benefits," HR World, May 19, 2009, http://www.hrworld.com/features/build-loyalty-unusual-benefits/.

57. "Winning Workplaces: Building a Fun Work Culture," *Small Business Review*, http://smallbusinessreview.com/human_resources/Building_a_fun_work_culture/.

58. Ritch L. Sorenson, Keith H. Brigham, Thomas E. Holubik, and Robert L. Phillips, "Predictors of Longevity in Small Family Firms: An Exploratory Study," United States Association for Entrepreneurship and Small Business National Conference, Dallas, Texas, 2004; Facts and Figures," Family Firm Institute, http://www.ffi.org/genTemplate.asp?cid=186#us; Pat Curry, "Measured Steps," *Prosales*, September 2002, http://www.findarticles.com/p/articles/mi_m0NTC/is_9_14/ai_100962585.

59. "Passing the Baton," *Fortune* Insert, May 28, 2008, p. 60; "Facts and Figures," Family Firm Institute, http://www.ffi.org/genTemplate.asp?cid=186#us.

60. "Facts and Perspectives on Family Business Around the World: United States," Family Business Institute, http://www.ffi.org/looking/fbfacts_us.pdf.

61. Leah Kristie, "The World's Oldest Family Companies," *Family Business*, September 2008, http://www.familybusinessmagazine.com/worldsoldest.html/

62. "Passing the Baton," *Fortune* Insert, May 28, 2008, p. 60; "Facts and Figures," Family Firm Institute, http://www.ffi.org/genTemplate.asp?cid=186#us.

63. Jeff Mesiner, "What Now?" *Entrepreneur*, December 2008, p. 75; "Company History," Mountain Madness, http://www.mountainmadness.com/news/cbcf.cfm.

64. *Laird Norton Tyee Family Business Survey: Family to Family 2007*, Laird Norton Tyee, Seattle, Washinton, 2007, pp. 12–15; *2007 American Family Business Survey*, MassMutual, 2007, p. 7.

65. Passing the Baton," *Fortune* Insert, May 28, 2008, p. 60.

66. Patricia B. Gray, "The Stranger Among Us," *FSB*, October 2008, pp. 86–90.

67. *Laird Norton Tyee Family Business Survey: Family to Family 2007*, Laird Norton Tyee, Seattle, Washington, 2007, p. 12.

68. *Laird Norton Tyee Family Business Survey: Family to Family 2007*, Laird Norton Tyee, Seattle, Washington, 2007, p. 15.
69. Julie Schlosser, "The Son Rises at Qualcomm," *Fortune*, April 18, 2005, p. 45.
70. Woody White, "Planning Eases Transfer of Control of Family Business," *Upstate Business*, October 8, 2000, p. 1.
71. H. G. Stern and Bob Vineyard, "Death of a Salesman (and His Business)," *Insureblog*, December 13, 21, 2005, http://insureblog.blogspot.com/2005/12/death-of-sales-man-and-his-business.html; Tim Tresslar, "Jeweler Jaffe Returning to Downtown . . . Temporarily," *Dayton Business Journal*, June 9, 2006, http://dayton.bizjournals.com/dayton/stories/2006/06/12/tidbits1.html.
72. *Laird Norton Tyee Family Business Survey: Family to Family 2007*, Laird Norton Tyee, Seattle, Washinton, 2007, p. 15.
73. "About Our Founder," Pampered Chef, http://www.pamperedchef.com/our_company/doris.html.
74. "Largest Study Yet Shows ESOPs Improve Performance and Employee Benefits," National Center for Employee Ownership, http://www.nceo.org/library/esop_perf.html .
75. Bruce Edwards, "Carris Reels Wins 'Company of the Year' Award," *Rutland Herald,* June 2, 2008, http://www.rutlandherald.com/apps/pbcs.dll/article?AID=/20080602/BUSINESS/806020301/1011/BUSINESS; "Carris Reels Named 2008 Company of the Year by the ESOP Association," ESOP Association, May 13, 2008, http://www.esopassociation.org/media/media_reels.asp; Loren Rodgers, "'Employee Owned and Governed,' The Carris Community of Companies,'" *ESOP Report*, March 2001, p. 3.

Appendix

1. http://www.ets.org/Media/onethird.pdf
2. http://www.stolaf.edu/people/steen/Papers/numeracy.html; John A. Dossey, Ina V.S. Mullis, Mary M. Lindquist, and Donald L. Chambers, The Mathematics Report Card: Are We Measuring Up? Princeton, New Jersey: Educational Testing Service, 1988.
3. http://nifl.gov/nifl/facts/reading_facts.html
4. http://money.cnn.com/magazines/fsb/fsb_archive/2005/11/01/8360973/index.htm
5. http://homeschooling.gomilpitas.com/weblinks/numbers.htm
6. http://www.hslda.org/docs/nche/000010/200410250.asp
7. http://www.eden.rutgers.edu/~auderey/Devine-Eller,%20Reasons%20Families%20Choose%20SAT%20Prep.pdf
8. http://www.time.com/time/nation/article/0,8599,1885239,00.html
9. Maria Glod, "U.S. Teens Trail Peers Around the World on Math-Science Test," *Washington Post*, December 5, 2007, http://www.washingtonpost.com/wp-dyn/content/article/2007/12/04/AR2007120400730.html.
10. Nicholas Johnson, Phil Oliff, and Jeremy Koulish, "An Update on State Budget Cuts," Center on Budget and Policy Priorities, May 13, 2009, http://www.cbpp.org/cms/?fa=view&id=1214.
11. *Knocking at the College Door: Projections of College Graduates by State and Race/Ethnicity, 1992–2022*, Western Interstate Commission for Higher Education (Boulder, Colorado: 2008), p. 6.

Name Index

A

A&W, 181, 184
AARP, 184–185
Abbruzzese, Mia, 486, 501
Abrams, Rhonda, 110
Abrams, Steven, 216
A. C. Nielsen Company, 107, 266
Access Markets International (AMI)
    Partners, 292–293
Acclaim Electronics, 452
Ace Hardware, 163
Acme Packet, 485
Acorn Food Services, 144
Acquireo, 197
Acton, Bill, 25
Adams, Jennifer, 505
Adams, Roger, 33
Adams Pressed Metals, 219
Adec Group, 537
Advanced Circuits, 533
Advanced Composite Materials
    (ACM), 73
Advanced Micro Devices (AMD), 103
Advent, 476
A. E. Schmidt Company, 19
Aero Flite Inc., 431
Agee, Jefferey, 461
Agrawal, Andy, 216
Ahmad, Ayasha, 276
Air Guitar Shirt, 258
Airstream, 8
Alabama International Trade Center, 500
Albertson's, 312
Albright, Tenley, 38
Alder, Nate, 119
Aldi, 473
Alexander, Bill, 542
Alexander, Jay, 542
Alexander Machinery, 542
Alibaba.com, 504
Allanival, Abbé D', 444
Allen, Cindy, 396
Allen, Paul, 151, 345
Allessandrini, Walter, 416
Alliance of Merger and Acquisition
    Advisors, 220
Allied Capital, 221
Allied Domecq Quick Service
    Restaurants, 181
AllState Insurance Company, 308–309
Altshuller, Genrich, 56–57
Amazon.com, 12, 33, 50, 59, 246, 308, 350,
    406–407, 413
American Association of Franchisees
    and Dealers, 176–177
American Collectors Association, 383–384
American Diabetes Association (ADA), 241
American Express OPEN Ages Survey, 4–5, 11
American Express OPEN Small Business
    Monitor, 368, 382
American Franchise Association, 177
American Management Association, 262
American Plume and Fancy Feather, 91
American Registry for Internet Numbers, 287
American Speedy Print, 173–174
America's Research Group, 253
A.M.E.'s Uniforms, 198
AmieStreet.com, 308
Anaya, Ana Maria, 117

Anaya, Hipolito, 117
Anaya, Ruben, 117
Anderson, Nate, 83
Anderson Valley Ranch, 230–231
Angel Capital Association, 409
Annan, Kofi, 484
Annenberg Public Policy Center, 308
Anton, John, 62–63
Anton Sport, 62–63
Anytime Fitness, 88
Anywhere Shoe Company, 198–199
AOL, 283
Appel, Jennifer, 216
Apple Inc., 12–13, 43, 61, 258, 304, 311, 322,
    407, 410, 429
Aqua Lights, 421
Arctic Wire Rope and Supply Inc., 331
Arick, Daniel, 431
Armstrong, Lance, 154
Arn, Jamin, 447
Around Your Neck, 184
Arrowhead Credit Union, 428
Artic Stud Poker Run, 261
Arvidson, Ed, 461
Arvig, Jamin, 288
Asbury, Neal, 490
Asherian, Philip, 426
Ask Achelle, 278
Ask.com, 283
Asterino, Christopher, 217
Asterino Associates, 217
AT&T Small Business Lending, 427
Atlanta Bread Company, 168
A-2-Z Scuba, 420
Aucent, 136
Auditors Inc., 395
Aussie, Andrew, 467
Auto City, 423
Automated Concepts, 521
Automatic Data Processing (ADP), 73
Autovent, 494
Axel, Jan, 376

B

Babson College, 170, 179, 196, 377
BabyGanics, 243
Backrub, 404
Baer, Max, 138
Bain and Company, 256, 485
Bain Capital, 413
Bakers Square, 344–345
Balon, Adam, 234
Band of Angels, 409
Bankers Association for Foreign
    Trade, 501
Barbara Butler Artist Builder Inc., 240
Barbie, 46
Bardow, Dick, 126–127
Barkingham Palace Doggie
    Daycare, 136
Bark Park Central, Dallas, 47
Barnes & Noble, 248, 473, 477
Barnett, Kenneth, 421
Barracuda Networks, 279
Barrato, Todd, 311
Basham, Robert, 429
Baskin-Robbins, 166, 181, 184
Batra, Sumita, 245
Batteries Plus, 91

Battina, Dann, 386
Baugh, Kenneth, 462
Bay Area Development Company, 435
Bay Area Discovery Museum, 240
Bayss, Nick, 44
BBBOnLine, 271, 280, 295
Bear Naked, 9
Beefjerky.com, 230–231
Behar, Jennifer, 422
Beijo Bags LLC, 260
Bell, Alexander Graham, 407
Bell, Andy, 527
Bella's Fat Cat, 434
Bell Telephone, 407
Beltmann Group, 386
Ben and Jerry's Homemade, Inc., 97,
    163, 418
Bennett, Laura, 25–26
Bennigan's, 167
Bennis, Warren, 34
Bergh, Arne, 90
Bergman, Ingrid, 308
Bergqvist, Yngve, 90
Berken, Riza, 451
Berkshire Hathaway, 546
Berry, Halle, 18
Bessemer Venture Partners, 413
Bezos, Jackie, 405
Bezos, Jeff, 12, 33, 50, 54, 407
Bezos, Mike, 405
Bhidé, Amar, 6
Bickoff, Darius, 216
Bidwell, Chuck, 346–347
Bill Heard Enterprises (BHE), 342
Billings, Josh, 159, 189
Birch, David, 10, 23
Bisbee, Bob, 240
Bisbee's Black and Blue
    Tournament, 240
BizBuySell, 197
BizPlan Builder, 112
BizQuest, 197
Bizstats, 357
BKI, 512
Black, Jerry, 301
Blackboard, Inc., 523
Blackfin Technology, 383
Blackshaw, Pete, 246
Blackwave Inc., 410
Blackwell, Steve, 280
Blanchard, Ken, 74
Blanchard, Mike, 470
Blau, Georgette, 14
Blendtec, 247
Blimpie Subs and Salads, 184
Blip.tv, 234
Blockbuster, 78
Bloomsbury, 48
Bluefly.com, 284
Blue Gecko, 535
BlueLithium, 203
Bob Howard Chrysler-Jeep-Dodge, 347
Bobker, Zach, 274
Body Shop, 407
Bogart, Humphrey, 308
Bonneville Seabase, 7
Bonney, Tom, 521
Book Bin, 241
Boots, 492
Booz Hamilton, 73

Subject Index